THE OXFORD ENCYCLOPEDIA OF

ARCHAEOLOGY IN THE NEAR E

.

THE OXFORD
ENCYCLOPEDIA OF
ARCHAEOLOGY
IN THE NEAR EAST

PREPARED UNDER THE AUSPICES OF THE
AMERICAN SCHOOLS OF ORIENTAL RESEARCH

Eric M. Meyers

EDITOR IN CHIEF

VOLUME 1

New York   Oxford
OXFORD UNIVERSITY PRESS
1997

Oxford University Press

Oxford   New York
Athens   Auckland   Bangkok   Bogotá
Bombay   Buenos Aires   Calcutta   Cape Town
Dar es Salaam   Delhi   Florence   Hong Kong   Istanbul
Karachi   Kuala Lumpur   Madras   Madrid   Melbourne
Mexico City   Nairobi   Paris   Singapore
Taipei   Tokyo   Toronto

and associated companies in
Berlin   Ibadan

Published by Oxford University Press, Inc.,
198 Madison Avenue, New York, New York 10016

Oxford is a registered trademark of Oxford University Press

Library of Congress Cataloging-in-Publication Data
The Oxford encyclopedia of archaeology in the Near East / prepared
under the auspices of the American Schools of Oriental Research;
Eric M. Meyers, editor in chief.
p.   cm.
Includes bibliographical references (p.   ) and index.
1. Middle East—Antiquities—Encyclopedias. 2. Africa, North—Antiquities—
Encyclopedias. I. Meyers, Eric M. II. American Schools of Oriental Research.
DS56.09   1996   96-17152   939'.4—dc20   CIP

ISBN 0-19-506512-3 (set)
ISBN 0-19-511215-6 (vol. 1)

*Many photographs and line drawings used herein were supplied by contributors to the work. Others
were drawn from the archives of the American Schools of Oriental Research, from commercial
photographic archives, and from the holdings of major museums and cultural institutions.
The publisher has made every effort to ascertain that necessary permissions to reprint
materials have been secured. Sources of all photographs and line drawings
are given in the captions to illustrations.*

EDITORIAL AND PRODUCTION STAFF

COMMISSIONING EDITOR: Elizabeth Maguire
DEVELOPMENT EDITOR: Mark D. Cummings

MANAGING EDITOR: Jeffrey P. Edelstein

ASSISTANT PROJECT EDITOR: Paul Arthur
COPYEDITORS AND PROOFREADERS: Roberta Maltese, Sandra Buch,
Karen Fraley, Donald Spanel, Leslie Watkins
BIBLIOGRAPHIC AND TECHNICAL RESEARCHERS: Stephen Goranson,
John S. Jorgensen, Eric C. Lapp, Philomena Mariani
INDEXER: Cynthia Crippen, AEIOU, Inc.
CARTOGRAPHER: Philip Schwartzberg, Meridian Mapping
MANUFACTURING CONTROLLER: Michelle Levesque
BOOK DESIGNER: Joan Greenfield

Printing (last digit): 9 8 7 6 5 4 3 2 1

Printed in the United States of America on acid-free paper

CONTENTS

Editorial Board

vol. 1, p. vii

Preface

ix

Abbreviations

xv

THE OXFORD ENCYCLOPEDIA OF

ARCHAEOLOGY IN THE NEAR EAST

EDITORIAL BOARD

PREFACE

The genesis of this work was in 1988 when the American Schools of Oriental Research (ASOR) moved its headquarters from Philadelphia to the campus of the Johns Hopkins University in Baltimore. As first vice president for publications I was encouraged by the ASOR Board of Trustees to establish a closer working relationship with the Johns Hopkins University Press. In that context I developed a project entitled *The ASOR Handbook of Biblical Archaeology,* which was to be an authoritative one-volume reference work on all aspects of the material culture of the lands of the Bible in antiquity. The geographical region to be covered was Syria-Palestine, or the modern territories of Israel, Jordan, Syria, and Lebanon. The chronological range was to have been the Early Bronze Age to the Byzantine period. The idea was to make available and easily accessible the results of modern archaeological scholarship to readers interested in the ancient Near East and biblical studies. A major motivating factor was the absence of such a work in the existing literature.

The model for the ASOR handbook was a German classic in the field, Kurt Galling's *Biblisches Reallexikon,* largely unavailable to English readers and long ago out of print. From the outset, the ASOR handbook was to have endeavored to bring together the results of archaeological fieldwork, epigraphy, and literary-historical studies. Archaeological fieldwork was also understood as something more than site reports. Rather, it was viewed as a means of securing data that would lead to a better understanding of aspects of everyday life such as agriculture, family life, medicine and public health, clothing, diet, and architecture; it was a way of examining how different sorts of material culture shaped and were shaped by the environment. Similarly, a major concern was to have been the economy of the peoples of the Levant; their industries, such as the production of agricultural commodities, glassmaking, shipbuilding, metallurgy, and so forth, were to be considered. The more familiar quest to determine the social world as well as the political setting of the peoples and cultures of the ancient Near East remained a basic aim from the outset. In addition, true to the tradition of W. F. Albright—preeminent archaeologist and orientalist, former professor of Near Eastern Studies at the Johns Hopkins University and long-term director of ASOR's Jerusalem school—the handbook would deal with the full range of written materials that have survived from Syria-Palestine, from the origins of alphabetic writing to the development of elaborate scribal practices and varied literatures. Finally, the project would embrace the challenge of explaining archaeological techniques, theory, methods, and practice including all matters pertaining to science and archaeology.

It soon became apparent to me and my counterparts at the Johns Hopkins University Press that such an undertaking was far too ambitious for ASOR and Hopkins and that what I envisioned fell squarely into the area of encyclopedic reference works. It was then, in seeking a publisher with a strong reference department, that ASOR and Oxford University Press came together.

After a few consultations with members of the reference department it became abundantly clear that there were many conceptual issues to be resolved before such a project could commence. The first issue to be considered was that of length. After several meetings I was convinced that the only way that the wide variety of issues to be covered could be properly accommodated was through a multivolume approach. The idea of bringing texts into dialogue with archaeological realia was appealing to all of us. No less important was the hope that this project would bring scholars from all countries of the region into dialogue with one another for the first time. Given the reality, at that time, of the Israeli-Palestinian conflict, which separated Israel from the rest of the Arab world, this was to be one of the greatest challenges but one that ASOR, with its historic position of neutrality in political matters and with research centers in both worlds, and Oxford University Press were particularly capable of meeting.

In organizing the editorial board I was mindful of all of these concerns. The inclusion of James A. Sauer, with his long experience in Jordan and the rest of the Arab world and knowledge of the sites there, was intended to ensure the participation of scholars from those countries where Americans have had only limited experience and even less familiarity with the data uncovered. The combination of William G. Dever's extensive field experience in Israel with my own work there as well as that of Carol Meyers was designed to attract our distinguished Israeli colleagues. James Muhly's expertise in several important areas—ancient history, the archaeology of the Aegean, and aspects of scientific approaches to the discipline—was deemed valuable to the project. Dennis Pardee seemed uniquely qualified to handle matters concerning ancient Near Eastern languages and literatures, especially Semitics, linguistics, and epigraphy. Carol Meyers's participation was enlisted in addition to her work in Israel, for her particular interest in methodology, theory, and social science aspects of the archaeological enterprise. My own focus on the classical periods and on the history of the discipline were considered beneficial and sufficient to guide us through those areas.

When the editorial board first met, we were of course aware that work was proceeding on the Israel Exploration Society's *New Encyclopedia of Archaeological Excavations in the Holy Land*; indeed, those of us who had contributed to the society's previous encyclopedia, published in English in 1975-1978, had been asked to revise and update our articles. The anticipated publication of their project was hardly a deterrent to us in our planning because theirs was to be strictly an encyclopedia of sites, virtually all of which are in Israel. As the development of our table of contents progressed, we learned that another multivolume work, titled *Civilizations of the Ancient Near East*, was being planned. Although comprehensive in its intended coverage of the region and its ancient cultures, the work was to be a collection of about two hundred lengthy and somewhat idiosyncratic topical essays, thematically organized, which would make it far less useful as a reference work than a standard encyclopedia, with its more specific, alphabetically arranged articles. Both works eventually were published, the former in 1993 (English edition) and the latter in 1995.

As the editorial team began the serious work of laying out a general plan, it became clear that we did not want to limit our geographical locations to the Levant. Rather, we were interested in the archaeology of the entire Near East, from the eastern Mediterranean to Iran, from Anatolia to the Arabian Peninsula; we also wanted to include Egypt, Cyprus, and parts of North and East Africa. Because of ASOR's particular role in the archaeology of Cyprus there was hardly any argument there. What soon became a very real problem for all of us was the classical world and the question of sites relating to the New Testament. In thinking about the Hellenistic world or the Roman Empire it became very difficult to limit our scope to the territories associated with the Near East. What would we do with Rome or Athens, the Italian Peninsula and Greece? If we would deal only with sites relating to the New Testament world how would that section stand up vis-à-vis the other conceptual categories in the encyclopedia?

In the end, we opted for the geographical principle and added places such as Malta and Sardinia where Semitic culture had been strong since antiquity, the Aegean world, and North Africa as far as Morocco. Anatolia would be our northern boundary, Iran our eastern boundary, and Ethiopia and the Arabian Peninsula our southern limits. In a way we adopted Albright's inclusive geographical view of the ancient Near East and decided to employ a broader chronological range as well. Since so much important new archaeological work is being done in periods prior to the Bronze Age, we felt that any new archaeological reference work could not fail to treat the newest discoveries in prehistory.

At the other end of the chronological spectrum it seemed less and less acceptable to end our studies in the Byzantine period, especially given the recent upsurge of interest and discoveries in the field of Islamic archaeology. In the end we decided to extend our coverage through the Crusades while allowing for individual authors to discuss some sites and some aspects of material culture of even later periods where appropriate. It should be noted, however, that many subjects and sites do not fall easily into the categories or parameters of the project. In some regions or countries certain periods of human history simply have not received as much attention as others. Islamic archaeology is stronger, as might be expected, in the Arab world. Iron Age archaeology is stronger in Israel because of interest in the Bible and the ancient kingdom of Israel. More extensive digging in Israel, for example, has resulted in the fact that more is known about its antiquity than about most other ancient societies. Correspondingly, the relatively fewer excavations in Arabia and East Africa and the current political situation in those areas means that our knowledge of their ancient cultures is more limited. Our coverage of individual countries thus varies considerably. For all areas we have tried to engage scholars with firsthand knowledge of the site, region, or topic to present available data with the idea of being as current and accurate as possible. Needless to say we have been more successful in some cases than in others.

Given the major reconceptualization of the project after our initial meetings with the Oxford University Press reference editors, it was impossible for us to title our project anything but what we in truth had become, an encyclopedia of Near Eastern archaeology. While some of us had some nostalgic feelings for titles such as *Encyclopedia of Archaeology in the Biblical World* or some variant of that, in the end we were all more comfortable with the more descriptive, geographical nomenclature, which we also believed was more appropriate, less political, and more inclusive: *The Oxford Encyclopedia of Archaeology in the Near East*. With our larger geographical and chronological scope there was no disposition or reason whatever to use the term *Syro-Palestinian* in the title of what was to be a multivolume work. Although Syria-Palestine remains very much at the core of these volumes, it is largely the result of the fact that there has been more historic interest, and consequently, more fieldwork in that area.

The cultures of both ancient Egypt and Mesopotamia, which have held such places of pride in Western consciousness since the beginning of the nineteenth century, especially after the decipherment of hieroglyphics and cuneiform (see "History of the Field," *overview article*), presented us with special problems as we planned our coverage. Both cultures have enormous literatures and complex histories that cannot be comprehensively presented even in a five-volume work such as this encyclopedia, which includes so many individual site entries. Nonetheless, we have aimed to provide sufficient coverage of these cultures so that the interested student or scholar can use our entries and their accompanying bibliographies as suitable entry points for further study. Similarly, given the limited access of Westerners, especially English speakers, to Iraq and Iran, we have only been able to highlight the most important sites there, although we have also included broader entries on all the significant historical peoples and cultures in those countries.

In pointing out some of the problems encountered in dealing with different ancient cultures, I must also mention other factors that have led to what might appear to be an unevenness in the amount of coverage and nature of the material presented for the various regions and cultures covered. Many subfields have their own audiences, and individual scholars in those fields do not necessarily know the work of other scholars engaged in similar projects in a nearby country. Egyptologists, for example, focus closely on their own subject. That is not to say that Egyptian archaeologists are uninformed about neighboring cultures or that a specialist in hieroglyphics is ignorant of Semitic languages, but in general the crossover from Egyptology to other fields is limited. Similarly, biblical archaeologists in general are not well informed about the larger ancient Near Eastern environment, in part because of contemporary regional politics but perhaps owing more to the tradition of scholarship that favors the Bible over the literatures of other Near Eastern cultures. Mesopotamian archaeologists, especially those working in Iran or Iraq, are still struggling to establish chronologies for certain periods; in other regions such efforts are no longer essential. It is only very recently that Jordanians and Israelis have had complete access to each other's published research or enjoyed the possibility of visiting each other's sites; despite the proximity of one area to the next there has been very little collaboration among local scholars in the region. In 1990 none of us had any inkling that many age-old political barriers that had so hindered synthetic thinking about the Near East region in the past would come tumbling down in the mid-1990s. These volumes do not in any sense reflect the scholarly fruits or potential benefits that will ultimately emerge as a result of the recent breakthroughs in the peace process. In this connection it is important to note also that different countries have different standards and laws for archaeological preservation and for reporting of data to the government antiquities authority. These variations have perforce affected the nature of the discipline of archaeology as practiced in individual countries or regions; it is the purpose of numerous entries in the encyclopedia to examine the implications of this reality (see, for example, "Nationalism and Archaeology").

One of the major areas of complexity has been the question of periodization and its nomenclature. Any serious reader in Near Eastern archaeology knows how heated debates can be over matters of chronology and period names. Though the editorial board considered developing its own neutral or common terminology that might be utilized by all contributors, it ultimately decided to allow the traditions of particular scholarly groups or specializations to stand. For example, the subperiods for the Iron Age used in Cyprus and in the Aegean reflect the longtime involvement and continuing influence of classical archaeologists. In general, the Arab world has eschewed certain classifications or designations that are common in Israel. For example, in the Arab world one would not encounter such expressions as *First Temple period* (a reference to Solomon's Temple from its construction in the tenth century until its destruction in 587/6 BCE) or *Israelite period*, which refers to the period of Israelite political autonomy. For obvious reasons it is more common in the Arab world than elsewhere to designate the period after the time of the prophet Muhammad as the *Islamic period* and to label the field that specializes in those periods *Islamic archaeology*. Similarly, the use by some scholars of the term *Crusader period* to designate the nearly two centuries of medieval history greatly influenced by the Crusades does not necessarily mean that it is appropriate to use such a term for the Near East as a whole.

The reader is thus alerted to such divergences and inconsistencies and should consult the chronological charts in volume 5 for assistance in terminology and the relevant individual entries for the distinctive chronological treatments by country, culture, or region. Some of the disagreements about nomenclature, it must be said, arise out of different scholarly trends in the country of the researcher rather than of the area being studied. So, for example, the British treat the transition between the Early Bronze Age and the Middle Bronze Age in their own way, referring to it as the *Intermediate Bronze Age*. Some American and Israeli scholars would call this period *Middle Bronze I*, others *Early Bronze IV*. Hence the reader is cautioned that what might be designated *late Early Bronze Age* in one culture may not be so designated in another setting. The French, whose presence has been especially strong in Egypt, North Africa, Syria, and Iraq, have their own scholarly traditions in this regard as well. The reader is referred to the regional survey entries (e.g., "Palestine," "Transjordan," "Cyprus") and their numerous sections organized by periods, and to the article "Periodization" for assistance in understanding this issue.

The attentive reader will also note that there are wide discrepancies in the periodization of what we call prehistory, roughly from the Stone Age to the Chalcolithic period. These discrepancies reflect the various levels of sophistication and refinement in establishing the chronologies of prehistoric archaeology in different countries. Like the ones already noted, the differences are indicative of the developing nature of the discipline and should serve as an incentive to further serious inquiry.

The presentation of sites stands at the very core of the present work and represents the first time that site reports of the archaeology of the entire Near East have been brought together in a single work. It has of course been necessary to be selective in choosing which sites would receive treatment in independent entries; despite this selectivity, site entries number almost 450 of the 1,100 entries in the encyclopedia. The editors have endeavored to include entries on all of the most significant sites; others are discussed within the context of the more general entries on regions, countries, or peoples. A careful use of the index together with the synoptic outline of contents (both at the back of volume 5) should lead the interested student or scholar to the discussion of the site in question even if it is not the subject of a separate entry. However, readers may not find coverage within the encyclopedia on relatively obscure sites, information on which is likely to be found only in more specialized scholarly literature.

Some might wonder about the illustrations program and its rationale. The editorial committee relied first on the submissions of individual contributors and second on the ASOR photographic archives. We particularly wished to illustrate places and sites that are not well known, especially in such areas as Syria, Jordan, and the Arabian Peninsula. Although we ultimately had to abandon our efforts to illustrate certain articles, particularly those for which contributors were unable to provide materials, in the end we found that we had included 650 drawings, plans, and photographs, a significant increase over the 450 originally planned. In addition, there is a separate series of regional maps in volume 5 that are designed to assist the reader in locating all sites that are the subject of independent entries; the less detailed maps accompanying individual entries on empires and peoples enable the reader to understand individual cultural and political entities (e.g., ʿAbbasid Caliphate, Arameans, Roman Empire).

Just as archaeologists from different countries and different scholarly traditions have different standards and modes of communications, so too do our colleagues in the fields of linguistics, language, literature, and epigraphy. Though we have attempted to render their presentations somewhat more accessible to the nonspecialist reader through certain editorial conventions, we have not attempted to alter their fundamental mode of scholarly discourse, which for some may seem a bit technical in places. Nonetheless, this practice is entirely in keeping with the editorial policy of inviting state-of-the-art presentations from experts in the field. In an age of specialization it should come as no surprise that both archaeologists and linguists have their own technical modes of discourse.

It has been especially difficult to develop a common system of spelling. Where a proper name is used commonly in the literature we have adopted the most frequently used spelling. So, for example, in Hebrew we have preferred *Beth-Shean* to the more precise *Beth She'an*. Where a strict transliteration rendered awkward or unfamiliar a fairly common Greek name, such as *Seleukos* following Greek convention rather than the more frequently encountered *Seleucus*, we opted for the more familiar latinized form, as we did for sites and individuals bearing Semitic names.

For place names in Israel we tended to be strict in utilizing diacritical marks with consonants, though we eschewed using macrons and other indications of vowel length. This general rule of thumb, however, was not adhered to for such common place names as *Bethlehem* (more properly *Beth-Leḥem*). For Hebrew site names that include the element *tell*, the spelling *tel* was employed to reflect the Hebrew spelling, while for those places within Israel bearing Arabic names the spelling *tell* was used. In this way we were able to remain sensitive to both Arabic and Hebrew conventions rather than leveling through and opting for one spelling over the other (e.g., *Tell Beit Mirsim* vs. *Tel Miqne*). We did try to be consistent in rendering the Hebrew *ṣade* using *ṣ*, though there are instances where we used *z* following a more common spelling from the primary publications (e.g., *Nazareth,*

'Ein-Zippori). For the common element meaning "spring/well" in Hebrew place names we chose the construct state spelling *'Ein* with the dipthong *ei* to indicate the long *ṣere* vowel as opposed to the alternate spelling *'En*, which is more frequently used by Israeli scholars; thus, we have preferred the spellings *'Ein-Besor* and *'Ein-Gedi* to *'En Besor* and *'En Gedi*. This we contrast with the absolute state spelling, *'Ayin*. While as a rule we did not indicate aspiration of the *begadkepat* consonants (e.g., *'Atlit* rather than *'Athlit*), we maintained the common spelling *Beth-* as in *Beth-Shean* and *Beth-Shemesh*, and so forth. For technical terms, we have usually included indications of vowel length as well, for example, *maṣṣēbâ, bāmâ*.

In deciding on spellings for Arabic place names we generally deferred to the spellings utilized in the primary publications (i.e., the formal excavation reports), since we did not wish to create conflicts with officially accepted forms, though again, as with the Hebrew names, normally we did not include indications of vowel length. We were perhaps less innovative here than in our choice for Hebrew place names. As with Hebrew place names, where a common spelling existed we maintained that spelling, as in *San'a* (contrast with the more proper *San'a'*). Note that in this context we spell "spring/well" *'Ain* (e.g., *'Ain Ghazal*).

Since Turkish is written in Latin characters with only slight modifications, we tried as best as possible to adhere to standard Turkish spellings. For instance the site name *Boghazkoy* is spelled *Boğazköy*. We employed the dotless i (*ı*) where appropriate; any inconsistency in its use is inadvertent.

For personal names, we generally tended simplify the names with little use of diacriticals. Thus, for instance, although we used the spelling *Aššur* for the Assyrian capital, we used *Ashurbanipal* for the name of the Assyrian king. This rule applies to most personal names.

Finally, since it was nearly impossible to be completely consistent in our spellings, we often provided variant spellings parenthetically in the opening lines of a site article or on first mention of a name in an article. Readers should be aware of the frequency of name changes for sites through time, resulting in a single location having an ancient name, a Roman name, and modern names (sometimes both Hebrew and Arabic). Variant spellings appear in the index; we have attempted to be thorough in linking these variant spellings so that readers will find all mentions of a particular site, regardless of the spelling used.

Readers seeking information about a particular subject are referred to the index and synoptic outline of the work in volume 5; as mentioned above, specific sites for which we have independent entries may be generally located on the regional maps. Such topics as scientific techniques and archaeology, biographies of prominent archaeologists now deceased; histories of all the major archaeological institutes and organizations in the Near East; and discussion of peoples, places, and languages as well as individual artifacts and their decoration and industries may be readily located by utilizing one of these reference tools. In locating the discussion on certain specialties such as glassmaking (see "Vitreous Materials") or shipbuilding (see "Underwater Archaeology," "Seafaring," or "Ships and Boats") the reader will have to pay attention to our system of internal cross-referencing, which is designed to make the encyclopedia user-friendly, leading readers from a particular entry into a vast network of related topics.

There are several kinds of specialty article in this work that distinguish it from all other presentations; the issues involved in these articles are at the cutting edge of the field of Near Eastern and world archaeology. In the area of theory or history of the discipline I would call attention to the multipart entry "History of the Field," which, following a general overview, is organized as ten articles that cover all the countries and regions of the Near East (Syria, Israel, Jordan, Mesopotamia, Persia, the Anatolian Plateau, Egypt, Cyprus, the Aegean Islands, and the Arabian Peninsula). The special role of "biblical archaeology" becomes clear within the larger context of Near Eastern archaeology. To round out the broad geographical perspective the reader should consult the entries "Ethiopia," "Nubia," and "North Africa." Other entries such as "New Archaeology," "Underwater Archaeology," "Survey, Archaeological," and "Salvage Excavation" will also indicate the rich diversity of archaeological theory and method. While there have been numerous works on the history of archaeology, there is nothing in the existing literature that can quite compare to this treatment, which has the benefit of being site specific and up to date in terms of actual fieldwork while treating archaeology historically and in general terms.

It is only in the broader Near Eastern context and setting that we also may fully appreciate the distinctive contributions of specialists who have written on "Ceramics," "Bone, Ivory, and Shell," or "Building Materials and Techniques." In this broader context, too, the role of various kinds of settlements or a particular kind of fortification or weapon may be better appreciated and understood.

I would also like to mention a number of special entries planned within the category of Theory and Practice: "Development and Archaeology," "Museums and Museology," "Ethics and Archaeology," "Ideology and Archaeology," "Nationalism and Archaeology," and "Tourism and Archaeology." Each of these articles is designed to call attention to the place and plight of archaeology in the individual countries in which it is practiced. Moreover, these entries focus on the results of archaeological work and the influence those results have on both the national culture and consciousness of people at home and abroad. How the stories of peoples and places of long ago are recovered and told anew brings us closer to the contemporary issue of how modern nation-states define themselves and their cultures in the multicultural universe of contemporary society. These articles allow the reader to reflect on the impact of the field of archaeology on the citizens of the modern countries located in the territories of ancient civilizations, on the tourists who visit there, and on the students who read their ancient literatures.

When Edward Robinson, the United States's pioneer explorer and first historical geographer of ancient Palestine, and David Roberts, England's premier landscape artist, set out to explore and illustrate the Holy Land in 1839, neither individual had an inkling of how his scientific achievement or artistic genius would so capture the imagination and hearts of the West. Yet the enthusiasm that they generated at home and throughout Europe was only a prelude to what was to come in the latter part of the nineteenth century: the beginning of a systematic and scientific exploration of all the countries of the region. The canvas of the artist was ultimately replaced by the lens of the camera, which ironically also came to Palestine in 1839 when the first landscape pictures of Palestine were taken with the daguerreotype process by the French painter Horace Vernet. The beginnings of the scientific exploration and excavation of the Near East followed closely the establishment of the national schools of archaeology (see "American Schools of Oriental Research," "École Biblique et Archéologique Française," "Institut Français d'Archéologie du Proche Orient," "Israel Exploration Society," "British School of Archaeology in Jerusalem," "British School of Archaeology in Iraq," "Deutsche Orient-Gesellschaft," etc.), which were ultimately the leading sponsors of actual fieldwork in nearly all of the countries of the region. The breakup of the Ottoman Empire and the assignment to individual countries of "mandates" to administer vast territories only strengthened the forces of national interest, which are reflected in the archaeology of the contemporary Middle East even today.

Bringing together the work of a wide array of scholars from all over the world has been a real challenge; by the time we had completed the commissioning of articles, we had enlisted 560 contributors from more than two dozen countries. The encyclopedia contains more than 1,100 entries, and the sheer logistics of communicating in a variety of languages with individuals from so many countries has been enormously complicated. During the course of the evolution of this project the editors have witnessed the electronic mail revolution. Unfortunately, although in the later stages of the project this improved communications with our American contributors considerably, it has not yet been established in most of the countries of the Middle East, nor is it yet widely used in Europe. Thus we have had to rely on mail, phone, and fax for most of our communications. The efforts of the dedicated staff of the Scholarly and Professional Reference Department at Oxford University Press have enabled the editors to overcome many of these logistical barriers. It has been a privilege to work with them.

This project could not have been launched and completed without the encouragement, support, and wisdom of Oxford's Claude Conyers, whose input at the conceptual planning stage was essential and determinative. Also involved at the earliest stage and extraordinarily helpful in conceptual matters was Mark Cummings, who served as the encyclopedia's development editor until his departure from the press in June 1991. It was at that point that Jeffrey Edelstein assumed direct administrative and editorial responsibility as project editor, later managing editor. Jeffrey's indefatigable work ethic, keen eye, and versatile editorial skills enabled the project to progress with great efficiency and care. I have benefited in so many ways from collaboration with these editors that it is almost impossible to offer words that can express adequate appreciation. Nonetheless, I do so on a personal level and on behalf of all the members of the editorial board.

Our assistants in New York and Durham, Paul Arthur of Oxford University Press and John S. Jorgensen of Duke University, have also helped greatly in a variety of matters, but especially in locating illustrations and preparing captions, checking spellings and bibliographies, and assisting in the preparation of maps, charts, and other such materials. Roberta Maltese, bringing to the project valuable editorial experience with the writings of archaeologists, served as principal copyeditor, adding a level of clarity and consistency and establishing standards for the presentation of information that we could not otherwise have achieved. All of us are indebted to them for their tireless efforts.

Eric M. Meyers
Durham, North Carolina
February 1996

ABBREVIATIONS AND SYMBOLS

ACOR	American Center of Oriental Research	BSAJ	British School of Archaeology in Jerusalem
AD	*anno Domini*, in the year of the (our) Lord	B.T.	Babylonian Talmud
AH	*anno Hegirae*, in the year of the Hijrah	c.	*circa*, about, approximately
AIA	Archaeological Institute of America	CAARI	Cyprus American Archaeological Research Institute
AIAR	(W. F.) Albright Institute of Archaeological Research	CAD	computer-aided design/drafting
AJA	*American Journal of Archaeology*	CAORC	Council of American Overseas Research Centers
Akk.	Akkadian	CE	of the common era
Am.	*Amos*	cf.	*confer*, compare
ANEP	J. B. Pritchard, ed., *Ancient Near East in Pictures*	chap., chaps.	chapter, chapters
ANET	J. B. Pritchard, ed., *Ancient Near Eastern Texts*	*1 Chr.*	*1 Chronicles*
		2 Chr.	*2 Chronicles*
AOS	American Oriental Society	*CIG*	*Corpus Inscriptionum Graecarum*
APES	American Palestine Exploration Society	*CIS*	Corpus Inscriptionum Semiticarum
Ar.	Arabic	cm	centimeters
'Arakh.	*'Arakhin*	CNRS	Centre National de la Recherche Scientifique
Aram.	Aramaic	col., cols.	column, columns
ASOR	American Schools of Oriental Research	*Col.*	*Colossians*
Assyr.	Assyrian	*1 Cor.*	*1 Corinthians*
A.Z.	*'Avodah Zarah*	*2 Cor.*	*2 Corinthians*
b.	born	*CTA*	A. Herdner, *Corpus des tablettes en cunéiformes alphabétiques*
B.A.	Bachelor of Arts	cu	cubic
Bab.	Babylonian	d.	died
BASOR	*Bulletin of the American Schools of Oriental Research*	DAI	Deutsches Archäologisches Institut
B.B.	*Bava' Batra'*	diss.	dissertation
BC	before Christ	*Dn.*	*Daniel*
BCE	before the common era	DOG	Deutche Orient-Gesellschaft
Bekh.	*Bekhorot*	D.Sc.	Doctor of Science
Ber.	*Berakhot*	*Dt.*	*Deuteronomy*
Bik.	*Bikkurim*	EB	Early Bronze
BP	before the present	*Eccl.*	*Ecclesiastes*
BSAE	British School of Archaeology in Egypt	ed., eds.	editor, editors; edition
		ED	Early Dynastic
BSAI	British School of Archaeology in Iraq	EEF	Egyptian Exploration Fund
		e.g.	*exempli gratia*, for example

Egyp.	Egyptian
Elam.	Elamite
En.	*Enoch*
Eng.	English
enl.	enlarged
esp.	especially
et al.	*et alii*, and others
etc.	*et cetera*, and so forth
Eth.	Ethiopic
et seq.	*et sequens*, and the following
Ex.	*Exodus*
exp.	expanded
Ez.	*Ezekiel*
Ezr.	*Ezra*
fasc.	fascicle
fem.	feminine
ff.	and following
fig.	figure
fl.	*floruit*, flourished
ft.	feet
frag., frags.	fragment, fragments
gal., gals.	gallon, gallons
Geog.	Ptolemy, *Geographica*
Ger.	German
GIS	Geographic Information Systems
Gk.	Greek
Gn.	*Genesis*
ha	hectares
Heb.	Hebrew
Hg.	*Haggai*
Hist.	Herodotus, *History*
Hitt.	Hittite
Hos.	*Hosea*
Hur.	Hurrian
IAA	Israel Antiquities Authority
ibid.	*ibidem*, in the same place (as the one immediately preceding)
IDA(M)	Israel Department of Antiquities (and Museums)
i.e.	*id est*, that is

IEJ	*Israel Exploration Journal*	*Meg.*	*Megillah*	*SEG*	*Supplementum Epigraphicum Graecum*
IES	Israel Exploration Society	mi.	miles	ser.	series
IFAPO	Institut Français d'Archéologie du Proche-Orient	*Mk.*	*Mark*	sg.	singular
Is.	*Isaiah*	mm	millimeter	*Sg.*	*Song of Songs*
IsMEO	Istituto Italiano per il Medio ed Estremo Oriente	mod.	modern	*Shab.*	*Shabbath*
Jb.	*Job*	Mt.	Mount	s.J.	Societas Jesu, Society of Jesus (Jesuits)
Jer.	*Jeremiah*	*Mt.*	*Matthew*		
Jgs.	*Judges*	n.	note	*1 Sm.*	*1 Samuel*
Jn.	*John*	NAA	Neutron Activation Analysis	*2 Sm.*	*2 Samuel*
Jon.	*Jonah*	*Nat. Hist.*	Pliny, *Naturalis Historia* (Natural History)	sq	square
Jos.	*Joshua*	n.b.	*nota bene*, note well	St., Sts.	Saint, Saints
JPOS	*Journal of the Palestine Oriental Society*	n.d.	no date	Sum.	Sumerian
JRA	*Journal of Roman Archaeology*	*Nm.*	*Numbers*	supp.	supplement
J.T.	Jerusalem Talmud	no., nos.	number, numbers	Syr.	Syriac
KAI	H. Donner and W. Röllig, *Kanaanäische und aramäische Inschriften*	n.p.	no place	*Ta'an.*	*Ta'anit*
		n.s.	new series	Th.D.	Theologicae Doctor, Doctor of Theology
Kel.	*Kelim*	O.P.	Ordo Praedicatorum, Order of Preachers (Dominicans)	*Ti.*	*Titus*
Ket.	*Ketubbot*	p., pp.	page, pages	Tk.	Turkish
kg	kilogram	para.	paragraph	*1 Tm.*	*1 Timothy*
1 Kgs.	*1 Kings*	PEF	Palestine Exploration Fund	*2 Tm.*	*2 Timothy*
2 Kgs.	*2 Kings*	Pers.	Persian	trans.	translated by
km	kilometers	Ph.D.	Philosophiae Doctor, Doctor of Philosophy	Ugar.	Ugaritic
KTU	M. Dietrich and O. Lorentz, *Die keilalphabetischen Texte aus Ugarit*	*Phil.*	*Philippians*	v.	verse
		pl.	plate; plural	viz.	*videlicet*, namely
l	liter	PN	Pottery Neolithic	vol., vols.	volume, volumes
l., ll.	line, lines	ppm	parts per million	vs.	versus
Lat.	Latin	PPN	Pre-Pottery Neolithic	*Yad.*	*Yadayim*
lb.	pounds	*Prv.*	*Proverbs*	*ZDPV*	*Zeitschrift des Deutschen Palästina-Vereins*
LB	Late Bronze	*Ps.*	*Psalms*		
lit.	literally	pt., pts.	part, parts	*Zec.*	*Zechariah*
Lk.	*Luke*	*1 Pt.*	*1 Peter*	*	hypothetical; in bibliographic citations, English language pages in Hebrew journals
LM	Late Minoan	*2 Pt.*	*2 Peter*		
Lv.	*Leviticus*	r.	reigned, ruled	?	uncertain; possibly; perhaps
m	meters	*RCEA*	*Répertoire chronologique d'epigraphie arabe*	°	degrees
M.A.	Master of Arts	*Rev.*	*Revelations*	′	minutes; feet
masc.	masculine	rev.	revised	″	seconds; inches
Mal.	*Malachi*	*Ru.*	*Ruth*	+	plus
MB	Middle Bronze	SBF	Studium Biblicum Franciscanum	−	minus
Mc.	*Maccabees*			±	plus or minus
M.Div.	Master of Divinity	SBL	Society of Biblical Literature	=	equals; is equivalent to
				×	by
				→	yields

A

'ABBASID CALIPHATE. As the result of a revolution that culminated in 750 CE in the defeat of the last Umayyad caliph, Marwan ibn Muhammad, on the River Zab in northern Iraq, the 'Abbasid family came to power. This real revolution stemmed from the profound social stresses of the Umayyad period: the imposition of new cultural values on the Middle East, the privileged position of Arab Muslims over others, the perceived irreligious lifestyle of the Umayyads, exemplified by their desert castles, and finally the constant in-fighting of the Arab tribes. Like all revolutions, the constitution of the new state did not initially differ much from the old but was rather affected by environmental factors. Although the 'Abbasid family had lived at Humeima in Jordan, the revolutionary army, the Khurasaniyah, was recruited on the frontier in eastern Iran, and the 'Abbasids found their support in the former territories of the Sasanian empire, notably in Iraq.

The 'Abbasids first settled near Kufah, but in 762 the second 'Abbasid caliph, al-Mansur, founded a new capital, Baghdad, only 30 km (19 mi.) from the Sasanian capital of Ctesiphon. The centralized administrative traditions of the late Sasanian Empire were taken as a model for an imperial state, a phase which in its original form lasted for half a century until the death of Harun al-Rashid in 809. [*See* Sasanians.] The subsequent civil war, including the siege of Baghdad in 811–813, destroyed much of the state's infrastructure and led to the increasing recruitment of peoples from the eastern frontier in the army, notably Central Asian Iranians and Turks. Reliance on the Turks led to alienation of the state from the Muslim population; in particular disturbances between the Turks and the Baghdadis led to the foundation of a new capital, Samarra, by al-Mu'tasim in 836. In spite of the success of al-Mu'tasim himself in reforming the state, the isolation of the caliphs with their army in Samarra exposed the ruler to control by the soldiery, culminating in a decade of troubles in the 860s, and gravely weakened the prestige of the state. Already existing tendencies were given free rein: the increasingly successful attempts by the provinces to gain independence, a separation of the religious institution of Islam from the control of the caliph, and the evolution of a commercial economy that was uncontrolled by the state.

Although the state's prestige was reestablished under the regent al-Muwaffaq (d. 891) and his son al-Mu'tadid, who settled again at Baghdad in 892, the disastrous reign of al-Muqtadir (d. 932) led to a complete loss of power by the regime from 937 and a takeover of Baghdad by an Iranian Shi'i tribal dynasty, the Buyids, in 945. The 'Abbasids remained virtual prisoners in their palaces even after the Sunni reconquest by the Seljuks in 1055. Nevertheless, the idea of a unified Islamic world did not disappear, and the 'Abbasids gave legitimacy to independent dynasts. Notably under al-Muqtafi (1136–1160) and al-Nasir li-Din Allah (1180–1225), an independent 'Abbasid state reemerged in central Iraq, only to be extinguished finally by the Mongols under Hülegü in 1258. Even subsequently, the Mamluks installed an 'Abbasid prince as caliph in the Cairo Citadel, a line that continued until the Ottoman conquest in 1517.

The 'Abbasids never controlled the extensive territories lightly governed by the Umayyads; the 'Abbasid empire extended from Tunisia to Samarkand. The problem of control over far distant provinces was solved at the beginning of the ninth century by hereditary dynasties of autonomous governors: the Aghlabids in Tunisia and the Tahirids in Khurasan (eastern Iran), who continued to contribute to the central treasury. In the era of Samarra, however, genuinely independent rulers, such as the Saffarids of Sistan, ceased to pay, and much confusion was caused by the slave revolt of the Zanj in the marshes of southern Iraq for fifteen years until 883. Removal of Arabs from the pay registers of the army (c. 833) equally alienated the tribes, and control over the Arabian Peninsula was increasingly lost, apart from the Holy Cities of Mecca and Medina.

The economic basis of the 'Abbasid state was the land tax on agriculture, initially calculated in cash, and later as a proportion of the crop. By far the largest sums were contributed by Iraq, but Egypt and western Iran were also significant. The importance of Iraq stemmed from the high degree of development of irrigation under the Sasanians, which has been well illustrated by the area surveys of Robert McC. Adams in the Diyala region (Adams, 1965), and south central Iraq (Adams, 1981). [*See* Diyala.] Although it is difficult to date the construction of canals, the full elaboration of the system seems to date to the later Sasanian period in the sixth

1

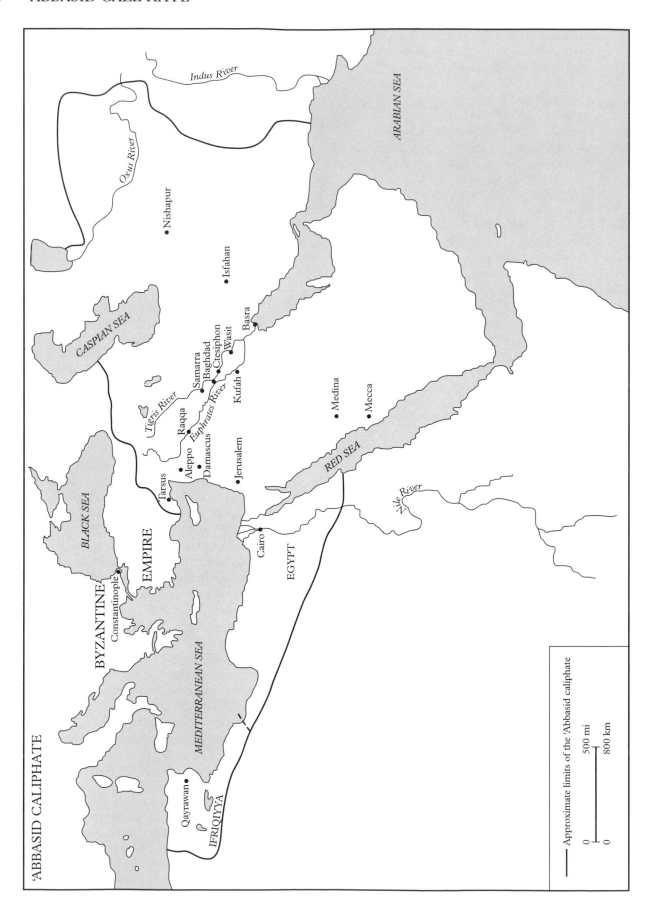

'ABBASID CALIPHATE

Indus River

Oxus River

ARABIAN SEA

• Nishapur

• Isfahan

CASPIAN SEA

Basra

Tigris River

Samarra
Baghdad Ctesiphon
Wasit

Medina •   • Mecca

Raqqa *Euphrates River* Kufah •

BLACK SEA

Aleppo
Damascus •
Tarsus •   • Jerusalem

RED SEA

Nile River

BYZANTINE
EMPIRE
Constantinople •

Cairo •

EGYPT

MEDITERRANEAN SEA

Qayrawan •

IFRIQIYYA

———— Approximate limits of the 'Abbasid caliphate

0   500 mi
0   800 km

century, probably under the centralizing monarch Khusrau Anushirvan (531–578). Particularly the northern extension of the Nahrawan canal east of Baghdad (Ar., al-Qatul al-Kisrawi) with its offtakes from the Tigris River in the region of Samarra increased the availability of irrigation water considerably. The early 'Abbasids, al-Rashid and al-Ma'mun (813–833), took care to add to the system. However, this achievement carried within it the seeds of its own decay: according to Adams, the sharp increase in the availability of water leads to rapid salinization and, after a certain length of time, decline in land productivity (Adams, 1981, p. 20). Even if this were not so, the long and massive Sasanian irrigation canals of Iraq—the Nahrawan canal is 225 km (139.5 mi.) long—required a large investment to excavate, and a centralized administration to maintain, a degree of organization that did not exist before the sixth century or after the ninth century. It was impossible, then, later to replace canals ruined by warfare, sedimentation or, more importantly, the regrettably frequent tendency of the Tigris and the Euphrates to change their courses. According to both archaeological surveys and historical sources, there was a severe retrenchment in the cultivated area of Iraq from the mid-tenth century onward. Although the decline of Iraq, one of the most striking phenomena of the economic history of Islam, remains a puzzle, it may be that the explanation lies in this area.

There is no doubt that the fortunes of the 'Abbasid state paralleled the economic fortunes of Iraqi agriculture. In its first century the 'Abbasid caliphate was a great world power. The system was established by al-Mansur (754–775), based upon the bureaucracy inherited from the Sasanians and an aristocracy of the Khurasani Arabs. Monumental architecture played a significant role. The new capital of Baghdad (founded 762–766) was dominated by the Round City, the circular fortified palace and administrative quarter, which is the first fully developed example of an Islamic royal city (Northedge, 1994). The 'Abbasid army, the Khurasaniyah, were settled in a cantonment in al-Harbiyah, and the crown prince, al-Mahdi, had his own establishment on the east bank in Rusafa. The markets were centered around a pre-Islamic settlement at al-Karkh. Although we have no archaeological trace of early Baghdad, the plan was very influential, and the same general pattern can be seen repeated over the following century. After the abandoned construction of an octagonal city on the pattern of the Round City at Qadisiyah in 796, Harun al-Rashid (786–809) built a palace quarter at Raqqa in Syria, outside the walls of a horseshoe-plan city built by al-Mansur in 772 apparently as a garrison center. [See Raqqa, ar-.]

The construction of caliphal cities reached its greatest extent at Samarra (836–892), where 57 sq km (22 sq. mi.) of construction in pisé, mud brick and baked brick in a steppe zone on the bank of the Tigris included two caliphal establishments, Surra Man Ra'a and al-Mutawakkiliyah, six major military cantonments and a moderate-sized town. The two main military cantonments (Ar., qati'a), of the Turks at al-Karkh, and the Central Asian Iranians at al-Matira, were placed apart from Surra Man Ra'a, at a distance of 2 farsakhs each (c. 10 km [6 mi.]), although Matira was later engulfed by the development of the city, and there were further cantonments in the city itself. The caliphal establishments and military cantonments consisted of a main palace, minor palaces, a grand avenue, and a grid of streets with houses. Significant differences from Roman practices in military settlement lay in the freedom of 'Abbasid troops to marry, personal allegiance to generals, and ethnic division of units. The imperial character of the city is emphasized by the lack of fortifications and the monumental provision for sports—race courses and polo grounds. According to the extravagant textual descriptions, the tenth-century palace complex in Baghdad (Dar al-Khilafah) was similar, but the economic collapse of the caliphate suggests a reality of more limited dimensions.

The planning of the palaces revolved around the four iwan plan—according to E. J. Keall (1974) the iwan is first found as an open-fronted vaulted hall in Parthian Mesopotamia. The original pattern of four iwans facing onto a courtyard gave way to a central dome chamber with four iwans opening to the exterior. Samarra and Raqqa are typically Mesopotamian, vast complexes of rooms and courtyards, with provision at Samarra for sunken basins to avoid the heat of summer. In Iraq and Iran the Sasanian tradition of carved stucco revetments was further developed with new inspiration in the designs, suggested to be of Indian, Central Asian, and Byzantine origin—a sign of wider cultural horizons.

This dynastic concentration on the capital diverts our attention from the growing islamization of the provinces; apart from Syria, many of the congregational mosques in cities were first built in the ninth century, such as at Isfahan. The pattern was established of a courtyard mosque with a hypostyle or basilical prayer hall, and a minaret opposite to the mihrab (the niche indicating the direction of Mecca), a plan built differently according to local architectural traditions. At Kairouan (Qayrawan) in Tunisia the mosque has a square brick minaret, horseshoe arches, and square external buttresses; at Samarra the minaret is helicoidal, apparently after the pattern of Assyrian ziggurats, the buttresses semicircular, and the arches pointed.

The defenses of the Byzantine frontier in southeastern Anatolia, stretching from Tarsus to Malatya, and Erzurum, were based on series of fortified cities, in which the frontier troops were settled. It was only at the end of the eighth century and the beginning of the ninth that the Roman concept of the frontier fort was introduced in the ribats of the Tunisian coast and Central Asia. With the collapse of the secular authority of the 'Abbasid Caliphate, the ribats were manned by volunteers for religious reasons, and in the tenth century they developed into religious centers, or caravanserais, if located on a main route.

During the early part of the 'Abbasid period, especially in the reigns of al-Mahdi and Harun al-Rashid, the transdesert pilgrim road from Baghdad and Kufah to Mecca was built up in a monumental form, known today as Darb Zubaydah [See Darb Zubaydah.] The *hajj* was sometimes led by the caliph and nearly always by a leading man of state. Long stretches of the road were cleared of boulders, and in places the road was walled and drainage ditches were dug. The road stations in Iraq and Saudi Arabia have been surveyed, and the station at ar-Rabadha has been excavated. The arrangements seem to have fallen into decay in the tenth century.

Apart from state activity, a thriving commercial economy begins to be visible in the archaeological evidence. In part this was related to the growth of maritime trade with the Far East. Although the Sasanians had taken care to control Indian Ocean trade, a substantial increase in quantity occurred about 800, based on Basra and the Gulf. Excavations at Siraf on the Iranian coast recorded the first appearance of Chinese stoneware and, later, porcelain, the first of a long line of Chinese ceramic imports that came to dominate the Middle East. However, distribution patterns show that in fact Chinese pottery did not penetrate in quantity far from the ports or river transport to the capital cities of Iraq. Ceramics are also only the most visible element of trade in the archaeological record; spices and teakwood were also important. From the tenth century onward, after the sack of Basra by the Qaramita, the trade moved elsewhere, notably the Red Sea and Egypt.

The consequences of this trade were fundamental. On the simplest level, it is remarkable that the introduction of polychrome-glaze pottery in Iraq, and thus in Islam, closely postdates the first large-scale Chinese imports. Although some copying of Chinese white stoneware and splash-lead glazes took place, original Islamic techniques played a more important role—cobalt-blue painting, luster painting, and glazed-relief molded wares. The evidence appears to show that the idea of polychromy spread immediately to Syria, Egypt, and Iran, and polychrome-glaze pottery quickly became the staple of fine ceramics. The stimulation to the pottery industry was not limited to glazed wares: Brittle-Ware cooking pots from North Syria, and unglazed barbotine and molded vessels were also traded widely.

However, as demonstrated for later periods by K. N. Chaudhuri (1985), although there was a risk of shipwreck, even a single successful eastern voyage could lead to enormous profits. The availability of large quantities of investment capital among Basran and other merchants is the best explanation of phenomena in the historical sources and the archaeological record. Gangs of imported East African slaves (Zanj) put to clearing saline land for agricultural estates around Basra, revolted, but particularly there was economic development in the Arabian Peninsula. Large-scale development of copper mining in Oman during the ninth century has been demonstrated, and the Saudi Arabian archaeological survey has found mining sites east of Medina for gold and chlorite-schist for cooking pots, lamps, and incense burners. Produced around Sa'dah in Yemen even today, chlorite-schist is found in most archaeological deposits in the Fertile Crescent between the mid-eighth and ninth centuries, and the central Arabian production represents an expansion. Investment in Arabia may have been sentimental, but peaceful conditions there opened up possibilities that did not exist later.

At any rate the political collapse of the 'Abbasid regime in the second quarter of the tenth century brought an end to promising developments. Political and economic power (including also the centers of production, most visibly of ceramics) was subsequently in Egypt (the Fatimids from 969) and Iran–Central Asia (the Buyids, Samanids and Seljuks). The agriculture of these regions depends on short-distance, easily maintained irrigation systems, which could survive independently of the low level of organization of a medieval state.

[See also Arabian Peninsula, *article on* Arabian Peninsula in Islamic Times; Baghdad; Fatimid Dynasty; Mesopotamia, *article on* Mesopotamia in the Islamic Period; Samarra, *article on* Islamic Period; *and* Umayyad Caliphate.]

BIBLIOGRAPHY

Adams, Robert McC. *Land behind Baghdad: A History of Settlement on the Diyala Plains.* Chicago, 1965.

Adams, Robert McC. *Heartland of Cities: Surveys of Ancient Settlement and Land use on the Central Floodplain of the Euphrates.* Chicago, 1981.

Chaudhuri, K. N. *Trade and Civilisation in the Indian Ocean: An Economic History from the Rise of Islam to 1750.* Cambridge, 1985.

Costa, Paolo M., and T. J. Wilkinson. "The Hinterland of Sohar." *Journal of Oman Studies* 9 (1987).

Creswell, K. A. C. *Early Muslim Architecture,* vol. 2, *Umayyads, Early 'Abbasids, and Tulunids.* Oxford, 1940.

De Jesus, P. S., et al. "Preliminary Report of the Ancient Mining Survey, 1981 (1401)." *Atlal* 6 (1981): 63–96.

Keall, E. J. "Some Thoughts on the Early Eyvar." In *Near Eastern Numismatics: Iconography, Epigraphy, and History,* edited by D. K. Kouymjian, pp. 122–136. Beirut, 1974.

Kennedy, Hugh. *The Early 'Abbasid Caliphate: A Political History.* London, 1981.

Kennedy, Hugh. *The Prophet and the Age of the Caliphates: The Islamic Near East from the Sixth to the Eleventh Century.* London, 1986.

Kervran, Monik. "Les niveaux islamiques du secteur oriental du tépé de l'Apadana." *Cahiers de la Délégation Archéologique Française en Iran* 7 (1977): 75–162.

Lassner, Jacob. "The Caliph's Personal Domain: The City Plan of Baghdad Reexamined." In *The Islamic City,* edited by Albert Hourani and S. M. Stern, pp. 103–118. Oxford, 1970.

Lassner, Jacob. *The Topography of Baghdad in the Early Middle Ages: Text and Studies.* Detroit, 1970.

Morony, Michael. "Continuity and Change in the Administrative Geography of Late Sasanian and Early Islamic al-'Irāq." *Iran* 20 (1982): 1–49.

Popovic, Alexandre. *La révolte des esclaves en Iraq au IIIe/IXe siècle.* Paris, 1976.

Rashid, Saʿad al-. *Darb Zubaydah: The Pilgrim Road from Kufa to Makkah.* Riyadh, 1980.

Rashid, Saʿad al-. *Al-Rabadhah: A Portrait of Early Islamic Civilisation in Saudi Arabia.* London, 1986.

Samarrai, Husam Q. *Agriculture in Iraq during the Third Century A. H.* Beirut, 1972.

Sarre, Friedrich P. T. *Ausgrabungen von Samarra*, vol. 2, *Die Keramik von Samarra.* Berlin, 1925.

Waines, David. "The Third-Century Internal Crisis of the ʿAbbasids." *Journal of the Economic and Social History of the Orient* 20 (1977): 282–306.

Watson, Andrew M. *Agricultural Innovation in the Early Islamic World: The Diffusion of Crops and Farming Techniques, 700–1100.* Cambridge, 1983.

Whitehouse, David. "Sirāf: A Medieval Port on the Persian Gulf." *World Archaeology* 2 (1970): 141–158.

ALASTAIR NORTHEDGE

ABEL, FÉLIX-MARIE

ABEL, FÉLIX-MARIE (1878–1953), professor of history and geography at the École Biblique et Archéologique Française in Jerusalem from 1905 to 1953. Abel went to Jerusalem as a novice in the Dominician Order in 1900. Even as a student he participated in the scientific activity of the École Biblique, where he was to spend his entire career.

From his debut in the pages of the *Revue Biblique* in 1903, Abel systematically published dozens of detailed studies of different areas in the regions, from the Orontes River to the Sinai Desert and from Cyprus to Jordan. He eventually synthesized in his two-volume *Géographie de la Palestine* (Paris, 1933–1938), which deals in exemplary detail with physical, historical, and political geography from earliest times to the Byzantine period. The ten maps he prepared have served as the prime, but often unacknowledged, source of much subsequent topographical identification.

Abel's mastery of the whole range of Greek sources is displayed in his *Grammaire du Grec biblique suivie d'un choix de Papyrus* (Paris, 1927), his major commentary on *1* and *2 Maccabees* (1949), and his two-volume *Histoire de la Palestine depuis la conquête d'Alexandre jusqu'à l'invasion arabe* (Paris, 1952). He had an uncanny ability to identify the key questions in texts, and the vast majority of his proposed answers—for example, his location of Pilate's praetorium in Herod the Great's palace, rather than at the Antonia fortress—have stood the test of time.

Inevitably L.-H. Vincent, also of the École Biblique, called on him to contribute the documentary evidence to the magisterial studies of Bethlehem, Hebron, Jerusalem, and Emmaus on which they collaborated (Paris, 1914, 1923, 1926, 1932, respectively). His extraordinary erudition facilitated the ease with which he tracked down the most esoteric data, even for individual buildings. It is his insights rather than Vincent's conclusions that give these volumes their permanent value.

[*See also* École Biblique et Archéologique Française; *and the biography of Vincent.*]

BIBLIOGRAPHY

Abel, Félix-Marie. *Grammaire du Grec biblique suivie d'un choix de Papyrus.* Paris, 1927.

Abel, Félix-Marie. *Géographie de la Palestine.* 2 vols. Paris, 1933–1938.

Abel, Félix-Marie. *Les livres des Maccabées.* Paris, 1949.

Abel, Félix-Marie. *Histoire de la Palestine depuis la conquête d'Alexandre jusqu'à l'invasion arabe.* Paris, 1952.

Vincent, L.-H., and Félix-Marie Abel. *Bethléem, le sanctuaire de la nativité.* Paris, 1914.

Vincent, L.-H., and Félix-Marie Abel. *Hébron: Le Haram el-Khalîl, sépulture des patriarches.* Paris, 1923.

Vincent, L.-H., and Félix-Marie Abel. *Jérusalem: Recherches de topographie, d'archéologie et d'histoire*, vol. 2, *Jérusalem nouvelle.* Paris, 1926.

Vincent, L.-H., and Félix-Marie Abel. *Emmaüs, sa basilique et son histoire.* Paris, 1932.

JEROME MURPHY-O'CONNOR, O.P.

ABILA

ABILA, city of the Decapolis, located about 15 km (9 mi.) north–northeast of Irbid in northern Jordan. Abila has an occupational history that extends from the fourth millennium to 1500 CE. It is identified in numerous ancient sources: Polybius (second century BCE) mentions that Antiochus III (218 BCE) conquered Abila along with Pella and Gadara/Umm Qeis (*Historiae* 5.69–70). It is later conquered by Alexander Jannaeus (first century BCE), as reported by Georgios Synkellos (*Chronographia*, 294 D–295 A). An inscription (133/144 CE) at Tayibeh, northeast of Palmyra, Syria, speaks of an *agathangelos Abilenos tēs Dekapoleōs* ("good messenger, or well-heralded Abila of the Decapolis;" *CIG* 4501 or LeBas-Waddington, *Inscriptiones III*, 2, no. 2631 = *OGIS* 631). In the second century CE, Ptolemy (*Geography* 5.14) identifies this Abila separately from the Abila of Lysanias just north of Damascus, Syria. Hierokles (sixth century CE) in *Synekdemos* (pp. 720–721) lists this Abila as part of the Provincia Secunda, along with the nearby sites of Scythopolis, Sella (Pella), Gadara, and Capitolias. Jerome identifies an Abila 12 Roman miles from Gadara (Carl Ritter, *Erdkunde*, Berlin, 1832–1858, vol. 15, p. 1060), the same city (Abel) Eusebius had earlier located 12 Roman miles east of Gadara (*Onomasticon*, 32.16; Spijkerman, 1978, pp. 48–49, n. 5; cf. Johann L. Burckhardt, *Travels in Syria and the Holy Land*, rpt. New York, 1983, vol. 1, p. 537, note to p. 425). In 1888 Gottlieb Schumacher (1889, pp. 18, 21) found that the nationals at this site still called the north tell Tell Abil. The 1984 excavation on Tell Abila produced an inscription in Greek with the name cut in the second line; in the fourth line Emma[tha] (Ḥammath-Gader), a site 18 km (11 mi.) west of Abila (Michael Avi-Yonah, *The Holy Land*, Grand Rapids, Mich., 1977, pp. 166, 170) is mentioned, further verifying that this is Abila of the Decapolis. In the Bronze and Iron Ages the site's name may have carried the prefixed noun, ʾābēl (Heb., "meadow"; Ar., "green"). It is similar to the Semitic noun used in several other sites in the Jordan River system: Abel Beth-Maacah (*2 Kgs.* 15:29); Abel

Meholah (*Jgs.* 7:22); Abel Shittim (*Nm.* 33:49); and Abel Keramim (*Jgs.* 11:33). *Matthew* 4:25 and *Mark* 5:20 and 7:31 mention the Decapolis but without specifying Abila or any other individual city.

In the modern period, in 1806, Ulrich Jasper Seetzen (*Reisen durch Syrien*, ed. Fr. Kruse, Berlin, 1854–1859, vol. 1, p. 371, vol. 4, pp. 190–191) rediscovered Abila. He was followed by Schumacher (see above) who described the ruins and drew a map of the site, today called Quailibah. In 1978 W. Harold Mare of Covenant Theological Seminary, St. Louis, revisited the site; he began excavating there in 1980, with subsequent seasons in 1982, 1984, 1986, 1988, 1990, 1992, 1994, and 1995.

Abila of the Decapolis is about one mile north–south and a half-mile east–west in area. The site consists of Tell Abila to the north and Tell Umm el-ʿAmad to the south. It is protected by deep wadis on the north, east, and south and by a saddle depression between the two tells. The site is surrounded by rich farmlands and has a generous water supply. Ancient building remains are visible over the entire site. Its occupational history begins in the Neolithic period and goes through the Early Bronze, Middle Bronze, Late Bronze, and Iron Ages and the Hellenistic period, concentrated particularly on the acropolis of Tell Abila. Occupation in the Roman, Byzantine, and Islamic periods (especially Umayyad and ʿAbbasid, a bit of Fatimid, and some Ayyubid/Mamluk) is evident throughout the site. Occasional Ottoman sherds are also found, indicating more recent Turkish hegemony.

Excavations (1982–1990) on the acropolis of Tell Abila uncovered a large sixth-century triapsidal Christian basilica (19 × 34.5 m) in area A. It shows evidence of two rows of twelve columns dividing the nave from the side aisles. The nave is paved with an opus sectile floor and the atrium in the west with mosaics. The church was built on the foundations of an earlier possibly fourth–fifth-century Christian basilica or Greco-Roman temple. Just to the northeast of the basilica, in deep trenches (area AA), pottery and walls point to Roman, Hellenistic, and Iron and Bronze Age occupations. EB and MB pottery appeared extensively in area AA.

Excavation on Tell Umm el-ʿAmad revealed a seventh-century triapsidal Christian basilica (20 × 41 m), with two rows of twelve columns each. It, too, was paved with an opus sectile floor and had mosaics in its auxiliary rooms, colonnaded porch, and atrium. The excavated remains of this basilica were restored in 1988 (see figure 1).

In the terraced depression between the two tells a large civic center existed in the Roman and Byzantine periods. It included what seems to have been a theater built into the northeast slope of Umm el-ʿAmad. Most of the theater's remains were reused both recently and in antiquity. Schumacher (1889, p. 30) saw some of the seats in 1888. In the Umayyad period a large building (palace?) was constructed within the theater's cavea. Part of the cavea was used in the ʿAbbasid and Ayyubid/Mamluk periods. An extended Byzantine basalt street existed just in front (north) of the Islamic building. Its eastern segment at least lay over an earlier lime-

ABILA. Figure 1. *Restored seventh-century basilica.* The basilica, partially restored in 1988, is located on Umm el-ʿAmad, the southern tell at Abila. (Courtesy W. H. Mare)

stone street or plaza with an entranceway. North of this plaza excavation was begun in 1990 in what seems to have been a bath/nymphaeum complex; a channel cut into a vault at the east end of the complex indicates that water was brought there from springs ('Ain Quailibah at the southern foot of Umm el-'Amad and Khuraybah, farther south) through an intricate system of underground aqueducts. These aqueducts, which have been excavated, studied, and mapped, were used to bring water to the site to provide for the needs of industry, civic installations, and private citizens. In the civic center farther to the northeast, near the Roman bridge, excavation was begun in 1990, and has continued, on another large Christian basilica, cruciform in design (32 m × 29.25 m); at the extremities of the arms of the central apse, large basalt piers with Ionic capitals were found, as well as another north row and also a south row of basalt columns.

Extensive burial sites were cut into the wadis. Between 1982 and 1994, eighty-five burial sites (mostly tombs, but some graves) were excavated. The burials date mainly from the Late Hellenistic, Roman, and Byzantine periods, but a few Iron Age and MB/LB period tombs were also excavated. The grave goods, the embellishment of the tombs and their architectural style, food offerings, and religious iconography indicate three levels of society: the wealthy, the middle class, and the poor.

Excavation thus far of the Iron and Bronze Age levels has produced evidence of a fairly well-developed society, with a variety of pottery types and buildings with small rooms. Excavation of the Roman and Byzantine levels points to a considerably well-developed city of seven thousand–eight thousand inhabitants, with a strong agricultural base, thriving commercial activity, and a strong emphasis on cultural and religious activities.

BIBLIOGRAPHY

Corpus Inscriptionem Graecarum (CIG). 5 vols., 13 faces. Berlin, 1828–1877, no. 450.
Dittenberger, W. Orientis Graecae Inscriptiones Selectae (OGIS). Leipzig, 1903–1905.
Le Bas, Philippe, and William Henry Waddington. Inscriptiones grecques et latines recueilles en Asie Mineure. Hildesheim and New York, 1972. III, 2, no. 2631.
Mare, W. Harold, et al. Preliminary Reports. Near East Archaeological Society Bulletin 17 (1980): 5–25; 21 (1983): 5–68; 22 (1983): 5–64; 24 (1985): 7–108; 25 (1985): 35–90; 26 (1985): 5–70; 27 (1985): 25–60; 28 (1987): 35–76; 29 (1987): 31–88; 30 (1987): 27–106; 31 (1988): 19–66; 32–33 (1988): 2–64; 34 (1991): 2–41; 35 (1991): 2–41.
Mare, W. Harold, et al. "The Decapolis Survey Project: Abila 1980." Annual of the Department of Antiquities of Jordan 26 (1982): 37–65.
Mare, W. Harold, et al. "The 1982 Season at Abila of the Decapolis." Annual of the Department of Antiquities of Jordan 28 (1984): 39–54.
Mare, W. Harold, et al. "The 1984 Season at Abila of the Decapolis." Annual of the Department of Antiquities of Jordan 29 (1985): 221–237.
Mare, W. Harold, "Quwailiba: Abila of the Decapolis." Archiv für Orientforschung 33 (1986): 206–209.
Mare, W. Harold, et al. "The 1986 Season at Abila of the Decapolis." Annual of the Department of Antiquities of Jordan 31 (1987): 205–219.
Mare, W. Harold, "Quweilbeh (Abila)." In Archaeology of Jordan, vol. 2, Field Reports, edited by Denyse Homès-Fredericq and J. Basil Hennessy, pp. 472–486. Louvain, 1989.
Mare, W. Harold, "The 1988 Season of Excavation at Abila of the Decapolis." Annual of the Department of Antiquities of Jordan 35 (1991): 203–220.
Mare, W. Harold, "Abila." In The New Encyclopedia of Archaeological Excavations in the Holy Land, vol. 1, pp. 1–3. Jerusalem and New York, 1993.
Schumacher, Gottlieb. Abila of the Decapolis. London, 1889.
Smith, Robert Houston, and Leslie P. Day. Final Report on the College of Wooster Excavations in Area IX, the Civic Complex, 1979–1985. Pella of the Decapolis, vol. 2. Wooster, Ohio, 1989.
Spijkerman, Augusto. The Coins of the Decapolis and Provincia Arabia. Jerusalem, 1978.

W. HAROLD MARE

ABU ḤAMID, TELL, site located in the Jordan Valley, at 240 m below sea level, on Lisan marl deposits between two small wadis (32°19′ N, 35°33′ E). It originally covered an area of 1,400 m east–west and 400 m north–south. Since 1975 and the development of modern agriculture, it has suffered from intensive leveling, and most of the site has disappeared.

The site was first surveyed in 1975 (Ibrahim, Sauer, and Yassine, 1975), and revisited in 1982 by Zeidan Kafafi (Kafafi, 1982). In 1984 an international research project was initiated by the Institute of Archaeology and Anthropology of Yarmouk University, Jordan; the Institut Français d'Archéologie du Proche Orient (IFAPO, Amman); and the Centre National de la Recherche Scientifique, with the cooperation of the Department of Antiquities of Jordan. Research was focused on the Jordan Valley and the northern Jordanian plateau in the seventh–fifth millennia BP. The first stage of the project was the excavation of Abu Ḥamid. The five seasons carried out from 1986 to 1992 provided a firm stratigraphic and chronological sequence: 350–2,000 sq m were exposed, and long north–south and east–west sections were established. The stratigraphic sequence and the chronology of the occupation of the site can now be combined with the sequence at Munhata (30 km, or 19 mi., to the north, on the west bank of the Jordan River) to provide a clear picture of the history of the middle Jordan Valley region. [See Munhata; Jordan Valley.]

At Abu Ḥamid no significant hiatus is presented in the stratigraphic sequence; however, small gaps were observed that were caused by occasional abandonment or by the use of the site by seasonal groups (Dollfus and Kafafi, 1993). At the beginning of the occupation, in the early seventh millennium BP, the group lived in circular or oval shelters partially dug into the soil (up to 1.50 m deep, 1.80–3 m in diameter); some are lined with roughly made bricks along the sides. The inhabitants used various kinds of pits and gypsum basins to store and process food. Their handmade pottery includes a small percentage of painted ware (bowls with interior and/or exterior decoration, such as chevrons or diagonal lines; jars with sun motifs and criss-crossed lines). In terms of subsistence, the inhabitants were beyond merely exploiting natural resources; they employed strategies to exploit their livestock and grew wheat, barley, lentils, and peas. These levels are certainly postclassical Yarmukian, as defined at Shaʿar ha-Golan by Moshe Stekelis; at Munḥata 2b by Jean Perrot, Avi Gopher, and Yosef Garfinkel; at Abu Thawwab; at ʿAin Rahub; and at Wadi Shuʿeib by Kafafi (1993). [See Shaʿar ha-Golan; Shuʿeib, Wadi.] In some strata ashy floors, pits, and hearths were observed, but no dwelling remains.

During the next occupation, which, according to the stratigraphy and the associated cultural remains could be dated to the second part of the seventh millennium BP, the houses were built with well-made plano-convex mud bricks and most are pluricellular. Their rooms are rectangular and, in some instances, their interior walls were plastered with gypsum. At least one structure had a wall painting, of which some fragments were uncovered. Its design is linear, broad, straight lines in yellow and red, with a series of narrower vertical and curved lines in red. [See Wall Paintings.]

The occupants either heated their houses or cooked inside (cf. some small oval pits with ashes), but most domestic activities took place outside, as suggested by the many gypsum plastered basins, oval fire pits, and hearths found in one of the dwelling complexes. In that same complex, the large rectangular living room is clearly separated from a storage building comprised of two small rectangular rooms and a brick platform.

The ceramic evidence shows new techniques, especially in decoration: incisions, impressions, deep punctures, combing and such plastic decoration as incised or finger-impressed bands in relief; an applied snake decoration appears for the first time. Painted sherds as well as some sherds of extremely finely made dark- and red-faced burnished ware were found. Shapes that played an important role in the following periods, such as churns and pedestal vessels, make their debut here. From a chronological point of view, these levels undoubtedly pertain to the Wadi Rabah chronological horizon (cf. Wadi Rabah, Munḥata 2a, Hazoreaʿ). Differences do exist, for at Abu Ḥamid there is an absence of carinated vessels and bow rims.

In the early sixth millennium BP, the village compound was comprised of a series of houses. Most of them were originally unicellular, but during their occupation partitions were made in some; in others, small rooms were added. The houses differ in building technique. Some are made completely of mud bricks, while others have walls with stone bases. As at the beginning of the occupation, the group raised animals: sheep, goats, pigs, and cattle. [See Sheep and Goats; Pigs; Cattle and Oxen.] Its material culture represents a regional facies—northern Middle Jordan Valley, Upper Jordan Valley, Djaulan, Irbid plateau—of the Ghassu-

ABU ḤAMID, TELL. *Rectangular living room from a late fifth-millennium dwelling.* (Courtesy Z. Kafafi)

lian/Beersheba culture, evident in aspects of its pottery and artifacts (large storage jars, flint perforated disks, "pillar mortars"). As the violin figurines and large zoomorphological vessel (bull) recovered at Tel Abu Ḥamid suggest, the group certainly had links with others living in the south (Negev); moreover there also were ties with the inhabitants of the Wadi ʿArabah, indicated by the copper used in some pins from Wadi Feinan copper ores.

[See also Institut Français d'Archéologie du Proche Orient.]

BIBLIOGRAPHY

Dollfus, Genevieve, and Zeidan A. Kafafi et al. "Preliminary Results of the First Season of the Joint Jordano-French Project at Abu Hamid." *Annual of the Department of Antiquities of Jordan* 30 (1986): 353–380.

Dollfus, Genevieve, and Zeidan A. Kafafi et al. "Abu Hamid, an Early Fourth Millennium Site in the Jordan Valley: Preliminary Results." In *The Prehistory of Jordan: The State of Research in 1986*, edited by A. N. Garrard and Hans Georg Gebel, pp. 567–601. Oxford, 1988.

Dollfus, Genevieve, and Zeidan A. Kafafi. "Recent Research at Abu Hamid." *Annual of the Department of Antiquities of Jordan* 38 (1993): 241–262.

Dollfus, Genevieve, and Zeidan A. Kafafi. "Representatins humaines et animales sur le site d'Abu Hamid (MI–7E–D'ebut 6E Millenaire

BP).” *Studies in the History and Archaeology of Jordan* 5 (1995): 449–457.

Ibrahim, Moawiyah, James A. Sauer, and Khair Yassine. “The East Jordan Valley Survey, 1975.” *Bulletin of the American Schools of Oriental Research*, no. 222 (1976): 41–66.
Kafafi, Zeidan A. “The Neolithic of Jordan (East Bank).” Ph.D. diss., Freie Universität Berlin, 1982.
Kafafi, Zeidan A. “The Yarmoukians in Jordan.” *Paleorient* 19.1 (1993): 101–115.

ZEIDAN A. KAFAFI and GENEVIEVE DOLLFUS

ABU HAWAM, TELL, 10-acre mound on the Mediterranean coast near where the Kishon River empties into the bay of Haifa (map reference 151 × 144). It may be identified with Bronze–Iron Age Achshaph, or biblical Shihor-Libnah (*Jos.* 19:26). Within the Haifa city limits, the site was the focus of several salvage excavations by the British Mandatory Department of Antiquities (1922–1933), and later by the Israeli archaeologists Emanuel Anati, Yaacov Olami, and Moshe Prausnitz (1952, 1963). More modern stratigraphic work was carried out in 1984–1989 by French and Israeli archaeologists. They also investigated the ancient harbor area, which was responsible for Tell Abu Hawam's relative abundance of imported wares and commercial prominence.

The earlier stratigraphic sequence, mostly derived by R. W. Hamilton (1932, 1933), has been much debated in the literature. Jacqueline Balensi (1980) has revised the strata and dates (1985, 1986) based on the latest excavations.

The town was founded at the end of the Middle Bronze Age (stratum VI; sixteenth–fifteenth century BCE), then fortified and equipped with a citadel and sanctuary when it became a major entrepôt during the Late Bronze Age (stratum VA–C; mid-fifteenth–twelfth century). The material belonging to the latter horizon is exceptionally fine and often imported; the older view that Tell Abu Hawam was an Egyptian nineteenth-dynasty naval base has now been largely abandoned (Weinstein, 1980). The destruction that ended stratum VC was probably caused by invading “Sea Peoples” in about 1200 BCE, as at other sites along the Levantine coast. [*See* Philistines, *article on* Early Philistines.] A gap posited by Hamilton at the end of stratum V seems not to have existed.

Stratum IVA–B (eleventh–tenth century) represents an Iron I reoccupation, characterized by reuse of temple 30, three-room houses, and some Phoenician bichrome wares. This stratum ended in a great conflagration.

Stratum IIIA–B (tenth–eighth century) belongs to the Iron II period and seems to represent a mixed Israelite-Phoenician culture, in which some of the earlier cyclopean walls and other installations were reused. The pottery included late Cypro-Phoenician wares; some “Samaria” wares; Cypriot White-Painted III wares, and Greek imports. This stratum either declined, perhaps as a result of the silting

up of the harbor, or was destroyed in the Assyrian invasions in the eighth century BCE. [*See* Phoenicians; Assyrians.]

Stratum IIA–B (fifth–fourth century) produced a Persian-period settlement, with substantial fortifications and considerable imported pottery. Tell Abu Hawam was subsequently largely abandoned. Many of the tombs in the nearby cemetery on the northern slope of Mt. Carmel belong to this Persian horizon.

BIBLIOGRAPHY

Balensi, Jacqueline. “Les fouilles de R. W. Hamilton à Tell Abu Hawam, Niveaux IV et V.” Ph.D. diss., University of Strassburg, 1980.
Balensi, Jacqueline, et al. “Abu Hawam, Tell.” In *The New Encyclopedia of Archaeological Excavations in the Holy Land,* vol. 1, pp. 7–14. Jerusalem and New York, 1993.
Weinstein, James M. “Was Tell Abu Hawam a Nineteenth Dynasty Egyptian Naval Base?” *Bulletin of the American Schools of Oriental Research*, no. 238 (1980): 43–46.

WILLIAM G. DEVER

ABU SALABIKH (modern name, Ar., Tell or Īšān Abū es-Ṣalābīḫ [“father of clinker”]), city of the fourth and third millennia in southern Iraq, located at the center of the Mesopotamian alluvial plain between the Euphrates and Tigris Rivers (32°15′ N, 45°3′ E). The site's modern name comes from the quantities of overfired ceramic slag found on its surface. Settlement distribution and geomorphology suggest that in antiquity the site lay on a principal arm of the Euphrates, flowing from Kish toward Nippur, which lies only some 16 km (about 10 mi.) to the southeast and can be seen from Abu Salabikh on a clear day.

The site's ancient name remains uncertain. Kesh (*kèš*), which was initially proposed, seems likelier to be near Adab, farther east (perhaps at Tell al-Wilayah). At present, Eresh counts as the best candidate, which would be significant in that its patron deity was Nisaba, goddess of reeds and hence of scribal craft.

The mounds on the site are scattered over an area of about 2 × 1 km. None rises more than 5 m above the surrounding plain, but their lower parts are shrouded by 2–3 m of silt that has accumulated since the first settlement here. The earliest occupation is hinted at by a few Late Ubaid painted potsherds from unstratified contexts. Uruk levels are represented on the Southwest (“Uruk”), West, and Northwest Mounds but are not yet identified elsewhere. The Northeast Mound and compounds laid out on the flattened surface of the West Mound date from the beginning of Early Dynastic (ED) I (c. 2900 BC). The occupation of the Main Mound may not predate the later ED I. All that is known of the South Mound is that its surface levels were occupied in ED III. The very low-lying area known as the East Mounds may be Ur III, on the evidence of an unstratified Amar-Suen brick. Dates of abandonment are more difficult to establish because of massive erosion. There is no reason to think that the main part of the Uruk Mound was occupied after the Uruk period, or the West Mound after ED I. The highest buildings surviving on the Main Mound are ED III, but the evidence of potsherds used as packing around drains, in pits and in tip lines outside the city wall proves Akkadian and probably Ur III occupation. There is no artifactual evidence for the second millennium BC or later.

Archaeological notice of the site was first published by Albrecht Goetze and Vaughn E. Crawford, as part of the Akkad survey carried out by the American Schools of Oriental Research. Crawford initiated excavations in 1963–1965, assisted by Donald P. Hansen. Several soundings were made: of principal interest was the unexpected discovery of about five hundred pieces of Pre-Sargonic cuneiform tablets scattered through the rooms of a building in area E on the Main Mound, probably part of a temple complex. Published by Robert D. Biggs in 1974, they revolutionized our view of early Mesopotamian literature. Of particular interest are versions of the Instructions of Shuruppak and the Kesh Temple Hymn. Old Babylonian copies of these texts help us to understand them. In addition to lexical and geographical lists, some now duplicated by texts from Ebla in Syria, there are literary and religious pieces and a few public administrative documents. Later work at the site yielded additional tablets, some from other buildings on the Main Mound, including administrative tablets and an incantation.

A contour survey was carried out in 1973 and excavation was resumed in 1975 by the British School of Archaeology in Iraq, under the direction of J. N. Postgate. The work continued with occasional fallow years until 1989 and will be resumed if circumstances permit. The principal results include the recovery of more than 4 ha (10 acres) of the city layout as a result of surface clearing: on the main mound this revealed the street and lane network, the line of the city wall, the probable location of gates, and many individual buildings. On the West Mound it showed that the ED I settlement was laid out in compounds divided by heavy walls.

In areas A and E of the Main Mound, buildings excavated by the earlier excavators were further investigated. This entailed excavating numerous graves, furnished with considerable amounts of pottery, jewelry, and other goods, including equids presumably harnessed to wheeled vehicles. Some of the graves were demonstrably intramural having been dug from within the houses. Against the southeastern side of the area E complex a massive refuse tip was identified that was more than 6 m deep. It contained many door sealings, figurines, and other items suggestive of temple discard. Two large ED III domestic buildings were excavated on the Main Mound, with particular attention, given to defining the use of space through quantitatively controlled recovery and micromorphological examination of the stratification.

Susan M. Pollock undertook excavation and other work on the Uruk Mound between 1985 and 1990. Her work confirmed an occupation from Early to Late Uruk, with a small ED occupation on the mound's southeastern sector. A Late Uruk city wall 20 m thick was located. Detailed observation of its surface remains has illuminated the distribution of activities throughout the settlement.

[See also Mesopotamia, article on Ancient Mesopotamia.]

BIBLIOGRAPHY

Biggs, Robert D. Inscriptions from Tell Abū Ṣalābīkh. University of Chicago Oriental Institute Publications, no. 99. Chicago, 1974. Definitive publication of the inscriptions from 1963 to 1965, with a report on the excavations by Donald P. Hansen.
Green, A. R., et al. Abu Salabikh Excavations, vol. 4, The 6G Ash-Tip and Its Contents. London, 1993. See below for the first three volumes of this report; two additional volumes are in preparation.
Martin, Harriet P., Jane Moon, and J. N. Postgate. Abu Salabikh Excavations, vol. 2, Graves 1 to 99. London, 1985.
Moon, Jane. Abu Salabikh Excavations, vol. 3, Catalogue of Early Dynastic Pottery. London, 1987.
Pollock, Susan. "Abu Salabikh, the Uruk Mound, 1985–86." Iraq 49 (1987): 121–141.
Pollock, Susan. "Archaeological Investigations on the Uruk Mound, Abu Salabikh." Iraq 52 (1990): 85–93.
Pollock, Susan, Caroline Steele, and Melody Pope. "Investigations on the Uruk Mound, Abu Salabikh, 1990." Iraq 53 (1991): 59–68.
Postgate, J. N. "Excavations at Abu Salabikh" (1976–1979). Iraq 39.2 (1977): 269–299; 40.2 (1978): 77–87; 42.2 (1980): 87–104.
Postgate, J. N. Abu Salabikh Excavations, vol. 1, The West Mound Surface Clearance. London, 1983.
Postgate, J. N. "Excavations at Abu Salabikh, 1988–89." Iraq 52 (1990): 95–106.
Postgate, J. N., and Jane Moon. "Excavations at Abu Salabikh, 1981." Iraq 44.2 (1982): 103–136.
Postgate, J. N., and P. R. S. Moorey. "Excavations at Abu Salabikh, 1975." Iraq 38.2 (1976): 133–169. For other articles on the inscriptions, animal and fish bones, fire installations, pottery, the flint industry, and geomorphology, see various authors in Iraq, vols. 40–52.

J. N. POSTGATE

ABU SIMBEL, colossal temple complex located in the northern Sudan about 200 km (186 mi.) up the Nile from Aswan (22°21′ N, 31°38′ E). Built in Nubia by the Egyptian pharaoh Rameses II (1279–1213 BCE), the complex consists of two rock-cut temples, a large structure for the pharaoh and a small one for him and his queen, Nefertari. Begun after 1274, both temples were officially opened for cult purposes in 1255; the officials responsible for the work were two successive viceroys of Kush (Nubia), Iuny and Hekanakht, and a royal cupbearer, Ashahebsed. In 1238 Abu Simbel experienced a severe earthquake. Viceroy Paser carried out extensive repairs, but the upper part of one of four great colossi of Rameses II that fronted the Great Temple had to be left where it had fallen. The colossi, and the Great Temple itself, were already partly buried under encroaching sand in 593, when Greek, Carian, and Phoenician mercenaries serving in an invading army of Psammetik II (595–589) left graffiti relatively high up on the legs of the colossi. Eventually both temples were largely buried under sand; the Great Temple was rediscovered by the Swiss traveler Johann Burckhardt in 1813 and first entered by the early Egyptologist Giovanni Belzoni in 1817.

The two temples of Abu Simbel are the best-preserved examples of the grandiose art and architecture typical of the reign of Rameses II. Each was cut into separate, high sandstone bluffs. Nefertari's structure lay northeast of the Great Temple. The Great Temple's facade is cut directly into the cliff face (over 26 m [85 ft.] high and recalling a temple pylon in form). Four colossal figures (over 19.8 m [65 ft.] high) of an enthroned Rameses stand in front, and over the entrance a statue of Re-Harakhti, a solar god, set in a recess, receives offerings from figures of Rameses cut in relief on either side. A frieze of baboons along the top of the facade represents those creatures of the "eastern horizon" who adore the rising sun. The Great Temple's maximum depth is 62.85 m (206.2 ft.); on each side, also rock cut, are long chambers, which housed temple utensils and furniture.

Within is a large columned hall lined with eight colossal figures of Rameses standing in both royal regalia and Osiride pose. The reliefs covering the walls focus mostly on royal victories; in particular, the north wall is occupied by the best-preserved depiction of the famous battle of Rameses II against the Hittites at Qadesh (1274). More conventional scenes involving Syrians, Libyans, and Nubians are found on the south wall. Beyond, a smaller columned hall is embellished with cult scenes, and further in (after a small vestibule) is the sanctuary, which contains an altar or barque stand (at festival times, images of gods were carried outside the temple in a boat-shaped palanquin) and, along the rear wall, four seated statues representing Ptah and Amun on the south side and the deified Rameses and Re-Harakhti on the north side. In the New Kingdom (eighteenth to twentieth dynasties, 1550–1069) a pharaoh could be understood as being both a mortal earthly ruler and simultaneously a divine being capable of receiving cult like a god.

Nefertari's temple is markedly smaller; its facade is only 12 m (39 ft.) high, and its total depth about 20 m (66 ft.). Six colossal standing figures (all 9.9 m [32.4 ft.] high) front the temple. On each side, Nefertari is depicted as the goddess Hathor and is flanked by figures of Rameses. A columned hall with six Hathoric columns within is decorated mainly with cult scenes, and a small chamber before the sanctuary celebrates in its reliefs deities associated with femininity and birth. Hathor in cow form emerges from the marshes, and Taweret, protector of women in childbirth, appears. In the sanctuary is a statue of Hathor as a cow protecting the king. Implicitly he is her maturing son, although he is shown as an adult.

The temples of Abu Simbel are of manifold significance; they are best understood as a conceptual, as much as an architectural, whole. On one level, the temples link Rameses with the gods of Nubia and Egypt, specifically the Nubian gods Horus of Meh and Hathor of Ibshek, and the four Egyptian deities Ptah, Amun, Re-Harakhti, and the deified Rameses himself. They also provide the context for a cult of the divine Rameses. However, the mythic dimensions of kingship are also involved. The Nefertari temple is conceptually a secluded arena for conception, gestation, birth, and creation, and Nefertari and four individualized hypostases (essential natures) of Rameses (the six colossi) literally stride out from it. These same four hypostases take their place as the four colossi of the Great Temple, which celebrates Rameses as virtual embodiment of the sun god on earth and ruler of Egypt and the world. The Nefertari temple was aligned so that its' most direct solar illumination would occur at about the winter solstice. Sunlight penetrated the Great Temple most deeply about a month and a half before or after the solstice. These schedules suggest that Nefertari's temple was ritually most significant during the period of growth and emergence, and the Great Temple was most prominent at the time of increasing heat and at the inundation.

As a result of the flooding of Nubia by the Lake Nasser reservoir, both temples were cut into segments and rebuilt at a higher location between 1964 and 1968, a spectacularly successful example of salvage archaeology.

[*See also* Nubia.]

BIBLIOGRAPHY

Desroches-Noblecourt, Christiane, and Charles Kuentz. *Le petit temple d'Abou Simbel*. 2 vols. Centre de Documentation et d'Étude sur l'Ancienne Égypte, Mémoires, vols. 1–2. Cairo, 1968.
Desroches-Noblecourt, Christiane, and Georg Gerster. *The World Saves Abu Simbel*. Vienna, 1968.
Héry, François-Xavier, and Thierry Enel. *Abou Simbel & les temples de Nubie*. Aix-en-Provence, 1994.
Save-Soderbergh, Torgny, ed. *Temples and Tombs of Ancient Nubia: The International Rescue Campaign at Abou Simbel, Philae, and Other Sites.* London, 1987.

DAVID O'CONNOR

ABYDOS, one of ancient Egypt's most sacred sites, located in the eighth Upper Egyptian nome, or province (26°11′ N, 31°55′ E). Archaeological survey indicates that along with This (Thinis) it was one of two prominent towns within this administrative district. Initially, Khentiamentiu, a protector of cemeteries, was the local god, but by the late Old Kingdom (c. 2350 BCE), he had been syncretized with Osiris, the powerful god of the underworld. Most likely, Osiris came to be associated with Abydos because the ancient Egyptians believed the underworld's entrance was there. By the twelfth dynasty (c. 1991–1783 BCE), annual rites included a procession from the temple at the edge of the flood plain to Osiris's supposed tomb at Umm el-Qa'ab, the Early

Dynastic royal cemetery at the foot of the high desert escarpment.

In ancient Egypt the name *Abydos* applied only to the town in which the Osiris temple was located. Today the designation *Abydos* refers to the town as well as a number of settlements, cemeteries, and monuments located along a narrow 4 km (2.5 mi.) stretch of low desert. Additionally, several other Abydos cemeteries, including Umm el-Qa'ab, are found beyond this zone, into the low desert along a small wadi whose mouth was located behind the town of Abydos.

The first person to excavate at Abydos was Auguste Mariette around 1858–1859. He focused on the necropoleis, labeling the largest ones the North, Middle, and South Cemeteries. He was principally interested in acquiring funerary stelae, (commemorative tablets), although he undertook a substantial amount of excavation in the northwest corner of Kom es-Sultan (the modern name for the ancient town site), searching for the "tomb of Osiris." The ancient Egyptians believed that Abydos was the burial place of Osiris, hence Mariette's search for that tomb.

Between 1895 and 1897, Émile Amélineau conducted the first excavations at Umm el-Qa'ab, uncovering tombs of early kings. A considerable body of early archaeological work was conducted under the auspices of the Egypt Exploration Fund (EEF) of London. William Matthew Flinders Petrie was responsible for the largest and most systematic body of early EEF excavations. Although Amélineau had already dug at Umm el-Qa'ab, Petrie's more detailed research on the tombs and Amélineau's dumps allowed him to outline the Early Dynastic period. Also he excavated the Osiris temple, some of the early town, as well as the Middle Cemetery; much of this work has yet to be improved upon. Other archaeologists worked there as well: T. Eric Peet and Henri Frankfort (Middle Cemetery); E. R. Ayrton and C. T. Currelly (South Abydos); and Arthur C. Mace (North Cemetery). John Garstang dug in the North and Middle Cemeteries as well but published little.

Abydos continues to be a rich source of data. Since 1979, the Pennsylvania–Yale Expedition to Abydos has regularly and systematically explored the ancient town and nearby funerary remains, especially Middle Kingdom cenotaphs of private persons and the mud-brick funerary enclosures of the first and second dynasties. At the latter, numerous mud-brick structures have been discovered that house wooden boats. Recent work at Cemetery U near Umm el-Qa'ab by the German Archaeological Institute in Cairo has uncovered tombs belonging to high-ranking individuals, possibly kings, whose remains date prior to Narmer of Dynasty 0 (c. 3150 BCE).

The earliest predynastic remains date to the late Naqada I and early Naqada II periods (Cemeteries φ/C, E, U, and S/Salmani and a settlement east of the Ahmose cenotaph). Numerous cemeteries (x/B, E, U, and S/Salmani) and several small settlements (west of the Osireion [elaborate cenotoptah built by Seti I] and under Cemetery D) have been assigned to the subsequent late Naqada II and III periods. The stratigraphic remains from Kom es-Sultan suggest that the town was occupied by the end of the Predynastic period, but the earliest stratified levels in the Osiris temple cannot be documented prior to the late Old Kingdom. Caches of objects and several burials within the town site (M series), generally agreed to be principally of Early Dynastic date, suggest, however, that the temple flourished earlier.

The ten royal tombs at Umm el-Qa'ab and their funerary enclosures in the Middle Cemetery are the most significant early dynastic remains. The Old Kingdom is represented by tombs (most in Mariette's North and Middle cemeteries), temple architecture, and a settlement (both in Kom es-Sultan). The increasing importance of Abydos to the Middle Kingdom Egyptians can be seen in the growth of the cemetery zone. In addition to traditional burials, cenotaphs (or more precisely, memorial chapels) became fashionable. The private cenotaphs are located in the easternmost portion of the North Cemetery, but large royal cenotaph-temples, such as those of Senwosret (Sesostris) III and Ahmose, were built farther south (now known as South Abydos). Particularly well known are the nineteenth-dynasty structures, including one dedicated to Rameses I, the large, well-preserved example built by Seti I, and the small Rameses II temple.

The North and Middle Cemeteries were used extensively from the New Kingdom through the Roman period, and the south cemetery is certainly of a late date. As of the Ptolemaic period, the wadi bed, previously taboo for burial purposes, became a heavily exploited cemetery zone. The cemeteries for animals—predominantly ibis, dog, and hawk—date to the Late period and subsequent phases of Egyptian history.

The Osiris temple was expanded in the Middle Kingdom, and in the later New Kingdom, it was leveled and rebuilt. Numerous rulers of the New Kingdom (eighteenth–twentieth dynasties) decorated and added onto the revamped temple. Rameses II built a new temple, the portal, to the west. Finds of private and royal statuary, dating through the end of the twenty-sixth dynasty, testify to the Osiris temple's continued use. Fragments bore a dedication to Nectanebo, suggesting that building continued in the thirtieth Dynasty, and the same structure was probably used in the Ptolemaic and Roman periods.

[*See also* Egypt, *article on* Predynastic Egypt; Egypt Exploration Society; *and the biographies of Frankfort, Garstang, Mariette, and Petrie.*]

BIBLIOGRAPHY

Dreyer, Günter. "Recent Discoveries at Abydos Cemetery U." In *The Nile Delta in Transition: 4th–3rd Millennium B.C.*, edited by Edwin C. M. van den Brink, pp. 293–299. Tel Aviv, 1992. Brief summary of the newly discovered burials of the earliest rulers.

Kees, Hermann. *Ancient Egypt: A Cultural Topography.* Translated by Ian F. D. Morrow. Edited by T. G. H. James. London, 1961. Chapter 9 is devoted to a very readable discussion of the significance of Abydos in ancient Egyptian culture.

Kemp, Barry J. "The Egyptian 1st Dynasty Royal Cemetery." *Antiquity* 41 (1967): 22–32. Important discussion of the evidence that leads most scholars to accept the structures of Umm el-Qa'ab as the tombs of Egypt's first kings not cenotaphs.

Kemp, Barry J. "Abydos." In *Lexikon der Ägyptologie*, vol. 1, cols. 28–41. Wiesbaden, 1972. Excellent summary of the archaeological remains at Abydos.

Kemp, Barry J. "Abydos." In *Excavating in Egypt: The Egypt Exploration Society, 1882–1982*, edited by T. G. H. James, pp. 71–88. London, 1982. Summarizes the archaeological excavations conducted at Abydos under the auspices of the Egypt Exploration Society.

O'Connor, David. "The 'Cenotaphs' of the Middle Kingdom at Abydos." In *Mélanges Gamal Eddin Mokhtar*, vol. 2, pp. 161–177. Cairo, 1985. Clear, detailed discussion of the Pennsylvania-Yale Expedition's excavations of private cenotaphs of the Middle Kingdom.

O'Connor, David. "The Earliest Pharaohs and The University Museum." *Expedition* 29.1 (1987): 27–39. Excellent summary of known Early Dynastic sites at Abydos, with information about the personalities of the individuals responsible for some of the archaeological excavations there at the turn of the century.

O'Connor, David. "Boat Graves and Pyramid Origins: New Discoveries at Abydos, Egypt." *Expedition* 33.3 (1992): 5–17. O'Connor discusses his most recent find of boats in the vicinity of an Early Dynastic funerary enclosure.

DIANA CRAIG PATCH

ACHAEMENID DYNASTY. *See* Persians.

ACHZIV (or Akhzib; Ar., Ez-Zib; Assyr., Accipu), site located on the Mediterranean coast of Israel, 15 km (9 mi.) north of Akko and 25 km (15 mi.) south of Tyre (33°02′08″ N, 35°06′ E). The tell, a double mound, is located on a *kurkar* (sandstone) ridge that overlooks the Mediterranean Sea and is south of the estuary of the Kesib River. To the south a deep riverbed is usable as an anchorage. Beyond the southern bay, a well-protected and sizable harbor (Minat ez-Zib) can accommodate a considerable number of boats. An underwater survey revealed rock installations used in growing crops of the Murex snail that produces the purple and blue dyes so valued in antiquity.

Achziv is mentioned in the Hebrew Bible as a town on the northern coast of Canaan bordering the land of the Sidonians and allotted to the tribe of Asher (*Jos.* 19:29). Greek and Roman writers, among them Josephus, knew Ekdippa, a city on the Phoenician coast (*War* 1.257). Travelers and historians in Roman, Byzantine, and Arab times also mention Achziv on the road to Tyre, 16 km (9 mi.) from Akko. The Crusaders built a fortress, the Casal Umberti, on the higher mound of the tell. The native Arabic-speaking population continues to call the village Ekziv/ez-Zib.

In 1963–1964, excavations were undertaken jointly by the Istituto de Vicino Oriente of the University of Rome and the Israel Department of Antiquities, directed by Moshe W. Prausnitz. Four contemporary, or overlapping, Iron Age cemeteries were excavated: the central cemetery (CCA) at the foot of the defenses on the eastern slope; the northern cemetery (NCA) on the northern bank of the Kesib River; the southern cemetery (SCA) overlooking Minat ez-Zib; and the eastern cemetery (ECA), dug into a second *kurkar* ridge east of and parallel to the coastal ridge. According to Jewish tradition, this is the northwest border of the ancient land of Israel.

Achziv's strategic position on the coastal main artery, the Via Maris, from Tyre to Akko and on to Philistia, was coveted by the Asherites and the Tyrians. In antiquity the harbor was regularly visited by Levantine, as well as Cypriot, coastal vessels. The Sidonians focused all their resources on maintaining control of the harbor. Their flourishing arts and crafts survived the aftermath of the collapse of eastern Mediterranean trade in the twelfth century BCE (see below).

The site's earthworks—its rampart and glacis—and towers were built in the Middle Bronze IIA period. The peninsula was turned into an island city by cutting the fosse to join the creek with the mouth of the Kesib River. At the beginning of the Late Bronze Age I, the site's defenses were destroyed and then rebuilt, only to be destroyed again at the end of LB II.

Inside the city, the excavators discontinued a test trench when it reached the final LB destruction layers. Among the few remains belonging to the transitional Iron Age IA, pits, fireplaces, and occasional walls were excavated. Inside the pits, wall brackets and Philistine-style pottery were discovered. Achziv recovered in the eleventh century BCE (Iron IB). The town proceeded to develop rapidly, and during the eighth century BCE reached its largest size, some 20 acres. Sennacherib of Assyria conquered a prosperous town in 701 BCE. The excavations on the northern part of the mound uncovered a number of storerooms adjacent to the Late Iron Age and Persian-period fortifications. Inside the storerooms were jars given as tax payments "to my lord the king," incised in Aramaic *Adonimelech*. The town's prosperity continued throughout the Hellenistic and Early Roman periods. The higher, small central mound contained levels from the Byzantine to the Arab and Crusader periods.

Four phases of activity in the northern cemetery were discerned. Stratum 4, the earliest, revealed part of a floor of an open area—a "high place"—that had a cultic use. It was founded on sand and covered with thick layers of plaster, indicating frequent reuse during the eighth–seventh centuries BCE. A *maṣṣēbâ*, or stela (1.5 × 1 m), used as an altar was found lying on the floor. Subsequently, this "high place" was enclosed by a wall. The wall remained in use throughout stratum 3. Jars with ashes and kraters containing cremation burials, juglets, and Achziv-ware vessels had been placed around the high place and beneath its foundations. Graves first appear in stratum 3, with small baetyls (upright stones signifying Heb., *bêt-ēl*, "house of God") marking each burial. Until recently, this type of baetyl was known only in Punic North Africa. A tophet was discovered nearby—the first instance of a tophet related to a central high place discovered in the Phoenician homeland.

The central cemetery contained cist graves dated to Early Iron IB. Single or pairs of skeletons were buried in a supine position. They were found with cylinder seals, a bronze bowl, a small ivory bowl with a lion couchant on the rim, and numerous locally made bichrome pilgrim flasks—burnished and decorated with vertical, concentric circles. A bronze double axhead, a spear, and a fibula date the cists to the eleventh century BCE. [*See* Seals; Tombs; Grave Goods.]

The eastern cemetery began to be used at the end of Iron IB. Many rock-hewn burial chambers with shafts were found in a family vault that was in use for 250–300 years. These chamber tombs are identical with contemporary Israelite burials. In them, a sequence of proto–Black-on-Red and Black-on-Red I wares was found along with red-burnished and red-polished jugs of typical Achziv ware. Only a few early bichrome vessels and pilgrim flasks were found.

A different range of Iron II pottery appeared with most of the burials in the southern cemetery. Bichrome, black-on-red, and black-on-pink pilgrim flasks represent the overwhelming majority of pottery in this cemetery's early phase, which was dated by its ceramics, scarabs, and seals to the eleventh–tenth centuries BCE. A recently excavated built tomb illustrates funerary architecture and this cemetery's three phases. A short dromos led to the entrance of a rectangular chamber dug into the earth and hewn into the rock. Its roof, visible aboveground, was covered with large stone slabs sealed by a stepped, upper structure of clay bricks, to form a high place. The dromos and the chamber were arranged on an east–west axis. This was a family tomb in which the bodies were placed on their back facing the entrance in the southern corner of the east wall. The cemetery's middle phase (end of the tenth to end of the eighth century BCE) is marked by the first appearance of red-polished Achziv jugs and bowls. The final phase (seventh century BCE) is noteworthy for the large imported storage jars used as receptacles for funerary gifts. During all three phases, valuable metals (lead net weights, bronze armrings, and other ornaments of gold), ivories, amber beads and seals, and votive figurines were buried with the deceased. These finds bear witness to the range of Sidonian trade throughout the Mediterranean basin and the rest of the Near East.

BIBLIOGRAPHY

Giveon, Raphael. *Scarabs from Recent Excavations in Israel.* Fribourg, 1988. See pages 22–39 (nos. 5–28).

Oren, Eliezer D. "The Pottery from the Achzib Defence System, Area D, 1963 and 1964 Seasons." *Israel Exploration Journal* 25 (1975): 211–225.

Prausnitz, M. W. "Notes and News." *Israel Exploration Journal* 9 (1959): 271; 10 (1960): 260–261; 13 (1963): 337–338; 15 (1965): 256–258.

Prausnitz, M. W. "Red-Polish and Black-on-Red Wares of Akhziv." In *The First International Congress of Cypriot Studies*, pp. 151–156. Nicosia, 1969.

Prausnitz, M. W. "Israelite and Sidonian Burial Rites at Akhziv." In *Proceedings of the Fifth World Congress of Jewish Studies*, vol. 1, pp. 85–89. Jerusalem, 1972.

Prausnitz, M. W. "The Planning of the Middle Bronze Age Town of Achzib and Its Defences." *Israel Exploration Journal* 25 (1975): 202–210.

Prausnitz, M. W. "Die Nekropolen von Akhziv und die Entwicklung der Keramik vom 10. bis zum 7. Jahrhundert v. Chr. in Akhziv, Samaria und Ashdad." In *Phönizier im Westen*, edited by Hans-Georg Niemeyer, pp. 31–44. Madrider Beiträge, 8. Mainz, 1982.

Prausnitz, M. W. "Akhziv (North)." *Excavations and Surveys in Israel* 4 (1985): 2.

Smith, Patricia M., et al. "Human Remains from the Iron Age Cemeteries at Akhziv." *Revista di Studi Fenici* 18.2 (1990): 137–150.

M. W. PRAUSNITZ

ACOR. *See* American Center of Oriental Research.

ADAB (modern Bism[a]ya), mounds located in a desert area of southern Iraq about 40 km (25 mi.) due east of the modern town of Diwaniya and about 30 km (19 mi.) southeast of the ancient religious capital of Nippur (31°54′ N, 45°36′ E) The identification of the site with ancient Adab was made by Edgar James Banks at the beginning of the twentieth century on the basis of inscriptions from the main temple, which named it as the E-Sar, known to be the main temple of Adab. In 1885 J. P. Peters, the excavator of Nippur, visited the site and noted its main features. Banks carried out the first full-scale excavations in 1903–1904, which he described in his book (1912). It remains the major source of information about the site.

Adab is roughly rectangular in shape and is approximately a mile long by half a mile wide. It is surrounded by a double wall that, at least in part, is third-millennium in date and is bisected by the bed of a dried-out canal, a branch of the Shatt-an-Nil, which linked it to Nippur. Inside the walls are a number of mounds, one of which Banks identified as a temenos with a ziggurat and temple; others contained a palace and an area of domestic dwelling. Additional low mounds lay outside the walls and may represent the remains of suburbs and gardens.

The town was inhabited from at least the early third millennium and appears in the Sumerian King List where the dynasty of Adab contains the name of a single king, Lugal-anne-Munda, credited with a reign of ninety years. He is thought to have lived at the end of the Early Dynastic III period. The importance of the town in the third millennium is confirmed by the archaeological finds, which include the statue of another ruler of similar date, Lugal Da-udu, and an area of well-preserved private houses which included one fine courtyard house with a brick-paved floor. Banks identified the house as the residence of the local governor, on the basis of cuneiform tablets found in it. Bricks stamped with the names of Early Dynastic and Agade (Akkadian) kings, including Sargon I and Naram-Sin, were recovered from the temenos; bricks stamped with the name of Shulgi came from the top levels of the ziggurat. Hammurabi claims, in the prologue to his law code, to have (re)built the temple and the city. Part of a palace thought to date to this period was found on mound 1. Occasional bricks stamped with the name of Kurigalzu indicate that the city was still inhabited, and of some importance, in the Kassite period.

Small finds include a collection of about three hundred cuneiform clay tablets from the so-called palace, and some of a late third-millennium date from the private houses. A magnificent collection of inscribed and decorated sherds from a wide variety of stone bowls was found in the temple dump. Some of the finest are of steatite, or chlorite, elaborately decorated with geometric and figurative designs. Many of the designs can be matched on similar vessels from Iran and Arabia, as well as from Mesopotamian cities such as Nippur, Ur, and Mari. It has been suggested that Adab may have been a distribution point for this type of imported vessel. Provenience analyses of the stone have also indicated a number of different sources for them in southeast Iran and the Arabian Peninsula. A fine alabaster head of a man, with a close-trimmed beard and inlaid eyes, only 10 cm high, is dated to the Akkadian period on stylistic grounds and on the basis of its stratigraphic association with an inscription thought to be of that date. It is the finest of a number of heads and other fragments of statuary. Adab undoubtedly is one of the most important third-millennium sites in southern Iraq, still to be fully explored.

[See also Nippur; Sumerians; and the biography of Peters.]

BIBLIOGRAPHY

Banks, Edgar James. *Bismya, or, The Lost City of Adab.* New York and London, 1912.
Unger, Eckhard. "Adab." In *Reallexikon der Assyriologie*, vol. 1, pp. 21–22. Berlin, 1932.

HARRIET CRAWFORD

ADEN, since antiquity a major port city (12°46′ N, 45°02′ E) on the Gulf of Aden, now in Yemen. Modern Aden is associated with the northwestern port on Bandar Tawahi, but the ancient and medieval port appears to have been on Sira Bay, on the eastern side of the irregular oval volcanic promontory known as Aden ('Adan). The ancient city was located at Crater, the hollow of the volcano washed by the waters of Sira Bay. In antiquity, Aden may have been an island intermittently, especially at high tide. Ancient land

and sea communications routes met at Aden, as known primarily from deductions and later sources. The very few inscriptions found in Aden may not come from there originally, and South Arabian texts name many cities called Aden. It is not clear when the present name came to be associated with this particular city. The principal pieces of direct evidence concerning Aden are the famous water tanks and the ancient text the *Periplus of the Erythraean Sea.*

From prehistoric until modern times, the city at the present location of Aden has been an emporium, importing and exporting, serving the masters of the interior, rather than becoming a power in its own right. Historically the port of Aden served the frankincense trade of the kingdom of 'Awsan in Wadi Markha in the first half of the first millennium BCE and then the kingdom of Saba (Sheba) in the following centuries, before falling into the hands of the kingdom of Qataban and later Himyar. Informed speculation suggests that the historic role mirrored a prehistoric precedent—the importation of frankincense from Dhufar and Somalia and the transshipment by the overland trade route heading north.

During the first centuries of Islam, apart from continuing to serve as an emporium, Aden may have become a primary source of glass, which was exported to the Levant and the Far East, again perhaps in continuation of an earlier tradition. During the Rasulid period (thirteenth century), Aden imported Chinese products and exported horses. It would seem that the temporary decline of ancient Aden in the first centuries CE can be associated with the rise of the Himyarite port Muza (near modern Mocha, on the Red Sea coast) and the Hadhramaut port Qana' (modern Bir 'Ali, 500 km [310 mi.] farther east), which flourished from roughly the first century BCE until well after the demise of the Hadhramaut kingdom. Historically, Aden probably dominated the seaborne import-export frankincense trade during the entire first millennium BCE.

The *Periplus of the Erythraean Sea,* a shipping guide dating to the first–third century, describes all of the ports in the region, defining the South Arabian coast as "Ausanic" (thus associated with the kingdom of 'Awsan) and reports that the port of Aden (Eudaimon Arabia or Arabia Felix) was sacked, possibly by the Roman Emperor Claudius (41–54 CE). It has been equally plausibly argued, however, that the plundering was the work of a Himyarite king. Because the date of the *Periplus* itself is not certain, the destruction may have occurred anywhere from first to the third centuries CE. Regardless of the date, the eclipse was only temporary; and Eudaimon Arabia was flourishing again soon thereafter.

The most overwhelming archaeological feature of Aden consists of the famous Tawila tanks. Carved into the rock of a narrow cleft on the southern edge of Crater, they have a combined capacity of some 136,500,000 l (30 million imperial gals.) of water. They were filled completely in 1993, showing that the capacity corresponded to the extraordinarily irregular rainfall patterns of Aden, where 70 mm (2.8 in.) annual rainfall was the mean in the 1980s. That the tanks were remodeled by Islamic and British rulers is clear, but the date of their conception is not.

Apart from random soundings and an attempt to reestablish the ancient coastline, archaeological research in Aden itself has never been undertaken, and the objects supposedly coming from the city and neighboring regions cannot be regarded as reliable sources. The column capitals found 3 m (10 ft.) beneath the surface in the city are medieval and not ancient.

Dating to the third and early second millennia and revealing parallels to both Africa and the rest of the peninsula, the pottery from the sites of Ṣubr and Bir Nasser, some 25–30 km (15.5–18.6 mi.) north, suggests, however, that Aden was indeed a trading center in prehistoric times. Prehistoric import pieces can have reached Ṣubr only after passing through Aden, and the same route applies to the Greco-Roman finds from the district northwest of Ṣubr. The Qatabanian material from Bir Fadhl, one of the mainland suburbs of the modern city, underlines the continuous importance of the site. Thus, despite the dearth of material, dispersed artifacts and written South Arabian and medieval sources indicate that Aden always served as a major port despite occasional periods of decline, such as that mentioned in the *Periplus*.

[*See also* Ḥadhramaut; Ḥimyar; Mocha; Qataban; *and* Yemen.]

BIBLIOGRAPHY

Casson, Lionel, ed. and trans. *The "Periplus Maris Erythraei": Text with Introduction, Translation, and Commentary.* Princeton, 1989.
Doe, Brian. *Southern Arabia.* London, 1971. Guide to the most important published sources relating to Aden.

DAVID A. WARBURTON

ADULIS, important ancient coastal trading center in Ethiopia (now in Eritrea; 15°17′ N, 39°40′ E). Located on the deep Gulf of Zula (Annesley Bay), Adulis was the Red Sea port of ancient Axum. This was where Roman traders transshipped goods to vessels headed for southern India. From Adulis, ivory collected in northern Ethiopia was shipped to the eastern Mediterranean. Although the site was occupied before the Aksumite period, the period of its activity as a trading center was from the first through the eighth century CE.

The first extensive note about Adulis and the first mention of Axum appears in a Greek merchant's handbook, the *Periplus of the Erythraean [Red] Sea*, datable to 40–70 CE. According to this source, the journey from Adulis to Koloē, an inland city and the first trading post for ivory, took three days. From there it was five days to the metropolis called Axōmitēs. The ruler of these regions was Zōskalēs, who was well versed in reading and writing Greek. Major exports of Adulis were ivory, tortoise shell, and rhinocerus horn; imports included clothing from Egypt, millefiori glass, brass, iron, wine, olive oil, Indian iron, and steel (*Periplus*, 4–6).

The land route went up the northern Ethiopian escarpment to Koloē of the *Periplus* (perhaps the site known currently as Maṭara) and then west to Axum. Fragments of Mediterranean amphorae, glass, and iron in later chronological levels at Adulis, Axum, and Maṭara demonstrate the continued importance of Axum's import trade.

The author of the *Christian Topography* (recently identified as Costantine of Antioch) visited Adulis about 520 CE. The port of the Axumites, he wrote, was visited by merchants of Alexandria and Eilat [Aila]. At Adulis he copied the Greek inscription of a marble victory throne of an unidentified Axumite ruler (the *Monumentum Adulitanum*) and the Greek inscription of a basalt stele of Ptolemy III. The search for the *Monumentum Adulitanum* inspired nineteenth-century interest in the ruins of Adulis.

Roberto Paribeni excavated at Adulis in 1906, followed by Francis Anfray in 1961 and 1962. Like Axum and Maṭara, Adulis was unwalled. The monumental architecture complexes of the northern and northeastern portions of the site reveal characteristic traits of Axumite architecture—stepped podia platforms with projecting and re-entrant walls, and adjacent annex constructions. Anfray's excavations revealed specific similarities between Adulis and Maṭara. He uncovered an area at the western part of the site with popular two- to three-room dwellings that appear to have been part of a much larger architectural complex.

Unlike the churches at inland Axumite sites, those at Adulis yielded fragments of prefabricated marble ecclesiastical furnishings from the eastern Mediterranean (see figure 1). These are datable to the sixth century. Fragments of similar or identical marble chancel panels and posts are found at Constantinople and Ravenna as well as at churches in Byzantine Palestine. The prefabricated marbles found at Adulis must have been carved at eastern Mediterranean quarries, sent overland through the Negev, and shipped from a port at the northern end of the Red Sea, probably Aila.

These marble fragments found at Adulis are associated with churches built in Axumite style. Their plan (like the church in complex F at Maṭara) is a basilica with an inscribed eastern apse. The latter feature is typical of sixth-century churches in Byzantine Palestine. In the complex that includes the northern church, Paribeni found fragments of marble reliefs carved with a six-armed star disk. This design prompted him to identify the architectural mass below the church as a pagan *ara del sole* ("altar of the sun"). However, the six-armed star disk is typical of the repertoire of designs carved on prefabricated marble chancel and ambo (pulpit) furnishings; these fragments should also be dated to the sixth century.

Ash layers and charcoal provide ample evidence of fire at Adulis, but the port city was not destroyed in the second quarter of the seventh century as some have assumed. International trade routes were deflected from the Red Sea from the late sixth century onward, and the importance of Adulis waned.

[*See also* Axum; Ethiopia; Maṭara.]

BIBLIOGRAPHY

Anfray, Francis. "Deux villes axoumites: Adoulis et Matara." In *IV Congresso Internazionale di Studi Ethiopici – Rome 1972*, pp. 745–766, pls. 1–6. Accademia Nazionale dei Lincei, Quaderno no. 191. Rome, 1974. Includes a discussion of the findings of the 1961–1962 mission of the Ethiopian Institute of Archaeology (led by Anfray).

Casson, Lionel. *The "Periplus Maris Erythraei": Text with Introduction, Translation, and Commentary*. Princeton, 1989. Presents the most recent discussion of the date of the *Periplus*.

Heldman, Marilyn E. "Early Byzantine Sculptural Fragments from Adulis." In *Études éthiopiennes, Actes de la Xe conférence internaitonale des études éthiopiennes – Paris 1988*, edited by Claude Lepage, vol. 1, pp. 239–252 Paris, 1994.

Munro-Hay, Stuart. "The British Museum Excavations at Adulis, 1868." *Antiquaries Journal* 69.1 (1989): 43–52 pls. 3–6 With an inclusive bibliography.

MARILYN E. HELDMAN

AEGEAN ISLANDS.

The purpose of this essay is to situate the Aegean Islands in their own social, economic and cultural milieu as well as in a Near Eastern context. Links between the Aegean Islands and the ancient Near East were influenced by the ever-changing array of states and cultures that dominated the eastern Mediterranean—in Syria-Palestine, Anatolia, and Egypt. To discuss these island cultures and their relationship to Near Eastern societies, it is important to move back and forth between between historical and archaeological records, always keeping each distinct but placing one in counterpoint to the other wherever appropriate. Such an approach will facilitate our understanding of the political ties, economic relationships, and cultural associations between the major polities of the mainland Near East and the dominant island cultures of the Aegean.

By the beginning of the Early Bronze Age, about 3000 BCE, most of the Aegean Islands had been settled for the better part of a millennium, but Crete had been occupied for several millennia. Our understanding of island developments during the third millennium is based exclusively on archaeological evidence. Documentary materials do not come into play before the Middle Bronze Age (about 2000–1600). By the Late Bronze Age (about 1600–1200/1100), the developing international spirit in the Aegean and eastern Mediterranean led to much closer connections within the Mediterranean islands and between those islands and the ancient Near East. Such developments fostered a need for more detailed records of commercial transactions or political alliances and divisions.

The absolute chronology of the Aegean Early Bronze Age has improved markedly in recent years, and yet, because it is difficult to establish chronological connections among so many islands, cultural sequences still remain vague, and economic or social developments can only be assessed in the broadest of terms. By the Middle and Late Bronze Ages (about 2000–1200), more detailed cultural sequences help to characterize many of the Aegean Islands. One result is

ADULIS. Figure 1. *Marble chancel posts and panels.* Sixth century CE. Archaeological Museum, Asmara. (Courtesy M. E. Heldman)

that the chronological framework and the relative chronological sequences in the Aegean and eastern Mediterranean are well known. Absolute dating, however, and the radiocarbon dating method are still much debated.

The two following reasons underlie the improved situation for dating: (1) The international contacts that developed on an unprecedented scale between about 1800 and 1100 BCE brought distinctive Aegean pottery or metal products into reasonably secure stratigraphic contexts in Egypt or western Asia, where astronomically derived dates have enhanced possibilities for closer dating; (2) the spectacular Bronze Age eruption on the Cycladic island of Thera not only buried the site of Akrotiri but also preserved crucial evidence for radiocarbon dating.

Still the chronological debate continues. The best radiocarbon-based approximation for the cataclysmic event associated with the Thera eruption is 1728 BCE a date which *may* correlate with other types of scientific evidence. Yet there remain considerable problems associated with laboratory error, interlaboratory comparisons, and the statistical approximation of calibrated radiocarbon-date ranges. Unlike most archaeologists elsewhere, many Aegean prehistorians do not accept radiocarbon-dating evidence. One consequence is the notable disparity of up to 150 years between their favored date for the eruption of Thera (about 1550) and the best estimate that current scientific evidence can provide. Despite the wide range of scholarly expertise and high-tech equipment brought to bear on the problem, such discrepancies persist: they are typical of archaeology the world over.

Cyclades and Crete. Although limited in size, most Cycladic islands were colonized by the Bronze Age, not least because water and arable land were available. The role of the Cyclades in Bronze Age regional trade networks was perhaps even more important in their permanent settlement. Early mariners used islands as landmarks (or "stepping stones") to avoid crossing open stretches of sea. The location of the Cyclades within the Aegean allowed them to serve as bridges linking mainland Greece, Crete and Anatolia.

During the Early Cycladic period (about 3000–1800 BCE), these islands were at the forefront of cultural and artistic developments in the Aegean, only to give way in the subsequent Middle and Late Cycladic periods to their increasingly influential neighbors, the Minoans and the Mycenaeans. In comparison with Crete, the Cyclades show less archaeological evidence for contact with areas beyond the Aegean. The final settlement at Thera in the late Middle Bronze Age is an exception. Links between Minoan Crete and Cyprus, the eastern Mediterranean, and the Near East (including Egypt) increased through time and reached a peak during the Late Bronze Age. Whereas the likelihood of some Near Eastern influence on Minoan Crete is still debated, recent finds of Minoan-style frescoes (Egypt) and painted-plaster floors (Israel) leave no doubt that Aegean influences traveled in the opposite direction.

Aegean prehistorians work in a nearly "prehistoric" context with a very limited range of documentary evidence (Linear A and Linear B) at their disposal. This factor combined with the inherent chronological imprecision for Bronze Age Crete and the Cyclades (from 50 to 200 years) makes it difficult to provide reliable narrative accounts for much of the Bronze Age. Given the nature of the evidence, the best that Aegean prehistorians can do is to outline patterns of human activity, development, or change. To reflect this situation, the chronological terms used here are based on the most obvious material development in the Aegean world: the emergence, development, and decline of palatial civilization on Middle–Late Bronze Crete.

The *Pre-Palatial Period* corresponds to the Early Bronze Age (EBA) and spans the period from 3000 to about 2000/1950 BCE.

The *Old Palatial Period* corresponds to the Middle Bronze Age (MBA), covering the period 1950–1700 BCE.

The *New Palatial Period* marks the transition from Middle to Late Bronze, about 1700–1400 BCE.

The *Post-Palatial Period* corresponds to the later phases of the Late Bronze Age (LBA), extending from 1400 to 1200 BCE.

The final period is the *Sub-Minoan/Mycenaean*, from 1200 to 1000 BCE.

During the third millennium BCE, innovations in maritime transport and the earliest cultivation of olives and vines had a striking effect on social and economic developments. Heretofore isolated from the broader Mediterranean world, Aegean islanders began to manufacture distinctive artifacts, to participate in overseas trade, and to construct the earliest towns in the Mediterranean. Most Cycladic sites (farming settlements) were no more than an acre in size, but their spread throughout the islands is a notable feature of the Early Bronze Age archaeological record. At the same time, the advent and spread of copper and silver metallurgy permitted some Aegean islanders to acquire wealth and prestige, which promoted social stratification. A multitude of harbors and the potential diversity of trading routes further promoted international contacts.

These interrelated developments represent a sharp break with earlier patterns. On Crete in the Early Bronze Age, several new, widely dispersed settlements arose. Before larger sites such as Knossos, Mallia, or Phaistos—all situated in agriculturally favorable positions and all destined to become palace centers—could be constructed and maintained (along with their dependent personnel), society had to be reoriented, and a labor force mobilized. It is still difficult to reconstruct this social reorganization from the archaeological record.

How did these developments promote long-distance trade, and how did that trade help to stabilize the new palatial regimes? The Aegean generally and Crete in particular were obvious nodes for trade and communications between the east and central Mediterranean, and between Europe and the Near East. Although Early Bronze Age trade in the Aegean was chiefly local or regional, it had an international aspect concerned with the acquisition of luxury items or basic resources. Such "prestige goods" singled out the social groups that increasingly maintained centralized control over Crete and developed the Aegean palatial system. Because the palaces not only maintained production for export but at the same time controlled imports, they played a key role in overseas trade. In the return trade, Crete offered its Near Eastern partners finished goods—textiles, metal, semiprecious stones, organic goods, and dyes.

The material evidence of contact with the ancient Near East, therefore, is clear, but the nature of this contact is a problematic issue that the archaeological record cannot resolve easily. How were goods exchanged? Who actually conducted trade? Some scholars who study the later, Minoan Linear B tablets maintain that the palaces could not have controlled overseas trade because it is never mentioned as such in the tablets.

Given the evidence for contacts between Minoan Crete and the Levant during the Old Palatial period, is it possible that Minoan palatial civilization evolved as a result of interaction between the Aegean and the Near East? Because certain functional (drainage systems), technical, and stylistic aspects (ashlar masonry, wall paintings) in the two areas are similar, some archaeologists have argued for a direct technological and artistic exchange of ideas. Several new features apparent in the Minoan palaces (pottery shapes, monumentality of the palaces, iconography, use of writing, and complexity of Minoan production and communication systems) are not random occurrences. They may reflect a close knowledge of Near Eastern ideas of kingship. The ceremonial and administrative aspects, however, appear as early on Crete as they do in the Near East, and there is little that is specifically Near Eastern about their adoption in Minoan bureaucracies. Each Minoan palace reveals unique elements, and in overall design they focus on a central court in a manner distinct from Near Eastern palaces (Mari or Alalakh), or from Egyptian urban centers (Tell el-Amarna). In other words, the form of the Minoan palaces is clearly not derived from Near Eastern prototypes.

In an era of increasing internationalism, cultural interconnections between the Near East and the Aegean are not especially remarkable. It is likely, therefore, that the intensification of long-distance trade during the twentieth-seventeenth centuries BCE (including gift exchanges between palace centers in both regions) may have led Crete's rulers to emulate what they learned about Near Eastern royal institutions, particularly those aspects that may have helped to consolidate their own rule. Acquiring "prestige goods" from abroad helped to confer higher status on Minoan elites, which in turn led to further social inequalities. In sum, exposure to the ideas and institutions of the ancient Near East did not lead directly to the rise of the Minoan palaces, although it may have initiated some level of competition among elites in neighboring Minoan polities and thereby led to intensified production, as well as social and organizational change.

Crete's Neo-Palatial Period. About 1700 BCE, an earthquake or series of quakes destroyed Crete's first palaces. In the elaborate reconstructions that followed, the magnificent frescoes widely recognized as an important hallmark of Minoan civilization were applied to the new palace walls. Unprecedented wealth is further indicated by fine painted pottery, jewelry, engraved gems, bronze items, and ivory figurines. Self-supporting in food and most other basic resources except metals, the inhabitants of Minoan Crete intensified their agricultural and textile production. Combined with the extensive trade contacts that funneled luxury items and other goods into the economy, these factors brought Crete to the apex of prosperity by about 1600.

Even if land and agriculture-pastoralism formed the economic basis of the palatial system, centralized control over foreign trade provided much of the extraordinary wealth and prestige items that helped to solidify political and economic power. Merchants or mariners, moreover, would have indulged in other forms of (private) trade and barter. Through such mechanisms, Minoan goods began to appear in increasing numbers throughout the Aegean and western Anatolia, and in Cyprus, the Levant, and Egypt. Documentary and pictorial evidence related to *Keftiu/Kaptaru* (Crete, or the Aegean world generally) suggests that this trade was much more extensive than the archaeological evidence alone would imply. The "cultural imperialism" suggested by the presence of Minoan goods overseas, however, does not mean that the Minoans also exercised political or even economic dominion.

Toward the end of what Aegean prehistorians term the Late Minoan (LM) IB period, when "marine-style" pottery flourished on Crete, there is evidence of damage, desertion, or destruction at several Minoan sites with the possible exception of Knossos. The immediate and extensive rebuilding that followed was almost as elaborate as that of the palatial period, but Minoan settlement overall contracted during the LM II period. Knossos, extensively remodeled at the same time, remained the only functioning palatial center. Mycenaean (i.e., Greek mainland) influence became more evident on Crete at the same time. Sometime within the post-palatial period (the date is disputed) Knossos's grand palace was destroyed by fire. Afterward, although Minoan culture flourished at sites such as Khania in the west and

Kommos on the south coast, palatial life on Crete along with Minoan power and influence in the Aegean ceased to exist.

The political and economic collapse of Minoan Crete came at a time when Minoan power, in archaeological terms, seemed to be at its peak. Over recent decades the LM IB destructions and the Minoan collapse have been attributed exclusively to such factors as the cataclysmic eruption of a volcano on Thera, earthquakes and fires, a Mycenaean invasion, or an internal revolution. Yet we know that the collapse of dominant early states at the peak of their power is not uncommon—witness Mesopotamia during the Old Babylonian or Neo-Assyrian periods or Egypt during its New Kingdom. It is much more likely that Crete's political and economic preeminence was disrupted by several interrelated factors, among them the Theran eruption, the later LM IB earthquakes, and Mycenaean incursions. External factors such as increased Mycenaean power and Hittite expansion in Anatolia and north Syria may also have upset the balance of Minoan power, and disrupted long-standing Minoan links with those areas. Once Minoan power was shattered, an internal revolution may have temporarily concentrated power at Knossos. Crete never regained its position of dominance, and like all other states in the eastern Mediterranean, it suffered further economic stress at the end of the Late Bronze Age.

Thera. Nowhere is the extent of Minoan cultural contacts overseas more apparent than at the site of Akrotiri in Thera. Excavations at Akrotiri (a Bronze Age Pompeii in the Aegean) have uncovered hundreds of examples of Minoan pottery, as well as "Minoanizing" features and iconography in pottery, frescoes, spindle whorls, lamps, and other items. When the Minoans emerged as a major economic force in the Aegean during the early second millennium BCE, other islands like Thera may have accrued prestige or power simply by possessing Minoan products.

In the final two phases of its occupation, the inhabitants of Akrotiri had rebuilt their town in a manner reminiscent of the dominant Minoan centers on Crete. Throughout the island there are signs of dispersed settlement—farmsteads, villages, perhaps "country houses"—similar to that of contemporary Minoan Crete. Akrotiri's multistoried architecture, however, is unique, and its pottery and other fine arts represent a high Cycladic standard.

The site of Akrotiri would have been an important bureaucratic center with a maritime location ideally situated for inter-Aegean communications. Sailing ships, which are depicted on Thera's "Miniature Fresco," would have helped to regularize intra-Aegean trade, and to facilitate an increased movement of local, surplus, and luxury goods. As in Crete, the incentive may have come from the elite desire to acquire prestige goods (on Thera, often of Minoan origin or style) in order to concentrate and legitimize power and from the ability of that elite to control a labor force that produced finished goods for trade.

The cataclysmic destruction suffered by the town of Akrotiri toward the end of LM IA buried it in more than 30 m (98 ft.) of volcanic ash and debris. The entire island of Thera was devastated. Throughout the Aegean area, ash fallout, if not tidal waves, wreaked further havoc. Shipping and trading within the Aegean must have been curtailed as a result, and some scholars argue that this hypothetical series of related events must have broken Minoan control over Aegean seas. Even if earthquakes connected with the eruption caused localized destructions on Crete, the series of catastrophes on Crete, which served to undermine its preeminence within the Aegean, occurred during the LM IB (not the LM IA) pottery phase. In other words, however disruptive the Theran eruption may have been to Aegean society and commerce, it did not cause the demise of Minoan cultural and political dominion.

Rhodes. Throughout the Dodecanese group of islands, which includes Rhodes, archaeological evidence for the Early and Middle Bronze Ages is still limited. The heaviest concentration of sites on Rhodes is found along the fertile northwest coastal plain, where two key Late Bronze Age sites—Trianda and Ialysos—were situated. The earliest middle Bronze Age settlement at Trianda reveals a local character peppered with northwest Anatolian influence. A subsequent Late Minoan IA town covered more than 12 ha (29.6 acres) and revealed so much evidence of Minoan contact that LM IA Trianda is widely regarded as a Minoan colony. This classification masks the fact that the inhabitants of Trianda like those of contemporary Akrotiri and of many Minoan settlements had greatly expanded and elaborated their towns during the LM IA period.

After what appears to be earthquake damage, Trianda underwent some renovations, which were disrupted and left unfinished. Perhaps this was yet another outcome of the massive volcanic eruption on Thera (tephra from several places in northwest Rhodes has been analyzed as Theran in origin). Trianda was partially reconstructed in LM IB, but the new town was reduced in size and more limited in habitation. The LM IB and Late Cypriot I pottery found in this stratum indicates that overseas links remained open, and the increasing occurrence of Mycenaean pottery (Late Helladic II–IIIA2) in the upper layers may indicate changing economic orientations. Evidence for Late Bronze Age settlements on Rhodes ends with the apparent abandonment of the site of Trianda during the fourteenth century BCE.

The mortuary evidence for the following centuries is overwhelmingly based on the massive cemetery site at nearby Ialysos. The presence in the Ialysos tombs of a variety of metal artifacts, amber, glass ornaments, beads of semiprecious stones, and rock crystal, and even the odd seal and Egyptian scarab, attests to far-flung economic relations. Like Trianda before it, Ialysos would have been an ideal point for transshipping cargo from eastern Mediterranean bottoms onto local craft and may therefore have controlled much of the eastern trade coming into the Aegean. The current archaeological record of Late Bronze Age Rhodes suggests that a group of Minoan or Mycenaean merchants ensconced at Trianda or Ialysos may have managed the transshipment of goods to and from the eastern Mediterranean. In this scenario, Rhodian elites would have emulated and sought to acquire certain prestige goods from the Aegean core area.

The Aegean World and the Ancient Near East. Cuneiform, hieroglyphic, and hieratic documents dated primarily to the second millennium BCE refer only sporadically to the Aegean Islands. Even then, the geographic identifications proposed—Ahhijawa=Achaean; Keftiu/Kaphtor=Crete or the Aegean—are not universally accepted. These texts are not only limited in number, they are also uneven in nature and concerned with idiosyncratic matters that often have little relevance for historical reconstruction. Many have little bearing on the archaeological record of the Bronze Age Aegean world.

Cultural associations between the Aegean Islands and the ancient Near East are best demonstrated by archaeological materials, which show particularly close contacts on the part of Minoan Crete during the Middle and Late Bronze Ages. The documentary evidence associated with the terms *Ahhijawa*, *Keftiu*, and *Kaptaru* provides insight into certain types of island-mainland contacts, usually economic or geopolitical in nature. What we can learn from textual evidence about relations between Ahhijawa and Hittite Anatolia, for example, is decidedly geopolitical or military in outlook. Yet we also know that the people of Ahhijawa were able to ply the eastern Mediterranean Sea to their economic advantage. By contrast, documentary materials that refer to Keftiu/Kaptaru are decidedly economic in nature. Yet we also learn that Keftiu was ranked politically with powerful states such as Babylon, Hatti, Assur, Ugarit, and Cyprus.

Our understanding of the relationships between the Bronze Age Aegean and Egypt or the Levant has been colored by nineteenth-century preconceptions that discounted the notion of Semitic cultural impact upon the Bronze Age precursors of classical Greek civilization. These views have now altered dramatically, not least because of Martin Bernal's controversial study *Black Athena* (1987). Bernal believes that Egypto-Levantine cultural and linguistic influences on the Aegean world began as early as 2000 BCE and played a central role in the formation of Greek civilization. The present study has suggested, quite to the contrary, that some rulers of Minoan Crete, as an adjunct to commercial trade, came to emulate various aspects of Near Eastern ideology in order to enhance their own political roles.

The Keftiu evidence makes it clear that Aegean traders visited Egypt during the mid-second millennium, while the evidence of the Tell ed-Dab'a frescos indicates that contacts between Egypt and the Aegean went beyond the purely commercial. The Egyptians chose to describe their own relationship with the Keftiu as tributary—and thus politically motivated. Although a statue base of Amenophis III may well have recorded a fourteenth-century Egyptian ambassadorial visit to the Aegean, it cannot be interpreted (following Bernal) as indicating Egyptian suzerainty over the Aegean. In sum, whereas Bernal's challenge to the orthodoxy about the nature of second millennium Aegean-Near Eastern relations may force scholars to reevaluate earlier colonial and racist notions, his concept of Egyptian or Levantine colonizations in the Aegean is ill founded and confuses the nature of economic and ideological processes at work in the Bronze Age eastern Mediterranean.

The Keftiu/Kaptaru documents show that the Aegean world had a recognized political status among contemporary Near Eastern states and enjoyed economic relations with Egypt, Mari, and Ugarit. Crete's active involvement in this trade enriched its own culture, vitalized the palatial economy, and expanded its horizons far beyond the Aegean area. If the Ahhijawa-Achaiwa equation is accepted, the geopolitical status of the Aegean world indicated by the Keftiu/Kaptaru records finds further substantiation. Mycenaean trading ventures correspond closely in time and space to the economic and political activities of the Ahhijawa. The Ahhijawa-Achaiwa correspondence seems eminently defensible. It hints at Aegean military and political maneuvers in western Anatolia, reveals that diplomatic relations existed between the two areas, and makes it feasible to reconsider the quasi-historical aspects of the Trojan war.

The elaborate commercial networks of the Bronze Age Mediterranean involved a multitude of trade mechanisms and a variety of trading partners. Together they defined the nature and intensity of Mediterranean contacts with the ancient Near East. Although some have argued for a state-controlled Minoan thalassocracy, there are good reasons to think that localized trade predominated in the Cycladic and Dodecanese islands. In either case, centralized control over some aspects of trade does not preclude private initiative in others. The ethnicity of the merchants and mariners who conducted Mediterranean trade has been deduced from archaeological evidence or presumed on the basis of personal names found in documentary records. Together they indicate that Semites, Hurrians, Anatolians, Egyptians, Minoans, Cypriotes, and probably Mycenaean Greeks were involved. Yet there is no final way to determine who controlled or directed trade. A Canaanite thalassocracy is no more plausible than a Minoan one. The picture that emerges from the foregoing suggests that ruling elites, royal merchants, itinerant tinkers, and private individuals were all involved in the long-term political and economic interconnections between the Aegean Islands and the ancient Near East.

[*See also* Crete; Minoans.]

BIBLIOGRAPHY

Bietak, Manfred, et al. "Neue Grabungsergebnisse aus Tell el Dab'a und 'Ezbet Helmi im östlichen Nildelta 1989–1991." *Ägypten und Levante* 4 (1994): 9–81.

Bietak, Manfred, et al. *Pharaonen und Fremde: Dynastien im Dunkel.* Vienna, 1994.

Bernal, Martin. *Black Athena: The Afroasiatic Roots of Classical Civilization*, vol. 1, *The Fabrication of Ancient Greece, 1785–1985*; vol. 2, *The Archaeological and Documentary Evidence*. New Brunswick, N.J., 1987–1991. The first two of four projected volumes, detailing Bernal's ideas concerning Egypto-Levantine influence on the Bronze Age Aegean.

Cherry, John F. "Polities and Palaces: Some Problems in Minoan State Formation." In *Peer Polity Interaction and Socio-Political Change*, edited by Colin Renfrew and John F. Cherry, pp. 19–45. Cambridge, 1986. Detailed theoretical study of the possible impact of Near Eastern political and ideological factors on the formation of the Minoan palaces.

Dietz, Soren, and Ioannes Papachristodoulou, eds. *Archaeology in the Dodecanese.* Copenhagen, 1988. Provides up-to-date reports on sites and artifactual material from Rhodes and other Dodecanese islands (prehistoric to Classical).

Doumas, Christos. *Santorini: A Guide to the Island and Its Archaeological Treasures.* Athens, 1985. Up-to-date, general archaeological study and guide to the excavations on Thera.

Forrer, E. O. "Vorhomerische Griechen in den Keilschrifttexten von Boghazkoi." *Mitteilungen des deutschen Orient Gesellschaft* 63 (1924): 1–22. Forrer's original publication, equating Aḫḫiyawa and Achaiwa. See also Sommer and Huxley.

Gale, N. H., ed. *Bronze Age Trade in the Mediterranean.* Studies in Mediterranean Archaeology, vol. 90. [Göteborg], 1991. Publication of a 1988 conference held in Oxford, featuring several important papers dealing with various aspects of trade in the Bronze Age Aegean and adjacent areas.

Güterbock, Hans G., Machteld J. Mellink, and Emily Townsend Vermeule. "The Hittites and the Aegean World." *American Journal of Archaeology* 87 (1983): 133–143. Reasonably up-to-date discussion of the Aḫḫiyawa-Aegean debate, by a Hittitologist, an Anatolian archaeologist, and an Aegean archaeologist, respectively.

Hardy, D. A., et al., eds. *Thera and the Aegean World*, vol. 3.1, *Archaeology*. London, 1990. Published proceedings of a 1989 conference, detailing the latest archaeological work on the island of Thera. Indispensable for any extended study of Aegean prehistory.

Hardy, D. A., and Colin Renfrew, eds. *Thera and the Aegean World*, vol. 3.3, *Chronology*. London, 1990. Published proceedings of a 1989 conference, with several important chronological studies relating to Thera. Indispensable for research on Bronze Age Aegean chronology.

Huxley, George L. *Achaeans and Hittites.* Oxford, 1960. The best English-language discussion of the corpus of cuneiform Hittite texts on the *Aḫḫijawa*. See also Güterbock et al.

Manning, Sturt. "The Bronze Age Eruption of Thera: Absolute Dating, Aegean Chronology, and Mediterranean Cultural Interrelations." *Journal of Mediterranean Archaeology* 1.1 (1988): 17–82. The most detailed discussion available of the archaeological, radiocarbon, and other scientific factors involved in the higher Aegean Bronze Age chronology. See also Manning (1992).

Manning, Sturt. "The Emergence of Divergence: Bronze Age Crete and the Cyclades." In *Development and Decline in the Bronze Age Mediterranean*, edited by Clay Mathers and Simon Stoddart, pp. 221–270. Sheffield, 1994. Comprehensive and up-to-date discussion of a vast range of Aegean Bronze Age sites and materials within a sophisticated theoretical (social) framework.

Manning, Sturt. *The Absolute Chronology of the Aegean Early Bronze Age.* Monographs in Mediterranean Archaeology, vol. 1. Sheffield, 1995. Comprehensive study, updated just before publication, establishing an accurate chronological framework for the Aegean during the Early Bronze Age. Replaces Warren and Hankey and contains an appendix treating the higher Aegean chronology.

Mee, Christopher. *Rhodes in the Bronze Age.* Warminster, 1982. Still the only book in English that deals with Bronze Age Rhodes in detail, heavily weighted toward description and study of the Mycenaean pottery from the tombs at Ialysos.

Renfrew, Colin. *The Emergence of Civilisation: The Cyclades and the Aegean in the Third Millennium B.C.* London, 1972. Still the most comprehensive archaeological study of the Cycladic islands during the Bronze Age, and unlikely to be superseded in the immediate future.

Sherratt, Andrew G., and Susan Sherratt. From Luxuries to Commodities: The Nature of Mediterranean Bronze Age Trading Systems." In *Bronze Age Trade in the Mediterranean*, edited by N. H. Gale, pp. 351–386. Studies in Mediterranean Archaeology, vol. 90. [Göteborg], 1991. The most sophisticated theoretical article ever written on the topic of Bronze Age trade in the Mediterranean, and the standard-bearer for the Oxford conference where it was first presented.

Sommer, Ferdinand. *Die Ahhijawa–Urkunden.* Abhandlungen der Bayerische Akademie der Wissenschaften, Historische-Philosophische Abteilung 6. Munich, 1932. Sommer's publication of twenty-odd Hittite cuneiform texts concerning the *Aḫḫiyawa*. See also Forrer and Huxley.

Strange, John. *Caphtor/Keftiu: A New Investigation.* Acta Theologica Danica, vol. 14. Leiden, 1980. Detailed philological study of all textual evidence for *Kaphtor/Keftiu*, flawed by its identification of that place name with Cyprus. See also Vercoutter.

Vercoutter, Jean. *L'Égypte et le monde égéen préhellénique.* Bibliothèque des Études, vol. 22. Cairo, 1956. Still the most comprehensive study of all Egyptian material, especially of Kaphtor/Keftiu, related to the Bronze Age Aegean.

Wachsmann, Shelley. *Aegeans in the Theban Tombs.* Orientalia Lovaniensia Analecta, vol. 20. Louvain, 1987. Comprehensive, up-to-date, descriptive study of all Theban tomb paintings thought to depict Bronze Age Aegean peoples, including a discussion of *Keftiu*-related issues.

Warren, Peter M., and Vronwy Hankey. *Aegean Bronze Age Chronology.* Bristol, 1989. The most detailed recent publication of the traditional (lower) chronology in the Aegean, which rejects the updating necessitated by the radiocarbon dates from Thera. See Manning (1988).

Watrous, L. Vance. "The Role of the Near East in the Rise of the Cretan Palaces." In *The Function of the Minoan Palaces*, edited by Robin Hägg and Nanno Marinatos, pp. 65–70.. Skrifter Utgivna av Svenska Institutet i Athen, vol. 35. Stockholm, 1987. Comprehensive, traditional archaeological discussion of possible Near Eastern influences on the art and architecture of the Minoan palaces.

A. BERNARD KNAPP

AGRICULTURE. The broad array of activities and knowledge whereby human communities exploit plants to produce food and other crops (fibers and oils), agriculture, literally means the cultivation of fields. In the Near East, agriculture-based subsistence nearly always included a component of pastoralism. The nature of agricultural systems is determined by the complex interaction of environment, population, and technology. Technology includes tools and techniques as well as cultural traditions—knowledge and social organization—for dealing with the material and social environment. Population size determines the number of hands available for agricultural tasks. The influence of population on the conduct of agriculture is also shaped by its distribution on the landscape, both in terms of density and its location relative to particular environmental conditions and lines of communication. The environmental determinant itself embraces both the physical environment—climate, soil, vegetation, and topography—and the cultural/historical environment, including the configuration of interregional political power. The interrelatedness of these three parameters bears emphasizing. The study of agriculture in the Near East has periodically highlighted either technological innovation, environmental change, or population growth as the key to explain the ebb and flow of farming. Yet none of these determinants can be isolated from the others. Environment is no static dictator, but responds to technological treatment. Technologies generally depend upon economic feasibility, largely a matter of labor supply in the ancient world. Population is not a straightforward measure of available labor because a constellation of cultural traditions and historical circumstances affects the weight of per capita labor burdens.

Origins of Agriculture. Archaeological data relating to the origins of agriculture have mushroomed since Robert Braidwood's expedition to Jarmo in Iraq began a systematic gathering of botanical evidence for plant domestication (Braidwood, 1960). [See Jarmo.] The transition from the foraging cultures of the late Epipaleolithic (c. 11,000–9000 BCE) to the farming cultures of the Neolithic (c. 9000–5000 BCE) is documented by vegetal and animal remains recovered in excavations, by artifacts—prehistoric tools and facilities—and by human skeletal remains. Village life preceded farming. At sites such as Hayonim, Mureybet, and Abu Hureyra in the southern Levant and Syria, villagers gathered wild cereals and pulses. [See Hayonim; Mureybet.] Centuries of harvesting wild cereals altered their characteristics, selecting for larger heads that did not burst when harvested. So, too, generations of year-round communal life forged new forms of social organization. Early foragers paved the way for the development of agriculture.

Current models of the origins of agriculture diverge significantly from V. Gordon Childe's mid-century portrait of domestication driven by the opportunity and necessity of advancing aridity (Childe, 1969). One key element of current theory is the recognition that dense stands of wild cereals offered an attractive subsistence source for early foragers on a seasonal basis. Explanations of what motivated the shift from gathering bountiful wild harvests to conscious cultivation call upon climatic deterioration, more permanent and populous settlements and the resulting pressure on local resources, as well as the emergence of new social forms and cultural traditions. All explanations still suffer from an insubstantial database. Knowledge of ancient environmental

conditions and preagricultural subsistence patterns has not stretched to the point of being able to tie the emergence of village life or the appearance of domesticated crops to local changes in environment and resource use.

Remains of domesticated crops first appear in the southern Levant in about 9000 BCE. Usually preserved through carbonization by fire, domesticated cereal seeds possess plumper kernels than their wild counterparts and less brittle ears that resist shattering when ripe. Such morphological indicators of domestication do not exist for lentils, peas, bitter vetch, and chick-peas. Yet, these pulses routinely join barley, emmer wheat, and einkorn wheat in the archaeobotanical material from this period of incipient farming villages (Pre-Pottery, or Aceramic, Neolithic, c. 9000–6000 BCE). Grains and legumes were complementary crops at an early stage of agricultural development. Botanical finds at Jericho (Jordan Valley), Aswad (near Damascus), Abu Hureyra (western Syria), Çayönü (southeastern Anatolia), Yiftahel (Galilee), and 'Ain Ghazal (near Amman) represent the spread of agricultural life. [See Jericho; Çayönü; Yiftahel; 'Ain Ghazal.] Though hunting mammals such as gazelle and gathering wild fruits and seeds continued alongside farming, settled life in these mud-brick villages was thoroughly committed to crop cultivation. A number of sites attain sizable proportions and show signs of social differentiation (e.g., 'Ain Ghazal). They witness technological developments as well, including the building of rectilinear houses, some employing lime plaster and timber in their construction. Flax, harvested for its fiber (linen) as well as its oil, also shows up in the plant medleys of Pre-Pottery Neolithic (PPN) villages. Many sites evidence herding sheep and goats as well. Because these animals were domesticated in the region of the Zagros Mountains, their place in the subsistence systems of the Levant manifests interregional exchange. Sheep and goats represent the other side of the exchange network that sent domesticated cereals northward from the Levant. [See Sheep and Goats.]

By about 6000 BCE, the agricultural village was well established in the Near East. Farming cereals and pulses and herding sheep, goats, pigs (sporadically), and cattle formed its economic basis, initiating an enduring pattern of mixed subsistence. [See Pigs; Cattle and Oxen.] Subsistence security was enhanced by the proliferation of free-threshing wheat (where the kernel is freed from its hull during threshing, obviating pounding before use) and six-row barley. Though data from the Pottery Neolithic (PN) period remain sparse, changes in the distribution of settlements reflected the increasing reliability of subsistence systems. A particularly important expansion of the population landscape occurred outside the rainfall agriculture zone in southern Mesopotamia. At the eastern edge of the Mesopotamian plain, Choga Mami has produced traces of an irrigation canal as well as botanical indicators—plump flax seeds—of crop irrigation. Sketchy data awkwardly cramp knowledge of this period subsequent to the origins of agriculture and prior to the third-millennium BCE emergence of irrigation-based Mesopotamian civilization. [*See* Irrigation.]

In the Levant, the Chalcolithic period (5000–3500 BCE) added a crucial component to the subsistence repertoire: the cultivation of fruit trees. Fruit pips preserved outside the natural range of wild trees and vines offer the first signs of horticulture. The olive and the date palm appeared earliest. [*See* Olives.] The domestication of the fig, also a native species, probably waited until the Early Bronze Age. The same holds for the imported pomegranate and grape vine (Eurasian natives). Domestication of fruit trees required substituting vegetative for sexual propagation, and these five fruits—olive, date, fig, pomegranate, and grape—shared the capacity to be multiplied by simple cuttings, rootings, or transplanting of offshoots. More technically demanding grafting enabled the taming of apple, pear, and other trees, but only much later. The earliest examples of olives and dates materialized at the large fourth-millennium Jordan Valley site of Teleilat el-Ghassul. [*See* Teleilat el-Ghassul.] These same two fruits also showed up in the botanical remains excavated from the Cave of the Treasure (Naḥal Mishmar) in the Judean Desert. [*See* Judean Desert Caves.] While it is possible that the fruits were imported at both sites from zones where they grew wild, Chalcolithic sites in the Golan have produced numerous finds of olive wood, demonstrating the cultivation of the tree. [*See* Golan.] Spouted craters at the sites make sense as tentative separator vats for the production of olive oil. Fruits have not appeared among the Beersheba culture sites, where evidence points toward a greater commitment to pastoral pursuits. Animal kill-off patterns, multitudinous ceramic churns, and artistic motifs together portray communities devoted to animals not only for their meat, but for their secondary products as well. [*See* Beersheba.]

Agriculture in Urbanized Mesopotamia. The emergence of the world's first urban civilization in southern Mesopotamia's Uruk period is linked inextricably to the bounty of irrigated grain fields. Yet scholars of early Mesopotamia have moved away from the commanding hypothesis of Karl Wittfogel in *Oriental Despotism* (1957) that explained the rise of social complexity by the need to create administrative structures to manage the irrigation works. Because data place control of irrigation at the local rather than regional level, the administration of large-scale irrigation projects was not the prime agent in urbanization. The emergence of stratified society was nonetheless dependent upon the potential surplus in the reliable cereal harvests produced by the irrigation of this otherwise uncultivable alluvial plain. The increased conflict inherent in the landscape's burgeoning population density—clearly manifest in the settlement patterns—set the scene for the birth of a new political order. From multitiered settlement patterns to systems of writing, monumental art and architecture to delicately

carved cylinder seals, an urban-based, rivertine civilization took shape.

A "managerial revolution" did overtake agriculture in early Mesopotamia. The interrelated complexities of bringing water to the fields, capturing it, draining away unwanted water, and protecting arable plots from floods called for management. The fact that the flow of the Tigris and Euphrates Rivers is not synchronized with the needs of farming (the rivers are low at planting time in the fall and reach flood stage after crops are well grown) exposes the need for careful coordination. Texts mention a local official, the *gugallum*, the "canal inspector," who may have served this function as well as seeing to canal maintenance. Construction of irrigation facilities would also require planning and collaboration and might entail the cooperation of one or more villages. Records and inscriptions advertise royal accomplishments in sluice construction, canal digging, and even alterations in river courses. The advantages of scale in irrigation agriculture—from planning to production—were apparently recognized early on and resulted in numerous grandiose state initiatives.

The third-millennium managers of this agrarian society left records outlining the farming system. One Ur III text, the so-called Farmer's Instruction, apparently intended to disseminate practicable information. It detailed fieldwork from initial preparation through harvest. Its outline of agricultural practice fits readily within the boundaries of ethnographically documented traditional irrigated cereal production. Flooding the bone-dry field from the adjacent irrigation ditch launched the agricultural year in the fall. The plot was grazed over and hoed to loosen the ground. Plowing followed. Use of the plow in the Near East dates to the Uruk period, as plow marks in the soil and representations of plows on seals attest; third-millennium cultivators were meticulous in its deployment. The Instructions specifies furrow spacing, signaling close attention to growing conditions and their effect on yield. Other records contained precise calculations of seed rates. The seed was planted, not sown, with the help of a seed drill attached to the plow. A timetable enumerated the ideal delivery of irrigation water to the field. Nearly one-third of the text's lines profile the harvest and crop-handling season. Harvest represented a crunch point in the farming calendar and was a time of economic reckoning. Landlord-tenant farmer contracts and loan documents took crop failure as well as pre- and postharvest price variation into account. [*See* Ur.]

Wheat and barley were the key crops, occupied the lion's share of the irrigated arable land, and figure most prominently in the documents. [*See* Cereals.] Contracts and administrative records also mention lentils, pea and bean species, onions and garlic, flax, and sesame. Non-native sesame was likely introduced from the Indus Valley during the third millennium. Grown for its oil, sesame became an extremely important commercial crop in this region outside the range of olive-oil production. Gardens offered cucumbers, some root vegetables, and lettuce as well. Orchards boasted tall date palms, pomegranates, apples, figs, vines, and tamarisk trees cultivated for their timber. Of these, the date palm occupied the position of greatest importance, parallel to the olive in Mediterranean lands. The date produced a storable crop of great nutritional value as well as wood, fiber, and leaves used in roofing.

Sheep and goats dominated the animal holdings detailed by temple offering lists and household property inventories. Contracts between herd owners and shepherds specified flock compositions, terms of employment, and the expected productivity of the herd. [See Animal Husbandry.] The huge volume of texts continues to provide the primary source of information on the animal and crop inventory of early Mesopotamia. The strictly archaeological contribution of recovering botanical and zoological data remains minimal in comparison. Nevertheless, paleobotanists have identified a host of agricultural plants from third-millennium contexts: of the grains einkorn, emmer, and naked wheat and six- and two-row barley; lentil, pea, chick-pea, grass pea, horse bean, bitter vetch, date and grape; as well as tamarisk and willow trees.

Mediterranean Mixed Economy. Civilization sprinted ahead in Mesopotamia (and Egypt). By the Early Bronze Age (contemporaneous with the Mesopotamian Late Uruk through the Third Dynasty at Ur), Palestinian societies had decisively assembled all the elements of what has come to be known as the Mediterranean mixed economy. The emergence of full-fledged Mediterranean agriculture and pastoralism coincided with Palestine's first urban period. The region experienced fundamentally the same dynamic as in Mesopotamia: urbanization, intensification of agricultural production, and interregional trade. The population landscape showed the first signs of this transformation. Palestine witnessed a dramatic growth in the numbers of settlements and a conspicuous shift toward less arid plains and valleys, encompassing the highland region as well. Minimally two-tiered settlement patterns constellated villages around walled cities in the Levant as they had previously in Mesopotamia.

Botanical remains from Bab edh-Dhra‘ and Numeira on the eastern shore of the Dead Sea illustrate the changed economic regime. [See Bab edh-Dhra‘.] The major crop, barley, included the bounteous six-row variety, which was better represented than the two-row. Figs and grapes joined the olive in the fruit assemblage. Flax was grown, and the large size of the preserved seeds suggests that it was an irrigated crop. Coupled with the large amounts of linen discovered in burials, the flax seeds suggest the appearance of a local textile industry. [See Textiles, article on Textiles of the Neolithic through Iron Ages.] Faunal remains extended beyond the predominate sheep and goats to include the donkey, a crucial pack animal.

Increasingly productive grain fields, expanding invest-

ment in horticulture, intensified production of selected crops, local industry, and advancing trade—in sum, intensified agriculture yielding a greatly augmented total economic product—are in evidence throughout the Levant. The ceramic repertoire included transport containers for liquids—notably Abydos ware and metallic comb ware. Metallic comb ware has been associated with olive oil and wine production. Its particular clay and high temperature firing served to seal otherwise porous walls. Moreover, storejars of metallic ware have been found in conjunction with an elaborate oil press at Early Bronze Age Ugarit. [See Ugarit.] Abydos jugs were widely distributed, ranging from southern Egypt to the northern coastland of Syria. [See Abydos.] The vessels likely carried Palestinian oils and ointments for elite consumption. Trade connections were particularly strong between Egypt and the southern Levant. An impressive array of goods was already flowing by the initial phase of the Early Bronze period. To the north, the growth and strength and the exceptional durability of Levantine cities such as Byblos already demonstrate in the Early Bronze Age the central importance of seafaring and especially seaborne trade for the shape and conduct of agricultural subsistence. [See Byblos.] Cyprus and the islands of the Aegean were already participating in a Mediterranean maritime economic system. Cypriot copper ores were exchanged with the Near East and Egypt, as were manufactured goods and agricultural products from the Cyclades and Crete. Farming settlements spread widely on the islands, forming the foundations for the emergence of the palatial periods. [See Cyprus; Aegean Islands.]

AGRICULTURE. *Room with sixteen grindstones in situ.* Ebla. (Courtesy ASOR Archives)

The granary at Beth-Yeraḥ (near the Sea of Galilee), with its capacity of approximately one and one-half tons of grain, illustrates the expansion of grain production. [*See* Beth-Yeraḥ; Granaries and Silos.] Animal bone remains point to a likely contributor to this augmented capacity; the increased incidence of ox bones calls attention to the first widespread appearance of this draft animal in Palestine. The thousand-year old scratch plow (ard) must have cut furrows behind this source of traction. Although textual sources do not exist, the collection and distribution of such quantities of grain demands no less of a managerial revolution than transpired in Mesopotamia. The mechanisms by which this grain was produced for storage may have included elements of elite "stimulation" of increased production, such as was argued years ago by Childe, the "urban revolution's" original theorist (see above). More crucial were the growing abilities of an urban-based elite to "extract" or appropriate the product of subsistence cultivators, including the "normal" surplus produced as a buffer by village agriculturalists. During the Early Bronze Age, interaction between urban and rural spheres constituted the emergent economic context in which subsistence strategies developed over thousands of years bent to new urban-based demands. Typically for the Syro-Palestinian region, this process took place in the context of increasing relations with more highly organized and more powerful neighbors, in this case, a unified Egypt.

The basic structure of the Mediterranean mixed economy rests on the region's sharp climatic biseasonality. The beginning of the agricultural year finds the fields hard baked by five months of rainless summer, during which high insolation rates drain the soil of all its moisture. The winter rains must fall to inaugurate the plowing of the fields. Throughout most of the region precipitation is ample, above the 200 mm level necessary for dry farming. Yet, squeezed into the short rainy season (October–April, with most rain falling in three months), rain falls intensely and much precious water is lost to agriculture through runoff. Moveover, the precipitation is highly erratic both with respect to its annual accumulation and its pattern throughout the season. Because crops depend entirely on the rain that falls during their growth, they are vulnerable both to precipitation deficiencies and to skewed patterns that may delay the opening of the sowing season or strand germinated crops beneath rainless skies. The strictly limited possibilities of assuring water supplies to cereal fields through irrigation offer no relief from rainfall dependency.

To cope with the frustrating rainfall regime, farmers staggered their field preparation and broadcast sowing so as not to depend too heavily on any particular pattern of rainfall. The plowing and sowing season stretched well into the winter as the Iron Age "Gezer calendar" indicates by devoting four months to the operation. [*See* Gezer Calendar.] Beginning in early summer, the cereal harvest embodied the period of greatest labor intensity, a peak in the curve of annual labor demand. Arduous tasks and a high degree of attention were required to bring in the wheat and barley. Harvesting per se was accomplished by reaping with a hand sickle or hand picking. The harvested stalks were then transported to

AGRICULTURE. *Threshing floor with piles of grain.* East Delta region, Egypt. (Photograph courtesy J. S. Jorgensen)

AGRICULTURE.   *Agricultural terraces.* (Courtesy Pictorial Archive)

the threshing floor, dried, and threshed to disarticulate the spikelets and remove the hulls. Winnowing and sieving separated the chaff from the grain, which was finally measured and stored.

Cereals were by no means the sole focus of agricultural energy. A variety of crops diversified the productive base, spreading risk and optimizing labor resources. Pulses (e.g., lentils and chick-peas) were planted predominantly as field crops, while other vegetables (onions, melons, leeks) were likely tended in garden plots near residential zones. Vine and tree crops provided the most significant spreading of risk without competing for the labor needed for field crops. Cultivators opened orchards and vineyards to the rain by hoeing and plowing during breaks in the field sowing season. Likewise, pruning was accomplished at in-between times. Most importantly, the harvest from grape vines, fig trees, and olive trees meshed advantageously with the cereal harvest. The fig ripened incrementally at both ends of summer. Grape harvest and processing were intensive. Grapes were tread or pressed in shallow, rock-cut depressions and the juice decanted through one or more basins, then ladeled off into ceramic jugs. Grapes had to be processed expeditiously, yet wine production occupied vintners after wheat and barley had already been put away. [See Viticulture.] Olive picking and oil manufacture were also concentrated and laborious. Ripe olives were picked or beaten from tree branches, pounded or crushed with some type of stone, and pressed. The resultant oil was decanted from the surface of the aggregate extracts. Though demanding, olive oil manufacture transpired before the onset of the winter rains and the return to grain field preparation.

All told, the annual agricultural calendar was a full one, as the Gezer tablet outlines:

line 1: two months of [olive] harvest;
line 1–2: two months of sowing;
line 2: two months of late sowing;
line 3: a month of hoeing weeds;
line 4: a month of harvesting barley;
line 5: a month of harvesting and [measur]ing;
line 6: two months of cutting [grapes];
line 7: a month of [collecting] summer fruit.

The diversification of the agricultural base accomplished especially by the cultivation of tree and vine crops served indispensably in a geographically fractured region with limited expanses of level land. Plains and valley bottoms—from the Madaba Plains of central Jordan to the basin of the Orontes River in Syria—had long been the focus of profuse agricultural efforts. [See Jordan Valley.] Farming must often manage in the sometimes mountainous highland terrain. This terrain was perfectly suited to horticulture. Heavier rainfall and hilly terrain, however, demanded attempts to preserve the highlands' nutrient-rich but easily eroded terra rossa soils. Terrace construction represents the chief strategy to stabilize hillside soils, and terraces offer the further advantage of controlling runoff and augmenting rainwater infiltration. Archaeological documentation of terrace construction, though still sporadic, stretches back to the Early Bronze Age. Yet, the widespread adoption of terraces was regularly limited by the high labor costs demanded by their construction and maintenance. Short-term challenges alone preoccupied subsistence-oriented agriculturalists, leaving precious time left for investments in long-term stability. "Soil mining" often resulted: the terracing accomplished during the most intensive periods of agricultural development often faced the need to import colluvial soil from valley floors to fill hillside terraces above.

Terraced-based horticultural development held the key to any long-term highland agricultural tenancy. Like pastoralism, it complemented rain-fed grain cultivation. Many of its products were storable (wine and raisins, olive oil, and fig cakes) and made essential dietary contributions (e.g., sugar and fat). Horticulture provided a resource subject to a somewhat different set of environmental hazards than field crops, whose yields were not only erratic, but notably meager. With wheat and barley yields stagnant at ten to fifteen fold, the olives, grapes, figs, and pomegranates of the hillsides were indispensable. Moreover, the transportability of tree and vine products facilitated the creation of regional economies and interregional exchange.

Subsistence-Pattern Oscillations. The building, dismantling, and rebuilding of the Mediterranean mixed economy has stamped the ebb and flow of Syro-Palestinian civilization since it was achieved by the Early Bronze Age. Thus, after realizing a plateau of urban life and sway over the hinterlands, the collapse of Early Bronze culture opened a period of agricultural abatement. Over the course of several centuries, the relative proportion of agriculturalists decreased, and nomadic pastoralists multiplied on the landscape. [See Pastoral Nomadism.] The Middle Bronze reemergence of more intensive subsistence patterns is well illustrated in the Egyptian tale of Sinuhe (mid-twentieth century BCE), who testifies regarding his allotment of land somewhere in northern Syria-Palestine: "It was a good land, named Yaa. Figs were in it, and grapes. It had more wine than water. Plentiful was its honey, abundant its olives. Every kind of fruit was on its trees. Barley was there, and emmer. There was no limit to any [kind of] cattle" (ANET, p. 19, ll. 81–84). Such subsistence-pattern oscillations represent movements along an increasingly well understood and documented pastoral-agricultural continuum. At one end of this spectrum, periods of high-intensity agriculture manifest relatively higher population densities; settlement patterns with recognizable central places; specialization of production in agricultural, industrial, and pastoral pursuits, including the production of market-oriented goods; integration into interregional and international trading networks; and heightened investments in permanent production facilities, transportation, food storage, and water and soil management. [See Food Storage.] At the spectrum's other end, periods of agricultural abatement produce low-intensity constellations dominated by subsistence-oriented nomadic pastoralists. A relatively lower sedentary population density clings to a decentralized landscape with fewer settled towns and villages, while nonsedentary folk spread out in seasonal encampments. Regional isolation dampens trade, and production for autoconsumption produces few large-scale permanent facilities.

The basic principle underlying movement along this agricultural-pastoral continuum relates to contrast in the elasticity of the two modes of production. Pastoral productivity and its demands for land (pasturage) and labor fluctuate considerably: boom years see tremendous increases but are matched by the precipitous declines of bust years. Farming, on the other hand, is more inelastic: land and labor needs remain relatively constant and do not rise and fall with the success of each crop. These contrary tendencies provide incentives for the security-conscious integration of pastoral and agricultural pursuits. They also associate the florescence of agriculture with periods of well-organized central authority, which provides the stability, institutions, and capital necessary for agricultural growth. The predominance of pastoralism is associated with weak rule and disordered social conditions. Under such risky conditions, the selection of resilient and mobile pastoralism offers an adaptive advantage.

Many factors are associated with movement along this continuum. Agricultural intensification is propelled by population growth, centralization, expanding markets and international trade, bureaucratic direction, and innovation. Abatement is connected to environmental degradation, population decline, loss of trading opportunities, political disintegration, and military defeat.

Empire and Agricultural Intensification. The Iron Age in Palestine marks a particularly sharp and well-documented spike in the course of Levantine and Near Eastern agricultural history. Regional settlement patterns signal a throughgoing intensification of agricultural subsistence. The crucial context of this agricultural trajectory was the expansion of the Assyrian Empire and the florescence of Mediterranean trade. Galvanized by the maritime expertise and urban-oriented manufacturing advantage of the Phoenicians, trade connections began to weave a web of interregional exchange and regional specialization across the Mediterranean world. By the first two centuries of the first millennium, Tyrian and other Phoenician traders plied the main artery of east–west trade from Cyprus along the southern Anatolian coast to the Aegean, Crete, and the Cyclades, and as far west as Sardinia. The long-distance routes linked up with existing regional exchange networks, stimulating the growth of local centers. In the eighth century BCE, Assyrian expansion westward to the Levant sought to establish and control trade with the lands of the Mediterranean as well as with Egypt and Arabia. Assyria also aimed to enrich itself by gathering spoil and extracting regular tribute. Most of the tributary goods were not indigenous to subjugated regions: according to Assyrian sources, the Judean king Hezekiah's postrevolt tribute (mentioned in 2 Kgs. 18:13–16) included gold, silver, gems, ivory-inlaid couches, elephant hides, African blackwood, boxwood, and human beings (ANET, p. 288).

The luxury goods demanded as tribute payments held more consequences for agricultural economies than short-term impoverishment; they incited the search for high-value materials. These commodities (preciosities) had to be procured on the international trade network. To enter this network demanded intensive investments in exportable agricultural products. Thus, Assyrian power pushed dependent polities to produce more and pulled them toward specific products. These influences were joined by increasing population densities, urbanization, and political centralization in spurring agricultural industrialization and commercialization. In Israel and Judah, the intensification of olive oil and wine production stands out. [See Judah.] Terrace technology advanced, reclaiming denuded hillside slopes. The terraces were accompanied by hundreds of rock-cut presses throughout highland regions where wine production progressed at both industrial sites (Gibeon north of Jerusalem) and dispersed farmsteads (e.g., Khirbet er-Ras). [See Gibeon.] The addition of a beam advanced existing pressing technology, adding leverage to extract grape juice and olive oil more proficiently. In Judah, signs of bureaucratic management of wine production and distribution took the form of royally stamped wine jar handles. The enormous concentration of olive-oil production facilities at seventh-century BCE Tel Miqne/Ekron on the southern Palestinian coast superbly manifested the economic benefits of proximity to the sea and the access it afforded into Mediterranean commerce. More than 100 olive-oil production units have been excavated or surveyed thus far, making the site the largest such constellation of industrial facilities in the ancient Near East (Heltzer and Eitam, 1987). The overall agricultural intensification stretched as far as the arid lands of the Negev desert, where runoff farming created costly wadi terraces, catchments, and even diversion systems to trap a meager rainfall. [See Miqne, Tel; Negev.]

With its emphasis on commodity production, Iron Age agricultural intensification supplies a signal instance of urban manipulation of the economy counter to the subsistence-oriented objectives of villages. Villages cope with the two major constraints of erratic environment (physical as well as political) and demographic fragility by diversifying their productive regimes. Farmers seek to spread the risk inherent in settled agriculture by planting a variety of crops in scattered locations and by a scattered timetable. Herds are maintained as part of the village enterprise, a complementary pursuit that adds greatly to household productivity as well as resilience. Such subsistence-oriented objectives are not sustainable when urban-based direction of the productive activities sets the agricultural agenda for rural life. The governors demanded the most readily exchangeable and exportable commodities—wine and olive oil in the Levant—and encouraged their production through polices of taxation and procurement, judicial regulation, and land development. These forces pushed village agriculture toward specialization. Rural life found itself making investments in long-term improvements (such as water reservoirs and terracing), producing marketable goods, and depending upon regional networks of exchange. Thus, agricultural intensification severed village life from its traditional subsistence moorings as urban rule fashioned a "command" or "mobilization" economy. Dependent upon maladroit administrative structures, tenuous politically secured access to maritime trade, and the erratic nature of the Palestinian natural environment, such a structured economic system was highly fragile.

Agricultural Data. Charting the dynamic relationship between urban and rural zones is one area that benefits from emergent archaeological strategies pursuing quantitative reconstructions of ancient agricultural economies. [See Paleoenvironmental Reconstruction; Paleobotany.] In the absence of ancient agricultural records, researchers turn to data from preindustrial economies to posit levels of yields, proportions of various crops (especially grains and fruits), and animals (sheep, goats, and cattle), as well as human dietary needs. These data are collected in ethnoarchaeological fieldwork or are mined from the census figures of the late premodern and even the earlier Ottoman periods. [See Ethnoarchaeology.] Admittedly relative and approximate, such data join with site-catchment analysis and other regional studies to offer assessments of field and pasture potential (carrying capacity). Placed next to other archaeological indicators (e.g., settlement patterns, site areas, and processing installations), such calculations fuel assessments of agricultural intensity and reconstructions of the relationship between agricultural production and its larger political and economic environment. Thus, for example, the olive presses at Tel Miqne might have produced 1,000 tons of oil each season. Based on yields from olive groves planted and tended under preindustrial conditions (kilograms per tree and trees per hectare), Miqne's demand for raw olives would have required orchards ranging over 5,000 ha (12,350 acres), encompassing a radius of 10–20 km (6–12 mi.) surrounding the site. The control of such a vast territory raises political questions and points to the role of the Assyrian Empire in creating conditions for or sponsoring the massive industrial center.

Paleoosteological analysis of faunal remains offers crucial assistance to reconstructions of ancient agricultural economies. Analysis of stratified bone refuse permits characterizations of animal production systems and their temporal development. [See Paleozoology.] Because of the interdependence between pastoralism and agriculture in the Near East, these data permit inferences about the nature of the agricultural systems. Thus, an increase in the relative frequencies of cattle and pig bones at the expense of sheep/goat bones may manifest the waxing of agricultural intensity. Land development around a site reduces the amount of small-animal pasturage available, forcing sheep and goat pastoralism more into the periphery. Cattle can be kept more easily in close proximity to agricultural operations, and their traction is crucial for field crops. Pigs find their place as town scavengers. Among sheep and goats, kill-off patterns provide a complementary barometer of the delocalization of pastoral production: greater distances between the loci of consumption and herding spell higher ages at death, as nomadic pastoralists sell older animals to town dwellers. Increasing proportions of sheep/goats and younger ages at death may signal a less intensive economy with a less dichotomized agricultural-pastoral continuum. Thus, faunal remains offer the possibility of charting the ebb and flow of agricultural life.

[*See also* Farmsteads.]

BIBLIOGRAPHY

Borowski, Oded. *Agriculture in Iron Age Israel.* Winona Lake, Ind., 1987. Catalog of the components of Israelite agriculture, with special emphasis on their Hebrew Bible terminology.

Braidwood, Robert J., and Bruce Howe, eds. *Prehistoric Investigations in Iraqi Kurdistan.* Studies in Ancient Oriental Civilization, vol. 31. Chicago, 1960.

Bulletin on Sumerian Agriculture. Vols. 1–7. Cambridge, 1984–1993. Indispensable collections of articles by archaeologists, philologists, agronomists, and ethnographers. Individual volumes focus on cereals, field crops, fruits, irrigation, trees, and domestic animals.

Childe, V. Gordon. *New Light on the Most Ancient East* (1952). 2d ed. New York, 1969.

Dalman, Gustaf. *Arbeit und Sitte in Palästina.* 7 vols. in 8. Gütersloh, 1928–1942. Rich compendium of Palestinian village life as Dalman observed it in the early twentieth century.

Finkelstein, Israel. *The Archaeology of the Israelite Settlement.* Jerusalem, 1988. Presentation and analysis of the settlement pattern and material culture of Early Iron Age Palestine, focusing on the central hill country and utilizing 1945 village statistics to portray the demography and economy of premodern settlement.

Halstead, Paul, and John O'Shea, eds. *Bad Year Economics: Cultural Responses to Risk and Uncertainty.* New York, 1989. Collection of essays on culturally and historically diverse contexts regarding how human communities secure their food supplies in the face of environmental variability.

Heltzer, Michael, and David Eitam, eds. *Olive Oil in Antiquity: Israel and Neighboring Countries from Neolith [sic] to Early Arab Period.* Haifa, 1987. Several articles on the olive-oil production facilities at Tel Miqne highlight a wide-ranging collection on this most important fruit of the Mediterranean basin.

Hesse, Brian, and Paula Wapnish. *Animal Bone Archaeology: From Objectives to Analysis.* Washington, D.C., 1985. Exacting, detailed, and superbly illustrated presentation of faunal analysis, covering specimen identification, the nature of bone preservation, sampling strategies, and analysis.

Hesse, Brian. "Animal Use at Tel Miqne-Ekron in the Bronze Age and Iron Age." *Bulletin of the American Schools of Oriental Research,* no. 264 (1986): 17–27. Animal bone statistics depict shifts in the animal-husbandry systems that supported Tel Miqne/Ekron.

Hopkins, David C. *The Highlands of Canaan: Agricultural Life in the Early Iron Age.* Sheffield, 1985. A systematic, anthropologically oriented presentation of the nature of agriculture and its particular manifestations in Early Iron Age Palestine.

LaBianca, Øystein S. *Hesban,* vol. 1, *Sedentarization and Nomadization: Food System Cycles at Hesban and Vicinity in Transjordan.* Berrien Springs, Mich., 1990. Outlines the idea of a "food system," including relevant concepts of intensification and abatement and sedentarization and nomadization as integrating principles for archaeological investigation. Describes the successive food-system configurations for the Hesban (Heshbon) region of Jordan based on excavated animal-bone refuse and carbonized seeds and survey data.

Miller, Naomi F. "The Near East." In *Progress in Old World Palaeoethnobotany,* edited by Willem van Zeist et al., pp. 133–160. Rotterdam, 1991. Up-to-date survey of the archaeobotanical record of the Near East.

Nissen, Hans J. *The Early History of the Ancient Near East, 9000–2000 B.C.* Translated by Elizabeth Lutzeier and Kenneth J. Northcott. Chicago, 1988. Readable survey that includes a discussion (based on settlement patterns) of the beginnings of food production, permanent settlement, and the emergence of high civilization through the third millennium. Relies too heavily on an insecure reconstruction of climate change to explain developments.

Postgate, J. N. *Early Mesopotamia: Society and Economy at the Dawn of History.* Rev. ed. London, 1994. Artful integration of literary and archaeological data, creating a lively narrative of the social world of Mesopotamia, 3000–1500 BCE.

Renfrew, Jane M. *Palaeoethnobotany: The Prehistoric Food Plants of the Near East and Europe.* New York, 1973. Classic text with illustrations of each of the major genera and species of domesticated and edible wild plants, their origins, identification, cultivation, and use.

Sherratt, Susan, and Andrew G. Sherratt. "The Growth of the Mediterranean Economy in the Early First Millennium BC." *World Archaeology* 24.3 (1993): 361–378. Outlines the development of Iron Age trading systems in the Mediterranean against Bronze Age patterns from the perspective of world systems theory. Maps the interaction of Assyrian, eastern, central, and western Mediterranean, and European economic arenas.

Stager, Lawrence E. "The First Fruits of Civilization." In *Palestine in the Bronze and Iron Ages: Papers in Honour of Olga Tufnell,* edited by Jonathan N. Tubb, pp. 172–187. University of London, Institute of Archaeology, Occasional Publication, no. 11. London, 1985. Lucid chronicle and explanation of EB domestication of the olive, grape, date, fig, and pomegranate.

Zohary, Daniel, and Maria Hopf. *The Domestication of Plants in the Old World: The Origin and Spread of Cultivated Plants in West Asia, Europe, and the Nile Valley.* 2d ed. Oxford, 1993. Synthesis of crop-plant evolution combining data from archaeology and the distribution of living plants. Covers cereals, pulses, oil and fiber crops, fruit trees and nuts, vegetables and tubers, condiments and dyes, as well as wild fruits.

DAVID C. HOPKINS

AHARONI, YOHANAN (1919–1976), Israeli biblical archaeologist and historical geographer. Born in Germany, Aharoni went to Palestine as a young man. His character and his desire to explore Israel were formed in the Zionist youth movement and the kibbutz. He earned his Ph.D. in 1957 at the Hebrew University of Jerusalem, where he studied under Benjamin Mazar. Aharoni's doctoral dissertation, almost unknown outside of Israel, outlined an important direction for biblical archaeology, which had been foreseen by the German biblical scholar Albrecht Alt in 1925: regional research combined with biblical-historical data in a critical synthesis. This was the first archaeological challenge to the "Albright-Glueck-Yadin school" of biblical archaeology.

[*See the biographies of Mazar; Albright, Alt, Glueck, and Yadin.*] Aharoni's untimely death left his regional research in the Negev desert unfinished. His emphasis on a regional approach was developed by his students, however—mainly by Moshe Kochavi and his students in turn—in projects in the Galilee, the Golan, Manasseh, Ephraim, and Judah. These projects have had a major impact on biblical history and the archaeology of Israel. Better-known outside Israel are Aharoni's syntheses (1962–1964) of the historical geography of the biblical period. These works are still among the main handbooks for this field. They combine a wide range of archaeological and historical data for the ancient Near East, with a semicritical use of biblical materials.

Aharoni excavated at Ramat Raḥel, Lachish, Arad, and Tel Beersheba. He developed an Israeli method of excavation that emphasizes the importance of digging large areas, in addition to recording sections, for a better understanding of a site. This strategy was a response to the Wheeler-Kenyon method. [*See the biographies of Kenyon and Wheeler.*] Aharoni published the Arad inscriptions, an important contribution to the history and paleography of late Iron Age Judah. Noteworthy also is his participation in the exploration of the caves in the Judean Desert and of Masada, his work at Hazor, and his study of Iron Age Megiddo.

In 1968 Aharoni founded the Institute of Archaeology at Tel Aviv University. He gathered scholars in archaeology, ancient Near East studies, and related disciplines, ensuring progress toward current interdisciplinary research. Along with Yigael Yadin, his everlasting adversary, Aharoni shaped the character of Israeli biblical archaeology.

[*See also* Arad Inscriptions; Beersheba; Biblical Archaeology; Historical Geography; Judah; *and* Ramat Raḥel.]

BIBLIOGRAPHY

Aharoni, Yohanan. *The Settlement of the Israelite Tribes in the Upper Galilee* (in Hebrew). Jerusalem, 1957. Aharoni's first regional research, based on his Ph.D. dissertation. Most of his conclusions are no longer valid, but this study is a methodological turning point in the archaeology of Israel and in biblical history.

Aharoni, Yohanan. *Excavations at Ramat Rahel.* 2 vols. Rome, 1962–1964. Covers the 1959–1960 and 1961–1962 excavation seasons.

Aharoni, Yohanan. *The Land of the Bible: A Historical Geography* (1967). 2d ed. Philadelphia, 1979. Still the most comprehensive description and primary handbook for the historical geography of biblical Israel and Judah. Much of what was out of date was replaced in the posthumous editions, edited by Anson F. Rainey.

Aharoni, Yohanan, ed. *Beer-Sheba I: Excavations at Tel Beer-Sheba, 1969–1971 Seasons.* Tel Aviv, 1973.

Aharoni, Yohanan. *Investigations at Lachish: The Sanctuary and the Residency (Lachish V).* Tel Aviv, 1975.

Aharoni, Yohanan, with contributions by Joseph Naveh. *Arad Inscriptions.* Translated by Judith Ben-Or. Jerusalem, 1981.

Aharoni, Yohanan, and Michael Avi-Yonah. *The Macmillan Bible Atlas.* 3d ed., completely revised by Anson F. Rainey and Zeev Safrai. New York, 1993. Detailed maps of the biblical and Roman-Byzantine periods. The material by Aharoni, up to the Persian period, is a useful supplement to his *Historical Geography* (see above).

Bachi, Gabriella, comp. "Bibliography of Y. Aharoni." *Tel Aviv* 3 (1976): 161–184.

Kochavi, Moshe. "Professor Yohanan Aharoni, 1919–1976: In Memoriam." *Tel Aviv* 3 (1976): 2–4.

AVI OFER

AHIRAM INSCRIPTION.

The sarcophagus of Ahiram found in Byblos, in Lebanon, by French archaeologists in 1923 is one of the most important works of art from the Levant. [*See Byblos.*] Its inscription can be considered the oldest meaningful document so far known in Phoenician. The text, in two lines of unequal length, is carved on the lid of the sarcophagus. Words and syntactic units are separated by a small vertical stroke, but the technical execution of the writing leaves a bit to be desired. Analysis of the inscription shows that orthographic practice at the end of the second millennium BCE did not include the use of matres lectionis. The script presents a number of peculiar features: the *aleph*, the upright stance of *gimel*, the horizontal crossbars of *ḥet*, and the archaic *ayin*. The inscription is dated on paleographic grounds to about 1000 BCE. The text runs as follows: "Coffin which Itthobaal son of Ahiram, king of Byblos, made for Ahiram, his father, when he placed him in eternity: if a king from among kings or a governor from among governors or the commander of an army should come up against Byblos and uncover this coffin, may the scepter of his rule be broken, may the throne of his kingship be overturned, and may peace flee Byblos, and (as for) him, may his inscription be effaced (from) before Byblos."

The decoration on the lid portrays two figures, a father and son. The dead father holds a drooping flower in one hand and raises the other in a gesture of benediction. On the main body of the sarcophagus, the father is enthroned, and before him is a table laden with food; on the other side of the table a standing courtier is followed by two men with cups and four others with both hands raised. Mourning women, persons carrying baskets on their heads, and a single man leading an animal are carved on the narrow and long sides of the sarcophagus. The strong Egyptian influence in the iconography of these scenes reflects the connections this ancient city-state always had with Egypt. The decoration allows for a date at the end of the eleventh century BCE, which accords well with the paleography of the inscription. The royal name *Ahiram*, which means "My brother [god] is exalted," appears very frequently in Phoenicia, but less so the name *Itthobaal*, "Baal is with him."

BIBLIOGRAPHY

Dussaud, René. "Les inscriptions phéniciennes du tombeau d'Ahiram, roi de Byblos." *Syria* 5 (1924): 135–159. Contains the *editio princeps* of the principal Ahiram inscription (pp. 135–142).

Gibson, John C. L. *Textbook of Syrian Semitic Inscriptions*, vol. 3, *Phoenician Inscriptions.* Oxford, 1982. See pages 12–16.

Porada, Edith. "Notes on the Sarcophagus of Ahiram." *Journal of the*

Ancient Near Eastern Society of Columbia University 5 (1973): 355–372.

Teixidor, Javier. "L'inscription d'Ahiram à nouveau." *Syria* 64 (1987): 137–140.

JAVIER TEIXIDOR

AHMAR, TELL. *See* Til Barsip.

AI, biblical site located east of Bethel (*Gn.* 12:8, *Jos.* 7:2). Three sites on the perimeter of modern Deir Dibwan, 3 km (2 mi.) east of Beitin (Bethel) have been suggested as the location of biblical Ai: Khirbet Haiyan, to the south, Khirbet Khudriya, to the east; and et-Tell, to the northwest. The first two have been excavated and found to be Byzantine settlements. Et-Tell (map reference 71385 × 53365), a polygon-shaped mound of 27.5 acres, situated on the south side of the deep Wadi el-Jaya, which leads east toward Jericho, has been extensively excavated. It yielded cultural material from as early as 3100 BCE. Et-Tell is generally accepted as biblical Ai; both the Hebrew and Arabic names for the site mean "the ruin heap."

The first excavations at et-Tell were undertaken by John Garstang for the Department of Antiquities of Palestine in 1928 but were brief and involved only eight trenches. The work yielded a three-page summary report and the sketch of a plan. Judith Marquet-Krause, with the support of Baron Edmond de Rothschild, directed the second excavation project in 1933–1935. Her work focused on the highest part of the mound and the Early Bronze Age necropolis east of it. The Rothschild expedition excavated several significant EB structures, including the temple-palace (Marquet-Krauser's *palais*) and the sanctuary on the acropolis with its splendid alabaster and pottery cult objects; the nearby Iron Age village, where finds demonstrated that the village had been built directly on top of the EB city; and the lower city, whose fortifications included a postern and towers.

The third excavation project at et-Tell was a joint expedition of several research institutions that was in the field for nine seasons (1964–1976) under the direction of Joseph A. Callaway. The joint expedition expanded the Marquet-Krause excavations to include the citadel fortifications; the expanded Iron Age village; the lower-city residential area; fortifications with gates; and a reservoir. In addition, it excavated three sites in the vicinity of et-Tell to address further the location of biblical Ai and to secure comparative materials from the region for the study of et-Tell. In 1964 and 1969, Khirbet Haiyan was excavated to bedrock and was found to be a Byzantine settlement. Tombs and a Byzantine settlement were also excavated at Khirbet Khudriya in 1966 and 1968. Both sites may represent the location of monasteries. The third site in the regional study was Khirbet Raddanah, at the northern perimeter of modern Ramallah. An unfortified village with pillared houses was excavated that is contemporary with the Iron Age village at et-Tell.

The major evidence from et-Tell points to five settlement phases with abundant cultural remains. The original settlement (EB IB, 3250–3100 BCE) is an unwalled village 220 m long and located on the upper terraces of the site. The artifacts indicate a mixture of local and foreign elements. Local Chalcolithic traits of the indigenous population include angular jar neck and rim forms, as well as angular bowl forms. "Foreign" influence has been seen in carinated platters, holemouth jars with their rims rolled inward, and painted designs of groups of lines. Callaway (1964) thought these new forms might have been the result of migrations of populations from Anatolia and Syria, but most scholars dissent from that view. The dead were buried in caves along the slopes of the hill, and the burial goods reflect the cultural varieties of the mixed settlement population.

The second settlement phase (EB IC, 3100–2950 BCE) was a well-planned, walled city enclosing 27.5 acres. Massive fortifications were constructed over the homes in the unwalled village, following the site's natural contours. Four city-gate complexes were discovered: three of them were one meter wide and went straight through the wall; the fourth, which appears to be larger than the others, was only partially excavated. All the gates were fortified by towers constructed on the wall's exterior. These fortifications enclosed significant functional areas, including the impressive acropolis complex, the citadel and sanctuary, and a market and residential area. A large building (25 m long) of uncut stones with structures attached may represent the temple-palace complex of the acropolis and the center of urban life. Callaway argued again that the changes in material culture and settlement plans suggest that the indigenous population was absorbed by newcomers, possibly from Anatolia and Syria (Callaway, 1972). These newcomers imposed new leadership forms and a changed lifestyle from village to urban life, with creative city planning for the new settlement. In any case, this settlement ended in destruction—a blanket of ashes being mute testimony to the violent event.

The settlement was rebuilt in the third major phase (EB II, 2950–2775 BCE) of its history. The inhabitants repaired and modified buildings and widened and strengthened the fortifications, all inferior to those of the original city. New pottery forms include a carinated bowl with an outward-curving rim and a jug with a tall cylindrical neck and high loop handles. A massive destruction of this city may have been caused by an earthquake, as evidenced by rifts in the bedrock and associated walls, with stones tilting into the fissures. The destruction was accompanied by an intense fire.

Egyptian involvement in the rebuilding of the fourth settlement (EB III, 2775–2400 BCE) is evident in the temple-palace and in the corner-gate area of the fortifications. Column bases in the temple-palace were reworked with copper saws like those used by Egyptian craftsmen. The walls were built of hammer-dressed stones laid like bricks. The interior of the walls was plastered, and the rooms contained Egyptian imports of alabaster and stone vessels. At the southeast corner of the cities' fortifications, a kidney-shaped reservoir was constructed to capture rainwater from the upper city. [*See* Reservoirs.] Estimates of its capacity range from 1,800 to 2,000 cu m. Major changes appear about midway in this fourth period of settlement (c. 2550 BCE). Walls were rebuilt, the temple was redesigned as a royal residence, and a sanctuary was constructed against the citadel. Khirbet Kerak pottery and new objects seem to imply a new influence from the north of Canaan. This phase was ended by another violent destruction (c. 2400 BCE), and the site was abandoned and left in ruins for more than a millennium.

The fifth and final settlement phase (Iron Age I, 1200–1050 BCE) was established on the terraces below the acropolis by newcomers. The new villagers, probably "Proto-Israelites," did not fortify their settlement, and their houses were characterized by pillars or piers that supported the roof and divided the space. Streets were paved with cobblestones, and the houses shared common walls—suggesting that the population was made up of extended families. Two new technologies were evident: cisterns were dug for a water supply (see figure 1) and the hillslopes were terraced for

AI. Figure 1. *Three cisterns in the courtyard of a house.* (Erich Lessing/Art Resource, NY)

crop planting. [*See* Cisterns; Agriculture.] These settlers were farmers and shepherds, as indicated by the stone saddles, querns, mortars, pestles, iron implements, and numerous bones of goats and sheep. [*See* Sheep and Goats.] Two phases of the Iron Age village are seen in the rebuilt houses and the different pottery forms. The original houses were modified by relocating their doors, repairing walls, and resurfacing floors. The long collared-rim storejar distinguishes the first-phase pottery form from the low collared-rim jar of the second phase. Slingstones were found on the floors of the rebuilt houses, suggesting that the settlement may have been abandoned after a minor battle. The excavator has suggested that this Iron I settlement represented the Early Israelite villagers described in the *Book of Judges*.

[*See also* Ceramics, *article on* Syro-Palestinian Ceramics of the Neolithic, Bronze, and Iron Ages; *and the biographies of Callaway, Garstang, and Marquet-Krause.*]

BIBLIOGRAPHY

Callaway, Joseph A. *Pottery from the Tombs at Ai (ēt-Tell).* Colt Archaeological Institute, Monograph Series, 2. London, 1964.
Callaway, Joseph A. "The 1964 'Ai (et-Tell) Excavations." *Bulletin of the American Schools of Oriental Research,* no. 178 (1965): 13–40.
Callaway, Joseph A., and M. B. Nicol. "A Sounding at Khirbet Haiyân." *Bulletin of the American Schools of Oriental Research,* no. 183 (1966): 12–19.
Callaway, Joseph A. "New Evidence on the Conquest of 'Ai." *Journal of Biblical Literature* 87 (1968): 312–320.
Callaway, Joseph A. "The 1966 'Ai (et-Tell) Excavations." *Bulletin of the American Schools of Oriental Research,* no. 196 (1969): 2–16.
Callaway, Joseph A. "The 1968–1969 'Ai (et-Tell) Excavations." *Bulletin of the American Schools of Oriental Research,* no. 198 (1970): 7–31.
Callaway, Joseph A. *The Early Bronze Age Sanctuary at Ai (et-Tell).* London, 1972.
Callaway, Joseph A., and Kermit Schoonover. "The Early Bronze Age Citadel at Ai (et-Tell)." *Bulletin of the American Schools of Oriental Research,* no. 207 (1972): 41–53.
Callaway, Joseph A. *The Early Bronze Age Citadel and Lower City at Ai (et-Tell).* Cambridge, Mass., 1980.
Marquet-Krause, Judith. *Les fouilles de 'Ay (et-Tell), 1933–1935.* 2 vols. Paris, 1949.

ROBERT E. COOLEY

AIA. *See* Archaeological Institute of America.

'AIN DARA', site located in Syria's 'Afrin valley, upstream from the 'Amuq plain, about 67 km (42 mi.) northwest of Aleppo and 7 km (4 mi.) south of the new city of 'Afrin (36°56' N, 36°55' E). It is not far from the archaeological site of Ha-za-za/A-za-za, modern I'azaz, about 25 km (15.5 mi.) to the northeast, and from Tell Rifa'at/Arpad, about 30 km (18 mi.) to the east. 'Ain Dara' is named after a spring about 700 m east of the mound. The tell is enormous. Its citadel rises about 30 m from the level of the plain; its lower city covers an area of 24 ha (59 acres).

'Ain Dara' is not mentioned often in the scholarly literature. Some researchers passed through the area while studying the ancient city of Kunulua. It was generally ignored, however, until the chance discovery of a monumental basalt lion in 1955. The Department of Antiquities of Aleppo then initiated a series of seasons of excavation on the tell.

Excavations at its southern corner and on the northwestern edge of the summit were conducted in 1956, 1962, and in 1964 under the direction of Feisal Seirafe, assisted by the French archaeologist Maurice Dunand. [*See the biography of Dunand.*] In 1976 and again in 1978, an expedition from the Syrian Department of Antiquities and Museums, under the direction of Ali Abou Assaf, excavated at the site.

In seasons 6–11 (1980–1985) a temple was uncovered. In 1983 and 1984, Paul Zimansky and Elizabeth Stone made soundings in the lower city near the western and northern corner. From surface exploration and a sounding in the citadel and the lower city it appears that the lower city was settled from the end of the Late Bronze Age (c. thirteenth century BCE) until the Iron Age II (c.740 BCE). Except for the Roman period, the citadel was settled from the Chalcolithic through the Ottoman periods.

The following levels, dated by their artifacts, were distinguished in the area above and around the temple, which belongs to level VII (three phases: 1300–1000 BCE; 1000–900 BCE; and 900–740 BCE).

Level I: Seljuk period (1100–1400 CE)
Level II: Late Byzantine period (650 CE)
Level III: Umayyad and 'Abbasid period (650–900 CE)
Level IV: Hellenistic period (330–75 BCE)
Level V: Late Aramean and Achaemenid periods (530–330 BCE)
Level VI: Aramean and Neo-Babylonian periods (740–530 BCE).

The temple, oriented to the southeast, consists of six architectural components.

1. *Paved courtyard.* A well and a basin for washing hands before entering the sanctuary for prayers were found in the courtyard.

2. *Entrance.* Three basalt steps decorated with a guilloche pattern led to the entrance, which was a portico with two columns. Two huge limestone threshold blocks were situated in the successive doorways; there are impressions of two footprints on the first, and the print of a left foot on the second (97 × 31 cm). Two towers or rooms may have flanked the entrance. Through a room on the right a staircase between the anticella and the corridor was reached. Two sphinxes and four colossal lions flank the entrance, guarding the portico.

3. *Facade.* Reliefs of lions and sphinxes arranged in two levels decorated the facade. The upper level was comprised of huge lions in protome, and the lower of opposing lions and sphinxes.

4. *Anticella.* The decoration of the oblong anticella is very impressive. Above the floor on the lower part of the wall is a series of orthostats decorated with a pair of guilloches. Large basalt slabs are decorated with figures of mountain gods; the ornamentation above the orthostats is geometric.

'AIN DARA'. *Basalt bas-relief on a socle, depicting a mountain god and two bulls with human heads and arms.* National Museum, Aleppo, Syria. (Erich Lessing/Art Resource, NY)

5. *Stairway.* Three steps of a stairway join the anticella with the cella. The cella must have once have been very impressive. Only a few orthostats decorated with guilloches remain. The podium opposite the door was badly destroyed. Its profile is only suggested by the series of facing basalt orthostats, decorated with figures of mountain gods and geniuses (see below).

6. *Raised corridor.* In the latest phase of the temple the builder surrounded it with a raised corridor. Orthostats of opposing lions and sphinxes grace its exterior, and lions flank its entrance. On both sides of the corridor the builders originally erected thirty opposing stelae with different scenes (e.g., a throned king, a palm tree, a standing god, offerings).

The sculpture in the temple at 'Ain Dara' is integrated into the building's design: lions line the passage through the gates, lions and sphinxes are carved in protome on the slabs in the anticella and on the socle in the niche of the podium in the cella. The stelae on both sides of corridor exhibit the same technique: eighty-two reliefs form a dado around the sides of the temple terrace. The repertoire is very limited—only lions and sphinxes. It is well known that the lion is an attribute of the goddess Ishtar, and it is known from Phoenician works of art that the sphinx is an attribute of that goddess. Ishtar-Šawuška, the lover of the mountain god, ruled the mountains in northern Syria and southern Anatolia. [*See* Phoenicians.] Because the mountain god is dipicted on the orthostats and socles in the cella and anticella, it can be assumed that the temple was dedicated to the goddess Ishtar. In its plan the temple at 'Ain Dara' repeats the main features of temples at Tell Chuera, Munbaqa, Emar, Ebla, Hazor, and Tell Ta'yinat. [*See* Chuera, Tell; Emar; Ebla; Hazor.] At 'Ain Dara', however, the following principal changes appear: the platform is higher, a corridor is situated on three sides of the temple, the decorations include more than 168 reliefs and sculptures in protome, and a deep well and a large chalkstone basin opposite the east corner were found in the paved courtyard. The lions and sphinxes on the main facade and the facade of the cella resemble those guarding the gates at Boğazköy and Alaca Höyük and may be said to follow Canaanite and Hittite prototypes. [*See* Boğazköy; Hittites.]

[*See also* Temples, *article on* Syro-Palestinian Temples.]

BIBLIOGRAPHY

Abdul-Hak, Sélim. "Les musées syriens et l'éducation." *Annales Archéologiques Arabes Syriennes* 15 (1965): 3–12.
Abou Assaf, Ali. *Der Tempel von 'Ain Dārā.* Mainz am Rhein, 1990.
Annales Archéologiques Arabes Syriennes 10 (1960): 87–103.

ALI ABOU ASSAF

'AIN ES-SAMIYEH, an exceptionally strong, perennial spring some 19 km (12 mi.) north-northeast of Jerusalem, at the northeastern foot of Ba'al Hazor, one of the highest peaks in the Judean mountains (31°59′ N, 35°20′ E). The spring arises in a deep ravine surrounded by cliffs pockmarked with caves and grottoes. William Foxwell Albright, Amihai Mazar, and others have suggested plausibly that this lush area was a sanctuary in antiquity. The spring irrigates a system of small valleys that converge into the Wadi Auja, which cuts all the way down from the Judean hills, at 457 m (1,500 ft.), to the Jordan Valley. The spring still provides copious water for the town of Ramallah, from the modern pumping station at the site.

It is not surprising that there are a number of archaeological sites of many periods in the vicinity. (1) Khirbet Samiyeh lies 275 m (900 ft.) to the southeast, apparently a relatively late ruin, mostly Byzantine and Arab. (2) Khirbet el-Marjameh ("Ruin of the Heaps of Stones") is a large, rocky ruin on a promontory just northeast of the spring, with sherds from the Early Bronze, Middle Bronze, and Late Bronze Ages, as well as major ruins from the Iron I–II periods. (3) The long, narrow Dhahr Mirzbaneh ridge, some 730 m (2,400 ft.) north-northeast of the spring, has a few remains from an EB IV settlement and a complex of much-robbed cemeteries that is known to have more than one thousand tombs.

The antiquities of 'Ain es-Samiyeh have long been known to topographers and archaeologists, but the area's settlement history was only elucidated recently. David G. Lyon acquired Early Bronze IV pottery from robbed shaft tombs while director of the American School of Oriental Research in 1906–1907, and similar material found its way into many other collections from Jerusalem and elsewhere. Albright surveyed Khirbet el-Marjameh in 1923, identifying it with biblical Ephraim (*2 Sm.* 13:23). Paul W. Lapp excavated forty-five Early Bronze IV tombs on the Dhahr Mirzbaneh in 1963–1964, but he failed to locate any settlement. Bakizah Shantur and Yusuf Labidi dug another forty-four Early Bronze IV tombs in 1970; and William G. Dever published still more material from robbed tombs in 1972. Z. Kallai surveyed Khirbet el-Marjameh in 1968, opposing Albright's identification and suggesting an alternative identification with Baal Shalisha (*1 Sm.* 9:4; *2 Kgs.* 4:42). Mazar cleared portions of the Iron Age town in 1975 and 1978. Finally, in 1987 Israel Finkelstein located many more Early Bronze IV tombs on the Dhahr Mirzbaneh, as well as a fairly extensive settlement from the same period.

The two best-known periods of occupation in the vicinity of 'Ain es-Samiyeh are the Early Bronze IV and Iron I–II. During the Early Bronze IV (c. 2300–2000 BCE), the site attracted large numbers of migratory pastoralists, as well as transitory settlements. The Dhahr Mirzbaneh shaft-tomb cemetery, with several differing groups of tombs, is the largest such cemetery known in Palestine, with eleven hundred tombs in evidence and many more no doubt yet undiscovered. The pottery belongs to Dever's Central Hills type but has clear links with Jericho, the Jordan Valley, and the southern Hebron hills. One tomb produced a unique silver goblet of Syrian origin, with an embossed scene in the Ur III style. The settlement on the ridge at Dhahr Mirzbaneh, partly enclosed, covers some 4 acres and has remains of both crude dwellings and a possible cult area, possibly with two phases.

The Iron Age occupation, concentrated at Khirbet el-Marjameh, may extend from the tenth to the late eighth century BCE. The earliest phase of occupation at the 10-acre site may have been in the tenth century BCE, for there is material known from robbed tombs of that period in the vicinity. Somewhat later, in the ninth–eighth centuries BCE, a town grew up, with well-laid-out lanes and densely built-up courtyard houses of the "Israelite" type, surrounded by a stone wall 4 m wide with a massive tower, or citadel, at its northern end. The existence of a large fortified town during the Monarchy in such an isolated site may seem surprising, but it is explicable given the strategic importance of and attractive conditions for settlement at 'Ain es-Samiyeh.

BIBLIOGRAPHY

Albright, William F. "The Ephraim of the Old and New Testaments." *Journal of the Palestine Oriental Society* 3 (1923): 36–40.
Dever, William G. "Middle Bronze Age I Cemeteries at Mirzbâneh and 'Ain-Sâmiya." *Israel Exploration Journal* 22.2–3 (1972): 95–112.
Dever, William G. "MB IIA Cemeteries at 'Ain es-Sâmiyeh and Sinjil." *Bulletin of the American Schools of Oriental Research*, no. 217 (February 1975): 23–36.
Finkelstein, Israel. "The Central Hill Country in the Intermediate Bronze Age." *Israel Exploration Journal* 41.1 (1991): 19–45.
Kallai, Zecharia. "Baal-Shalisha and Ephraim." In *HaMikra' weToledot Yiśra'el: Essays in Memory of Ron Yishai*, edited by Benjamin Uffenheimer, pp. 60–71. Tel Aviv, 1972.
Lapp, Paul W. *The Dhahr Mirzbâneh Tombs: Three Intermediate Bronze Age Cemeteries in Jordan.* New Haven, 1966.
Mazar, Amihai. "Three Israelite Sites in the Hills of Judah and Ephraim." *Biblical Archaeologist* 45.3 (1982): 167–178.
Shantur, Bakizah, and Yusuf Labadi. "Tomb 204 at 'Ain Samiya." *Israel Exploration Journal* 21.2–3 (1971): 73–77.

WILLIAM G. DEVER

'AIN GHAZAL, site located in the Wadi Zerqa, at the northeast edge of Amman, Jordan (31°59' N, 35°58' E). Highway construction in 1974 bared a continuous exposure of archaeological settlement. Six seasons of excavations and site survey were conducted under the auspices of Yarmouk University, the University of Kansas, San Diego State University, the Desert Research Institute of the University of Nevada, and the Jordanian Department of Antiquities from 1982 to 1985 and in 1988–1989 (cf. Rollefson, Simmons, and Kafafi, 1992), and a regional survey around the settlement was undertaken in 1987 by Alan H. Simmons and Zeidan A. Kafafi (1988).

More than forty radiocarbon dates from the site have shown that settlement was continuous for more than two thousand years. Coupled with major changes in architec-

ture, ritual, economic base, and ceramic technology, four major stages of cultural development have been identified.

Middle Pre-Pottery Neolithic B (MPPNB) Period. In the earliest phase at 'Ain Ghazal (c. 7200–6500 BCE), cereals and pulses were farmed and goat husbandry developed. By the middle of the seventh millennium, the settlement had grown from a small hamlet of about 2 ha (5 acres) to a village of nearly 5 ha (12 acres). Hunting still played a vital role in the diet, contributing half of the meat protein; domesticated goats provided the other half. Houses were large (up to 40–50 sq m), with the number of rooms increasing from one at the beginning of the period to two and three rooms by the end of the phase. Walls were of undressed fieldstone, coated with mud mortar and finished with lime plaster. Floors were made of a fine layer of lime plaster applied over a lime-and-gravel base. Red pigment was used to decorate the floors and walls; a few fragments indicate specific designs: stylized birds and perhaps other animals among them.

MPPNB ritual practices were particularly striking at 'Ain Ghazal. Subfloor house burials of both adults and children were the norm, although courtyard burials were also common. All burials were individual (except for females with newborns or still births). The common regional MPPNB practice of decapitating the corpses of children and adults and interring their skulls elsewhere was followed (in some cases the skulls were treated with special reverence, see below). A significant number of "trash burials" of adults with skulls intact was also found, suggesting that social divisions existed in the early seventh millennium BCE.

Although the appearance of numbers of small baked and unbaked clay figurines of humans and animals is a characteristic of the MPPNB, only a few specimens of the economically important goats were found at 'Ain Ghazal. Cattle, on the other hand, dominated the identifiable animal figurines, including two examples of "ritually killed" cows buried beneath a house floor and several others with twisted fiber imprints behind their head that suggest halters. The human figurines are headless or lack a body, perhaps reflecting a close parallel to the predominant burial mode. Fertility figurines at 'Ain Ghazal are very distinct: obviously pregnant females with distended abdomens and enlarged breasts are also decorated with rocker-stamped "tattooing."

The most impressive aspects of ritual activity at 'Ain Ghazal are plastered skulls and plaster human statuary. Six plastered skulls and two caches of statues have been recovered. Three plastered skulls have been dated to before 7100 BCE, and a cache of twenty-five statues and busts dates to about 6750 BCE; a second cache of statues may date to about 6,500 BCE, at the transition of the MPPNB and the Late Pre-Pottery Neolithic B (LPPNB).

Late Pre-Pottery Neolithic B Period (LPPNB). At 'Ain Ghazal the Late Pre-Pottery Neolithic B period lasts from about 6500 to about 6000 BCE. Within this period the site more than doubled in size, reaching 10 ha (25 acres) in extent. House design changed radically, from the spacious

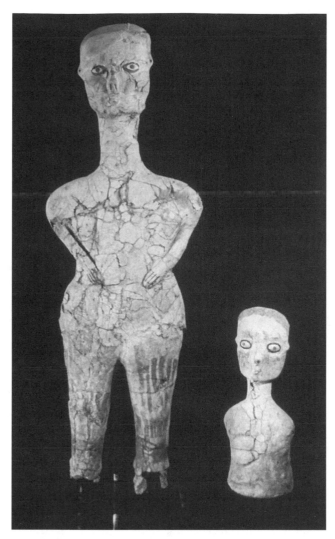

'AIN GHAZAL. *Human figurines.* (Photograph by Dorrell and Stuart Laidlaw; courtesy G. Rollefson)

two- to three-room MPPNB settings to multiple small cells (approximately 2 × 2 m each) around a central hall or chamber of unknown dimensions. Lime-plaster floors decorated with red ocher continued to characterize the buildings.

The site's economic base remained agricultural. Domesticated dogs are evident early in the phase, and at its close cattle and pigs were probably domesticated. It is clear that hunted wild species began to decline dramatically after 6500 BCE, signaling a major environmental change for the settlement and its vicinity. There appear to be no major ritual changes in human burials from those in the MPPNB; the number of human and animal figurines recovered from the restricted areas of excavation also was the same.

Pre-Pottery Neolithic C Period (PNNC). The end of the seventh millennium in ancient Palestine witnessed the demise of all known large agricultural settlements. However, during the Pre-Pottery Neolithic C period (6000–c. 5500

BCE) 'Ain Ghazal grew to more than 12 ha (30 acres; and, possibly, to more than 14 ha or 34 acres). Although details of that period's agricultural pursuits are lacking, a farming base for the settlement is undeniable. Hunting, on the other hand, was severely restricted to steppe and desert fauna, with domesticated goats, cattle, pigs, and sheep constituting the bulk (90 percent) of recovered animal bones.

Beyond differences in animal husbandry, hunting, and implied environmental change, the PPNC period at 'Ain Ghazal suggests in other critical ways that a major cultural change was underway. Architecturally, houses included semisubterranean structures founded on MPPNB and/or LPPNB lime-plaster floors, as well as similar surface structures that differed dramatically from MPPNB and LPPNB times. Buildings were smaller (approximately 3.5–4 m on a side), with small rectangular chambers (approximately 3 times 1 m) bisected by a central corridor that created cells too small for normal domestic functions, such as living or sleeping areas. Altogether, the PPNC structures suggest permanent storage features with flimsy superstructures.

The ritual aspects of the first half of the sixth millennium contrast with the LPPNB as strongly as the architectural elements. PPNC burials occur as subfloor and courtyard interments, but in every case the skull remains intact with the skeleton. The consistent occurrence of pig remains with PPNC burials is also a major departure from PPNB practices.

The appearance of pottery has long been taken to be a watershed of cultural development in the Levant, and in the south it has been conventionally assumed that this was a technological innovation introduced by populations migrating from the north (Mellaart, 1975, p. 238). The evidence from 'Ain Ghazal argues against this view however. Several examples of modifications of PPNC architecture are associated with crude fired pottery, followed soon thereafter by typical Yarmukian ceramics. This development indicates that the transition from the aceramic to the ceramic Neolithic was a local phenomenon (Rollefson, Kafafi, and Simmons, 1993).

Yarmukian Pottery Neolithic. The gradual changes from the PPNC to the Yarmukian Pottery Neolithic are also expressed in other ways. Hunting and herding evidence from animal remains is similar for both periods. The earliest Yarmukian inhabitants modified standing PPNC structures, but slightly later, Yarmukians built permanent rectangular structures very different from PPNC norms. These structures included large open spaces enclosed by stone walls, with floors made of puddled mud or *huwwar*, a "plaster" composed of mud and pounded chalk. The latest preserved Yarmukian architectural remains are curvilinear stone arrangements around the repeated appearance of puddled-mud floors. The indication is that 'Ain Ghazal had ceased to function as a permanent settlement, offering instead a seasonal camp for pastoral nomadic groups, probably during the dry summer months. The evidence from 'Ain Ghazal

(Köhler-Rollefson, 1988; Köhler-Rollefson and Rollefson, 1990), as well as from the eastern deserts of Jordan (e.g., Betts, 1986, p. 303) strongly suggests that an increasing reliance on pastoral nomadism began during the PPNC and that pastoral and agricultural economic systems were completely segregated shortly after the beginning of the Yarmukian period.

In its ritual practices the Yarmukian period differed vastly from its aceramic forebears: not a single Yarmukian burial has been identified at 'Ain Ghazal and animal figurines are rare, although a bird (?) has been found; human figurines are also few, but the head of a typical "coffee-bean" fertility figurine (Rollefson, Kafafi, and Simmons, 1993) was recovered (cf. Perrot, 1964, pl. XXIII).

Interpretation of the Data. The changes witnessed in the long, unbroken occupational sequence at 'Ain Ghazal can be understood in terms of responses to the demands of increasing population growth on what was a lucrative but delicate habitat. The MPPNB strategy of a combined hunting, goat herding, and agricultural subsistence base permitted an unprecedented population growth. By the onset of the LPPNB, the effects of these increasing demands is seen in the decrease of animal species variability. This decrease culminated during the PPNC period, when faunal diversity collapsed to a handful of wild species. Continued environmental degradation during the Yarmukian period finally led to the collapse of 'Ain Ghazal as a permanent settlement (Köhler-Rollefson and Rollefson 1990).

Climate change had little to do with the demise of 'Ain Ghazal (and other settlements in the southern Levant). The large demands on tree stands for fuel to produce MPPNB and LPPNB lime plaster deforested an area within a radius of several kilometers; exacerbated by the appetite of increasingly large herds of goats, the landscape around 'Ain Ghazal was exposed to continual erosion by the winter rains and summer winds. Logs and branches became scarcer for construction through time, and wood was increasingly difficult to collect for hearths. Agricultural fields within a reasonable distance from the spring at 'Ain Ghazal became so distant that it was no longer feasible to use the settlement as a home base. By the PPNC period the cultural degradation of the environment was probably already irreversible, and late PPNC and Yarmukian efforts to accommodate those changes were too little and too late for the long-term stable continuation of a permanent community.

[*See also* Cattle and Oxen; Paleoenvironmental Reconstruction; Pigs; *and* Sheep and Goats.]

BIBLIOGRAPHY

Betts, Alison V. G. "The Prehistory of the Basalt Desert, Transjordan: An Analysis." Ph. D. diss., University of London, 1986.
Köhler-Rollefson, Ilse. "The Aftermath of the Levantine Neolithic Revolution in the Light of Ecological and Ethnographic Evidence." *Paléorient* 14.1 (1988): 87–93.
Köhler-Rollefson, Ilse, and Gary O. Rollefson. "The Impact of Neolithic Subsistence Strategies on the Environment: The Case of 'Ain Ghazal, Jordan." In *Man's Role in the Shaping of the Eastern Mediterranean Landscape*, edited by Sytze Bottema et al., pp. 3–14. Rotterdam, 1990.
Mellaart, James. *The Neolithic of the Near East.* New York, 1975.
Perrot, Jean. "Les deux premières campagnes de fouilles à Munhata, 1962–1963: Premiers résultats." Syria 41 (1964): 323–345.
Rollefson, Gary O., Zeidan A. Kafafi, and Alan H. Simmons. "The Neolithic Village of 'Ain Ghazal, Jordan: Preliminary Report on the 1989 Season." In *Preliminary Excavation Reports: Sardis, Paphos, Caesarea Maritima, Shiqmim, 'Ain Ghazal*, edited by William G. Dever, pp. 107–126. Annual of the American Schools of Oriental Research, no. 51. Baltimore, 1993.
Rollefson, Gary O., Alan H. Simmons, and Zeidan A. Kafafi. "Neolithic Cultures at 'Ain Ghazal, Jordan." *Journal of Field Archaeology* 19 (1992): 443–470.
Simmons, Alan H., and Zeidan A. Kafafi. "Preliminary Report on the 'Ain Ghazal Archaeological Survey, 1987." *Annual of the Department of Antiquities of Jordan* 32 (1988): 27–39.

GARY O. ROLLEFSON

'AJJUL, TELL EL- (Ar., "the mound of the calf"), site located on the northern bank of Wadi Gaza, 2 km (1.2 mi.) from the Mediterranean coast and 6 km (3.6 mi.) southwest of modern Gaza (31°29' N, 34°28' E; map reference 0934 × 0976). The site is poorly preserved as a result of encroaching dunes and seasonal flooding; it is at least 8 ha (20 acres) in size and rectangular in shape.

William M. Flinders Petrie excavated Tell el-'Ajjul for the British School of Archaeology from 1930 to 1934. Ernest H. Mackay and Margaret A. Murray briefly continued the excavation in 1938. Less than 5 percent of the site has been excavated. Petrie claimed that Tell el-'Ajjul was ancient Gaza. However, Aharon Kempinski (1974) notes that ancient Gaza was probably located within the confines of the modern city and correctly suggests that Tell el-'Ajjul is the city of Sharuhen, mentioned in both biblical and Egyptian sources. The size of Tell el-'Ajjul, along with its great quantity of Hyksos scarabs and the wealth of its gold hoards, supports this identification. Petrie's excavation and publication of the site are, thus, problematic, and basic aspects of stratigraphy and chronology remain confusing and controversial. William Foxwell Albright (1938), James R. Stewart (1974), Kempinski (1993), and William G. Dever (1992) have all attempted to rework the dating of Tell el-'Ajjul. [*See the biographies of Petrie and Albright.*]

Except for the site's Early Bronze IV tombs, there are scant traces of early settlement. Tell el-'Ajjul reached its zenith during the Middle Bronze Age. In the Late Bronze Age, occupation was limited, but new cemeteries appeared. There are a few Iron Age II burials and a smattering of material that dates to the Hellenistic, Roman, and Late Arab periods.

Cemeteries. Cemetery 1500 (EB IV) is located west of the tell and includes approximately forty-two single, articulated burials in rectangular tombs with square shafts. [*See Burial Sites; Tombs.*] Grave goods were often limited to a single bronze dagger. [*See Grave Goods.*] Kathleen M. Kenyon (1956) suggests that only the earliest tombs contained daggers. Cemetery 100–200 (EB IV) is located east of the tell and contained approximately fifty burials. Its tombs shafts and chambers tend to be rounded. Grave goods included ceramic bowls and deep cups but very few daggers.

The earliest material from the tell itself comes from the Courtyard Cemetery. Its tombs were cut into the soft marl in the northern corner of the site. There is a total of twenty-five human burials and evidence of eighty animals. Burials were usually of single individuals. Six phases of burial types have been identified dating to MB IIA. Noteworthy is the burial of a child wearing gold jewelry found beneath palace II.

The Canaanite city ceased to function in the Late Bronze Age and a series of three large cemeteries began to develop to the north and east of the tell. The lower cemetery to the north of the site, the eighteenth-dynasty cemetery to the northeast, and the eastern cemetery to the east contained three hundred and five simple pit burials and eight elaborate pit burials. The pit burials were simple shallow rectangular or oval pits dug into the ground.

The practice of pit burials continued from the Middle Bronze Age, but the MB burials were intramural, whereas the LB cemeteries were not. However, there are a few LB intramural burials on the tell. The pit burials contain a high percentage of imported Cypriot pottery. Other grave goods include Mycenaean IIIA pottery, gold and bronze jewelry, metal objects (e.g., toggle pins, needles, daggers, arrowheads, a blade, razor, adzer, and axe), and Egyptian objects, especially scarabs. The cemeteries decline in use in LB IIB.

Eight elaborate pit tombs that include a dromos and a stone-lined cist are unique to Tell el-'Ajjul and date to LB II. This evolution from simple pit burials probably accommodated elite families. Both the structure of the tombs and the grave goods are more elaborate. The grave goods included a great number of weapons, Egyptian objects (a gold ring, scarabs), and Egyptian-inspired objects (lead fishing-net weights, duck-shaped bowl). The "governor's tomb" is particularly outstanding and was reused several times throughout the Late Bronze Age. It has a stepped dromos, walls lined with sandstone slabs, and a gabled roof. Grave goods include a gold ring with the name of Tutankhamun, a scarab of Rameses II, thirty-five arrowheads, a bronze wine set, fishing weights, and an duck-shaped ivory bowl.

Other LB burial types include cave burials and loculi burials. Rivka Gonen (1992) considers the limited use of these burial types to be evidence of foreign populations, with pit burials reserved for the indigenous population. A group of loculi burials was found in the eastern cemetery. Each cave had a wide entrance and the loculi were carved into the walls. The caves measured at least 3.5 m in diameter, with the largest measuring 3.5 × 6 m. They may have had vaulted ceilings. Each loculus had the remains of at least two individuals and several contained the dismembered skeleton of an equid (tomb 411 contained the remains of an entire

horse). A cache of limbs from a variety of species including ass, gazelle, horse, and ox, as well as human bones, was found near the entrance to these loculi. Gonen (1992; p. 131) compares the horse burials to one from Marathon in Greece. An odd use of a burial cave is one cut into the MB fosse: a shaft leads to a central chamber, off of which two burial niches contained the remains of four distinct burial groups. A total of fourteen people was found.

There is some indication of Phoenician-style cremation burials in cemetery 1000. Thirteen simple graves contained cremation urns along with metal (bronze and iron) and Egyptian objects (faience cup, scarabs, amulets). Cypro-Phoenician vessels, Cypriot vessels, and some Philistine pottery were also found. The cremation jar burials date to the tenth–eighth centuries BCE.

Fortifications. The site was protected by a fosse that surrounded the mound on three sides and was up to 6 m deep. The fosse was created by digging out the soft marl and sandstone, which in turn was used to build a steep rampart. The fosse and rampart date to late MB IIA. There is some evidence for a mud-brick wall crowning the rampart that would have been contemporary with palace III. Entrance to the site was from the northeast, where a strip of marl was left intact, acting as a causeway across the fosse. A series of enigmatic shallow tunnels emerged from the causeway and continued out to the coastal plain. Olga Tufnell (1993) suggests that these tunnels may be part of an irrigation system. [See Irrigation.]

Palaces. A planned city was constructed inside the ramparts in the MB IIB. A ring road encircles the inside of its fosse, and a major southeast–northwest road runs through the center of the tell. Palace I (43 × 55 m) is located in the northwest part of the mound. A rectangular structure, it consists of a large central courtyard surrounded by rooms and is constructed of large blocks of sandstone, probably cuttings from the fosse. Palace I bears some similarities in plan and construction to the MB palace at Lachish, including embedded orthostats in the lower part of plastered walls—a Canaanite architectural tradition. [See Lachish.] City III was partially destroyed in the early sixteenth century BCE.

City II was built along the same general plan as City III and dates to MB IIC. The residential quarter, in the southeast part of the mound, is divided by long streets that create an orthogonal plan similar to MB Megiddo. Houses had several rooms and often included a small interior courtyard. Patrician houses ranged in size from 190 to 270 sq m and sometimes had second stories; the houses belonging to individuals of lower status were one story and only 70–100 sq m in size. Palace II is built above palace I, but it is smaller and made entirely of mud brick, without orthostats.

Several very significant gold hoards were found in contexts most likely associated with City II prior to its destruction. These hoards suggest that Tell el-'Ajjul was a wealthy city. These particular hoards may reflect the stress felt by the inhabitants during Ahmose's campaign in Canaan, when the Egyptians besieged the city of Sharuhen for three years. The City II palace was thus probably destroyed in about 1530 BCE.

The city declined steadily in the Late Bronze Age, when a series of large cemeteries was in use. The palace, which was rebuilt several times throughout the Late Bronze Age, was converted into an Egyptian fortress that controlled the coastal road to Gaza. Palace III dates to LB IB, Palace IV to LB IIA, and Palace V to LB IIB. There is some evidence of an Iron Age occupation. Albright (1938) suggested that Palace V might date to the tenth century BCE. [See Palace.]

Material Culture. The use of bichrome decoration, the arrangement of motifs, and the vessel morphology at Tell el-'Ajjul all reflect Canaanite ceramic traditions. A bichrome ware sometimes referred to as 'Ajjul Painted Ware is distinctive because red and black paint were used to depict both geometric and anthropomorphic motifs. The decoration is frequently arranged in a frieze of metopes or triglyphs in which bulls, birds, and fish are depicted. Typical ceramic forms at the site include the krater, jug, and bowl. Some forms are more typically Cypriot, however, as are the anthropomorphic motifs.

Bichrome Ware begins in MB IIC and continues in use until LB IA. It has a wide distribution in the eastern Mediterranean but is found primarily along the southern coast of Palestine, in the Shephelah, along the Syrian coast, on Cyprus, in the Egyptian Delta, and in Cilicia. Neutron activation analysis has demonstrated that most of the Tell el-'Ajjul Bichrome Ware was produced in eastern Cyprus, which was a major production center for this ceramic type (Artzy et al., 1973). [See Neutron Activation Analysis.] Some of the Bichrome Ware from Tell el-'Ajjul was also produced locally. Other imported Cypriot pottery found at Tell el-'Ajjul includes Red-on-Black, Black-Slip II, Monochrome, Black Lustrous, Base-Ring I and II, White-Slip I and II, and White-Painted IV and V Wares.

Tell el-'Ajjul is well known for gold jewelry found in several hoards and in tombs. Unique gold crescents, pendants, earrings, toggle pins, and bracelets were made in a variety of sophisticated techniques such as granulation, cloisonné, and repoussé. [See Jewelry.] Gold-foil pendants with schematic representations of a fertility goddess, similar to examples from Gezer, were also found. [See Gezer.] The gold itself was probably imported from Nubia. [See Nubia.] The jewelry found is also made of silver, electrum, and lead. The floruit of jewelry production was in MB IIC.

Tell el-'Ajjul has produced scores of fifteenth-dynasty, or Hyksos, scarabs and eighteenth-dynasty scarabs. [See Hyksos.] Egyptian royal seals from several kings were found, including Amenemhet III, Neferhotep I, and Ma-ib Re Sheshi. Other Egyptian artifacts include a jar with cartouches of Hatshepsut and Thutmosis III, a gold signet ring with the name of Tutankhamun, and scarabs of Thutmosis III. The last royal name found is that of Rameses II, indicating that the cemeteries were used until 1200 BCE.

[See also Ceramics, article on Syro-Palestinian Ceramics of the Neolithic, Bronze, and Iron Ages; and Fortifications, article on Fortifications of the Bronze and Iron Ages.]

BIBLIOGRAPHY

Albright, William Foxwell. "The Chronology of a South Palestinian City, Tell el-'Ajjul." *American Journal of Semitic Languages and Literature* 55.4 (1938): 337–359.
Artzy, Michal, et al. "The Origin of the 'Palestinian' Bichrome Ware." *Journal of the American Oriental Society* 93.4 (1973): 446–461.
Dever, William G. "The Chronology of Syria-Palestine in the Second Millennium B.C.E.: A Review of Current Issues." *Bulletin of the American Schools of Oriental Research*, no. 288 (1992): 1–25.
Epstein, Claire. *Palestinian Bichrome Ware.* Leiden, 1966. The most comprehensive analysis of bichrome pottery from a stylistic perspective. Though a bit dated and written prior to Artzy et al.'s important work, this is still worthwhile.
Gonen, Rivka. *Burial Patterns and Cultural Diversity in Late Bronze Age Canaan.* American Schools of Oriental Research, Dissertation Series, 7. Winona Lake, Ind., 1992. See especially pages 70–82, 118ff.
Heurtley, W. A. "A Palestinian Vase-Painter of the Sixteenth Century B.C." *Quarterly of the Department of Antiquities in Palestine* 8 (1938): 21–37. The first comprehensive look at bichrome pottery; remains valuable for its stylistic analysis.
Kempinski, Aharon. "Tell el-'Ajjûl—Beth-Aglayim or Sharuhen?" *Israel Exploration Journal* 24.3–4 (1974): 145–152.
Kempinski, Aharon. "The Middle Bronze Age." In *The Archaeology of Ancient Israel,* edited by Amnon Ben-Tor, pp. 159–210. New Haven, 1992. Kempinski's overviews of Tell el-'Ajjul are invaluable for understanding the importance of the site and the material's broad implications (see esp. pp. 189ff, 203ff).
Kempinski, Aharon. "Tell el-'Ajjûl." In *The New Encyclopedia of Archaeological Excavations in the Holy Land,* vol. 1, pp. 52–53. Jerusalem and New York, 1993.
Kenyon, Kathleen M. "Tombs of the Intermediate Early Bronze–Middle Bronze Age at Tell Ajjul." *Annual of the Department of Antiquities of Jordan* 3 (1956): 41–55.
McGovern, Patrick E. *Late Bronze Age Palestinian Pendants: Innovation in a Cosmopolitan Age.* Sheffield, 1985. Excellent detailed treatment of Canaanite pendants; Tell el-'Ajjul's many such pendants are prominent.
Negbi, Ora. *The Hoards of Goldwork from Tell el-Ajjul.* Studies in Mediterranean Archaeology, vol. 25. Göteborg, 1970. Valuable overview of the gold jewelry from the site, with important commentary on its dating and stylistic influences.
Petrie, W. M. Flinders. *Ancient Gaza.* 4 vols. London, 1931–1934.
Petrie, W. M. Flinders. *City of Shepherd Kings and Ancient Gaza V.* London, 1952. Excavation reports by Petrie to be read as catalogs.
Stewart, James R. *Tell el-'Ajjul: The Middle Bronze Age Remains.* Studies in Mediterranean Archaeology, 38. Göteborg, 1974.
Tufnell, Olga. "The Courtyard Cemetery at Tell el-'Ajjul, Palestine." *Bulletin of the Institute of Archaeology* 3 (1962): 1–37.
Tufnell, Olga. "A Review of the Contents of Cave 303 at Tell el-'Ajjul." *'Atiqot* 14 (1980): 37–48. This and the article by Tufnell above represent some of the best analyses of the Tell el-'Ajjul material by someone who was present at the excavations.
Tufnell, Olga. "Tell el-'Ajjûl." In *The New Encyclopedia of Archaeological Excavations in the Holy Land,* vol. 1, pp. 49–52. Jerusalem and New York, 1993.

J. P. DESSEL

'AJLUN, site located above Wadi Kafranja, one of three valleys between the two lakes which climb from the Jordan Valley up to the Transjordanian plateau (32°20′ N, 35°45′ E). 'Ajlun has the best preserved Ayyubid mosque in Jordan. An inscription of al-Malik al-Mu'azzam (*RCEA* 3970) demonstrates that it was founded in or before 1218–1227. The minaret was built under Baybars I in 1264 (*RCEA* 4528), and the doorway was repaired in 1332 (*RCEA* 5618).

'Ajlun castle, called *Qal'at al-Rabad* ("citadel of the suburb") after the suburb which grew up around it, occupies the last high point in the northern part of the valley. It was extensively restored by the Department of Antiquities of Transjordan in 1927–1929. The castle was founded in 1184–1145 by 'Izz ad-Din Usama by order of Salah ad-Din (Saladin) to counter the threat posed by the Crusaders' Belvoir castle on the opposite side of the Jordan Valley. It may also have served to check Reynald de Châtillon, lord of Kerak, and to protect the region's rich iron ore deposits.

The nucleus of the castle was a four-towered keep on the site's highest point, flanked by two baileys on its eastern and southern sides. The main entrance lay beneath the southeast corner of the keep, protected by a machicoulis on two corbels (dismantled in 1927). The whole complex was surrounded by a deep rock-cut ditch.

The castle was extensively refortified in about 1214 by Aybak b. 'Abd Allah, chamberlain (Ar., *ustādh al-dār*) to al-Malik al-Mu'azzam 'Isa. He built the south tower to protect the reflex angle between the two baileys (*RCEA* 3746), added a ward to its east, constructed two outer gates (one decorated with zoomorphic carvings), and heightened much of the older structure.

Some restoration to the east wall was carried out in about 1253–1260 (*RCEA* 4463), before the castle was surrendered to the Mongols (in 1260). Crude repairs to the keep and the southwest corner are postmedieval. The castle was still inhabited when J. L. Burckhardt visited it in 1812, and Ibrahim Pasha installed a small Egyptian garrison there in 1831–1841.

[*See also* Crusader Period; Kerak.]

BIBLIOGRAPHY

Johns, C. N. "Medieval 'Ajlūn: The Castle." *Quarterly of the Department of Antiquities of Palestine* 1 (1932): 21–33. Good account of the castle's history and construction.

Répertoire chronologique d'épigraphie arabe (RCEA). 18 vols. to date. Edited by Étienne Combe, Jean Sauvaget, and Gaston Wiet. Cairo, 1931–. Standard collection of Arabic epigraphy.

JEREMY JOHNS

AKKADE, capital city, location unknown, of the Akkadian Empire (c. 2290–2200 BCE), created and maintained by Sargon and his dynastic successors. The city of Akkade and the Akkadian Empire are at the nexus of several interrelated problems: the location of the city; why and how southern Mesopotamia underwent a centralization of regional power, passing from a loose urban confederation in the early third millennium to tight politicoeconomic imperialization under one city in the late third millennium; whether the third-millennium cities of southern Mesopotamia were self-sustaining or were dependent on adjacent regions for essential resources; the reason for the regional extensions of southern Mesopotamian political and economic power in the mid-third millennium; and how the empire functioned and the reasons for its collapse. These historical questions surrounding Akkade make the city the most important ancient West Asian site as yet to be located and excavated.

Knowledge of the city and the empire is mostly derived from settlements and material and epigraphic remains from regions imperialized by the Akkadians, and from Akkadian-period documents copied by later scribes. However, the earliest reference to Akkade occurs in a year date of Enšaku-šanna (second dynasty of Uruk), who probably ruled within the generation prior to Sargon, founder of the Akkadian dynasty. [*See* Uruk-Warka.] This singular datum indicates that Akkade was not founded *ab novo* by Sargon and suggests the limitations of data presently available for understanding the early history of the city and its rise to regional political power.

Contemporary Akkadian-period references, as well as later copies of historical inscriptions, describe Akkade as a bustling imperial capital with temples and palaces, a busy harbor, a large imperial bureaucracy, merchants traveling to distant realms acquiring and dispatching exotic goods, as well as an army capable of marches to the Mediterranean Sea, to the sources of the Tigris and the Euphrates, and the conquest of the urban centers in its path. The most famous of the Mesopotamian "city laments," the Curse of Akkade, composed within a hundred years of the Akkadian imperial collapse, describes the collapse and abandonment of Akkade as symbolic of the collapse of the Akkadian Empire.

Historical references indicate, however, that Akkade was occupied for seventeen hundred years following the collapse of the empire. In the Ur III period the city was the seat of a provincial governor, while the prologue to the Code of Hammurabi mentions the still-functioning Eulmaš Temple of Ištar (Ishtar) within "broad-marted" Akkade. Parts of the ancient city were still settled in the Kassite, Neo-Assyrian, and Neo-Babylonian periods, during which archaeological expeditions were repeatedly undertaken in search of Akkadian-period treasure. [*See* Kassites; Assyrians; Babylonians.] The most famous of these excavations, a program that lasted three years, was directed by a scribe of King Nabonidus of Babylon (r. 555–539) who took an impression of a commemorative inscription excavated within a palace of Sargon's grandson Naram-Sin; the excavator labeled the impression with its provenience as well as his name. The city is last mentioned in a document dated to year 29 of the reign of Darius.

V. Gordon Childe's early characterization of the Akkadian Empire stressed its campaigns of conquest for the acquisition of resources unavailable in southern Mesopotamia, such as metals and timber. Childe's sketch, although still influential among archaeologists, could not consider the progression and the context of expansionary activities directed from Akkade that are now documented in the archaeological and epigraphic records, nor the still earlier sequence of repeated southern Mesopotamian expansions documented in the Late Ubaid, Late Uruk, and Late Early Dynastic II/early Early Dynastic III periods (Childe, 1951).

The detailed Akkadian data suggest that Sargon's long-distance military campaigns were but one stage of the Akkadian expansionary process. These early military campaigns focused on conquest of distant urban centers and the retrieval of plunder. Subsequent military campaigns led by Sargon's successors, particularly Naram-Sin, conquered and then imperialized both irrigation-agriculture southern Mesopotamia and dry-farming northern Mesopotamia. In this second stage of Akkadian expansion, the forces from Akkade first conquered local states and then constructed fortresses and temples for resident Akkadian administrators and functionaries.

Acting in each imperialized province, these Akkadian forces systematically implemented five imperial strategies on behalf of the capital:

1. Reorganized the administrative structure of agricultural production by establishing a streamlined administrative command responsible to authorities in Akkade;

2. Reorganized the spatial structure of regional agricultural production by vacating second- and third-level population centers; concentrated labor forces in urban centers; and constructed city walls to enclose relocated populations;

3. Intensified agro-production by creating imperial domains in Sumer and Akkad for the exclusive production of Akkade-directed taxes and by extended, and perhaps irrigated, cereal production in the imperialized dry-farming regions;

4. Introduced and enforced imperial-standard units of measure for ration-labor work gangs and for regional agricultural production;

5. Extracted imperial taxes, as much as 70 percent of the intensified agro-production, from each reorganized administrative unit, and shipped these agricultural goods by water transport to Akkade.

This flow of administrators, military forces, and imperialized agricultural produce into and out of Akkade can be modeled (see figure 1) to illustrate the imperial accumulation of agricultural wealth from both Sumer in southern Mesopotamia and Subir, the dry-farming Khabur plains of northern Mesopotamia. [See Sumerians.] Similar relationships were structured at the five other high-productivity dry-farming regions (Susa, Gasur/Nuzi, Erbil, Nineveh, Diyarbakir) surrounding Akkade, where urbanized polities with nucleated labor forces already comprised a preadaptation for Akkadian agricultural imperialism. [See Susa; Nuzi; Nineveh.]

The water-born course of imperialized and convertible agricultural wealth into Akkade from adjacent regions underlies the ideal of regional unification upheld by the Akkadians and successor Mesopotamian empires. It also emphasizes the still-problematic goals of the earlier southern Mesopotamian expansions into these same regions, although the form and regional structure of earlier expansions differed considerably.

The description of the fall of Akkade in the poetic Curse of Akkade portrays a city suffering from reduced Euphrates flow, desiccated irrigation fields, famine, and the incursions of neighboring "barbarians" into the Akkadian heartland. These descriptions have been understood as poetic metaphors by many Assyriologists, but a few have ventured that the descriptions, while poetic, are not necessarily metaphoric. Southern Mesopotamian irrigation agriculture was dependent upon the frequently variable flow of the Euphrates. The documentary evidence for Late Akkadian-period agricultural failure in southern Mesopotamia, and for extended drought in northern Mesopotamia, conforms to the independent data for hemispheric aridification, probably an abrupt climate change, beginning in about 2200 BCE. The gradual aridification and decrease in Euphrates flow that had begun about seven hundred years earlier may explain in part the stages of conflict, unification, and expansion that culminated in Akkade's ascension to regional and transregional power.

The publication in 1972 of two surface surveys of the region of Akkad raised anew the longstanding question of the location of Akkad. The associations of Sargon and Akkade with the city of Kish made these surface reconnaissance observations particularly important for locating the city. [See Kish.] These associations include the paramountcy of Kish within southern Mesopotamia in the pre-Akkadian period, Sargon's service as cupbearer to Ur-zababa, king of Kish, and the historiographic traditions of Sargon's construction of a new city opposite Babylon, which is adjacent to Kish. [See Babylon.]

Ishan Mizyad, one site identified in the Akkad surveys, is located between Kish and Babylon, beside the ancient course of the Euphrates River. It presents several locational, topographic, and settlement-history features that can be associated with Akkade. Recent Iraqi government soundings at the site produced evidence for the Ur III settlement there, and cuneiform texts mentioning Bab-Ea, but did not extend to the site's Akkadian levels (Mahdi, 1986). Bab-Ea, an otherwise unknown toponym, is a likely name for an urban

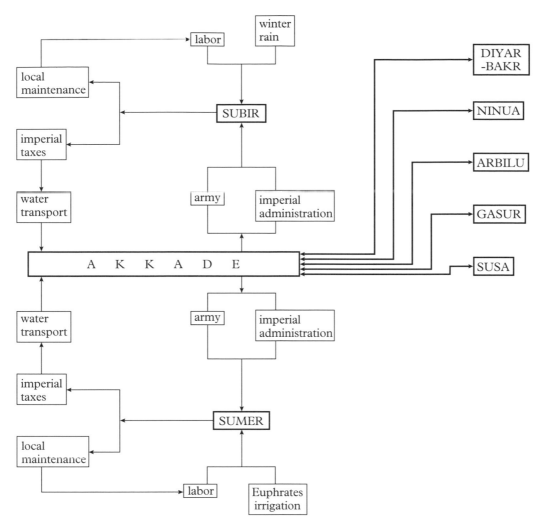

AKKADE. Figure 1. *Flow chart schematizing Akkadian agro-imperialism.*

quarter or "gate." More recent reviews of historical occurrences of the city strongly suggest a location about 50 km (31 mi.) to the northeast, at or near the confluence of the Tigris and the Diyala Rivers. These locational suggestions, if accurate, may require a major reconsideration of the role of the Tigris River in third-millennium southern Mesopotamian history.

[*See also* Agriculture; Akkadians; *and* Mesopotamia, *article on* Ancient Mesopotamia.]

BIBLIOGRAPHY

Attinger, Pascal. "Remarques à propos de la 'Malediction d'Accad.'" *Revue d'Assyriologie et d'Archéologie Orientale* 78 (1984): 99–121. Full translation of the Curse of Akkade, with an illuminating discussion of its ambiguous or difficult-to-translate passages.

Childe, V. Gordon. *Man Makes Himself.* New York, 1951. Influential sketch of Near Eastern prehistory and early historic developments, including the origins of Mesopotamian cities and empires.

Foster, Benjamin R. "Management and Administration in the Sargonic Period." In *Akkad, the First World Empire,* edited by Mario Liverani,

pp. 25–39. Padua, 1993. Summary of the epigraphic data for Akkadian imperial activity.

Gibson, McGuire. *The City and Area of Kish.* Miami, 1972. Archaeological surface reconnaissance, including an appendix by Robert Adams presenting the settlement data from his earlier Akkade survey.

Glassner, J.-J. "La fin d'Akkadé: Approche chronologique." *Nouvelles Assyriologiques Brèves et Utilitaires* 1 (1994): 8–9. Outline of the sequence, chronology, and actors within the Akkadian collapse events.

Mahdi, A. M. "Ishan Mizyad: Important centre agadéene." *Histoire et Archéologie* 103 (1986): 65–67. Summary description of brief Iraqi excavations at a site hypothesized to be Akkade.

McEwan, G. J. P. "Agade after the Gutian Destruction: The Afterlife of a Mesopotamian City." *Archiv für Orientforschung* 29 (1982): 8–15. Synthesis of cuneiform references to Akkade after the imperial collapse.

Wall-Romana, Christophe. "An Areal Location of Agade." *Journal of Near Eastern Studies* 49.3 (1990): 205–245. Collection of epigraphic data for a Tigris-region location for Akkade.

Weiss, Harvey. "Kish, Akkad, and Agade." *Journal of the American Oriental Society* 95.3 (1975): 434–453. Analysis of Kish-area settlement data for the Akkadian period and comparison with epigraphic data for the location of Akkade.

Weiss, Harvey, and M.-A. Courty. "The Genesis and Collapse of the

Akkadian Empire." In *Akkad, the First World Empire,* edited by Mario Liverani, pp. 131–156. Padua, 1993. A model for the development, function, and collapse of the Akkadian Empire, with an emphasis on late third-millennium abrupt climate change and third-millennium variability in Tigris-Euphrates flow.

HARVEY WEISS

Old Assyrian	2000–1500	Old Babylonian
Middle Assyrian	1500–1000	Middle Babylonian
Neo-Assyrian	1000–600	Neo-Babylonian
	600 BCE–100 CE	Late Babylonian

AKKADIAN. The language of the ancient Assyrians and Babylonians of Mesopotamia, Akkadian, subsumes both Assyrian and Babylonian dialects within it. The earliest attested Semitic language, Akkadian comprises the more important member of the eastern branch of the Semitic family (the other member being Eblaite). The name *Akkadian* (*akkadû*) derives from Akkad(e), the capital city built by king Sargon in about 2300 BCE. It is not known when speakers of Akkadian or its linguistic predecessor(s) first arrived in Mesopotamia, nor is it known when the last speakers of the language died out; the first written attestations date to the 26th century BCE (in Semitic names; connected texts somewhat later) and the latest to the first century CE. Several hundred thousand texts have been discovered in excavations, many of which remain unpublished.

Dialects and Genres. Old Akkadian refers to texts from the earliest attestation of Akkadian down to about the beginning of the second millennium, thus including documents dating to the reigns of Sargon and Naram-Sin of Akkad and to the Ur III period; although the term is used collectively for all such texts, dialectal distinctions, both geographical and chronological, are evident within this corpus. Old Akkadian is attested in letters, legal texts, economic dockets, royal inscriptions, and a few literary texts (such as a love incantation). To the middle of the Old Akkadian period as well date the thousands of texts found recently at Ebla, in Syria, some of which are also partly written in a Semitic language, referred to as Eblaite or Eblaic. Formerly thought to be an early representative of West Semitic, Eblaite is now considered to be a close linguistic relative of Akkadian (or even, though this is less likely, a dialect of Akkadian). [*See* Ebla Texts.]

In the second and first millennia, two major geographical dialects are attested, Assyrian in northern Mesopotamia and Babylonian in the south. Linguistically these are distinguished by a number of phonological differences, by minor morphological variations, and by certain lexical items. The Assyrian and Babylonian scripts also developed somewhat independently of one another. As is true in all languages, numerous linguistic changes occurred over the many centuries in which Assyrian and Babylonian were spoken, and these appeared (eventually) in the texts. Although these developments arose continuously, so that there are no neat chronological divisions, scholars refer for the sake of convenience to the following subphases, which correspond roughly with political periods:

Old Assyrian is known from approximately fifteen thousand letters and legal and economic documents dating from the mid-twentieth to the mid-eighteenth centuries BCE, most of which have been found in Cappodocia (eastern Turkey) at the site of Kaneš (modern Kültepe), although other sites in Anatolia and Assyria have also produced a few similar texts. The majority of these documents concern the business activities of Assyrian merchant houses and their trade with outposts in Anatolia. (The majority of these texts are unpublished.) Also attested are a number of royal inscriptions of rulers of the city of Aššur, commemorative and dedicatory in nature, and a few magical texts. [*See* Kültepe Texts.]

Middle Assyrian is sparsely attested, although it is known from a variety of genres, including letters, legal texts, economic texts, and inscriptions of the early kings of the nation and nascent empire of Assyria, and a set of harem decrees. Perhaps most famous, however, are the fourteen tablets containing the Middle Assyrian laws, discovered in the city of Aššur.

Neo-Assyrian is the spoken language of the period of the Assyrian Empire in the first millennium until its demise late in the seventh century BCE. There are a great many letters and administrative texts, of both the court and private individuals. Many royal inscriptions and scholarly writings are also attested; as in all periods, literary texts exhibit considerable linguistic influence of the more prestigious Bablyonian dialect.

Old Babylonian is the language of several tens of thousands of texts, dating to the first half of the second millennium, from the first dynasty of Babylon, from the Isin and Larsa dynasties, and from other southern Mesopotamian sites, as well as from sites outside Mesopotamia, such as Mari and Susa. Not surprisingly, texts from such a range of sites exhibit numerous minor dialectal differences. The best-studied form of Old Babylonian is that of the court of King Hammurabi of Babylon. An extremely diverse variety of genres has been preserved; in addition to thousands of letters, contracts, economic texts, and royal inscriptions, these include the famous "code" of laws of Hammurabi (the longest single Old Babylonian document), and many kinds of scholarly and school texts such as medical, mathematical, and grammatical texts, encyclopedic lists of words (lexical texts), and omens. There are also hymns, prayers, and epic and mythological works of literature, of which the best known are Gilgamesh, Atraḥasis (the flood story), and Anzû (the theft of the "tablets of destiny"); these latter texts, as well as royal inscriptions, are often written in a high literary language full of archaic forms and archaisms.

In later times, Old Babylonian was regarded as the classical period of Akkadian language and literature, and scribes in both Babylonia and Assyria attempted to duplicate it in a purely literary (i.e., unspoken) language called Standard Babylonian (though usually with mixed results, as their own linguistic forms frequently intervened). This is the dialect in which such important works as *Enuma elish* and the later version of Gilgamesh are written—indeed, all of the literary texts of the first millennium, as well as many royal inscriptions.

Middle Babylonian is the language of texts from the Kassite period. Like Middle Assyrian, it is less well represented than the dialects that precede and follow it. It is known from letters, legal texts, economic texts, a few royal inscriptions, and inscribed boundary stones (*kudurru*s).

Already in the Middle Bronze period, but especially in the Late Bronze, Akkadian, particularly Babylonian, was used as an international lingua franca; Akkadian texts have been found at a great many sites outside Mesopotamia, including Alalakh, Emar, and Ugarit in Syria, Ḫattuša in Anatolia (modern Boğazköy, the capital of the Hittite land), and el-Amarna in Egypt, to name a few. The language of these texts, which was written by non-native speakers, is usually termed Peripheral Akkadian; the texts vary considerably in their fidelity to normative grammar and frequently betray the influence of the scribes' own languages. [*See* Emar Texts; Alalakh Texts; Ugarit Inscriptions; Amarna Tablets.]

Neo-Babylonian refers to the spoken, nonliterary language of southern Mesopotamia until the end of the Assyrian Empire, after which the term Late Babylonian is used for the final period of texts written in Akkadian. These dialects comprise large numbers of letters and administrative documents. For literary and monumental texts, Standard Babylonian (see above) was employed.

Writing System. Akkadian was written in cuneiform, a system of wedge-shaped characters usually pressed into moist clay tablets with a reed stylus. (Other media for inscriptions were wax, metal, and, especially for monumental texts, stone.) The system was borrowed from Sumerian, the other language of Mesopotamia and the language for which it was devised. The writing was at first pictographic, with fairly representational drawings; early on, however, it became more and more stylized until the pictographs ultimately became unrecognizable. As the Old Babylonian (code of Hammurabi) forms in figure 1 show, individual signs may consist of one wedge (such as AŠ and U), of a few wedges (such as BAD and MAŠ), or of many wedges (such as IN and IG). As already noted above, forms of signs continued to change throughout the history of Akkadian, and Assyrian and Babylonian forms differed from one another: the histories of a representative sample of signs appear in figure 2. There are three types of signs:

1. *Phonetic signs.* Syllables or parts of syllables to be pronounced are indicated by phonetic signs that may represent a simple vowel (such as "a"), a consonant plus a vowel

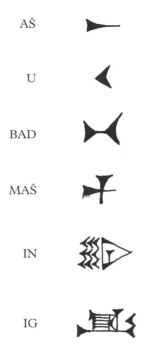

AŠ

U

BAD

MAŠ

IN

IG

AKKADIAN. Figure 1. *Cuneiform writing (Old Babylonian Code of Hammurabi).* (Courtesy J. Huehnergard)

("ba"), a vowel plus a consonant ("ab"), or a consonant-vowel-consonant sequence ("bad"). Individual consonants cannot be written.

2. *Logograms.* These may be used to represent whole words.

3. *Determinatives.* A few signs that serve as classifiers indicating semantic ranges are known as determinatives. One determinative, for example, may precede words for items made of wood, while another precedes names of gods.

The three types of signs are formally indistinguishable and, in fact, some signs are used in all three ways; an example is the sign KI, which, in any given context may, among other possibilities, represent the (part-)syllable "ki," denote the word for "earth," or indicate that the word preceding it is a place name. To illustrate the writing system, the beginning of Law 8 of Hammurabi's code is reproduced in figure 3 with a standard Assyriological transliteration, in which phonetic values appear in italics, logograms in roman capital letters (with their Sumerian pronunciation), and a determinative in superscript letters. As the sample in figure 3 indicates, cuneiform is written from left to right.

Two additional complicating aspects of the writing system are homophony and polyphony. Homophony describes the fact that several discrete signs may have the same phonological value, such as /sa/; these are distinguished in transliteration by diacritical marks as follows: the most common sign found for a particular value receives no special mark, the second an acute accent over the vowel, and the third a grave accent, whereas the fourth and following receive sub-

Sign Name and Meaning	Pictogram	Old Akk.		Old Bab./Assyr.	Middle Bab./Assyr.	Neo-Bab./Assyr.
DINGER "star"	✳	✳	Bab.	𒀭	𒀭	𒀭
			Assyr.	𒀭	𒀭	𒀭
KA "mouth"			Bab.	𒅗	𒅗	𒅗
			Assyr.		𒅗	𒅗
LUGAL "king"			Bab.	𒈗	𒈗	𒈗
			Assyr.		𒈗	𒈗
GUD "ox"			Bab.	𒄞	𒄞	𒄞
			Assyr.	𒄞	𒄞	𒄞

AKKADIAN. Figure 2. *Comparison of Old Akkadian, Assyrian, and Babylonian Cuneiform Signs.* (After Labat, 1988)

script numbers (thus, *sa, sá, sà, sa₄*, etc.; called sa-one, sa-two, sa-three, sa-four, etc.). Many signs are polyphonous—that is, they may represent more than one phonetic value; for example, the sign used to write the value *ud* may also be used to write the values *tam* and *pir*.

Grammatical Summary. The original number of twenty-nine Proto-Semitic consonants was considerably reduced in Akkadian, probably through constant contact with Sumerian, to only twenty, as shown in table 1. Naturally the precise pronunciation of these phonemes is unknown; modern scholars base their pronunciation on parallels with living Semitic languages. The phoneme *š* is pronounced as "sh" and *ḫ* as "ch" in the German *ach* or Scottish *loch*; the so-called "emphatic" consonants *q, ṣ, ṭ* were either pharyngealized (as in Arabic) or, more likely, glottalized (as in Amharic and modern South Arabian languages). It is likely that Old-Akkadian preserved more of the original Semitic consonants, especially the interdental $\star\Theta$ and some of the so-called guttural phonemes, such as *ḫ* and *ᶜ*; the writing system was poorly equipped to expressed such sounds, however.

Early Semitic had three short vowels, (*a, i, u*) and three corresponding long vowels ($\bar{a}, \bar{\iota}, \bar{u}$); most dialects of Akka-

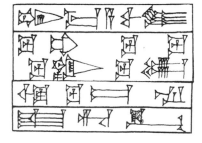

Šum-ma a-wi-lum	if man
lu GUD lu UDU	or ox or sheep
lu ANŠE lu ŠAḪ	or donkey or pig
ù lu ᵍⁱˢ MÁ	or else ᵂᵒᵒᵈ boat
iš-ri-iq	stole

"If a man stole an ox, a sheep, a donkey, a pig, or a boat,..."

AKKADIAN. Figure 3. *Sample Akkadian text from Code of Hammurabi.* (Courtesy J. Huehnergard)

TABLE 1. *Akkadian Consonants*

	Bilabial	Dental	Palato-Alveolar	Velar	Glottal
Stops					
Voiced	*b*	*d*		*g*	
Voiceless	*p*	*t*		*k*	ʾ
Emphatic		*ṭ*		*q*	
Fricatives					
Voiced		*z*			
Voiceless		*s*	*š*		*ḫ*
Emphatic		*ṣ*			
Nasal	*m*	*n*			
Trill				*r*	
Approximant	*w*			*l, y*	

dian preserve these and add a fourth vowel quality, *e* and long *ē*. Most Assyriologists distinguish two types of long vowels, marking those inherited as long vowels with a macron (*ā, ē, ī, ū*) and those that result from the contraction of two adjacent vowels with a circumflex (*â, ê, î, û*). It has recently been proposed that Akkadian also had a fifth phonemic vowel quality, *o* (Westenholz, 1991).

Akkadian phonology is marked by a number of sound changes vis-à-vis common Semitic, in addition to the loss of consonants and the addition of the vowel *e* already described. All dialects exhibit a phenomenon called vowel syncope, in which the second of two short vowels in open syllables is deleted, as in *damqum*, "good (masculine)," from **da/mi/qum* (cf. the feminine counterpart, *damiqtum*) or in *napšātum*, from **na/pi/šā/tum*, the plural of *napištum*, "life." Also common to Akkadian is Geer's law, according to which two emphatic consonants may not cooccur in one word: thus, for example, Semitic **qaṣārum* became Akkadian *kaṣārum*, "to bind"; Semitic **ṣabāṭum* became Akkadian *ṣabātum*, "to seize"; and Semitic **qaṭārum* became *qatārum*, "to billow (of smoke)." In Barth's law, the initial *m* of noun prefixes became *n* in words in which a labial consonant (*b*,

m, p) followed: *narkabtum*, "chariot;" *narāmum*, "beloved"; *našpakum*, "storage area." Both Assyrian and Babylonian forms of Akkadian also exhibit distinctive types of vowel harmony: in Assyrian, short *a* in an unaccented open syllable is replaced by a short-vowel that mimics the vowel of the following syllable, as in *iṣbat*, "he seized," but *taṣbitī* (vs. Babylonian *taṣbatī*), "you (feminine) seized," and *iṣbutū* (vs. Babylonian *iṣbatū*), "they (masculine) seized"; in Babylonian, the presence of an *e* vowel tends to cause an *a* vowel in the same word to become *e*, as in *bēlētum*, "ladies" (from *bēlātum*; cf. *šarrātum*, "queens").

The basic morphological categories of pronouns, nouns, and verbs generally exhibit two genders (masculine and feminine) and three numbers (singular, dual, and plural), although the use of the dual is considerably circumscribed after the Old Akkadian period.

As in other Semitic languages, there is a set of independent personal pronouns and there are also sets of pronominal suffixes that indicate possession (when used on nouns and prepositions) or direct or indirect objects (on verbs); the Old Babylonian and Old Assyrian forms are shown in table 2. Indirect object forms are also attested in Eblaite but are not found in other branches of Semitic; they probably represent an innovation within East Semitic (Akkadian and Eblaite).

In early dialects of Akkadian (Old Akkadian, Old Babylonian, Old Assyrian), as in other morphologically conservative Semitic languages, nouns and adjectives exhibit three cases, marked with distinct vowels: nominative, for the subject of a clause (marked with *u*; in the dual with *ā*); genitive, indicating possession and also used after prepositions (marked with *i*); and accusative, for the direct object and various adverbial uses (marked with *a*). In dual and plural forms the genitive and accusative merge into a single form, termed the oblique (marked with *i*). In addition to endings that indicate the case, the regular, or free, forms of nouns also bear a final -*m* in the singular and the feminine plural (but not in the masculine plural) and a final -*n* in the dual.

TABLE 2. *Old Babylonian (OB) and Old Assyrian (OA) Pronoun Forms* (1, 2, 3 = first, second, third person; m = masculine; f = feminine; c = common gender; s = singular; p = plural; dual forms are omitted).

	Independent		Possessive	Direct Object		Indirect Object	
	OB	OA	OB/OA	OB	OA	OB	OA
1cs	*anāku*	*anāku*	*-ī, ya*	*-ni*	*-ni, -ī*	*-nim*	*-nim*
2ms	*atta*	*atta*	*-ka*	*-ka*	*-ka*	*-kum*	*-kum*
2fs	*atti*	*atti*	*-ki*	*-ki*	*-ki*	*-kim*	*-kim*
3ms	*šū*	*šūt*	*-šu*	*-šu*	*-šu*	*-šum*	*-šum*
3fs	*šī*	*šīt*	*-ša*	*-ši*	*-ši*	*-šim*	*-šim*
1cp	*nīnu*	*nēnu*	*-ni*	*-niāti*	*-niāti*	*-niāšim*	*-niāti*
2mp	*attunu*	*attunu*	*-kunu*	*-kunūti*	*-kunu*	*-kunūšim*	*-kunūti*
2fp	*attina*	*attina*	*-kina*	*-kināti*	*-kina*	*-kināšim*	*-kināti*
3mp	*šunu*	*šunu*	*-šunu*	*-šunūti*	*-šunu*	*-šunūšim*	*-šunūti*
3fp	*šina*	*šina*	*-šina*	*-šināti*	*-šina*	*-šināšim*	*-šināti*

Feminine nouns and feminine forms of adjectives are usually marked with either -t- or -at- after the base and before the case vowel: *bēlum*, "lord"; *bēltum*, "lady"; *šarrum*, "king"; *šarratum*, "queen"; *ṭābum* (masc.) and *ṭābtum* (fem.), "pleasant"; *dannum* (masc.) and *dannatum* (fem.), "strong." Besides the regular, or free, form of the noun there is also the bound form (or construct form), used when a noun syntactically governs another noun or a pronominal suffix; the bound form generally lacks both the final -m/-n and the case vowel: *šarratum*, "queen," and *mātum*, "land" (both nominative case); but *šarrat mātim*, "queen of the land" (with "land" appropriately in the genitive case), and *šarratni*, "our queen." Adjectives are for the most part declined like substantives, although they exhibit a distinctive ending in masculine-plural forms. Table 3 shows the regular (free form) declensions of the substantives *šarrum*, "king," and *šarratum*, "queen," and the adjective *ṭābum*, "pleasant," in Old Babylonian. Final -m/-n were lost in the late stages of both Old Assyrian and Old Babylonian, so that in later phases of Akkadian the singular *šarru/šarri/šarra* is found, for example. Still later in the history of Akkadian, the case system itself became defunct as final vowels were lost. (In the literary dialect called Standard Babylonian, the nominative and the accusative are both usually written *šarru*; one form, the earlier oblique, is usually written for plurals regardless of case.)

In addition to their free and bound forms, substantives and adjectives also enter into a syntactic construction called the predicative form (also called the stative, with adjectives), in which the base of a substantive or adjective is followed by a special set of pronominal suffixes; the two elements constitute a verbless clause, with the substantive or adjective as predicate and the pronominal suffix as subject: *šarrāku*, "I (-āku) am king (šarr-)"; *ṭābat*, "it (feminine; -at) is pleasant (ṭāb-)"; *rabiānu*, "we (-ānu) are great (rabi-)." That this is an ancient construction is suggested by the appearance of a similar construction in Old Egyptian; in other Semitic languages, however, it fell out of use except in restricted circumstances.

TABLE 3. *Old Babylonian Noun Declension*

	"King"	"Queen"	"Pleasant" Masc.	"Pleasant" Fem.
Singular				
Nominative	šarrum	šarratum	ṭābum	ṭābtum
Genitive	šarrim	šarratim	ṭābim	ṭābtim
Accusative	šarram	šarratam	ṭābam	ṭābtam
Dual				
Nominative	šarrān	šarratān		
Oblique	šarrīn	šarratīn		
Plural				
Nominative	šarrū	šarrātum	ṭābūtum	ṭābātum
Oblique	šarrī	šarrātim	ṭābūtim	ṭābātim

Akkadian verbal morphology is complex, as in other Semitic languages. The verbal "root" usually consists of three consonants, as in r-k-b, "ride." There are four main finite forms (or tenses, or aspects): (1) an imperfective form denoting the present, the future, the habitual or circumstantial past, and a variety of modal functions, that is characterized by doubling in the second of the three root consonants, as in *arakkab*, "I ride/am riding/will ride/used to ride (etc.)," in which the prefix a- denotes "I" (cf. *nirakkab*, "we ride," with ni- for "we"); (2) a punctive form called the preterite, for the past, as in *arkab*, "I rode, did ride"; (3) the perfect, a form in which -t- is infixed after the first root consonant, as in *artakab*, "I have ridden"; and (4) the imperative *rikab*, "ride!". The imperfective form *arakkab* and the preterite *arkab* were undoubtedly inherited essentially unchanged from common Semitic. Akkadian shares the *arakkab* form with Ethiopian and modern South Arabian Semitic languages (compare classical Ethiopic *ʾərakkəb*, "I attain"), but the form was lost in the Central Semitic languages (such as Arabic, Hebrew, and Aramaic). The preterite form *arkab* is found in most other Semitic languages in restricted uses, but has been replaced as the main past-tense form by a conjugation in which the subject pronouns are indicated by suffixes rather than prefixes (derived ultimately from the predicative form of Akkadian, discussed above), as in Arabic *rakibtu* or Hebrew *rɔkabti*, "I rode." The form called the perfect is not found in other Semitic languages and is generally considered an Akkadian innovation. Finite verbs may be marked with a morpheme called the ventive, which indicates motion or activity in the direction or proximity of the speaker: *illik*, "he went," but *illikam*, "he came"; *tuṣi*, "you went forth," but *tuṣiam*, "you came forth." The ventive is unknown in other Semitic languages and its presence in Akkadian may reflect the influence of Sumerian.

In addition to the finite forms there is a verbal noun or infinitive, *rakābum*, "to ride"; an active participle *rākibum*, "riding, rider"; and a verbal adjective *rakbum*, "ridden." These forms have analogues or parallels in the other Semitic languages.

In common with other Semitic tongues, Akkadian exhibits the modification of verbal roots, by means of prefixes or other changes, to produce a series of augmented stems with meanings derived more-or-less predictably from that of the basic stem; for example, from the basic form *parāsum*, "to separate," are derived a passive verb with a prefixed n, *naprusum*, "to be separated"; a causative verb with a prefixed š, *šuprusum*, "to cause to separate"; and an iterative verb with an infixed syllable, *pitarrusum*, "to separate repeatedly." The last of these is an Akkadian innovation, unknown elsewhere in Semitic.

In many features of syntax Akkadian resembles other Semitic languages closely. For example, attributive adjectives follow their head nouns and must agree with them in gender, number, and case; and verbs must agree with their subjects in gender and number. Akkadian makes frequent use of a genitive chain involving juxtaposition of two nouns to indicate governance of one by the other, the lead or governing noun appearing in the bound (construct) form, as in *šarrat mātim*, "queen of the land" (see above); but a pronominal form, *ša*, also evolved for the expression of the same relationship, as in *šarratum ša mātim*, "queen of the land" (a similar development occurred in many other Semitic languages).

In other syntactic features Akkadian deviates markedly from its Semitic relatives. In all prose dialects and texts, the verb occupies the final position in the sentence, a feature undoubtedly borrowed from Sumerian: *šarrum ekallam ina ālim ibni*, "king-palace-in-city-built" (i.e., "the king built a palace in the city"). Already noted above was the use of the predicative construction in verbless sentences in which the predicate is an adjective or a noun: *Ḥammurapi rabi*, "Hammurabi is great"; *šarrāku*, "I am king." There are two main clause coordinators: *u* (Semitic *wa-*) connects nouns in phrases (*šarrum u šarratum*, "king and queen") and clauses that are not semantically connected (*abni u arkab*, "I built and I [also] rode"), whereas the enclitic particle *-ma* connects clauses in which the first is logically subordinate to the second (*allikam-ma abni*, "I came and then built" or "having come, I built"). The use of *-ma* is so common that the wide range of subordinating conjunctions is used only infrequently (subordinate clauses, like other parts of speech, usually precede the main-clause verb). The syntax of the infinitive is complex; for example, the phrase "on reaching the town" may appear in the following three forms: *ina kašād ālim* (lit., "in the reaching of the town"), *ina ālim kašādim* ("in town-reaching"), *ālam ina kašādim* ("the town in reaching").

The majority of the lexicon in all Akkadian dialects is inherited from common Semitic. In the earliest period, however, there are already many loanwords from Sumerian, nearly all of which are nouns, covering a wide semantic range. Beginning in the Neo-Assyrian and Neo-Babylonian periods, many Aramaic words begin to enter the language as well.

[*See also* Akkadians.]

BIBLIOGRAPHY

Aro, Jussi. *Studien zur mittelbabylonischen Grammatik*. Studia Orientalia, 20. Helsinki, 1955. The most recent monograph-length treatment of Middle Babylonian grammar.

Borger, Rykle. *Handbuch der Keilschriftliteratur*. 3 vols. Berlin, 1967–1975. Indispensable guide to the publication of Akkadian and Sumerian texts and all matters pertaining to the reading of cuneiform texts, updated in the periodical *Archiv für Orientforschung*.

Borger, Rykle. *Assyrisch-babylonische Zeichenliste*. 4th ed. Kevelaer, 1988. One of two sign lists that give both phonological and logographic values and histories of individual signs (the other is Labat, 1988; see below).

Ebeling, Erich, et al., eds. *Reallexikon der Assyriologie und Vorderasiatischen Archäologie*. Berlin, 1932–. Encyclopedic reference work of all things Assyriological.

Gelb, Ignace J., et al. *The Assyrian Dictionary of the Oriental Institute of the University of Chicago*. Chicago, 1956–. Encyclopedic reference work, devoting one volume to each "letter" of the Akkadian phonological system; sixteen of twenty-one volumes have appeared to date.

Gelb, Ignace J. *Old Akkadian Writing and Grammar*. Materials for the Assyrian Dictionary, 2. 2d ed. Chicago, 1961. Description of the earliest phase of Akkadian.

Groneberg, Brigitte. *Syntax, Morphologie und Stil der jungbabylonischen "hymnischen" Literatur*. 2 vols. Wiesbaden, 1987. Up-to-date description of the important literary dialect known in English as Standard Babylonian.

Hecker, Karl. *Grammatik der Kültepe-Texte*. Analecta Orientalia, 44. Rome, 1968. Comprehensive description of the Old Assyrian dialect.

Labat, René. *Manuel d'épigraphie akkadienne*. 6th ed. by Florence Malbran-Labat. Paris, 1988. One of two sign lists that give both phonological and logographic values and histories of individual signs (the other is Borger, 1988; see above).

Mayer, Walter. *Untersuchungen zur Grammatik des Mittelassyrischen*. Kevelaer, 1971. The most thorough treatment of the Middle Assyrian dialect.

Reiner, Erica. *A Linguistic Analysis of Akkadian*. The Hague, 1966. The most competent linguistic presentation of Akkadian yet published.

Reiner, Erica. "Akkadian." In *Current Trends in Linguistics*, vol. 6, *Linguistics in South West Asia and North Africa*, edited by Thomas A. Sebeok, pp. 274–303. The Hague, 1970. History of Akkadian grammatical and lexical research, and a review of topics requiring new or additional research.

Reiner, Erica. "Die akkadische Literatur." In *Altorientalische Literaturen: Neues Handbuch der Literaturwissenschaft*, edited by Wolfgang Röllig, pp. 151–210. Wiesbaden, 1978. Comprehensive review of the types of Akkadian literature.

Röllig, Wolfgang. "Überblick über die akkadische Literatur." In *Reallexikon der Assyriologie und Vorderasiatischen Archäologie*, vol. 7, pp. 48–66. Berlin, 1987. Survey of Akkadian literary works.

Soden, Wolfram von. *Akkadisches Handwörterbuch*. 3 vols. Wiesbaden, 1965–1981. The only complete modern dictionary of Akkadian.

Soden, Wolfram von. *Grundriss der akkadischen Grammatik samt Ergänzungsheft*. Rome, 1969. Standard reference grammar of Akkadian.

Soden, Wolfram von, and Wolfgang Röllig. *Das akkadische Syllabar*. 4th ed. Rome, 1991. Authoritative reference for phonetic sign values in Akkadian.

Westenholz, Aage. "The Phoneme /o/ in Akkadian." *Zeitschrift für Assyriologie* 81 (1991): 10–19.

JOHN HUEHNERGARD

AKKADIANS. Although the origin of the term is unknown, *Akkadians* refers to a Semitic-speaking people living in northern Babylonia in about 2400–2100 BCE. The term may derive from a city and its surrounding territory, for which the earliest spellings are Agade or Aggide, later Akkade or Akkad. By the end of the third millennium, the land of Akkad meant northern Babylonia, from north of Nippur to Sippar. However, during the early second millennium BCE, the name *Akkadians* broadened to mean the indigenous population of all of Babylonia, as opposed to Amorites. By the first millennium BCE, Akkad had become a literary synonym for Babylonia. Modern scholars call the language of the Akkadians Old Akkadian, to distinguish it from *Akkadian, the ancient name, used from the early second millennium onward, for the Semitic language of Assyria and Babylonia and its numerous dialects. The term *Akkadian period* usually refers to the 150 years (c. 2334–2193 BCE) defined by the reign of five kings of the Akkadian, or Sargonic, dynasty (hence also called the Sargonic period). Some scholars add another fifty years to this to include later kings of the city Agade (Akkade), thus overlapping the Late Akkadian and Post-Akkadian, or Gutian, periods. The broader meanings of *Akkad* and *Akkadian* were consequences of political and military expansion of the Sargonic dynasty. *Babylonian* and *Assyrian* expanded from local to regional terms, with their respective empires, are later examples of the same process.

Prior to the Sargonic dynasty, northern Babylonia was part of a larger Semitic-speaking cultural horizon that stretched west into northern Syria from its Mesopotamian center at Kish, perhaps as early as the Early Dynastic I period. The Akkadians may have been an eastern group of this population, perhaps centered around the confluence of the Diyala and the Tigris Rivers. This is only a hypothesis, for, according to surface surveys, the Diyala region was only sparsely populated in the Akkadian period. The relationship between the Akkadians and the earlier, more widely distributed Semitic-speaking population of greater northern Mesopotamia remains obscure.

In the absence of epigraphic data, Akkadian period sites are often difficult to distinguish from those of earlier or later periods; as a result, analysis of settlement patterns may be based on sketchy evidence. Archaeological surveys suggest that during the Akkadian period the population of northern Babylonian cities and towns increased at the expense of villages. These findings could imply centralization of government and production. In contrast, the central Euphrates floodplain witnessed a decline in the number and size of large urban centers but an increase in the number and size of medium-sized towns and smaller villages (Robert McC. Adams, *Heartland of Cities*, Chicago, 1981, p. 139). Although this can be viewed as a long-term natural development, a contributing factor could have been aggression by the Akkadian dynasty against the older city states in this region, with the creation of extraurban administrative centers. The resulting pattern—centralization of rural landscapes and decentralization of potentially competitive urban landscapes—needs verification.

Topographic lists of northern Babylonian settlements permit reconstruction of nine important waterways branching southward from the area of Sippar, between the modern courses of the Euphrates and Tigris Rivers, with a string of towns along each and a sparsely populated hinterland between (Douglas Frayne, *The Early Dynastic List of Geographical Names*, American Oriental Series; vol. 74, New Haven, 1992). Communication northwest followed the Euphrates upstream; one route east led to the Iranian plateau through the Hamrin Valley, where extensive remains of the Akkadian period have been found.

Northern Babylonia depended on a mixed economy of agriculture and husbandry. During the Akkadian period there is substantial epigraphic evidence for control of production through local centers of collection, preparation, and redistribution of food for workers; production, storage, and distribution of implements; and coordination of agriculture. Fields were allocated to plowing teams; seed and feed used for draft animals and the collection, distribution, and transport of the harvest, locally and to the capital, were recorded; and flocks and herds were maintained (shearing, culling, counting, fattening).

The history and culture of the Akkadians are mostly associated with the Sargonic Empire, a military, political, and cultural unification of Mesopotamia and North Syria that is often considered the first of the great empires or territorial states in Mesopotamian history. The founder of the dynasty was Sargon (Sharrukin) of Akkad (so called to distinguish him from the two later Assyrian kings referred to as Sargon I and II). According to one legendary account, he was cupbearer to a king of Kish. Thwarting a murder plot by his master, Sargon made himself king, taking the title "king of Kish," which implied suzerainty over northern Babylonia and perhaps beyond. He defeated the principal ruler in Sumer, Lugalzagesi king of Uruk, and thereby united Babylonia under one rule. He invaded southwestern Iran in several campaigns and turned north and northwest to Syria and Anatolia, stating in his inscriptions that Mari and Ebla became subordinate to him. He is credited with building up a capital city, Akkade (often spelled Agade in modern books, to distinguish it from the region of Akkad). The city's location has not been identified, but it may lie east of the confluence of the Tigris and Diyala Rivers, although a location near Kish has been proposed. In an inscription he boasts that he made Akkadians governors throughout his conquered lands. Sargon's life, reign, and exploits became the subjects of a richly embroidered literary tradition in later Mesopotamia, including epic poetry and a tale that he was born in secret to a priestess and set adrift in a basket. A stela, now in the Louvre, is the major surviving monument of his reign; his commemorative inscriptions are best known from copies prepared by Babylonian scholars centuries after his death. Sargon was remembered in later ages as the archtypical successful warrior-king; it is for him that the dynasty is named Sargonic (to be distinguished from Sargonid, referring to Sargon II of Assyria and his successors).

Sargon's son and successor, Rimush, devoted much of his nine-year reign to suppressing revolts in Sumerian cities. His inscriptions claim the execution and enslavement of tens of thousands of people. Fragmentary stelae showing marching soldiers, parading and killing captives may date to this reign or later (e.g., the Victory Stela from Telloh at the Louvre, a fragment at the Boston Museum of Fine Arts, and the Nasiriyyah stela, the last perhaps commemorating an Anatolian campaign by a later king). Rimush was murdered in

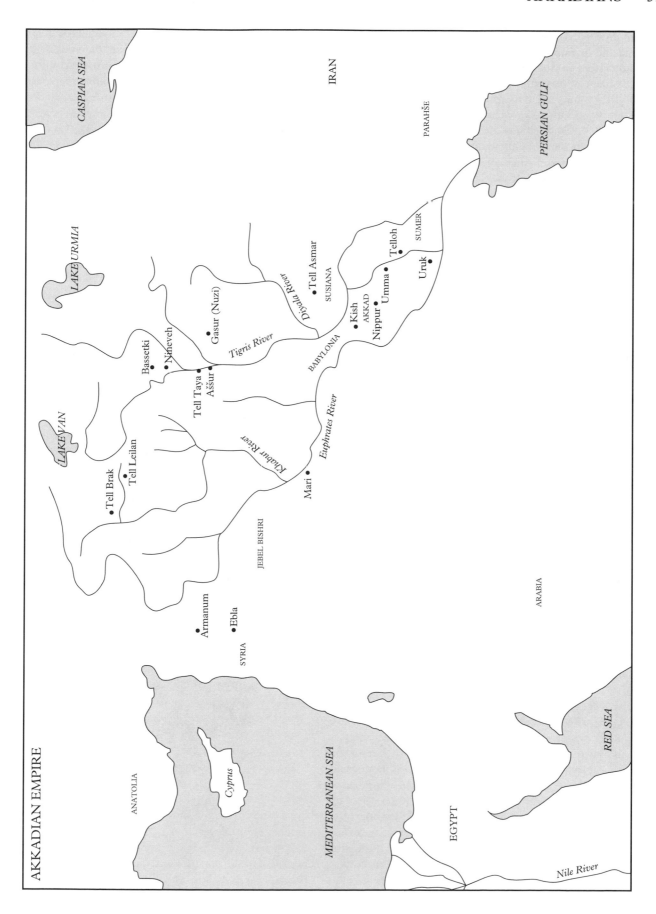

AKKADIAN EMPIRE

a palace conspiracy and succeeded by his brother, Manish-tushu.

Manishtushu restored his father's control over south-western Iran, where an expansionist state, Parahše (Mar-haši), had established itself. He also launched a naval campaign in the Gulf, among the results of which was the importation of blocks of diorite. A group of statues from his reign carved in this hard medium marks the emergence of what is called the Akkadian style in sculpture: life-sized or larger naturalistic, but idealized portraits of the ruler that convey a sense of serene muscular strength and unchallenged power. The style and medium were imitated for centuries thereafter. Another important monument of his reign, called the Obelisk of Manishtushu, records the king's purchase of large tracts of land from families in western Babylonia, presumably for redistribution to his officers and household in return for their service. He too was murdered in a palace conspiracy after a reign of fifteen years, to be succeeded by his son, Naram-Sin.

Like Sargon, Naram-Sin became the subject of legendary and monitory literature after his death, so that the events of his thirty-seven(?)-year reign are difficult to interpret. He was a successful warrior-king whose conquests established his hegemony over the upper Gulf, southwestern Iran, Assyria, the Upper Euphrates and Tigris into Anatolia, and North Syria to the Mediterranean coast. In his inscriptions he claims to be the first to destroy Ebla and Armanum, the latter a heavily fortified city in the same region, perhaps modern Aleppo. Major religious and administrative structures of this period at Tell Brak in the Khabur region show that his policy was one of direct rule in this area, perhaps intending to develop its agricultural potential. Mass production of standardized pottery at Tell Leilan, also in the Khabur, suggests the use of a rationed labor force or garrison there at about this time; changes in local settlement patterns could be the result of enforced centralization. [*See* Brak, Tell; Leilan, Tell.]

Throughout his reign, Naram-Sin faced important rebellions and external attacks, some on a scale that gained supernatural character in later literature. One was led by a Sumerian city, the name of which is uncertain, and included Amorite tribesmen and perhaps the land of Magan (Oman and the Iranian coastline opposite); it thus seemed a worldwide event to Mesopotamian contemporaries. Another rebellion was centered on a pretender at Kish, with support at Nippur, Uruk, and elsewhere. In nine battles, Naram-Sin defeated a coalition of foreign rulers and Mesopotamian allies. These dramatic events were retold as cautionary tales in later literature, while in his own lifetime they resulted in his deification as savior of his city, Agade. He led an expedition to the sources of the Tigris and reconquered Susiana, imposing a treaty on the ruler there. His reign marks the apogee of the Sargonic state. A standardized bureaucracy spread throughout Mesopotamia, where former city-states were reorganized as provinces and Naram-Sin's progeny served as governors and priestesses. His rebuilding of the Temple of Enlil at Nippur may have inspired a Sumerian narrative poem called the Curse of Agade, which attributes the later fall of the empire to Naram-Sin's hubris and falsely projects it to his reign.

The art of this period is exemplified by a stela of Naram-Sin, now also in the Louvre, that shows the deified king invading a mountainous region. Its brilliant design and execution make it one of the most significant works of art of its millennium to have survived. [*See* Stelae.] This and various other rock reliefs projected the authority of the ruler and the death and enslavement in store for his enemies. Cylinder seals used by courtiers were exquisitely engraved with combat scenes and representations of wild beasts in heraldic poses. A mutilated nude male figure, found at Bassetki, was

AKKADIANS. Figure 1. *Bronze head from Nineveh.* Iraq Museum, Baghdad. (Scala/Art Resource, NY)

cast in more than 160 kg of copper, proof of the extraordinary artistic and technical achievements of the period, further exemplified by a bronze head of an Akkadian ruler found at Nineveh (see figure 1). A later poetic narrative speaks of the treasures accumulated in the capital; the wealth and resources available to the royal establishment are reflected in administrative documents of the period as well, some of which list magnificent gifts to the royal family.

Naram-Sin was succeeded by his son, Sharkalisharri, the events of whose twenty-five-year reign are obscure. He may have faced a rebellion at his accession. As crown prince he directed the reconstruction of the Temple of Enlil at Nippur, whose work he may have completed as king. His territories shrank, although he claimed victory over the Elamites in the Diyala region. Sargonic administrators must have left Susiana by this time and the former governor of the area, Epir-mupi, may have set up an independent kingdom. Sharkalisharri also fought the Amorites near Jebel Bishri, as well as the Gutians, a people of uncertain origin whom the Mesopotamians considered barbarians. The picture is of an embattled state falling back toward its capital. Its final collapse may have been the result of internal weaknesses, rebellion, and foreign attack, especially, according to Sumerian tradition, by the Gutians. Dessication and abandonment of former Akkadian centers in the Khabur, such as Tell Leilan, may also have been a significant factor (Harvey Weiss et al., "The Genesis and Collapse of Third Millennium North Mesopotamian Civilization," *Science* 261 [1993]: 995–1004).

There followed a short interregnum: a letter, apparently from a ruler of this period, asserts "There is a king in Agade," whereas the Sumerian King List says "Who was king, who was not king?" A local dynasty was established at Agade that ruled for about forty years. One of its kings, Dudu, campaigned against Umma and Susa, but Agade was thereafter an unimportant place, although attested into the Achaemenid period.

One major legacy of the Sargonic dynasty to Mesopotamia was the realization of the political and economic possibilities of a territorial state, transcending the city-state pattern typical of Sumer previously. Along with this came political vocabulary, military and management strategies, and a grandiose ideology of the ruler that were to be emulated, denounced, and admired for fifteen hundred years.

Prior to the Sargonic dynasty, the Akkadians presumably shared the religious convictions of the Semites of northern Mesopotamia and Syria, which often accorded special veneration to the sun (Shamash), the moon (Sin), and the planet Venus (Ishtar), especially as "lady of combat" (Annunitum). The inclusion of Sumer in the Sargonic state brought with it the Sumerian city-states' pantheon, including Enlil, chief god of Sumer, thereafter used as a term for "supreme deity." Sumerian Inanna, a goddess of reproduction and fertility, was fused with Ishtar to create a complex,

contradictory persona. Some deities important in North Syria, such as Adad (the thunder god) and Dagan (popular in the Upper Euphrates region) were less important in northern Babylonia, suggesting greater Sumerian than Syrian influence there. A deity referred to simply as God (Il or Ilum) is sometimes compared to the western El or the later Babylonian Ilum, in the sense of "personal god." Local deities in northern Babylonia included Zababa (at Kish); Ilaba, a patron deity of the dynasty; and Nergal (at Cutha). Save for Nergal, little or no mythology is known of these figures.

The most important religious compositions of the period are attributed to Enheduanna, daughter of Sargon and high priestess of the moon god Sin at Ur. These include a cycle of Sumerian hymns in honor of important Sumerian sanctuaries, perhaps with the intent of promoting Sumero-Akkadian syncretism. Among her other works is a narrative poem describing her personal humiliation at the hands of a local pretender and her appeal to Ishtar, who reinstates her and destroys her enemies. This is but one example of many where Ishtar is regarded as holding the royal family in special favor: both Sargon and Naram-Sin are said to have been loved by Ishtar, and the Sargonic dynasty is sometimes referred to in later sources as Ishtar's period of ascendancy.

Mesopotamian religious architecture of this period is poorly known, and, where identified, shows no significant changes in plan from previous phases of established temples. A religious structure at Tell Brak contained a large courtyard that may have been used for some important public event. Naram-Sin introduced religious veneration of the living ruler by proclaiming himself god of his city, Agade.

Secular architecture is also poorly known, for various buildings formerly considered Sargonic in date, such as the northern palace at Tell Asmar, the palace at Tell al-Wilayah, and the Old Palace at Aššur, are now generally dated to earlier or later periods. A large building at Tell Brak, which incorporated some bricks stamped with the name of Naram-Sin, remains the most securely dated building of the Akkadian period. Tell Taya is a town-sized settlement of this period, allowing the reconstruction of house and street plans and a group of administrative buildings.

Akkadian society may originally have been articulated by extended families reckoning their descent from a common male ancestor and holding large areas of arable land in communal ownership, with shares allotted to individuals and nuclear families. An innovation of the Sargonic dynasty was the creation of royal estates and their distribution to members of the royal family and ruling elite. These elites in turn leased and subleased parcels for rental payments in cash and kind. Akkadian estates have been identified at Gasur (Nuzi), in Akkad (Umm el-Jir), in Sumer (Mesag Estate, near Umma), and Susa. An Akkadian stela from Girsu (Telloh) records distribution of an immense area of land to Sargonic officials, including towns and villages.

Records of internal commerce show the free circulation

of silver in private hands and government establishments and its use as a standard of valuation and medium of exchange. Commodities bought and sold included foodstuffs, slaves, real estate, aromatics, metals, and finished products such as wagons and boats. There are hints of international venture trade by commercial families that took advantage of the Sargonic occupation of such entrepôts as Susa to purchase foreign commodities such as copper, tin, and semiprecious stones. Sargonic weights and measures spread, with the empire, to Syria and Anatolia. Foreign trade is known to Dilmun, Magan, and Meluḫḫa.

Extensive archival remains from all parts of Mesopotamia and from Susa illuminate management and recordkeeping techniques, using a distinctive calligraphy for official purposes. These archives shed light on such subjects as labor, animal husbandry, fishing, agriculture, and production (sometimes on a gigantic scale); on commodities such as pottery; and on comestibles such as bread and beer. These archives mostly date to the reigns of Naram-Sin and Sharkalisharri and include records of Akkadian estates, as well as urban and regional administrative centers. Family and private archives include records of buying, selling, and leasing land; making loans at interest; depositing valuables; managing livestock; and contracting to carry out government services. Sargonic letters make requests and orders for goods and services, bring news, and make complaints and petitions.

The Akkadian rulers drew from their northern environment traditions of statecraft dating to the earliest kings of Kish. These they introduced to Sumer, along with Akkadian ideas of nobility, land tenure, and military organization. On the other hand, much of Akkadian literate and scholastic tradition was drawn from Sumer, either directly through conquest, or indirectly through long-standing Sumerian cultural influence in the north. This means that a north–south influence went in both directions over many centuries.

The Akkadian achievement was to be an important ideological concern in later Mesopotamia. The rulers of the successor state of the third dynasty of Ur distanced themselves from it, although they adopted its management techniques, whereas the dynasty of Eshnunna adopted Sargonic royal names. To the Mesopotamians, the Sargonic, or Akkadian, period was a turning point in their history.

[See also Akkade; Diyala; Ebla; Kish; Mari; Mesopotamia; article on Mesopotamia; Nippur; Taya, Tell; Ur; and Uruk-Warka.]

BIBLIOGRAPHY

Amiet, Pierre. L'art d'Agadé au Musée du Louvre. Paris, 1976. Detailed study of the large collection of Sargonic sculpture in the Louvre.
Boehmer, Rainer Michael. Die Entwicklung der Glyptic während der Akkad-Zeit. Berlin, 1965. Major publication and study of cylinder seals of the Akkadian period.
Cooper, Jerrold S. The Curse of Agade. Baltimore, 1983. Edition of a Sumerian narrative poem about the destruction of the Sargonic empire, with a discussion of the historical background.
Foster, Benjamin R. "Archives and Empire in Sargonic Mesopotamia." In Cuneiform Archives and Libraries, edited by Klaas R. Veenhof, pp. 46–52. Leiden, 1986. Survey of historical uses of administrative documents of the Akkadian period; with a bibliography.
Foster, Benjamin R. "Select Bibliography of the Sargonic Period." In Akkad, the First World Empire: Structure, Ideology, Traditions, edited by Mario Liverani, pp. 171–182. Padua, 1993. Annotated bibliography for archaeology, art, language, literature, and archival and inscriptional sources for the Akkadian period, as well as studies of the history and economy of the Sargonic Empire.
Frayne, Douglas. The Royal Inscriptions of Mesopotamia: Early Periods, vol. 2, Sargonic and Gutian Periods, 2334–2113 BC. Toronto, 1993. Commemorative inscriptions of the Akkadian period, with historical commentary.
Glassner, J.-J. La chute d'Akkadé: L'événement et sa mémoire. Berliner Beiträge zum Vorderen Orient, 5. Berlin, 1986. Historical survey of the period, with a bibliography.
Hallor, William W., and J. J. A. Van Dijk. The Exaltation of Inama. Yale Near Eastern Researchers, 3. New Haven, 1968. Edition and Commentary on a poem by Enheduanna, daughter of Sargon.
Liverani, Mario, ed. Akkad, the First World Empire. Padua, 1993. Essays on the history, archaeology, administration, and tradition of the Akkadian Empire.
Nissen, Hans J. "'Sumerian' vs. 'Akkadian' Art: Art and Politics in Babylonia of the Mid-Third Millennium B.C." In Insight through Images: Studies in Honor of Edith Porada, edited by Marilyn Kelly-Buccellati, pp. 189–196. Malibu, 1986.
Porada, Edith. "The Period of Akkad." In Chronologies in Old World Archaeology, vol. 1, edited by Robert W. Ehrich, pp. 113–116. 3d ed. Chicago, 1992. Archaeological evidence for Akkadian chronology.
Westenholz, Aage. "The Sargonic Period." In Circulation of Goods in Non-Palatial Context in the Ancient Near East, edited by Alfonso Archi, pp. 17–30. Incunabula Graeca, 82. Rome, 1984. Surveys records of commercial activity.

BENJAMIN R. FOSTER

AKKO (Ar., Tell el-Fukhar), a prominent 50-acre tell on the northern bank of the Na'aman River in Israel, near its debouchment into the Mediterranean Sea at the medieval-modern port of Akko (map reference 1585 × 2585). It was excavated from 1973 to 1989 by Moshe Dothan on behalf of Haifa University, with the participation of the University of Marburg, Germany. Occupation levels from the Middle Bronze Age to the Roman era were revealed.

Tel Akko was evidently a major port in the Middle Bronze Age, heavily defended by a massive terre pisée embankment and glacis connected with a cyclopean wall 3.5 m wide with towers. A large fortress with a nearby elite tomb is associated with those early defenses, all dated by the excavator to the late MB I. To this horizon apparently belong sherds of Cypriot White Painted III–IV pottery, among the earliest such imports known in the Levant.

Early in MB II the embankment and ramparts were augmented, and a three-entryway sea gate, was constructed down along the northwest slopes. In MB III, Akko seems to have declined, and some of the defenses, including the gate, were abandoned. However, a number of tombs belonging to this period have been found, both constructed and pit burials, as well as a rare type of stone-vaulted tomb. These tombs produced ceramic imports (some from Anatolia), weapons, scarabs, and jewelry.

In the Late Bronze Age some of the ramparts were reconstructed. From the first phase, in the early fifteenth century BCE, there is an elaborate tomb of ashlar construction, with Bichrome and Chocolate-on-White pottery. The phase seems to end in a destruction. LB II is witnessed by large, well-planned buildings, as well as numerous Cypriot and Mycenaean imports that point to prosperous trade. The site remained largely unfortified, although, according to a relief at Karnak, Rameses II destroyed a gate at Akko. The final LB levels are characterized by burials found in the abandoned fortress (building A), followed by silos and industrial installations of several types. Late Cypriot and Mycenaean IIIB pottery places this phase in the late thirteenth century BCE.

The beginning of the Iron Age appears to be marked by new settlers, although the remains consist largely of pits and workshops, with flimsy dwellings. Late Mycenaean IIIC: 1b pottery, as well as a scarab of Tawosert, queen of Egypt in about 1207–1200 BCE, places this occupation mainly in the early twelfth century BCE. The excavator suggests that the inhabitants were the Sherden, one group of the Sea Peoples known from the onomasticon of Amenemopet (c. 1000 BCE), who are said to have occupied the coast north of the *škl*. The eleventh and tenth centuries BCE are poorly attested.

There are more extensive remains from the Iron II period, including residences and several large public buildings. The site was destroyed by fire, probably by the Assyrians in the late eighth century BCE. Only scant remains survive from the Babylonian period, but in the Persian period Akko recovered, probably as a port again and an administrative center. Attic imports and some Phoenician inscriptions belong to this era. The Hellenistic period reveals a well-planned town, preserving the Persian building technique of ashlar construction interspersed with rubble fill: Roman, Byzantine, and Crusader remains have either been severely disturbed or have largely disappeared.

BIBLIOGRAPHY

Dothan, Moshe, and Diethelm Conrad. "Accho." *Israel Exploration Journal* 23 (1973): 257–258; 24 (1974): 276–279; 25 (1975): 163–166; 26 (1976): 207–208; 27 (1977): 241–242; 28 (1978): 264–266; 29 (1979): 227–228; 31 (1981): 110–112; 33 (1983): 113–114; 34 (1984): 189–190.

Dothan, Moshe. "A Sign of Tanit from Tel 'Akko." *Israel Exploration Journal* 24 (1974): 44–49.

Dothan, Moshe. "'Akko: Interim Excavation Report, First Season, 1973/4." *Bulletin of the American Schools of Oriental Research,* no. 224 (1976): 1–48.

Dothan, Moshe. "An Attic Red-Figured Bell-Krater from Tel 'Akko." *Israel Exploration Journal* 29 (1979): 148–151.

Dothan, Moshe. "A Phoenician Inscription from 'Akko." *Israel Exploration Journal* 35 (1985): 81–94.

Dothan, Moshe. "Archaeological Evidence for Movements of the Early 'Sea Peoples' in Canaan." In *Recent Excavations in Israel: Studies in Iron Age Archaeology,* edited by Seymour Gitin and William G. Dever, pp. 59–70. Annual of the American Schools of Oriental Research, 49. Winona Lake, Ind., 1989.

WILLIAM G. DEVER

ALALAKH (modern Tell 'Atchana), site located in the Turkish province of Hatay, near the mouth of the Orontes River, in the 'Amuq plain (36°19′ N, 36°29′ E). The site commanded the area's principal trade routes and was selected by C. Leonard Woolley in 1936 as a link between the early cultures of the Aegean and the Asiatic mainland.

The mound (750 × 300 m) is an oval, its axis being roughly northwest by southeast. The elevation slopes from about 9 m at the northwestern end to the level of the plain on the southwest. Horizontal excavation was concentrated in the north and northwestern parts of the mound, with several deep soundings providing a continuous sequence of seventeen architectural levels reaching back to the early second millennium BCE. The succession of temples, palaces, and town defenses confirmed the city's prominence, particularly during levels VII and IV. Those periods are noted for their royal archives, which identify the ancient site as Alalakh, capital of the province Mukish, vassal to the kingdoms of Yamhad (modern Aleppo) in the eighteenth–sixteenth centuries BCE and Mitanni in the fifteenth–fourteenth centuries BCE. [*See* Alalakh Texts; Aleppo; Mitanni.] Providing key synchonisms with the kings of Yamhad, Mari, Babylon, Hatti, Mitanni, and Egypt, these archives are central to discussions of absolute chronology for the second millennium BCE and have been cited, in particular, in support of the "middle" chronology. [*See* Mari; Babylon.] The two archives also reveal changes in social structure and ethnic composition that, combined with the material remains, bear, in particular, on the problem of Hurrian infiltration and culture. [*See* Hurrians.] Subsequent spells under Hittite suzerainty between levels III and I ended in the city's final destruction, tentatively correlated with the onslaught of the Sea Peoples. [*See* Hittites.] Level O represents a brief attempt at recolonization in the twelfth century BCE.

History of Excavation. Woolley, on behalf of the British Museum in London, conducted eight seasons of excavation between 1937 and 1939 and 1946 and 1949. His first exploratory soundings, begun as an offshoot of the excavations at the Mediterranean port of Tell al-Mina, were followed in 1937 by more extensive investigations of the level I–IV residential houses and associated citadel wall. The level IV palace and archives, discovered at the end of this season, were fully excavated in 1938, when investigations along the northern and northwestern ridge of the tell exposed older fortifications of VI and V as well as the city gate of VII. The fourth season (1939) was marked by the discovery of palace VII and its archives beneath the private houses of IV–VI. Directly west of the palace. Woolley encountered the temple precinct, which became the focus of the first postwar season in 1946. By the end of the fifth season, most of levels I–VII had been uncovered, and a sounding below palace VII exposed precursors in levels VIII and IX. Extended down to the water table in 1947, this deep sounding produced seven further levels, X–XVI; a second sounding in the temple precinct reached virgin soil below level XVII, under the present water table. The last two seasons were devoted to problems of stratigraphy in the temple sounding and the fortifications of levels I–VII. [*See the biography of Woolley.*]

The finds were divided mainly between the British Museum in London and the Hatay Museum in Antakya, but some also went to the Ashmolean Museum at Oxford University and to the Universities of Sydney and Melbourne, Australia. The field notes and negatives are stored at the Institute of Archaeology, London. The results of the excavations were published in preliminary reports between 1936 and 1950. Woolley's final publication in 1955 followed two volumes on epigraphy by Sidney Smith (1949) and Donald J. Wiseman (1953). Much of the secondary literature is devoted to problems of stratigraphy and chronology.

Stratigraphy and Chronology. The absolute chronology at Alalakh hinges on the dating of the archives in levels VII and IV. That dating, in turn, depends on the reconstruction of the local genealogy and on synchronisms with external king lists as well as ceramic and glyptic assemblages.

Level VII constitutes an architectural phase represented by a city gate, ramparts, a temple, and a palace. Archaeologically, level VII is considered coterminous with the palace, whose archive of 175 tablets spans at least two rulers at Alalakh, coinciding with at least five rulers at Yamhad. Both the palace archive and architecture suggest a short occupation of fifty to seventy-five years. Originally, Smith (1940), followed by Woolley (1953, 1955), fixed the time span of VII at 1780–1750 BCE. In his assessment, based on ceramic and glyptic evidence as well as the Venus tablets of Ammisaduqa, Smith assumes a synchronism between Yarimlim of level VII, Hammurabi of Babylon, and Zimrilim of Mari.

Following the publication of the texts in 1953, it transpired that the contemporary of Hammurabi and Zimrilim was Yarimlim of Yamhad, grandfather of Yarimlim of Alalakh to whom the oldest palace records pertain. The dates were revised to about 1720–1650 BCE by advocates of the "middle" chronology (see above). Following Benno Landsberger ("Assyrische Königsliste und 'dunkles Zeitalter,' " *Journal of Cuneiform Studies* 8 [1954], p. 8), Albrecht Goetze (1957, p. 23) linked the destruction of VII with Muršili I and the sack of Babylon during the reign of Samsuditana. However, texts found at Boğazköy in 1957 reveal that it was Hattušili I who destroyed Alalakh during his second Syrian campaign. [*See* Boğazköy.] Proponents of the "low" chronology question the accuracy of the Venus tablets and dispute the glyptic

and ceramic parallels between Alalakh VII and Egypt's twelfth dynasty. Instead, they would correlate them with Middle Bronze IIB/C material in Palestine. The introduction of Bichrome ware, Base Ring I, and Cypriot Monochrome in VIB suggests a destruction date of about 1575 BCE or later for VII, which would thus span the late seventeenth–early sixteenth centuries BCE. Despite reservations about the dating of Bichrome Ware based on its presence in Megiddo stratum IX, which ended in destruction supposedly at the hands of Thutmose III in 1468/67 BCE, recent evaluations of historical and archaeological data support the "low" chronology.

Woolley's proposed hiatus between the destruction of level VII and the beginning of level VI is also questioned. Levels VI and V were associated by Woolley with two rebuildings of the fortress, each of which comprised two distinct phases: VIA and B, VA and B. The correlation of VI–V with the MB IIC and Late Bronze I period (c. 1575–1460 BCE) is supported by ceramic parallels from recent excavations at Tell Hadidi and Mumbaqat. [*See* Hadidi, Tell.]

The beginning of level IV, according to Woolley, is marked by the construction of the Niqmepa palace, which was destroyed in the reign of Niqmepa's son, Ilimilimma, before the end of level IV. Because, contrary to Woolley's assumption, six of the three hundred tablets in the palace archive pertain to Idrimi (once considered to be Niqmepa's grandson but now recognized as his father), it is uncertain who built the palace. Idrimi's date derives from his inscribed statue, although the text, if composed posthumously, has little historical value. Vassal to Parrattarna, king of the Hurrians, and indirectly linked with the Hittite king Zidanta, Idrimi is now dated to about 1470 BCE. In recent studies (Gates, 1981, pp. 8–9; Gates, 1987, p. 76; Heinz, 1992) he is associated with the southeastern wing (C1–9) of the palace and the triple *serai* (Tk. [orig., Pers.], "palace") gate, both assigned to level VB. Woolley's 1460/50 BCE date for the start of level IV conforms with the relative dating of the Mitannian rulers and the dates of Mediterranean imports in IV. Niqmepa is vassal to Sauštatar, king of Mitanni, whose seal occurs at Nuzi, where it may have been used as an heirloom. [*See* Seals; Nuzi.] The absence of Bichrome Ware in Alalakh IV, combined with the presence of Cypriot Base-ring II Wares and a Mycenaean IIIA sherd, places the destruction of palace IV after 1425 BCE. The end of level IV, attributed to an invasion by Šuppiluliuma I, was once dated 1370 BCE but might be as late as 1340 BCE, according to the "low" chronology.

Level VII provides an end date for levels XVII–VIII encountered in two deep soundings. Woolley's correlation between these two soundings, however, was based on the sequence of structures below VII and is currently challenged by a comparative study of the pottery (Heinz, 1992). In both soundings, levels IX–VIII represent subphases of VII. Whereas in the palace sounding, levels XVI–XIV = XIII, in the temple sounding, levels XVI–XV = XIV and XI = X.

Woolley's original fourth-millennium date for the beginning of the "Archaic" levels was questioned as long ago as 1957 by Machteld J. Mellink (review of Woolley, *Alalakh*, in *American Journal of Archaeology* 61 [1957]: 395–400). Her observation that the uniform ceramic assemblage of XVII–VIII matches the early MB repertoire has since been confirmed by several studies drawing on comparative evidence from recent excavations, in particular at Tell ed-Dabʿa in the Egyptian Delta, and Tell Mardikh/Ebla, Tell Habuba Kabira, Tell Hadidi, and Mumbaqat in Syria. [*See* Dabʿa, Tell ed-; Ebla; Habuba Kabira.]

The uppermost levels, III–I, share ceramic elements. The destruction following level II, which contained Late Cypriot IIB ware, signals the end of a period of Hittite domination (c. 1350/40–1275 BCE). Level I is dated by the presence of Late Minoan IIIB pottery to the late thirteenth–early twelfth centuries BCE, preceding the arrival of the Sea Peoples.

Architecture. A circuit wall, city gate, and fortress enclosed a palace, a temple, and residential houses. Of these, only the palace and temple were traced down through the Archaic levels. While the temple location remained more or less fixed, the palace moved from the temple area to the city gate in the mid-second millennium BCE.

Middle Bronze IIA (levels XVII–X). The temple was traced back to level XIV, but best known is the temple plan of XIIA–B. Considered a precursor to the Neo-Hittite *bit ḫilani*, this multistoried temple included a cella and an anteroom fronted by a courtyard. In the palace sounding, level XII also produced the earliest remains of a monumental building with a colonnade, followed in levels XI–X by an imposing structure with a stairway and courtyard.

Middle Bronze IIB (levels IX–VII). The sparse architectural remains of levels IX–VIII are considered subphases of the temple and palace of level VII, which also includes a rampart, gate, and "fortress." The so-called Yarimlim palace is built in three sections on a terraced terrain along the city wall. The official quarter (rooms 1–13), embellished by basalt orthostats, contains the main entrance, courtyard, audience chamber, and archive room. It rises to the central block in which a stairway leads to the living quarters above. Both the audience chamber and the upper living room were divided by wooden columns on basalt bases between two projecting piers, a feature that recurs in levels IV–I. The walls were decorated by frescoes of architectural and naturalistic designs of Cretan inspiration. Stairs lead down to a possible hypogeum, which remains an enigma. The southern section probably served a domestic function.

The adjoining temple contained related tablets. Its unusually thick walls suggest an upper story; its plan, which consists of a shallow antechamber and deep cella with an altar aligned on a central axis with the entrance, is related to third-millennium North Syrian prototypes.

Also typical of Syria and Palestine in the MB II period is the "three-entrance" city gate framed by lateral towers crowning an earthern rampart or glacis. The gate's association with level VII is based on its relative position below the fort/fortress of level IV.

Middle Bronze IIC–Late Bronze I (levels VI–IV). Although the remains of levels VI and V were encountered in all areas of excavation, their subphases, A and B, were less apparent outside the fortress. The first major construction is the nine-room palace and triple (*serai*) gate of level VB, now associated with Idrimi, that were later incorporated as the south wing in Niqmepa's level IV palace. The separation of the palace from the temple and its relocation near the city gate indicate major social or political change. Its plan, comprising a central hearth room surrounded by smaller utility and storage rooms, is in the tradition of contemporary houses. Its main distinguishing feature is its monumental entrance with stairs and a columned portico. Polished basalt orthostats line the walls of the entrance and anteroom leading to stairs and an upper story. Like temple XII, this arrangement is seen as a precursor of the earlier *bit ḫilani* plan. Columned porticoes also mark two ceremonial rooms of the later extension built by Niqmepa's son, Ilimilimma, and recur in the fort. The level IV temple, superimposed on the sunken cella of temple V, resembles the axial plan of temple VII, which conformed to a local North Syrian tradition.

The town defenses, traced to levels V and VI, were only partially remodeled in level IV. The entrance leads through a narrow passage with two right-angle turns. It opens into a courtyard bordered on the northwest by the fortress, which is integrated with the gate buildings and contains formal rooms with columned porticoes.

Late Bronze IIA–B (levels III–I). Following the destruction of level IV, the fort and temple were rebuilt on a massive scale by the Hittite conquerers. It occupied the entire northwest quarter of the citadel, including the old palace area. Its destruction at the end of level II was succeded by a rebuilding on a smaller scale.

Temple III comprised two double-storied shrines with opposite orientations. In shrine A, the altar is located in the courtyard, with the cella, presumably, upstairs. Temple II marks a reversion to the axial plan of levels IV and VII. Temple I is a one-story building consisting of a large cella, antechamber, and courtyard. Apart from porticoed doors, its distinguishing features include a triple-niched cella in phase A and an annex in phase B.

Pottery. The ceramic evidence comes from all levels at Alalakh and supplements the tablets from levels VII and IV as a chronological index. Attempts to subject this material to statistical analysis have been thwarted by lack of information in the final report (McClellan, 1989), but comparative studies of the pottery assemblage have led to adjustments in Woolley's correlation between levels at Alalakh and their association with dated assemblages in Mesopotamia, Palestine, and the Aegean.

Middle Bronze IIA (levels XVII–X). The type index of levels XVII–X is "ʿAmuq-Cilician" ware, with its characteristic trefoil-mouthed jugs, carinated bowls, and high-footed vessels decorated with a painted triglyph-metope frieze containing geometric, plant, and animal motifs. Dated parallels from northern Syria, Cilicia, and Anatolia range within the MB IIA period. From level XII comes a solitary "red-cross bowl," whose far-flung analogs date to the EB III period. Level X saw the introduction of Khabur Ware and gray burnished Ware, both characteristic of the MB IIB period.

Middle Bronze IIB (levels IX–VII). The burnished gray ware that began in level X is characteristic of IX–VIII but also occurs in levels VII–V. Khabur Ware, too, continues through VIII. The ceramic assemblage of VII is marked by the absence of painted pottery and by bowls and handleless pots with carinations and flaring rims.

Middle Bronze IIC–Late Bronze I (level VI A–B). The main feature of VI is the abrupt influx of Syro-Palestinian wares (black lustrous juglets, painted craters, and footed goblets), which together with Cypriot imports (Bichrome, Red-on-Black, and Monochrome ware in VIA; White Slip I and Base Ring I in VIB), provide a chronological indicator of the transition from the Middle to the Late Bronze Age.

Late Bronze IA–B (levels V–IV). Level V is marked by imported White Slip I and II, Base Ring I, late Khabur Ware, and Black Impressed Ware. The disappearance of Bichrome Ware and Khabur Ware in level IV and the introduction of Nuzi Ware have long overshadowed the transitional character of this level. In it, Cypriot imports (White Slip I and II, Base Ring II) increased, while new types appeared that became more common in levels III–I.

Late Bronze IIA–B (levels III–I). The white-painted Nuzi Ware blends into "Aṭchana Ware," a local variation whose shapes and decoration show strong Aegean affinities. In level II, the fashion for Cypriot wares is superceded by Mycenaean IIIA and B imports, the main ceramic element of level I.

Glyptic. The glyptic material from Alalakh comprises cylinder seals mainly but also scarabs. Actual cylinder seals span a broader time range and show greater variety. They are, however, qualitatively inferior to the seal impressions, which occur mainly on envelopes in VII and on tablets and jars in IV. These include seal impressions of the rulers of Alalakh, Yamḥad, and Mitanni. In VII, the standard compositional scheme comprises an inscription and three standing figures: the king/seal owner, a deity, and an interceding goddess. The style evolves from solid, delicately modeled figures (baroque) toward thinner, elongated figures executed in flat relief (rococo). Although locally produced, the designs show Egyptian, Babylonian, and Cappadocian as well as Aegean and Cypriot inspiration. The seal impressions from IV are in contrast with contemporary seals. Whereas the former reveal a preference for recut older or foreign products with distinctive designs, the latter, made of sintered quartz, are uniformly drill decorated, which characterizes the widespread Mitannian Common Style. There are local variations, of which the Alalakh group appears to be one.

The oldest cylinder seals belong to the late fourth–early third millennia. Once cited as evidence for the early dating of the Archaic levels, they are now recognized as antiques. The latest seals, showing figures with raised arms supporting the winged disk, are related to Hittite iconography, which, ultimately, however, derived from northern Syria.

Small Finds. As a result of numerous violent destructions followed by looting, few of the small finds were found in situ and their dates are largely open to debate. Composite statues were popular during VII, to judge by the stone heads and fragments from the floor of the temple. Most remarkable is the black diorite "head of Yarimlim," a priestly figure, whose beard and moustache may have been highlighted by paint or incrustation. Two crude basalt figures found in the northeast gate tower of level V belong to a growing number of statuettes from Syria, northern Mesopotamia, and the Levantine coast. They date to the middle and late second millennium BCE, and their contexts suggest a guardian function. The well-known seated statue of Idrimi, identified by its autobiographical inscription, was found broken and buried in the temple IB annex. Thought to have survived several centuries as an object of veneration, it is unclear whether the statue was ever mounted on the basalt lion throne found nearby. Made of white stone, with eyes and eyebrows inlaid in black stone, the statue's striking frontality was once considered characteristic of Hurro-Mitannian art. However, its tall hat and wraparound cloak with its thick rolled hem place it firmly in the Old Syrian tradition. Egyptian influence is seen in the somber facial expression and the position of the hands. More puzzling is the abstract sculpture of a ram's head from palace IV, whose only parallel comes from Nuzi. Evidence of Hittite supremacy during level III is manifested by the basalt slab of a Hittite royal relief showing Tudḥaliya and his wife, which was found inverted as a paving slab in temple I. Also of this general period, but considered typically North Syrian, are two cornerstone lion sculptures with the head, chest, and forelegs carved in the round; the body is rendered in relief.

Most noteworthy is a bronze god seated on an eagle from the level VII gate and a bronze goddess from temple V. A ritual spearhead with molded lions gripping the blade is considered to be of Hittite inspiration. This and a ceremonial sword with an inlayed hilt and a lunate handle were found in level I and are difficult to date.

Alalakh's location at the heart of the ivory trade network is evidenced by the store of elephant tusks found in palace VII. Used primarily for appliqué or inlay, the raw material was worked by local craftsmen, although Egyptian and Hittite inspiration is apparent. The repertoire of luxury products includes statuettes, toilet boxes, and bowls from the temple, palace, and graves.

The discovery of faience vessels and polychrome glass beads in the level VII temple and palace is consistent with the MB glass and faience industry in Syria and Anatolia. [*See* Glass.] These precede the earliest glass vessels and the first vessels of glazed terra cotta found in level VI. The glaze is alkaline, not lead, as once thought. Woolley's discovery of sherds of polychrome, core-formed glass vessels in level VI must be cited with caution: examples found outside Alalakh date to the mid-fifth century BCE. Other cast or molded glass objects reported from level VI, notably a nude-female plaque, are in keeping with external finds.

BIBLIOGRAPHY

Primary Sources

Collon, Dominique. *The Seal Impressions from Tell Atchana/Alalakh.* Alter Orient und Altes Testament, 27. Kevelaer, 1975. Comprehensive publication of the seal impressions from Alalakh, with a critical examination of their chronological and sociological role, combined with an art historical study of style and iconography. Collon's dating of level VII is now obsolete.

Collon, Dominique. *The Alalakh Cylinder Seals.* British Archaeological Reports, International Series, no. 132. Oxford, 1982. Valuable catalog with much information on dating, iconography, and distribution included with the descriptions in the individual entries.

Dietrich, Manfried, and Oswald Loretz. "Die Inschrift der Statue des Königs Idrimi von Alalah." *Ugarit Forschungen* 13 (1981): 201–269.

Oller, Gary Howard. "The Autobiography of Idrimi: A New Text Edition with Philological and Historical Commentary." Ph.D. diss., University of Pennsylvania, 1977. Reedition of the text with a useful summary of existing theories on the inscription and a critical evaluation of its historical significance.

Smith, Sidney. *The Statue of Idri-mi.* Occasional Publications of the British Institute of Archaeology in Ankara, no. 1. London, 1949. The original translation and evaluation of the Idrimi inscription, which has been amended and augmented by newer readings, notably Oller (1977) and Dietrich and Loretz (1981).

Wiseman, D. J. *The Alalakh Tablets.* Occasional Publications of the British Institute of Archaeology in Ankara, no. 2. New York, 1953. Primary reference work for most of the 460 tablets from Alalakh, with a useful introduction and synopsis of key developments in population, social structure, religion, and literature. Additional tablets were published by Wiseman in "Supplementary Copies of Alalakh Tablets," *Journal of Cuneiform Studies* 8 (1954): 1–30.

Woolley, C. Leonard. *A Forgotten Kingdom.* London, 1953. Popular account of the excavations.

Woolley, C. Leonard. *Alalakh: An Account of the Excavations at Tell Atchana in the Hatay, 1937–1949.* Oxford, 1955. The final publication of Woolley's last excavation, an overview of the general results. On the whole, the chronology is outdated and Woolley's interpretation of the lower strata, in particular, is doubtful. Recent studies on the pottery, small finds, and glyptic have been frustrated by inadequacies and inaccuracies with regard to information on findspots, types, and quantities. Best used in conjunction with the field notes and actual objects.

Secondary Sources

Albright, William Foxwell. "Stratigraphic Confirmation of the Low Mesopotamian Chronology." *Bulletin of the American Schools of Oriental Research*, no. 144 (1956): 26–30. Pioneering study of the low chronology, which has recently gained favor.

Gates, Marie H. C. *Alalakh Levels VI and V: A Chronological Reassessment.* Syro-Mesopotamian Studies, 4.2. Malibu, 1981. Novel approach to the dating of Alalakh VII and IV by means of the LB assemblages of the intervening levels VI and V, which support the low chronology.

Gates, Marie H. C. "Alalakh and Chronology Again." In *High, Middle, or Low? International Colloquium on Absolute Chronology Held at the University of Gothenburg, 20–22 August 1987*, edited by Paul Åström, pp. 60–86. Gothenburg, 1987. Updated version of her 1981 work.

Götze, Albrecht. "Alalah and Hittite Chronology." *Bulletin of the American Schools of Oriental Research*, no. 146 (1957): 20–26.

Heinz, Marlies. *Tell Atchana/Alalakh: Die Schichten VII–XVII.* Alter Orient und Altes Testament, 41. Neukirchen-Vluyn, 1992. The most recent in-depth investigation of the early ceramic assemblage, with a view toward defining its date and context. Drawing on comparative material from recent excavations, Heinz proposes adjustments to Woolley's stratigraphic correlations and supports the MB horizon suggested by Mellink and others.

McClellan, Thomas L. "The Chronology and Ceramic Assemblages of Alalakh." In *Essays in Ancient Civilization Presented to Helene J. Kantor*, edited by Albert Leonard, Jr., and Bruce B. Williams, pp. 181–212. Studies in Ancient Oriental Civilization, no. 47. Chicago, 1989. Lucid discussion of the central issues affecting the chronology of Alalakh, which the author attempts to solve by means of a statistical analysis of pottery types in various levels. Relying heavily on Woolley's publication, McClellan's results are perhaps less reliable than those of Heinz (1992), which are based on her inspection of the actual sherds. See the comments on McClellan by Heinz in *Akkadica* 83 (1993): 1–25.

Smith, Sidney. *Alalakh and Chronology.* London, 1940. The basis for the middle chronology, which gained a wide following and is still prevalent in textbooks despite the faulty synchronisms between the kings of Alalakh and Babylon.

DIANA L. STEIN

ALALAKH TEXTS. British-led archaeological teams, directed by C. Leonard Woolley from 1937 to 1939 and again from 1946 to 1949, excavated more than 515 texts and fragments at Tell 'Atchana, in northwestern Syria, the site of the ancient city of Alalakh. Of the seventeen levels of occupation found, dated from about 2400 to about 1195 BCE, two yielded nearly all the texts: level VII (mid-eighteenth–mid-seventeenth centuries) synchronized with the First Dynasty of Babylon; and level IV (fifteenth century) synchronized with the kingdom of Mitanni. Almost two hundred texts date to level VII, about three hundred to level IV, and about twenty to the succeeding levels.

All but a few of the texts are written in Akkadian cuneiform on clay tablets. A letter and a lengthy divination text are in Hittite, and an inscription of King Idrimi is written in Akkadian on a statue (see below). Nearly all the Akkadian texts were written locally in a western form of the language that betrays a Hurrian influence and, to a lesser degree, of the local West Semitic languages.

A few of the Akkadian texts were published preliminarily by Sidney Smith in 1939. The Hittite letter was published by H. Eheholf in the same year. The statue inscription of Idrimi was published in a separate volume by Smith in 1949; it has been reedited by Edward L. Greenstein and David Marcus, by Gary H. Oller, and by Manfried Dietrich and Oswald Loretz. More than 460 texts were cataloged and most of them published in a handwritten copy and/or transliteration by Donald J. Wiseman in a 1953 volume, which included Oliver R. Gurney's transliteration of a lengthy Hittite divination report, and in a series of subsequent articles.

Forty-three additional, fragmentary documents from level IV were published in transliteration by Dietrich and Loretz in three articles appearing in 1969–1970. One text, a name list, remains altogether unpublished. The majority of the tablets are held by the Antakya Museum in Turkey; most of the rest are held by the British Museum.

The level VII tablets, mainly from the reign of Yarim-lim and his son Ammitaqum, were, for the most part, discovered in the palace archive and in the temple. Most of the level IV tablets were found in the palace of Niqmepa, but outside the archive, strewn about the floors as though they were being removed to safety at the time the palace was burned.

The majority of the texts are lists: censuses by name and in some cases also by place and occupation; inventories; ration lists; landholdings; and others. Two level IV texts list women. There are contracts of town purchases, mainly from level VII, and deeds of the exchange of villages, mainly from level IV. Several contracts, issuing loans or giving credit—many by the king or his agent—take persons as surety, as at Nuzi. The king serves as magistrate, but in level IV he must also appear as a litigant before the Mitanni overlord. The last king of level IV, Ilimilimma II, adopts a man as his "father," providing him a son's service in life and death in return for a father's inheritance. A level IV marriage contract permits a man to designate a son other than the firstborn as principal heir, in accordance with practices at Nuzi and Ugarit. The presence of parts of the Mesopotamian lexical series ḪAR-*ra*=*ḫubullu* attests to a Babylonian scribal tradition.

The texts furnish an excellent picture of level VII and IV societies with respect to ethnicity, economic structure, and size. A substantial Hurrian sector in level VII becomes the predominant population group in level IV. The latter society is stratified into a small aristocracy, a middle class of "free(d) persons," and a heterogeneous lower class, including peasants and rootless 'Apiru.

In the level VII texts we find references to a certain Abban (or Abba-'Il), king of the north-central domain of Yamḫad, who granted Alalakh to his son Yarimlim as part of a division of power to decrease the chances of revolt. Yarimlim's gifts to the temple, apparently upon his accession, are also documented. Two treaties governing the extradition of fugitives are present in the corpus, one from level VII and another from level IV. In the latter treaty the Hurrian overlord, Barrattarna, oversees the agreement between two vassals, Pilliya, apparently of Kizzuwatna (Cilicia) and Idrimi of Alalakh.

The pseudoautobiography of King Idrimi was inscribed in 104 lines across the front of a statue of the subject that had stood, enthroned, in the sanctuary, and was securely buried nearby, apparently to protect it from the coming destruction that took place in level I. The text, which was composed in the mid-15th century by a well-known scribe in the palace of Idrimi's son Niqmepa, provides invaluable historical information within a unique specimen of ancient Syrian narrative prose. Its closest parallels are the Egyptian tale of Sinuhe and the biblical stories of Jacob, Joseph, Moses, and David. It tells how Idrimi, who escaped calamity in his native Aleppo with his older brothers, went on to live among 'Apiru in northern Canaan until he could return to the land of Mukish and, by the assent of Barrattarna, assume the kingship of Alalakh.

This and other level IV Alalakh texts are of particular value, for they illuminate what would have otherwise been a continuation of the "dark age" created by the lack of epigraphic sources for the sixteenth century BCE.

[*See also* Akkadian; Alalakh; Hurrians; *and* Nuzi.]

BIBLIOGRAPHY

Hess (see below) provides a key to the various primary publications of texts, and these references are not repeated here:

Dietrich, Manfried, and Oswald Loretz. "Die Inschrift der Statue des Königs Idrmi von Alalaḫ." *Ugarit-Forschugen* 13 (1981,): 201–268. Thorough re-edition of the inscription based on a new collation with some improvements in interpretation.

Draffkorn, Ann. "Hurrians and Hurrian at Alalaḫ: An Ethno-Linguistic Analysis." Ph.D. diss., University of Pennsylvania, 1959. The most comprehensive investigation of Hurrian names and terminology in the Alalakh texts from levels VII and IV; it has a tendency to maximize the Hurrian presence and influence where evidence is lacking or ambiguous.

Drower, Margaret S. "Syria c. 1550–1400 B.C." In *The Cambridge Ancient History*, vol. 2, pt. 1, *History of the Middle East and the Aegean Region c. 1800–1380 B.C.*, edited by I. E. S. Edwards et al., pp. 417–525. 3d ed. Cambridge, 1973. Sound interpretation of the historical context and significance of level IV at Alalakh. The reader must follow the bibliographic references for documentation.

Greenstein, Edward L., and David Marcus. "The Akkadian Inscription of Idrimi." *Journal of the Ancient Near Eastern Society of Columbia University* 8 (1976): 59–96. Detailed linguistic and philological commentary, but a few of its suggestions are not sustained by a collation of the text.

Hess, Richard S. "A Preliminary List of the Published Alalakh Texts." *Ugarit-Forschungen* 20 (1988): 69–87. Catalog of all published texts and fragments, except the Idrimi inscription, with reference to places where hand copies, transliterations, and translations may be found. Thorough, but lacks some data.

Hess, Richard S. "Observations on Some Unpublished Alalakh Texts, Probably from Level IV." *Ugarit-Forschungen* 24 (1992): 113–115. Note 2 provides references to additional transliterations and translations of texts, courtesy of Nadav Na'aman.

Klengel, Horst. *Geschichte Syriens im 2. Jahrtausend v.u.Z.*, vol. 1, *Nordsyrien*. Berlin, 1965. Comprehensive presentation and analysis of the pertinent historical sources, which benefits from comparison with other, later discussions because of the often difficult nature of the material.

Kupper, J.-R. "Northern Mesopotamia and Syria." In *The Cambridge Ancient History*, vol. 2, pt. 1, *History of the Middle East and the Aegean Region c. 1800–1380 B.C.*, edited by I. E. S. Edwards, pp. 1–41. 3d ed. Cambridge, 1973. Sound interpretation of the historical context and significance of the level VII Alalakh texts. The reader must follow the bibliographic references for documentation.

Oller, Gary H. "The Autobiography of Idrimi." Ph.D. diss., University of Pennsylvania, 1977. Transcription, translation, and interpretation based on a new collation, with good discussion of historical and literary matters.

Smith, Sidney. "A Preliminary Account of the Tablets from Atchana." *Antiquaries Journal* 19.1 (1939): 38–48. Initial sampling of diverse texts, superseded for the most part by later publications.

Smith, Sidney. *The Statue of Idri-mi.* Occasional Publications of the British Institute of Archaeology in Ankara, no. 1. London, 1949. Initial publication of Alalakh's most remarkable text. Still valuable for hand copies and photographs, but many of Smith's readings and interpretations have been superseded.

Wiseman, Donald J., and Richard S. Hess. "Alalakh Text 457." *Ugarit-Forschungen* 26 (1994): 501–508. Publication and discussion of this list of personal names and their geographic locations.

Woolley, Leonard. *A Forgotten Kingdom.* London, 1953. Popular, authoritative account of Tell 'Atchana and neighboring excavations, providing historical background and interpretation. The history of level IV Alalakh is distorted by the author's acceptance of Sidney Smith's dating of Idrimi to the end, rather than the beginning, of the dynasty.

Woolley, Leonard. *Alalakh: An Account of the Excavations at Tell Atchana in the Hatay, 1937–1949.* Oxford, 1955. Fundamental, comprehensive excavation report; the conclusions (especially concerning chronology) must be balanced by later, critical discussions.

EDWARD L. GREENSTEIN

ALBRIGHT, WILLIAM FOXWELL

ALBRIGHT, WILLIAM FOXWELL (1891–1971), the acknowledged "dean of biblical archaeology." Born to self-supporting missionary parents in Chile, Albright grew up in a strict, frugal Methodist family as the oldest of four boys and two girls. At the age of five, on furlough with his parents at his grandmother's Iowa farm, the nearsighted William caught hold of a machine rope that drew his left hand up into a pulley, injuring it severely. Thus handicapped, the boy, on returning to Chile, and unable to engage in sports, devoured his father's history and theology books. By age eleven he wanted to become an archaeologist but feared that by the time he was old enough everything would have been discovered.

The family returned to Iowa in 1903, and William attended a regular school instead of being tutored at home. In 1912 he was graduated from Upper Iowa University and spent the next year as a teacher in and principal of a high school in Menno, South Dakota, a Volga-German farming community. Realizing that he had no gift for teaching young pupils, he sent an application to Paul Haupt at Johns Hopkins University in Baltimore, Maryland. He enclosed proofs of an article of his that had been accepted by a German scholarly journal. The article dealt with an Akkadian word—he had in college taught himself Akkadian as well as Hebrew, and knew Spanish, French, German, Latin, and Greek. Haupt granted him a modest scholarship that enabled him to begin four years of study in Baltimore that he was to pass with brilliance.

Albright won the Thayer Fellowship for study in Jerusalem but was unable to use it until the end of World War I. In 1916, after earning his Ph.D., he received research grants and taught in Haupt's Oriental Seminary at Johns Hopkins. Late in 1918, he endured six painful months as a clerk in the army. Returned at last to his beloved books and teaching, he met his future wife, Ruth Norton, who subsequently earned her Ph.D. in Sanskrit literature in the Classical Seminary at Hopkins.

Albright arrived in Jerusalem at the beginning of 1920 for a decade of fruitful study, teaching, exploration, and excavation. He made his home at the American School of Oriental Research, now the William F. Albright Institute of Archaeological Research, where he and Ruth Norton were married in 1921. His three boyhood years spent living in the Atacama Desert of northern Chile were excellent preparation for life in the Near East, the place that had so early become the focus of his interest, study, and lifework.

Under Paul Haupt, Albright had been trained in higher criticism and a mythological approach to biblical subjects. The impact of being in the land of the Bible, as he led his students on walking and horseback tours, convinced him of the Bible's basic historicity, changing his focus and his writing. The *Bulletin of the American Schools of Oriental Research* (*BASOR*) was begun the same month he arrived, and for years its main content was his reports of his explorations and excavations, written in a popular style to generate interest and support. He was its editor from 1930 to 1968.

Albright first excavated at Tell el-Ful, the palace of King Saul at Gibeah. He also excavated at Tell Beit Mirsim for four seasons (1926–1932), which he believed to be biblical Debir (Israeli and other scholars prefer nearby Khirbet Rabud). Tell Beit Mirsim proved ideal for ascertaining a pottery chronology for western Palestine, as its layers of occupation were clearly separated by destruction levels. Albright's chronology is still standard. From 1929 to 1935, he also conducted "shoestring" excavations at Bethel and Beth-Zur—while commuting half-yearly between Baltimore and Jerusalem—and later excavated in South Arabia. He was chairman of the Oriental Seminary at Hopkins from 1929 until his retirement in 1958. At Hopkins he produced a cadre of scholars who became specialists in the numerous fields in which this giant had pioneered and made himself expert.

Albright published prolifically—his lifetime bibliographic total is more than eleven hundred books and articles. He received medals and other awards, and about thirty honorary doctorates in the United States and in many European countries. In 1969, on his last visit, he was given the honorary title of "Worthy [One] of Jerusalem," which had never before been given to a non-Jew. He had played a part in such "revolutionary" (his word) discoveries as the Ugaritic tablets (1929) and the Dead Sea Scrolls (beginning in 1947) and was founding coeditor, with David Noel Freedman, of the Anchor Bible project.

Albright died from multiple strokes just a few months after celebrating his eightieth birthday and receiving his final *Fest-*

schrift. He had been a legend in his own time, a pioneer archaeologist, and a historian of ideas, especially of religion, in the ancient Near East, and truly a genius.

[*See also* American Schools of Oriental Research; Beit Mirsim, Tell; Beth-Zur; Dead Sea Scrolls; Historical Geography; Rabud, Khirbet; *and* Ugarit Inscriptions.]

BIBLIOGRAPHY

Albright, William Foxwell. *The Archaeology of Palestine and the Bible* (1932). Cambridge, Mass., 1974.

Albright, William Foxwell. *From the Stone Age to Christianity: Monotheism and the Historical Process.* Baltimore, 1940.

Albright, William Foxwell. *Archaeology and the Religion of Israel.* Baltimore, 1942.

Albright, William Foxwell. *History, Archaeology, and Christian Humanism.* New York, 1964.

Albright, William Foxwell. *Yahweh and the Gods of Canaan: A Historical Analysis of Two Contrasting Faiths.* Garden City, N.Y., 1968.

Bulletin of the American Schools of Oriental Research, no. 122 (April 1951): In Honor of William Foxwell Albright on His Sixtieth Birthday, May 24, 1951 (guest editor: Ephraim Avigdor Speiser).

Freedman, David Noel, ed. *The Published Works of William Foxwell Albright: A Comprehensive Bibliography.* Cambridge, Mass., 1975.

Goedicke, Hans, ed. *Near Eastern Studies in Honor of William Foxwell Albright.* Baltimore, 1971.

Malamat, Abraham, ed. *W. F. Albright Volume.* Eretz-Israel, vol. 9. Jerusalem, 1969.

Running, Leona Glidden, and David Noel Freedman. *William Foxwell Albright: A Twentieth-Century Genius.* New York, 1975; centennial ed., Berrien Springs, Mich., 1991.

Van Beek, Gus W. *The Scholarship of William Foxwell Albright: An Appraisal.* Atlanta, 1989.

Wright, G. Ernest, ed. *The Bible and the Ancient Near East: Essays in Honor of William Foxwell Albright.* Garden City, N.Y., 1961.

LEONA GLIDDEN RUNNING
and DAVID NOEL FREEDMAN

ALBRIGHT INSTITUTE OF ARCHAEOLOGICAL RESEARCH.

The W. F. Albright Institute of Archaeological Research (AIAR) in Jerusalem is the oldest American research center for ancient Near Eastern studies in the Middle East. Founded in 1900 as the American School of Oriental Research (ASOR) by its parent organizations—the American Oriental Society, the Society for Biblical Literature, and the Archaeological Institute of America—its purpose was to create an institutional base in Palestine in which scholars could pursue more efficiently and productively their research on issues relating to the Levant. In 1970, under the leadership of then ASOR president G. Ernest Wright, the school was separately incorporated and renamed after its most distinguished director, William Foxwell Albright. Today, AIAR is one of three institutes affiliated with ASOR, the others being in Amman and Nicosia. Support for AIAR is provided by its trustees, alumni, and a large constituency within the ASOR consortium of 150 institutions.

The present AIAR facility, constructed in 1925 for ASOR, is located 500 meters north of the old walled city of Jerusalem. It is within walking distance of the École Biblique et Archéologique Française; the British, German, and Spanish Schools of Archaeology; the Institute of Islamic Archaeology; the Nelson Glueck School of Biblical Archaeology of the Hebrew Union College–Jewish Institute of Religion; the Hebrew University's Institute of Archaeology; the Rockefeller Museum; and the Israel Antiquities Authority. This grouping of scholarly resources is an unparalleled concentration of human, bibliographic, and artifactual resources in Near Eastern studies.

The main objectives of the institute, with its long-standing tradition of academic freedom and excellence in scholarship, are to provide a comprehensive scholarly environment for qualified students and scholars in ancient Near Eastern studies; to advance the study of the literature, history, and culture of the ancient Near East, with an emphasis on the disciplines of the archaeology of Palestine and biblical studies; and to help educate the next generation of American scholars in ancient Near Eastern studies, with an emphasis on the training of archaeologists.

The importance of AIAR is measured by its critical contributions to the development of the discipline of Syro-Palestinian archaeology, in particular the archaeology of ancient Israel. These include advancements in excavation methodology, archaeological periodization, and stratigraphic and material culture analyses. They also include the results of the institute's major excavations and surveys, its pivotal role in the study of the Dead Sea Scrolls, and the impact of its distinguished alumni on the fields of ancient Near Eastern, biblical, and Judaic studies.

The institute's most productive periods have been under its five long-term directors. William Foxwell Albright (1920–1926, 1927–1929, 1933–1936) is considered the father of the discipline of Palestinian, or biblical, archaeology. Albright's Tell Beit Mirsim excavation reports (1932–1943) produced a pottery dating sequence that gave the emerging field of Palestinian archaeology a chronological foundation that is still used. The framework for this new discipline and the stimulus for its growth were provided by Albright's synthetic volumes on the archaeology of Palestine and religion of Israel (1942; 1949), and by his seminal articles on Hebrew and Phoenician epigraphy.

Nelson Glueck (1932–1933, 1936–1940, 1942–1947) identified more than 1,000 sites in his survey of Transjordan and produced the first scientific demographic synthesis of Moab, Ammon, and Edom, published in four volumes (1934–1951). This is still a primary textbook of the archaeology of Jordan, as is his volume on the Nabateans (1966), based on his excavation of Khirbet et-Tannur.

Paul Lapp (1961–1965) made a major contribution to the study of Palestinian pottery in his pioneering volume on the Late Hellenistic and Early Roman periods (1961). Also, his excavations at 'Iraq el-Amir, Tell er-Rumeith, Wadi ed-Daliyeh, Dhahr Mirzbaneh, Tell el-Ful, and Tell Ta'anach produced significant results for the Bronze and Iron Ages and the Hellenistic and Early Roman periods.

William G. Dever (1971–1975) is best known for his work at Tell Gezer and on three of the Gezer report volumes (1970–1986). His long-term research projects and publications on the material culture of the Early Bronze IV (Middle Bronze I) period, the chronology of Middle Bronze Age II, the Late Bronze II/Iron I transition, and his integrative studies emphasizing new directions in archaeology have become a major focus of study in the archaeology of ancient Israel. Continuing one of Albright's legacies, Dever has trained many of the new generation of American archaeologists presently working in the Middle East.

The AIAR's current director, Seymour Gitin, appointed in 1980, was a student of both Glueck's and Dever's and is known for his publications on the first millennium BCE at Tell Gezer (1990) and on the Iron II period at Tel Miqne/Ekron (1981–1995). Based on the work of his predecessors, he has built an extensive program that offers pre- and post-doctoral researchers multicultural experiences spanning the broad spectrum of Near Eastern studies. The program provides a unique opportunity for the exchange of ideas between the forty annual AIAR appointees, primarily from North America and Europe, and hundreds of researchers living and working in Israel and in other countries in the eastern Mediterranean basin. For many, including Palestinian and foreign scholars working in Arab countries, the institute is their primary contact with colleagues in Israel. The program, which annually involves more than three thousands participants, includes a series of eighty lectures, reports, seminars, workshops, field trips (local and abroad) and social events, and support for twenty-one ASOR-affiliated excavation and publication projects, among which are the long-term projects at Ashkelon, Caesarea, Lahav, Sepphoris, and the institute's excavation at Tel Miqne/Ekron, jointly sponsored with the Institute of Archaeology of the Hebrew University of Jerusalem. The AIAR also has a publications program, an extensive research library, laboratories, and living accommodations for thirty-four people.

To further expand the scope of interregional scholarly collaboration, AIAR recently initiated an international research project, "The Neo-Assyrian Empire in the Seventh Century BC: A Study of the Interactions between Center and Periphery." Designed to investigate the growth and development of the Assyrian Empire, its participants include researchers who have worked on Cyprus and in Egypt, Greece, Iran, Iraq, Israel, Jordan, Spain, Syria, and Turkey. The institute has also created a long-term joint research, lecture, field trip, and fellowship program with the American School of Classical Studies at Athens, a program it plans to extend to other American research centers in the Mediterranean basin.

For almost one hundred years, AIAR has been at the forefront of archaeological and historical scholarship in the Middle East. It is this tradition that has made the Albright Institute a renowned international research center.

[*See also* American Schools of Oriental Research; Biblical Archaeology; *and the biographies of Albright, Glueck, and Lapp. In addition, all sites mentioned are the subject of independent entries.*]

BIBLIOGRAPHY

Albright, William Foxwell, ed. *The Excavation of Tell Beit Mirsim.* 4 vols. Annual of the American Schools of Oriental Research, 12, 13, 17, 21/22. New Haven, 1932–1943.

Albright, William Foxwell. *Archaeology and the Religion of Israel.* Baltimore, 1942.

Albright, William Foxwell. *The Archaeology of Palestine.* Harmondsworth, 1949.

Dever, William G., et al. *Gezer I: Preliminary Report of the 1964–66 Seasons.* Jerusalem, 1970.

Dever, William G., et al. *Gezer II: Preliminary Report of the 1967–70 Seasons in Field I and II.* Jerusalem, 1974.

Dever, William G., et al. *Gezer IV: The 1969–71 Seasons in Field VI, the "Acropolis."* Jerusalem, 1986.

Gitin, Seymour. "Tel Miqne-Ekron: A Type-Site for the Inner Coastal Plain in the Iron Age II Period." In *Recent Excavations in Israel: Studies in Iron Age Archaeology*, edited by Seymour Gitin and William G. Dever. Annual of the American Schools of Oriental Research 49 (1989), pp. 23–58.

Gitin, Seymour. *Gezer III: A Ceramic Typology of the Late Iron II, Persian, and Hellenistic Periods at Tell Gezer.* Jerusalem, 1990.

Gitin, Seymour, ed. *Tel Miqne (Ekron) Excavation Project.* 6 vols. Jerusalem, 1981–1995.

Glueck, Nelson. *Explorations in Eastern Palestine.* 4 vols. Annual of the American Schools of Oriental Research, 14, 15, 18/19, 25/28. New Haven, 1934–1951.

Glueck, Nelson. *Deities and Dolphins: The Story of the Nabataens.* London, 1966.

King, Philip J. *American Archaeology in the Mideast: A History of the American Schools of Oriental Research.* Philadelphia, 1983.

Lapp, Paul W. *Palestinian Ceramic Chronology, 200 B.C.–A.D. 70.* New Haven, 1961.

SEYMOUR GITIN

ALEPPO (Ar., Ḥalab), the second largest city in Syria, located in the northern part of the country (40°12′ N, 38°68′5″ E). It has been occupied since remote antiquity and played a very important role in Near Eastern history during the second millennium BCE.

It is likely that Aleppo has existed since at least the Early Bronze Age, although the evidence is indirect and uncertain. Excavations of a small site in the southwest part of modern Aleppo (al-Ansari) exposed Early Bronze IV levels and show at least that the outskirts of the area were occupied in the latter part of the millennium (see Antoine Suleiman, "Excavations at Ansari-Aleppo for the Seasons 1973–1980: Early and Middle Bronze Ages," *Akkadica* 40 [1984]: 1–16; and idem., "Fouilles d'Alep (Al-Ansari)," *Syria* 62 [1985]: 135). Aleppo may be mentioned under the name Ḥalam in tablets from Ebla and Early Dynastic Mari (see W. G. Lambert, "Ḥalam, Il-Ḥalam and Aleppo," *Mari: Annales de Recherches Interdisciplinaires* 6 [1990]: 641–643.).

During the first half of the second millennium, Aleppo was the capital of the important state of Yamḥad, which played a leading role in the political development of northern Syria and Upper Mesopotamia. During the eighteenth century BCE, Yamḥad was the most powerful state in Syria and could resist the expansionist attempts of Shamshi-Adad I of Assyria. The Hittites, who rose to power in Anatolia during the seventeenth century BCE, referred to Yamḥad as having a "great kingship." Aleppo prospered until the opening years of the sixteenth century BCE, when Muršili I of Ḥatti attacked and destroyed the city.

During the Late Bronze Age, Aleppo no longer held its previous, dominant position; instead, it became a strategic pawn in the imperial conflicts between Ḥatti and Mitanni over the control of northern Syria, eventually coming firmly under Hittite rule. During the first millennium BCE, Aleppo appears to have been reduced to political insignificance, but it retained its ancient religious status as a major center of the worship of Hadad, the storm god.

In the early third century BCE, Seleucus I Nicator settled a colony of Macedonians at Aleppo, renamed it Beroea, and rebuilt the town as a Hellenistic city, probably with a squarish city wall and rectilinear streets, some of which can still be discerned in the current layout of the "Old City." Evidence for the Roman period is extremely slim, but the city is likely to have prospered, as did most of northern Syria, although not as a major city. Aleppo remained a secondary city under the shadow of Antioch until the latter was destroyed in 539/40 CE. It is likely that Aleppo began to develop into a major trade center at this point.

In 636 CE, Aleppo came under Muslim control, and in the early eighth centuy CE, a major mosque was built by either al-Walid I (r. 705–715) or his successor, Sulayman (r. 715–717). Unfortunately, none of this mosque has survived the several destructions and disastrous fires that befell it. Following the demise of the Umayyad dynasty in the mid-eighth century, Aleppo, like most of Syria, slipped into a deep decline, from which it did not recover until the twelfth century.

Because the city has been continuously occupied for millennia, little archaeological work has been done in Aleppo. It is not yet certain where the earliest occupation of the town actually occurred, although most scholars believe that a tell in the western part of the current Old City, called el-ʿAqabe, represents the original settlement. It is assumed that the site expanded eventually to include the high hill now occupied by the great medieval citadel (see figure 1). Limited excavations early in this century by G. Ploix de Rotrou on the citadel showed that this high hill was occupied at least by the first millennium BCE. The excavators found the wall of a major public building, along with ornamented orthostats, two basalt lions, and a relief sculpture dating to the ninth/eighth centuries BCE.

Remains of the Hellenistic and Roman periods are few. As mentioned above, the area east and south of the tell, el-ʿAqabe, preserves the lines of the rectilineal streets of the Hellenistic city. The streets divided the area into rectangular blocks roughly 48 m north–south and 124 m east–west, the

ALEPPO.   Figure 1.   *Medieval citadel.* (Courtesy W. T. Pitard)

typical arrangement in cities founded during the Seleucid period. Nothing of the original city wall has been found, but scholars have generally thought that the preserved medieval wall runs along the ancient line. No building remains of the Hellenistic and Roman periods have been recovered on the citadel hill, although numerous small finds indicate a substantial occupation there during this time.

During the Byzantine period the city expanded outside the old walls, and records mention the construction of several churches. However, remains of only one church survive, the city's sumptuous and beautiful cathedral, located just south of where the great mosque was eventually built and the *madrasah Halawiyeh*, an Islamic school, now stands. A few vestiges of the Great Synagogue built during this period by Aleppo's then large and prosperous Jewish community have also survived.

No overwhelming changes took place in the city during the Umayyad period. Its most significant building was, of course, the Great Mosque, whose construction began in about 715. It is not certain whether Caliph al-Walid or his successor Sulayman actually inaugurated the project. Although none of the original exists, records show that it was built on the same general plan as the Great Mosque of Damascus, but on a more modest scale.

From the mid-eighth until the mid-twelfth century, Aleppo suffered a significant decline. Repairs were made to the major structures of earlier periods, but little new development took place in the city.

BIBLIOGRAPHY

Gaube, Heinz, and Eugen Wirth. *Aleppo: Historische und geographische Beiträge zur baulichen Gestaltung, zur sozialen Organisation und zur wirtschaftlichen Dynamik einer vorderasiatischen Fernhandelsmetropole.* Beihefte zum Tübinger Atlas des Vorderen Orients, 58. Wiesbaden, 1984. Excellent study of the city; a very different interpretation of its growth from the Hellenistic through Byzantine periods from that of Sauvaget (see below).
Klengel, Horst. *Geschichte Syriens im 2. Jahrtausend v.u.Z. Teil 1–Nordsyrien.* Berlin, 1965. By far the best (though now somewhat dated) study of the city during its early period of greatness. Chapters 7–10 deal with Aleppo during the second millennium BCE.
Klengel, Horst. *Syria: 3000 to 300 B.C. A Handbook of Political History.* Berlin, 1992. A less detailed, but more current study. See especially chapter 2.
Sauvaget, Jean. *Alep: Essai sur le développement d'une grande ville syrienne, des origines au milieu de XIXe siècle.* Paris, 1941. Classic study of the city, which should now be read in conjunction with the volume by Gaube and Wirth. Because of the meager evidence for the early periods, Sauvaget depends heavily on parallels from other Syrian cities.

WAYNE T. PITARD

ALEXANDRIA, city in Egypt, the most important of many by that name founded by Alexander the Great (d. 323 BCE). Alexandria (Gk., Alexandreia) was built on a ridge of land between the Mediterranean Sea and Lake Mareotis at the western end of the Nile Delta (31°12′ N, 29°53′ E), where there was already a native Egyptian village, Rhakotis. Rhakotis was the name given to the quarter of the city occupied chiefly by native Egyptians and was later retained as a designation for the city as a whole in Coptic sources (Rakote, Rakoti). Its modern Arabic name is el-Iskandariya.

History. Alexandria was founded in the spring of 331 BCE. Its first architect was Deinokrates of Rhodes; Kleomenes of Naukratis was its first governor. In 323 Egypt came under the rule of the Macedonian Ptolemy I Soter, who had been a general and companion of Alexander. The city became the capital of Ptolemaic Egypt and quickly prospered, eventually becoming the cultural and educational center of the Hellenistic world. A multiethnic city, Alexandria became the home of the most important Jewish community of the Diaspora (Jews living outside of Palestine). Later, from the third to the fifth centuries CE, the Alexandrian church was the leading intellectual and theological center of Christendom.

Alexandria came under Roman rule in 30 BCE. After a series of disasters—riots and pogroms against the Jews in 38 and 66 CE; the Jewish revolt of 115–117; and attacks on the city by Caracalla in 215, Aurelian in 273, and Diocletian in 295—the city declined in population and in area. Further devastation was visited on the city by the Persians in 617 and by the Arabs in 641, after which Egypt as a whole came under Muslim Arab rule. Alexandria was then eclipsed by the new Arab capital at Fustat (Old Cairo) and by the maritime city of Rashid (Rosetta) on the mouth of the western bank of the Nile. In 1798 Napoleon and his forces encountered Alexandria as a small village of a few thousand inhabitants. The city's modern development began under Muhammad 'Ali (1805–1848), and it is now a major city with a population estimated as high as four million.

Topography. The dominant geographical feature of Alexandria was the bay formed by a promontory called Lochias (modern Silsila), protected by the island of Pharos offshore. A dike joining the island to the mainland, the Heptastadion (Gk., "seven stades" long), built soon after the city's founding, divided the bay into two main harbors. This structure has silted up over the centuries; by Napoleon's time the city's population was concentrated on the resulting land area.

The best and most extensive description of Alexandria at the end of the Ptolemaic period is that of Strabo in book 17 of his *Geography,* which was based on personal observations made during a residence about 24–20 BCE. Strabo begins his description by giving the dimensions of the city: 30 stades (5.5 km or 3.5 mi.) in length (east–west) and approximately 8 stades (1.5 km or 1 mi.) in width (north–south). Of the wide streets intersecting the city, the two broadest cut one another at right angles (17.1.8). The long one, Via Canopica (corresponding roughly to the modern Sharia el-Horreya) ran from the necropolis (cemetery) in the west to the Canopic Gate in the east. Strabo reports that up to a third of the city consisted of an area called the Palaces, resplendent with beautiful buildings, the most prominent of which were the Mouseion (presumably including the famous Library) and the Sema (the tomb of Alexander and some of his successors). Concentrated on and near Cape Lochias was a smaller part of the Palaces neighborhood called the inner palaces (17.1.9).

Strabo then describes the city as one would encounter it sailing into the "great" (eastern) harbor. To the right lay Pharos with its famous lighthouse (one of the seven wonders of the ancient world). To the left were the reefs and promontory of Lochias with its royal palace and private royal harbor. Opposite that harbor was Antirrhodos, an island with a palace and another small harbor. The Theater occupied a prominent place on the mainland above. An elbow of land extended from the shore on which was a temple of Poseidon. From there Mark Antony had extended a mole or breakwater out into the harbor, where on an artificial island he built a palace, the Timonium (17.1.9).

Structures further west included the Caesarium, which was a temple begun by Cleopatra VII for Julius Caesar and completed as a temple dedicated to Augustus. Nearby were the Emporium (market) with its warehouses and ship buildings extending as far as the Heptastadion. Beyond lay the western harbor, the Eunostos (now the main harbor of Alexandria) within which was a smaller harbor, the Kibotos, used for Nile traffic and connected to a canal leading to Lake Mareotis. A necropolis lay outside the city to the west. Within the city east of the canal were the Serapeum (temple of the god Serapis) and other sanctuaries.

In the central part of the city were the Gymnasium, a center for athletic training and education, which was situated on Via Canopica, and the Paneion (a sanctuary of the god Pan) on a hill nearby. Outside of the Canopic Gate to the east lay the Hippodrome (racetrack) and beyond that, 5.5 km (3.5 mi.) from Alexandria, the suburb Nikopolis founded by Augustus in commemoration of his victory over Mark Antony and Cleopatra (17.1.10).

Absent from Strabo's account is any mention of the city's walls, the older eastern necropoleis, the fortified acropolis, the city's agora, assorted other public buildings and temples, and its division into five quarters named for the first five letters of the Greek alphabet, details known from other ancient sources. Philo reports that two of the "letters" were predominantly Jewish (*Flaccus*, 55).

Archaeological History. Alexandria presents daunting problems for the archaeologist, because of geological factors and the results of urban development since the nineteenth century. Because the coastal area of the city has subsided some 4 m (15.7 ft.) over the centuries, the ancient structures along the coast have been swallowed up by the sea, leaving only foundations sometimes visible beneath the surface. This subsidence plus intensive building activity, with much

cutting and filling, has resulted in the virtual obliteration of the contours of the ancient city. Numerous ancient structures were demolished at the time of the construction of the corniche (completed in 1906), and the present coastline facing the harbors is completely artificial.

The first modern archaeological excavation of any consequence was carried out by Mahmud Bey "el-Falaki," court astronomer of Khedive Ismail, whose goal was to prepare a map of the ancient city. On the basis of many soundings Mahmud Bey prepared a plan of the ancient streets and walls, published in 1872, which is still in use today. Unfortunately, he had no qualifications as an archaeologist, and the accuracy of his work has often been questioned. Where modern excavations have confirmed the existence of some of his streets, for example, at Kom el-Dik, these turn out to belong to the late Roman period. Their orientation differs in the main from the streets of the Ptolemaic era.

Scientific excavations began with the appointment of Giuseppe Botti in 1891 to the directorship of the newly formed Greco-Roman Museum. His work in the city and in the ancient necropoleis was published in numerous monographs and in several volumes of the *Bulletin de la Société (royale) archéologique d'Alexandrie*.

In 1895, the Egypt Exploration Fund of London sent D. G. Hogarth, E. F. Benson, and E. R. Bevan to Alexandria to carry out some excavations in the city and in the eastern cemeteries. Hogarth's report was very pessimistic, concluding that the city's greatest monuments stood within the area covered by the occupied quarters of Alexandria (then recently built) or by the encroaching sea, except for the Serapeum then under excavation by Botti. He expressed doubts as to the possibility of reaching Ptolemaic levels owing to the rise of the water table resulting from the city's subsidence. Hogarth advised against any further work by foreign societies in Alexandria, advice fortunately not heeded. A German expedition sponsored by Ernst von Sieglin worked in Alexandria from 1898 to 1902.

Botti was succeeded by Evaristo Breccia (curator of the museum, 1904–1933), who expanded upon Botti's efforts. Achille Adriani followed Breccia in 1932 (curator, 1933–1939; 1947–1953). Adriani's directorship of the museum was interrupted during the war years, when Alan Rowe served as curator (1941–1947) and worked during that time on the Serapeum hill and at the Kom el-Shogafa necropolis nearby.

Apart from the excavation of the Serapeum and the necropoleis of Alexandria, much of the archaeological work in the city until 1960 consisted of narrowly confined soundings or salvage work connected with innumerable building projects. The many artifacts that have turned up are housed mainly in the Greco-Roman Museum. Unfortunately much has also been destroyed.

The most extensive archaeological project ever mounted in Alexandria is that of the Polish Center of Mediterranean

Archaeology in the Kom el-Dik neighborhood, virtually in the center of the city. The excavations began under Kazimierz Michałowski in 1960 and are ongoing. A late Roman theater discovered in 1964 has been restored and now serves as the centerpiece of an archaeological park (see figure 1). Other finds at Kom el-Dik include a large bath complex (second–sixth century CE), a group of early Roman houses, a second-century school building, and a part of a Ptolemaic pavement.

It has not been possible to obtain a complete stratigraphic record of the city's archaeological history apart from the partial results obtained at isolated locations. Contrary to Hogarth's expectations, however, Ptolemaic levels have been identified, principally at four areas. In addition to the finds at Kom el-Dik, three areas associated with the ancient royal quarter have been excavated: (1) several sites in the area around the government hospital, (2) near the Medical Faculty of the University of Alexandria, and, most recently, (3) at the site of the new Alexandria Library, opposite Silsila. In addition, Ptolemaic foundations have been found just south of Horreya Street, near Kom el-Dik. Farther west along the same street foundations of a temple of Sarapis and Isis (identified as such by an inscription of Ptolemy IV and Queen Arsinoe III) were found already in 1895, but this find was not associated with a scientific archaeological excavation.

The only structure mentioned by Strabo that has so far been confirmed archaeologically is the Serapeum (Gk., Serapeion). Located in the Rhakotis district (modern Kharmuz), it is a temple that also served as a daughter library to the Mouseion. It is now covered over by a hillock dominated by a column 26.85 m (88 ft.) high referred to erroneously as "Pompey's Pillar"—it was actually dedicated to Emperor Diocletian (see figure 2). The Serapeum was excavated first by Giuseppi Botti (1894–1896) and then by Alan Rowe (1943–1945, 1956). Excavations revealed evidence of a major Ptolemaic temple built by Ptolemy III, and possibly an earlier one built by Ptolemy I. These structures were enclosed within a much larger sanctuary built in the early Roman period. The sack of the Serapeum by Christians in 391 apparently did not result in the temple's complete destruction at that time, contrary to an often repeated claim.

The Pharos tower and lighthouse, which was built early in the third century BCE, was severly damaged by an earthquake in 956 CE and incurred further damage by subsequent earthquakes. By the fourteenth century it was in ruins. In 1480 Sultan Ashraf Qait Bey built a fortress upon its foundations. Traces of the temple of Isis Pharia (not mentioned by Strabo) and a colossal statue of Isis have been found by divers off the north coast of Pharos near the Qait Bey fort. Structures associated with Antirrhodos and Mark Antony's Timonium have been spotted by divers in the eastern Harbor, but no underwater excavations have been carried out there as yet. No remains of the Heptastadion have been identified, nor is its exact location known.

As for the famous Mouseion and Sema, no trace of these monuments has been found. There is a long-standing but unconfirmed rumor to the effect that Alexander's tomb is located under the mosque of Nebi Daniel, near Kom el-Dik. On the other hand, some have argued unconvincingly that

ALEXANDRIA. Figure 1. *Late Roman theater.* Fourth–sixth century CE. (Courtesy B. A. Pearson)

the "Alabaster Tomb" found in the Latin Cemetery is actually Alexander's tomb. It is a Macedonian-style tomb, originally covered by a tumulus, of the Ptolemaic period, but its original owner remains unknown.

The Theater described by Strabo was probably located near the modern government hospital, but the excavations in that vicinity have turned up no convincing traces. Remains of other Ptolemaic buildings have been found there. There is no archaeological evidence of the Gymnasium or the Paneion. The approximate location of the Caesarium is well known because the obelisks associated with it remained, one standing and one fallen, until the 1870s. (These obelisks are now located respectively in Central Park in New York City and on the Thames Embankment in London.) The lavish description of the temple and its precincts provided by Philo (*Embassy to Gaius* 151) has not been confirmed by archaeology, though it is not inconceivable that excavations begun in 1992 at the site of the old Majestic Theater may turn up some trace of it. The Caesarium was rebuilt as a church in the fourth century and was finally destroyed in 912.

Mention should be made of the synagogues and churches known from literary sources. Philo cites numerous synagogues (*proseuchai*) existing in Alexandria (*Embassy to Gaius*, 132), including one near the Gymnasium that he calls "the largest and most notable" (134–135), presumably to be identified with the double-colonnaded basilica described in rabbinic sources (Tosefta *Suk.* 4.6; J.T. *Suk* 5.1; B.T. *Suk* 51b) that also report its destruction under Trajan during the revolt of 115–117. No traces of this or other synagogues have

been identified within the city, though an isolated dedicatory inscription of 37 BCE was found in Gabbari (part of the western necropolis area), and another of the second century BCE in Hadra (part of the eastern necropolis area).

Epiphanius of Salamis lists the churches in Alexandria known to him (*Panarion* 69.2), all of them datable to the fourth century except that of Theonas (bishop, 282–300). This, the earliest attested church in Alexandria, is said to have become part of the Mosque of a Thousand Pillars, damaged by the French in 1798 and destroyed in 1829. Another church-become-mosque is that built by St. Athanasius near a temple called Bendidion (or Mendidion), which was rebuilt as the Mosque of the Souq al-Attarin (destroyed in 1830). Hundreds of stone fragments from churches datable to the fourth–seventh centuries have been found—belonging to architectural features such as capitals, column bases, and decorative elements—but unfortunately none of these objects was found in situ. Thus, although locations of some ancient churches are well established, not one has ever been identified by excavation.

The best preserved evidence of Ptolemaic and Roman art and architecture is that associated with the necropoleis of Alexandria. The oldest of these cemeteries were located east of the early Ptolemaic city and were left unmentioned by Strabo, presumably because they were no longer in use. The city had extended eastward by his time. The most important necropoleis are in the Shatby district (fourth–third century BCE), excavated by Breccia; several areas of Hadra (mainly third–second century BCE, some later); Ibrahimiya; and, farther east, Mustafa Pasha. A small, late Ptolemaic hypogeum

ALEXANDRIA.   Figure 2.   *Pompey's pillar.* (Courtesy B. A. Pearson)

(subterranean burial chamber) was also found in the Antoniadis Garden. Of these only the Shatby necropolis can be visited.

The island of Pharos had a substantial native population in the Ptolemaic and early Roman periods, and several late Ptolemaic–early Roman hypogaea have been found there, that is, those of Ras el-Tin and Anfouchi. The latter is accessible. Probably the most remarkable of Alexandria's necropoleis is the magnificent three-level hypogeum complex at Kom el-Shogafa (mainly second century CE) near the Serapeum. A popular tourist attraction, it has carved tomb chambers featuring bas-relief decorations of mixed Egyptian and Greek inspiration.

The western necropolis mentioned by Strabo corresponds to finds made in the modern industrial areas of Mafrusa, Gabbari, and Wardian—hypogaea and other tombs datable to the late Ptolemaic and early Roman periods. Most of these burials have been destroyed, although some discoveries have been made by the Egyptian Antiquities Organization at Wardian, including a second-century BCE hypogeum with well-preserved wall paintings.

Thus, a hundred years of archaeological work in Alexandria has produced mixed results. Perhaps the richest possibilities for future work are underwater, principally in the eastern harbor and off Shatby beach east of Silsila. The latter area corresponds to Alexandria's main Jewish quarter in antiquity, as attested by Josephus (*Against Apion 2.33–36*).

BIBLIOGRAPHY

Adriani, Achille. "Saggio di una pianta archeologica di Alessandria." *Annuario del Museo Greco-Romano* 1 (1934): 55–96, map. Guide to archaeological discoveries made in Alexandria to 1931.

Adriani, Achille. *Repertorio d'arte dell'Egitto greco-romano*. Series C. 2 vols. Palermo, 1966. Essential work on the topography of ancient Alexandria and reports on excavations in the city and its necropoleis, with bibliographies.

Bonacasa, Nicola, and Antonino Di Vita, eds. *Alessandria e il mondo ellenistico-romano: Studi in onore di Achille Adriani*. 3 vols. Rome, 1983. Contains essays by leading scholars on the history, topography, art, and architecture of ancient Alexandria.

Botti, Giuseppe. *Plan de la ville d'Alexandrie à l'époque ptolémaïque*. Alexandria, 1898. Discussion of the ancient testimonies of Alexandria's topography and monuments in the Ptolemaic period in light of archaeological discoveries.

Breccia, Evaristo. *Alexandria and Aegyptum: A Guide to an Ancient and Modern Town, and to Its Graeco-Roman Museum*. Bergamo, 1922. Expanded English edition of the historical and topographical account of ancient Alexandria, with a guide to the Graeco-Roman Museum. Originally published in French (1914), and still very useful.

Breccia, Evaristo, ed. *Inscriptiones Graecae Aegypti*, vol. 2, *Inscriptiones nunc Alexandriae in Museo* (1911). Chicago, 1978. Useful but dated collection of the Greek inscriptions found in Alexandria, with commentary.

Butler, Alfred J. *The Arab Conquest of Egypt and the Last Thirty Years of the Roman Domain*. Edited by P. M. Fraser. 2d ed. Oxford, 1978. See the valuable chapter, "Alexandria at the Conquest" (pp. 368–400).

Description de l'Égypte. 21 vols. Paris, 1809–1828. Rare multi-volume report of the studies of Egypt carried out by the scientific staff of Napoleon's expedition. Contains descriptions of the antiquities of Alexandria by B. Saint-Genis (in vol. 2 of *Antiquités: Descriptions*) and of the "modern state" by G. Le Père (in vol. 2 of *État moderne: Texte*). The five volumes of *Antiquités: Planches* have been reproduced in *Monuments of Egypt: The Napoleonic Edition*, 2 vols., edited by Charles Coulston Gillispie and Michel Dewachter (Princeton, 1987). For Alexandrian monuments see volume 1, plates (= *Planches*, vol. 5, pls. 32, 34–39, 41–42), and volume 2, double plates (= *Planches*, vol. 5, pls. 31, 33, 40).

Fraser, P. M. *Ptolemaic Alexandria*. 3 vols. Oxford, 1972. Absolutely indispensable study of Alexandria in the Ptolemaic period, with extensive accounts of topography and archaeology (see vol. 1, pp. 3–37; vol. 2, pp. 1 111).

Hogarth, D. G., and E. F. Benson. "Report on Prospects of Research in Alexandria." In *Egypt Exploration Fund: Archaeological Report, 1894–1895*, pp. 1–33. London, 1895. Contains a report of work in Alexandria and the eastern cemeteries.

Horbury, W., and D. Noy, eds. *Jewish Inscriptions of Graeco-Roman Egypt*. Cambridge, 1992. Contains all of the Jewish inscriptions of the Graeco-Roman period found in Egypt. Nos. 1–21 (pp. 1–24) are the Alexandrian ones. Nos. 125–134, of uncertain origin (pp. 212–226), may include inscriptions of Alexandrian origin.

Jondet, M. Gaston. *Atlas historique de la ville et des ports d'Alexandrie*. Cairo, 1921. Contains reproductions of maps of Alexandria from the fifteenth to twentieth centuries, invaluable for topographical research.

Mahmoud-Bey, Al-Falaki. *Mémoire sur l'antique Alexandrie, ses fauborgs et environs*. Copenhagen, 1872. Contains the famous map of ancient Alexandria and its streets.

Pagenstecher, Rudolf. *Nekropolis: Untersuchungen über Gestalt und Entwicklung der Alexandrinischen Grabanlagen und ihrer Malereien*. Leipzig, 1919. Valuable discussion of Alexandrian art and architecture as revealed in the city's cemeteries, comprising part of a report of the Sieglin expedition.

Pearson, Birger A. "The New Alexandria Library: An Update." *Biblical Archaeologist* 56 (1993): 221. Brief account of the excavations begun in May 1993 at the site of the new Alexandria Library, part of the "Palaces" area of Ptolemaic Alexandria.

Rodziewicz, Mieczyslaw. *Les habitations romaines tardives d'Alexandrie: À la lumière des fouilles polonaises à Kôm el Dikka*. Alexandrie, 3. Warsaw, 1984. Valuable study of the results of excavations at Kom el-Dik by the project's former director, concentrating chiefly on the Roman houses, with numerous photographs, plans, and drawings.

Sieglin, Ernst von. *Die Nekropole von Kom-esch-Schukafa*. 2 vols. Leipzig, 1908. Complete account of the most impressive of Alexandria's tomb complexes, comprising part of a report of the Sieglin expedition.

Swelim, Nabil, ed. *Alexandrian Studies in Memoriam Daoud Abdu Daoud*. Alexandria, 1993. Collection of essays on the history, topography, archaeology, and art of ancient Alexandria.

Tkaczow, Barbara. "Archaeological Sources for the Earliest Churches in Alexandria." In *Coptic Studies: Acts of the Third International Congress of Coptic Studies, Warsaw, 20–25 August 1984*, edited by Wlodzimierz Godlewski, pp. 431–435. Warsaw, 1990. Contains a discussion of Alexandria's churches of the fourth–seventh centuries, and architectural fragments associated with them.

The ancient literary and documentary references to Alexandria, its topographical features, and its monuments are far too numerous to list here, but are conveniently collected in Aristide Calderini's invaluable work, *Dizionario dei nomi geografici e topografici dell'Egitto greco-romano*, vol. 1.1, *Alexandreia*, pp. 55–206 (Milan, 1935). See also *Supplemento*, vol. 1, 1935–1986, edited by Sergio Daris, pp. 18–22 (Milan, 1988).

BIRGER A. PEARSON

ALEXANDRIAN EMPIRE. Under the hegemony of King Philip II of Macedonia and, later, his son Alexander III (the Great), the Greek city-states bound themselves to a military alliance (the League of Corinth) for the purpose of invading the Achaemenid Empire. This Pan-Hellenic crusade was meant to rescue the Aegean world from a long history of Persian influence and to avenge the fifth-century BCE invasion by Xerxes, which had destroyed much of Athens. In 336, Philip II was assassinated on the eve of the Greek advance, but his young son Alexander (356–323) took up the cause after securing his position on the Macedonian throne.

In 334 BCE the new Macedonian king led nearly 40,000 troops across the Hellespont into Achaemenid Anatolia. He quickly defeated a satrapal (Persian provincial) army at the battle of the Granicus River and then systematically captured the coastal strongholds of the Persian fleet from the Hellespont to Cilicia. The Achaemenid king, Darius III (r. 336–330), personally commanded his troops in a move to halt the Greek advance into Syria. At the battle of Issus (late 333), Alexander defeated, but did not capture, the king of Persia. While Darius regrouped in Mesopotamia, Alexander continued his coastal campaign down the eastern Mediterranean. The offshore fortress of Tyre resisted for seven months but fell in a brutal assault when Alexander's forces completed a 1,600-meter siege mole out to the island. After besieging the city of Gaza in late 332, the Greeks marched unopposed into Egypt.

Alexander was seen by the Egyptians as a liberator who respected their ancestral customs and religion. He undertook an arduous journey to consult the oracle of Zeus-Ammon at Siwah in the Libyan Desert, where he was supposedly assured of world conquest. Alexander's most enduring achievement in Egypt was the construction of a city, bearing his name (Alexandria) and destined to become an unrivaled intellectual and commercial success under the patronage of his successors.

In early summer 331, Alexander's forces marched back to Phoenicia and then east toward Mesopotamia for a showdown with Darius. The Persian king had not been idle. His forces numbered over 100,000, and he had carefully prepared a battlefield near Arbela. On 1 October 331 Alexander's army routed the Persians at the battle of Gaugamela. Again Darius escaped eastward, hoping to rally a defense of Bactria (Afghanistan), but he had lost the heart of his empire. The major cities of Mesopotamia lay open to Alexander, who marched triumphantly into Babylon, Susa, and finally Persepolis in January 330. The vast Achaemenid treasures were seized and the palace destroyed. The Greeks were avenged for the sack of Athens a century and a half before. [*See* Persians; Babylon; Susa; Persepolis.]

Alexander soon resumed his pursuit of Darius. Near Hecatompylos (modern Shahr-i Qumis), however, a desperate group of Iranian nobles led by Bessus, satrap of Bactria,

assassinated Darius. As successor to the Achaemenid throne, Alexander gave Darius a royal burial, but Bessus tried to undermine Alexander's legitimacy by declaring himself the rightful Persian king. Thus, Alexander was compelled to continue his advance eastward against this new adversary. These next campaigns carried Alexander's army beyond the Near East into Central Asia (329–327) and the Indus Valley (326–325). On their return, a fleet commanded by Nearchus explored the coastline from Pattala to the Persian Gulf while Alexander led the land forces on a disastrous desert march through Gedrosia back to Babylon.

Alexander encountered many military hardships during these years in the distant east, and he faced a growing tide of related problems: opposition of his high command to acts of reconciliation with the defeated Iranian nobility, sagging morale of his troops because of physical and emotional strain, limited resources to occupy and administer the eastern empire, and misconduct among the senior officials in charge of the Near Eastern satrapies during Alexander's absence in India.

When Alexander returned to Mesopotamia in 324, he began to address the emerging crisis in his newly won empire. He punished some officials and pardoned others, paid his army handsomely from the revenues earlier stockpiled after the plunder of Susa and Persepolis. He arranged a massive wedding ceremony at Susa in which senior officers took noble Persian brides, and 10,000 Macedonian soldiers formalized their liaisons with native women. When Alexander then organized a force of indigenous soldiers to help meet his military needs, he had to face down at Opis in 324 the mutinous insubordination of his Macedonian veterans who opposed an ethnically mixed military system.

In the midst of plans for future conquests, including an expedition to Arabia, Alexander fell ill and died at Babylon in early June 323. The army and its officers soon quarreled over the issue of succession. A compromise provided for a dual monarchy shared by two nonentities: Philip III Arrhidaeus, Alexander's infirm half brother, and Alexander IV, Alexander's posthumous son. In truth, the empire was governed by ambitious generals down to 306/05. First, Perdiccas asserted authority as regent for the kings but was assassinated in 320. In Macedonia, the aging general Antipater served as the next regent until his death a year later.

The fragile unity of the empire endured as the *diadochoi* ('successors') competed for the regency, often in shifting coalitions sealed by marriage alliances and satrapal appointments. Until his defeat at the battle of Ipsus in 301, the lead in this struggle was taken by Antigonus the One-Eyed, along with his son Demetrius the City-Sacker. Those not aiming for supreme power staked out smaller domains for that day when the empire would splinter beyond a single man's grasp. As expected, the assassination of the two kings, Philip III (317/16) and Alexander IV (311/10), exhausted the bloodline of Alexander the Great and opened the way for

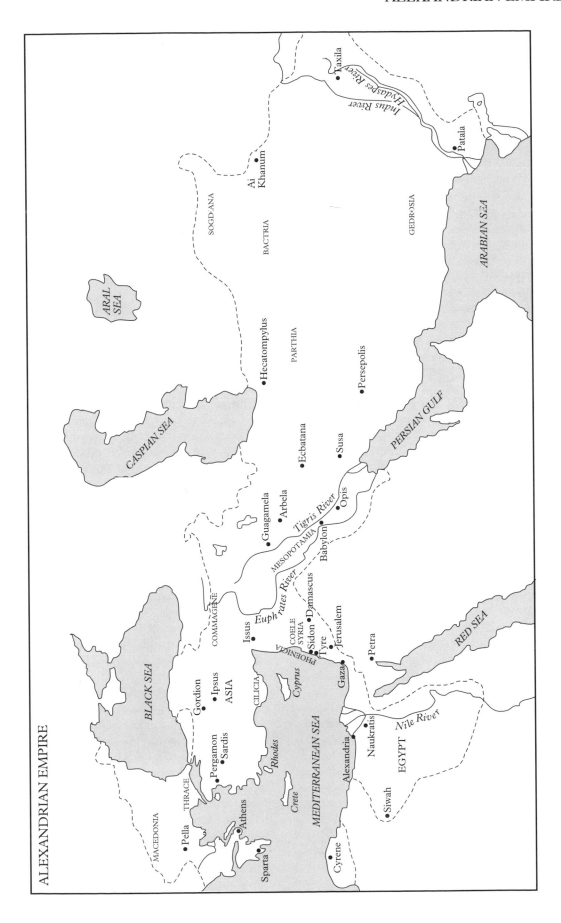

ALEXANDRIAN EMPIRE

the formation of new royal dynasties in the Near East headed by Ptolemy (Egypt), and Seleucus (Syria).

The political unity of the Alexandrian Empire had not long survived the fall of the Achaemenids, as the competition for greatness inspired by Alexander led to an unprecedented period of kingmaking among the Macedonians and, later, the local nobility of the Near East as well. Generally known as the Hellenistic Age, the three centuries following Alexander's death (323–30) witnessed the reigns of fourteen Ptolemies in Egypt, capped by the remarkable career of Queen Cleopatra VII (r. 51–30). In addition to the Nile Valley, the Ptolemies controlled a few Aegean ports, Cyprus, and Cyrene; they fought five major Syrian wars against the Seleucids for dominion over Coele-Syria (Palestine) down to 200. [See Ptolemies; Cyrene; Coele-Syria.]

The Seleucid dynasty produced over two dozen kings and numerous usurpers. In addition, the slow dissolution of this vast state, which under Seleucus I (312–281) had stretched from Anatolia to Afghanistan, allowed the rise of many local dynasties in areas such as Bactria, Parthia, Commagene, Pergamon, Judea, Iturea, Nabatea, and Characene; smaller principalities and numerous cities also gained their independence, most notably in Phoenicia. By the time that Rome annexed the remains of the Seleucid Empire in 63, only the region around Antioch was left in Macedonian hands. [See Seleucids; Pergamon; Antioch.]

This Near Eastern world gradually absorbed into the Roman Empire was very different from the Achaemenid world rapidly absorbed into the Alexandrian Empire some three centuries earlier. These differences give measure to the impact of Alexander the Great upon this region. We may here summarize that legacy in its archaeological context.

First, the rise of an Alexandrian Empire introduced a strong and lasting Hellenic influence into the rich cultural milieu of the Near East. This is not to say that Greek culture wholly dominated the area during the Hellenistic Age nor that some Greek influence had not already been felt in the Near East long before Alexander's invasion. Greek mercenaries had been recruited earlier into the armies of the Achaemenid kings, and Greek merchants had long plied their trade in the ports of the eastern Mediterranean. A Greek trading colony had existed at Naukratis (Egypt) since the seventh century. [See Naukratis.] The degree of Hellenic influence clearly intensified, however, no longer incrementally, but exponentially, in the wake of Alexander's wars. Rather than a few thousand Greek mercenaries, the Near East witnessed a wave of Greek military colonists (klēroukoi) that crested in the hundreds of thousands. Wherever there were permanent camps of Greek soldier-settlers, there were now islands of Hellenism in the Semitic Near East. Of course, non Greeks inhabited these "islands" as well, some as soldiers or support personnel, others as wives or workers. Recent excavations on Ikaros (modern Failaka) reveal a Seleucid military settlement where traditional Mesopotamian

artifacts and non Greek graffiti exist side by side with dedications to Greek gods made by the garrison commander and his troops. [See Failaka.] From Anatolia as far east as Ai Khanum (Afghanistan), evidence of this type demonstrates how immigrant Greek soldiers introduced a new but not overwhelming cultural element in terms of their language, religion, art, and architecture. In Egypt, where papyrus documents tell the story more fully, we can follow the family histories of some of these settlers. In some cases, the colonists held doggedly to their Hellenic background and insulated themselves as far as possible from native influences; others married Egyptian wives, worshiped local deities, and raised bilingual children. Whatever the degree of cultural "fusion" in a given klērouchia, the rather sudden and sustained presence of Greek soldiers occupying the Near East contributed greatly to the changes wrought by Alexander the Great.

Second, the number of Hellenistic urban centers grew. The one Greek entrepôt at Naukratis was quickly supplanted by dozens of full-fledged cities founded throughout the Near East by Alexander and his successors. Alexandria in Egypt blossomed under the Ptolemies into a major Mediterranean city that attracted Greek artists, intellectuals, administrators, merchants, and many others into its population. Although non-Greeks certainly played a vital role in the city's history, the Hellenic element under Ptolemaic patronage enjoyed a privileged position both politically and culturally. [See Alexandria.] The same occurred at Antioch, one of the capitals of the Seleucid Empire, and many other places. The administration of these Hellenistic cities was generally Greek, though we can trace in the documentary sources the appointment of some officials bearing non-Greek names and titles; some city business was conducted in native languages and according to local customs. Babylon provides a well-known example of how traditional Mesopotamian temple and civic practices survived the intrusion of the Greeks. In the main, however, the Greek language and Hellenic political institutions took root in these new foundations. Care was often taken by the Macedonian dynasts to give these cities a Greek appearance to go along with their Greek names (usually dynastic, but occasionally transplanted place-names from Greece) and institutions (e.g., boule [council] and agora [assembly]). Though often adapted to local building methods and materials (e.g., mud brick), Hellenic structures such as gymnasia and theaters rose on Near Eastern soil. Greek terra cottas, column drums and capitals, propylaea [entrance structures], and Macedonian palaces could be seen in many of these cities, along with Greek pottery and other Greek domestic items in private houses built of Greek design. Even burial practices and tomb construction were influenced by Hellenic models, as at Jerusalem, Marisa (Mareshah), Deir ed-Derb in Samaria, Suweida in Syria, Hermel and Kalat Fakra in Lebanon, and of course Petra in the Negev. Clearly, places such as Babylon and Jerusalem did not become thoroughly hellenized, but a substantial Greek presence could easily be seen there by any visitor, and some cultural interaction and blending was inevitable over the course of three centuries. [*See* Jerusalem; Mareshah; Suweida; Petra.]

Through military occupation and city founding, then, Greek culture made a lasting impact upon the Near East. The Greek language, in the Koine (common Greek) dialect of the Hellenistic world, became the lingua franca of the Near East, a role previously played by Aramaic under the Achaemenids. Yet, when the Romans arrived on the scene in the first century BCE, they could still hear spoken a variety of Semitic languages and local dialects. They could see in the Seleucid archives recent cuneiform texts, or in Egypt the ongoing use of hieroglyphs and demotic script on monuments and inscriptions such as the famous Rosetta Stone from the reign of Ptolemy V (205–180). But the language of the Hellenistic rulers was Greek (only the last of the Ptolemies, Cleopatra VII (51–30), learned the Egyptian language), and court life required Koine for business and pleasure. The educated elite seldom strayed into the languages or literatures of the Near Eastern peoples. Native works of note had to be translated into Greek for further study, as in the case of the Septuagint, the Egyptian history preserved by Manetho, or the Babylonian lore translated by Berossos. When Alexander invaded the Near East, interpreters were required to make it possible for Greeks and non-Greeks to communicate. When the Romans arrived, Greek was a second language throughout the region, at least among the privileged classes. That did not change, even through centuries of Roman rule. The New Testament took form in Koine, Roman coinage in the Near East employed Greek inscriptions, and Byzantium inherited from the Alexandrian Empire an administrative system based on Greek rather than Latin. [*See* Greek.]

Third, the Alexandrian Empire increased the production of coins, which made trade easier. Greeks, especially merchants and mercenaries, were long accustomed to the convenience of coinage. The Achaemenids had established mints, therefore, in those regions where Greeks were normally recruited and stationed, but had not pressed to have a monetized economy replace traditional barter in other areas of their empire. Trading centers, such as Phoenicia and Egypt, had been compelled to import Greek coinage or to mint locally. Alexander and his successors changed this situation very rapidly, not so much as part of a grand economic scheme to stimulate the "stagnant" Near East (an old view that still holds too much influence), but rather to meet the immediate needs of a massive invasion and occupation. To pay his troops, Alexander operated nearly two dozen royal mints in Anatolia, Cyprus, Syria, Phoenicia, Egypt, and Mesopotamia. These mints produced a homogeneous, "imperial" coinage on the Attic Greek standard (see figure 1). Massive supplies of bullion came to hand when Alexander

ALEXANDRIAN EMPIRE. Figure 1. *Macedonian tetradrachm.* Figure of Alexander III is seated on right. Dated to 320 BCE. (Courtesy American Numismatic Society)

captured the treasuries of the Achaemenid palaces; Persepolis alone yielded some 120,000 talents' worth (more than 3 million kg or 6.8 million lbs.) of silver. Most, but not all, of this plunder was converted into coins to meet the military expenses of Alexander and the *diadochoi*. Over time, a monetary economy replaced barter in most parts of the Near East, particularly the urbanized areas. This is especially evident in the increased production of bronze fiduciary currencies, and the striking of Greek-style coinage in areas beyond the control of the Ptolemies and Seleucids. All of the native dynasties that broke free of the Seleucids minted Hellenistic coinage. Widespread monetary production facilitated trade. Archaeology confirms this development through coin finds, the diffusion of Mediterranean amphorae, and the luxury goods that flowed in and out of the Near East. From the death of Alexander down to 167 BCE, when punished by Rome with crippling economic sanctions, Rhodes served as the wealthy center of East Mediterranean maritime trade; its amphorae have been found from the British Isles to India. [*See* Coins.]

In spite of economic growth in the Hellenistic Age, war still provided the usual means of expanding royal wealth. Taxes, tolls, and tribute seldom met the exorbitant needs of the kings, for whom conspicuous consumption on a grand scale was a hallmark of Hellenistic monarchy. If not by trade, then by conquest, these kings sought luxury goods to put on parade. On one famous occasion, Ptolemy II (285/82–246) marched through Alexandria an astounding display of prestige items, including exotic animals from India, Ethiopia, and Arabia. There was also competition among the kings either to develop the largest warships or to field the largest elephant corps. Everywhere in the Near East, the Macedonian military system took hold. Beginning with Alexander, levies of local troops were armed and trained in the Macedonian manner, a practice expanded by the successors from the late third century BCE onward. Advanced siege engines and artillery, not to mention the counterforce of intensive fortification, became standard features of Near Eastern warfare. Hellenistic armies were naturally the heirs of the Alexandrian Empire rather than of the Achaemenid. In fact, all processes of hellenization were essentially military in origin, from colonization to monetization. The legacy of the Alexandrian Empire remained imperialist and colonial in nature.

When looking so deliberately for Alexander's impact on the Near East, we must not leave the false impression that earlier patterns of social, cultural, political, religious, military, and economic life were totally swept away. In many ways, the Hellenic customs of the conquerors were held at bay by the resilient and often better-suited traditions of the indigenous peoples. Recall that local languages were not effaced by Greek and that many Greeks adopted Near Eastern religious practices or, at the very least, adapted them to their own use through syncretism. Even in warfare, the Greeks grew fond of the elephants and scythed chariots employed by the Achaemenids. In fact, Seleucus I traded India to Chandragupta Maurya for five hundred elephants, which proved a good investment at the battle of Ipsus in 301.

No reign or region of the Hellenistic Near East was thoroughly Greek. The important political institutions of the Greeks, most notably those of the *polis* (city), functioned within an administrative system that was largely Achaemenid. Alexander had retained the successful bureaucratic structure of the Near East, with its diverse collection of "temple-states", semi-independent cities and tribes, tributary kings, and satraps. Before becoming kings, all of the eastern *diadochoi* had first been satraps. When, for example, the Seleucids later established their royal dynasty, they appointed satraps of their own, some of whom in turn became independent kings who straightaway divided their former satrapies into smaller satrapies. Clearly, the Greeks could find nothing better than the old Achaemenid structure within which to build their new Hellenistic states.

The hellenization of the Semitic East was, therefore, a long, complex process that did not touch all areas nor all classes with the same effect. The aggressive measures to compel cultural change in Judea under Antiochus IV (175–164), for example, sparked intensive resistance that, itself, divided many non-Greeks over the issue of hellenization. Everywhere in the Near East, Alexander's legacy was a patchwork of languages and cultures that included for the first time a substantial Greek element that clearly inspired some and incensed others.

BIBLIOGRAPHY

Austin, M. M., ed. *The Hellenistic World from Alexander to the Roman Conquest: A Selection of Ancient Sources in Translation.* Cambridge, 1981. Convenient collection of 279 items, including literary sources as well as documentary evidence.

Bosworth, A. B. *Conquest and Empire: The Reign of Alexander the Great.* Cambridge, 1988. The best recent biography, meticulously researched with excellent chapters on administration and the army.

Burstein, Stanley B., ed. and trans. *The Hellenistic Age from the Battle of Ipsos to the Death of Kleopatra VII.* Translated Documents of Greece and Rome, vol. 3. Cambridge, 1985. Well-chosen selection of 112 documents, with first-rate commentary and bibliographical references.

Downey, Susan B. *Mesopotamian Religious Architecture: Alexander through the Parthians.* Princeton, 1988. Close scholarly examination of how Near Eastern traditions endured under foreign occupation.

Eddy, Samuel K. *The King Is Dead: Studies in Near-East Resistance to Hellenism, 334–31 B.C.* Lincoln, Neb., 1961. Classic attempt to see the Near Eastern side of the Hellenistic world.

Fedak, Janos. *Monumental Tombs of the Hellenistic Age: A Study of Selected Tombs from the Pre-Classical to the Early Imperial Era.* Toronto, 1990. The best work of its kind, covering tomb architecture from pre-Classical to Roman periods.

Grainger, John D. *The Cities of Seleukid Syria.* Oxford, 1990. Useful case study of Hellenistic city-founding in the heart of the Seleucid Empire, with summaries of excavations and surveys.

Green, Peter. *Alexander to Actium: The Historical Evolution of the Hellenistic Age.* Berkeley, 1990. Opinionated but expert essay of nearly a thousand pages that minimizes the geniune interaction of Greek and non-Greek cultures.

Green, Peter, ed. *Hellenistic History and Culture.* Berkeley, 1993. Eight articles on important aspects of Hellenistic studies, with an excellent balance of critical responses and discussion.

Hengel, Martin. *Jews, Greeks, and Barbarians: Aspects of the Hellenization of Judaism in the Pre-Christian Period.* London, 1980.

Kuhrt, Amélie, and Susan Sherwin-White, eds. *Hellenism in the East: The Interaction of Greek and Non-Greek Civilizations from Syria to Central Asia after Alexander.* Berkeley, 1987. Six studies giving much needed attention to the non-Greek side of Hellenistic history and making effective use of new archaeological evidence.

Lewis, Naphtali. *Greeks in Ptolemaic Egypt: Case Studies in the Social History of the Hellenistic World.* Oxford, 1986. Uses papyrological evidence to explore cultural interaction on the personal level.

Momigliano, Arnaldo. *Alien Wisdom: The Limits of Hellenization.* Cambridge, 1975. Based on a series of lectures at Cambridge, this work examines the intellectual meeting ground of Greeks, Romans, Persians, Jews, and Celtic tribes.

Rostovtzeff, Michael. *The Social and Economic History of the Hellenistic World.* 3 vols. 2d ed. Oxford, 1953. Venerable and still valuable treatment of the scattered evidence; nothing is likely to replace its scope.

Samuel, Alan E. *From Athens to Alexandria: Hellenism and Social Goals in Ptolemaic Egypt.* Series Studia Hellenistica, vol. 26. Louvain, 1983. Careful analysis of all phases of contact and conflict between Greek and Egyptian cultures in the Hellenistic Age.

Samuel, Alan E. *The Shifting Sands of History: Interpretations of Ptolemaic Egypt.* Publications of the Association of Ancient Historians, vol. 2. Lanham, Md., 1989. Rich historiographical survey for the educated nonspecialist.

Sherwin-White, Susan, and Amélie Kuhrt. *From Samarkhand to Sardis: A New Approach to the Seleucid Empire.* Berkeley, 1993. The best single volume now available on the Seleucids, with detailed regional surveys and up-to-date archaeological evidence.

Thompson, Dorothy. *Memphis under the Ptolemies.* Princeton, 1988. Very detailed but readable account of a key Egyptian city, fully documented and illustrated.

Walbank, F. W., and A. E. Astin, et al. *The Cambridge Ancient History*, vol. 7.1, *The Hellenistic World.* 2d ed. Cambridge, 1984. The best starting point for all aspects of Hellenistic history. Note also the article on later Seleucid history by Christian Habicht, "The Seleucids and Their Rivals," in *The Cambridge Ancient History*, vol. 8, *Rome and the Mediterranean to 133 B.C.*, edited by A. E. Astin et al., pp. 324–387 (Cambridge, 1989).

FRANK L. HOLT

ALI KOSH, a small prehistoric site located on the Deh Luran plain in southwestern Iran at an elevation of about 170 m (32°30′ N, 47°20′ E). The plain, covering approximately 169 sq km (100 sq. mi.) is enclosed by the Zagros Mountains on the north, a low line of hills and the vast Mesopotamian plain on the south, and by two small streams on the east and west.

In 1903 the French archaeologists, Joseph E. Gautier and Georges Lampre, representing the Mission Archéologique de Perse, excavated a small trench at the site that they called Tepe Mohammed Jaffar (the name of a local tribal leader). When they found only remains of "reed and branch huts," along with some flints and crude ceramics, they abandoned work. Nearly sixty years later, Robert Braidwood and Richard Watson of the Oriental Institute Prehistoric Project collected some flints there and, on their advice, in 1961 Frank Hole and Kent Flannery (Rice University–Oriental Institute) undertook a 3-by-5-meter excavation. The upper layers of the site were found to contain Early Neolithic pottery, but the lower layers were aceramic. According to local villagers, the site had two names, Bus Mordeh (Pers., "dead goat") and Ali Kosh (Pers., "the place where Ali was killed"). Unaware at the time that the French had named the site Mohammed Jaffar, the excavators called it Ali Kosh.

On the basis of the initial results, and especially on finding charred seeds in ashy material collected for radiocarbon dating, Hole and Flannery returned to the site in 1963 for more extensive excavations. Guided by Braidwood's previous research into the origins of domestication, the renewed excavation was focused on recovering plant remains and animal bones. Hans Helbaek, a Danish paleobotanist who had worked with Braidwood, an authority on ancient plant remains, joined the team in the field to study the samples as they were excavated. To extract seeds from the soil, the excavators used flotation (the first time the technique was employed in Southwest Asia). The technique separates charred organic remains from soil by immersing them in water with the aid of machines. At Ali Kosh, a tedious hand method was used, with water trucked to the site.

There are three archaeological phases at Ali Kosh, each given local site names: Bus Mordeh for the oldest, Ali Kosh for the second aceramic phase, and Mohammed Jaffar for the ceramic Neolithic. Fifteen radiocarbon dates were originally obtained for the site, but they gave highly variable and ambiguous results. On the basis of dates from other sites, as well as additional accelerator mass spectroscopy AMS dates on charred bone from the Bus Mordeh and Ali Kosh phases, it is now estimated that the site was founded in about 7000 BCE.

The first settlers at Ali Kosh lived near a permanent marsh from which they harvested fish, turtles, clams, and waterfowl. Hunters stalked wild gazelle, onager, cattle, and pigs that grazed the surrounding plain, and herders kept small flocks of domestic goats. [*See* Cattle and Oxen; Pigs; Sheep and Goats.] They supplemented these foods by harvesting seasonally abundant wild plant foods and cultivating wheat and barley. [*See* Cereals.] The successive layers at Ali Kosh document the increasing dependence on domesticated herds and agriculture until 6000 BCE, when the marsh dried and the villagers moved to one of the other sites on the plain, such as Chogha Sefid.

[*See also* Persia, *article on* Prehistoric Persia.]

BIBLIOGRAPHY

Gautier, Joseph, and Georges Lampre. "Fouilles de Moussian." *Mémoires de la Délégation en Perse* 8 (1905): 59–149. The first mention of Ali Kosh, here called Tepe Mohammad-Djaffar (see pp. 81–83).

Hole, Frank, et al., eds. *Prehistory and Human Ecology of the Deh Luran Plain: An Early Village Sequence from Khuzistan, Iran.* University of Michigan, Memoirs of the Museum of Anthropology, no. 1. Ann Arbor, 1969. Final report of the excavations, with specialist studies of botanical and faunal remains.

Hole, Frank, ed. *The Archaeology of Western Iran.* Washington, D.C., 1987. See chapters 2 and 3 for discussions of Ali Kosh and other contemporary sites.

FRANK HOLE

ALPHABET. [*This entry treats the origins and development of what is traditionally termed the "alphabet," that is, the stages termed "abjad" and "alphabet." For definitions and further discussion, see* Writing and Writing Systems.]

The alphabet began as a system of symbols, each of which represented a consonantal phoneme. Because in the earliest attested stages the signs are quasi-pictographic and the form of the sign corresponds in several cases to the name of the letter known from later periods, it is plausible that each of the earliest sign forms bore a name beginning with the phoneme represented by the sign. For example, the name of the {b}-sign would have been *baytu*, the Semitic word for "house," and it would have represented the consonantal phoneme /b/. This is the so-called acrophonic principle.

More than a millennium after writing had come into use in Mesopotamia and in Egypt, the alphabetic principle was devised somewhere in the Levant between these two early centers of civilization. Because of the representational character of the earliest signs, the invention probably took place under Egyptian rather than under Mesopotamian influence, for hieroglyphs maintained pictographic forms for millennia, even while cursive scripts developed. [*See* Egyptian; Hieroglyphs.] On the other hand, although a system of quasi-alphabetic signs was developed in Egyptian, used principally to represent foreign names, each Egyptian sign continued to note one, two, or three consonants until the Greek alphabet was adopted for Coptic. [*See* Hieroglyphs; Greek; Coptic.] The earliest alphabet clearly did not originate in a simple borrowing of the Egyptian quasi-alphabetic signs, for no single correspondence between the two systems has been proven. Rather, even though the idea may well have been born under the influence of the Egyptian usage (Sznycer, 1974; Sass, 1991), the true invention is the idea of noting the consonantal segment only, for that resulted in the radical reduction of the number of signs: from the large number required for a syllabic system to a much small number required for an alphabetic system. It is estimated that a working Mesopotamian scribe needed an active knowledge of approximately two hundred signs, but the earliest alphabets probably did not have more than twenty-nine signs at the most. The imitation of the Egyptian iconic principle of writing also resulted in a set of relatively simple symbols; the Mesopotamian cuneiform system, by contrast, included many signs that consisted of a large number of wedges (ten or more in the archaic period) and that required much practice to produce and to recognize. [See Cuneiform.] It can be debated whether the consonantal writing system merits the name *alphabet*, but the simplification of the writing process it represented makes it the decisive step toward the full alphabet as devised by the Greeks. [See Writing and Writing Systems.]

Because of the small number of extant early alphabetic inscriptions and the difficulties in dating them, it is uncertain just where the alphabet was invented. Because the earliest known examples are arguably the Proto-Sinaitic texts, it is tempting to see in them the texts for the writing of which the alphabet was invented. That temptation must be resisted, however, for it is presently impossible to determine whether the social conditions requisite for the invention of a writing system existed in the Sinai then—that is, the presence of a scribe of the language for which the alphabet was invented who was also well acquainted with Egyptian. It is in any case likely that the invention was only accomplished once and spread throughout the Levant. In theory, it could have occurred anywhere there was an Egyptian influence in the late Middle Kingdom—from Egypt itself through Canaan into Syria. The concentration of early texts in Sinai and the various inscriptions from sites in southern Canaan, however, make the most plausible hypothesis that of a southern origin.

If the hypothesis be accepted that the above Proto-Sinaitic and Proto-Canaanite inscriptions represent the earliest alphabetic writings, a necessary corollary is that the alphabet was invented to write a West Semitic language. [See Proto-Sinaitic; Proto-Canaanite.] Unfortunately, problems of overall decipherment and of the identification of individual signs and their variants make it impossible at present to determine the precise characteristics of the language(s) represented by the earliest inscriptions. The data available indicate an early dialect of Canaanite.

Ugaritic Alphabet. The earliest West Semitic language represented in an alphabetic script and with an important body of decipherable inscriptions is Ugaritic. [See Ugarit; Ugaritic; Ugarit Inscriptions.] These texts date to the four-

teenth–thirteenth centuries BCE, although the greatest number are probably from the last few decades before the destruction of the site in the early twelfth century BCE.

Ugaritic made two major contributions to the early history of the alphabet: it is the only West Semitic alphabetic writing system that is cuneiform and a significant number of abecedaries exist (an *abecedary* is the conventional name for the writing out of an alphabet according to an established order).

For reasons presently unknown (the prestige of Mesopotamian cuneiform, a temporary shortage of papyrus?), the West Semitic alphabet was reduced to wedge forms and written on clay at Ugarit. [See Papyrus; Writing Materials.] Various considerations—chronological, formal, and structural—make it highly unlikely that the Ugaritic writing system represents a local invention of the alphabet: it appeared too late (fourteenth century BCE), there are several plausible correspondences of sign forms between it and the known linear writing systems, and it does not correspond perfectly to the Ugaritic phonological system.

The Ugaritic abecedaries have established several valuable reference points in the history of the alphabet.

- They prove that the order of the letters later known as the standard Northwest Semitic order (Hebrew, Phoenician-Punic, Aramaic) was in use in the fourteenth century BCE in Syria. [See Hebrew Language and Literature; Phoenician-Punic; Aramaic Language and Literature.] Abecedaries are attested in Palestine and in Phoenicia by the late thirteenth century BCE and on into the first millennium BCE (Cross, 1980, pp. 8–15; Lemaire, 1978). The early date of the Ugaritic examples and the wide spread of the later languages attesting this order make it plausible that the inventor of the alphabet had conventionally used this order for pedagogic purposes.

- Comparison between the Ugaritic abecedaries and the order of letters in the later Northwest Semitic languages shows that a "long" alphabet was in use in the fourteenth century BCE. The basic consonantal inventory of Ugaritic was represented by twenty-seven signs, whereas the basic southern Canaanite alphabet consisted of twenty-two signs. The five extra Ugaritic signs are interspersed among the signs known from the southern Canaanite alphabet as follows:

Canaanite	$\tilde{}$	b	g		d	h	w	z	ḥ	ṭ	y	k	
Ugaritic	à	b	g	ḫ	d	h	w	z	ḥ	ṭ	y	k	š

Canaanite	l	m		n		s	ʿ	p	ṣ	q	r	š		t	
Ugaritic	l	m	ḏ	n	ẓ	s	ʿ	p	ṣ	q	r	ṯ	ġ	t	(ì ù ś)

- If the inventor of the Ugaritic cuneiform system had been imitating a "short" alphabet, he would in all likelihood have tacked the extra signs he needed on the end of the alphabet, as he did with the three extra signs that he did devise ({í, ú, ś})—and as the Greeks did when they borrowed and adapted the West Semitic alphabet; or he would have adapted existing signs in groups, as the Arabs did when they revised the Northwest Semitic alphabet. Rather, he seems to have been following an established order in which {ḫ} followed {g}, {š} followed {k}, et cetera. Because the Ugaritic phonological system does not perfectly match the writing system (e.g., is used inconsistently), it is likely that the alphabet was originally borrowed from a West Semitic language with a slightly different consonantal inventory and/or that the use of the long linear alphabet already had a history at Ugarit.

- The order of the long alphabet, as illustrated by the Ugaritic abecedaries, makes the hypothesis plausible that the short alphabet is a simplification of the longer one: that is, certain sign forms were dropped from usage when not needed (probably in the process of adoption from one language to another, rather than by alphabet reform in a given community), for alphabet usage tends to be conservative.

- The recent discovery at Ugarit of an abecedary in the South Semitic order and with variant sign forms (Caquot, forthcoming; Bordreuil and Pardee, forthcoming), and the earlier decipherment of a cuneiform tablet from Beth-Shemesh as an abecedary in the South Semitic order (Loundin, 1987; further bibliography in Bordreuil and Pardee, forthcoming), prove the widespread use of a different alphabetic order coupled with variant sign forms. [See Beth-Shemesh.] These abecedaries must reflect the use of a language of the South Semitic type in Canaan, although they and a few signs on sherds from Kamid el-Loz (Röllig and Mansfeld, 1969–1970) are the only present evidence for that usage. [See Kamid el-Loz.]

Spread of the Semitic Alphabet. The date of the earliest Phoenician inscriptions has been much debated. The Ahiram inscription is the earliest continuous text in a Phoenician dialect, but arrowhead inscriptions from about 1100–900 BCE and a few very brief inscriptions from Byblos and other sites illustrate the use of the alphabet in the Early Iron period. [See Ahiram Inscription; Byblos.] It is also clear that the Ugaritic cuneiform system was occasionally used to write Canaanite at the very end of the Late Bronze Age (the language of a late thirteenth-century BCE inscription from Sarepta in Ugaritic script has been classified as Phoenician: see Greenstein, 1976, and Bordreuil, 1979). [See Sarepta.]

By the late tenth–early ninth centuries BCE, inscriptions in Aramaic and Hebrew illustrate the spread of the Phoenician alphabet inland. It is clear that the Aramaeans borrowed the alphabet from the Phoenicians because the sign forms in the earliest inscriptions are Phoenician and because there were major phonological differences between the two languages that affected the development of Aramaic orthography. [See Arameans; Phoenicians.] For example, /ḏ/ and /ṣ/ had coalesced in Proto-Phoenician and only one sign remained; Aramaic, on the other hand, had a phoneme, /ḏ/, the scribes represented by means of {q}; at a later point, the pronunciation of /ḏ/ shifted and the scribes began representing it by {ʿ}: for example, "earth" {ʾrṣ} in Phoenician is written {ʾrq} in Old Aramaic, {ʾrʿ} in the Persian period.

Because /ś/ survived as a phoneme in Hebrew but without a corresponding sign in the Hebrew alphabet, it is clear that the Hebrews borrowed the standard short alphabet from the Phoenicians or from speakers of another Northwest Semitic language who used the same alphabet. (For the possibility that other consonantal phonemes had survived in the Hebrew of the biblical period that were not noted in the writing system, see Kutscher, 1982, pp. 17–18.) All that can be said for the present is that the Hebrew alphabet does not represent an independent adaptation of the short alphabet to the peculiarities of the Hebrew language (cf. Cross, 1980, pp. 13–15).

Within the Levant the various linguistic/political/geographic entities adopted the alphabet, and the sign forms underwent local evolutions (Naveh, 1982/1987; Cross, 1980). The alphabet spread throughout the Semitic world and to its colonies (Phoenicians in the West). After Aramaic was adopted as a lingua franca by the Achaemenids, its usage spread throughout the Near East and beyond; Aramaic even seems to have been used logographically in areas corresponding to modern Turkmenistan and Georgia (Naveh, 1982/1987, pp. 127–130). The short alphabet was eventually borrowed by Arabic speakers and adapted in a different order to express the fuller consonantal inventory of Arabic—twenty-eight phonemes (Naveh, 1982/1987, pp. 153–162). [See Arabic.]

Contribution of Greek. There has been a long controversy about the date at which the Greeks borrowed the West Semitic consonantal alphabet, with proposals ranging over several centuries—from the middle of the second millennium BCE to the early eighth century BCE. Phoenician and Aramaic inscriptions from as early as about 900 BCE (Bisi, 1991) are rare in the West, and the earliest Greek inscriptions date to the early eighth century BCE; thus, a hypothetical earlier borrowing of the alphabet must be based on the typology of letter forms: the earliest Greek letters most clearly resemble West Semitic signs from what period? Viewed abstractly, denying a date significantly earlier than the first inscriptions is essentially an argument from silence: because no examples exist of Greek writing earlier than the eighth century BCE, the writing system was adopted relatively shortly before that date. Following Rhys Carpenter's 1933 article of fundamental importance, P. Kyle McCarter (1975) and Maria Giulia Amadasi Guzzo (1991) have made very strong arguments from sign typology that essentially back up the argument from silence, to the effect that archaic Greek letters look like West Semitic forms from the late ninth/early eighth centuries BCE.

A less heated debate has been carried on with regard to the place where the alphabet was borrowed, with proposals tending to fit the date being argued. Because of the varieties of letter forms and alphabetic configurations attested among the Greeks, there are even those who favor multiple borrowings: while refusing to choose a particular place of borrowing, Amadasi Guzzo (1991, p. 309) makes an essential methodological point: the sophistication shown in recognizing phonetic equivalences between the Greek borrower's language, the Phoenician system being borrowed, and the adaptations to Greek needs requires that the place of borrowing be a metropolitan center with significant groups of both Greeks and Phoenicians, including well-trained scribes. [*See* Scribes and Scribal Techniques.]

The alphabet borrowed by the Greeks was of the Phoenician type, consisting of twenty-two consonantal signs. This is clear both from early Greek abecedaries and from the numerical value of the Greek letters (Piérart, 1991, pp. 571–573, figs. 1, 2). Most scholars assume that the Phoenicians themselves were the transmitters—in no small part because of the many contacts between Greeks and Phoenicians on their common Mediterranean waters. It cannot be ruled out that the Arameans were involved, but because the Arameans were not known as seafarers, this theory usually involves overland transmission across Asia Minor (Amadasi Guzzo, 1991). The strongest basis for this theory remains the Greeks names of the letters, such as *alpha* and *delta,* for they seem to reflect Aramaic pronunciation, not Phoenician (which would be *'alp* and *dalt*). It has been counterargued that forms like *alpha* only represent the Greek pronunciation of consonantal clusters such as /-lp/ at the end of the word, whereas some letter names, such as *iota,* presuppose a non-Aramaic origin (Naveh, 1982/1987, p. 183).

By inventing the notation of vowels, the Greeks made their own contribution to the history of the alphabet. On the Semitic side, a start in this direction had been made that has become systematized in Hebrew and in Arabic: the use of matres lectionis. The consonants *'aleph, hē, wāw,* and *yōd* were first used by Arameans and Hebrews to indicate a long vowel. The usage may have arisen by analogy from historical writings (e.g., if/bayt/becomes/bêt/, the tendency is to continue writing the word with {y}, even though the consonant is no longer pronounced). It never became a rigid system in any of the Hebrew or Aramaic dialects of the pre-Christian era, but in time more and more *matres lectionis* are found in the texts. They are used, for example, more frequently in the so-called sectarian documents from Qumran than in the received text of the Pentateuch, which represents a stage of the text dating a few centuries earlier than the Dead Sea Scrolls. [*See* Qumran; Dead Sea Scrolls.]

It is for the present a moot point whether the Greeks knew about such usages—they certainly did not if the alphabet was borrowed from the Phoenicians, for matres lectionis were not a part of normative Phoenician orthography in the eighth century BCE. What the Greeks did, in any case, was to give vocalic values to certain Phoenician consonants that did not correspond to consonantal phonemes in the Greek language, beginning with the first letter of the alphabet: the sign for the West Semitic consonant /'/ was used to represent the vowel /a/ by the Greeks. The signs for all the Semitic gutturals (/', h, ḥ, ʿ/) were so adapted, as were those for the two continuants /w/ and /y/.

The addition of vowel signs made the alphabet more explicitly expressive, for it provided a more complete pronunciation of a word than did the notation of consonants only. The notation of vowels made the Greek alphabet a stronger pedagogic tool, allowing for a decrease in the importance of oral tradition in teaching. This increased expressivity not only gave a more complete rendition of words in a given language, but also facilitated reading and understanding a foreign language. Greek also had a series of consonantal phonemes that did not have correspondences in Phoenician. New signs were invented or existing ones were transmuted for those sounds and they were added to the end of the alphabet—whence come several of the letters that occur in the English alphabet after {t}, the last sign of the West Semitic alphabet. The transmission of the alphabet to the Greeks permitted the writing down of Greek traditions that have by this means become part of modern culture. For example, the Homeric traditions plausibly began being committed to writing in the eighth century BCE, shortly after the full alphabet was devised (Amadasi Guzzo, 1991, pp. 307–308; Powell, 1991).

The invention of the consonantal alphabet by the Semites and its transformation by the Greeks for the notation of vowels are often cited as important factors in the democratization of writing. Although widespread literacy did not follow immediately upon the invention of the alphabet, a more rapid spread of literacy can be seen after the invention of the vowels. [*See* Literacy.] There is certainly a good deal of truth in linking democratization and the alphabet: to the extent that the growth of democracy required an educated middle class to deal with the complexities of growing societies, the ease of use of the alphabet may be thought to have facilitated, by the principle of efficient use of resources, this process.

Owing to the spread of alphabetic usage throughout the Mediterranean world and eastward during the last centuries of the pre-Christian era, the major writings of the three great Western religions have, with relatively few exceptions (e.g., Ethiopic), been transmitted in alphabetic scripts (e.g., Hebrew, Greek, Latin, Syriac, Coptic, Arabic, Armenian). [*See* Ethiopic; Latin; Syriac; Coptic; Armenian.]

BIBLIOGRAPHY

Amadasi Guzzo, Maria Giulia. "'The Shadow Line': Réflexions sur l'introduction de l'alphabet en Grèce." In *Phoinikeia Grammata, lire et écrire en Méditerranée: Actes du colloque de Liège, 15–18 novembre 1989,* edited by Claude Baurain et al., pp. 293–311. Namur, 1991. Excellent, brief overview of the origin of the alphabet and its transmission to the Greeks, with a good presentation of methodological factors. The essential bibliography is provided in footnotes.

Bisi, Anna M. "Les plus anciens objets inscrits en phénicien et en araméen retrouvés en Grèce: Leur typologie et leur rôle." In *Phoinikeia Grammata, lire et écrire en Méditerranée: Actes du colloque de Liège, 15–18 novembre 1989,* edited by Claude Baurain et al., pp. 277–282. Namur, 1991. Discusses the implications of the presence of Phoenician- and Aramaic-transcribed objects in the West.

Bordreuil, Pierre. "L'inscription phénicienne de Sarafand en cunéiformes alphabétiques." *Ugarit Forschungen* 11 (1979): 63–68. Improved reading of the Sarepta inscription in Ugaritic script.

Bordreuil, Pierre, and Dennis Pardee. "Les textes ougaritiques." Forthcoming in the edition of texts discovered at Ras Shamra from 1986 to 1992. Includes the *editio princeps* of the abecedary in South Semitic order.

Caquot, André. "Un abécédaire du type sud-sémitique découvert en 1992 dans les fouilles archéologiques françaises de Ras Shamra-Ougarit." *Comptes Rendus de l'Académie des Inscriptions et des Belles Lettres.* Forthcoming. First announcement of the discovery of an abecedary of South Semitic type at Ras Shamra.

Carpenter, Rhys. "The Antiquity of the Greek Alphabet." *American Journal of Archaeology* 37 (1933): 8–29. Fundamental article on the methodology of dating the borrowing of the alphabet by the Greeks. More recent discoveries have moved the date a bit earlier, but the basic arguments still stand.

Cross, Frank Moore. "Newly Found Inscriptions in Old Canaanite and Early Phoenician Scripts." *Bulletin of the American Schools of Oriental Research,* no. 238 (1980): 1–20. Reappraisal of alphabetic origins and developments which accepts an early borrowing of the alphabet by the Greeks (eleventh century).

Greenstein, Edward L. "A Phoenician Inscription in Ugaritic Script?" *Journal of the Ancient Near Eastern Society of Columbia University* 8 (1976): 49–57. Identifies the language of the Sarepta inscription in Ugaritic script as Phoenician.

Kutscher, Eduard Y. *A History of the Hebrew Language.* Jerusalem, 1982. Includes a discussion of the relationship of graphemes to phonemes in Biblical Hebrew.

Lemaire, André. "Fragment d'un alphabet ouest-sémitique du VIIIe siècle av. J.-C." *Semitica* 28 (1978): 7–10. Edition of a partial abecedary purchased on the antiquities market.

Lunden [Loundine], A. G. "L'abécédaire de Beth Shemesh." *Le Muséon* 100 (1987): 243–250.

McCarter, P. Kyle, Jr. *The Antiquity of the Greek Alphabet and the Early Phoenician Scripts.* Harvard Semitic Monographs, 9. Missoula, 1975. The basic work accepting a late borrowing of the alphabet by the Greeks (though it leaves open the possibility of earlier experiments). Competent treatment of both the Semitic and the Greek sides of the question.

Naveh, Joseph. *An Early History of the Alphabet: An Introduction to West Semitic Epigraphy and Palaeography.* 2d ed. Jerusalem, 1987. Good overview of alphabetic origins and developments, though one may query the late dating of the Proto-Sinaitic inscriptions (fifteenth century) and the early borrowing of the alphabet by the Greeks (eleventh century). Generally more thorough on graphic evolutions than on correlations between graphemes and phonemes.

Piérart, Marcel. "Écriture et identité culturelle: Les cités du Péloponnèse nord-oriental." In *Phoinikeia Grammata, lire et écrire en Méditerranée: Actes du colloque de Liège, 15–18 novembre 1989,* edited by Claude Baurain et al., pp. 565–576. Namur, 1991. Discussion of the contribution of Greek abecedaries to the early history of the alphabet among the Greeks.

Powell, B. P. "The Origins of Alphabetic Literacy among the Greeks." In *Phoinikeia Grammata, lire et écrire en Méditerranée: Actes du colloque de Liège, 15–19 novembre 1989,* edited by Claude Baurain et al., pp. 357–370. Namur, 1991. Sees the origin of vowel notation by the Greeks in the requirements of representing the hexameter in writing.

Röllig, Wolfgang, and G. Mansfeld. "Zwei Ostraka vom Tell Kamid-el-Loz und ein neuer Aspekt für die Entstehung des kanaanäischen Alphabets." *Die Welt des Orients* 5 (1969–1970): 265–270.

Sass, Benjamin. *Studia Alphabetica: On the Origin and Early History of the Northwest Semitic, South Semitic, and Greek Alphabets.* Orbis Biblicus et Orientalis, 102. Freiburg, 1991. Overview of various crucial points in the origin and transmission of the alphabet.

Sznycer, Maurice. "Quelques remarques à propos de la formation de l'alphabet phénicien." *Semitica* 24 (1974): 5–12. Brief but systematic treatment of alphabetic origins.

DENNIS PARDEE

ALT, ALBRECHT (1883–1956), Hebrew Bible scholar and founder of the discipline of historical geography. Alt was born in Stübach, near Neustadt/Aisch, in Bavaria. After finishing the gymnasium in Ansbach, he studied theology in Erlangen and in Leipzig. In 1909 he received a doctorate of theology for his thesis "Israel und Ägypten." In that same year, he received a promotion to lecturer at the University of Greifswald, where he served as associate professor of Old Testament studies. He became a full professor at Basel in 1914 and at Halle in 1921. He held the Old Testament chair at Leipzig from 1923 until shortly before his death. Alt was a very gifted teacher, and many of the most important scholars in the field of Old Testament studies were his pupils: Martin Noth, Gerhard von Rad, Herbert Donner, and Siegfried Herrmann. He was also closely affiliated with the Evangelisches Institut für die Altertumswissenschaft des Heiligen Landes. He made two long visits to Palestine in 1908 and 1912–1913 and directed the institute's scientific research and field trips there from 1924 until 1931. In 1925 he became president of the Deutscher Verein zur Erforschung Palästinas and in 1927 editor of the *Palästina Jahrbuch.*

Alt had a profound knowledge of the texts dealing with the history of Palestine in all periods, as well as an intimate knowledge of the country itself. He developed the history of its territories in the biblical period (*Territorialgeschichte*) as a special subject area in the discipline of the historical geography of the Holy Land, with far-reaching results. Although he never published a book summarizing his work, many of his papers became the focus of further research and advanced theories. His critical studies of the lists of the cities in the Hebrew Bible were used as primary sources for the many different periods of Israel's history. Developing the critical view of German scholarship toward the historicity of the *Book of Joshua,* Alt articulated a new theory of the conquest of the land by the tribes of Israel: the immigration, or infiltration, theory. Even though some of his ideas are no longer accepted, many others remain of fundamental importance to the fields of archaeology and biblical studies, especially in the areas of biblical law and social development. He influenced not only his own pupils, but scholars all over the world. His collected papers appeared in 1953 and 1959 in three volumes, the last one edited by Noth. A selection of his work in English translation appeared in 1966 under the title *Essays on Old Testament History and Religion*.

Alt has been praised by those who studied with him as a stimulating teacher who encouraged his pupils to do original work. His knowledge of topographical and historical details exceeded that of all his colleagues and enabled him to develop new views for certain regions and whole epochs. Although he never participated in an excavation, Alt closely followed the progress of archaeological fieldwork. In his own work, he used pottery as a key indicator for chronology, combining surface exploration with text interpretation in a unique way. This new approach to the material advanced specialized research into the territories and regions of ancient Palestine.

[*See also* Historical Geography; *and the biography of Noth.*]

BIBLIOGRAPHY

Bardtke, Hans. "Albrecht Alt: Leben und Werk." *Theologische Literaturzeitung* 81 (1956): 513–522.
Noth, Martin. "Albrecht Alt zum Gedächtnis." *Zeitschrift des Deutschen Palästina-Vereins* 72 (1956): 1–8.

VOLKMAR FRITZ

ALTARS. In the ancient Near East, altars are typically classified on the basis of their material and style of construction. However, the flexibility and comprehensiveness of a typology based on function and location allows altars to be described within an archaeological context useful in analysing written sources such as the Hebrew Bible. The term *altar* refers to any surface on which an offering to a deity is placed. The use of altars is widespread geographically and chronologically throughout the Near East, with types ranging from plain rock surfaces to elaborate installations within temple complexes. Although altars were associated with the presence of a deity, their location was not limited to the area of temples. Altars were often located on hilltops, raised platforms, and rooftops, as well as in a range of settings not characterized by height. The term *altar* should not be applied to the interior raised platform, or "dais," found opposite the entry to many temples, on which the image of the deity was displayed.

A distinction is made archaeologically between altars found outside structures (type I) and those found within structures (type II), both having a number of subtypes.

1. *Rock altars: type Ia.* An example of a rock altar is the stepped stone block with channels and cup marks found at Tel Sera', west of Jerusalem. This installation has been associated with the account of the sacrifice of Manoah in *Judges* 13. It is often impossible to verify the date or religious function of this type of altar because of the lack of associated artifacts. It should also be noted that seemingly "secular" installations, such as threshing floors, may have had religious/cultic connections in ancient times. [*See* Sera', Tel.]

2. *Open altars: type Ib.* Installations known as open altars had clear cultic functions but were not located within temple complexes. An example is the Early Bronze Age structure (4017) at Megiddo, in ancient Palestine, a large altar (8 m diameter) mounted via steps. [*See* Megiddo.] In later periods this type of installation is found surrounded by a number of temples (although it does not afford direct access to them). Other buildings sometimes found near open altars may have had a function within the cult, but they are not considered temples. Throughout the Near East evidence of open altars comes primarily from the Bronze Age.

3. *Enclosed altars: type Ic.* Found commonly throughout the Bronze and Iron Ages, enclosed altars were located within the forecourt of temple complexes. Examples of this type may be seen in the temple areas at Kition on Cyprus. [*See* Kition.] Another prominent example is the stone and earth altar of the Judahite temple at Arad. [*See* Arad.] Biblical evidence (1 *Kgs*. 9:25, for example) indicates a similarly located altar in the courtyard of the Solomonic Temple in Jerusalem, but this has not been verified archaeologically. Both the archaeological and written evidence identify open and enclosed altars (Heb., *mizbēaḥ*), often with "horns," as the site of burnt offerings. The written evidence suggests that the materials used in the construction of these altars included earth, stone, and metal, although there are no known excavated examples of metal.

4. *Incense altars: type IIa.* It is unlikely that altars found within buildings were used for the burning of animal sacrifices. It was the practice within temples, however, to burn several types of incense. A variety of stone and ceramic stands have been identified as incense altars, and a number of the former, which may have had a religious function, have also been identified in "secular" contexts. Incense altars became ubiquitous in the southern Levant during the Persian period.

5. *Presentation altars: type IIb.* The "presentation" altar is found within temples and related buildings but is not associated with burning. It is a surface upon which offerings to the deity, such as grain, could be placed. At times, presentation altars took the form of benches (often plastered mud brick); stone "tables" or ceramic stands also served this function.

6. *Libation altars: type IIc.* Offerings to deities also included liquids, such as water, wine, and oil. Installations with depressions—plastered mud brick or large stone basins (e.g., the Gezer stelae field), detached stone tables with carved depressions (e.g., Hazor, area H), or bowls placed on ceramic stands—held such offerings. This type of altar is often found within the temple itself (cf. Lachish Palace Temple) or in its courtyard (e.g. 'Ein-Gedi). [*See* Gezer; Hazor; Lachish; 'Ein-Gedi.]

Altars were the focal point of communication between the human and divine realms and are ubiquitous in those areas of the Near East where religious practice included the transmission of foodstuffs to the gods.

[*See also* Cult; Incense; *and* Temples.]

BIBLIOGRAPHY

Barrick, W. Boyd. "High Place." In *The Anchor Bible Dictionary*, vol. 3, pp. 196–200. New York, 1992. Summary of an important study that distinguishes altars from cultic areas known as high places.

Bergquist, Birgitta. "Bronze Age Sacrificial *Koine* in the Eastern Mediterranean? A Study of Animal Sacrifice in the Ancient Near East." In *Ritual and Sacrifice in the Ancient Near East*, edited by J. Quaegebeur, pp. 11–43. Orientalia Lovaniensia Analecta 55. Leuven, 1993.

DeVries, Lamoine R. "Cult Stands: A Bewildering Variety of Shapes and Sizes." *Biblical Archaeology Review* 13 (1987): 26–37. Popular presentation of information about ceramic stands, especially in cultic contexts.

Galling, Kurt. *Der Altar in den Kulturen des alten Orients eine archäologische Studie*. Berlin, 1925. Classic study of the phenomenon of altars in the ancient Near East.

Gitin, Seymour. "Incense Altars from Ekron, Israel, and Judah: Context and Typology." *Eretz-Israel* 20 (1989): 52*–67*. Authoritative study of four-horned incense altars in the Iron Age.

Haak, Robert D. "Altar." In *The Anchor Bible Dictionary*, vol. 1, pp. 162–167. New York, 1992. Convenient summary of information concerning altars in the written and archaeological record.

Hägg, Robin. "Open Cult Places in the Bronze Age Aegean." In *Biblical Archaeology Today, 1990: Proceedings of the Second International Congress on Biblical Archaeology, Jerusalem June–July 1990*, edited by Avraham Biran and Joseph Aviram, pp.188–195. Jerusalem, 1993.

Meyers, Carol L. "Altar." In *Harper's Bible Dictionary*, pp. 22–24. San Francisco, 1985. Overview of the types and functions of altars mentioned in the Hebrew Bible.

Stendebach, Franz Josef. "Altarformen im kanaanäisch-israelitischen Raum." Biblische Zeitschrift 20 (1976): 180–196.

Weiner, Harold M. *The Altars of the Old Testament*. Leipzig, 1927.

ROBERT D. HAAK

AMARNA, TELL EL-, site of the capital of the heretic Egyptian king Akhenaten, built to honor his sole god, Aten, located in Middle Egypt (27°38′ N, 30°53′ E). The large mud-brick and stone expanse of the city, as well as the cuneiform clay tablets found there within a state archival office, have made Tell el-Amarna important to archaeologists and essential to historians of the Near East in the Late Bronze Age.

Identification. The remains of Tell el-Amarna today stretch some 10 km (10 mi.) north to south on the east side of the Nile River. The ancient city and environs occupied nearly twice that distance on both sides of the river and were together called *Akhetaten*, "the Horizon of the Aten (sun disk)." The name was given by the city's founder, Akhenaten, on a series of stelae placed to delimit Tell el-Amarna. The city within Akhetaten may have had a separate designation or more than one, and the monumental buildings that Akhenaten placed within the city likewise had discreet appellations (for some of these see below).

ALTARS. *Limestone incense altars.* Tel Miqne, Iron II period. (Courtesy ASOR Archives)

AMARNA, TELL EL-. Figure 1. *Limestone bust of Queen Nefertiti.* New Kingdom, eighteenth dynasty, Amarna period, c. 1340 BCE. Height, 50 cm. Egyptian Museum, Berlin. (Erich Lessing/Art Resource, NY)

The name *Tell el-Amarna* is a misnomer, for the site has no visible mound that characterize tells in the Near East generally. Modern names and spellings have shifted since Western expeditions arrived there in the late eighteenth century. First designated with the name of the village of El-Tell by the Napoleonic expedition of 1798, the site was called by several names, for example, Till Bene Amran, used by Robert Hay in 1829. European travelers conflated the villages of et-Tell (or Till) and el-Amariya with a tribe settled in the region called Ben Amran. The name *Tel(l) el-Amarna* first appeared on a publication by Sir John Gardner Wilkinson, who mapped the site and published his map in 1830.

Occupational History. Tell el-Amarna, or el-Amarna as it is now more commonly termed, consists principally of the capital built for King Akhenaten, about 1350 BCE, on land that he believed to be previously unsettled. (Son of Amenhotep III, Akhenaten had ascended the throne as Amenhotep IV, but changed his name a few years later.) A few areas

of the site were occupied, however, during other ancient eras. Earliest remains are known from several Paleolithic sites with flint concentrations, and a few Neolithic (predynastic) artifacts suggest pre-third millennium occupation in the region.

Akhenaten's city within Akhetaten was largely abandoned within a dozen years of his death. The ruler who succeeded Akhenaten for a year or two, Smenkhkare, appears to have resided in el-Amarna, and Tutankhaten, who soon changed his name to the more familiar Tutankhamun, is well attested at the site for at least another two years. Building activity is documented also in a worker's village in the period following Tutankhamun's abandonment of Middle Egypt and return to the region of Thebes. The full seventeen years of Akhenaten's reign, together with the dozen or so years comprising Smenkhkare's, Tutankhamun's, and Ay's rules, are often referred to as the "Amarna Period," although el-Amarna was not inhabited during all of it.

In one region of southern el-Amarna, near the river, are the remains of a town that survived the abandonment of the main city. Fragmentary architecture of late New Kingdom date or later are mixed there with sherds of the Amarna period. Although originally identified as the "river temple," the bits of structures have recently been relabeled as house remains. A few burials of the twenty-second–twenty-third dynasties were found in the early 1920s near the worker's village, and in 1984 a burial of the twentieth–twenty-first dynasties was excavated in the same area. Sherds of the Late Period (end of eighth century–332 BCE) were found near the southern tombs of Akhenaten's nobles. These may have belonged to burials of a population living in the general vicinity (possibly the river town) or may indicate transient activity through the area for various purposes, possibly even illicit ones, that is, tomb robbery. In the Roman period several settlements existed at the site of el-Amarna, and Coptic Christians later converted tombs there for housing and worship.

Research and Excavation. The largest of the few preserved Egyptian cities, el-Amarna has been frequently explored and studied. Recent surveys and comparisons with the earliest maps of the region indicate that el-Amarna has always been visible to interested visitors. Areas destroyed by illicit digging appear to have been only slightly less disturbed 150 ago than today.

As early as 1714 Father Claude Sicard, a French Jesuit missionary, published a drawing of Amarna Boundary Stela A at Tuna el-Gebel. The Napoleonic scientific expedition visited the region in 1799, and Edmé Jomard produced a plan of El Tell in the pioneering study *Description de l'Égypte,* published in 1817. Sir John Gardner Wilkinson visited el-Amarna in 1824 and 1826 to draw, plan, and copy the buildings and tombs and he produced plans of the entire city. Other travelers in the 1820s and 1830s, such as Robert Hay, James Burton, and Nestor L'Hôte, made copies of the tombs of Akhenaten's nobles. The royal Prussian expedition led by Richard Lepsius drew plans of the city of el-Amarna between 1843 and 1845.

The first modern archaeological work at el-Amarna took place in 1891–1892 when Sir William Matthew Flinders Petrie opened excavations in a variety of locations at the site. Several expeditions followed in rapid succession, culminating in the methodical survey and excavations of Ludwig Borchardt (1907, 1911–1914), carried out for the Deutsche Orient-Gesellschaft. Some of the best-known works of Amarna art were uncovered during this period, including the famous bust of Nefertiti (see figure 1), which is now in the Egyptian Museum in Berlin (Charlottenburg), and numerous other statues found in the house and workshop of the sculptor Thutmose in the main city/south suburb. The Egypt Exploration Fund (now Society) of London copied and published the private tombs and boundary stelae between 1901 and 1907. They resumed work at the site in 1921 under a succession of well-known directors, including Thomas Eric Peet, Henri Frankfort, Francis Llewellyn Griffith, and John D. S. Pendlebury. The EEF explored nearly all areas of the site, moving from peripheral regions such as the worker's village, the "river temple," and the northern palace to later extensive excavations in the central city lasting until 1936.

In the early 1970s Geoffrey T. Martin reinvestigated the royal tomb at el-Amarna and published in addition the numerous but fragmentary objects from the tomb associated with Akhenaten and Nefertiti. In 1977 the Egypt Exploration Society resumed work under the direction of Barry J. Kemp and has worked at the site since. Kemp commenced excavation at the worker's village that once housed artisans employed in the royal tomb. His team found that the village may have been abandoned and then reinhabited in the time of Tutankhamun by guardians of the royal and private necropoleis. Research has focused on identifying patterns of activity sited within the village, as well as the interdependence between the village and the central city. Kemp has moved his investigations into the main city area since 1987 but continues to be interested in the interrelationships between public and private buildings and their peripheral economic dependencies.

Remains. The fifteen boundary stelae of Akhenaten delimiting the territory of el-Amarna, like the remains of the city they describe, are important monuments. Some of these boundary markers consist only of a stela and others of an actual rock shrine containing statuary. They provide further information vis-à-vis the site, however, for three of them preserve the text of a proclamation made by Akhenaten in the first months of his fifth regnal year, in which he describes and names numerous buildings and complexes to be constructed at Akhetaten. Some of these (e.g., the great Aten temple, the "mansion of the Aten," the royal tomb) can be identified with excavated structures; some cannot with cer-

tainty (e.g., the "house of rejoicing and sunshade of the great queen"), and some others appear never to have been completed (e.g., the tomb of the Mnevis bull of Heliopolis). The identifiable buildings correspond to complexes and tombs built throughout much of the 10-kilometer north–south stretch of el-Amarna, a fact that confirms the original design of the city as a long narrow town accommodated to the Nile and the eastern bay of limestone cliffs by a royal road. This road was later redirected in part but remained the primary route linking north areas to the central city.

At its northern end, el-Amarna had a mud-brick northern river palace oriented on its west side to the royal road that travels southward for 6 km (3.7 mi). This palace may have been the principal residence of the king. A group of administrative buildings lies just south of it along with a residential quarter likewise oriented to the road. Farther south is the northern palace, also built to face the royal road and a tourist attraction today. Here, around courts with pools and shaded garden porticoes, lived at least two queens, including Meretaten, Akhenaten's daughter, who resided there after a predecessor, perhaps Nefertiti or Kiya.

The northern suburb is located to the east of the royal road orientation, and the parts excavated (those farthest north from the central city) appear to have been a late addition. Areas of residence between the northern suburb and the central city have not been excavated but could reveal in time whether this is a natural northern extension from the central city or grew up later in a separate but parallel fashion.

The central city contains most of the buildings whose material remains, architecture, and preserved decoration may suggest a center planned for state administration and worship. Oriented to the royal road, it contained from north to south, the enormous precinct of the great Aten temple ("house" or "estate of the Aten"); the king's house, connected by a bridge to the great palace; the smaller Aten temple (the "Mansion of the Aten"); and the Smenkhkare hall. On the east side of the road, the king's house and smaller Aten temple were the westernmost of a complex of buildings that were crucial to state functions. Kemp considers the King's house to be the most likely siting for the "window of appearance" pictured in numerous private tombs of Akhenaten's officials (Kemp and Garfi, 1993, p. 59). A series of scribal offices lay east of the king's house, including one identified by stamped bricks as the "place of the pharaoh's correspondence." In this archival office were found the majority of the Amarna Letters, famous as the correspondence between the Egyptian rulers Amenhotep III, Akhenaten, and Tutankhamun with kings and city-state rulers from Mesopotamia and the Levant. To the east of the offices lies a garrison block with animal stalls and barracks, as well as separate storage areas for rations. This security complex is not oriented toward the royal road. Being on the eastern edge of the city, it may have had more association with the desert and the wadi due east leading to the royal tomb.

The best-known compound in the central city, the great Aten temple, likewise comprised several structures. The Gempaaten ("the Aten is found") was a multicourted stone building near the western end of the temple precinct. It was entered from a western gateway through high pylons giving on to stone colonnades that themselves led to a series of unroofed courtyards. Within and beside these courts were arranged bread-offering altars, made of stone (within the courts) or brick (south of the courts). More than 750 altars were placed within the Gempaaten, and some 920 brick tables lay to the south of the building. Another 920 may once have existed on the northern side. The formal colonnaded setting appears to have been the primary offering area for Aten state worship but not the actual sanctuary of the temple. Between Gempaaten and a second stone structure to the east, the sanctuary, was a "butcher's yard" with tethering stones and an enormous open area. A separate northern entrance to the open area before the sanctuary was elaborated as a gateway pavilion. A stela of quartzite, perhaps evoking the Heliopolitan *benben* stone, was set up on a line with this entrance. The sanctuary building was flanked to the north by more bread-offering altars, but excavations to the south of the building and just outside the enclosure wall have revealed indications of different ritual activities as well. In a dump Petrie and Pendlebury found plain everted rim bowls with burnt resins inside. In 1986 Kemp confirmed that the bowls with burned "incense" were common in the dump area along with "beer-jar" shapes and other offering vessel types (Kemp, 1989, vol. 4, pp. 116–121). He found fragments of storage jars, and Pendlebury had found seals and labels in the area. Kemp has identified this dump as a significant locale for the sanctuary's refuse. It provides evidence for the libations and offerings of incense made within the neighboring building. Kemp has noted the placement of large bakeries on the south side of the enclosure wall opposite the Gempaaten. The hundreds of altars there would have held loaves from those bakeries; Kemp believes that a segment of the city's populace offered to the Aten on the brick tables to the south of the Gempaaten while the king and family officiated inside the temple proper (Kemp and Garfi, 1993, p. 55). Despite Kemp's contributions, the ritual connection between the sanctuary and the Gempaaten, as well as the use patterns for the complex generally, remain uncertain.

In the main city or south suburb are residential and administrative quarters. Large-scale unexcavated complexes of undoubted administrative nature lie in this sector, largely to the west of more domestic structures. The state and temple institutions operated their own economies and necessarily housed the resources, both perishable and nonperishable. Kemp believes that government workshops may have been situated in these large centers, but he also notes that large institutions appear to have been made up of a number of complexes, often not located together. The designation of industrial centers without inscription as "royal," "temple," or "private" thus becomes problematic (Kemp and Garfi, 1993, pp. 67–69; Kemp, 1989, vol. 5, pp. 56–63).

The house and workshop of the sculptor Thutmose, famous for the many statues and plaster masks of royal family, are located in the south suburb near other sculptors' shops (see figure 2). Thutmose's precise economic and administrative association with his patrons is difficult to ascertain. Whether individual artisans were contracted directly by the court, through court-sanctioned patrons, or both is un-

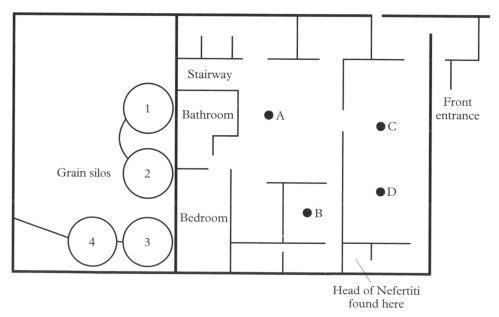

AMARNA, TELL EL-. Figure 2. *Floor plan of the house of the sculptor Thutmose.* (After Kemp, 1989)

known. For example, some obviously nonroyal estates appear to have housed royal workshops, perhaps as a subcontract from the crown.

Architecture is not always a clear indicator of function. Archaeological research has demonstrated the often diverse patterns of use for both residences and specialized buildings, such as "magazines," which, as Kemp has found, were used both for production and for storage (Kemp and Garfi, 1993, pp. 67–69). Nearly all areas of el-Amarna held residences (royal, temple, private), and those residences nearly always contained separate storage facilities, wells, often industrial centers. The degree to which these separate facilities indicate independent economic behavior is unknown.

To the south of the main city/south suburb is Kom el-Nana, oriented to the original royal road as it was laid out before the growth of the main city. Kom el-Nana is a temple complex with supporting buildings for food production and storage. Kemp believes that this is the third of three major institutions described in the early proclamation, the "sunshade of the great queen" (Kemp and Garfi, 1993, p. 79). Even farther south and entirely isolated is the Maruaten, a site that houses enclosures with altars and shrines along with pools and surrounding gardens. It is clearly linked with queens, including Akhenaten's daughter Meretaten.

Other areas of southern el-Amarna include the above-mentioned river settlement, which is a residential area and el-Hawata in the far south also near the Nile. Little remains in this sector. On the opposite end of the site are a number of architectural remains not part of the city proper. Three large desert altars in the northeastern desert, nearly opposite the north palace, are oriented toward the royal road. These mud-brick structures with ramps once held pavilions, perhaps for large-scale royal receptions of dignitaries, such as are pictured in two private tombs. Above these altars are the northern tombs of private residents of el-Amarna. A second set of such tombs exists in the southern cliffs. A total of forty-three tombs was excavated in whole or part. The most elaborate had colonnaded inner halls, and in those that were decorated (many were left incomplete) the royal family and the architecture of Akhetaten figured prominently in painted relief sculpture.

The royal tomb and a few uninscribed smaller tombs were located in a wadi reached through a larger wadi running eastward opposite the central city. Unusual relief scenes of mourning over corpses on beds appear on the walls of the royal burial chamber and on a side chamber used for the burial of Akhenaten's daughter Meketaten, who may have died in childbirth. The royal funerary goods left at the site were smashed into pieces, but remains of the royal sarcophagus and canopic box have been studied (Martin, 1974). At the mouth of eastern wadi was the worker's village, which was apparently used for the building of the royal tomb and later, during the reign of Tutankhamun, for guarding the same area. Residents at this village in the time of Tutan-

khamun had not only self-sufficient residences but also shrines where families gathered to eat and commune with recently deceased relatives. These shrines would also have been memorial chapels for a household or several related households. The second phase in the worker's village is one of the latest excavated, representing the later reign of Akhenaten through the reign of Tutankhamun, including the time after the court's departure from el-Amarna. The activity of the guards living in the village in the last phase therefore reflects a mixture of religious beliefs with various traditional gods reappearing in shrine images. Following the abandonment of the worker's village, the city of Amarna was both used as a quarry, especially for the Ramesside temple at Hermopolis, and deliberately mutilated. Statuary was destroyed in situ or dragged away and dumped. A similar pattern of reuse and destruction can be seen in the earlier complex at East Karnak, which Akhenaten built both before and after his change of name from Amenhotep.

BIBLIOGRAPHY

Aldred, Cyril. *Akhenaten, Pharaoh of Egypt: A New Study*. London, 1968. Pioneering historical and art historical study of the ruler, presenting Aldred's arguments for a prolonged co-regency between Akhenaten and his father Amenhotep III. Revised and reissued in 1988.

Bomann, Ann H. *The Private Chapel in Ancient Egypt: A Study of the Chapels in the Workmen's Village at El Amarna with Special Reference to Deir el Medina and Other Sites*. London, 1991. Identifies the close relationship between el-Amarna chapels and Deir el-Medineh private chapels used for personal cult worship, differentiating these from chapels strictly attached to tombs, which the author considers to be for the Ka of the deceased.

Kemp, Barry J. *Amarna Reports*. 5 vols. London, 1984–1989. Annual reports of work by the Egypt Exploration Society under Kemp's direction. Each volume includes contributions by expedition members on topics such as pottery analysis, ancient wells, survey work, ancient ovens, faunal and botanical remains, etc. Kemp's offerings are always written with the reader in mind, but some authors allow the technical side to dominate.

Kemp, Barry J. "Tell el-Amarna." In *Lexikon der Ägyptologie*, vol. 6, cols. 309–319. Wiesbaden, 1985. Encyclopedia article encapsulating work at the site, with references to 1985.

Kemp, Barry J. *Ancient Egypt: Anatomy of a Civilization*. London, 1989. General work on the cultural life of ancient Egypt, with a lengthy chapter using el-Amarna as "Egypt in microcosm." Contains analysis of work up to 1988.

Kemp, Barry J., and Salvatore Garfi. *A Survey of the Ancient City of El-'Amarna*. London, 1993. Survey sheets of the site with accompanying text. Kemp offers a number of recent thoughts, particularly on provisioning within el-Amarna, and provides summaries of earlier analyses within the technical descriptions of the sheets.

Martin, Geoffrey T. *The Royal Tomb at el-Amarna I*. London, 1974. The tomb objects from museums all over the world gathered together for study.

Martin, Geoffrey T. *A Bibliography of the Amarna Period and Its Aftermath*. London, 1991.

Moran, William L. *The Amarna Letters*. Baltimore, 1992. Retranslation and annotation of the famous correspondence between the rulers of el-Amarna, Mesopotamia, and the Levant. Eminently readable.

Murnane, William J., and Charles C. Van Siclen III. *The Boundary*

Stelae of Akhenaten. London, 1993. Publication of the refound, re-collated, and researched boundary stelae, forming an important reference work for historians and philologists of el-Amarna.

Redford, Donald B. *Akhenaten the Heretic King.* Princeton, 1984. Chapter 7 contains Redford's summation of the city. Archaeologically much has been revised since that time, but Redford has a spirited style and links the site with East Karnak, where he excavated Akhenaten's early temples.

Van de Walle, Baudouin. "La découverte d'Amarna et d'Akhenaton." *Revue d'Égyptologie* 28 (1976): 7–24. History of the early researches at el-Amarna.

BETSY M. BRYAN

AMARNA TABLETS. Tell el-Amarna (ancient Akhetaten) in middle Egypt was, in the fourteenth century BCE, the capital city of Akhenaten, or Amenophis IV. In 1887 local inhabitants discovered cuneiform tablets there while digging in the mounds. The tablets eventually found their way to antique dealers and museums. Subsequently, more tablets were unearthed in organized excavations. The existing corpus consists of 380 tablets now primarily in the British Museum in London, the Vorderasiatisches Museum in Berlin, and the Egyptian Museum in Cairo.

The corpus of the Amarna tablets mainly includes letters sent to the courts of the Egyptian pharaohs Amenophis III and his son Akhenaten. The senders were other kings—namely of Babylonia, Assyria, Ḫatti, Mitanni, and Alashiya—and some minor princes and rulers in the Near East. The majority of the extant letters are from vassals of the Egyptian Empire in the Levant. Some copies or drafts of letters from the pharaohs are also preserved. Another part of the corpus consists of scholarly tablets (e.g., literary texts, vocabularies, and scribal exercises). Most of the Amarna texts were written in Akkadian, the diplomatic language of the ancient Near East in the second millennium BCE (two of the letters were written in Hittite and one in Hurrian). The letters from Canaan reflect a language that is a mixture of the Akkadian lingua franca and the local Canaanite, the mother tongue of their scribes. The Amarna letters from Canaan are thus a unique, and invaluable source for understanding the Canaanite dialects of the second millenium BCE.

The international correspondence is usually concerned with exchanges of gifts; some letters deal with diplomatic marriages and thus give the impression of a time of peaceful relationships among the great political powers of that period. However, the rising power of the Hittites was already threatening the northern border of the Egyptian Empire, which is clearly reflected in the letters from Egypt's vassals in the northern Levant. A considerable number of letters from Byblos (in Lebanon) tell of the pressure put on the coastal plain by Adbi-Aširta and his sons after him. These letters, along with others from the northern Levant, and letters from the Amurrite kings themselves, tell the story of the rise of the state of Amurru, and the shift of allegiance of Aziru, the Amurrite king and son of Abdi-Aširta, from Egypt to the Hittites. Letters from local kings in most areas of Syria and Palestine reflect an almost constant state of conflict and requests to the pharaoh to intervene. Inner-city rebels and pressure from the ʿapiru, a class of outsiders, are also commonly mentioned. For example, ÌR-ḫeba, king of Jerusalem, complains about a coalition of other southern Canaanite kings against him led by Milkilu, king of Gezer. Later, in Gezer, Yapaʿu, a successor of Milkilu, complains that his brother rebelled against him and joined the ʿapiru. Similar descriptions of unsteady situations come from all over the area dominated by Egypt.

Through the Amarna letters we learn about the relationship both between the empires and among the local Canaanite rulers; about the ways the Egyptian Empire dominated its territories in the Levant; about the social diversity in Syria-Palestine; and about the political structure and struggles between the Hittite and the Egyptian empires at their borders in the northern Levant. The Amarna letters constitute a unique corpus for studying the social and political structure of Syria-Palestine in the second half of the fourteenth century BCE, a time that has accordingly been termed, the Amarna age.

Shortly after their discovery, all of the Amarna texts were published in cuneiform copies, in transliteration, and in translation. Jørgen A. Knudtzon (1915) compiled a full edition of the texts that is still authoritative with regard to their Akkadian texts. The second volume of this edition includes a historical commentary by Otto Weber and an analytic vocabulary by Erich Ebeling. The texts discovered later were published by Anson F. Rainey in 1970 (revised edition, 1978). The language of the Canaanite Amarna letters posited many difficulties, but William L. Moran achieved a breakthrough in 1950 in understanding it as a mixed language. This breakthrough and subsequent research by Moran, Rainey, and others have established the study of the Amarna letters on solid philological grounds. A new, authoritative translation of the Amarna letters by Moran appeared in French in 1987 (English edition, 1992). Historical research has concentrated mainly on the relationships between the great powers and much less on the internal affairs of Syria-Palestine. The first major attempt to tackle the complicated chronological disposition of the letters was made by Edward F. Campbell (1964). This paved the way for Nadav Naʾaman's pioneering history of Palestine in the Amarna period (1975). Horst Klengel (1965–1970) was the first to handle comprehensively internal affairs in Syria.

[See also Akkadian; and Amarna, Tell el-.]

BIBLIOGRAPHY

Campbell, Edward F. *The Chronology of the Amarna Letters: With Special Reference to the Hypothetical Coregency of Amenophis III and Akhenaten.* Baltimore, 1964.

Kitchen, K. A. *Suppiluliuma and the Amarna Pharaos: A Study in Rel-*

ative Chronology. Liverpool Monographs in Archaeology and Oriental Studies, no. 5. Liverpool, 1962.

Klengel, Horst. *Geschichte Syriens im 2. Jahrtausend v.u.Z.* 3 vols. Berlin, 1965–1970.

Knudtzon, Jørgen A. *Die el-Amarna-Tafeln* (1915). Vorderasiatische Bibliothek, 2. Leipzig, 1964.

Kühne, Cord. *Die Chronologie der internationalen Korrespondenz von El-Amarna.* Alter Orient und Altes Testament, vol. 17. Kevelaer, 1973.

Moran, William L. "A Syntactical Study of the Dialect of Byblos as Reflected in the Amarna Tablets." Ph.D. diss., Johns Hopkins University, 1950. The first breakthrough for the understanding of the language of the Canaanite Amarna letters. Available from University Microfilms International, Ann Arbor.

Moran, William L. *The Amarna Letters.* Baltimore, 1992.

Na'aman, Nadav. "The Historical Disposition and Historical Development of Eretz-Israel according to the Amarna Letters." Ph.D. diss., Tel Aviv University, 1975. In Hebrew with English summary.

Rainey, Anson F. *Tell el-Amarna Tablets, 359–379.* 2d ed., rev. Alter Orient und Altes Testament, vol. 8. Kevelaer, 1978.

SHLOMO IZRE'EL

AMATHUS, city on the south coast of Cyprus, approximately 10 km (6.2 mi.) east of modern Limassol, capital of one of the small kingdoms of the island until the end of the fourth century BCE (34°41′25″ N, 33°12′5″ E). The principal part of the site occupies a small hill 88 m (289 ft.) high; toward the south the hill descends in a gentle slope to the sea, but on the other three sides the site is protected by a natural cliff. To the southeast of the acropolis there is the lower city occupied principally during the Roman period, and the port built at the end of the fourth century. The necropoleis extend all around these populated areas, but the unexcavated summit of the hill, called Viklaes, to the east of the acropolis, seems to have been occupied by a Phoenician sanctuary.

The Greek and Latin literary texts concerning ancient Amathus are not numerous. According to the historian Theopompos (fourth century BCE), the city was home to the descendants of the "companions of Kinyras who had been put to flight by the Greeks who accompanied Agamemnon." Pseudo-Skylax on the other hand describes the Amathusians as "autochthonous." The inscriptions discovered at the site confirm that until the beginning of the Hellenistic period the Amathusians wrote and very probably spoke a language that was neither Indo-European nor Semitic, but one that is conventionally called "eteocyprian." However, the dearth of available inscriptions makes translation impossible. Until 1975 the archaeological exploration of Amathus involved only the necropoleis: in 1874–1875 the American consul Luigi Palma di Cesnola had discovered a few spectacular pieces, such as a grand limestone sarcophagus at the New York Metropolitan Museum or a silver cup at the British Museum. The first scientific excavations were carried out in 1893–1894 by a British expedition, followed in 1930 by those of a Swedish expedition directed by Einar Gjerstad. Since 1975, an expedition from the French School of Archaeology

in Athens has opened many sites on the acropolis, in the port, and in many places on the ramparts of the city; these excavations have been concluded by a survey of the territory of this small realm. For its part, the Department of Antiquities of Cyprus has taken charge of the excavation of the lower city and associated tombs, especially in those areas, where sites are threatened by constructions prompted by tourism. [*See the biographies of di Cesnola and Gjerstad.*]

Many sites located close to the city testify to an occupation of the region since the Pre-Pottery Neolithic but, curiously, no important settlement has yet been attested in the Late Bronze Period, when the south coast of Cyprus knew its most important development (despite Cesnola's claims to have discovered oriental cylinder seals and Mycenaean pottery at Amathus). The earliest evidence of occupation of the site dates to the eleventh century, but this consists of no more than a small deposit of pottery found on the slope of the acropolis and, perhaps, of the tomb situated at the very top of the hill, in the future sanctuary of Aphrodite. The other oldest tombs currently known date no further back than the late Cypro-Geometric I (i.e., the beginning of the tenth century BCE), and a more dense occupation of the site, characterized by the exchanges with Phoenicia and the Aegean world, is attested only in Cypro-Geometric II and III (end of the tenth–eighth century). On the acropolis, the first phases of the sanctuary of Aphrodite and the palace do not date back further than the eighth century.

Regarding the occupation of Amathus in the Cypro-Geometric II–III and at the beginning of the Cypro-Archaic, it is necessary to consider the problem of the identification of the kingdom of Qartihadasht, the Carthage of Cyprus, mentioned both in the dedication of a bronze bowl discovered in the last century in the area of Amathus/Limassol (object offered to Baal of Lebanon by a "governor of Carthage, servant of Hiram, king of the Sidonians," eighth century), and in the list of the Cypriot kings subject to Esarhaddon and Ashurbanipal (seventh century). Given the importance of the Phoenician influence on the material culture and religion of Amathus, it is altogether possible that this "Carthage of Cyprus" referred to Amathus, even if the Phoenicians exerted only a tenuous power there and the majority of the population was made up of "Eteocyprians." To the arguments that result from the studies already published one must add the discovery in 1992, in the west part of the necropolis by the edge of the sea, of a great mass of burials in vases placed on the bare earth. These hundreds of vases, which contain the remains of children or adults, seem to date between the end of Cypro-Geometric and the Cypro-Archaic. This was very probably the Phoenician necropolis of Amathus. In the fifth and fourth centuries, when Cyprus was a part of the Achaemenid Empire, the Phoenician presence at Amathus was visibly limited: all the kings had Greek names. In the absence of inscriptions, only isolated monuments such as anthropoid sarcophagi, brought to light in the necropolis, and fragments of the "throne of Astarte" discovered on the hill of Viklaes, to the east of the acropolis, still testify to the role played in the city by the Phoenicians.

On the acropolis, two sites opened by the French expedition have revealed important information on the history and civilization of Amathus. The first, situated half-way up the hill, explored a large building of which the first two levels date to the end of the Cypro-Geometric and the Cypro-Archaic; these levels are followed by a reconstruction of the whole at the end of the sixth century or the beginning of the fifth and then a destruction around 300. At the moment only the area of the warehouses has been excavated, but there are numerous similarities with the palace of Vouni, on the north coast of Cyprus, excavated by the Swedish expedition of Gjerstad, and consequently there is a good chance that this building on the acropolis is the palace of the kings of Amathus, destroyed no later than the war between Ptolemy I and Demetrios Poliorcete. [*See* Vouni.] The pottery imported from Athens and the quality of the limestone sculpture (among which it is necessary to mention the Hathoric column capital dated around 480, the loveliest example of this type discovered at Cyprus) testify to the wealth of the local princes in the fifth century after the victory of their allies, the Persians, over the Cypriots who joined the revolution on the side of the Ionians (499–497).

Currently the best-known site at Amathus is the sanctuary of Aphrodite, situated at the summit of the acropolis. Cited by the Roman historian Tacitus (*Annals* 3.62) as one of the most important on Cyprus, it was definitely identified in 1979 owing to the discovery of two dedications made by king Androkles, a contemporary of Alexander the Great. These dedications were addressed to "the Cypriot" (Kypria) and to "the Cypriot Aphrodite" (Aphrodite Kypria). The sanctuary developed beginning in the eighth century, no doubt on the site of an older tomb, perhaps that of Ariana-Aphrodite mentioned by Plutarch (*Life of Theseus* 20.30–34, citing the Amathusian historian Paion). Although the ancient cities were devastated in the Roman period and, above all, in the early years of Christianity, some characteristics of the primitive sanctuary can be discerned. There was a large court open to the sky, into which a small natural cave opened. This area was dedicated to the cult down to the fifth century. Two large monolithic vases made of local limestone were also found here, one of which was taken to the Louvre in Paris in 1865; weighing approximately 13,000 kg (14 tons), it has four handles, one of which bears an Eteocypriot inscription. Beneath these handles the vase is decorated with bulls. The water that these vases contained was perhaps used in ablutions of the faithful during rituals practiced in the sanctuary. In the sixth to fifth century a fair number of figurines of the Greek Kore or of the breast-holding Phoenician "Astarte" type were offered. Furthermore, a Hathoric column capital made of limestone, which was found in a

Christian wall near the vases, shows that the local goddess was equivalent to the Egyptian cow-headed Hathor, who was also a goddess of love and fertility. In the Hellenistic period, an inscription suggests that the cult of Isis and Serapis was associated with that of Aphrodite. This association was illustrated by the discovery just under the palace of many terra-cotta figurines, from the end of the Hellenistic period, representing Aphrodite and Isis. In the last quarter of the first century CE a monumental Greek temple was constructed, but with "Nabatean" column capitals of great quality. At the beginning of the seventh century CE the surviving pagan buildings were destroyed for the construction of a church and other Christian buildings. The site was abandoned at the end of the seventh century, when Limassol became the principal urban center of the region.

BIBLIOGRAPHY

Each year a report on the work of the French expedition and the Department of Antiquities is published in the *Bulletin de Correspondance Hellénique*. For monographs on the results of the French expedition, see Pierre Aupert et al., *Amathonte I. Testimonia 1: Auteurs anciens, monnayage, voyageurs, fouilles, origines, géographie* (Paris, 1984), which contains all the literary sources concerning Amathus; Antoine Hermary, with Veronica Tatton-Brown, *Amathonte II. Testamonia 2: Les sculptures découvertes avant 1975* (Paris, 1981); Robert Laffineur et al., *Amathonte III. Testimonia 3: L'orfèvrerie* (Paris, 1986); and Anne Queyel, *Amathonte IV: Les figurines hellénistiques de terre cuite* (Paris, 1988). Antoine Hermary provides a synthesis in French and English, with a detailed bibliography, in "Les fouilles françaises d'Amathonte/The French Excavations at Amathus," in *Kinyras: L'archéologie française à Chypre*, pp. 167–193 (Lyon, 1993). The excavations of the Department of Antiquities are covered in Vassos Karageorghis et al., eds., *La nécropole d'Amathonte: Tombes 110–385*, 6 vols. (Nicosia, 1987–1992). For the early periods and relations with the East, the reader should consult Antoine Hermary, "Amathonte de Chypre et les Phéniciens," in *Phoenicia and the East Mediterranean in the First Millennium B.C.*, edited by Éduard Lipiński, pp. 375–388 (Louvain, 1987); and Vassos Karageorghis and M. Iacovou, "Amathus Tomb 521: A Cypro-Geometric I Group," *Report of the Department of Antiquities of Cyprus* (1990): 75–100, pls. 4–11. A guide of the site, edited by Pierre Aupert, is in press.

ANTOINE HERMARY

Translated from French by Melissa Kaprelian

AMERICAN CENTER OF ORIENTAL RESEARCH.

Located in Amman, Jordan, the American Center of Oriental Research (ACOR) was established in 1968, but its origins belong to the turn of the century. In 1900 the American School of Oriental Research (ASOR) was established in Jerusalem as a permanent research center that would facilitate regional biblical, historical, linguistic, and archaeological studies. After 1967 the school became known as the Albright Institute of Archaeological Research. In the aftermath of the 1967 War, because it is situated in East Jerusalem, it became logistically impossible to continue using the institute as a base of operations for archaeological field projects in Jordan and neighboring Arab countries. Dr. G. Ernest Wright, then president of ASOR, called for the establishment of a new research institute in Amman, and in 1968 an apartment was rented near the first traffic circle on Jebel Amman. Like its predecessor in Jerusalem, the future of the Amman institute was very uncertain at its genesis. Funding was minimal and the new center had neither a library nor other assets.

In 1971 ACOR was legally incorporated and registered in both the United States and Jordan as a nonprofit educational and cultural organization. It is governed by a board of trustees in accordance with its charter and bylaws. Although ACOR is technically an independent organization, it has always maintained a close working relationship with its parent organization, ASOR.

For the first seven years of its existence, ACOR operated with a modest annual budget of less than $25,000 provided by grants from the U.S. Information Agency (USIA), ASOR, and private contributions. Its directorship was a one-year appointment that also carried with it the title "annual professor." In addition to facilitating the research projects of U.S. and Canadian scholars, the directors also taught courses at the University of Jordan and were instrumental in setting up the master's program in archaeology there. The ACOR directors in order of their terms of service between 1968 and 1975 were Rudolph Dornemann, Murray Nichol, Bastiaan van Elderen, Siegfried Horn, Henry Thompson, and George Mendenhall. During those early years a cook was the only full-time employee.

In 1971, the center moved to somewhat larger quarters near the third circle on Jebel Amman and a small library collection was established. The appointment of James Sauer as director in 1975 marked an important turning point for ACOR. Sauer was the first long-term appointment, serving from 1975 to 1981. During his tenure, a hostel was established to provide accommodations for visiting scholars, and the number of research projects working through the center more than doubled. The operating budget tripled and income generated from the hostel and equipment rental made the institute less dependent on external funding sources. By 1977 ACOR had outgrown the third-circle facility and a newly constructed two-story house was rented near the sixth circle on Jebel Amman. In 1980 new fellowships were established with funding from the National Endowment for the Humanities.

The rapid growth of ACOR's projects and program, along with rising rental costs in Amman, spawned a discussion in the late 1970s about the advisability of constructing a permanent facility for ACOR. Crown Prince Hasan ibn Talal encouraged this course of action, pledging his government's support in securing land.

The task of overseeing the fund-raising and construction projects was undertaken by David McCreery, who served as director from 1981 to 1988. Throughout the 1980s, the number of field projects working through ACOR, of long-term appointees, of library volumes, and of resident scholars continued to increase. The public lecture series and field trips to archaeological sites initiated by Sauer grew in popularity.

In June 1986 the new ACOR facility, located at the western edge of Amman, near the university and the British and German archaeological Institutes, opened its doors. The 25,000-square-foot facility comfortably accommodates thirty people, a library, private study carrels, a conservation lab, workrooms, storage rooms, and a lecture room.

Between 1988 and 1994, ACOR was directed by Bert de Vries (1988–1991) and Pierre Bikai (since 1991). Under these most recent directors a Cultural Resource Management program was established in cooperation with the Jordanian Department of Antiquities to protect and conserve endangered sites. ACOR works closely with Jordanian and U.S. governmental agencies to coordinate the interests of the international scholarly community and governmental agencies interested in developing archaeological sites for their touristic and economic value to the country. The ACOR library holds more than twenty thousand volumes, making it one of the best in the region. In 1994, a newly equipped conservation lab was inaugurated and immediately put to use by a U.S./Finnish/Jordanian team working on the fifth–sixth-century Petra papyri. [*See* Petra, *article on* Recent Finds.]

Approximately forty archaeological field projects are currently associated with ACOR. ACOR is today actively promoting the investigation of Jordan's prehistoric and postclassical (Islamic) periods. Although archaeological research has always been the focal point of the institute, throughout the early 1990s the scope of ACOR-sponsored research was broadened dramatically. The institute now offers fellowships in a variety of disciplines under the overall rubric of Near Eastern Studies. The institute houses up to thirty scholars and students on a regular basis and has an overflow capacity of up to seventy during the peak excavation season. ACOR has become a truly international institute.

In 1992 ACOR initiated a new program with the goal of producing high-quality archaeological publications in Jordan. With funding from the U.S. Agency for International Development, the first major ACOR publication—*The Mosaics of Jordan*—appeared in 1993, followed by volumes on the architecture of the Great Temple of Amman and the Jordan Antiquities Database and Information System. A publications endowment has been established to ensure the longevity of ACOR's publication program. In its brief twenty-five-year history, ACOR has undergone several transformations, to take its place, despite political and financial obstacles, as a dynamic research institute in the Near East.

[*See also* Albright Institute of Archaeological Research; American Schools of Oriental Research; *and the biography of Wright.*]

BIBLIOGRAPHY

Bikai, Pierre, ed. *ACOR, the First Twenty-Five Years: The American Center of Oriental Research, 1968–1993.* Amman, 1993.

Kanellopoulos, Chrysanthos. *The Great Temple of Amman: The Architecture.* Amman, 1994.

King, Philip J. *American Archaeology in the Mideast: A History of the American Schools of Oriental Research.* Winona Lake, Ind., 1983.

Palumbo, Gaetano, ed. *JADIS, the Jordan Antiquities Database and Information System: A Summary of the Data.* Amman, 1994.

Piccirillo, Michele. *The Mosaics of Jordan.* Amman, 1993.

DAVID W. MCCREERY

AMERICAN INSTITUTE FOR MAGHREB STUDIES.

Founded in 1984 as a private, nonprofit association to foster research and promote scholarly cooperation between the United States and countries in North Africa known collectively as the Maghreb (Algeria, Libya, Mauritania, Morocco, and Tunisia), the American Institute for Maghreb Studies (AIMS) is supported financially by individual and institutional memberships, as well as by public and private grants. AIMS meets annually in conjunction with the Middle East Studies Association.

AIMS operates an overseas center, the Center for Maghrebi Studies in Tunis (Centre d'Études Maghrébines à Tunis, or CEMAT). CEMAT was established in 1985 under an agreement between AIMS and the Tunisian Ministry of Higher Education and Scientific Research. The ministry provides CEMAT's premises and administrative support, while AIMS contributes an American resident director. CEMAT assists visiting researchers in making contact with local scholars, gaining access to research resources, and securing permissions for fieldwork. It also sponsors lectures and seminars by local and foreign scholars and museum and archaeological site tours. CEMAT maintains a reference library of works in English on the Maghreb, especially American and British dissertations not otherwise readily available in the region. It also possesses a large collection of World War II–vintage topographic maps of the Maghreb.

AIMS sponsors an annual regional conference on a specific topic held on a rotating basis in one of the Maghreb countries. In developing its programs and planning its annual conference, AIMS and CEMAT work closely with an advisory commission composed of Tunisian, Moroccan, Algerian, and American members. AIMS offers grants for travel and research in the Maghreb, mainly for topics in the humanities and social sciences. AIMS also publishes proceedings of its annual conferences and occasional papers. AIMS is a member of the Council of American Overseas Research Centers (CAORC) and is associated with the Tangier American Legation Museum in Morocco.

[*See also* Council of American Overseas Research Centers; Libya; Middle East Studies Association; *and* North Africa.]

JOSEPH A. GREENE

AMERICAN INSTITUTE FOR YEMENI STUDIES.

Until the early 1970s, Yemen, land of the fabled Queen of Sheba and a rich source for classical and Islamic Near Eastern history, was effectively closed to foreigners. In 1970, although a new modernizing government there changed this policy, Western scholars found that fieldwork was being severely hampered by the lack of research facilities and materials. In 1978 the American Institute for Yemeni Studies (AIYS) was founded in Toronto to provide such field support for international scholars in all disciplines and to act as an international clearinghouse for research related to Yemen. By the 1990s other national research institutes had been established in Yemen, notably by the Italian, French, and German governments. AIYS differs from them in its broad scope of disciplinary interest and deliberately international scholarly support.

AIYS is housed at the University of Chicago's Oriental Institute. Its individual membership as of 1995 was 190, drawing from scholars from around the world; there are thirty-six university and museum institutional members.

Archaeology has been a primary beneficiary of the institute. Its lead founding member and first and current president is McGuire Gibson, a Near Eastern archaeologist. The institute has undertaken archaeological projects on its own: in 1993 it carried out an archaeological survey of the proposed highway route between Marib and Shabwa and continued a second season of excavation in the vicinity of Shabwa. Its key role, however, is in providing logistic and liaison support for the numerous member teams working in the country. Several of these groups already figure prominently in the history of archaeology in Yemen. Between 1981 and 1986 the American Foundation for the Study of Man (AFSM), under Chief Archaeologist James Sauer, carried out the first modern excavation in northern Yemen (at Wadi el-Jubah) since the brief 1951 expedition of Wendell Phillips, the founder of AFSM. Under the direction of Edward Keall, in 1982 Toronto's Royal Ontario Museum began the broadest multiseason archaeological survey to date in Yemen, that of the coastal city of Zabid; excavation continued there in 1993.

AIYS also plays a major support role in UNESCO's efforts to conserve the Old City district of Yemen's capital, San'a. AIYS publishes both a Translations and a Development monograph series. Its semiannual bulletin, *Yemen Update* (Chicago, 1979–) reports on all on-going archaeological research in and concerning Yemen.

[*See also* Jubah, Wadi el-; Marib; San'a; Shabwa; Yemen; *and* Zabid.]

BIBLIOGRAPHY

Buringa. Joke. *Bibliography on Women in Yemen.* Editcd by Marta Coll-
    win. AIYS, Yemen Development Series, no. 2. Portland, Ore., 1992.
Croken, Barbara, et al. *Libraries and Scholarly Resources in the Yemen
    Arab Republic.* AIYS, Yemen Guide Series, no. 2. DeKalb, Ill.,
    c.1985.
Tutwiler, Richard, and Sheila Casapico. *Yemeni Agriculture and Eco-
    nomic Change.* AIYS, Yemen Development Series, no. 1. San'a,
    1981.
Wenner, Manfred W., and Leila N. Swanson. *An Introduction to Yemen
    for Researchers and Scholars.* AIYS, Yemen Guide Series, no. 1.
    DeKalb, Ill., c. 1984.

JON MANDAVILLE

AMERICAN INSTITUTE OF IRANIAN STUDIES. Established in 1967 as a nonprofit educational organization to encourage and facilitate Iranian studies, the American Institute of Iranian Studies was founded by a committee composed of Robert H. Dyson, Jr., Richard N. Frye, and Jacob C. Hurewitz. The institute was supported by some twenty universities and museums, each of which nominated a trustee to the governing board, which elected officers to administer the institute.

From 1969 until 1979 the institute operated a center in Tehran, which served as a liaison between North American scholars and the Iranian government. The Tehran center also maintained a small library, issued a quarterly newsletter, hosted informal seminars on current research, and maintained a hostel to provide temporary housing for scholars. During the years the Tehran center was open there was a virtual explosion of research in Iran. Numerous archaeological excavations and regional surveys were conducted, and graduate students and established scholars in almost all humanistic and social science disciplines were well represented in the country. The center was a focal point for interdisciplinary discourse that created a remarkable sense of camaraderie.

Since 1979 the institute has continued to foster research on Iranian topics by offering dissertation grants, essay and translation prizes, and publication subvention. It has supported a bibliographic inventory of resources for Iranian studies in North American libraries and commissioned a survey of the state of Iranian studies in North American universities. In January 1989, the institute convened a conference on Iranian studies at the Arthur M. Sackler Gallery at the Smithsonian Institution in Washington, D.C. Papers were delivered on the state of studies in the following disciplines: literature, history, linguistics, economics, sociology, political science, geography, anthropology, archaeology, and art history. The proceedings of the conference will be published in a special issue of the journal *Iranian Studies.* The archives of the institute are held in the University Museum Archives at the University Museum, University of Pennsylvania.

WILLIAM M. SUMNER

AMERICAN PALESTINE EXPLORATION SOCIETY. A privately funded society for the geographical and archaeological exploration of the Holy Land, the American Palestine Exploration Society (APES) was founded in New York city in 1870. The society's leaders, including Roswell Hitchcock of Union Theological Seminary and J. Henry Thayer of Harvard University, highlighted the conservative theological orientation of the APES in their hope that archaeology would help verify the historical authenticity of the Bible. With that goal in mind, funds were solicited from American universities and church groups and an expedition was recruited to undertake a survey of Transjordan. The work was coordinated with the survey work of the British-sponsored Palestine Exploration Fund in western Palestine.

From the start, the American expedition was plagued by a lack of funds and poor communication with society headquarters in New York. Led by U.S. Cavalry Lieutenant Edgar Z. Steever and naturalist John A. Paine of New York, the American team proceeded to Moab from Beirut in spring 1873. The result was a preliminary (and only roughly triangulated) field map of approximately 500 square miles extending southward from Hesban (Heshbon). Following Steever's resignation in 1874, the APES turned to James C. Lane, a former railroad planner and Civil War hero, to command its subsequent exploration parties. Also appointed at this time was the Reverend Selah Merrill of Andover, Massachusetts as expedition archaeologist.

The second APES expedition departed from Beirut in September 1875 and was considerably more successful than the first. The goal of detailed mapping was abandoned; instead, the team took hundreds of photographs and collected thousands of artifacts and natural specimens. After Lane's resignation in a disagreement over funding, Merrill was placed in charge of APES explorations and led three more expeditions. These were the APES's final expeditions; the organization was never able to muster the resources or trained personnel of its British counterpart. The American Palestine Exploration Society published its last *Statement* in 1877.

[*See also the biographies of Merrill and Thayer.*]

BIBLIOGRAPHY

King, Philip J. *American Archaeology in the Mideast: A History of the
    American Schools of Oriental Research.* Philadelphia, 1983.
Moulton, Warren J. "The American Palestine Exploration Society."
    Annual of the American Schools of Oriental Research 8 (1928): 55–69.
Silberman, Neil Asher. *Digging for God and Country: Exploration, Ar-
    chaeology, and the Secret Struggle for the Holy Land, 1799–1917.* New
    York, 1982.

NEIL ASHER SILBERMAN

AMERICAN RESEARCH CENTER IN EGYPT. Founded in 1948, the American Research Center in Egypt (ARCE) is an organization that assists American institutions conducting archaeological projects in Egypt. Since 1951, an office has been maintained in Garden City, Cairo, where the staff assists resident scholars and fellows and manages ARCE's programs in Egypt. Over the years, many American archaeological projects, such as the Epigraphic Survey of the Oriental Institute of the University of Chicago and the Theban Mapping Project, have worked in Egypt under ARCE's aegis.

Although ARCE's attention first focused on ancient Egypt, its board soon recognized that Egypt had an important role in the modern Middle East. This realization led to a broadening of ARCE's agenda to embrace scholars interested in all aspects of medieval and modern Egypt, resulting, for example, in support for the American University in Cairo's excavations in Fustat, an early Islamic settlement. [*See* Fustat.] ARCE thus aims to provide its members with a better understanding of Egypt, both ancient and modern.

In the past three decades, ARCE has pursued several major initiatives: advancing American and Egyptian collaboration, encouraging research, and assisting scholarly publication. The importance of American and Egyptian cooperation is a high priority. An early and important example of such teamwork was ARCE's involvement in the Nubian salvage operation, and since then restoration of the Sphinx has been the subject of collaboration. The second goal is successfully addressed through the fellowship program, bringing both new and established scholars to Egypt under ARCE's sponsorship. Recently, ARCE has begun the reverse process, sending Egyptian researchers to the United States.

The initial step toward a program of scholarly publication was taken in 1951 when the first issue of the *Newsletter* appeared. It communicated to ARCE's members information about the recent responsibilities and travels of its directors and officers. Now ARCE fellows present the preliminary reports of their projects in this format. The initial volume of the annual *Journal of the American Research Center in Egypt*, a periodical presenting scholarly research on all Egypt's history and culture, was published in 1962. Since then ARCE has expanded its publication program to include monographs and catalogs.

ARCE's headquarters is located in New York City. Members of the board of governors include representatives from research-supporting institutions and scholars and non-academics, who are all elected from a membership that in the early 1990s stood at twelve hundred. In 1985, the first of five regional chapters was formed. These chapters have contributed to a growing membership and expanded ARCE's public programming in the United States.

BIBLIOGRAPHY

American Research Center in Egypt. *Forty Years of Bridging Time and Culture.* New York, 1987. Interesting summary of the organization's goals and accomplishments.

American Research Center in Egypt. Informational pamphlet. New York, 1992. Basic information about the Center's current direction.

DIANA CRAIG PATCH

AMERICAN RESEARCH INSTITUTE IN TURKEY.

Americans have participated in the archaeological exploration of Turkey since the 1881–83 excavations at Assos in the Troad, sponsored by the Archaeological Institute of America just two years after its foundation. Following the establishment of the Republic of Turkey in 1923, archaeologists were joined by scholars in many other disciplines, including historians of all periods, political and social scientists, philologists, anthropologists, and Turcologists. By the early 1960s, it was clear that an organization was needed to assist scholars conducting research in the country.

The American Research Institute in Turkey (ARIT) was founded in 1964 "to promote research on Turkey in ancient, medieval, and modern times in all fields of the social sciences and the humanities." ARIT, the primary representative of American higher education within Turkey, is supported and governed by a consortium of thirty-five universities, museums, and research institutions in the United States and Canada. ARIT's branches in Istanbul and in Ankara, each with a resident director, specialized library, and hostel, provide a wide range of scholarly support services.

From its inception, ARIT has concentrated its resources on a fellowship program that has enabled more than one thousand pre- and postdoctoral researchers to work in Turkey. This includes fellowships to Turkish scholars, awarded through ARIT's in-country counterpart, the *Türk-Amerikan İlmi Araştırmalar Derneği* (Turkish-American Academic Research Association). ARIT also administers an intensive summer program of advanced Turkish-language instruction at Bosphorus University.

Throughout its existence, ARIT has strongly supported archaeological research in Turkey, and four of its six presidents have been prominent in this field: Hans G. Güterbock, who guided the institute through much of its formative decade; Cecil L. Striker; Machteld J. Mellink; and G. Kenneth Sams. In 1993, at the request of the Turkish Ministry of Culture, ARIT assumed responsibility for conducting an annual primary review of all applications from the United States for archaeological excavations and surveys within Turkey.

TONI M. CROSS

AMERICAN SCHOOL OF ORIENTAL RESEARCH IN BAGHDAD.

The idea of an American school of Mesopotamian archaeology in Baghdad was proposed in 1913 by George Aaron Barton to the Archaeological Institute of America (AIA). The AIA appointed a committee with Barton as chair to study the matter and, if feasible, organize the school. In 1919–1920, Albert T. Clay, annual professor at the American School for Oriental Research (ASOR) in Jerusalem, was sent to Baghdad jointly by the AIA committee and the ASOR executive committee to prepare the way for the new school; he arranged for it initially to be sheltered by the American consulate. In 1921, the Mesopotamian committee of the AIA and the executive committee of ASOR in Jerusalem jointly incorporated as the American Schools of Oriental Research, the plural "schools" being an intentional recognition of the planned Baghdad enterprise and other possible undertakings elsewhere in the Near East. In that same year, Mesopotamian committee member Morris Jastrow, Jr., died, and his widow presented the Assyriological portion of his library to the planned school; it reached Baghdad in 1924, where it formed the core of the new school's library. An earlier bequest of books from pioneer Orientalist William Ward for an anticipated American school in Baghdad seems never to have gotten beyond Philadelphia.

On 2 November 1923, Albert T. Clay inaugurated the American School of Oriental Research in Baghdad in the presence of the American consul and officials of the Iraqi and British governments. The school's first-year's program included public lectures on Babylonian history, outreach sessions with Iraqi schoolmasters, and archaeological survey work.

The Baghdad school was always more a research concept than a place. In 1926, Gertrude Bell, honorary director of antiquities for Iraq, offered the school a room for its library in the new Iraq Museum; it remains in that museum, still serving, as ASOR intended in 1926, as "the first nucleus of an archaeological library in that part of the world" (Dougherty, 1926). Despite sporadic plans and hopes, the school would have no building of its own in Baghdad; yet, it managed, over a fifty-year period, to assemble an impressive record of scholarly achievement.

The school was led by a long-term director and staffed by a variety of annual appointees, the most important being the annual professor and the (more junior) fellow. Barton, the first director, (1922–1934), was resident in the United States; subsequent directors spent varying lengths of time in Baghdad when conditions permitted: Ephraim A. Speiser (1934–1947), Albrecht Goetze (1947–1956), Vaughn Crawford (1956–1968), and Robert McC. Adams (1968–1970). Annual professors and fellows included, among others, Adams, Robert Biggs, J. A. Brinkman, Giorgio Buccellatti, Briggs Buchanan, George Cameron, Edward Chiera, A. T. Clay, Crawford, George Dales, Raymond Dougherty, Richard Ellis, McGuire Gibson, Goetze, Cyrus Gordon, Donald Hansen, Alexander Heidel, Bruce Howe, Thorkild Jacobsen, Samuel N. Kramer, Theophile Meek, Albert T. Olmstead, Edith Porada, Speiser, and Leroy Waterman. Beginning in about 1931, the school was overseen by a standing committee of the ASOR board of trustees. The school's

main source of income was an endowment fund bequeathed by James B. Nies.

The school was conceived as an engine for American archaeological activity in Mesopotamia. It played that role both by enabling its directors, annual professors, and fellows to be in Iraq participating in various digs and projects and by directly sponsoring excavations, preferably with other institutions. Between the wars, the Baghdad school jointly supported work at Nuzi with the Iraq Museum and Harvard University; at Tepe Gawra with the University Museum of the University of Pennsylvania and Dropsie College; at Tell Billa and Khafajeh with the University Museum; and at Tell 'Umar with the University of Michigan. After World War II, the school sponsored, with the Oriental Institute of the University of Chicago, several campaigns at Nippur and the Iraq Prehistoric Project (together with related projects in Iran and Turkey) and the Iraq Surface Survey, as well as excavations at al-Hiba with New York University and the Metropolitan Museum of Art (New York City).

Publications sponsored or cosponsored by the school include numerous volumes of Nuzi tablets; the excavations of Nuzi and Gawra; Neugebauer and Sachs (1945); and the following AASOR volumes: Speiser (1941); Kramer (1944); Porada (1947); and Goetze (1956). In 1947, ASOR, at the urging of the Baghdad school committee, began publishing the *Journal of Cuneiform Studies*, which immediately established itself as a leading Assyriological journal. It was founded by Goetze and edited by him until his death in 1971; from 1972 to 1990 it was edited by Erle Leichty. Since 1990 the editor has been Piotr Michalowski of the University of Michigan.

After 1970, as access to Iraq became more restricted and the notion of an ASOR school (or center, as it had come to be called) and professor in Baghdad less tenable, the Baghdad school committee became the committee on Mesopotamian civilization, or, as it is more commonly known, the Baghdad committee. It awards an annual Mesopotamian fellowship to pre- and postdoctoral scholars for research on ancient Mesopotamian civilization, preferably involving some residence in the Near East. It continues to oversee the publication of the *Journal of Cuneiform Studies* and publishes a newsletter, *Mar Šipri*. For several years before the Gulf war, the Committee's McAllister Fund supported excavations at Mashkan-shapir, Abu Salabikh, Tell Hamida, and Deylam.

[*See also* Abu Salabikh; American Schools of Oriental Research; Khafajeh; Mashkan-shapir; Nippur; Nuzi; Tepe Gawra; *and the biography of Speiser.*]

BIBLIOGRAPHY

Dougherty, Raymond. "Reports." *Bulletin of the American Schools of Oriental Research*, no. 22 (1926): 1.

Goetze, Albrecht. *The Laws of Eshnunna*. Annual of the American Schools of Oriental Research, 31. New Haven, 1956.

King, Philip J. *American Archaeology in the Mideast: A History of the American Schools of Oriental Research*. Philadelphia, 1983.

Kramer, Samuel Noah. *Sumerian Literary Texts*. Annual of the American Schools of Oriental Research, 23. New Haven, 1944.

Neugebauer, Otto, and Abraham Sachs. *Mathematical Cuneiform Texts*. American Oriental Series, 29. New Haven, 1945.

Porada, Edith. *Seal Impressions from Nuzi*. Annual of the American Schools of Oriental Research, 24. New Haven, 1947.

Speiser, Ephraim Avigdor. *Introduction to Hurrian*. Annual of the American Schools of Oriental Research, 20. New Haven, 1941.

JERROLD S. COOPER

AMERICAN SCHOOLS OF ORIENTAL RESEARCH.

The history and tradition of the American Schools of Oriental Research (ASOR) are linked to the parent societies that called for its founding more than a century ago. The first academic organization to press for the establishment of a new society with an archaeological focus was the Society of Biblical Literature (SBL), originally founded as the Society for Biblical Literature and Exegesis in 1880. On 13 June 1895, its president, J. Henry Thayer, a specialist in the New Testament at Harvard University, urged the society to establish a school in Palestine that would be able to promote the study of scripture in the very land in which it had taken shape. It was to be called an American School for Oriental Study and Research. Others, notably Henry W. Hulbert, wanted such a school to be located in Beirut and had referred to it as a school of biblical archaeology and philology in the East. [*See the biography of Thayer.*]

Thayer's suggestion to establish a school in Palestine was referred to committee, which consequently published a circular to win the support and confidence of both theological schools and universities. In that document Thayer's colleagues expressed the rationale for establishing an overseas center in this way: "The object of the school would be to afford graduates of American theological seminaries, and other similarly qualified persons, opportunity to prosecute biblical and linguistic investigations under more favorable conditions that can be secured at a distance from the Holy Land; . . . to gather material for the illustration of the biblical narratives; to settle doubtful points in biblical topography; to identify historic localities; to explore and, if possible, excavate sacred sites" (King, 1983, p. 26).

The tone and direction of SBL's 1895 circular clearly express the overriding interest of the founding fathers, which remains to this day, although ASOR's purpose was soon broadened to include nonbiblical aspects of Near Eastern studies. The circular also illustrates the Western bias of "Orientalism," a certain disregard of indigenous culture by those who study a region only in terms of Western and colonial values. At any rate, by 1890 eleven institutions had pledged one hundred dollars each annually, for a period of five years, until a plan for a new school could be implemented.

Another strong supporter of the idea of establishing an overseas research center in the Near East was the American Oriental Society, which formally endorsed the idea in 1896. In 1898 the Archaeological Institute of America (AIA) not only endorsed the proposal, but also pledged an annual subsidy. The AIA had established its own American School of Classical Studies at Athens in 1882 and a comparable school in Rome in 1895, which in 1913 was consolidated with the American Academy in Rome, formerly a fine arts school and enterprise devoted to humanistic research. The president of the AIA in 1899 was Charles Eliot Norton, professor of Fine Arts at Harvard; he pledged his complete support to a school of biblical studies that would soon be established in Jerusalem on the model of the American institutes in Athens and Rome.

By 1900 twenty-one institutions of higher learning—colleges, seminaries, and universities—had been organized into ASOR's first academic consortium. Although most of those institutions were secular universities, theological interest and support were key from the outset. The organizing committee's restatement of goals and objectives, which became the basis of ASOR's future bylaws, reflected a broadened intellectual horizon that would enable ASOR to extend its purview beyond the Levant into the greater Near East and to extend its historical reach and interest beyond the mere "biblical." Its charter also contained an inclusive statement that resonates with an entirely modern spirit: "The School shall be open to duly qualified applicants of all races and both sexes, and shall be kept wholly free from obligations or preferences as respects any religious denomination or literary institution." ASOR's ties with the AIA and SBL were so strong that in the early years all research studies conducted under ASOR auspices were to be published in the journal of either affiliated society—the former publishing archaeological and nonbiblical material, the latter the biblical.

Jerusalem. ASOR's first overseas institute was opened in 1900 in Jerusalem, with Charles C. Torrey, an Old Testament scholar at Yale University, serving as its first director for that year. Torrey, supported by the U.S. consul in Jerusalem, Selah Merrill, himself a distinguished Orientalist, established ASOR's first headquarters in a large room in a hotel in the Jaffa Gate area, launched a lecture program, and began his own series of field explorations. These activities became hallmarks of ASOR institutes' future programs. Without a permanent ASOR facility, American scholars in Jerusalem at the time were dependent on other institutes for library resources. [*See the biography of Merrill.*]

Palestine's unstable political situation at the beginning of the twentieth century, with the emergence of Arab nationalism clashing with Zionism and signaling the collapse of the Ottoman Empire, made significant progress for the Jerusalem school difficult. The political instability, lack of a permanent facility, and annual rotation of directors meant that a program of activities along the lines established by Torrey and his successors was the correct and most stable course for the school. The character of the program, except for excavation, remained intact until 1920, when William Foxwell Albright became the school's first long-term director, serving until 1929, and then again from 1933 to 1936. ASOR's first major field project in the years prior to Albright was the expedition to Samaria (1908–1910) led by George A. Reisner, Clarence S. Fisher, and David G. Lyon, and in 1908 by Gottlieb Schumacher. The report of this project, delayed by World War I, appeared in 1924. [*See* Samaria; *and the biographies of Albright, Reisner, Fisher, and Schumacher.*]

During those years, the Jerusalem school was managed in the United States by committee. Reports on the school's activities and research were given at special meetings or at ASOR meetings held in conjunction with the annual meeting of the SBL or AIA. To all intents and purposes, ASOR and the Jerusalem school were one and the same. In 1907 the Ottoman government recognized the school in Jerusalem as the "American School of Archaeology at Jerusalem." In 1910 the managing committee changed its official name to The American School of Oriental Research in Jerusalem. In 1917 Torrey announced the promise of a gift of $50,000 by Jane Orr Nies to erect a permanent facility in Jerusalem on land that had been purchased in 1909. James A. Montgomery of the University of Pennsylvania and the Protestant Episcopal Divinity School, the Jerusalem school's annual director in 1914–1915, became the chairman of ASOR's managing committee in 1918. At its annual meeting the committee voted to reopen the Jerusalem school the following year (it had been temporarily closed during the war from (1916 to 1918). At that 1918 meeting, Albright was elected Thayer Fellow for 1919. The school reopened in October 1919, with William H. Worrell as director. The first issue of the *Bulletin of the American Schools of Oriental Research (BASOR)*, the journal that was to become the central organ of scholarly communication for ASOR, also appeared in that year. The first issue of ASOR's *Annual* appeared in 1920, edited by four former directors of the Jerusalem school.

The legal incorporation of ASOR in the District of Columbia in 1921 reiterated the plural "Schools" in the title, correctly anticipating the future of other institutes in the Near East, but specifically the imminent start of the school in Baghdad. In 1923 the Egyptian ankh, the symbol of life, inside of which was the eight-pointed Babylonian star, the sign of deity, became the logo of ASOR.

ASOR Presidents. ASOR's presidents form an illustrious group. The work of these individuals represents the height of scholarship in their respective fields.

1921–1933	James A. Montgomery, University of Pennsylvania
1934–1948	Millar Burrows, Yale University
1949–1954	Carl H. Kraeling, University of Chicago
1955–1965	A. Henry Detweiler, Cornell University
1966–1974	G. Ernest Wright, Harvard University
1975–1976	Frank Moore Cross, Harvard University
1976–1982	Philip J. King, Boston College
1982–1988	James A. Sauer, University of Pennsylvania
1988–1989	P. Kyle McCarter, Johns Hopkins University
1990–1996	Eric M. Meyers, Duke University
1996–	Joe D. Seger, Mississippi State University

[*See the biographies of Montgomery, Burrows, Kraeling, and Wright.*]

Baghdad. With the long-term appointment of Albright as director in Jerusalem in 1920, archaeological activities there expanded and the school's future was secured in a way that had not been possible before. Such stability also allowed ASOR to enlarge its horizons to Mesopotamia, where the Baghdad school, originally called the American School of Mesopotamian Archaeology, opened officially in 1923. That school was the first American academic institution in Baghdad; it was housed in a space provided by the American consulate. The Baghdad school, although not a full-fledged institute, had an outstanding library, and from its inception provided an important base from which researchers conducted field surveys and on-site examination of the most important sites in Mesopotamia. Among the best-known excavations conducted from the school were the ASOR-Harvard excavations at Nuzi, particularly from 1925 to 1931. [*See* Nuzi.] Other noteworthy excavations include Tell Billa, Tepe Gawra, Tarkhalan, and Tell Oman. [*See* Tepe Gawra.] Baghdad's first publication, Edward Chiera's *The Joint Expedition with the Iraq Museum at Nuzi*, appeared in 1927.

It soon became clear that there were not sufficient financial resources to support a permanent facility in Jerusalem and a new one in Baghdad. Hence, ASOR's academic managing committee was reorganized in 1929 to include nonacademic, lay members on a board of trustees to broaden its financial base.

The Baghdad school attracted a series of distinguished scholars as annual professors until 1970. Then, for political reasons, it was no longer possible for Americans to be in residence there. Among those who worked out of Baghdad were Ephraim Speiser (1926–1927, 1931–1932), Nelson Glueck (1933–1934, 1942–1946), Samuel Noah Kramer (1946–1947), Thorkild Jacobsen (1953–1954, 1968–1969), Robert McC. Adams (1968–1969), Albrecht Goetze (1955–1956), and McGuire Gibson (1969–1970). [*See the biographies of Speiser, Glueck, and Jacobsen.*] From 1947 to 1956 Goetze served as director of the school; among his most notable achievements was the founding of the *Journal of Cuneiform Studies* in 1947. The 1967 Arab-Israeli War made any future significant ASOR presence in Iraq doubtful. ASOR's last field project prior to the war had been in 1963, but it renewed its fieldwork there in the 1980s. The 1991 Gulf War ended that activity as well.

The annual professorship in Baghdad was converted to a Mesopotamia fellowship following the termination of a physical presence at the school in Baghdad. Today, a committee supervises ASOR's interests in the region and oversees publication of the *Journal of Cuneiform Studies*.

Interwar Period (1919–1945). A remark made by Millar Burrows when he served as director of the Jerusalem school (1931–1932) provides insight into the period between the world wars and is remarkably relevant. Noting the dearth of American archaeologists and the plethora of archaeological activities in Palestine, he observed that most of the funding was American, that most of the leadership of excavations was non-American, and that chief among ASOR's goals was to raise a cadre of "young Americans who would like to take up the fascinating work." The interwar years produced a new generation of leaders in the field in the Near East, yet there was a genuine shortage of qualified Americans to carry forward the aims of ASOR's founders, as well as a shortage of funds to carry them out. Despite the considerable achievements of the Jerusalem and Baghdad schools, politics soon again interfered in the progress of the first half of the twentieth century.

A major figure to emerge during this period was Nelson Glueck, explorer par excellence. Trained in biblical studies at Jena in Germany, Glueck came under the influence of Albright in the late 1920s while digging at Tell Beit Mirsim. There he learned the essentials of stratigraphic archaeology and the basis of ceramic typology. Glueck succeeded Albright as director of the school in Jerusalem in 1936, a position he held three times, first in 1932–1933, again from 1936 to 1940, and finally from 1942 to 1947.

Glueck's major contribution to work in the region was his extensive explorations in Transjordan and the Negev desert. As a result of this enterprise he became fascinated with the history and material culture of the Nabateans. Glueck conducted his surveys while serving as director of the Jerusalem school. He developed his expertise in Nabatean studies from 1952 to 1964, while based at Hebrew Union College (HUC) in Cincinnati, Ohio; he had been a faculty member there since 1928 and became president in 1948. One of his major accomplishments as an administrator was the building of the HUC campus in Jerusalem, which opened in 1963 with an archaeological component he envisioned as the successor to ASOR's Jerusalem school, which had been cut off from Israel as a result of the 1948 War of Independence.

The irony of the situation cannot be overstated. Glueck, president of a theological school for training American Reform rabbis, had explored the territories that largely became part of the Kingdom of Jordan. He founded an archaeological school in Israeli Jerusalem largely because Arab lands had been cut off from Jewish archaeologists after 1948.

However, following the 1967 war and the reunification of Jerusalem, there were two schools in the city devoted to archaeological work, ASOR's Jerusalem school and HUC, later to be renamed the Nelson Glueck School of Biblical Archaeology. [*See* Nelson Glueck School of Biblical Archaeology.] The 1967 war, however, had even far greater implications for ASOR.

ASOR and Its Overseas Centers: 1967–1978. One of the major results of the 1967 war was the Arab boycott of all scholars working in Israeli territory, former territory or newly held, which effectively meant that archaeologists and Near Eastern specialists in other disciplines had to decide whether to continue to work in Israel. If they had worked in Israel they could choose to work in Arab lands, especially in the Hashemite Kingdom of Jordan or in Syria, but could not then continue to work in Israel as well. Because the Baghdad school was defunct, to all intents and purposes, the ASOR board of trustees, headed by G. Ernest Wright of Harvard University, president at the time, decided that the only way for ASOR scholars to continue working on both sides of the Jordan River was to create separate institutes: a separately incorporated Amman center in Jordan administered by its own board of trustees, so that ASOR's historic aims and goals could continue to be pursued unimpeded, and the Jerusalem school to be reorganized along these same lines. The ASOR trustees approved the move in December 1969. The Jerusalem school was renamed the W. F. Albright Institute of Archaeological Research (AIAR); it still occupies the building whose construction was begun in 1924, completed in 1931, and designated a historical landmark by the State of Israel. The Amman center was named the American Center of Oriental Research (ACOR); it moved into a spacious, state-of-the-art facility in 1986.

Both institutes, newly constituted with their own boards of trustees, began their operations in spring 1970. The ASOR board continued to subsidize in part the activities at both schools, but increasingly turned its attention to generating funds for new overseas field projects, publications, and other programmatic activities relating to its annual convention held in conjunction with the SBL and the American Academy of Religion (AAR).

In creating a decentralized ASOR, Wright and the trustees had averted the political repercussions of the Arab-Israeli conflict. The parent organization was, however, still expected to seek and secure funds as before for both centers and to fund field projects on both sides of the Jordan River. ASOR subsidies to the centers continued through the 1980s, but responsibility for raising funds for the overseas centers, their programs, and their buildings began to shift to their own boards.

During the tumultuous period in the region between the 1967 and 1973 wars, ASOR entertained the idea of establishing a center in Beirut that would focus scholarly attention on Lebanon's special heritage of Phoenician culture, in addition to other aspects of its rich material remains. Although the Civil War in Lebanon and ASOR's increased financial responsibilities ultimately precluded undertaking the project, interest in Phoenicia led ASOR scholars to look to two of Phoenicia's principal colonies, Cyprus and Carthage, for the recovery of new data through archaeological excavation. [See Cyprus; Carthage.]

At Carthage, ASOR fulfilled its field objectives from 1975 to 1979 by sponsoring a series of excavations, financed with U.S. federal funds, at Punic and Roman Carthage. During this limited period ASOR supported a new center nearby, the Carthage Research Institute, which served as a base for the excavation and survey work at the site. The western Mediterranean region could not maintain its hold on ASOR's historic constituency, however, which was far more oriented to the east, and the institute closed upon the completion of fieldwork.

Cyprus, the other important Phoenician colony, attracted ASOR's attention in the early 1970s. Encouraged by Wright to engage in fieldwork that would shed further light on Phoenician culture and also establish a definitive typology of Cypriot ceramics, ASOR scholars began excavations at the Cypriot site of Idalion in 1971. Preliminary work at Idalion had involved Wright and three of his former students: Paul Lapp, until his untimely death in 1970; Lawrence Stager; and Anita Walker. Wright's interest in establishing a permanent ASOR facility away from the center of the ancient Near Eastern mainland was further stimulated by his own work at Idalion. Wright died in 1974, four years before the founding of the most recent of ASOR's overseas centers, the Cyprus American Archaeological Research Institute (CAARI), in Nicosia. [See Idalion; and the biography of Lapp.]

Establishing a research center on the island of Cyprus enabled ASOR at long last to enter institutionally into the world of classical archaeology and to provide a bridge between it and Near Eastern archaeology. In fact, Near Eastern sites are replete with remains from the classical period, and ASOR field projects had long dealt with material originating in or influenced by Aegean cultures. The new institute in Nicosia brought formal recognition to ASOR's broader interest in the classical and pre-classical Aegean worlds, for Cyprus in nearly all its periods of human occupation exhibits a meeting or synthesis between Near Eastern and Aegean cultures. Because there was no university on Cyprus until 1993, CAARI had and continues to have a special role in the intellectual life of the country. Like ASOR's other institutes, CAARI cooperates closely with the local department of antiquities and invites scholars of all countries to use its library and facilities. Although ASOR-sponsored excavations on Cyprus have thus far been few, CAARI's presence has nonetheless been influential. The institute's facility is a meeting ground for scholars from all over the world. CAARI moved into elegant renovated quarters in 1991 and, like AIAR and ACOR, is managed by an independent board of trustees and received subsidies from ASOR until 1990.

The establishment of ACOR in 1970, initially a way of continuing traditional patterns of Near Eastern archaeology with a strong biblical focus, also led to a significant widening of ASOR's perspective on archaeology in general and on several subfields in particular. Far more digs were carried out in Jordan at prehistoric sites by Americans than in Israel (where the biblical focus remained a constraint), a reality paralleled also on Cyprus. Archaeology in Jordan began to prosper in new and unanticipated ways. The Late Antique floruit of Transjordanian Christianity, for example, which extended well into the Early Islamic period, has become a special field along with Islamic archaeology, which is also flourishing. With its abundance of U.S. federal funding, ACOR has also enabled cultural resource management—the excavation and restoration of antiquities sites for national and touristic purposes—to set the standard for the entire region. [See Restoration and Conservation; Conservation Archaeology.]

New Directions: 1978–1995. With the decentralization of ASOR and with the operations and programs of the overseas centers run entirely by separate boards, ASOR's historic role in fostering excavations and scholarship has changed. ASOR's home office continues to assist the overseas centers in building their libraries through book and journal exchanges, in communicating with U.S. trustees and scholars, in some banking activities, in preparing and auditing federal grants, and in some fund raising. The approximately 150 colleges, universities, seminaries, and museums that constitute the ASOR consortium of corporate members are by and large the same institutions that send volunteers and students to digs and that support scholars in their academic pursuits at each of the centers.

ASOR's annual convention and its publications are the two major vehicles for facilitating interaction among scholars in the field of ancient Near Eastern archaeological studies. ASOR remains the premier international scholarly organization dedicated to fostering research in the modern Near East. Its record of sustaining its projects through periods of war and political tension has won it valued admiration in the region. The realization of peace treaties between Israel and its neighbors makes the future seem brighter than ever before and should result in new projects in Near Eastern research. Current developments within ASOR and its overseas centers can be followed in its quarterly Newsletter, or more generally in its quarterly journal, The Biblical Archaeologist. ASOR's home office was located on the Johns Hopkins University campus in Baltimore, Maryland; as of July 1996 the office, together with those of the three overseas centers, was relocated to the campus of Boston University, adjacent to the headquarters of the Archaeological Institute of America.

[*See also* Albright Institute of Archaeological Research; American Center for Oriental Research; American School of Oriental Research in Baghdad; Archaeological Institute of America; Cyprus American Archaeological Research Institute; Periodical Literature; *and* Society of Biblical Literature.]

BIBLIOGRAPHY

King, Philip J. *American Archaeology in the Mideast: A History of the American Schools of Oriental Research.* Philadelphia, 1983. The definitive work on ASOR's history, prepared by a past president and commissioned by the ASOR trustees.

ERIC M. MEYERS

AMMAN, capital city of the Hashemite Kingdom of Jordan, located about 88 km (55 mi.) east of Jerusalem, 206 km (128 mi.) south of Damascus, and 335 km (208 mi.) north of ʿAqaba (31°57′ N, 35°56′ E; map reference 238 × 152). In the earliest references, it is designated as ʿAmmān of the Benē ʿAmmôn or as Rabbat Benē ʿAmmôn and is referred to as Bit Ammānu in Assyrian texts. It was renamed Philadelphia at the time of Ptolemy II Philadelphus (283–246 BCE); its earliest name was revived as ʿAmmān in the Islamic period. The Amman district is a fertile area that drops down through rough terrain and occasionally forested hillsides to the Jordan Valley to the west and merges gradually into the steppelike desert to the east. [*See* Jordan Valley.]

The city has a long history dating back to the sixth millennium; remains found in its vicinity date back even earlier, to the Paleolithic period. Jebel Qalʿa, Amman's citadel, was the focus of settlement for thousands of years (see figure 1); numerous sites occupied in many different periods are scattered around the city. Some—Sahab, Tell el-ʿUmeiri, ʿAin Ghazal, and Ṣafut—were significant settlements in size, strategic location, and preserved artifacts. Amman was still flourishing in the tenth century CE according to the Arab historian al-Muqaddasi, but by the fifteenth century it was described as a field of ruins.

Amman was a spectacular Roman, Byzantine, and Umayyad ruin for many centuries until late in the Ottoman period, with impressive stretches of fortification walls, colonnaded streets, and many substantially preserved buildings. Although adventurers made the trip to ancient ruins

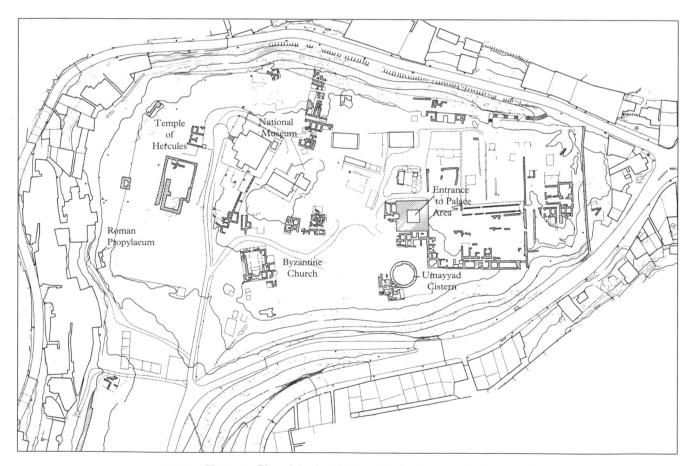

AMMAN.   Figure 1. *Plan of the citadel, Jebel el-Qalʿa.* (Courtesy R. Dornemann)

east of the Jordan River late in that period, serious surveys of sites such as Amman were not initiated until the nineteenth century. Claude R. Conder visited Amman in 1880 and Howard Crosby Butler published the results of the Princeton Archaeological Survey there in 1921. The survey included the careful mapping and examination of ruins in Amman and elsewhere in Transjordan. The gradual resettlement of Amman began in 1878, as a small village among the ruins, with a group of Circassians relocated by Ottoman Turkish authorities. The village expanded after Prince Abdullah chose Amman as the seat of government in 1921 and the Hashemite Kingdom of Jordan was established in 1946. Another expansion of the city took place in the 1970s and 1980s. It now covers more than 900 sq km (558 sq. mi.), with a population approaching two million.

Throughout history, the communication essential to the prosperity of Amman and the surrounding area traversed the desert highway and the Kings Highway. Nelson Glueck's extensive Transjordanian survey (1932–1949) has recently been augmented by surveys connected with the Cultural Resource Management program in Jordan and by the Madaba Plains Project. This has led to a better understanding of land-use patterns and the interrelationships between remains in the countryside (farmsteads, storage towers, and forts) and occupation on the region's tells.

Earliest Remains. The earliest major settlement around Amman is the Neolithic village of 'Ain Ghazal. [See 'Ain Ghazal.] Its occupation extended from the Natufian and Pre-Pottery Neolithic (PPN) periods through an early pottery phase of the Yarmukian culture. The site's most remarkable remains are rectilinear structures with plastered walls from the PPNB that are associated with burials of plastered skulls and caches of the earliest known reed-and-plaster human statuary.

Occupation on the citadel, Jebel Qal'a, can be traced to the Neolithic as well, but, except for Chalcolithic pottery found in a cave on its second plateau, remains are extremely scanty for any period before the Middle Bronze Age. Early Bronze Age tombs have been found on Jebel Qal'a, Jebel et-Taj, Jebel Abdali, and other nearby sites like Umm el-Bighal. The traditions recorded in the biblical accounts of Lot and Abraham indicate an early political Ammonite entity (Gn. 19:28).

Walls of substantial MB buildings and stretches of the fortifications have been excavated on the citadel, but the remains are scattered and do not provide information about how the site was organized then. The importance of the MB settlement is demonstrated by the many rich tomb groups excavated on Jebel Qal'a and in the nearby hills. The assemblage includes distinctive, well-made vessels; scarabs; cylinder seals; metal pins and implements; ivory inlays; beads; and alabaster jars. The chocolate-on-white wares and the white burnished wares from the end of the period and the beginning of the Late Bronze Age are exceptionally finely made. Bronze Age remains have been found on the highest and second plateau of Jebel Qal'a, indicating that the city (at least 20 ha [49 acres] in extent) was probably as large and important as the Iron Age city (see below). Little is known about the periods of occupation on the lowest, or third, plateau in any period because it is covered with modern houses.

The richest remains from Late Bronze Age in the Amman district come at present from the temple at the old airport, northeast of the city. [See Amman Airport Temple.] Excavation of this substantial, isolated building yielded significant quantities of foreign, Cypriot and Mycenaean and luxury wares, and important small finds such as cylinder seals, jewelry, Egyptian scarabs, amulets, and alabaster vessels. Similar artifacts have been found in lesser quantities in Amman-area tombs. An architecturally similar structure was discovered nearby at el-Mabrak (Yassine, 1988, pp. 61–64).

Iron Age. Remains of the Iron Age occupation on Jebel Qal'a have been excavated in more areas and in larger exposures than for earlier periods, but still not enough to reveal a coherent plan. Several centuries of Iron II occupation are represented, but they only give limited insight into the nature of the settlement. Portions of fortification walls and a possible gateway were excavated from the tenth and ninth centuries BCE (Dornemann, 1983, pp. 90–92) and sections of defense walls have been found in several other areas (Humbert and Zayadine, 1992). A large building of late Iron II date has been excavated on the second plateau (Humbert and Zayadine, 1992). The first excavators, an Italian expedition in 1934 (Bartoccini, 1933–1934), suggested that temple remains existed in what was later the precinct of the Roman Temple of Hercules. However, the "temple" was badly destroyed by the Roman construction, making the designation questionable. A large number of rich Iron Age tombs have been excavated in Amman and its vicinity. A tomb near the royal palace provided evidence that spanned the end of the Bronze Age and Iron I and II. This supplements the meager evidence from Jebel Qal'a for the beginning of the Iron Age. The early pottery traditions of the Iron Age show limited examples of the decorated pottery with an Aegean influence that is so characteristic in coastal assemblages from the period. Although a variety of painted pottery is present, the assemblage is dominated by plain wares that show a transition in form and technique from the Bronze Age to Iron II materials. A long list of neighboring sites has now been investigated to help develop a picture of the area's material culture in the Iron Age. Excavation has now been carried out or tombs excavated at Tell el-'Umeiri, Tell Jawa, Tell Safut, Tell Siran, Khilda, Khirbet el-Hajjar, Meqabelein, Rujm el-Malfuf, and Tell Sahab. [See 'Umeiri, Tell el-; Safut, Tell; and Sahab.]

Many of the excavated tomb groups and much of the pottery encountered on the site date to the seventh and sixth centuries BCE. The pottery tradition is impressive for its sophistication. Red-burnished ware is the most distinctive Iron

II feature, with some very sophisticated, finely made examples of bowls and jars. These traditions can be established in a broader regional context with examples that rival the best production in neighboring lands, particularly the Phoenician coast, if they are not examples of imports. A characteristic corpus of simple painted pottery also exists. The tombs demonstrate a burial tradition that includes anthropoid coffins. One of the Ammonite kings, 'Ammi-Nadab, is mentioned on the seal of one of his officers that was found in one of these tombs, in a rich assemblage that also contained gold and silver jewelry and decorated seals. Handmade and mold-made figurines illustrate the period's artistic conventions, with horse and rider figurines predominating that apparently enjoyed special significance locally, at least in the Amman District.

Rabbat Ammon was the capital of an Iron Age state that at times stretched from the modern Wadi Mujib (biblical Arnon River) to the Wadi Zerqa (biblical Jabbok River), from the Jordan River to the desert, and at times beyond. Its relationships with the neighboring states of Moab and Israel, as well as the mighty Assyrian, Neo-Babylonian, and Persian empires shifted constantly and dramatically from peaceful and cooperative to hostile. Amman is first mentioned as a state in the Jephthah stories in *Judges* 3 and 11 and played an important role in the time of David and Solomon. It fought as a member of a coalition of Syrian and neighboring states against Assyrian advances in the ninth century BCE but eventually was incorporated into the Assyrian provincial administration under Tiglath-Pileser III. Two Ammonite rulers of the seventh century BCE are mentioned in an inscription on a Bronze bottle from Tell Siran, adding to the still incomplete series of royal names that extends from the late eleventh through the sixth centuries BCE. Amman came successively under Neo-Babylonian and then Persian rule (under the Persian governorship of Arabia). The Tobiad family, powerful Jewish landowners in the Ammonite area connected with the Jerusalemite priesthood, was influential in Amman in the Persian and Hellenistic periods.

A small corpus of Ammonite inscriptions and an extensive collection of inscribed seals exist. The Amman citadel inscription and the inscribed bottle from Tell Siran are the longest texts. They illustrate an Ammonite language, but it is difficult to translate because the corpus is so limited. Ammonite script is related to Hebrew, Phoenician, Aramaic, and Moabite. [*See* Ammonite Inscriptions.]

A rich collection of sculpture and other small finds indicates many elements incorporated from a variety of sources, particularly Egyptian, Phoenician, Syrian, Assyrian, and Cypriot. The corpus of Ammonite limestone and basalt sculpture continues to grow and is quite distinctive: small freestanding sculptures in the round with unusual and unrealistic proportions, frequently with oversized heads, feet, and other body parts. Some pieces are very polished in their rendering and others heavily stylized (see figure 2).

AMMAN. Figure 2. *Double-faced stone female head.* Iron Age. (Courtesy R. Dornemann)

Hellenistic, Roman, and Early Islamic Periods. Following the conquests of Alexander the Great, Amman was included in the sphere of control of the Ptolemies. Ptolemy II Philadelphus (285–247 BCE) rebuilt the city and renamed it Philadelphia. Amman later came under the control of the Seleucid dynasty of Syria. Only scattered building remains of this period have been encountered so far on the two upper plateaus of the citadel, but the ceramic remains, coins, and other small finds again indicate a rich and prosperous city.

Amman became part of the Roman Empire in the first century BCE, a result of Pompey's victories. Marcus Antonius took the Ammonite area from Nabatean control and gave it to Egypt. With his defeat at Actium (31 BCE), the city regained its independence in the Roman world. A new height in the city's prosperity was reached in the second century BCE, when Trajan's annexation of the Nabatean kingdom reduced competition for trade. Amman was associated with the Decapolis league of cities and was an important stop on a newly established road system, the Via Nova Trajana. [*See* Decapolis.]

Amman's expansion and prosperity in the Roman period (second century CE) entitled it to all of the trappings of a major city in the empire: temples adorned its acropolis and a theater/odeum complex and other impressive structures,

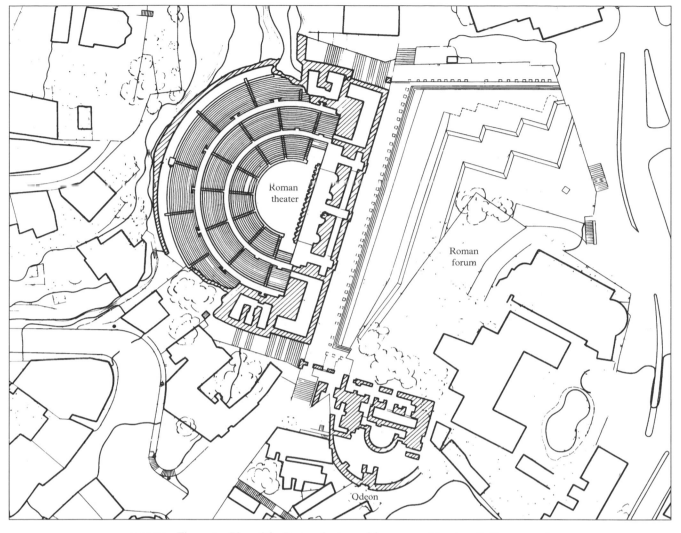

AMMAN.   Figure 3.   *Plan of the Roman theater and forum area.* (Courtesy R. Dornemann)

such as the nymphaeum on the banks of the stream, the Seil Ammon, adorned the downtown area (see figure 3). A system of colonnaded streets organized the city's areas: its *cardo* ran down the main wadi along the Seil Ammon, which was vaulted; its *decumanus* intersected the *cardo* near the present-day Husseni mosque in the downtown area; and another street extended up the slopes of the citadel through a monumental gateway. The partly restored temple on the citadel is now securely attributed to Hercules by two fragments of an inscription on the architrave of the portico that dedicates the building to the emperors Marcus Aurelius Antonius and Lucius Aurelius Verus (161–169 CE), during the governorship of P. Julius Geminius Mercianus (see figure 4).

Philadelphia was the seat of a bishopric in the Byzantine period. Remains of several churches were recorded on early twentieth century maps of the downtown area and a church dedicated to St. Elianos (a third-century Christian martyr from Amman) stands excavated on the citadel. The traditional location of the Cave of the Seven Sleepers, on the outskirts of Amman, at Rajib, near Saḥab, still venerated, traces its origins to Byzantine legends. The Roman city was rebuilt in both the Byzantine and Islamic periods. The ancient name *Amman* was again given to a burgeoning city substantially renewed by walls, streets, and an impressive palace complex on the citadel in the Islamic period. Amman prospered under the Umayyad dynasty and was the granary of the ʿAbbasid province. Following the Islamic period, the city waned in importance, its decline hastened by the shift of major administrative functions to other cities— to Kerak, Ḥeṣban, and Salt, in turn. By the fourteenth century, Abul Fida, an Arab writer, described the city as a ruin.

[*See also* Amman Airport Temple.]

AMMAN. Figure 4. *Temple of Hercules.* (Photograph by Gaetano Palumbo, courtesy ACOR)

BIBLIOGRAPHY

Almagro, Gorbea Antonio. "The Photogrammetric Survey of the Citadel of Amman and Other Archaeological Sites in Jordan." *Annual of the Department of Antiquities of Jordan* 24 (1980); 111–119.

Bartoccini, Renato. "Scavi ad Ammàn della missione archeologica italiana." *Bollettino dell' Associazione interna degli studi mediterranei* 4 (1933–1934): fasc. 4–5, pp. 10–15.

Butler, Howard Crosby. *Ancient Architecture in Syria.* Publications of the Princeton University Archaeological Expedition to Syria, 1904–1905 and 1909, Division 2, Section A. Leiden, 1907. Includes a survey of Amman when major ruins were still visible (see pp. 34–62).

Dornemann, Rudolph H. *The Archaeology of the Transjordan in the Bronze and Iron Ages.* Milwaukee, 1983. Major synthesis of archaeological remains in the Transjordan concentrating on remains from Amman.

Geraty, Lawrence T., et al. "Madeba Plains Project: A Preliminary Report of the 1987 Season at Tell 'Umeiri and Vicinity." *Bulletin of the American Schools of Oriental Research,* no. 26 (1990): 59–88. Report of an ongoing project that is doing major work in the area and integrating remains from stratigraphic excavation with systematic survey of the surroundings.

Glueck, Nelson. *Explorations in Eastern Palestine.* Vol. 3. Annual of the American Schools of Oriental Research, 18/19. New Haven, 1939. One of four volumes in a landmark survey covering all of the Transjordan, including materials from the Amman area.

Harding, G. Lankester. *The Antiquities of Jordan.* London, 1959. Excellent overview of the cultural remains of Jordan.

Homès–Fredericq, Denyse, and J. Basil Hennessy, eds. *Archaeology of Jordan,* vol. 1, *Bibliography and Gazetteer of Surveys and Sites.* Louvain, 1986. Very useful summary of sites and excavations in Jordan.

Humbert, Jean–Baptiste, and Fawzi Zayadine. "Trois campagnes de fouilles à Ammân (1988–1991). Trosième Terrasse de la citadelle (Mission Franco-Jordanienne)." *Revue Biblique* 99 (1992): 214–260.

LaBianca, Øystein S. *Hesban,* vol. 1, *Sedentarization and Nomadization: Food System Cycles at Hesban and Vicinity in Transjordan.* Berrien Springs, Mich., 1990. Innovative work interpreting the remains encountered in surveys of the Hesban and Amman areas.

Landes, George M. "The Material Civilization of the Ammonites." *Biblical Archaeologist* 24 (1961): 65–86. Important synthesis of Ammonite culture and history.

Northedge, Alastair. *Studies on Roman and Islamic Amman: The Excavations of Mrs. C.-M. Bennett and Other Investigations.* Oxford, 1992. Major study of the architecture and other remains of the Roman and Islamic periods in Amman.

Yassine, Khair. *Archaeology of Jordan: Essays and Reports.* Amman, 1988.

RUDOLPH H. DORNEMANN

AMMAN AIRPORT TEMPLE, located at the former Amman Civil Airport in Markeh, Jordan, a northern suburb of Amman. The site lies immediately east of the apron runway, where it joins the first of the main runways, and about 300 m south of the terminal. This single-period site was discovered in 1955 while bulldozers were expanding the runway area. A salvage excavation by M. Salih cleared a square structure to its stone-paved floor; G. Lankester Harding reported on it in 1956 (*Annual of the Department of Antiquities of Jordan* 3:80). Later, Harding identified the structure as an isolated Late Bronze Age temple (*Palestine Exploration Quarterly* 90 [1958]: 10–12). J. Basil Hennessy (1966) subsequently excavated beneath the floor and in probes outside the structure. He interpreted the site as a temple where human sacrifice had taken place and confirmed the structure's isolation (Hennessy, 1985). In 1976, when the site was again threatened by expansion, Larry G. Herr expanded Hennessy's probes in the north. Herr uncovered a square stone structure he interpreted as a platform for cremation, used with the main building, which he suggested had functioned as a mortuary temple ("The Amman Airport Structure and the Geopolitics of Ancient Transjordan," *Biblical Archaeologist* 46 [1983]: 223–229).

The plan of the building was virtually a perfect square, approximately 15 m on a side (see figure 1). A narrow door led through the two-meter-thick north wall to a series of six interconnected, rectangular rooms, of roughly the same size, surrounding a central square room. In the middle of the central room was a circular pillar base or platform/incense altar. All the rooms were paved with flat stones. A shallow earth surface extended about 2 m north of the structures

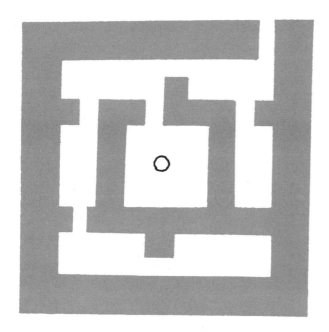

AMMAN AIRPORT TEMPLE. Figure 1. *Plan of the Amman airport temple, based on 1966 excavation plans.* At the northeast is a very small entrance. In the center room is the circular "incense altar" or "column base." (Courtesy ASOR Archives)

doorway, but no other external surface could be distinguished. Six meters to the north was a square stone structure measuring about 4 m per side.

The finds from inside and outside the structure comprised an extremely large proportion of imported finds, including Mycenaean pottery, Egyptian stone vessels and scarabs, and Cypriot pottery. Other objects included hundreds of beads made of semiprecious stones, small strips of gold, bronze and silver jewelry, and bronze weapons. Such items are normally rare at contemporary sites in Jordan. Moreover, in 1976 Herr (1983) collected a total of 1,127 burned adult human bone fragments. Hennessy (1966) had also collected burned human bones in foundation deposits beneath the floors of the structure.

The imported remains span the late Middle Bronze Age through the Late Bronze Age (c. 1700–1200 BCE). Many of them must have been curated in antiquity and preserved through generations as special objects because the local pottery seems to date exclusively to the 13th century BCE, the end of the Late Bronze Age.

Because the burned bones were from adults, the practice of cremation has been suggested, not human sacrifice because that usually involved children. Furthermore, the curated imported objects are typical of Late Bronze tomb deposits, suggesting that the whole site was dedicated to

mortuary activities, which would have included, among other possible activities, cremation and the storage of tomb offerings. Although Semites did not generally practice cremation, Hittites apparently did, which suggests their presence in the region at the time.

BIBLIOGRAPHY

Hankey, Vronwy. "A Late Bronze Age Temple at Amman: I. The Aegean Pottery." *Levant* 6 (1974): 131–159. Technical publication of fifty to sixty imported Mycenaean pots from the 1955 and 1966 excavations studied in the context of other Mycenaean finds from ancient Palestine.

Hankey, Vronwy. "A Late Bronze Age Temple at Amman: II. Vases and Objects Made of Stone." *Levant* 6 (1974): 160–178. Does for the stone vessels what she does for the Mycenaean pottery (see above).

Hennessy, J. Basil. "Excavation of a Late Bronze Age Temple at Amman." *Palestine Exploration Quarterly* 98 (1966): 155–162. In the absence of a final report, the best publication on the 1966 excavations, although it appeared almost immediately after the excavations were completed, leaving many finds unstudied.

Hennessy, J. Basil. "Thirteenth Century B.C. Temple of Human Sacrifice at Amman." *Studia Phoenicia* 3 (1985): 85–104.

Herr, Larry G., ed. *The Amman Airport Excavations, 1976.* Annual of the American Schools of Oriental Research, 48. Winona Lake, Ind., 1983. Final publication of the small 1976 excavations, the most complete synthesis to date.

LARRY G. HERR

AMMON. Ammon and the Ammonites make up one of the national groups east of the Jordan River mentioned by the Bible as enemies or subjects of Israel during the time of the Israelite monarchy, the Iron II period. They are best known from the seventh and sixth centuries BCE, when a large portion of the biblical and Assyrian sources that mention them were written and when their material culture flourished in the archaeological record.

History. According to the Bible (*Gn.* 19:38), the eponymous ancestor of the Ammonites was the son of Abraham's nephew Lot, who had an incestuous relationship with his daughter while fleeing from the destruction of Sodom and Gomorrah. They probably first appeared toward the end of the Late Bronze Age or in the Early Iron I period (c. 1300 BCE), however, when a cluster of sites in the Amman region began to be settled by them or by others perhaps related to them (Amman, Baq'ah Valley, 'Umeiri, Jawa, Hesban, Jalul, Madaba). [*See* Amman; Baq'ah Valley; 'Umeiri, Tell el-; Jawa; Hesban; Madaba.] More such sites will probably be found in the future. These and subsequent settlements display a continuity of material culture throughout Iron I, Iron II, and the Persian period that indicates an ethnic and national continuum (Herr, 1992). National awareness reached its height in the seventh century BCE, when the Pax Assyriaca allowed the greatest intensification of settlement before Roman times and the development of a distinctive material culture that can be called Ammonite.

Several Ammonite kings (or chiefs) are known from a variety of literary evidence. The Israelite chief Saul fought with a corresponding leader in Ammon whom the Bible calls Nahash ("snake"), perhaps in the late eleventh century (*1 Sm.* 11:1–12); and King David dealt with an insult from Hanun the son of Nahash (*2 Sm.* 10:1–4). Tiglath-Pileser III mentions a Shanib as king in a text dated to about 733 BCE (*ANET* 282), and two statues from Amman dated to the eighth–seventh centuries BCE, now in the Amman Museum, may represent kings: they claim to be of Zakur the son of Shanib and Yarih-Ezer. The Assyrian kings Sennacherib and Esarhaddon (early seventh century BCE) mention Budu'il (Assyr., Pudu-Ilu; Riekele Borger, *Die Inschriften Asarhaddons Königs von Assyrien*, Graz, 1956); and Ashurbanipal lists 'Ammi-Nadab in about 667 BCE (*ANET* 294). A small bronze bottle from Tell Siran near Amman lists several kings, including 'Ammi-Nadab I, his son Hissal'il, and 'Ammi-Nadab II, the son of Hissal'il. Finally, a seal impression from Tell el-'Umeiri was made from a seal belonging to a royal official who served a king named Ba'alyasha', undoubtedly the Ba'alis of *Jeremiah* 40:14, who appears in a story dated to about 582 BCE (Herr, 1985).

Probably as a result of Ammonite complicity in the murder of Gedeliah, the Babylonian-appointed governor of Judah, the Babylonians conquered Ammon and made it a part of their empire, but retained the Ammonite king (Josephus, *Antiq.* 10.9:7). The monarchy seems to have lasted through the Babylonian period but was replaced by a Persian provincial system similar to the one in Judah (Herr, 1993). The biblical reference to Tobiah (e.g., *Neh.* 2:10) as a Persian official in Ammon has created the mistaken assumption by some that he was an Ammonite ruler of the Persian government—however, no Ammonite would give his child a Yahwistic (Hebrew) name. Based on the occurrence of the name in two Aramaic tomb inscriptions at 'Iraq el-Amir, the presence of a dynasty of Tobiads in the well-watered Wadi es-Sir west of Amman must be accepted. [*See* 'Iraq el-Amir.] They may have been descendents of Nehemiah's Tobiah. It is possible that this family descended from the renegade prince of Judah, Ishmael, who escaped the Babylonian destruction of Judah by fleeing to Ammon and soon thereafter murdered Gedeliah (*Jer.* 40). The Ammonite presence apparently continued behind the scenes during the classical and Islamic periods, remembered in the name of modern Jordan's capital city, Amman.

Geographical Borders. The territory of Ammon centered around its central city, called Rabbat Ammon in the Bible. The ancient city is still preserved in downtown Amman, Jordan, on the hill called el-Qal'a ("the Citadel"). Although the Iron Age I and Early Iron II territory of Ammon may have had slightly different borders, a common material culture—including pottery, script, and language—has been found at sites from Wadi Zerqa in the north to the southern edge of the hilly region north of Madaba and from the eastern desert to the Jordan Valley (late seventh and sixth centuries BCE), undoubtedly representing the Ammonite culture at its greatest extent (Herr, 1992). Biblical evidence suggests that Moab may have controlled the southern edge of this territory for a time (Hübner, 1992, pp. 131–157). Ammonite holdings in the Jordan Valley may have occurred only during the seventh and early sixth centuries BCE as well.

Settlement Pattern. For most of its history, Ammon was probably little more than a city-state—that is, the capital city ruled a small territory on the central Transjordan plateau with satellite towns and villages in a relatively small hinterland. The finds from small excavations on the citadel of Amman reflect a major urban center (Geraty and Willis, 1986, pp. 11–17). Stone statues of kings or divinities, royal inscriptions such as the Amman Citadel Inscription (Horn, 1969), many small finds of superior quality, and the large size of the site all point to its central importance. Smaller towns in the surrounding hinterland fed the capital with agricultural produce gathered from their own territories. Several have been excavated: Tell Safut, Umm ad-Dananir, Sahab, Jawa, Tell el-'Umeiri, and Hesban. [*See* Safut, Tell; Sahab.] Throughout the region are many small, isolated structures often built of megalithic stones. Early explorers interpreted them as towers for the defense of the capital, but the location of most of them (on spurs of hills with poor visibility above agricultural fields) suggests they were farmsteads. [*See* Farmsteads.] The few larger ones on hilltops may have served as military watchtowers.

The scores of farmsteads in the Ammonite region seem to have produced grain in the valley bottoms and fruit on the slopes. Strong evidence for wine production was found at several farmsteads in the 'Umeiri region. [*See* Viticulture.] Together with an administrative center dating to the seventh–fifth centuries BCE at Tell el-'Umeiri, the Ammonite monarchy seems to have helped farmers construct these farmsteads to produce wine for tribute to Babylon. The farmsteads continued into the Persian period. Along with agriculture, most families kept mixed flocks of sheep and goats, some cattle and a few donkeys and horses.

Social and Political Organization. As was true of most of the tribal groups in the southern Levant during the early stages of the Iron Age, when they originated, individual loyalties were stronger to family and clan than they were to a cohesive "national" entity. The name *běnê 'ammôn*, "sons of Ammon" (e.g., *Gn.* 19:38), seems to suggest an allied group of tribes or clans that, by Iron II, when the biblical name was used, had coalesced into a coherent and permanent tribal confederation with a chief or "king" as head (LaBianca and Younker, 1994). By that time national awareness was developing rapidly, facilitated by a national deity, Milkom, and the development of an Ammonite script out of Aramaic and a dialect (or language) related to other Northwest Semitic language groups (Phoenician, Aramaic, Hebrew, Moabite, and Edomite). Ammon appears as the name of a Persian province on three seals found at Tell el-ʿUmeiri (Larry G. Herr, "Two Stamped Jar Impressions of the Persian Province of Ammon from Tell el-ʿUmeiri," *Annual of the Department of Antiquities of Jordan* 36 [1992]: 163–166).

Ethnicity and Material Culture. Excavations have uncovered a strong similarity in the material culture within the boundaries mentioned above during the Late Iron II and Persian periods. Pottery forms frequently found in the Ammonite region are rare or unknown elsewhere (Lugenbeal and Sauer, 1972). Figurines, although similar to those found all over the southern Levant, have unique features that allow researchers to pinpoint them to the Ammonite region. Inscriptions are written in an alphabetic script similar to that of other Northwest Semitic peoples but with easily definable characteristics that can be isolated to Ammon (Herr, 1978; Aufrecht, 1989). Personal names from inscriptions found in Ammon also reflect typical patterns. Use of the theophoric element *'Il* (or *'El*) is almost universal, in spite of the practice elsewhere of using national deities most of the time. Certain personal names are found more frequently in the Ammonite region than elsewhere, such as Tamakʾil or 'Ilnadab (Aufrecht, 1989, pp. 356–376; Hübner, 1992, pp. 125–129). Many short inscriptions allow a basic description of the Ammonite dialect (Jackson, 1983; Aufrecht, 1987). All of these cultural features indicate that, by the eighth and seventh centuries BCE, Ammonites saw themselves as a distinctive ethnos even though Ammonite pottery may be related more to regional technologies than to ethnic practices.

Religion. Ammonite religion can be characterized as a limited polytheism or heterotheism centered on the deity Milkom, who seems to have been an 'Il (or 'El) divinity based on the bull imagery in Ammonite iconography (especially the seals) and the use of 'Il in the Ammonite onomasticon (Aufrecht, 1989). The few Ammonite names with the theophoric title *baʿal* ("lord") probably refer to Milkom. The Ammonite deity should not be equated with Molek, as 1 Kings 11:7 seems to do (*mlk* is the result of a scribal error for *mlkm*); therefore, Milkom should not be connected with rites of child sacrifice, as the mistaken connection of Molek with Milkom has suggested to some.

The Ammonites were one of the few peoples of the southern Levant to depict deities in statues. Several stone busts wearing crowns formed of the Egyptian atef symbol may depict Milkom (Piotr Bienkowski, *The Art of Jordan*, Liverpool, 1991, p. 41). The large Roman Temple of Hercules on the Ammonite citadel has led some researchers to suggest an identification with that Greek deity (Hübner, 1992, p. 259). The primary goddess was Astarte, probably seen as the consort of Milkom. One seal in typical Ammonite script even mentions a pious worshiper of the goddess at Sidon (Aufrecht, 1989, pp. 145–148). Scores of figurines of nude fertility goddesses probably are meant to depict her.

[*See also* Edom; Moab; *and* Transjordan, *article on* Transjordan in the Bronze and Iron Ages.]

BIBLIOGRAPHY

Aufrecht, Walter E. "The Ammonite Language of the Iron Age." *Bulletin of the American Schools of Oriental Research,* no. 266 (1987): 85–95.

Aufrecht, Walter E. *A Corpus of Ammonite Inscriptions.* Lewiston, N.Y., 1989.

Geraty, Lawrence T., and Lloyd A. Willis. "Archaeological Research in Transjordan." In *The Archaeology of Jordan and Other Studies Presented to Siegfried H. Horn,* edited by Lawrence T. Geraty and Larry G. Herr, pp. 3–72. Berrien Springs, Mich., 1986.

Herr, Larry G. *The Scripts of Ancient Northwest Semitic Seals.* Harvard Semitic Monographs, 18. Missoula, 1978.

Herr, Larry G., ed. *The Amman Airport Excavations, 1976.* Annual of the American Schools of Oriental Research, 48. Winona Lake, Ind., 1983.

Herr, Larry G. "The Servant of Baalis." *Biblical Archaeologist* 48 (1985): 169–172.

Herr, Larry G. "Shifts in Settlement Patterns of Late Bronze and Iron Age Ammon." In *Studies in the History and Archaeology of Jordan,* vol. 4, edited by Ghazi Bisheh, pp. 175–178. Amman, 1992.

Herr, Larry G. "What Ever Happened to the Ammonites?" *Biblical Archaeology Review* 19.6 (1993): 26–35.

Horn, S. H. "The Ammān Citadel Inscription." *Bulletin of the American Schools of Oriental Research,* no. 193 (1969): 2–13.

Hübner, Ulrich. *Die Ammoniter.* Abhandlungen des Deutschen Palästinavereins, 16. Wiesbaden, 1992.

Jackson, Kent P. *The Ammonite Language of the Iron Age.* Harvard Semitic Monographs, 27. Chico, Calif., 1983.

LaBianca, Øystein S., and Randy W. Younker. "The Kingdoms of Ammon, Moab, and Edom: The Archaeology of Society in Late Bronze/Iron Age Transjordan, ca. 1400–500 BCE." In *The Archaeology of Society in the Holy Land,* edited by Thomas E. Levy, pp. 399–415. London, 1994.

Lugenbeal, Edward N., and James A. Sauer. "Seventh–Sixth Century B.C. Pottery from Area B at Heshbon." *Andrews University Seminary Studies* 10 (1972): 21–69.

McGovern, Patrick E. *The Late Bronze and Early Iron Ages of Central Transjordan: The Baqʿah Valley Project, 1977–1981.* University Museum, Monograph 65. Philadelphia, 1986.

LARRY G. HERR

AMMONITE INSCRIPTIONS. Ammonite texts are inscribed on various materials: stone (e.g., from the Amman Citadel), metal (e.g., on a bottle from Tell Siran), pottery (engraved, e.g., from Sahab; or with ink on ostraca, e.g., from Tell Hesban), semiprecious stones (seals), and clay (seal impressions, known as bullae). [*See* Amman; Sahab; Ostraca; Hesban; Seals.] An inscription may be defined as Ammonite according to several categories of criteria: geographic (i.e., the text was found in territory ascribed to the Ammonites), cultural (e.g., iconographic, religious), technical (e.g., paleographic), and linguistic (i.e., grammatical and lexical). Unfortunately, so few inscriptions of significant length are attested, the presently known linguistic features differentiating the Ammonite language from Moabite and Edomite are rather few in number. Thus, other criteria have been used more extensively in defining the Ammonite corpus, for example, iconography and onomastics (Israel, 1979; Naveh, 1982/1987, pp. 105–111; Jackson, 1983; Aufrecht, 1987).

Seals. The largest number of extant Ammonite inscriptions are on seals (Hübner, 1993; pp. 154–155) and date to the eighth–sixth centuries BCE. The earlier ones are classified as Ammonite primarily on the basis of the script and the discovery site; the later ones are classified on the basis of language, onomastics, or iconography but not on the script, which is Aramaic. [*See* Aramaic Language and Literature.] Only a small number have been found in systematic excavations, and it is difficult without scientific analysis to establish which of the objects obtained on the antiquities market are authentic (Hübner, 1993, pp. 132–133; Bordreuil, 1992, pp. 13–38). The history of research and the criteria that directed the formation of the extant corpus of Ammonite seals are listed by Felice Israel (1991, pp. 227–231, and Pierre Bordreuil (1992, pp. 157–159).

Monumental Inscriptions. The circumstances of discovery of the Amman Citadel inscription (*CAI* 59) remain unclear. The beginnings and endings of all of its lines have disappeared but paleographic analysis indicates a date for it at the beginning of the eighth century BCE. Several tempting hypotheses regarding its purpose (bibliography in *CAI*) have been rejected because they are based on incorrect readings. Most probably the inscription refers to an order from the Ammonite national god, Milkom, to build some *mb't*, "entrances." A salvation oracle appears at the end of the inscription.

Because it was reused in Amman's Roman theater and probably conceived by its author as a building inscription, *CAI* 58 is known as the Amman Theater inscription. Unfortunately, the disappearance of the beginning and endings of its lines impedes understanding the text, which is dated only paleographically to the sixth century BCE.

A now damaged inscription of the eighth century BCE (*CAI* 43) is engraved on the base of the statue of *Yrh'zr*, the grandson of the Ammonite king Shanibu. The use of *br* for "son" indicates that the language of the inscription is Aramaic.

Produced as a part of monumental artworks, but nonmonumental in character, are letters and religious symbols engraved on the reverse of eyes fixed in the heads of female statues found on the Amman Acropolis (*CAI* 73). The purpose of these brief inscriptions was to indicate their correct placement to the builders or craftsmen. They have been dated to the seventh century BCE, but on archaeological evidence rather than by paleographic comparisons.

Inscriptions on Metal. An Ammonite inscription, probably royal, from Tell Siran near Amman (*CAI* 78), is engraved on a metal bottle (Hübner, 1992, p. 29). The text contains stylistic literary features known from other Northwest Semitic literature. A cup found in an Iron II tomb at Khirbet Udeinah, also near Amman (Hübner, 1992, pp. 30–31), is engraved with the name of its owner. The inscription is dated to the sixth century BCE on archaeological and paleographic grounds. Two inscribed weights are known whose Ammonite identification remains in doubt (Hübner, 1992, pp. 31–32).

Inscriptions on Clay. Ammonite ostraca have been found at Tell Hesban (*CAI* 65, 80, 94, 137), Tell el-Mazar (*CAI* 144–147), and Tell el-'Umeiri (Herr, 1992). [*See* Mazar, Tell el-; 'Umeiri, Tell el-.] Ulrich Hübner (1992, p. 136) disputes the classification of the Tell Hesban ostraca as Ammonite for topographic reasons. The validity of the geographic argument is doubtful, however, for the oracle of *Jeremiah* 49:1–3 shows that during the sixth century BCE Heshbon/Hesban was under Ammonite control (Lemaire, 1992). In any case, the language and script of these texts is not Moabite. They have been dated on paleographic grounds to the sixth century BCE by Frank M. Cross (1986, pp. 480–484). The Hesban IV ostracon (*CAI* 80) is noteworthy for its grammatical features, which are characteristic of the Ammonite language. Also of note are Tell Mazar ostraca no. 3 (*CAI* 144), a letter from the sixth century BCE that contains a typical epistolary formula, and no. 7 (*CAI* 147), a list of personal names dating to the fifth century BCE that demonstrates the continuity of the traditional Ammonite onomasticon (Heltzer, 1989). Other documents from the site refer to agricultural life and are to be ascribed to the Hellenistic period.

The ostraca from Tell el-'Umeiri remain undeciphered for the most part because of their poor state of preservation. One fragmentary inscription from that site may be classified as sacred (Herr, 1992, pp. 195–196). The ostraca from Deir 'Alla are still unpublished (see the list in Franken and Ibrahim, 1977–1978, p. 79). [*See* Deir 'Alla Inscriptions.] The scholarly consensus that ostracon no. 6231 from Nimrud (*CAI* 47) is a list of typical Ammonite personal names was recently rejected by Bob Becking (1988) and Hübner (1992, pp. 35–37). [*See* Nimrud.] However, the presence of Ammonites at Nimrud has been proved by the discovery of Ammonite pottery on the site (Israel, 1990, p. 234). The possibility of ascribing the document to the Ammonite world therefore remains open. Excavations at Amman (*CAI* 77), Hesban (*CAI* 81), Sahab (Hübner, 1992, p. 39, no. 4), and Khirbet Umm ad-Dananir (Hübner 1992, p. 39, no. 5) have produced pottery engraved with personal names that are more or less fragmentary.

BIBLIOGRAPHY

Aufrecht, Walter E. "The Ammonite Language of the Iron Age." *Bulletin of the American Schools of Oriental Research,* no. 266 (1987): 85–95. Review of Jackson (1983).

Aufrecht, Walter E. *A Corpus of Ammonite Inscriptions (CAI)*. Lewiston, N.Y., 1989. Includes extensive bibliography and photographs.

Becking, Bob. "Kann das Ostrakon ND 6231 von *Nimrūd* für ammonitisch gehalten werden?" *Zeitschrift des Deutschen Palästina-Vereins* 104 (1988): 59–67. Rejects the Nimrud ostracon as Ammonite.

Bordreuil, Pierre. "Sceaux inscrits des pays du Levant." In *Supplément au Dictionnaire de la Bible*, vol. 12, cols. 86–212. Paris, 1992. Detailed overview of inscribed seals from the Levantine area.

Cross, Frank Moore. "An Unpublished Ammonite Ostracon from Hesban." In *The Archaeology of Jordan and Other Studies Presented to Siegfried H. Horn*, edited by Lawrence T. Geraty and Larry G. Herr, pp. 475–489. Berrien Springs, Mich., 1986.

Franken, H. J., and Mo'awiyah Ibrahim. "Two Seasons of Excavations at Deir 'Alla, 1976–1978." *Annual of the Department of Antiquities of Jordan* 22 (1977–1978): 57–79.

Heltzer, Michael. "The Tell el-Mazār Inscription n° 7 and Some Historical and Literary Problems of the Vth Satrapy." *Transeuphratène* 1 (1989): 111–118.

Herr, Larry G. "Epigraphic Finds from Tell el-'Umeiri during the 1989 Season." *Andrews University Seminary Studies* 30 (1992): 187–200.

Hübner, Ulrich. *Die Ammoniter: Untersuchungen zur Geschichte, Kultur und Religion eines transjordanischen Volkes im 1. Jahrtausend. v. Chr.* Abhandlungen des Deutschen Palästinavereins, 16. Wiesbaden, 1992. Extensive bibliography, with particular attention to Ammonite culture.

Hübner, Ulrich. "Das ikonographische Repertoire der ammonitischen Siegel und seine Entwicklung." In *Studies in the Iconography of Northwest Semitic Inscribed Seals: Proceedings of a Symposium Held in Fribourg on April 17–20, 1991*, edited by Benjamin Sass and Christoph Uehlinger, pp. 130–160. Orbis Biblicus et Orientalis, 125. Freiburg, 1993. Overview of Ammonite seals, particularly from the iconographic perspective.

Israel, Felice. "The Language of the Ammonites." *Orientalia Lovaniensia Periodica* 10 (1979): 143–159. Brief overview of the Ammonite language problem, with extensive bibliography.

Israel, Felice. "Note Ammonite II: La religione degli Ammoniti attraverso le fonti epigrafiche." *Studi e Materiali Storico-Religiosi* 56 (1990): 307–337. Ammonite religion as revealed by Ammonite inscriptions.

Israel, Felice. "Note Ammonite III: Problemi di epigrafia sigillare ammonita." In *Phoinikeia Grammata, lire et écrire en Méditerranée: Actes du colloque de Liège, 15–18 novembre 1989*, edited by Claude Baurain et al., pp. 215–241. Namur, 1991. Overview of Ammonite seals.

Israel, Felice. "Note di onomastica semitica 7/2. Rassegna critico-bibliografica ed epigrafica su alcune onomastiche palestinesi: La Transgiordania." *Studi Epigrafici e Linguistici* 9 (1992): 95–114. Transjordanian onomastics, including Ammonite.

Jackson, Kent P. *The Ammonite Language of the Iron Age*. Harvard Semitic Monographs, 27. Chico, Calif., 1983. Attempt to gather all the data for defining the Ammonite language (see Aufrecht 1987).

Lemaire, André. "Heshbôn = Hisbân?" *Eretz-Israel* 23 (1992): 64–70.

Naveh, Joseph. *An Early History of the Alphabet: An Introduction to West Semitic Epigraphy and Palaeography*. 2d ed. Jerusalem, 1987. Discussion of the Ammonite script.

FELICE ISRAEL

AMORITES. The term *Amorite* is the English rendering of the Hebrew word *'ĕmorî*, which is derived in turn from the Akkadian *Amurrūm* or *Amurr-ī-um*. This gentilic is derived from the term *Amurrum*, which corresponds to *mardú* in Sumerian (written MAR.TU), of unknown origin. The Hebrew form is a gentilic from a name such as **'emôr*,

which is otherwise unattested in Hebrew. The English term *Amurrite*, derived directly from the Akkadian version of the word, is preferred by some scholars.

No distinctive archaeological evidence can be convincingly associated with the Amorites. The material culture found in the urban centers where they were active does not exhibit stylistic traits that could positively be identified with them; this holds true even for smaller provincial cities closer to their home ground, such as Terqa. [*See* Terqa.] Nor has any site been identified in the steppe that could even be dated to the period in question. What is left are only tantalizing textual clues that speak of weapons and garments fashioned in the Amorite style and that indicate that they were the suppliers of products associated with herding and with the steppe (salt and a special kind of truffle, both resources still being exploited).

The pertinent textual documentation falls into three major periods:

1. *Second half of the third millennium (2500–2000 BCE):* The relatively few explicit references to Amorites are primarily from southern Mesopotamia and Ebla. [*See* Ebla.] The few individuals so identified are generally labeled in the texts by the Sumerian appellative MAR.TU.

2. *Old Babylonian period (c. 1900–1600).* Large numbers of individuals are mentioned in cuneiform texts of the Old Babylonian period (which corresponds in part to the Middle Bronze Age) who bear names identifiable linguistically as Amorite; they are not, however, explicitly labeled MAR.TU. Besides personal names there are also names for larger social groups and a few words referring to the landscape and the material culture. The majority of the texts were found at Mari. [*See* Mari; Mari Texts.]

3. *Late Bronze Age.* No trace is left of the Amorites in LB Mesopotamia, except that the term *Amurrum* is still in use to denote the west. In Syria there is an important kingdom that bears the name *Amurrum* (written as either MAR.TU or *A-mur-ri* in Akkadian texts from el-Amarna, Ugarit, and Boğazköy and as *'mrr* in Ugaritic texts). [*See* Amarna Tablets; Boğazköy; Ugaritic Inscriptions.]

Origin and Ethnolinguistic Identification. The widespread opinion among scholars is that the Amorites spoke a West Semitic language and were essentially a nomadic population interacting with the urban centers of Syro-Mesopotamia. The nature of this interaction has been variously defined as representing a gradual infiltration (Kupper, 1957; Anbar, 1991) or a symbiosis based especially on economic factors (Rowton, 1987). Their origin would be in the Syrian steppe, and this would have shaped their ethnic identity as essentially nomadic, whatever nuance is placed on this definition.

An alternative interpretation views the Amorites as peasants originally at home in the narrow valley of the Middle Euphrates River (Buccellati, 1992; a preliminary suggestion in this sense was advanced by George Mendenhall and by his student, John T. Luke [Luke, 1965]). From their restricted home base, they would have moved toward the steppe in a successful effort to gain control of the vast steppe rangeland for their flocks. In the process, they would have acquired nomadic traits and developed considerable social and political autonomy. In this perspective, their language represents the rural Semitic counterpart of urban Semitic (Akkadian/Eblaite), vis-à-vis which it retained more archaic traits.

The Amorite language is known almost exclusively from personal names (more than four thousand text occurrences; Gelb, 1980). Like all Semitic names, they consist of recognizable sentences and noun phrases, so that much can be said about phonemics and morphology. Some traits are most distinctive, in comparison to Akkadian, the other Semitic language with which it is contemporary in (Buccellati, 1966; Huffmon, 1965).

1. The phonemic inventory includes more consonants than Akkadian, which is most likely the result of the retention of archaic traits (rather than an innovation); see, for example, the retention of ʿayn, as in ʿammu-rapi, "the paternal uncle has healed."

2. Several morphophonemic alternations are also indicative of archaism: the retention of the middle vowel in šalamatum (compare Akk. šalimtum), "well-being."

3. The third person of the verb retains the original vowel in first position: Yasmaʿ-Dagan, "Dagan hears" (compare Akk. Išmē-Dagan).

4. A possible innovation in the verbal system is the development of a perfect with suffixed pronominal elements: Mutu-malaka, "the man has ruled."

5. The word order retains for the most part the sequence verb–subject, as in Yantin-Erah, "the moon god gives" (compare the semantically equivalent Akkadian name Sîn-iddinam where the word order is inverted).

The few Amorite words that have survived outside onomastics include some toponyms that refer to the local landscape. Thus, nawû connotes the specific perception of the Syrian steppe, dotted with wells and herding camps. As such, it may be an Amorite word (borrowed in Akkadian), while sērum is the proper Akkadian term for the southern steppe, more sharply differentiated from the irrigated agricultural areas. Similarly, the Amorite term yamina refers to the "right (bank of the river)," looking at the Euphrates flowing downstream (only secondarily did it acquire the meaning "south"). Also Amorite are the terms ʾaḫaratum/ʾaqdamatum, which refer, respectively, to "the region behind" or "in front," looking at the river from the western side, where the major cities were located.

Geographic Background. The Amorites represent one of the better-known nonurban societies of the ancient Near East. The question about their origin has a bearing on a proper understanding of their socioeconomic institutions. If they were nomads, or seminomads, on their way to sedentarization, a well-established social organization would have to be assumed that had developed apart from urban civilization and came to face it full blown from a position of outright distinctiveness—and from a distant location that did not allow contact. As indicated above, some scholars prefer to see them instead as peasants in an incipient stage of nomadization, with a persistent geographic and institutional link to the urban setting from which they originated. Like the other rural classes more directly under the sway of city influence, they were essentially "paraurban" at the same time that they were developing antiurban tendencies. It is this perspective that is followed here.

The area of the Middle Euphrates is well within the arid zone (below the 200-millimeter rainfall line), so that agriculture is impossible without irrigation. [See Irrigation.] However, the bed of the river has cut a deep trough in the steppe, and the irrigable area is limited to a narrow strip that is for the most part no more than 10 km (6 mi.) wide; it is called zôr in Arabic, and in Akkadian aḫ Purattim. The urban density in the area of the Middle Euphrates is correspondingly much lower than either in the irrigable alluvium to the south or the rain-fed plains to the north and the west. As a result, a single political center (Mari, for most of the Amorite period) controlled a much vaster territory (comprising valley floor and steppe) than any other Syro-Mesopotamian kingdom.

The exploitation of the steppe as a rangeland for herding turned out to be of major economic benefit: this was possible through the development of a network of wells that provided water for animals (not for cultivation, much less for humans, because it was too brackish). The peasants of the valley floor seized on this opportunity and expanded immeasurably the territorial boundaries and the economic base of the kingdom to which they belonged. Even though it remained without urban settlements until the latter part of the second millennium BCE, the entire steppe was the domain of the Mari herders, who were in direct contact with the cities from the Orontes valley to the Khabur plains.

Social and Economic Institutions. The peasant-herders acquired a high degree of autonomy, simply because the steppe, however temporary a residence it might have remained for them, provided a safe distance from the forces of the central government, which was aiming to enforce regulations pertaining especially to military conscription and taxation. Certainly the government never undertook the task of imposing direct central controls in the steppe: it is significant that of the several military confrontations between the urban government and the various Amorite groups, only those initiated by the kings of the Old Akkadian dynasty speak of battles in the steppe; those involving the kings of Mari take place at or near the cities by the riverbanks.

From this perspective it may be said that the Amorites extended beyond the limits of territorial contiguity the ties that, in the urban and rural settlements, had grown to be intimately dependent on just such contiguity. The *'ibrum* is the smallest unit to transcend the village and function as an extended nonterritorial neighborhood, a "clan." (The term *'ābirum*, could then be understood as "the one who joins the *'ibrum*," referring to an individual escaping from a city to a clan and in this respect it would be semantically, though not morphologically, equivalent to the Hebrew gentilic form *'ibr-î*). The clustering of clans into higher units would result in a tribe, to which the Amorite term *gayum* seems to apply.

The larger tribal families were defined by proper names: Amorites in the earlier periods and then, as a result of demographic increases, a variety of other names, including especially the Haneans and the Suteans. (Mention is found of the "dynasty of Amurrum," referring to the Hammurabi line in Babylon.) The term *mārū yamina*, on the other hand, which is generally interpreted as the name of an analogous tribal family, can best be interpreted as the generic, and potentially derogatory, term for tribal people—literally, "sons of (the steppe on) the right (bank)"—much as *mārū ugārim* and *mārū ālim*—literally, "sons of the irrigation district" and "of the city"—mean, respectively, "peasants" and "urban dwellers." Only clans and tribes were associated with specific geographic areas, but not the larger tribal families.

Political Consolidation. The development of a tribal structure had significant political ramifications. In the first place, the tribe became the major alternative to the territorial state as a factor in providing political cohesion. In other words, while the city had been the first major state organization, which built on the solidarity deriving from territorial contiguity, the tribe achieved similar goals without presupposing such contiguity. What little is known about Amorite tribal history is, therefore, of great consequence in typological terms. The development of putative kinship ties (as evidenced, among other things, by the prominent role played in the onomastics by kinship terms such as *'ammu*, "paternal uncle") bears evidence to this. More important, however, is the ability to retain the cohesion of a large human group over the vastness of the steppe, which was the last region of the Near East to become urbanized. The term *chiefdom* might be used, but such political units had very special dimensions. It is out of this experiment with tribal institutions, which the Amorites were the first to undertake, that the political configuration of a national state eventually arose (as distinct from city-states and expanded territorial states).

A clear indication of the degree of political autonomy achieved comes from the titulary of the leaders. The office of village headman *(sugāgum)* was extended to provide leadership, beyond the village, to the clan. The title *king* (LUGAL or *šarrum*) was used for the leader of the tribe *(gayum)*. It is important to note that only the name of an individual tribe, and never the name of a major tribal family, appears in the royal titulary of these tribal "kings," with the following qualifications.

1. The plural "kings of Hana" and "kings of the sons of *yamina*" (alternating with "fathers of . . .") is not properly a royal title, but rather a descriptive designation for the leaders of individual Hanean or nomadic tribes.

2. The title "king of Hana" (assumed by the rulers of Mari and possibly Terqa, but never used by individual tribal leaders) may be understood as programmatic in that it proclaimed the broad authority of the king of the city-state over the entire tribal family, rather than over any single tribe.

3. The Old Babylonian title *wakil Amurrim*, "leader of Amurrum" (translated as "general"), may be a carry-over into the urban sphere of the position of the minor tribal kings after their political and military integration had taken place: a "king of Amnanum," for instance, would be called leader of Amurrum after he was absorbed within the military cadre of Babylon. From there the title would have assumed the generic connotation of "military leader, general."

4. The title "king of Amurrum," as found at a later date in Syria, would represent a parallel development, with the added dimension of political independence.

The situation may be summarized as shown in table 1.

Expansion and Assimilation. The tribal entities under the rule of these kings acquired sufficient military strength to pose a threat to the established territorial states. Eventually, in fact, most of these kingdoms of ancient Syro-Mesopotamia were overrun by Amorites. The full dimension of this danger became apparent by the end of the third millennium, when Shulgi and Shu-Sin of the third dynasty of Ur built a defensive system called—presumably in a mixture of Sumerian and Akkadian—BÀD-*murīq-Tidnim*, "the wall (or fortress) that repels Tidnum" (another general name for the Amorites). This may have been a line of watchtowers stretching "like a net" into the steppe on either side of the Euphrates and Tigris Rivers, for a length of some 280 km, or 174 mi. (cf. Wilcke, 1969, p. 9). By the second century

TABLE 1. *Socio-political Categories*

	Generic	Tribal Family	Tribe	Clan
Group	Amurrum, mārū yamina	Hana, Sutū	gayu	hibrum
Leadership				
Tribal			šarrum	sugāgum
Urban		šar Hana	wakil Amurrim	

of the following millennium, most of the royal dynasties of Syro-Mesopotamian city-states were Amorite, least in terms of the linguistic affiliation of the names of their kings. Because it is unlikely that this was purely on account of stylistic preferences, it can be assumed that the name bearers were Amorite not just onomastically, but ethnically.

The counterpart of the political takeover was a thorough "urbanization" of the Amorites—a complete assimilation into the culture of the Syro-Mesopotamian cities. It may not be necessary to speak of the Amorites becoming Mesopotamians if it is accepted that, as a local rural class, they had in fact been Mesopotamian all along. Thus, it may be assumed that those Amorite elements who established themselves as the new ruling dynasties simply became fully urban, from the paraurban that they were, while other segments of the same population remained just as rural and paraurban as they had been. This is the picture that the Mari texts, in particular, paint.

In the area of the Middle Euphrates, the steppe remained the exclusive domain of the peasant population, without the urban leadership ever trying to intervene there directly. After the fall of Mari and then of Terqa as the capital of the Middle Euphrates (by the middle of the second millennium BCE), the entire region underwent a devolution process of deurbanization. The tribes moved their geographic focus to the west, where they eventually established (by about 1300 BCE) the first true steppe-based state, the kingdom of Amurrum. Because of its unique typological traits, this final efflorescence of the Amorites may be regarded as their first true state formation; the other kingdoms called Amorite are so only in terms of the origin of their dynasties and part of the population, but not institutionally.

Ideology and Intellectual History. In the early stages of the confrontation between the Amorites and the southern city-states, Sumerian characterizations are found of the Amorites as nomadic: they "do not bend their knee" (no organized temple cult), they "do not bury their dead" (no permanent cemeteries), they "do not grow grain" (no agriculture—at least at the point of contact in southern Mesopotamia). However, no convincing, independent trace of their culture, and in particular their ideology, was transferred to the urban culture into which they became assimilated.

It is only in the west that such traces may be found, possibly transmitted over the intermediary of the kingdom of Amurru. It has long since been argued that the patriarchal tradition of the Bible can be understood against the setting of Amorite expansion. Because several scholars tend to accept a much later date for the patriarchal tradition, this interpretation is now generally downplayed. There are still, nevertheless, good reasons in its favor, such as the close parallels in onomastics (e.g., Amorite *Yaʿqubum* and Hebrew *Yaʿqob*) and institutions (e.g., the agropastoralist economic

base, the rejection of the urban milieu, the significance of wells).

There is also, however, a more generic argument that bears mentioning. The figures of the patriarchs are relatively modest from the point of view of the court and temple that sanctioned their introduction in the canon. A later process of literary invention would have been likely to present grander figures and more heroic events. If that is not so, it is very likely because the Amorite conquest of the steppe was indeed perceived as epic in its proportions by those who had carried it out in the first place. Similar echoes are found in Mesopotamia—in, for example, the Assyrian king list, which gives the names of earlier kings "who dwelt in tents" and in the retention of Amorite personal names for rulers who had long since lost their nomadic identity. These are, however, no more than echoes; the interaction of the pastoralists with urban culture was too close, and the cultural weight of urban tradition too massive, to allow for the crystallization of any true internal Amorite ideology. The distance (in time and space) resulting from the relocation in the west, and the eventual establishment of a culturally autonomous steppe kingdom, that of Amurru, were possibly the catalysts for such crystallization. If so, the "Amorite" steppe, having remained the last empty, nonurban space of the Fertile Crescent, was to prove, by virtue of its very barrenness, one of the most fruitful bridges across space and time in ancient Near Eastern history.

[*See also* Akkadian; Hebrew Language and Literature; Mesopotamia, *article on* Ancient Mesopotamia; *and* Syria, *article on* Syria in the Bronze Age.]

BIBLIOGRAPHY

Anbar, Moshé. *Les tribus amurrites de Mari*. Orbis Biblicus et Orientalis, 108. Fribourg, 1991. Methodologically in line with Kupper's work; presents an up-to-date, reliable review of the philological evidence.

Archi, Alfonso, et al. *I nomi di luogo dei testi di Ebla (ARET I–IV, VII–X e altri documenti editi e inediti)*. Rome, 1993. Complete list, with a discussion, of all the references from the texts of Ebla to MAR.TU(M).

Buccellati, Giorgio. *The Amorites of the Ur III Period*. Pubblicazioni del Seminario di Semitistica, Richerche 1. Naples, 1966. Historical and linguistic analysis of the earliest phase of Amorite.

Buccellati, Giorgio. "'River Bank,' 'High Country,' and 'Pasture Land': The Growth of Nomadism on the Middle Euphrates and the Khabur." In *Tall al-Hamīdīya 2*, by Seyarre Eichler et al., pp. 87–117. Göttingen, 1990. Presents the evidence from "perceptual" geography as gleaned from the ancient texts and the contemporary landscape.

Buccellati, Giorgio. "Ebla and the Amorites." In *Eblaitica*, vol. 3, edited by Cyrus H. Gordon et al., pp. 85–106. Winona Lake, Ind., 1992. The last in a series of articles dealing with the hypothesis that the Amorites were originally peasants in the process of nomadization.

Gelb, Ignace J. *Computer-Aided Analysis of Amorite*. Chicago, 1980. The most comprehensive and authoritative collection of personal names, each one parsed grammatically, and a variety of alternative listings according to different grammatical categories.

Huffmon, H. B. *Amorite Personal Names in the Mari Texts: A Structural and Lexical Study.* Baltimore, 1965. Still the most detailed and balanced reconstruction of the Amorite language.

Izre'el, Shlomo. *Amurru Akkadian: A Linguistic Study.* 2 vols. Harvard Semitic Studies, 40–41. Atlanta, 1991. Thorough investigation of the second millennium BCE kingdom of Amurru, including an appendix of the history of Amurru by Itamar Singer.

Kupper, J.-R. *Les nomades en Mesopotamie au temps des rois de Mari.* Paris, 1957. Modern classic on the subject.

Kupper, J.-R. *L'iconographie du dieu Amurru dans la glyptique de la Ire dynastie babylonienne.* Brussels, 1961. Argues for a Mesopotamian origin of the eponym divinity of the Amorites.

Luke, John Tracy. "Pastoralism and Politics in the Mari Period." Ph.D. diss., University of Michigan, 1965. Influential dissertation based on George Mendenhall's theory.

Matthews, Victor H. *Pastoral Nomadism in the Mari Kingdom, ca. 1830–1760 B.C.* American Schools of Oriental Research, Dissertation Series, 3. Cambridge, Mass., 1978.

Podany, A. H. "A Middle Babylonian Date for the Ḫana Kingdom." *Journal of Cuneiform Studies* 43–45 (1991–1993): 53–62. Argues that the cities of Ḫana were located on the Kabur, not the Euphrates.

Rowton, M. B. "The Role of Ethnic Invasion and the Chiefdom Regime in Dimorphic Interaction: The Post Kassite Period." In *Language, Literature, and History: Philological and Historical Studies Presented to Erica Reiner*, edited by Francesca Rochberg-Halton, pp. 367–378. New Haven, 1987. The last in a series of influential articles on the question of nomadism in southwestern Asia at the time of the Amorites.

Wilcke, Claus. "Zur Geschichte der Amurriter in der Ur-III-Zeit." *Die Welt des Orients* 5 (1969): 1–31. The historical evidence for the Amorite invasions in the south at the end of the third millennium.

GIORGIO BUCCELLATI

'AMRIT (ancient Marathus), site located 7 km (4 mi.) south of Tartus, Syria, and 700 m inland from the Mediterranean Sea, behind tall sand dunes, where recent discoveries from the Hellenistic and Roman periods were made. East of the dunes the plain is dominated by a rocky plateau. The dimensions of the ancient town were 3 × 2 km (2 × 1 mi.). Two springs, 1,300 m apart, about 1.5 km from the sea, feed the Nahr 'Amrit to the north and Nahr al-Qubleh to the south. Both flow toward the sea, the first one directly; the second one, which forms an angle to the north, runs along the coast before it joins Nahr 'Amrit close to its estuary.

'Amrit served as the continental port for the island of Aradus/Phoenician Ruad (Arwad). Recent excavations recovered a simple harbor that had sheltered ships. The rocky and arid island of Aradus faces the continent 2.5 km (1.5 mi.) away; it has two large, well-protected deep-water bays that form a natural harbor. When Ugarit declined, Aradus became the principal commercial and naval power on the Syrian coast, as important as Phoenician Sidon to the south. Until Roman times, the entire region depended on the harbors of Aradus and 'Amrit. Ancient historians recount that Alexander the Great spent four days at Marathus while his army conquered Damascus. [*See* Arwad.]

Prior to excavation, the only visible monuments were from the Persian period: funerary towers, two of them called the spindles by the local population and a third that is cube shaped (see below). In addition, two temples were built around a spring: the Ma'abed and a temple at the "spring of the serpents." The latter, although visible long ago, has disappeared entirely: early visitors to the site, M. Maundrell (1697), Richard Pococke (1743), and Ernest Renan (1860), described two sanctuaries there. A small archaeological investigation was undertaken by Maurice Dunand in 1926 at the Ma'abed, but it is only since 1954 that major explorations of the tell and stadium have taken place. The Ma'abed was partly excavated in 1957 and a hypogeum in 1976. [*See the biographies of Renan and Dunand.*]

Led by Dunand, excavations were begun at the tell east of the Ma'abed and south of Nahr 'Amrit. The tell is rectangular, measuring 110 m at its north–south axis and 140 m at the east–west axis. The summit platform is 16.25 m above sea level and the bedrock about 10–11 m. The archaeological occupational layer is about 7–8 m thick. At the northern side of the tell, a main building came to light that is preserved on 24.2 m east–west and to a width of 21.8 m; only the southern wall is preserved in its entire length. The most significant objects from the building date to the end of the Persian period (end of the fifth and the first half of the fourth centuries BCE). During the excavations on the tell, a deep test trench indicated the earliest levels (dated by the ceramics) to be from the end of the third millennium: jugs with small handles and short necks that are decorated with clear, closely spaced horizontal lines.

In the excavated area, eight corbeled tombs were discovered. Small stones formed a circular dome that closed a pit 2.5–3.5 m deep. The skeletons found in the better-preserved tombs were folded over on themselves because the tomb's diameter was not large enough to accommodate an extended body. Among the grave goods were a bronze pin, a fenestrated ax, a semicircular ax, a dagger blade, a terra-cotta cup, a spearpoint, a jug, cream-colored goblets with incised lines, and decorated jars. [*See* Burial Techniques; Grave Goods.]

These silo tombs can now be added to the known forms of burial in Phoenician Syria: their dates vary between the Middle Bronze III and Late Bronze I or II. [*See* Tombs.] These dates are interesting for their potential connection with the Amorite invasion of Phoenicia. 'Amrit lies at the maritime outlet of the Eleutherus valley, which served as one of the main routes of the Amorite invasion.

The site's porticoed temple is known to the local population by the name *Ma'abed*. Excavations were undertaken in 1955 to clarify a few problems resulting from Renan's *Mission de Phénicie* (1864). The Ma'abed was excavated from the rocky slope of gravel near Nahr Marathus. The temple site was completely covered with rubble; only the T-shaped corner pillars and the sanctuary at the center of the building were visible. The 1957 excavation reached the bottom of the basin at a depth of 3 m below the floor level of the portico. The temple's maximum dimensions were 56.23 m in length and 49.5 m in width; the basin was 46.7 × 38.5 m; the total height is 7.7–8 m at the northwestern corner. A channel running northwest carried the water out of the basin.

The excavation removed massive architectural fragments that had rolled into the basin: all were portico elements—pillars, architraves, friezes, and leonine gargoyles—in the Achaemenid Persian style. Among the recovered pottery were fragments of amphorae from Rhodes, stamped handles, and large Megarian bowls as well as incised Pergamon pottery; in the northern section were found numerous fragments of globe-shaped flat-bottom jugs with a small pouring lip on the shoulder and a short neck ending in a strainer, usually with two–five holes, sometimes seven. These jugs may have been receptacles for holy water from the temple.

The pillars recovered are 3 m tall, 1 m × 55–60 cm in section. In addition, blocks of architrave and blind merlons from the crowning, as well as bossage from the covering,

were recovered. These fragments permitted a reconstruction of the *naos* in the center of the basin, where it would have served as a shelter for the idol (see figure 1). This temple, with its wide entrance, flanked by two square towers on the north, and an altar in its middle, is unique. It dates to the time of the Achaemenid expansion into Syria after Cyrus the Great conquered Babylon (539 BCE). It was dedicated to the savior gods Melqart and Eshmun.

The remains from the favissa Dunand discovered in 1926 also date to the two centuries of Persian rule. The favissa is situated 100 m west of the Ma'abed, where it forms an embankment (70 m × 60 m). Until very recently, the local population exploited the favissa for building materials. Dunand found several limestone statues, some of them dressed in the style of the time of Rameses II; others represent Heracles and are similar to the statues at the stairs at Persepolis (Dunand, 1944–1945; 1946–1948). The 1957 excavation added a number of fragments that could be joined to the statuary found in 1926. The statues date to the sixth–fourth centuries BCE. [*See* Persepolis.]

'AMRIT. Figure 1. *The sanctuary after restoration.* (Courtesy N. Saliby)

The stadium at 'Amrit has been known since Renan's excavations (see above). It stands at the northern bend of the Nahr and is 230 m long and 30 m wide. There are seven tiers of seats (each 55 cm deep) on both sides that end in a semicircle with two corridors for passage. On the southern side were foundations for small houses. Stamped handles from Rhodian amphorae were found in test trenches. Roman tombs were hollowed out of the rock. The stadium dates to the fourth century BCE, with continued use through the third century BCE.

The spindles are hypogea topped by funerary monuments. The pyramidal hypogeum consists of a cubic base on which stands a cylinder topped by an eight-sided pyramid. Two irregular steps descend into it, followed by three more leading to the bottom. The interior consists of two chambers, the first with loculi and the second meant to hold the founder of the hypogeum. The pyramidal hypogeum is contemporary with the 'Amrit temple, but the objects found in it date to the period between the fourth and first centuries BCE, indicating that the hypogeum was in use for a long period of time.

The dome hypogeum is a 5.5-meter-high cylinder flanked by four lions and topped by a dome. The upper part has decorative friezes similar to those from the temple. It is 9.5 m high, plus the base. The interior is reached via a slope ending in three steps before the entrance. The internal organization is similar to that of the pyramidal hypogeum. A plan and a section executed during the 1976 restoration rectified the results previously published by Renan (1864).

Across the centuries the builders of the town of 'Amrit found their stone at a quarry whose material is golden in color. The ruins of the town later served as a quarry for construction at Ruad and Tartus. 'Amrit was destroyed in the first century BCE. What remains constitutes a unique Phoenician site, which clearly shows the assimilation of Orient and Occident in its architecture and ceramic artifacts.

BIBLIOGRAPHY

Bordreuil, Pierre. "Le dieu Echmoun dans la région d'Amrith." In *Studia Phoenicia*, vol. 3, edited by Eric Gubel and Éduard Lipiński, pp. 221–230. Louvain, 1985.
Dunand, Maurice. "Les sculptures de la favissa du temple d'Amrit." *Bulletin du Musée de Beyrouth* 7 (1944–1945): 99–107; 8 (1946–1948): 81–107.
Dunand, Maurice. "Recherches archéologiques dans la région de Marathus: Note préliminaire." *Annales Archéologiques Arabes Syriennes* 3 (1953): 165–170.
Dunand, Maurice, et al. "Les fouilles d'Amrith en 1954: Rapport préliminaire." *Annales Archéologiques Arabes Syriennes* 4–5 (1954–1955): 189–204.
Dunand, Maurice, and Nassib Saliby. "Rapport préliminaire sur les fouilles d'Amrith en 1955." *Annales Archéologiques Arabes Syriennes* 6 (1956): 3–10.
Dunand, Maurice, and Nassib Saliby. "Le sanctuaire d'Amrit: Rapport préliminaire." *Annales Archéologiques Arabes Syriennes* 11–12 (1961–1962): 3–12.
Dunand, Maurice, and Raymond Duru. *Oumm el-'Amed.* Paris, 1962.
Dunand, Maurice. "Phénicie." In *Dictionnaire de la Bible, Supplement,* vol. 7, cols. 1141–1204. Paris, 1966.
Dunand, Maurice, and Nassib Saliby. *Le temple d'Amrith dans la Pérée d'Aradus.* Bibliothèque Archéologique et Historique, vol. 121. Paris, 1985.
Dussaud, René. *Topographie historique de la Syrie antique et médiévale.* Bibliothèque Archéologique et Historique, vol. 4. Paris, 1927.
Gawlikowski, Michal. *Monuments funéraires de Palmyre.* Warsaw, 1970.
Maundrell, Henry. *Journey from Aleppo to Jerusalem at Easter, A.D. 1697.* London, 1810.
Renan, Ernest. *Mission de Phénicie.* Paris, 1864.
Rey-Coquais, Jean-Paul. *Arados et sa Pérée aux époques grecque, romaine et byzantine.* Bibliothèque Archéologique et Historique, vol. 97. Paris, 1974.
Saliby, Nassib. "Essai de restitution du temple d'Amrit." *Annales Archéologiques Arabes Syriennes* 21 (1971): 283–288.
Saliby, Nassib. Article in *Congrès international du verre provenant de la côte phenicïenne,* pp. 133–143. London, 1979.
Saliby, Nassib. *Archéologie et histoire de la Syrie.* Vol. 2. Liège, 1989.
Seyrig, Henri. "Aradus et sa Pérée sous les rois Séleucides." *Syria* 28 (1951): 206–220.

NASSIB SALIBY
Translated from French by Ulla Kasten

AMULETS. The Latin term *amuletum* ("an object used as a charm to avert evil") was possibly derived from the Arabic word *hamilet* (something "carried, worn") by the first century CE because the term first appears in the work of Pliny the Elder (*Nat. Hist.* 29.66, 83; 37.50, 118). Amulets are objects made of various types of material, either uninscribed or inscribed, and supposedly charged with supernatural power. The magical properties believed to be inherent in particular plants, animals, stones, and metals often determined the selection of a certain material for an amulet. Amulets function like prayers; they are intended to offer protection from disease, misfortune, or attacks from supernatural beings or to guarantee wealth, success, and victory. In the ancient Near East, they were usually worn on the neck on a cord or chain, but some types of amulets were affixed to houses and places of business. *Lamellae,* a special type of amulet, are thin pieces of inscribed tin, lead, bronze, silver, or gold that were rolled up, placed in small tubes, and then worn on a cord around the neck. Frequently magical letters, words, symbols, or pictures were engraved on semiprecious stones (e.g., hematite, chalcedony, quartz), which are generally called "magical gems." Amulets were also made of perishable animal and vegetable material, such as leather, bone, wax, wood, herbs, roots, linen, and papyrus, and many of these have also survived because of the very dry climate.

Amulets of various types were widely used throughout the ancient Near East, although it is frequently difficult to determine whether small uninscribed objects and statuettes actually functioned as amulets. Furthermore, some items may have had dual functions, serving as amulets in addition to their original function. For example, cylinder seals (engraved with designs, inscriptions, or both), sometimes worn suspended on a cord around the owner's neck occasionally functioned as amulets. Mitannian faience seals from the last half of second millennium BCE probably functioned as both jewelry and amulets. On the other hand, the function of two small seventh-century BCE rectangular limestone plaques with Aramaic inscriptions from Arslan Tash (between Carchemish and Harran in Syria) is clear. One depicts a winged sphinx and a crouching lioness with a serpent's tale swallowing a man and is inscribed with an incantation to protect the house of the strangling nocturnal demons, while the other depicts a person with big eyes and scorpion feet and has two inscriptions, one for protection against the evil eye, and the other to obtain rain. (translations in Beyerlin, 1978, pp. 247–250; pictured in Pritchard, 1969, p. 216, no. 662). During the Persian period (539–330 BCE), many glass amulets in the shape of human heads (both bearded male and female), have been found in tombs in Cyprus, Egypt, and the Syro-Palestinian coast (as well as Spain, Carthage, and Sardinia). This distribution suggests that they were produced and distributed by Phoenicians.

Egyptian Amulets. More amulets are preserved from ancient Egypt than from anywhere else in the ancient Near East. Three Egyptian terms for amulet are *sa* ("protection"), *meket* ("protector") and *uedjau* ("health-maintaining object"). Amulets for the dead were essential features of Egyptian funerary practice. The *Book of the Dead* contains incantations that, when recited, were thought to endow the amulets with magical powers. Sometimes larger than amulets worn by the living, funerary amulets were found on different parts of the body, not just around the neck. Many amulets were wrapped under the bandages. There was an appropriate amulet for each limb of the deceased. There were at least 275 types (Petrie, 1914).

Ushebtis were small funerary statuettes inscribed with the name of the deceased and a magical spell from the *Book of the Dead*. These statuettes were intended to take the place of the deceased when the gods desired work in their fields to be performed. *Scarabs*, representing a type of beetle, made from many materials but typically stone or faience (glazed blue, green, or turquoise), were symbols of the god Khepri (the rising sun), promising the renewal of life in the next world. Other Egyptian amulets represented various parts of the human body and were intended to protect those parts from misfortune or disease.

Greco-Roman Amulets. The three general Greek terms for amulets are *phylakterion* ("safeguard," "preservative") *periapton*, and *periamma* (both meaning "attached," "tied on"). Thousands of Greco-Roman amulets from the first few centuries CE have survived, primarily inscribed on gemstones. These gemstone amulets have been frequently, though mistakenly, called "Gnostic" amulets in the past because of the use of bizarre images (such as a commonly occurring rooster-headed, snake-footed figure) and of *voces*

magicae, that is, "magical words" made up of meaningless, though traditional, strings of vowels and consonants that make no sense in Greek (e.g., "ablathanalba"). These gemstone amulets were worn in rings, bracelets, or as parts of necklaces (Bonner, 1950; Delatte and Derchain, 1964). Some of these amulets consist of an incised image on the obverse and a magical inscription on the reverse, and others have only a magical inscription. The strong influence of Egyptian religion on Greco-Roman magical practices meant that gods like Osiris, Sarapis, Isis, Anubis, and Horus occur frequently on amulets. Favored by magical practitioners were the rooster-headed, snake-footed god and a headless figure variously identified as Iao (a divine name derived from Judaism), Seth, Atum, or Osiris (the last three of Egyptian origin). This iconography is not known from ancient cults. The strong influence of Judaism on ancient magic had a profound effect on the divine names inscribed on amulets, including Iao, Adonai, Sabaoth, and Elohim. The Greek magical papyri contains many spells in which careful instructions are given regarding how to prepare amulets properly and what should be inscribed on them.

Jewish Amulets. The primary Hebrew term for amulet, *qmʿ* comes from a root meaning "to bind", "to tie." The Hebrew Bible has surprisingly few real or imagined references to amulets (*Gn.* 35:4; *Ex.* 32:3; *Jgs.* 8:21, 26; *Is.* 3:18–20; *Zech.* 14:20); only in the fourth reference are they viewed pejoratively, but nowhere are they forbidden. Although most surviving Jewish amulets are from the Roman period, two silver amulets dating from the late seventh century BCE were found at Ketef Hinnom in the vicinity of Jerusalem (Davies, 1991, p. 72, 4.301, 302). [*See* Ketef Hinnom.] One contains the entire priestly blessing in *Numbers* 6:24–26, and the other has an abbreviated form of the same text, which contains the divine name YHWH three times, a text often used or alluded to on later Jewish amulets (Schrire, 1966, pp. 82, 97).

According to *2 Maccabees* 12:40, when Judas examined the bodies of Jews who had fallen in battle, he discovered that "all" of them were wearing *hieromata*, "sacred objects" or "amulets" consecrated to the idols of Jamnia. Phylacteries (from the Greek word *phylakterion*, "means of protection") or *tĕfillîn*, from *tĕfillâ*, "prayer" (*Ex.* 13:9, 16; *Dt.* 6:8; cf. *Mt.* 23:5) are containers holding four Biblical passages: *Ex.* 13:1–10, 11–16; *Dt.* 6:4–9, 11:13–20. The phylactery that is placed on the upper part of the left arm contains just one roll of parchment on which all four passages are written, and that put on the upper forehead contains four separate rolls of parchment. They are traditionally worn by Jewish males during prayer, except on Sabbaths and holy days. Although *tĕfillîn* are distinguished from amulets in the Mishnah (*Shab.* 6.2; 8.3; *Sheq.* 3.2), they are called phylacteries, and they were assumed to exert protective powers on the wearers. The *mĕzûzôt*, which still function as apotropaic amulets, are small containers fixed on doorposts (*Dt.* 6:9). They contain the Biblical texts *Deuteronomy* 6:4–9 and 11:13–20, which mention the name of God ten times, including the tetragrammaton (the four consonants of the Hebrew name for God—YHWH) seven times. Two Jewish magical handbooks, the first from the Talmudic era and the second not later than the eleventh century, are the *Sefer ha-Razim* ("Book of Mysteries"), and the *Harba de Mosheh* ("Sword of Moses") containing instructions for the preparation of amulets.

BIBLIOGRAPHY

Andrews, Carol. *Amulets of Ancient Egypt*. Austin, 1994.
Barkay, Gabriel. "The Divine Name Found in Jerusalem." *Biblical Archaeology Review* 9.2 (1983): 14–19. Popular, illustrated discussion of the two silver amulets covered in more detail in Yardeni (below).
Benoit, Pierre, et al. *Les grottes de Murabba'at*. Discoveries in the Judaean Desert, vol. 2 Oxford, 1961. See pages 80–86 for phylactery and *mezuza* from Wadi Murabba'at, with references to earlier publications of phylacteries among the Dead Sea Scrolls.
Beyerlin, Walter, ed. *Near Eastern Religious Texts Relating to the Old Testament*. Philadelphia, 1978.
Bonner, Campbell. *Studies in Magical Amulets, Chiefly Graeco-Egyptian*. Ann Arbor, Mich., 1950. Important discussion of Greco-Roman amulets and magical gems dating primarily from ca. 100–500 CE.
Bonner, Campbell. "Amulets Chiefly in the British Museum: A Supplementary Article." *Hesperia* 20 (1951): 301–345.
Budge, E. A. Wallis. *Amulets and Superstitions*. London, 1930.
Dauphin, Claudine. "A Graeco-Egyptian Magical Amulet from Mazzuvah." *'Atiqot* 22 (1993): 145–147.
Davies, Graham I. *Ancient Hebrew Inscriptions: Corpus and Concordance*. Cambridge, 1991.
Delatte, Armand, and Phillippe Derchain. *Les intailles magiques gréco-égyptiennes*. Paris, 1964. Important study of Greco-Roman magical gems.
Gager, John G., ed. *Curse Tablets and Binding Spells from Antiquity and the Ancient World*. New York, 1992.
Lise, Giorgio. *Amuleti Egizi/Egyptian Amulets*. Milan, 1988.
Montgomery, James A. "Some Early Amulets from Palestine." *Journal of the American Oriental Society* 31 (1911): 272–281.
Müller-Winkler, Claudia. *Die ägyptischen Objekt-Amulette*. Freiburg, 1987.
Naveh, Joseph, and Shaul Shaked. *Amulets and Magic Bowls: Aramaic Incantations of Late Antiquity*. Jerusalem and Leiden, 1985. Collection of and commentary on all Hebrew and Aramaic amulets from the first to the fourth centuries CE from Syria-Palestine, except those published in Montgomery (above).
Petrie, W. M. Flinders. *Amulets: Illustrated by the Egyptian Collection in University College, London*. London, 1914. Important study of Egyptian amulets, lavishly illustrated.
Pritchard, James B. *The Ancient Near East in Pictures Relating to the Old Testament*. 2d ed. Princeton, 1969.
Reiner, Erica. "Plague Amulets and House Blessings." *Journal of Near Eastern Studies* 19 (1960): 148–155.
Schrire, Theodore. *Hebrew Amulets: Their Decipherment and Interpretation*. London, 1966.
Trachtenberg, Joshua. *Jewish Magic and Superstition*. New York, 1939. Contains a chapter devoted to late Talmudic and medieval Jewish amulets (pp. 132–152).
Waegeman, Maryse. *Amulet and Alphabet: Magical Amulets in the First Book of Cyranides*. Amsterdam, 1987. The *Cyranides* is an ancient encyclopedia of magical lore composed in the first or second century CE.
Yardeni, Ada. "Remarks on the Priestly Blessing on Two Ancient Amulets from Jerusalem." *Vetus Testamentum* 41 (1991): 176–185.
Zwierlein-Diehl, Erika, ed. *Magische Amulette*. Opladen, 1992.

DAVID E. AUNE

'AMUQ, a well-watered and extremely fertile plain more than 1,400 sq km (868 sq. mi.) in area, bounded on the north by the Taurus Mountains and on the west by the Kızıldağ extension of the Amanus Mountains. To the northeast the Kürt Dağı rises to the Anatolian plateau, on the east and south the hills of Jebel Sima'an and Jebel 'Ala rise to the Aleppo plateau; and on the southwest, behind the ruins of Antioch on Orontes, rises Jebel Akra. The 'Afrin and Kara Su Rivers flow into the 'Amuq from the east, where they reach a marshy area around the Lake of Antioch. That point is north of a major bend in the Orontes River that flows for more than 644 km (400 mi.) from the south and makes a sharp bend there to the sea. Major connecting roads traverse the area and are well documented throughout history—from the Aleppo area and points south and east, to the coast along the course of the Orontes River. Connections to the Anatolian plateau and Cilicia are made possible through the Bailan Pass through the Amanus Mountains.

The 'Amuq plain is dotted with numerous tells, a strategic selection of which have been investigated. Archaeological remains before the Neolithic period are not well documented at present, but a series of rich cultural sequences continues from that period to the present. The archaeological sequence has been blocked out in phases by the excavations of the Oriental Institute of the University of Chicago carried out between 1933 and 1937 at the important sites of Tell Ta'yinat (36°15' N, 36°22'30" E) on the Orontes 2 km (1 mi.) northwest of Tell 'Atchana and 20 km (12 mi.) east-northeast of Antioch (36°17' N, 36°22'11" E); Tell el-Judeideh; Çatal Höyük, Tell Dhahab, and Tell Kurdu. The excavators designated phases A–Q from the Neolithic through the Hellenistic periods. The ancient capital of Alalakh was excavated by a British expedition in 1937–1939 and 1946–1949 that highlighted the occupation of the Middle and Late Bronze Ages (within phases K–L of the Oriental Institute excavation sequence). [*See* Alalakh.] The British expedition also excavated at Tabara el-Akrad, Tell esh-Sheikh, and al-Mina on the Mediterranean coast. The classical periods were documented primarily through the efforts of the Princeton University excavations at Antioch. [*See* Antioch on Orontes.] Excavations farther south along the Orontes at Qarqur and at 'Ain Dara' to the east on the Afrin have yielded by assemblages very closely related culturally to the 'Amuq in the specific periods that have so far been investigated there. [*See* Qarqur, Tell; 'Ain Dara'.]

The Neolithic sequence in the 'Amuq begins with the Pottery Neolithic. The flint inventory and such pottery as coarse simple wares; dark-faced burnished wares with incised, impressed, and washed variants; and brittle and other painted wares characterize the assemblage. It is further articulated by period-typical pendants and stamp seals, stone tools, and worked bone.

The sequence continues through the Halaf and Ubaid periods, again well documented by rich ceramic traditions. A tremendous variety of monochrome and bichrome painted wares, characteristic of these phases, represents strong local traditions as well as typical Halaf and Ubaid painted traditions. The latter have wide-ranging connections to well-documented cultures across northern Syria, into the Assyrian heartland, and reaching south into southern Mesopotamia. The long tradition of dark-faced burnished ware ended in phase E, at the end of the Ubaid period. Small finds include both chipped and ground-stone tools, in a decreased quantity from before, and includes a significant quantity of well-made stone bowls, as well as stamp seals, beads, and pendants.

New ceramic and stone-tool traditions are present in 'Amuq phase F, and metal objects are present for the first time and in significant quantities. Flint tools characteristic of the Canaanean industry occur from phase F through phase H. Characteristic ceramic indicators of foreign connections are included among the rich local assemblage of the fourth millennium. The beveled-rim bowls, triangular-lug handles, bent spouts, and other distinctive features of the Late Uruk–Jemdet Nasr period in Mesopotamia are clearly represented in 'Amuq phase F and continue to be present at the beginning of phase G. In phase G the variety of pottery increases, as cultural connections become broader. In addition to the Mesopotamian ceramic influences already mentioned, there are cylinder seals and reserved-slip wares. In addition to the local stamp seals, locally produced cylinder seats also show Mesopotamian influence. Similar definitive features are found in a Gerzean context in Egypt, including multiple-brush painted pottery, incised and impressed wares, and 'Syrian bottles.' Palestinian connections are demonstrated with platter forms, red-surfaced wares with simple and patterned burnished decorations, and comb-impressed surface treatment on hard, high-fired wares.

The third-millennium sequence is represented in exceptional detail. The plain simple wares of phases G–J, including a variety of cup or goblet forms, are established with basic similarities but some geographic variation over a broad area of northern Syria. Red-black burnished ware with connections to southeastern Turkey, also known as Khirbet Kerak ware, is well represented in phases G–I. In phase I, and particularly in phase J, a new, sophisticated painted tradition, characteristic of the end of the Early Bronze Age, is well represented. A good sampling of small finds was also excavated in these phases, ranging from beads, a variety of stone tools, metal implements, and terra-cotta figurines to surprisingly sophisticated human figurines from phase G that were cast in copper by a lost-wax process.

A drastic change occurred in the 'Amuq at the beginning of the second millennium BCE with radical political and cultural shifts. The flourishing EB cultural tradition, well represented at Tell Ta'yinat, ended, and the nearby site of Tell 'Atchana rose to prominence. The ceramic traditions changed significantly at that time. Comb-incised decoration became the most commonly used, though beautiful pieces of painted "Cilician ware" jars, jugs, and bowls are present in limited quantity. Spectacular remains from the middle of the second millennium BCE were preserved at Tell 'Atchana, the site of ancient Alalakh, capital of a region within the kingdom of Yamḫad that had its capital at Aleppo. [See Aleppo.] Palace complexes were excavated in levels VII and IV. The level VII palace dates to the end of the Middle Bronze, primarily to the eighteenth century BCE and is attributed to Yarimlim by C. Leonard Woolley (1955), the site's excavator. The level IV palace dates to early in the Late Bronze Age, primarily in the late fifteenth and early fourteenth centuries BCE, and was labeled the palace of Niqmepa by Woolley, (1955). Rich artistic remains were preserved in the palaces and associated temples, as well as significant archives of cuneiform tablets and the inscribed statue of the seated king Idrimi. This written documentation gives an insight into the history, diplomacy, trade, administrative structures, and many other details of the culture of the period. [See Alalakh Texts.]

The long, continuous sequence of temples was located adjacent to the palaces and not far from a major city gate that is best preserved in level VII and covered by a fortress in levels III–II. Interestingly, the architectural traditions represented in the temple plans changed radically in its rebuildings. Typical Syrian direct-access temples occur but others, including some that seem to have Anatolian inspiration, are also present.

International connections are also demonstrated in the decorated Nuzi and "'Atchana" pottery found in levels IV–II and in the imported Mycenaean and Cypriot wares in the same time range and later. Also, imported Egyptian, Cretan, and Anatolian objects were found in these contexts. The well-built palaces once stood several stories high and were decorated with frescoes. Basalt or limestone orthostats faced the walls of major rooms and courtyards, and wood was heavily used in the construction. The half-timber construction in the level IV palace is particularly well documented.

When Alalakh was destroyed at the end of the Late Bronze Age, political power in the region shifted and again became established at nearby Ta'yinat, as it had apparently shifted from Ta'yinat to Alalakh earlier. The transition period in the twelfth–eleventh centuries BCE is not well represented at either site but is well documented at Tell el-Judeideh and Çatal Höyük. Aegean influence is very clear in the painted pottery of phase N, particularly in its very distinctive shapes and painted designs. There is some development within this pottery tradition down to the eleventh century BCE, but another tradition, characterized by red-washed and burnished pottery, became dominant in about 1000 BCE. That new tradition is also well documented to the south at Tell Qarqur and to the west at 'Ain Dara'. At Ta'yinat it occurs through several phases of a citadel complex characterized by a series of typically Syrian *hilani* buildings and a small temple of direct-axis type but proportioned longer than wide. Luwian hieroglyphic and other inscriptions date the complex to the Neo-Assyrian period, continuing well beyond the reign of Tiglath-Pileser III. Eight- and seventh-century BCE Egyptian, Greek, and Cypriot pottery are better documented in the latest layers of this complex than earlier. In another area of the site a palatial Assyrian building of the seventh and sixth centuries BCE was excavated by the Oriental Institute expedition (Haines, 1971, pp. 61–63, pls. 84, 85, and 109) and "Assyrian palace ware" was among the ceramic materials found in its remains.

The British expedition to Alalakh also excavated a site on the coast that was considered to be the outlet to the sea for the 'Amuq area in the Iron Age. This site, al-Mina, was occupied primarily from the mid-eighth century BCE until the beginning of the Hellenistic period, but also subsequently in the Byzantine and later periods. Iron Age storerooms at al-Mina contained quantities of imported Aegean and Cypriot wares that are also represented in the 'Amuq, but not in the same quantities. As in the 'Amuq, the sequence continues unbroken into the Hellenistic period.

The founding of the city of Antioch by Seleucus I in 300 BCE caused a major political shift in the area. As the city grew to become one of the most important in the ancient world, the 'Amuq plain clearly shifted to a supporting but integral role in its success. The 'Amuq plain was now known by a new designation, the plain of Antioch. The rich culture of the area relied on the newly constructed ports of Seleucia and Laodocia. Antioch was renowned for its beauty in antiquity, though its physical appearance was altered several times by major earthquakes. The Princeton Expedition to Antioch has provided a hint of the greatness of this center in the rich architectural and artistic remains that are part of the cultural materials that were uncovered (Downey, 1961). Antioch continued beyond the classical period as an important Byzantine and then Crusader city. Its fortunes only declined drastically after the destructions suffered at the hands of Muslim and Mongol forces in the thirteenth century.

BIBLIOGRAPHY

Braidwood, Robert J., and Linda S. Braidwood. *Excavations in the Plain of Antioch,* vol. 1, *The Earlier Assemblages, Phases A-J.* Oriental Institute Publications, 61. Chicago, 1960. Major resource detailing the archaeological assemblages of the 'Amuq from the Neolithic through the Early Bronze Age.

Downey, Glanville. *A History of Antioch in Syria: From Seleucus to the Arab Conquest.* Princeton, 1961. Excellent summary of the history of Antioch, reviewing the finds of the Princeton Archaeological Expedition in their historical context.

Haines, Richard C. *Excavations in the Plain of Antioch,* vol. 2, *The Structural Remains of the Later Phases.* Oriental Institute Publications, 95. Chicago, 1971. Final architectural study of the later phases excavated by the Oriental Institute.

Smith, Sidney. *Alalakh and Chronology.* London, 1940. Basic publication and commentary on the cuneiform texts found at Alalakh.

Woolley, C. Leonard. *A Forgotten Kingdom.* London, 1953. Interesting discussion of the excavations at Tell 'Atchana, for a general audience. Must be used with caution because the chronological discussion for the period prior to 2000 BCE has been completely revised.

Woolley, C. Leonard. *Alalakh: An Account of the Excavations at Tell Atchana in the Hatay, 1937–1949.* Oxford, 1955. Major documentation of the archaeological materials and architecture excavated at Tell 'Atchana, but also must be used with caution for the discussion of materials dated before 2000 BCE because the chronology has been completely revised.

RUDOLPH H. DORNEMANN

ANAFA, TEL, small site in the northeastern corner of modern Israel (map reference 2105 × 2869). The site was first excavated between 1968 and 1973 by the Museum of Art and Archaeology of the University of Missouri, under the directorship of Saul Weinberg. These excavations revealed evidence for occupation from the Early Bronze II period through the first century BCE. The remains of the Late Hellenistic era were the best preserved and were striking for the numbers of imported luxury products—fragments of thousands of cast-glass bowls and the red-gloss pottery known as Eastern Sigillata A, as well as hundreds of mold-made lamps and coins of Tyre and Sidon. The principal building uncovered was lavishly decorated with gilded and painted stucco in the manner of the Hellenistic buildings on Delos. Indeed, the variety of finds led Weinberg to speculate that the Late Hellenistic settlement might have been a trade emporium providing amenities for those plying the caravan route from Damascus to Tyre and that was abandoned, never to be reoccupied, when the campaigns of Alexander Jannaeus made the area too dangerous for trade. Study seasons between 1974 and 1977 cast some doubts on these hypotheses and led to the reopening of the site for a second series of excavations between 1978 and 1986. This series was jointly sponsored by the Missouri Museum and the Kelsey Museum of the University of Michigan with Sharon Herbert and Weinberg serving as co-directors. The excavations were funded by the sponsoring universities, the Smithsonian Institution, the National Endowment for the Humanities, and private donors. The first of three projected volumes of final reports on the site appeared in 1994 (Herbert et. al., 1994). There is still no evidence for the ancient name of the settlement. G. Fuks (*Scripta Classica Israelica,* 1979–1980, pp. 178–184) has argued it to be Arsinoe of

Coele-Syria. Arguments against this identification appear in *Tel Anafa* (vol. 1.i, p. 10, note 25).

The second series of excavations at Tel Anafa focused on two issues: the form and function of the Late Hellenistic stuccoed building, only a corner of which had been exposed in the first series; and the date of the final phase of occupation in antiquity. Study had shown substantial numbers of early Roman artifacts at the site but no clearly Roman buildings. With the exposure of more than 50 percent of the stuccoed building by 1986, it was established that this structure was modeled after Greek peristyle private houses. Significant variations from the prototype include Phoenican masonry techniques, an elaborate bath complex, and its large size. All these variations might be attributed to lingering Phoenician customs of the residents of nearby Tyre into whose territory the Late Hellenistic site can be argued to fall. Tyrians are, in fact, the most likely candidates to have built and lived in the structure now thought to be a private country villa rather than a trade center. The Roman occupation was also clarified with the exposure of eleven small dwellings datable to the first century CE. Unlike the Hellenistic remains, the Roman levels showed little evidence of contact with Tyre but were much more closely connected with the economy of the Galilee and Herod Philip's nearby capital of Caesarea Philippi. In summary, the richness of the site and controlled stratigraphic contexts of the finds allow Tel Anafa to serve as a Hellenistic type-site for the Levant, presenting a broader and more closely dated range of Hellenistic artifacts than ever before possible. Its location in the border area between Phoenicia, the Galilee, and the Golan also makes it an important site for studying changing interactions between Greeks, Phoenicians, Ituraeans, and Jews in the Hellenistic and Roman eras.

[*See also* Galilee, *article on* Galilee in the Hellenistic through Byzantine Periods; Golan; Phoenicians; *and* Tyre.]

BIBLIOGRAPHY

Fuks, Gideon. "Tel Anafa: A Proposed Identification." *Scripta Classica Israelica* 5 (1979–1980): 178–184.
Herbert, Sharon C. "The Greco-Phoenician Settlement at Tel Anafa: A Case Study in the Limits of Hellenization." In *Biblical Archaeology Today, 1990: Proceedings of the Second International Congress on Biblical Archaeology, Jerusalem, June–July 1990*, edited by Avraham Biran and Joseph Aviram. Jerusalem, 1993.
Herbert, Sharon C., et al. *Tel Anafa I: Final Report on Ten Years of Excavation at a Hellenistic and Roman Settlement in Northern Israel.* 2 vols. Journal of Roman Archaeology, Supplementary Series, 10.1. Ann Arbor, Mich., 1994. Includes an introduction and chapters on occupational history and stratigraphy, stamped amphora handles, coins, a Tyrian sealing, the geological setting, and vertebrate fauna.
Naveh, Joseph. "Unpublished Phoenician Inscriptions from Palestine." *Israel Exploration Journal* 37 (1987): 25–30.
Weinberg, Saul S. "Tel Anafa: The Hellenistic Town." Brochure for an excavation exhibit, Rockefeller Museum. Jerusalem, 1970.
Weinberg, Saul S. "Tel Anafa: The Hellenistic Town." *Israel Exploration Journal* 21 (1971): 86–109.

SHARON C. HERBERT

ANALYTICAL TECHNIQUES. The traditional archaeological methods of classification and seriation were developed on the basis of the physical appearance of archaeological artifacts, but it is increasingly acknowledged that the material of the artifact also carries information. There is usually no difficulty, for example, describing pottery by its color and texture; it is, however, more difficult to describe artifacts made of rock or metal in this way without being inaccurate (e.g., "green stone") or even wrong. The possibility of identifying the nature of certain materials only by scientific analysis inevitably arises. To extract the maximum information locked in the material of archaeological remains it is often necessary to proceed one step farther to employ a variety of scientific techniques to establish, for example, the identity and geographic sources of the raw materials used or the techniques of manufacture. Thus, applying scientific methods to archaeological objects can simply be regarded as an extension to the sort of visual examination the magnifying lens or binocular microscope do.

Determining chemical components (or elemental analysis) is nowadays rarely accomplished by the classical wet chemical methods (i.e., gravimetric or volumetric quantification by chemical reactions in aqueous solution); it is carried out rather by applying physical techniques based on the properties of molecules, atoms, and atomic nuclei. The common principle of these analytical techniques is the exposure of the sample to some form of energy input (thermal or by irradiation with photons or particles). Exposure results in the excitation of molecules and atoms that either emit, scatter, absorb, or reemit various forms of radiation analyzable with spectroscopic methods.

The choice of any method usually depends on a variety of factors such as sensitivity, selectivity, precision, accuracy, speed, availability, or cost of analysis. Their applicability may depend on the sample matrix, sample size, or on another specific component being absent. Even more important is the sampling step. It has to be ascertained that the sample is truly representative of the whole that it represents. With archaeological objects it is often not possible to remove a sample, so that the application of nondestructive techniques becomes necessary. Sometimes it may not be possible to obtain a pure sample from a heterogeneous object. In this case, it is better to apply a microanalytical method with high lateral resolution. On the other hand, if knowing the average composition of a heterogeneous sample will suffice, the bulk analysis of a relatively large sample may provide more reliable results than any microanalytical method.

Optical Methods. The range of colors to which the human eye is sensitive is only a very narrow range of the electromagnetic spectrum of radiation. Of progressively decreasing wavelength and, hence, increasing energy are the ultraviolet, X-ray, and γ-ray regions of the spectrum, while the infrared and microwave regions have longer wavelengths than visible light. All these regions are used in chemical analysis.

UV-VIS spectroscopy (also called colorimetry) involves measuring the intensity of absorption of visible light. It is therefore restricted to colored substances, usually in solution. Often, not the substance itself but a colored derivative is measured by comparison with standard solutions. Concentrations of elements can be determined in the parts per million range in solutions (1 ppm = 1 $\mu g/g$ = 0.0001%) as well as their valency states and complex species (speciation). This method is regaining importance because it is rather inexpensive and can be applied in the field (e.g., for environmental monitoring and phosphate analysis).

In optical emission spectrometry (OES) the sample to be analyzed is vaporized at high temperatures by means of combustion flames, an electric discharge between electrodes, a laser beam, or a plasma torch. Such a treatment breaks most chemical bonds and excites the outer electrons of some atoms to higher energy levels that emit light in the visible and near ultraviolet region on their return to the ground state. This light consists of a number of sharply defined wavelengths or spectral lines that are characteristic of the particular element excited. Consequently, the determination of the constituent wavelengths in the light emitted by the sample provides the basis for identifying the elements present in the sample while the intensity of the light, at a particular wavelength, provides an estimate of the concentration of the associated element. By comparison with standards of known composition it allows, in principle, the simultaneous determination of up to seventy elements in the range of between 1 ppm and 10 percent with detection limits varying between 1 and 100 ppm in the solid sample.

Although some materials, like metals, can be used directly as electrodes, the method cannot be regarded as nondestructive. For analysis, a small sample, typically 10 mg, has to be removed from the object. The sample is either dissolved or mixed directly with pure graphite powder and placed in a graphite cup, which forms the lower electrode. An electric arc or a spark discharge is struck between this and an upper graphite electrode, thus completely volatilizing the sample and exciting its constituent atoms. A more elegant method of direct analysis is the excitation with an intense laser beam of about 100 μm in diameter. A brief burst of intense light is sufficient to vaporize a few micrograms of material and leaves behind only a very small and hardly visible crater on the surface of the object. The small cloud of sample vapor needs an auxiliary spark discharge to excite the emission spectrum used for analysis. Although this laser-induced OES may appear to be a much better technique than the first one, it has the decisive disadvantage that its reproducibility is much lower and that it can only be used for qualitative or semiquantitative analyses.

Further improvement of the technique has been made by the introduction of a plasma torch for the vaporization and excitation of the sample instead of the electric discharge. It has only relatively recently been possible to obtain a stable plasma (a completely ionized gas) under laboratory conditions. The most widely employed plasma for analytical purposes consists of argon flowing through a quartz tube placed with its upper end into a high-frequency (about 30 MHz) magnetic field. Once ignited to plant a "seed" of electrons in the gas, the electron are accelerated by the oscillating field and obtain enough energy to ionize all other argon atoms within a very short time. The result is a very high-temperature flame (up to 10,000°C) through which the solution of the dissolved sample is transported as an aerosol. This technique is called inductively coupled plasma-OES (ICP-OES) and is a highly reliable method for the analysis of many elements in the parts per billion (ppb) range in solutions (1 ppb=1 ng/g=0.0000001%). Because solids have to be dissolved for analysis, elemental concentrations in the ppm range can be determined in the solid sample. A disadvantage is that the dissolution step is very critical for the accuracy of the method and the sample is lost on analysis.

In atomic absorption spectrometry (AAS) the sample, usually in the form of a solution, is also volatilized and atomized with combustion flames or by electrothermal heating in a small graphite tube. This method utilizes the fact that free atoms can absorb radiation at the same wavelength that they would emit on excitation. If copper is being determined, a copper-containing light source is used to pass a beam through the atomized sample. The amount of light absorbed can be detected electronically and is directly proportional to the number of atoms present. Comparison with standard solutions yields elemental concentrations. The instrumentation of AAS is cheaper than that of OES and the method is less sensitive to interelement interferences. Detection limits are roughly comparable. However, only one element can be determined with one measurement, whereas with OES all detectable elements are measured simultaneously. Only elemental concentrations can be determined with both methods.

The methods discussed so far are based on the fact that electrons of the outer shells of atoms can be excited, which results in absorption and emission of light in the visible and UV range of the electromagnetic spectrum. The energy of infrared radiation is too low for such processes, but it can excite oscillations and vibrations in molecules. Certain specific wavelengths that depend on the structure of the compound being tested are absorbed when a beam of infrared radiation is passed through a suitably prepared specimen of almost any inorganic or organic compound. The greatest use of this technique (IRS) is in the qualitative identification of organic compounds. Structural information on the presence or absence of certain functional groups is obtained. It is thus a typical method for species analysis. Many compounds exhibit typical infrared spectra that can be used as a "fingerprint." Resonance raman spectroscopy (RRS) is a complementary technique to IRS in that the radiation scattered and partly reemitted in a direction perpendicular to that of the incident beam is measured.

X-Ray Methods. When an element is irradiated with X-rays of appropriate wavelength, X-rays of different but smaller wavelength, characteristic of the element, are emitted. The underlying process is the displacement of an electron of one of the inner shells of the atom followed by filling of the vacancy by one of the outer electrons combined with simultaneous emission of a photon. Complex mixtures can usually be analyzed without prior separation of the components by the spectroscopy of the secondary radiation with diffracting crystals or semiconductor detectors and—most important—the method is virtually nondestructive (only some glasses and gemstones may change color on irradiation with X-rays, but this can be reverted by gentle heating). However, the depth of analysis is only in the range of 0.1 mm in silicates and even less in metals, so that the surface of an object has to be representative of the bulk composition, which is not always the case. Therefore, it may often be better to take a representative sample and perform the analysis on that.

The sensitivity of the method depends on the matrix and the element to be analyzed, but typical detection limits are around 10–100 ppm. XRF is the standard method for rock analysis in geology, and it is also widely employed for analyzing metals and alloys. The analyzed area is usually about 1 cm in diameter but can be reduced with appropriate slits; however, these also reduce the intensity of the primary beam and accordingly extend the necessary measurement time.

X-rays can also be excited by energetic electrons that can be focused with magnetic lenses. In the electron probe microanalyzer, a fine electron beam is focused on the surface of the sample (approximately 1 μm in diameter); the position of the beam can be changed systematically. Thus, it is possible to obtain information on the concentrations and distribution of the elements within a small area of the sample. For quantitative analysis the sample is mounted in a resin and the surface polished. Accordingly, strictly nondestructive analysis is not possible, but small objects like coins can be investigated with little damage. Electrons induce more background radiation in the sample. Therefore, detection limits are somewhat higher ($>$ 100 ppm) than with XRF.

Protons produce much less background and can also be focused so that proton-induced X-ray analysis (PIXE) combines lower detection levels and high lateral resolution. However, the instrumental effort to produce a proton beam is much larger than for electrons. Accordingly, this method is rarely available and comparatively expensive.

With X-ray diffraction analysis (XRD), crystal structures (and thus mineral compounds) can be identified. This method is very useful to complement chemical analysis when different materials have similar chemical composition.

Nuclear Methods. While the preceding methods make use of physical processes taking place in the molecules or in the electron shells of atoms, nuclear methods are based on reactions that occur between nuclei and neutrons or charged particles. Such reactions are usually accompanied or followed by the emission of radiation that is phenomenologically largely identical with the radiation emitted by the electron shells—with the difference that it originates from the nucleus. The most important of these techniques is neutron activation analysis (NAA), in which a sample is irradiated with thermal neutrons to interact with the atomic nuclei of the constituent elements, transforming them into unstable radioactive isotopes. The decay of these isotopes is often accompanied by the emission of γ-rays, which can be used for identifying and quantifying the elements in question. The spectroscopic techniques for γ-rays are similar to the ones used for X-rays. Because radioactivity can be measured very sensitively, this method offers an unparalleled combination of selectivity and sensitivity for simultaneously determining many elements. Typically, about 40 elements can be determined in rock samples from major components to the ppb range. For several elements this is the most sensitive method of analysis altogether. Depending on their major compositions, small objects can be analyzed nondestructively, if no long-lived isotopes are produced. In any case, the sample is preserved and can be used for other investigations after the decay of the radioactivity. The major disadvantage of this method is the low and diminishing availability of strong neutron sources—that is, nuclear research reactors.

Analogous to AAS, Mössbauer effect spectroscopy (MES) involves the absorption of γ-rays of characteristic energies within a very narrow energy range by specific nuclei in the sample. This method is mainly used for the speciation of iron in various matrices or, more generally, provides information on the immediate crystallographic environment of the isotope under investigation. Typically, it is the ratio of Fe^{2+}/Fe^{3+} in minerals that is of interest because it bears on the ambient conditions during the formation of iron-containing minerals.

A mass spectrometer is an instrument that will sort out charged gas molecules (ions) according to their masses by accelerating them electrically to form a beam that is deflected magnetically into separate beams according to the mass-to-charge ratio of the ions involved. These beams can be made to pass through a series of slits to reach separate detectors where they are individually counted. In thermal-ionization mass spectrometry (TIMS) the element sought has to be separated from the sample and is then evaporated and ionized from an array of hot filaments. Quantification is achieved by adding known amounts of different isotopes of the same element (isotope dilution). For many elements this is the most sensitive technique available, but it is rather time consuming and usually only one element can be measured at a time. The major advantage is that not only the concentration of an element can be determined, but also its isotopic composition—which is especially important for elements with varying abundances of their constituent stable isotopes. Most elements on Earth have a uniform isotopic composition regardless of their location or chemical form. Variations can be induced in light elements (from hydrogen to sulfur) by physical processes such as diffusion that are sensitive to isotopic differences (e.g., "heavy" water, D_2O can be enriched by repeated evaporation of ordinary water) or by the decay of radioactive elements occurring in nature. A typical example is the decay of uranium and thorium to lead, so that the isotopic composition of lead varies according to which geochemical environment it derives.

There are also alternative ways to produce ions from the sample: One is the direct atomization and ionization by an electric spark similar to OES (spark-source mass spectrometry, or SSMS) or the introduction of a sample solution into a plasma torch (ICP-MS). Both combine the high sensitivity of MS with multielement detection. However, especially SSMS can only be regarded as a semiquantitative method unless a tedious multielement isotope dilution technique is applied. If a sample is directly evaporated by a narrow laser beam and then introduced into an ICP-MS, high lateral resolution is also possible. Even better resolution is achieved by ionization with a primary beam of ions (secondary-ion mass spectrometry, or SIMS), so that the features of the EMPA are combined with high sensitivity and isotopic analysis. Unfortunately, precision and accuracy of all these methods is not yet competitive with conventional instrumental methods (e.g., XRF or NAA) because of interelement effects that are as yet difficult to correct. However, with their increased use, these new techniques will certainly become powerful and reliable analytical tools.

The main field of application of MS in analytical chemistry is actually the analysis of complex organic molecules. To increase its selectivity, it is now common practice to separate the individual components first in a gas chromatograph (GC) by differential adsorption on a solid stationary phase (GC-MS). Because of these differences, each component diffuses at a different speed through a narrow column packed with, for example, silica gel, so that at the end of the column the components are completely separated and introduced into a MS one after the other.

Selected Archaeological Applications. OES was the first widely employed physical method of chemical analysis; thus, most of the analytical data published since 1930 was, until recently, derived from this technique. Most noteworthy are the many thousands of analyses of prehistoric metal objects from Europe, the eastern Mediterranean, and the Near East carried out at the Württembergisches Landesmuseum in Stuttgart, Germany. These data are still the primary source for studying the development of alloying techniques in various regions and have frequently been discussed in terms of the provenance of raw materials. The method is still in use but XRF, AAS, NAA, and ICP-OES are replacing it increasingly in determining major and trace elements. A significant methodical extension has been the introduction of TIMS for determining lead isotope ratios not affected by production processes.

Obsidian, a naturally occurring volcanic glass that has been used widely for blades from Paleolithic periods through the Bronze Age, is a much better material for provenance studies because the production of artifacts does not alter its chemical composition in any way and it is also very resistant to chemical weathering. OES has been used to characterize many obsidian sources in the Aegean, in central and eastern Anatolia, in Armenia, and in Ethiopia, as well as obsidian artifacts from Near Eastern sites. It appears that the Levant was mainly supplied from Cappadocian sources, whereas obsidian from eastern Anatolia was dominant along the Zagros flanks. Today, the most widely applied analytical methods for this purpose are NAA and RFA, although the latter is not applicable for very small samples. So far, TIMS has offered little advantage over these methods.

In a similar approach, OES has also been used for the chemical analysis of pottery; however, characterizing clay sources presents more difficulties than obsidian. There is a very large number of potential clay sources, and the variation within a source is likely to be larger than with obsidian. On the other hand, for mineralogical reasons, the variation between sources is rather small; as a result, they can hardly be distinguished with the relatively low precision of OES. Progress, thus, came only after the introduction of NAA, which is now the standard method for pottery analysis.

Stone artifacts have also been studied extensively, particularly marble, starting with isotope analysis of carbon and oxygen. As with all studies where many sources have to be considered, various overlapping parameters prevent the unique assignment of an artifact to any source. Better resolution between sources can only be achieved by increasing the number of geochemical parameters. Hence, isotope analysis is now routinely complemented by trace element and petrographic analysis.

Of organic materials, amber has been the most extensively studied, especially by IRS, with the aim of localizing raw-material sources and establishing trade routes in the Late Bronze Age. A promising field seems to be the analysis of food residues by GC-MS.

[See also Dating Techniques; Microscopy; Neutron Activation Analysis; Spectroscopy; and X-Ray Diffraction Analysis.]

BIBLIOGRAPHY

Beck, Curt W., Constance A. Fellows, and Edith MacKennan. "Nuclear Magnetic Resonance Spectrometry in Archaeology." In *Archaeological Chemistry: A Symposium Sponsored by the Division of the History of Chemistry at the 165th Meeting of the American Chemical Society, Dallas, Texas, April 9–10, 1973*, edited by Curt W. Beck, pp. 226–235. American Chemical Society, Advances in Chemistry Series, no. 138. Washington, D.C., 1974. Good introduction to an important technique (not covered in this article) for analyzing organic materials in archaeology.

Boumans, Paul W. J. M., ed. *Inductively Coupled Plasma Emission Spectroscopy*. New York, 1987. Comprehensive overview of this relatively new analytical technique.

Ehmann, William D., and Diane E. Vance, eds. *Radiochemistry and Nuclear Methods in Analysis*. New York, 1991. The most readable modern treatment of analytical radiochemistry.

Harbottle, Garman. "Chemical Characterization in Archaeology." In *Contexts for Prehistoric Exchange: Studies in Archaeology*, edited by Jonathan E. Ericson and Timothy K. Earle, pp. 13–51. New York, 1982. Useful review of the application of chemical analyses in archaeology.

Kolthoff, I. M., and Philip J. Elving, eds. *Treatise on Analytical Chemistry*. 2d ed. New York, 1978–. Authoritative series on analytical chemistry that treats the field comprehensively.

Pollard, A. M., ed. *New Developments in Archaeological Science: A Joint Symposium of the Royal Society and the British Academy, February 1991*. Proceedings of the British Academy, 77. Oxford, 1992. The most recent collection of specific applications of scientific methods to archaeological problems.

Potts, P. J. *A Handbook of Silicate Rock Analysis*. Glasgow, 1987. Summarizes the principles and experimental techniques of all analytical methods discussed in this text with the exception of IRS, RRS, and GC-MS.

Tite, Michael S. *Methods of Physical Examination in Archaeology*. London and New York, 1972. Concise overview of physical methods applied for the location, dating, and compositional analysis of archaeological artifacts.

Wagner, U., F. E. Wagner, and J. Riederer. "The Use of Mössbauer Spectroscopy in Archaeometric Studies." In *Proceedings of the 24th International Archaeometry Symposium*, edited by Jacqueline S. Olin and M. J. Blackman, pp. 129–142. Washington, D.C., 1986. Useful introduction to the principles of the method, with an archaeological application.

Zussman, J., ed. *Physical Methods in Determinative Mineralogy*. 2d ed. New York and London, 1977. Somewhat dated but detailed and authoritative review of OES, XRF, XRD, AAS, IRS, and SSMS.

ERNST PERNICKA

ANATOLIA. [*This entry provides a broad survey of the history of Anatolia as known primarily from archaeological discoveries. It is chronologically divided into four articles:*

Prehistoric Anatolia

Ancient Anatolia

Anatolia from Alexander to the Rise of Islam

Anatolia in the Islamic Period

In addition to the related articles on specific subregions and sites referred to in this entry, see also History of the Field, *article on* Archaeology in the Anatolian Plateau.]

Prehistoric Anatolia

V. Gordon Childe places the origins of his Neolithic Revolution in hypothesized "nuclear zones" where climate, environment, and human experience came together to catalyze the transition of human society from a food-gathering organism to a food-producing one (Childe, 1952, p. 23). These nuclear zones were limited to an arc of land from Egypt to Mesopotamia, the so-called Fertile Crescent. Although later scholarship considered Anatolian sites such as Çatal Höyük and Çayönü to be peripheral developments of the Levantine Neolithic tradition, the growing evidence from sites such as Aşıklı Höyük points to an autochthonous development within Anatolia. [*See* Çatal Höyük; Çayönü.] As a result, Anatolia has begun to take its place as one of the primary areas of prehistoric investigation in the Near East. It was in the Neolithic and Chalcolithic periods that humans acquired the capacity to manipulate their surroundings in ways still observable in the archaeological record.

Climate, Environment, and Domestication. Much of Anatolia is situated along a broad plateau that stretches from the Aegean Sea to Iran. While this plateau may seem, at first glance, to be little more than monotonous highlands, careful inspection reveals a complex landscape composed of numerous microenvironments, each with its own peculiar set of ecological features (Yakar, 1991). Within the context of this ecological framework, the basic elements of soil, temperature, and precipitation had much to do with the success or failure of human habitation on the plateau (cf. Gorny, 1995b). Environmental studies indicate that the climate of Anatolia in the era preceding the Neolithic may have differed significantly from what it is today, with large areas inhospitable to human habitation (Butzer, 1970, 1982; Cohen, 1971). Climatic conditions seem to have ameliorated in Anatolia during the eighth millennium, making it conducive to settlement at sites such as Hacılar and Çatal Höyük. [*See* Hacılar.] Whether this climatic change was the prime catalyst behind the innovations of the Neolithic period is still uncertain, but what stands out is the dramatically different direction human culture took from that point onward.

Although humans had already begun to observe and experiment with the plants (and animals) in their environment, it was not until this moderating change in climate occurred that the "incipient agriculture" of the Epipaleolithic period finally gave way to a more formalized system of settlement and cultivation. [*See* Agriculture.] The system was characterized by dry-farming communities in which the inhabitants practiced cereal cultivation and animal husbandry. [*See* Cereals.] While village communities apparently sprang up before the development of plant domestication, there are indications that, in at least some cases (see below), animal domestication also preceded that of plants, especially in central Anatolia (cf. Yakar, 1991; M. Özdoğan, 1995). [*See* Villages.] Other developments in social organization, ideology, architecture, and craftmanship followed on the heels of the food-producing revolution; exchange is also evident, even from earliest times. These cultural developments, however, represent only a small segment on a long and not necessarily straight continuum.

Neolithic Period (c. 11000–5500 BCE). The earliest evidence of settled life in Anatolia dates to the Neolithic period (Singh, 1974; Mellaart, 1975; Todd, 1980; Yakar, 1991; Joukowsky, forthcoming), with settlement divided into two phases based on the absence or presence of pottery technology. Prepottery or aceramic settlements have been identified at Çayönü, Hallan Çemi, Nevalı Çori, Gritille, Aşıklı Höyük, and Suberde, with additional evidence coming from surveys (cf. Voigt, 1985; Todd, 1980; Meriç, 1993; Algaze, 1994; M. Özdoğan 1995). [*See* Nevalı Çori.] Together they provide a broadening vista of Neolithic settlement in Anatolia.

Radiocarbon dating of the evidence of the Neolithic at Hallan Çemi places it in the ninth millennium, making it the oldest known permanent settlement in Anatolia (Rosenberg, 1994). Circular houses appeared in each of the two levels of occupation, whose economy was typical of a food-collecting site. Nearly all the faunal and botanical remains appear to have come from wild species—the exception being the pig, which may have been domesticated. [*See* Pigs.] This suggests that, contrary to earlier opinions, animal domestication probably occurred here (in the form of pig domestication) prior to the domestication of plants. Querns, grinding stones, and pestles, many of which were festooned with zoomorphic decorations, demonstrate that wild grains were processed. Other evidence points to fishing and nut and legume gathering supplementing the diet. [*See* Fishing.] While most of the chipped-stone industry is to be attributed to obsidian derived from the Van region, the microlithic repertoire has little in common with contemporary cultures—which may point to outside influences. Obsidian, copper (or perhaps just copper ore), and Mediterranean shells suggest that exchange also formed part of the Hallan Çemi economy.

The well-documented settlement at Çayönü (c. 8000 BCE) provides revealing data regarding the shift from a hunter-gatherer society to a village-farming economy (cf. Braidwood and Braidwood, 1982; A. Özdoğan, 1995). Four phases of settlement cover some five hundred years and display unusual standardization in their plans. The phase I prehistoric settlement covered approximately 30,000 sq m at its peak and was occupied by several thousand inhabitants. The earliest structures in subphase I were primarily oval and set on virgin soil. Subphase II showed evidence of town planning, with a central square and buildings on a south–southeasterly axis. The dominant building style is the so-called grill building, which encourages ventilation. A terrazzo floor found in subphase III represents another innovation of the Çayönü inhabitants, and the "cell building" is the featured architectural type. The advanced style and arrangement of these architectural types may eventually provide some of the first real evidence of stratification and specialization (their architectural antecedents are still to be discovered).

Phases I and II at Çayönü yielded wild cereals, vetch, and nuts, supplemented by wild pig, goat, sheep, and deer. [*See* Sheep and Goats.] Evidence of domestication begins to appear by phases III–IV, with plants such as peas, lentils, and emmer joined by domesticated animals such as sheep, goat, and pig. The economy of Çayönü may have been augmented by copper production from a nearby mine. The site's pins, awls, and fishhooks represent the first known use of copper for fashioning tools; whether this copper was used in trade is unclear, but the increased use of obsidian from the Nemrud Dağı region in phase IV does suggest that it could have been imported in the exchange.

Evidence regarding mortality for the site's inhabitants comes from the remains of more than five hundred individuals found at Çayönü. Of interest are the skeletal remains found associated with the so-called skull house, where the discovery of numerous skulls suggests a cult in which the skull played an important role. [*See* Cult.] Additional evidence revealing the religious and artistic sensibilities of the inhabitants is demonstrated by clay figurines found at the site, especially those that are early manifestations of the mother-goddess motif so prominent in later cultures. Although true pottery was absent, white plaster vessels occurred in the upper levels.

Nevalı Çori is the site of an aceramic village whose excavation was occasioned by the Atatürk dam project on the Euphrates River (Hauptmann, 1993). [*See* Euphrates.] Four levels of aceramic remains were recovered. Many of the twenty-seven tripartite structures excavated are of interest, but several are of particular note. House 13 yielded a terrazzo floor with several limestone stelae, one of which is 2.50 m high and portrays a human figure. The preceding level of the house produced several more carved stelae. The monumental sculptures are said to indicate the presence of a sanctuary. Several other buildings were constructed with cross channels running under the walls. Cattle was domesticated and cereals cultivated. [*See* Cattle and Oxen.] Flint was the stone of choice, but no obsidian has been discovered. Artistic motifs on several stone vessels may link the site with Pre-Pottery Neolithic B sites on the Levantine coast.

Farther to the west, in the heart of the plateau, is Aşıklı Höyük, one of Anatolia's most important Neolithic sites (Esin, 1991, 1995). The settlement displays thickly clustered houses and a double wall, one of stone and one of mud brick. Faunal remains indicate that wild sheep and goat were consumed, but there is no evidence of agriculture in the 15-

meter-deep deposit. Ceramics were introduced in its later levels. The sophistication of the Aşıklı assemblage is evidence that Neolithic settlement in Anatolia was more than just an afterthought of Levantine developments.

The appearance of pottery at Neolithic sites in Anatolia is dated to about 6500 BCE. Çatal Höyük (East), perhaps the best-known site of the Ceramic Neolithic (Mellaart, 1967), was composed of buildings with contiguous walls and entryways through the roof. The solid exterior face of the village probably served as a simple defensive device. Utilitarian pottery is found in all thirteen of its excavated levels. Aceramic levels were not found but are thought to lie beneath the ceramic levels. The chipped-stone assemblage from Çatal Höyük is notable because the inhabitants made exclusive use of obsidian from local sources. The importance of this obsidian resource cannot be overemphasized, as discoveries of central Anatolian obsidian in places such as Jericho in Syria-Palestine are indicative of Early Neolithic exchange. [See Jericho.] Mediterranean shells, metal ores, and pigments not found locally provide additional evidence of an exchange network. Animal husbandry appears to have been important to the town's overall economy, with most of its meat coming from cattle. Hunting was still an important factor, however, as indicated by the bones of wild animals and hunt scenes depicted on the walls of buildings. [See Hunting; Wall Paintings.] Cult figurines, shrines with bucrania, plaster reliefs, and wall paintings reflect the town's religious disposition. The site comes to an end in about 5400 BCE but is succeeded by a settlement in the Early Chalcolithic period.

Hacılar (Mellaart, 1970) illustrates a Late Neolithic tradition somewhat farther west of Çatal Höyük and provides a key link with other Late Neolithic traditions. The Early Aceramic period (of which there were seven sublevels that ended in about 6700 BCE) ended with an abandonment of approximately one thousand years. The succeeding six levels (IX–VI), which span a period from about 5700 to 5600 BCE) represent typical Neolithic agricultural settlements that cultivated wheat and barley along with lentils. Only the dog was domesticated, and hunting still provided a supplement to the local diet. Pottery appears for the first time in level IX, and exquisite clay figurines, probable domestic cult statues, appear in Neolithic levels IX–VI.

In Cilicia the sites of Mersin and Tarsus maintained their close links with the Syro-Mesopotamian plain. [See Cilicia.] Central Anatolian obsidian found at Mersin illustrates the contact between Cilicia and the plateau. Köşk Höyük, located near Niğde, is again close to the obsidian sources (Silistreli, 1989). Not surprisingly, 90 percent of its chipped-stone assemblage is composed of obsidian. Its strategic situation leading to the Cilician gates, along with the obsidian and crafted pottery and figurines that parallel the Çatal Höyük assemblage, suggests an exchange of materials and ideas among Cilicia, the 'Amuq, and the Levant. [See

'Amuq; Levant.] Höyücek, near Lake Burdur, is important as a site that was a predecessor to the Late Neolithic (levels IX–VI) at Hacılar (Duru 1993). In the northwest, the earliest levels at Hoca Çeşme Höyük in Thrace also show connections with Hacılar levels IX–VI and provide clues about the widespread character of the Anatolian Late Neolithic (Özdoğan, 1993).

Neolithic innovations occurred in Anatolia over an extended period and in widely differing regions—establishing a tradition that was both rich and complex. Early on, settlements practiced a mixed economy composed of food gathering, food production, and exchange, with surplus goods leading to social complexity at places like Çayönü and Çatal Höyük. Pyrotechnological industries were in their initial stage of development, as evidenced by metals and pottery (Esin, 1995; Schmandt-Besserat, 1977). Artistic representations at Çatal Höyük and Nevalı Çori provide evidence of religious sensibilities and the ability to think in the abstract. Evidence of exchange provides a window to a complex extraregional perspective that must already have been taking shape at this early date (Yakar, 1991).

Chalcolithic Period. The innovations and technologies that originated in the Neolithic period were expanded in the Chalcolithic period. Excavations and surveys bear witness to a widening network of settlements across a broad range of environmental settings (cf. Yakar, 1985; Summers, 1993; Efe, 1993; Parzinger, 1993; Algaze, 1994; Gorny et al., 1995c). The Chalcolithic is generally delineated into three chronological phases: Early (5500–5000 BCE), Middle (5000–4500 BCE), and Late (4500–3000 BCE). The emergence of the Anatolian plateau as an important center of settlement in the prehistoric period means that discussions regarding the Anatolian Chalcolithic must take into account not only chronological factors, but an expanded geographic range in which contemporary developments occur alongside each other on both the Syro-Mesopotamian plain and in the Euro-Anatolian regions.

Anatolia and the Syro-Mesopotamian plain. The three phases of the Chalcolithic period in the Syro-Anatolian region developed gradually from the Neolithic period onward, with no indication of cultural upheaval. Hacılar I–V (Mellaart, 1970) remains the principle site for the Anatolian Early Chalcolithic. Animal husbandry probably existed at Hacılar just as it did at Can Hasan, where sheep, goats, cattle, and perhaps pigs were kept (French, 1972). The dog is the only animal for which there is evidence of domestication. Paleobotanical research discovered emmer and einkorn wheat, along with barley, lentils, pea, bitter vetch, pistachio, and almond. What set Chalcolithic Hacılar apart from other Anatolian settlements, however, was the red-on-cream pottery of levels II–V; its quality is unparalled throughout both Anatolia and the ancient Near East until much later times. In addition to the ceramics, a later phase of figurines was uncovered at Chalcolithic Hacılar. They lack the creativity and zest found in the earlier Neolithic examples and eventually degenerated into schematized violin-shaped examples in level I. The early levels remained unprotected, but a defensive perimeter was formed in level II by the construction of a fortification wall 1.5–3 m thick. The village showed evidence of specialization, with various industries located in their own sectors. Shrines in the site's northeast corner, along with the presence of mother-goddess figurines, indicate continuing religious sensibilities. The settlement was destroyed and then resettled. Its new inhabitants built an even stronger fortification wall. Hacılar I came to a violent end in about 4800 BCE and appears to have left no heirs to its rich traditions.

The Cilician towns of Mersin and Tarsus again represent the northernmost extension of the Syro-Mesopotamian cultural zone and provide a potential interface for connecting the Syro-Mesopotamian and Euro-Anatolian worlds. Early Chalcolithic Mersin (levels XXIII–XX) shows Halaf inspiration in its ceramic sequence, but the Middle Chalcolithic is poorly represented. The ceramic repertoire begins to show Ubaid influences in the Late Chalcolithic (level XVI), when the town was defended by a wall, a fortified gate, and a glaci (Garstang, 1953). A large residence and outbuildings give the settlement the appearance of a military quarters. The town was leveled by attack in about 4300 BCE.

The Middle Chalcolithic, is best represented by a string of settlements stretching along the Euphrates River from Lower Mesopotamia to the Middle Euphrates. Late Ubaid evidence found at sites along this route, such as at Değirmentepe, suggests that Mesopotamians expanded into the area in order to exploit the resources of the Middle Euphrates (Esin, 1989; Hendrickson and Thuesen, 1989). While the Taurus Mountains are generally considered to have been a barrier to intercourse between the Syro-Mesopotamian and Euro-Anatolian cultural zones, the presence of Ubaid pottery at Fraktin suggests that Mesopotamian influences could have penetrated into central Anatolia at this very early date. [See Taurus Mountains.]

In northeastern Anatolia there is increasing evidence of Trans-Caucasian culture by the end of the Late Chalcolithic (Sagona, 1984). The group's unique red-black polished pottery provides a reliable means of tracing this culture from the Caucasus into Anatolia; however, the sparcity of secure data makes it difficult to provide assess the group's impact on Anatolia's cultural development. The Late Chalcolithic period is best documented by another Mesopotamian intrusion. Following the lead of their Ubaid predecessors, Uruk elements settled in Anatolia as far north as the Middle Euphrates, at numerous sites along the river: at Habuba Kabira, Carchemish, Kurban Höyük, Samsat Höyük, Hacinebi Tepe, Norşuntepe, and most notably at Arslantepe (Frangipane, 1988–1989). [See Habuba Kabira; Carchemish; Arslantepe.] The widespread Uruk system collapsed suddenly in about 3000 BCE (Algaze, 1993; cf. Stein, forthcoming).

Euro-Anatolian zone. Some studies postulate that at roughly the same time in which important developments were shaping Neolithic and Chalcolithic traditions on the Syro-Mesopotamian plain, intensive interaction between Europe and Anatolia was establishing independent links between the two regions. Prehistoric connections between Anatolia and the Balkans assume internal development rather than external influence, with a geographic range extending from the Hungarian plain to the southeastern stretches of Anatolia, where it is effectively cut off from contact with Mesopotamia by the Taurus Mountains (Özdoğan, 1993).

Evidence suggests two phases of contact: the first, beginning in about 5500 BCE (Thissen, 1993; Todorova, 1993)—or roughly contemporary with the Early Chalcolithic of the Syro-Mesopotamian region—and continuing until the beginning of the fourth millennium, when several elements may have been responsible for a cultural break. Among these elements were tectonic activity, higher temperatures resulting from climatic change, long periods of drought, erosion, changing sea levels, and/or nomadic invasions (Todorova, 1993; Lichardus-Itten, 1993). The resulting breakdown of existing social structures lasted approximately eight hundred years, during which time the affected areas witnessed mostly local development (Makkey, 1993; Todorova, 1993). The second phase, beginning at the end of the fourth millennium, saw a stabilization of environmental conditions, which led to the renewal of cultural interaction between southeast Europe and Anatolia (Todorova, 1993).

Evidence for the spread of Euro-Anatolian culture into central Anatolia comes first from sites in the northwest, such as Yarımburgaz (Özdoğan, 1991) and Ilıpinar (Roodenberg, 1993). It is also apparent at central Anatolian sites such as Alişar Höyük and Gelveri, where curvilinear-decorated pottery of the so-called *fruchenstich* technique is dated to between 4000 and 3500 BCE (Esin, 1993; Thissen, 1993; Gorny, 1995a). Graphite-slipped pottery found at Çadır Höyük and Alişar is linked with the Karanova VI Vinça D culture and provides a date between 3000 and 3500 BCE for settlement at both Alişar and Çadır (Thissen, 1993; Gorny, 1995a). Further evidence for the breadth of Late Chalcolithic culture comes from southwestern sites such as Elmalı (Eslick, 1992), Beycesultan (Mellaart, 1962), and Aphrodisias (Joukowsky, 1986), where cultural development may have some connection with earlier influences from Hacılar. [See Aphrodisias.]

The Chalcolithic period witnessed the dramatic development of earlier Neolithic themes. Food production began to take on a standard appearance across the plateau, with most of the major categories of plants and animals domesticated. Horticulture, however, does not seem to have made its appearance until the third millennium (Gorny, 1995a). The hunting and gathering of foodstuffs still augmented the Anatolian diet, but they were declining. Artistic expression reached a height in the pottery of Hacılar, and cosmological themes are recognizable in such religious motifs as mother-goddess figurines. Increasing social complexity seems to have fueled the competition for limited resources, which may account for the evidence of fortifications and major defensive systems at Mersin and Hacılar—evidence that betrays an ability to coordinate massive amounts of labor and capital.

By the beginning of the third millennium (Early Bronze Age I) there were increasing points of contact along the Euro-Anatolian and Syro-Mesopotamian interface. That barrier gradually broke down, however, and an increasing orientalization of the Anatolian plateau took place that greatly influenced interaction between Anatolia, Syria, and Mesopotamia in the historical periods.

BIBLIOGRAPHY

Algaze, Guillermo. *The Uruk World System: The Dynamics of Early Mesopotamian Civilization.* Chicago, 1993.

Algaze, Guillermo, et al. "The Tigris-Euphrates Archaeological Reconnaissance Project: Final Report of the Birecik and Carchemish Dam Survey Areas." *Anatolica* 20 (1994): 1–144.

Bordaz, J. "Current Research in the Neolithic of South Central Turkey: Suberde, Erbaba, and Their Chronological Implications." *American Journal of Archaeology* 77 (1973): 282–288.

Bordaz, J. "Erbaba: The 1977 and 1978 Excavations in Perspective." *Türk Arkeoloji Dergisi* 26 (1982): 85–93.

Braidwood, Linda S., and Robert J. Braidwood, eds. *Prehistoric Village Archaeology in South-Eastern Turkey.* British Archaeological Reports, International Series, no. 138. Oxford, 1982.

Butzer, Karl W. "Physical Conditions in Eastern Europe, Western Asia, and Egypt before the Period of Agricultural and Urban Settlement." In *The Cambridge Ancient History,* vol. 1.1, edited by I. E. S. Edwards et al., pp. 35–69. Cambridge, 1970.

Butzer, Karl W. *Archaeology as Human Ecology: Method and Theory for a Contextual Approach.* Cambridge, 1982.

Childe, V. Gordon. *New Light on the Most Ancient East.* 4th ed. New York, 1952.

Cohen, H. "The Paleoecology of South Central Anatolia at the End of the Pleistocene and the Beginning of the Holocene." *Anatolian Studies* 20 (1971): 119–137.

Duru, Refik. "Höyücek Kazılan." *Kazı Sonuçları Toplantısı* 14.1 (1993): 147–153.

Efe, Turhan. "Chalcolithic Pottery from the Mounds of Aslanapa and Kınık." *Anatolica* 19 (1993): 9–31.

Esin, Ufuk. "An Early Trading Center in Eastern Anatolia." In *Anatolia and the Ancient Near East: Studies in Honor of Tahsin Özgüç,* edited by Kutlu Emre et al., pp. 135–141. Ankara, 1989.

Esin, Ufuk. "Salvage Excavations at the Pre-Pottery Site of Aşıklı Höyük in Central Anatolia." *Anatolica* 17 (1991): 124–174.

Esin, Ufuk. "Gelveri: Ein Beispiel für die kulturellen Bezeihungen zwischen Zentralanatolien und Südosteuropa während des Chalcolithikums." *Anatolica* 19 (1993): 47–56.

Esin, Ufuk. "Metallurgy at the Prehistoric Site of Aşıklı." In *Prehistorya Yazıları: Readings in Prehistory,* pp. 61–78. Istanbul, 1995.

Eslick, Christine M. *Elmalı-Karataş I, the Neolithic and Chalcolithic Periods: Bağbaşı and Other Sites.* Bryn Mawr, Pa., 1992.

Frangipane, Marcella. "Aspects of Centralization in the Late Uruk Period in the Mesopotamian Periphery." *Origini* 14 (1988–199): 535–560.

French, David H. "Excavations at Can Hasan II, 1969–70." In *Papers in Economic Prehistory,* edited by David H. French et al., pp. 180–190. Cambridge, 1972.

Garstang, John. *Prehistoric Mersin: Yümük Tepe in Southern Turkey.* Oxford, 1953.

Goldman, Hetty, ed. *Excavations at Gözlü Kule, Tarsus.* Princeton, 1956.

Gorny, Ronald L. Review essay on *Anatolica* 19 (special issue on "Anatolia and the Balkans"). *Biblical Archaeologist* 58 (1995a): 119–122.

Gorny, Ronald L. "Viticulture and Ancient Anatolia." In *The Ancient Origins of Wine,* edited by Patrick E. McGovern, pp. 133–174. Newark, 1995b.

Gorny, Ronald L., et al. "The Alisar Regional Project, 1994 Season." *Anatolica* 21 (1995c): 68–100.

Hauptmann, Harald. "Ein Kultgebäude in Nevali Çori." In *Between the Rivers and over the Mountains: Archaeologica Anatolica et Mesopotamica, Alba Palmieri Dedicata,* edited by Marcella Frangipane et al., pp. 37–69. Rome, 1993.

Henrickson, Elizabeth F., and Ingolf Thuesen, eds. *Upon This Foundation: The 'Ubaid Reconsidered.* Carsten Niebuhr Institute of Ancient Near East Studies, 10. Copenhagen, 1989. See the introduction by Henrickson and Thuesen.

Joukowsky, Martha Sharpe. *Prehistoric Aphrodisias: An Account of the Excavations and Artifact Studies.* 2 vols. Archaeologia Transatlantica, 3.39. Providence, R.I., 1986.

Joukowsky, Martha Sharpe. *Early Turkey: An Introduction to the Archaeology of Anatolia from Prehistory through the Lydian Period.* Forthcoming.

Lichardus-Itten, Marion. "Zum Beginn des Neolithikums im Tal der Struma." *Anatolica* 19 (1993): 99–116.

Makkay, Janos. "Pottery Links between Late Neolithic Cultures of the NW Pontic and Anatolia and the Origins of the Hittites." *Anatolica* 19 (1993): 117–128.

Mellaart, James. *Beycesultan I: The Late Chalcolithic and Early Bronze Age Levels.* London, 1962.

Mellaart, James. *Çatal Höyük: A Neolithic Town in Anatolia.* London, 1967.

Mellaart, James. *Excavations at Hacılar.* 2 vols. Edinburgh, 1970.

Mellaart, James. *The Neolithic of the Near East.* London, 1975.

Meriç, R. "Pre-Bronze Age Settlements of West-Central Anatolia." *Anatolica* 19 (1993): 143–147.

Osten, Hans Henning. *The Alişar Höyük: Seasons of 1930–32.* Oriental Institute Publications, 28.1. Chicago, 1937.

Özdoğan, Aslı. "Life at Çayönü during the Pre-Pottery Neolithic Period." In *Prehistorya Yazıları: Readings in Prehistory,* pp. 79–100. Istanbul, 1995.

Özdoğan, Mehmet. "An Interim Report on the Excavations at Yarımburgaz and Toptepe in Eastern Thrace." *Anatolica* 17 (1991): 59–120.

Özdoğan, Mehmet. "Vinca and Anatolia: A New Look at a Very Old Problem." *Anatolica* 19 (1993): 173–193.

Özdoğan, Mehmet. "Neolithic Anatolia: The State of Current Research." In *Prehistorya Yazıları: Readings in Prehistory,* pp. 41–60. Istanbul, 1995.

Özdoğan, Mehmet. "Pre-Bronze Age Sequence of Central Anatolia: An Alternative Approach." In *Beran Festschrift.* Forthcoming.

Parzinger, H. "Zur Zeitstellung der Büyükkaya-ware: Bemerkungen zur vorbronzezeitlichen Kulturfolge Zentralanatoliens." *Anatolica* 19 (1993): 211–229.

Roodenberg, J. "Ilıpınar X to VI: Links and Chronology." *Anatolica* 19 (1993): 251–267.

Rosenberg, M. "Hallan Çemi Tepisi, An Early Aceramic Neolithic Site in Eastern Anatolia: Some Preliminary Observations Concerning Material Culture." *Anatolica* 20 (1994): 1–18.

Sagona, A. G. *The Caucasian Region in the Early Bronze Age.* British Archaeological Reports, International Series, no. 214. Oxford, 1984.

Schmandt-Besserat, Denise. "The Beginnings of the Use of Clay in Turkey." *Anatolian Studies* 27 (1977): 133–150.

Silistreli, Uğur. "Les fouilles de Köşk Höyük." In *Anatolia and the Ancient Near East: Studies in Honor of Tahsin Özgüç,* edited by Kutlu Emre et al., pp. 461–463. Ankara, 1989.

Singh, Purushottam. *The Neolithic Cultures of Western Asia.* London, 1974.

Stein, G. "Uruk Colonial Expansion and Anatolian Communities: An Interim Report on the 1992-3 Excavations at Hacırebı, Turkey." *American Journal of Archaeology.* Forthcoming.

Summers, G. D. "The Chalcolithic Period in Central Anatolia." In *The Fourth Millennium B.C.: Proceedings of the International Symposium, Nessebur, 28–30 August 1992,* edited by Petya Georgieva, pp. 29–48. Sofia, 1993.

Thissen, L. "New Insights in Balkan-Anatolian Connections in the Late Chalcolithic: Old Evidence from the Turkish Black Sea Littoral." *Anatolian Studies* 43 (1993): 207–237.

Todd, Ian A. *The Prehistory of Central Anatolia,* vol. 1, *The Neolithic Period.* Studies in Mediterranean Archaeology, vol. 60. Göteborg, 1980.

Todorova, Henrietta. "Die Protobronzezeit auf der Balkanhalpinsel." *Anatolica* 19 (1993): 307–318.

Voigt, Mary M. "Village on the Euphrates: Excavations at Neolithic Gritille in Turkey." *Expedition* 27 (1985): 10–24.

Yakar, Jak. *The Later Prehistory of Anatolia: The Late Chalcolithic and the Early Bronze Age.* British Archaeological Reports, International Series, no. 268. Oxford, 1985.

Yakar, Jak. *Prehistoric Anatolia: The Neolithic Transformation and the Early Chalcolithic Period.* Tel Aviv, 1991.

RONALD L. GORNY

Ancient Anatolia

Archaeological discoveries in the modern era have brought to light a remarkable series of indigenous civilizations that arose in Anatolia during the Bronze Age (c. 3000–1200 BCE) and in subsequent centuries before the conquests of Alexander the Great in the 330s BCE. Nourished by the region's rich subsistence base and coveted metal resources, these civilizations developed distinctive forms of material culture, religion, and writing. At the same time, they were influenced and enriched by ongoing contacts with their neighbors. As with other areas of the Near East and Aegean, the initial impetus for exploring Anatolia's pre-Roman past came from European and American interest in tracing civilizations known from the Bible or from Greek epic and historical tradition. Organized archaeological investigations thus began in the nineteenth century with searches for Homer's Troy, the Greek cities and Anatolian kingdoms of Herodotus's accounts, and the biblical Hittites. The rediscovery and documentation of other native and of prehistoric cultures followed during the twentieth century, together with efforts to explore areas once considered peripheral or provincial.

Writing, and hence the earliest evidence for linguistic, ethnic, and historical labels, is first attested in Anatolia shortly after 2000 BCE. [*See* Writing and Writing Systems.] These records, the archives of Assyrian merchants from northern Mesopotamia, document several ethnic and linguistic groups residing in central Anatolia, and they also tie the archaeological sequences of the region to Mesopotamian absolute chronologies. For the Early Bronze Age (c. 3000–2000 BCE), dates in years are obtained by radiocarbon dating and by cross-dating sites using isolated artifacts that supply synchronisms with the absolute chronologies of Mesopotamia, Syria, and Egypt. Throughout the period, archaeological sequences recovered from stratified sites furnish relative chronologies.

Bronze Age metal technologies had a profound impact on the location and organization of settlements, material culture, and commercial networks in Anatolia. [*See* Metals, *article on* Artifacts of the Bronze and Iron Ages.] Bronze, silver, and gold were highly prized for weapons, tools, and personal ornaments, and the influence of these prestige materials can be seen in the metallic shapes, colors, and highly burnished surfaces of contemporary ceramic vessels. Stimulated by the demand for metals, trade in both raw materials and finished goods supplemented the settled subsistence economy based on dry farming and animal husbandry already established in Neolithic times.

Sites of this period display distinctive regional styles in architecture, ceramics, metalwork, and burial customs, perhaps reflecting different ethnic groups organized in small states. The site of Hisarlik, near Çanakkale, illustrates the material culture of northwestern Anatolia in this period. Long identified as the Troy of Homer's *Iliad,* the site is located in rich farmland, with access to the sea; its fortified citadel enclosed several buildings of a particular plan known as a megaron. [*See the biography of Schliemann.*]

Quantities of gold and silver vessels and jewelry preserved in a number of "treasures" testify to a highly developed metalworking industry and a wealthy elite. [*See* Jewelry.] Many of Troy's important commercial and cultural contacts were clearly by sea, for similar forms of architecture, ceramics, and metalwork are found at sites along the western coast and on offshore islands. On the southern coast, at the site of Karataş-Semayük near Elmalı, west of Antalya, a fortified citadel enclosed structures of megaron plan. In contrast to Troy, where no third-millennium burials have yet been found, Karataş yielded an extensive cemetery of inhumations placed in large ceramic storage jars, or pithoi. This form of burial was also customary in west-central Anatolia, where it continued into the early second millennium BCE. [*See* Jar Burials.] Still farther east, at the coastal site of Tarsus (Gözlü Kule), near Adana, architecture, ceramics, and metalwork similar to styles attested at Troy and Karataş demonstrate the range and importance of seagoing contacts in this period. [*See* Seafaring.] In north-central Anatolia, at the site of Alaca Höyük, stone-lined cist burials richly equipped with metal vessels, jewelry, and weapons probably belonged to the ruling elite. Elsewhere in central Anatolia, as at Alişar Höyük and Kültepe, fortification walls enclosed settlements with modest architecture and simple inhumation burials; large-scale buildings served as residences and administrative centers for the rulers or communal functions, such as temples. In eastern Anatolia, little-known archaeologically in this period, ceramics and metalwork reveal links with northern Mesopotamia and the Caucasus Mountains.

No written records explain the religious beliefs or practices of EB Anatolian cultures. Ceramic or metal sculptures of bulls, stags, and felines, among other animals, are often interpreted as representations of deities or of animals associated with particular deities. Illustrations of deities and their animals, or textual descriptions of such images, are found in central Anatolia in the second millennium BCE. Some of the same animals appear to have been worshipped in central Anatolia in Neolithic and Chalcolithic times, indicating a remarkable continuity in cultic expression over a period of several millennia.

A series of destruction levels at sites in western Anatolia from the mid- and late third millennium has been thought by some scholars to indicate the arrival of peoples speaking Indo-European languages, whose presence in central Anatolia is first documented by personal names mentioned in the Assyrian merchants' archives. [See Indo-European Languages.] However, where the homeland of the Indo-European speakers was located, and hence the route or routes by which they entered Anatolia, and when, are issues currently under debate.

Beginning in the Middle Bronze Age (2000–1600 BCE), and continuing into the Late Bronze Age (1600–1200 BCE), written records supplement archaeology in documenting political and economic organization, as well as ethnic and linguistic makeup. The earliest written records found in Anatolia are the commercial archives of merchants from northern Mesopotamia. Written in the Old Assyrian dialect of Akkadian, one of the Semitic languages of Mesopotamia, in cuneiform script, the records consist of small clay tablets and the clay envelopes in which they were originally enclosed. [See Cuneiform.] By far the largest merchant archives have been excavated at Kültepe, ancient Kaneš, near Kayseri in central Anatolia, furnishing evidence for the organization of the trade. [See Kültepe Texts; Kaneš.] Private, family-based firms established in Aššur, the capital of the Assyrian state of northern Mesopotamia, arranged for the export via donkey caravan of textiles and garments and a metal, probably tin, in exchange for silver and gold. [See Aššur; Textiles; Transportation.] This trade was conducted by Assyrian commercial representatives, who established permanent residence at some twenty centers in central and southeastern Anatolia and northern Syria; the trade continued for at least three generations. [See Assyrians.] The texts also provide a glimpse of the local communities with whom the foreign merchants did business and occasionally inter-

married. References to local Anatolian rulers suggest a political framework of small, independent states, occasionally united in temporary alliances through the efforts of a powerful individual. The merchants and their families lived in houses and used furnishings and utensils indistinguishable from those of the local residents.

Imported from Mesopotamia, the Akkadian language and cuneiform script seem not to have been adopted for use by native Anatolians. Many documents are sealed with cylinder seals, however, a Mesopotamian invention that spawned a native Anatolian style depicting local deities and scenes of worship. [See Seals.] Impressions of these seals are found on clay envelopes alongside those of Mesopotamian and North Syrian glyptic styles. The indigenous form of seal was the stamp, which was used along with the cylinder, and continued after trade with Assyria ended.

In about 1750 BCE, the merchant settlements and local communities were destroyed and abandoned. Perhaps a century later, a people known as the Hittites established a new political order from their capital city, Ḫattuša, today called Boğazköy. [See Hittites; Boğazköy.] Earlier the site of an Assyrian merchant colony and local settlement, Ḫattuša served as the capital of the Hittite Old Kingdom (1650–1400 BCE) and Empire (1400–1200 BCE) almost continuously for more than four hundred years. From this regional base, the Hittite kings gradually expanded their domain by frequent military campaigns and came to rule over most of central and southeastern Anatolia.

The language of the Hittites has been preserved in extensive cuneiform records on clay tablets recovered from Ḫattuša. Known in the texts as Neshite, it belongs to the Indo-European family of languages. Two other languages preserved in the archives, Luwian and Palaic, are closely related to Hittite. [See Luwians.] The archives also include texts written in Akkadian, the Semitic language of Mesopotamia; Hurrian, a non-Indo-European language spoken by the Hittites' neighbors to the southeast; and Hattian, another non-Indo-European language apparently spoken by the pre-Hittite inhabitants of central Anatolia. [See Akkadian; Hurrian.] Among the contents of the archives are royal laws, decrees, edicts, treaties, and letters; annals; literary works, epics, and myths; and a vast number of religious texts relating to festivals, rituals, and incantations. The cuneiform script continued as the principal writing system until the end of the empire. In addition to cuneiform, the Hittites also employed a hieroglyphic writing consisting of pictographic signs. A writing system of Anatolian invention, the hieroglyphic script was used on personal seals and on stone monuments carved with figured scenes. The language of the hieroglyphic script was not Hittite but Luwian, its close kin also written in cuneiform script on texts found at Ḫattuša.

From their political heartland in north-central Anatolia, the Hittite kings ruled over an ethnically and linguistically diverse empire. At its maximum extent, in the thirteenth century BCE, Hittite influence—if not outright political control—reached far into west-central Anatolia. In this region, the Hittites came into conflict with a power called the kingdom of Arzawa, which seems to have occupied the coastal regions of western and southern Anatolia, and whose language was Luwian. Arzawa was destroyed by the Hittites in about 1350 BCE. Farther west lay the state known in Hittite texts as Aḫḫiyawa, which has long been identified by some with the Mycenaean (Achaean) Greeks. The Hittite kings maintained active diplomatic exchanges with the great empires to the south and east: the Mitanni, centered in northern Syria and Mesopotamia; Egypt; Babylonia; and Assyria. Egyptian doctors and Babylonian sculptors were invited to the Hittite court by the king himself, and diplomatic marriages were arranged among the immediate members of these empires' ruling families. The close relationships the kings enjoyed with their counterparts in neighboring empires are richly illustrated by the Amarna letters, royal correspondence written in Akkadian and found at the site of Amarna in Egypt, dating principally from the reigns of pharaohs Amenhotep III and Akhenaten (c. 1360–1330 BCE). [See Amarna Tablets.] Yet, at the same time, the Hittites fought with Egypt over control of Syria's rich farmlands and thriving coastal ports. Finds of raw materials, such as ingots, together with luxury finished goods, demonstrate that extensive trade and perhaps also diplomatic contacts flourished in the Aegean region. The Hittite Empire, through its important port at Ugarit, was an active participant. [See Ugarit.]

Ḫattuša housed impressive buildings of administrative and religious function, surrounded by monumental fortification walls pierced by a few elaborate gates with carved sculptural decoration. Massive stone foundations, hewn with harder stones or iron tools, also secured mud-brick walls with timber framework for palace structures, in which the extensive archives mentioned previously were found. On higher ground, above the palace-citadel, a religious precinct housed some thirty temples almost identical in plan, probably built in one massive phase of construction during the thirteenth century BCE. Below the palace-citadel a monumental temple adjoined by extensive storage facilities was apparently dedicated to the Hittites' chief deities, the storm god, Tešub, and sun goddess, Hepat (see below). Outside the capital few sites have been intensively excavated, but at least several smaller cities boasted architecture and sculpture emulating imperial fashions: modest palaces, city walls decorated with figural relief sculptures, and guardian gate figures. Ceramic styles throughout the empire are virtually identical to those found at Ḫattuša, perhaps suggesting a centrally administered industry.

Texts found in the Ḫattuša archives, together with remains of temples and other cult sites, furnish information on the religion of the Hittites. Their pantheon consisted of male and female deities personifying forces of nature, but it also included deities of the Syrian and Mesopotamian religions. The iconography of the pantheon is known from relief preserved at cult sites, especially the rock sanctuary of Yazılıkaya, near Ḫattuša. The deities were often associated with a particular animal, whose image could be worshipped as a representative of the deity. Iconographically, some are closely related to deities depicted in the native Anatolian seals of the Assyrian merchant colonies (see above). Cult sites, usually consisting of a stone monument or rock face carved with a scene of worship, have been found over a wide area of Anatolia, supplementing textual documentation for an extraordinarily active calendar of religious festivals celebrated by the Hittite king and queen throughout the empire.

In about 1200 BCE, Ḫattuša was destroyed. The reasons for the destruction of this and other Hittite cities, and the subsequent collapse of the empire, are not well understood. Presumably, there were significant movements of peoples throughout Anatolia that succeeded in disrupting the empire's established political and military authority. Whatever the cause, the site of Ḫattuša was virtually abandoned for some time and never again supported a major city.

For the period beginning in about 1200 BCE, known in archaeological terms as the Iron Age, almost everywhere in Anatolia a "dark age" followed the end of the Hittite Empire. Yet, many imperial traditions lived on in southeastern Anatolia and northern Syria, formerly border provinces. There, small kingdoms were established, probably by 1000 BCE, when hieroglyphic inscriptions in the Luwian language again appeared on stone monuments. As with the hieroglyphic script of Hittite imperial times, these texts were mostly official and highly restricted in content, consisting primarily of commemorative and dedicatory inscriptions, boundary markers, and land grants. The Neo-Hittite states also continued imperial traditions of monumental stone architecture and reliefs decorating city walls and gates. Also beginning in about 1000 BCE, the Arameans, a Semitic-speaking people, moved into northwest Syria and established neighboring, and sometimes rival, states. [See Arameans.] The Arameans wrote their language using the Phoenician alphabetic script, but drew on Hittite traditions for monumental stone architecture and sculpture. [See Phoenician-Punic.] Located on or near the Euphrates River and in control of the lucrative trade routes between Mesopotamia and the Syrian coast, the Neo-Hittite and Aramean states were well suited to prosper. Beginning in the ninth century BCE, they came under the influence and then the political control of the Neo-Assyrian Empire centered in northern Mesopotamia. By the end of the eighth century BCE, the states were forced to pay tribute to the Assyrians.

In eastern Anatolia, the Bronze Age traditions of cuneiform script and interaction with Mesopotamia and Syria continued in the first millennium BCE in the kingdom of Urartu. [See Urartu.] Centered around Lake Van, this kingdom came to power in the early first millennium BCE, a rival state on the northern frontier of the Neo-Assyrian Empire. Its non-Indo-European language, apparently related to Hurrian, was written in cuneiform and has survived in many official and commemorative inscriptions. At its greatest extent, in the ninth century BCE, Urartu extended well into the regions occupied now by the Republic of Armenia and Iranian Azerbaijan. Like the Neo-Hittite states, Urartu was conquered and destroyed as a political entity by Assyrian armies in the eighth century BCE. Urartu also engaged in diplomatic and commercial exchanges with Phrygia, and perhaps also with North Syria.

By contrast, in the first millennium BCE, the kingdoms of central and western Anatolia borrowed alphabetic scripts to write their Anatolian languages. Inscriptions in Phrygian, Lydian, Lycian, and Carian are mostly dedicatory or commemorative, and for narrative accounts scholars depend on the writings of Herodotus (fifth century BCE), a native of the Greek town of Halikarnassos on the southwest coast of Anatolia. [See Lycia.] During the early first millennium BCE, settlers from mainland Greece established colonies on the western and southern coasts of Anatolia, and later along the Black Sea coast. While closely tied to their mother cities, these colonies prospered through their economic interaction with Anatolian states, with whom they were also linked culturally.

West-central Anatolia came under the control of the Phrygians, an Indo-European-speaking group that seems to have migrated there from the far northwest, probably originally from Thrace, reaching central Anatolia perhaps in about 1100 BCE. Phrygian inscriptions, mostly votive, are found on rock facades, altars, and small objects. Excavations at the Phrygian capital of Gordion, west of Ankara, have uncovered remains of fortifications, monumental buildings, and impressive tumulus burials whose rich contents suggest that their occupants were members of the ruling family. [See Gordion; Tumulus.] Cremation seems to have been the more typical burial form. Herodotus and later Greek tradition are the principal written sources on the Phrygians and their kings, especially Midas, who may also be the ruler, Mita, mentioned in Neo-Assyrian records. In outdoor cult places and in city temples, the Phrygians worshiped above all Cybele, an earth goddess of longstanding Anatolian tradition. Gordion was destroyed in about 700 BCE, apparently by invading Cimmerians from the north, whose attacks on Anatolia were recorded in both Greek and Neo-Assyrian sources.

The downfall of the Phrygians enabled another Anatolian kingdom to extend its domination toward the plateau. Until its conquest by the Achaemenid Persians in the 540s BCE, the Lydian kingdom of western Anatolia was ruled from its capital at Sardis, east of Izmir. [See Sardis.] During the seventh century and into the first half of the sixth century BCE, the kings of Lydia, especially Croesus, acquired wealth and status that became legendary in later Greek tradition. The

history of Lydia and its links with the coastal Greek cities under its control are known principally through Herodotus's accounts; inscriptions in the native language are few and mostly votive in content. Lydia also exchanged diplomatic envoys with the Neo-Assyrian court.

After Croesus's defeat by Cyrus, king of Persia, the Achaemenid Empire acquired the vast and rich region of Anatolia. The Achaemenid domination of Anatolia introduced new cultural elements, including languages and scripts, religion, and artistic traditions. Aramaic, the bureaucratic language of the Achaemenid Empire, has been preserved in the form of inscriptions carved on grave stelai or on small objects such as cylinder seals. [See Aramaic Language and Literature.] Inscriptions naming Iranian deities or their amalgamations with Anatolian or Greek counterparts demonstrate that Iranian religious beliefs were also introduced into the region. Under Darius (r. 520–486 BCE), the empire was organized into provinces called satrapies, ruled by a governor, or satrap, usually a member of the royal family. In western Anatolia, the satrapies centered at Sardis and Daskyleion are known in part through Greek accounts describing the conflict between the Greeks and Persians. Archaeology has contributed additional information, showing that the satrapal capitals fostered a rich and varied artistic mix combining Greek, native, and Iranian traditions. Farther south, in Lycia, inscriptions in Lycian, Greek, and Aramaic, together with extensive archaeological remains, document a similar cultural flowering under local dynasts who ruled for the Achaemenid Empire.

The invasion of Macedonian armies led by Alexander the Great, which began with the empire's westernmost possessions in Anatolia in the 330s BCE, brought the Achaemenid Empire to an end. In his sweep through western Asia, Alexander attacked and burned many of Anatolia's great cities. In 333 BCE he defeated the last Achaemenid ruler, Darius III, at the battle of Issus, near modern Iskanderun.

[See also Alexandrian Empire; and Persia, article on Ancient Persia.]

BIBLIOGRAPHY

Akurgal, Ekrem. *Die Kunst Anatoliens von Homer bis Alexander*. Berlin, 1961. Well-illustrated survey of the native arts of Anatolia in the first millennium BCE, with special reference to central and western Anatolia.

American Journal of Archaeology. Includes a yearly illustrated newsletter reporting on excavation and survey results in Turkey, covering the Palaeolithic through Byzantine periods. Initiated by Machteld J. Mellink, "Archaeology in Asia Minor/Anatolia" (1955–1993), the newsletter is now written by Marie-Henriette C. Gates, "Archaeology in Turkey" (1994–).

Bittel, Kurt. *Die Hethiter: Die Kunst Anatoliens vom Ende des 3. bis zum Anfang des 1. Jahrtausends vor Christus*. Munich, 1976. Richly illustrated survey focusing on art and architecture, beginning with cultural developments of the Early Bronze Age.

The Cambridge Ancient History. Vols. 1–3.2, 4. Cambridge, 1971–1988. Contains authoritative chapters on the archaeology and history of

Anatolia from the Early Bronze Age through the Achaemenid period. See essays by James Mellaart, Hildegard Lewy, R. A. Crossland, Albrecht Götze, R. D. Barnett, Carl W. Blegen, Machteld J. Mellink, J. D. Hawkins, J. M. Cook, and Olivier Masson. Contributions treating the Bronze Age, especially archaeological topics, are out of date and need to be supplemented by preliminary or final publications mentioned in the yearly newsletter of the *American Journal of Archaeology* (see above).

Gurney, O. R. *The Hittites*. Rev. ed. London, 1990. Highly readable and useful introduction to the history, languages, and archaeological remains.

Haas, Volkert. *Geschichte der hethitischen Religion*. Leiden, 1994. Detailed scholarly synthesis.

Sasson, Jack M., et al., eds. *Civilizations of the Ancient Near East*. New York, 1995. Articles on Anatolian history, art, and archaeology, written by specialists for a general readership; illustrated, with annotated bibliographies.

van Loon, Maurits N. *Anatolia in the Second Millennium B.C.* Leiden, 1985.

van Loon, Maurits N. *Anatolia in the Earlier First Millennium B.C.* Leiden, 1991. This and van Loon's volume above examine the rich repertoire of religious iconography in the light of archaeological and textual sources; abundantly illustrated and full of insights.

ANN C. GUNTER

Anatolia From Alexander to the Rise of Islam

The Hellenistic age in Anatolia opens with the arrival of Alexander the Great, king of Macedon, at Troy in 334 BCE, from whence he launched his conquest of the Persians and united the Greeks, or Hellenes, on both sides of the Aegean Sea. Final victory against Darius III was achieved at the battle of Issus, near Syrian Antioch, in 333 BCE. [*See* Antioch.] Henceforth, Greek culture and institutions, already established to some extent in the western cities, predominated in Anatolia. A uniform culture and the Greek language supplanted local styles and dialects. Predominant was the foundation of cities governed by Greek political institutions, a council, popular assembly, and college of magistrates. The *gymnasion* was the key cultural and educational institution. The Persian oligarchy was supplanted by principles that were democratic by the standards of the day.

Alexander died in 323 BCE. Within twenty years his empire was divided into four kingdoms ruled by his successors *(diadochoi)* and Hellenistic monarchy emerged. The attributes of kingship appear on coins and sculpture. [*See* Coins.] Anatolia north of the Taurus Mountains was ruled by the Seleucids, descendants of Seleucus, one of Alexander's generals. [*See* Seleucids.] The ruler of Thrace, Lysimachos, rivaled Seleucid control in Anatolia until he was defeated by Seleucus I at the battle of Korupedion in 281 BCE. South of the Taurus, Lycia and Pamphylia belonged to the Ptolemies, who ruled Egypt. [*See* Lycia; Ptolemies.] The cities on the Aegean coast, descendents of the Greek colonies, remained nominally free. Cappadocia, Pontus, and Bithynia remained independent kingdoms. [*See* Cappadocia.] In the early third century (c. 280 BCE), a semi-independent kingdom arose in the west, ruled by the local Attalid dynasty established at Pergamon. [*See* Pergamon.]

These changes had profound cultural effects strongly elucidated by the archaeological record. Inscriptions, many collected before the era of controlled excavation and published in a systematic corpus, *Monumenta Asiae Minoris Antiqua,* are as important as historical texts in revealing the major players, social and political organization, and changes in religion and occurrence of festivals. The network of roads the Persians established was expanded both for the movement of troops and for travel and trade. [*See* Roads; Transportation.] Coins were minted by kings and by cities. A single standard for silver and gold prevailed over much of the Hellenistic world, and the issuance of bronze coins in small denominations led to a monetary economy. Coins were also used as propaganda: for example, coins show Alexander with the power and attributes of Zeus. Patterns of overseas trade have been established through analysis of ceramics, their stamps, and graffiti.

A Celtic tribe from Europe, the Gauls, or Galatians, invaded Anatolia in 278 BCE. Within ten years the Galatians had acquired extensive territories and wealth through plunder and extracting protection money from cities. In the mid-third century BCE, the Galatians and their allies in Bythinia were defeated in a decisive battle by the king of Pergamon, Attalus I. In celebration of this victory, a great altar decorated with reliefs and two sculptures—a dying Gaul by Epigonus and a warrior and his wife committing suicide—were set up in the precinct of the Temple of Athena at Pergamon, establishing it as an artistic center that rivaled Athens and extended far-reaching influence into the Roman imperial period.

The majority of the Gauls moved into Phrygia, which was renamed Galatia. Although partially hellenized, they retained their own material culture, a distinctive political and social organization, and their own language, still spoken in Late Antiquity. Their customs included human and animal sacrifice, which has been graphically confirmed by skeletal finds at Gordion. [*See* Gordion.]

Hellenistic Cities. In the Troad, Alexander instructed that Ilyum be rebuilt. It was later overshadowed by Alexander Troas and joined in the Ilian foundation with Assos, Parium, and Lampsacus. Cyme, Myrina, Gryneum, and Elea (the port of Pergamon) were established. The Ionian cities of Ephesus, Smyrna, Priene, and Colophon were moved, largely because silt had filled in the harbors and created unhealthy marshes. [*See* Assos; Ephesus; Priene.] The new cities show the development of planned complexes in which individual buildings were designed to fit a visually unified whole and the streets followed the rectilinear grid plan named for Hippodamus of Miletus. Open spaces were provided by sanctuaries, the palaestras of the gymnasia, and rectilinear agoras with stoas, often two-storied, on all four sides, except where they were built into the hillside, as at

Assos and Pergamon. In some cases shops were built behind the colonnade; the east stoa of the South Agora at Miletus has back-to-back shops and at Alinda and Aigai shops and storerooms were built below the colonnade on the downhill side of the agora. [See Miletus.]

The classical orders were used freely for nonstructural decoration. [See Architectural Orders.] The Temple of Zeus at Olba in Cilicia, begun in about 170 BCE by Antiochus IV, ranks with the Olympeion in Athens as the earliest Corinthian temples. The Council House at Miletus exemplifies the new secular architecture and the use of composite orders. All cities had a theater with stage buildings and a stadium with seating supported by stone vaulting. [See Theaters; Stadiums; Building Materials and Techniques, article on Materials and Techniques of the Persian through Roman Periods.] Portrait statues stood in the theater, in the agoras, and along the streets, a reversal of earlier custom, which prohibited the representation of an individual before death. [See Architectural Decoration.] Although few statues have survived, many bases and dedicatory inscriptions remain to tell of the benefactions of individual citizens. [See Inscriptions, article on Inscriptions of the Hellenistic and Roman Periods.]

As a wealthy class of merchants and officials arose, grand residences were built, typically focused on an inner court and decorated with mosaic pavements, painted walls, and marble statues and furnishings. [See Mosaics; Wall Paintings.] These are known best through the well-preserved houses excavated at Priene. Furnishings were lavish, with marble stands and tables, ivory inlay, and bronze and silver embellishment. Terra-cotta figurines were much favored as ornaments and as dedications, and they reveal a great deal about styles of dress and daily activities (Myrina).

Post-and-lintel construction remained basic, but the arch and vault were introduced. [See Arches.] Sloping vaults covered the interior passages in the Temple of Apollo at Didyma. [See Didyma.] The tradition of fitted stone masonry without the use of mortar persisted.

A new style of city planning developed that was rooted in the ancient Anatolian acropolis palace. [See Palace.] It featured vertical planning and conformity rather than resistance to the topography. Pergamon demonstrates the most adventurous and dramatic development of this new concept of exploiting the terrain but regularizing it with terraces supported by retaining walls of large ashlars—once believed to be a Hellenistic innovation but now known to have occurred much earlier, at Sardis. [See Sardis.]

The deification of kings and the heroization of nobles and local potentates gave rise to the building of grand tombs. [See Tombs.] The most splendid is the tomb at Belevi, near Ephesus, begun after 300 BCE, possibly for Lysimachos. The tomb was reused by Antiochus II. In Lycia, rock-cut tomb chambers are faced with Greek facades, some showing Persian burial customs combined with Greek figural styles. [See Burial Techniques.]

Each city controlled the surrounding territory with farms, towns, sanctuaries, and landed estates. On the coast and along the east–west river valleys these territories were contiguous, but the density of urbanization diminished inland. Although many surveys have been carried out, analysis of country life is the area least elucidated by archaeology.

Hellenistic Temples and Religion. Temples and their estates were central to the religious and economic life of Anatolia; temple states, ruled by priests, became strong centers of settlement in the interior and in the south, where cities were slow to develop. Temple estates were not secularized until the Roman period, but under Seleucid rule land was often taken from them to found cities. The ancient fertility gods worshiped at these cult centers gradually acquired Greek names and associations: for example, Attis at Pessinus, Zeus of Olba, and the many shrines to Artemis. [See Cult.]

In the west, cult centers flourished, some traditionally attached to the cities. One of the largest building projects was the Temple of Apollo, patron deity of the Seleucid kings, at Didyma (see above). The rebuilding of the huge Temple of Artemis at Ephesus was to make it one of the Seven Wonders of the World.

Roman Rule. The pressure of the expanding power of Rome was felt as early as 200 BCE, and by the first century BCE, after the conquest of Pompey, the remaining Hellenistic kingdoms were vassal states. Augustus annexed most of Anatolia to Rome, and under his reign the growth of urban institutions, a permanent military presence, and radical changes in the pattern of land ownership were witnessed. The institutions and ideals of the Hellenistic monarchs were continued and evolved as Anatolia was integrated into the social and economic organization of the Roman empire. Although Latin was the language of empire, the language of the educated classes in which official notices and dedications were inscribed remained Greek. [See Latin; Greek.]

From 25 BCE to 235 CE, Anatolia was organized into five major provinces—Asia, Bithynia and Pontus, Galatia, and Cappadocia, from which Tres Eparchiae was split in 140 CE—with the Euphrates River forming the eastern frontier. [See Euphrates.] The boundaries of the province of Asia remained firm, but the others, especially Galatia's, fluctuated. Administration depended on a network of cities and their dependent territories. Tax collection, provision of supplies, and transport for the armies and officials were all organized through the administration of the cities. Urbanization spread through the imperial foundation of cities and the consolidation of their territories. By the end of the Julio-Claudian period (68 CE), a network of cities was established in central Anatolia for the first time. For two centuries thereafter, the Anatolian cities grew in size and importance and became the wealthiest in the empire.

The wealth of the Anatolian cities was, however, always derived from the land and the expansion of agriculture and stock raising. [See Agriculture.] Timber was brought down from the mountains and marble was one of the principle exports throughout the empire. Both the sculptors and sculpture from the workshops at Aphrodisias were found at Rome and other centers. [*See* Aphrodisias.] Salted fish (tunny), olives, grapes, and wine (Cappadocian wine rivaled that from Greece), grain, wool and skins from stock raising, and flax and linen woven in Cilicia were all widely exported. [*See* Olives; Viticulture; Cilicia.] Additional wealth was derived from silver and iron deposits, semiprecious stones, mica, and other mineral resources. [*See* Metals, *article on* Artifacts of the Persian through Roman Periods.] The huge harbor buildings at Aegean and Mediterranean ports bear witness to the extent of maritime trade. Underwater archaeology has just begun to reveal rich information from shipwrecks and submerged harbors. [*See* Seafaring.]

In the Taurus/Pisidia, the Julio-Claudian emperors built roads to link the highland cities with the coast. By the end of the first century CE, a network of paved roads that was maintained until the fourth century crisscrossed the peninsula. The roads were built primarily by Vespasian for the military, but they facilitated travel and trade. In the second and third centuries, a system of rest houses and post stations developed. Vespasian established the limes on the frontier— forts linked by paved highways and auxiliary forts between them—and established garrisons, the most important at Ancyra.

Roman cities. There was absolute continuity of the Hellenistic tradition in architecture and city planning under Roman rule, but the emphasis was more on secular than religious building. [*See* Cities, *article on* Cities of the Hellenistic and Roman Periods.] Changes in construction materials especially the use of vaulting and concrete, were not as dramatic as in the West. The notable contribution of Roman planners was to connect urban spaces with colonnaded thoroughfares that transected the city between well-defined gateways. Sagalassos exemplifies the Roman embellishment of the city with monumental entrances added to both agoras under Tiberius and Claudius, the building of a sanctuary of Apollo Clarius, probably under Augustus, and the building of triumphal arches, symbolic of Roman rule.

In 17 CE, an earthquake leveled twelve of the great cities in the west; hardest hit was Sardis. Rebuilding was on a strictly Roman plan under imperial direction. As the cities grew, new buildings and neighborhoods were connected by major streets having colonnaded sidewalks with shops behind them. The streets opened into colonnaded plazas that served as the commercial agoras and as gathering places. Statuary in every conceivable context—along the roadways, on facades and monuments, and on tombs and sarcophagi— celebrated the power of the emperor and the prestige of rich citizens. [*See* Sarcophagus.] Portrait sculpture became a major industry (e.g., at Aphrodisias). Recent evidence suggests Sagalassos was an equally important center for sculpture. Stonecutters of all types were required to chisel inscriptions and elaborate architectural ornament and to cut marble and

other colored stones to be set in patterns on walls and floors. Schools of painters and mosaicists appear to have moved from city to city.

By the end of the second century every throughway had a fountain, some set in exedras (as at the great *nymphaion* at Miletus), some with elaborate aedicular buildings (e.g., at Hierapolis, Side). The bath-gymnasium became the architectural symbol of imperial culture. [*See* Baths.] Baths and fountains required vast amounts of water, which were provided by aqueducts. [*See* Aqueducts.] Placing the water supply outside the fortification walls was only made possible by the *pax romana*. Adequate drainage and waste disposal were the responsibility of the civic administration.

Entertainment was taken for granted by the populace. Theaters were modified to accommodate animal contests and many cities had an amphitheater. The best-preserved theater, at Aspendos, has a seating capacity for seventy-five hundred spectators.

Housing, needed for a vastly increased population, is best studied at Ephesus, where terraced houses reached five stories and were arranged in blocks, or insulae. They were richly furnished and decorated with mosaics, paintings, and cut-marble inlay.

Inscriptions document some key aspects of city life. Patriotism is revealed by dedications to the *patris*. Family members were celebrated through the naming of privately donated buildings, as the libraries at Sagalassos and Ephesus demonstrate. [*See* Libraries and Archives.] Pre-Roman cultural heritage was often celebrated: Tarsus and Aigai in Cilicia claimed Perseus as their founder, Nicaea was founded by Herakles, other cities claimed relationships with Argos, Athens, and Sparta. Under the Severan emperors building reached a zenith, and the network of cities attained its maximum geographic extent.

Imperial cult. The imperial cult played an important role in the development of urbanism. In newly annexed areas the cult provided traditions that unified the populous: public sacrifices, festivals, games, wild-animal fights *(venationes),* and gladiatorial shows at which feasts were enjoyed and corn and oil distributed. Before taking the name of Augustus in 27 BCE, Octavian authorized dedications to Rome and the deified Julius Caesar at Ephesus and Nicaea and to himself at Pergamon and Nicomedia. At Aphrodisias the Sebasteion, the most elaborate temple complex to the imperial cult presently known, was established during the reign of Claudius (41–54 CE) through a private donation. The temple itself and the public buildings connected to it were often the first Greco-Roman buildings in the new cities of the interior.

Later Empire. In the mid-third century, incursions by the Goths from the north and the Sasanian Persians and breakaway dynasts of Palmyra from the east and south caused the collapse of the empire's frontiers. [*See* Sasanians; Persians; Palmyra.] Throughout the peninsula hasty fortifications were built around the cities, often with material taken from public buildings. Widespread plague also contributed to an economic crisis. In response, Diocletian, who ruled from Nicomedia (284–305, instituted radical administrative changes: he created smaller provinces composed of the contiguous territories of the cities. Frontiers were strengthened and troops, who were paid in kind as well as in coin, were stationed in and near the cities. The authority of the city councilors gradually diminished under the strain of increased taxation, and the ancient autonomy of the cities was gradually lost. The transfer of lands to the church and consequent loss of taxes also contributed to urban decline.

The countryside, with its villages and landed estates, became the key factor in economic recovery in the fourth century. [See Villages.] When grain supplies from Egypt were inadequate, the capital was supplied from Anatolia, especially from Bithynia and Phrygia. Stock raising continued to be the predominant use of land on the central plateau. Neither erosion nor deforestation from the overexploitation of the land appears to have altered settlement patterns—the only geomorphological change to have done so was the silting up of the great harbors.

Scholarship has relinquished the old concept of "decline and fall," largely as a result of the archaeological evidence, which shows continued urban life and even growth during the fourth and fifth centuries. The survival of classical culture is seen in writing and in the arts, especially sculpture (e.g., at Nicomedia, Nicaea, Ephesus, and Sardis). In the sixth century, the picture changed. Plague struck again and pressure from the Persians intensified. Treaties with them were made at an enormous price in gold. Justinian's building programs caused a further strain on local economies and manpower, while earthquakes disrupted the water supply and the aqueducts fell into disrepair. In general, the subdivision of and encroachment on monumental buildings and thoroughfares was widespread (e.g., at Sagalassos, Sardis, Ancyra). However, streets were repaired late into the century and a lively local commerce and small industry continued with the manufacture of pottery, glass, gilded jewelry, and utilitarian metal items—albeit often from recycled materials (e.g., at Sardis, Sagalassos). [See Glass; Jewelry.] Of continued scholarly debate is whether the evidence demonstrates an actual decline in society or a new pattern of settlement that was concentrated less in the city, foreshadowing the medieval society that emerged after the dark age that followed the Persian invasions in the seventh century (see below).

Judaism and Christianity. The single most provocative development in Late Antiquity was the rise of Christianity, which was introduced into Anatolia by St. Paul in the first century CE. After the Christian church was legalized in the early fourth century, churches and other ecclesiastical buildings were built rapidly, sometimes preempting civic space such as the agora (e.g., at Sagalassos). [See Churches.] Pagan temples slowly went out of use or were converted to churches (e.g., at Aphrodisias). Burials were made in and around the churches, a change from the Roman prohibition

of burial within the city. [See Burial Sites.] Political power transferred from the civic centers to the ecclesiastical realm. Excavation has enhanced the picture of personal piety through rich finds of seals and amulets, small flasks from pilgrimage sites, and Christian symbols on domestic pottery, glass, metal, gravestones, and sarcophagi. The material culture also demonstrates the persistence of pagan cult and superstition, especially the practice of magic.

The conditions under which Christianity spread so rapidly in Anatolia are complex. Archaeological evidence has illuminated the size and civil status of Jewish communities (e.g., the great synagogue at Sardis, an inscription at Aphrodisias, coins from Apamea in Phrygia showing Noah's ark). Jews had been resettled in Lydia and Phrygia by Antiochus III at the end of the third century BCE, and imperial directives had protected Jewish law and customs since the reign of Caesar. As is clear from the story of Paul's visits to Galatia, related in *Acts,* the status of the Jewish communities was undoubtedly basic to the spread of the Christian message. Concurrently, a strong tendency to monotheism had developed in paganism with the rise of a "super god" (*Theos Hipsistos,* a term used also by the Jews to describe their God). Thus, the worship of an abstract god who dwelt above or replaced the anthropomorphic pantheon was fertile ground for the spread of Christianity even before Constantine, when it was accepted as the official religion, supplanting the imperial cult.

End of Antiquity. The Sasanian Persians, under Chosroes II, took Antioch and Jerusalem in 614 CE, Alexandria in 617, and then turned on Anatolia. [See Jerusalem; Alexandria.] Coin finds at several Anatolian cities stop with the issues of 616/17, and there is evidence of destruction, burning, and population dispersal. Heraclius counterattacked and reestablished the eastern frontier, but the cities of Anatolia had suffered to such an extent they never recovered.

The history of central Anatolia during the seventh and eighth centuries is little known; excavation shows that churches were repaired and enlarged (e.g., at Amorium, Sardis, Aphrodisias), but little is known about the life of the inhabitants. A genuine dark age apparently ensued until the ninth century, for which some evidence is available. When recovery did occur, the cities that survived had retracted to walled *acropoleis.* The vast urban culture established under Greco-Roman domination was to some extent a thin veneer that disappeared after imperial rule was weakened and Anatolia became once again a land of villages and country estates.

[See also Alexandrian Empire; and Roman Empire.]

BIBLIOGRAPHY

Brown, Peter. *The World of Late Antiquity.* New York, 1971. Social history, especially the deep effects of religious change rooted in Anatolia.

The Cambridge Ancient History. Vols. 7.1, 8, and 9. 2d ed. Cambridge, 1984–1994. The best historical overview of the Hellenistic and early

Roman period; the relevant sections are clear from the outline/contents. The separate plates to volume 7.1 provide notes and illustrations on sites and finds. Additional volumes of this edition are planned. Extensive bibliography.

Cameron, Averil. *The Mediterranean World in Late Antiquity, 395–600.* London, 1993. Provides extensive critical bibliography and analysis of the state of scholarship, situating Anatolia in a broader context.

Foss, Clive. *History and Archaeology of Byzantine Asia Minor.* Aldershot, 1990. The articles reprinted here form the seminal study of the "disappearance" of the great Greco-Roman cities and the importance of archaeological evidence to historical reconstruction.

Gates, Marie-Henriette. "Archaeology in Turkey." *American Journal of Archaeology* 99 (1995): 207–255. The most recent summary of current fieldwork and new bibliography for sites in Anatolia, published annually (previously "Archaeology in Asia Minor" by Machteld Mellink).

Hanfmann, George M. A. *From Croesus to Constantine: The Cities of Western Asia Minor and Their Arts in Greek and Roman Times.* Ann Arbor, 1975. Still a stimulating treatment of the creative synthesis of Greek and Anatolian contributions to the plastic arts and city planning.

Lloyd, Seton. *Ancient Turkey: A Traveller's History of Anatolia.* London, 1989. Extraordinarily clear narrative history imbued with the author's close experience of the ancient sites, routes, and countryside. See especially chapters 12–20.

MacDonald, William L. *The Architecture of the Roman Empire,* vol. 2, *An Urban Appraisal.* New Haven, 1986. The reciprocal relationship of Rome and its provinces in the development of urbanism and the imagery of empire. Limited in its point of view; see the review by Frank B. Sear, *Journal of Roman Archaeology* 1 (1988): 160–165.

Magie, David. *Roman Rule in Asia Minor to the End of the Third Century after Christ.* 2 vols. Princeton, 1950. Fundamental to the study of the Roman period.

Mitchell, Stephen. *Anatolia: Land, Men, and Gods in Asia Minor,* vol. 1, *The Celts and the Impact of Roman Rule;* vol. 2, *The Rise of the Church.* New York, 1993. Definitive treatment of the period from the conquest of Alexander through the fourth century CE. Thorough synthesis of textual and archaeological evidence, concentrating on central Anatolia. Extensive bibliography.

Price, S. R. F. *Rituals of Power: The Roman Imperial Cult in Asia Minor.* Cambridge, 1984. Remains the basic work.

Ramage, N. H., and Andrew Ramage. *Roman Art: Romulus to Constantine.* Englewood Cliffs, N.J., 1991. Lucid and well-illustrated account. The authors' long experience working in Turkey results in more than usual emphasis on the artistic centers in Anatolia. A new edition is in press.

Syme, Ronald. *Anatolica: Studies in Strabo.* Edited and completed posthumously by Anthony R. Birley. Oxford, 1995. Studies in the historical geography of Anatolia and adjacent regions, with reference to the *Geography* of Strabo.

JANE AYER SCOTT

Anatolia in the Islamic Period

Three phases mark the history of medieval Anatolia. From the seventh to the ninth century CE urban life and economic exchange shrank drastically; from the tenth until the twelfth century recovery occurred in towns, cities, and the countryside until the disruptions of Turkish immigration; and from the twelfth century onward an influx of pastoral nomads, a growth of regional trade, and the processes of conversion to Islam accompanied the splintering of political authority and the end of Byzantine power in the peninsula. During the first era, Byzantium ruled the peninsula supreme; in the second, central Anatolia became the home of the Seljuks of Rum; and in the third, Byzantium lost control over the coastal lands and the Seljuks ultimately disappeared before the Mongols and the Turkish *beyliks* (area ruled by a *bey*).

Despite the utility of such public works as the great bridge over the Sangarius (completed in 560) and the church of St. John at Ephesus of the emperor Justinian (527–565), the cost of his campaigns, as well as outbreaks of plague (beginning in 542), burdened his subjects and led to a pause in the prosperity of towns and cities. This prosperity came to an end following the destructive invasions of the Persians (613–626), who practically ended classical urban life in this corner of the Mediterranean. Once prosperous cities (Sardis [c. 616] Ephesus [c. 614], Ankara [622], Pergamon, for example) shrank to fortifications and villages, occasionally on nearby hills. Coin finds and the evidence from such sites as have been excavated or surveyed point to a substantial decline in economic life and the end of public works and social services.

A full recovery from the Persian devastation remained impossible for two full centuries because of Muslim raids that began in 641. Ankara in the center and Amorion in the southwest became centers of Byzantine defense, and many cities became walled or had their existing walls strengthened. The raids were disruptive but did not result in Muslim occupation of lands north and west of the Taurus range, and in areas untouched by Muslim raids there was a relative continuity, as in the monastic communities in Bithynia. Nonetheless, there is little Byzantine construction on the plateau beyond repairs that may be securely dated to the period from the Persian invasions to the Macedonian dynasty, and thus the era is justly termed a "dark age." Cities became fortified, housing shrank in size and quality, and many settlements removed to better defensible hills: external threat and internal defense became key concepts.

Beginning in the mid-ninth century, the emperors of the Macedonian dynasty managed to stop the raids (after 863 they went on the offensive) and to restore peace and predictability to life on the plateau. Consequently, there is evidence of economic expansion and urban revival. A broad recovery may be posited from the restoration of the church of the Dormition at Nicaea (after 843), the church of St. Nicholas at Myra, the building, perhaps in the late ninth century, of the (pilgrimage?) church at Dereağzı (Lycia), a very large building for a remote hill country, and the tenth- or eleventh-century church of Üçayak. In the ninth century there also began an era of construction and elaboration of the rock-cut churches and monasteries of Cappadocia, in the Peristrema valley near Aksaray and the area centered on Göreme, where new building flourished from around 900 to about 1060.

Turkish migration into Anatolia began in the mid-eleventh century, and after the Seljuk sultan Alp Arslan (1063–1073) defeated the Byzantines at Manzikert (1071) no line of defense prevented the Turks from raiding the plateau and even establishing a short-lived emirate at Nicaea. During the First Crusade, Alexios Komnenos (1081–1118) managed to reconquer Nicaea and to retrieve the coastal plains and the hill country of western Anatolia for Byzantium. During the twelfth century Seljuk and Danishmend leaders warred over the possession of central Anatolia, and only after the defeat of the Danishmendids (1178) and the crushing of a Byzantine army at Myriocephalon (1176) were the Seljuks, now established at Iconium/Konya under the leadership of Kılıj Arslan II (1155–1192), able to devote themselves fully to the elaboration of Perso-Islamic civilization in the peninsula; in 1156 the construction of the 'Ala ed-Din mosque at Konya began, but no great resources were available for monumental building. The Seljuks began to strike silver *dirham*s in the 1180s, and their silver coinage, of a fineness superior to other Muslim coinages in the Levant, continued to expand until the end of the thirteenth century. To their west, during the early and middle years of the twelfth century the Komneni built a number of fortifications and walled many of their Anatolian towns (e.g., Achyraous 1139, Dorylaion 1175, Laodikeia [Laodicea] c. 1119, Lopadion 1130), and as the frontier stabilized on the western confines of the plateau after the Fourth Crusade, there was further economic development, including the growth of long-distance trade throughout the peninsula and across the political frontiers. Even during the period of Byzantine exile in Anatolia, from 1204 to 1261, there is evidence of an increase in wealth both in the "empires" of Nicaea and Trebizond: building of churches (e.g., Nicaea) and fortifications (such as Nymphaion, Pegai) resumed on a modest scale. There was, however, much more Turkish than Byzantine construction in Anatolia.

The fullest flowering of Seljuk civilization in Anatolia occurred in the generation before the Mongol defeat of the Seljuk armies at Köse Dağı (1243). The monumental constructions of the Seljuks, superior in number, quality, and size to Byzantine Anatolian architecture, reflect the wealth of their society; indeed, no fewer than ten Anatolian silver mines were in operation (and were Seljuk mint sites) during the century. The Seljuks conquered important ports (Antalya in 1207, Sinope in 1214) that allowed them to establish and reinforce commercial routes. The extent of trade, and its extension across the peninsula from Constantinople to Konya and from Konya to the Mediterranean or to Sivas and the east is best measured by the forty or more caravanserais built during this era (no Byzantine caravanserai is known). There was a great deal of mosque and tomb construction, and excavation of the country palaces of the Seljuks at Kubadiya and Kubadabad has begun (M. Zeki-Oral, 1949–1951; Katharina Otto-Dorn and Mehmet Önder, 1965–1966). The Rum Seljuk constructions of this era are known for their extensive use of calligraphic ornamentation and "stalactites" *(muqarnas)*. During the entire century much of the monumental architecture was ordered by high officials of the government, and there was a good deal of building (besides at Konya) in Sivas, Tokat, Amasya, and Erzurum. The patronage of the sultans was either military or devoted to commercial use; and there was some patronage from the women of the royal family. The Mongols extracted an enormous tribute from the Seljuks, and after 1277 administered eastern Anatolia as a province of the Ilkhanate, but the economic expansion of the peninsula did not suffer greatly; in 1299 there were well over thirty mints striking silver *dirham*s, a figure not attained before or since. After 1243, however, there is little architectural patronage from the sultans, and most comes from the officials of state; there was, then, no letting up in construction. The Mongols were able to control eastern Anatolia into the fourteenth century, but the collapse of Byzantine defenses at the edge of the plateau after the recovery of Constantinople in 1261 led to the Turkish infiltration of the entire coastal areas, except for Trebizond and the eastern shores of the Marmara, by 1300, and the division of Anatolia into a number of *beylik*s, usually founded by independent chiefs, which lasted until the later Ottoman conquests. The mosques and other structures of the early *beylik* era are small, and among early Ottoman monuments they display Byzantine influence in building style ("Byzlamic," in the terminology of Clive Foss).

Despite the political, cultural, and religious changes during this era, there were some constants. The incursions of the Turks before and with the Mongols strengthened the pastoral segment of Anatolian agriculture, but it had long been polycultural. Agricultural technology remained based upon earlier practices. By 1300, the conversion of Greek Christians to Islam was well under way but by no means complete, and there were inheritances from Christianity in the form of Islam practiced in the countryside.

[*See also* Byzantine Empire.]

BIBLIOGRAPHY

Cahen, Claude. *La Turquie pré-Ottomane*. Paris and Istanbul, 1988. Standard survey of the Seljuks of Rum; the English version (New York, 1968) has fuller coverage but lacks documentation.

Crane, Howard. "Notes on Saldjūq Architectural Patronage in Thirteenth-Century Anatolia." *Journal of the Economic and Social History of the Orient* 36 (1993): 1–57. Contains a full list of patrons and buildings, with helpful commentary.

Foss, Clive. "Archaeology and the 'Twenty Cities' of Byzantine Asia." *American Journal of Archaeology* 81 (1977): 469–486. Convenient summary of important work published in detail in later articles and monographs.

Foss, Clive, and David Winfield. *Byzantine Fortifications: An Introduction*. Pretoria, 1986. Important study of method.

Hendy, Michael. *Studies in the Byzantine Monetary Economy c. 300–1450*. Cambridge, 1985. Landmark study (to be used with caution) of the interaction of Byzantine economic, social, and monetary history.

Mango, Cyril. *Byzantine Architecture*. New York, 1976. Authoritative, well-illustrated survey.

Meinecke, Michael. "Kubādābād." In *Encyclopaedia of Islam,* new ed., vol. 5, pp. 285–286. Leiden, 1986.

The Oxford Dictionary of Byzantium. 3 vols. Oxford, 1991. The best digest of information on individual sites. The *Encyclopaedia of Islam* is uneven, as is its Turkish version, the *Islam Ansiklopedisi,* which is fuller on Anatolian cities.

Rodley, Lyn. *Cave Monasteries of Byzantine Cappadocia.* Cambridge, 1985. Emphasizes architecture rather than decoration.

Tabula imperii byzantini. Vienna, 1976–. The best site surveys and discussions of sources bearing upon particular locales; profusely illustrated with excellent maps.

RUDI PAUL LINDNER

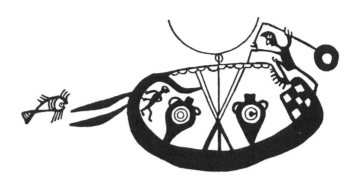

ANCHORS. Figure 1. *Depiction of a figure on a ship handling a stone anchor.* Painting from a seventh-century BCE Cypriot jug. (After Karageorghis and des Gagniers, 1974, p. 123, no. 11.2)

ANCHORS. In antiquity, those who sailed utilized stones as the earliest anchoring devices. As anchors found on the seabed assume the passing of a ship, these stones provide valuable clues about ancient routes and seafaring practices. Defining the nationalities of stone anchor types can thus lead researchers to determining the range and directions of ancient seafarers. A ship's home port also may be identifiable from the anchors it carried.

As the last hope for a storm-tossed ship, anchors also took on a religious significance—and many have been found in temples and other cultic locations. Because anchors found on the seabed are unlikely to have a stratigraphic context, their dating depends largely on anchors found at archaeologically excavated land sites.

Stone Anchors. Along the shores of the eastern Mediterranean during the Bronze and the Iron Ages, anchor stones were pierced to secure the hawsers (ropes). Typologically, pierced-stone anchors fall into three categories: weight anchors, in which the stone's weight acts as the anchoring device; sand anchors, which are relatively lightweight and contain one or more additional piercings to secure wooden slats that grasp the seabed; and composite anchors, which hold the seabed both by means of their weight and by wooden "arms" inserted through additional piercings.

Stone anchors are often asymmetrical. Erect anchors positioned at the bow are sometimes depicted in illustrations of seagoing ships in Old Kingdom Egypt. This design may have permitted the anchors to stand upright on a tilting deck. If so, bars must have been used to lock them in place against the bulwarks to prevent their shifting in heavy seas.

Although the heaviest recorded Bronze Age stone anchor, from Kition, weighs 1,350 kg, it is unlikely to have been used at sea. [*See* Kition.] Half-ton stone anchors found on the Mediterranean sea floor probably indicate the upper limits of functional weight. How such heavy anchors were raised without a capstan is unclear. Two seventh-century BCE Cypriot jugs depict the handling of stone anchors (figure 1). One scene shows the anchor's hawser going through a sheave at the top of the mast, while the other seems to be an exploded view of a similar operation. Alternately, cargo derricks may have been used for maneuvering anchors.

Ancient ships employed a complement of anchors. The Uluburun shipwreck off the coast of Turkey carried twenty-four weight anchors, totaling more than 4 tons. Two-thirds of the ship's anchors were stationed at the bow, while the remainder had been stowed amidships. [*See* Uluburun.] A group of fifteen Byblian anchors, undoubtedly from a single ship, were found in Israel at Neveh Yam. Curiously, only one anchor has been found on the Cape Gelidonya shipwreck off Turkey, perhaps indicating that not all of the ship has been located. [*See* Cape Gelidonya.]

Studies in the typologies of Bronze Age stone anchors have permitted the differentiation of several regional types. Egyptian anchors often have a second, L-shaped piercing near the anchor's base, perhaps for the attachment of a line with a float to indicate the anchor's location on the sea bed (see below). Examples have been found at Mirgissa on the Upper Nile River, at Wadi Gawasis on Egypt's Red Sea coast, and as far afield as Byblos in Lebanon and Ugarit in Syria.

Stone anchors abound underwater along Israel's Mediterranean coast. Several anchors from the Carmel coast bear markings, some in relief. The earliest datable stone, anchorlike objects in the Near East are *shfifonim* (Heb., "vipers"), found in the region immediately south of the Sea of Galilee. [*See* Shfifonim.] Numerous stone anchors have also been found at Byblos and Ugarit. Among those found at Byblos were several that have a distinctly triangular shape. Although anchors with this shape are commonly termed Byblian, the majority have been found in Israeli waters (figure 2).

Cyprus is rich in stone anchors—147 were found at Kition alone. Few stone anchors have been recovered from Turkish waters, however, and they are so rare in the Aegean Sea that a different form of anchoring device may have been in use there. Aegean Bronze Age cultures may have employed killiks—devices that use undressed stones as weights for

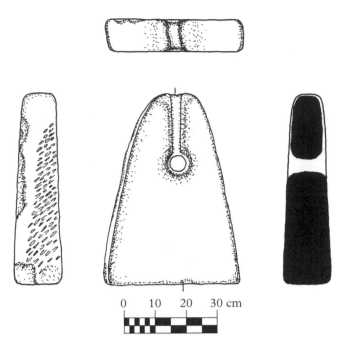

ANCHORS. Figure 2. *Stone anchor.* Byblian anchor found in the ancient harbor of Dor, in Tantura Lagoon, Israel. (Courtesy S. Wachsmann)

wooden anchoring devices. Once the wood disintegrated, the anchor-stone would be indistinguishable from other stones (see below). On Crete, some stone anchors have been found at Mallia and Kommos. An anchor-shaped porphyry stone from Knossos, with a relief carving of an octopus, may have been a weight, or a cultic object. It is unlikely to have ever been employed at sea.

Small stone anchors have continued in use into modern times. Large stone anchors—those that required more than one person to handle them—apparently went out of use as new types of anchors were introduced, toward the end of the Iron Age.

Wooden Anchors. Dramatic changes in anchor shape probably occurred toward the end of the seventh century BCE when the word *ankura* ("bent") first appears in Greek texts (Kapitän, 1984; pp. 33–36). Four types of wooden anchor stocks were used in the Greco-Roman period (figure 3): stone (type I); wood with lead cores (II); lead (III), occasionally with wooden cores (C), and removable lead stocks (IV). Lead stocks continued to be known as stones long after their typological forebears fell into disuse (Durrbach and Roussel, 1926–1935, vol. 1, 443.92, vol. 3;1417, pp. 163–65).

In general, Greeks used stone-stocked anchors (type I), whereas Romans used solid lead (type III) stocks. Type II represents a transition from stone to lead stocks, and type IV a more drastic change from wooden anchors to iron anchors. Both transitions were products of historical and tech-

nological developments. Stone stocks often broke on rocky sea bottoms. Lead-cored wooden stocks were not as fragile, but their number was directly linked to the supply of lead. Lead was in short supply until the late third-century BCE, when the Romans gained control of rich Spanish silver mines and produced silver, and its by-product, lead, on a grand scale. When the price of lead fell, type-III solid-lead stocks appeared almost simultaneously. Type-IV removable stocks are frequently found in the eastern Mediterranean. These collapsible anchors were designed for an economy of space and suggest the use of smaller ships. The versatile removable-stock wooden anchors heralded increasing use of removable-stock iron anchors.

Greeks called anchors hanging gear (probably because they hung from bows and sterns [Casson, 1971, p. 265]), stays (Athanaeus, *Diepnosophists* 3.99D), or even holders (Lucian, *Lex.* 15). The largest anchor was the "sacred anchor" which was thrown in times of desperation (Lucian, *Jup. Trag.* 51). Roman authors made more specific references to anchor parts. Arms (figure 3.3) or even entire anchors were known as hooks (Virgil, *Aeneid* 1.169.3). The conical iron or bronze caps that reinforced arm ends (figure 3.2) were called teeth (Livy 37.30.9–10), because of their toothlike shape, or claws (Plutarch, *de mul.* 8.247E).

Pliny credited invention of the one-armed anchor to Eupalamus and of the two-armed anchor to Anacharsis (*Nat. Hist.* 7.56.209). References like Pliny's were thought apocryphal until a reinforcement collar (figure 3.4) for a one-armed anchor was found near Brindisi, Italy (Kapitän, 1984; Rosloff, 1991). One-armed iron anchors also existed (*P. Lond.* 1164h 11.7–11).

Scholars learned more about anchor arm construction with the discovery of a fragmentary anchor on the Chrétienne "C" wreck (Joncheray, 1975). Arms were bound fastened to anchor shanks with Z-shaped hook joints that were, in turn, secured by mortise-and-tenon joints (figure 3.5). Pegs placed perpendicularly through tenons in anchor arms locked them in position. When arm/shank joints loosened with wear, reinforcement collars (figure 3.4) poured onto anchors held the anchor arms in position (Haldane, 1986).

Pliny records cork floats on lines used to mark an anchor's location on the sea bottom (*Nat. Hist.* 16.13.34). These lines, tied to wooden-anchor crown notches (figure 3.6) or iron anchor crown rings, also freed anchors stuck in the seabed.

Iron Anchors. Herodotus (9.74) makes the first recorded reference to iron anchors in the early fifth century BCE. Iron was scarce, however, and iron anchors do not commonly appear on shipwrecks until the first century CE. As iron-working technology developed in the Mediterranean, the use of wooden anchors diminished.

The first conclusive evidence of anchor manufacture to predetermined specifications can be seen in iron anchors. The first-century CE iron anchor found at Lake Nemi, Italy,

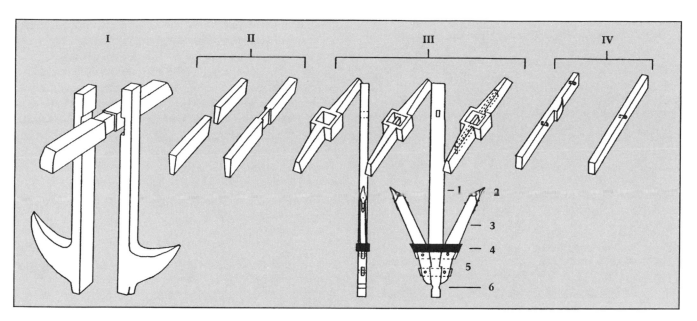

ANCHORS. Figure 3. *Wooden anchors.* Stock types for wooden anchors. Type I is a stone stock; Type II is a wood stock with a lead core; Type III stocks are lead; Type IV stocks have removable lead cores. The pieces of the Type III anchor are numbered: (1) shank; (2) teeth; (3) arm; (4) reinforcement collar; (5) mortise and tenon joints; (6) crown. (Courtesy ASOR Archives)

has its weight inscribed in Roman pounds on its shank (Speziale, 1931). The anchor complement of the seventh-century CE Yassıada Byzantine shipwreck found off the coast of Turkey may have ranged from smallest to largest in increments of 50 Roman pounds (Bass and van Doorninck, 1982, p. 134). [*See* Yassıada Wrecks.]

Anchor arm configurations also show a progressive evolution. Iron anchor arms first imitated the sharp V pattern of wooden anchors but gradually relaxed to the lunate shape of the Nemi iron anchor (B); they continue to open from the first to the fourth centuries CE in the Dramont D and F anchors. The cruciform shape of the seventh-century Yassıada anchors reflects the christianization of the Roman Empire. Anchor arm angles relative to shanks increased until they reached the Y shape of the eleventh-century Serçe Limanı anchors. [*See* Serçe Limanı.]

Increasingly unstable economic and political conditions in the medieval Mediterranean dictated the use of smaller, faster ships. Deck space was at a premium, and the use of durable, removable-stock iron anchors aboard ships became the rule.

[*See also* Ships and Boats.]

BIBLIOGRAPHY

Stone Anchors

Frost, Honor. "The Stone Anchors of Ugarit." *Ugaritica* 6 (1969a): 235–245.

Frost, Honor. "The Stone Anchors of Byblos." *Mélanges de l'Université Saint-Joseph* 45 (1969b): 425–442.

Frost, Honor. "Anchors, the Potsherds of Marine Archaeology: On the Recording of Pierced Stones from the Mediterranean." In *Marine Archaeology: Proceedings of the XXIII Symposium of the Colston Research Society Held in the University of Bristol, April 4th to 8th, 1971,* edited by D. J. Blackman, pp. 397–406. Colston Papers, no. 32. London, 1973.

Frost, Honor. "Egypt and Stone Anchors: Some Recent Discoveries." *Mariner's Mirror* 65 (1979): 137–161.

Frost, Honor. "Appendix I: The Kition Anchors." In *Excavations at Kition 5,* vol. 1, *The Pre-Phoenician Levels, Areas I and II,* edited by Vassos Karageorghis and Martha Demas, pp. 281–321, pls. A–N. Nicosia, 1986.

Frost, Honor. "Anchors Sacred and Profane: Ugarit–Ras Shamra, 1986, the Stone Anchors Revised and Compared." In *Arts et industries de la pierre,* edited by Marguerite Yon, pp. 355–410. Ras Shamra–Ougarit, 6. Paris, 1991.

Galili, Ehud. "A Group of Stone Anchors from Newe-Yam." *International Journal of Nautical Archaeology and Underwater Exploration* 14 (1985): 143–153.

Galili, Ehud, and Kurt Raveh. "Stone Anchors with Carvings from the Sea off Megadim." *Sefunim* 7 (1988): 41–47, pl. 5.

Karageorghis, Vassos, and Jean des Gagniers. *La céramique chypriote de style figuré, Âge du fer (1050–500 Av. J.-C.).* Rome, 1974.

Sayed, A. M. A. H. "Discovery of the Site of the Twelfth-Dynasty Port at Wadi Gawasis on the Red Sea Shore." *Revue d'Égyptologie* 29 (1977): 138–178.

Wachsmann, Shelley. *Seagoing Ships and Seamanship in the Bronze Age Levant.* College Station, Texas, in press.

Wood and Iron Anchors

Babbitt, Frank C., trans. *Plutarch's Moralia.* Vol. 3: 172a–263c. Loeb Classical Library. Cambridge, Mass., 1961.

Bass, George F., and Frederick H. van Doorninck, Jr. *Yassi Ada,* vol. 1, *A Seventh-Century Byzantine Shipwreck.* College Station, Texas, 1982.

Casson, Lionel. *Ships and Seamanship in the Ancient World*. Princeton, 1971. Definitive work on ancient ships and seafaring.

Durrbach, Félix, and Pierre Roussel. *Inscriptions de Delos*. Vols. 1 and 3. Paris, 1926–1935.

Godley, Alfred D., trans. *Herodotus*. Vol. 4, Books 8–9. Loeb Classical Library. Cambridge, Mass., 1924.

Gulick, C. B., trans. *Athanaeus: The Deipnosophists*. Vol. 1, Books 1–3. Loeb Classical Library. Cambridge, Mass., 1927.

Haldane, Douglas. "Wooden Anchor Arm Construction." *International Journal of Nautical Archaeology and Underwater Exploration* 15 (1986): 163–166.

Harmon, Austin M., trans. *Lucian*. Vol. 5. Loeb Classical Library. Cambridge, Mass., 1936.

Harmon, Austin M., trans. *Lucian*. Vol. 2. Loeb Classical Library. Cambridge, Mass., 1960.

Joncheray, J.-P. "L'épave 'C' de la chrétienne." *Cahiers d'Archéologie Subaquatique*, supp. 1 (1975).

Kapitan, Gerhard. "Ancient Anchors: Technology and Classification." *International Journal of Nautical Archaeology and Underwater Exploration* 13 (1984): 33–44.

Kenyon, Frederic, and H. Idris Bell. *Greek Papyri in the British Museum*. Vol. 3. London, 1907.

Rackham, Harris, trans. *Pliny: Natural History*. Vol. 2, Books 3–7. Loeb Classical Library. Cambridge, Mass., 1942.

Rackham, Harris, trans. *Pliny: Natural History*. Vol. 4, Books 12–16. Loeb Classical Library. Cambridge, Mass., 1945.

Rosloff, Jay. "A One-Armed Anchor of c. 400 B.C.E. from Ma'agan Michael Vessel, Israel: A Preliminary Report." *International Journal of Nautical Archaeology and Underwater Exploration* 20.3 (1991): 223–226.

Sage, E. T., trans. *Livy: From the Founding of the City*. Vol. 10, Books 35–37. Loeb Classical Library. Cambridge, Mass., 1935.

Speziale, G. C. "The Roman Anchors Found at Nemi." *Mariner's Mirror* 17 (1931): 300–320.

SHELLEY WACHSMANN and DOUGLAS HALDANE

ANDRAE, WALTER (1875–1956), archaeologist, scholar, and museologist. Andrae was born in Anger, near Leipzig, Germany. After finishing school at Gimma (the school of the princes of Saxony), he studied architecture for four years at the Technical University in Dresden. Andrae was only twenty-three when, in 1898, he set off for the Near East with the Deutsche Orient-Gesellschaft's Babylon Expedition. In Babylon Andrae learned excavation techniques from the expedition's leader, Robert Koldewey, the most prominent excavator of that time. In 1903, Andrae undertook the first excavation of his own, at Aššur, the capital of Assyria. He worked there until 1914. Andrae also worked at Shuruppak (modern Fara) and Kisurra (Abu Hatab), both south of Babylon, and at Hatra, the Parthian city of the sun god northwest of Aššur.

During World War I, Andrae served as a German army officer in the Near East. After the war he was employed by the Berlin Museum, where he succeeded Koldewey as curator of the Near East collection. In 1928 he became director of the Near East department of the State Museum of Berlin, a position he held until the 1950s. After World War II, Andrae became a professor of the history of architecture at the Technical University in Berlin. Toward the end of his life, an accident caused his almost complete blindness.

At Aššur, Andrae first introduced the system of examining levels: in the area of the Temple of Ishtar, the oldest building at Aššur, he named building levels by letter, designating A for the uppermost and H for the lowest level. He also developed Koldewey's methods of archaeological work for the coming generations. At the Berlin Museum, Andrae was responsible for the reconstruction work on the Procession Street, the Ishtar Gate, and other monuments from Aššur and Uruk.

[*See also* Aššur; Deutsche Orient-Gesellschaft; *and the biography of Koldewey*.]

BIBLIOGRAPHY

Andrae, Ernst Walter, and Rainer Michael Boehmer. *Sketches by an Excavator: Walter Andrae im Orient, 1898–1919*. Berlin, 1989.

Andrae, Walter. *Lebenserinnerungen eines Ausgräbers*. Berlin, 1961.

Andrae, Walter. *Das wiedererstandene Assur*. 2d ed. Munich,, 1977.

BARTHEL HROUDA

ANIMAL HUSBANDRY. The domestication of animals is a component of the "Neolithic Revolution" and a process that had an impact both on the biology of the tamed and the culture of the tamers. One of the main centers for the evolution of husbandry was the ancient Near East, where its beginnings, in the early Holocene c. 9000 BCE, can be found in Iran, Iraq, Anatolia, Syria, and the Levant, within the hilly zones adjacent to the Fertile Crescent. There, within a relatively short period of time—a few thousand years at most—mobile hunting and gathering, a strategy that had been successful for millennia, was replaced by sedentary farming and animal husbandry as the primary mode of subsistence for most communities. These three aspects of the Neolithic Revolution—sedentism, husbandry, and agriculture—are interwoven but independent components of the process; thus, evidence for the presence of one is not certain proof for the existence of the others. For this reason, the primary evidence for animal husbandry is to be sought in the bones of animals recovered at archaeological sites.

Bones reflect domestication in two ways. One is the impact the process had on the wild species that came under human control; the other is its impact on human values and social organizations. Shifts in the selective forces affecting the small populations of animals initially tamed gradually changed the appearance of their descendants: most became smaller, neotenous features were retained, and coat color and texture as well as other morphological features became more variable. These changes were likely not intentional goals of the first herders but emerged from the process of selecting animals who were easiest to manage and maintain. Some novel morphological and behavioral features did come to have economic significance: the wooly coat of sheep or a more docile personality in cattle; others, such as the corkscrew horns of goats or the shortened faces of pigs, although perhaps culturally salient, did not contribute obvious material benefits to the husbanders' new adaptation to the environment.

Morphological features produced through unconscious human intervention are visible in skeletons and can be used to demonstrate the presence of domestic stock at an archaeological site. At Ali Kosh, in southwestern Iran, the presence of domestic sheep c. 7500–7000 BCE is evidenced by the skull of a hornless ewe; domestic goats are deduced from horncore morphology (the horns of bovids, which are not shed like antlers, are keratinous sheaths covering bone spikes that project from the frontal bone of the skull). At Hallan Çemi, in eastern Anatolia, domestic pigs can be demonstrated in about 8000 BCE on the basis of the discovery of teeth smaller than their wild ancestors'. The existence of domestic cattle in central Anatolia in the late sixth millennium has been argued on the basis of the small overall size of the animals. Morphological evidence alone, however, is insufficient to trace the process of domestication. The earliest stages of husbandry—those that occurred before morphological changes appeared—will be missed. Moreover, the remains of domestic stock at a site is not certain proof that the people who slaughtered and consumed the animals also raised them. Thus, the second way in which bones reflect domestication is crucial.

Domestication is the incorporation of living animals into human society. Domestication not only produces domestic animals, it encourages the adoption of different values and social organizations by the societies that employ it. A major adjustment is required: an increased sense of property becomes a measure of social status. The term *husbandry* means to conserve, keep, and alienate resources. The route to success is through resisting the impulse to slaughter stock so that herd growth can be encouraged. This way of thinking is anathema to many foraging societies in which there is strong pressure to share the game from a successful hunt across the whole community. The demographics of pastoral societies are shaped by the ratio between the number of herders and the size of the flock, a relatively rigid relationship that fosters segmentation within communities on household lines and discourages the free flow of personnel between camps or settlements that is characteristic of hunters. The events of the early Holocene in the Near East therefore produced significant changes in the values and social organization of the emergent communities. The new attitudes can only be inferred indirectly. A key component of husbandry is the decision to cull. The proportions of the different ages and sexes in the animals that herders choose to slaughter to feed their families are distinct from those seen in the animals hunters are likely to kill. Thus, evaluation of the mortality of potentially domesticable animals at a site is a key technique in determining whether the human behav-

iors associated with pastoralism are present. Though other information is supportive, demographic information is central to the conclusions that sheep were domestic by about 8500 BCE at Zawi Chemi and Shanidar cave in northern Iraq and goats husbanded at Tepe Ganj Dareh in western Iran by 7000 BCE.

What motivated the incorporation of animals into human society? Most theories have argued that the reliable production of meat was the incentive. It is widely agreed that human population was increasing in the Early Holocene, forcing marginal habitats (from a hunter-forager perspective) to be occupied—lands with less game, where those communities with domestic herds would more easily survive. Because some of these marginal habitats are outside the range of the wild ancestors of sheep, the discovery of their remains at such Pre-Pottery Neolithic sites as Jericho in the Jordan Valley, Beidha in Jordan, and Abu Hureyra on the Euphrates River in Syria has been taken as direct evidence of domestication. For what, then, were they being raised? At the same time marginal habitats were being invaded, the environment of the Early Holocene was both spatially variable and temporally erratic—conditions ethnology tells us promote storage as a buffering mechanism, and husbandry is a form of storage on the hoof. The difficulty with these models has been the lack of an explanation for how hunters can avoid killing the animals they encounter and instead treat them more like gathered resources—which, again ethnology reports, are shared within the household, not the community at large. One controversial explanation for the motivation is the milk even wild caprines yield. Small numbers of tame stock maintained by households for dairy products could have served as the basis for the development of larger herds capable of producing meat. A second factor is the behavior of two of the wild species first domesticated—sheep and goats. Both of these animals are "vertical migrators," adapting to the change of the season by moving up and down precipitous terrain. They contrast with "horizontal migrators," such as gazelles and equids, which deal with variable climate by traversing great distances. Sheep and goats also have a considerable attachment to their home ranges. Exploiting them, rather than the horizontal migrators, would have given a new definition to the concept of hunting territory because sheep and goat habitat is productive year-round rather than just seasonally. It is more worth defending. Game-management techniques, which mimic some herding strategies and so are hard to distinguish in the archaeological record, would have had value and offered another potential pathway to more intensive husbandry.

Although husbandry was underway by about 9000 BCE, it took nearly eight thousands years for the list of Near Eastern domesticates to be complete. Sheep, goats, and probably pigs were first, domesticated across southwest Asia by 7000 BCE. By 6000 BCE, the first sites with multiple species of domestic livestock are recorded (e.g., Erbaba in Anatolia and

Jarmo in Iraq, among many others). At about the same time or a little earlier, a figurine found at the western Iranian site of Sarab indicates that woolly sheep were known. Hunting had not died out as an important subsistence pursuit—though at sites where the important domesticates belonged to the same species as the wild animals hunting might also have been pursued—but there is presently no way to estimate its contribution accurately. However, at the site of Umm Dabaghiyeh, a sixth-millennium settlement in Iraq, onagers (a wild relative of the horse) were hunted intensively. A scattering of domestic donkeys is found in various parts of the Near East in about 3000 BCE, in Mesopotamia often in ritual contexts. Shortly thereafter, the animal became a mainstay as a beast of burden. The horse was domesticated in central Asia by the fourth millennium and seems to have appeared in the Near East by the third millennium, although a Chalcolithic horse bone has been found in Israel's Negev desert. Cattle entered the barnyard at the end of the sixth millennium and were used for motive power and milk by the fourth.

The centuries just before 3000 BCE have been referred to as the period of the Secondary Products Revolution—a time when donkeys not only entered the work force, but sheep, goats, and cattle began to be managed for their fiber and dairy products. In fact, the management for secondary products probably began much earlier; it is more correct to say that the effort invested in these forms of husbandry increased with the advent of complex society.

The complex political organization associated with the rise of the state reshaped animal husbandry in the Near East. One development was specialized nomadic pastoralism, an adaptation dependent on the economic infrastructure the state provides. It is not, as some would have it, a simpler subsistence mode into which people slip during the intermittent periods of social disintegration brought on by the collapse of states and empires. Nomadic pastoralism has the capacity to generate considerable political power. Though it is counterintuitive, the successes and failures of individual pastoralists do not even out over time. Instead, some succeed enormously and are able to employ or otherwise attach their luckless fellows to manage their ever-increasing herds. These arrangements are capable of multiplying to produce nomadic "kingdoms" of considerable power. Under the state, animal production was managed either through bureaucrats or the action of markets. In either case, husbanders were encouraged by the demands made or the opportunities provided by these institutions to redirect their efforts away from household production and toward the creation of animal products for exchange. For example, in the Levant, at Tel Ḥalif, donkeys were produced on a large scale, presumably to serve a regional need for transport animals. This principle also is visible in the transformation of culling strategies for sheep and goats. Effective multipurpose management of these animals for household consumption focuses on dairy production as the most efficient method of producing calories. Evidence for herding techniques aimed at the production of meat or wool implies that the exchange value associated with these products was sufficient to outweigh the overall decrease in total production. These are recorded in all parts of the Near East. In Mesopotamia, cuneiform documents indicate that by the end of the third millennium extensive centralized sheep herding was underway. Unfortunately, the documentary record refers almost exclusively to state-directed activities and provides no picture of the rural domestic production of animal products, which must have been enormous.

The textual record also indicates that local "breeds" had developed. It is a mistake to view these as distinctive morphologies produced by deliberate isolation and selection, as is practiced in modern husbandry. Instead, subregional economic, political, and physical boundaries produced isolated populations of domestic stock that, either through adaptation to local conditions or the effects of genetic drift, attained distinctive and recognizable qualities. In these circumstances, local herds, even though named, actually contain a wide range of morphologies. *Genesis* 31 provides a clear example of the principle. While Jacob believes that the characteristics of the male goats in his flock will turn up in the next generation of kids, the flock itself is very diverse in appearance, hardly the modern idea of a breed.

In Egypt, domestic sheep and goats seem to have been imports from southwest Asia. In the case of cattle, the case is not settled. A center of domestication, independent of the one in Anatolia and southeast Europe, may have existed in northeast Africa. Certainly in the pharaonic era, extensive experimentation with a wide range of animals was practiced. While most ventures never went beyond taming, some birds, notably geese, became significant domesticates, as they did in Mesopotamia.

The date the camel entered the register of domestic stock is unknown. Though most authorities would place the event in Arabia and eastern Iran sometime in the third millennium or a little earlier, the evidence is extremely thin and subject to alternative explanations. As important contributors to the economy, however, the evidence for camels points certainly to the early first and perhaps to the middle of the second millennium BCE.

Other animals deserve some mention. The humped Zebu cattle, especially well adapted to arid conditions, is present in Jordan by the Late Bronze Age, although the difficulty associated with identifying its remains means that it may be present elsewhere earlier, but unrecognized among the bones of the more common taurine cattle. The same problem faces the identification of the contribution of the water buffalo, presumably wild examples of which have been found in Halafian deposits. Faunal evidence shows that the animal was domesticated in the Indus Valley by the third millennium, and a seal impression places the animal in Mesopotamia at about the same time. Little more is known. The indigenous hare of the Near East was not domesticated, and rabbits were not introduced until Roman times. Fish were raised in ponds in Mesopotamia but do not seem to have been true domesticates. Bees were kept in Egypt beginning in the Old Kingdom (third millennium), but the technology does not seem to have spread to Asia.

The elephant presents an especially complex problem. The discovery of ivory at such workshops as Bir es-Safadi in the northern Negev indicates the presence of the animal in the Chalcolithic period. Scattered bone and tusk finds together with textual records of imperial hunting suggest that a relict population of an as yet undetermined species of elephant was present in Syria as late as the beginning of the first millennium BCE. However, at least one authority has argued that these animals were actually transported from India for royal sport and so technically would be domesticates.

Finally, the chicken has been reported from occasional finds as early as the Early Bronze Age. The scarcity of these reports and the possibility of contamination associated with most of them contrasts with the explosion of chicken husbandry that begins in the Persian and particularly the Hellenistic period. The evidence now points to an original domestication of the chicken in China during the Neolithic, followed by an extremely slow diffusion west.

[See also Camels; Cattle and Oxen; Equids; Paleozoology; Pigs; and Sheep and Goats.]

BIBLIOGRAPHY

Boessneck, Joachim. *Die Tierwelt des Alten Ägypten: Untersucht anhand Kulturgeschichtlicher und Zoologischer.* Munich, 1988. Encyclopedic survey of animal domestication in Egypt.

Clutton-Brock, Juliet, ed. *The Walking Larder: Patterns of Domestication, Pastoralism, and Predation.* London, 1989. Presents important studies by Pierre Ducos and Sandor Bökönyi from a social and instrumental perspective, as well as a survey by Richard H. Meadow of the methods of determining animal domestication in the Near East.

Crabtree, Pam J. "Early Animal Domestication in the Middle East and Europe." In *Archaeological Method and Theory,* edited by Michael B. Schiffer, pp. 201–245. Tucson, 1993. Clearly written summary of the evidence for animal domestication, although it does not emphasize social process.

Gautier, Achilles. *La domestication: Et l'homme créa ses animaux.* Paris, 1990. Important European perspective on the process of animal domestication.

Grigson, Caroline. "Plough and Pasture in the Early Economy of the Southern Levant." In *The Archaeology of Society in the Holy Land,* edited by Thomas E. Levy, pp. 245–268. New York, 1995. Recent review of the process of domestication in the western Near East. Emphasizes a critical review of the evidence within an ecological model.

Redding, R. W. "A General Explanation of Subsistence Change: From Hunting and Gathering to Food Production." *Journal of Anthropological Archaeology* 7 (1988): 56–97. Utilizes a systems approach to explain the advent of domestication.

Russell, Kenneth. *After Eden.* British Archaeological Reports, International Series, no. 391. Oxford, 1988. Important statement from the perspective of optimization theory on the process of domestication, providing the argument for the early exploitation of dairy products.

Tchernov, Eitan, and Liora K. Horwitz. "Body Size Diminution under Domestication: Unconscious Selection in Primeval Domesticates." *Journal of Anthropological Archaeology* 10 (1991): 54–75. Sophisticated analysis of the coevolution of domesticators and domesticated.

Zeder, Melinda A. *Feeding Cities: Specialized Animal Economy in the Ancient Near East.* Washington, D. C., 1991. Based on a study of Tal-e Malyan in Iran, providing a systems view of the impact of complex society on animal production systems in southwest Asia.

BRIAN HESSE

'ANJAR ('Andjar, 'Ain al-Jarr), site located in Lebanon, in the eastern foothills of the Biqa' (Bekaa) Valley, south of Baalbek, halfway between Beirut and Damascus (35°56' N, 33°44' E). Some ruins in the area of 'Anjar, in particular a quadrangular fortification wall, were described by nineteenth-century travelers and biblical scholars, such as Johann L. Burckhardt and Edward Robinson. The first exploration of the site, carried out by the German Archaeological Expedition excavating at Baalbek, was published in 1938 by Daniel M. Krencker and Willy Zschietzschmann. In 1939, Jean Sauvaget identified the ruins as Umayyad 'Ain al-Jarr. In 1953, Maurice Chéhab began to excavate 'Anjar, publishing preliminary reports in 1957 and 1963. In 1967, Solange Ory published the site's Arabic inscriptions and graffiti, and Jean-Paul Rey-Coquais published the few Greek inscriptions excavated. In 1969, K. A. C. Creswell included 'Anjar in his second edition of *Early Muslim Architecture* (1969). In 1993, Hafez K. Chehab commented on Greek and Syriac texts that attribute the construction of 'Anjar respectively to al-Walid I (r. 705–715 CE), and his son al-'Abbas (in 709 CE); Chehab also discussed 'Anjar's identification with Chalcis ad Libanum, its pre-Islamic origin, and the problems created because the material culture excavated at 'Anjar has not been studied. It is still unclear whether the site is an Islamic foundation reusing architectural structures from nearby Roman and Byzantine sites, or the Islamic reconstruction of a previous settlement. It is even less certain that the Iturean and Herodian Chalcis was at 'Anjar.

The excavations at 'Anjar carried out by Maurice Chéhab cleared a quadrangular defense wall (310 × 370 m) that was buttressed with semicircular towers and had a monumental gate in the middle of each side. Two colonnaded avenues link the gates and intersect at right angles under a monumental tetrapylum. Two palaces, a mosque (with a *miḥrab* added later), and two baths (the larger with mosaic and marble floors) were cleared and partially rebuilt. The foundations of three other palaces with inner courts were found along the east-west colonnaded avenue. The overall plan of this walled town, which recalls plans of Roman and Byzantine castra, appears to have been laid out all at once: the foundation masonry, using a hard mortar, is of the same type for all the large structures. The southwest quadrant is covered with smaller dwellings. Drainage channels were found all over the site, converging toward sewers built under the colonnaded avenues. Reused architectural structures, in particular capitals of Roman and Byzantine types, were found in the larger palace and along the porticoes. A column with a Greek Christian inscription that belonged to a church dedicated to "Our Lady Mother of God" can be seen in the court of the larger palace. Many stone elements of archivolts and friezes (with vegetal, floral, and geometric motifs) and pillar and pilaster capitals (some with figures) were uncovered in the palaces. It remains to be seen whether this part of the architectural decoration is Islamic or pre-Islamic. It is certain, however, that ʿAnjar, called ʿAin al-Jarr in Islamic sources, was inhabited from at least 741 CE until its destruction, reported by the Muslim geographer Abu al-Fida', in 1321.

BIBLIOGRAPHY

Burckhardt, Johann L. *Travels in Syria and the Holy Land.* London, 1822. See pages 8–9.

Chehab, Hafez. "On the Identification of ʿAnjar (ʿAyn al-Jarr) as an Umayyad Foundation." *Muqarnas* 10 (1993): 42–48.

Chéhab, Maurice. "The Umayyad Palace at ʿAnjar." *Ars Orientalis* 5 (1963): 17–25.

Creswell, K. A. C. *Early Muslim Architecture*, vol. 1, *Umayyads A. D. 622–750.* 2d ed. Oxford, 1969. See pages 478–481.

Krencker, Daniel M., and Willy Zschietzschmann. *Römische Tempel in Syrien.* Vol. 1. Berlin, 1938. See pages 192–194.

Ory, Solange. "Les graffiti Umayyades de ʿAyn al-Ğarr." *Bulletin du Musée Beyrouth* 20 (1967): 97–148.

Rey-Coquais, Jean-Paul. *Inscriptions grecques et latines de la Syrie*, vol. 6, *Baalbek et Béqa.* Institute Français d'Archéologie de Beyrouth, Bibliothèque Archéologique et Historique, 78. Paris, 1967. See pages 229–232.

Robinson, Edward, et al. *Biblical Researches in Palestine and the Adjacent Regions: A Journal of Travels in the Years 1838 and 1852*, vol. 3, *Later Biblical Researches in Palestine.* 2d ed. London, 1856. See pages 495–500.

Sauvaget, Jean. "Les ruines omeyyades de ʿAndjar." *Bulletin du Musée de Beyrouth* 3 (1939): 5–11.

HAFEZ CHEHAB

ANTIOCH ON ORONTES,

ANTIOCH ON ORONTES, site identified with Antakya, modern Hatay, founded on the course of the Orontes River (36°12' N, 36°10' E). One of the greatest cities in the ancient world, Antioch is now a town of moderate importance, incorporated into Turkey in 1938. Antioch was originally founded in 330 BCE by Seleucus I. Henri Seyrig has demonstrated that the cities that preceded it on the plain of Antioch, Alalakh, and later Antigonia, the short-lived city founded by Antigonus I (the One-Eyed), were situated within the plain and drew the bulk of their resources from the fertility of the ʿAmuq and the proximity of inland Syria. In contrast, Antioch is on the Orontes River, where its channels run into the sea. It was located directly on the great trade route that runs from the Persian Gulf to the Mediterranean Sea by way of the Euphrates River valley. It is notable that among the three cities founded in the same period by Seleucus, two—Seleucia of Pieria and Laodicea—were sited on the sea and served as trading outlets. It may seem that the true capital of the Seleucid Empire was Seleucia of Pieria rather than Antioch. Seleucia, however, was exposed and occasionally succumbed to external threats which gave the advantage to Antioch.

Of ancient Antioch, nothing remains on the surface except for a few traces of walls. The city suffered numerous earthquakes and was reconstructed each time upon the ruins of the preceding epoch. Thanks to ancient authors, principally Libanios and Julian in the fourth century and Malalas in the sixth, its topography is known with such precision that the German philologist Carl Otfried Müller gave a fairly precise view of the city in his *Antiquitates Antiochenae* published in 1839. The excavations carried out between 1932 and 1939 by Princeton University updated and refined what was known of the city. The earliest levels occur at a depth of 11 m; the city of Justinian (sixth century CE) was found at 6 m. Because of the continuous occupation of the city, it was not possible to proceed with extensive excavations. In addition, the rise in the level of the Orontes and the surrounding water table as a result of alluviation has resulted in the submersion of the earliest Hellenistic levels. The great north-south road that traversed the city could be thoroughly excavated, however. Because all the city streets connected to the main road, the excavators were able to advance our understanding of the city's general organization and evolution.

Our knowledge of the city founded by Seleucus is restricted to a record of its modest size. Situated entirely on the left bank of the Orontes, it was surrounded by a wall that extended to the east along a cart track on which a great colonnaded road was later installed. According to the texts, it included a Greco-Macedonian and an Aramean quarter. As the capital of the Seleucid kingdom, which, at the end of the third century, extended as far as India and included Asia Minor, Antioch experienced rapid growth. Its area more than doubled under Antiochus IV, with the construction of the Epiphania quarter to the east. The city did not yet have the wealth it later acquired. The ancient road that ran along the wall of Seleucus certainly existed in the center of the city, but it was unpaved and remained so and without a gate until the beginning of the first century.

Antioch participated in the urban expansion that resulted from the Roman annexation of Syria. Under Augustus, thanks to the intervention and financing of Agrippa and Herod, the city's great road was flanked by broad walkways. Tiberius installed the colonnade. The road was transected by alleys and lined with shops, at least on its east side. The city was destroyed by the terrible earthquake of 115 CE. Trajan, who was present in the city, escaped by taking refuge in the Hippodrome. Reconstruction was planned on a grand scale and completed in the time of Antoninus. Land was expropriated on both sides of the roadway, and a new, wider (33 m) road was constructed that was more monumental than the preceding one. The roadway was 9 m wide, each lateral gate was 9 wide, and the shops were 6 m deep. It was the most impressive road in all the Syrian cities, except for the one at Apamea.

No major modification of the city plan was undertaken until the sixth century. Libanios and Malalas and a mosaic executed in about 460 at Yakto inform us that the city enjoyed a continuous increase in its population and monumental ornamentation. For several decades, the city's growth was interrupted only by its capture by the Persians (in 256 and 260) and the deportation in each case of a portion of the population. At the end of the fourth century, suburbs were built outside the city walls. After the Edict of Milan, several churches were constructed, including an octagonal building notable for its scale and gilded wood cupola. It was attributed to Constantine and called the *domus aurea*, the "house of gold." The city was lighted through the night. Even though the population was known as boisterous, pleasure loving, and argumentative, Julian the Apostate displeased the people with his paganism and his lack of interest in games.

The wealthy inhabitants of Antioch had country houses in the vicinity of Daphne. In the third century, this little town, celebrated for the abundance of its waters, acquired an urban organization: narrow lanes appear to have separated the modest properties, and subterranean channels supplied them with water. A number of pagan sanctuaries were installed at Daphne, including one dedicated to oracular Apollo. The Christians succeeded in dislodging them.

In the fifth and sixth centuries, the life of the city was marked by the contests that opposed the factions of the Blues and the Greens in the Hippodrome, but especially by the confrontation of the Chalcedonians and the Monophysites. The sixth century was marked by great disasters. Earthquakes struck Antioch in 526 and 528 that killed between 250,000 and 300,000 victims; another earthquake struck in 551 and at Daphne in 577. In 528, el-Mundhir the Lakhmidian, a Persian ally, captured and sacked the city and deported a significant portion of the population. Antioch suffered a similar attack by the Persians in 540. Epidemics of plague struck from 542 to 573. After the destructions of 526 and 528, well documented by excavation, Justin and then Justinian reconsecrated the city as Theopolis and dedicated considerable resources to its reconstruction. In spite of what Procopius says, the destruction debris could not be completely cleared away. In the reconstruction of the new city, most of the rubble was reused. The great road was reconstructed one meter higher, with basalt paving. Some monuments were restored and others were newly con-structed. The city wall, which had been destroyed several times, was rebuilt but with a shorter perimeter. In sum, the city was restored—if not to its ancient splendor, at least approaching it.

Disasters were renewed in the seventh century. Antioch was captured by the Persians in 606, 607, and again in 611 and remained occupied until 622. Earthquakes followed the pillage. When the Arabs arrived in 636, the city was in a pitiful state and was taken without resistance. The city never recovered her former metropolitan role. Antioch reverted again to Byzantine control in the second half of the tenth century. It fell to Philarete, the Armenian adventurer, in the last third of the eleventh century, and then to the Franks, at the very end of the same century. Taken by the Crusaders in 1098, Antioch ceased to be the capital of Syria because of the decline in the number and activity of its inhabitants and its status. In the twelfth and thirteenth centuries, it again became a capital, but of a state much reduced in size, the principality of Antioch.

BIBLIOGRAPHY

Downey, Glanville. *A History of Antioch in Syria*. Princeton, 1961.
Kennedy, Hugh. "The Last Century of Byzantine Syria." *Byzantinische Forschungen* 10, pp. 141–183.
Lassus, Jean. *Les portiques d'Antioche*. Princeton, 1977.
Levi, Doro. *Antioch Mosaic Pavements*. 2 vols. Princeton, 1947.
Liebeschuetz, J. H. W. G. *Antioch, City and Imperial Administration in the Later Roman Empire*. Oxford, 1972.
Stillwell, Richard. *Antioche-on-the-Orontes: The Excavations, 1933–1936*. Princeton, 1938.
Stillwell, Richard. *Antioche-on-the-Orontes: The Excavations, 1937–1938*. Princeton, 1941.
Tate, Georges. *Les campagnes de la Syrie du Nord du IIe au VIIe siècle*. Vol. 1. Bibliothèque Archéologique et Historique, vol. 133. Paris, 1992.
Tchalenko, Georges. *Villages antiques de la Syrie du Nord: Le massif du Bélus à l'époque romaine*. 3 vols. Bibliothèque Archéologique et Historique, vol. 50. Paris, 1953–1958.

GEORGES TATE
Translated from French by Nancy Leinwand

APAMEA (Gk., Apameia; Lat., Apamea; Ar., Afamiya, Famiya; Old Fr., Fémie), Hellenistic, Roman, Byzantine, and Early Islamic city in the Middle Orontes valley, one of the four main cities of the North Syrian *tetrapolis* (Strabo 16.2.10). Once thought to be at Hama (Epiphaneia) because of an erroneous identification with the Syriac Euphemia, ʿwpymyʿ (P. della Valle, 1614), it has been located at Qalʿat el-Muḍiq in the province of Hama, Syria (35°25′ N, 36°24′ E) at least since Carsten Niebuhr's visit in 1766, C.-F. Volney's from 1783 to 1785, and Johann L. Burckhardt's in 1812. [*See* Hama.] The city was founded in 300/299 BCE by Seleucus I Nicator with the dynastic name *Apamea*, related to that of the sovereign's wife, Apama. It was the headquarters of the Seleucid army, with five hundred war elephants, a pay corps checking office, and a stud farm that comprised no fewer than thirty thousand mares and three hundred stallions. "Riding masters, masters-at-arms and anyone who was paid to teach the art of warfare were also stationed there" (Strabo 16.2.10). The town, like Antioch, which also lies in a seismic region, suffered many earthquakes in its history, among which those of 115, 526, 528, 1157, and 1170 CE were the most disastrous. Definitively abandoned after these last two, the town was superseded by the citadel on the tell, was reconstructed by Nur ad-Din, and encloses the modern village.

Foreign travelers to the site noted some scattered Greek and Latin inscriptions, the remains of a magnificent colonnaded street that once crossed the site, and an agora, a cathedral, and a theater. Cumont, who visited the ruins on his way to Dura-Europos (1922), recommended the site to the Belgian Fonds National de la Recherche Scientifique for excavation. After a survey in 1928, F. Mayence led seven campaigns there (1930–1938), with the help of the architect H. Lacoste. The work was interrupted by World War II, resumed for two years (1947, 1953), and then resumed every year from 1965 onward, with a new staff, in cooperation with the Syrian Directorate General of Antiquities and Museums, which is responsible for restoration.

Although especially interested in the city's wide spectrum of historical periods, the Belgian expedition has also surveyed Middle Paleolithic encampments and workshops where flints were knapped, collected Neolithic material that fell from the top of the tell, and excavated rich Bronze Age tombs. It has systematically uncovered and studied various monuments belonging to the later periods of occupation. Soundings made on the southern slope of the tell in 1970 revealed Late Ubeid sherds (square A 1) and some thirty successive strata of the Middle Bronze Age and the transitional phase to the Late Bronze (square B 1). Inaccessible until now on the slopes of the medieval citadel, the second millennium BCE and the first half of the first millennium BCE remain mostly unknown. However, the discovery of a Neo-Hittite stela of King Urhilina of Hama (c. 850–840 BCE) in the foundation of a Christian church on the plateau attests to the city's importance at that time.

By comparing Apamea to the other Seleucid towns of the tetrapolis and making soundings on the main street and at the foot of the city wall, the Hellenistic town planning is now better understood. Unearthing the rampart on its northern, eastern, and southern sides (1984–1986) confirmed that the city wall, perhaps not earlier than the end of the third century BCE, enclosed a city of about 230 ha (568 acres). The town developed within this framework, divided into quarters of varying importance and character, in a cross-of-Lorraine pattern, of its main *plateiai*. The insulae seem to have measured approximately 55 × 110 m, just as at Antioch and Laodicea, its sister cities. [*See* Antioch on Orontes.] Recent

discoveries at the northern gate have shown that in the Hellenistic period a colonnaded avenue, in a "Dorico-Toscan" composite style, preceded the Corinthian porticoes built after the earthquake of 115 CE (some of these capitals were found reused in private houses). In the center of the city, west of the main axis and between the two principal east–west arteries, was the huge peribolos of a temple dedicated to Zeus Belos, the oracular god of Apamea. The monument stands on a high podium that occupied the highest point on the urban landscape, in front of the citadel, exactly where the temple of the *poliad* goddess Artemis dominates the city of Gerasa/Jerash. [*See* Jerash.] It is not possible to recover anything of the Hellenistic buildings because they were extensively rebuilt in the second century CE.

The Corinthian colonnaded avenue (north–south), where smooth columns alternate with columns with vertical and sometimes rare spiral fluting, attests to the grandeur of the restored city (3,750 m wide and about 1,850 m from its northern to its southern gate). Hundreds of shops and workshops, monumental baths (e.g., the North Baths, dedicated by L. Julius Agrippa, 116/17 CE), a large public latrine, a two-story nymphaeum decorated with statues of gods and heroes (?), the courtyards of some temples and a synagogue, and, later, the entrances to many churches (Northwest Basilica, Atrium Church, and Rotunda) opened onto the avenue. Private houses (excavated since 1973) are numerous on the other streets. Of special interest, because of their spectacular proportions (from 1,500 sq m sometimes to 4,500 sq m), the houses, with their peristyles with wide openings and their beautifully ornamented reception halls (paved with mosaics or opus sectile), confirm that an aristocracy of rich landowners lived in the city. Apamea had been, since Numenius settled his school there in the second century CE, the seat of various philosophic schools—Epicureans and especially Neo-Platonists—whose importance ceased only as a consequence of the Theodosian edicts, when the Belos Temple, the oracle Hadrian, Septimius Severus, and Macrinus had earlier consulted, was destroyed by Bishop Marchellus (c. 376 CE). A marvelous series of mosaics, found under the pavement of the cathedral that was to seal the Neo-Platonic school (now in the Musées Royaux d'Art et d'Histoire in Brussels and in the local museum at Apamea) reveals much of the temples iconographic program: Socrates as one of the Seven Wise Men of Greece, the return of Ulysses to Ithaca as a symbol of the soul recovering Philosophy at the end of its life, the crowning of Cassiopeia as Beauty itself in the competition with the Nereids. The mosaics may have been commissioned in the time of Emperor Julian by Sopatros II, in the very last years of the school's life. [*See* Mosaics.]

Apamea's proximity to Antioch, where Roman emperors so often prepared their eastern campaigns against the Parthians and later the Sasanians, led to its being the winter quarters of the Legio II Parthica in the third century CE. This special elite corps accompanied Caracalla, Severus Alexander, and Gordian III to the East and was stationed near the city for a few years each time. Numerous gravestones of its soldiers, reused in one of the towers of the city wall, are incomparable documentation of these events and their participants, as are the stelae of riders of two cavalry alae (Ulpia Contariorum and Flavia Britannica) dispatched there from the Balkans in 252 CE to stop the first Sasanian raid into the empire's territory.

Churches were built throughout the city, as elsewhere in the province (Tell Arr, 374 CE; Hass, 388 CE; Khirbet Muqa, 394/95 CE). Bishops were known there as early as 325 CE (Council of Nicaea). The monuments date mainly from the fifth and especially the sixth centuries, from the Justinianic rebuilding of the town after the earthquakes of 526 and 528 CE. This is true for the Atrium Church, where the cult of the martyrs developed around reliquaries of Sts. Cosmas and Damian and of St. Theodore; for the Rotunda; for the Cathedral (for whose decoration Archbishop Paul is responsible); and for a pillared basilica recently excavated at the northern gate.

Apamea was not destroyed when Chosroes I invaded Syria in 540 CE, and it was taken but also not destroyed in 613 CE by Chosroes II. The town suffered during the raid of Adaarmanes in 573 CE, who sent some 292,000 captives into exile in Persia. The city opened its doors to the conquering Arabs in 638 because of the Monophysite inclination of a great part of the population against Byzantine fiscal oppression. The city did not suffer any damage, but some of its richest inhabitants appear to have abandoned their houses. Their flight was not temporary, as they may have believed it would be, and the servants they left to protect their property retained it. As a result, deep social changes ensued. Ceramics and coins date this last phase in the city's history to the seventh–tenth centuries.

Apamea was retaken and reoccupied by the Byzantines in 975; it fell to the Fatimids in AH 388/998 CE and then to the Crusaders, who held the citadel between 1106 and 1149. At that time, the plateau was already mostly abandoned as a result of the period's increasing political instability. The severe earthquake of 1157 struck Apamea off the map. It is mentioned in Arabic sources in the list of the cities destroyed then but does not appear as one of the cities destroyed in 1170.

BIBLIOGRAPHY

Balty, Janine, et al., eds. *Apamée de Syrie: Bilan des recherches archéologiques, 1965–1968.* Brussels, 1969. The results of the first four campaigns, as well as a discussion with colleagues excavating other sites in Syria.

Balty, Janine, and Jean Ch. Balty, eds. *Apamée de Syrie: Bilan des recherches archéologiques, 1969–1971.* Brussels, 1972. The results of the 1969–1971 campaigns.

Balty, Janine, and Jean Ch. Balty. "Julien et Apamée: Aspects de la restauration de l'hellénisme et de la politique antichrétienne de l'empereur." *Dialogues d'Histoire Ancienne* 1 (1974): 267–304. The

links between Apamea and Emperor Julian through an analysis of the mosaics of the Neo-Platonic school discovered under the cathedral.

Balty, Janine, and Jean Ch. Balty. "Apamée de Syrie, archéologie et histoire. I. Des origines à la Tétrarchie." In *Aufstieg und Niedergang der römischen Welt*, vol. II.8, edited by Hildegard Temporini, pp. 103–134. Berlin, 1977. Ancient sources and archaeological monuments combined to present a history of Apamea.

Balty, Janine, ed. *Apamée de Syrie: Bilan des recherches archéologiques, 1973–1979.* Brussels, 1984. Focuses on domestic architecture, presenting the results of the 1973–1979 campaigns in five different houses within the context of extensive comparative material from other sites in Syria and the Near East.

Balty, Janine, and Jean Ch. Balty. "Un programme philosophique sous la cathédrale d'Apamée: L'ensemble néo-platonicien de l'Empereur Julien." In *Texte et image: Actes du colloque international de Chantilly, 13 au 15 octobre 1982*, pp. 167–176. Paris, 1984. Attempts a global analysis of the mosaics of the Neo-Platonic school.

Balty, Jean Ch., and Jacqueline Napoleone-Lemaire. *L'église à atrium de la Grande Colonnade.* Brussels, 1969. The church through its successive architectural phases.

Balty, Jean Ch. "L'évêque Paul et le programme architectural et décoratif de la cathédrale d'Apamée." In *Mélanges d'histoire ancienne et d'archéologie offerts à Paul Collart*, edited by Pierre Ducrey et al., pp. 31–46. Cahier's d'Archéologie Romande de la Bibliothèque Historique Vaudoise, vol. 5. Lausanne, 1976. Interprets the program of the cathedral's mosaics as influenced by the patronage of Bishop Paul in the 630s.

Balty, Jean Ch. "Les grandes étapes de l'urbanisme d'Apamée-sur-l'Oronte." *Ktèma* 2 (1977): 3–16. Sketches the evolution of town planning through its four major phases (Hellenistic, Roman, Byzantine, and Early Islamic).

Balty, Jean Ch. *Guide d'Apamée.* Brussels, 1981. Intended primarily as a guide to the monuments at Apamea, this book also provides an extensive bibliography and numerous illustrations; the best introduction to the city.

JEAN CH. BALTY

APHEK (Gk., Antipatris; Ar., Tell Ras el-'Ain), site located in Israel at the headwaters of the Yarkon River on the Sharon plain (32°06′ N, 34°56′ E; map reference 143 × 168). Tel Aphek, one of five different places by the name of *Aphek* (Heb., 'aphik, "riverbed") mentioned in the Hebrew Bible, is situated on one of the country's most important ancient crossroads. It is about 30 acres in size and was continuously inhabited from the Chalcolithic to the Ottoman period.

Aphek is first mentioned in the Egyptian Execration texts of the nineteenth century BCE as 'APQM. In the topographical lists of Thutmose III it is mentioned as number 66, on the Via Maris, between Ono to the south and Socoh to the north. The location was instrumental in establishing its identification, first proposed by Albrecht Alt and William Foxwell Albright in 1923. Aphek is also mentioned in the annals of Amenhotep II as a city that surrendered to him on his march to the northern Sharon. In the Septuagint it is called Aphek of the Sharon in the list of conquered Canaanite cities in *Joshua* 12. It served twice as a base for the Philistines in their war against Israel (*1 Sm.* 4:21, 29:1). David covered

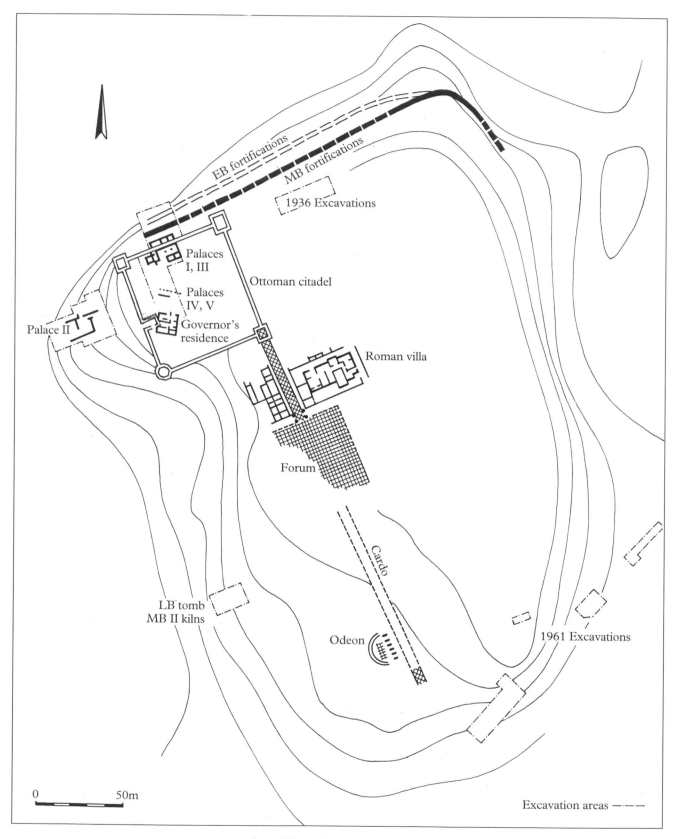

APHEK. *General plan of the site.* (Courtesy M. Kochavi)

the distance between Aphek and Ziklag in three days, a reasonable walking time between Aphek and southern Philistia (*1 Sm.* 30:1).

Aphek/Antipatris marked the border between the country's northern and the southern regions. It is mentioned in this context in Esarhaddon's campaign to Egypt; in an Aramaic letter from Egypt warning against Babylonian troops appearing as far as Aphek; and in several Jewish laws and legends in which Antipatris is the northernmost town of Judah. [*See* Judah.] The building of Antipatris by Herod the Great in 9 BCE, in memory of his father, Antipater, is reported by Josephus (*War* 1.21.9), as is its destruction during the First Jewish Revolt (*War* 2.29.1). [*See* First Jewish Revolt.] Late Roman Antipatris was one of the towns completely ruined in the 363 earthquake. An eighth-century Umayyad fort and an Ottoman fortress by the name of Binar Bashi, built in 1572, mark the only major later occupation of the site.

Two rescue excavations and a planned excavation project have been carried out at Aphek. The first rescue operation was conducted in 1934–1936 by Jacob Ory on behalf of the Palestine Department of Antiquities. The second one took place in 1961, under the direction of Avraham Eitan on behalf of the Israel Department of Antiquities. The Aphek-Antipatris Expedition, directed by Pirhiya Beck and Moshe Kochavi of Tel Aviv University, was carried out in thirteen seasons of excavation, from 1972 to 1985. The archaeology and history of the site are recounted here in chronological order, utilizing the results of all three expeditions.

Chalcolithic and Early Bronze Ages. A nodule of grayish soil containing Chalcolithic sherds was found in a section cut at the southeastern slope of the tell. It represents the earliest settlement at the site, near a large body of water formed by the Yarkon springs, one of several Chalcolithic settlements known in the vicinity. Remains from the Early Bronze Age were uncovered in all the excavated areas. EB IB private buildings were uncovered near the northern city wall. The wall (2.5 m wide), which also forms the northeastern corner of the tell in Ory's excavation, was laid in three even courses of fieldstones followed by layers of crushed-*kurkar* sun-dried mud bricks. A substantial building with rounded corners was uncovered at the southeastern edge of the site. At this early date the settled area already comprised all of the tell. A section of the EB II town at the northeast edge of the site contained several broad houses arranged on both sides of two streets. Very few EB III pottery sherds were detected, suggesting a decrease in the town's importance then. In the EB IV (Intermediate Bronze period), the site was totally deserted.

Middle Bronze Age. Aphek was rebuilt at the very beginning of the Middle Bronze Age. As in the earlier urban period, its remains were found in all areas of excavation, but far more of them were exposed, thus enabling their phasing into six stages of occupation.

Stage 1. Private buildings, tombs, and pottery were found in the acropolis fill. The pottery included simple bowls and whitewashed storage jars decorated with bichrome painting, incised decoration, or applied relief.

Stage 2. The first palace (palace I) was constructed on the acropolis fill. Exposure of its north wing revealed a large hall containing storejars and an adjacent courtyard with two cooking ovens. Intramural burials, typical of all the MB phases, were found beneath the courtyard floor. (The pottery resembles that found in the cist graves Ory excavated.) These burials may belong to Aphek's royal cemetery. The new MB city wall (3.5 m wide) was erected several meters uphill from the EB city wall.

Stage 3. Palace II, with its three large courtyards with plaster floors, was built on the western slope of the tell, not on the acropolis. A major restoration of the city wall took place during this phase. The pottery's elegant shapes and lustrous red slip (palace ware)—carinated bowls and jugs with perfect finish—represent a zenith in terms of style and craftsmanship.

Stage 4. Palace II was abandoned and a residential quarter with many infant burials in jars took its place. The pottery has MB II affinities.

Stage 5. Palace III, the largest of Aphek's palaces was built on the acropolis. Its 2-meter-wide walls, with foundations 2 m deep, enclosed an area of about 4,000 sq m. Its "reception hall" was 150 sq m in size; two one-meter-wide columns supported the ceiling.

Stage 6. Many modifications occurred in the palace III plan. The hall was divided into small rooms, one of which was a cultic area comprising a monolithic round altar and a cistern. The palace was destroyed in a huge conflagration at the end of the Middle Bronze Age.

Besides the acropolis and its vicinity, only the far southeastern part of the tell was excavated at MB levels. This area was first used to fire pottery in pottery kilns; three more or less complete kilns were excavated. The area was subsequently turned into a burial ground. During most of the Middle Bronze Age, Aphek was the central city in the southern Sharon.

Late Bronze Age. During the Late Bronze Age, three more palaces were built on Aphek's acropolis. Palace IV (fifteenth century BCE) was built on the remains of palace III, reusing its cultic installation. Palace V (fourteenth century BCE) was built on a new orientation, with large paved courtyards. A stone-lined family grave and two large plastered wine presses belong to the thirteenth century BCE. Palace VI, the last of Aphek's palaces was an Egyptian fortified residency, built on the southwestern wing of the previous palace. It had solid stone walls (1.4 m wide, 2 m high) and was 400 sq m in area. Its ground floor consisted of two small rooms, two storage halls, a corridor, and a stone and brick staircase leading to an upper floor. A monolithic trough was located at the main entrance. The residency was destroyed

APHEK. *Palace VI, the Egyptian governor's residence.* (Courtesy M. Kochavi)

by a fire that consumed its upper floor and sealed the ground floor with its debris. Several inscribed items were found under the debris:

Two unique cuneiform lexical tablets, one of which mentions kinds of liquids in Sumerian, Akkadian, and Canaanite; the second is bilingual, in Sumerian and Akkadian or Canaanite [*See* Sumerian; Akkadian; Proto-Canaanite.]

A fragmentary business letter, in cuneiform Akkadian [*See* Cuneiform.]

A Hittite seal impression with the name of a royal prince or princess [*See* Hittites; Seals.]

Three administrative fragments written in Akkadian

An Egyptian faience ring inscribed with a blessing to Amun-Re and an Egyptian faience foundation deposit plaque dedicated by Rameses II to the goddess Isis

A complete cuneiform clay tablet containing a letter from Takuhlinu, the prefect of Ugarit, to Haya, the Egyptian high commissioner of Canaan. [*See* Ugarit.] The synchronism between the careers of these personalities fixes the date of the destruction of LB Aphek to 1240/30 BCE.

Iron Age. After a gap in occupation, the acropolis of Aphek was resettled in the twelfth century BCE. Two residential quarters with different characters were uncovered: fine square buildings with paved courtyards—the elite section—and haphazardly built dwellings—the poorer quarter. Fishhooks, lead net weights, and turtle shells were found in

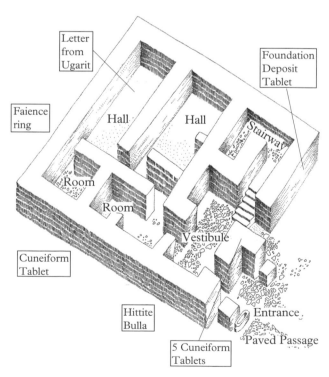

APHEK. *Plan of Palace VI, the Egyptian governor's residence.* (Drawing by Judith Dekel; courtesy M. Kochavi)

the poorer houses, indicating that their inhabitants were fishermen. [*See* Fishing.] Philistine pottery, several figurine heads of the Philistine goddess Ashdoda and a clay tablet inscribed in an as yet undeciphered script indicate a Philistine presence at Aphek in the eleventh century BCE. [*See* Philistines, *article on* Early Philistines.] Stone-lined silos typical at Israelite sites were dug into the debris of the first Iron Age strata which may indicate the arrival of the Israelites at Aphek. Several four-room houses from the tenth century BCE were also excavated. [*See* Four-room House.] Most of the later strata on the acropolis were wiped out during leveling operations to construct a fort in the Ottoman period.

Hellenistic and Roman Periods. Excavation south of the acropolis penetrated only to the Hellenistic level. Private buildings, arranged on both sides of a road, were excavated. The western part of a Hellenistic fort, erected on the acropolis, was saved from the Ottoman leveling operations. These remains suggest locating the Hellenistic town of Pegae at Aphek, rather than at the ruins of Fejja, its namesake, 2 km to the southwest.

Herodian Antipatris was built on the same plan as the Hellenistic town. A section of its marketplace, with shops arranged on both sides of a 9-meter-wide paved *cardo,* was excavated. The town's destruction by Vespasian in 68 is well attested. The shops and their merchandise were burned and hoards of coins and unused oil lamps were found on the floors.

The restoration of Antipatris during the second–third centuries nearly doubled the limits of the city toward the south. Several mansions, some with elaborately decorated mosaic floors, were built then; public buildings were added around the forum; and an odeum was constructed near the town's southern gate. [*See* Mosaics; Odeum.] This prosperous town was completely destroyed, probably in the earthquake of 363. Only fragmentary remains from the Byzantine period were found, and no town has been built on the tell since. The fort that crowns the tell today was built in the sixteenth century by the Ottoman Turks as a cavalry base, guarding that segment of the Via Maris between Gaza and the Megiddo pass. Its gate, mosque, and barracks have been excavated.

BIBLIOGRAPHY

Albright, William Foxwell. "The Site of Aphek in the Sharon." *Journal of the Palestine Oriental Society* 3 (1923): 50–53.

Beck, Pirhiya. "An Early Bronze Age 'Family' of Bowls from Tel Aphek." *Tel Aviv* 12 (1985): 17–28. Analyzes a class of pottery found at Aphek and suggests Aphek as its production center.

Beck, Pirhiya. "The Middle Bronze Age IIA Pottery from Aphek, 1972–1984: First Summary." *Tel Aviv* 12 (1985): 181–203. Definitive work on the chronology of MB IIA pottery based on the Aphek stratigraphy.

Eitan, Avraham. "Excavations at the Foot of Tel Rosh Ha 'Ayin" (in Hebrew). *'Atiqot* 5 (1969): 49–68. Report on the 1961 excavations.

Hellwing, Salo [Shlomo], and Ram Gophna. "The Animal Remains from the Early and Middle Bronze Ages at Tel Aphek and Tel Dalit: A Comparative Study." *Tel Aviv* 11 (1984): 48–59.

Iliffe, J. H. "Pottery from Rās el-'Ain." *Quarterly of the Department of Antiquities in Palestine* 5 (1936): 113–126. Important for the pottery from the MB IIA cist graves.

Kindler, Arie. "The Coins of Antipatris" (in Hebrew). *Eretz-Israel* 19 (1987): 125–131. Catalog of the coins minted in Antipatris.

Kochavi, Moshe, and Pirhiya Beck. *Aphek-Antipatris, 1972–1973: Preliminary Report.* Tel Aviv, 1976. The first two seasons of excavation and an analysis of the chronology and typology of the Aphek MB IIA pottery.

Kochavi, Moshe, et al. *Aphek-Antipatris, 1974–1977: The Inscriptions.* Tel Aviv, 1978. *Prima lectiones* of the Aphek inscriptions.

Kochavi, Moshe, et al. "Aphek-Antipatris, Tēl Pōlēg, Tēl Zerōr, and Tēl Burgā: Four Fortified Sites of the Middle Bronze IIA in the Sharon Plain." *Zeitschrift des Deutschen Palästina-Vereins* 95 (1979): 121–165. Establishes the existence of fortified cities in this period on the basis of MB IIA Aphek and other sites (see Yadin below).

Kochavi, Moshe. "The History and Archaeology of Aphek-Antipatris, a Biblical City in the Sharon Plain." *Biblical Archaeologist* 44 (1981): 75–86. Concise review based on information available by 1980.

Kochavi, Moshe. *Aphek-Antipatris: Five Thousand Years of History* (in Hebrew). Tel Aviv, 1989. The most complete synthesis on the subject, with a comprehensive bibliography.

Kochavi, Moshe. *Aphek in Canaan: The Egyptian Governor's Residence and Its Finds.* Israel Museum Catalogue, no. 312. Jerusalem, 1990. Hebrew and English text with numerous illustrations.

Neidinger, William. "A Typology of Oil Lamps from the Mercantile Quarter of Antipatris." *Tel Aviv* 9 (1982): 157–169. Report on the Hellenistic and Roman periods.

Ory, J. "Excavations at Rās el-'Ain." *Quarterly of the Department of Antiquities in Palestine* 5 (1936): 111–112; 6 (1937): 99–120. Report on the first rescue excavation at the site.

Owen, David I., et al. *Aphek-Antipatris, 1978–1985: The Letter from Ugarit—Philological, Historical, and Archaeological Considerations.* Tel Aviv, 1987. Establishes the date of the end of LB Aphek.

Yadin, Yigael. "The Nature of Settlement in the Middle Bronze IIA Period in Israel and the Problem of the Aphek Fortifications." *Zeitschrift des Deutschen Palästina-Vereins* 94 (1978): 1–23. Argues against the dating of the Aphek city wall to MB IIA.

MOSHE KOCHAVI

APHRODISIAS, site located in a fertile upland plain south of the Maeander River valley, about 200 km (124 mi) southeast of Izmir, in modern Turkey (37°43′ N, 28°44′ E). The city was part of ancient Caria and was best known for its cult of Aphrodite and the high-quality work of its sculptors in marble. The site was visited in the eighteenth and nineteenth centuries by such learned travelers as William Sherard, the Dilettante, and Charles Texier). Excavations were first conducted in 1914 by Paul Gaudin and in 1937 by Giulio Jacopi. Systematic investigation has been carried out since 1961 by New York University, led, until his death in 1990, by Kenan T. Erim.

The site's buildings and monuments, predominantly of the Roman period, are exceptionally well preserved and unusually well documented by inscriptions. This material gives a detailed picture of the city and its people from the first to the sixth century.

Aphrodisias was founded, according to a legend recorded by Stephanus of Byzantium, by the Babylonian king Ninos, husband of Semiramis. There are considerable prehistoric and Bronze Age remains, but fewer for the archaic and classical periods. The town grew up around its sanctuary of Aphrodite in the second century BCE and began rapid urbanization in the mid-first century BCE. Sulla and Caesar patronized the sanctuary, and in 39 BCE the city gained lasting favor and privileges through Octavian. Loyalty to Rome in the War of Labienus (41/40 BCE) was rewarded by the granting of autonomy, tax-free status, and new asylum rights for the Temple of Aphrodite. The nearby marble quarries were opened and, during the first and second centuries, the city saw continuous building.

Aphrodisias retained its urban vitality far into late antiquity, when it was the seat of the Roman governor of the new (Diocletianic) province of Caria. For a long period, Aphrodite and the old religion remained strong alongside rising Christianity. The city had a Christian bishop in the fourth century, and in the fifth century it was still home to a leading school of pagan Neoplatonic philosophy.

The North Agora and Portico of Tiberius were two great colonnaded piazzas that together defined the orthogonal center of the city's urban plan, laid out probably in the late first century BCE and under construction throughout the first century CE. The Council House (Odeion, first–second century CE) formed, with the North Agora, an agora-bouleuterion complex typical of civic planning of the early imperial period in Asia Minor. It was decorated with a *scaenae frons* and a rich display of marble statuary.

The Temple of Aphrodite, rebuilt in the 30s BCE as a prostyle temple, was surrounded during the first century CE with a great Ionic peripteral colonnade (8 × 13 m). It was later turned into a Christian basilica, with considerable care and economy, and is one of the best examples of such a temple-church conversion. A monumental columnar Tetrapylon (mid-second century CE), in the style of the Antonine baroque, formed the entrance gate to the sanctuary area. Its full restoration, using 85% of its original blocks, was completed in 1991.

The Sebasteion, built in the mid-first century CE, was a remarkable temple complex dedicated to Aphrodite and the Julio-Claudian emperors. It was excavated between 1979 and 1982. The complex consisted of a raised prostyle Corinthian temple approached by a narrow processional way flanked by two porticos 90 m long, each three-storied and decorated with a series of figural marble reliefs. The more than eighty surviving reliefs represent scenes both from Greek mythology and of Roman imperial subjects.

The Hadrianic Baths, built across the end of the Portico of Tiberius, were a massive construction and have been standing since antiquity. They are composed of five great barrel-vaulted parallel chambers, with an imposing colonnaded court in front. A stadium, built in the first–second

centuries CE, was encompassed by the later city wall (mid-fourth century), and is virtually intact. It is 262 m long with thirty tiers of seats and could hold up to thirty thousand people.

The theater, built into the site's main prehistoric *höyük* in the later Hellenistic period, was equipped in the 30s BCE with an elaborate columnar stage facade donated by a powerful local benefactor, one C. Julius Zoilos, an ex-slave and agent of the emperor Augustus, as recorded in the inscribed dedication of the building. Marble seating and other monumental work were added in the first century CE. The building remained in use until the seventh century, when the theater hill was converted into a fort.

Aphrodisian sculptors were well known abroad—they provided sculpture for Hadrian's villa at Tivoli, for example—and held in high repute at home. A large sculptor's workshop has been excavated in the heart of the city (between the Council House and the Temple), and the range of fine statuary recovered from other buildings gives a complete cross section of the sculpture production of a Greek city in the Roman period. The sculptures range from second-century BCE grave reliefs to fifth-century CE statues of Late Roman governors.

BIBLIOGRAPHY

Erim, Kenan T. *Aphrodisias: City of Venus Aphrodite.* London and New York, 1986. A well-illustrated introduction to the history and monuments of the site, with full bibliography of earlier work.

Joukowsky, Martha S. *Prehistoric Aphrodisias.* 2 vols. Rhode Island and Louvain, 1986. Detailed publication of all aspects of the site in the Bronze Age and earlier.

Reynolds, J. M. *Aphrodisias and Rome.* London, 1983. Publication of an important series of inscriptions, including several imperial letters, detailing the city's special relationship with Rome.

Roueché, Charlotte. *Aphrodisias in Late Antiquity.* London, 1989. Publication of the Late Antique inscriptions (after 250 CE), with full historical commentary on the city in this period.

Roueché, Charlotte. *Performers and Partisans at Aphrodisias.* London, 1993. A publication of inscriptions and graffiti relating to the athletic festivals and games held in the city.

Roueché, Charlotte, and Kenan T. Erim, eds. *Aphrodisias Papers 1.* Journal of Roman Archaeology Supplementary Series, no. 1. Ann Arbor, 1990. Studies on the temple of Aphrodite and various groups of sculpture.

Smith, R. R. R. *Aphrodisias I. The Monument of C. Julius Zoilos.* Mainz, 1993. A detailed publication of the allegorical frieze from the tomb of Zoilos, the freedman and agent of Octavian in the city in the 30s BCE. The first in a new series publishing the major monuments of the site.

Smith, R. R. R., and Kenan T. Erim, eds. *Aphrodisias Papers 2.* Journal of Roman Archaeology Supplementary Series, no. 2. Ann Arbor, 1991. Studies on the theater, coins, and further groups of sculpture.

R. R. R. SMITH

APLIKI, important copper-mining and smelting site on Cyprus. Located approximately 6.5 km (4 mi.) south of the modern village of Lefka on the east bank of the Marathasa River in the foothills of the Troodos Mountains (35°04′39″

N, 32°50′34″ E), Apliki-*Karamallos* was a Late Bronze Age miners' village in the copper-mining region of northwest Cyprus. The discovery of Late Bronze Age ceramics by the Cyprus Mines Corporation led to limited excavations in 1938 and 1939 under direction of Joan duPlat Taylor on behalf of the Cyprus Department of Antiquities.

The site occupies an area of perhaps two ha (5 acres) on a high plateau. Several trenches were opened, designated areas A–H. Architectural remains were uncovered in areas A (roughly 270 sq m or 2,905 sq. ft.) and B (125 sq m or 1,345 sq. ft.); other trenches were smaller and revealed fragmentary walls or pits and Late Bronze Age sherd material. The remains in area A comprise a well-built stone and mudbrick L-shaped structure of at least eight rooms opening onto a courtyard, some provided with benches and hearths. Taylor identified two periods of occupation, distinguished by two floor levels and architectural rearrangements. This complex was destroyed by fire. Area B revealed remains of at least five houses with one period of occupation, which were abandoned but not burnt. Principal pottery types from these buildings include White Slip II, Base Ring II, Plain White Wheelmade, imported Mycenaean, White-Painted Wheelmade III, Coarse Monochrome (Apliki) wares and large storage jars (pithoi). This ceramic evidence suggests that the site was constructed during Late Cypriot IIC (thirteenth century BCE) and destroyed and abandoned early in Late Cypriot IIIA (early twelfth century BCE).

The site is of greatest interest for its evidence for metallurgical activity. Quantities of black slag, with ropy surface, a type formerly thought to belong to the Roman period, were found in areas A and B, along with crucible fragments and tuyères (pipes for channeling air into a furnace), including D-shaped and elbow types, in stratified Late Bronze Age contexts within the houses. The location of the site and the massive size of the slag (blocks weighing up to 14 kg or 30.8 lbs.) and tuyères suggest that it was a major copper-mining and smelting center. Mine shafts and galleries noted in the nearby copper-rich hills may have been associated with this settlement, although independent archaeological dating evidence for them is lacking.

Other objects from the rooms include loom weights, spindle whorls, and wall brackets for hanging lamps; stone querns, pestles, and bowls; bronze chisels, drills, and knives; terra-cotta bull and female figurines; unengraved cylinders of ivory and steatite; fragments of a wooden comb; a gold lunate earring; and a large serpentine stamp seal carved with a bull's head and Cypro-Minoan sign. Burnt vegetable remains from area A include barley, wheat, horsebean, lentil, almond, grape, olive, and coriander. They were probably not cultivated at the site, which is badly suited for farming, but may have been exchanged for the copper produced there. A large slag heap and Late Roman–Byzantine remains have been found at the foot of the hill.

[*See also* Mines and Mining.]

BIBLIOGRAPHY

Helbaek, Hans. "Late Cypriote Vegetable Diet at Apliki." *Opuscula Atheniensia* 4 (1962): 171–186. Detailed discussion of the plant remains, their place in Near Eastern agriculture, and possible trade in agricultural products.

Kling, Barbara. *Mycenaean IIIC:1b and Related Pottery in Cyprus*. Studies in Mediterranean Archaeology, vol. 87. Göteborg, 1989. Reassessment of the site's chronology in the light of recent discussions of the ceramics of the LC IIC and LC IIIA periods (see pp. 85–86); accepts Taylor's original dating.

Muhly, James D. "The Organisation of the Copper Industry in Late Bronze Age Cyprus." In *Early Society in Cyprus*, edited by Edgar Peltenburg, pp. 298–314. Edinburgh, 1989. Discussion of metallurgical remains based on recent reexamination of the material, and consideration of the place of Apliki within the larger context of the Late Cypriot copper industry.

Taylor, Joan duPlat. "A Late Bronze Age Settlement at Apliki, Cyprus." *Antiquaries Journal* 32 (1952): 133–167. Original excavation report containing good descriptions of the architecture, pottery, and small finds.

BARBARA KLING

'AQABA, port in modern Jordan overlying the ancient cities of Roman Aila and early Islamic Ayla (29°31′ N, 35°0′ E). The biblical sites of Eilat and Ezion-Geber were presumably also located somewhere in the vicinity. Situated at the north end of the Gulf of 'Aqaba, on an arm of the Red Sea, 'Aqaba lies at the nexus of important trade routes. The port serviced sea traffic with Egypt, South Arabia, Africa, and India. Several land routes intersected at 'Aqaba, including roads northeast through Transjordan to Syria, north via Wadi 'Arabah to the Dead Sea and Jordan Valley, northwest via the Negev to Gaza on the Mediterranean, west across Sinai to Egypt, and southeast into the Arabian Peninsula. Copper from important mines at Feinan and Timna', just to the north in Wadi 'Arabah, was transshipped via this port. Several Chalcolithic sites are attested in the region. One, the small mound of Tell Maquss near the modern 'Aqaba airport, was excavated by Lufti Khalil in 1985 and yielded evidence of copper processing from the mid-fourth millennium (Khalil, 1987, 1992).

The biblical tradition asserts that Eilat was the port of departure for Solomon's merchant fleet to Ophir (*1 Kgs.* 9:26–28; *2 Chr.* 8:17–18). A later king of Judah, Jehoshaphat, also planned to send a fleet to Ophir, but it was wrecked at Ezion-Geber (*1 Kgs.* 22:48; *2 Chr.* 20:36–37). Eilat was later ceded by Judah to the Edomites in the late eighth century BCE (*2 Kgs.* 16:2). [*See* Judah.] Inspired by the biblical traditions, Nelson Glueck excavated Tell el-Kheleifeh (1938–1940), a low mound just northwest of modern 'Aqaba. [*See* Kheleifeh, Tell el-.] Glueck (1965) claimed to have found Eilat/Ezion-Geber, but his results were never adequately published. A reexamination by Gary Pratico (1993) of Glueck's evidence suggests, rather, an Edomite settlement occupied from the late eighth through the fourth centuries BCE. The walled site, apparently a caravanserai, yielded evidence of grain storage, copper smelting, and trade with southern Arabia. [*See the biography of Glueck.*]

The next major ancient settlement was Aila, a city at the head of the gulf attested in various literary sources during the Roman and Byzantine periods. Its origin is unclear, but presumably Aila began as a Nabatean settlement in the first century BCE. [*See* Nabateans.] Strabo (*Geog.* 16.2.30), writing in the early first century CE, already refers to Aila as a city (polis). Merchants from Aila traveled to South Arabia to obtain frankincense and myrrh (*Geog.* 16.4.4). The city passed under direct Roman rule with the annexation of Nabatea as the Roman province of Arabia in 106 CE. Aila then became the southern terminus of the Via Nova Trajana, a major trunk road between southern Syria and the Red Sea completed in 111–114 CE. The strategic importance of the city is suggested by the transfer of the Legio X Fretensis from Jerusalem to Aila in about 300 CE (Eusebius, *Onomasticon* 6.17). A fragmentary monumental Latin building inscription of the early fourth century may relate to this legion, which remained garrisoned until at least the turn of the fifth century (*Notitia Dignitatum Oriens* 34.30). Christian bishops from Aila are attested beginning in 325. Various sources suggest that significant seaborne trade continued between Aila and the Indian Ocean littoral through the Byzantine period. The city made a treaty with the prophet Muhammad himself in 630 that guaranteed protection of its commerce at the beginning of the Muslim conquest.

Richard Burton identified the remains of Nabatean and Roman Aila in 1878. The classical site, now within the modern city of 'Aqaba, was rediscovered by John L. Meloy in 1989. An excavation launched by S. Thomas Parker of North Carolina State University in 1994 uncovered significant portions of Aila. The earliest excavated evidence dates to the first centuries BCE/CE, including amphorae from the western Mediterranean, terra sigillata, and painted Nabatean fine ware. This Early Roman pottery was associated with mud-brick domestic structures. Farther south, the city wall was erected in stone in the late fourth century. The excavated segment is about 30 m long, survives to nearly 2 m in height, and was defended by a projecting rectangular tower. The wall was built over an earlier massive mud-brick structure, apparently once vaulted. Just north of the city wall was a mud-brick domestic complex consisting of rooms built around a paved courtyard. The complex was apparently occupied from the sixth/seventh to the eighth centuries. North of the domestic complex was a cemetery of mud-brick tombs. [*See* Tombs.] Three excavated tombs each contained a single articulated skeleton and date to the fourth century. Continued international trade during the Byzantine period is evidenced by fine glossy red pottery imported from North Africa, the Aegean, Cyprus, and Egypt. South of the Byzantine city wall (i.e., within the city walls), two other areas yielded substantial evidence of Early Islamic occupation. This suggests that the Byzantine city survived for a time alongside the new Early Islamic city founded just to the southeast.

Archaeological investigation of the early Islamic city at 'Aqaba began in 1986 and continued through 1993 under Donald Whitcomb. T. E. Lawrence (Lawrence of Arabia) provided the earliest description of the site in 1914 as a "settlement of some luxury in the early Middle Ages" (Woolley and Lawrence, 1936). The Early Islamic city was probably founded under 'Uthman ibn 'Affan (c. 650). Beneath the slightly mounded surface is about 4.5 m of occupation from the mid-seventh century until the arrival of the Crusaders in 1116. The city wall is defended by U-shaped towers and was entered via four gates, now named the Egyptian, Syrian, Hijazi, and Sea Gates. The plan of the city (165 × 140 m) is marked by axial streets dividing the town into four quadrants. The central crossing had a tetrapylon, like the early Islamic city of 'Anjar in southern Lebanon. The plan may have been modeled on that of the fortress of the Legio X Fretensis, presumably located nearby. In addition to the streets and residences of the later periods (see below), several functional institutions have been discovered. The central pavilion became a wealthy merchant's residence, which might be associated with the governor's palace. The changes associated with the 'Abbasid reorganization of the city after 750 included the use of the sea wall as the backdrop of an extensive suq, or "market," with numerous small shops (some composed of converted towers) lined up along the beach. During the 1993 season, the city's congregational mosque was discovered, a hypostyle hall in the Syrian style and an important addition to excavated mosques of the early Islamic period. [*See* Mosque.] This mosque is oriented southwest, possibly a misconception of the direction of Mecca (Ar., *qiblah*).

The stratigraphic evidence gives an artifactual sequence that amplifies the meager historical information on Aila. The most recent levels (phase E, 1050–1100 CE) belong to the Late 'Abbasid or Fatimid period and are marked by the aftermath of the 1068 earthquake. The limited reconstruction amid the rubble ended with the arrival of a band of Crusaders; the people of Aila fled in their boats, returning much later to resettle around the 'Aqaba castle, one kilometer to the south. The century before this (phase D, 950–1050) was not much better. The Fatimids of Egypt established some control, but increasingly southern Palestine was a war zone where the Fatimids exchanged lands with Byzantines, Seljuks, and a local bedouin confederation. In 1024 the town was sacked by the Banu Jarrah, a catastrophe in which a hoard of gold was abandoned. The hoard, of thirty-two dinars, was composed mainly of issues from Sijilmasa in Morocco, suggesting a merchant's or a pilgrim's loss. The pottery may point to this social instability: fine luster, decorated, and other glazed wares occur with a crude, handmade pottery. The preceding phase C (850–950) is a mystery century at 'Aqaba, when apparently nothing dra-

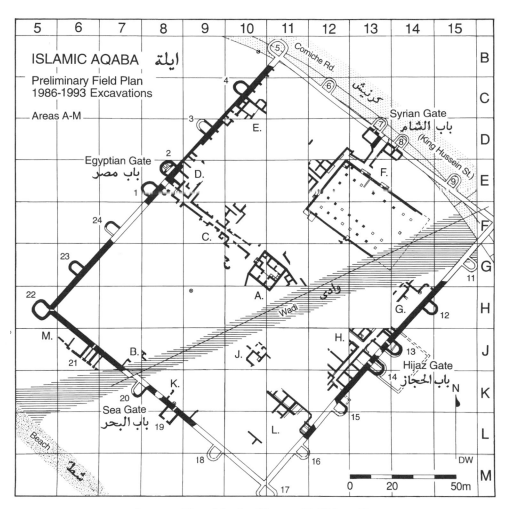

'AQABA. *Plan of the site.* (Courtesy D. Whitcomb)

matic happened—neither political nor natural events marred its tranquility.

The 'Abbasid period (phase B, 750–850) began with a catastrophe, the earthquake of 748; an energetic reconstruction and reorganization resulted in a new, more prosperous town that became an important center for the study of religious law. The pottery again reflects these changes: the transition introduced an unglazed cream ware (Mahesh ware), abandoning the earlier Byzantine/Umayyad tradition and revealing stylistic attributes typical of 'Abbasid Iraq. Other artifacts reveal the cultural leadership of the Hijaz during this period, when Aila participated in the active commercial world of the Indian Ocean via South Arabia and Ethiopia. These patterns began in the initial phase A (650–750) and endured even though the most prominent cultural influence of that period was from Early Islamic Egypt. The earliest glazed ceramics at 'Aqaba (Coptic glazed ware) were produced in Egypt (probably at Alexandria) in the early eighth century; the finds at 'Aqaba have confirmed the identification of this ceramic tradition. The city plan and artifacts

of this phase testify to the transformation from Late Byzantine to Early Islamic styles, paralleling the emergence of Islamic political and cultural identity in the time of the first caliphs and the Umayyad dynasty.

BIBLIOGRAPHY

Burton, Richard F. *The Land of Midian (Revisited).* Vol. 2. London, 1879. See pages 240–241.

Glueck, Nelson. "Ezion-Geber." *Biblical Archaeologist* 28 (1965): 70–87. Glueck's final interpretation of Tell el-Kheleifeh, revising some of his earlier views.

Khalil, Lufti. "Preliminary Report on the 1985 Season of Excavation at el-Maqass—'Aqaba." *Annual of the Department of Antiquities of Jordan* 31 (1987): 481–483.

Khalil, Lufti. "Some Technological Features from a Chalcolithic Site at Magass—'Aqaba." In *Studies in the History and Archaeology of Jordan IV*, pp. 143–148. Amman, 1992.

MacAdam, Henry I. "Fragments of a Latin Building Inscription from 'Aqaba, Jordan." *Zeitschrift für Papyrologie und Epigraphik* 79 (1989): 163–172.

Meloy, John L. "Results of an Archaeological Reconnaissance in West 'Aqaba: Evidence of the Pre-Islamic Settlement." *Annual of the Department of Antiquities of Jordan* 35 (1991): 397–414.

Parker, S. Thomas. "The Roman 'Aqaba Project: Aila Rediscovered." *Biblical Archaeologist* 57 (1994): 172. Short summary of results from the first field season.

Parker, S. Thomas. "Preliminary Report on the 1994 Season of the Roman 'Aqaba Project." *Bulletin of the American Schools of Oriental Research.* Forthcoming.

Pratico, Gary D. *Nelson Glueck's 1938–1940 Excavations at Tell el-Kheleifeh: A Reappraisal.* American Schools of Oriental Research Archaeological Reports, 3. Atlanta, 1993. This study, based on a re-examination of Glueck's artifacts and field records, casts doubt on Glueck's claim that the site was Solomon's Ezion-Geber.

Whitcomb, Donald S. "Excavations in 'Aqaba: First Preliminary Report." *Annual of the Department of Antiquities of Jordan* 31 (1987): 247–266.

Whitcomb, Donald S. *'Aqaba: Port of Palestine on the China Sea.* Amman, 1988. Excellent introductory guide to the site, although now somewhat dated.

Whitcomb, Donald S. "Coptic Glazed Ceramics from the Excavations at 'Aqaba, Jordan." *Journal of the American Research Center in Egypt* 26 (1989): 167–182.

Whitcomb, Donald S. "Evidence of the Umayyad Period from the 'Aqaba Excavations." In *The History of Bilād al-Sham during the Umayyad Period: Proceedings of the Fourth International Conference,* vol. 2, edited by Muhammad Adnan al-Bakhit and Robert Schick, pp. 164–184. Amman, 1989.

Whitcomb, Donald S. "Diocletian's *Miṣr* at 'Aqaba." *Zeitschrift des Deutschen Palästina-Vereins* 106 (1990): 156–161. Debunks the view that the Early Islamic fortified town was actually a rebuilt version of an earlier Roman legionary fortress.

Whitcomb, Donald S. "The Fourth Gate at Ayla: A Report on the 1992 Excavations at 'Aqaba." *Annual of the Department of Antiquities of Jordan* 37 (1993): 533–543.

Whitcomb, Donald S. *Ayla: Art and Industry in the Islamic Port of 'Aqaba.* Chicago, 1994.

Whitcomb, Donald S. "The *Miṣr* of Ayla: Settlement at al-'Aqaba in the Early Islamic Period." In *The Byzantine and Early Islamic Near East,* vol. 2, *Land Use and Settlement Patterns,* edited by G. R. D. King and Averil Cameron, pp. 155–170. Princeton, 1994.

Woolley, C. Leonard, and T. E. Lawrence. *The Wilderness of Zin.* New York, 1936. See pages 141–145.

S. Thomas Parker and Donald S. Whitcomb

'AQAR QUF (Dur Kurigalzu), site located about 30 km (19 mi.) west of Baghdad, Iraq (33°21' N, 44°21' E), and situated on an outcrop of the limestone terrace of the Euphrates River adjoining the Patti-Enlil canal in the east, connecting it with the Babylonian city of Sippar. It was identified by Henry Creswicke Rawlinson on the basis of bricks inscribed with the name of the Kassite residence/capital Dur Kurigalzu (H. C. Rawlinson, *A Selection from the Historical Inscriptions of Chaldaea, Assyria, and Babylonia,* The Cuneiform Inscriptions of Western Asia, 1, London, 1861, pl. 4.14). The town was founded by the Kassite king Kurigalzu I at the end of the fifteenth or the beginning of the fourteenth century BCE. There are traces of an older settlement from the fifteenth century. Following the fall of the Kassite dynasty during the twelfth century BCE, the site was abandoned

and never reoccupied. It was, however, occasionally used for burials. The overall occupation area seems to have been about 225 ha (556 acres) with an enclosure wall, parts of which could be distinguished topographically in the east. Within this area several hills diversify the otherwise flat ground; the highest of those hills is 'Aqar Quf. Another hill, 1 km to the west, is Tell al-Abyad; a third mound, A, lies between them, but only 100 m to the west of the ziggurat at 'Aqar Quf. Excavation results point to a clear functional separation of the two main areas—'Aqar Quf being the religious district and Tell al-Abyad the palace and administrative center. Both were excavated by a joint Iraqi-British mission directed by Seton Lloyd and Taha Baqir under the auspices of the British School of Archaeology in Iraq and the Iraqi Directorate-General of Antiquities between 1942 and 1945. [*See the biography of Lloyd.*]

The ziggurat, É-GI-KIL, is part of the temple quarter, which is devoted to the god Enlil, the main god in the Babylonian pantheon. Its ground plan is almost square, covering an area of 69 × 67.6 m. Three main staircases led up to the first terrace, which must have been about 33 m high. The two lateral staircases spread around the corners to meet the main central staircase. Only a small part of the temple complex was excavated. It consisted originally of three almost square courtyards, each of which was enclosed by a single row of rooms. The main temple is not preserved but must have been situated between the central courtyard and the main staircase of the ziggurat. According to inscriptions found in each unit, the central one was devoted to the god Enlil; the one on the northeast to his wife, the goddess Ninlil; and the one on the southwest to the war god Ninurta. On mound A another temple, possibly also dedicated to Ninlil, was discovered.

The palace consisted of several units, not all contemporary. In the main unit, A, four stages were distinguished. Unit H, with wall paintings in situ, was the latest addition. [*See* Wall Paintings.] The palace was in use until the end of the Kassite dynasty (mid-twelfth century BCE). Unit A consisted of three *mittelsaalhäuser* (a building with a large central hall flanked on each long side by a row of smaller rooms connected with it) adjoining a square courtyard. The ground plans of all but the one on the northeast are very similar; it seems to have been the throne room used in connection with a ceremonial room. Other remarkable features of the palace are a treasury on the east, which consisted of small vaulted rooms along a corridor. [*See* Palace.]

Many of the known major works of art of the Kassite period were found in the palace at Dur Kurigalzu. A sculptured terra-cotta head of a bearded man, an almost completely preserved sculpture of a hyena, a relief mace head of limestone, some glass inlays, gold jewelry, and gold ornaments and overlays are among the small finds. Only interim reports on the excavations at 'Aqar Quf have been published

(Baqir, 1944–1946). Much of the unpublished material is in the Baghdad Museum.

[*See also* Kassites; Mesopotamia, *article on* Ancient Mesopotamia; Sippar; Temples, *article on* Mesopotamian Temples; Ziggurat; *and the biography of Rawlinson.*]

BIBLIOGRAPHY

Balkan, Kemal. "Kassitenstudien 1. Die Sprache der Kassiten." *American Oriental Series* 37 (1954): 93.

Baqir, Taha. *Iraq Government Excavations at 'Aqar Qūf, 1942–1943.* Iraq Supplement. London, 1944.

Baqir, Taha. *Iraq Government Excavations at 'Aqar Qūf: Second Interim Report, 1943–1944.* Iraq Supplement. London, 1945.

Baqir, Taha. "Iraq Government Excavations at 'Aqar Qūf: Third Interim Report, 1944–1945." *Iraq* 8 (1946): 73–93.

Heinrich, Ernst. *Die Tempel und Heiligtümer im alten Mesopotamien.* Denkmäler Antiker Architektur, 14. Berlin, 1982. See pages 223–225.

Heinrich, Ernst. *Die Paläste im alten Mesopotamien.* Denkmäler Antiker Architektur, 15. Berlin, 1984. See pages 89–91.

Nashef, Khaled. *Die Orts- und Gewässernamen der mittelbabylonischen und mittelassyrischen Zeit.* Répertoire Géographique des Textes Cunéiformes, 5. Wiesbaden, 1982. See "Dūr-Kurigalzu."

Tomabechi, Yoko. "Wall Paintings from Dur Kurigalzu." *Journal of Near Eastern Studies* 42 (1983): 123–131.

HARTMUT KÜHNE

AQUEDUCTS.

In antiquity, aqueducts transported spring water or running water to communities, principally to cities, but also to palaces, fortresses, monasteries, and farms. These water systems supplied fresh water for individual everyday use, for pools in private residences, and for public use in bathhouses, fountains, and reservoirs. They transported water from a high place to a low place according to the law of gravity. Aqueducts begin at springs, a few of which were enhanced by built structures: at Jerusalem, Caesarea, Emmaus, Sebaste, Beth-Guvrin, and 'Ein-Boqeq in Palestine. At first, channels for the moving water were dug into the ground, but eventually they were hewn or built of field stone, sealed with waterproof plaster, and covered with flat stone slabs that prevented the water from becoming polluted. In a number of places, pits were dug, into which residue from the sediments in the water could settle. The channels in which the water flowed were generally cut in a rectangular shape; some narrowed at the bottom, to become trapezoidal. The dimensions of the channels were determined by the amount of water they were designed to carry: from 1.4 × 1.8 m long (the lower aqueduct at Caesarea) to 0.1 × 0.14 m long (the lower aqueduct at Emmaus) and generally about 0.3–0.5 m wide and 0.5–0.8 m deep. The aqueducts themselves were usually built from small stones that did not exceed 0.2 m in length; the stones were held together with mortar. In order to cross valleys and mountain chains, arched bridges were built and tunnels were dug. Tunnels first appeared in the Iron Age in Jerusalem in Palestine and at Erbil in Syria. Many were dug in the Hellenistic, Roman, and Byzantine periods, several of which had shafts 33–56 m apart. Such a system allowed the digging to be carried out simultaneously in all the shafts, so that work on the tunnel could proceed more quickly. Tunnels constructed in this manner were used at Akko, Beth-ha-'Emek, Gaaton, Jerusalem, Caesarea, and Sepphoris. Shorter tunnels without shafts were found at Susita, Sebaste, Jerusalem, Jericho, Qumran, and Hyrkania.

From the Hellenistic period onward, it was customary in deep valleys to use an inverted siphon to move water. This consisted of a lead or clay pipe that could be closed off. This important invention conveyed water to cities on high hills (at Pergamon the ridge was about 200 m high). To regulate the flow of water, pools and reservoirs were built along the path of the aqueducts. Near the city or inside it, the water entered a large reservoir (Sepphoris, Susita) or an enclosed pool (Sepphoris, Tiberias, Jericho, Petra, Humeima) or entered into large water pits (Masada, Cypros, Sartaba, Hyrkania).

In the Roman period, an inverted siphon built of stone links was in use at Jerusalem, Susita, and Beth-Yerah. Linked stones were used in building the arched bridges that appear for the first time in the first century BCE. These bridges are considered the most impressive structures associated with the aqueducts; together with the inverted siphon (sometimes also in combination, as at Aspendos in Anatolia) and the tunnels, they mark the high point in the development of aqueducts.

The earliest aqueduct is Menua's canal dug at Urartu in Turkey, at the beginning of the eighth century BCE. It conveyed spring water for a distance of about 56 km (about 35 mi) to the foot of the settlement at the citadel of Urartu. Knowledge of this technology traveled from Urartu to Assyria, where, at the end of the eighth century BCE, Sennacherib built two aqueducts for the cities of Nineveh and Erbil. The aqueduct at Nineveh was about 55 km long and included a number of tunnels and bridges. Inscriptions glorifying Sennacherib have been discovered on the largest of the bridges (approximately 300 m long and about 12 m wide). A shaft tunnel was dug for the aqueduct at Erbil. Hezekiah's Tunnel (533 m long) was built in Jerusalem in the same period. It passed under the city, to the other side of the ridge, going east to southwest, in order to bring water into the city. The technique of conveying water by means of aqueducts also reached classical Greece, where, in the sixth century BCE, Eupalinos constructed a tunnel 1,040 m long to bring water to the city of Samos. Hezekiah's Tunnel and the tunnel of Eupalinos, both of which were built without trenches, are considered the greatest works of water-engineering technology in the preclassical period. The techniques developed by the Greeks for building aqueducts arose from the need to hide their water systems from their enemies. As a result, they constructed underground tunnels. Just such a water system in Palestine brought water from a distance of about 14 km (8.75 mi.) to the city of Ptolemais/Akko, at the beginning of the third century BCE; it is the first aqueduct to bring water from such a distance.

In the second century BCE, in the desert of Palestine, aqueducts gathered floodwaters into gigantic water pits located in palaces and fortresses. These aqueducts are distinguished by a deeply cut channel. At Sartaba and Hyrkania, an inverted siphon was built that allowed water to be conveyed to the pits situated along the slope of the fortress, according to the principle that water in a pipe will always rise to its original height. An aqueduct was built from the springs at Wadi Qelt to the palaces of the Hasmoneans in Jericho; in it a clay pipe was installed that was used as an inverted siphon to raise water to the fortress. The lower aqueduct to Jerusalem is dated to this same period.

In the Roman period, aqueducts were built in most of the cities of the ancient Near East. The most important ones were in Palestine, at Caesarea and in Jerusalem. The upper aqueduct at Caesarea, first built either by Herod the Great or by his followers, rests on impressive arches to keep water at the desirable height. Thus, the water could reach every part of the city by force of gravitation. At the time of the emperor Hadrian, a second aqueduct was affixed to it that bears no fewer than nine imperial inscriptions glorifying the emperor for building the structure. Jerusalem's aqueduct in this period is an arrangement of four aqueducts whose total length is about 80 km (about 50 mi.). Additional aqueducts were built at Antioch, Tyre, Tadmor/Palmyra, Banias, Susita (three aqueducts), Gadara/Umm Qeis, Tiberias (two), Sepphoris (two), Beth-Shean (three), Abila (three), Dor (two), Legio, Sha'ar ha-'Amaqim (two), Sebaste/Samaria (two), Shechem, Emmaus (two), Beth-Guvrin (two), Humeima, and Petra (two), among others. An inverted siphon built of stone links is found on the ridge (about 45 m deep) at Susita and in the valley of Bethlehem, on the high (about 40 m deep) aqueduct to Jerusalem. The aqueduct at Tiberias has a secondary water line (about 20 m deep) that leads to the bathhouse at Beth-Yerah. Stone inverted siphons such as these are widespread in many Roman cities in western Anatolia.

Bridges support aqueducts in only a few places: at Cypros and Hyrkania and in Wadi Qelt, Samaria, Tiberias, Jerusalem, and Na'aran, near Jericho. There probably was a bridge at Sepphoris, but it has been completely destroyed. In other places, high support walls were built to guard the aqueduct as it passed through low-lying regions: at Cypros, Hyrkania, and Sepphoris. Aqueducts were used late into the Byzantine period. In the Early Arab period, an aqueduct was built at Ramla, then the capital of Palestine.

Jerusalem's aqueducts continued to operate in the Mamluk and Ottoman periods. In the Ottoman period, two aqueducts were built at Akko; the later one dates to the reign of the Pasha Süleyman and operated from 1814 to 1948. The Biar aqueduct, one of the four aqueducts to Jerusalem, was repaired by the British and still operates, as do the ones in Wadi Qelt and Wadi Auja, which were built in the twentieth century on the foundations of aqueducts from the Hasmonean period.

[See also Baths; Cisterns; Dams; Hydrology; Pools; Reservoirs; Sewers; and Water Tunnels. In addition, many of the sites mentioned are the subject of independent entries.]

BIBLIOGRAPHY

'Amit, David, Yizhar Hirschfeld, and Joseph Patrich, eds. *The Aqueducts of Ancient Palestine* (in Hebrew). Jerusalem, 1989.
Olami, Yaacov, and Yehudah Peleg. "The Water Supply System of Caesarea Maritima." *Israel Exploration Journal* 27.2–3 (1977): 127–137, pls. 16–17.
Stenton, E. C., and J. J. Coulton. "Oinoanda: The Water Supply and Aqueduct." *Anatolian Studies* 36 (1986): 15–59.
Tsuk, Tsvika. "The Aqueducts to Sepphoris." M.A. thesis, Tel Aviv University, 1985. In Hebrew, with English summary.
Tsuk, Tsvika. "The Aqueduct to Legio and the Location of the Camp of the VIth Roman Legion." *Tel Aviv* 15–16 (1988–1989): 92–97, pls. 13–14.
Vitruvius, Pollio. *De Architectura*. Book 8. Cambridge, 1934.

TSVIKA TSUK
Translated from Hebrew by Eric S. Cohen

ARABIAN PENINSULA. [*This entry provides a broad survey of the history of the Arabian Peninsula as known primarily from archaeological discoveries. It is chronologically divided into three articles:*
    The Arabian Peninsula in Prehistoric Times
    The Arabian Peninsula before the Time of Islam
    The Arabian Peninsula in Islamic Times
In addition to the related articles on specific countries, subregions, and sites referred to in this entry, see History of the Field, *article on* Archaeology in the Arabian Peninsula.]

The Arabian Peninsula in Prehistoric Times

The earliest hominoid finds from the Arabian Peninsula are fossil remains of dryopithecine type recovered in northeastern Saudi Arabia and dated to the Lower Miocene (c. seventeen–fourteen million years BCE). Eastern Arabia must have been a relatively lush environment then, for the fossil record contains evidence for the presence of various members of the giraffe, bovine, pig, crocodile, and rhinoceros families. A great quantity of important fossil remains has also recently been discovered in western Abu Dhabi, but thus far no remains of hominoids. The earliest traces of artifactual remains, possibly of hominid origin, come from a site north of Hail in Saudi Arabia, where a pre-Acheulean industry, thought to be related to Oldowan B in East Africa, has been identified. Much of northern, western, and southwestern Arabia, in what is geologically part of the Arabian shield formation, has yielded remains of Lower Pleistocene date (c. 1.2 million–100,000 BP), where a population using a variety of Lower, Middle, and Upper Acheulean industries lived. Typical Acheulean handaxes, bifaces, chopping tools, and flakes have been found throughout this region. The Middle Pleistocene is equally, if not better represented by sites with Middle Paleolithic tools of Mousterian or Mousterian of Acheulean tradition, dating to about 75,000–30,000 BP. Sites in the Rub al-Khali were recently studied that contain an industry typologically related to the Aterian of North Africa, and that probably date to about 35,000–20,000 BP. The existence of human occupation in presently desertic areas such as this was made possible by considerably moister conditions during the Late Pleistocene, probably as a result of a northward displacement of the monsoon at that time. The Rub al-Khali was an area of savannahlike grassland then.

It is noteworthy, however, that Upper Paleolithic remains of Late Pleistocene date are rare in northern Arabia. No evidence of Lower, Middle, or Upper Paleolithic industries has yet been recovered anywhere on the Arabian shelf—that is, in eastern Arabia (Oman included), where the earliest industries found date to about 5000 BCE. Sites dating to this period were first identified in Qatar, where they were assigned to the so-called Qatar B group. More recently, contemporary and, to a limited extent, typologically related sites belonging to the Wadi Wutayya facies have been found on the coast of Oman. The blade arrowheads that characterize the Qatar sites show a clear affinity to Levantine types. This suggests that the southward spread of pastoral groups from the Levant, via northern Arabia, may have occurred then, perhaps coinciding with what has been described as an early/mid-Holocene "climatic optimum" in the region. Moister conditions throughout eastern Arabia probably prevailed through the fifth millennium, when a veritable explosion in the number of late prehistoric sites belonging to the "Arabian bifacial tradition" (i.e., characterized by stone tools flaked with fine retouch on two sides) occurred. Fine pressure flaking, and the use of tanged and/or barbed arrowheads in northeastern Arabia, Qatar, the Rub al-Khali, Yemen, and the coast of the United Arab Emirates (UAE), are common features, whereas arrowheads are absent on the coast of Oman proper in the so-called Saruq facies.

In spite of the fact that the prominence of the arrowhead in their tool kit might argue otherwise, the bearers of this culture were not exclusively or even primarily hunters. Sites in eastern Arabia of this period routinely contain remains of domesticated sheep and goat, neither of which was, in its wild state, native to the region. (They may have been introduced by those Levantine/North Arabian immigrants who brought with them the blade-arrowhead technology of the Qatar B sites.) Moreover, the coastal sites always show evidence for extensive shellfish gathering as well as fishing, routinely yielding ovoid and subrectangular stone crushing platforms, often deeply pitted in the center, that were probably used, together with a particular kind of stone chisel, to open shellfish. Various forms of net sinkers are also common on these sites. Thus, sites of the Arabian bifacial tradition probably represent the remains of pastoralists who moved seasonally between the coast, where they did some shellfish gathering and fishing, and the interior, where they could graze their herds during the winter. Hunting was an option and helped to conserve their herds (perhaps used principally for milk products, hair, and fleece) by providing another source of protein. [See Pastoral Nomadism; Sheep and Goats; Fishing; Hunting.]

Some of the coastal Arabian bifacial sites in Saudi Arabia, Qatar (Qatar groups A, C, D), Bahrain, and the UAE have also yielded small amounts of imported Mesopotamian pottery of Ubaid 3–4 type. Those sherds that have been analyzed come almost certainly from Ur and al-'Ubaid in southern Iraq, presumably from vessels traded to the local inhabitants by Mesopotamians in return for local products, perhaps pearls, dried fish, and copper. It appears, however, that this contact did not lead to the birth of an indigenous ceramic tradition in eastern Arabia. Some sites in eastern Saudi Arabia on which painted Ubaid sherds have been found also contained examples of a coarse, red, chaff-tempered pottery; however, as this tends not to occur on sites without the imported ware, it would not seem to be an indigenous product. Certainly there is no indication of an evolution of local ceramic technology postdating the period of Ubaid contact with the area. [See Ur; Ubaid.]

The archaeological record of Oman, northeastern Arabia, and Yemen shows conclusively that sites of the Arabian bifacial tradition continued to exist right down to the third millennium. The latest sites of this type on the coast of Oman (Bandar Jissa facies), although aceramic, do contain small amounts of copper or bronze but would never be classified as Bronze Age sites. Thus, the users of the Arabian bifacial tradition presumably represent a segment of the local population that coexisted with those other, sedentary groups, yet did not move down a social evolutionary path leading ultimately toward a complex, "Bronze Age" way of life. To what extent the Arabian bifacial groups were part-time agriculturalists is an open question. Some sites in the desertic regions of eastern Saudi Arabia have yielded grinding stones, though these need not have been used to grind domesticated cereals. The site of Ras al-Hamra 5, on the coast of Oman near Muscat, may have the earliest evidence of domesticated sorghum—during the fourth millennium—but this was recently disputed. At Hili 8, in the interior of Abu Dhabi, domesticated cereals and dates are present by about 3100 BCE, along with domesticated sheep, goats, and cattle; however, the origins of the cereals (the date [i.e., datepalm] was indigenous) is unknown.

[See also Agriculture; Cereals; Kuwait; Oman; Qatar; United Arab Emirates; and Yemen.]

BIBLIOGRAPHY

Amirkhanov, Khizri A. *Paleolit Iuga Aravii* (The Paleolithic in South Arabia). Moscow, 1991. The most extensive account of the subject ever written, with an English summary.

Andrews, Peter, et al. "Dryopithecines from the Miocene of Saudi Arabia." *Nature* 274 (1978): 249–251.

Di Mario, Francesco. "A New Lithic Inventory from Arabian Peninsula: The North Yemen Industry in Bronze Age." *Oriens Antiquus* 26 (1987): 89–107. To be read in conjunction with the article by Uerpmann (below) for lithic facies of the Bronze Age.

Di Mario, Francesco. "The Western ar-Rub' al-Khali 'Neolithic': New Data from the Ramlat Sab'atayn (Yemen Arab Republic)." *Annali dell'Istituto Orientale di Napoli* 49 (1989): 109–148. The most recent statement on the western Rub al-Khali Neolithic.

Edens, Christopher. "The Rub al-Khali 'Neolithic' Revisited: The View from Nadqan." In *Araby the Blest: Studies in Arabian Archaeology*, edited by Daniel T. Potts, pp. 15–43. Carsten Niebuhr Institute Publication, 7. Copenhagen, 1988. Comprehensive study of the Late Prehistoric stone-tool assemblages from the Rub al-Khali; an excellent bibliography refers to earlier works on the subject.

Inizan, Marie-Louise. *Préhistoire à Qatar*. Mission Archéologique Française à Qatar, vol. 2. Paris, 1980. Final publication of the work of the French mission under Jacques Tixier on the Qatar peninsula. Supersedes all earlier publications on the prehistory of Qatar by the Danish, British, and French missions.

Inizan, Marie-Louise, and Luc Ortlieb. "Préhistoire dans la région de Shabwa au Yemen du sud (R.D.P. Yemen)." *Paléorient* 13.1 (1987): 5–22.

McClure, Harold A. "Late Quaternary Palaeogeography and Landscape Evolution of the Rub' al-Khali." In *Araby the Blest: Studies in Arabian Archaeology*, edited by Daniel T. Potts, pp. 9–13. Carsten Niebuhr Institute Publication, 7. Copenhagen, 1988. Brief survey of the environmental history of the Rub al-Khali in the period 35,000–20,000 BCE.

Potts, Daniel T. *The Arabian Gulf in Antiquity*. Vol. 1. Oxford, 1990. The entire prehistoric record of eastern Arabia, from the earliest hominoid finds through the late prehistoric period.

Tosi, Maurizio. "The Emerging Picture of Prehistoric Arabia." *Annual Review of Anthropology* 15 (1986): 461–490. Synthetic look at the peninsula in prehistory, emphasizing processes of cultural evolution.

Uerpmann, Margarethe. "Structuring the Late Stone Age of Southeastern Arabia." *Arabian Archaeology and Epigraphy* 3 (1992): 65–109. The first comprehensive presentation of the late prehistoric stone-tool assemblages on the Oman peninsula.

DANIEL T. POTTS

The Arabian Peninsula before the Time of Islam

Although a number of early European visitors wrote valuable descriptions of the visible ancient monuments on the Arabian Peninsula, it is only during the last generation that systematic archaeological research has been carried out there, and then only in limited areas. Compared with other parts of Southwest Asia, therefore, current knowledge of Arabia is meager and uneven; much of the archaeological map remains blank, and problems of chronology and interpretation abound. Many of the blanks are doubtless a true reflection of the absence of permanent settlement, both ancient and modern, in those vast barren areas of desert which occupy much of the central and eastern parts of Arabia.

Even those areas, however, usually have sufficient vegetation to support nomads and their flocks (who leave little sign of their presence in the archaeological record). The desert is, after all, scattered with oases which form staging posts on the cross-peninsular routes. Other parts of Arabia are more fertile and attractive to human settlement, and it is in them that the major developments in pre-Islamic Arabian civilization took place: the mountains and valleys of Asir, Yemen, and Hadhramaut in the southwest (the Arabia Felix of the classical authors); Dhofar in the south and Oman in the southeast; and the lagoons and islands along the coast of the Arabian (Persian) Gulf in the east. [*See* Yemen; Hadhramaut; Oman.] Some of these same regions are also rich in natural resources: copper in Oman, aromatic gums (frankincense and myrrh) in Yemen and Dhofar; and fish and pearls from the Gulf. Probably the most important factor in the historical development of the Arabian Peninsula has been the exploitation of these natural resources by more powerful neighbors—first Mesopotamia and Egypt and then Greece, Rome, and Persia—from whom the Arabian peoples received cultural stimuli, both material and spiritual. They assimilated and refashioned those influences to suit their own needs and tastes.

Sporadic contact between the inhabitants of eastern Arabia and southern Mesopotamia began at least as early as the fifth millennium. It is demonstrated by the presence at a number of small Arabian coastal sites of the distinctive painted Ubaid pottery that was manufactured in Mesopotamia and brought to Arabia by seasonal fishermen. Archaeological evidence for this contact ceases for the early part of the fourth millennium but occurs again after about 3000 BCE, in the form of another type of Mesopotamian pottery, the Jemdet Nasr style, found at certain sites in inland Oman, such as Hafit. This distribution may indicate that the Omani copper deposits were already being exploited. By this time the advanced, literate Sumerian civilization had been established in Mesopotamia. [*See* Sumerians.] It was greatly dependent for its wealth and power upon foreign trade, both for the supply of those raw materials—metals, semiprecious stones, good building stone, and timber—Mesopotamia itself lacked and for the profits to be made from the export of the foodstuffs, textiles, and manufactured items it produced in abundance. The Sumerians were thus a trading people, and throughout the third millennium the gulf and the seas beyond, toward India, were the scene of intense commercial activity. As a result, eastern Arabia, the source of some of the raw materials in demand and well provided with harbors and fresh water, prospered. This is documented in the Mesopotamian textual sources, where two places in particular are mentioned in connection with this activity: Dilmun and Magan (or Makkan). [*See* Dilmun.] The former can confidently be identified with the island of Bahrain and neighboring parts of the northern gulf, while Magan is almost certainly Oman. [*See* Bahrain.] It was there that, in the third and early second millennia BCE, what can be termed true civilization first developed on the peninsula.

Two distinct but closely related Arabian cultures emerged in this period. One, the Umm en-Nar culture, named for the island off the coast of Abu Dhabi, where it was first discovered, is spread throughout Oman and is clearly to be equated with Magan. Although many small settlements are known, most of the archaeological material comes from the distinctive Umm en-Nar tombs. The tombs are circular stone structures, often with excellent masonry, designed for multiple successive burials. [See Tombs.] It seems that Oman was then inhabited by a tall people who cultivated wheat, barley, dates, and sorghum (some form of simple run-off irrigation may have been practiced). [See Agriculture; Cereals; Irrigation.] They raised sheep, goat, and cattle, and the domesticated donkey and camel were probably also known. [See Sheep and Goats; Cattle and Oxen; Camels.] Hunting gazelle, oryx, and various birds was also important, while at coastal settlements fishing and the capture of large sea mammals such as the turtle and dugong were customary. [See Fishing.] The mining and smelting of the local copper ore appears to have been well established, and some sites (e.g., Maysar) have been interpreted as specialized industrial centers. Arsenic and tin found in some of the bronze objects were probably brought from Afghanistan or Iran.

Such mercantile contacts with the East are confirmed by some of the pottery, which is influenced by the ceramic tradition of those countries and even, occasionally, by that of the Indus River Valley civilization. Commercial contacts were probably strongest with Sumer, however, either directly or, more likely, indirectly, via Dilmun. Some pottery of the Umm en-Nar type has been found at the northern end of the gulf. The corresponding culture is that of Dilmun, probably originating in about 3000 BCE on the mainland of Arabia, but best known during the late third and the early second millennium BCE from excavations on the islands of Bahrain and Failaka (Kuwait). [See Failaka; Kuwait.]

At Qal'at al-Bahrain a sequence of five "cities" has been uncovered between 1953 and 1969 by a team of Danish archaeologists, directed by Geoffrey Bibby, of which cities I (c. 2400–2000 BCE) and II (c. 2000–1600 BCE) are relevant here; the excavations produced a wealth of material, particularly distinct types of pottery and stamp seals (Bibby, 1969; Højlund and Andersen, 1994). [See Qal'at al-Bahrain; Seals.] The finds have enabled archaeologists to establish cultural and chronological links throughout the region—from southern Mesopotamia and the Gulf of Iran, Baluchistan, and the Indus Valley—thus confirming the picture of widespread trade activity provided by contemporary Mesopotamian texts. Little architecture of this period survived at Qal'at al-Bahrain, although city II was provided with a substantial town wall. For this aspect of Dilmun civilization, the sites of Barbar, Diraz, and Sar, all on Bahrain, are more

informative. At Sar, recent excavations (Crawford, 1993) revealed a regular plan of standard houses lining a street. Their occupants (judging from the number of seals, seal impressions, and imported materials and objects) were engaged in commercial activities. However, the economy of the settlement seems, from a study of the excavated bones and plant remains, to have been mainly based on agriculture and fishing. A small temple was also excavated there and at Diraz. The major Dilmun sacred building known is at Barbar, though. It is a finely constructed of stone and incorporates a sacred well; it is itself enclosed by an oval perimeter wall recalling the temple ovals at Khatajeh and Ubaid in Mesopotamia. It has been suggested that the Barbar temple may have been dedicated to the Sumerian god Enki, whose special element was water. Nothing is known of the rituals conducted in these temples, or of the organization of religious life in Dilmun; however, the hundreds of burial mounds of this period with which Bahrain is covered, and which have produced large quantities of rich grave goods, testify to the amount of resources invested in provising the afterlife. [See Grave Goods.]

The precocious Umm en-Nar and Dilmun cultures, dependent as they were upon a thriving maritime trade, seem not to have spread very far inland from the gulf and the Oman peninsula. Nor did these regions continue to flourish to the same extent after about the middle of the second millennium BCE. Although the gap once thought to exist in the archaeological record there during the second half of that millennium and the first half of the next is gradually being filled, it is clear that gulf trade was in decline. Mesopotamian merchants increasingly favored the northern routes along the Tigris and Euphrates Rivers toward Anatolia, Syria, and the Mediterranean (where, e.g., Cyprus was then the main source of copper). Dilmun continued to be mentioned in the literary sources and was probably incorporated into the Kassite and, later, Neo-Assyrian Empires; Qal'at al-Bahrain itself maintained its urban character (cities III, IV). Elsewhere, however, cultural standards seem to have declined, perhaps also partly because of a slight deterioration in the climate. For whatever reason, on present evidence it seems that it was not until the end of the first millennium BCE that a real cultural revival took place in eastern Arabia.

Until recently very little was known of conditions on the rest of the peninsula in the third and second millennium BCE. It was generally assumed that the area was mostly uninhabited except, perhaps, by a few survivors of the Stone Age hunters who had once lived there in climatically more favorable times. This picture has now begun to change. Recent surveys, particularly in Saudi Arabia (for preliminary reports, see the journal *Atlal* 1 [1977] and following years), have located the remains of many hundreds of small settlements and burial grounds. Although it is currently impossible to date most of these, archaeological research in Yemen indicates, on the basis of radiocarbon dating, that similar sites there were occupied as early as the second or even the third millennium BCE. Little can be said as yet about the lifestyles of the inhabitants, although agriculture and stock rearing were practiced and simple copper metallurgy known. It is claimed (Maigret, 1990) that some of the pottery in use has similarities with that of contemporary Palestine. If this is so, it may point to the direction from which cultural influences, and perhaps elements of the population itself, reached southwestern Arabia.

The most important aspect of recent work in Yemen is that it has at last provided an acceptable background against which the spectacular cultural development there in the first millennium BCE may be set. The substantial architectural monuments of ancient southwestern Arabia—walled towns, temples, dams—have long been known. In addition, the many inscriptions associated with them or carved on natural rock faces indicate that this was an advanced, literate civilization. The inscriptions have enabled scholars to reconstruct, in outline, the complex political history of the region. It reflects the rivalries of the various tribal federations (each of which spoke and wrote a distinct branch of a Semitic language known as Old South Arabian) as they struggled for control of the trade routes. It was the export of frankincense and myrrh (which grew only there and in neighboring East Africa) which provided the chief source of wealth for the South Arabian states. There were four of these states, each centered on a city on the inland slopes of the high coastal mountains. These states were protected from the destructive summer monsoon and were close to the edge of the desert, where caravan travel was comparatively easy and the runoff could be utilized for agriculture. The date of the emergence of these states is the subject of intense debate (see K. A. Kitchen, *Documentation for Ancient Arabia, Part I*, Liverpool, 1994, chaps. 1–4). The earliest was certainly Saba' (Sheba), with its capital at Marib. [*See* Sheba; Marib.] The first reference to a king of Sheba, Yith''amara, occurs in an inscription of the Assyrian king Tiglath-Pileser III (r. c. 745–727 BCE). It was once generally agreed that this marked the approximate date of the beginning of a developed culture in the region. However, some scholars have accepted the account in the Hebrew Bible of the visit of Sheba's queen to King Solomon in the tenth century BCE as a reliable indication of its importance this early. Recent geoarchaeological work on the Marib dam and associated field systems has led scientists to conclude that major hydraulic engineering works were being built there at the beginning of the first millennium BCE, and that some form of irrigation had been in use a thousand or more years earlier (Jürgen Schmidt in Daum, 1988, pp. 55–62). A date no later than the end of the second millennium BCE for the appearance of an advanced civilization in South Arabia is now also supported by most epigraphists, on the grounds that the script in which the inscriptions are written could only have been derived from the Canaanite linear alphabet of the twelfth–eleventh cen-

turies BCE—and not from later Phoenician or Aramean versions. Suggestions that it was inspired by the Greek script of the sixth–fifth centuries BCE have been completely discounted (see the discussion in Maigret and Robin, 1989).

So powerful and rich was Saba' that its name became synonymous in Greco-Roman times with all of southwest Arabia. Well before that, the kingdom had yielded pride of place to states which had once been its vassals: Ma'in, centered at Qarnaw in the north (fl. fifth–fourth centuries BCE); Hadhramaut in the east, where it controlled the main frankincense-producing region of Dhofar (fourth–second centuries BCE); and Qataban in the southeast (third–second centuries BCE). In the second century BCE, however, an important shift of power took place, away from the inland valleys and oases bordering the desert and toward the coast, closer to the sea lanes. After the discovery by western sailors of the value of shipping in the Indian Ocean during the monsoon winds, the sea lanes began to play a greater part in the transport of both the locally produced aromatics and of the spices and other precious commodities from India and Southeast Asia. This trade is vividly described in the sailors' handbook known as the *Periplus of the Erythraean Sea* (see the edition by Lionel Casson, Princeton, 1989) written in the middle of the first century CE. The beneficiary of this shift of power was the kingdom of Himyar, whose capital, Zafar, is situated on the crest of the mountains at the head of routes running down to the coastal plain. [*See* Himyar; Zafar.] It was under the Himyarite kings in the fourth and fifth centuries CE that both Judaism and Christianity were established in Yemen, leading to internal religious strife as well as to conflict with the Christian state of Abyssinia across the Red Sea. It was for help against Abyssinia that the Himyarites appealed successfully to the Sasanian Persians, who were in effective control of South Arabia at the time of its conversion to Islam in the mid-seventh century. [*See* Sasanians.]

Although tomb robbing and illicit excavations have filled the museums and private collections of the world with South Arabian antiquities (especially the small alabaster statues, votive plaques, and vessels in which the region seems to have specialized), very little scientific archaeology had been undertaken. Apart from the three capital cities of Timna' (Qataban), Marib (Saba'), and Shabwa (Hadhramaut) none of the major sites has been excavated, and very few have been even properly surveyed and recorded. [*See* Timna' (Arabia); Qataban; Shabwa.] That they were normally provided with massive stone fortifications is obvious on the ground, but none have been studied. Dams, both of stone and of earth, and associated irrigation works are also common, although only those at Marib have received attention. Domestic and minor public buildings seem mostly to have been of unbaked mud brick; one excavated house at Shabwa is of reinforced timber and several stories high, foreshadowing the typical tall houses of medieval and modern Yemen.

The most monumental and best-known buildings are the temples, which, in an essentially theocratic society, were not only the homes of the gods and places for cultic ritual, but also played an important secular role in administration, tax collection, and judicial activities. In their surviving forms, the temples are the result of long periods of renovation and elaboration. It is likely that the earliest cult place was little more than an open-air enclosure with a standing stone representing the deity, perhaps under a simple canopy. The most common basic plan of the later temples, particularly in the Sabaean region, remained that of an enclosed rectangular courtyard with a more elaborate chamber at one end, although regional variations are found. Particularly striking in these temples is the abundant use of square monolithic columns in the courtyard, either as an interior peristyle or completely filling the open area. Monumental entrance buildings (or gateways, reminiscent of the Greek/Roman propylaeum, and leading to a sacred enclosure, as at Marib) with similar massive columns are also found. Ornamentation is typically ascetic and abstract. Bull-headed gargoyles and friezes of ibex heads do appear, but always expressed in a rigid geometric style. The only concessions to naturalism are the simple vine scrolls and palmettes found on architraves and wall panels. Standards of craftsmanship are on the whole excellent, however, with the ashlar limestone masonry particularly noteworthy.

The origins of this advanced civilization remain uncertain, as do the dates of the appearance of its various components. Masonry styles have been compared with those of Phoenicia and Israel in the late second–early first millennia BCE, thereby reinforcing the links suggested by the script and by the story of the Queen of Sheba. Such styles had a long history in Assyria and Persia as well, however. The influence of Achaemenid Persia (sixth–fourth centuries BCE) has been seen in the prolific use of massive columns, especially in hypostyle halls, but this was also always a feature of Egyptian religious architecture. The austere, massive nature of the architecture and its decoration is also suggestive of Egypt, although no typically Egyptian motifs occur. The vine scrolls are undoubtedly of Mediterranean inspiration but could equally well have come by way of Hellenistic Egypt, the Levant, Mesopotamia, or Persia. South Arabia was inevitably brought into contact with all of these regions through the aromatic and spice trade. It would be natural for its material culture to reflect those contacts. Nevertheless, South Arabian civilization was not cosmopolitan—in the sense that it was an undigested mixture of foreign elements. Rather, it was a distinctive blend of Arabian and non-Arabian themes, selected and assimilated by what was clearly a highly creative people, and fully worthy of the fame it achieved in both the ancient and modern worlds.

With the notable exception of Abyssinia, where contemporary developments in institutions, religion, and material culture largely paralleled those in South Arabia, this flourishing civilization seems to have had little direct influence on the rest of the peninsula. Other parts of Arabia were certainly affected by the incense trade, however. As early as the thirteenth–eleventh centuries BCE, northwest Arabia—the Hijaz—had seen the establishment of urban settlements at oases such as Qurayyah and Tayma'. [*See* Qurayyah; Tayma'.] It is possible that these sites were already involved in the trade, perhaps under Egyptian (Midian) initiative. [*See* Midian.] If so, they must have been in contact with the producing regions of the south and played a role in transmitting those Syro-Palestinian elements (script and masonry and pottery styles) discernible in South Arabian civilization. Although this remains controversial, it is certain from the Assyrian and Babylonian texts that, by the mid-first millennium BCE, the inhabitants of northern Arabia were profiting from the aromatic trade and that Tayma' and al-'Ula/Dedan had become the centers of small kingdoms. [*See* Dedan.] At Dedan, Minaean inscriptions and sculptural fragments survive from a small colony founded there by merchants from South Arabia in the fourth century BCE. Of these North Arabian kingdoms the most important was that of the Nabateans, established at Petra, in modern Jordan, probably in the third century, and with a strongly hellenized material culture. [*See* Nabateans; Petra.] Nabatean pottery has been found in Yemen, and it may well have been through the southern Nabatean center of Meda'in Saleh that some of the Greco-Roman features of the later phases of South Arabian civilization arrived. [*See* Meda'in Saleh.]

The east–west routes across the peninsula were also assuming importance at this time. A few Nabatean sherds have been found at Thaj, probably the important emporium of Gerrha mentioned by classical authors, about 100 km (62 mi.) inland from the gulf coast between Kuwait and Bahrain. [*See* Thaj.] After what appears to have been a cultural decline throughout much of the first millennium BCE, eastern Arabia and the Gulf experienced an economic revival. It was brought about largely by the establishment of a wealthy Hellenistic (Seleucid) state in Mesopotamia and Persia following the death of Alexander the Great in 323 BCE. [*See* Seleucids.] The culture of the entire region became rapidly infused with Western elements, as shown by the discovery of a Greek temple at Failaka/Kuwait and Greek inscriptions, pottery, and jewelry there and at Qal'at al-Bahrain, Thaj, and many smaller sites.

Little is known of the effects of the substitution of Parthian for Seleucid power in the region in the mid-third century BCE. It is not until the Sasanian period (224–642 CE) that the picture becomes clearer—although even then only in the southern gulf. The Sasanians created a maritime empire encompassing virtually all the Indian Ocean. While it was naturally the eastern (Persian) side of the gulf which benefited mostly from this, Oman and its chief port, Mazum (modern Sohar), played a crucial strategic role also. [*See* Sohar.] Nor was Sasanian involvement restricted to the coast; the interior of the Oman peninsula was colonized by the Persians, who, among other enterprises, began fully to exploit its copper deposits again and probably introduced new irrigation technology. Their political ambitions led them even farther west: Yathrib (modern Medina) was devastated by the Sasanian army in the fourth century CE and they were in effective control of southwest Arabia in the sixth (see above) [*See* Medina.] Most of the evidence for this comes at present from literary rather than archaeological sources. However, sites of the period are beginning to be investigated, especially in Oman and the Arab Emirates. Nevertheless, it is clear that Persia had a profound effect on the culture of eastern and southern Arabia, the legacy of which was to be an important factor in the history of the peninsula in the medieval period.

[*See also* Mesopotamia; *articles on* Ancient Mesopotamia *and* Mesopotamia from Alexander to the Rise of Islam; *and* Persia, *articles on* Ancient Persia *and* Persia from Alexander to the Rise of Islam.]

BIBLIOGRAPHY

Bibby, Geoffrey. *Looking for Dilmun.* New York, 1969. Immensely readable and evocative account by the man chiefly responsible for the Danish excavations which marked the real beginning of scientific archaeology in the Gulf and East Arabia in the 1950s and 1960s. A classic of archaeological literature.

Bowen, Richard Le Baron, and Frank P. Albright, eds. *Archaeological Discoveries in South Arabia.* Baltimore, 1958. The first volume of the report on the pioneering work at Marib in the 1950s.

Crawford, Harriet. "London-Bahrain Archaeological Expedition: Excavations at Saar, 1991." *Arabian Archaeology and Epigraphy* 4 (1993): 1–19.

Daum, Werner, ed. *Yemen: Three Thousand Years of Art and Civilization in Arabia Felix.* Innsbruck, 1988. Originally an exhibition catalog, this is now the best concise survey of South Arabian history and culture; authoritative contributions by most of the leading workers in the field and excellent illustrations.

Doe, Brian. *Southern Arabia.* London, 1971. Informative though rather poorly organized account of the archaeology of the region, concentrating on sites in the former British colony and protectorate of Aden, where the author was director of antiquities.

Doe, Brian. *Monuments of South Arabia.* New York, 1983. Similar to Doe (1971) but with a more extensive geographic coverage, including the southern Gulf and Oman.

Groom, Nigel. *Frankincense and Myrrh.* London, 1981. Excellent treatment, although the argument (p. 37) that the incense trade was of little importance in South Arabia before the middle of the first millennium BCE has lost much of its force.

Højlund, Flemming, and H. Hellmuth Andersen. *Qala'at al-Bahrain,* vol. 1, *The Northern City Wall and the Islamic Fortress.* Moesgaard, 1994. The first detailed publication of some aspects of the important Danish excavations.

Khalifa, Shaikha Haya A. al-, and Michael Rice, eds. *Bahrain through the Ages: The Archaeology.* London, 1986. Collection of conference papers, varying in quality but mostly of importance, particularly those summarizing recent fieldwork.

Larsen, Curtis E. *Life and Land Use on the Bahrain Islands: The Geoarchaeology of an Ancient Society.* Chicago, 1983. Somewhat outdated archaeological evidence but an excellent and stimulating review of the environmental factors affecting the prehistory and history of Bahrain, based largely on the author's original research.

Maigret, Alessandro de, and C. Robin. "Les Fouilles Italiennes de Yalā: Nouvelles données sur le chronologie de l'Arabie du Sud Prèislamique." *Contes Rendus de l'Academic des Inscriptions et Belles Lettres* (April–June 1989).

Maigret, Alessandro de, ed. *The Bronze Age Culture of Ḥawlān aṭ-Ṭiyāl and al-Hadā.* Instituto Italiano per il Medio ed Estremo Oriente, Centro Studi e Scavi Archeologici, Reports and Memoirs, vol. 24. Rome, 1990. Detailed account of the evidence from recent Italian excavations of third- and second-millennium BCE occupations in South Arabia.

Nayeem, Muhammad Abdul. *Prehistory and Protohistory of the Arabian Peninsula,* vol. 1, *Saudi Arabia.* Hyderabad, 1990. The only survey of its kind for Saudi Arabia; contains many facts but is somewhat uncritical.

Potts, Daniel T. *The Arabian Gulf in Antiquity.* 2 vols. Oxford, 1990. The most comprehensive survey of the subject in English, from prehistoric times to the coming of Islam, by a leading expert. Incorporates the evidence from recent fieldwork (otherwise only available in specialist journals). Full bibliography.

Rice, Michael. *Search for the Paradise Land.* New York, 1985. Popular and generally reliable introduction to the archaeology of the Gulf and Bahrain, from the earliest times to the death of Alexander. Well illustrated with a good bibliography.

Van Beek, Gus W. *Hajar Bin Ḥumeid: Investigations at a Pre-Islamic Site in South Arabia.* Publications of the American Foundation for the Study of Man, vol. 5. Baltimore, 1969. Report of the first excavation of a deeply stratified urban site in the Yemen which provided reliable archaeological evidence for the chronology of South Arabian civilization.

Vine, Peter, ed. *Bahrain National Museum.* London and Bahrain, 1993. Well-illustrated guide to the museum, with a brief but reliable text.

PETER J. PARR

The Arabian Peninsula in Islamic Times

The mission of the prophet Muhammad ibn 'Abd Allah of Quraysh was to unite a divided people through the force of a new monotheistic religion. He received divine revelations after 610 and assumed prophethood. His teachings aroused opposition by the conservative Meccans (Makkans), which led to the emigration of Muslims first to Abyssinia in 614 and then, in 622 (the beginning of the Islamic era), to Yathrib, renamed Medina (Madina al-Munawwara), capital of the first Islamic state. The state was a political community of people *(ummah)* bonded by the Constitution of Medina that had been laid down by the Prophet and held together by the religion of Islam under the Prophet's leadership. Gradually, the Prophet attempted to build a political and socioeconomic system among Muslims based on the divine revelations. The new Islamic order, or polity, forged under the principles of equality among all, the right to an adequate livelihood, courteous treatment, the security of life and property, and community stability, attracted groups of nomads. They accepted Islam and gave allegiance to the Prophet. Thus, Islam spread gradually and peacefully through far-flung Arabia, unifying the Arabs and establishing Islamic institutions. Mecca (Makkah) for instance, was conquered without a struggle because Islam propagates peace, all-embracing tolerance, and social equality. The institutions of Islam, derived from the Qur'an and the Prophet's traditions, altered both the religious and domestic life of its believers. Some of its features are prayer five times a day, fasting, the pilgrimage to Mecca, circumcision, and almsgiving. Islamic law *(shari'ah)* abolished slavery, limits a Muslim man to four wives at a time, and prohibits usury, intoxicating beverages, certain types of food, and representational art. Islam has a particular system of taxation, contractual law, and inheritance rules, and its own calendar and rules of manners and moral conduct. In places where Islam was embraced, the Prophet allowed the existing official/governor to continue to rule. Thus, when Yemen accepted Islam in 628, the Prophet allowed Budhan, the fifth Persian governor, whose capital was San'a, to continue in this capacity. [*See* San'a.]

The Four Caliphs (632–661). The Prophet died in 632, without making provisions for a successor. Abu Bakr, one of his companions, who had represented the Prophet during his illness, was choosen as successor. The institution of the caliphate, which lasted for centuries, thus emerged. During Abu Bakr's caliphate, some tribal revolts, or apostasy *(ridda)*, arose and were suppressed. Before his death in 634, Abu Bakr urged his companions to elect 'Umar ibn al-Khattab as his successor, which they readily did. To the title *caliph* was added that of *amir al-mu'minin* ("commander of the faithful").

In addition to the conquest and expansion of Islam outside Arabia, 'Umar's greatest contribution during his ten-year tenure was to organize a form of government that was followed for centuries. Before his death 'Umar appointed an elective committee *(shura)* of six from Quraysh for selecting the caliph. They elected 'Uthman. After 'Uthman's twelve-year rule, 'Ali ibn Abi Talib succeeded him as caliph in 656. A struggle for the caliphate soon ensued that 'Ali suppressed.

Islam's expansion outside Arabia made control difficult from al-Medina. Thus, to administer the conquered lands properly and meet the challenge of his adversary Mu'awiyah ibn Abi Sufyan, the governor of Syria, 'Ali, in 657, shifted the capital from Medina to al-Kufah. Factions formed among the Muslims: one rebellious group from the Kharijis ("outgoers") assassinated 'Ali at al-Kufah in AH 40/661 CE. 'Ali's son al-Hasan was immediately proclaimed caliph, but for reasons of political expediency renounced his claim in favor of Mu'awiyah.

Umayyads (692–750) **and 'Abbasids** (750–1171). Under the Umayyads, Damascus became the capital of Islam, governors were appointed at Mecca and al-Medina, and nominal rule was extended to other parts of Arabia. [*See* Damascus.] The Hijaz became a separate province; Najd, al-Yamamah, al-Bahrain, and Oman became parts of the eastern province; and Yemen and South Arabia formed another province. Subsequently, for purposes of proper administration, the Hijaz, Yemen, and central Arabia were combined into a single province and were ruled by a viceroy of the caliph. Mu'awiyah, in order to maintain tribal support in the provinces, gave them a certain degree of autonomy. The factional rivalry between the 'Alids (descendents of 'Ali and Fatimah, the Prophet's daughter) and Umayyads continued for decades. The caliphate underwent a change from the prophetic to something like sovereignty. The hereditary principle of succession to the caliphate was introduced in 679, when Mu'awiyah nominated his son as his successor. Subsequently, this Umayyad practice was followed by the 'Abbasids and other Muslim dynasties.

Islamic coins (gold dinars and silver dirhams) were minted for the first time by Caliph 'Abd al-Malik in 695. Politically, life at Mecca and al-Medina then was tranquil; intellectuals gathered there to study and propagate the traditions of the Prophet. The expansion of Islam and the many pilgrims visiting al-Medina and Mecca brought great wealth from all parts of Arabia and neighboring Muslim countries.

The 'Abbasids ruled over Arabia from Baghdad for nearly five centuries, in two separate periods, beginning with Caliph Abu al-'Abbas in 750. [*See* Baghdad.] During the first century of their rule, an era of great prosperity, they maintained authority in Arabia by appointing governors at Mecca, al-Medina, Yemen, and the central and eastern regions. However, the second period, which began with Mutawakkil (847), was one of rapid decline. The reign of Harun al-Rashid (786–809) is reckoned as the golden age of the caliphate. The archaeological remains and finds along the pilgrim road (Darb Zubaydah), from al-Kufah to Mecca, established during his period, testify to the favorable socioeconomic conditions of the people in Arabia in general and Mecca and al-Medina in particular. [*See* Darb Zubaydah.]

Saudi Arabia is replete with Early Islamic monuments and sites, especially at Mecca and al-Medina and the pilgrim attractions in their vicinity. While the main mosque is at Mecca (Masjid al-Haram), mosques are named after the companions of the Prophet: Bilal bi Rabah, Abu Bakr as-Siddiq, Hamza ibn al-Muttalib, ar-Raiya, al-Jin, and al-Ijaba. At al-Medina, there is the Mosque of the Prophet, Masjid Quba (the first mosque built after the Prophet moved to al-Medina), Masjid al-Juma, Masjid at Qiblatain, and Masjid 'Umar ibn al-Khattab, among others. The mountains associated with the prophetic revelations are Jebel Thor and Jebel Hara', or Noor, at Mecca. [*See* Mosque.]

Archaeological excavations in Arabia have brought to light Early Islamic settled sites with characteristic features. Traces of a Friday mosque have been found at Jawatha, near Hafuf, and dated to the first century of the Islamic era. Early and Middle Islamic sites are characterized by mud-brick architecture. Early Islamic sites are characterized by green-glazed and incised wares. Slightly later sites display 'Abbasid glazed, painted, and luster wares. Impressive Islamic architectural remains—pottery, soft-stone and glass vessels, bracelets, copper, and slag—have been recovered from several sites in central Arabia.

In the Ṭa'if area of the Hijaz, dams were built during Mu'awiyah's reign (AH 58/677–78 CE), as attested by Kufic inscriptions. Dams (at Sadd al-Qusaybah, Sadd al-Hasid, and Sadd az-Zaydia) dated to the Early Islamic period are also found in the Khaybar area in northwest Arabia. Besides dams, several reservoirs from the 'Abbasid period, especially along the pilgrim roads, have survived. Caliph 'Umar's mosque at Domat al-Jendal is one of the earliest stone-built mosques with a towerlike minaret. It is dated to 634–644. 'Abbasid-period towns (Khaybar al-Qadim, Rafhe-Linah) and forts (Qal'at al-Muazzam) are found in northwest Arabia.

In the vicinity of Riyadh, near Ammariyah, well-planned buildings with courtyards date to the 'Abbasid period. They are dated by their characteristic glazed ceramics and steatite and glass objects. Traces of settlements—including houses and mosques—have also been found in other parts of the peninsula—at Bahrain, Oman, and Yemen and in the United Arab Emirates.

In Bahrain, at Rasal-Qal'at, remains of an Early Islamic city have been excavated that were built over cities of earlier periods. There, during the second–fourth centuries AH, a fort (qal'at) was built whose remains are preserved. It is one of the oldest examples of Early Islamic architecture. Its square plan (each side measures 52.50 m) resembles the Umayyad residences in Syria and Palestine and the Qasr al-Kharanah in Jordan. Its features suggest that the building's function was military. Built of limestone, it has corner towers.

For the two decades following AH 317/930 CE, Bahrain had the privilege of housing the Black Stone of the Ka'bah, after it was removed from Mecca by the Qarmatians. Tradition dates the building of the Masjid al-Khamis in Bahrain to 992, the time of Umayyad caliph 'Umar ibn Abdul Aziz. However, an inscription found in the mosque dates it to the second half of the eleventh century and attributes it to Abu Sinan Muhammad al-Fadl Abdullah, the third ruler in the al-'Auni family that ruled Bahrain then.

The earliest Islamic monument in Yemen is the al-Jami' al-Kabir (the Great Mosque) at San'a, which was built on the orders of the Prophet during his lifetime. It was expanded by Ayyub ibn Yahya ath-Thaqafi, the Umayyad governor of San'a, on the orders of Caliph al-Walid Marwan. However, it was the 'Abbasid governor 'Umar ibn 'Abd al-Majid al-'Adwi who provided doors for the mosque for first time in the mid-eighth century. It has undergone several phases of renovation and rebuilding.

In the UAE, remains of many Islamic buildings survive in the al-'Ain area (Hili, Qaṭṭara, Ma'sudi). In the emirate of Sharjah Islamic-period settlements are also found at Muwaylih, between the village of Falah and the eastern limits of the town of Sharjah.

[*See also* 'Abbasid Caliphate; Bahrain; Kuwait; Mecca; Medina; Oman; Umayyad Caliphate; *and* Yemen.]

BIBLIOGRAPHY

Atlal: The Journal of Saudi Arabian Archaeology 1–13 (1977–1990).
Balādhurī, Ahmad ibn Yaḥyā al-. *Kitāb futūḥ al-buldān.* Cairo, 1901.
Ibn al-Kalbī. *Kitāb al-aṣnām.* Cairo, 1914.
Ibn Hishām, 'Abd al-Malik. *Al-sira al-nabaweya.* Cairo, 1914.
Ibn Isḥāq, Muḥammad. *Sīrat Rasūl Allāh.* Lahore, 1967.
Ibn Sa'd, Muhammad. *Al-tabaqāt al-kubrā.* 10 vols. Beirut, 1957–1968.
Rashid, Sa'ad al-. *Al-Rabadhah: A Portrait of Early Islamic Civilisation in Saudi Arabia.* London, 1986.
Rentz, George. "'Arab, Djazīrat al-.'" In *Encyclopaedia of Islam,* new ed., vol. 1, pp. 533–556. Leiden, 1960–.
Shibli Numani, Muhammad. *Sirat al-Nabi.* 2 vols. Translated by Fazlur Rahman. Karachi, 1970–1971.
Von Grunebaum, G. E. *Classical Islam: A History, 600–1258.* London, 1970.
Watt, W. Montgomery. *Muhammad at Medina.* Oxford, 1956.
Watt, W. Montgomery. *The Majesty That Was Islam: The Islamic World, 661–1100.* London, 1974.

ABDUL RAHMAN T. AL-ANSARY

ARABIC. The most widely spoken language in the Middle East and North Africa today, spoken by more than 160 million people, Arabic is the language of the Qur'an and is therefore used in the prayers of 800 million Muslims the world over. Arabic belongs to the Semitic family of languages; its closest relatives are South Arabian and Ethiopic.

Two varieties of Arabic are in use today—literary Arabic and colloquial Arabic. Literary is used for all forms of writing, such as fiction, nonfiction, and advertisements. This Arabic is remarkably uniform throughout the Arab world. The language used in a newspaper from Morocco is the same as that used in a newspaper from Iraq. Literary Arabic is also used for formal speech, such as news broadcasts, lectures, interviews, academic instruction, and sermons.

The Arabic used in everyday communication is colloquial Arabic and consists of hundreds of dialects. The closer two communities are geographically, the closer their Arabic; the farther apart, the more divergent their Arabic. Thus a Palestinian and a Jordanian can understand each other readily, but an Iraqi and a Libyan will encounter problems. When educated Arabs who speak fairly different varieties of colloquial Arabic get together, they shift their Arabic toward the literary mode.

The differences between literary Arabic and colloquial Arabic range from minimal to striking. The most visible difference is that literary Arabic utilizes a series of case markers on nouns and mood markers on verbs that have disappeared in colloquial Arabic.

Such a situation, in which two divergent forms of a language exist, each with its own social function, is known as *diglossia*. Thus, literary Arabic has its role—writing and formal speech—and colloquial Arabic has its role—everyday conversation. The two roles are not mixed. Using the literary language in a taxicab would provoke amusement, and delivering a news broadcast in the colloquial form would get the announcer fired. The two forms of the language are also learned differently. Colloquial Arabic is a native, first language, learned by children from parents and friends. It is never studied at school. Literary Arabic is learned at school; there are no native speakers of this form.

Although literary Arabic and colloquial Arabic are frequently said to be polar opposites, the situation is actually more complex. Various forms of in-between Arabic exist. The literary and colloquial languages form two end points of a continuum; for this reason, the term *multiglossia* is sometimes used. A radio broadcast, for example, may include every case and mood vowel, whereas a lecture may be basically in the literary form but without most case vowels, thus verging toward the colloquial variety.

The term "classical Arabic" is here used for the Arabic written prior to Napoleon's invasion of Egypt (1798); the term "literary" Arabic is used for later written Arabic, and particularly for the modern period. Many scholars use "classical" to include what is here called literary. The use of the one term ("classical") stresses the continuity of the language, emphasizing that the grammar of the Qur'an is essentially the same as that of a modern newspaper. However, neither the stylistic differences over thirteen centuries nor the changes of vocabulary (including much borrowing from Western languages) can be denied. The use of only one term glosses over these differences.

History. Arabic is first attested in the form of proper names. At the battle of Qarqar (Carchemish) in 853 BCE, a few Arab chieftains allied themselves with some Syrian and Palestinian kingdoms (including Ahab of Israel) against the Assyrians, who were expanding south. The names of these chieftains, preserved in cuneiform script, are recognizably Arabic, for example, Gindibu. A number of such names occur in Neo-Assyrian and later annals.

The first written Arabic consists of thousands of graffiti written in a form of Arabic called Preclassical Northern Arabic, which is first attested in the seventh century BCE. The last inscriptions date to perhaps 500 CE or even later. The number of such inscriptions, in what must have been a largely illiterate society, is surprising. They consist mainly of personal and place names, but also include curses, reminiscences of the past, and memorials of the dead. Pre-classical Northern Arabic is not one language but comprises four or five closely related languages or dialects. It was not spoken throughout the entire Arabian Peninsula, but its exact geographical distribution is uncertain.

At the time of Muhammad's birth (570 CE), there was no unifying political structure in the Arabian Peninsula; rather, hundreds of tribes, varying greatly in size, lived throughout the area. Some tribes spoke forms of Preclassical Northern Arabic, but most tribes spoke other varieties of Arabic. Some of the linguistic features of these latter tribes are known because they have been recorded by medieval Arab and Persian grammarians.

Alongside these spoken varieties of Arabic, there existed a literary variety, the poetic koine. This was a supradialectal variety, which drew features (especially vocabulary) from all the various spoken dialects. It was used primarily for poetry, not for everyday speech. The origins of this koine are unknown, but it presumably originated with one of the spoken dialects, perhaps based on the dialect of a commercial or cultic center.

This interpretation means that at the time of Muhammad's birth, a type of diglossia already existed in the peninsula. However, it is very difficult to determine how the dialects of the time differed from the poetic koine. The basic question is: what was the status of the case endings at the time of, say, the birth of Muhammad? One view is that the case endings were still in use in both the poetic koine and the contemporaneous dialects but only disappeared later from the dialects through contact with languages lacking these grammatical distinctions (such as Persian). The opposing view holds that the case vowels had already disappeared from the spoken dialects and that they may indeed have disappeared centuries before the birth of Muhammad. They were, however, preserved in the literary language, primarily because of metrical considerations.

No literature from the pre-Islamic period is directly preserved. Society in the peninsula was largely nomadic. In such an environment, oral poetry developed as the art form par excellence. The custom of memorization played a key role in preserving this poetry. Composed in the two or more centuries preceding the birth of Muhammad, it was written down on a systematic basis in the middle of the eighth century; a vast array has been preserved. Because the poetic *koine* was the language regularly used for literary expression, the Qur'an was delivered in this language.

The poetic *koine* and the related contemporaneous spoken dialects are categorized as Northern Arabic. The relationship of Northern Arabic to Preclassical Northern Arabic is uncertain. Both coexisted as spoken languages for some time, but their geographical distribution is not known. Most likely, both Northern Arabic and Preclassical Northern Arabic go back to a common ancestor. Curiously, the medieval grammarians do not mention Preclassical Northern Arabic forms, and it appears to have died out soon after the Arab conquests.

The first text in Northern Arabic is a funeral inscription from Nemara in Syria dating to 328 CE. Only a handful of inscriptions in Northern Arabic from before 600 CE are preserved. Although written in prose, not poetry, they are in the same poetic koine used for pre-Islamic poetry and the Qur'an or in some spoken dialect close to it.

Northern Arabic had been largely restricted to the peninsula and the regions bordering upon Syria. The Arab conquests, however, carried Arabic throughout all of North Africa and most of the Middle East. The most widely spoken language in the Middle East (outside the peninsula) on the eve of the Arab conquests was Aramaic, which today is spoken in only a few places. Similarly, in Egypt Coptic became displaced as a spoken language. In some areas, such as Iran, the Arabic language did not take root, but the Arabic script (the script used for the Qur'an) did. Thus, Persian is today written in Arabic script. Several other non-Semitic languages have been written in Arabic script, such as Ottoman Turkish.

After the Arab conquests, the medieval Arab and Persian grammarians studied the language of the Qur'an and the language of pre-Islamic poetry. Using primarily these two sources, the grammarians defined the grammatical rules of Arabic. Classical Arabic is the language as specified by these grammarians. Because of the sanctity accorded the language of the Qur'an, the grammatical structure of classical Arabic became relatively fixed.

The Qur'an was the first large-scale prose composition in Arabic. The expansion of Islam brought the Arabs into contact with other cultures, and the resultant cross-fertilization of ideas along with the adoption by non-Arab Muslims of Arabic as a written language led to an explosion in scholarship and literary activity. There is a vast body of literature written in classical Arabic during the medieval and premodern periods. Much of this has not been edited or published. Every major Middle Eastern city has large collections of manuscripts, often only incompletely cataloged. A systematic but by no means complete catalog of published and manuscript works for the early medieval period (up to about 1050 CE) by Fuat Sezgin includes separate volumes for the following genres: (1) Qur'an, religious sciences, history; (2) poetry; (3) medicine, pharmacology, zoology, veterinary science; (4) alchemy, chemistry, botany, agriculture; (5) mathematics; (6) astronomy; (7) astrology, meteorology; (8) lexicography; and (9) grammar. Each volume comprises thousands of entries.

Contact with the West during the early modern period led to the importing of new literary genres, including the short story, novel, and drama. All three are actively practiced today. In 1988 the Egyptian novelist and short-story writer Naguib Mahfouz won the Nobel Prize in literature. A small amount of fiction is now written in colloquial Arabic, particularly in Egypt.

Origin of Colloquial Arabic. Since classical Arabic was purely a literary language (even if rooted in a spoken dialect), the modern dialects cannot be regarded as its lineal descendants. Rather, they are descendants of the Northern Arabic dialects spoken in the peninsula at the time of the conquests. Exactly how they came into existence is still unresolved. A process of leveling of dialects probably took place after the conquests as Arab soldiers from different tribes came together in the Arab military camps. There was also widespread contact with non-Semitic languages.

Because colloquial Arabic was not regarded with the same sanctity as the classical form, it was never subject to the normative forces of the grammarians and consequently has continued to evolve. The colloquial language of today is very different from that of a thousand years ago.

Script. The script used to write Arabic derives from that of the Nabateans, an Arabic-speaking people centered around Petra. Although ethnic Arabs, the Nabateans wrote in Aramaic because this was the prestige language of the time. Their form of the Aramaic script was adopted by the Arabs. The previously mentioned inscription from Nemara is Arabic in grammar but the script still looks Nabatean. As time passed, the external form of the script changed rapidly. Since Arabic had more phonemes than Nabatean, and since several letters had begun to fall together in shape, the Arabs had to develop new symbols. This was done by marking some letters with dots. [*See* Nabateans; Aramaic Language and Literature.]

Classical Arabic uses a series of super- and sublinear marks to indicate vowels; these strokes are not part of the consonantal text. They were developed to preserve the correct and full pronunciation of the Qur'an. They are not in everyday use but appear only in the Qur'an and occasionally in religious literature or poetry.

Since the dots distinguishing certain consonants can easily be misplaced or left out, and since the vowel marks are usually omitted, the Arabic script contains a certain measure of inherent ambiguity. Arab scholars have occasionally suggested modifications to the script, including the possibility of replacing it by the Latin script. Given the sanctity of the writing system, however, it is hard to imagine this happening.

The script used to write Preclassical Northern Arabic is quite different from that used for the classical form; it may have branched off from the paleoalphabet by the thirteenth century BCE. The same script was also employed for Epigraphic South Arabic and Ethiopic.

Future of Arabic. With its long and complex history, Arabic offers several interesting future scenarios. Many Arabs believe that with the spread of education, the literary form will take over the functions of the colloquial, which will thus disappear. Most Western linguists doubt this development will occur. They do believe, on the other hand, that many of the village-level dialects will disappear and that dialects based on the capital cities will spread. Thus the colloquial dialect of Cairo will displace other Egyptian varieties. The state of diglossia, however, with all its attendant problems, may persist for a very long time.

[*See also* Semitic Languages; South Arabian.]

BIBLIOGRAPHY

Abboud, Peter, et al. *Elementary Modern Standard Arabic.* 2 vols. 2d ed. Cambridge, 1983. The most widely used teaching grammar of Arabic.

The Cambridge History of Arabic Literature. Cambridge, 1983–. The most recent large-scale treatment of Arabic literature; the quality of individual contributions varies. Four volumes have appeared to date: *Arabic Literature to the End of the Umayyad Period,* edited by A. F. L. Beeston et al. (1983); *Abbasid Belles-Lettres,* edited by Julia Ashtiany (1990); *Religion, Learning, and Science in the Abbasid Period,* edited by M. J. L. Young et al. (1990); and *Modern Arabic Literature,* edited by Muhammad Mustafa Badawi (1992).

Ferguson, Charles A. "Diglossia." *Word* 15 (1959): 325–340. The first work to systematically define and characterize diglossia in Arabic and other languages.

Fischer, Wolfdietrich, and Otto Jastrow. *Handbuch der arabischen Dialekte.* Porta Linguarum Orientalium, n.s. 16. Wiesbaden, 1980. Survey of Arabic dialectology, with texts transcribed from several different dialects.

Fischer, Wolfdietrich. *Grundriss der arabischen Philologie,* vol. 1, *Sprachwissenschaft.* Wiesbaden, 1982. Studies of the different varieties of Arabic in their Semitic context.

Hopkins, Simon. *Studies in the Grammar of Early Arabic Based upon Papyri Datable to before A.H. 300/A.D. 912.* London Oriental Series, 37. Oxford, 1984. Detailed analysis of the earliest dated texts; for specialists.

Kaye, Alan S. "Arabic." In *The World's Major Languages,* edited by Bernard Comrie, pp. 664–685. Oxford, 1987. Short description of the major linguistic characteristics of Arabic, with a bibliography including grammars on the major dialects.

Negev, Avraham. "Obodas the God." *Israel Exploration Journal* 36 (1986): 56–60. Publication of a Nabatean inscription which apparently contains two lines in Northern Arabic, dating to before 150 CE, thus predating the Nemara inscription by centuries.

Sezgin, Fuat. *Geschichte des arabischen Schrifttums.* 9 vols. Leiden, 1967–1984. Catalogue of published and unpublished texts of many different genres.

Stetkevych, Jaroslav. *The Modern Arabic Literary Language: Lexical and Stylistic Developments.* Chicago, 1970. Discusses the changes taking place in Literary Arabic.

Versteegh, Kees. *Pidginization and Creolization: The Case of Arabic.* Amsterdam, 1984. Argues that the modern dialects result from a pidginization process, as the inhabitants of lands conquered by the Arabs attempted to learn Arabic.

Wansbrough, John. *Quranic Studies: Sources and Methods of Scriptural Interpretation.* London Oriental Series, 31. Oxford, 1977. Controversial view of the development of Classical Arabic and of the text of the Qur'an, which considers both to have crystallized only some two centuries after the birth of Muhammad.

Zwettler, Michael. *The Oral Tradition of Classical Arabic Poetry: Its Character and Implications.* Columbus, Ohio, 1978. Studies the oral nature of Classical poetry, and the characteristics it shares with other such poetries of the world. Prompted much heated discussion.

JOHN L. HAYES

ARAD. [*This entry comprises two articles treating the remains of the Bronze Age and Iron Age, respectively.*]

Bronze Age Period

Tel Arad lies 576 m above sea level, in Israel's northeastern Negev desert (map reference 162 × 075). The 10-ha (25 acre) tell is bowl shaped, facilitating the drainage of runoff into its center, where a reservoir was located in the Early Bronze Age II. At present, annual rainfall averages 170 mm at Tel Arad, classifying the climate as semiarid. However, there is much evidence to suggest a more humid climate for the Chalcolithic and Early Bronze Ages, up to the mid-third millennium.

The city was found to have five principal strata, with varying local sequences and sublevels. Because the main objective of the excavations at Arad was to obtain a comprehensive picture of the site in its uppermost urban phase (stratum II), the picture gained of the earlier strata (V–III) is more fragmentary.

Stratum V. The stratum V settlement (c. 4000–3400 BCE) resembled contemporaneous ones in the Beersheba valley: non-nucleated remains dispersed over the tell and its neighboring hills. Though assigned to the Beersheba culture, no cavelike, subterranean occupation was found—only pit dwellings—possibly because the loess layer at Arad is very shallow. The pits may be the lower sections of structures whose upper walls were made of perishable materials. Stratum V produced evidence of two phases. It now seems clear that a gap in occupation occured between strata V and IV because the material found in stratum IV belongs to EB IB, and EB IA finds are absent.

Stratum IV. An unfortified "village," whose remains were found wherever stratum III remains were removed, represents stratum IV (3200–3000 BCE). Its full extent is unknown. Finds under the subsequent stratum III city-wall foundations were of particular significance for chronological and urban development. Dated to EB IB, the settlement's traces were found both in rock caves and in building remains. No remains of larger, public buildings were discerned. This small community was one of several similar ones that coexisted in the Arad basin in EB IB. It is not clear whether Arad already served as a central place at this time.

The Egyptian pottery from stratum IV indicates that trade between Egypt and Canaan, well-known from the southern coastal plain, also involved Arad. The most important find of this kind was an Egyptian jar fragment bearing the *serekh* (the pharaoh's name in a rectangular frame) of Narmer, the last king of dynasty 0, at the end of the Egyptian predynastic period (Amiran, 1974, 1976). This inscription provided a synchronism of Canaanite and Egyptian chronologies: the EB I, coeval on the whole with the Naqada II and III periods,

ARAD: Bronze Age. *Excavations in progress.* (Courtesy O. Ilan)

included the reigns of the last pharaohs of dynasty 0 (Narmer and Hor-Aha). EB II began in the reign of Pharaoh Djer of the first dynasty. Trade with Egypt continued throughout the city's history (see below).

The only burial cave found at Arad so far belongs to stratum IV. Located northwest of (i.e., outside) the later stratum III city wall, the cave contained sixteen skeletons of men, women, and children; pottery, stone, and copper vessels; and beads of various materials. [*See* Burial Sites; Grave Goods.] One skull was trephinated (a small section of the skull was removed while the person was alive)—one of the earliest of such surgeries known (Smith, 1990).

Stratum III. There appears to be no hiatus between strata IV and III. The city wall, sacred precinct, palace, and other structures throughout the tell were erected in stratum III, the earliest "urban" stratum at Tel Arad. The reservoir was also installed, surrounded by a complex of public buildings. Thick conflagration layers found throughout the site, and the breaching and subsequent reconstruction of the city wall, attest to stratum III's destruction by enemy attack in about 2800 BCE.

Stratum II. The destruction of stratum III was probably followed immediately by the stratum II settlement. Its architectural style, building techniques, material culture, and social structure all show continuity. Below is a more detailed description of the finds from strata II and III.

Fortifications. The city wall, 1,176 m long, contained gates, posterns, and towers. It ran along the watershed and was founded partly on bedrock and partly on stone bedding. The wall was 2–2.5 m thick, constructed of twin stone courses filled with rubble, and estimated to have been 4–5 m high. The original stratum III towers were semicircular. Two of these were replaced in stratum II with rectangular ones. Their total number has been estimated at between thirty-five and forty, but the distances between them are not uniform. The two gates discovered were somewhat dissimilar, the western one having a wider opening and an adjoining semicircular tower on its north side, while the southwestern gate had a square tower flanking it. Posterns (narrow openings in the city wall) were also uncovered; they seem to have been additional openings that could be easily plugged when necessary.

Domestic architecture. Now termed the Arad House in the archaeological literature, the typical building at Arad, for both public and private purposes, was a broadroom—a rectangular structure with an entrance in the long wall. Its features recur with great regularity: benches along the walls, a stone pillar base in the center to support the roof, one to three steps down from the street outside, and a stone doorpost socket to the left of the entrance to the house. The location of the pillar bases, together with a pottery model of an Arad House discovered in excavation, indicate a flat roof. This basic structure was usually one part of a walled compound that typically included a courtyard and a smaller subsidiary room or two that may have served as storage facilities. The courtyards contained square or round platforms used as silo bases or work surfaces. Residential compounds usually contained great quantities of restorable pottery vessels; implements of flint, bone, copper, and stone; and charred grain, flax and legume seeds, olive pits, and animal bones, all of which allowed for a detailed reconstruction of daily life. Clear residential quarters were identified in areas T-east, T-north, H, and K.

Public and elite areas. The tract between the western gate and the reservoir was designated for public and elite activities. Four distinct zones were discerned: the "market" area, the palace, the sacred precinct, and the reservoir district. This discussion proceeds from the western gate to the reservoir on the east.

Market area. Located just inside the western gate, the market area was a large open space with two large, atypical buildings with flimsy walls. Fragments of mostly large pithoi (storage vessels) were recovered from the two buildings.

Palace. A large enclosed complex of interconnected rooms, courts, and passages, the palace had a large entrance on the north that provided access from the main street. Smaller entrances existed to the south and east. A large room appended by an antechamber and two courtyards formed the core of the palace. Numerous other rooms, cells, and courts contained considerable evidence for the storage, preparation, and cooking of food in large quantities. Other unusual features included large stone basins, monolithic "tables," and a cultic stela (see below). These elements and the location of the complex between the western gate and the reservoir, next to the sacred precinct, gave rise to the conjecture that this was the town's administrative center. [*See* Palace.]

Sacred precinct. Just below and across the street from the palace and separated from the reservoir complex by an open square was another self-contained complex. Three of its components were discerned in stratum II: a large twin temple, a small twin temple, and another large, single-roomed cultic structure. Several buildings and courtyards were only partially excavated north of the sacred precinct; their connection to the precinct remains unclear. The large twin temples each opened onto courtyards that themselves opened

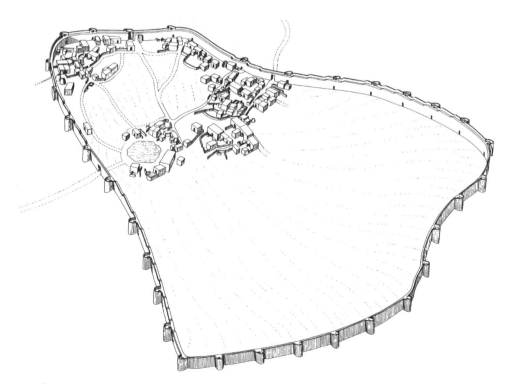

ARAD: Bronze Age. *Reconstruction of the early Canaanite city.* (Drawing by L. Ritmeyer; courtesy O. Ilan)

ARAD: Bronze Age. *Reconstruction of domestic area K.* (Drawing by L. Ritmeyer; courtesy O. Ilan)

onto a type of piazza. One of the courtyards contained a large altar with an adjacent basin. The southern chamber contained a stone *maṣṣēbâ*, or stela. Large quantities of pottery and carbonized seeds were recovered there. The smaller twin temples were much like the large ones in plan. The courtyard of the northern hall contained another stone altar and a group of complete vessels, and chunks of bitumen found beneath the floor of the southern hall may have been a ritual offering. These twin temple units have much in common with the EB I twin temples at Megiddo, while the broadroom type itself is found at the Chalcolithic temple at 'Ein-Gedi and the EB acropolis Temple at Ai. [*See* Megiddo; 'Ein-Gedi; Ai.]

Reservoir quarter. Located in a depression in the town's center, the reservoir quarter was comprised of a ring of structures surrounding the reservoir on three sides. The reservoir was an open pool of approximately 1,000 sq m, into which runoff drained from all parts of the town by way of its radial streets. A dam must have existed on the east side, where no architectural remains were preserved. The surrounding buildings differ from those in the residential quarters; they can be divided into five blocks whose sequence of construction can be traced. Worthy of note are the Water Citadel, with its massive walls and unique plan of five parallel chambers, and the Water Commissioner's House,

which includes the only true stone paving at EB Arad. [*See* Reservoirs.]

Religious beliefs. There are some clues to the religious beliefs held by the denizens of Arad, but they remain somewhat of a mystery. The stela in the main room of the palace was inscribed with two anthropomorphic figures with grain-like heads, one in a prone and the other in an upright position. The iconography is thought to represent the cyclical nature of the agricultural seasons and of life and death (cf. the Dumuzi/Inanna tales of Sumerian literature). [*See* Agriculture; Sumerians.] Cultic practice may also be inherent in the numerous stone and clay animal figurines found in various rooms. In general, it appears that the forces of nature were a dominant motif in the cult of Arad. [*See* Cult.]

Economy and urbanism. Considering its arid location, the economy of EB Arad was highly diversified. Sickle blades and a plethora of carbonized grain (barley and wheat), peas, lentils, chickpeas, flax seeds, and olive pits from all parts of the settlement testify to a thriving agricultural base. Sheep and goat bones were ubiquitous and represent the production of dairy products, meat, skins, and wool. Cattle bones indicate the use of the plow, and ass bones are indicative of the major form of transportation. [*See* Cereals; Olives; Sheep and Goats; Cattle and Oxen; Transportation.]

Food processing seems to have been the most common pursuit: grinding stones and mortars were found in almost every house. Evidence of other domestic activities exists as well: spindle whorls, shuttles, and needles for spinning, weaving, and sewing. Flint tools—sickle blades, tabular scrapers, drills, and awls—were still widely used in this period. Special flint objects, such as tabular scrapers and Canaanean blades, were imported to Arad as finished products, probably from the central Negev. Jewelry manufacture is indicated by beads and shells in various stages of modification, found with copper and flint awls and drills. The shells were from both the Mediterranean and the Red Seas. Two jewelry hoards were discovered—in a jug and jar, respectively—in a quarter that produced evidence for the existence of specialized artisans. [See Jewelry.] A number of cylinder and stamp seals were uncovered, all made of local chalk. Their style and technique are reminiscent of examples from North Syria and Mesopotamia.

Long-distance exchange relations were maintained with Sinai, Egypt, and the northern Canaanite heartland. The study of pottery fabrics (petrography) has revealed pottery exchanges between Arad and Canaanite centers to the north. Petrography has also documented ties with southern Sinai by disclosing that many of the cooking pots at Arad were made with minerals found exclusively in the former region. The material culture of contemporary sites in Sinai is also remarkably similar to that of Arad. The Sinai copper deposits seem to have been the underpinning for this interconnection and it is suggested that desert peoples used Arad as a trade emporium (Ilan and Sebbane, 1989; Finkelstein, 1990), bringing copper to exchange for northern products such as olive oil and grain. Arad seems to have been the main supplier of copper to the north throughout EB I and EB II.

Some kind of connection with Egypt is also attested to by the Egyptian pottery found at Arad. It is not known what Egyptian produce was sent to Arad in these vessels, but the Egyptians may well have imported copper, salt, and bitumen (the latter two from the nearby Dead Sea) from Arad. (In general, the Egyptians would have been primarily interested in olive oil and wine from Canaan.)

Archaeological survey has revealed that Arad was encompassed by small rural settlements it is assumed were economically and politically associated, and perhaps dominated, by the town (Amiran et al., 1980). Arad was, in fact, the only urban entity in the Negev during EB II and probably functioned as the focal point for much of the region's commercial and political activity.

The destruction of the stratum II city may be attributable to any combination of causes: a gradual decline in annual precipitation toward the middle of the third millennium, Egyptian encroachment in southern Sinai in the early years of the third dynasty (undermining Arad's primacy as a major trading center), or a version of the general political unrest and collapse such as afflicted the rest of Canaan somewhat later.

Stratum I. The stratum I settlement was much smaller and more sparse than the earlier ones, made up, perhaps, of squatters who occupied the ruined city after its destruction.

Following its abandonment in about 2650 BCE, Arad remained uninhabited until the Iron Age. Even then, most of the lower town remained unsettled and relatively undisturbed. This resulted in well-preserved remains near the surface, which have allowed for a wide exposure and a detailed reconstruction of the ancient town's economy and social life. The excavations at Arad are of paramount importance for understanding processes of urbanization, the nature of the relationship between the desert and the sown, patterns of exchange, and the nuances of everyday life in the Early Bronze Age.

[See also Building Materials and Techniques, article on Building Materials and Techniques of the Bronze and Iron Ages; Cities, article on Cities of the Bronze and Iron Ages; and Temples, article on Syro-Palestinian Temples.]

BIBLIOGRAPHY

Amiran, Ruth. "An Egyptian Jar Fragment with the Name of Narmer from Arad." *Israel Exploration Journal* 24 (1974): 4–12. Explains the nature of the synchronism between Egyptian and Canaanite chronologies.

Amiran, Ruth. "The Narmer Jar Fragment from Arad: An Addendum." *Israel Exploration Journal* 26 (1976): 45–46. Important supplemental information to the previous paper.

Amiran, Ruth, et al. *Early Arad I: The Chalcolithic Settlement and Early Bronze Age City, First–Fifth Seasons of Excavations, 1962–1966.* Jerusalem, 1978. The first final scholarly report. Several conclusions have been modified in the subsequent final reports (see below).

Amiran, Ruth, et al. "The Arad Countryside." *Levant* 12 (1980): 22–29.

Amiran, Ruth, and Ornit Ilan. *Arad: Eine 5000 Jahre alte Stadt in der Wuste Negev, Israel.* Neumunster, 1992. The only comprehensive popular account of the finds from ancient Arad, includings many photographs in color.

Amiran, Ruth, and Ornit Ilan. *Early Arad II: The Chalcolithic and Early Bronze IB Settlements and the Early Bronze II City—Architecture and Town Planning, Sixth to Eighteenth Seasons of Excavations, 1971–1978, 1980–1984.* Jerusalem, 1996. The second detailed scholarly account of the Arad excavations, focusing on building techniques, with plans, reconstructions, and analysis.

Amiran, Ruth, Ornit Ilan, and Michael Sebbane. *Early Arad III: Finds of the Sixth–Eighteenth Seasons, 1971–1978, 1980–1984.* Jerusalem, forthcoming. The third and final scholarly account, covering the small finds (pottery, crafts, agricultural implements, trade techniques), their uses, and their social implications.

Finkelstein, Israel. "Arad: Urbanism of the Nomads." *Zeitschrift des Deutschen Palästina Vereins* 106 (1990): 34–50. Interesting interpretation of EB Arad as the northernmost manifestation of desert peoples, rather than as the southernmost outpost of the northern Canaanite culture.

Ilan, Ornit, and Michael Sebbane. "Metallurgy, Trade, and the Urbanization of Southern Canaan in the Chalcolithic and Early Bronze Age." In *L'urbanisation de la Palestine à l'âge du Bronze ancien: Bilan et perspectives des recherches actuelles; Actes du Colloque d'Emmaüs, 20–24 octobre 1986*, vol. 1, edited by Pierre de Miroschedji, pp. 139–162. British Archaeological Reports, International Series, no. 527. Oxford, 1989. Data-based inquiry into the crucial role of copper mining and trade between Arad and the Arava valley and Sinai. Includes a broad citation of relevant literature.

Smith, Patricia M. "The Trephined Skull from the Early Bronze Age Period at Arad." *Eretz-Israel* 21 (1990): 89–93.

ORNIT ILAN and RUTH AMIRAN

Iron Age Period

The Iron Age settlement at Arad was erected on the northeastern hill of the Early Bronze Age II city, following a gap of one and a half millennia. The excavation of the site's fortress and tell was conducted during five seasons (1962–1965, 1967) under the directorship of Yohanan Aharoni (in 1962, with Ruth Amiran). After 1977, limited excavations were carried out under the supervision of Ze'ev Herzog, in conjunction with the National Parks Authority, which is conducting restoration work at the site. Some of this summary includes reassessments of the work at Iron Age Arad—stratigraphic and chronological conclusions that differ from earlier views. The fortress and tell at Arad provide a unique archaeological sequence for the period of the Judean monarchy. The discoveries of the Judean temple and numerous Hebrew ostraca also contribute to the site's importance.

The site's Arabic name (Tell Arad) affirms its identification. It is also located at the distance from Hebron and Moleatha cited by Eusebius (*Onomasticon* 14. 1–3). Finally, the name *Arad* is inscribed four times (in mirror image) on a pottery sherd found at the site.

Arad is mentioned in the Bible: the Canaanite king of Arad foils the Israelite attempt to enter the country from the south (*Nm.* 21:1, 33:40); it is on the list of conquered Canaanite cities (*Jos.* 12:14); the Kenites settled in the wilderness of Judah at "Negev Arad" (*Jgs.* 1:16); it is listed (misspelled as Eder) among the cities of Judah (*Jos.* 15:21); and the name *Arad* is mentioned twice on Shishak's (Sheshonq) list of 925 BCE (nos. 107–112): *Hgrm 'Arad rbt 'Arad n-bt Yrhm.* The prevailing interpretation of the text is "the citadels of greater Arad and Arad of the house of Yeruham" (Aharoni, 1993). Another view recognizes three names in this text: *Hagraim, Greater Arad,* and *Arad* (of the family) *nbt* (Na'aman, 1985). "Greater Arad" is unanimously identified by scholars as Tel Arad.

Iron Age I Village: Stratum XII. The first settlement (stratum XII) was built over the deserted ruins of the EB II city. In fact, the new occupants reused some of the old houses. Most of the stratum XII remains were uncovered to the west of the citadel, buried under a later glacis. Pillared walls and storage bins were attached to two of the EB II broad rooms. A fence bordered the houses on the west, where a steep rock cliff is exposed. The preserved section, as well as sporadic finds uncovered under the later remains, allow the reconstruction of the small village in the form of an enclosed settlement. In some spots, several stratum XII living surfaces were noted. The objects recovered date to the eleventh century BCE. There was no sign of a violent destruction, and the same community may have erected the fortress of the succeeding occupational stage, in the tenth century BCE.

The initial publications of the finds from stratum XII presented a reconstruction of a cultic temenos in the center of the site, with an altar and a round high place (Herzog et al., 1984; Aharoni, 1993). These interpretations followed the view, first suggested by Benjamin Mazar, that the religious tradition at the site stemmed from the settlement of the Kenites, who had family ties (Hobab the Kenite) with Moses as mentioned in *Judges* 1:16 (Mazar, 1965). A more critical opinion suggests that these elements were ordinary domestic installations: a wall and a circular silo (Herzog, 1994). [*See* Granaries and Silos.]

First Fortress: Stratum XI. The fortress (55 × 50 m) was carefully planned: it was surrounded by a casemate wall and reinforced by projecting towers. The remains of four towers were detected on the western side. Except on the east, the casemate wall was rebuilt in the succeeding stage as a solid wall. The only exposed casemate room was at the northwest corner. The outer wall is 1.60 m wide and the inner wall 1.40 m wide. On the east, the casemate rooms were significantly wider, perhaps serving as barracks for the fort's guards. The citadels' gate was at the northern end of the eastern side (blocked by a later solid wall). The approach into the gate chamber was protected by two towers.

The assumed presence of a temple in stratum XI was not validated by the evidence. A probe under the sacrificial altar disproved the assumption that the step at its southern side belonged to an older altar. Remains of a substantial structure were observed in the northern part of the fortress, but they do not indicate a cultic use. It seems safer to attribute the construction of the temple only to stratum X.

Several domestic structures were uncovered on the southern side of the fortress. Some stone-lined granaries found to the west of the fort indicate that the glacis had been laid in stratum X, whose structures were destroyed in a conflagration. Numerous pottery vessels found in the destruction layer clearly date to the tenth century BCE, affirming the identification of the fortress with the one on Shishak's list (cf. Zimhoni, 1985).

Solid-Wall Fortress: Strata X–VI. The fortress rebuilt in stratum X was protected by a solid wall with only two gate towers. The builders filled in the space in the casemates on three sides, but on the east the new wall was constructed over the inner casemate wall. The wall was staggered at small angles in a sawtooth pattern. The fort was then square, with an area of 52 m (or 100 cubits). A new gate with two long halls inside the wall and two projecting towers was built in the center of the eastern wing. The fortifications were reinforced by a wide glacis laid around the fortress and retained by a low wall at its base.

An additional defensive feature was the construction of a water system. It consisted of underground cisterns hewn deep into the bedrock and plastered. [*See* Cisterns.] Water was directed into the system through a channel cut into the rock on the western side of the hill. The channel was covered with stones and concealed by the glacis. The cisterns were intended for use during a siege, when water could not be drawn from the well outside the fortress in the lower city and carried by jars or waterskins to the channel opening. A passage in the solid wall, above the cover stones, may have served as a secret postern.

The casemate fortifications first attributed to this horizon were constructed of ashlars worked with a toothed chisel. Their attribution to strata VII or VI was strongly criticized by various scholars (Nylander, 1967; Yadin, 1965). A re-examination of the stratigraphic data leads to the conclusion that the casemates were, rather, part of a Hellenistic fortress that was never completed. The solid wall was thus utilized throughout the Iron Age II, in strata X–VI. Each stratum is represented by definite architectural alterations, such as the raising of floor levels, and by a large collection of pottery vessels found in destruction layers. The time span of these strata is between the ninth and early sixth centuries BCE.

Temple. The erection of the temple in stratum X in the northwest quadrant of the fortress was the only major modification made in the interior. The temple itself consisted of a main broadroom hall with plastered benches along its walls and a small compartment attached to the center of the western long wall. The compartment served as the naos, identified with the *debir* of the Temple in Jerusalem. A stela made from an oblong stone with rounded edges and showing traces of red paint was found lying next to a low stone podium. Four shallow steps led into the naos; flanking them were two limestone incense altars. These objects date to the latest use of the temple (in stratum IX), but their first use phase may belong to the early shrine.

In front of the sanctuary was a rectangular courtyard (12.00 × 7.50 m) with a stone pavement. Rooms flanked the courtyard on its other three sides, and a large sacrificial altar was found on the east. The altar (2.40 × 2.20 m) was raised approximately 1.50 m above the floor of stratum X. It was built from unhewn fieldstones laid in mud mortar. A stone step, or bench, had been placed at the foot of its southern side. A large flint flagstone, girdled by plastered channels, covered the top of the altar, and a small compartment was found adjacent to the altar on the west. A red-slipped clay incense burner, comprised of two parts, was found inside the room, attesting to the room's use as a storage area for ceremonial articles.

In stratum IX, the floor of the temple's courtyard was elevated by about 1.20 m, so that the sacrificial alter projected only 0.40 m. Another innovation related to the area's ceremonial role was the addition of a stone-built basin in the courtyard, 2 m south of the altar.

Unlike the other buildings, no indication of violent destruction is observable in the temple area. The vertical disposition of the altars and the stela and the superb preservation of the limestone incense altars and the top of the sacrificial altar indicate that the temple was intentionally dismantled. The upper parts of the walls were torn down and the whole area was buried under a thick layer of soil. The abolition of the temple is attributed to the cultic reform carried out by King Hezekiah in 715 BCE (*2 Kgs.* 18:22).

Dwellings, storerooms, and workshops. The remaining area inside the fortress was allocated to residential dwellings in the southern wing, storage units in the northern quadrant, and the workshops of craftsmen on the southwest. The house of Eliashib, the commander of the Arad fortress, was uncovered at the eastern end of the southern wing. His letters and personal seals were found in two successive layers. Crafts are evident from a hoard of unworked silver and broken jewelry that surely belonged to a local silversmith; the dozens of juglets recovered suggest the production of perfume.

Inscriptions. More than one hundred Hebrew inscriptions were uncovered at Arad. They comprise one of the largest epigraphic collections dating to the Iron Age II (Aharoni, 1981). Most of the inscriptions are on sherds (ostraca); a few are inscribed on whole pottery vessels. [*See* Arad Inscriptions; Ostracon.] The ostraca are administrative in character. Many are letters concerned with the delivery of the food supply (flour or bread, wine, oil) to military units or to *kittim*, apparently Phoenician merchants (originating from Kition on Cyprus) in the service of the kingdom. Others record taxes in kind sent from villages in southern Judah. Some historical information is hinted at the letters: the inauguration of a new king (no. 88), and threat of an Edomite attack on Ramot Negev (no. 25). Nineteen inscriptions were found in one room, in the house of Elyashib, the commander of Arad in stratum VI (see above). Three of his personal seals were uncovered in stratum VII, indicating a short time span between the end of both strata.

Post-Iron Age Phases: Strata V–I. Numerous pits, in which eighty-five Aramaic ostraca were found, characterize the Persian period (stratum V). A casemate fortress was initiated later, in the Hellenistic period, but was never completed (see above). Instead, a small fort was erected within a fenced-in camp (stratum IV). A new fort was erected in the Roman period (stratum III), in the first century BCE, and existed for about two hundred years. Following a long period of abandonment, the remains of the fort were partially reused and incorporated into a way station in the Early Arab period, in the seventh and eighth centuries CE (stratum II). A bedouin cemetery (stratum I) of the thirteenth–nineteenth centuries concludes the stratigraphic sequence.

[*See also* Fortifications, *article on* Fortifications of the Bronze and Iron Ages; *and* Temples, *article on* Syro-Palestinian Temples.]

BIBLIOGRAPHY

Aharoni, Miriam. "The Israelite Citadels." In *The New Encyclopedia of Archaeological Excavations in the Holy Land,* vol. 1, pp. 82–87. Jerusalem and New York, 1993.

176 ARAD INSCRIPTIONS

Aharoni, Yohanan, in collaboration with Joseph Naveh. *Arad Inscriptions.* Translated by Judith Ben-Or. Jerusalem, 1981.

Aharoni, Yohanan. "Arad: Identification and History." In *The New Encyclopedia of Archaeological Excavations in the Holy Land,* vol. 1, p. 75. Jerusalem and New York, 1993.

Herzog, Ze'ev, et al. "The Israelite Fortress at Arad." *Bulletin of the American Schools of Oriental Research,* no. 254 (1984): 1–34.

Herzog, Ze'ev. "The Beer-Sheba Valley: From Nomadism to Monarchy." In *From Nomadism to Monarchy: Archaeological and Historical Aspects of Early Israel,* edited by Israel Finkelstein and Nadav Na'aman, pp. 122–149. Jerusalem and Washington, D.C., 1994.

Mazar, Benjamin. "The Sanctuary of Arad and the Family of Hobab the Kenite." *Journal of Near Eastern Studies* 24 (1965): 297–303.

Na'aman, Nadav. "Arad in the Topographical List of Shishak." *Tel Aviv* 12 (1985): 91–92.

Nylander, Carl. "A Note on the Stonecutting and Masonry of Tel Arad." *Israel Exploration Journal* 17 (1967): 56–59.

Yadin, Yigael. "A Note on the Stratigraphy of Arad." *Israel Exploration Journal* 15 (1965): 180.

Zimhoni, Orna. "The Iron Age Pottery of Tell 'Eton and Its Relation to the Lachish, Tell Beit Mirsim, and Arad Assemblages." *Tel Aviv* 12 (1985): 63–90.

ZE'EV HERZOG

ARAD INSCRIPTIONS. The excavation of the citadel of Arad in the Judean Negev (about 32 km [20 mi.] south of Hebron), carried out between 1962 and 1967 by Yohanan Aharoni, was made famous by the discovery there of numerous inscriptions, most of them written on sherds in carbon black ink. Their preservation was made possible by the Negev's dry climate and the care with which they were excavated. This small site (about 50 sq m) produced 131 Hebrew, 85 Aramaic, 2 Greek, and 5 Arabic inscriptions.

Hebrew Inscriptions. All of the Hebrew inscriptions are from the Iron Age II and are written in Paleo-Hebrew. Those found in stratified contexts are said to come from strata VI–XI (c. 600 BCE–tenth century BCE). Inscriptions from earlier strata (XI–X) are rare and almost illegible; in addition, the stratigraphy of Iron Age II Arad is disputed. The final publication has not yet appeared, and the proposed dating, particularly for the earlier inscriptions, should be considered tentative. In any case, various groups of inscriptions can be discerned based on their date and content:

1. *Elyashib archives.* Ostraca 1–18 are short messages sent to the commander of the fortress, Elyashib son of Eshiyahu (cf. item 10, below, on seals), or to his lieutenant, Nahum (no. 17 in the corpus). Several are complete and most are orders to give food (flour/bread, oil, and wine) to people designated as Kittim (*ktym*)—probably Cypriot or Greek mercenaries in the Judean army. According to the quantity of food, there were probably about twenty-five Kittim who generally received their food every four or six days. These inscriptions offer clues about the bookkeeping done for the storeroom in the fortress. Apparently, these ostraca were kept for one month and, at the beginning of the next month, were registered on a papyrus scroll. The Elyashib ostraca seem to date to the tenth month—Tebet—starting on 16

January 597 BCE, when Nebuchadrezzar was either on his way to attack Jerusalem or was already besieging it. The month was probably the last in the fortress's existence.

2. *Two probable royal ostraca.* Ostraca 24 and 88 may be from the royal court in Jerusalem. Both are broken, but number 24, with at least nine complete lines, is evidence of the Edomite threat against Ramat Negev, the capital of the Judean Negev (probably Khirbet Ghara/Tel 'Ira). This ostracon contains an order to send soldiers from the small fortresses of Arad and Qinah (probably Khirbet Ghazza/Horvat 'Uza) to the threatened town. Ostracon 88 is a royal declaration, probably of a new king of Judah ("I have come to reign/*'ny mlkty*") mentioning also the "king of Egypt/*mlk mṣrym.*" If it is not a schoolboy's exercise, it may be attributable to the new king Jehoahaz son of Josiah (*2 Kgs.* 23:31–32) or, more likely, to Jehoiachin son of Jehoiakim (*2 Kgs.* 24:8) and be dated to December 598 or January 597 BCE. In that case, both ostraca may also date from the last month(s) of the Judean fortress.

3. *Name lists.* Many ostraca from various strata are lists of names (nos. 22, 23, 27, 30?, 31, 35, 36, 38, 39, 41?, 42?, 49, 58, 59, 64?, 67, 69?, 72, 74, 76?, 80, 110), with or without symbols (of capacity?) and ciphers. It is very difficult to determine the precise purpose of these lists, although some may have been connected with the distribution of rations (cf. *ḥṭm,* "wheat," in no. 31). In the latest ostraca, most of the names are Yahwistic, with the theophoric element *yhw.*

4. *Military reports with a formulaic greeting.* A few ostraca contain some kind of a formulaic greeting: "Your son(s)" or "your brother" N . . . and "I bless you by *YHWH/brktk lyhwh*" (nos. 21, 40; cf. nos. 16 and 111?).

5. *Single personal names.* Eight ostraca (nos. 50–57) are small sherds with a single personal name (occasionally including the patronym). These ostraca may have been used as lots cast for priestly duties in the Arad sanctuary.

6. *Hieratic symbols.* A few ostraca are account notes with (hieratic?) symbols that are difficult to interpret (nos. 34, 112). The ostraca may be connected with the collection of grain (cf. *ḥṭm* in no. 33) from various towns (cf. no. 25: 'Anim and Ma'on).

7. *Inscriptions on whole jars.* Three inscriptions on whole jars mention a date, a personal name, and a place name (nos. 19, 20, 32?).

8. *Incised inscriptions.* Other inscriptions, on whole vessels usually, indicate the name of the owner (nos. 89, 91–98, 100, 101?). Two incised inscriptions on small plates (nos. 102–103, probably to be read *q<d>š*) and one preserved on a body sherd (no. 104, *qdš,* "holy") apparently connect these vessels with a sanctuary.

9. *Writing exercises.* Two inscriptions may have been a writing exercise: a plate incised several times with the name Arad (no. 99) and a small fragment of an incised abecedary (no. 90).

10. *Seals.* There are five Hebrew seals (nos. 105–109), among them three (nos. 105–107) with the name of the com-

mander of the fortress, Elyashib son of Eshiyahu/'*lyšb bn 'šyhw*, and one (no. 108) with three lines (name + patronym + name of the grandfather). They are all aniconic, conforming thereby to the general pattern of seals in Judah in about 600 BCE.

11. *Royal seals.* Nine royal seal impressions (*lmlk hbrn*; *lmlk šwkh*) from the end of the eighth century BCE were discovered, all on broken jar handles.

12. *Inscribed weights.* Thirteen inscribed weights from the seventh century BCE were recovered: two *pym* weights, a one-shekel weight, three two-shekel weights, and four eight-shekel weights.

All of the Hebrew inscriptions shed vivid light on the organization and life of a small Judean fortress in the late seventh century BCE. They are evidence that writing was in common use in a small fortress of the Negev before the first Nebudchadrezzar campaign.

Aramaic Inscriptions. Eighty-five Aramaic ostraca were found at Tel Arad. Most are very poorly preserved and half are practically illegible. Except for numbers 38?, 44, and 45, they are probably to be dated paleographically to the fourth century BCE and may be witnesses to the Persian political reorganization of the Negev at the beginning of that century (cf. André Lemaire, "Populations et territoires de la Palestine à l'époque perse," *Transeuphratène* 3 (1990): 31–74, esp. 51–53; and Lemaire, in *La Palestine à l'époque perse*, edited by E. M. Laperroosaz and A. Lemaire, Paris, 1992, pp. 29–30).

The ostraca frequently mention horses (*swsh*) or donkeys (*hmr*), barley, measures (in an abbreviated form), personal names, and sometimes a date (*b* + number). Ostracon 12 specifies that "donkey drivers?" came "from the province of . . . (*mdnt*)" and "belong to the regiment of Abdnanay (*ldgl 'bdnny*)." It is thus clear that some of these inscriptions at least are connected with military organization; judging from the numerous occurrences of the name on other ostraca, the local commander may have been Yaddua (*ydw'*).

In addition to these ostraca there is an inscription on a bone (no. 33) and another on a jar (no. 43). The onomastic evidence from these inscriptions gives some hint of the ethnic composition of the settlement at Arad in the fourth century BCE: Hebrew names are in the majority, but there are also several Edomite (with the theophoric element *qws*) and Arabic (with the ending *-w*) names, as well as a Babylonian name.

Greek and Arabic Inscriptions. From later periods, there are inscriptions in Greek and Arabic. Two fragmentary Greek ostraca were discovered that are difficult to read and interpret. They are probably from the Roman period. Four of the fragmentary Arabic ostraca are probably to be dated to the ninth century CE. A fifth sherd is incised twice with the beginning of the formula: "In the name of Allah. . . ."

[*See also* Arad; Ostracon; Seals.]

BIBLIOGRAPHY

Aharoni, Yohanan, in collaboration with Joseph Naveh. *Arad Inscriptions.* Translated by Judith Ben-Or. Jerusalem, 1981. *Editio princeps* of all the inscriptions discussed here.

Ahituv, Shmuel. *Handbook of Ancient Hebrew Inscriptions* (in Hebrew). Biblical Encyclopedia Library, 7. Jerusalem, 1992. See pages 54–96. Illustrated.

Davies, Graham I. *Ancient Hebrew Inscriptions: Corpus and Concordance.* Cambridge, 1991. See pages 11–38.

Dion, P. E. "Les KTYM de Tel Arad: Grecs ou Phéniciens?" *Revue Biblique* 99 (1992): 70–97.

Lemaire, André. *Inscriptions hébraïques*, vol. 1, *Les ostraca.* Littératures Anciennes du Proche-Orient, 9. Paris, 1977. See pages 145–235.

Mittmann, Siegfried. " 'Gib den Kittäern 3 *b(at)* Wein.' Mengen und Güter in den Arad-Briefen." *Zeitschrift des Deutschen Palästina-Vereins* 109 (1993): 39–48.

Naveh, Joseph. "The Numbers of *Bat* in the Arad Ostraca." *Israel Exploration Journal* 42 (1992): 52–54.

Pardee, Dennis, et al. *Handbook of Ancient Hebrew Letters.* Society of Biblical Literature, Sources for Biblical Study, vol. 15. Chico, Calif., 1982. See pages 28–67.

ANDRÉ LEMAIRE

'ARA'IR (Khirbet, 'Arā'ir), biblical Aroer (not to be confused with Aroer in Judea), site situated to the east of Dibon (Dhiban), 4 km (2.5 mi.) from the Madaba-Kerak road, following the path that borders the northern slope of Wadi el-Mujib (the biblical Arnon River). Its present location coincides with the references in the Hebrew Bible (*Dt.* 2:36, 3:12, 4:48; *Jos.* 12:2; *2 Kgs.* 10:33; *Jer.* 48:19) and in the Mesha inscription (l. 26). [*See* Moabite Stone.] From the site's relatively small size (50 × 50 m) and the durability of its structural remains, it appears that Aroer was built as a solid fortress to control the King's Highway crossing the Arnon. According to *1 Chronicles* 5:8, it was assigned to the tribe of Reuben after the Israelite conquest, remaining in possession of the Israelites until the reign of Solomon (*Jgs.* 11:26). King Mesha conquered and rebuilt it in about 850 BCE, annexing it to the kingdom of Moab (Mesha inscription, l. 26). Shortly thereafter, Aroer passes on to the kings of Damascus (*2 Kgs.* 10:33), until the conquest of Tiglath-Pileser III (732 BCE). Josephus (*Antiq.* 10.181) attributes its definitive destruction to the armies of the king of Babylon, Nebuchadrezzar (c. 582 BCE). Afterward, 'Ara'ir is inhabited only occasionally, during the Hellenistic and Nabatean periods.

Excavation at 'Ara'ir were undertaken by Emilio Olávarri for the Casa Santiago of Jerusalem from 1964 to 1966. Six archaeological levels were uncovered, corresponding to as many periods of occupation. Level VI, the earliest, has two phases: VIB (Intermediate Bronze Age I, c. 2250–2050 BCE), with remains of seminomadic occupation in which agriculture is practiced; and VIA (Intermediate Bronze Age II, c. 2050–1900 BCE), with very rudimentary stone houses.

After a long period of abandonment, corresponding to the Middle Bronze Age (c. 1900–1250 BCE), 'Ara'ir was again occupied at the end of the Late Bronze Age and the beginning of the Iron Age I (level V, c. 1250 BCE), as a well-built fortress belonging to the Israelite settlement. King Mesha of Moab (c. 850 BCE) rebuilt the by then ancient structure as a solid new fortress, using monumental stones for the outers walls. The square building (50 × 50 m) was protected by three parallel walls: an interior wall that served as a buttress for the fortress's central area, an exterior wall 2 m wide, and an intermediate wall 1.5 m wide. The inner corridors running between each of these three walls were filled with the debris of earlier buildings. On the northwest side, which faces the surrounding plain and is therefore more vulnerable, was a double defensive wall and in front of it a reservoir to collect and store water from rainfall. Following another period of abandonment, ʿAraʿir was reoccupied, in the second and third centuries BCE (level III). A few houses were built inside the ancient fortress; they do not appear to have been constructed for permanence, suggesting that their inhabitants were seminomadic. The Nabatean occupation (level II) in the first century BCE and first century CE has little more consistency. To this period belong four houses excavated within the ancient fortress and several pits in the surrounding plain, some of them still in use. By this time, ʿAraʿir had already lost its strategic and military character. After the Roman conquest of the Nabatean kingdom by Cornelius Palma (106 CE), several more houses were built (level I), in the second and third centuries CE. They were scattered over the site and also do not appear to have been built for permanence.

[*See also* Dibon; Moab.]

BIBLIOGRAPHY

Olávarri, Emilio. "Sondages à ʿARŌʿER sur l'Arnon." *Revue Biblique* 72 (1965): 77–94, pls. 1–4.
Olávarri, Emilio. "Fouilles à ʿARŌʿER sur l'Arnon: Les Niveaux du Bronze Intermédiaire." *Revue Biblique* 76 (1969): 230–259, pls. 1–4.

EMILIO OLÁVARRI

ARAMAIC LANGUAGE AND LITERATURE.

One of the two branches of the later Northwest group of Semitic languages, the other being Canaanite (Phoenician and Hebrew), "Aramaic" actually encompasses a number of closely related dialects. They probably emerged in Syria at the end of the Late Bronze Age; the first written traces date from the tenth century BCE. The Aramaic dialects have been in continual use since that time in some form. The importance of Aramaic lies in its long history and the geographic extent of its influence. Many of the cultures of the region employed Aramaic for civil, literary, or religious use even when the vernacular was another language. The formative periods of Christianity and Judaism occurred when Aramaic was in wide use, and it has left its mark on much of their literature. There is no consensus on the periodization of Aramaic, but the categories developed by Joseph A. Fitzmyer (1979) are widely used: Old Aramaic, the dialects of the Iron Age inscriptions from Syria, Palestine, and Mesopotamia (tenth–seventh centuries BCE), Imperial Aramaic (sixth–third centuries BCE), Middle Aramaic (second century BCE–second century CE), Late Aramaic (third–eighth centuries CE), and Modern Aramaic (present day).

Grammar. Aramaic grammar, the description of its phonology (meaningful sounds), morphology (formation and inflection of words), and syntax (meaningful arrangement of words in clauses and sentences), shares many features with the other Semitic languages.

Alphabet. The Arameans borrowed the twenty-two-letter Phoenician alphabet sometime in the eleventh or tenth century BCE. The letter forms of the earliest inscriptions are the same as contemporary Phoenician ones. Aramaic forms of the letters began to develop in the eighth century BCE. The intensive use of Aramaic in the Persian Empire (539–332 BCE) resulted in a widely used Aramiac cursive. The geographic extent of Aramaic writing triggered—by borrowing or imitation—the development of alphabetic writing in non-Aramaic languages such as Brahmi (in northwestern India), Armenian, and Georgian.

Local varieties of the script emerged in the Hellenistic period for writing the indigenous dialects, such as Palestinian, Nabatean, and Palmyrene. Jewish scribes modified each letter to fit within an imaginary square frame; this "square script" was eventually used for Hebrew as well as Aramaic, and much later was adapted for Yiddish. The Nabatean script eventually evolved into the Arabic cursive.

Orthography. When the Arameans adopted the alphabet, they had twenty-seven phonemes to fit to the twenty-two Phoenician letters. Several of the letters had to represent two phonemes (see table 1). This breach of the one-letter/one-phoneme principle may have expedited an important Aramaic innovation: using the letters /ʾ/, /h/, /w/, and /y/ to represent the long vowels /ā/, /ē/, /ū/, and /ī/, respectively. At first used mostly for final vowels, these matres lectionis ("mothers of reading") could also be used within a word, and conceivably for short as well as long vowels. Some later dialects fully exploit these possibilities; for example, Mandaic indicates every vowel by a *mater*. [*See* Mandaic.] However, the ambiguity inherent in a primarily consonantal system was not resolved until Syriac grammarians in the fourth century CE invented symbols written above and below the consonants to express the vowels. [*See* Syriac.] Jewish scribes adopted the principle (and some of the diacritics) for the various vocalization systems developed for the square script. The Tiberian Masoretic system is still in use.

Phonology. The consonants and vowels of Aramaic have undergone a number of important changes throughout history.

Consonants. The oldest Aramaic texts have a consonantal inventory little changed from Proto-Semitic. One peculiarity is the indication of etymological *ḍ* by /q/; for examples, the

TABLE 1. *Aramaic Phonemes.*   The Aramaic phonemes are given, by point of articulation, in standard transcription. The square-script equivalent is also given, as well as the phonemic changes that become standard in later dialects.

	Old Aramaic	Later Dialects
Laryngeals		
Glottal stop	', written א	
Voiceless spirant	h, written ה	
Pharyngeals		
Voiceless spirant	ḥ, written ח	
Voiced spirant	ʿ, written ע	
Postvelars		
Voiceless spirant	ḫ, written ח	ḥ (ח)
Voiced spirant	ġ, written ע	ʿ (ע)
Palatovelars		
Emphatic stop	q, written ק	
Voiced stop	g, written ג	
Voiceless stop	k, written כ	
Prepalatals		
Voiceless sibilant	š, written ש	
Lateral(?) sibilant	ś, written ש	s (ס)
Alveolars		
Emphatic sibilant	ṣ, written צ	
Voiced sibilant	z, written ז	
Voiceless sibilant	s, written ס	
Interdentals		
Emphatic spirant	ṭ, written צ	ṭ (ט)
Voiced spirant	ḏ, written ז	d (ד)
Voiceless spirant	ṯ, written ס/ש	t (ת)
Voiced emphatic stop	ḍ (?), written ק	ʿ (ע)
Dentals		
Emphatic stop	ṭ, written ט	
Voiced stop	d, written ד	
Voiceless stop	t, written ת	
Bilabials		
Voiced stop	b, written ב	
Voiceless stop	p, written פ	
Sonorants		
Lateral	l, written ל	
Flap(?)	r, written ר	
Dental nasal	n, written נ	
Bilabial nasal	m, written מ	

TABLE 2a. *Inflection of Nouns*

	Masculine	Feminine
Singular Nouns		
Absolute	—	-ā
Construct	—	-at
Emphatic	-â	-tâ
Plural Nouns		
Absolute	-în	-ân[1]
Construct	-ê[2]	-ât
Emphatic	-ayyâ[3]	-âtâ

[1]Old Aramaic also -āt. [2]Syriac -ay. [3]Syriac, JBA, Mandaic -ē.

/h/). The position of word stress affected the vowels: During the Middle Aramaic period and after, short vowels in unstressed open syllables were eliminated or reduced to the semivowel shewa (ə). In some late dialects, unstressed final long vowels were dropped.

Morphology. Morphology is the analysis of word structure. Aramaic words can be analyzed according to their formation (the production of lexical items) or their inflection (elements added to words to indicate various nonlexical relations, such as number, gender, person, and so on).

Nouns: Inflection and formation. Nouns are inflected for three "states": absolute, construct, and emphatic (or determined). The absolute state is the unmarked state, while the emphatic state (indicated by final -â) signifies definiteness, similar to a definite article. (The Old Aramaic inscriptions from Zincirli, Turkey, and the Deir ʿAlla plaster text do not use the emphatic state; it may have been a later innovation that spread to all the dialects.) [*See* Deir ʿAlla Inscriptions.] In Syriac and Late Eastern Aramaic, the emphatic state is the normal state, while the absolute is used only in certain contexts. (See table 2a–b.)

Nouns in the construct state are the head words of genitive constructions (see below). In addition to the states, most nouns are marked for number (singular, plural, and sometimes dual) and gender (masculine, feminine). Most nouns are formed by combining a triconsonantal root and a vocalic or vocalic-consonantal pattern, as in other Semitic languages. Some of the nominal patterns have a regular func-

TABLE 2b. *Example Showing Inflection of* ṭâb, *"good"*

	Masculine	Feminine
Singular		
Absolute	ṭâb	ṭâbā
Construct	ṭâb	ṭâbat
Emphatic	ṭâbâ	ṭâbᵉtâ
Plural		
Absolute	ṭâbîn	ṭâbân
Construct	ṭâbê	ṭâbât
Emphatic	ṭâbayyâ	ṭâbâtâ

original *ʾarḍ, "earth," is spelled /ʾrq/ (later dialects ʾrʿ). The articulation is not known, but in later periods the consonant is written with ayin (/ʿ/). In Imperial Aramaic, the original interdentals (ḏ, ṯ, ṯ) become the corresponding dentals (d, t, ṭ). All later dialects reflect this change. The merger of ḫ with ḥ and of ś with s occurred in the Middle Aramaic period. (See table 1.)

Vowels. By the time Old Aramaic emerged, all final short vowels had disappeared. The other vowels, only partially indicated orthographically, show some development away from the Proto-Semitic system of six vowels (long and short i a u): for example, unstressed final î becomes ê (written

TABLE 3. *The Aramaic Verb.* A good impression of the similarities and differences between the dialects can be gained from a synoptic table of verb conjugations. This table presents the conjugation of the root *ktb*, "to write," in the G-stem (basic stem), perfect and imperfect tenses. The sample dialects are those for which dependable traditions of vocalization exist. "Proto-Aramaic," the putative ancestor language, is purely hypothetical. Superscript letters represent consonants written but not pronounced.

	Proto-Aramaic	Targum Onkelos	JPA	Samaritan	Syriac	Mandaic
Perfect, Singular						
3d masc.	kataba	kətab	kətab	kātab	ktav	ktab
3d fem.	katabat	kətabat	katəbat	kātābat	katvat	kitbat
2d masc.	katabtā	kətabtā	kətabt	kātabt	ktavt	ktabt
2d fem.	katabtī	kətabt	kətabt	kātabt	ktavt^y	ktabt
1st (com.)	katabt(u)	kətabit	katəbet	katbət	kitvet	kitbit
Perfect, Plural						
3d masc.	katabû	kətabû	kətabu	kātābu	ktav^w	ktab, ktabyun
3d fem.	katabâ	kətabâ	katben	kātābi	ktav^y, ktaven	ktab, ktabyan
2d masc.	katabtuma	kətabton	kətabton	kātabton	ktavtun	ktabtun
2d fem.	katabtina	kətabten	kətabten	kātabt^{e}n	ktavten	ktabtin
1st (com.)	katabnâ	kətabnâ	kətabnan	kātabnan	ktavn	ktabnin
Imperfect (indicative), Singular						
3d masc.	yaktubu	yiktob	yektob	yiktab	nektuv	niktub
3d fem.	taktubu	tiktob	tektob	tiktab	tektuv	tiktub
2d masc.	taktubu	tiktob	tektob	tiktab	tektuv	tiktub
2d fem.	taktubina	tiktəbîn	tektəbin	tiktābi	tektvin	tiktub
1st (com.)	'aktubu	'ektob	'ektob, nektob	iktab	ektuv	iktub
Imperfect (indicative), Plural						
3d masc.	yaktubûna	yiktəbûn	yektəbun	yiktābon	nektvun	nikitbun
3d fem.	yaktubnâ	yiktəbân	yektəban	yiktāban	nektvân	nikitban
2d masc.	taktubûna	tiktəbûn	tektəbun	tiktābon	tektvun	tikitbun
2d fem.	taktubnâ	tiktəbân	tektəban	tiktāban	tektvân	tikitbun
1st (com.)	naktubu	niktob	nektob	niktab	nektuv	niktub
Infinitives						
G-stem	katâb	miktab	mektob	maktab	mektav	miktab
D-stem	kattâb?	kattâbā	məkattaba	amkattaba	mkattâvu	katobi
C-stem	haktâb?	'aktâbā	maktaba	miktāba	maktâvu	aktobi

tion, such as the adjectival pattern *kattîb* (e.g., *qaddîš,* "holy," from *qdš; raššî',* "wicked," from *rš'*), or the *kâtôb* agentive (e.g., *pârôq,* "savior," from *prq*), but many patterns have no systematic function. Compound words are very rare.

Verbs: Inflection and formation. Verbs have two conjugations, one with suffixes (the "perfect") and one with prefixes and sometimes suffixes (the "imperfect"). The conjugational affixes indicate person, number, and gender. In Old and Imperial Aramaic, the imperfect distinguished between the indicative and jussive moods, but the later dialects made their paradigms uniform, leveling through the indicative type (Western Aramaic) or the jussive type (Syriac, Eastern). Infinitives and active/passive participles complete the system. (See table 3.)

Like nouns, root/pattern combinations form verbal "stems." Unlike nouns, the stems form a limited but productive system and differentiate certain kinds of action. The three principal stems are the simple, or G stem for simple or unmarked action; the D-stem (with a doubled middle root letter) for repetitive, factitive, or pluritive action; and the C-stem for causative action. Each stem has a corresponding stem with prefixed *'it-* (Gt, Dt, Ct), usually indicating the passive voice. Early Aramaic used an internal causative passive instead of the Ct-stem; it also had an internal G-stem passive. The verb stems in the perfect conjugation with the root *ktb* are as follows (using Biblical Aramaic):

G-stem	*kətab*	Gt-stem	*'itkətib*
D-stem	*kattēb*	Dt-stem	*'itkattab*
C-stem	*haktēb*	C-passive	*huktab*

In later dialects, the C-passive *huktab* was replaced by *'ittaktab.*

Syntax. Syntax examines the combination of words into phrases, clauses, and sentences. Only a few important syntactic features are discussed here.

Genitive phrase. The oldest type is the construct chain, in which a noun in the construct state is prosodically bound to a following noun to produce a genitive construction: *bayt,* "house" + *malkâ,* "the king" > *bêt malkâ,* "the house of the king." In Old Aramaic the construct phrase begins to be replaced, under Akkadian influence, by nouns joined by the particle *dî* (later *d-*): *bêtâ dî malkâ* (same meaning). Such constructions become the rule in the later dialects. A common subtype has a suffix on the head-word: *bêtēh dî malkâ,* "his house of the king," or "the king's house."

Verbal function. The perfect conjugation is commonly used for the historical past or the perfect. The imperfect has a more complicated development. In the older texts, it has an iterative, durative, future, or precative reference. When used as a precative, some dialects used a preformative *l-* instead of the usual *y-*. In Eastern Aramaic and Syriac, the precative came to replace the indicative (with the preformative *l-* becoming *n-* in Syriac and Mandaic). At the same time, the active participle came to be used as a present tense and, with the root *hwy,* "to be," to denote past or future continuous action. In Syriac and Late Eastern Aramaic, the participle often denotes futurity, and the imperfect, modality, while in the West a three-tense system formed: past (perfect), present (participle), and future (imperfect).

Word order. The oldest word order in the verbal clause is verb-subject-object (VSO), with a subject-verb-object (SVO) as a common variant; both orders are common in the later dialects. Some Imperial Aramaic texts, as well as Biblical Aramaic, also use an SOV order, apparently under Akkadian or Persian influence.

Vocabulary. Despite significant dialect differences, a pervasive unity is seen in common Aramaic vocabulary. The most frequently used verbal roots are shared by all dialects: *slq,* "to go up"; *nht,* "to go down"; *'ll,* "to enter"; *npq,* "to exit"; *'bd,* "to do, make"; *mll,* "to speak"; *'zl,* "to go"; *yhb,* "to give"; *ntl,* "to lift up"; and so on. The same is true of nouns, numerals, and adjectives—for example, *had,* "one"; *rab,* "great"; *'órah,* "way"; *'atar,* "place"; *saggî,* "many." Such unity must derive from a common divergence from a single ancestor dialect, or from a convergence of dialects fostered by constant contact. Probably both elements contributed to Aramaic uniformity.

Contact with other languages. Aramaic was used alongside other languages throughout its history, and it both absorbed features from them and influenced them. Akkadian had great influence, particularly on the shape of Imperial and Eastern Aramaic (see above), and it borrowed freely from Aramaic as well. Persian also contributed many lexemes and some grammatical features. Greek loanwords and constructions became increasingly common in the Byzantine period, especially in Syriac. [*See* Greek.] In Jewish circles, Aramaic greatly altered Hebrew; postbiblical Hebrew owes many of its characteristic features to Aramaic, and Aramaic in turn borrowed various religious words from Hebrew. Finally, Arabic owes its alphabet and a significant number of loanwords to Aramaic. [*See* Hebrew Language and Literature; Arabic.]

Aramaic dialects. No texts in the hypothetical ancestor language of the Aramaic dialects ("Proto-Aramaic") have survived. From its earliest written appearances, Aramaic is characterized by dialect divisions.

Old Aramaic. The earliest Old Aramaic text is a one-line inscription on an altar found at Tell Halaf on the upper Khabur River (*KAI* 231), possibly from the tenth century BCE. [*See* Halaf, Tell.] From a nearby site and from a slightly later time is the Tell Fakhariyah bilingual, a statue bearing inscriptions in Akkadian and Old Aramaic. [*See* Fakhariyah Aramaic Inscription.] The oldest text from Syria is the Melqart stela (*KAI* 201), a votive inscription to Melqart from "Bar-Hadad, king of Aram," probably from the ninth century BCE. Although found north of Aleppo, it probably originated in the kingdom of Damascus. The longest texts, the Sefire treaty inscriptions (*KAI* 222–224), appear on three stelae discovered at Sefire, south of Aleppo. They contain the text of a treaty made between Mati''el of Arpad and a certain Bar-Ga'yah of KTK (the Assyrian Shamshi-Ilu, according to André Lemaire and J.–M. Durand, *Les inscriptions araméennes de Sfiré et l'Assyrie de Shamshi-ilu,* Geneva, Paris, 1984). The texts date from the mid-eighth century BCE. [*See* Sefire Aramaic Inscriptions.]

Two eighth-century BCE inscriptions, the Hadad and Panammu inscriptions (*KAI* 214, 215) were discovered at Zincirli (ancient Sam'al). The first is on a statue of Hadad dedicated by Panammu I of Sam'al; the second is on a broken statue, dedicated to Panammu II by his son Bar-Rakkab (c. 730 BCE). The inscriptions are the only evidence for the Sam'alian dialect of Aramaic, which evinces a number of archaisms and unusual features, leading some to doubt its classification as Aramaic. Bar-Rakkab also left six other texts, not written in Sam'alian, of which the so-called *Bauinschrift* (*KAI* 216), detailing his building activities, is the longest and best preserved.

From the ancient kingdom of Hamath comes the Zakkur stela (*KAI* 202), a fragmentary inscription from Afis south of Aleppo. [*See* Zakkur Inscription.] It narrates the rise to kingship of Zakkur, "a humble man" (l.2), and how, having fought off a coalition of foreign kings, he embarked on building projects to the glory of his god Iluwer. It probably dates from the early eighth century BCE. Two funerary inscriptions from Nerab probably date from the beginning of the seventh century BCE: the Sin-zer-ibni inscription (*KAI* 225) and the Si-gabbar inscription (*KAI* 226), commemorating two priests of the god Śahr. [*See* Nerab Inscriptions.]

Modern Jordan and Israel are the sites of two important recent discoveries. The most interesting (and perplexing) is the Deir 'Alla plaster text, an inscription in ink painted on plaster discovered in 1967 at Tell Deir 'Alla in Jordan. Only fragments are preserved, and the reconstruction of the text as a whole is provisional. It is certain, however, that it tells of a vision seen by Balaam son of Beor, known from *Numbers* 22–24. The connections with the biblical text are intriguing. Equally as controversial is the classification of the language: despite some features that link it to the local Canaanite languages (Hebrew or Moabite), the language of the text should be considered Aramaic. The newest Aramaic discovery is the Tel Dan stela, a stone fragment containing 13 incomplete lines discovered in northern Israel in 1993. The fragments tell of the victory of an Aramean king, probably Hazael (eighth century BCE), over the "king of Israel" and the "king of the house of David"—that is, Judah—in what, apparently, is the first reference to David outside the Hebrew Bible. Additional fragments were discovered in 1994.

Imperial Aramaic. Assyria dominated the Near East in the 8th and 7th centuries BCE, and the texts from this period reflect a growing standardization of Aramaic—the beginning of "Imperial Aramaic," an Aramaic koine that left its mark on all subsequent dialects. The widespread use and influence of Aramaic dates to the period of Assyrian hegemony. A narrative from the Hebrew Bible depicts the knowledge of Aramaic at this time as a possession of the Israelite scribes but not of the common people. The emissary of Sennacherib of Assyria came to Jerusalem in 710 BCE to demand surrender. During the parley, the Judeans said, "Please speak to your servants in Aramaic, for we understand it. But do not speak with us in Judean in the hearing of the people" (*2 Kgs.* 18:26). Written and pictorial remains testify to the presence of Arameans and Aramaic scribes in official capacities throughout the region.

The extant Aramaic texts from the Assyrian period, however, are brief. They include 14 inscribed weights from Nineveh (*CIS* 1–14), dockets, labels, and brief records written or scratched into clay tablets from Aššur, Nimrud, Tell Halaf, and elsewhere. The Aššur ostracon (*KAI* 233) is a fragmentary letter sent from Babylonia and dated to about 650 BCE. [*See* Nineveh; Aššur; Nimrud.]

Aramaic texts from the Neo-Babylonian period (612–539 BCE) are also few and brief, comprising a few dockets, and one fragmentary papyrus, the 6th-century Adon letter (*KAI* 266), from the ruler of Ekron (Tel Miqne) in Palestine to the Pharaoh. [*See* Miqne, Tel.] The original of the Uruk incantation may date to the same period. Its magical text contains an archaic form of Eastern Aramaic written in syllabic cuneiform on a tablet dating to the third century BCE.

The high point of Imperial Aramaic is in the Persian period (539–332 BCE). The Achaemenid dynasty continued the practice of using Aramaic as a lingua franca, and textual remains from every point of the far-flung Persian Empire attest to its use in law, administration, and literature. The largest and most significant remains have come from Egypt, where the climate is ideal for preserving writings on leather and papyrus. One of the most important manuscript finds of the century was the discovery in 1906 of the archives of the Jewish colony at Elephantine, comprising more than one hundred relatively intact papyri. Dating from the fifth century BCE, they include ten official letters to and from the head of the community, several family archives, and numerous administrative, legal, epistolary, and literary documents. [*See* Papyrus; Elephantine.]

The most important literary text is a copy of the Words of Ahiqar, later versions of which are known from other languages. It is the story of how the sage Ahiqar, advisor to Assyrian royalty, was betrayed by his nephew Nadan and later restored to favor. The "proverbs" of Ahiqar contained in the document are a significant example of Near Eastern wisdom literature. Also found at Elephantine was an ancient translation of the Bisitun inscription of Darius. [*See* Bisitun.] Other significant documents from Egypt are the correspondence of Arsham, the Persian satrap of Egypt; the Hermopolis letters, private letters written in a nonstandard dialect; papyri and inscriptions from Memphis Saqqara, Abydos, Giza, Luxor, Edfu, and elsewhere. [*See* Memphis; Saqqara; Abydos; Giza.] One of the most remarkable documents is the Amherst demotic papyrus, a long, fragmentary scroll of religious and narrative texts in Aramaic written in Egyptian demotic script. Still only partially published, the often idiosyncratic use of demotic characters makes the papyrus difficult to understand. Other Imperial Aramaic documents from Syria-Palestine, Mesopotamia, Asia Minor, Iran (especially Persepolis), Afghanistan, and Arabia (Tayma'), show its widespread use. [*See* Persepolis; Tayma'.] The Aramaic sections of the *Book of Ezra* in the Hebrew Bible, putatively dating from the Persian period, are written in Imperial Aramaic.

Middle Aramaic. When the Greeks came to power in the Near East in the fourth century BCE, Aramaic lost its official status. However, its long career as a lingua franca left its mark on every dialect, and the local vernaculars continued to play major roles. The "post-Imperial" period, during which the local dialects developed as literary standards in their own right, is called Middle Aramaic.

Nabatean was used in North Arabia, Sinai, and Petra in Jordan. Archaeologists have found thousands of Nabatean graffiti and burial inscriptions dating from the second century BCE to the fourth century CE. Several Nabatean legal texts have been discovered in caves in the Judean wilderness. In general, Nabatean is conservative, being much influenced by Imperial Aramaic. It contains a number of loans from Arabic, the region's principal vernacular. The Nabateans developed a highly individual cursive script that was the direct ancestor of the Arabic script. [*See* Nabatean Inscriptions; Sinai; Petra.]

To the west, Jewish Palestinian Aramaic is attested from the finds from the Dead Sea wilderness, principally Wadi Qumran. [*See* Qumran.] About 25 percent of the Dead Sea Scrolls were written in Aramaic, including the oldest targum (Aramaic Bible translation), the Targum of Job. Other important texts include the *Genesis Apocryphon* (a retelling of the patriarchal narratives), the *Book of Tobit*, the *Book of Enoch*, and the *Testament of Levi*. Other texts, including apocalypses, stories, and legal texts, have recently been published, and testify to a rich Aramaic literary culture in the centuries from about 200 BCE to the mid-first century CE. The Aramaic sections of the *Book of Daniel* probably belong to this period, although in some respects its language is more archaic than that in the Qumran documents. Inscriptional material is sparse, but there are some burial texts and graffiti on ossuaries. Letters and legal documents from the Second Jewish Revolt against Rome (132–35 CE) found in other cave sites near the Dead Sea include letters (some in Aramaic) written by the revolt's leader, Shimʿon bar Koseba/Bar Kokhba. [*See* Judean Desert Caves; Dead Sea Scrolls; Bar Kokhba Revolt.] The Qumran dialect itself is conservative, but less so than Nabatean. By the time of the Second Revolt, the vernacular was beginning to shake off the influence of the old Imperial dialect, particularly in the Bar Kokhba letters. The legal texts often preserve the formularies of earlier centuries.

From the same period, the Greek New Testament preserves a few words and brief sentences in Aramaic; this, combined with other evidence, has given Aramaic a reputation as the "language of Jesus." Although Aramaic was commonly used, it is not certain that Jesus and the early Palestinian church used it exclusively because Hebrew and Greek were also widely spoken at the time.

The oasis of Palmyra (Tadmor) in the Syrian desert yielded thousands of inscriptions in its national script dating from 44 BCE to 272 CE, including the longest Aramaic inscription known, the Tariff Bilingual in Greek and Palmyrene (137 CE). [*See* Palmyrene Inscriptions.] Palmyrene is a transitional dialect sharing both Western and Eastern features. Farther north, about seventy votive and funerary inscriptions in Edessene (Old Syriac) survive from the first and second centuries CE. As its name indicates, this literary dialect originated in Edessa (modern Urfa). The oldest inscription is dated to 6 CE.

Finally, the Aramaic of the Parthian Empire is found on hundreds of votive inscriptions from Hatra, an oasis on the upper Tigris River, from Aššur and a few other sites. They date from the first–third centuries CE. The morphology of Hatran already displays the traits of the later Eastern dialects. [*See* Hatra Inscriptions.]

Late Aramaic. The late dialects (200 CE–700 CE) are generally associated with the national or religious groups that used them. They are typically divided geographically into Eastern (Mesopotamian) and Western (Palestinian) dialects. This division is simplistic and should be revised to include Central Aramaic (see below), which is comprised of classical Syriac and other dialects not clearly falling into the East–West categories.

Western Aramaic includes the dialects used by the three principal religious groups of Palestine in the Byzantine period: Jewish Palestinian Aramaic, Christian Palestinian Aramaic, and Samaritan Aramaic. Jewish Palestinian Aramaic (JPA) is used in the Palestinian targum, a translation of the Pentateuch preserved in various recensions, including texts from the Cairo geniza, liturgical selections known as the Fragment-Targum, and the virtually complete Targum Neofiti. A somewhat different (later?) dialect is used in the Palestinian Talmud and the Palestinian rabbinic commentaries (midrashim). Although JPA developed from dialects spoken in an earlier period, occasional efforts to study it simply as the first-century-CE vernacular (and therefore the language of Jesus) have not been successful. Christian Palestinian Aramaic (CPA) is preserved in inscriptions and manuscripts of the Melkite Christians, primarily from the third–ninth centuries CE. Almost all of the literature is translated from Greek and includes biblical texts, liturgies, sermons, and biographies. CPA is written in a form of the Syriac script, and indeed Syriac was an important influence on it. Samaritan Aramaic was used by the Samaritan sect of Judaism. The Samaritans had their own targum (in two recensions) and religious literature, including chronicles, sermons, and liturgical poetry. [*See* Samaritans.]

Eastern Aramaic is comprised of Jewish Babylonian Aramaic (JBA) and Mandaic. JBA was the language of the Mesopotamian Jewish community. The Aramaic portions of the Babylonian Talmud are the most important witness to this dialect. Hundreds of bowls bearing magical incantations in JBA from excavations at Nippur and other sites in Lower Mesopotamia constitute crucial nonliterary evidence for JBA. Mandaic was used by the Mandaeans, a Gnostic sect living in parts of Iran and Iraq since Late Antiquity. Mandaic, used in their voluminous religious literature (also including incantation bowls and other magical texts), is very close to JBA in its grammar and vocabulary but has its own distinctive script and orthography.

Central Aramaic is virtually equivalent to Syriac, the written variety of the standard Aramaic of Syria-Upper Mesopotamia during the Byzantine period. There is more surviving literature in Syriac than in any other Aramaic dialect because it was used by a vast portion of Eastern Christianity for liturgy, translations of secular works, and religious literature, including one of the oldest Bible translations, the Peshitta.

Syriac Christianity, divided by doctrinal controversies, split into two groups during the fifth and sixth centuries CE. The Western (Jacobite) branch, centered on Edessa in the Byzantine Empire, and the Eastern (Nestorian) branch, centered at Nisibis in the Persian sphere, evolved their own scripts, pronunciation, and literary traditions. In both forms, Syriac continued to be a creative medium of literature until around the fourteenth century CE. It still survives in its classical form as a liturgical and scholarly language. The language of Targum Onkelos and Targum Jonathan, the most widely used targums in Judaism, has proved difficult to classify. Although many consider it to belong to Middle Palestinian Aramaic, it may be a Jewish variety of early Central Aramaic.

Late literary dialects. Aramaic declined as a spoken language after the rise of Arab power and prestige under Islam, but the literary dialects continued in use. Syriac, as noted, endured as a literary medium to modern times. A number of Jewish Bible translations were written in late Jewish Literary Aramaic, a dialect combining Eastern, Western, and Syriac features. CPA's second principal literary period occurred during the eleventh–thirteenth centuries CE.

Modern Aramaic. Some forms of Aramaic are still spoken in various ethnic enclaves of the Near East. Western Aramaic is represented by the language of the Syrian town of Ma'lula and other nearby villages and Eastern Aramaic by a number of dialects spoken in parts of Turkey, Iraq, and Iran. The phonology and vocabulary of the modern dialects are heavily influenced by Arabic, Turkish, and Persian.

[*See also* Arameans; Imperial Aramaic; *and* Palestinian Aramaic.]

BIBLIOGRAPHY

Beyer, Klaus. *Die aramäischen Texte vom Toten Meer.* Göttingen, 1984. Collection of Dead Sea documents as well as other texts from the period, along with a general description and history of Aramaic, an outline grammar, and lexicon. An ambitious but idiosyncratic study. An *Ergänzungsband* appeared in 1994.

Brockelmann, Carl. *Lexicon Syriacum.* 2d ed. Halle, 1928.

Degen, Rainer. *Altaramäische Grammatik der Inschriften des 10.–18. Jh. v. Chr.* Wiesbaden, 1969. Complete text and grammatical description of Old Aramaic texts known to 1969.

Donner, Herbert, and Wolfgang Röllig. *Kanaanäische und aramäische Inschriften* (KAI). 3 vols. 2d ed. Wiesbaden, 1969. Useful collection of most of the major Aramaic inscriptions, including bibliography, commentary, and glossary.

Fitzmyer, Joseph A. "The Phases of the Aramaic Language." In Fitzmyer's *A Wandering Aramean: Collected Aramaic Essays,* pp. 57–84. Missoula, 1979. Description and defense of Fitzmyer's periodization of Aramaic.

Fitzmyer, Joseph A., and Stephen A. Kaufman. *An Aramaic Bibliography,* part 1, *Old, Official, and Biblical Aramaic.* Baltimore and London, 1992. Indispensable tool for studying the early dialects of Aramaic.

Garr, W. Randall. *Dialect Geography of Syria-Palestine, 1000–586 B.C.E.* Philadelphia, 1985. Methodologically significant study of dialect relationships, including Old Aramaic.

Hoftijzer, Jacob, and Karel Jongeling. *Dictionary of the North-West Semitic Inscriptions.* Leiden, 1995. An able and comprehensive two-volume lexicon incorporating all the Old and Imperial Aramaic inscriptions (as well as Palmyrene, Hatran, and Nabatean). Includes R. C. Steiner and A. M. Mashawi, "A Selective Glossary of Northwest Semitic Texts in Egyptian Script."

Kaufman, Stephen A. *The Akkadian Influences on Aramaic.* Chicago, 1974. One of the few works to provide extensive treatment of the major linguistic influences on Aramaic.

Kutscher, Eduard Y. "Aramaic." In *Current Trends in Linguistics,* vol. 6, *Linguistics in South West Asia and North Africa,* edited by Thomas A. Sebeok, pp. 347–412. The Hague, 1970. Presents a comprehensive summary of research and suggests directions for inquiry into the earlier dialects.

Macuch, Rudolf. *Handbook of Classical and Modern Mandaic.* Berlin, 1965.

Macuch, Rudolf. *Grammatik des samaritanischen Aramäisch.* Berlin, 1982.

Müller-Kessler, Christa. *Grammatik des Christlich-Palästinisch-Aramäischen,* vol. 1, *Schriftlehre, Lautlehre, Formenlehre.* Hildesheim, 1991. Comprehensive grammar based on a reexamination of the manuscripts and inscriptions.

Muraoka, Takamitsu, ed. *Studies in Qumran Aramaic.* Abr-Nahrain, Supplement Series, vol. 3. Leiden, 1992. Essays on general and particular linguistic issues raised by the Aramaic dialect of the Dead Sea Scrolls.

Nöldeke, Theodor. *Compendious Syriac Grammar.* Translated by James A. Crichton. Rev. ed. London, 1904. This research grammar has not been equaled for its grasp of detail, especially in syntax.

Porten, Bezalel, and Ada Yardeni. *Textbook of Ancient Aramaic Documents from Ancient Egypt,* vol. 1, *Letters*; vol. 2, *Contracts*; vol. 3, *Literature, Accounts, Lists.* Jerusalem, 1986–1992. New edition of all the Elephantine papyri and other important Imperial Aramaic texts, including excellent facsimiles by Yardeni.

Rosenthal, Franz. *Die aramäistische Forschung seit Th. Nöldekes Veröffentlichungen.* Leiden, 1939. Classic study of early linguistic research on Aramaic.

Rosenthal, Franz. *A Grammar of Biblical Aramaic.* Porta Linguarum Orientalium, n.s. 5. Wiesbaden, 1974.

Segert, Stanislav. *Altaramäische Grammatik mit Bibliographie, Chrestomathie und Glossar.* Leipzig, 1975. Detailed structural study of Old, Imperial, and Biblical Aramaic.

Sokoloff, Michael. *A Dictionary of Jewish Palestinian Aramaic of the Byzantine Period.* Ramat Gan, 1990. The first lexicon devoted solely to JPA, compiled on the basis of the best manuscript evidence.

Vogüé, Melchior de. *Corpus inscriptionum semiticarum,* part 2, *Inscriptiones aramaicae.* Paris, 1889. Monumental collection of more than four thousand texts, sketchy for Old and Imperial Aramaic (both then little known) but admirably comprehensive for Nabatean and Palmyrene inscriptions.

EDWARD M. COOK

ARAMEANS designates a number of linguistically related ethnic groups who spoke the West Semitic language called Aramaic and who inhabited a considerable part of the Near East, particularly Syria and Mesopotamia, in the first millennium BCE. A number of Aramean nation-states developed in Syria in the late eleventh and the tenth centuries BCE that became influential in the political and cultural development of the Levant. Aramean tribes also became a major population element in both Assyria and Babylonia in the first half of the first millennium BCE, so that eventually Aramaic became the primary spoken language of the Fertile Crescent, largely replacing Akkadian in the east and the local West Semitic dialects, such as Hebrew, in the west.

The origins of the Arameans are obscure. They make their first certain appearance in historical texts only in the early eleventh century BCE. Some scholars believe that they were pastoralist tribes living on the borders of the Syrian desert who swept northward into northern Syria and Upper Mesopotamia during the last years of the second millen-

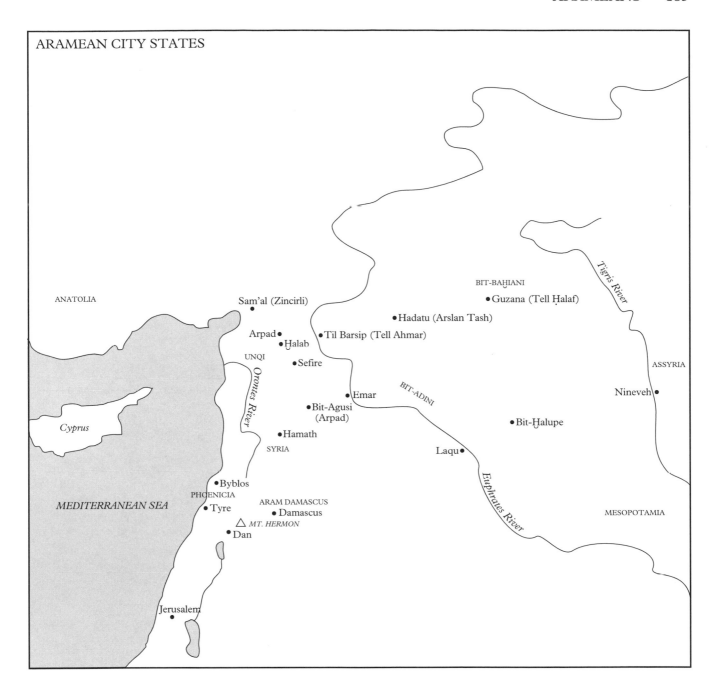

ARAMEAN CITY STATES

nium. After establishing themselves there, the tribes migrated both toward the southwest, into central and southern Syria, and southeastward, into central and southern Mesopotamia. Those scholars who disagree with this model suggest that the Arameans were simply the descendants of the West Semitic population of Syria, known from earlier second-millennium sources as Amorites and Aḫlamu. Although political power in northern Syria had been held by the Hurrians in the Late Bronze Age, the Iron Age saw a resurgence of Semitic aristocracies (i.e., Arameans) in control of many areas.

The Arameans never developed a unified culture or po-litical entity. Numerous small states developed throughout Syria and flourished between the eleventh and the late eighth centuries BCE, alongside other states whose aristocracies belonged to Luwian-speaking groups that had migrated into northern Syria after the collapse of the Hittite Empire. The Aramean states were eventually demolished, both economically and ethnically, by the Assyrians, through brutal military suppression and mass deportation of populations.

Although dozens of Aramean tribes and states existed throughout Syria, only a few of them became politically significant and played major roles in that region's political history.

1. *Bit-Zamani, Bit-Baḥiani, Bit-Ḥalupe, and Laqu.* Four Aramean states developed quite early along the western border with Assyria, but they came under Assyrian domination by the ninth century BCE. The important city of Guzana (Tell Ḥalaf) was the capital of one of these states, Bit-Baḥiani. The excavations there provided significant evidence of early Aramean public art and architecture.

2. *Bit-Adini.* Located in the great bend of the Euphrates River, Bit-Adini was a formidable opponent to Assyrian expansion during the early ninth century BCE. Excavations have taken place at two important cities of Bit-Adini—Til Barsip (Tell Ahmar), which may not actually have come under Aramean control until the reign of Aḫuni, the last king of Bit-Adini, and Hadatu (Arslan Tash), which became an important Assyrian outpost in the region after Bit-Adini was annexed.

3. *Bit-Agusi.* In the region surrounding Aleppo, the state of Bit-Agusi was called Yaḫan early in the ninth century BCE, and, sometimes, Arpad, after its capital city, in the eighth century. This state, under vigorous kings, became a primary power in northern Syria in the ninth and eighth centuries BCE and was not fully subdued by the Assyrians until 743 BCE, during the reign of Tiglath-Pileser III. Limited excavations have been undertaken at Arpad (Tell Rifaʿat), and an important Aramaic treaty between king Matiʿʿel of Bit-Agusi and one Bar-Gaʾya of the land of *ktk*, inscribed on stone stelae, was found at the site of Sefire, in the southern part of the kingdom.

4. *Aram Damascus.* In southern Syria, Aram Damascus played a major role in the Levant in the ninth and eight centuries BCE, with the peak of its power occurring in the mid and late ninth century, under its kings Hadad-idri and Hazael. No excavations have reached Iron Age levels at Damascus.

5. *Samʾal (Zincirli).* Mention should also be made of the small city-state of Samʾal (Zincirli). Excavations at this site produced considerable sculpture, architecture, and inscriptions that are an important source of study for north Aramean culture.

6. *Other states in Syria.* There were certainly large populations of Arameans in other states in Syria, although they were often ruled by members of the Neo-Hittite aristocracy. Some states had both a Luwian and an Aramaic name, such as Pattina/Unqi. The important kingdom of Hamath was ruled in the tenth and ninth centuries BCE by dynasts with Neo-Hittite names, but by kings with Aramaic names in the eighth century BCE.

Literary remains of the Iron Age Aramean states are very limited. A few Aramaic inscriptions on stone are known, but most of the historical information available about these kingdoms comes from Assyrian texts and the Hebrew Bible. These two sources, while helpful, are of limited value, however, because they deal almost exclusively with the conflicts between their own nations and the Aramean states. They offer little or no insight into the internal structure of the Aramean kingdoms. In addition, remarkably little archaeological work has been done on the important sites, and most of the large-scale excavations that have taken place, such as at Arslan Tash, Tell Ahmar, Tell Halaf, and Zincirli, were in the late nineteenth or early twentieth centuries, before reliable field and recording techniques were developed.

Not much can be said about Aramean culture because so little archaeological and literary data has been recovered so far. The Arameans do not appear to have made major contributions either to political or social practices in the Levant; and their styles of art and architecture are largely based on those of others. In northern Syria, the artistic and architectural traditions of the Arameans were heavily influenced first by the Neo-Hittite states, which preserved many cultural elements of the Late Bronze Age Hittite civilization, and later by the Assyrians. The few artistic pieces from southern Syria show a strong cultural influence from Phoenicia. The Arameans in Babylonia appear to have adapted to Babylonian styles.

Aramaic inscriptions indicate that Aramean religion descended from the West Semitic religion of the second millennium. The weather/fertility god, Hadad, appears to have been the head of the pantheon in several of the Aramean states, while the moon god Sin/Shahar, El, Rakib-el, Shamash, and Resheph seem to have played significant roles.

The major legacy of the Arameans was their language and script. Because they were probably the largest population group in Syria, their language came to dominate that area early in the first millennium BCE. The mass deportations of Arameans into Assyria in the ninth and eighth centuries resulted in the spread of the language into northern Mesopotamia; by the late eighth century it was being used as a diplomatic language by the Assyrians themselves. In the Neo-Babylonian period, Aramaic became the most common language in Babylonia as well. The Persian government adopted Aramaic as its international language, so that it came to be used commonly across southwest Asia. Thus, archives of Aramaic papyri from Egypt in the Persian period, Aramaic documents from Palestine in the fourth century BCE, and inscriptions from Turkey, Iran, and even Afghanistan have been found. Eventually, Palestine's local West Semitic dialects, including Hebrew, died away and were replaced with Aramaic. By the last two centuries BCE, Aramaic had become an important language for Jewish literature, and Syriac, an Aramaic dialect, played an important role in the Eastern church in the Roman and Byzantine periods.

The Arameans borrowed their script from the Phoenicians, probably in the late eleventh or early tenth century. However, they made a significant adaptation to Phoenician writing customs: they were the first to use some of the alphabetic letters to indicate vowel sounds (the so-called *matres lectionis*). This important contribution to orthography was slowly adopted by other cultures, including Israel. Eventually, the Aramaic script itself came to replace the other national scripts of Syria-Palestine, including that of Hebrew. The square script commonly used in Judea (Judah) by the third century BCE, which is the ancestor of the Hebrew book script used today, is actually a descendant of Aramaic script.

[*See also* Aramaic Language and Literature; Damascus; Halaf, Tell; *and* Syria, *article on* Syria in the Bronze and Iron Ages.]

BIBLIOGRAPHY

Brinkman, John A. *A Political History of Post-Kassite Babylonia, 1158–722 B.C.* Rome, 1968. See this and the following for information about the Aramean tribes in Babylonia.

Brinkman, John A. *Prelude to Empire: Babylonian Society and Politics, 747–626 B.C.* Philadelphia, 1984.

Fitzmyer, Joseph A., and Stephen A. Kaufman. *An Aramaic Bibliography,* part 1, *Old, Official, and Biblical Aramaic.* Baltimore and London, 1992. Monumental, comprehensive bibliography of all published Aramaic inscriptions and papyri.

Gibson, John C. L. *Textbook of Syrian Semitic Inscriptions,* vol. 2, *Aramaic Inscriptions.* Oxford, 1975. Convenient English translation of the major Aramaic inscriptions.

Greenfield, Jonas C. "Aspects of Aramean Religion." In *Ancient Israelite Religion: Essays in Honor of Frank Moore Cross,* edited by Patrick D. Miller, Jr., et al., pp. 67–78. Philadelphia, 1987. Brief, helpful discussion of a topic that has barely been examined in print.

Hawkins, J. D. "The Neo-Hittite States in Syria and Anatolia." In *The Cambridge Ancient History,* vol. 3.1, edited by John Boardman et al., pp. 372–441. Cambridge, 1982. Thorough, rather technical survey of the history and culture of Iron Age Syrian states.

Layton, Scott C. "Old Aramaic Inscriptions." *Biblical Archaeologist* 51 (1988,): 172–189. Fine, recent survey of the earliest known Aramaic inscriptions.

Pitard, Wayne T. *Ancient Damascus: A Historical Study of the Syrian City-State from Earliest Times until Its Fall to the Assyrians in 732 B.C.E.* Winona Lake, Ind., 1987. Detailed account of this important southern Syrian state.

Pitard, Wayne T. "The Aramaeans." In *Peoples of the Old Testament World,* edited by Alfred J. Hoerth, Gerald L. Mattingly and Edwin Yamauchi, pp. 207–230. Grand Rapids, Mich., 1994. General introduction to Aramean history and culture.

Sader, Hélène. *Les états araméens de Syrie depuis leur fondation jusqu'à leur transformation en provinces assyriennes.* Beirut, 1987. Deals in detail with Bit-Baḥiani, Bit-Adini, Bit-Agusi, Sam'al, Hamath, and Aram-Damascus.

WAYNE T. PITARD

ARARAT. *See* Urartu.

ARCE. *See* American Research Center in Egypt.

ARCHAEOLOGICAL INSTITUTE OF AMERICA. Founded in 1879 by Charles Eliot Norton, the Archaeological Institute of America (AIA) is a not-for-profit, scientific and educational organization chartered through the Smithsonian Institution by the U.S. Congress. The following act of incorporation was approved by President Theodore Roosevelt for the Archaelogical Institute of America on 26 May 1906: "[The Institute] shall have perpetual succession for the purpose of promoting archaeological studies by investigation and research in the United States and foreign countries . . . by aiding the efforts of the independent explorers, by publication of archaeological papers, and reports of the results of the expeditions. . . ."

The institute is the oldest archaeological institution in North America, whose governing board was elected in 1929 to safeguard its endowment. The AIA administrative offices are located at Boston University. The central mission of the AIA is to encourage and promote archaeological research and to increase public knowledge and awareness through the conservation, preservation, and publication of the world's patrimony for the benefit of all.

The institute remains a paradigm for combining both a professional and public focus on archaeology. Its programs and activities are designed to meet the needs and interests of its members and the public. The institute has initiated educational outreach in archaeology for schoolchildren through its Youth Education Program, which has successfully implemented programs in St. Louis, Minneapolis, Los Angeles, and Chicago. Since 1967, expert archaeologists have guided travelers around the world with the institute-sponsored tours.

The institute inaugurated its scholarly journal, the *American Journal of Archaeology (AJA),* in 1882. During World War II, the *AJA* published articles by European scholars, and the institute assisted in preparing maps of monuments it hoped would be spared from bombing raids. Published quarterly and with a circulation of four thousand, it is devoted to the archaeology and art of ancient Europe and the Mediterranean world, including the Near East and Egypt, from prehistory to late antiquity.

The institute actively promotes research and fieldwork and annually publishes the *Fieldwork Opportunities Bulletin* for students and amateurs; the publication lists opportunities and programs supplied by excavation directors and institutions. The institute's other publications include abstracts from its annual meeting (held, for ninety-three years, in conjunction with the American Philological Association) and its *Newsletter,* founded in 1989. Its annual report, the *Bulletin,* has been published since 1910. Between 1948 and 1973, the institute published thirteen monographs in the AIA Monograph Series; since 1944 it has supported the publication of the International Committee on the *Corpus Vasorum Antiquorum.*

The institute responded to the interests of nonspecialists by publishing *Archaeology* magazine (originally *Art and Archaeology*), beginning in 1914. Revitalized in 1948 (after the Depression in the 1930s), it has followed a steady rate of growth to a present-day circulation of 150,000. *Archaeology* continues to inform the public about the latest discoveries in archaeology worldwide, with richly illustrated articles written by professionals.

In 1884, the institute established local societies in Boston, New York, Baltimore, and Philadelphia; by 1890 they were joined by societies in Chicago, Detroit, Madison, and Minneapolis. Today, with 11,400 members in 87 societies, the institute is one of the largest in the world. Members of the AIA who belong to a local society enjoy lectures, field trips, tours, and museum visits, as well as serve on local committees.

The institute founded the American School of Classical Studies in Athens in 1882. In 1895 it founded what became the American Academy in Rome and in 1899–1900 was instrumental in establishing the American Schools of Oriental Research. In 1907 the institute established the School of American Archaeology in Santa Fe, New Mexico, for the study of the Native American past, and in 1921 joined with the American Anthropological Association to create the American School of Prehistoric Research, devoted to Stone Age studies.

In 1951 the institute founded the American Research Center in Egypt and in the mid-1960s supported the founding of the American Research Institute in Turkey and the American Institute of Iranian Studies. In 1974, it supported the creation of the American Institute of Nautical Archaeology.

An annual Charles Eliot Norton Memorial Lectureship was founded in 1895 for presentations by a distinguished scholar. Three additional lectureships were established in 1986: the Anna Marguerite McCann and Robert D. Taggart Lectureship in Underwater Archaeology, the Homer A. and Dorothy B. Thompson Lectureship, and the George M. A. Hanfmann Lectureship. In 1990 the President's Lectureship was inaugurated. These special lectures are supplemented by prominent scholars who share their research results with the public by delivering a total of 250 lectures annually throughout North America.

The institute offers a placement service for archaeologists and scholars in related fields as well as direct support for research and travel to five students per year; the promotion and support of graduate fellowships began in 1961 with the Olivia James Travel Fellowship, followed by the Harriet Pomerance Fellowship in 1971 and the Anna C. and Oliver C. Colburn Fellowship in 1990. In addition, the institute also awards the Helen M. Woodruff Fellowship and the Kenan T. Erim Aphrodisias Fellowship.

The institute is committed to recognizing distinguished scholars and archaeologists whose research has made an outstanding contribution to the field. To this end, the institute established the James R. Wiseman Book Award, the Gold Medal Award for Distinguished Archaeological Achievement, and the Pomerance Award for Scientific Contributions to Archaeology. In addition, foreign scholars of distinction are nominated as Foreign Honorary Members to the governing board and council.

The AIA is at the forefront in shaping such national public policy issues as artifact ownership, ethics, the environment, and the future of archaeology. In a period of unprecedented looting of archaelogical sites and dealing in stolen antiquities, the Professional Responsibilities Committee acts as the steward of the institute's mission. In 1990, the institute adopted a *Code of Ethics* now followed by many other organizations.

[*See also* American Schools of Oriental Research.]

MARTHA SHARP JOUKOWSKY

ARCHES. The arch is one of four basic structural devices for bridging architectural spaces. The other three are the corbel, post and lintel, and truss. Both corbeling and post and lintel rely exlusively on the vertical stacking of architectural members. Trussing and arching overcame this limitation. Trussing uses the principle of triangular distribution of vertical force in a horizontal direction, to enable the bridging of larger spans. Though this provided a solution for opening spaces in pedimented Greek temples and Christian and Jewish basilicas, the complex mathematics involved in truss design were not well understood until recently, and its use in antiquity remained tentative. [*See* Basilicas.] That leaves the arch, which uses the principle of the wedge to transpose vertical forces to horizontal planes. Arch construction is more cumbersome than post and lintel because it requires centering—erecting supportive filler on which to set the voussoirs until the keystone locks them in place. Nevertheless, it proved to be the most successful device of classical, Late Antique, and medieval architecture.

The basic arch is a semicircle of masonry with its center at the midpoint of the base line (see figure 1). Its component blocks are voussoirs, each of which is cut in a wedge shape, so that its joining side is aligned with the radius of the semicircle. The inner edge of a voussoir is usually dressed as an arc of the interior circle of the arch (the intrados or soffit). The upper edge, the extrados, may also receive circular dressing but may be left rough if the masonry above it is not smoothly dressed. The base stones of an arch are called springers and are sometimes set directly into a wall or onto a projecting pier. However, the transition from vertical to circular is often defined by placing the springer on an impost, a wall stone or pier cap with a molding defining the setting of the arch. The keystone is set at the top, or crown, of the arch and serves as the wedge that holds all the other voussoirs in position.

To have the components of the arch stably locked in place, it needs to be loaded, which means that the weight of the wall above firmly wedges the voussoirs into the arc of the circle. The thrust created by this weight onto the crown is deflected sideways through the lower components of the

ARCHES.   Figure 1.   *Arch for ceiling support in great room of house* 35 *at Umm el-Jimal.* (a) load; (b) keystone; (c) intrados or soffit; (d) extrados; (e) haunch; (f) springer; (g) impost; (h) voussoir. (Drawing by Tania Hobbs; courtesy B. de Vries)

arch. At the haunch, the area midway between the keystone and the springer, that thrust is directed about 45° downward and outward—namely, onto the vertical wall or pier and into the adjacent masonry. This is why an arch needs not only a strong vertical base, but also buttressing. Such buttressing may be achieved variously by thickening the wall into which it is built, having a balancing arch spring out of the opposite wall face (as in an adjacent room, or in the rows of arches in Roman raised aqueducts and the side aisle partitions of basilical churches and synagogues), or having a buttress brace the exterior wall face. In Roman commemorative arches (like that of Hadrian at Jerash in Jordan) the smaller flanking arches serve as buttresses for the huge central one. [*See* Aqueducts.]

When properly loaded, an arch is stronger than a solid wall. However, when it has lost its load, it becomes very unstable, and the voussoirs at the haunch, where the side thrust is the greatest, have a tendency to pop up and out.

The crown then flattens and becomes lower, the keystone looses its grip, and the arch collapses.

The voussoirs of fallen arches are usually readily recognizable in collapse debris. They will appear in a regular order that differs from an ordinary wall because they form a single row of equal width "headers" that are not as neatly aligned as in situ masonry. Individual pieces are readily identified because of their wedge shape and circularity on the narrow side. This is true especially of Roman arches, which tended to be of very high quality. In later construction, that of the Crusaders, for example, some arches were constructed of a combination of undressed fieldstones, chink stones, and mortar. If an arched partition was bonded into the wall from which it was sprung, collapse of the arch would result in a vertical damage line in that wall. Evidence of its use can also be surmised from the surviving piers from which an arch was sprung.

The arch's bridging function was used in various ways.

Most simply it created openings like doorways and windows. The stepped arch, a series of arches with reduced heights (as in the vomitoria of the South Theater at Jerash) can be a graceful transition from one type of space to another. Rows of arches could be used to support superstructure when solid partitions were undesirable (curtain walls of Roman theaters, Ottoman railroad bridges). [*See* Theaters.] Transverse arches set in a parallel row were used to support the flat roofs over large auditoria (like the "hall" churches in Levantine villages) or over underground cisterns (Ḥumeima, Umm el-Jimal, the Negev). [*See* Cisterns.] Continuous arches in a linear direction form vaults, and those in a circular direction, domes. Relieving arches were commonly used over lintels (the gate at Qaṣr Bshir) to discharge their thrust or in solid walls to bridge weak areas in the foundation bedrock (north wall of the Ḥesban acropolis church).

Although the circular arch was known but used only slightly in ancient Egypt, Mesopotamia, and Greece, it was basic to Etruscan design and became the basic structural component (alongside the Hellenistic post and lintel) of Roman architecture. It remained a common feature of domestic house design from the Byzantine–Umayyad to the Ayyubid–Mamluk and Late Ottoman periods in the Levant. Islamic architects pioneered major innovations in various arch shapes, among them variations on the circular arch, but especially diverse forms of the pointed arch. Though the pointed arch may predate Islam, it became a regular feature of monumental architecture sponsored by Umayyad caliphs (like the Dome of the Rock in Jerusalem, where it occurs tentatively alongside the circular arch) and was the trademark of classical Muslim design. Thus, it may be considered a major technological breakthrough of the Late Antique and Early Islamic cultural eras, contributing greatly to ease of construction, structural simplification, and elaboration of design aesthetics.

[*Many of the sites mentioned are the subject of independent entries.*]

BIBLIOGRAPHY

Adam, Jean-Pierre. *Roman Building: Materials and Techniques.* Bloomington, Ind., 1994. Chapter 6, "Arches and Vaults," gives an excellent illustrated history.
Fletcher, Banister, and John Musgrove, eds. *History of Architecture.* 19th ed. London and Boston; 1987. In a history such as this the historical uses of arches can easily be traced from the index.

BERT DE VRIES

ARCHITECTURAL DECORATION. In most regions of the Near East the local limestone is of good quality, especially on Syria's limestone massif and in Baalbek, Palmyra, Palestine, and Egypt, which allowed artisans to work in deep relief and with "light and shadow." [*See* Baalbek; Palmyra.] In the case of hard stone, such as basalt in the Golan and southern Syria and porphyry in the Sinai desert, decorative motifs were executed in bas-relief. [*See* Golan; Sinai.]

It was not until the beginning of the second century CE that the massive quarrying, working, and trading of marble and architectural elements in marble began. This became an important means for the distribution of a more or less uniform imperial art and architecture. Throughout the Roman and the Byzantine periods marble was imported into the Near East, mainly from Aphrodisias in Caria and Proconnesus in the Sea of Marmara. [*See* Aphrodisias.] Marble replaced the local limestone, enabling more impressive and finer achievements in architectural molding and sculpture.

Even before the conquest of Alexander the Great in 333–331 BCE decorations in a Greek style appeared in a funerary context on the Phoenician coast (the sarcophagi of the mourning women, of the satraps, of Alexander, and related finds in the necropolis at Sidon). [*See* Phoenicia; Sarcophagus; Necropolis; Sidon.] With the advent of the Hellenistic age, however, when a Greek regime was established in the Near East under the Ptolemies, these territories were open to the introduction and spread of Greek styles in architecture on a large scale. [*See* Ptolemies.] The styles, all of them trabeated, can be differentiated according to the shape of the base, column, capital, and entablature. Each component had a systematic set of moldings, and there was a correspondence between each molding and the motif carved on it in relief. Three were these styles, which go back to the Archaic and Classical Greek world: Doric, Ionic, and Corinthian. The last one, recognized mainly in the Corinthian capital and cornice and by the Attic base, became increasingly popular in the Hellenistic and Roman periods. Another common process in the Hellenistic period was a blend of orders: a Doric frieze above an Ionic or Corinthian capital was not unusual.

In the Hellenistic and Early Roman periods, decorated edifices were mainly temples, tombs, palaces, and the mansions of the wealthy: the rock-carved facades in Petra and Jerusalem, the painted tombs of Alexandria and Marisa/Mareshah, the palaces of the Hasmoneans and Herod. [*See* Tombs; Palace; Petra; Jerusalem; Mareshah; Hasmoneans.] Local traditions and Oriental influences—Egyptian, Syro-Palestinian, Mesopotamian, and Iranian—were always at work, forming undercurrents that emerged periodically in one region or another. They more and more took the lead in the Byzantine period, establishing the Coptic style in Egypt and the Greco-Syrian style. The religio-nationalistic response of the Jews and the Nabateans to foreign influences and their rejection of figurative art resulted in the emergence of two indigenous decorative approaches (Avi-Yonah, 1961; Hachlili, 1988; Patrich, 1990). [*See* Nabateans.] Everywhere in the region the city was more hellenized and romanized than the countryside.

During the Antonine and Severan periods (second and third centuries), with the large-scale spread of Roman urbanization in the Near East, stone-molded architectural decorations in the Greco-Roman spirit were found in all the cities. The main thoroughfares in a typical Roman city were colonnaded streets (cf. Gerasa/Jerash, Scythopolis/Beth-Shean, Apamea, Palmyra). [See Jerash; Beth-Shean; Apamea.] Fora and other public piazzas at the intersections of streets were surrounded by colonnades and adorned with tetrapyla (Gerasa, Bosra), *tetrakionia* (four columns on a common pedestal; Gerasa, Palmyra, Antinoe), "triumphal" arches with single or triple openings (Palmyra, Scythopolis, Jerusalem, Petra), memorial columns (Jerusalem), or pedestals with statues. Even city gates, incorporated in sober wall lines, were made to resemble triumphal arches. The steady visual rhythm of the street columns was broken by facades of a larger order of magnitude: the huge propylaea of temples, thermae, basilicae, and other public buildings. [See Basilicas.] The emphasis was on the exterior, on the facades. The *scena frons*, an inner wall in the Roman theater, inspired the decorations of the public nymphea: a decorative wall of two or three stories, adorned with niches holding statues and with an apse (Philadelphia/Amman, Gerasa, Bosra, Scythopolis, Petra). [See Theaters; Amman; Bosra.] This baroque system of niches arranged in several stories, inspired by Hellenistic Alexandria (see below), was carried even to the interior and exterior of temples (cf. the Temple of Bacchus in Baalbek, the Temple of Zeus in Gerasa). The inner courts of temples and the palaestra of thermae, gymnasia, and stadia were surrounded by a stoa with one or two rows of columns and by exedrae.

The first marble capitals appeared in the Near East in the late first or early second century CE. Later, during the second and early third centuries, Corinthian marble capitals of the "normal" type became widespread throughout the Mediterranean, forming an important common feature of imperial art and reflecting a renaissance of the Greek art. Above the two regular rows of acanthus leaves on the "normal" Corinthian capital are corner volutes and inner helices springing from an acanthus calyx, set on top of a fluted sheath known as a caulicole. The abacus is decorated with a central fleuron. Corinthian "normal" capitals (either in marble or in local stone) have been found throughout the Near East: at Gerasa, Bosra, Palmyra, Caesarea, Beth-Shean, and in Egypt (Fischer, 1990; Kautzsch, 1936; Pensabene, 1993). [See Caesarea.] Subtypes of marble capitals are defined based on the extent to which the leaves of the lower row remain independent, approach, or touch each other in a geometric pattern of rhomboids and oblongs—contributing to the light-and-shadow effect. With the increased touching zone between the leaves of the lower row, the calathus became covered, more and more, by a net of geometric patterns, causing the capital to lose its plasticity; the way was thus prepared to the schematically decorated Byzantine capital (see below).

Important production centers for marble were the workshops at Ephesus, Pergamon (active since Hellenistic times), and Aphrodisias; the latter was a new, and the most active, center in the Roman empire. [See Ephesus; Pergamon.] Their products were exported and served as models for local workshops in the Near Eastern provinces, where the details were then worked out on blocks of imported marble or imitated in local limestones. The crisis of the third century brought about a decline in marble architecture everywhere and a revival of local traditions expressed in local stone.

In the cities of the Byzantine period, architectural members were commonly taken from Roman structures and re-used. Churches were the primary new addition to the urban landscape. As assembly halls, there is a clear tendency in their architecture to adorn the interior at the expense of the exterior. [See Churches.] Instead of decorated, stone-molded facades, the emphasis was placed on floor and wall mosaics, capitals in the colonnades or arcades of the basilicae, the triumphal arch, and the string course. [See Mosaics.] The liturgical furniture (e.g., the altar and its cyborium, the ambo, and the chancel screen) also received attention from artists and sculptors. Marble was the preferred material for these furnishings as well as for the plates used for wall revetment and paving. Yet, on Syria's limestone massif architectural stone molding continued, reaching a floruit in monuments such as Qal'at Sim'an and the church at Qalb Louzeh (Strube, 1977; 1993). [See Qal'at Sim'an.] The notion of an architectural order in its Greco-Roman sense was lost, however, and decoration was adapted to new architectural forms. On the exterior the emphasis was on the frames of doors and windows, rather than on the lintel alone. Cornices reappeared under roofs, and moldings underlined the stories on the facade and surrounded buildings. External apses were decorated on their exterior by attached columns, as at Qal'at Sim'an and associated churches, such as at Turin and Fasuq on Jebel Wastani (Biscop and Sodini, 1984). A Greco-Syrian style developed and became established in which human and animal figures are almost entirely absent and whose vegetal motifs are never naturalistic. The acanthus in particular became just a decorative motif.

In the Near East in the Byzantine period, the Corinthian capital appeared in a rich variety of types and subtypes (Kautzsch, 1936; Pensabene, 1993, pp. 157–177). The components of the upper zone (six helices and volutes) are reduced in size or disappear, at the expense of the acanthus leaves. The leaves are variegated in treatment and shape. The fine dressing, done with a drill, of the so-called Theodosian capital is especially delicate. Tilted, or "windblown" leaves, first seen in the Severan period, reappeared. The bi-zone capital had variants, including wild beasts in the upper zone and a tendril or a basket in the lower zone. The Ionic capital with a springstone (an impost block) attached at the top became one unit—the Ionic impost capital. Its lower, Ionic member was greatly simplified and gradually reduced in size until it disappeared entirely. The impost became a capital on its own, in either a trapezoidal or folded form, whose surface was covered with rich foliage, finely cut with a drill, or with ribbons arranged in a zigzag pattern.

Egypt. Alexandria and a few other urban centers were more receptive to Greek culture than the vast rural zone along the Nile River and in the Delta, where the pharaonic tradition had been preserved for centuries. [See Alexandria; Delta.] A final blending of traditions is reflected in the Coptic art and architecture of the Christian Byzantine period.

Ptolemaic Alexandria became a leading Hellenistic center of architectural decoration and painting. [See Wall Paintings.] Although the remains are very fragmentary and scattered, their features have been defined as baroque: they broke away from a post-and-lintel system, demonstrating a nontectonic use of structural members (Adriani, 1966; Breccia, 1926; McKenzie, 1990; Pensabene, 1993). Alexandria's Hellenistic architectural finds are mainly from its various necropoleis (Shatby, Mustafa Pasha, the Alabaster Tomb, Sidi Gaber, Minet el-Bassal, Mafrousa, Gabbari, Anfoushy, Ras el-Tine, Antonides Garden, Suq el-Wardian, Kom el-Shoqafa, Hadra) and from Tuna el-Gebel (the necropolis of Hermopolis Magna), and from temple remains (mainly the Serapea at Alexandria and Canopus, the Ptolemaic-cult sanctuary of Hermopolis Magna, and the Serapeum[?] there). [See Cult.] Many architectural fragments are preserved in the Greco-Roman Museum in Alexandria. Two other important sources of data are Kallixeinos's description of the pavilion of Ptolemy II, raised in Alexandria between 274 and 270 BCE to house a symposium held in connection with a great religious procession in honor of Dionysus (Athenaeus 5.196–197), and Athenaeus's description of the palatial Nile barge (Gk., *thalamegos*) of Ptolemy IV (Athenaeus 5.203–206).

All three Greek orders were represented in Hellenistic Egypt (Pensabene, 1993). The Ionic-Corinthian cornice, with modillions under the corona, appeared with both Doric and Ionic trabeation. The Alexandrian examples of a "free" (heterodox) Corinthian capital differed from the "Hellenistic" type found in Asia Minor (inspired by the capital of the tholos at Epidauros) and the "normal" type found in Italy. The last type did not appear in Alexandria until the second century CE. Most capitals were heterodox; "normal" capitals were very rare; and a mixed Greco-Egyptian group introduced lotus flowers, palmettes, and papyrus buds over the calathos. Sometimes the leaves were left plain, *en bosse*. Greek and Asiatic type marble capitals were imported only during the Roman period. The style of most bases was simple Attic. Bases on a square or an octagonal pedestal appeared only in the Roman period.

The structural features of baroque architecture recognized in Alexandria, all appearing before 100 BCE, include segmented, hollow, and broken pediments; the so-called Syrian pediment; entablatures broken forward, arched or curved vertically, or horizontal and curved inward; projected pedestals; engaged columns, pilasters, and quarter columns; coupled quarter columns; *tholoi*; and apsidal niches decorated with shells or coffering (McKenzie, 1990). Sculpted conchs were popular in Egypt down to the Byzantine period (Kitzinger, 1937; Török, 1990).

There were Hellenistic decorative elements other than the Corinthian capital: architraves of two fasciae and of even one fascia (unlike the three fasciae of later Roman architecture); new types of cornices with dentils or with flat modillions (without the consoles of Roman architecture); acanthus column bases (an example from the Roman period is preserved in the tetrapylon of Alexander Severus at Antinoe); floral or animal acroteria that slope to the side, unlike the vertically positioned Greek and Roman acroteria.

Most of the Ptolemaic features and elements mentioned above were carried into the first, second, and early third centuries, under the Romans, even beyond Egypt. They shaped Roman baroque architecture, like that seen at Baalbek (Lyttelton, 1974). Besides canonical entablature—composed of architrave, frieze, and cornice variants existed without an architrave or without a frieze especially in the Roman baroque. Hellenistic painting was influenced by the Alexandrian style (Brown, 1957).

Some surviving Hellenistic and Roman temples in Upper Egypt were constructed according to ancient pharaonic tradition (e.g., Dendera, Edfu, Kom Ombo, Philae), evidently a living practice. The influence of this indigenous architecture is also expressed in some types of bell-shaped capitals decorated with lotus flowers or papyrus buds, papyrus bases, and in the so-called Egyptian cornice (a cavetto cornice above a torus), prevalent also in the "Oriental" facade types at Petra, in some of the monumental tombs in Jerusalem (Tomb of Zechariah, Absalom's Tomb), and in some Late Persian and Early Hellenistic structures in Phoenicia. The pyramid, found in some monumental tombs in Jerusalem and in 'Amrit (Phoenicia), is another motif derived from ancient Egyptian architecture. [See 'Amrit.]

Israel and Jordan. The palace known as Qasr el-'Abd at 'Iraq el-Amir demonstrates a blend of Greek elements that are decisively Alexandrian in origin and Oriental elements of Mesopotamian or Iranian origin: a Greek interpretation of a monument in the Oriental tradition. Although unfinished, it is a well-preserved example of Hellenistic architecture in the Syro-Palestinian regime in the early second century BCE (Dentzer-Feydy, 1991). More than ten architectural orders have been counted, of different types and sizes, superimposed or set one next to the other. Yet, the decoration exhibits a homogenous character. The orders are composed of freestanding columns as well as quarter, half, and three-quarter engaged columns and engaged pilasters. The half columns may be engaged to a portal frame, window jamb, or wall face. There is a single model, in several variations, of the Corinthian capital and a single model of the Ionian capital. The Corinthian capitals are "free" (heterodox), related to the Alexandrian Corinthian capital. Pilasters had capitals of their own, with Attic bases; the columns of the upper loggia had an acanthus base. There is a single model of Doric entablement and one of Ionic entablement. The Ionic one appears, as is normal, on top of a Corinthian column, while the Doric example exhibits a blend of orders common to the Hellenistic period and is placed on top of Corinthian as well as Ionic capitals. The inner walls had crown moldings. Figural motifs—of panthers, lions, and eagles—are superimposed on the architectural orders, as decorative accents, at the corners of the building and its fountains. Fragments of stucco work were found in the building as well.

The influence of Alexandrian architecture on the layout and decorations of the principal monuments at Petra, in Jordan, can be seen in the temples—the Qaṣr Bint Faraun and the Temple of the Winged Lions (McKenzie, 1990) and in the more recently excavated Southern Temple. Some of Petra's monumental tomb facades reflect a decisive Greco-Roman architectural influence. However, most of them are Oriental in style, crowned by one or two rows of crenellations (crowsteps) or by two sets of five corner steps that face each other. The crenellations, or merlons, are an Oriental motif of Assyrian origin, popular in Phoenicia in the Late Persian and Early Hellenistic periods, that survived in interior Syria up to the Roman period (cf. the square altars on Mt. Lebanon; the Temple of Bel in Palmyra; the peribolos of the great temple in Damascus; and the temple at Dmeir, in southern Syria). [See Assyrians; Altars; Damascus.]

The Nabatean plain-faced, blocked-out capital is derived from the Nabatean Corinthian capital—a heterodox floral capital (Patrich, 1984). Stucco work and frescoes of the First and Second Pompeiian styles decorated Petra's temples and houses (Kohl, 1910; Zayadine, 1987).

The art of decorative stucco work is of Iranian-Central Asian origin; it spread to the west and became popular there in the Hellenistic period. The stucco work on a mansion at Tel Anafa in Israel demonstrates the Late Hellenistic achievements in this domain in Syria-Palestine under the Seleucids (Gordon, 1977). Stucco fragments of a large, engaged Corinthian order and of an attic zone have been retrieved. The main order includes pieces of white fluted shafts, smooth red shafts, bases, capitals, and fragments of such entablature members as dentils, cornice, and cyma. The components of the attic zone include fragments of pilasters, colonnettes, small capitals, and a lozenge pattern. A limestone capital was found as well. Four variants of the Corinthian capital are of Syrian rather than Alexandrian Hellenistic stock, while the lozenges reflect an Egyptian influence. The Hellenistic masonry style of the stucco work reflected in the Tel Anafa finds survived on Masada in a better state of preservation (Foerster, 1995). [See Anafa, Tel; Masada.]

The masonry style (sometimes referred to as incrustation, or structural style) is characterized by its use of stucco as a medium for stimulating ashlars and other architectural elements by molding them in relief. A wall was divided into five horizontal zones: plinth (about 20–30 cm high); drafted orthostats (about 1 m high); frieze (string course); isodomic courses of drafted rectangular blocks—the largest portion of the wall; and a top zone, or wall crown. Generally, this stucco work was subsequently covered with polychrome paint, but at Masada, Herodium, and in a large mansion excavated in the Jewish Quarter in Jerusalem (decorated in the First Pompeiian style, closely related to, although different from, the masonry style), the wall, including the orthostats, was painted white. [See Heroduim.] Painted surfaces, or frescoes, on flat, nonstuccoed walls have also been found on Masada, however, as well as in other Herodian palaces (Herodium, Jericho), sometimes in conjunction with engaged columns, or pilasters, and at Tel Anafa. [See Jericho.] Actually, the Northern Palace on Masada is considered to be an example of built architecture that inspired the Second Pompeiian style in painting. Its relationship to Alexandrian palace architecture, on the one hand, and to Augustan architecture in Rome, on the other, has been noted (Foerster, 1995). It may have been introduced into Judea (Judah) under the influence (if not by the very hands) of an Augustan Roman imperial workshop (Foerster, 1995). In addition to these survivals of the Hellenistic masonry style, the Second Pompeiian style in wall painting (fresco) is represented at the above-mentioned Judean sites as well, where fragments of ceiling stucco have been recovered.

The Masada columns are built of separate drums, covered by a thick layer of stucco in a fluted pattern. Columns in other Herodian palaces were constructed similarly. It has also been suggested that the entablature was partially made of wood and then stuccoed. The floors were of plaster, mosaic, or opus sectile (colored stone tiles). Opus sectile floors have also been found at Jericho, Cypros, Herodium, and in the Herodian quarter in Jerusalem. The orchestra floor of the Herodian theater at Caesarca was of painted plaster, depicting various geometric patterns.

The Herodian Temple Mount in Jerusalem is the most prestigious Herodian project of monumental architecture. The reliefs on the shallow domes of the Hulda Gates, depicting a network of geometric and vegetal patterns, are exceptionally elegant.

The "normal" types of Corinthian capital, introduced by Herod under Roman influence, replaced the heterodox capitals that predominated in the Hellenistic period. The Herodian Corinthian capital is built of two blocks, like the Augustan one seen in Rome (Fischer, 1990, pp. 12–20). The contemporary Nabatean floral capital is similarly built of two blocks, but it shows affinities derived from Alexandria (Patrich, 1984). At times, Hellenistic and Early Roman Corinthian capitals were plastered with a thin layer of stucco and then painted (e.g., at Tel Anafa, Masada, Cypros, Alexandria, Edfu). At Masada the colors used were white and purple, in addition to gilding. A peculiar feature of the Herodium capitals is a central leaf below the calyx that is worked as a detail *en bosse*. "Normal" Corinthian capitals, with plain, *en bosse* leaves, were common in Jerusalem in the first century CE (e.g., on the Mount Temple, in the Jewish Quarter, in the Tombs of the Kings). The blocked-out Corinthian capitals found on Masada are derived from the Herodian Corinthian capital, which was a "normal" type. Plain-faced or blocked-out capitals have also been found on Cyprus and in Egypt.

Jewish art in the post-70 CE period is expressed mainly in funerary architecture (e.g., in the necropolis at Beth-She'arim) and in synagogues. [*See* Beth-She'arim; Synagogues.] It was influenced to a large extent by that of non-Jewish society: in the pagan Late Roman period it is extroverted and stone carved (Foerster, 1987); in the Christian Byzantine period it is introverted, appearing as floor and wall mosaics and wall paintings (Tsafrir, 1987). Components that were decorated were facades, portals, and windows; capitals and entablature; the Torah ark; floors (mosaics); and walls (frescoes). Three types of ornate portals, or entrance frames (Ionic, with moldings parallel to the opening frame and with two consols flanking the lintel; Attic, with lintel moldings wider than the opening; and a lintel supported by pilasters), and nine types of ornamental lintels have been documented (Hachlili, 1988). The Corinthian capital, of local manufacture, was the most prevalent type. Jewish motifs—mainly the menorah and other liturgical objects—may adorn one of its faces. Heart-shaped columns were crowned by heart-shaped capitals. The best-known synagogue paintings are the third-century frescoes at Dura-Europos in Syria. [*See* Dura-Europos.] Fragmentary frescoes and drawings of lesser quality have also been found in some Galilean synagogues (e.g., at Reḥov, Ḥusifah, Ma'oz Ḥayyim, Hammath Tiberias, Beth Alpha). [*See* Hammath Tiberias; Beth Alpha.]

Syria. In geographic and cultural terms, Syria encompasses three different regions: the Phoenician coast; the interior, or central, region, including the Biqa'; and the Mesopotamian region, a transition zone between the western regions and Iran and Central Asia.

Excellent surveys have been made of decorative art throughout Syria in the Hellenistic and Roman periods (Dentzer-Feydy, 1989) and for the Byzantine period (Naccache and Sodini, 1989). What is known about the Seleucid period and the art of Antioch and of Seleucia on the Tigris is meager because their Hellenistic infrastructure has entirely disappeared—perhaps having been replaced by Roman imperial structures (as in Damascus and Apamea). [*See* Seleucids; Antioch on Orontes; Seleucia on the Tigris; Damascus.] The process by which Syrian decorative art developed can be traced for the periods following Pompey's establishment of the Roman province of Syria. However, it is only from the Flavian period onward that it shows signs of homogeneity and a coherent evolution, both chronological and regional. Architectural decoration at Baalbek and Palmyra is provincial; it demonstrates a virtuous and profuse combination of the Greco-Roman decorative grammar in use in the eastern Mediterranean basin: a fondness for geometric and vegetal surfaces or band covering, filled with figures, fruits, and flowers and arranged in endless patterning.

In addition to the three classical orders, a Tuscan order, with a particular capital type, was recognized. This form of capital often has a sharp-pointed leaf beneath each angle of the abacus and the astragal at the neck is often omitted.

Hellenistic period. Remains from the Hellenistic period in Syria are preserved mainly in the Mesopotamian zone—at Dura-Europos (lintels, moldings; Shoe, 1948) and Seleucia on the Tigris—and in the Phoenician zone. In Seleucia, where good building stone is rare, Seleucid decorative architecture in terra cotta (common in the Greek world since Archaic times), was replaced under the Parthians by molded stucco, which was popular in Central Asia. The recognized motifs are western (e.g., palmettes, acanthus leaves), eastern (geometric surfaces), and hybrid (heterodox capitals with human heads and busts).

Hellenistic remains in Phoenicia are few and diverse, reflecting a composite character of foreign origins. The use of crenellations, or stepcrow, to crown the Ma'abed at 'Amrit, the square altars on Mt. Lebanon, the Temple of Bel at Palmyra, and the Temple of Dmeir in southern Syria is Mesopotamian in origin and survived into the Roman period. An Egyptian influence on the Ma'abed can be seen in its cornice, while its dentils reflect a Greek influence. One of the aedicules at 'Ain al-Hayat has a uraeus frieze. An "Egyptian cornice" is found in the third-century BCE sanctuary at Umm el-'Amad, along with hellenized elements—Doric capitals, members of an Ionic order (including capitals with a collar decorated with palmettes that seem to be inspired by the ones on the northern portico of the Erechtheion in Athens), and an Ionic cornice resembling one at 'Iraq el-Amir.

Roman period (first–third centuries). Archaic decorated blocks found at Palmyra belong to the frames of niches in the Temples of Bel and of Ba'al Shamin. The blocks are covered with vegetal decorations arranged in bands of endless, repetitive patterns, a style derived from Iran and Central Asia (Seyrig, 1934; 1940). Most popular is a sinusoidal vine tendril with individual leaves, tiny vine bunches, and various interlacings and bundles of leaves; the upper bands contain figural reliefs. Hellenized motifs were apparently less popular—they are distorted and set on improper moldings. The Corinthian heterodox capitals at Palmyra, which lack helices also belong to this Archaic Palmyrene style (Schlumberger, 1933). The basalt heterodox capitals of the Hauran (e.g., at Si, Qanawat, and Suweida) have busts above the acanthus leaves, and the structure and motifs of the door frames recall the Archaic Palmyrene style (Dentzer-Feydy, 1985; 1990; 1992). The column bases in the Ba'al Shamin temple at Si have a corona of acanthus leaves.

The architectural decorations in the Temple of Bel at Palmyra (erected under Tiberius between 19 and 32 CE) were cut in the local limestone. The temple is considered to reflect the magnificence of Seleucid architecture at Antioch (Will, 1975). The homogeneous and coherent Palmyrene style is distinguished in the Temple of Bel by a variety and abundance of decoration. Its motifs belong to the central Syrian tradition revealed in Archaic Palmyrene sculpture: rich geometric, vegetal, and figurative decorations, arranged in bands or as surface cover—as in the ceiling coffers of the peristyle, displaying an "endless pattern." These local motifs are a blend of elements and motifs from the classical repertoire. The decorative elements include Corinthian and Ionic capitals and fluted shafts, walls with an Attic base; three plain fasciae on the architrave, whose frieze is decorated with garlands held by putti; and a Corinthian cornice. The motifs include egg and tongue, Lesbian cymation, interlaces, bead and reel, dentils, modillions, rosettes, palmettes, laurel bunches, stems with leaves, bands of dressed leaves, and of floral scrolls (mainly acanthus, but vine and ivy as well). There are also indications of paintings and of metal decoration, including bronze capitals.

Baalbek/Heliopolis became a Roman colony in about 15 BCE under Augustus, thus opening it to direct influences from Rome. The temples of Baalbek represent the grandeur of Roman architecture in Syria. The Corinthian columns of the great Temple of Jupiter (first century CE) are monolithic and its Corinthian entablature is densely covered with uniform vegetal decoration: beads and reels on the architrave, palmettes on its crowning cavetto, a frieze with consoles and animal protomes, and a cornice extravagantly covered with ornamentation. A close look at its capitals, niches, and other decorative elements (Weigand, 1914, 1924; Schlumberger, 1933; Lyttelton, 1974) reveals a coexistence of western and eastern Syrian types: only some of its "normal" Corinthian capitals are derived from Rome; the others display affinities typical of the Oriental production seen at other sites in Syria and Asia Minor during the empire—affinities that seem, rather, to be derived from Late Hellenistic examples. Similarly, in the Temple of Bacchus at Baalbek (second century), several models of capital can be recognized: a Roman, pre-Flavian model, some of the Epheso-Pergamene school, and others in the Palmyrene style. A motif derived directly from Rome is the shell or conch shape that adorns the temple's semicircular niches. In the forecourt the shell is placed with its base upward (in the Roman style), while at other Syrian sites it is generally found with the base at the bottom. Examples of Roman types at Baalbek were isolated and do not appear to constitute a factor dictating the Syrian decorative style under the empire (Dentzer-Feydy, 1989). The coexistence of three decorative styles can also be seen in the ceiling coffers of the great altar at Baalbek (Collart and Coupel, 1951).

The Baalbek style is reflected at temples in the Biqaʿ, on Mt. Lebanon, in the Anti-Lebanon range (Niha, Hosn Niha, Hosn Soleiman), and in southern Syria (Sleim). Ionic capitals, "peopled" or vacant acanthus scrolls, and other standard motifs of imperial decorative art in Syria (including the "Syrian gable"), also demonstrate similarities with motifs and types from Asia Minor rather than with those from Rome (Dentzer-Feydy, 1989, pp. 467–470; Lyttelton, 1974).

The traits of the Antonine and Severan periods that are peculiar to Syria include the meander motif placed in unusual locations, such as on the fasciae of the architraves; the vine motif that, in the second century, continued to cover—as a single or double tendril—portal frames, friezes, and pilasters; the excessive density of sculptured decorations framing the niches and portals of cult edifices; figural reliefs on the soffits or on the vertical surface of lintels; and ceiling coffers decorated with busts set in an intricate geometric pattern. This common cultural stock of interior Syria was already encountered at the beginning of the imperial period but may have much older origins.

In southern Syria, second-century portal lintels retained their figural decoration, which in the north had moved to the soffits, in order not to distort the Greco-Roman architectural order. The third century is represented mainly by the imperial building activity at Shahba-Philippopolis and adjacent sites. The simplification of decorative forms and a departure from the imperial models that were used in the other regions are evident. Ionic capitals with local traits became more popular, and there was a resurgence of local art in a domestic context.

Byzantine period. The cross, in a rich variety of forms, became a dominant motif in the Byzantine period. Otherwise, the decorative grammar and scheme were derived from the classical repertoire of the Roman period, combined with indigenous originality. In the basaltic region, sculpture underwent a process of schematization and simplification, while the local Syrian, Oriental decorative art in limestone flourished. Ecclesiastical decorative art affected domestic embellishment (doors, windows, porticoes), resulting in regional architectural homogeneity for the limestone massif, in which two local schools are recognized: the Antiochene in the north and the Apamene in the south. In porticoes, for example, a square monolithic pier was commonly used in the north, where a column would be employed in the south.

Two architects—Julianus and Markianos Kyris—were active in about 390 in Brad and at Jebel Simʿan and Jebel Barisha. They influenced the Syrian decorative art of later generations, creating new types of capitals decorated with ribbons or divided into two zones. Markianos Kyris built four churches in about thirty years (c. 390–420) and introduced new plans and decoration. He revived the Palmyrene Archaic architectural decoration after 450 years.

The imperial architectural project of Qalʿat Simʿan was also very influential in the development of Syrian decorative art in the sixth century. It is rich with moldings and motifs, including new forms of the acanthus leaf and a windblown Corinthian capital, which reappeared two hundred years after it first emerged in Severan art. Among its most distinguished representatives are the basilica at Qalb Louzeh, and the capitals at Qaṣr Ibn Wardan (Strube, 1983).

Altogether, there is a large variety of Corinthian and Syrian Byzantine capitals. The Byzantine Corinthian capital is bell shaped, but shorter than the "normal" type. At times the volutes are omitted; in others, deeply carved, flowing leaves are twisted into a whorl. The most usual form is the uncut Corinthian, in which the leaves are only blocked out. This form continued to be used in sixth-century churches and was the most common form found in small churches of late date in the region.

The most popular form of molding was the cyma recta, with a fillet above and below. It was used for the cornices of all kinds of buildings throughout the period. The cyma reversa is rarely found in Syria and then only in the early dates. The moldings of doorways have a classic profile consisting of two or three narrow fasciae, an ovolo, a cyma recta, and a flat band; the position of the ovolo and the cyma is frequently reversed. The architraves were often perfectly plain and composed of two or three fasciae. Broad moldings carried vegetal bands and disks and narrow moldings were also often carved in patterns. Pulvinated friezes were usually ornamented with elaborate rinceaux of highly conventional and geometric acanthus leaves, interspersed with symbolic disks. The dated monuments of the fifth century nearly all have the same profile in their main cornices: a cyma recta with a beveled fillet at the top; dated buildings of the sixth century have a more S-shaped profile in the cymatium. Below this there are one, two, or even three narrow bands, a form also used in the string courses. After reaching an apogee in decoration under Justinian, further geometrization and a lessening use of moldings and motives are seen.

In many cases where an opening was rectangular, the moldings describe a semicircle on the lintel above it, giving the effect of a round-headed window. In Antiochene the window moldings were curved upward and carried over the next opening, presenting a wavy succession of curves, instead of being returned at a right angle on the string course at the sill level. These curved moldings were often terminated on either side of a window or at the end of a row of windows by two volutes.

[See also Arches; Architectural Drafting and Drawing; Architectural Orders; Building Materials and Techniques; Public Buildings; and Temples.]

BIBLIOGRAPHY

Egypt

Adriani, Achille. *Repertorio d'arte dell'Egitto greco-romano*. Series C, vols. 1–2. Palermo, 1966.

Badawy, Alexander. *Coptic Art and Archaeology: The Art of the Christian Egyptians from the Late Antique to the Middle Ages*. Cambridge, Mass., 1978.

Bernand, André. "Un inventaire des monuments d'Alexandrie gréco-romaine." *Revue des Études Grecques* 85 (1972): 139–154.

Breccia, Evaristo. *Monuments de l'Égypte gréco-romaine*, vol. 1, *Le rovine e i monumenti di Canopo*. Bergamo, 1926.

Brown, Blanche R. *Ptolemaic Paintings and Mosaics and the Alexandrian Style*. Cambridge, Mass., 1957.

Crema, Luigi. "La formazione del 'Frontone siriaco.' " In *Scritti di storia dell'arte in onore di Mario Salmi*, vol. 1, edited by Valentino Martinelli, pp. 1–13. Rome, 1961.

Duthuit, Georges. *La sculpture Copte*. Paris, 1931.

Effenberger, Arne. *Koptische Kunst*. Vienna, 1975.

Fakharani, Fawzi el-. "Semi-Dome Decoration in Greco-Roman Egypt." *American Journal of Archaeology* 69 (1965): 57–62.

Grimm, Günter, et al. *Das römisch-byzantinische Ägypten*. Aegyptiaca Treverensia, 2. Mainz, 1983.

Hesberg, Henner von. "Zur Entwicklung der griechischen Architektur im ptolemäischen Reich." In *Das ptolemäische Ägypten: Akten des internationalen Symposions, 27.–29. Sept. 1976 in Berlin*, edited by Herwig Maehler and Volker M. Strocka, pp. 137–145. Mainz am Rhein, 1978.

Kautzsch, Rudolf. *Kapitellstudien: Beiträge zu einer Geschichte des spätantiken kapitells im Osten vom 4. bis ins 7. Jahrhundert*. Berlin, 1936.

Kitzinger, Ernst. "Notes on Early Coptic Sculpture." *Archaeologia* 87 (1937): 181–215.

Lyttelton, Margaret. *Baroque Architecture in Classical Antiquity*. London, 1974.

Makowiecka, Elzbieta. "Acanthus-Base: Alexandrian Form of Architectural Decoration at Ptolemaic and Roman Period." *Études et Travaux* 3 (1969): 115–131.

Michalowski, Kazmierz. *The Art of Ancient Egypt*. London, 1969.

Noshy, Ibrahim. *The Arts in Ptolemaic Egypt*. London, 1937.

Pensabene, Patrizio. *Elementi architettonici di Alessandria e di altri siti egiziani*. Repertorio d'Arte dell'Egitto Greco-Romano, ser. C, vol. 3. Rome, 1993.

Ronczewski, Konstantin. "Les chapiteaux corinthiens et variés du Musée Gréco-Romain d'Alexandrie." *Acta Universitatis Latviensis* 16 (1927): 3–32.

Schmidt-Colinet, Andreas. "Der Ptolemäische Eckgiebel: Ursprung und Wirkung eines Architekturmotivs." In *Arabia Antiqua: Hellenistic Centers around Arabia*, edited by Antonio Invernizzi and Jean-François Salles, pp. 1–14. Rome, 1993.

Török, László. "Notes on the Chronology of Late Antique Stone Sculpture in Egypt." In *Coptic Studies: Acts of the Third International Congress of Coptic Studies, Warsaw, 20–25 August 1984*, edited by Wlodzimierz Godlewski, pp. 437–484. Warsaw, 1990.

Wace, A. J. B., et al. *Hermopolis Magna, Ashmunein: The Ptolemaic Sanctuary and the Basilica*. Alexandria, 1959.

Israel and Jordan

Avigad, Nahman. "The Rock-Carved Facades of the Jerusalem Necropolis." *Israel Exploration Journal* 1 (1950–1951): 96–106.

Avigad, Nahman. *Discovering Jerusalem*. Nashville, 1980.

Avi-Yonah, Michael. *Oriental Art in Roman Palestine*. Rome, 1961.

Avi-Yonah, Michael. *Art in Ancient Palestine: Selected Studies*. Jerusalem, 1981.

Crowfoot, J. W. *Early Churches in Palestine*. London, 1941. See pages 146–156.

Dentzer-Feydy, Jacqueline. "Les linteaux à figures divines en Syrie méridionale." *Revue Archéologique* 1 (1992): 65–102.

Fischer, Moshe L. *Das korinthische Kapitell im Alten Israel in der hellenistischen und römischen Periode*. Mainz am Rhein, 1990.

Fischer, Moshe L. "Figural Capitals in Roman Palestine, Marble Imports and Local Stones: Some Aspects of 'Imperial' and 'Provincial' Art." *Archäologischer Anzeiger* (1991): 119–144.

Foerster, Gideon. "Architectural Fragments from Jason's Tomb Reconsidered." *Israel Exploration Journal* 28 (1978): 152–156.

Foerster, Gideon. "The Art and Architecture of the Synagogue in Its

Late Roman Setting." In *The Synagogue in Late Antiquity*, edited by Lee I. Levine, pp. 139–146. Philadelphia, 1987.

Foerster, Gideon. *Masada V: The Yigael Yadin Excavations, 1963–1965, Final Reports: Art and Architecture*. Jerusalem, 1995.

Gordon, Robert L. "Late Hellenistic Wall Decoration of Tel Anafa." Ph.D. diss., Columbia University, 1977.

Hachlili, Rachel. *Ancient Jewish Art and Archaeology in the Land of Israel*. Leiden, 1988.

Ismail, Z. "Les chapiteaux de Pétra." *Le Monde de la Bible* 14 (1980): 27–29.

Kohl, Heinrich. *Kasr Firaun in Petra*. Leipzig, 1910.

Ma'oz, Zvi. "The Art and Architecture of the Synagogues of the Golan." In *Ancient Synagogues Revealed*, edited by Lee I. Levine, pp. 98–115. Jerusalem, 1981.

McKenzie, Judith. *The Architecture of Petra*. British Academy Monographs in Archaeology, 1. London, 1990.

Negev, Avraham. "Nabatean Capitals in the Towns of the Negev." *Israel Exploration Journal* 24 (1974): 153–159.

Ovadiah, Asher, and Yehudit Turnheim. *"Peopled" Scrolls in Roman Architectural Decoration in Israel*. Rivista di Archeologia, Supplementi 12. Rome, 1994.

Patrich, Joseph. "The Development of the Nabatean Capital" (in Hebrew). *Eretz-Israel* 17 (1984): 291–304.

Patrich, Joseph. *The Formation of Nabatean Art*. Leiden, 1990.

Peters, John P., and Hermann Thiersch. *Painted Tombs in the Necropolis of Marissa*. London, 1905.

Ronczewski, Konstantin. "Kapitelle des El Hazne in Petra." *Archäologischer Anzeiger* (1932): 37–90.

Schmidt-Colinet, Andreas. "Dorisierende nabatäische Kapitelle." *Damaszener Mitteilungen* 1 (1983): 307–312.

Tsafrir, Yoram. "The Byzantine Setting and Its Influence on Ancient Synagogues." In *The Synagogue in Late Antiquity*, edited by Lee I. Levine, pp. 147–157. Philadelphia, 1987.

Turnheim, Yehudit. "Architectural Decoration in Northern Eretz-Israel in the Roman and Byzantine Periods" (in Hebrew). Ph.D. diss., Tel Aviv University, 1987.

Turnheim, Yehudit. "The Corinthian Cornice in Northern Eretz-Israel in the Roman and Byzantine Periods." In *Homenaje a José María Blázquez*, edited by Julio Mangas and Jamie Alvar. Madrid, 1993–.

Watzinger, Carl. *Denkmäler Palästinas*. Vol. 2. Leipzig, 1935.

Weigand, Edmund. "Das Theodosiuskloster: Zur kunstgeschichtlichen Stellung Palästinas vom 4.–7. Jahrhundert." *Byzantinische Zeitschrift* 23 (1914): 167–216.

Zayadine, Fawzi. "Decorative Stucco at Petra and Other Hellenistic Sites." In *Studies in the History and Archaeology of Jordan*, vol. 3, edited by Adnan Hadidi, pp. 131–142. Amman, 1987.

Syria

Biscop, Jean-Luc, and Jean-Pierre Sodini. "Qal'at Sem'an et les chevets à colonnes de Syrie du Nord." *Syria* 61 (1984): 267–330.

Butler, Howard Crosby. *Architecture and Other Arts*. Publications of an American Archaeological Expedition to Syria in 1899–1900, Part 2. New York, 1903.

Collart, Paul, et al. *Sanctuaire de Baalshamîn à Palmyre*. 6 vols. Neuchatel, 1969–1975.

Collart, Paul, and Pierre Coupel. *L'autel monumental de Baalbek*. Paris, 1951.

Debevoise, Neilson C. "The Origin of Decorative Stucco." *American Journal of Archaeology* 45 (1941): 45–61.

Dentzer-Feydy, Jacqueline. "Décor architectural et développement du Hauran du Ier siècle avant J.-C. au VIIe siècle après J.-C." In *Hauran I*, edited by Jean-Marie Dentzer, pp. 261–310. Paris, 1985.

Dentzer-Feydy, Jacqueline. "Le décor architectural en Syrie aux époques hellénistique et romaine." In *Archéologie et histoire de la Syrie*, vol. 2, *La Syrie de l'époque achéménide à l'avènement de l'Islam*, edited by Jean-Marie Dentzer and Winfried Orthmann, pp. 457–476. Saarbrücken, 1989.

Dentzer-Feydy, Jacqueline. "Les chapiteaux corinthiens normaux de Syrie méridionale." *Syria* 67 (1990a): 633–663.

Dentzer-Feydy, Jacqueline. "Les chapiteaux ioniques de Syrie méridionale." *Syria* 67 (1990b): 143–181.

Dentzer-Feydy, Jacqueline. "Le décor architectural." In *Iraq al Amir, le château du Tobiade Hyrcan*, by Ernest Will et al., pp. 141–208. Paris, 1991.

Filarska, Barbara. "Remarques sur le décor architectural de la voie prétorienne au camp de Dioclétien à Palmyre, et Nouveaux chapiteaux de Palmyre." *Études et Travaux* 3 (1966): 108ff., 124ff.

Gawlikowski, Michal, and Michal Pietrzykowski. "Les sculptures du temple de Baalshamîn à Palmyre." *Syria* 57 (1980): 421–452.

Naccache, Alice, and Jean-Pierre Sodini. "Le décor architectural en Syrie byzantine." In *Archéologie et histoire de la Syrie*, vol. 2, *La Syrie de l'époque achéménide à l'avènement de l'Islam*, edited by Jean-Marie Dentzer and Winfried Orthmann, pp. 477–490. Saarbrücken, 1989.

Rostovtzeff, Michael. *Dura-Europos and Its Art*. Oxford, 1938.

Schlumberger, Daniel. "Les formes anciennes du chapiteaux corinthien en Syrie, en Palestine et en Arabie." *Syria* 14 (1933): 283–317.

Schlumberger, Daniel. "Note sur le décor architectural des colonnades des rues et du camp de Dioclétien." *Berytus* 2 (1935): 163–167.

Schlumberger, Daniel. "Descendants non-méditerranéens de l'art grec." *Syria* 37 (1960): 253–318.

Seyrig, Henri. "Bas relief monumentaux du temple du Bel à Palmyre." *Syria* 15 (1934): 155–186.

Seyrig, Henri. "Ornamenta palmyrena antiquiora." *Syria* 21 (1940): 277–328.

Shoe, Lucy T. "Architectural Mouldings of Dura-Europos." *Berytus* 9 (1948): 1–40.

Strube, Christine. "Die Formgebung der Apsisdekoration in Qalbloze und Qalat Siman." *Jahrbuch für Antike und Christentum* 20 (1977): 181–191.

Strube, Christine. "Die Kapitelle von Qasr Ibn Wardan." *Jahrbuch für Antike und Christentum* 26 (1983): 59–106.

Strube, Christine. *Baudekoration im Nordsyrischen Kalksteinmassiv*, vol. 1, *Kapitell-, Tür- und Gesimsformen der Kirchen des 4. und 5. Jahrhunderts n. Chr.* Mainz am Rhein, 1993.

Tanabe, Katsumi, ed. *Sculptures of Palmyra*. Tokyo, 1986–.

Weigand, Edmund. "Baalbek und Rom: Die römische Reichskunst in ihrer Entwickelung und Differenzierung." *Jahrbuch des Deutschen Archäologischen Instituts* 29 (1914): 37–91.

Weigand, Edmund. "Baalbek: Datierung und kunstgeschichtliche Stellung seiner Bauten." *Jahrbuch für Kunstwissenschaft* (1924): 77–99.

Will, Ernest. "IX congrès international d'archéologie classique, Damas 1969." *Annales Archéologiques Arabes Syriennes* 21 (1971): 261–268.

Will, Ernest. "Le monument: Son histoire, ses caractères, son architecte." In *Le temple de Bêl à Palmyre*, vol. 2, by Henri Seyrig et al., pp. 147–223. Paris, 1975.

JOSEPH PATRICH

ARCHITECTURAL DRAFTING AND DRAWING.

By providing scientifically measured graphic description and analysis to complement verbal and numeric recording, architectural drafting and drawing play an important role in the visual depiction of the human environment. The archaeologist's notebook usually includes lined and graph paper interleaved, and every field archaeologist must be skilled in both verbal and graphic recording.

In addition, well-staffed field projects include a team of specialists adept at using surveying instruments and trained in architecture and architectural drawing.

Although photography, like architectural drawing, provides a three-dimensional visualization of a site or building, the roles are quite different, but complementary. Photography presents structures from a perspective; architectural drawing presents them, not as seen, but as measured in horizontal (plan) and vertical (section, elevation) components. As a result, these components of three-dimensional shape can be reproduced accurately to a consistent scale on the flat plane of the drawing surface. A photographer is forced to record all the details within the image framed by the lens; the architect selects only those features salient to understanding the shape being represented. For example, a ruin whose masonry is overgrown with brambles may show up only as a wild thicket in a photograph. In a drawing, however, the brambles can be ignored and only the in situ masonry selected from among the rubble, so that a viable building appears on paper.

Hence, the best visual depiction of an object or structure is achieved by publishing both photographs and drawings: one gives a close approximation of what is to be seen, the other of what the original shape was or was intended to be. Artistic renderings and sketches, so popular before photography was commonly used, are, in a way, a middle ground, allowing the perspective of the camera and the selectivity of the drawing instrument. Good artistic renderings can add valuable insights that may be missed by the camera or architectural drawing. [See Photography, article on Photography of Fieldwork and Artifacts.]

Architectural drawing relies on precise measurement and scale reproduction of the features and objects on a site. A primary goal is to provide a three-dimensional framework in which everything excavated can be located, including both the site's stratigraphic features and the artifacts found within its strata. In this sense, architectural drawing is akin to mapping, and the various drawings are integral components of a master site map. Vertically, all features and objects are locatable on sitewide sections related to their distance above sea level (a.s.l.). Such a three-dimensional framework gives accurate locations for everything on the site in question and makes it possible to determine their comparative dimensional relationship to features at other sites.

In a broad sense architecture suggests the adaptation of space for human habitation. An entire site is therefore like a structure in which natural and hand-worked elements function to form a cohesive settlement. Considered in this way, the preparation of sitewide maps is an aspect of architectural drawing. In a narrow sense architecture is the art of building, the creation of enclosed spaces in which humans live and function (barns, houses, temples, palaces, forts). In this sense architectural drawing becomes the comprehensive assembly on paper of fragmentary building remains in order to understand their structure and function. This requires careful measurements and a knowledge of ancient building design and construction methods. As with pottery typologies, building typologies make it possible to identify styles, determine dates, and reconstruct the whole from fragments. As such, architectural drawing joins with other archaeological specializations to contribute to the overall interpretive process and to conservation.

Taking Measurements. Measuring techniques used on archaeological projects are identical to those used by surveyors for modern platting of a subdivision. They can be learned from a standard textbook on surveying or from chapters on surveying included in archaeological field manuals. [See Site Survey.]

The distance between two points is usually determined by taping, for which 20–50-meter steel or vinyl tapes are used for large areas and 3–5-meter steel tapes for small ones. All measurements must be taken in horizontal and vertical components in order to be able to record them to scale on the drawing board. For horizontal measurements the tape must be held level and a plumb bob used at the lower point. For distances longer than 30–50 m (the limit of the tape length), it is necessary to establish a "chain" of intermediate points. Such chaining requires the use of a transit or theodolite to align the survey pins set on the series of intermediate points.

A faster, but less accurate, alternative to taping is to use the 1:100 ratio between the transit's stadia hair readings on the leveling rod and the distance along the line of sight. On adequately funded projects both these methods have been obviated by the electronic distance meter (EDM), a device that gauges distance by measuring the time it takes to bounce a laser beam shot from point a off of a crystal target set at point b. Readings are correct to a fraction of a millimeter over distances of hundreds of meters. Vertical measurement, or leveling, is best done by using a dumpy level, transit, or theodolite with the telescope set level and a leveling rod (a 4-m pole with centimeter calibrations) held vertically on the points between which the difference in height is desired.

The final key element in measurement is triangulation, which allows the accurate position of three or more points to be determined in relation to each other. This process combines assessing linear distance (see above) with the measurement of angles between sets of points. For example, once the distance between points a and b and angles abc and bac is known, distances ac and bc and angle acb can be determined by geometric plotting or trigonometric solution. For long-distance measurement, horizontal angles are best read with a transit or theodolite. However, for small spaces, astute use of a measuring tape will suffice. For example, to determine the exact relationships among the four corners of a room, measuring the four sides and the two diagonal distances enables very precise plotting on paper.

For survey work in an excavation area, taping and triangulation can be combined by using a plane table, a device that enables the plotting of both distances and angles directly onto a drawing as measurements are being taken. This traditional equipment has been replaced, for those who can afford it, by a combination of theodolite, EDM, and data recorder, which allows the direct transfer of data to a computer with computer-aided design (CAD) software. [See Computer Mapping.]

Activities in the Field. The architect's responsibilities during fieldwork can be divided into sitewide and excavation-related activities. Sitewide activities include producing a contour map with natural features and maps with artificial features, including ancient structures visible above ground as well as modern buildings. In many cases, much of this work has already been done, and the information is available on regional maps and aerial photographs from national land survey departments or geographic societies, municipal development maps from local municipal offices that will show existing houses and street systems on or near the site, maps done by earlier archaeological projects, and satellite photos from French (Spotimage) and American (Landsat) sources. The ground survey can also be greatly enhanced by low-altitude aerial balloon photos, such as those taken by Wilson Myers and Ellie Myers over Greece, Crete, Jordan, and Israel.

Excavation-related activities begin with the establishment of a predetermined excavation grid and the layout of the units (squares) to be excavated. In conjunction with the site contour survey, benchmarks with known a.s.l. elevations, from which the excavators take their levels, are established in or near excavation units. With the grid and benchmarks in place, it is possible to maintain a three-dimensional control for recording all finds. To ensure ongoing accuracy, this system needs regular maintenance (strings and benchmarks often get moved or disappear), and excavators need to be advised on and checked on the correct use of the survey information.

As an excavation proceeds, the architect serves as a consultant to interpret building features as they surface, to predict where still-unexcavated portions of a structure may be, and to develop excavation strategy accordingly. After sufficient masonry appears, detailed (stone-for-stone) field drawings are produced in plan and elevations. As the components of a building extending over several excavation units come together in a single drawing, the integral nature of the structure will usually emerge. It is then possible for the architect to advise the excavator on where other components of the structure may be located. Field drawing requires a portable drawing board and theodolite, or a plane table, and is most efficiently performed with a team of three people, with one drawing and two involved in taping and sighting. [See Excavation Strategy.]

Given the complexity of this set of field assignments, it is essential to have in place a well-organized and archivable recording and filing system to be adapted and followed for the duration of the field project. If a project goes on for a number of seasons, with possible changes in the staff of architects, these records are especially essential in reestablishing the grid and the benchmarks at the inception of each new season. Also, over multiple seasons the array of drawings will become cumbersome and confusing unless the drawings are carefully numbered and cataloged. It is even important to adopt a standard paper size for ease of transportation, storage, and future access. All the data produced in the field—survey notes, layouts of excavation units, benchmarks, calculations of levels preliminary sketches, architectural drawings—windblown and soiled though they may be, are considered primary information and should be cataloged and stored for subsequent interpretive work.

Interpretating Data. To enable the preparation of publication drawings, the goal is to come out of the field with a set of sufficiently complete data and drawings. This is a job that often continues beyond the field season, possibly an ocean's distance from a site, so that it is impossible to retake a missing measurement. To avoid such frustration it is recommended that at least the publication drawings to be used in preliminary reports be completed at the excavation camp during the field season. This adds a quality-control factor to the fieldwork because the process of tracing and assembling portions of different field drawings will lead readily to the discovery of missing data—which can then be easily supplied, especially if the camp is at the excavation site. This also puts the final product into the hands of the author of the preliminary report immediately. Doing the same work after the return home can stretch over months.

It is therefore necessary to have an adequate, dust-free work space equipped with tables and tools with which high-quality ink drawings and illustrations can be produced. With CAD and GIS (Geographic Information Systems) software, the computer drafting of maps and buildings can also be done on location. The use of CAD enables the instant production of publication-quality drawings and the reconstruction and manipulation of field drawings to create simulations, from any selected point of view, of buildings and sites as they may have looked in antiquity. GIS allows the use of a base map to store various layers (categories) of data that can be retrieved by using a mouse to "click on" a point of the map with which the data are associated. [See Computer Recording, Analysis, and Interpretation.]

The aftermath of the field season involves an array of follow-up research before the final publication of drawings and analyses of material culture: from analyzing construction techniques, finding parallels for the site's building designs and settlement plans, and determining the use and function of the buildings to preparing plans for site restoration. Drawings for final publication will include, among others, those of the actual remains (already completed during the field season), reconstructions showing the complete structure as it was in the various phases of its use, artistic renderings, and studies of construction methods, design techniques, and architectural details.

BIBLIOGRAPHY

Allen, Kathleen M. S., S. W. Green, and E. B. W. Zubrow, eds. *Interpreting Space: GIS and Archaeology.* New York, 1990.

Detweiler, A. Henry. *Manual of Archaeological Surveying.* New Haven, 1948. This ASOR manual applies the regular principles of surveying to archaeology, and is still a good beginning point, especially for those working with a manual theodolite or transit. For greater detail and use of electronic and computerized equipment, up to date manuals on standard and electronic surveying, available in libraries of universities with engineering departments, should be consulted.

Dillon, Brain, ed. *The Student's Guide to Archaeological Illustrating.* Vol. 1, *Archaeological Research Tools.* 2d rev. ed. Los Angeles, 1985. A useful introduction that includes chapters on maps, plans, sections and reconstruction drawings.

Harris, Edward C. *Principles of archaeological stratigraphy.* 2d ed. London and New York, 1989. Chapter 9, "Archaeological Plans," gives a good theoretical discussion of the role of precise excavation plans and their difference from sections.

Hobbs, A. H. A. *Surveying for Archaeologists and Other Fieldworkers.* New York, 1980. Includes an excellent section on mapping from oblique aerial photographs.

BERT DE VRIES

ARCHITECTURAL ORDERS.

The two types of Greek trabeation—Doric and Ionic—apparently were themselves created as adaptations of Near Eastern architectural ornaments in about 600 and 560 BCE, respectively (Doric as an adaptive imitation of the so-called Proto-Doric columns of type at Deir el-Baḥari, Ionic as assemblage of Mesopotamian and Levantine motifs). Although they do exercise some influence on Near Eastern architecture after the sixth century BCE (especially Achaemenid and Cypriot), on the whole they do not appear in the Near East before the conquests of Alexander. The Greek colonies (e.g., Naukratis) and the Anatolian coastlands, which remain part of the Greek homelands proper throughout the Hellenistic period, are the exceptions. [*See* Naukratis.]

The principal conservative tradition of monumental architecture in the Anatolian coastlands is the Ionic tradition of temple design codified by Pytheos (Temple of Athena at Priene, c. 340 BCE) and later by Hermogenes (Temple of Artemis Leukophryne at Magnesia ad Maeandrum, c. 220/200 BCE). This consisted of a refined system of proportions (Vitruvius 3.3.1–13) based on a regular spacing of columns on a grid often determined by the plinth module. The principal monuments of this tradition are a number of peripteral and pseudodipteral temples (at Magnesia, Chryse, Teos, Alabanda, and Lagina, third–second centuries BCE). The other major monuments are the "Ionian" agoras and temple temene surrounded on all four sides by regularly spaced colonnades, usually one story with Doric on the exterior and Ionic on the interior and with the passage through the agora placed along one side rather than axially (Miletus, Magnesia, and Priene). [*See* Miletus; Priene.]

The other tradition in Anatolia centers around Pergamon in the second century BCE and involves the development of earlier innovations in the syntax of the orders, with the use of engaged pier columns for corners of colonnades and upper stories (Pergamene stoas at Athens and Aigai). There is also some use of screens of engaged orders as articulation for wall surfaces (the bouleuteria at Miletus and Termessos) and the development of buildings with real (the Maussoleion [Mausoleum] at Halikarnassos and Belevi) or engaged (the Lion Monument at Knidos) orders on a podium in the Greek and non-Greek lands of the southwest Anatolian coast. The earliest use of the engaged column on a projecting pedestal seems to be the Gymnasium at Stratonikeia (mid-second century BCE). [*See* Pergamon; Halikarnassos.]

The extent to which Hellenic types of columns supplanted native architectural forms in the Hellenistic period in the Near East, and the nature of their development, is very uncertain. There are almost no preserved interpretable architectural remains until the early imperial period, even in the principal centers, such as Antioch. [*See* Antioch on Orontes.] It has been speculated that the architecture of the Syrian coastlands was dominated by the East Greek (Anatolian) Ionic tradition because in the Roman period the Ionic rather than the Corinthian order predominates. It is clear that Doric and Ionic buildings were built by Greek colonists as far east as Ai Khanum.

However, recent scholarship has largely settled the point that Hellenistic Alexandria was the major creative center in the development of so-called baroque aedicular screen architecture and that this is the architecture depicted in Second Style Pompeiian wall painting (McKenzie, 1990). This architecture must therefore have developed in Alexandrian palace architecture in the third and second centuries BCE. Individual features are noticeable in fragments in tombs in Alexandria and at the Alexandria Museum: pier columns (from Shatby, Mustafa Pasha, third century BCE); segmental pediments (from Anfoushy, Hypogeum 2, third century BCE); modillion cornices and coffered conches (Alexandria Museum). To some extent, the creativity of this architecture was clearly a product of the mixing of Hellenic and native forms (e.g., segmental pediments and foliate bases, the latter attestable for the Egyptian seventeenth dynasty). [*See* Alexandria.]

This architecture begins to appear in the evidence of preserved buildings at the end of the first century BCE and spreads rapidly across the entire Mediterranean in the course of the first century CE. The earliest preserved buildings with a complete repertoire of baroque aedicular screen facades (broken and hollow pediments, columns on pedestals, foliate bases, broken forward and curved entablatures, framed tholoi, coffered conch niches) are the temple tombs at Petra (e.g., the Khasne, now dated to late first century

BCE) and the Palazzo delle Colonne in Ptolemais, Cyrenaica (first century BCE or first century CE). By the second half of the first century and the early second century CE in Anatolia, this is established as the basic formal vocabulary of theater scene buildings (e.g., the Domitianic scene at Ephesus); of screen walls in the imperial cult chambers of gymnasia (at Ephesus, Sardis, and Miletus); of nymphaea (the Trajanic nymphaeum at Miletus); and of other public buildings (the Celsus library at Ephesus, c. 117 CE). The conservative tradition of temple design derived from Hermogenes does persist in Asia Minor into the early second century (at Aizanoi) but seems to end by the time of the peripteral colonnade at Sardis (in Antonine baroque). [See Petra; Ptolemais; Ephesus; Sardis.]

The colonnaded street seems to originate in the Syrian coastlands in Augustan times (first attested in Herod's project at Antioch), as does the arcuated or "Syrian" pediment between twin towers (the Augustan Temple of Dushara at Si). Arcades (archivolts on columns) may exist in the Alexandrian-inspired repertoire before the imperial era.

Relatively little further change occurs in the use of the orders in Anatolia and the Near East in the second and third centuries CE. In the second century, the so-called marble style dominates the production of ornament in Anatolia, Syria, and North Africa, based on production from the Proconnesus quarries. By Severan times, the production of ornament is dominated by a type of brittle carving with simple faceted surfaces that create abrupt contrasts of light and

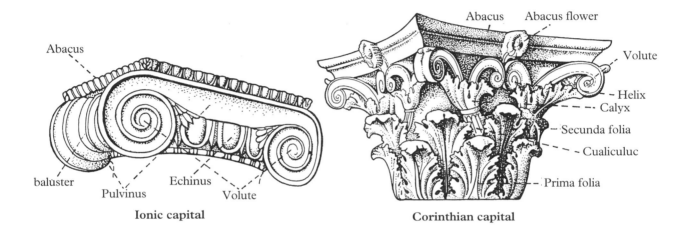

Ionic capital

Corinthian capital

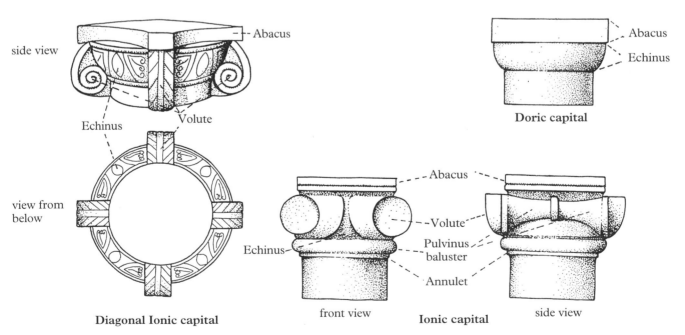

Diagonal Ionic capital

Doric capital

Ionic capital

ARCHITECTURAL ORDERS. *Classical capitals.* Doric, Ionic, and Corinthian styles. (Courtesy T. N. Howe)

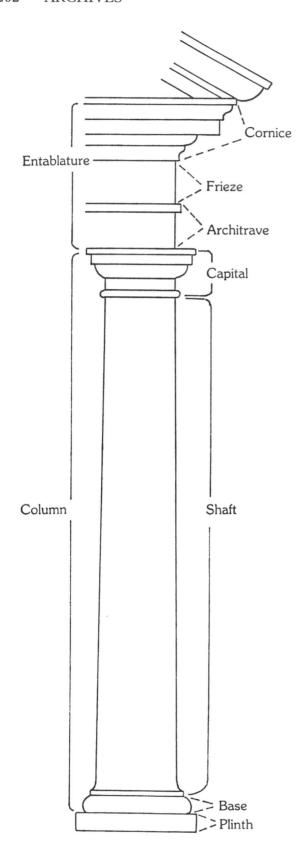

ARCHITECTURAL ORDERS. *Diagram of various architectural features of public buildings.* (Courtesy T. N. Howe)

shade; this aesthetic forms the basis of Late Antique and Byzantine ornament.

The hybrid use of Hellenic types of columns and Near Eastern elements continues throughout the Roman period. The Trajanic kiosk at Philae is in a fully traditional Egyptian form, whereas the temple tombs at Petra and the Temple of Bel at Palmyra combine canonical orders with "Assyrian" crowstep merlons and Egyptian cavetto cornices. At a number of centers, buildings with partially or fully native plans adapt the architecture of the edicular screen or arcade as engaged or low-relief surface patterning, but without the fixed relative proportions or syntactical rules of Hellenic types (e.g., the Temple of Gareus at Uruk; the "peripteros" and the "Freitreppenbau" at Aššur).

[*See also* Architectural Decoration.]

BIBLIOGRAPHY

Boëthius, Axel, and J. B. Ward-Perkins. *Etruscan and Roman Architecture.* Harmondsworth, 1970. The section by Ward-Perkins (reprinted as *Roman Imperial Architecture* [1981]) is still the standard survey of all imperial age Roman architecture.

Browning, Iain. *Petra.* 2d ed. London, 1973. 3d ed. London, 1989. General survey of Petra.

Dentzer-Feydy, Jacqueline. "Décor architectural et développement du Hauran du Ier siècle avant J.-C. au VIIe siècle après J.-C." In *Hauran I,* edited by Jean-Marie Dentzer, vol. 1, pp. 261–310. Bibliothèque Archèologique et Historique, vol. 124. Paris, 1985. Survey for the specialist.

Downey, Susan. *Mesopotamian Religious Architecture: Alexander through the Parthians.* Princeton, 1988. Focuses on the continuation of Mesopotamian tradition but with some consideration and illustration of Hellenic hybrid elements, particularly at Dura and Aššur.

Lauter, Hans. *Die Architektur des Hellenismus.* Darmstadt, 1986. The only recent attempt at a general history of Hellenistic architecture, limited largely to Greek cultural areas but with some consideration of the Near East. Well illustrated in a compact format.

Lyttelton, Margaret. *Baroque Architecture in Classical Antiquity.* London, 1974. Well-illustrated, compendious attempt to chronicle the development of baroque aedicular screen architecture.

McKenzie, Judith. *The Architecture of Petra.* London, 1990. Well-illustrated study of one site, which establishes that so-called baroque aedicular architecture developed in Alexandria in the third and second centuries BCE and is essentially that which is represented in Pompeiian second style painting.

THOMAS NOBLE HOWE

ARCHIVES. *See* Libraries and Archives.

ARMENIA. Any study of Armenian archaeology is hampered from the start by fundamental handicaps: the chronology remains insufficiently precise and not yet universally accepted, so that terminologies used by local and foreign scholars vary. Despite the extensive work done in eastern Anatolia and northwestern Iran, the majority of the evidence comes from the present Republic of Armenia, comprising, at best, one-fifth of historic Armenia, which covered all of the Armenian plateau. Consequently, serious geographic and chronological lacunae remain, distorting our understanding of the existing material. This is especially so because the Armenian plateau at times entered into larger cultural units. Most conclusions are therefore rendered tentative and possibly inaccurate.

Archaeological evidence on the Armenian plateau begins with the Early Paleolithic period. The earliest finds in Armenia, and indeed in all of the former USSR to date, were made in 1946–1948 by S. A. Sardaryan and M. Z. Panichkina (Mongait, 1961, pp. 56–57; Panichkina, 1950) at Satani dar on the southwestern slopes of Mt. Aragac, near the Armeno-Turkish border. These consisted of typical Chellean and Early Achulean artifacts, made of obsidian, which is plentiful in this volcanic region. Somewhat later, more developed Middle and Late Paleolithic sites also occur in the gorge of the Hrazdan River, just north of the present Armenian capital of Erevan on the Middle Araxes River. A number of petroglyphs representing long-horned animals and hunting scenes, found on Mt. Aragac and elsewhere in Armenia and neighboring Azerbaijan, may also go back to the Paleolithic period, although their chronology remains uncertain.

The stratigraphy of more permanent settlements—rather than mere encampments—found on the southwestern slopes of Mt. Aragac demonstrates a direct succession from food-gathering to food-producing levels not yet attested elsewhere in Transcaucasia. A local evolution derived from the neighboring hills (and leading to Neolithic settlements in the plain of Erevan as early as 6000 BCE) has consequently

been postulated (Burney and Lang, 1971, p. 34). The agricultural basis of the economy in the earliest level of these new settlements is clearly attested by the presence of querns, mortars, obsidian sickle blades, and storage jars; stock raising is reflected in rock reliefs of domesticated animals. Various forms of round-bottomed vessels and cups made of sand and straw-tempered clay, occasionally decorated with an incised motif, mark the appearance of pottery. These early settlements apparently shared a common tradition with those of mid-sixth–fifth-millennium Georgia: a small, circular house plan occurs both there and at Tełut, west of Erevan.

The transition from stone to metal late in the fourth millennium is still obscure, but the period from about 3250 to about 1750 BCE is of particular note in Armenia. Called Kuro-Araxes by local scholars, but also known under a variety of other names (e.g., Early Transcaucasian), it spanned both the Chalcolithic (Soviet Eneolithic) and Early Bronze Ages. Geographically, its culture reached from the Caucasus to eastern Anatolia, northwestern Iran, and beyond to Syria-Palestine. Its remarkable stability and uniformity, despite a gradual evolution and the development of local particularism in its last phase, led Charles Burney to conclude that "Never again was there a culture in the highland zone both so far-flung and so long-lived" (Burney and Lang, 1971, p. 85).

The hallmark used to identify the Kuro-Araxes culture is a distinctive, high-quality, dark-monochrome (usually black or red) burnished pottery in various shapes that is decorated with grooved, or occasionally raised, hatched triangles, sin-

ARMENIA. Figure 1. *Round house at Šengawił displaying the base of a central post.* Third millennium BCE. (Courtesy N. G. Garsoïan)

gle or double spirals, zigzags, or incipient floral or bird motifs. The superior technical level and sophistication reached by this style in the Araxes valley during the third millennium has lent credence to the hypothesis that this may well have been its center. Variations of the type can be traced throughout the cultural area—particularly in the slightly later Khirbet Kerak ware of Syro-Palestine, whose style seemingly originated in Transcaucasia. With some tendency toward more elongated forms, the Kuro-Araxes tradition lasted through the Early BronzeAge and even beyond the mid-second millennium BCE in some areas.

Šengawit̀, a southern suburb of Erevan on the high left bank of the Hrazdan, has often been selected, among many others, as a typical Kuro-Araxes site, although it was probably founded even earlier. It was a permanent settlement, surrounded by a protective wall of large, undressed stones, with an underground passage to the river. Within it were grouped numerous, usually single-room, round houses some 7–8 m in diameter. They are similar to ones found in Georgia, in Karabagh, and near Naxčawan on the lower Araxes. Composed of several stone courses surmounted by thin wattle and clay walls, their inward curvature suggests a beehive shape. According to Aṙak'elyan (1976, p. 14), the interiors were usually painted blue. Rectangular annexes often flanked the central room, and the larger houses had a central wooden post (see figure 1). All examples included a storage bin for grain and an elaborate and highly ornamented clay hearth (some ram shaped or with ram heads and movable parts) that may have served religious as well as practical purposes. The growing importance of animal husbandry is reflected by petroglyphs and multiple figurines or amulets of tiny bulls, probably also with a religious significance. Burials from this period are rare, but Šengawit̀ had a largely intramural cemetery, with early communal burials in rectangular graves containing up to ten bodies. Grave goods included stone and copper weapons, amulets, personal ornaments, bone implements, and fragments of textiles. [See Burial Sites; Grave Goods; Weapons; and Textiles, article on Textiles of the Neolithic through Iron Ages.]

Certain regions display signs of stagnation in the last, EB phase of this culture, beginning in about 2300 BCE. However, the activity in northern and central Armenia did not abate. Many new settlements developed in the hill country (Gaṙni, Elar, and Lčašēn in the north, Haṙič in the west) as the predominance of animal husbandry and population pressure began to require additional space. Of particular importance is the appearance of a major metallurgical center at Mecamōr, west of Erevan. Even though the technique used had probably been brought from Mesopotamia, and Mecamōr did not reach its apogee before the second half of the second millennium BCE, it may be the earliest such center in Transcaucasia. Bronze slag, together with casserite ore and animal-matter briquettes containing the phosphorus required to extract tin from this ore, were found in Mecamōr's earliest phase, together with Kuro-Araxes pottery.

Considerable continuity from this culture can be traced in the subsequent Middle Bronze (twentieth–fourteenth centuries BCE) and Late Bronze (thirteenth–tenth centuries BCE) periods, though some sites were temporarily abandoned. Even so, Armenia in the second millennium BCE presents a complex picture, continually supplemented by ongoing excavations and the identification of new western sites through recent air surveys and the work by Philip Kohl and Hermann Gasche under the auspices of the Institutes of Archaeology of the Academies of Sciences of the Armenian and Georgian Republics. Most of the material for this period derives from burials and shows a fairly unified culture, including both Transcaucasia and northwestern Iran by the end of the fourteenth century BCE. Numerous barrows of the northern steppe type, similar to those from Trialeti in southern Georgia, have come to light in the Armenian Republic: at Kirovakan (c. 1500 BCE) and Tazekend in the north, as well as at Karabagh in Azerbaijan. In 1950, at Lčašēn, the lowering of the water level of Lake Sevan revealed a major cemetery in use from the third millennium to about 1200 BCE. Its richest tombs, however, approached by dromi and lined as well as roofed with massive stone slabs, have been attributed to the thirteenth century BCE. [See Tombs.] Near Artik, on the western slopes of Mt. Aragac, a vast complex of some 640 catacomb tombs with vertical shafts and oval burial chambers filled with stones and earth was uncovered beginning in 1959 by T. S. Xačatryan (Khachatrian, 1963). These have been dated to between the fourteenth and the tenth centuries BCE, with the majority of burials belonging to the middle phase (twelfth–eleventh centuries). In both types of cemeteries, single burials (the contracted body lies on its side with no particular orientation) are the norm, although twin and even some communal burials occasionally appear in the last phase.

The great development of metallurgy, evidenced by the presence of some twenty-four smelting furnaces at Mecamōr dating to before 1000 BCE, is also reflected in the diversity and wealth of the grave furnishings. The richest and best known are those from Kirovakan: a gold bowl decorated with pairs of repoussé lions, silver cups similar to those found in the Trialeti barrows, a wooden couch with silver-plated ends, bronze bowls and weapons, and a gold and carnelian necklace adorning the corpse. Similar bronze tools, weapons, and ornaments—daggers with openwork pommels, spearheads, axes, swords with decorated blades (some with a copper-snake inlay), bronze and obsidian arrowheads, horse bits and wheeled cheek pieces, decorated belts, bracelets with spirals and granulation, earrings, hairpins with decorated heads, and pendants with openwork bells and birds were found with bronze, glass paste, and carnelian beads at Artik, Lčašēn and elsewhere. All testify to the mastery of Armenian metalwork in this period. [See Metals, article on Artifacts of the Neolithic, Bronze, and Iron Ages; Jewelry.]

Foreign influences on Armenia have been argued for the

late second millennium BCE. Parallels are manifest in the northern barrow-type burials, in the ceramics with corded decoration (similar to those of the later steppe kurgans found in the earlier MB burials at Lčašēn), and perhaps in the remarkable group of open and covered wooden vehicles with disk and spoked wheels also recovered from Lčašēn. These correspond to examples in Trialeti, though Mitannian influence from the south has also been postulated. [See Mitanni.] The profusion of polychrome ceramics occurring at numerous sites—Tazekend (with which a red-on-black type has been identified), Gaṙni, Mecamōr, and Lčašēn, among others points southward, to northwestern Iran. The same holds for the Mitanni-type cylinder seals discovered in the earlier Artik tombs. Even so, most artifacts are of local origin, as is the gold. The earlier Lčašēn tombs are characterized by their own monochrome pottery with a punctuated decoration. Similarly, all levels at Artik contain only black-decorated ceramics, at times crude, at times burnished to a nearly mirrorlike luster.

The bulk of the MB and LB evidence is, then, derived from cemeteries. However, cyclopean fortresses, known as *berdšēn*, dating to the millennium preceding the eighth-century BCE appearance of the Urartians in the region, have increasingly been detected throughout the Armenian Republic and in neighboring Karabagh (four in the immediate vicinity of Gaṙni). [See Urartu.] Large groups of LB megalithic monuments have also been recorded near Sisian, in the eastern region of Zangezur. Of special interest are those known as *višaps*, "monsters, or dragons." Up to 2–3 m long, with large fish mouths and eyes, as well as crude indications of scales and gills, and erected upright in the mountains at the head of springs, *višaps* may well indicate widespread water worship, just as the presence of small amulets point to the probability of fertility cults. [See Cult.] Shrines with curious clay altars with hearths and multiple cups, presumably for libations and sacrifices, found near the metalworks of late second-millennium BCE Mecamōr, must have some religious significance. An artificial open-air platform at Mecamōr is marked with hieroglyphic signs, for which an astral significance has been suggested.

With the opening of the first millennium BCE, iron objects begin to appear in graves. The new technology may have caused the gradual decline of Mecamōr, even though evidence demonstrates the survival of second-millennium BCE Transcaucasian culture to the ninth century BCE at least. Elegant bronze belts with running spiral borders framing lively animal figures, chariots, and hunting scenes have been attributed to the immediately pre-Urartian period (c. 1100–900 BCE). Hence, for millennia, and down to the Urartian conquest in the early eighth century BCE, the Araxes valley and much of north-central Armenia had already experienced a continuous, and at times brilliant, evolution—of which it may even have been the center during the long Kuro-Araxes period.

In sharp contrast to the growing wealth of evidence from earlier periods, material securely datable to the millennium from the sixth century BCE to the fourth century CE is puzzlingly meager. Its scarcity presents one of the major unsolved problems in Armenian archaeology. Some Urartian survivals occur at Armawir/Argištihinili and at Erebuni, within the limits of modern Erevan; except for a few silver rhyta, a hypostyle hall and a fire altar at Erebuni, and the unfinished inscription of King Xerxes at Van, however, the period of Achaemenid domination of Armenia (sixth–fourth centuries BCE) must still be reconstructed from literary sources, primarily Xenophon.

Alexander the Great himself never visited Armenia, and the Seleucid hold on the plateau ruled by a native dynasty was precarious. [See Seleucids.] By the late third–early second centuries BCE, eponymous cities appeared, presumably modeled on the ubiquitous Alexandrias: Artaxata/Artašat, the northern capital on the middle Araxes founded by Artaxias/Artašēs; Zarišat; Zarehawan; and Arsamosata in southwestern Sophene; eventually the new capital of Tigranakert. Only Artašat and Armawir have been excavated to date, and even the site of Tigranakert remains disputed. Nevertheless, preliminary work shows generally Hellenistic urban plans with an acropolis, a temple at Armawir, hypocaust baths, shops, and dwellings. [See Baths.] Greek inscriptions, or rather graffiti, from Armawir show a familiarity with Greek classical literature. [See Greek.] A small statuette of the Praxitelean Aphrodite type was found in the excavations at Artašat (Aṙak'elyan, 1976, pl. xxii–xxiii), but the dating of the material from this city destroyed by the Romans in 59 CE and reconstructed with the permission of the emperor Nero (whose name it briefly took after 66) is not clear.

The apogee of Greek influence came during the reign of Tigran II (95–55 BCE). Literary sources describe the Hellenistic character of his capital, Tigranakert, and of his court. Handsome silver tetradrachms celebrating his taking of Antioch on the Orontes River in 84 BCE follow the Hellenistic model: they represent the profile of the king on the coin's obverse and the city's Tyche as a crowned woman enthroned above the Orontes River on its reverse, and they display Greek legends. [See Antioch on Orontes.] Similar coins of lesser quality continued this type in Sophene until the first years of the Christian period. Under the Romans, a few inscriptions of Trajan and particularly from the reign of Marcus Aurelius at Vaḷaršapat/Kainē Polis ("new city") west of Erevan, attest the presence of Roman troops.

The major classical monument in Armenia is the complex at Gaṙni. Its fortress was begun in the third/second century BCE. It was rebuilt in the eleventh year of King Trdat (c. 77), according to a Greek inscription discovered there in 1945. Within it the ruins of a palace and of a small Ionic peripteros on a high podium were found. They are now reconstructed as a temple, though this identification has been challenged. Despite some attributions to the third century, derived from later literature, this structure is usually dated to the first century on the basis of its style and use of a dry-masonry technique with swallowtail clamps, rather than the later mortar binder. A hypocaust bath nearby produced a floor mosaic of classical sea gods and creatures in a somewhat crude opus vermiculatum and sectile (Aṙak'elyan, 1976, pl. xxiii–xxvii). [*See* Mosaics.]

Iranian aspects continued to manifest themselves beyond the fourth century BCE in clay plaques representing a Mithraic heroic rider found at Artašat and in the pearl diadem worn by Tigran II on his coinage. The mixed Greco-Iranian type of this coinage similarly characterizes the classical bronze head of the Iranian goddess Anahita now in the British Museum and in small statuettes of birds and stags on a stepped pedestal discovered at Sisian. Most interesting of all are boundary stones of Artašēs I (189–c. 160 BCE), whose Aramaic inscriptions confirm the continuation of the local Orontid dynasty in this period, and the hunting scenes that decorate the hypogeum of the Christian Arsacid kings at Ałck', northwest of Erevan. [*See* Aramaic Language and Literature; Hunting.] The presence of Iranian fire altars under the main altar of the patriarchal cathedral of Ējmiacin and at Kasax, farther north, mark the Sasanian occupation of Armenia in the late fourth century. [*See* Sasanians.]

The long hiatus of the Armenian archaeological dark ages came to a close with the appearance of Christian monuments, probably in the fifth century. Numerous single- and three-aisled basilicas, seemingly related to Syrian or Anatolian types, were built throughout Armenia and in Georgia. [*See* Basilicas.] Some of these were monumental and of remarkable quality, such as the one at Ereruk, on the western border of the Armenian Republic, which has been compared to the one at Qalb Louzeh in northern Syria. By the early seventh century, a multitude of domed basilicas, and especially cruciform churches with a central dome on squinches, appeared in both Armenia and Georgia, together with a few circular and polygonal types, of which the best known is the one at Zuartnoc', near Ējmiacin. [*See* Churches.] Historiated stelae, often depicting figures in Parthian dress, were erected—alone or within double-arched monuments, such as the one at Ōjun, in the north, and possibly at Ałudi in the east (see figure 2). [*See* Parthians.] Some of the churches (e.g., at Ptłni, Mren, Ōjun, and At'eni in Georgia) have figured relief decorations, but most rely on the harmony of their proportions and the perfection of their dressed-stone surfaces enclosing a mortar inner core and minimal architectural decoration around windows and cornices for their effect. They range in size from the minute princely chapels at Aštarak, T'alin, and Bjni (belonging to the parafeudal aristocracy of the period) to the vast domed basilicas of St. Gayanē at Ējmiacin, Aruč, T'alin, and Ōjun to the monumental cruciform churches of Gaṙnahovit, St. Hṙip'simē, and Sisian. The endless variety and sophistication of their types and proportions, as well as the subtlety of their decoration, testify to the mastery of the artists and the wealth of their patrons, the ruins of whose palaces are still visible in the countryside. The earlier cities, unsuited to contemporary military and aristocratic society, did not revive, except for the administrative center of Duin near Artašat. Recent excavations there have uncovered a patriarchal residence and cathedral from the seventh century built over earlier structures. Steady architectural activity continued through most of the seventh century, despite the Arab conquest of the Armenian plateau. It was halted for nearly two hundred years, however, along with most cultural activity, when the occupation became more oppressive later in the eighth century.

[*See also* Armenian.]

ARMENIA. **Figure 2.** *Kars stele showing a male figure in Parthian dress.* (Courtesy N. G. Garsoïan)

BIBLIOGRAPHY

Alekseev, V. P., et al. *Contributions to the Archaeology of Armenia.* Translated by Arlene Krimgold. Harvard University, Peabody Museum, Russian Translation Series, vol. 3.3. Cambridge, Mass., 1968.

Aṙak'elyan, Babken N. *Očerki istorii iskusstva drevneĭ Armenii.* Erevan, 1976.

Arutiunian, V. M. *Kamennaja letopis' armjanskogo naroda.* Erevan, 1985.

Burney, Charles, and David Lang. *The Peoples of the Hills.* London, 1971. See chapters 1–5.

Burney, Charles. "The Khirbet Kerak Question and the Early Trans-Caucasian Background." In *L'urbanisation de la Palestine à l'âge du Bronze ancien: Bilan et perspectives des recherches actuelles; Actes du Colloque d'Emmaüs, 20–24 octobre 1986,* edited by Pierre de Miroschedji, pp. 331–339. British Archaeological Reports, International Series, no. 527. Oxford, 1989.

Chaumont, M.-L. "Tigranocerte: Données du problème et état des recherches." *Revue des Études Arméniennes* 16 (1982): 89–110.

Der Nersessian, Sirarpie. *Armenian Art.* London, 1978.

Esaian, S. A. *Drevnjaja kul'tura plemen severo-vostočnoĭ Armenii.* Erevan, 1976.

Khachatrian/Xačatryan, Telemak S. *Material'naja kul'tura drevnego Artika.* Erevan, 1963.

Kušnareva, Karine X., and T. N. Chubinishvili. *Drevnie kul'tury južnogo kavkaza, V–III tys. do N.Ē.* Leningrad, 1970.

Maddin, R. "Early Iron Metallurgy in the Near East." *Transactions of the Iron and Steel Institute of Japan* 55 (1975): 59–68. Discusses Mecamōr (or Metsamor).

Martirosyan, Arutiun A. *Armenija v ēpoxu bronzy i rannego železa.* Erevan, 1964.

Mnatsakanyan, Stepan K., et al. *Očerki po istorii arxitektury drevneĭ i srednevekovoĭ Armenii.* Erevan, 1978.

Mongait, Aleksandr. *Archaeology in the USSR.* London, 1961.

Munchaev, Rauf M. *Kavkaz na zare bronzovogo veka.* Moscow, 1975.

Panichkina, M. Z. *Paleolit Armenii.* Leningrad, 1950.

Perikhanian, Anahit G. "Une inscription araméenne du roi Artašēs trouvée à Zanguézour (Siwnikʿ)." *Revue des Études Arméniennes* 3 (1966): 17–29.

Piggott, Stuart. *The Earliest Wheeled Transport: From the Atlantic Coast to the Caspian Sea.* London, 1983. See especially pages 70–78 for a discussion of chariot burials at Trialeti and Lčašēn (or Lchashen).

Sardaryan, S. A. *Primitive Society in Armenia.* Erevan, 1967. In Armenian with a long English summary.

Thierry, Jean-Michel, and Patrick Donabédian. *Armenian Art.* New York, 1989.

Trever, Kamilla V. *Očerki po istorii kul'tury drevneĭ Armenii.* Moscow, 1953.

Wilkinson, R. D. "A Fresh Look at the Iconic Building at Garni." *Revue des Études Arméniennes* 16 (1982): 221–244.

NINA G. GARSOÏAN

ARMENIAN.

ARMENIAN. Although sharing many of the linguistic features and characteristics of the contiguous Indo-European dialects that once spread between Greek in the south and Balto-Slavic in the north, the position of Armenian among the Indo-European languages appears to be highly archaic, judging from the phonetic system of stops. The prehistory of Armenian is invariably connected with the spatial linguistic interrelationships of the ancient Indo-European dialects and the geographical origin of the Armenians and their migration. However, there is no scholarly consensus on this subject. Some favor the traditional view that Armenians reached Asia Minor from Europe, a view based on the testimonies of the classical Greek historians and the linguistic affinities with the Pontic branch of Indo-European, that is, Greek and the Paleo-Balkan group (Thraco-Phrygian in particular). Others hold that the very cradle of Proto-Indo-European is to be found in eastern Anatolia and the southern Caucasus in or near Armenia. Whether or not Proto-Armenian originated in the area where we find it later, the language retains some one thousand words of Indo-European origin, making it an important source for the study of Indo-European roots.

The early development of the language seems to have included considerable borrowings from neighboring languages: from Hitto-Luwian and Hurro-Urartian proper names (theonyms, anthroponyms, and toponyms) to Indo-Iranian words of everyday life. The archaic contacts among the various peoples of the Armenian highlands account for a rich stock of common terms, and this development has given rise to passionate debates over etymologies and loan words from one or another of the languages of the region—from the Kartvelian family and other Caucasian languages farther north to the various Iranian languages. There is also some lexical evidence suggesting possible early contacts with Semitic languages. The complexity of the question of influences and counterinfluences notwithstanding, the early impact of Armenian on neighboring lands, such as Georgia and Albania, has long been recognized. Many Iranian loanwords also made their way into these regions through Armenian. Yet Armenian possesses with Kartvelian and Albanian components such as consonant shifts that go back to one or another of the ancient dialects found in the Balkan languages as substrata.

The subsequent history of the language can be divided into four major periods: (1) preliterate, that is, prior to the formulation of the Armenian alphabet early in the fifth century; (2) Old Armenian, which is known through the classical sources of early Armenian literature in the fifth–tenth centuries; (3) Middle Armenian, as developed primarily in the Cilician kingdom in the eleventh–fifteenth centuries, a period to which most of the current dialectal phonetic splits can be traced; and (4) Modern Armenian, which is divided into Eastern and Western Armenian following two major dialectal groupings. One has flourished in and around Armenia and Iran with substantial literary development in Tbilisi since the beginning of the nineteenth century and in Erevan since the beginning of the twentieth century. The other has flourished simultaneously among Armenian communities in Anatolia, the rest of the Middle East, and the Western world with its literary capital at Istanbul in the last century and Beirut in the twentieth century. The Eastern dialect retains the pronunciation of Old Armenian, and the Western dialect its orthography. The grammars differ throughout.

Before the introduction of the Armenian script by broad modifications of the Greek alphabet and to a lesser extent of the Syriac alphabet, Armenians used Greek and Aramaic for coinage and inscriptions. The coins of the independent Armenian kingdom of Sophene, founded by Aršam (260–228), and those of the Artaxiads, widespread after the conquests of Tigran II (95–55), have Greek legends. However, the landmark inscriptions from the reign of Artašēs I (190–159), the founder of the Artaxiad dynasty, are in an unusual form of Aramaic script. A royal dedicatory inscription at Garni, from the eleventh year of Trdat I (66 BCE–c. 100 CE), the founder of the Arsacid dynasty in Armenia, is in Greek. There are few Latin inscriptions from the Roman occupation of the second century CE. The earliest Christian texts used in Armenia were in Syriac, and the ecclesiastical correspondence in the early decades of the Armenian Church was primarily in Greek. Very little of this correspondence survives in later translation. Unfortunately, in their zeal for Christianity and as the native historians of the fifth century attest, Armenians made a conscious effort to eradicate every relic of their pagan past. This was accomplished under the leadership of Grigor the Illuminator, the saint largely responsible for the conversion of the nation to Christianity in 314. Under his descendants the nascent church took an increasingly pro-Byzantine stance and did away with much of the early Syriac elements in Armenian Christianity. Moreover, natural conditions and constant ravages by hostile invaders also had a devastating effect. Consequently, there are no documentary remains from this period; a few lines of epic songs survived orally and were committed to writing by later generations, the last being in the eleventh century.

From the first four centuries of scribal activity employing the Armenian script there are only fragments that are preserved for the most part as end gatherings used to reinforce the binding of later codices. The oldest surviving Armenian manuscript is a set of the Gospels from the year 887, now in Erevan (Matenadaran Library, no. 6200). As for the epigraphic evidence, few Armenian inscriptions survive from these early centuries. The oldest is the late fifth-century inscription of the Tekor basilica. The best examples of sixth-century script and iconography come from mosaic floors found in and around Jerusalem. Numerous fine inscriptions from churches and monuments built in Armenia in subsequent centuries and other texts in the form of graffiti, are found throughout the land. Graffiti are found also in distant places like the Sinai, left by pilgrims en route to the monastery of St. Catherine. Numerous graffiti were left in Cilicia and Palestine during the Crusades. Before the eleventh century, writing was only in uncials. Thereafter, a significant paleographical development occurred with the introduction of minuscules. The earliest inscriptions of this period have a mixed script, partly uncial and partly minuscule, but uncials continue to be the common script for inscriptions. Prior to the use of minuscules Armenian paleography may be described as somewhat uniform; its study, however, is not firmly established.

The invention of the native script in 405 CE is credited to Maštoc' (d. 439), a learned cleric who was determined to have the Bible translated into Armenian. Maštoc' experimented briefly with a script that had been developed by a Syrian bishop named Daniel, but rejected it for its insufficiency and also excluded the use of a predominantly Semitic alphabet. Other existing alphabets must have been inadequate for transcribing certain Armenian consonants by a single sign; hence, there is no evidence for writing Armenian in either Greek, Syriac, or Latin script prior to Maštoc'. His alphabet of thirty-six characters, which was refined by a calligrapher named Rufinus at Samosata permitted a phonetically perfect transcription of the language (see figure 1). Pupils were sent to Edessa and Constantinople to study Syriac and Greek, to acquire choice manuscripts, and to translate. Later on, in keeping with his missionary endeavors, Maštoc' devised alphabets for the Georgians and the Caucasian Albanians.

Koriwn, a pupil of Maštoc', details the efforts of his tireless teacher in *The Life of Maštoc'*, the first work composed in Armenian (c. 443). The work conforms to the requirements for encomium in the classical tradition (a later, shorter version omits the essential proem). Another pupil, Eznik of Kołb, later bishop of Bagrewand, wrote *Refutation of the Sects*. This four-part polemic, employing traditional arguments on Divine Providence vis-à-vis evil and free will, was directed against what the author considered to be false religious movements because of their rivalry with Christianity—paganism in general, Zoroastrianism, Greek philosophy, and Marcionism. A collection of twenty-three homilies and a few hymns have been traditionally attributed to Maštoc' himself. Likewise, another collection of liturgical compositions, especially for the Holy Week, together with a

Uncials	Minuscules	Transliteration	Uncials	Minuscules	Transliteration
Ա	ա	a	Մ	մ	m
Բ	բ	b	Յ	յ	y
Գ	գ	g	Ն	ն	n
Դ	դ	d	Շ	շ	š
Ե	ե	e	Ո	ո	o
Զ	զ	z	Չ	չ	č̌
Է	է	ē	Պ	պ	p
Ը	ը	ə	Ջ	ջ	ǰ
Թ	թ	t'	Ռ	ռ	ṙ
Ժ	ժ	ž	Ս	ս	s
Ի	ի	i	Վ	վ	v
Լ	լ	l	Տ	տ	t
Խ	խ	x	Ր	ր	r
Ծ	ծ	c	Ց	ց	c'
Կ	կ	k	Ւ	ւ	w
Հ	հ	h	Փ	փ	p'
Ձ	ձ	j	Ք	ք	k'
Ղ	ղ	ł	Օ	օ	ō
Ճ	ճ	č	Ֆ	ֆ	f

ARMENIAN. Figure 1. *The Armenian alphabet.* The last two letters are Middle Armenian additions. The vowel ու / ու is transliterated u. The transliteration follows the standard international practice, that of Hübschmann-Meillet-Benveniste.

six-part *Constitution* governing the hierarchy of the church, has been ascribed to the patriarch Sahak, who held the hereditary leadership of the Armenian Church for about fifty years (386–428, 435–438), the last of the lineage of Grigor the Illuminator to hold that office. According to Koriwn, Sahak was the foremost patron of the activities pursued by Maštocʿ and his pupils and was the translator of numerous patristic works. He was also responsible for the revision of the first translation of the Bible.

The Old Testament was translated from Greek, and the New Testament was translated apparently from the Old Syriac version first and then revised by the same translators, following a Caesarean-type Greek text (traces of a later revision prior to the eighth century are also discernible). The Armenian version, however, offers more than the usual contribution to the understanding of the development of the textual tradition of the Bible. Numerous Armenian manuscripts containing the Old Testament preserve many of Origen's Hexaplaric signs (asterisks, obeli, and metobeli), which are important elements for Septuagintal studies. New Testament manuscripts yield traces of the mostly lost Old Syriac version, attested also in certain patristic quotations. As for the textual tradition of the Old Testament Pseudepigrapha (noncanonical works), the Armenian often preserves readings superior to those extant in Greek, as in the case of the *Testaments of the Twelve Patriarchs*. Certain of the New Testament apocryphal works have peculiar versions in Armenian, such as the amplified *Gospel of the Infancy*.

With the exception of the Latin Vulgate, there are more Armenian biblical manuscripts than of any other early version. Such manuscripts, whether whole or partial Bibles, constitute nearly a tenth of all medieval Armenian manuscripts. There is but one Armenian-Greek bilingual text, containing *Acts*, the Pauline corpus, and the Catholic epistles (Paris, Bibliothèque Nationale, Arm. 9, c. eleventh–twelfth century). Altogether there are more than thirty thousand ancient Armenian manuscripts, two-thirds of which are at the Matenadaran Library in Erevan. Other major collections are at the St. James Monastery in Jerusalem and the Mekhitarist monasteries in Venice and Vienna. Lesser collections are found in several national and university libraries in Europe, the Middle East, and the United States. Scores of biblical commentaries also exist, covering almost every book of the Bible.

The most popular primary source on the conversion of Armenia from Zoroastrianism to Christianity very early in the fourth century is the *History of the Armenians* by Agathangelos. The importance of this work is attested by early translations into several languages—Greek, Georgian, Arabic, Latin, and Ethiopian, with two distinct versions in each of the first three languages. The fifth-century Armenian author purports to be a Roman scribe and an eyewitness of the conversion of King Trdat III (298–c. 330), at whose command he wrote the *History*. Notwithstanding his use and adaptation of earlier sources, the pseudonymous author seems to have transmitted some reliable information regarding the events surrounding the conversion of the King and the life and teachings of Grigor, the Illuminator of Armenia. Among the earlier sources used by him are Koriwn's *Life of Maštocʿ* and the anonymous collection of oral histories of Greater Armenia during the fourth century, compiled in the year 470 and transmitted under the title *Epic Histories (Buzandaran Patmutʿiwnk)*. It contains earlier and conceivably more trustworthy traditions. A clear evidence for the latter is the observation that Grigor is called neither "saint" nor "illuminator" in the *Buzandaran*, thus reflecting a very early period of the tradition—when such titles were not yet in vogue. The *Buzandaran* in its own way chronicles the history of Armenia during the long reign of Shapur II of Persia (309–379) and concludes with the official partition of the land under his successor, Shapur III, in 387. The compilation attempts to fill the historical gap between the conversion of Armenia at the hand of Grigor and the formulation of the alphabet by Maštocʿ. The author makes ample use of the Armenian Bible with which he was thoroughly familiar.

The next century, from 387 to 485, is covered by Łazar Pʿarpecʿi and Ełiše Vardapet. In a letter to a noble friend, and overseer for the Sasanian overlords, the *marzpan* Vahan Mamikonean (485–505), Łazar defends himself against rival clergy because of whom he had sought exile in Amid (modern Diyarbakir). Thereupon, he was called by Vahan to head the monastery at Vałaršapat and was commissioned by him to write the *History*. In it he acknowledges the works of the shadowy Agathangelos and the *Buzandaran* and considers his own contribution as the third historical writing (Koriwn's encomium is deemed sacred biography). Łazar is the first Armenian historian of the fifth century whose identity is known. The central part of his *History* focuses on the revolt of 451 and the ensuing battle against the Sasanian king Yazdgird II (438–457) for pressing the Armenians to return to Zoroastrianism. Łazar gives no details of the battle led by Vardan Mamikonean, the hero of the patron's clan, and is often less elaborate than Ełiše, the other exponent of the event. The *History of Vardan and the Armenian War* by Ełiše amplifies that event, especially the battle. There are numerous other differences between the two accounts, however, beginning with the circumstances leading to the conflict that led to the revolt and to war. These differences notwithstanding, Ełiše's more passionate retelling has endeared his version to the point of allowing little hearing for the other account on which he depends. He wrote at the request of the priest Dawitʿ Mamikonean likewise to glorify the hero of the patron's clan. There is some doubt about Ełiše's claim to have been an eyewitness to the events recorded by him. He employs well-established martyrological elements, especially when recounting the speeches he attributes to Vardan and the priest Łewond just before the fateful battle.

The most noted historian, however, is the enigmatic Movsēs Xorenac'i, whose *History of the Armenians* is deemed extremely valuable especially for providing a coherent and systematic view of the nation's history from mythical times to the Persian period (Book 1) and an apologetic interpretation of the Armenian dynastic history from the time of Alexander the Great to the early fifth century in favor of the patronizing Bagratids (Books 2–3). Book 1 includes some rare examples of pre-Christian oral poetry. In it the author reflects keen awareness of the Hellenistic historiographical emphasis on antiquity as found in the national histories of Eastern historians writing in Greek: Berossus, Manetho, Josephus, and Philo of Byblos (these he encountered in the works of Eusebius of Caesarea—his major source—and followed their apologetic commonplaces). In Books 2 and 3 he relies on various other literary and historical sources, including the earlier histories of Łazar and the *Buzandaran* collection, which he modifies as necessary for his transparent intentions.

Following the religious awakening brought about by the early translations and the literary-historical development started by Koriwn, there came yet another period of enlightenment, generated by the translation of philosophical works from the classical period and late antiquity. This was achieved by the "Hellenophile School" of the sixth–eighth centuries noted for its retention of Greek syntax. Collectively, these translations are an outgrowth of the classical curriculum consisting of the seven liberal arts that fell into two groups: the *Trivium*, consisting of grammar, rhetoric, and dialectic; and the *Quadrivium*, consisting of music, arithmetic, geometry, and astronomy. The first comprised the elements of general liberal education, the best representative of which in the Armenian literary tradition is the late sixth-century Neoplatonist philosopher Dawit', surnamed "Invincible." Because of his contemporaniety with the early activities of the school, he may have been instrumental in its founding. Four of his works were translated from Greek into Armenian, possibly during his lifetime (*Definitions of Philosophy, Commentary on Porphyry's Isagoge, Interpretation of Aristotle's Analytics,* and *Interpretation of Aristotle's Categories*). Indicative of these grammatical, rhetorical, and philosophical/theological interests are the numerous elaborations on the *Ars grammatica* of Dionysius Thrax and the more than three hundred Aristotelian and almost one hundred Philonic manuscripts (thanks to these translations, several philosophical and theological works now survive only in Armenian, including a fifth of the works of Philo of Alexandria). The second curricular division consisted of the technical disciplines or the sciences, the best representative of which is Anania Širakac'i, a prolific author of the seventh century. He wrote some twenty treatises, covering every aspect of the sciences known in the early Middle Ages.

History, however, continued to dominate the literary output for the rest of the millennium. The rise of Islam and the extent to which Arab rule affected Armenia is the subject of several historical works, the foremost of which is ascribed to a certain Sebēos. In his *History of Herakleios* the seventh-century author accounts for the Byzantine-Persian wars from the reign of Maurice (582–602) to the accession of Mu'awiyah as caliph (661–680). Łewond (c. 730–790), an apologist for the princely Bagratids (soon to become a royal dynasty, 885–1045), covers the years 632–788. T'ovmas Arcruni (c. 840–906), an apologist for the princely Arcrunis, describes life under the caliphate in the ninth century. Throughout, however, he shows dependence on all earlier Armenian historians. His younger contemporary, the patriarch Yovhannes V Drasxanakertc'i (897–925), follows Xorenac'i rather closely both in his *apologia* for the Bagratids and in his beginning from mythical times. The ethos of the time, however, is depicted best in the national epic *Sasunci Dawit'*. Later historians limit themselves to chronicles of current events, such as Aristakes Lastiverc'i (c. 1000–1073), who tells of the fall of the Bagratid capital, Ani, and Matt'eos Uṙhayec'i (i.e., Edessene, c. 1070–1140), who details the coming of the Turks and of the Crusaders. There are also poetic laments over the fall of Edessa to Nur ad-Din in 1146 (by the patriarch Nerses IV Šnorhali, 1166–1173), Jerusalem to Salaḥ ad-Din in 1187 (by the patriarch Grigor IV Pahlawuni, 1173–1193), and Constantinople to Mehmed II in 1453 (by Aṙak'el Bałišec'i, c. 1390–1454).

In spite of the dominance of the historical genre in literature, the Bible continued as the primary source of inspiration, as evidenced by the mystical soliloquies of Grigor Narekac'i (c. 945–1003) and the first literary epic, a recounting of the Bible in verse by Grigor Magistros (c. 990–1059), a work that inspired the more elaborate *Jesus the Son* by the patriarch Nerses IV Šnorhali a century later. Nerses was the most prominant figure of a new era of literary enlightenment that characterized the Armenian kingdom of Cilicia in the eleventh–fifteenth centuries. Thousands of illuminated manuscripts, mostly Bibles, and scores of commentaries on various books of the Bible survive from this period. Most of these biblical commentaries were inspired by the earlier translations of such works from Syriac and Greek. Some of these early commentaries now survive only in Armenian: Ephrem the Syrian's *Commentary on the Acts of the Apostles* and his *Commentaries on the Epistles of Paul,* John Chrysostom's *Commentary on Isaiah,* and Hesychius of Jerusalem's *Commentary on Job.*

Lexicography likewise thrived with increasingly expanded compilations when Middle Armenian was the current stage of the language. By far the most exhaustive of the Armenian lexica is the somewhat later *Nor Baṙgirk' Haykazean Lezui* (New Dictionary of the Armenian Language), published in two volumes by the Venetian Mekhitarists (1836–1837). The work encompasses all words found in medieval Armenian literature, from the fifth to the fifteenth century. Although the coverage of the earlier literature is thorough, the coverage of works written after the tenth century is rather sketchy, perhaps intentionally, to avoid what was perceived to be Cilician corruptions. No lexicon of Middle or Cilician Armenian exists. Such a work should necessarily include words found outside published religious texts and should account for unpublished manuscripts with secular contents.

[See also Armenia.]

BIBLIOGRAPHY

Abełyan, Manuk. *Hayoc' hin grakanut'yan patmut'yun* (History of Ancient Armenian Literature). 2 vols. Erevan, 1944–1946. Authoritative survey of ancient Armenian literature, organized by genre.

Abrahamyan, A. G. *Hay gri ev grč'ut'yan patmut'yun* (History of the Armenian Script and Writing). Erevan, 1959. The best treatment of the subject, in the absence of a definitive work that would include recent discoveries in the Sinai and Jerusalem.

Ačařyan, Hrač'eay. *Classification des dialectes arméniens.* Paris, 1909. Handy guide to the Armenian regional dialects, unsurpassed by recent works.

Ačařyan, Hrač'eay. *Hayerēn armatakan baŕaran* (Etymological Dictionary of Armenian). 7 vols. Erevan, 1926–1935. Standard reference.

Ačařyan, Hrač'eay. *Hayoc' lezvi patmut'yun* (History of the Armenian Language). 2 vols. Erevan, 1926–1935. Classic source, in spite of more recent works.

Amalyan, H. M. *Mijnadaryan Hayastani baŕaranagrakan hušarjannerĕ* (The Lexicographical Masterpieces of Medieval Armenia). 2 vols. Erevan, 1966–1971. Provides thorough, topical coverage of Armenian lexicography through the middle ages.

Benveniste, Émile. *Origines de la formation des noms en indo-européen.* Paris, 1935. Establishes the Classical Armenian voiced stops to be the unchanged Indo-European voiced (aspirated) stops.

Etmekjian, James. *History of Armenian Literature: Fifth to Thirteenth Centuries.* New York, 1985. The best English-language survey available, although uncritical and marred by noticeable omissions.

Godel, Robert. *An Introduction to the Study of Classical Armenian.* Wiesbaden, 1975. Good primer for the beginner.

Hübschmann, Heinrich. *Kleine Schriften zum Armenischen.* Edited by Rüdiger Schmidt. Hildesheim and New York, 1976. Pioneering studies, establishing the archaic place of Armenian among the Indo-European languages, independent from Iranian. This view, however, originated with Johan Joachim Schröder in 1711.

Jensen, Hans. *Altarmenische Grammatik.* Heidelberg, 1959. One of the best Armenian grammars in the West.

Karst, Josef. *Historische Grammatik des Kilikisch-Armenischen.* Strassburg, 1901. The only work on Middle Armenian grammar.

Mann, Stuart E. *An Armenian Historical Grammar in Latin Characters (Morphology, Etymology, Old Texts).* London, 1968. Fine interpretation of the grammatical facts of the language.

Markey, T. L., and John A. C. Greppin, eds. *When Worlds Collide: The Indo-Europeans and the Pre–Indo-Europeans.* Linguistica Extranea, Studia 19. Ann Arbor, Mich., 1990. Collection of interdisciplinary papers from a 1988 conference held in Bellagio, dealing with the roots of Indo-European culture(s) and the Indo-Europeanization of large parts of Eurasia. Substantial attention is given to Armenian and the question of the original homeland of the Proto–Indo-Europeans.

Meillet, Antoine. *Esquisse d'une grammaire comparée de l'arménien classique.* 2d ed. Vienna, 1936. Standard work in a European language.

Pedersen, Holger. *Kleine Schriften zum Armenischen.* Edited by Rüdiger Schmidt. Hildesheim and New York, 1982. Significant studies, especially on the Classical Armenian voiced stops, establishing them to be the unchanged Indo-European voiced (aspirated) stops—as independently demonstrated by Benveniste.

Stone, Michael E. *The Armenian Inscriptions from the Sinai with Appendixes on the Georgian and Latin Inscriptions by Michel van Esbroeck and W. Adler.* Harvard Armenian Texts and Studies, no. 6. Cambridge, Mass., 1982. Middle Armenian rock inscriptions and graffiti;

constitutes a major contribution to Armenian epigraphy and paleography.

Terian, Abraham. "The Hellenizing School: Its Time, Place, and Scope of Activities Reconsidered." In *East of Byzantium: Syria and Armenia in the Formative Period,* edited by Nina G. Garsoïan et al., pp. 175–186. Washington, D.C., 1982. Surveys the mostly philosophical translations of the Hellenophile School of the sixth to eighth centuries and its formation.

Thomson, Robert W. "The Formation of the Armenian Literary Tradition." In *East of Byzantium: Syria and Armenia in the Formative Period,* edited by Nina G. Garsoïan et al., pp. 135–150. Washington, D.C., 1982. Treats the development of Armenian literary productions and other literary works from the formative period to the ninth century.

Thomson, Robert W. *An Introduction to Classical Armenian.* 2d ed. Delmar, N.Y., 1989. Good textbook for the English reader.

ABRAHAM TERIAN

'ARO'ER

'ARO'ER (Ar., Ar'arah), site located on a low ridge overlooking a broad wadi in Israel's Negev desert, some 22 km (13 mi.) southeast of Beersheba (map reference 1479 × 0623). In *1 Samuel* 30:28, David sends the spoils of war to 'Aro'er's elders. It appears also in *Joshua* 15:22, defining the borders of Judah. It is written *Adada* in the Masoretic text. Guided by the Arabic pronunciation, the site was first identified as 'Aro'er by Edward Robinson in 1838. Excavations were carried out between 1975 and 1982 by Avraham Biran of the Nelson Glueck School of Biblical Archaeology of the Hebrew Union College in Jerusalem and Rudolph Cohen of the Israel Antiquities Authority.

Six areas were opened: areas A, B, D, and Y on the mound's summit; area C at the base of its southeastern slope; and area F on a terrace in the Naḥal 'Aro'er drainage at the southwest foot of the tell. The tell, or acropolis, occupied an area of approximately 1 ha (2.5 acres), but in the Iron Age the settlement also occupied another hectare or so outside the early acropolis wall (stratum IV). Four main strata were identified:

Stratum I: Herodian (50 BCE–135 CE)
Stratum II: Iron III (late seventh–early sixth centuries BCE)
Stratum III: Iron III (mid- to late seventh century BCE)
Stratum IV: Iron II–III (late eighth or early seventh–mid-seventh centuries BCE)

The founding layer, stratum IV, featured a solid offset-inset wall as the dominant feature. Its surfaces were plastered, and an earthen, stone-lined glacis was built against it from the outside. Some indications point to a gateway on the southwest. Structures were erected against this wall along its inner face and toward the interior of the settlement. The area outside the walls was also occupied by architectural remains dating to this phase over an area of approximately one hectare. This stratum has been attributed by the excavators to a fortification project ostensibly carried out by Manasseh, king of Judah, which included a number of sites.

However, the pottery and certain other artifacts—three *lamelekh* seals in particular—suggest a possible earlier date, perhaps during the reign of Hezekiah.

In stratum III the acropolis wall and gateway went out of use; structures were built over it and the upper mound's area was expanded by terracing. The lower slopes were also built up intensely during this period, and many round, stone-lined silos were constructed. In stratum II, the last Iron Age stratum, a small fort was built over the remains of the stratum IV gateway on the acropolis. The settlement was reoccupied around this fort, much as before, often using existing walls.

The cosmopolitan nature of strata III and II is accented by Edomite epigraphic material and pottery, as well as by pottery, glass, and a commercial weight in the Assyrian style—all of which coexisted with the dominant Judahite material: pottery, pillar figurines, a shekel weight, and three *lamelekh* impressions. Located on a prominent transversal route between the King's Highway on the Transjordan plateau and the coast, 'Aro'er was probably a major trade center and provisioning station. For most of its history it seems to have been controlled by Judah (under the larger Assyrian umbrella), though at a later stage the area may have come under Edomite dominion. [*See* Edom.]

Stratum I was comprised of two phases: the earlier dated to the late Second Temple period (first century BCE–first century CE) and the last to the period between the destruction of the Temple and the Bar Kokhba rebellion (c. 70–135 CE). The settlement was confined to the acropolis and featured a small square, two-story fortress to which a large square courtyard was appended (in area D) and domestic structures with bread ovens in areas H and B. The finds include a well-preserved and diagnostic pottery assemblage; Nabatean wares; a moratarium with the potter's name stamped on its rim; an Aramaic inscription listing workers' salaries; chalkstone vessels; glass vessels, including an inscribed Sidonian cup; and a bronze *umbo*, or "shield boss." This small settlement may have been established under Herod the Great, or, more likely, in light of the numismatic evidence, Agrippa (38–44 CE). The excavations at 'Aro'er resulted in three significant contributions to the field.

1. The three Iron Age strata (II–IV) represent discrete, well-defined material-culture assemblages that show typological development and changing cultural affinities over a relatively short time (about 100–150 years). The ceramic repertoires of these strata can be used as points of reference and comparison for more poorly defined assemblages in southern Judah, Edom, and Moab. [*See* Moab.] Relative chronologies can thus be fine tuned to within approximately fifty years.

2. The combination of Judahite, Edomite, and Assyrian attributes in the material culture allows scholars to make inferences about economic ties, cultural affiliations, and political control in the Negev in the Iron Age.

3. The stratum I artifactual assemblage is a classic one of much utility for comparative purposes. The final phase, closely dated to about 70–135 CE, is also significant for pinning down the dating and historical context of contemporary settlements at other sites.

BIBLIOGRAPHY

Biran, Avraham. " 'And David Sent Spoils . . . to the Elders in Aroer' (I Sam. 30:26–28): Excavators Bring Life to Ancient Negev Fortress but Find No Remains of David's Time." *Biblical Archaeology Review* 9 (1983): 28–37. Popular account of the excavations—including good color photos—with a more detailed discussion of the biblical associations.

Biran, Avraham, and Rudolph Cohen. "Aroer in the Negev." *Eretz-Israel* 15 (1981): 250–273. The most complete publication to date, including detailed plans, sections, and stratigraphically organized material culture plates (though stratum IV is not represented in the latter). See page 84* for an English summary.

Biran, Avraham. "Aroer (in Judea)." In *The New Encyclopedia of Archaeological Excavations in the Holy Land*, vol. 1, pp. 89–92. Jerusalem and New York, 1993. The most comprehensive English publication to date.

Hershkovitz, Malka. "Aroer at the End of the Second Temple Period." *Eretz-Israel* 23 (1992): 309–319. Good summary of the finds from a closely dated context, making it one of the type-sites for the period. Illustrations are useful for comparative purposes. See page 156* for an English summary.

DAVID ILAN

ARSLANTEPE, tell *(höyük)* located in eastern Turkey, 6 km (4 mi.) northeast of the town of Malatya and 4 km (2.5 mi.) south of the town of Eski Malatya (Old Malatya), the ancient Roman settlement, in the modern village of Orduzu, 15 km (9 mi.) from the right bank of the Euphrates River. The site, which is about 30 m high, dominated the Malatya plain from the fifth millennium to the Neo-Hittite age (1200–700 BCE), evident from the interrupted succession of many settlement levels, some with monumental architecture. After the conquest of the Assyrian king Sargon II in 712 BCE, the site declined for the first time in millennia. However, it seems to have been occupied as a simple rural village in Roman times, between the fourth and sixth centuries CE, even once the main center had moved to Eski Malatya, the ancient town of Melitene.

The earliest historical reference to the town, known as Mal(i)dija, was in the final phase of the Middle Hittite Kingdom in about 1400 BCE, when it submitted to a Hittite king. When it appears in later Assyrian, Neo-Assyrian, and Babylonian sources, the name *Mi/Melidia, Mi/Melidu,* or *Mi/Melid* is used (see Hawkins, 1993, pp. 35–36) for one of the flourishing Neo-Hittite centers that sprang up in the eastern regions following the breakup of the Hittite Empire. [*See* Hittites.]

It is the Neo-Hittite period stone reliefs, identified on the mound by late nineteenth- and early twentieth-century travelers, that led the French scholar Louis Delaporte to conduct

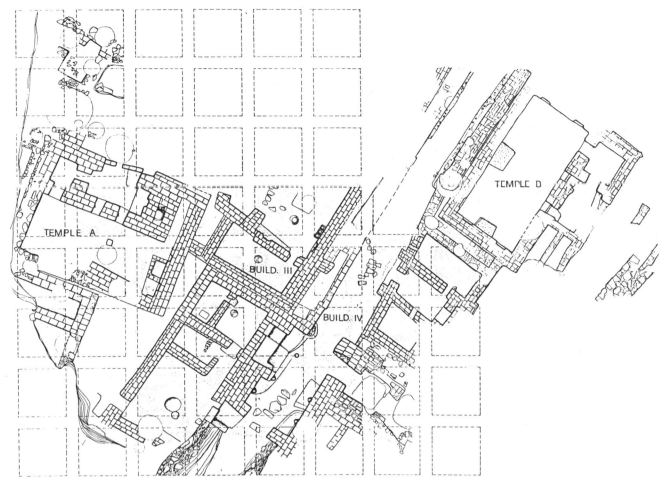

ARSLANTEPE. *Plan of the site.* (Courtesy M. Frangipane)

the first archaeological work there (1932–1939). Delaporte's excavations unearthed a tenth-century BCE palace with an entry gate flanked by two sculpted lions (the Lion Gate) and a paved courtyard, both with limestone bas-reliefs decorating their walls. Together with the large statue of a ruler erected after the construction of the gate, this is one of the most important Neo-Hittite art complexes.

Claude F.-A. Schaeffer carried out some deep soundings at the site in the early 1950s. An Italian archaeological mission has been systematically excavating there since 1961. Begun by Piero Meriggi, from Pavia University, the excavation was directed initially by Salvatore Puglisi and then by Alba Palmieri, both from Rome University. [*See the biography of Schaeffer.*]

The Italian mission began excavating on the northeast part of the mound, where the structures Delaporte brought to light lay. In addition to identifying other Neo-Hittite and imperial Hittite buildings, a sequence of walls and town gates belonging to the various phases of Hittite influence from between 1500 and 900 BCE were identified, superimposed on the outermost parts of the Late Chalcolithic and

Early Bronze Age settlements. In the early 1970s, the mission began work in the southwest zone, where the main nuclei of the third- and fourth-millennium settlements seemed to be. Extensive excavations in this zone, and more recently on the western part of the mound, have revealed wide areas of many superimposed settlements. As a result, it is now possible to reconstruct thoroughly the history of the site and the region from the late fifth to the early second millennium BCE.

The earliest level reached so far, which is carbon-14 dated to the end of the fifth millennium (4300–4000 BCE; period VIII in the site's internal sequencing), refers to a little-known cultural aspect of the region from the end of the Ubaid period. (Schaeffer seems to have reached a typical Ubaid horizon with painted pottery in a deep sounding.) While this aspect was represented by domestic structures, at least in the small area excavated, it was in the later period (VII), in the first half of the fourth millennium, that monumental structures were built. The settlement, which covered the whole area presently occupied by the tell, had functionally different sectors: the northeast zone was covered by dwell-

ARSLANTEPE. *Excavated site.* (Courtesy M. Frangipane)

ings with varying floor plans, and domestic structures such as ovens, basins, and burials under the floor; the western zone contained large, imposing buildings, with thick mudbrick walls coated in white plaster and distinctive floor plans and decorative features, built at a much higher level, on what must have been the top of the ancient mound. A building with several adjacent rooms had some of the walls painted red and black, with what were probably geometric designs, and mud-plastered mud-brick columns arranged along the walls. Whatever activities were performed there, the building must have been important and used by the emerging elites.

This community's handicrafts show an increasingly complex organization of labor, judging from the abundant massproduced pottery, the widespread use of the wheel and potters' marks, and the many metal slag and copper ore fragments and finished copper objects (pins, awls, chisels) found on the site. This Late Chalcolithic aspect belongs to a broader cultural horizon that, with significant local differences, covers all the Upper Euphrates valley and the 'Amuq plain (Antiochia), where it is represented by phase F. [*See* 'Amuq.]

A central power became fully established in the next period (VIA), between 3300 and 3000 BCE, when the Late Uruk Mesopotamian culture expanded northward, and Arslantepe entered an extended exchange network. In this period, a new large building was erected on the ruins of the Late Chalcolithic building in the western area of the mound, in a topographically preeminent position; at the same time, a large public area with monumental buildings was constructed on the southwest slope. Three buildings were unearthed there whose function was religious, in addition to being used for centralized economic and administrative activities. The oldest of these (building IV) was also the most complex and most monumental: it comprised a large bipartite temple (temple B) surrounded by wide corridors and bordered on the south by a row of adjacent storerooms. Entrance was through a monumental rectangular gate. The walls around the openings and in the most interior part of the main corridor leading to the temple were decorated with red and black wall paintings. Particularly noteworthy are the paintings, covering two of the walls in the central room leading to the storerooms, where a stylized human figure with raised arms standing before a table or an altar under a kind of canopy is repeatedly depicted. The corridor and the rooms surrounding the cella of the temple were decorated with plastic concentric lozenges applied with a stamp, very similar to a related decoration in one of the Uruk-Warka level III temples. [*See* Wall Paintings.]

Apart from the ideological-religious sphere, the central institutions, which were certainly very powerful by this time, probably controlled most economic activities through a sophisticated administrative system. This is evidenced from the thousands of clay sealings found both in situ in one of the storerooms in building IV and piled in a set order in a kind of dumping place in one of the walls in the large corridor, where they had been discarded, probably after being checked and recorded. [*See* Seals.] The system must have been quite complex, which the great many officials inferred from the repeated impressions of more than 150 different seals suggest. These consist mainly of stamp seals with rich figurative motifs depicted in different styles, evidence of flourishing local glyptics. A few cylinder seals, sometimes bearing motifs of Mesopotamian style, are also present. Metallurgy was considerably developed at this time, as well. Twenty-one weapons of arsenical copper, swords and spearheads, plus a quadruple spiral plaque in another cult building (building III) to the west of building IV, on a higher terrace, were discovered.

Another temple (temple A) was built later toward the western edge of the mound. It also was bipartite and followed almost the same floorplan as temple B, showing that there existed a typical Arslantepe temple design at the end of the fourth millennium. The walls in one of rooms adjacent to the cella also were decorated with plastic geometric motifs, in this case concentric ovals. Again, a large number of discarded clay sealings were found, even though activity was evidently on a much smaller scale. The decreasing dimensions of the public buildings and the declining scale of activities performed are perhaps indications of the crisis that was to strike. The public area was abandoned and this early state system, which had been strongly influenced by the Late Uruk culture, while remaining markedly original, collapsed.

Following the destruction of temple A, at the beginning of the third millennium (period VIB1), the site was inhabited by groups of an Eastern Anatolian/Transcaucasian culture using a typical handmade red-black ware; they built a village of huts on the ruins of the late fourth millennium monumental buildings. The close links with the south were severed, except for a short period of contact with the northern Syro-Mesopotamian area immediately afterward (VIB2). The evidence at Arslantepe is of a village of mud-brick houses, with plain, wheelmade pottery in the Late Uruk tradition.

The new links with northeastern Anatolia underlay the development of a new local culture throughout the whole of the third millennium, beginning in 2700 BCE (Early Bronze II and III period, phases VIC and VID), which was restricted to the regions of Malatya and Elazig, with characteristic handmade painted pottery in addition to a more abundant red-black ware. During the second part of this period, a new urban structure of Anatolian tradition was established at Arslantepe. A walled town with a well-planned urban layout was constructed, exploiting the sharp slope of the tell with impressive terracing works.

This local cultural characterization remained almost unchanged even during the Middle Bronze Age (phase VA, 2000–1700 BCE). New links in pottery production with the areas south of the Taurus Mountains and, to a lesser degree, central Anatolia, are evidence, however, of the new international relations then being established between the emerging political entities on the Anatolian highlands and the states of Upper Mesopotamia. Soon, though, the eastward expansion of the Hittite kingdom brought the region of Malatya into the sphere of influence of central Anatolia.

BIBLIOGRAPHY

Delaporte, Louis. *Malatya, Arslantepe.* Paris, 1940. Final report on the Neo-Hittite palace and reliefs excavated by the French expedition in the 1930s.

Frangipane, Marcella, and Alba Palmieri, eds. "Perspectives on Protourbanization in Eastern Anatolia: Arslantepe (Malatya), an Interim Report on the 1975–1983 Campaigns." *Origini* 12.2 (1983): 287–668. The most complete report on the archaeology, geomorphology, archaeozoology, paleobotany, dating, and archaeometallurgy of the EB IA and B levels (phases VIA and VIB).

Frangipane, Marcella, and Alba Palmieri. "Urbanization in Perimesopotamian Areas: The Case of Eastern Anatolia." In *Studies in the Neolithic and Urban Revolutions,* edited by Linda Manzanilla, pp. 295–318. British Archaeological Reports, International Series, no. 349. Oxford, 1987. Remarks on the cultural relations shown by the site with southern Mesopotamia and other Mesopotamian-related northern sites in the Late Uruk period. Some suggestions are given on the role of external relations in early urban developments at Arslantepe.

Frangipane, Marcella. "Dipinti murali in un edificio 'palaziale' di Arslantepe-Malatya: Aspetti ideologici nelle prime forme di centralizzarione economica." *Studi Miceni ed Egeo-Anatolici* 30 (1992): 143–154. Preliminary publication of the wall paintings at the site.

Frangipane, Marcella. "Arslantepe-Melid-Malatya." In *Scavi archeologici italiani in Turchia,* pp. 31–103. Venice, 1993. Up-to-date general presentation of the archaeology of the site, with color plates.

Frangipane, Marcella. "Melid (Malatya, Arslan-Tepe). Archäologisch." In *Reallexikon der Assyriologie und Vorderasiatischen Archäologie,* vol. 8.1–2, pp. 42–52. Berlin, 1993. General synthesis of the site's cultural sequence, taking into account the results obtained up to the 1989 campaign. In English.

Frangipane, Marcella. "The Record Function of Clay Sealings in Early Administrative Systems as Seen from Arslantepe-Malatya." In *Archives before Writing,* edited by Piera Ferioli et al., pp. 125–147. Turin, 1994.

Hawkins, J. D. "Melid (Malatya, Arslan-Tepe). Historisch." In *Reallexikon der Assyriologie und Vorderasiatischen Archäologie,* vol. 8.1–2, pp. 35–41. Berlin, 1993. General presentation of data on the name, historical sources, and inscriptions concerning the site. In English.

Palmieri, Alba. "Scavi nell'area sud-occidentale di Arslantepe: Ritrovamento di una struttura templare dell'Antica Età del Bronzo." *Origini* 7 (1973): 55–182. Exhaustive report on the EB levels up to 1973.

Palmieri, Alba. "Excavations at Arslantepe (Malatya)." *Anatolian Studies* 31 (1981): 101–119. First presentation of the public buildings from the end of the fourth millennium (phase VIA) with metal weapons and clay sealings, including a discussion of their significance and a short analysis of the successive developments in EB IB.

Palmieri, Alba. "Storage and Distribution at Arslantepe-Malatya in the Late Uruk Period." In *Anatolia and the Ancient Near East: Studies in Honor of Tahsin Ozguc,* edited by Kutlu Emre et al., pp. 419–430. Ankara, 1989. Analysis of the functional organization of centralized storerooms in period VIA building IV and a preliminary presentation of wall paintings in the entrance room.

Pecorella, Paolo E. *Malatya III: Il livello eteo imperiale e quelli neoetei.* Orientis Antiqui Collectio, 12. Rome, 1975. General report on the archaeological remains of the Hittite period excavated by the original Italian expedition.

Puglisi, Salvatore M., and Piero Meriggi. *Malatya I: Rapporto preliminare delle campagne 1961 e 1962.* Orientis Antiqui Collectio, 3. Rome, 1964. Preliminary report on the first two campaigns carried out at the site by the Italian group.

Schneider Equini, Eugenia. *Malatya II: Il livello romano bizantino e le testimonianze islamiche.* Orientis Antiqui Collectio, 10. Rome, 1970. Report on the Roman-Byzantine remains found at the site.

MARCELLA FRANGIPANE

ARTIFACT CONSERVATION. Archaeological artifacts provide a unique record of human behavior. As the tangible remains of past societies, reflecting their ideas, beliefs, and activities, artifacts can be regarded as primary documents of human behavior. At all times, their integrity and research potential must be kept in mind. Preservation, or stabilization, rather than restoration, should be the primary and ethical aim of archaeological conservation. Whenever possible, noninvasive procedures should be selected and intervention kept to a minimum because intervention can lessen the research potential of artifacts. Each subsequent treatment moves the artifact farther from its original state.

Treating an artifact is not necessarily restricted to preserving its appearance or its essential material(s). The technological information an artifact embodies such as repairs or modifications made in antiquity, must also be preserved.

Conservation consists of two main functions: preservation and restoration. The goal of preservation is to stabilize, or arrest, damage to and the deterioration of artifacts. It usually involves controlling an artifact's immediate environment and the conditions of its use, but can also involve treatment when done to stabilize an object. The purpose of restoration, a term frequently but erroneously used interchangeably with conservation, is to return an artifact to its original or a previous appearance. Restoration involves carefully considering the modification of an object's material and structure. While generally done for exhibition or educational purposes to aid in the process of interpretation, restoration can also be used to stabilize an artifact.

The underlying precept guiding all conservation work is respect for an artifact's aesthetic, historical, and physical integrity. For most archaeological materials, historical and physical integrity may be of greater concern than the aesthetic. An artifact's history should be preserved and not sacrificed in returning it to its original condition or in restoring it for solely aesthetic reasons. For example, if a vessel was repaired with rivets in antiquity, those modifications should not be removed today, no matter how unsightly. Respect for an object's integrity also involves not imposing on it the conservator's own cultural values and assumptions about how it should look.

Conservation treatment includes examination, analysis of the materials used to create artifacts, active treatment involving stabilization and restoration, passive treatment involving environmental controls, and documentation. Conservators strive to use only reversible materials when they actively treat artifacts. Reversibility means that any treatment applied must be capable of being reversed or removed at a later date, without damaging or changing the object. The idea of reversibility recognizes that conservation knowledge is constantly developing. Future analytical methods will surpass current techniques, perhaps enabling the extraction of new information from uncompromised artifacts.

Some treatments by their very nature are not reversible. For example, if an object has lost so much of its cohesiveness that it cannot be lifted out of the ground safely, it may be necessary to strengthen it by adding a consolidant, even though this process is not fully reversible. Thus, the concept of reversibility is of particular significance to on-site conservation, where often procedures must be carried out under less than ideal conditions. What is done in the field more often than not has to be redone in the laboratory.

Striving for reversibility ensures that conservators use only quality materials that will endure. Pure materials are used rather than their proprietary equivalents, which contain, potentially harmful additives that extend their shelf life or modify their properties.

Minimal intervention has become a realistic tenet in conservation work: treatment should not be more extensive than absolutely necessary, and it should leave an artifact as close to its original condition as possible. If an artifact appears to be sound and has a good chance of survival without treatment, then nothing should be done. When treatment is necessary, the conservation materials applied should be used minimally. Minimal intervention is particularly important when treatment may alter or destroy technological information.

Documentation is a vital part of any conservation treatment. Written and photographic records maintain all the technological data gleaned about an artifact during treatment, fully describing the materials and methods involved for future researchers and conservators.

Minimal intervention and full documentation take on particular importance when treating artifacts to be analyzed. Any treatment an artifact receives, including mere cleaning, can contaminate it and invalidate subsequent analysis, whether for dating, elemental analysis, or identifying use residues. While most of the added treatment material can be removed to the extent that it may no longer be visible, traces will always remain to compromise it. Thus, artifacts to be analyzed are often best left untreated. At the very least, part of the artifact should be left untreated or samples taken before treatment.

There are other ways in which conservation treatment can invalidate research potential. Frequently, valuable information is embodied in the dirt or encrustations on the surface of an artifact, and, removing them can be just as damaging as adding foreign materials. Even handling can compromise future analytical work, as is the case with samples taken for carbon-14 dating. The conservator must work closely with the archaeologist to ensure that research potential is not compromised.

Conservation efforts have shifted in favor of passive, or preventive, techniques. The concept underlying this approach is that deterioration can be reduced by controlling its causes. The proper handling, storing, and exhibiting of artifacts can prevent deterioration and thus reduces the need for active, or remedial, treatment.

While most active treatment in archaeological conservation should be done by a trained conservator, preventive conservation techniques can be performed effectively by the archaeologist, particularly on site. Proper handling procedures, for example, prevent breakage and damage. The natural deterioration processes of materials can be forestalled or reduced by ensuring that artifacts are properly packed with suitable materials.

The examination of objects is an important aspect of archaeological conservation. Its goal is to extract as much information as possible to elucidate ongoing research about technology, provenance, and authenticity. A background in materials science, along with extensive experience with a wide variety of materials and artifacts, invests conservators with the knowledge and skills they need to recognize materials and determine an artifact's components. While they do not themselves undertake sophisticated analytical tests, they are familiar with the capabilities of different analytical techniques and can act as liaisons between archaeologists and other scientists.

Most archaeological conservators understand ancient

technological procedures and can thus provide information about objects that might otherwise be missed. For example, evidence of organic materials is frequently preserved by or in corrosion products on metal artifacts. In cleaning these artifacts, an experienced conservator can recognize, document, and preserve such evidence, where chemical cleaning by a nonconservator might inadvertently destroy it.

Restoration is generally not an important aspect of archaeological conservation, but at times it is appropriate. For example, restoring the missing parts of an artifact can increase its educational value or facilitate its interpretation. Restoration should be done as obviously and honestly as possible, making a clear demarcation between what is original and what has been added. Repairs or restoration should be visible and not make the artifact appear to be in better condition than it actually is.

In restoring artifacts, conservators must be careful not to impose their own aesthetic or cultural values. Missing elements, such as handles, should not be added unless there is unassailable evidence for their shape and position. Neither should the extent of decoration on an object be left to guesswork. If, for example, the decoration on an object is repetitive and symmetrical, the conservator must have clear evidence that the design continues in the same way before restoring large sections of it. Similarly, if an object's decorative elements appear randomly or are asymmetrical, only its basic shape can then be restored. Even when an artifact is part of a group, it cannot be assumed that it is just like the others. For all of these reasons, restoration is a conservation procedure that requires the collaboration of conservator and archaeologist to maintain the ethics of restoration and the information the artifacts contain.

[See also Conservation Archaeology; Field Conservation; and Museums and Museology.]

BIBLIOGRAPHY

Cronyn, J. M. *The Elements of Archaeological Conservation.* London, 1990. The only text on this topic, a good overview but should be used with caution as not all the procedures described are to be recommended.

Foley, K. "The Role of the Objects Conservator in Field Archaeology." In *Conservation on Archaeological Excavations,* edited by N. P. Stanley Price, pp. 11–20. Rome, 1984. Good discussion of the difference between conservation and restoration and of the function of an archaeological conservator.

Plenderleith, Harold J., and A. E. A. Werner. *The Conservation of Antiquities and Works of Art.* 2d ed. London, 1971. Standard text, now out of date, which must be used with caution.

Pye, E., and J. M. Cronyn. "The Archaeological Conservator Reexamined: A Personal View." In *Recent Advances in the Conservation and Analysis of Artifacts,* edited by James Black, pp. 355–357. London, 1987. British perspective on archaeological conservation and the role of the conservator, including a discussion of ethical considerations governing conservation work.

Sease, Catherine. *A Conservation Manual for the Field Archaeologist.* 2d ed. Los Angeles, 1992. Up-to-date information on the handling and treatment of artifacts on site, including methodology, bibliography, and lists of materials and suppliers.

Seeley, N. J. "Archaeological Conservation: The Development of a Discipline." *Bulletin of the Institute of Archaeology, University of London* 24 (1987): 161–175. Interesting outline of the history of archaeological conservation in Britain, including a good discussion of all basic aspects of archaeological conservation.

CATHERINE SEASE

ARTIFACT DRAFTING AND DRAWING.

Field archaeology is a destructive endeavor in the sense that the removal of occupational debris and material culture destroys certain of a site's physical features and remains. An essential component of modern excavation methodology is careful recording, so that what has been removed can be reconstructed and studied with a view to historical and cultural interpretation.

In that context, one of the important tasks of architectural drafting and drawing is to create, and thereby preserve, a visual record of the archaeological features or structures that have been partially or completely removed. The terms *feature* and *structure* have specific connotations in archaeology. A feature is a major coherent element on a site, such as a room, courtyard, or an industrial installation. A structure is a group of features that, taken together, constitute a major architectural unit in one of its phases (such as a city gate, house, or water system). The component element(s) that define a physical feature or structure are called loci (sg., locus). Most loci are real structural or architectural features.

On a daily basis, archaeologists are occupied with creating this visual record through drafting numerous plans (top plans and phase plans) and sections that record all layers and loci in horizontal and vertical relationship with one another. A top plan documents the excavation's progress, and each one is a record of the excavated area at a point in modern time during the excavation. A phase plan documents the loci and features of a given occupational level, thereby creating a record of the excavated area at some point in its history. A section drawing documents vertical relationships and represents a scale drawing of one of the sides or balks of an excavated area. This three-dimensional and descriptive recording is the basis of modern recording methodology. In theory, if plans and sections accurately reflect an excavation, it should be possible to reconstruct, with a high degree of precision, what has been removed.

Architectural drafting also plays a crucial role in the final phase of a project because plans, sections, and drawings of archaeological features and structures are published in preliminary and final reports. The architectural drafting may take one or more of three basic forms: flat line drawing, pictorial drawing, or orthographic projection. Plans and sections usually appear as flat line drawings. Features and structures are usually presented in this format but may be represented three-dimensionally in a pictorial drawing. There are three types of pictorial drawing: axonometric (including isometric projections), oblique, and perspective projections. Orthographic projections are not often used in field recording and publication.

[*See also* Architectural Drawing; Artifact Conservation; *and* Photography; *article on* Photography of Field Work and Artifacts.]

GARY D. PRATICO

ART SITES. Isolated monuments, most frequently paintings and relief sculpture, for which there is no known context are designated art sites. The best known are found in Iran and date from the Elamite period (c. 1925–1120 BCE) through the third century CE. Four groups of Elamite reliefs are carved into the rocky ravines at Izeh (formerly Malamir), east of Susiana. The Kul-i Farah ravine has six reliefs, the principle one representing King Hanni and his minister, Shutruru, attending a sacrifice in the presence of musicians. A twenty-four-line inscription runs along the width of the relief. The Shakaf-i-Salman ravine has four reliefs, two of which represent King Hanni and his spouse. A similar relief was carved into the rocky face of the mountain at Naqsh-i Rustam, four miles north of Persepolis, during the Neo-Elamite period. Naqsh-i Rustam, which became the royal necropolis of the Achaemenids in the time of Darius I (522–486 BCE), has four tombs cut into the vertical rock that are adorned with reliefs. In the third century CE, the Sasanian king Shapur I (241–272 CE) had a victory relief carved in the rock below the Achaemenid tomb, where other reliefs also celebrate Sasanian victories. [*See* Izeh; Naqsh-i Rustam; Elamites; Sasanians.]

Less sophisticated in style and conception are the thousands of rock drawings and rock inscriptions in the southern Sinai Desert. The rock drawings, which are impossible to date, were probably engraved by desert people and pilgrims. Their subjects are predominantly local animals, mostly camels and ibex, but occasionally more exotic ones, such as oryxes and ostriches. A few hunting scenes are known. The most extensive of the rock paintings is one found in Jordan, east of Amman, that depicts an antelope hunt inside an enclosure, or desert "kite." A rock drawing representing a man with his arms raised over his head, perhaps a cultic gesture, has been found at Timna' in the Negev. [*See* Timna' (Negev).]

BIBLIOGRAPHY

Berghe, Louis Vanden. "Les reliefs élamites de Mālamīr." *Iranica Antiqua* 3 (1963): 22–39.

Berghe, Louis Vanden. *Reliefs rupestres de l'Iran ancien.* Brussels, 1983. Most recent and authoritative work on the Iranian reliefs. There are no English-language works devoted exclusively to the Iranian reliefs.

Meshel, Zeev. "New Data about the 'Desert Kites.'" *Tel Aviv* I (1974): 129–143.

Meshel, Zeev, and Israel Finkelstein, eds. *Sinai in Antiquity: Researches in the History and Archaeology of the Peninsula* (in Hebrew). Tel Aviv, 1980.

LUCILLE A. ROUSSIN

ARWAD, a small island located 2.5 km (16 mi.) from Syria's Mediterranean coast, facing the city of Tortose ancient Antarados. The city of Arwad was built on the largest island of a chain of very small islands extending south to Tripoli. Oval in shape, it measures 800 × 500 m. As noted by Strabo (16.2.13), its surface area was so limited that houses had to be built several stories high. The site's name in Phoenician, *'rwd,* means "refuge." The name also appears in Eblaitic as *A-ra-wa-ad* in the Ebla archives of the second millennium BCE; in Akkadian as *Ar-wa-da, A-ru-da, A-ru-ad-da* in the Alalakh and Amarna tablets; as *Arados* in Greek and Latin; and as *Arwad* in Arabic.

The island has probably been inhabited since the Neolithic period (occupational remains of this period have been found on the mainland), but continuous human occupation at the site has erased all remains except for those belonging to the Roman period. In the fifteenth century BCE, the people of Arwad reached Ugarit and other Palestinian and Phoenician cities (Astour, 1959, 70–76). According to the Amarna letters (fourteenth century BCE), the sailors of Arwad frequently traveled to Egypt and the eastern Mediterannean. At the end of the second millennium BCE, with the invasion of the Sea Peoples, the concept of unity among Phoenician cities developed. Mutual interest led to their occasional alliance under the authority of one or the other of them for a limited period in order avoid the rivalry of the great powers. These cities, however, remained basically independent city-states. [*See* Phoenicia; Phoenicians.]

The cuneiform sources related to the campaigns of Tiglath-Pileser (1115–1077 BCE) mention the continental area of Arwad, which probably provided food for the island and also served as its cemetery. This idea is strengthened by the recent discovery of a necropolis of royal character southeast of Tortose dating to the fifth century BCE. (The cemetery is not yet published, but the sarcophagi are in the Tortose Museum.) Toward the mid-ninth century BCE, Arwad was only a small city-state, compared with the large neighboring kingdoms of Siyannu and Irqata (Tell 'Arqa). Arwad and Ushatu sent two hundred soldiers each to Qarqar against Shalmaneser III in 853 BCE, while Siyannu and Irqata each contributed ten thousand. (Pritchard, *ANET,* p. 279). It is also at about this time that the Greeks established their settlements south of Arwad (Riis, 1970, p. 161). At the beginning of the eighth century BCE, Arwad flourished as a result of its shipbuilding trade. The skill of its builders helped expand the kingdom onto the mainland; the Aramean presence marked Arwad's inland boundaries. [*See* Arameans.] Arwad soon lost its continental provinces to Sumur, however, which became the capital of Amurru.

In 701 BCE, Abdil'ti, king of Arwad, paid tribute to Sennacherib. His successor, Matanba'al, is mentioned among the twelve kings of the seacoast who were ordered by Esarhaddon (680–669 BCE) to transport "building material" to Nineveh (Pritchard, *ANET,* no. 297). In administrative documents found in Babylon, the king of Arwad is mentioned among others who belonged to the court of Nebuchadrezzar II (605–562 BCE), where carpenters from Arwad were employed. The shipbuilding craft continues on Arwad to the present day. [*See* Ships and Boats.]

During the Persian period, the Persian king owned a sumptuous palace on the island, and the Aradian navy, led by Merbal son of Agbal, joined Xerxes's expedition against the Greeks. With Alexander the Great's conquest of Syria, Gerastratos, king of Arwad, surrendered his kingdom to the conqueror. Later, however, the Seleucids offered the Aradian confederation autonomy.

Documentation related to Arwad in the Roman period is scarce. Silver coins disappear in 46/45 BCE, and gradually Arados ceases to be mentioned. The few remaining monuments on the island include a huge rampart built to protect it both from its enemies and from stormy winter seas. This wall dates to the Hellenistic or Roman period.

[*See also the biography of Seyrig.*]

BIBLIOGRAPHY

Astour, Michael. "Les étrangers à Ougarit et le statut juridique des Habim." *Revue d'Assyriologie et d'Archéologie Orientale* 59 (1959): 70–76.

Pritchard, James B. *Ancient Near Eastern Texts Relating to the Old Testament (ANET).* Princeton, 1969.

Rey-Coquais, Jean-Paul. *Arados et sa pérée aux époques grecque, romaine et byzantine.* Paris, 1974.

Riis, Paul J. *Sūkas I. The North-East Sanctuary and the First Settling of the Greeks in Syria and Palestine.* Copenhagen, 1970.

Seyrig, Henri. "Aradus et sa pérée sous les rois Séleucides." *Syria* 28 (1951): 206–220.

LEILA BADRE

ASHDOD, large mound of some 70 acres, located on the Mediterranean coast north of Ashkelon, that was a major seaport in the Late Bronze and Iron Ages (map reference 118 × 129). The site was excavated from 1962 to 1972 for the Israel Department of Antiquities, under the direction of Moshe Dothan. Twenty-three strata were discerned, from the late Middle Bronze to the Byzantine period.

The first fortified city began in MB III (stratum XXIII), with defenses that included city walls, an earthen glacis, and a rare two-entryway gate (rather than the usual three-entryway type). There follow five ephemeral LB phases (strata XVIII–XXII).

The main LB phase (LB IIA–B) is represented by strata XIV–XVII, all showing strong continuity. Its substantial mud-brick buildings may even be fortified. One large, multiroomed courtyard structure may be an example of the Egyptian-style "residences" known at other Amarna Age sites in Canaan. A fragmentary doorpost that may have originated in this building is inscribed with a name that may be that of an Egyptian governor. There are also imports from Cyprus and the Mycenaean world. The city of stratum XIV was violently destroyed by fire toward the end of the thirteenth century BCE and covered by a thick ash layer, apparently by the "Sea Peoples."

Stratum XIIIA–B marks a major change at Ashdod. Stratum XIIIB is transitional, with new constructions, some partially built over the earlier fortifications. Characteristic imported Mycenaean IIIC:1 sherds date this brief occupation to about 1225–1175 BCE. Stratum XIIIA represents the first substantial Philistine settlement, which then continues through to its main phase in strata XII–XI. Ashdod was one of the five cities of the Philistine Pentapolis known from the Bible (the others being Gaza, Ashkelon, Ekron/Tel Miqne and Gath/Tel 'Erani). [*See* Ashkelon; Miqne, Tel; 'Erani, Tel.] A large fortress constructed in stratum XI in area A, marked by Philistine Bichrome ware, continued in use into the early tenth century BCE. In area G, stratum XII was represented by heavy structures, some forming a "casemate" line of defense. Several of the rooms were used as workshops. In one of them, stacks of painted bowls of Mycenaean IIIC type were found, some possibly imported, the forerunners of the full-blown Philistine Bichrome ware. In area H a distinctive apsidal structure belonging to stratum XII may have had a cultic function, to judge from a terra cotta representing a female goddess seated on a couch, similar to the well known Mycenaean "mourner" figurines. There were also two seals, one with signs similar to the Cypro-Minoan script used on Cyprus and in the eastern Mediterranean in the thirteenth–twelfth centuries BCE, the other with signs and a pictorial representation in the Aegean style. [*See* Seals; Minoans.] These are so far the only examples of a possible Philistine script. In area M, there was evidence of the expansion of Philistine occupation beyond the acropolis to the lower city in the mid-eleventh century BCE (stratum XB). A two-chambered mud-brick city gate attached to a section of city wall is attributed by the excavator to stratum XA; it is thought to have been destroyed in the early tenth century BCE, in the campaigns of King David.

The Iron II period is represented by strata IX–VI, mostly in the lower city. Near the area M gate a new city gate was built, of the four-entryway type familiar at Israelite sites of the tenth century BCE (e.g., at Hazor, Megiddo, Gezer) connected to a solid rather than a casemate wall. [*See* Hazor; Megiddo; Gezer.] A variant of the typical Israelite red-burnished pottery now begins to appear at Ashdod—red burnished but with bands of black; Philistine Bichrome ware is now extinct. A fortress was built in stratum IX that is connected with this pottery. In stratum VIII a small temple with several rooms was found with a considerable number of anthropomorphic and zoomorphic figurines, many of them from Kernoi. The scattered skeletal remains of some three thousand humans were also found, some with funerary offerings, most in secondary burials. The excavators suggest that these remains testify to the destruction by Sargon II in

711 BCE, known from both Assyrian and biblical texts. Two fragments of a basalt relief of Sargon were recovered, similar to victory stelae found at Khorsabad. [*See* Khorsabad.] Stratum VII belongs to the early seventh century BCE. Ashdod is probably best understood then not as a Judean site, but as part of the "Neo-Philistine" culture that still flourished along the southern coast—as Late Iron Age Ashkelon, Miqne/Ekron, and several other sites also seem to be. Yet, some Hebrew ostraca, inscribed weights, and a few royal stamped jar handles attest to trade with Judah. Stratum VI lasts until the end of the seventh century BCE and the rise of Babylon.

Stratum V has remains of a large public building of the Persian period, some fine jewelry, and an Aramaic ostracon reading "wine delivered in the name of Zebadiah." Hellenistic remains (stratum IV) reveal a well-planned town. Strata III–I represent the Roman, Byzantine, and Early Arab periods at Ashdod. Following the First Jewish Revolt against Rome and the destruction of Jerusalem in 70 CE, Ashdod was of little importance, however.

BIBLIOGRAPHY

Dothan, Moshe, and David Noel Freedman. *Ashdod I: The First Season of Excavations, 1962.* 'Atiqot, 7. Jerusalem, 1967.
Dothan, Moshe. *Ashdod II–III: The Second and Third Seasons of Excavations, 1963, 1965.* 'Atiqot, 9–10. Jerusalem, 1971.
Dothan, Moshe, and Yosef Porath. *Ashdod IV: Excavation of Area M.* 'Atiqot, 15. Jerusalem, 1982.
Dothan, Moshe, and Yosef Porath. *Ashdod V: Excavation of Area G, the Fourth–Sixth Seasons of Excavations, 1968–1970.* 'Atiqot, 23. Jerusalem, 1993.
Dothan, Trude, and Moshe Dothan. *People of the Sea: The Search for the Philistines.* New York, 1992.

WILLIAM G. DEVER

ASHKELON, site located on Israel's Mediterranean coast, some 63 km (39 mi.) south of Tel Aviv and 16 km (10 mi.) north to Gaza (31°40' N, 34°33' E; map reference 107 × 119). The ruins of the ancient city, now a national park, form a 150-acre semicircle that faces the sea. Archaeological excavations have revealed evidence of occupation beginning as early as the Neolithic period and ending with the final abandonment of the site in Crusader times. The aquifer running under the site made it a favored spot for settlement, and it became an important seaport at an early date. The name Ashkelon itself is attested in historical records (the Egyptian Execration texts) as early as the nineteenth century BCE. It probably reflects the Semitic root *tql, "to weigh," and so is related to the Hebrew word *shekel*. Ashkelon flourished as a center of trade under this name—transmuted to Ascalon during the Hellenistic period—from about 2000 BCE (if not earlier) until its demise in 1270 CE.

During the Late Bronze Age, Ashkelon was part of the Egyptian Empire in Canaan. Several letters from its ruler to the pharaoh were found in the el-Amarna archive. Toward the end of the Late Bronze Age (c. 1200 BCE), Pharaoh Merneptah commemorated his suppression of a revolt by Ashkelon and other groups in Canaan. Ashkelon did not remain in Egyptian hands much longer, however; it fell to the Sea Peoples in about 1175 BCE. Ashkelon became a member of the Philistine pentapolis, along with Gaza, Ashdod, Gath, and Ekron. This is how it is known in the story of Samson (*Jgs.* 14:19) and in other biblical texts dealing with the period of the Judges and the rise of David in Israel (*Jos.* 13:3; *Jgs.* 1:18; *I Sm.* 6:17; *2 Sm.* 1:20).

Ashkelon is not mentioned again in historical sources until the time of Tiglath-Pileser III of Assyria, who conquered Philistia in 734 BCE (cf. *Am.* 1:6–8). Some years later, at the time of Sennacherib's campaign against Jerusalem in 701 BCE, the Assyrian army suppressed a rebellion in which Ashkelon was involved. For the remainder of the Neo-Assyrian period in the seventh century, we hear only that Ashkelon paid tribute to Esarhaddon and Ashurbanipal. The Philistine period at Ashkelon finally came to an end in 604 BCE, when the Neo-Babylonian army under Nebuchadrezzar destroyed the city and deported its rulers (cf. *Jer.* 47:4–7).

During the Persian period, Ashkelon was ruled by Phoenicians from Tyre (according to the fourth-century BCE Greek geographer Pseudo-Scylax) under ultimate Persian suzerainty. It prospered under this arrangement as one of the major ports of Palestine. After Alexander's conquest of the Persian Empire, Ashkelon (now Ascalon) became a thoroughly hellenized city and flourished as a center of commerce and of the arts throughout the Hellenistic and Roman periods. Under both the Maccabees and the Romans, in fact, Ascalon enjoyed autonomy as a free city, even minting its own coins. Eventually, the pagan city of Ascalon became a Byzantine Christian stronghold, the seat of a bishopric. In 636 CE it passed from Byzantine to Muslim rule, but it remained a prominent and wealthy seaport. The Crusaders managed to capture Ascalon in 1153 but lost it to Saladin in 1187, who ordered its destruction in 1191, lest it fall intact into the hands of a new army of Crusaders led by Richard the Lion Heart. The city was partially rebuilt and served for a time as a Crusader fortress; its fate was sealed in 1270, however, when it was destroyed for the last time by the Mamluk sultan Baybars. Since then the site has been uninhabited.

Lady Hester Stanhope, an Englishwoman living in Syria, mounted a treasure-hunting expedition to Ashkelon in 1815. Her workmen found no treasure but did unearth a Roman-era building, probably a basilica, and a large headless statue. Proper excavation of the site was not attempted until 1920–1921, when John Garstang, under the auspices of the Palestine Department of Antiquities and the Palestine Exploration Fund, uncovered more Roman architecture and his assistant, W. J. Phythian-Adams, dug two step trenches in the southern part of the tell, revealing a cultural sequence extending back into the Iron and Bronze Ages. Some fine are evident in the earthen rampart that encloses the city. The glacis, or outer face, of the rampart initially consisted of mud bricks, but it was later composed of *kurkar* fieldstones sealed with clay. Contemporary with the earliest phases of the rampart is a 7-meter-wide street (resurfaced several times) and a gate possessing the oldest monumental arch yet found in the Near East. Two phases of construction are evident in the gate (the earliest in c. 2000 BCE), which enclosed a passageway 2.5 m wide and had a second-story superstructure flanked by mud-brick towers preserved to a height of 6 m (see figure 1).

By the end of the Middle Bronze Age (in about 1550/BCE), the rampart was 15 m high and 30 m thick at its base, with a 40-degree slope on its outer face. Contemporary with the last phase of the rampart is a structure the excavator named the Sanctuary of the Silver Calf; it lies near the bottom of the outer slope, along a roadway leading up from the sea

ASHKELON. Figure 1. *The Middle Bronze Age gate.* (Photograph by Carl Andrews, courtesy Leon Levy Expedition to Ashkelon)

examples of Philistine pottery came to light at this time. [*See the biographies of Stanhope and Garstang.*]

It was not until 1985, however, that extensive excavations were begun on the tell of ancient Ashkelon by the Leon Levy Expedition, sponsored by the Semitic Museum of Harvard University, under the direction of Lawrence E. Stager. The project, still underway, has made significant discoveries from all periods of occupation in various parts of the site. The following summary of excavation results is based largely on this expedition's findings.

Neolithic and Chalcolithic Periods. A small Neolithic settlement was excavated on the beach in 1955 by Jean Perrot and John Hévesy. No architectural remains from the Chalcolithic period have yet been discovered, but a number of cornets were found during the recent excavations in a secondary context in the southeastern part of the tell.

Early Bronze Age. Ashkelon continued to be inhabited throughout the Early Bronze Age I–III, judging by pottery from this period found in later fills. Part of an EB II–III mud-brick building has been excavated at the north end of the tell. During the EB IV period there appears to have been a gap in occupation at Ashkelon, as at other urban sites in Palestine.

Middle Bronze Age. The most striking remains of the Middle Bronze Age found so far are the massive fortifications discovered at the north end of the tell. During the MB I alone, at least four cumulative stages of construction

ASHKELON. Figure 2. *Bronze bull calf and shrine.* (Photograph by Carl Andrews, courtesy Leon Levy Expedition to Ashkelon)

into the city. In it was found a finely crafted bronze statuette of a bull calf (originally covered with silver) 10 cm long and 11 cm high and weighing about 400 gm (see figure 2).

Middle Bronze Age pottery has also been found on the southern part of the tell, suggesting that Canaanite Ashkelon already occupied the entire area (about 150 acres) within the arc of the earthworks surrounding the site. Excavation at the north end of the tell has shown that the MB rampart was reused in later periods, which may be the case elsewhere along the perimeter of the tell, where only the final, Crusader fortifications are now visible.

Late Bronze Age. Remains from the Late Bronze Age are so far confined to a small area on the southern part of the tell and consist of a few courtyard surfaces and silos and, more notably, two burials in brick-lined vaults dating to about 1500 BCE. These vaults are reminiscent of an earlier "Hyksos" burial tradition, now known also at Tell ed-Dabʿa (ancient Avaris) in the Nile Delta. One of the burials at Ashkelon is that of an adolescent girl surrounded by imported pottery, including two bowls that once contained food offerings; in the other, a small child was interred.

Iron Age. The Philistine period at Ashkelon lasted from about 1175 BCE until Nebuchadrezzar's destruction of the city in 604 BCE. A Philistine mud-brick tower was in place on the northern rampart by 1100 BCE, indicating that the Philistine city was not confined to the southern part of the tell, as had once been thought. On the south tell evidence has been found of the earliest Philistine pottery sequence, involving a transition from a monochrome style based on Mycenaean antecedents to the familiar Philistine bichrome decoration. Another indication of Mycenaean or Aegean connections is the presence of a large number of unperforated cylindrical loom weights made of unbaked clay, quite different from the common Levantine type but known from Cyprus and Greece during this period.

Finds from the latter part of the Iron Age include an architectural complex containing several shallow, well-plastered vats, most likely used in wine production. Evidence has also been found of the final fiery destruction of Philistine Ashkelon in 604 BCE, including the complete skeleton of one of the victims of the disaster lying amid the burnt debris.

Persian Period. The excavated remains of the Persian period at Ashkelon are 2–3 m thick on the southern part of the tell. In most places there is evidence of several phases of construction, ending in a large-scale destruction in about 300 BCE. A sequence of large warehouses (see figure 3) built successively in one area near the sea was interrupted for a time in the fifth century BCE by an unusual burial ground that contained hundreds of individually interred dogs, most of which apparently died of natural causes. These animals

ASHKELON. Figure 3. *View of the excavated Persian-period warehouses.* (Photograph by Carl Andrews, courtesy Leon Levy Expedition to Ashkelon)

may have had a role to play in some local cult and may therefore have been regarded as sacred. [*See* Dogs.]

The material culture of Ashkelon in the Persian period reflects imports and influences from both Phoenicia and the Aegean, including Attic black-figured and red-figured wares. As for Persian imports, little has been found except for a carved ivory comb depicting a hunting scene.

Hellenistic and Roman Periods. A number of impressive Greco-Roman buildings were erected at Ashkelon. Garstang excavated a large, rectangular, columned structure near the center of the tell that Stager identifies as a forum from the third century CE. A basilica found by Lady Hester Stanhope lies just north of the forum and dates to the same period. The recent excavations have uncovered, in addition to these public buildings, private villas occupying three insulae that were built early in the Hellenistic period but whose architectural plan remained unchanged until Byzantine times.

Byzantine Period. The Roman villas were replaced by a bathhouse in the fourth century. Here the excavators found nearly a hundred skeletons of newborn infants in the sewer of the bath, grisly evidence of the practice of infanticide. Another notable aspect of Byzantine Ashkelon was the trade in wine, shipped in distinctive amphorae (including the so-called Gaza jar) to destinations all over the Christian world, where wine from the Holy Land was highly prized.

Arab and Crusader Periods. Ashkelon was fortified for the last time under the Fatimids (who ruled from the tenth through twelfth centuries), and parts of those fortifications are still visible. At the north end of the tell, near what would have been the Jaffa Gate (it opened to the route leading to Jaffa), a lengthy Arabic inscription, engraved on a limestone slab (now broken) measuring 149 × 63 × 10 cm, was recently fished from debris filling a stone-lined dry moat. It commemorates the construction of a tower and bears a date 2 March 1150. Three years later the Crusaders captured the city and defaced the inscription, engraving five heraldic shields over the Arabic text.

Elsewhere on the tell, evidence of the prosperity of the Arab period at Ashkelon is found in well-built private houses, near one of which four pieces of gold filigree jewelry were unearthed. On the east side of the city, just inside the Jerusalem Gate, excavators uncovered a church that was constructed as a basilica in the fifth century, converted into a mosque under the Fatimids, and restored as a church by the Crusaders in the twelfth century.

BIBLIOGRAPHY

The first systematic excavations at Ashkelon in 1920–1921 are covered in several reports by John Garstang and W. J. Phythian-Adams, all published in the *Palestine Exploration Fund Quarterly Statement* (PEFQS). See Garstang, "The Fund's Excavation of Askalon," PEFQS (1921): 12–16, 73–75, 162–163; "The Excavations at Askalon," PEFQS (1922): 112–119; and "Askalon," PEFQS (1924): 24–35. Reports by Phythian-Adams include the discovery of a pottery sequence at Ashkelon extending back to the Philistine and Canaanite periods; see "History of Askalon," PEFQS (1921): 76–90; "Askalon Reports," PEFQS (1921): 163–171; and "Report on the Stratification of Askalon," PEFQS (1923): 60–84. Jean Perrot provides a brief description of a Neolithic settlement found on the beach at Ashkelon in "Notes and News: Ashkelon," *Israel Exploration Journal* 5 (1955): 270–271. For an overview of work at the site, see Lawrence E. Stager, "Ashkelon," in *The New Encyclopedia of Archaeological Excavations in the Holy Land*, vol. 1, pp. 103–112 (Jerusalem and New York, 1993). Although quite condensed, this entry is now the most complete discussion of the archaeological excavations, pending publication of the final report.

A brief discussion of the first two seasons of work by the Leon Levy Expedition may be found in Lawrence Stager and Douglas Hesse, "Notes and News: Ashkelon, 1985–1986," *Israel Exploration Journal* 37 (1987): 68–72. Stager, the current excavator, has also published a number of interesting studies on specific aspects of Ashkelon history and culture. See, in particular, "When Canaanites and Philistines Ruled Ashkelon," "Why Were Hundreds of Dogs Buried at Ashkelon?," and "Eroticism and Infanticide at Ashkelon," all in *Biblical Archaeology Review* 17.2 (1991): 24–37, 40–43; 17.3 (1991): 26–42; and 17.4 (1991): 34–53, 72. Written for a broad audience, these articles provide detailed descriptions and interpretations of the most important discoveries made at Ashkelon by the Leon Levy Expedition and include many color photographs. For further information on the enigmatic dog burials, consult Paula Wapnish and Brian Hesse, "Pampered Pooches or Plain Pariahs?," *Biblical Archaeologist* 56.2 (June 1993): 55–80, the most detailed study to date on the subject, by two leading zooarchaeologists.

Wine amphorae are discussed in Barbara L. Johnson and Lawrence E. Stager, "Ashkelon: Wine Emporium of the Holy Land," in *Recent Excavations in Israel*, edited by Seymour Gitin, pp. 95–109 (Boston, 1995), a study of the types and distribution of Late Roman/Early Byzantine amphorae used to ship wine from Ashkelon and Gaza to the rest of the Christian world. See as well Philip Mayerson's interesting studies of the differences between Ascalon and Gaza wine and the amphorae in which they were shipped during the Byzantine period: "The Gaza 'Wine' Jar (*Gazition*) and the 'Lost' Ashkelon Jar (*Askalônion*)" and "The Use of Ascalon Wine in the Medical Writers of the Fourth to the Seventh Centuries," both in *Israel Exploration Journal* 42 (1992): 76–80, and 43 (1993): 169–173. Mayerson's sources include papyri, ostraca, and literary and medical texts.

DAVID SCHLOEN

ASHUR. *See* Aššur.

ASOR. *See* American Schools of Oriental Research.

ASSOS, Greek city in Anatolia rising a precipitous 234 m (768 ft.) from the sea to the summit of a volcanic citadel on the southern coast of the Troad (modern Turkey; 39°29′ N; 26°21′ E). The site is unequivocally identified by Strabo's description of a naturally fortified, well-walled city with a steep ascent from the harbor, set between Cape Lekton and Gargara (*Geography* 13.1.51, 57–58). Pliny notes that it was also called Apollonia (*Natural History* 5.32). Attempts to assign to Assos a Bronze Age name and history remain unsubstantiated by the literary and archaeological record. Proposals include Heinrich Schliemann's suggestion that the site was the original Chryse of the *Iliad*, and Joseph Thatcher Clarke's conviction, followed by Walter Leaf, that Assos was Homeric Pedasos (contra Strabo 13.1.59; see Clarke, 1882, pp. 60–63; Leaf, 1923, p. 295). Assos acquired its Turkish name, Behram (also Mahram, Menherein, or Préheram), at the time of the Ottoman conquest (c. 1330), as a corruption of the last Byzantine leader's name, Machrames. Today the village is called Behramkale.

According to Myrsilos and Hellanikos (Strabo 13.1.58), colonists from Aeolian Methyma on Lesbos founded Assos in the seventh century BCE. The city served as the strategic and commercial center of the southern Troad for it commanded a superb view of the Gulf of Adramyttium and Lesbos, was naturally defensible, and had the best harbor on the northern side of the Gulf. Just inland of the citadel stretched fertile wheat plains watered by the Touzla River (possibly the Homeric Satnioeis). The physical remains document vigorous activity from the early Archaic through the early Christian periods (seventh century BCE to fifth century CE). Assos remained a viable Byzantine city, despite serious assault and occupation by the Seljuk Turks in 1080 CE, the Franks in the first quarter of the thirteenth century, and finally the Ottoman Turks in the first quarter of the fourteenth century. Its significance declined rapidly thereafter.

The ruins of Assos (identified as Behram) were first noted from the sea by the Turkish cartographer Piri Re' is in 1521. The English chaplain John T. Covel, stopping at Assos in 1677, wrote a fairly detailed account of the agora and western necropolis, and the French count Marie-Gabriel-Auguste-Florent Choiseul-Gouffier included a hasty description of the site in his geographical survey of the Turkish coast made in 1785. During the first third of the nineteenth century, a steady stream of European aristocrats, archaeologists, and architects visited Assos, writing descriptions that document the dramatic situation of the city and its then remarkably well-preserved civic structures and monuments. Based on its setting, urban plan, and architectural remains, Colonel William Martin Leake declared that Assos gave "the most perfect idea of a Greek city that anywhere exists" (Leake, 1820, pp. 253–255).

The French architect Charles Texier carried out the first brief excavations on the acropolis in 1835, where he unearthed part of the archaic Doric temple's foundation. Désiré Raoul-Rochette returned three years later to take thirteen architectural reliefs and one capital from the temple to the Musée du Louvre in Paris. Systematic quarrying of monuments to provide cut stone for the docks of the arsenal in Istanbul during the 1860s left the city gates, gymnasium, and theater greatly diminished.

The first excavations sponsored by the Archaeological Institute of America were conducted at Assos between 1881–1883. American architects Joseph Thatcher Clarke and Francis Henry Bacon, aided in the second and third seasons by German architect Robert Koldewey, exposed most of the major monuments of the city. [*See the biography of Koldewey.*] The archaic temple on the acropolis received greatest attention, but enough excavation was conducted in the lower city to reveal the plan of the agora, gymnasium, city gates, and many funerary monuments. Finds from the excavation were deposited in the Archaeological Museum in Istanbul and the Museum of Fine Arts in Boston.

A hiatus of nearly one hundred years followed the American excavations. An international team under the direction of Ümit Serdaroğlu resumed archaeological work in 1980, concentrating on the acropolis and western necropolis. Additional sculpture from the archaic temple has been recovered, and finds from the necropolis, including seventh-century pottery, confirm early activity at the site.

The urban plan of Assos follows the contours of the site with monuments set on a series of partially excavated terraces on the seaward-facing side of the citadel. All of the buildings are constructed of local volcanic andesite. The mid-sixth-century temple crowning the acropolis remains the only known archaic Doric temple in Asia Minor and is distinctive for the program of architectural sculpture decorating its architrave. Below, two multi-storied stoas, one built into the scarp of the acropolis and the other with one story facing the agora and two additional stories reaching to a lower terrace, frame a long, trapezoidal agora with a prostyle temple at one end and a bouleuterion (council chamber) at the other. A gymnasium with cisterns lies between the agora and the chief city gate. The theater, as well as numerous smaller buildings not fully excavated, occupy lower terraces to the south and east. The city walls of the fourth century encircling the acropolis and southern region of the city, as well as a Hellenistic northern extension with salient round and square towers, are of excellent workmanship and have well-preserved main and lesser gates (see figure 1). Early archaic burials have been found in the same region as the elaborate Hellenistic and Roman funerary monuments that line the streets leading to the eastern and western city gates. Both within and outside the walls, several early Christian churches have been identified. Good evidence exists for Roman and Byzantine domestic quarters to the southeast of the akropolis, but the civic and domestic quarters of the archaic and classical town have not yet been located. Numerous architectural elements presumably belonging to moles of the ancient harbor lie underwater at the port.

Famous sons of Assos include the stoic philosopher Kleanthes. Aristotle and Xenokrates resided in Assos (c. 348–345) upon the invitation of the ruler Hermias, himself a student of Plato; Theophraster probably joined them. St. Paul stopped there en route from Alexandria Troas to Mitylene. Important ancient sources noting Assos include

ASSOS.   Figure 1.   *The city gate.* (Erich Lessing/Art Resource, NY)

Strabo, *Geography* (13.1.51, 57–58, 66); Theophrastos, *On Fire* (46–47); Pliny, *Natural History* (2.211, 5.32, 36.131–33); and *Acts* 20.13, 14.

BIBLIOGRAPHY

Clarke, Joseph Thatcher. *Report on the Excavations at Assos.* 2 vols. Boston and New York, 1882–1898. Volume 1 includes a history of Assos, a record of early travelers to the site, a description of the first season, and a preliminary analysis of the major monuments with appendices on inscriptions, other sites in the southern Troad, and the local geology. Volume 2 concentrates on the architecture and sculpture of the archaic temple. The proposed date of mid-fifth century BCE is not accepted.

Clarke, Joseph Thatcher, et al. *Investigations at Assos.* Cambridge, Mass., 1902–1921. Folio volume (issued in two parts) with text condensed from the *Reports* and invaluable illustrations of the actual state, individual elements, and restored views of most major monuments, providing the best overview of the site.

Finster-Hotz, Ursula. *Der Bauschmuck des Athenatempels von Assos: Studien zur Ikonographie.* Rome, 1984. Iconographic study of the sculpture from the temple, not including new finds.

Leaf, Walter. *Strabo on the Troad.* Cambridge, 1923. See pp. 289–300; a topographical study of the Troad based on the work of the ancient geographer Strabo.

Leake, William Martin, as printed in Robert Walpole, *Travels in Various Countries of the East*, pp. 253–255. London, 1820. See also William M. Leake, *Journal of a Tour in Asia Minor.* London, 1824.

Sartiaux, Félix. *Les sculptures et la restauration du temple d'Assos en Troade.* Paris, 1915. Discerning view of Clarke's work on the archaic temple, largely superseded by Finster-Hotz and Wescoat.

Serdaroğlu, Ümit, et al. *Ausgrabungen in Assos.* Bonn, 1990. Reports by several authors on recent discoveries from the western necropolis.

Wescoat, Bonna D. *The Temple of Athena at Assos.* Oxford, forthcoming. Investigation of the architecture, iconography, and reconstruction of the archaic temple based on new excavation and fieldwork.

BONNA D. WESCOAT

AŠŠUR (also Ashur; modern Qal'at Šerqat), site located approximately 110 km (68 mi.) south of Mosul, on the west bank of the Tigris river in northern Iraq (35°28′ N, 43°14′ E). The ancient settlement is situated some 40 m above the alluvial plain of Šerqat on a natural, nearly triangular eminence at the junction of two branches of the Tigris. This location provided the site with natural protection on two sides. On the third, the landward side, its defenses were completed by a crescent-shaped array of mighty walls enclosing an area of nearly 65 ha (161 acres). Inside the fortification walls the settlement was subdivided into two parts: the Old City (about 40 ha or 99 acres), with temples, palaces, and some "private" buildings in the north, and the so-called New City (about 15 ha or 37 acres) whose function has not yet been identified but which is most probably a dwelling area. It is adjacent to the Old City in the settlements' extreme southeast.

The first archaeological investigations at the site were carried out in the nineteenth century by Austen Henry Layard, Hormuzd Rassam, and Victor Place. Although hardly scientific, their work was of considerable importance in identifying Qala'at Šerqat with the first Assyrian capital, Aššur. Well-known objects associated with these early excavations are a statue of Shalmaneser III (854–824 BCE) and a clay prism of Tiglath-Pileser I (1115–1077 BCE). The latter was of considerable importance in deciphering cuneiform writing. [*See* Cuneiform.] What is known of the city's archaeology, however, belongs almost exclusively to the work of the German excavators who began their investigations at Aššur in 1903. From then onward, until 1914, Walter Andrae carried out large-scale excavations at the site on behalf of the Deutsche Orient-Gesellschaft. Andrae's combined achievements, in recovering historical information and perfecting archaeological method, have since come to be generally recognized. No further work took place at the site until 1945. Apart from some investigations in the following decades by the Department of Antiquities of Iraq, two more German campaigns, but on a much smaller scale, took place in 1988–1989, conducted by the Free University of Berlin under the direction of Reinhard Dittmann, and in 1989–1990, by the University of Munich under the direction of Barthel Hrouda. In attempting to resolve specific details and problems, the recent work has provided new topographical plan and, for the first time, a ceramic sequence ranging from the Ur III-period (2112–2004 BCE) down to Parthian times (250 BCE–256 CE).

Andrae's principal excavations took place in the elevated part of the Old City to the north and northwest, where most of its temples and palaces are situated. Because, successive kings had contributed to the restoration and multiplication of these public buildings and fortifications, the chronological sequence of their building levels could only be determined with the help of associated inscriptions. These showed, for example, that many of the excavated buildings continued to be rebuilt over a period of some two thousand years, even after the city had ceased to be the administrative capital of Assyria (beginning of the first millenium BCE).

The latest architectural remains Andrae encountered in his excavations date to the final phase of the Parthian period (c. 250 CE). The main excavated buildings of this period are the so-called Parthian Palace in the southern part of the city and an Aššur-Šerua Temple in the extreme north. The most important buildings of the Assyrian era (c. 1813–614 BCE), the city's main occupation level, are the Aššur Temple, Aššur Ziggurat, Old Palace, Temple of Sin and Shamash (the moon and sun gods), Temple of Ishtar, Temple of Anu and Adad (the sky and weather god's), New Palace, and a full circuit of fortification walls including gates, riverside quays, and other features. The deepest levels reached during the 1903–1914 campaigns were in a sounding that revealed the "pre-Sargonic" (before 2300 BCE) foundation of the Ishtar Temple. However, traces of "pre-Assyrian" occupation there, as well as in other parts of the city, are very scarce. The origin of the settlement is still unknown. Some traces of handmade (?) pottery found below the Aššur Temple may be of Early Chalcolithic (c. 5500 BCE) date. Hrouda's claim of an Ubaid sherd (c. 4000 BCE) in Aššur has to be considered with caution as well. [See Ubaid.] Indications of an Uruk or Ninevite V horizon (c. 3500–3000 BCE)—the latter present at a small tell in the modern city of Šerqat—have never been found in excavations or on the surface at Aššur. [See Uruk-Warka; Nineveh.]

The earliest remains, excavated in level H of the Ishtar Temple sounding, belong to the Early Dynastic III period (c. 2500 BCE). Material from this period is also present below the Old Palace, dated to the second millenium BCE. The style of the few sculptural remains found in these levels is comparable to artifacts from Mari and Kish. [See Mari; Kish.] For the Akkadian period (2334–2154 BCE) which followed, the city of Aššur is known to have been under the hegemony of the Akkadian Empire. [See Akkade; Akkadians.] Only level G of the previously mentioned Ishtar Temple sequence, with its sculptural finds, and, according to Olof Pedersén, the so-called archive O1 found below the schotterhofbau (a building with a gravel courtyard) can be dated to this period with any certainty. An Akkadian date for the so-called Old Akkadian house below the later Temple of Sin

and Shamash is possible but not proven. The dating of two fragments belonging to one sculpture, one a male torso found next to the later Temple of Anu and Adad and the other a male head found by the Iraqis in 1982 in the area of the Aššur Temple, also remains uncertain. Although an early second-millennium BCE date should not be excluded, Evelyn Klengel Brandt dates this sculpture to the Akkadian period, either to King Rimush or to Manishtushu. According to Peter A. Miglus (1989) the schotterhofbau itself, which is part of a large structure underneath the foundation trenches of the Old Palace, should be dated to the following Ur III period. Levels F and early E of the Ishtar Temple sounding most probably date to the same period of time. Zariqum, a local ruler of Aššur, probably represented by a fragment of a sculpture, calls himself a servant of Amar-Suen, one of the kings of the third dynasty of Ur. [See Ur.] In the latest phase of Ishtar E, a sealing was found of a servant of the šakkanakku (an official of the state) Isi-Dagan of Mari, who, according to Jean Marie Durand, is a contemporary of Ishbi-Erra (c. 2017–1985 BCE) of Isin, the founder of the Isin I dynasty. [See Isin.]

In the beginning of the second millennium BCE, Assyria was officially declared a state, and the city of Aššur was transformed into the religious and administrative center of the so-called Old Assyrian Empire. It was at that time that merchants from Aššur organized a long-distance trade with Anatolia known as the kārum trade. Brick inscriptions of the third and fourth king of the local Puzur-Aššur dynasty already mention the Aššur Temple. Even the existence of fortification walls and Adad and Ishtar temples is not out of the question for this early period of Assyrian history. Nevertheless, the first really notable Assyrian king was Shamshi-Adad I (1813–1781 BCE), a prominent rival of Hammurabi of Babylon. [See Babylon.] After he defeated the local king and usurped the throne, he extended the territory of Assyria and created a formidable kingdom. Among other things, this ruler is known for his intense building activities in and around Aššur. Important buildings founded by Shamshi-Adad I are the Enlil Ziggurrat which was later also identified with the god Ashur and, according to Miglus, the Old Palace. The first entirely recorded ground plan of the Aššur Temple, which was not much altered by later kings, was created by him. Also associated with his reign is a special kind of painted pottery, the so-called Khabur Ware found in northern Mesopotamia as well as in northwestern Iran. The end of Shamshi-Adad's reign is more or less unknown.

After the fall of the Babylonian Hammurabi dynasty (c. 1595 BCE), which, in its later days, controlled much of Assyria, the political vacuum was filled by the Mitanni rulers, who controlled major parts of Syria and northern Mesopotamia. [See Mitanni.] Not much is known about the history and archaeology of Aššur for this period. Only the Temple of Sin and Shamash, which was erected in the reign of Ashurnirari I is notable. According to the inscriptions, this local ruler of Aššur was also engaged in building activities in the Aššur Temple area.

It was only with Eriba-Adad I (1392–1366 BCE) and his successor Ashur-Uballit I (1365–1330 BCE) that Assyria, still with its capital at Aššur, freed itself from Hurri-Mitannian domination. An interesting archaeological find dating to this period is the so-called *stelenreihe* ("row of stelae"), a kind of Assyrian calendarium. Starting with Eriba-Adad I and continuing to a wife of King Ashurbanipal (668–667 BCE), each stela mentions an Assyrian king or the name of a state official. As one able ruler followed another, Assyria began to reappear as a major power at the beginning of the thirteenth century BCE; by the end of that century it was again one of the strongest powers in the Near East. The Assyrian kings associated with the emergence of the so-called Middle Assyrian Empire are Adad-Nirari I (1307–1275 BCE), his son Shalmaneser I (1274–1245 BCE), and his grandson Tukulti-Ninurta I (1244–1208 BCE). All of them contributed to the restoration and rebuilding of Aššur.

Under the reign of Adad-Nirari I, the Old Palace was rebuilt and restoration work was performed at the Temple of Sin and Shamash. Shalmaneser I is known to have rebuilt the partly burnt Aššur Temple, and Tukulti-Ninurta I initiated a completely new building program. During his reign a deep moat was dug around the fortification walls and its old posterns, some kind of tunnel, were abandoned. In the northwestern angle of the Old City he erected an artificial terrace (some 29,000 sq m) which was used as a foundation platform for his New Palace. Unfortunately, because of later building activities, only traces of the stone foundations remained of the structure built on top of it. He also built a new Temple of Ishtar, now called Ishtar-Ashuritu ("Ishtar of the city of Aššur"). In contrast to the earlier Ishtar temples, the alignment of the ground plan, which dated back to archaic times, was altered by approximately 90 degrees, and a second, smaller shrine of a goddess called Dinitu was added to the temple. Even though the previously mentioned building activities at Aššur were considerable, it is assumed that early in his reign Tukulti-Ninurta I built a new residence, called Kar-Tukulti-Ninurta, on the opposite side of the Tigris, some 3 km (2 mi.) north of Aššur. [See Kar-Tukulti-Ninurta.] Among the finds at Aššur associated with the Middle Assyrian period are an altar of Tukulti-Ninurta I with a relief in which homage is paid to the symbol of a god and some cylinder seals carved in a characteristic Middle Assyrian style.

The period following Tukulti-Ninurta I's violent death is, archaeologically speaking, almost terra incognita. Although Aššur most probably did not lose its importance, it is only with Ashur-resh-ishi I (1133–1116 BCE) and his successors that further building activities are attested at Aššur. It was Ashur-resh-ishi I who built a new Ishtar Temple—but neither on top of the early structures founded by Ilushuma in the nineteenth century BCE, nor on Tukulti-Ninurta I's con-

struction. The Temple of Anu and Adad as well was most probably founded by this king. A characteristic feature of this temple are two small ziggurats, towerlike constructions, attached to the sanctuaries. According to Miglus the extensive building activities evidenced at the Aššur Ziggurat should be attributed to the largely unknown kings Ashurnasirpal I (1049–1031 BCE) and Shalmaneser II (1030–1019 BCE). In a gate between the Anu-Adad complex and the Old Palace, which was devoted to the dispensation of justice, several unfortunately heavily damaged fragments of sculptures, perhaps parts of winged and human-headed bulls or lions guarding an entrance, were found. Apart from fragments like these, evidence concerning the facade ornament and external appearance of buildings at that time is very scarce. Occasional clues are to be found only among contemporary seal designs. In general, the account of buildings at Aššur must be confined, at least for the Old and Middle Assyrian periods, to variations in their ground plans.

Early in the tenth century BCE at Aššur, a new dynasty was founded by a king called Ashur-Rabi II. In a sense the founding of this dynasty marked the beginning of a period at the end of which Assyria was at the apex of its power. From an archaeological viewpoint, however, it was only with Ashurnasirpal II (883–859 BCE) and his successors that the so-called Late Assyrian Empire (c. 883–609 BCE) was born. It was Ashurnasirpal II who transferred the center of government from Aššur to Kalhu/Nimrud, the Calah of the *Book of Genesis*. [See Nimrud.] It was also this king or one of his predecessors who rebuilt and converted the Old Palace, still in use at the time of Tiglath-Pileser I, into a mausoleum, in which some of the elegant tomb chambers and monolithic sarcophagi of the Assyrian kings were found. Although Aššur ceased to be the administrative capital, the subsequent kings did not cease their building activities in the city. Shalmaneser III (858–824 BCE), for example, strengthened the fortifications, rebuilt the Temple of Anu and Adad, and erected a new Ishtar Temple, now dedicated to Belit-nipha. In contrast to his predecessors, his plan of the latter was again in the tradition of the archaic sanctuaries. From the archaeological objects associated with his reign and that of his predecessors and successors, the glazed and colorfully decorated tiles (Assyrian, *zigatti*) and clay orthostats, both used as some kind of facade ornament, are notable.

While the administrative capital of the ever-growing Assyrian Empire was transferred for a second and third time from Kalhu/Nimrud to Dur Sharrukin/Khorsabad by Sargon II (721–705 BCE) and finally to Nineveh/Kuyunjik by Sennacherib (704–681 BCE), not much is known archaeologically about Aššur itself in the eighth–early seventh centuries BCE. It was only with Sennacherib that the so-called *Neujahrsfesthaus*, a cultic building situated west of Aššur outside the city walls, and the Prince Palace, a structure dedicated to his son in the southeast, were founded. Fundamental changes in the ground plan of the Sin-Shamash and

Aššur temples are attributed to this king as well. On the other hand, fragments of a large, heavily damaged water basin (?) recovered in the Old Palace are the only noteworthy archaeological finds associated with his reign at Aššur. The Aššur Temple as well as the Aššur-Enlil Ziggurat are known to have been subject to some restoration work by his successors Esarhaddon (680–669 BCE) and Ashurbanipal (668–627 BCE). During the reign of Sin-shar-ishkun (623–612 BCE), the last of the Late Assyrian kings, the Ishtar Temple became part of an adjacent sanctuary dedicated to Nabu, the god of writing and writers, and his wife, Tashmetu. Finally, in 614 BCE, a Median army invaded the Assyrian homeland and destroyed the city of Aššur completely.

Traces of a post-Assyrian occupation at Aššur are scarce. It is only with the beginning of the first century BCE that Aššur regained some significance as a residence of a Parthian satrap. The Parthian name of the city is still unknown, but, according to the most recent investigations by Stefan Hauser (1994), it was not Libanae, as hitherto assumed. Some of the main excavated buildings dating to this period are the Aššur-Sherua Temple erected on top of the former Aššur Temple and the Parthian Palace in the south decorated with colored paintings on plaster. After the destruction of "Aššur" in the third century CE by Shapur I (241–272 CE), the former Assyrian capital was neither rebuilt nor resettled.

[See also Assyrians; Deutsche Orient-Gesellschaft; Ziggurat; and the biographies of Andrae and Layard.]

BIBLIOGRAPHY

Andrae, Walter. Das wiedererstandene Assur. 2d ed., revised by Barthel Hrouda. Munich, 1977. Essential summary for anyone interested in the archaeology and history of Aššur; extensive bibliography.

Dittmann, Reinhard. "Ausgrabungen der Freien Universität Berlin in Assur und Kār-Tukultī-Ninurta in den Jahren 1986–1989." Mitteilungen der Deutschen Orient-Gesellschaft 122 (1990): 157–171. Preliminary report on work at the site.

Dittmann, Reinhard. "Assur and Kār-Tukultī-Ninurta." American Journal of Archaeology 96 (1992): 307–312. Second preliminary report on the new excavations carried out by the Free University of Berlin, 1986, 1988–1989.

Finkbeiner, Uwe, and Beate, Pongratz-Leisten. Examples of Near Eastern Cities—Residences of the Assyrian Empire—Assur. Map B IV, 21, edited by Sonderforschungsbereich des Tübinger Atlas des Vorderen Orients der Universität Tübingen. Wiesbaden, 1992. The most up-to-date map of Aššur, showing the historical development of the archaeological remains.

Hauser, Stefan, "Chronologische und historisch-politische untersuchungen zu örtlichen Ḡerīsa in vorislamische zeit." Ph.D. diss., Freie Universität Berlin, 1994.

Hrouda, Barthel. "Vorläufiger Bericht über die neuen Ausgrabungen in Aššur Frühjahr 1990." Mitteilungen der Deutschen Orient-Gesellschaft 123 (1991): 95–109. Preliminary report on the new investigations under Hrouda.

Larsen, Mogens T. The Old Assyrian City-State and Its Colonies. Copenhagen, 1976.

Miglus, Peter A. "Zur Grossen Ziqqurrat in Assur." Mitteilungen der Deutschen Orient-Gesellschaft 117 (1985): 21–45. New information on the Aššur-Enlil ziggurat.

Miglus, Peter A. "Untersuchungen zum Alten Palast in Assur." Mitteilungen der Deutschen Orient-Gesellschaft 121 (1989): 93–133. Useful information about the pre-Assyrian history of Aššur in the area of the Old Palace.

Oates, David. Studies in the Ancient History of Northern Iraq. London, 1968. Useful information about the history of Aššur.

Pedersén, Olof. Archives and Libraries in the City of Assur. 2 vols. Survey of the Material from the German Excavations, vols. 1–2. Uppsala, 1985–1986. Overview and systematic summary of the textual finds and their corresponding archives.

Pedersén, Olof. "Die Assur-Texte in ihren archäologischen Zusammenhängen." Mitteilungen der Deutschen Orient-Gesellschaft 121 (1989): 153–167. Attempt to reconstruct the original setting of some of the textual finds.

ROLAND W. LAMPRICHS

ASSYRIANS. Little is known about population groups and settlement patterns in Assyria before about 2000 BCE. By this date the people were speaking a dialect of Akkadian and writing it in the cuneiform script. A people called Amorites, who had been seminomads living in the Syro-Arabian desert, made major inroads into all of Mesopotamia. They took over many city-states, founded new dynasties, and gradually intermarried with the older population and adopted its culture. This is certainly what happened in Assyria; therefore, the "Assyrians" after around 2000 were a mixture of Amorites, who spoke a Semitic language, and the older population, which spoke Akkadian, also a Semitic language. About 1200 BCE the Arameans, another group of Semitic-speaking seminomads from the Syro-Arabian desert, began to make significant incursions into Assyria, and over the next several centuries they intermingled with the Assyrians, thus making the "Assyrians" an even more mixed population group.

The Assyrian population was concentrated in a few cities in what is now Iraq, mainly Aššur, Arbela, Nineveh, and, after the mid-ninth century, Kalḫu (Nimrud). The rural population clustered in numerous villages from which they would venture each day to till their fields and tend their flocks. As the empire was created, Assyrians were settled in some provincial regions where they remained sometimes for centuries. Around 1900 the city-state of Aššur established some Assyrian merchant colonies in Anatolia to facilitate trade between the two regions.

Political History. The Assyrians not only developed a powerful and profitable empire, but also sponsored and protected the activities of the religious and cultural communities. It is because of the Assyrians that so much of the earlier Sumerian and Babylonian civilizations have been recovered by modern archaeology. The political history of the Assyrians is divided by modern scholars into the Old (c. 2000–1750), Middle (c. 1750–1000), and Neo-Assyrian (c. 1000–609) periods. There was no unified nation "Assyria" at the beginning of the Old Assyrian period. There were just independent city-states, which shared a common

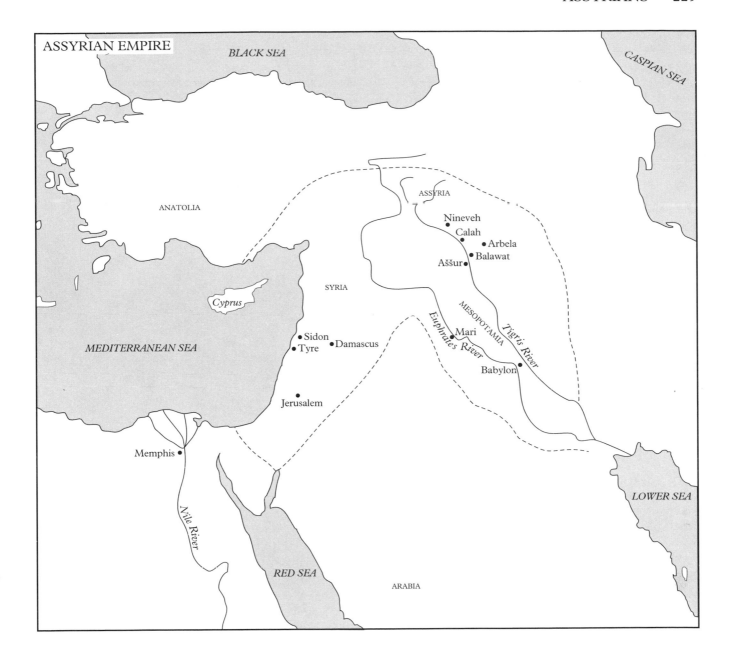

culture, and nomadic tribes in the surrounding hills and mountains. Shamshi-Adad I (c. 1813–1781), whose ancestors were Amorites, led his forces slowly up the Tigris River to conquer Aššur and then the surrounding region as far as Mari on the middle Euphrates River. [See Mari.] He was the first to establish some political solidarity in the region. This unity collapsed, however, shortly after his death, and for over three centuries (c. 1740–1400) little is known about the region and its people. During this "dark" age, a revolution in warfare, the light horse-drawn chariot, was introduced into southwestern Asia by Indo-Aryan warriors. The Assyrians seized this new device and used it in their building of a militaristic state. [See Chariots.]

The power of the Middle Assyrian monarchs, notably Tukulti-Ninurta I (1243–1207) and Tiglath-Pileser I (1114–1076), was unprecedented. They not only ruled over a united Assyria, but they also led their armies on vigorous campaigns abroad, conquering Babylonia to the south and Syria to the west as far as the Mediterranean Sea. In the process the principles of an absolute monarchy, ruling from Aššur, were established, and the idea of imperialism was given practical expression.

After a period of confusion and temporary eclipse of Assyrian might (c. 1000–900), the greatest period of the Assyrian empire emerged. Outstanding among the warrior kings of the early phase of this era were Ashurnasirpal II (883–859) and Shalmaneser III (858–824). During their reigns the Assyrian armies thundered once again to the west, reaching the Mediterranean and then moving both north and south along the Levantine coast. There was, however, little interference in Babylonian affairs. The exotic items such as gold, silver, ivory, and cedar that they brought back from the western expeditions were used to build and decorate new palaces and temples. Masses of foreign captives, mainly Arameans, were transported to Assyria to work on these building projects or to develop uncultivated land in order to feed the expanding population of the Assyrian cities.

After another brief interval of weakness, a series of kings resumed the military expansion of the empire. At its height (c. 680) Assyria laid claim to an empire that embraced all of the Fertile Crescent, including Egypt, as well as central Anatolia and western Iran. By this time the capital had been moved to Nineveh, where the last great monarch, Ashurbanipal (668–627), resided. In 612 Nineveh fell to the Medes and Babylonians, and over the next few years the territory that had been the Assyrian Empire was taken over by the Babylonians.

Social Structure. Assyrian society was male dominated and militaristic in character. Every male in theory was required to perform military service when called upon by the king. Thus, the social structure was essentially based on army rank—the king at the top and the peasant infantry at the bottom. The role of women, who were confined to harems and had to be veiled, was to care for the men in their family, their children, and their homes. The men engaged in arduous activity on the battlefield, hunting ground, and fields and pastures. To a modern Western eye, Assyrian society appears harsh and cruel. Punishments for criminal acts were severe, commonly requiring physical mutilation, torture, and execution.

At the bottom of the social spectrum were slaves, but they did not play as vital a role in Assyrian society as they did in the Roman Empire. There were two kinds of slaves: (1) Assyrians who went bankrupt and so became debt slaves, and (2) foreign prisoners of war. The latter had no chance of freedom, except escape or death, but the debt slaves could regain their independence by gradually paying off their debts. Above the slaves were various levels of free citizens, from rank and file to archers to noncommissioned and commissioned officers, charioteers, and cavalry. Above these were the chief army commanders of which the most important was the field marshal, who was directly under the king. The chief officers came from the noble families of the Assyrians.

Political Structure. The king was an absolute monarch being the supreme commander of the army, the chief priest in religion, and the highest source of appeal in legal disputes. He ruled by personal decree, there being no legislative or consultative assembly. The only restraints on his authority were ancient customs and religious practices, which he had to observe, and the attitude of the nobility. He had to keep his nobles happy by providing them with high offices and the benefits which came therefrom.

The Assyrian king resided in a palace which was full of courtiers, many of whom were eunuchs, of various rank. Only one courtier, however, seems to have had regular direct access to the monarch. All messages, even from the royal family, had to be conveyed through the major domo. It appears that most Assyrians, including the king himself, were illiterate. There was a large corps of scribes of which the chief was one of the king's most important advisers. It was a hereditary monarchy, the legitimate successor normally being the eldest son of the previous king.

Warfare. The Assyrians regarded warfare as their most important activity. In return for the military service which, in theory, every male citizen had to perform, he was given the use of a plot of land under an arrangement called the *ilku*. "Captains" (*rab kiṣri*) lived in the various agricultural villages, and when the call to arms was sent out, it was their responsibility to rally and produce their companies at the appointed place and time. By the Neo-Assyrian period, the annual military campaign, led by the king, had become the norm and, later in the same era, a standing army, which served year round, was also established.

On the march, the army was preceded by the divine standards ("the colors") followed by the diviners, the king surrounded by his bodyguard, the cavalry and chariots, the infantry, the siege machines and other equipment, and the camp followers. Engineers were responsible for taking the army across rivers and for organizing sieges. Rafts were built to transport equipment across the rivers, and individual soldiers stripped their clothes off and swam with the aid of inflated goat skins. The Assyrians were experts both at open-field warfare and sieges. In the field their cavalry made the initial attack, followed by the chariots, and then the infantry. Siege warfare, which was costly and time consuming, was used only as a last resort. If a region refused to submit voluntarily and would not field an army to fight, the Assyrian army surrounded a strategic town. All traffic in and out of the city was cut off and, if this maneuver did not bring capitulation, the army would attempt to penetrate the walls by various techniques: tunneling, battering rams, or building earthen ramps up the wall. Once the town was taken, it was thoroughly pillaged, and the inhabitants either were taken prisoner or slaughtered in gruesome ways as an example to the other towns in the region. Excellent organization and tactics, together with metal (first bronze, later iron) weapons, the bow, and the light horse-drawn chariot, made the Assyrians the most successful fighting power the world had seen.

Religion. State religion in Assyria was cultic and polytheistic. There were a number of temples, including that of the god Ashur (Aššur) at the city of the same name, dedicated to a variety of deities. Each temple had a corps of priests and servants who carried out elaborate rituals and regularly cared for the gods by providing them with food and drink. There were numerous festivals, but the most important was for the new year (*akītu*), which was celebrated in the spring. Festivals often involved processions of the gods' statues through the city streets. Among the chief Assyrian gods were Ashur, Ninurta (god of war), Ishtar (goddess of love), Shamash (sun god and god of justice), Sin (moon god), and Adad (storm god).

Magic, both black (bad) and white (good), was practiced, and a large body of incantations and rituals, on a variety of themes, has been discovered on clay tablets. The Assyrians, like the Babylonians, believed in divination. According to them, the gods were constantly sending messages regarding the future to human beings through any number of vehicles. It was the task of humans to recognize and read these omens. The two most popular vehicles for omens were the entrails of a sacrificed animal, particularly a sheep's liver, and the movements of the stars and planets. An Assyrian king would not take any decisive action without consulting his diviners.

Economy. The economy of the Assyrians was founded on agriculture, animal husbandry, and foreign trade. In the rolling hills of the Assyrian homeland where rainfall was regular, the fertile fields lent themselves to abundant yields and the pasturing of sheep and goats. The crops were primarily barley (for bread and beer), linseed oil, and grapes, which were used for both fruit and wine. Goats were a source of milk, butter, and cheese, and their wool, like that of sheep, was used for textiles, which were major articles of export. The Assyrians participated in an extensive trading network, which brought them metal (silver, gold, tin, copper, and iron) precious stone (such as lapis lazuli), ivory, and various other items, both practical and luxurious.

The palace had considerable control of the economy, although it is impossible to give exact data because of scanty sources. The temples had a much smaller role to play in the economy, and by the Neo-Assyrian period they had become dependent on the king for much of their income through royal offerings and for the maintenance and construction of their buildings. Although the palace and, to a much lesser extent, the temples were directly involved with agriculture and animal husbandry, it appears that foreign trade was in the hands of private entrepreneurs. Nevertheless, the palace gained profit from the trade by means of taxation. As the empire was expanded, another major source of income became the annual tribute exacted from the provinces and territories. The tribute was of two types: (1) supplies for the military garrisons and armies on campaign in the form of grain and animals, and (2) luxury items for the construction and embellishment of monumental buildings.

Art and Architecture. The artists of Assyria were sponsored primarily by the state; therefore, most of their works related to the deeds of the king. The carved stone reliefs that lined the walls of the palaces portrayed the Assyrian monarch triumphantly fighting, hunting, and feasting (see figure

1). The scenes were accompanied by inscriptions explaining these activities. The quality of the human figures was high, even if the subject matter was repetitious. It was in the depiction of animals, however, that the Assyrian artists surpassed themselves. The reliefs were painted in various colors, which have now almost entirely disappeared. Scenes similar to those on the reliefs were incised on a number of bronze bands on gates discovered at Balawat near Nimrud. The palaces were also adorned with scenes set out with glazed ceramic bricks, clay knobs, and painted murals. A rich horde of finely carved ivories was excavated at Nimrud, as was a large amount of jewelry of superb craftsmanship. Note must also be taken of the mythological and legendary scenes carved on the stone stamp and cylinder seals.

The palaces were constructed on artificially created terraces and consisted of many rooms of various types. The central room was the audience chamber; colossal bulls and lions sculptured in stone towered over the palace entrances. Temples and temple towers (ziggurats) were also built on terraces. [*See* Ziggurat.] Stone statues of the king, large and small, were erected inside to indicate his continual worship of the gods.

Archaeological Recovery. First excavated in the early nineteenth century, Assyrian sites in Iraq were among the initial places of investigation in the whole of the Fertile Crescent. Émile Botta, a Frenchman, concentrated on Khorsabad (ancient Dur Sharrukin, "Fort Sargon") and Austen Henry Layard, an Englishman, began work at Nimrud (ancient Calah). The discoveries, which included colossal stone winged bulls and reliefs, were a sensation when they were transported to London and Paris. They generated increased support and also lured other Europeans into Assyrian archaeology. By modern standards, the techniques employed in these early excavations were primitive. Tunneling was common because the goal was to find as many interesting objects as possible.

A more scientific approach finally came with the German expedition to Aššur at the beginning of the twentieth century. Walter Andrae, leader of the team, recognized the importance of making a topographical map that divided the mound into small carefully labeled, squares. Andrae also paid attention to the different levels (strata) of the site. Avoiding tunneling, he dug systematically, section by section. Every object was assigned a number and photographed, and its provenance was carefully recorded. Another innovation was the division of the finds. Rather than taking all of the objects to Berlin, a significant portion was handed over by agreement to the sultan in Istanbul because northern Iraq (the core of Assyria) was at this time part of the Ottoman Turkish Empire.

Before Andrae had opened excavations at Aššur, the site of Nineveh (modern Mosul) had attracted the interest of successive British archaeologists. Expeditions from various nations have continued during the twentieth century to ex-

ASSYRIANS.   Figure 1.   *Relief showing warriors carrying heads of enemies and throwing them on a heap.* Battle of Til Tuba. Ashurbanipal and the Assyrians fight Teumman, king of Elam, on the Ulai River in 635 BCE. British Museum, London. (Erich Lessing/Art Resource, NY)

plore other tells in Assyria. Gradually Iraqi archaeologists have appeared on the scene, and in modern times they outnumber foreigners in the field. There is no longer a division of the finds from foreign expeditions; a strict ban on the export of any antiquities has enriched Iraqi museums, notably the Iraq Museum in Baghdad and the Mosul Museum.

A major change in the direction of archaeology in the Near East was brought about by modern irrigation projects, which involved the construction of dams and the flooding of plains which were full of ancient sites. This development led to "rescue archaeology"; the organization of numerous teams of archaeologists from various parts of the world to survey the area and excavate some of the most significant looking tells. In Assyria, one such project was in the Eski Mosul region on the upper Tigris River just north of Mosul. [*See* Eski Mosul Dam Salvage Project.] In concluding this

description of archaeological recovery of Assyrian remains, it must be stated that only a fraction of the ancient sites in this region has been explored, and even the excavated tells have not been fully investigated.

Inscriptions. A major product of archaeological activity in Assyria has been the discovery of a vast quantity of inscriptions. These are in the cuneiform (wedge-shaped) writing system, and the language is Akkadian. The Assyrians had their own dialect of Akkadian, but they often wrote in the Babylonian dialect because they were very much influenced by Babylonian culture. Cuneiform and the Akkadian language were deciphered about the same time that intensive archaeological activity began, that is around 1850.

The majority of inscriptions are on clay tablets. Hundreds of thousands have been recovered, but there are many texts inscribed on stone, metal, and other materials. The contents of the inscribed tablets vary considerably. On the one hand there are libraries of tablets; most notable are the libraries of Ashurbanipal (668–627). In these libraries are found myths (such as the creation stories), legends (such as the Flood story), epics (such as the Gilgamesh epic), hymns, prayers, magical incantations, medical texts, divinatory texts, astrological texts, and mathematical texts. There are also archives: the documents accumulated by the palace and merchant houses in the course of daily business. These include letters, contracts, and administrative records. Although efforts to edit and publish all these inscriptions, which are now in museums, have increased in recent years, a significant portion of them remains unpublished, and an unknown quantity are buried in ancient sites.

By the late period of Assyrian history, the spoken language had changed from Akkadian to Aramaic, which was written in an alphabetic script on parchment or papyrus. Because those two materials perished in the Assyrian climate, almost all Aramaic documentation has disappeared. References to it exist, however, in cuneiform inscriptions.

[*See also* Akkadian; Akkadians; Amorites; Aramaic Language and Literature; Aššur; Cuneiform; Nimrud; Nineveh; *and the biographies of Andrae, Botta, and Layard.*]

BIBLIOGRAPHY

Andrae, Walter. *Das wiedererstandene Assur.* 2d ed. Munich, 1977. Account of the excavations at Aššur and their results, written by the director of the expedition.

Barnett, Richard D., and Margarete Falkner. *The Sculptures of Aššurnāṣir-apli II, 883–859 BC, Tiglath-pileser III, 745–729 BC, Esarhaddon, 681–669 BC, from the Central and South-West Palaces at Nimrud.* London, 1962. Excellent collection of photographs and commentary on Assyrian sculptures; see as well Barnett and Lorenzini (below).

Barnett, Richard D., and Amleto Lorenzini. *Assyrian Sculpture in the British Museum.* Toronto, 1975.

The Cambridge Ancient History. Vols. 1.2–3.2. 2d and 3d eds. Cambridge, 1971–1991. The relevant chapters in these volumes vary in quality but in general are quite authoritative and include extensive bibliographies.

Collon, Dominique. *First Impressions: Cylinder Seals in the Ancient Near East.* Chicago, 1988. Comprehensive treatment of cylinder seals with fine illustrations and a sound commentary.

Dalley, Stephanie, and J. N. Postgate. *The Tablets from Fort Shalmaneser.* Cuneiform Texts from Nimrud, 3. London, 1984. The introduction to this book is one of the best treatments of administration and the army. See also Postgate (below).

Grayson, A. Kirk. *Assyrian Royal Inscriptions.* 2 vols. Wiesbaden, 1972–1976. English translation of all royal inscriptions and related texts from the beginning of Assyrian history to 859 BCE. See also Luckenbill (below).

Larsen, Mogens T. *The Old Assyrian City-State and Its Colonies.* Copenhagen Studies in Assyriology, 4. Copenhagen, 1976. Authoritative presentation of the Old Assyrian merchant colonies in Anatolia.

Luckenbill, Daniel D. *Ancient Records of Assyria and Babylonia.* 2 vols. Chicago, 1926–1927. Contains English translations of all Assyrian royal inscriptions known at the time of publication; dated but, except for the first volume (see Grayson above), there is nothing else yet available.

Mallowan, M. E. L. *Nimrud and Its Remains.* Vols. 1–2. London, 1966.
Final report of the excavations at Calah (Nimrud) conducted by the author in the 1950s and 1960s; extensively illustrated. The architecture was one of Mallowan's chief interests.

Oates, David. *Studies in the Ancient History of Northern Iraq.* London, 1968. The author excavated for many years in northern Iraq and this volume reflects his great knowledge of the region, its ancient history, and modern archaeology there.

Olmstead, Albert T. *History of Assyria.* Chicago and London, 1923. Olmstead was the first to write a proper history of Assyria and although the book is quite dated and ponderous, it is still well worth reading.

Postgate, J. N. *Taxation and Conscription in the Assyrian Empire.* Studia Pohl, Series Maior, 3. Rome, 1974. Thorough and reliable discussion.

Paley, Samuel M. *King of the World: Ashur-nasir-pal II of Assyria 883–859 B.C.* Brooklyn, 1976.

Reade, Julian. *Assyrian Sculpture.* Cambridge, Mass., 1983.

Russell, John M. *Sennacherib's Palace Without Rival at Nineveh.* Chicago, 1991.

The Royal Inscriptions of Mesopotamia: Assyrian Periods. Toronto, 1987–. Scholarly editions, including English translation, of all known Assyrian royal inscriptions. Three volumes have appeared and others are in preparation.

Saggs, H. W. F. *The Might That Was Assyria.* London, 1984. Comprehensive and up-to-date treatment of Assyrian history and civilization; good introduction for readers who know little or nothing of the subject.

State Archives of Assyria. Helsinki, 1987. Ongoing series of publications of Neo-Assyrian (nonroyal) inscriptions, in standard editions with English translations. The introductions to the volumes are particularly useful for the nonspecialist.

A. KIRK GRAYSON

ASYUT (also Gk., Lycopolis; 27°11′ N, 31°10′ E), capital of the thirteenth Upper Egyptian nome, or province. Although Anubis, Osiris, and eventually Hathor had cults in the city or at its necropolis, its principle deity was Wepwawet ("opener of the ways"), a jackal god, who held the title Lord of Asyut. The Greeks thought him a wolf, which explains the Hellenistic name, Lycopolis.

The nature of the local topography played a significant role in the importance of this site, where high cliffs demarcating the Libyan desert's eastern edge converge with the Nile River. These features effectively forced valley traffic to pass directly in front of Asyut, thus, allowing it to regulate river passage in either direction. Appropriately, the site's ancient Egyptian name was *S3wt(j)*, "sentinel" or "watchman"; the city's modern name, Asyut, derives from that word. The cliffs also provided an avenue into the Libyan desert, so that caravans traveling south to the oases and Sudan started from Asyut (in Islamic times, this route was the Darb el-Arba'in). Moreover, Bahr Yusuf, the only natural branch of the Nile River in Egypt, diverged from the main channel in the neighborhood of the city, flowing north toward the Faiyum.

Late Old Kingdom (c. 2465–2150 BCE) references indicate that Asyut was by then a recognized settlement, but it is during the First Intermediate period (c. 2150–2040 BCE) that Asyut first played a major role in Egyptian history. During that time, Asyut housed the thirteenth nome's local governors (nomarchs), whose personal armies fought with the Herakleopolitan rulers of the ninth and tenth dynasties in their wars against a Theban dynasty (the eleventh). Asyut's location helped these provincial leaders protect Herakleopolis from attack while they launched invasions south. Most of the information available on this period has been gleaned from biographical and funerary texts found on tomb walls of the nomarchs Khety I and II and Jtj-jb-j and on coffins from Asyut's necropolis.

In the twelfth dynasty (c. 1991–1783 BCE), the size of the local governor's tombs and the information contained in their inscriptions indicate that such men as Djefahepi I, II, and III enjoyed a high rank. Their status is confirmed by the quality of execution of the statue of Sennuwy, wife of Djefahepi I (reign of Senusert I, c. 1971–1926 BCE). Only powerful officials could have commissioned such funerary equipment. Regrettably, no more is known about Asyut's administrative role during this period, except that it remained the provincial capital. In Djefahepi I's tomb, however, detailed legal contracts for the maintenance of his pious foundation (personal cult) have provided Egyptologists with insights into the complexity of property ownership.

Post–Middle Kingdom archaeological remains indicate that the site was continuously inhabited throughout the remainder of the pharaonic and postpharaonic periods, but without its earlier distinction. During the eighteenth and early nineteenth centuries, European scholars touring Egypt began recognizing Asyut's historical importance. The team accompanying Napoleon's well-documented visit in 1799 were among the most important of these visitors. Later, archaeological and epigraphic work at Asyut was conducted exclusively in the provincial necropolis (*smjt nt s3wt*, or *r3 qrrt*). By the end of the nineteenth century, Egyptologists such as Gaston Maspero (1880), Adolf Erman (1882), and most importantly, F. Llewellyn Griffith (1886–1888) recorded the inscriptions on the walls of the necropolis's rock-cut tombs. In 1893, a local peasant discovered an important tomb, that of a First Intermediate period mayor, Mehesti. Two well-known wooden models from this burial depict provincial armies (Cairo Museum, CG 257 and 258), one of which represents Nubian soldiers.

Émile Chassinat and Charles Palanque conducted the cemetery's first major excavation in 1903. They discovered twenty-six largely intact graves containing more than sixty coffins. Thirty-five of these were inscribed and form an important corpus of funerary inscriptions from the First Intermediate period. They also uncovered the tomb of the wealthy "chancellor," Nakhti.

The French excavators were followed by Ernest Schiaparelli (1905–1913), working for the Museo Egizio in Turin, and D. G. Hogarth (1906–1907), who was acquiring objects for the British Museum. Both teams unearthed numerous burials containing objects dating from the Late Old Kingdom through the twelfth dynasty. Hogarth excavated more than 100 tombs, adding some 700 objects to the British Museum's collection, but little is known about Schiaparelli's work.

In 1922, Gerald Wainwright, while excavating in Djefahepi III's tomb, found a cache of stelae, dating from the New Kingdom through Roman times (c. 1550 BCE–495 CE), demotic papyri, and mummies of canines. He also discovered the twelfth dynasty grave of the "steward," Heny.

BIBLIOGRAPHY

Beinlich, Horst. "Assiut." In *Lexikon der Ägyptologie*, vol. 1, cols. 489–495. Wiesbaden, 1973. Brief summary (in German) of the site's significance.

Chassinat, Émile, and Charles Palanque. *Une campagne de fouilles dans la nécropole d'Assiout*. Mémoires de l'Institut Français d'Archéologie Orientale du Caire, vol 24. Cairo, 1911. An important source for the archaeology of the site, but not widely available.

Leospo, Enrichetta. "Gebelein and Asyut during the First Intermediate Period and the Middle Kingdom." In *Egyptian Civilization, Religious Beliefs*, edited by Anna Maria Donadoni Roveri, pp. 82–103. Turin, 1988. Uses objects in the Museo Egizio, Turin, to illustrate a discussion of ancient Egyptian religion. See pages 99–103 for a discussion of Schiaparelli's excavations at Asyut. *Daily Life* (1988), another publication in this series, is also useful.

Leospo, Enrichetta. "Assiut." In *Beyond the Pyramids: Egyptian Regional Art from the Museo Egizio, Turin*, edited by Gay Robins, pp. 34–38. Atlanta, 1990. Brief summary of the site's importance in a context in which the material from Asyut can be compared to objects from other sites of similar date.

Porter, Bertha, and Rosalind Moss. *Topographical Bibliography of Ancient Egyptian Hieroglyphic Texts: Reliefs and Paintings*, vol. 4, *Lower and Middle Egypt*. Oxford, 1934. Classic source listing finds from Middle and Upper Egyptian sites, including Asyut (see pp. 259–269).

Spalinger, Anthony J. "A Redistributive Pattern at Assiut." *Journal of the American Oriental Society* 105.1 (1985): 7–20. Detailed discussion of the mortuary contracts of Djefahepi with diagrams illustrating the economic redistributive systems involved in maintaining Djefahepi's personal cult.

DIANA CRAIG PATCH

'ATLIT RAM. A bronze warship ram and sixteen wooden bow fragments were all that survived the wreck of an ancient warship off the coast of northern Israel at 'Atlit, 19 km (12 mi.) south of Haifa. Yet, these spare remains have made important contributions to the subjects of naval warfare and logistics, metallurgy, shipbuilding, and art in antiquity. Discovered only 200 m from the shore, in the Mediterranean Sea, the ram was situated 3 m below the surface and was protected by an overburden of sand. A team of archaeologists from the University of Haifa excavated it in November 1980 and removed it to the National Maritime Museum in Haifa for conservation and study. Further examination of the site did not produce any additional material related to the 'Atlit warship.

The ram's external surface was in relatively good condi-

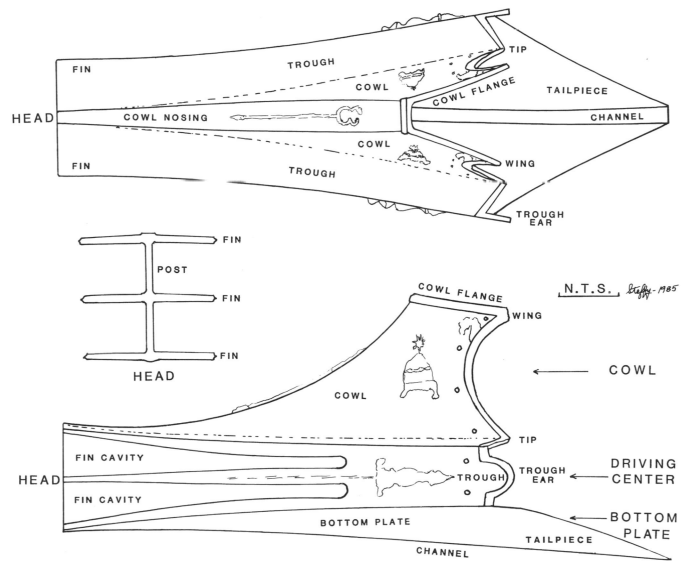

'ATLIT RAM. *Drawing of the ram and its features.* (Courtesy J. R. Steffy)

tion; its interior was completely filled with wood and concretion. Only one timber extended beyond the confines of the ram. Cobalt-source radiographs were used to examine the interior of the assembly to determine the methods by which the wood and concretion could be separated from the ram without damage.

Its superb workmanship and ingenious design make the ram a beautiful and functional weapon, the largest and most impressive ram yet discovered, and the only one of its type to be associated with the hull of a ship. The symbols on its surfaces suggest that it came from a Hellenistic warship, perhaps from a unit in one of the Ptolemaic Cypriot fleets of the late third or early second centuries BCE (Casson and Steffy, 1990, pp. 51–66). Literary and archaeological evidence reveal that it belonged to a vessel at least one or two classes larger than a trireme (Casson and Steffy, 1990, pp. 72–75).

The ram had an overall length of 2.26 m and a maximum height of 0.96 m. It was cast in 465 kg of high-grade bronze. Its head, or striking surface, consists of three horizontal fins joined by a vertical post; the post is 41.1 cm high while the fins had a maximum width of 44.2 cm and were only 2 cm thick at their outer ends. The shape of the fins and post changes aft of the head to form the driving center, a 76-centimeter-wide trough that housed the ship's main ramming timbers.

Above the driving center was the cowl, which curved gracefully upward and aftward from the head to house the stem and other vertical bow timbers. Beneath the driving center, an unadorned bottom plate protected the lower surfaces of the hull. The ram was attached to all the major hull timbers by means of bronze bolts.

The ram bears four different symbols. The first, a *kery-keion*, or "herald's staff," bound with a fillet, is located on the nosing of the cowl. It is the only one of the symbols that appears singly—the other three appear on both sides of the ram. The fins of the head merge to join a decorative handle on each side of the after end of the driving center's trough. These have been identified as triform thunderbolts, symbols representative of the Ptolemaic dynasty. Directly above the handle devices, on each side of the cowl, a wreathed helmet is mounted by an eight-pointed star. A fourth symbol in the upper, after corner of each cowl side has been identified as the eagle of Zeus.

A variety of sophisticated processes were employed to analyze the surprisingly advanced metallurgical expertise employed in casting the ram (Casson and Steffy, 1990, pp. 40–50). The bronze alloy (90 percent copper and 10 percent tin) was ideal for this military application. Based on radiograph analysis, the nature of various casting defects, and measurements taken at defect locations, the ram is believed to have been cast in a foundry consisting of thirty furnaces placed in a circle. With melt temperatures calculated at up to 1,350° C, these furnaces supplied the two-piece sand mold through an elaborate feeding and gating system.

The timber fragments, whose survival represented only a small fraction of the warship's bow, were all in their original orientation. The major timber, of a type that had not been recorded before the discovery of the 'Atlit wreck, was the centrally located, six-sided ramming timber; it survives for a length of more than 2.04 m. A keel and thick bottom planks were fastened to its bottom and sides, while vertical bow timbers were mounted on its upper surface. Fragments of side planking were still attached to the aftward raking stem. Although only fragmentary, the preserved wood provided new information about the construction of classical warships and confirmed that, like merchant vessels of the period, these ships had hulls made of thick planks whose edges were joined with strong, closely spaced mortise-and-tenon joints.

[*See also* Underwater Archaeology.]

BIBLIOGRAPHY

Basch, Lucien. *Le musée imaginaire de la marine antique.* Athens, 1987. The largest and best collection of illustrations of warship rams, along with extensive commentary and fresh ideas on the subject.

Casson, Lionel. *Ships and Seamanship in the Ancient World.* 2d ed. Princeton, 1986. Definitive work on ancient ships and seafaring.

Casson, Lionel, and J. Richard Steffy, eds. *The Athlit Ram.* College Station, Texas, 1990. The final project report on the 'Atlit wreck and the source for this entry.

Casson, Lionel. *The Ancient Mariners: Seafarers and Sea Fighters of the Mediterranean in Ancient Times.* 2d ed. Princeton, 1991. The best popular history of seafaring in the ancient Mediterranean.

Linder, Elisha, and Yehoshua Ramon. "A Bronze Ram from the Sea of Athlit, Israel." *Archaeology* 34.6 (1981): 62–64. Illustrated account of the discovery and excavation of the ram.

Morrison, J. S., and R. T. Williams. *Greek Oared Ships, 900–322 B.C.* London, 1968.

Morrison, J. S., and J. F. Coates. *The Athenian Trireme.* Cambridge, 1986. History and reconstruction of an ancient Greek warship.

Murray, William M., and Photios M. Petsas. *Octavian's Campsite Memorial for the Actian War.* Transactions of the American Philosophical Society, 79.4. Philadelphia, 1989. Analysis of the ram sockets at Octavian's memorial to the Battle of Actium in 31 BCE and comparisons with the shape of the 'Atlit ram.

J. RICHARD STEFFY

ATOMIC ABSORPTION ANALYSIS. *See* Neutron Activation Analysis.

AVDAT, or Oboda, founded as a Nabatean trade route site on a mountain ridge in the Negev desert, southwest of the Dead Sea, and identified with modern-day 'Abdah (map reference 120 × 020). The site was named for Oboda II (62/61–58 BCE), a Nabatean king who, according to Uranius (as cited by Stephen of Byzantium), was buried and venerated there as a god. His name is retained in the Arabic 'Abdah.

The first settlement appeared at the end of the fourth century BCE, when caravan traders from both Petra and Aila (Eilat) stopped at Avdat on their way to the Mediterranean sea at Gaza. By the end of the first century BCE, and into the mid-first century CE, Avdat was a major religious, military, and commercial center, the site of magnificent Nabatean temples. After the destruction of the settlement by fire, sometime between 40 and 70 CE, agriculture replaced trade as the primary source of revenue and Avdat became a center of sheep, goat, and camel breeding. Prosperity returned under the Romans, who, at the beginning of the fourth century, built a fortress there, making the town part of the eastern empire's overall defense system. During the fourth century, Christian churches replaced the Nabatean temples and wine production played an important role in the local economy. Avdat was destroyed in 636, during the Arab conquest of Palestine, and was subsequently abandoned.

Various explorers examined the site in the late nineteenth and early twentieth centuries, among them Edward H. Palmer in 1870 and Alois Musil in 1902 and 1904. The first comprehensive survey was conducted in 1904 by Antonin Jaussen, Raphael Savignac, and Louis-Hugues Vincent, who drew a detailed plan of the site. Further explorations were undertaken by C. Leonard Woolley and T. E. Lawrence in 1912 and by Theodor Wiegand in 1916. Large-scale excavations were conducted by Michael Avi-Yonah in 1958 on behalf of the Hebrew University of Jerusalem and by Avraham Negev from 1959 to 1961 and again in 1989 and by Negev and Rudolph Cohen from 1975 to 1977, also on behalf of the Hebrew University as well as the Israel Department of Antiquities.

Occupational evidence spanning the Nabatean through

the Byzantine periods has been uncovered. The remains from the Nabatean period have been assigned to three settlement phases. The first, Early Nabatean (early fourth century–early first century BCE), is characterized by imported pottery and minted coins but no architecture; the inhabitants probably dwelled in tents. This phase ended with abandonment, apparently in the wake of the Hasmonean conquest of Gaza by Alexander Jannaeus.

Public buildings were prominent features of the second phase, the Middle Nabatean period (50 BCE–50/70 CE). The most prominent was a temple complex (11 × 13.70 m) that consisted of a portico supported by four columns, a hall, and an adytum divided by a partition wall. The pantheon of Nabatean deities was worshiped in the larger area; Obodas, in the smaller area. The temple was plastered as well as painted and, as indicated by numerous Nabatean dedicatory inscriptions, was in use from the end of the first century BCE to the end of the third century CE. [See Nabatean Inscriptions.]

At a later stage of the middle period, the temple became part of a large sacred complex built on the acropolis. Supported by retaining walls on three sides (north, west, south), the acropolis could be entered through three passageways. One was a rectangular gatehouse (7 × 7 m) at the eastern edge of the northern retaining wall. Another, made up of a small court (10 × 6 m), an arched passageway, and a staircase tower (4 × 3.6 m), was built in the southwestern corner of the acropolis. Dedicatory inscriptions dating to the reign of Aretas IV (9 BCE–40 CE) were found among the ruins of this passageway, which led to the portico of the temple.

The remains of a military camp (100 × 100 m) located northeast of the acropolis also belong to the middle period. The main road leading in from the gate divided the camp in half, and another wide road divided it into quarters, each of which had barracks. There probably were camel sheds in the streets in front of the barrack, and halls and rooms had been built along the inside of the enclosure wall.

The end of the Middle Nabatean phase corresponds with the destruction of Avdat by pre-Islamic Arab invaders in the mid- to late first century CE. The Late Nabatean phase began with the reign of Rabel II (70–106 CE) and continues, from the second to the mid-fourth centuries, into what is historically termed Late Roman but can just as well be classified as Late Nabatean because the inhabitants remained culturally Nabatean even after 106 CE, when Avdat and the rest of the Negev were annexed by the Romans into the Provincia Arabia. The initial Late Nabatean settlement centered along the valleys to the south and west of the town, where the first private dwellings were located. Dedicatory inscriptions on pairs of limestone libation altars found in these valleys date to the reign of Rabel II and probably commemorate the beginning of Nabatean agriculture.

The subsequent Late Nabatean remains are concentrated in the Roman quarter situated to the southeast of the Middle Nabatean acropolis. Dwellings with enclosed courtyards were found within the quarter, and a three-story observation tower (9.6 × 9.6 m) was uncovered on its southwestern edge. Dated to 294 CE, the tower is the latest structure at Avdat to incorporate every component of Nabatean architecture. Also from this period are a burial cave (en-Nuṣrah, "cave of the Christian") found on the southwestern slope and a two-story khan, or rest house, situated northeast of the Nabatean settlement. The ashlar structure (22.5 × 31 m) had a large middle court (12 × 19 m) as well as rooms, halls, and a kitchen; it apparently remained in use until the mid-fourth century CE.

The beginning of the Byzantine period at Avdat seems to correspond to the devastating earthquake of 363, after which the primary structures on the acropolis were built. Dismantled stones from the Nabatean military camp were used to construct the Byzantine citadel on the eastern section of the acropolis. The rectangular fortress, comprising an area of about 0.5 acre, had thick outer walls (up to 2 m thick) that enclosed a large courtyard (61 × 41 m). Twelve towers of various sizes were positioned along the four walls (three towers on each wall); gates and entrances were situated on all sides. (Some entranceways had been blocked, perhaps to defend against Arab attacks in the mid-seventh century.)

Two Byzantine churches (north and south) were constructed on the western portion of the acropolis. The north church dates to the Early Byzantine period. Separated from the fortress by a large, unpaved square (51 × 40 m) that had belonged to the Nabatean sacred complex, it is situated just northeast of the Nabatean temple. It contains a basilica with a single apse and an abutting room that are adjoined on the south by a chapel and several service rooms. [See Basilicas.] Two projections (both enclosed by chancels) jutted out from the apse like shoulders. Inside of each were the truncated legs of small altars that supported containers filled with religious relics. To the west of the church, situated at one corner of the Nabatean portico, was a narrow baptistery that had a cross-shaped marble font (1.35 m per length) as well as a smaller font for infant baptisms. [See Baptisteries.]

The south church, constructed a century after the north church, was dedicated as the Martyrium of Saint Theodore. In addition to a basilica, this church contained a complex of rooms identified as a monastery. [See Monasteries.] Columns, capitals, and other architectural elements from the Nabatean temple were reused to decorate the atrium. Permanent reliquaries were found inside the large niches that had been carved into the rear walls of the two rooms flanking the single apse. In the sixth century the south church served as a burial ground.

The Byzantine occupants of Avdat lived in houses and adjoining caves built into the site's western slope. Several hundred of these house-cave units have been found. A cross carved into the ceiling of one cave suggests that the room served as a house chapel. Other Byzantine remains include five wine presses and associated storerooms, a large farmhouse (15 × 35 m) east of the Roman quarter, and a Roman bathhouse located at the bottom of the slope. [*See* Baths.] The bathhouse, which contained a cold bath, a tepid bath, and two hot rooms, was heated by flues leading to outside furnaces. Preserved with its roof, the structure is one of the best examples of a Roman bathhouse yet uncovered in the region.

[*See also* Churches; Nabateans; Petra, *and the biographies of Avi-Yonah, Lawrence, Palmer, Vincent, and Woolley.*]

BIBLIOGRAPHY

Negev, Avraham. "Nabatean Capitals in the Towns of the Negev." *Israel Exploration Journal* 24 (1974): 153–159.
Negev, Avraham. *The Nabatean Potter's Workshop at Oboda.* Bonn, 1974.
Negev, Avraham. "The Early Beginnings of the Nabatean Realm." *Palestine Exploration Quarterly* 108 (1976): 125–133.
Negev, Avraham, ed. "Die Nabatäer." *Antike Welt* 7, Sondernummer (1976). Thematic issue.
Negev, Avraham. "The Nabateans and the Provincia Arabia." In *Aufstieg und Niedergang der römischen Welt,* vol. II.8, edited by Hildegard Temporini and Wolfgang Haase, pp. 520–686. Berlin, 1977.
Negev, Avraham. "Housing and City-planning in the Ancient Negev and the Provincia Arabia." In *Housing in Arid Lands: Design and Planning,* edited by Gideon Golany, pp. 3–32. London, 1980.
Negev, Avraham. *The Greek Inscriptions from the Negev.* Jerusalem, 1981. See pages 11–45.
Negev, Avraham. "Christen und Christentum in der Wüste Negev." *Antike Welt* 13 (1982): 2–33.
Negev, Avraham. *Tempel, Kirchen und Zisternen.* Stuttgart, 1983.
Negev, Avraham. *The Late Hellenistic and Early Roman Pottery of Nabatean Oboda: Final Report.* Qedem, vol. 22. Jerusalem, 1986.
Negev, Avraham. *Nabatean Archaeology Today.* New York, 1986.
Negev, Avraham. "Obodas the God." *Israel Exploration Journal* 36 (1986): 56–60.
Negev, Avraham. "The Cathedral of Elusa and the New Typology and Chronology of the Byzantine Churches in the Negev." *Studium Biblicum Franciscanum/Liber Annuus* 39 (1989): 129–142.
Negev, Avraham. "The Temple of Obodas: Excavations at Oboda in July 1989." *Israel Exploration Journal* 41 (1991): 62–80.
Wenning, Robert. *Die Nabatäer: Denkmäler und Geschichte.* Göttingen, 1987. Contains a full bibliography (pp. 159–172).

AVRAHAM NEGEV

AVIGAD, NAHMAN (1905–1992), Israeli archaeologist, epigraphist, and paleographer. Born in Zawalow in Galicia, formerly Austria, today the Ukraine, Avigad studied architecture in Brno, Czechoslovakia, and then immigrated to Palestine in 1925. As a member of a Zionist youth group in Palestine he became enamored of archaeology as he hiked and camped around the country exploring the land and the physical remains of its long history. This field of study, known as *yedi'at ha'aretz,* "knowing the land," was the core of the absorption process for all newcomers to Palestine.

Avigad entered the Hebrew University of Jerusalem in 1929 and received his master's degree in 1949. The subject of his Ph.D. dissertation in 1952 was the ancient necropolis of Jerusalem, published in 1954 as a book, *Maṣṣebōt Qedumot be-Naḥal Qidron.* This work marked the beginning of his lifelong association with the archaeology of Jerusalem. His chief mentor in field archaeology was Eleazar L. Sukenik, with whom he worked at the synagogue sites of Beth Alpha (1929) and Hammath-Gader (1932). He also worked with Benjamin Mazar at Beth-She'arim, assuming the directorship of the elaborate catacomb excavations there in 1953. His work appeared as the third volume in that series, *Beth She'arim III: The Catacombs 12–23,* in 1971.

Avigad joined the faculty of the Institute of Archaeology at Hebrew University in 1949, later becoming a full professor. He specialized in epigraphy and paleography, focusing on Hebrew and Aramaic scripts. He also published a key text of the Dead Sea Scroll corpus, *The Genesis Apocryphon* (1956), jointly with Yigael Yadin. Avigad was the leading scholar for work on ancient seals, bullae, and jar stamps.

He was perhaps best known for his excavations in the Jewish Quarter of the Old City of Jerusalem, where he worked almost year-round from 1969 to 1983. During that time, he became emeritus professor in (1974). His semipopular report of his work in the Jewish Quarter, *Discovering Jerusalem* (Nashville, 1983), was widely acclaimed. He did not live to complete his final report, which will be written by a senior member of his staff. The areas he excavated now house the popular museums of The Burnt House, The Herodian Quarter, and Hezekiah's Wall.

Avigad received numerous prizes for his scholarship, including the Israel Prize (1977). He was especially honored when he was named "Yaqqir Yerushalayim," "Beloved One of Jerusalem" (1984), in recognition of his unique contributions to the city. His scholarship in all periods of antiquity, and his familiarity with ancient Near Eastern and biblical, classical, and rabbinic texts set him apart. It was Avigad's concern with their intersection that made his work important and enduring.

[*See also* Beth Alpha; Beth-She'arim; Dead Sea Scrolls; Hammath-Gader; Jerusalem; *and the biographies of Mazar, Sukenik, and Yadin.*]

BIBLIOGRAPHY

Meyers, Eric M. "Nahman Avigad, 1905–1992." *Proceedings of the American Academy for Jewish Research* 58 (1992): 1–5.
"Professor Nahman Avigad, 1905–1992: In Memoriam." *Israel Exploration Journal* 42 (1992): 1–3.

ERIC M. MEYERS

AVI-YONAH, MICHAEL (1904–1974), archaeologist and art historian best known for his synthetic studies establishing the foundations of classical and Byzantine archaeology in the land of Israel. Born in Lemberg (modern Lvov in western Ukraine), Avi-Yonah immigrated to Palestine as a child. He began his higher education at the University of London (1925–1928) in Classical archaeology and history; much later, after he had already established his career, he earned an M.A. (1943) and a Ph.D. (1953) from the same institution. Between 1931 and 1948 he served as the keeper of records in the Palestine Department of Antiquities, a position he continued in for the newly founded Israel Department of Antiquities (1948) until in 1953, he joined the Hebrew University of Jerusalem as a lecturer in archaeology and art history.

As an archaeologist, Avi-Yonah directed several small-scale excavations: the synagogue at 'Isfiya (1931); tombs in Nahariya (1941); the thermae at Beth-Yerah (1945–1946), the Roman site at Giv'at-Ram, Jerusalem (1949); and the synagogue at Caesarea (1956, 1962). He also participated in the first survey of Masada (1955).

Avi-Yonah's books on the history and historical geography of Palestine are significant contributions to the field. In addition, he was the editor of two of the leading journals of professional archaeology: from 1932 to 1950 he edited the *Quarterly of the Department of Antiquities in Palestine* (*QDAP*), publishing all fourteen of its issues; and he edited the *Israel Exploration Journal* (*IEJ*) for more than twenty years. As the author of a number of introductory books, dictionaries, and atlases, Avi-Yonah was an outstanding and responsible popularizer of the field of archaeology. He is also well known for his work on the scale model of Jerusalem of the Second Temple period on the grounds of the Holy Land Hotel in Jerusalem. The model is a graphic statement of Avi-Yonah's lifelong research on the topography of Jerusalem in the Second Temple, the Roman, and the Byzantine periods.

[*See also* Beth-Yerah; Caesarea; *and* Jerusalem.]

BIBLIOGRAPHY

Avi-Yonah, Michael. "Concise Bibliography of Excavations in Palestine." *Quarterly of the Department of Antiquities of Palestine* 1 (1932): 86–94, 139–149, 163–199.
Avi-Yonah, Michael. "Mosaic Pavements in Palestine." *Quarterly of the Department of Antiquities of Palestine* 2 (1932): 136–181; 3 (1933): 26–47, 49–73; 4 (1935): 187–193.
Avi-Yonah, Michael. "Map of Roman Palestine." *Quarterly of the Department of Antiquities of Palestine* 5 (1936): 139–193. Revised as a book (Jerusalem, 1940).
Avi-Yonah, Michael. *Abbreviations in Greek Inscriptions (the Near East, 200 BC–AD 1100)*. Quarterly of the Department of Antiquities of Palestine, Supplement to vol. 9. Jerusalem, 1940.
Avi-Yonah, Michael. "Oriental Elements in the Art of Palestine in the Roman and Byzantine Periods." *Quarterly of the Department of Antiquities of Palestine* 10 (1942): 105–151; 13 (1948): 128–165; 14 (1950): 49–80.
Avi-Yonah, Michael. *The Holy Land from the Persian to the Arab Conquests, 536 B.C.–A.D. 640: A Historical Geography*. Grand Rapids, Mich., 1966.
Avi-Yonah, Michael. *Gazetteer of Roman Palestine*. Qedem, vol. 5. Jerusalem, 1976.
Avi-Yonah, Michael. *The Jews of Palestine: A Political History from the Bar Kokhba War to the Arab Conquest*. Oxford, 1976.
"Bibliography of M. Avi-Yonah" (in Hebrew). *Bulletin of the Israel Exploration Society* 18 (1954): 113–120.
Salzmann, Milka C. "Bibliography of M. Avi-Yonah." *Israel Exploration Journal* 24 (1974): 287–315; 34 (1984): 184–186.

RONNY REICH

AXUM, ancient capital and important trading center in Ethiopia (14°10′ N, 38°45′ E). Located in the highland plateau of northern Ethiopia, Axum was a large urban center and the eponymous capital of a political state that flourished from the first through the seventh or eighth century CE. During the period of its greatest expansion, it controlled the highland plateau and coast of northern Ethiopia, southern Yemen, and part of the eastern Sudan.

Axum was the southernmost outpost of the hellenized Near East. Its economic strength depended upon its role in the international trade that passed through the Red Sea. This trade was diminished by Persia's conquest of South Arabia in the late sixth century; its decline continued with subsequent Islamic domination of the area. By the end of the seventh century the Axumite state had lost its international economic standing. Internally, deforestation and soil degradation around the urban center took their toll; between the eighth and tenth centuries Axum had ceased to be the capital of the Christian kingdom of highland Ethiopia.

Archaeological investigations have revealed the outlines of Axum's relative chronology, but its absolute chronology remains more problematic. King Ezana converted to Christianity about 333 and still reigned around the year 356. Kaleb reigned in 520 but had given up the throne before 543 when the Byzantine author Procopius in his *History of the Wars* (1.20.8) referred to Kaleb's successor. A merchant's handbook known as the *Periplus of the Erythraean [Red] Sea*, written in 40–70 CE, describes the Red Sea port of Adulis and names Axum as the metropolis.

The clearest indicator of Axum's position in the economy of the graecized Near East is its issue of gold coinage, beginning about 270 with the coins of King Endubis. Silver and bronze coins were issued for local use, and the gold coin issues were tied to the Roman standard. All coin issues, reflecting the design of Roman coinage, show a bust or half-length portrait of the ruler in profile, framed by stalks of barley or wheat (cereals being the basis of Axumite agriculture). Coins issued prior to the conversion of Ezana show a disc and crescent, and those issued after show the cross. Most coins are inscribed in Greek, but issues of the second half of the sixth and seventh centuries may be inscribed in Ge'ez, an Ethiopian Semitic language of the Afro-Asiatic linguistic family.

Monumental lapidary inscriptions offer royal propaganda in Greek language and script and in Ge'ez, written either in Epigraphic South Arabian or Ge'ez script. Although Ge'ez letter forms are related to those of the South Arabian scripts, a system of vocalization was invented, whereby vowel markers are joined to consonant letter forms. The first fully vocalized Ge'ez appears in a royal inscription of King Ezana. Royal victories were also commemorated by votive stone thrones. Remains of square throne bases, slotted on three sides, are visible at Axum. The stability of the centralized state (at least until the end of the sixth century) is reflected by the lack of defensive walls at Axum and other Axumite urban centers.

Little is known of Axumite religion prior to Ezana's conversion. His trilingual inscription mentions the deities Ashtar (Ishtar), Beher, and Meder, under whose protection he placed himself; it names him as the son of Mahrem, identified in the Greek Axumite inscriptions as Ares, god of war.

Excavations at Axum have revealed remains of several large elite mansions; foundations of the largest (in the Dungur area) measure 57 × 56.5 m (187 × 185 ft.). These mansions, dating from the late third to the late sixth century, incorporated distinctive features of Axumite architecture. Their central pavilions were built upon stepped podia (platforms) with monumental entrance stairs. Walls were constructed of stones laid in mud mortar, and corners of walls and podia were reinforced with dressed stone blocks. Walls and stepped podia were built with projecting and re-entrant sections, a design element that imparts greater strength. Dressed masonry was used for doorways, stairways, pillars, door jambs, and lintels. Wooden beams, round and square in cross-section, were used as roof supports.

These characteristic features of Axumite architecture—projecting wooden roof supports (so-called monkey heads), framed windows and doorways, and recessed facades—ornament the faces of six giant stelae at Axum's central necropolis. These monuments are datable to the fourth century. The great ornamented stela that still stands is 21 m (68 ft.) high (see figure 1). Contrary to legend, the giant stelae fell because of their inadequate foundations. Their suggestion of multiple stories (ten or more) is the sole fantastic element of an otherwise authentic facsimile of a monumental Axumite facade. Pottery house models, datable to the later third century, show rectangular houses with thatch roofs, which represent the ordinary dwellings of private individuals.

Earlier stelae at Axum were simple upright stones. After the fourth century, stelae were no longer erected. All were funerary. Those of the central necropolis are associated with platforms, terraces, and tombs that were either dug into rock or built in pits. Arches and vaults of baked brick were found in tombs datable to the fourth century. Excavations in this area by the British Institute in East Africa, led by Neville Chittick, were halted in 1974 because of the local political situation.

Tomb contents included a range of objects, imported Mediterranean luxury goods, and some glass fragments that suggest a local glass industry. Well-made Axumite pottery was produced by a local craft industry. Major ceramic types are the burnished Red Axumite ware, datable to the first or second through the fifth century, and Brown Axumite ware

AXUM. Figure 1. *Stelae at Axum.* (Werner Forman/Art Resource, NY)

that replaced Red Axumite ware during the sixth century. Axumite pottery is handmade, and glaze is rare.

The earliest Red Axumite ware shares sufficient elements with pre-Axumite pottery to suggest no discontinuity in local populations. Axum itself does not overlay earlier construction, although pre-Axumite sites, such as Yeha, are not far from Axum. The pre-Axumite period, dating to the second half of the first millennium BCE, is not well understood. Inscriptions demonstrate connections with South Arabia.

In 1993, programs of archaeological research at Axum and its environs resumed, including the work of the British Institute in East Africa led by David W. Phillipson and that of the Instituto Universitario Orientale and Boston University Archaeological Mission, led by Rodolfo Fattovich and Kathryn A. Bard.

[See also Ethiopia.]

BIBLIOGRAPHY

Munro-Hay, Stuart, et al. *Excavations at Aksum: An Account of Research at the Ancient Ethiopian Capital Directed in 1972–4 by the Late Dr. Neville Chittick.* Memoirs of the British Institute in Eastern Africa, no. 10. London, 1989. Authoritative monograph on the site of Axum, with extensive bibliography.

MARILYN E. HELDMAN

AYYUBID–MAMLUK DYNASTIES.

The Ayyubids (1169–1250) and the Mamluks (1250–1517) ruled with great impact over Egypt and Syria (i.e., Greater Syria: Palestine (modern Israel), Jordan, Lebanon, and modern Syria) for almost three hundred and fifty years. Toward the end of the Fatimid period (909–1169), Egypt was in chaos. Internal power struggles led to intervention by the Crusaders, who even controlled Cairo for a short time, and by the new rulers of Syria and northern Mesopotamia, the Zangids (1127/1146–1181). One of the Zangid generals, Salah ad-Din (the Saladin of Western sources), brought an end to the deteriorating situation in Cairo and to the Fatimids; came in control of Egypt (1169) and the holy cities of Islam (Mecca and Medina) and Yemen (1173); took Tripoli, in modern Lebanon, from the Normans (1172); and conquered Damascus (1174), Aleppo (1178), and, soon after, northern Mesopotamia.

Thus, Salah ad-Din, a ruler of Kurdish origin, was the king (sultan) of a state that stretched from the western borders of Egypt to the western borders of Iran. The only remaining enemy in the territory was the Crusaders, who controlled parts of the coastal regions of Syria and Jerusalem. In 1187 he took Jerusalem and conquered other Crusader states the following year. This led to the Third Crusade (1190–1192), which left the Crusaders with only a few sites and the right (if unarmed) to visit Jerusalem. [See Crusader Period.]

Salah ad-Din's political and military strength and his tolerance figure prominently in contemporary Western sources. Islamic sources place him next to a few other outstanding rulers in Islam, primarily because of his military achievements. He must have been an efficient ruler as well, but his political vision did not encompass a centralized state. Before his death in 1193, he divided his realm among members of his family, who ruled after him as kings in Egypt, Damascus, Aleppo, and elsewhere. The Ayyubid "federation" survived with some success into the middle of the thirteenth century.

Following a lengthy period of internal struggles for supremacy within the Ayyubid family, in Egypt a slave-soldier *(mamluk)* of Turkish origin named Aybak took power in 1250. He became the founder of the Mamluk dynasty, whose more than fifty sultans became the lords of Egypt and Syria for the next more than 250 years. In Syria the Ayyubid kingdoms were overrun by the Mongols of Hülegü in 1259, who in turn were defeated by the Mamluks in Palestine in the same year. This victory opened Syria to the Mamluks. The leader of this Mamluk army, Baybars, became the Mamluk sultan in 1260. It was during his long reign (for a Mamluk) of seventeen years that the foundations of the Mamluk state were established. An administrative system was laid out that used the pre-Mamluk structure in Syria. In it even an Ayyubid prince, the historian Abu al-Fida' of Hama, was retained. Baybars continued Salah ad-Din's policy of pushing back the Crusaders by military and political means and as a result, holds the same esteemed place in Islamic history as his predecessor. His quasi-successor, Kalaun (1279–1290), ended the Crusader presence in the Holy Land and built, on Baybars' foundations, the basic elements of the Mamluk state. The long reign of Kalaun's son Nasir Muhammad (1310–1341) benefited both the arts and political stability. Baybars, Kalaun, and Nasir are the most prominent Mamluk sultans of the so-called mainly Turkish Bahri dynasty, which in 1382 was overthrown by another Mamluk group, the mainly Circassian Burji dynasty. The Burjis remained in power until 1517, when a new and militarily advanced power the Ottomans, who introduced gunpowder to warfare in the Near East, conquered Syria and Egypt.

Few of the sultans who followed Baybars and Kalaun compare to them. Many ruled only for a short period and many suffered a violent death. It was the internal political structure of the Mamluk state that created instability. Whereas after Salah ad-Din members of the Ayyubid family ruled over small kingdoms in Syria and Egypt—Egypt being the most prominent—in which the ruler of Egypt, as a rule, was the overlord, patron, or "king of kings," the Mamluks had their own unique system of government and practice for choosing their sultan or king. Their system was oligarchic, even though there are a few exceptions where a son followed his father as sultan. In principle, only a slave-soldier who, as a boy or young man, had been brought as a slave from the Turkish areas north of the Black Sea and the

Caspian Sea—in general, a Kipchak Turk—or a Circassian slave-soldier who had been brought from the Caucasus were eligible to become sultan. After these young men were brought from the northeast, they went through thorough military and administrative training that sorted the weak from the strong. The strongest, within a very well-organized system, advanced themselves as military leaders and governors of the provinces in the Mamluk state. The strongest, most successful, most cunning, or most brutal advanced higher and higher in rank until they competed for sultanship. This system, for all its brutality, had one advantage: a weak son rarely followed a strong father. The sons of the Mamluks were not permitted to serve in the military, and were thus excluded from direct political power. They served in the lower ranks of government, where important (handling finances) posts were held by Christians, or in different trades. In this way a unique interrelated system developed between government and business that may have been the base of the longevity and relative economic prosperity of the Mamluk state.

The material evidence—remains of buildings and sherds classified as Ayyubid/Mamluk—demonstrates that in the Ayyubid and Mamluk periods in Syria large areas of land were recultivated that had not been used since Late Antiquity. Documents show that a rather efficient feudal system of land administration and land ownership existed in Egypt. Thus, enough surplus was produced to allow patronage in the arts and in building construction. Salah ad-Din built the citadel of Cairo, but no noteworthy architecture from his reign is left. Literary sources as well as inscriptions bear witness, however, that this sultan, who spent most of his time at war, was a patron of extensive construction projects. There were no innovations in style in Islamic art and architecture during his reign—nor is there an Ayyubid style in Islamic art and architecture. In Cairo, the few monuments remaining from the Ayyubid period are mature continuations of a Late Fatimid architecture. [See Fatimid Dynasty.] The best example is the Madrasah of Najmaddin (1240–1249). Like most buildings in Cairo, it was squeezed into a preexisting urban fabric. The style of the facade and the minaret in its (quasi) center have little to do with the architectural style of the building. The forms used are those of Late Fatimid buildings like the Mosque al-Akmar or the Mosque as-Salih Talai. The building's ground plan, however, determined the layout of future madrasahs in Cairo. Two large iwans (vaulted rooms open to the courtyard), elements taken from Iranian architecture via Zangid Syrian buildings, flank the courtyard. This future element in Islamic architecture in the west came from the east, with Syria the transmitter.

From pre-Ayyubid times, one of the finest examples of imported Iranian architecture is the Maristan an-Nuri, built by the Zangid Nur ad-Din, in Damascus, Syria. Nur ad-Din, the building's patron, came from the east and changed architectural forms in Syria. The most "classical" building in Mediterranean Islamic architecture is preserved in Aleppo, Syria: the Madrasah al-Firdaws. It was built in 1237 (?), toward the end of Ayyubid rule in Syria. A clear language of forms and a mature floor plan characterize it. The courtyard is framed by well-proportioned arcades and, in the north, a large iwan dominates. The integrated stonework of the *mihrab* hints at forms later taken up in Mamluk architecture in Syria and Egypt. Its polychrome execution (black and white stone) became a characteristic element of Mamluk and post-Mamluk architecture in Syria and Egypt, known as the *ablak* technique. The Zangid-Ayyubid "classical revival"—the tendency to return to pre-Islamic Mediterranean forms and concepts of proportion—was continued in Baybars' buildings in Damascus and Cairo. In Damascus, the Madrasah az-Zahiriya is a copy of the Ayyubid Madrasah al-Adiliya across the street. Imitations of the mosaics in the Umayyad mosque in Damascus (which Baybars ordered restored) reflect the tendency to link his sovereignty with the pre-Islamic past (the Umayyads in this case). In Cairo, Baybars built his Great Mosque following Fatimid examples—the mosque of al-Hakim and the mosque in Mahdiyah, in Tunisia, the first Fatimid capital. Older forms there were combined with a large dome in front of the mihrab, an eastern element, however.

More than three hundred years of shared history under the Ayyubids and the Mamluks mingled aesthetic concepts and practices in Egypt and Syria into a fruitful marriage of the "flat" Egyptian form and the use of space in Syrian forms. Examples are found in Cairo as well as in Damascus, Aleppo, and Jerusalem. The fragile structures found in Cairo and Jerusalem are in contrast to the monumental form of the Mosque of Sultan Hasan in Cairo (1356–1363) and the plump forms of the Great Mosque in Aleppo rebuilt by the Mamluks.

Characteristic elements of Mamluk architecture are the dome, the iwan, and polychromy in the facades and other parts of buildings. It is both a synthesis and development of earlier forms—a synthesis of pseudoclassical forms, of eastern, Crusader, and Zangid/Ayyubid traditions. It led (along with the dominant Ottoman dome) to what is understood to be "Islamic" architecture.

[See also Crusader Period; and Mosque. *In addition, many of the sites mentioned are the subject of independent entries.*]

BIBLIOGRAPHY

Ayalon, David. *Studies on the Mamluks of Egypt.* London, 1977.

Ayalon, David. *The Mamluk Military Society.* London, 1979.

Burgoyne, M. H. *Mamluk Jerusalem: An Architectural Study.* Buckhurst Hill, 1987.

Creswell, K. A. C. *Muslim Architecture of Egypt.* Vol. 2, *Ayyubids and Early Bahri Mamluks.* Oxford, 1959.

Herzfeld, Ernst. "Damascus: Studies in Architecture III: The Ayyubid Madrasa." *Ars Islamica* 11–12 (1946): 1–71.

Lapidus, Ira M. *Muslim Cities of the Later Middle Ages.* Cambridge, Mass., 1967.

Meinecke, Michael. *Die mamlukische Architektur in Ägypten und Syrien.* Glückstadt, 1992.

HEINZ GAUBE

'AZEKAH, a small one-acre site, situated on a high ridge of the Judean foothills overlooking the Elah Valley, 'Azekah (Tell Zakariya) is located 8 km (5 mi.) northeast of Beit Jibrin, 3.5 km (2 mi.) southwest of Tel Yarmut, and 6 km (4 mi.) southwest of Tel Beth-Shemesh (31°42' N, 34°54' E; map reference 1440 × 1230). Its strategic location, at 400 m above sea level, explains its description in Assyrian sources from the time of Sargon II as a "stronghold, which is situated in the mid[st of the mountains . . .] located on a mountain ridge like a pointed dagger" (British Museum 131-3–23; see Tadmor, 1958).

Tell Zakariya was first identified as biblical 'Azekah of the David and Goliath narrative (*1 Sm.* 17) by Jozeph Schwartz, in the nineteenth century. The site's excavator, Frederick J. Bliss, favored an identification with 'Azekah's sister city, Socoh. However, that site is now located at Khirbet Abad (near Khirbet Socoh), 5 km (3 mi.) to the southwest, and Zakariya's identification with Israelite 'Azekah is generally accepted. The later, Roman-period 'Azekah, mentioned by Eusebius (*Onomasticon* 18:10), is probably to be located at Khirbet el-'Almi, to the east.

Formal excavations at Tell Zakariya were conducted for only three seasons in 1898 and 1899, in work directed by Bliss, assisted by R. A. S. Macalister and sponsored by the Palestine Exploration Fund. On the southwest side of the site they explored foundations of three individual towers they initially dated to the Roman-Byzantine era. On the elevated southeast section, they uncovered the walls of a rectangular fortress (about 40 × 60 m) with towers at the corners and at midpoints along the northern and eastern sides. They subsequently excavated half of the fortress area to bedrock and dug another trial pit outside it, in the center of the mound to the north.

In the Bible 'Azekah is mentioned in *Joshua* 10:10–11 in connection with Joshua's defeat of the Amorite kings; in the Judean town lists in *Joshua* 15:35; and, subsequently, in the David and Goliath story in *1 Samuel* 17. In *2 Chronicles* 11:9, it is identified as one of the cities involved in King Rehoboam's refortification efforts, and in *Jeremiah* 34:7 it is cited, along with Lachish, as among the last fortresses to hold out against invading Babylonian forces in the early sixth century BCE. This last reference seems to be corroborated by the mention of 'Azekah in Lachish letter 4. The city is also mentioned in *Nehemiah* 11:30 as one of the homes of returning exiles.

Based on their excavations, Bliss and Macalister concluded that the site had been occupied almost continuously from before 1500 BCE until the Byzantine period; they attributed the construction of the southeast fortress to Rehoboam (922–915 BCE). Excavating to bedrock inside the fortress, they distinguished four main occupation periods: period A, early pre-Israelite (?–1500 BCE); period B, late pre-Israelite (1500–800 BCE); period C, Jewish (800–300 BCE); and period D, Seleucid (300–? CE).

Although in broad outline this sequence agrees with the mention of 'Azekah in the literary sources, the stratigraphic picture is very uncertain. The existence of some "pre-Israelite" component is attested by scarabs of Thutmose III and Amenhotep II assigned to period A. However, royal stamped jar handles were found on surfaces of both periods B and C within the fortress. This requires the ascription of both of these phases to the late eighth century BCE and admits the possibility that the fortress was constructed just before that time. Similar ninth- and eighth-century fortresses now excavated elsewhere in the region, as well as at Qadesh-Barnea and Arad, support this conclusion. Alternatively, Shmuel Yeivin (Avi-Yonah and Yeivin, 1955) has suggested that the fortress was initially constructed in the period of the Judges and the additional towers in the southwest represent Rehoboam's work.

[See also the biographies of Bliss and Macalister.]

BIBLIOGRAPHY

Albright, William Foxwell. *The Archaeology of Palestine.* Harmondsworth, 1949.

Avi-Yonah, Michael, and Shmuel Yeivin. *The Antiquities of Israel* (in Hebrew). Tel Aviv, 1955.

Bliss, Frederick Jones, and R. A. S. Macalister. *Excavations in Palestine during the Years 1898–1900.* London, 1902.

Horowitz, Gabriel. "Town Planning of Hellenistic Marisa: A Reappraisal of Excavations after Eighty Years." *Palestine Exploration Quarterly* 112 (1980): 93–111.

Mazar, Amihai. "Iron Age Fortresses in the Judean Hills." *Palestine Exploration Quarterly* 114 (1982): 87–109.

Tadmor, Hayim. "The Campaigns of Sargon II of Assur." *Journal of Cuneiform Studies* 12 (1958): 80–84.

JOE D. SEGER

AZRAQ. The Azraq oases lie at the center of an internal drainage basin (12,000 sq km [7,440 sq.mi.]) in north-central Jordan (31°50' N, 36°50' E). The basin formed within a geosyncline and contains Late Cretaceous and Early Tertiary limestones, marls, and cherts. The northern sector is overlain by a canopy of Late Tertiary and Quaternary basalts. Rainfall today varies from just over 200 mm along the basin's northern and western margins to less than 50 mm in the southeast. For this reason most of the region is dry steppe or subdesert and is only suited for seasonal pastoralism.

Irrigation cultivation is, however, practiced at Azraq where copious springs emerge from beneath the basalt. These formerly fed extensive tracts of marshland which attracted large numbers of migratory birds in spring and autumn (Nelson, 1973). During the last twenty years, water has been pumped from these springs to serve the population centers of Amman and Irbid, and the wetlands have largely dried out. In addition to the springs, there is also a large sabkha, or playa, at Azraq which serves as a central sump for runoff in the depression. This fills with water in the winter and dries out in the summer. The subsurface aquifer is highly saline and the villagers exploit this for salt production. There presently are two villages in the oases, both of which were established by refugees in the early part of the century: North Azraq, which was settled by Druze from southern Syria, and South Azraq, which was founded by Chechen from the Caucasus (Nelson, 1973).

The springs at Azraq have provided a focus for settlement since the Stone Age. In the 1950s, mechanical equipment uncovered two very rich late Acheulean (Lower Paleolithic) sites close to South Azraq which are likely to be more than 200,000 years old. Both were reinvestigated in the 1980s: Lion Spring ('Ain el-Assad) by Gary O. Rollefson (1983) and C Spring by Andrew N. Garrard (Copeland and Hours, 1989). The latter contained bones of an extinct rhinoceros and of camel, onager, wild ass, hartebeest, and cattle, in conjunction with handaxes, cleavers, and other flint tools.

During the 1980s, Garrard undertook an extensive survey of Epipaleolithic and Neolithic sites in the Azraq region and excavated at six of the localities (Garrard et al., 1994). Two of the most interesting were the Natufian occupation at Azraq 18 and the Neolithic settlement at Azraq 31, both lying close to South Azraq. Azraq 18 probably dates to between 10,000–9,000 BCE and is notable for containing a shallow burial pit with the disarticulated remains of at least eleven individuals. These represent the only Natufian burials known from east of the Jordan Valley. The burial pit was overlain by rich occupational levels containing the bones of wild cattle, ass, and gazelle and many stone tools (Garrard, 1991). Azraq 31 is thought to date to between 6300 and 5500 BCE. Remnants of semisubterranean circular or oval dwellings were found in the sixth-millennium levels. These were similar in design to those excavated in Wadi el-Jilat, 55 km (34 min.) to the southwest [See Jilat, Wadi el-.] The site documents a shift from the exploitation of the local wild fauna to imported sheep and goat (Baird et al., 1992). Traces of cultivated wheat and barley were also found.

Little research has been done on the later prehistoric sites of the Azraq region, but Alison Betts (1988) has undertaken extensive surveys in the lava country to the north and east, finding prehistoric hunting traps (desert "kites"), animal corrals, and settlement sites of various kinds. The classical period is better known as a result of the surveys of David L. Kennedy (1982) and others. An inscription indicates that Azraq may have been called Dasianis in Roman times (David L. Kennedy, personal communication). During the clas-

sical and Islamic periods the oases, which lie at the northwestern end of Wadi es-Sirhan, are likely to have been an important watering point on the caravan routes between the Levant and central Arabia. Two forts guard the approaches to the oases and a third stands close to the pools in North Azraq. The one lying 13 km (8 mi.) to the southwest, Qasr el-'Uweinid, stands on a basalt bluff overlooking Wadi el-'Uweynid. Its plan is trapezoidal with a projecting bastion containing a tower in its southern corner. It contains inscriptions indicating that it was built during the reign of Septimius Severus, probably in 201 CE. Names are given for the imperial governor of Arabia, L. Marius Perpetuus, and two consuls, M. Nonnius Arrius Mucianus and L. Annius Fabianus. Pottery indicates that the fort continued in use until the late third or early fourth centuries. The fort lying 13 km (8 mi.) northeast of the oases, Qasr Aseikhin, is situated on a commanding hilltop. It is square in plan and contains Late Roman and Byzantine pottery. The most impressive of the forts is that located in North Azraq, Qasr el-Azraq. It has been modified a number of times in its history: early aerial photographs show that it was erected within a much larger enclosure. The present structure (79 × 72 m) has angle towers at the corners and interval towers along the walls. Rooms were attached around the inside of the walls and there is a large central courtyard. Inscriptions have been found dating to the late 3rd and 4th centuries. The overall plan is comparable with other Late Roman forts. Modifications did occur in later periods however. An Arabic inscription above the main entrance indicates major building works by the Ayyubid governor Azzeddin Aybak in 1237. The mosque in the central courtyard may belong to this period.

Evidence for classical or Early Islamic building activity has also been found around the pools and marshes at South Azraq. A well-constructed and buttressed wall was erected around the main spring outlets, creating a large reservoir. A platform was erected at its eastern side and a number of animal sculptures were found in association with collapsed arches (Ghazi Bisheh, personal communication). An additional buttressed wall extended around the marshland to the south and east. No traces have been found on the north, but if the wall formed a complete circuit it would have enclosed an area of several square kilometers. An Umayyad farmhouse, Qasr 'Ain es-Sol, located 2 km northeast of the fort at Azraq. Roughly square in plan, its rooms are arranged around a central courtyard. Excavation has revealed ovens, olive presses, and an external bathhouse.

BIBLIOGRAPHY

Baird, Douglas, et al. "Prehistoric Environment and Settlement in the Azraq Basin: An Interim Report on the 1989, Excavation Season." *Levant* 24 (1992): 1–31. Description of a Neolithic site at Azraq.
Betts, Alison V. G. "The Black Desert Survey: Prehistoric Sites and Subsistence Strategies in Eastern Jordan." In *The Prehistory of Jor-

dan: *The State of Research in 1986,* edited by Andrew N. Garrard and Hans G. Gebel, pp. 369–391. British Archaeological Reports, International Series, no. 396. Oxford, 1988. Summary of prehistoric structures found in the lava country north and east of Azraq.

Bowersock, Glen W. *Roman Arabia.* Cambridge, Mass., 1983. Brief discussion of classical sites at Azraq.

Copeland, Lorraine, and Francis Hours. *The Hammer on the Rock: Studies in the Early Palaeolithic of Azraq, Jordan.* British Archaeological Reports, International Series, no. 540. Oxford, 1989. Detailed description of Lower and Middle Palaeolithic sites at Azraq.

Garrard, Andrew N. "Natufian Settlement in the Azraq Basin, Eastern Jordan." In *The Natufian Culture in the Levant,* edited by Ofer Bar-Yosef and François R. Valla, pp. 235–244. Ann Arbor, 1991. Description of a Natufian site at Azraq.

Garrard, Andrew N., et al. "The Chronological Basis and Significance of the Late Palaeolithic and Neolithic Sequence in the Azraq Basin, Jordan." In *Late Quaternary Chronology and Paleoclimates of the Eastern Mediterranean,* edited by Ofer Bar-Yosef and Renee S. Kra, pp. 177–199. Radiocarbon, Tucson, 1994. Summary of work on Epipaleolithic and Neolithic sites in the Azraq region.

Kennedy, David L. *Archaeological Explorations on the Roman Frontier in North-East Jordan.* British Archaeological Reports, International Series, no. 134. Oxford, 1982. Detailed descriptions of Classical sites in the Azraq region.

Nelson, Bryan. *Azraq, Desert Oasis.* London, 1973. Description of the environment and recent history of the Azraq region.

Rollefson, Gary. "Two Seasons of Excavations at 'Ain el-Assad near Azraq, Eastern Jordan." *Bulletin of the American Schools of Oriental Research,* no. 252 (1994): 25–34.

ANDREW N. GARRARD

B

BAALBEK, site located in the Biqaʻ (Bekaa) Valley, 85 km (53 mi.) from Beirut, Lebanon, at an elevation of about 12,540 m. The Biqaʻ Valley, known as Coele-Syria in classical times, is bordered on the west by the Lebanon mountain range and to the east by the Anti-Lebanon range. [*See* Coele-Syria.*] Two springs, Ras al-ʻAin and ʻAin Lejouj, a short distance away, provided caravans with water in antiquity. Baalbek is strategically placed at the highest point on a well-established trade route from Tripoli that led into the Biqaʻ before proceeding to Damascus or to Palmyra in Syria. Baalbek's name in Hebrew, *Baʻal biʻki,* means "Baal of tears"; its Greek name, Heliopolis, means "city of the sun."

The first survey and restoration work at the site was begun by the German Archaeological Mission in 1898 under the direction of Bruno Schulz and the supervision of Otto Puchstein. Later, in 1922, French scholars (René Dussaud, Sebastien Rouzevalle, Henri Seyrig, and Daniel Schlumberger) undertook extensive research and restoration work on the site's temples. The Lebanese Department of Antiquities subsequently continued excavation and restoration under the supervision of Emir Maurice Chehab, director general of Antiquities, and Haroutune Kalayan. [*See the biographies of Dussaud, Seyrig, and Schlumberger.*]

History. Test excavations at Baalbek in 1964–1965 revealed the Bronze Age tell beneath the Great Court of the Jupiter temple. Traces of settlements dating to the Middle Bronze Age (c. 1700 BCE) were found. Other minor remains were dated to the Early Bronze Age.

In the third century BCE, when Syria became a possession of the Lagid successors of Alexander the Great who ruled from Alexandria, Baalbek was given the Greek name *Heliopolis.* The Macedonians must have equated the Baal of the Bekaa with the Egyptian god Re and the Greek Helios, with the purpose of establishing closer religious ties between their new dynasty in Egypt and the eastern Mediterranean world. In the second century BCE, the Seleucids, successors of Alexander who ruled from Antioch, invaded Coele Syria and drove the Lagids back to Egypt. The podium of the Jupiter temple probably dates to this period. [*See* Seleucids.] Between 100 and 75 BCE, Baalbek was ruled by a hellenized Arab dynasty, the Itureans. In 63 BCE, the Roman emperor Pompey passed through Baalbek on his way to conquer Syria. He was succeeded by his son, who was put to death by Marc Antony. Marc Antony then gave all the Syrian territories, including Baalbek, to Cleopatra. In about 16 BCE, Augustus settled veterans of the same Roman legions in Beirut (Berytus) and Baalbek. It was then that building was begun on great Temple of Jupiter.

In the second century CE, the Great Court, with its porticoes, two altars, and two vast lustral basins, was added to the temple. At the same time construction of the Bacchus temple began. It was completed in the third century, at the same time that the Propylaea were erected and the Hexagonal Court added.

In about 330, Christianity became the official religion of the region and the Byzantine Emperor Constantine closed the temples. Emperor Theodosius destroyed them and tore down the Altar of Sacrifice and the Tower in the Great Court, replacing them with a Christian church in approximately 440. By this time the Temple of Jupiter was probably already in ruins as the result of an earthquake. Numerous architectural elements taken from the Heliopolitan Jupiter temple were reused in building the church.

In 636, after the battle of the Yarmuk River, the entire province of Syria fell to the Arabs. Muʻawiyah founded the Umayyad dynasty in 661 and took possession of the Byzantine mint at Baalbek, showing the name *Baalbek* inscribed in Arabic letters on the coins. Thus, the name *Heliopolis,* which had been in use for about a thousand years, was replaced with its original Semitic name. The temple area was transformed into a citadel and Baalbek fell successively into the hands of the ʻAbbasids, the Tulunids, and the Fatimids. [*See* Umayyad Caliphate; ʻAbbasid Caliphate; Fatimid Dynasty.]

During the eleventh–twelfth centuries, Baalbek suffered from floods and earthquakes and the passage of several plundering armies. The city fell to Salah ad-Din (Saladin), founder of the Ayyubid dynasty, in 1175. The Mongols arrived in Baalbek in about 1260, sacking it and destroying its mosques; they were soon overthrown by the Mamluks, however. (The Mamluks were enfranchised slaves purchased by the last Ayyubid ruler for his army. They constituted the bulk of his army in general and of his court in particular).

Under the Mamluks (and until the Ottoman occupation in the sixteenth century) Baalbek enjoyed a period of calm. The fine architecture of the city's Fortress must be attributed to this period. [*See* Ayyubid–Mamluk Dynasties.]

Monuments. The temples of Baalbek have an east–west orientation. A monumental stairway provides access to the platform of the Acropolis. When the Arabs turned this temple area into a fortress, they filled in the spaces between the columns of the portico, which is flanked by two towers. Three doors lead to the Hexagonal Court (see above), which may have been used for introductory rites for the pilgrims. This space was covered by a dome at the end of the third century, transforming it into the Church of the Virgin.

Three gates lead onto the Great Court (1,452 × 1,221 m), built in the second century CE. Important ceremonies and sacrifices were held in front of the facade of the Jupiter temple. The court is an artificial platform built over a huge area (6,600 m) of vaulted substructures that were used for stables and storage. The court contained two altars and two pools and was enclosed by a succession of rectangular and semicircular exedras decorated with niches that must have contained statues.

Temple of Jupiter Heliopolitan. All the temples of Baalbek are Roman in construction but show considerable Oriental influence in both their art and architecture. The huge Temple of Jupiter (950 × 495 m) was constructed during the Augustan era (first century CE), built as a high podium with mammoth blocks. It was reached by a monumental stairway 86 m above the courtyard. Until the earthquake of 1759, the temple had nine gigantic exterior Corinthian columns; only six remain. These columns and the entablature surmounting them, which consist of a frieze of bulls' and lions' heads connected by garlands, give some idea of the vast scale of the original temple. [*See* Temples, *article on* Syro-Palestinian Temples.]

Temple of Bacchus. The best-preserved Roman temple in the Near East, the Temple of Bacchus was built in the second century CE. There is no evidence for its attribution to Bacchus, except for some motifs in the gateway carvings (grapes and wine leaves) and of the adytum (dancing bacchanti). It was built on a high podium (746 × 386 m). A stairway with thirty-three steps divided into three stages leads to its pronaos. Its exterior portico is made of contrasting plain and fluted columns with Corinthian capitals. Large slabs form the ceiling, which is richly decorated with carved geometric patterns of triangles and hexagons. The latter are filled with busts or portraits.

The entrance to the cella through the monumental gate (more than 139 m high) is one of Baalbek's major beauties. The underside of the lintel depicts an eagle with a caduceus, the symbol of Mercury, in its claws. The interior of the cella is richly decorated with engaged fluted columns that divide the walls into compartments, each with two tiers of niches—the lower with arched pediments and the upper with trian-

gular ones. To the rear of the cella is the adytum, or holy of holies, which is on a higher level, following the Oriental Semitic tradition.

Temple of Venus. Located southeast of the Acropolis, the Temple of Venus has a unique circular design. Built in the third century CE, its podium and entablature are composed of five concave sections connected by Corinthian columns.

Byzantine modifications and remains. Toward the end of the third century, when Christianity was officially adopted, the open Hexagonal Court was covered with a dome and converted into the Church of the Virgin. At about the same time, under the rule of Theodosius (379–395), the two altars of the Great Court were removed to make room for the construction of a Christian basilica dedicated to St. Peter. Originally, the entrance was on the east and the apses were placed on the stairway of the Jupiter temple, but this order was later reversed in compliance with Christian tradition. [*See* Churches; Basilicas.]

Arab period remains. Within the Acropolis, the remains from the Arab period consist mainly of fortifications, including curtain walls, towers, and battlements that can be seen to the west of the Temple of Bacchus. Between the temple and the curtain walls are the remains of a mosque, living quarters, and storage rooms, all dating to the twelfth and thirteenth centuries. On the southeast of the temple stairway is a fortification tower of the Mamluk period (fifteenth century) with typical Islamic corbeled vaulting over the door.

East of the Acropolis the Great Mosque is on the original location of the Roman Forum. Built during the Umayyad period, it consists of three rows of columns (probably reused) that support arches on which the wooden roof must have rested. Remains of an octogonal minaret were found in the northwest angle of the courtyard.

BIBLIOGRAPHY

Jidejian, Nina. *Baalbek: Heliopolis "City of the Sun."* Beirut, 1975.
Kalayan, Haroutine. "Baalbek: Un ensemble récemment découvert (Les fouilles archéologiques en dehors de la qal'a)." *Les Dossiers de l'Archéologie* 12 (September–October 1975): 28–35.
Krencker, Daniel M., and Willy Zschietzschmann. *Römische Tempel in Syrien.* Vol. 1. Berlin, 1938.
Ragette, Friedrich. *Baalbek.* London, 1980. New panoramic guide with a detailed, step-by-step description, complete reconstruction, a bird's-eye-view of the city, and a comprehensive evaluation of the antiquities.

LEILA BADRE

BAB EDH-DHRAᶜ, Early Bronze Age (3300–2000 BCE) site on the plain southeast of the Dead Sea in Jordan (map reference 2006 × 0734). Because of its early time range, its size, and its location, some scholars have identified Bab edh-Dhraᶜ with the biblical traditions concerning

Sodom, the most prominent town of the Cities of the Plain (*Gn.* 19:25, 29; *Dt.* 29:23). Among all of the ancient sites recorded on the southeast Dead Sea plain before the Hellenistic period, Bab edh-Dhra' is the largest (the walled town is 12 acres: see figure 1) and has the longest occupational history (1,100 years). In addition to the town area the site includes an open settlement to the south and east and a large cemetery farther to the south. Although the biblical tradition locating the Cities of the Plain can also be interpreted as referring to a northern location (*Gn.* 13:10–13; *Dt.* 34:1–3), most of the biblical texts support a southern option (cf. e.g., *Gn.* 10:19, 14:1–12, 19:24–28; *Ez.* 16:46).

Early Greek writers (Diodorus and Strabo) vividly described the desolate nature of the region around the Dead Sea, and ever since a succession of historians, geographers, and travelers has noted its ruins, with widely varying degrees of detail. A 1924 survey, led by William Foxwell Albright, M. G. Kyle, and Alexis Mallon, was the first to describe with clarity and date the walled area of Bab edh-Dhra', interpreted by Albright as a sanctuary complex. Excavations under the direction of Paul W. Lapp (1965–1967) concentrated on the cemetery but also included some soundings in the area of the walled town. Following a survey in 1973 by Walter E. Rast and R. Thomas Schaub that identified several other EB settlements and cemeteries farther to the south, the Southeast Dead Sea Plain Expedition was formed to explore the relationship between the various towns and cemeteries (Schaub and Rast, 1989). At Bab edh-Dhra', the

expedition's interdisciplinary team explored both the town site and cemetery in four field seasons (1975–1981).

Excavations on high peripheral areas of the site and carefully chosen areas of the interior have determined the history of occupation and major activity areas. The earliest occupation within the town is associated with a village dated to EB IB (3150–3000 BCE). Remnants of mud-brick and stone structures above bed gravel and marl and associated with the distinctive line-group pottery of this period were found in all of the lowest areas of the site excavated. Evidence of the thriving EB II–III (3000–2300 BCE) urban culture of Bab edh-Dhra' is provided by a massive 7 meter wide stone wall, built on the site's natural marl ridges; a sanctuary area with a broadroom building; a courtyard with a circular stone altar; and domestic and industrial areas within the walls. The wall and gate area on the site's western edge underwent a major destruction near the end of EB III. Subsequent occupation in limited areas within the walls, including a sanctuary on the northern ridge, and to the south and east reflect a brief return to village life during EB IVA (2300–2200 BCE). The site was subsequently abandoned.

The use of the large cemetery area to the south basically parallels that of the town site. The area's soft marl and clay were cut into for deep shaft tombs in EB IA (3300–3150 BCE), apparently by seasonal pastoralists. Shafts 2–3 m deep lead to domed chamber tombs, varying in number from one to five, cut horizontally from the bottom of the shaft. The burial pattern in these chambers usually included a line of skulls to the left of a central disarticulated bone pile, sur-

BAB EDH-DHRA'. Figure 1. *Aerial view of the site.* The view looks south at the tower in the northeast corner of the walled town. (Courtesy R. T. Schaub)

BAB EDH-DHRA'.   Figure 2.   *A 111 North, an EB IA shaft tomb chamber of the Bab edh-Dhra' cemetery.* The typical placing of skulls in a line is shown to the left of the central disarticulated bone group. (Courtesy R. T. Schaub)

rounded by distinctive pottery groups of bowls, jars, and juglets (see figure 2). The second phase of the cemetery is signaled by the development of round mud-brick funerary buildings used for successive burials in EB IB. During the zenith of the town site (EB II–III), the funerary buildings became rectangular and increasingly larger, with several apparently in use simultaneously. Several of these mud-brick structures show signs of destruction and burning contemporary with the end of the town site. The last tombs excavated in the cemetery, dated to EB IV, were also shaft tombs, but usually stone-lined with single or double chambers, and contained both disarticulated and articulated skeletal material. [*See* Shaft Tombs; Burial Sites; Grave Goods.]

The cultural remains uncovered at Bab edh-Dhra' reflect the full development of ancient Palestine's EB culture. Many items suggest extensive trade with other urban centers, including Mesopotamia and Egypt. Among the more unusual finds are well-preserved textiles; copper and bronze weapons and tools, including some early tin/bronze weapons; slate palettes and combs; an extensive collection of cylinder-seal impressions, along with three cylinder seals; and a wide range of jewelry, including gold items. [*See* Textiles; Weapons; Seals; Jewelry.] Botanical samples reveal the predominant use of barley and include wheat, grapes, olives, figs, lentils, pistachios, and almonds. [*See* Cereals; Olives.] Faunal finds include the usually dominant sheep and goat and donkey and cow. [*See* Sheep and Goats; Cattle and Oxen.] Overall, the finds from the town site and cemetery at Bab edh-Dhra' allow for a reconstruction of the basic life and burial patterns of a thriving third-millennium urban culture that was not matched in the region until the Byzantine period, more than two thousand years later.

[*See also* Southeast Dead Sea Plain.]

BIBLIOGRAPHY

Howard, David M., Jr. "Sodom and Gomorrah Revisited." *Journal of the Evangelical Theological Society* 27 (1984): 385–400. Commentary on all of the pertinent biblical texts concerning the Cities of the Plains, with a discussion of the various theories about their location. The assessment of archaeological evidence needs to be supplemented with the article by Rast (1987a) below.

Rast, Walter E. "Bab edh-Dhra' and the Origin of the Sodom Saga." In *Archaeology and Biblical Interpretation: Essays in Memory of D. Glenn Rose*, edited by Leo G. Perdue et al., pp. 185–201. Atlanta, 1987a. Examines the Sodom tradition, integrating research on its origins with recent archaeological evidence. Excellent bibliography.

Rast, Walter E. "Bronze Age Cities along the Dead Sea." *Archaeology* 40.1 (1987b): 42–49. Excellent popular summary and discussion of the results of the excavations at Bab edh-Dhra', with a comparison with the neighboring town of Numeira.

Schaub, R. Thomas, and Walter E. Rast. *Bâb edh-Dhrâ': Excavations in the Cemetery Directed by Paul W. Lapp, 1965–67.* Reports of the Expedition to the Dead Sea Plain, Jordan, vol. 1. Winona Lake, Ind., 1989. Final report of Lapp's cemetery excavations, with analytical and synthetic studies of its artifacts and interpretation of its cultural and historical significance. Chapter 1 contains a summary of previous work in the southeast Dead Sea region. Includes a complete bibliography on the Early Bronze Age of the southeast Dead Sea plain.

Schaub, R. Thomas. "Bab edh-Dhra'." In *The New Encyclopedia of Ar-*

chaeological Excavations in the Holy Land, vol. 1, pp. 130–136. Jerusalem and New York, 1993. Detailed, up-to-date summary of the archaeological results for the site and cemetery.

R. THOMAS SCHAUB

BABYLON, site located on the bank of one of the branches of the Euphrates River, 90 km (59 mi.) southwest of Baghdad, in modern Iraq (32°33′ N, 44°26′ E). Babylon, as the name of a city and as a cultural concept, was transmitted to European culture through the Hebrew Bible and Greek and Roman authors. Christian cultures have used the concept of the Tower of Babel and the story of its destruction as synonyms for human arrogance and the punishing hand of God. Interest in rediscovering Babylon was primarily awakened by the biblical stories, on which numerous artistic representations of the Tower of Babel were based. The name Babel was associated with a large hill in the northern part of the ruined city of Babylon. The hill always linked the site with biblical Babylon, although the identification of the tower was strongly contested.

The name Babylon is traced to babil(a), a pre-Euphrates name (i.e., neither Sumerian nor Akkadian) and is interpreted as a place name. The designation was understood in the Sumerian period as ká-dingirra, first attested for the Akkadian king Sharkalisharri (2217–2193 BCE), who mentions two temples in the city. Presumably, this Sumerian spelling was used as a folk etymology, just as the Semitic Bab-ili has been translated as "gate of God." Beginning with the old Babylonian period, the spelling tintirki was also used. This probably had the same meaning as the other spellings or was a synonym. The spelling Babylon, still customary, was taken from the Greek name for the city.

History of Research. Some Islamic authors preserved the memory of Babylon; however, they knew little more than the name and a few almost legendary events. The scholar Ibn Hawqal, who probably visited Babylon in the tenth century, described it as a small village. In Jewish tradition, Babylon was the city hostile to God in which the Jews had been held captive. These memories as well as an interest in the Jewish communities still living there brought Rabbi Benjamin of Tudela to Babylon twice, between 1160 and 1173 (M. N. Adler, ed., The Itinerary of Benjamin of Tudela, London, 1907). He, like most later travelers, was primarily interested in the site of the tower described in the Bible. He mentions the ruins of the palace of Nebuchadrezzar and identified the tower ruins at Birs Nimrud/Borsippa as the biblical tower. Between 1573 and 1576, the German physician Leonard Rauwolff visited Babylon and described conditions there (Rauwolff, Itinerarium oder Raysbüchlein, Lauingen, 1583); ruins in ʿAqar Quf (actually ancient Dur Kurigalzu) were the remains of the tower. [See ʿAqar Quf.]

Toward the end of the sixteenth century, John Eldred, a merchant, who had a similar interpretation, described the tower (probably ʿAqar Quf) and its construction (see R. Hakluyt, The Principal Navigations, Voyages, Traffiques and Discoveries of the English Nation, London, 1589). The earliest detailed investigation was carried out by the Italian noble Pietro della Valle, who went to Babylon in 1616 while traveling in the Near East (Viaggi, Brighton, 1843). He considered the ruins of Babel to be the tower and provided measurements and a description. Della Valle brought the first bricks inscribed with cuneiform writing from Babylon and Ur to Europe, but they provoked no interest. When the famous traveler Carsten Niebuhr visited Babylon in 1765, he was prepared for the city by the reports of Herodotus, and expected that the city covered a huge area. He therefore believed that the ruins in Borsippa were the Babylonian tower (Niebuhr, Reisebeschreibungen nach Arabien und andern umliegenden Ländern, Copenhagen, 1774).

Of later travelers, only a few will be mentioned here. Abbé de Beauchamp, the papal vicar general who went to Babylon in 1780 and 1790, reported on the wholesale looting of baked bricks by the inhabitants of the surrounding areas (J. de Beauchamp, "Voyage de Bagdad à Bassora le long de l'Euphrate," Journal des Scavans, Paris, 1785; "Mémoire sur les Antiquités Babyloniennes qui se trouvent aux environs de Bagdad," Journal des Scavans, Paris, 1790). Local inhabitants described how walls with pictures made from glazed bricks as well as statues had been discovered during the looting. Beauchamp noted the existence of massive inscribed cylinders but was unable to obtain one. He dated the coins found in Babylon according to comparisons with examples from the Parthian period. With respect to identifying the Babylonian tower, he debated between the ruins of Babel and Borsippa. A resident of the East India Company, Hartford Jones Bridge, who visited Babylon briefly, succeeded in obtaining several bricks and the large stone inscription of Nebuchadrezzar II that became known as the East India House inscription.

Claudius James Rich, who knew Near Eastern languages and was interested in the cultures of antiquity, was in Baghdad as a resident of the East India Company. Beginning in 1811, he undertook the first systematic investigation of the area of the ruins, took measurements, and presented the results of his investigations in Memoir on the Ruins of Babylon (3d ed., London, 1818), which also contained drawings and plans. In this work, he describes the still visible walls of the city as well as the ruins on the individual hills, which he calls by their Arabic names. In his search for the Babylonian tower, he investigated the ruins of Babel, which was also called Mudshelibe by the inhabitants. There he discovered burials with small objects. Noteworthy among the objects he took back to England were some cylinder seals, now in the British Museum.

The English painter Robert Ker Porter went to Babylon in 1818 and was quite enchanted with its ruins. In a book that was very well received by the British public, he wrote about his impressions and illustrated them with romantic views of the ruins. He too was searching for the Babylonian tower, which he identified with Birs Nimrud. Like many of his predecessors, Porter adopted Herodotus's estimate of the city's size. In an area of the ruins at Kasr that contained pillars, scientist J. S. Buckingham believed that he had found the remains of the hanging gardens described by Greek authors. In the following years there was a considerable increase in knowledge concerning the ruins of Babylon. An officer employed by the East India Company, Robert Mignan, carried out some small excavations in Babylon, in the course of which he was able, among other things, to find an inscribed clay cylinder in situ. The English geologist William Kennett Loftus, who later became known for his excavations at Uruk/Warka and Kutalla/Tell Sifr, began his work in Babylon in 1849. However, he soon came to consider the work futile, rejecting the identification of individual mounds with buildings mentioned by Herodotus.

After Paul Émile Botta and Austen Henry Layard had initiated the first genuine excavations in northern Mesopotamia, the latter went to Babylon, in 1850, to begin archaeological investigations there. He began digging the mound of Babel where he found many, probably late, burials. He was unable to establish a clear picture of the construction in the huge ruins and uncovered only insignificant small objects. The situation was similar at the hill of Kasr, which the inhabitants of the villages had already thoroughly searched for baked bricks. Layard described the fragments of glazed bricks he discovered without recognizing their significance, and he mentioned the monumental basalt lion that had already been noted by other visitors. In the course of his investigations on the mound of Amran ibn Ali, he discovered some clay bowls with Aramaic inscriptions that he considered to be the work of the Jews taken to Babylon. Because of the paucity of the results, Layard soon decided to end his investigations. A collection of antiquities, mostly seals and inscriptions, found its way into the British Museum through Layard. [See the biography of Layard.]

A larger expedition under the leadership of the Frenchman Fulgence Fresnel, together with the Assyriologist Jules Oppert, arrived in Babylon in 1852. They found numerous inscriptions, especially on bricks. They were interested in the glazed and relief-bearing fragments of bricks in Kasr and tried to explain them. Fresnel and Oppert believed that the remains of the "hanging gardens" were hidden in the hill of Amran ibn Ali and that the mound of Babel was the grave of Belus (Bel, "Lord," was a title used for the highest god, Marduk). Oppert also busied himself with the mound of Homera, without, however, recognizing its significance (i.e., that the remains of ancient buildings might be from the Tower of Babel). His excavations of the ancient pier on the Euphrates, which he identified through the inscriptions of Nabonidus, were important. In 1853, using trigonometric measurements and observations, Oppert published the first relatively detailed map of Babylon. For the most part, the small objects the expedition discovered were lost while being transported on the Euphrates.

Following a brief excavation in 1854 by the diplomat and orientalist Henry Creswick Rawlinson and his assistant George Smith, the British Museum commissioned Hormuzd Rassam, a sometime British vice-consul from Mosul, who served as an assistant to Layard, to reopen excavations in Babylon in 1876. The agreement included the transfer of the finds to England. Rassam arranged with the Arabs who were digging for bricks and antiquities in the ruins that he would pay them for all significant finds. In the course of his excavations, numerous clay tablets came to light, including business contracts of the house of Egibi and a clay cylinder concerning the capture of Babylon by Cyrus of Persia. Rassam also investigated the portion of Babylon lying on the left bank of the Euphrates where he found a series of cuneiform tablets. The plundering of the ruins of Babylon continued to increase; in addition to the baked bricks, the locals also took stone monuments, which they burned for gypsum. In 1887 the British Museum sent Wallis Budge, who later was keeper of Egyptian and Western Asiatic Antiquities at the museum, to Babylon to seek an end to this practice. He reached an agreement with some of the native dealers, according to which all the clay tablets, seals, and significant small objects found were to be sold to the British Museum (the extraction of bricks would be tolerated). The destruction of the ruins did not end, however, and many important buildings were so thoroughly destroyed it was later impossible to identify their ground plans.

Excavations. In 1897–1898 a group of German researchers was sent to Mesopotamia to find a ruined site suitable for excavation. One of the members of the group was Robert Koldewey, to whom the direction of the excavation in Babylon was finally entrusted. From 1899 to 1914, the German excavations were carried out year-round with a small team, among whose members were Walter Andrae, Friedrich Wetzel, Oscar Reuther, and Georg Buddensieg. Some of the excavations goals were to uncover the city plan, to investigate Babylonian architecture, and to identify definitively the Babylonian tower (the Tower of Babel). [See the biographies of Koldewey and Andrae.]

One primary result of the excavation was the exposure of the layers of the Neo-Babylonian period, which document the time of Nebuchadrezzar and his dynasty. Because of the high level of the groundwater, the deeper layers of the Old Babylonian period could be reached only rarely. The periods of Achaemenid, Seleucid, and Parthian settlement were verified partially through excavation and by means of numerous surface finds. The plan in the Neo-Babylonian period reveals how strongly fortified the city was, with an outer ring of walls altogether 18 km (11 mi.) long. The fortifications consisted of an inner and an outer circuit of walls made of baked bricks and supplemented by a strong embankment and a moat. Herodotus had mentioned the unusual thickness of the walls and their circumference, which he gave as 120 stadia long (about 95 km or 59 mi.)—this contributed to many later errors in interpretation. The outer wall includes Nebuchadrezzar's summer palace, which covers the northern part of the mound of Babel. The inner circuit of walls forms a wide rectangle whose perimeter is 8,150 m; the Euphrates divides it into unequal halves.

It has been shown from inscriptions that the construction of the city walls dates back at least to the Neo-Assyrian period. Eight of its gates were located and partially excavated. Most of them are known by name on the basis of descriptions of the city transmitted in cuneiform. The network of streets was laid out in accordance with the wind directions (northeast, northwest, southeast, southwest). The most famous of the city's gates, because of its relief decoration in brick, is the Ishtar Gate, which has been partially reconstructed in the Vorderasiatisches Museum in Berlin (see figure 1). In this powerful double gate, reinforced with bastions, a number of construction phases could be

demonstrated, all of which probably belong to the Neo-Babylonian period. They are distinguished by the techniques used to decorate the walls. The first phase is decorated with figures of animals molded in relief in unglazed brick; the second has figures formed by glazed brick that are not in relief. The third construction phase, raised 15 m above the surrounding area on an embankment, is decorated with glazed figures of snakelike dragons (*mušḫuššu*) and bulls molded in relief (see figure 2).

A processional avenue about 250 m long and 20–24 m wide, coming from the north, led to the Ishtar Gate. The street was surrounded on both sides by high walls that delimited an outlying fortress on the east and the so-called citadel of Nebuchadrezzar on the west. The lower portion of the wall is decorated with glazed brick molded in relief that depicts lions surrounded by rosettes. According to an inscription, the citadel situated north of the city wall was constructed during the reign of Nebuchadrezzar. The citadel complex and the processional avenue were both set on a 15-meter embankment. A series of older sculptures that did not originate in Babylon was found in the citadel, along

BABYLON. Figure 1. *Reconstruction of the Ishtar Gate of Nebuchadrezzar II.* Pergamon Museum, Berlin. (Foto Marburg/Art Resource, NY)

BABYLON. Figure 2. *Detail of an enameled tile and ceramic brick bull from the Ishtar gate.* Period of Nebuchadrezzar II, 605-562 BCE. (Erich Lessing/Art Resource, NY)

with other artifacts, leading to the suggestion (now considered doubtful) that the rooms were a museum. The southern citadel lying inside the fortification walls dates back in part to the time of the Assyrian domination. It consisted of five large courtyard complexes that had served official and residential purposes. The throne room in the third courtyard had a 56-meter-long frontage decorated with stylized trees of life, rosettes, and a lion frieze of glazed bricks.

The center of Babylon was formed by the temple precinct Esagila, which contained the cult rooms of the chief god Marduk, of his wife, of Ea (god of water, wisdom) and Nabu (god of the scribal craft), and of other gods and goddesses. This precinct, which lies under the mound of Amran ibn Ali, was covered by more than 15 m of sand and rubble, so that only portions of it could be opened through tunneling. The temple precinct Etemenanki, lying to the north and surrounded by a temenos, houses the remains of the Babylonian tower, which had been sought for centuries. It was not until 1913 that the excavators, thanks to the low groundwater level at the time, succeeded in finding the building's mud-brick core, which was preserved to a height of only a few meters. The entire 15-meter-thick baked-brick facing had been looted. The tower itself, as the literary sources testify, had been torn down in the time of Alexander the Great with the intention of rebuilding it. It could be shown that the tower had covered a surface area of 91.48 × 91.66 m; it had consisted of six steps, each one set back from the one below it; on the top, as the seventh step, stood a high temple to the cult of Marduk. A monumental open staircase (51.61 m high and 9.35 m wide) and two side stairways led up the south side. The processional avenue coming from the Ishtar Gate, which was specially decorated for the cer-

emonial parade during the new year's celebration, ran to the southern corner of Etemenanki and then curved in the direction of the Euphrates, where a bridge (123 m long) crossed the river. Seven of its walled piers were documented. A few temples, including the Ninmah Temple and the Ishtar Temple, were located in the city area and excavated. In the course of the reconstruction of the ruins of Babylon by the Iraqi Antiquities Administration, the temple of Nabu sa hare, which borders on the Etemenanki precinct and contained a large library, was uncovered in 1978.

Architectural History. A description of the city of Babylon was compiled toward the end of the twelfth century BCE. Transmitted on numerous clay tablets it gives the names of ten city districts, eight gates, and at least fifty-three temples, as well as of numerous shrines and other buildings. Only a small number of these could be located and excavated. The history of the earlier settlements at Babylon is largely obscure and can almost only be reconstructed from literary sources. Sargon of Akkad is said to have destroyed Babylon in about 2340 BCE; two of its temples are known from the time of Sharkalisharri (c. 2270 BCE). Šulgi of Ur (2094–2047 BCE) carried off booty from Esagila during the course of a conquest of Babylon, which is so far the earliest mention of this temple.

The rise of Babylon, which also brought great architectural changes, began with the Amorite dynasty at the beginning of the second millennium BCE. Excavations in the ruins of the Merkes (inner city) uncovered several residential buildings, from which Old Babylonian documents were recovered. The year names of the kings of Babylon give evidence of the existence of city walls, gates, a cloister district, and numerous temples, among them Esagila, as well as temples for Ishtar, Adad, Shamash, Nanna, Enlil, Marduk, and other gods and goddesses. The center of Old Babylonian Babylon was surrounded by walls and was concentrated in the inner city; additional districts, among them the so-called eastern new city, were annexed.

Very little is known about the appearance of the city of Babylon during the time of the Kassite domination. Archaeological investigations were concentrated on some private houses and graves. The description in the texts of Tintir gives the impression that the general layout of the city seems to have been similar to that of later periods. The statue of Marduk that stood in the temple of Esagila was removed from Babylon as war booty and recaptured several times, first going to Hana in Syria, then to Aššur, and later to Susa. Opinions vary as to whether there was already a temple tower (or ziggurat) in the Old Babylonian period. Its earliest mention in a historical inscription, that of Sennacherib, who conquered Babylon in 689 BCE, says that he destroyed Esagila and the temple tower. The reconstruction of the holy structures followed under Esarhaddon (680–669 BCE) and Ashurbanipal (668–626 BCE). Presumably, the mud-brick core of the ziggurat dates from this period. Nabopolassar

(625–605 BCE) and Nebuchadrezzar (605–562 BCE) completed the work.

After the conquest of Babylon by the Persian king Cyrus II in 539 BCE, the city was elevated to a royal residence; the royal fortresses were rebuilt as citadels, and under Artaxerxes II (404–359 BCE) an apadanalike pillared building with colorful decorative brickwork was constructed there in addition to a palace for the crown prince. Even the summer palace continued to be used up until the time of Alexander the Great. After a number of revolts, the city walls were razed and various buildings destroyed. In scientific research it was assumed over the years that Xerxes (485–465 BCE) had torn down the main staircase of the tower and destroyed the statue of Marduk; probably the Euphrates also changed its course at that time and flowed through the residential section of the city in a large curve. These assumptions were based on the descriptions of Herodotus. Recently, however, scholars have published many arguments against this thesis and it is doubtful that Herodotus really did visit Babylon and described his own impressions. Herodotus had written about the hanging gardens, which Robert Koldewey located on the northeast corner of the great southern palace (this identification also seems doubtful; today scholars propose that the gardens were located not in Babylon but in Nineveh). As noted above, Herodotus also gave an exaggerated depiction of the length and breadth of the city walls, which are also doubtful.

In 331, Alexander the Great entered Babylon as conqueror and wanted to make it the capital of his world empire. He provided for the care of the traditional holy sites and planned to rebuild the dilapidated tower. The entire upper part of the construction was pulled down and the rubble transported to the northeast of Etemenanki, where construction was begun on a Greek theater made from decorated bricks; this construction was continued in the Seleucid period. The holy area, Esagila, was cared for as the stronghold of the tradition; the summer palace and the citadel continued to be inhabited. To judge from the small objects found, parts of the city remained thickly settled and kept their Near Eastern character.

The conquest by Mithridates I (171–138 BCE) was the start of the three-hundred-year Parthian domination of Babylon, during which the city gradually declined. Nevertheless, the Greek theater was remodeled, Nebuchadrezzar's summer palace was transformed into a fortress complex, and residential houses were built on the citadel. With the founding of Seleucia, Babylon lost some of its importance; buildings in the residential sector were simple and poor. During the visits of the Roman emperors Trajan (115 CE) and Septimius Severus (199 CE), Babylon seems to have been deserted. During the time of the Sasanian domination, Babylon is said to have still been a residence and to have had a city wall, something yet to be proven. From written records from the ninth and tenth centuries it is known that Babylon was a provincial capital and that the administrative district bore the name *Babel*.

Finds. Significant large sculptures from Babylon are attested only in fragments. In addition to monuments from Mari (statues of princes), from Ḥalab/Aleppo (weather god stela), and Suhi (reliefs), which came to light in the so-called museum in the citadel, is the monumental statue of a lion standing over a man (rediscovered by de Beauchamp in 1784; see above), whose date and origin are debated. Valuable small finds came from graves from all settlement periods. Ceramics and pottery make up the largest body of finds, and these serve primarily to illustrate daily life. In addition to building inscriptions on bricks and cylinders, thousands of commercial and legal inscriptions have been found, as well as all sorts of historical, cultural, and astronomical inscriptions that date all the way into Babylon's late period (early second millennium BCE to third/fourth century CE). Much about Babylon can be gleamed from cuneiform inscriptions from other regions, as well as from texts written in Aramaic, Persian, Greek, Hebrew, and Latin. Babylon was more than a city or a state; it was a cultural center of the ancient Near East, a religious center, and a scientific center whose influence reached Europe.

[*See also* Babylonians; *and* Mesopotamia, *article on* Ancient Mesopotamia.]

BIBLIOGRAPHY

Andrae, Walter. *Babylon: Die Versunkene Weltstadt und ihr Ausgräber Robert Koldewey.* Berlin, 1952.

Bergamini, Giovanni. "Levels of Babylon Reconsidered." *Mesopotamia* 12 (1977): 111–152.

Dalley, Stephanie. "Babylon and the Hanging Gardens: Cuneiform and Classical Sources Reconciled." *Iraq* 56 (1994): 45ff.

Fischer, Rudolf. *Babylon: Entdeckungsreisen in die Vergangenheit.* Stuttgart, 1985.

George, Andrew R. "The Topography of Babylon Reconsidered." *Sumer* 44 (1986): 7–24.

George, Andrew R. *Babylonian Topographical Texts.* Orientalia Lovaniensia Analecta, 40. Louvain, 1992.

George, Andrew R. "Babylon Revisited: Archaeology and Philology in Harness." *Antiquity* 67 (1993): 734–746.

Kienast, Burkhart. "The Name of the City of Babylon." *Sumer* 35 (1979): 246–248.

Klengel, Horst. "Babylon zur Zeit der Perser, Griechen und Parther." *Forschungen und Berichte* 5 (1962): 40–53.

Klengel, Horst. "Die östliche Neustadt Babylons in Texten altbabylonischer Zeit." In *Societies and Languages of the Ancient Near East: Studies in Honour of I. M. Diakonoff*, pp. 169–173. Warminster, 1982.

Klengel, Horst. *König Hammurapi und der Alltag Babylons.* Rev. ed. Zurich, 1991.

Klengel-Brandt, Evelyn. *Der Turm von Babylon.* 2d rev. ed. Berlin, 1992.

Kohlmeyer, Kay. *Wiedererstehendes Babylon: Eine antike Weltstadt im Blick der Forschung.* Berlin, 1991.

Koldewey, Robert. *Das Ischtar-Tor in Babylon.* Wissenschaftliche Veröffentlichungen der Deutschen Orientgesellschaft (WVDOG), 32. Leipzig, 1918.

Koldewey, Robert. *Die Königsburgen von Babylon*, vol. 1, *Die Südburg*; vol. 2, *Die Hauptburg und der Sommerpalaste Nebukadnezars im Hügel*

Babil. Edited by Friedrich Wetzel. WVDOG, 54–55. Leipzig, 1931–1932.

Koldewey, Robert. *Das Wieder erstehende Babylon.* 5th ed., rev. and exp. Munich, 1990. Contains an up-to-date bibliography.

Kuhrt, Amélie, and Susan Sherwin-White. "Xerxes' Destruction of Babylonian Temples." In *Achaemenid History,* vol. 2, *The Greek Sources,* edited by Heleen Sancisi-Weerdenburg and Amélie Kuhrt, pp. 69–78. Leiden, 1987.

Kuhrt, Amélie, and Susan Sherwin-White, eds. *Hellenism in the East.* Berkeley–Los Angeles, 1987.

Oates, Joan. *Babylon.* London, 1979. Rev. ed. London, 1986.

Reuther, Oscar. *Die Innenstadt von Babylon (Merkes).* WVDOG, 47. Leipzig, 1926.

Rollinger, Robert. *Herodots Babylonischer Logos: Eine kritische Untersuchung der Glaubwürdigkeitsdiskussion.* Innsbrucker Beiträge zur Kulturwissenschaft Sonderheft 84. Innsbruck, 1993.

Schmid, Georg. "Der Tempelturm Etemenanki zu Babylon." *Baghdader Forschungen* 17 (1995).

Unger, Eckhard. "Babylon." In *Reallexikon der Assyriologie,* vol. 1, pp. 330–369. Leipzig, 1928–.

Unger, Eckhard. *Babylon, die heilige Stadt nach der Beschreibung der Babylonier* (1931). 2d ed. Berlin, 1970.

Wetzel, Friedrich. *Die Stadtmauern von Babylon.* WVDOG, 48. Leipzig, 1930.

Wetzel, Friedrich, and F. H. Weissbach. *Das Hauptheiligtum des Marduk in Babylon: Esagila und Etemenanki.* WVDOG, 59. Leipzig, 1938.

Wetzel, Friedrich. "Babylon zur Zeit Herodots." In *Zeitschrift für Assyriologie und Vorderasiatische Archäologie* 48 (1944): 45–68.

Wetzel, Friedrich. *Das Babylon der Spätzeit.* WVDOG, 62. Leipzig, 1957.

EVELYN KLENGEL-BRANDT
Translated from German by Susan I. Schiedel

BABYLONIANS. The inhabitants of ancient southern Mesopotamia—that is, of the region extending approximately from modern-day Baghdad in Iraq, to the shore of the Persian Gulf—are designated Babylonians. The name is derived from the place name transmitted in cuneiform script as Babili (already misinterpreted in the late third millennium as "gate of God"); the Greek form of the name is Babylon. From the early second millennium BCE until into the Hellenistic period, this city southeast of modern Baghdad was a royal residence and one of the most important urban centers in Mesopotamia.

Origin and Chronology. The region of Babylonia belongs to the oldest, highly civilized areas in the world. Although Babylonia is part of the Old World desert belt, an urban culture based on irrigation systems constructed there had already developed in the fourth millennium. Beginning in the early third millennium, there is archaeological as well as written evidence for the existence of city-states in the area, which were developed by a population that spoke Sumerian (i.e., not Semitic; Sumer is the name for the southern portion of Babylonia). Semitic-speaking groups from middle Mesopotamia (Akkadians, after the source-language name for northern Babylonia) were increasingly added to this population. The origin of the Sumerians is unknown.

There is proof of Semitic-speaking groups as early as the so-called Early Dynastic period (c. 2800–2400 BCE); toward the end of this period they attained greater significance because of an increased rate of immigration from the peripheral areas of the Syrian desert steppe (possibly as the result of the onset of a dry period). At the time of Sargon (c. 2340–2284 BCE) the Akkadians became the political bearers of the earliest Mesopotamian territorial state (c. 2340–2100 BCE), which was simultaneously striving to gain control of the trade routes leading to the Mediterranean and to Anatolia. Following a period of domination by the mountain-dwelling Guti over parts of Babylonia, the (Neo-) Sumerian state of the third dynasty of Ur (2111–2003 BCE) was able to exercise control over almost all of Mesopotamia.

During the third dynasty of Ur, there was a renewed influx of Semitic-speaking groups from the northwest; they were called Amorites (Sumerian, *mar-tu,* "people of the west," from a Babylonian perspective). They achieved a ruling position in many places in Babylonia and founded dynasties that played a role in the Old Babylonian period (during the first half of the second millennium BCE), for example in Isin and Larsa, Babylon, Eshnunna, and Mari. [*See* Amorites.] After struggles for hegemony by Isin and Larsa, Babylon under Hammurabi (1792–1750 BCE, the "middle" chronology) was able to conquer all of Babylonia as well as parts of northern Mesopotamia in about 1760 BCE. Nevertheless, under Hammurabi's successors Babylon once again declined in importance; in about 1594 BCE the city was conquered by the Hittites, who were advancing from Asia Minor. After their departure Babylon became the residence of a dynasty of non-Semitic immigrants, the Kassites (sixteenth–twelfth centuries BCE) who, however, both linguistically and culturally rapidly attached themselves to the Babylonian tradition. [*See* Kassites.] In the thirteenth and twelfth centuries BCE, there were struggles between Babylon and the expanding Middle Assyrian kingdom, as well as renewed conflicts with Elam (the state bordering Babylonia on the southeast), during the course of which Babylon temporarily came under Assyrian rule.

In the late second millennium BCE, the regional political systems collapsed. In conjunction with this, there was an increased immigration of new Semitic-speaking population groups, the Arameans, from the northwest. They intermingled with the existing population of Babylonia, who increasingly used Aramaic as their everyday language, while Babylonian remained the language of official cuneiform inscriptions and the learned tradition. Beginning in the ninth century BCE, Babylonia was repeatedly the object of Assyrian military campaigns; after the middle of the eighth century BCE it became a part of the Neo-Assyrian Empire under its own kings; nevertheless, it repeatedly rebelled against its Assyrian overlords.

Babylon became the dominant power in the Near East under Nebuchadrezzar II (604–562 BCE), who was of Ara-

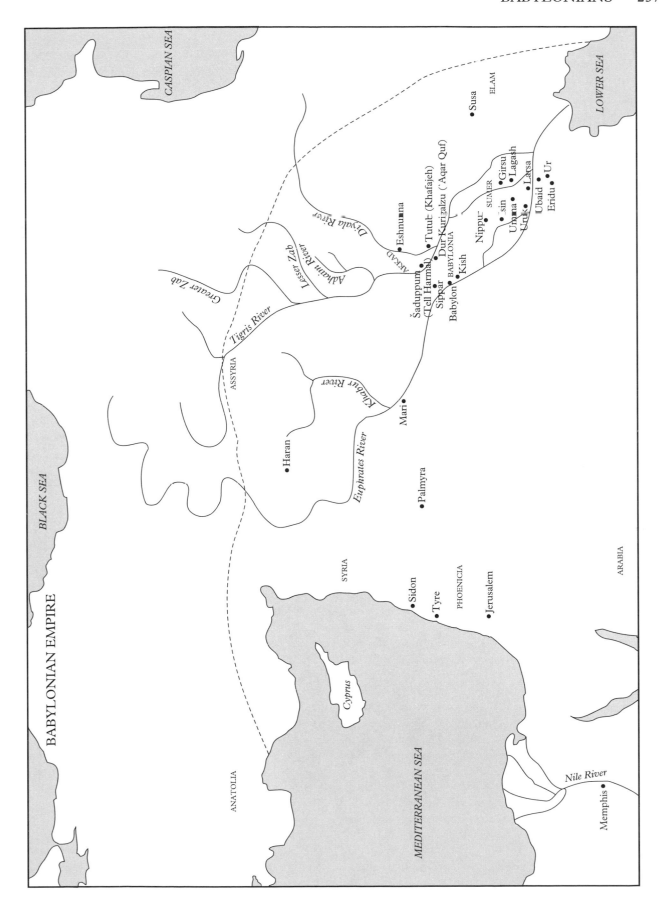

mean (Chaldean) origin. By conquering all of Mesopotamia, Syria, and Palestine, he became the founder of the Neo-Babylonian Empire; during his reign there was a large-scale expansion of his residence city, Babylon. In 539 BCE the troops of the Persian Achaemenid king Cyrus II conquered the city and all of Babylonia. Babylon remained a part of the Persian Empire until Alexander the Great conquered Babylonia in 331. In 323, Alexander died in Babylon, which he had wanted to make one of the capital cities of his empire. Even during the Seleucid and Parthian periods (third century BCE–second century CE) Babylonia was still able to preserve its own traditions, including the use of Babylonian and cuneiform writing (especially in mathematics and astronomy). Through the Greeks, Romans, and Byzantines, as well as through Europe's encounters with the Arab-Islamic world, the substance of Babylonian tradition even made its way into European culture.

Language and Writing. The history and culture of Babylonia were transmitted in a variety of languages and methods of writing. Sumerian and Semitic Akkadian (Babylonian-Assyrian) are the essential source languages. Whereas Sumerian began to die out as a colloquial language at the beginning of the second millennium, Akkadian continued to undergo further development through a series of stages: Old Babylonian (first half of the second millennium); Middle Babylonian (approximately the second half of the second millennium); Younger Babylonian (the literary language of the first half of the first millennium); New Babylonian (the language of the documents and letters in the first millennium up to about 625 BCE); and Late Babylonian (the language of learned texts during the Neo-Babylonian, Persian, Seleucid, and Arsacid/Parthian periods). Nevertheless, already in the early first millennium BCE, even in Babylonia, (West) Semitic Aramean began more and more to establish itself as the colloquial language; in the western Persian Empire it was used even for administrative purposes (Imperial Aramaic).

Both Sumerian and Akkadian used cuneiform writing (syllabic signs, word signs, and determiners). The three-dimensional cuneiform writing was pressed into wet clay with a stylus or chiseled into stone and metal. Aramaic, in contrast, used a linear system with an "alphabetic") script that had developed in Syria-Palestine. It was, thus, suitable for writing on other materials as well, such as skins/parchment and papyrus. Information, about Babylonia also comes from the Hittite tradition in Asia Minor, from Egyptian inscriptions, from the books of Hebrew Bible, and from ancient authors writing in Greek or Latin. The majority of the cuneiform texts from Babylonia were transmitted in archives or libraries as well as on monuments and archaeological finds. Aramaic texts were only preserved when they were written on clay, stone, or other materials durable enough to withstand the climate of Mesopotamia. [See Sumerian; Akkadian; Aramaic Language and Literature; Cuneiform.]

Excavations. The corpus of archaeological information about Babylonia and Babylonians essentially comes from the excavations that have been carried out in southern Mesopotamia since the middle of the nineteenth century. Especially in Babylon, Sippar, Isin, Larsa, Umma, Ur, Uruk, Nippur, and Girsu/Lagash, excavation has led to the discovery of textual materials, which have been supplemented by epigraphic finds from outside of Babylonia—from Mari on the Middle Euphrates and from Assyrian residences. Since the beginning of fieldwork, the methods of excavation—which originally were primarily concerned with obtaining interesting objects and often paid almost no attention to archaeological context—have been considerably refined. This is true not only for the exact scientific documentation but also with regard to the inclusion of research pertaining to the ancient environment, using methods from the natural sciences.

Economic Foundations. Archaeological discoveries and the testimony of the texts provide an insight not only into historical tradition, literature, and religion, but also into the means of subsistence. In contrast to the Assyrian north, Babylonia is an alluvial plain, in which the small amount of rainfall (under 250–300 mm per year) makes agriculture possible only through the use of river water. In order to enlarge the amount of usable area, canals were dug leading away from the course of the river. Even kings considered extending the land through canals to be one of their most important functions. The lack of dependence on rainfall and the fertility of the soil favored large, regular harvests; nevertheless, from an early date the increasing salinity of the soil as a result of an inadequate flushing out of the water-born minerals and the high level of groundwater proved to be a problem. Declining harvests and the abandonment of crops requiring high levels of care, such as wheat, in favor of the more resistant barley were often the result. The acquisition of new farmland was therefore also an attempt at solving this problem, which often led to military conflict.

In addition to hoes, cattle-drawn plows were also used for tilling the soil, leading to the development of breaking plows and plows with seed guides (the latter enabled a sparing and regular application of the seed). The date palm was added to grains (wheat, emmer, and barley) and vegetables (especially onions and leeks) and became an important crop; southern Iraq is still one of the largest date-growing regions in the world. Vegetables and other useful plants were often grown in the area underneath the date trees. Fertilization of the soil could occur in conjunction with the grazing of the harvested areas by herds of livestock belonging to the landowners or to seminomadic groups.

In the raising of livestock, sheep and cattle played the most important role. The sheep were primarily kept to provide wool. The use of camels as working animals is first attested in the late second millennium BCE; at that time they played an especially important role in transport because they can carry quite large loads and cover great distances without water. Camel breeding was primarily carried out by semi-nomadic groups. In the final analysis, it was the camel that provided these groups with considerable independence from the settled population and made them desert dwellers (bedouin). Beginning in the middle of the second millennium, horses were used in Babylonia for drawing war chariots; it was only later that they were ridden. Mostly, however, they were raised in the cooler mountain regions of the Near East.

In the third millennium, the Babylonians were already specializing in crafts, which can be demonstrated from the textual evidence; they were working indigenous materials (clay, reeds, leather) and, increasingly, imported material. Special mention should be made of their textile and leather production, pottery, metalworking, and stoneworking. Because Babylonia was poor in raw materials, metals and stone—including gemstones—had to be brought into the country either through trade or as war booty. Wood was also imported because the indigenous species (especially palms and tamarisk) did not provide suitable construction material for large buildings, such as palaces and temples.

The Babylonians exchanged products locally and regionally, without special markets, but an exchange system extending beyond the regional area was already in place in the prestate period (before the third millennium). Once the Babylonians were organized in a city-state, or territorial state, this exchange became a wide-reaching foreign trade documented in temple, palace, and private archives. Although Babylonia's trade was originally oriented toward the east—toward the mountain countries that were rich in raw materials or toward the countries on the Persian Gulf—in the early second millennium BCE there was a demonstrable shift of emphasis toward the Mediterranean. New partners had emerged there in the palace economies of Crete and through the exploitation of the copper deposits on Cyprus. As early as the fourth millennium, an important trade route from the Euphrates to Syria and Asia Minor included spurs that branched off to the west through the Syrian desert steppe to Syria and the Mediterranean. Beginning in the late second millennium, the use of the camel as a transport animal even made it possible to cross the desert steppe south of Palmyra and to reach the Phoenician coastal cities via a direct route from Babylon. The direction and intensity of this trade contributed significantly to cultural contacts for the Babylonians with the Mediterranean area.

Organization of Society. In the course of the approximately three millennia documented by the textual evidence, Babylonian society went through a considerable change, while preserving certain basic traits. The Early Dynastic period (c. 2800–2400 BCE) shows a city-state structure (a city with settlements on city territory) and a socially stratified population. Remnants of earlier political organizations, such

as councils of elders, were subordinated to and made to serve the growing monarchical power. The temples lost their role as the central economic and political institutions to the palace. At the time of the territorial states of Akkad and Ur (c. 2400–2000 BCE), the authority of the ruler succeeded in establishing itself even against the aristocracies of the former city-states that had been incorporated. The deification of the kings, attested from Naram-Sin of Akkad (2259–2223 BCE) until the Old Babylonian period (early second millennium), served firmly to establish monarchical rule—the king joined the local divinities as the god of the country. Royal legislation points to the establishment of newer, state regulated and controlled norms for community life, but at the same time hints at social tensions. The production of the means of earning a living was organized in the form of institutional (i.e., temple or palace) households, to which the individual "houses" were functionally and hierarchically assigned. The royal domains were at the same time centers for the distribution of goods in the form of rations (barley, oil, and other commodities).

The early Old Babylonian period (early second millennium) was characterized by the individualization of social relationships. From this time on, the palace economies represented themselves primarily as a sum total of smaller households, which worked parcels of land they had received subject to various conditions. In exchange they had to provide services in the form of work or produce. Payments in the form of produce could be excused for persons who paid corresponding sums of money to the palace as advance lump-sum payments. At the same time, the role of leasing land increased in the Old Babylonian period; family possession of land also seems to have expanded during then. The "edicts" (*mīšarū*) published by the Old Babylonian kings (generally at the beginning of their reigns) primarily signified debt relief, as well as the collection of laws into codices (especially the so-called code of Hammurabi). They should certainly also be understood as reactions to the economic and social problems that arose through the threat to the individual family as the foundation of production and the army.

In the Kassite period (c. second half of the second millennium), stone proclamations of gifts of land (*kudurrus*) point to the emergence of a larger private possession of land; nevertheless, this development does not seem to have advanced consistently. At any rate, in the Neo-Babylonian period (6th–5th centuries BCE) private possession of land did not play a dominant role. The temple and the palace controlled the possession of land and all important economic activities; but they left room for private involvement, as is expressed, for example, in the institution of general leasing, in which tenants of large estates (e.g., of temples) farmed out smaller areas to other tenants. Some of the Jews from Jerusalem who had been deported to Babylonia by Nebuchadrezzar II integrated themselves into this system at that time.

Art and Culture. The Babylonians' methods of earning a living, recording history, and cultivating imagination found expression in their artistic and literary legacy. The late fourth and early third millennia were among the most creative periods. Many of the artistic means of expression and stylistic devices that emerged then remained basic over the centuries that followed. The most lasting achievement was undoubtedly the development by the Babylonians of a system of writing, which enabled the transmission of entire bodies of knowledge. Their architecture reflects the emergence of large communities with central cult sites, such as have been excavated especially in Ubaid, Uruk, and Tutub (Khafajeh), where strong city walls suggest an increase in hostile attacks. The method of construction was determined by the sun-dried mud brick, which, in the Early Dynastic periods, appeared in the so-called plano-convex variety.

The walls in religious buildings consisted of projections and indentations (Ubaid period, fourth millennium). To stabilize and decorate walls, the Babylonians pressed patterns of colored clay pegs into the plaster on the walls (Uruk period, early third millennium). Their temples developed from small, single-roomed structures to monumental buildings, in which the central cult room was surrounded by symmetrically arranged subsidiary rooms (Uruk period). Beginning in the Early Dynastic period (first quarter of the third millennium), the cult rooms became separate spaces, often situated at the end of a rather large series of rooms; cult practice for the masses took place entirely in the courtyards, however. The Early Dynastic buildings in Kish, Eshnunna, and Eridu that contained reception rooms can be described as palaces.

In the Uruk period a rich artistic tradition developed that is attested by realistically formed small figurines of humans and animals as well as reliefs on stone vessels and other items. In the Early Dynastic period a change in stylistic devices took place. Babylonian artists began to depict human figures in a more strongly stylized way. They provided their cult statuettes of praying figures with a cuneiform dedication; they created dedicatory plaques with scenes of banqueting or supplication; and they carved the earliest historical depictions (of wars, victories, festivals) in relief on stone slabs (the vulture stela of Eanatum, ruler of Lagash). The burials of members of the ruling houses, especially the royal graves from Ur, bear witness to sophisticated craftsmanship in metalworking, which already had a long tradition. Craftsmen fashioned copper, often alloyed with arsenic or tin, as well as gold and silver, into jewelry, vessels, weapons, and other objects by means of a casting process (sometimes the lost-wax method); they frequently combined metals with semiprecious stones, especially lapis lazuli. Large sculptures were partially modeled over a bitumen or wood core and thinly plated with copper, bronze, or gold (Ur, Ubaid). Sol-

dering techniques were known and granulation techniques were developed.

During the Uruk period the Babylonians gradually replaced the stamp seal, which had been used since prehistoric times, with the cylinder seal, whose use spread into numerous regions of the Near East until the Neo-Babylonian period. The cylinder seal made it possible to represent many-figured scenes through a succession of pictures on a "rolling" seal. Sealing with clay allowed rooms and objects to be secured. Later, rolling a seal on a clay tablet became a technique of legal certification of one's personal presence or of one's office. The Babylonians took the design motifs of these seals, which changed throughout different periods of use, primarily from mythic and cultic realms. Archaeologists use them as "type-fossils" to date stratigraphic levels. [See Seals.]

Babylonian religious conceptualizations are mirrored in their visual arts and in inscriptions and mythical texts that were later committed to writing. Above all, to the Babylonians the gods incorporated whatever was necessary for the community's continued existence. The Babylonians conceived and depicted them anthropomorphically—as beings acting in human fashion. The epic tradition already told stories of heros who were, at the same time, or even predominantly, human beings (Gilgamesh stories). The contacts of the city-states with each other furthered the development of a pantheon, in which the local gods and goddesses were arranged according to rank and relationship; Enlil, son of the father of the gods; Anum, or god, rose to the top and ruled the universe with the help of "specialized" divinities. The Babylonians served their gods, providing them with food and drink and honored them in religious processions or through prayer; for this they expected a service in return. At the same time, however, they also sought to understand their natural environment and to arrange it in lists according to conceptual groups. The Babylonians observed the heavenly bodies in respect to the calendar. In laying out and measuring their fields for agriculture they used and developed their astronomical and mathematical knowledge.

In Babylonia the late third millennium was marked by the territorial states of Akkad and Ur. While the residence of the ruler of Akkad has not yet been discovered, Ur has provided proof of extensive building activity. The stepped temple (ziggurat) developed from temples on terraces and continued to be built until into the Neo-Babylonian period. The transition to a broad-room cella with an altar and a cult statue in a niche was an innovation. In contrast to the temple, the palaces appeared to be independent architectural complexes. Essentially they represent enlarged residential houses inasmuch as they, like the courtyard house, were oriented toward the inside with closed, windowless exteriors. Sun-dried clay remained the predominant building material, but formed into rectangular bricks. Figurines (terra cottas) of humans and animals were less and less frequently formed by hand, but were pressed in molds. Large-scale sculpture concentrated on representations of rulers; these show excellent knowledge of anatomy and a good mastery of stone-working techniques in such hard stone as diorite. Battle scenes predominate in Babylonian relief carvings (cf. the Naram-Sin stela) in which the heroic ruler is shown subjugating defeated peoples. In the Ur III period (late third millennium BCE), scenes of supplication once more came to the fore in increased numbers—a development also found in the glyptic arts. Frequently, an "initiation scene" is depicted, in which the worshiper is portrayed holding the hand of an intermediary protector god before the throne of the chief god. In literature, in addition to hymns to the gods, hymns to the kings appear as a new genre. From the time of Naram-Sin of Akkad until the Old Babylonian period, the deification of some rulers is also known. They appeared as the gods of the state in contrast to the local gods of the subjugated former city-states. Eventually, through the process of integration and merging, the number of gods in the Babylonian pantheon was gradually reduced.

The Old Babylonian period (first half of the second millennium) is still relatively poor in architectural remains. In Babylon itself, the high level of the groundwater has prevented the excavation of the architecture of Hammurabi's dynasty. Contemporary Mari, on the Middle Euphrates, may be the best-researched example for that period. Remains of palace buildings have been found in Old Babylonian Larsa, Uruk, and possibly also in Eshnunna. Temple buildings are demonstrated in many places, and at Šaduppum (Tell Harmal), near Baghdad, an Old Babylonian city, and at Ur, residential quarters are recognizable.

Three-dimensional sculpture and reliefs are still scantily represented; the best known is the stela of Hammurabi with the laws, which shows the king in a gesture of supplication before the sun god Shamash, a monument actually found in the Elamite city of Susa. The terra-cotta reliefs typical of the Old Babylonian period occur in great numbers, however, offering an impression of the treasure trove of motifs from this period and reflecting the literary transmissions. In the glyptic arts, it is interesting that initiation scenes more often show the worshiper directly before the enthroned godhead, suggesting perhaps a greater sense of self-worth on the part of the human being.

This concept may also be reflected in the literature of this period, above all in the Gilgamesh epic, in which the search for eternal youth is a leitmotif. That human beings, in contrast to the gods, grow old and die contributed to existential doubts and to the search for explanations in other compositions as well, leading to a fully developed omen literature as well as to doubts about the righteousness of the world order established by the gods. The city god of Babylon, Marduk, began to play an important role among the divinities of the Babylonian pantheon during the Old Babylonian period.

With respect to its architecture, the Kassite period in Babylonia (c. second half of the second millennium BCE) is best known through the excavations at Dur Kurigalzu (modern ʿAqar Quf), whose ziggurat is still an impressive ruin. From Kassite Uruk comes the temple facade of bricks that depicts the water divinities in high relief. In sculpture the so-called *kudurrus* are noteworthy; in addition to the text of a land transfer, these stone proclamations reproduce the symbols of the divine witnesses and also continue to be manufactured in the following period. In the literary tradition, the Kassite period primarily preserved and refined what had been handed down; the Gilgamesh stories, for example, were formatted into a coherent epic. The city god of Babylon, Marduk, rose to the top of the pantheon.

While there was already a recognizable separation between the literary language and the popular language of the Babylonians, in the Kassite period this development continued in the period of Assyrian dominance, as Aramaic probably more and more became the Babylonians' colloquial language. In their official inscriptions and learned tradition, however, the Babylonians continued to use the Babylonian language and cuneiform writing, the tradition, essentially, by which they are known today. It is not until the Neo-Babylonian period (604–539 BCE) that the architecture and art of the Babylonians are again better attested. At that time Nebuchadrezzar II had the city of Babylon rebuilt as his splendid residence city. In the process, large colored glazed bricks were used to cover the walls. In his official inscriptions, Nebuchadrezzar consciously affiliated himself with the Old Babylonian period, when a fairly sizable empire had similarly been ruled from Babylon.

[*See also* Akkade; ʿAqar Quf; Babylon; Eridu; Eshnunna; Girsu and Lagash; Isin; Kassites; Khafajeh; Kish; Larsa; Mari; Nippur; Sumerians; Ubaid; Ur; Uruk-Warka; *and* Ziggurat. *In addition, see* Mesopotamia, *article on* Ancient Mesopotamia.]

BIBLIOGRAPHY

Bottéro, Jean. *Mesopotamia: Writing, Reasoning, and the Gods*. Chicago, 1992.

Collon, Dominique. *First Impressions: Cylinder Seals in the Ancient Near East*. Chicago, 1988.

Dalley, Stephanie. *Myths from Mesopotamia: Creation, the Flood, Gilgamesh, and Others*. Oxford, 1989.

Frame, Grant. *Babylonia 689–627 B. C.: A Political History*. Istanbul, 1992.

Frayne, Douglas R. *Old Babylonian Period (2003–1595 B. C.)*. Toronto, 1990.

Hrouda, Barthel, ed. *Der Alte Orient: Geschichte und Kultur des alten Vorderasiens*. Munich, 1991.

Klengel, Horst, ed. *Kulturgeschichte des alten Vorderasien*. Berlin, 1989.

Klengel, Horst. *König Hammurapi und der Alltag Babylons*. Zurich, 1991.

Oates, Joan. *Babylon*. Rev. ed. London, 1986.

Orthmann, Winfried, ed. *Der Alte Orient*. Propyläen Kunstgeschichte, vol. 14. Berlin, 1975.

Postgate, J. N. *Early Mesopotamia: Society and Economy at the Dawn of History.* London, 1994.

Roaf, Michael. *Cultural Atlas of Mesopotamia and the Ancient Near East.* New York, 1990.

Westbrook, Raymond. "Cuneiform Law Codes and the Origins of Legislation." *Zeitschrift für Assyriologie und Vorderasiatische Archäologie* 79 (1989): 201–222.

EVELYN KLENGEL-BRANDT
Translated from German by Susan I. Schiedel

BADÈ, WILLIAM FREDERIC

BADÈ, WILLIAM FREDERIC (1871–1936), professor of Old Testament literature and Semitic languages and excavator of the site of Tell en-Naṣbeh northwest of Jerusalem (1926, 1927, 1929, 1932, and 1935). Badè taught at the Pacific School of Religion in Berkeley, California, from 1902 until his death. Although not trained as an archaeologist, Badè carried out his excavation at Tell en-Naṣbeh based on the highest standards of his day. He cleared about two thirds of the site, intending to test its identification with biblical Mizpah of Benjamin, which is now generally accepted. The method he employed was the so-called Reisner-Fisher method, dividing the tell into 10-meter squares and excavating in strips. Following the excavation, the strips were filled in. Badè kept meticulous records, including plans, photographs, and descriptions of about twenty-three-thousand artifacts, all of them drawn to scale. Badè's fieldwork ranks above the contemporary excavations at Beth-Shemesh and Beth-Shean, and below those at Megiddo and Tell Beit Mirsim.

Badè died after the final season at Tell en-Naṣbeh so that the excavation's final report was prepared by his colleague, Chester C. McCown, and chief recorder, Joseph C. Wampler (1947). Badè's publication of the site is generally limited to preliminary reports of the early campaigns and short articles on specific finds.

Although many excavators before him had written brief summaries of their methodologies as prefaces or appendices to their reports, Badè's *A Manual of Excavation in the Near East* was the first volume written as an independent account of the work of an excavation and the development of its methodology. Today, the Badè Institute of Biblical Archaeology in Berkeley houses a museum whose displays of Tell en-Naṣbeh materials illuminate daily life in the ancient Israel.

[*See also* Naṣbeh, Tell en-.]

BIBLIOGRAPHY

Albright, William Foxwell. "William Frederic Badè, Jan. 22, 1871–March 4, 1936." *Bulletin of the American Schools of Oriental Research*, no. 62 (1936): 4–5. Short critical review of Badè's life.

Badè, William Frederic. *A Manual of Excavation in the Near East.* Berkeley, 1934. A must for those interested in the development of archaeological methodology in Syria-Palestine, describing the state of the art in the 1930s.

McCown, Chester C. *Tell en-Nasbeh*, vol. 1, *Archaeological and Historical Results.* Berkeley, 1947.

Wampler, Joseph C. *Tell en-Nasbeh*, vol. 2, *The Pottery.* Berkeley, 1947.

Zorn, Jeffrey R. "The Badè Institute of Biblical Archaeology." *Biblical Archaeologist* 51.1 (1988): 36–45. Reviews the Institute's history, purpose, and displays, with many excellent illustrations.

Zorn, Jeffrey R. "William Frederic Badè." *Biblical Archaeologist* 51.1 (1988): 28–35. The latest and most comprehensive account of Badè's work, with a bibliography of his scholarly contributions.

JEFFREY R. ZORN

BADIAT ASH-SHAM, the steppe lands of southeastern Syria, eastern Jordan, and western Iraq. Rainfall in this region is insufficient for agriculture; as a result, the lands were, and still are, primarily used by nomadic herders, visited by hunters, and crossed by traders.

The region is divided into two distinct environmental zones, the *harra*, a rough, rock-strewn basaltic region, and the *hamad*, open, gravel-covered limestone plains. Water is scarce but there are three major oases, a number of wells, and also areas where water is held in pools for some months after the winter rains. The main oases are at al-Kowm in the north, Palmyra in central Syria, and al-Azraq in eastern Jordan.

The Badiat ash-Sham was used sporadically throughout the prehistoric periods. Paleolithic sites have been found around the oases, buried under several meters of later deposition. Kebaran camp sites (c. 15,000–10,000 BCE) are also found near major water sources. In the Natufian period (c. 10,000–9,500 BCE), when settlements in the verdant areas were becoming larger and more permanent, sites with stone huts and heavy grinding tools were established on the edges of the region, in areas where the rainfall was highest.

In the early Neolithic period (c. 8500–6000 BCE), the area was used by hunter-gatherers. Toward the end of that period, the groups developed sophisticated hunting techniques, using stone or brushwood enclosures to trap large herds of game. In the late Neolithic period (c. 6000–5000 BCE) sheep and goat herding were introduced to the region. Sheep and goat were already being kept as domesticated animals in villages of the verdant zone, but this expansion into the steppe marked the beginning of a pastoral nomadic way of life that has always been the economic mainstay of the peoples of the *badia*. [*See* Sheep and Goats; Pastoral Nomadism.] In the Chalcolithic and Early Bronze periods (fourth–third millennia BCE), villages were established on the western margins of the steppe, specifically in the Hauran region. By the beginning of the second millennium BCE, a series of fortified settlements and stations grew up on the more verdant fringes of the *badia*. Although the archaeological record for the early historic periods is still limited, these sites form a background to more extensive evidence from textual sources, particularly the archives of the Royal Palace at Mari on the Middle Euphrates River. In the early second millennium BCE, the kings of Mari ruled over lands used by seminomadic shepherd-farmers who grazed their flocks of sheep and goats in the *badia* down as far as Palmyra and the steppe to the east of Damascus and also raided Palmyra and north to Qatna. Farther south at this time, the *badia* was used in winter and spring by hunter-herders.

By the first millennium BCE, camel herding was introduced, and the *badia* became not only pastureland for camel breeders, but also the crossroads of several major trade routes between urban centers in Mesopotamia, Syria-Palestine, and Arabia. [*See* Camels.] By the time of the Roman conquest of western Asia, the nomads of the badia were economically sophisticated and many were literate, as is attested by numerous inscriptions and graffiti carved on rocks throughout the region. Relations between the Romans and the Arabs involved both conflict and cooperation. The Romans constructed frontier posts (*limes Arabicus*), such as the fort at al-Azraq, on the margins of the *badia*, to monitor the activities of the Arabs. [*See* Limes Arabicus.] By the sixth century CE, many of the tribes of the *badia* had converted to Christianity; some had entered into a client relationship with the Byzantine government, assuming control over the steppic borderlands with the Persians. These client "kings" (Ghassanids) began an ambitious building program throughout the area. During this time, monasteries and hermits' retreats were founded in the steppe. There may have been one such religious establishment at Qaṣr Burquʿ, deep in the steppe on the eastern edge of the *harra*. The coming of Islam saw further building activity in the *badia*, which produced the multipurpose desert castles, such as Qaṣr al-Hayr (East and West), Jebel Seys, the reconstruction at Qaṣr Burquʿ, and Qaṣr ʿAmra, among many others. After the early ʿAbbasid period, archaeological records are restricted to inscriptions, mostly of a religious nature, and sherd scatters at various sites.

[*See also* Azraq; Mari; Palmyra; Qaṣr al-Hayr al-Gharbi; Qaṣr al-Hayr ash-Sharqi; *and* Qaṣr Burquʿ.]

BIBLIOGRAPHY

Dentzer, Jean-Marie, ed. *Hauran I: Recherches archéologiques sur la Syrie du Sud à l'époque hellénistique et romaine.* Bibliothèque Archéologique et Historique, vol. 124. Paris, 1985. Study of the Hauran in the Roman period, including historical geography and data from surveys and excavations.

Grabar, Oleg, et al. *City in the Desert: Qasr al-Hayr East.* Cambridge, Mass., 1978. Detailed architectural report on one of the major monuments of the later historical periods in the Badiat ash-Sham.

Helms, S. W. *Early Islamic Architecture of the Desert: A Bedouin Station in Eastern Jordan.* Edinburgh, 1990. Study of an early Islamic station in the *badia*, with a useful account of the history of nomadic peoples in the Badiat ash-Sham.

Matthews, Victor H. *Pastoral Nomadism in the Mari Kingdom, ca. 1830–1760 B.C.* American Schools of Oriental Research, Dissertation Series, 3. Cambridge, Mass., 1978. Detailed discussion of the evidence for pastoral nomads in the Mari archives.

Parker, S. Thomas. *Romans and Saracens: A History of the Arabian Frontier.* American Schools of Oriental Research, Dissertation Series, 6. Winona Lake, Ind., 1986. Intensive and detailed survey of the *limes Arabicus*.

Poidebard, Antoine. *La trace de Rome dans le désert de Syrie.* Paris, 1934. Early aerial photographs of Roman and other sites in and around the Badiat ash-Sham. Many of the sites have now disappeared.

Sartre, Maurice. *Trois études sur l'Arabie romaine et byzantine.* Collection Latomus, vol. 178. Brussels, 1982. Detailed study of epigraphic and textual evidence for the pre-Islamic periods in Arabia.

ALISON V. G. BETTS

BAGATTI, BELLARMINO (1905–1990), Franciscan priest whose research and discoveries sparked a lively interest in Judaeo-Christianity and provided evidence for the Christian presence in the Holy Land before the era of Constantine. After obtaining a degree in Christian archaeology in Rome, Bagatti taught at the Studium Biblicum Franciscanum in Jerusalem for almost fifty years. He excavated at Commodilla's cemetery in Rome and in different parts of the Holy Land: the Beatitudes Shrine, the Visitation at ʿEin-Kerem, Emmaus/Qubeibeh, Bethlehem, the Mt. of Olives, Nazareth, Mt. Carmel, and Khirbet el-Mukhayyat (Mt. Nebo). His essays on the Churches of the Circumcision and of Gentility and on ancient Christian villages in Galilee, Samaria, Judea (Judah), and the Negev are indispensable for anyone interested in the history of Christianity in the Holy Land. Bagatti's methodological principle, ever present in his research, was an approach using both monuments and documents. This accounts for the numerous references to historical and literary sources in his work.

[*See also* Bethlehem; Emmaus; Franciscan Custody of the Holy Land; Jerusalem; Nazareth; *and* Nebo, Mount.]

BIBLIOGRAPHY

Bagatti, Bellarmino, and J. T. Milik. *Gli scavi del "Dominus Flevit" (Monte Oliveto).* Studium Biblicum Franciscanum (SBF), Collectio Maior, 13. Jerusalem, 1958. See Part 1, "La necropoli del periodo romano."

Bagatti, Bellarmino. *Excavations in Nazareth*, vol. 1, *From the Beginning till the XII Century.* SBF, Collectio Maior, 17. Jerusalem, 1969.

Bagatti, Bellarmino. *Ancient Christian Villages of Galilee* (1971). SBF, Collectio Minor, 13. Jerusalem, in press.

Bagatti, Bellarmino. *The Church from the Circumcision: History and Archaeology of Judaeo-Christians.* Translated by Eugene Hoade. SBF, Collectio Minor, 2. Jerusalem, 1971.

Bagatti, Bellarmino. *The Church from the Gentiles in Palestine: History and Archaeology.* Translated by Eugene Hoade. SBF, Collectio Minor, 4. Jerusalem, 1971.

Bagatti, Bellarmino, et al. *New Discoveries at the Tomb of Virgin Mary in Gethsemane.* SBF, Collectio Minor, 17. Jerusalem, 1975.

Bagatti, Bellarmino, and A. Battista. *Edizione critica del testo arabo "Historia Iosephi Fabri Lignarii" e ricerche sulla sua origine.* SBF, Collectio Minor, 20. Jerusalem, 1978.

Bagatti, Bellarmino, and Emmanuele Testa. *Il Golgota e la Croce: Ricerche storico-archeologiche.* SBF, Collectio Minor, 21. Jerusalem, 1978.

Bagatti, Bellarmino. *Ancient Christian Villages of Samaria* (1979). SBF, Collectio Minor, 19. Jerusalem, in press.

Bagatti, Bellarmino, and Donato Baldi. *Saint Jean-Baptiste dans les souvenirs de sa Patrie.* SBF, Collectio Minor, 27. Jerusalem, 1980.

Bagatti, Bellarmino. *Ancient Christian Villages of Judah and the Negeb* (1983). SBF, Collectio Minor, 24. Jerusalem, in press.

Bagatti, Bellarmino, and Eugenio Alliata. *Gli scavi di Nazaret,* vol. 2, *Dal secolo XII ad oggi.* SBF, Collectio Maior, 17. Jerusalem, 1984.

Bottini, Giovanni Claudio. "Bibliografia di Padre Bellarmino Bagatti, ofm." *Studium Biblicum Franciscanum/Liber Annuus* 40 (1990): 397–442.

Bottini, Giovanni Claudio. "In memoriam: Bellarmino Bagatti, ofm." *Studium Biblicum Franciscanum/Liber Annuus* 40 (1990): 538–540.

Padre Bellarmino Bagatti: Francescano, sacerdote, archeologo. SBF, Museum 9. Florence and Jerusalem, 1991. Includes a bibliography of Bagatti's work.

Testa, Emmanuele, et al., eds. *Studia Hierosolymitana in onore del P. Bellarmino Bagatti,* vol. 1, *Studi archeologici;* vol. 2, *Studi esegetici.* SBF, Collectio Maior, 22–23. Jerusalem, 1976.

GIOVANNI CLAUDIO BOTTINI

BAGHDAD, the major administrative center of the 'Abbasid caliphate (750–1258 CE) and the capital of the modern state of Iraq (33°26′18″ N, 44°23′9″ E). The city was founded in 762 CE by the second 'Abbasid caliph Abu Ja'far al-Mansur. Previously, the 'Abbasid rulers had established the center of their administration at a number of sites in Iraq, each of which was called al-Hashimiyyah. It would appear that the 'Abbasids preferred to build their administrative complexes in the vicinity of established urban centers, but they always left a discreet distance between an area reserved for the government and military and the urban population. In this way they hoped to provide for security while availing themselves of nearby goods and services. The pattern seems to have been employed at Baghdad as well.

The caliph's decision to seek a new location at which to build still another administrative center was conditioned by security needs. Al-Mansur's current administrative center was situated in the general vicinity of Kufah, a city known for its residual support of Shi'i causes. After a lengthy search, in which he followed the course of the Tigris River as far as Mosul, the caliph decided to construct a palace complex at the junction of the Tigris and the Sarat Canal, the latter a constructed waterway that bifurcated from the Euphrates River. This particular location offered certain strategic and geographic advantages. The Sarat, which was deep enough to allow for commercial traffic, enabled the caliph to utilize Iraq's two major river systems: the Tigris and the Euphrates. Moreover, the city was astride the major overland highways and pilgrimage routes. Baghdad thus became the commercial as well as geographic epicenter of the newly established 'Abbasid regime.

The palace complex itself was surrounded by three bodies of water: the Tigris and the upper and lower arms of the Sarat. The Tigris, a wide, undulating river, could not be forded at the site of the city. Throughout the history of Baghdad, movement across the Tigris was funneled through a series of pontoon bridges that could be cut from their moorings, denying potential enemies access to the caliph's flank. The built waterways similarly served as natural barriers in time of attack.

The first major structure to be erected was the Round City, called Madinat al-Salam. It was built on the site of an old hamlet on the west side of the river that was called Baghdad. That name was subsequently applied to the entire urban area. Before the founding of the 'Abbasid city, there were a number of villages in the general area. These were divided among four administrative districts on both sides of the Tigris: Qatrabbul, Baduraya, Nahr Buq, and Kalwadha. A small market area known as the Tuesday Market was situated on both sides of the river, to service the inhabitants of the four districts.

The construction of a major edifice on a sparsely settled site required an organized and highly efficient set of work procedures. It was not until a large labor force had been assembled that construction was actually begun, and it took four years to complete all the major elements of the Round City, thus allowing the caliph time to transfer his old capital from near Kufah. With tens of thousands of workers assembling from the outlying districts and from areas even farther removed, the skilled and unskilled laborers, the artisans, and the military who kept order all required housing and access to established markets for services. Al-Mansur's capital therefore assumed a quality of permanence in places beyond the walls, even before the Round City was completed. The urban area around its original walls eventually developed into a sprawling complex of interdependent elements with markets, mosques, and cemeteries. The area below the Sarat Canal, which contained the Tuesday Market, developed into the great commercial suburb called al-Karkh and was inhabited by the general populace. The area north of the Sarat and beyond the Round City was originally set aside for billeting the army.

The Round City was not a conventional city. It contained no economic infrastructure whatsoever, and strict precautions were taken to limit access by the general populace. It was more correctly an enormous palace complex that housed the residence and mosque of the caliph, the residences of his younger children, the agencies of government, and residences for the government bureaucracy that staffed the agencies of government as well as a skeleton force of security personnel. The size of the complex, 450 ha (1,132 acres) was unprecedented. Though only a palace complex, it was, in fact, larger than any urban settlement in the Diyala plains, the area that was the vast hinterland of Baghdad.

The Round City consisted of four architectural elements: outer fortifications, an inner residential area of symmetrically arranged streets, a second inner area of government agencies, and, moving toward the center of the circle, an inner courtyard in which the caliph's palace and the adjoining Friday mosque were situated. The outer fortifications were two concentric walls separated by an *intervallum*. The inner wall, the city's major protective wall, was flanked by roundels. Access to the residential area and the central court was gained through four elaborate gateways and arcades beginning at the outer wall and extending to the circular court. The four gate complexes were situated along the central axis of the caliph's residence and thus formed the city's northeast, northwest, southeast, and southwest quadrants. They originally contained security forces protecting the approaches to the central court. The arcade system was symbolically, as well as functionally, an extension of the caliph's domain. The purpose of the Round City was to combine the caliph's residence and mosque with the agencies of government, the residences of the regime's public servants, and security forces. Access to the general public was restricted and movement to the central court carefully monitored.

The very size of the palace complex, and the large and exclusive population it contained, made it difficult to service and supply. As a result, various distributive outlets were permitted within the walls, but following a breach of security, the merchants who had been permitted entry into the city were removed. The caliph, aware that his original plan for discrete government and private sectors had been compromised, moved to a more modest residence outside the Round City, along the Tigris. The caliph had previously begun construction of a second palace complex across the river. This construction on the east side of the Tigris was completed by his son and successor, al-Mahdi in 776 CE. The new area, called ar-Rusafah, or Askar al-Mahdi, contained a magnificent palace and Friday mosque that was to serve as the residence of the heir apparent. When al-Mahdi came to power, he took up residence in the palace built expressly for him. Unlike the Round City, which had been partly chosen for its advantageous location near the Tuesday Market, the situating of ar-Rusafah was determined primarily by its strategic location opposite the government sector on the upper west side of the river. This created two problems: a lack of water and a lack of services in the absence of a major nearby market area. Al-Mahdi therefore extended feeder channels from a canal north of the city and established a major market near the Main Bridge. It was called the Thirst Market and was likened to the markets of al-Karkh.

In time, two large private neighborhoods were developed nearby: Bab at-Taq, near the main bridge connecting ar-Rusafah with west Baghdad, and al-Mukharrim, which extended southeast along the river. Subsequent caliphs, al-Hadi (d. 786 CE) and Harun al-Rashid (d. 809 CE), lived in individual palaces rather than large complexes. The reign of al-Rashid is generally considered the zenith of growth in Baghdad. The city then reached its greatest limits in surface area and population.

The caliph's untimely death in 809 brought his son al-Amin to power and plunged the Islamic state into a debilitating civil war. A second son, the heir apparent, al-Ma'mun, dispatched an army against the capital and laid siege to it. The chronicles describe widespread devastation and suffering in graphic terms, but closer examination of these texts reveals that the damage is grossly overestimated: all the major structures that had been damaged were repaired and functioning shortly after the conflict ended.

Despite winning the battle for Baghdad, al-Ma'mun remained at his stronghold in the eastern province of Khurasan. When he finally did settle in the city, it was in a modest palace on the east side of the river. Even then, the caliph, who never felt comfortable in Baghdad, preferred to spend his time in Khurasan. When al-Ma'mun died in 833, he was succeeded by a third brother, Caliph al-Mu'tasim, who also resided in a modest residence. The latter relied heavily on military contingents recruited from among Turkish captives. The unruly behavior of the Turks resulted in several altercations with the local populace, causing al-Mu'tasim to leave the city altogether. The caliph then founded a rival administrative center at Samarra, about 96 km (60 mi.) upstream, along the Tigris. When the Caliph al-Mu'tadid returned to Baghdad in 892, he built the first of a series of new caliphal palaces, collectively called the Dar al-Khilafah.

The new caliphal enceinte, which was situated in the southeast section of the urban area, is described in the sources in great detail. Magnificent residences, exquisitely appointed, and featuring unusual elements are mentioned that include a zoological garden and fantastic mechanical devices. This impressive architectural achievement was to be the last major caliphal construction effort. With the caliphate's declining fortunes, the city began to shrink in size and population. Beginning with the Buyid hegemony in 945, the caliphs were increasingly reduced to the role of figureheads. The Buyids, indeed, went so far as to build a major series of palaces in the northeast section of the city above ar-Rusafah that was intended to rival the splendid residence of their de jure patrons. This construction was more than offset, however, by the breakdown of order and the decline of local neighborhoods. The chronicles describing the events of the tenth and eleventh centuries indicate a pattern of religious conflict, economic dislocation, and widespread decay. When Hülegü, the Mongol, conquered Baghdad in 1258, effectively ending the 'Abbasid regime, he conquered a hollow shell of a once-proud city. Writing about Baghdad, the great geographer Yaqut (d. 1225 CE) describes a series of truncated neighborhoods at some distance from one another, where there had at one time been a continuous line of occupation. This pattern continued until the twentieth century.

The dimensions of the medieval city and the extent of its population are difficult to gauge. The sources give exact figures for the surface area in varying meteorological systems. If these figures are accurate, the city would have covered more than 7,000 ha (17,290 acres). This would make

Baghdad five time larger than tenth-century Constantinople and thirteen times larger than Sasanian Ctesiphon, hitherto the largest city known in the Diyala plains. Although this figure reflects Baghdad's suburban districts as well, there is reason to believe that the greater metropolitan area was heavily occupied. There is no hint of any census in the sources, but various crude efforts were attempted to calculate the population, usually by the use of multipliers (i.e., the number of doctors, attendants at bathhouses, foods consumed, and so forth). The figures obtained from this method are, however, unreliable. In modern Baghdad, the density of occupation in the oldest neighborhoods is about 200 people per hectare, which agrees with the most conservative estimates for the population of medieval Constantinople. The physical and human dimensions of medieval Baghdad must have been vast by any standard of measurement, however, because the greater urban area did not represent a single city but a series of urban settlements collectively known as Baghdad.

BIBLIOGRAPHY

Creswell, K. A. C. *Early Muslim Architecture*, vol. 1, *Umayyads, A.D. 622–750* (1940). 2d ed. Oxford, 1969.
Herzfeld, Ernst, and Friedrich P. T. Sarre. *Archäologische Reise im Euphrat- und Tigris-Gebiet*. Vol. 2. Berlin, 1940.
Lassner, Jacob. *The Topography of Baghdad in the Early Middle Ages: Text and Studies*. Detroit, 1970.
Le Strange, Guy. *Baghdad during the 'Abbasid Caliphate*. Oxford, 1900.
Salmon, Georges. *L'introduction topographique à l'histoire de Baghdad*. Paris, 1904.

JACOB LASSNER

BAHRAIN. The State of Bahrain is an archipelago of thirty-three islands located in the Arabian Gulf, about 24 km (15 mi.) from the east coast of Saudi Arabia at roughly 26° N, 50°50′ E. Estimates of Bahrain's surface area vary considerably, but the Bahraini Central Statistics Organisation put the figure at 677.90 sq km (4,021 sq.mi.) in 1983. Although the climate of Bahrain is arid and rainfall is insufficient to support dry farming, the islands are underlain by one of the richest aquifer systems in the world, which endowed Bahrain with a permanent water supply throughout its history.

Geomorphological research and the study of sea-level changes in the Arabian Gulf have shown that the main island of Bahrain did not become separated from the Arabian mainland until about 5000–4000 BCE, when the trough between Bahrain, Saudi Arabia, and the Qatar peninsula became inundated at the presumed climax of the worldwide rise in sea level known as the Flandrian transgression. This accounts for the fact that the earliest occupants of Bahrain were the same late prehistoric, stone-tool using population as that found on the mainland in the fifth millennium. Although not abundant, lithic sites have been noted on Bahrain

since the first Danish reconnaissance in 1953 directed by P. V. Glob of the University of Aarhus. The industry is characterized by the use of pressure-flaked, tanged, and/or barbed arrowheads. A small encampment excavated at al-Markh has yielded evidence of intensive fishing, as well as 143 sherds of Terminal or Post-Ubaid 4 pottery, datable on stylistic grounds to about 3800 BCE. Interestingly, a later, aceramic phase at the site showed a substantial increase in sheep and goats (about 33 percent of the faunal collection), in hunted mammals such as dugong and hare, and nearly six times as much flint as found in the early deposit.

With the exception of a single sherd of painted Jemdet Nasr polychrome pottery from a context outside of the much later Barbar temple (see below), no evidence has been found of later fourth millennium occupation on Bahrain. Indeed, there is a gap in the occupational sequence of Bahrain until the middle of the third millennium, when Early Dynastic and/or Akkadian-related pottery appears in the basal levels of the major settlement Qal'at al-Bahrain. Dating to the same period is a *série ancienne*, or Intercultural Style, soft-stone vessel, of Mesopotamian or Iranian origin, from a grave in the burial complex at Saar (unpublished but illustrated in the Bahraini Ministry of Information's calendar for 1993).

By the late third millennium, pottery, Harappan weights, and glyptic evidence show that Bahrain was becoming integrated into an international network of trade linking Mesopotamia, the Gulf, Iran, Bactria, and the Indus Valley. It has been difficult to discover settlements of this period, but it appears that Qal'at al-Bahrain was the primary population center on Bahrain, while the temples at Barbar and Diraz, to the west, were important cult centers. It was at this time that the practice of burying the dead in above-ground mounds first became common. Some of the earliest graves at Rifa'a and Hamad Town contain imported painted Umm an-Nar pottery and soft-stone from the Oman peninsula.

Bahrain's importance grew during the early second millennium BCE, when it assumed the role of trade entrepôt for which it is so justly famous. Copper from Magan (Oman), and wood and ivory from Meluḫḫa (Indus Valley?), changed hands for silver, textiles, and sesame oil from Mesopotamia. Thousands of burial mounds bear witness to the thriving population inhabiting the island at this time. Several hundred years later, however, Bahrain fell prey to the Kassite state in Babylonia, at which time a governor (Akk., *šakkanakku*) was installed on the island. An important, but only partially excavated building complex at Qal'at al-Bahrain and many graves, particularly at al-Hajjar, are the main archaeological remains from this period. The presence of Mitanni Common Style cylinder seals and a handful of cuneiform tablets prove that Bahrain partook of the same pan-West Asian cultural trends at this time as its northern neighbors. Pottery with post-Kassite and Isin II parallels was discovered by a French team under the direction of Monique Kervran (CNRS, Paris) in new soundings on Qalʿat al-Bahrain between 1979 and 1982, but little is as yet known of the late second millennium BCE on Bahrain.

Indeed, there is no substantial body of data for Bahrain until the seventh or early sixth century BCE. A large residential complex on the Qalʿat al-Bahrain, sometimes incorrectly dubbed the palace of Uperi (the king of Dilmun attested in cuneiform sources from the reign of Sargon II), shows a ground plan that recalls Neo-Assyrian and Neo-Babylonian palatial and domestic architecture. Neo-Babylonian and/or early Achaemenid glazed ceramic bathtub coffins, one of which contained an Achaemenid-type bronze wine set, were dug into the building after it went out of use. A hoard of scrap silver found buried in the ruins of the Kassite-era building described above contained a pseudo-Egyptian scaraboid seal ring, probably of Phoenician manufacture; the hoard belongs to a category of silver hoard now well known at Iron Age sites in ancient Palestine, Mesopotamia, and Iran during the period just prior to the introduction of coinage.

The fate of Bahrain under the Achaemenids is a matter for speculation, and in spite of the large number of burials dating to the Hellenistic period, as well as building levels at Qalʿat al-Bahrain from that era, little is known of the political status of the island, known as Tylos (while the smaller Muharraq was called Arados), at the time. There are, however, accounts by writers such as Theophrastus that describe Bahrain's flora and water resources in great detail (*Historia Plantarum* 4.7.7–8, 5.4.7–8; *De Causis Plantarum* 2.5.5). Strabo (*Geog.* 16.3.4) and Pliny (*Nat. Hist.* 6.28.147; 12.21.38–23.40; 16.80.221) cover other topics, such as the origin of the Phoenicians on Bahrain and the location of the islands. In the second century CE, Bahrain was briefly ruled by a satrap of Meredat, the king of Characene, who may have been installed in a fortress located at Qalʿat al-Bahrain that was reused during the medieval era.

Bahrain, identified by the name Mešmahik or Mâsmahîg (cf. Samahiǧ, the modern name of a town on Muharraq Island), later became a part of the Sasanian Empire and was the seat of a Nestorian Christian bishopric (attested for the first time in 410 CE) that became involved in 676 CE in a revolt against the authority of the head of the Nestorian church (*catholicos*) Išoʾyahb III. Bahrain was known in Early Arabic sources as Awal, and it was not until the early eleventh century CE that the celebrated Persian traveler Nasr-i Khusrau called the island Bahrain. Little remains of the Early Islamic era on Bahrain, but the presence of Chinese coins and porcelain in the fortress attest to links with Southeast Asia and lively commerce prior to the coming of the Portuguese in the early sixteenth century.

[*See also* Qalʿat al-Bahrain.]

BAHRAIN. *Barbar Temple.* View of the ashlar masonry of the temple. (Courtesy D. Potts)

BIBLIOGRAPHY

Bibby, Geoffrey. *Looking for Dilmun.* New York, 1969. Popular account of the Danish Gulf expedition, with primary reference to the work carried out on Bahrain and the search for Dilmun.

Højlund, Flemming, and H. Hellmuth Andersen. *Qalaʿat al-Bahrain I. The Northern City Wall and the Islamic Fortress.* Aarhus, 1994. First volume of the final publication of the work of the Danish expedition.

Khalifa, Shaikha Haya A. al-, and Michael Rice, eds. *Bahrain through the Ages: The Archaeology.* London, 1986. Proceedings of a conference held in 1983; touches on most aspects of Bahraini archaeology.

Lombard, Pierre, and Monik Kervran, eds. *Bahrain National Museum Archaeological Collections,* vol. 1, *A Selection of Pre-Islamic Antiquities from Excavations, 1954–1975.* Bahrain, 1989. Catalog of objects in the Bahrain National Museum.

Potts, Daniel T. "Reflections on the History and Archaeology of Bahrain." *Journal of the American Oriental Society* 105 (1985): 675–710. Critical review of a number of studies in Bahraini archaeology that appeared in the early 1980s; contains a great deal of environmental and demographic information on Bahrain and extensive discussions of questions connected with Dilmun.

Potts, Daniel T. *The Arabian Gulf in Antiquity.* 2 vols. Oxford, 1990. General survey of the archaeology of the Gulf region, with reference to the occupation of Bahrain in all periods.

Sanlaville, Paul, et al. "Modification du tracé littoral sur la côte arabe du Golfe Persique en relation avec l'archéologie." In *Déplacements des lignes de rivage en Méditerranée*, pp. 211–222. Paris, 1987.

DANIEL T. POTTS

BALAWAT (Balāwāt), site of the ancient town of Imgur-Enlil ("The god Enlil was favourably inclined"), located about 15 km (9 mi.) northeast of Nimrud (ancient Kalḫu) in northern Iraq (36°09' N, 43°30' E). The town walls enclose an area nearly square in plan and approximately 52 ha (130 acres) in size. The main mound, where a palace and a temple dating to the Neo-Assyrian period have been uncovered, measures about 230 × 160 m. The primary occupation at the site dates to the ninth–seventh centuries BCE, although evidence of earlier settlement in the Ubaid, Uruk, and Middle Assyrian periods has been found on the main mound. Because the site was not a provincial capital in the Neo-Assyrian period, its substantial size and impressive remains at that time suggest that it functioned as a station on the road from Nineveh to Kirkuk (ancient Arrapḫa), possibly situated near junctions with two other routes. The site was apparently abandoned in the late seventh century BCE, when the most important Assyrian cities were destroyed. Evidence of later Hellenistic occupation has also been found on the summit of the main mound.

The site was first excavated in 1878 by the Iraqi Hormuzd Rassam, acting on behalf of the British Museum and prompted by the accidental discovery at the site of bronze relief fragments by a local gravedigger. Rassam uncovered parts of a palace and discovered sets of bronze bands that had been used to decorate two of its monumental doors. The bands depict military and hunting scenes and bear inscriptions indicating that one set dates to the reign to Ashurnasirpal II (883–859 BCE) and the other, more impressive set (currently on display in the British Museum) to the time of his son, Shalmaneser III (858–824 BCE). Rassam also excavated part of a temple, where stone foundation inscriptions of Ashurnasirpal were found. The king states that he refounded the town, gave it the name Imgur-Enlil, and built a palace and a temple dedicated to Mamu (the god of dreams). At the time, doubts were cast on Rassam's claim that the bronze bands came from this obscure site, but when the site was reexcavated for the British School of Archaeology in Iraq by M. E. L. Mallowan in 1956–1957, a third set of bronze door bands was found in the doorway leading into the anteroom of the temple of Mamu. This set bears an inscription dating it to the time of Ashurnasirpal II. An archive of forty legal and economic documents dating to the late eighth and the seventh centuries BCE, with the majority coming from 697–671 BCE, was found in one room of the temple. Work on the site was briefly resumed in 1989 by a British Museum team, with a surface survey of the area being carried out by D. J. Tucker.

[*See also* Assyrians; Libraries and Archives; Mesopotamia, *article on* Ancient Mesopotamia; Nineveh; *and the biography of Mallowan.*]

BIBLIOGRAPHY

Curtis, John E. "Balawat." In *Fifty Years of Mesopotamian Discovery: The Work of the British School of Archaeology in Iraq, 1932–1982*, edited by John E. Curtis, pp. 113–119. London, 1982.
Oates, David. "Balawat (Imgur Enlil): The Site and Its Buildings." *Iraq* 36 (1974): 173–178, pls. 24–27. Report of the 1956–1957 excavations.
Postgate, J. N. "Imgur-Enlil." In *Reallexikon der Assyriologie und Vorderasiatischen Archäologie*, edited by Dietz O. Edzard, vol. 5, pp. 66–67. Berlin and New York, 1976. Concise overview (with a good bibliography) by a noted English scholar, published in the standard reference work for Mesopotamian studies.
Rassam, Hormuzd. *Asshur and the Land of Nimrod* (1897). Rpt., Westmead, Eng., 1971. See pages 200–220.
Tucker, D. J. "Representations of Imgur-Enlil on the Balawat Gates." *Iraq* 56 (1994): 107–116.

GRANT FRAME

BALK. The vertical earth wall bordering and facing an area from which soil has been removed during an excavation is known as a balk. Its width between two excavated areas is usually one meter; its height increases as excavation proceeds downward. Once excavation has detected, defined, and removed the archaeological soils and their related features from a particular area, the adjacent balk contains and preserves a record of them—of their content, context, and sequence.

Balks initially help to understand and control the area under excavation. In addition, the top of the balk facilitates the movement of workers and the removal of excavated material. Balks are also a significant part of the survey grid, which enables the archaeologist to interconnect the various parts of the site under excavation. Most important is the record of human and geological activity that is preserved in the balk. The face of the balk is thus typically closely examined during the process of excavation.

In order for that record of activity to be observed accurately, interpreted, drawn, and photographed for future analysis, the balk face must be kept horizontally level and vertically plumb (this assures that the record is uniform). Frequent scraping with a trowel, putty knife, or even a broad, flat spade keeps it as smooth and even as possible.

Because lighting direction and angle play on the level and the plumb (or perpendicular) balk face, they are critical to the successful observation and accurate reading of a balk. Once it is drawn to scale and photographed under optimal lighting conditions, the balk face, or often an extended sequence of faces representing the side of a long trench or the cross-section of a building or succession of buildings, enters the archaeological record as a permanent key to interpreting a site. This visual recapitulation becomes the basis for an

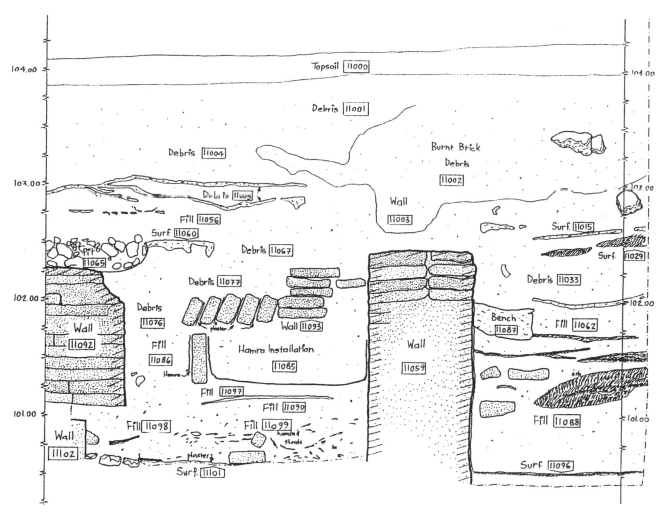

BALK. *Record of a balk face.* A sample balk face showing the spatial and chronological relationships between various archaeological features of a site, including walls, debris layers, pits, hard surfaces or floors, and various other artifacts. From Tel Miqne, field III, NE 11, east section, 1993. (Courtesy Tel Miqne-Ekron Excavation and Publication Project)

informed interpretation of the context and associations of any archaeological feature in the stratigraphic record.

[*See also* Excavation Strategy; Excavation Tools.]

BIBLIOGRAPHY

Dever, William G., and H. D. Lance eds. *A Manual of Field Excavation: Handbook For Field Archaeologists.* Cincinnati, 1978. Good advice and still in print, this valuable resource offers the most complete treatment of the care and breeding of balks.

McIntosh, J. *The Practical Archaeologist.* New York, 1986. An extremely well illustrated and readable introduction to the methods and practice of archaeology.

Renfrew, Colin, and Paul Bahn. *Archaeology: Theories, Methods and Practice.* New York, 1991. In an otherwise useful work which makes extensive use of section drawings, Renfrew and Bahn offer a limited and ill-considered view of the utility of balks (cf. pp. 92–93).

BARRY M. GITTLEN

BALU‘ (el-Bālū‘), site located south of Wadi el-Mujib and about 5 km (3 mi.) east of Jebel Shihan (elevation 1,063 m above sea level), in the district of Kerak, in central Jordan, ancient Moab. Balu‘ is the largest Iron Age ruin in the area, in which all periods of occupation are represented, from the Early Bronze Age to Mamluk times. The classical periods are not well represented in the site's southwestern quarter, where there are remains only of a large Mamluk village medieval Arab travelers called Shihan. Interest in Balu‘ was sparked with the discovery made by R. Head in 1930 of the Stela of Balu‘ (about 1.7 m high), which shows a Moabite "king" between two Egyptian gods. For iconographic reasons, the stela has been dated to the tenth century BCE. After the stela was found, three soundings by J. W. Crowfoot were carried out at the site (in 1933) but bore no specific results.

In 1986, an intensive surface survey of Balu‘ revealed that

the older part of the city (Late Bronze and Early Iron Ages) is the area immediately east and west of the impressive *qaṣr* (Ar., "castle"), which may date to the Iron Age and has undergone some rebuilding in the Nabatean or Early Roman period. The city had a defensive wall of the casemate type, with a small gate that faced east. During the Iron IIA–B period the city limits were extended eastward and another defense wall was built, enlarging the city by about 200 m. Soundings in this area brought to light an inscription (. . .]*tmlk*[. . .) on a basalt *mortarium*, or bowl. In the Iron II period the city expanded east–west for about 450–500 m.

The casemate wall runs up to a courtyard house that, based on its plan, the pottery found within it (including Assyrian-type carinated bowls), and a scaraboid Egyptian bulla (dated to c. 725 BCE and bearing the name *mn-k3rˤ*), can be dated to an Assyrian or Babylonian presence in ancient Palestine in the eighth–sixth centuries BCE. The excavated rooms had been used as a kitchen, reception hall, and a possible chapel, which was concluded from their finds (pilgrim flask, female figurine, small *maṣṣēbâ*?). Because the walls of the house are still standing (to a height of about 1.70 m), almost all the doors have their lintels in situ. At the western wall of the house in a temenos-like area, two standing stones (*maṣṣēbôt*) still in situ have been discovered. Wedging stones at the foot of each hold the stones in an upright position. Broken animal figurines, burnt ashes and bones from the immediate area suggest a religious meaning for these standing stones. In the partially excavated casemate wall west of the house, large storage jars and kraters were found, as well as several rims of collared-rim jars (of the late type)—the first found south of Wadi el-Mujib, but in an Iron II context.

West of the *qaṣr*, a farmhouse was partially excavated. One room and a courtyard represent the most recent occupational stratum. In the courtyard area a V-shaped enclosure apparently held goats and sheep during the night. A *tabun* was located in the yard where two additional unroofed cell-like units had been built adjacent to the north wall of the house. The chamber to the east contained many round stones, a grinder, and a trough. During a brief sounding in 1994 three figurines (two female, one male) were unearthed under and close to the threshold leading from the courtyard into the room. The most remarkable, almost complete, figurine is the "pillar-type figurine" holding a disk. The chamber to the west was empty, but it may have been used for storage.

The areas unearthed revealed the latest remains of the city of Baluˤ, which belong to the Iron IIB–C period. They indicate a flourishing city during Moab's vassalship under the Assyrians and Babylonians.

[*See also* Moab.]

BIBLIOGRAPHY

Crowfoot, J. W. "An Expedition to Baluˤah." *Palestine Exploration Fund Quarterly Statement* (1934): 76–84, pls. 1–3.

Horsfield, George, and L.-H. Vincent. "Chronique: Une stèle égypto-moabite au Balouˤa." *Revue Biblique* 41 (1932): 417–444, pls. 9–12.

Ward, William A., and M. F. Martin. "The Baluˤa Stele: A New Transcription with Palaeographic and Historical Notes." *Annual of the Department of Antiquities of Jordan* 8–9 (1964): 5–29.

Weippert, Helga. *Palästina in vorhellenistischer Zeit.* Handbuch der Archäologie, Vorderasien, 2.1. Munich, 1988. See pages 665–667.

Worschech, Udo F. Ch., et al. "The Fourth Survey Season in the North-West Ard el-Kerak, and Soundings at Baluˤ, 1986." *Annual of the Department of Antiquities of Jordan* 30 (1986): 285–310, pls. 57–65.

Worschech, Udo F. Ch. "Preliminary Report on the Second Campaign at the Ancient Site of el-Baluˤ in 1987." *Annual of the Department of Antiquities of Jordan* 33 (1989): 111–121, pls. 7–8.

Worschech, Udo F. Ch. *Die Beziehungen Moabs zu Israel und Ägypten in der Eisenzeit.* Ägypten und Altes Testament, vol. 18. Wiesbaden, 1990. See pages 71–90, 94–120.

Worschech, Udo F. Ch. "Ergebnisse der Grabung von *el-Bālū*, 1987: Ein Vorbericht." *Zeitschrift des Deutschen Palästina-Vereins* 106 (1990 [1991]): 86–113, pls. 1–6.

Worschech, Udo F. Ch. "Eine keilalphabetische Inschrift von *el-Bālū*?" *Ugarit-Forschungen* 23 (1992): 395–399.

Worschech, Udo F. Ch. "Collared-Rim Jars aus Moab: Anmerkungen zur Entwicklung und Verbreitung der Krüge mit 'Halswulst.' " *Zeitschrift des Deutschen Palästina-Vereins* 107 (1992): 149–170.

Worschech, Udo F. Ch. "Figurinen aus el-Baluˤ (Jordanien)." *Zeitschrift des Deutschen Palästina-Vereins* (forthcoming).

Worschech, Udo F. Ch. "Ar Moab." *Zeitschrift für die alttestamentliche Wissenschaft* (forthcoming).

UDO WORSCHECH

BANIAS, site of ancient Caesarea Philippi, located at the southern extremity of Mt. Hermon, between the northern Hula Valley and the western slope of the Golan Heights, in a region blessed with an abundance of water (map reference 2948 × 2150).

The copious amounts of precipitation that fall in this rocky region of soluble chalk penetrate deeply and burst forth in springs at the mountain's base. Where the Hermon, the Golan, and the northern Hula meet at Caesarea Philippi, springs gush forth from below a steep wall at the foot of a large cave that, according to Josephus, is the water's source (*War* 1.21.3). As early as the third century BCE, the cave was connected with the god Pan and, as such, was called Paneion, meaning "cave dedicated to Pan" (Polybius, *Historiae* 14.18.19:1–19).

Herod the Great, in 18 BCE, received the entire territory of the southern Hermon from the Romans and built a magnificent temple there that he dedicated to Augustus (Josephus, *Antiq.* 15.360). Following the division of Herod's kingdom, Paneion passed to his son Philip the Tetrarch (4 BCE–34 CE) who, because of the area's natural beauty and strategic importance, made it his capital city, changing the name to Caesarea Philippi, in honor of Augustus (Josephus, *War* 1.168). Philip's capital was also known as Paneas ("the city of Pan"), as the sanctuary of Pan continued to play a primary role in the city's cult rituals. During the reign of Agrippas II (53–93 CE), the city was renamed Neronias, in honor of the emperor Nero, Agrippas II's benefactor. Upon Nero's death, the city again was known both as Caesarea Philippi or Panias. Both names were retained throughout the Roman and Byzantine periods and up to the seventh century.

In 638 CE, following the Arab conquest, Panias passed from Byzantine into Muslim hands. The city's name became Banias, a distortion of the original Greek *Panias*. During the relatively short period of Crusader occupation (1129–1163), the city was reduced in size and fortified by massive citadels. Its name became the Bellina Citadel. When the last remnant of Crusader rule collapsed, the formerly magnificent Roman-Byzantine capital city Panias, or Caesarea Philippi, and the impressive fortified Crusader Bellina Citadel declined into a small and insignificant hamlet named Banias.

Archaeological and historical research at Banias received a powerful boost after the Arab-Israeli Six-Day War in 1967, when access to the area was renewed. Surveys, small rescue operations, and large-scale excavations were initiated. In progress are excavations directed by Zvi Uri Ma'oz at the cave sanctuary of Pan and at the center of the ancient city, where the public institutions and monumental buildings of Caesarea Philippi stood.

BIBLIOGRAPHY

Benvenisti, Meron. *The Crusaders in the Holy-Land.* Jerusalem, 1970. See pages 147–157.
Conder, Claude R., and H. H. Kitchener. *The Survey of Western Palestine: Memoirs of the Topography, Orography, Hydrography, and Archaeology,* vol. 1, *Galilee.* London, 1881. See pages 95–113.
Le Bas, Philippe, and W. H. Waddington. *Inscriptions grecques et latines de la Syrie.* Paris, 1870. See volume 3, part VII–3.
Meshorer, Ya'acov. "The Coins of Caesarea Paneas." *Israel Numismatic Journal* 8 (1984–1985): 37–58.
Tzaferis, Vassilios. "Banias, la Ville de Pan." *Le Monde de la Bible* 64 (May–June 1990): 50–53.
Tzaferis, Vassilios, and Avner Raban. "Excavations at Banias" (in Hebrew). *Qadmoniot* 23.3–4 (1990): 110–114.

VASSILIOS TZAFERIS

BAPTISTERIES. The term *baptistery* (Gk., *baptisterion*) denotes either a building or a pool (also called a font: Gk., *kolumbethra;* Lat., *fons* or *piscina*) for the performance of the Christian ritual of baptism. Because the practice of baptism among the earliest Christians has antecedents in both Jewish and pagan patterns of ritual washing, paradigms have often been suggested, such as in the Jewish *miqveh* (a pool for ritual ablutions known chiefly from Talmudic sources) or in the pools of the settlement at Qumran. [*See* Ritual Baths; Qumran.] Nevertheless, the bulk of the archaeological evidence for formal Jewish ablution installations in clearly religious or ritual contexts is later. Paradigms from ritual washings connected with the initiatory rites of the so-called pagan mystery cults also face difficulties because the washing was a preparatory purification rather than

the initiation proper. The beginnings of Christian baptism are, therefore, somewhat clouded. Nonetheless, it appears that the practice was already in use at least in some Christian groups by the middle of the first century CE, as reflected clearly in the letters of Paul (cf. *Rom.* 6:1–12; *Gal.* 3:27–28; *Col.* 2:10–12).

Going back to the tradition of John the Baptizer, who reportedly worked in the areas around the Jordan River (where, the Gospels say, Jesus came to him to be baptized), the earliest evidence seems to suggest that baptism was performed in streams or natural pools. By early in the second century, however, some alternative arrangements were allowed, as indicated in *Didache* 7, an early church order document (c. 100–140 CE) from Syria. By the middle of the second century, it appears that Christians used other regular sources of water, such as baths or fountains, at least in Rome (see Justin Martyr, *Apology* 1.61–66; cf. Tertullian, *On Baptism* 4), but there was no regularly designated place. [*See* Baths.] The earliest evidence that the ritual of baptism was being brought into the physical context of a church building comes only in the third century (cf. Tertullian, *On Baptism* 8–9; Hippolytus, *Apostolic Tradition* 21). Prior to this time there was little or no regularly identified church architecture because most Christians continued the earlier practice of meeting in unrenovated private buildings, such as houses. [*See* House Churches.] By the fourth–fifth centuries, an elaborate liturgical tradition had developed around the practice of baptism, and with it a regular architectural form.

The earliest archaeological evidence for a formal baptistery comes from the Christian building at Dura-Europos (c. 241–256 CE). [*See* Dura-Europos.] In the renovation of a typical house to form a *domus ecclesiae*, one room was set aside for baptism and a small font basin (0.955 m high, 2.57 m wide and 1.58–1.83 m deep) was installed in it. The basin was recessed slightly into the floor, the basin's interior was sealed with hydraulic plaster, and brick side walls were erected. The room's construction resembled that of the public baths at Dura-Europos. The formality of the ceremonies planned for this installation are further attested by the nature of the other decorations: an arched canopy over the font proper and an elaborate program of representational scenes around the walls. [*See* Wall Paintings.] The painted program contains a number of scenes drawn from the Gospels in which death or water symbolism is prominent. Analysis suggests also that there may have been a regular processual pattern attached to the performance of the ritual at Dura-Europos. A liturgical tradition like the one found in the Syriac *Didascalia* (a church order from c. 270) may be similar to that used at Dura, given its location in Roman Syria.

No other pre-Constantinian baptismal installations are known archaeologically, with the possible exception of the *domus ecclesiae* at Parentium, Istria. At least one other early church edifice in Rome (Ss. Giovnani e Paolo) was built around a building with a bath that might have been accessible to the Christians prior to the time of Constantine. At Aquileia, Istria, the first *aula ecclesiae* of Bishop Theodore (c. 317–319) seems to have been built over a house complex that continued to be used as the episcopal residence. These quarters included a bath, which appears to have served in some capacity related to the baptistery of the double-hall church. Of the two halls, the southernmost might have been especially designed with baptism in mind—as reflected in the elaborate mosaic pavement depicting the Jonah story and scenes of fishing and many forms of ocean life. [*See* Mosaics.] Even so, an elaborate baptismal font was not a part of the architectural form. At Philippi, Greece (Macedonia), the early fourth-century church edifice, the church of St. Paul beneath an octagonal complex, was built immediately adjacent to a Hellenistic hero cult tomb and an earlier Roman bathing establishment. In its later renovation (fifth century) to an octagonal form, one of the wings of the bath was annexed to the church and was used formally as its baptistery. A later basilica in Rome (S. Anastasia) was built over a public bath near the Circus Maximus, but there is no direct archaeological evidence that the bathing establishment was used by the Christiians prior to the construction of the basilica. [*See* Basilicas.]

Altogether, there are more than four hundred known sites for baptisteries from the third to the seventh centuries CE; most come from the later part of this span. There is a considerable diversity of architectural forms associated with baptism, ranging from small areas set aside within larger church buildings to elaborate freestanding buildings dedicated just to this act. The architectural iconography of these buildings was equally diverse. In a number of the Syrian churches of the fifth–seventh centuries, the baptistery in a separate building or complex of buildings in the form of a small basilica (e.g., at Dar Qita and Serğilla). [*See* Serğilla.] At Amwas/Emmaus in Israel, the baptistery was a slightly smaller basilical building beside and oriented on the same axis as the main basilical hall of the church (dating to the fifth century). [*See* Emmaus.] The baptismal font proper, a recessed pool cut into the floor in the shape of a cross, was set into the church's small apse. In these cases, the liturgical use of the architecture would seem to have been patterned directly on that of the main basilica. In other cases, the architecture developed on a central plan using either octagonal or domed construction. The octagonal plan has strong affinities with Roman funerary architecture; the church of Sta. Costanza in Rome was originally built as a mausoleum but was later converted into a church and used as a baptistery. [*See* Mausoleum.] The most elaborate baptisteries built on this octagonal plan are the Orthodox Baptistery in Ravenna, Italy (c. 450), and the baptistery of St. John Lateran in Rome. The latter also contains the largest font, a circular pool more than 8.5 m in diameter. Finally, the font basin itself tended, in later periods, to take one of two basic forms: either circular (or octagonal) or cruciform. Although they range in size, the average depth is just under one meter. It has been suggested that these forms were each associated with one of the dominant symbolizations of the baptismal ritual: the circle as a symbol of the womb and rebirth; the cross as a symbol of death and resurrection. In some cases, a combination of these architectural and artistic symbols was employed with conscious design to enhance the liturgical experience. For example, the plan of the Orthodox Baptistery in Ravenna was designed in such a way that the initiate was led through the antechambers and into the great domed room in order to approach the steps down into the font. The design placed the initiate so that he or she was looking directly up (and from the proper angle) at the magnificent ceiling mosaic of the baptism of Jesus in which he is surrounded by a procession of the twelve apostles.

[*See also* Churches; Martyrion.]

BIBLIOGRAPHY

Bedard, Walter M. *The Symbolism of the Baptismal Font in Early Christian Thought.* Washington, D.C., 1951.

Davies, John Gordon. *The Architectural Setting of Baptism.* London, 1962.

Deichmann, F. W. "Baptisterium." In *Reallexikon für Antike und Christentum,* vol. 1, pp. 1157–1167. Stuttgart, 1950–.

Khatchatrian, Armen. *Les baptistères paléochrétiens.* Paris, 1962.

Khatchatrian, Armen. *Origine et typologie des baptistères paléochrétiens.* Mulhouse, 1982.

Kostof, Spiro. *The Orthodox Baptistery of Ravenna.* New Haven, 1965.

Kraeling, Carl H. *The Christian Building.* The Excavations at Dura-Europos, Final Report 8, part 2. New Haven, 1967.

Krautheimer, Richard. *Early Christian and Byzantine Architecture.* 3d ed. Harmondsworth, 1981.

Lassus, Jean. *Sanctuaires chrétiens de Syrie.* Paris, 1947.

L. MICHAEL WHITE

BAQ'AH VALLEY, area located 15 km (9 mi.) northwest of Amman, Jordan, at 625 m above sea level on the Transjordanian plateau (32°5'10" N, 35°40'20" E; map reference 168 × 228). The region's earliest survey was conducted by Nelson Glueck in 1939. Since 1977 the Baq'ah has been the focus of ongoing excavations conducted by the University Museum of the University of Pennsylvania. The project is directed by Patrick E. McGovern and funded by the museum, its Applied Science Center for Archaeology (MASCA), the National Geographic Society, the Jordanian Department of Antiquities, and private sources.

The valley's central location, combined with its rich, arable soil, moderate climate, plentiful springs, and other natural resources, explain why the Baq'ah has been inhabited virtually without a gap for the last fifty thousand years—since the late Middle Paleolithic. Glueck stated that the Baq'ah was occupied only by nomadic peoples during the Late Bronze Age, but more recent evidence shows that there were numerous LB settlements in the region. Archaeological evidence points as well to occupation in the Early Bronze Age, the Early and Late Iron Age (into the Persian period), and the Early Roman period.

Most of the excavated sites—and exposed remains—are in the northwestern (Umm ad-Dananir) region of the Baqʿah, where there are more springs than in any other sector of the valley. Urban settlement is evidenced by the 3.5-hectare (9-acre) fortified hilltop site of al-Qaṣir ("the fortress"). Pottery vessels and grinding stones found crushed beneath a large, circular stone "hillock" date to EB II–III (c. 2900–2300 BCE), when occupation was most extensive. Many broadroom houses dating to this period also were found on the surface. By EB IV (c. 2300–1900 BCE), however, settlement had declined, and after 1900 BCE had ceased.

An overlapping sequence of LB (c. 1550–1200 BCE) burial caves on Jebel al-Qaṣir and Jebel al-Hawayah attest to the urban character of the Umm ad-Dananir culture, as well as to its international trade. Among the imports found in the caves were Mitannian Common Style cylinder seals; Egyptian scarabs and a ring; Mycenaean stirrup jars; Cypriot base-ring II and white-slip II wares; and numerous Mediterranean and Red Sea mollusk shells. In addition, pieces of wheel-made pottery uncovered at the site are comparable to those found at urban communities west of the Jordan River.

Another important LB settlement is situated on a series of terraces at Khirbet Umm ad-Dananir. Comprising about 2.5 ha (6 acres), the site overlooks Wadi Umm ad-Dananir. The earliest structure uncovered there is similar in plan to another LB structure, the Amman Airport building, located 15 km (9 mi.) to the southeast. [See Amman Airport Temple.] Of the Quadratbau type, both are laid out in a square with a central courtyard surrounded by outer rooms, and may have served a cultic purpose. At Umm ad-Dananir, for example, pottery, silicate jewelry items, and burned and unburned animal bones of cattle, donkeys, sheep and goats, mountain lions, and gazelles were found in a fill under the structure's plastered floor and in its foundation trenches. A freestanding altar (60 × 60 × 60 cm) with a limestone capstone was found near the center of the building, as was a fireplace that predates the building and that apparently was used in "sacrificing" the animals deposited in the fill. The destruction of the building has been dated to LB II, based on the pottery and animal bones (like those in the fill) found in pits dug into the destruction debris. Carbonized roof beams on the building's plastered floor indicate that the building was destroyed in a conflagration.

One of the largest Early Iron Age (c. 1200–1050 BCE) tombs yet discovered in the region is a circular burial cave on Jebel al-Hawayah. The bones of 227 men and women of various ages were found in the cave (4.5 m in diameter). The burial goods were poorer than in the Late Bronze Age and of local manufacture, suggesting that the standard of living was lower and that in the Iron Age trade was less widespread. [See Tombs; Grave Goods.] The few new pottery forms introduced in this period probably reflect a continuation of the coil-building technology begun in LB II.

Among the eleven complete pieces of mild-steel jewelry found in the tomb was an iron anklet or bracelet type; its similarity to one found in a nearby LB II burial cave suggests that iron metallurgy had already been developed.

A large number of structures dating to the Late Iron/Persian (c. 650–400 BCE) period have been found in central Transjordan. Among them, a building on the site of Rujm al-Henu (West) in the Baqʿah has been investigated. Probably a single-phase fortress with complementary domestic and agricultural functions, the building was constructed out of dry-laid, unhewn boulders. Its towers were circular and rectangular, and an inner courtyard was surrounded by casement rooms. The upper walls (some preserved as high as 2.5–3 m) collapsed onto the clay floor (over bedrock) sometime during this period. A contemporaneous level at Khirbet Umm ad-Dananir yielded an Ammonite inscription on a storage jar sidewall. The inscription reads shemaʿ ("to hear"), the first word in the traditional Hebrew declaration of faith (Dt. 6:4), but was more likely part of a name here. It was deeply incised in the clay before the jar was fired.

Also at Khirbet Umm ad-Dananir a large, Early Roman III (c. 4 BCE–73 CE) structure was excavated. The building was discovered just below the surface. Its central room was characterized by a northern wall with seven orthostats spaced about a half-meter apart, several with their overlying stretchers in place, and a beaten-earth floor. A collection of Early Roman III pottery and artifacts (including glass vessel and bracelet fragments, an intact iron sickle blade, and Herodian-type limestone vessels) help to date the structure, as does a coin of Antonius Felix (52–62 CE) recovered from under the building's floor.

The ancient identities of sites in the Baqʿah remain uncertain. In the list of Pharaoh Thutmosis III's Asiatic toponyms (c. 1450 BCE) that ostensibly lists sites and areas along the King's Highway (which probably ran through the middle of the Baqʿah), the Baqʿah Valley has been identified with mkrpwt ("fertile depression"). The Quadratbau-type building at Khirbet Umm ad-Dananir has affinities with late MB–early LB structures at Shechem. Later biblical tradition, as reflected in the Jacob-Laban cycle, the Israelite settlement narratives, and the story of the sacrifice of Jephthah's daughter, point to close ties between Gilead, where Khirbet Umm ad-Dananir (Mizpah Gilead?) is located, and Israel, where Shechem is located. [See Shechem; Gilead.]

BIBLIOGRAPHY

McGovern, Patrick E. "Test Soundings of Archaeological and Resistivity Survey Results at Rujm al-Henu." Annual of the Department of Antiquities of Jordan 27 (1983): 105–141. Preliminary reports on Late Iron buildings surveyed by geophysical prospecting instruments and excavated by test soundings.

McGovern, Patrick E. The Late Bronze and Early Iron Ages of Central Transjordan: The Baqʿah Valley Project, 1977–1981. University Museum, Monography 65. Philadelphia, 1986. Detailed archaeological and technological study of the LB and Early Iron Age cemetery, with preliminary findings on associated settlement sites.

McGovern, Patrick E. "Central Transjordan in the Late Bronze and Early Iron Ages: An Alternative Hypothesis of Socio-Economic Transformation and Collapse." In *Studies in the History and Archaeology of Jordan*, vol. 3, edited by Adnan Hadidi, pp. 267–273. Amman, 1987. Cultural and technological continuity evidenced from the LB into the Early Iron Age in central Transjordan.

McGovern, Patrick E. "Settlement Patterns of the Late Bronze and Iron Ages in the Greater Amman Area." In *Studies in the History and Archaeology of Jordan*, vol. 4, edited by Ghazi Bisheh, pp. 179–183. Amman, 1992. Overview of the area's archaeological and architectural traditions.

PATRICK E. MCGOVERN

BAR'AM, a Jewish settlement in the Upper Galilee in Late Antiquity, located approximately 11 km (7 mi.) northwest of Safed and 0.5 km south of Israel's modern border with Lebanon (map reference 1891 × 2701). This locale is not mentioned in ancient sources, but it appears as Kefar Bar'am in the itineraries of Jewish pilgrims, beginning in the fourteenth century. Numerous nineteenth-century explorers described the site, including Edward Robinson, Ernest Renan, Victor Guérin, and members of the British Survey of Western Palestine. Bar'am is one of only two settlements in this region (together with Gush Halav) that is known to have had two synagogues, which underscores its size and apparent importance. The larger of the two synagogues servicing this community was excavated by Heinrich Kohl and Carl Watzinger on behalf of the Deutsche Orient-Gesellschaft in 1905. Other areas of the village have not been excavated.

The large synagogue is the best preserved of all extant Galilean-type basilical synagogues. [*See* Synagogues.] Although Michael Avi-Yonah dated the Galilean type to the second century, it is now generally accepted that Galilean-type basilical synagogues date to the third–sixth centuries. [*See* Basilicas.] The building is constructed of local white limestone ashlars without mortar. The facade (15.2 × 20 m), which is aligned toward the south, is preserved to the upper cornice of the lower story. An exedra (5.35 m wide) supported by eight columns was constructed along the length of the facade. The building had three entrances: a large central portal that led into the nave and two smaller portals that led into the side aisles. The central entrance has molded jambs and a lintel bearing a wreath flanked by winged Victories that were intentionally mutilated. It is surmounted by a large Syrian arch. On the sill of a window above the eastern portal is a Hebrew dedicatory inscription that reads "Built by Eleazar son of Yudan." The central nave is surrounded by columns on three sides. A balcony may have been constructed above the nave on the northern, western, and eastern sides of the hall. The architecture of this building has much in common with contemporaneous Syrian church architecture. [*See* Churches.] During the late 1960s the site was cleared and partially restored.

Remains of the so-called small synagogue were still visible during the nineteenth century. Little is known of this building, although two doorways were apparently still in place in the sixteenth century. One of these monumental portals was still standing in the nineteenth century, when it was described by explorers and documented by photographers. These ruins were dismantled sometime before 1905. A portion of the lintel bearing a dedicatory inscription is preserved in the Louvre museum. This Hebrew inscription is particularly important for the history of synagogues in this region:

> May there be peace in this place and in all of the places of Israel. Yose the Levite son of Levi made (or donated) this lintel. May blessings come upon his deeds. Amen.

The artisan (or donor) of the lintel appears in a similar dedicatory inscription in Aramaic in the nearby Alma synagogue.

[*See also* Basilicas; Deutsche Orient-Gesellschaft; Galilee, *article on* Galilee in the Hellenistic through Byzantine Periods; Synagogue Inscriptions; *and the biographies of Avi-Yonah, Guérin, Renan, Robinson, and Watzinger.*]

BIBLIOGRAPHY

Avigad, Nahman. "Bar'am." In *The New Encyclopedia of Archaeological Excavations in the Holy Land*, vol. 1, pp. 147–149. Jerusalem and New York, 1993. Survey of the architectural history of Bar'am.

Chiat, Marilyn Joyce Segal. *Handbook of Synagogue Literature*. Chico, Calif., 1982. Surveys the architectural history of the Bar'am synagogues.

Hachlili, Rachel. *Ancient Jewish Art and Archaeology in the Land of Israel*. Leiden, 1988. The art and architecture of the synagogue in the context of Jewish and non-Jewish art in Late Antiquity (see the index under Baram).

Jacoby, Ruth. *The Synagogues of Baram: Jerusalem Ossuaries*. Jerusalem, 1987. Systematic and comprehensive presentation of the remains of the Bar'am synagogues, with a particularly useful bibliography.

STEVEN FINE

BARAMKI, DIMITRI CONSTANTINE (1909–1984), archaeologist and teacher. Born in Jerusalem, Baramki developed a keen interest in the cultural heritage of his homeland and city. After attending St. George's School in Jerusalem and the American University of Beirut, he received both his B.A. with honors and Ph.D. degrees from the University of London. In his dissertation, "The Culture and Architecture of the Umayyad Period," he drew upon the results of his excavation at Caliph Hisham's palace at Khirbat al-Mafjar near Jericho (1935–1948).

His career in the Department of Antiquities of Palestine began in 1927, and in 1945 he became senior archaeological officer. He served as acting curator of the Palestine Archaeological Museum (today the Rockefeller Museum) in Jerusalem (1948–1949). He was then appointed archaeological advisor and librarian at the American School of Oriental Research in Jerusalem. From 1951 until his retirement in

1975 he was curator of the Archaeological Museum of the American University in Beirut, where he also taught using the substantial collections for training in the study of artifacts.

Baramki's experience made him sensitive to the need to make knowledge of the past available to the public at large and to establish archaeology as an academic discipline in order to train local archaeologists. In 1952, the young Jordanian Department of Antiquities could only find one student of archaeology to send to the American University of Beirut. Subsequently, Baramki trained numerous Arab and foreign students in the program. As an archaeologist and teacher Baramki communicated with astonishing immediacy what he knew from direct contact with the archaeology of his homeland. In 1956 he introduced the vital aspect of fieldwork into the archaeology curriculum of the university by opening its first excavation site, the Bronze and Iron Age settlement of Tell el-Ghassil on the road to Baalbek.

The excavations at Umayyad Khirbat al-Mafjar made Baramki the first Arab archaeologist to deal with Islamic materials, at a time when the subject was the domain of art historians. His contributions to making the Islamic cultural heritage accessible to the public involved museum exhibits and activities and publications geared to a general audience.

[See also Mafjar, Khirbat al-.]

BIBLIOGRAPHY

Baramki contributed a series of articles to the *Quarterly of the Department of Antiquities in Palestine* beginning in 1935, as well as the *Dictionary of Biblical Archaeology* and the *Wycliffe Bible Encyclopaedia*. His popular publications have perhaps been more influential in spreading archaeological and heritage awareness than many scientific publications to which the general public has no or only difficult access. See, for example, *The Coins Exhibited in the Archaeological Museum of the American University of Beirut* (Beirut, 1968); *Phoenicia and the Phoenicians* (Beirut, 1961); *The Road to Petra: A Short Illustrated Guide to East Jordan* (Amman, 1947); and *The Art and Architecture of Ancient Palestine: A Survey of the Archaeology of Palestine from the Earliest Times to the Ottoman Conquest* (Beirut, 1969).

HELGA SEEDEN

BAR KOKHBA REVOLT. The hardships the Jews in Palestine endured at the hands of the Roman authorities after 70 CE were emphasized by the favorable attitude of the same authorities to the non-Jews there. This behavior sharpened even more the dichotomy existing between the two segments of the population. The non-Jews were in fact the major beneficiaries of the First Revolt against Rome (66–70 CE). [See First Jewish Revolt.] When Emperor Hadrian removed the hated governor Quietus and perhaps—if a late Jewish tradition is to be believed—even toyed with the idea of rebuilding the Temple and Jerusalem, the Jews felt more hopeful, as they regarded the emperor as "Cyrus Redivivus." When the emperor later decided not to go through with his plans (according to the same legend), their frustration was deep and strengthened the resolve of radical Jews to go to war.

In autumn 129, Hadrian arrived in Palestine as part of his visit to the provinces of the East, which he hoped would promote the process of hellenization there. This brought him into conflict with the Jews of Palestine. Although some specific reasons for the revolt can be found, they should be considered with caution. It is claimed that during Hadrian's visit it became clear that he had decided not to exempt the Jewish people from the law against castration, which for the Jews meant a ban on circumcision. It also became clear, probably at this juncture, that the emperor wished to rebuild Jerusalem as Aelia Capitolina, a pagan city. However, the information about the ban on circumcision comes from an unreliable source (the *Scriptores Historiae Augustae, Life of Hadrian*, 14.2). Cassius Dio, who does not mention the ban on circumcision but does mention Hadrian's scheme to build Aelia Capitolina on the Temple Mount, is also unreliable as a result of the abridgement of this source made by Xiphilinus in the eleventh century. The coinage of Aelia Capitolina does not help much because the series of Aelia Capitolina can only be dated to the span of time 131–135 CE. Thus, it is possible that both the above literary source retrojected Hadrian's punitive actions from the quelling of the revolt in 135 to its start. This would support the suggestion that the cause of Bar Kokhba's revolt was the revival of zealotism rather than initial Roman suppression. Be that as it may, some sort of provocation induced many Jews to start a rebellion under the leadership of Shim'on (Simeon) Bar Kokhba in spring 132 CE.

The war lasted three and a half years, but no historical survey is available analogous to the ones for the Maccabean Revolt and the First Jewish Revolt. The rabbinical sources contain some information about the events, but their reliability as historical sources is questionable. Greek and Latin sources are helpful but brief.

The war started in 132 CE after preparations were made by the rebels (Kloner and Tepper, 1987). The Bar Kokhba letters reveal that he had a well-organized, disciplined Jewish army, apparently organized hierarchically, with different ranks of commanders—a "head of the camp" is known, and even the names of some of the commanders. Judah bar Manasseh was the commander at Kiryath Arabaya, and Jonathan bar Be'ayan and Masabala bar Shim'on were the commanders at 'Ein-Gedi. From the letters it appears that Bar Kokhba's soldiers were God-fearing Jews. (There is one reference to non-Jews who participated alongside the Jews.) Bar Kokhba's official title was *nasi'*, which had already been associated with the king in the Hebrew Bible (*Ez.* 12:10) (Yadin, 1971; Lewis, 1989). In rabbinic literature there is a debate as to whether Bar Kokhba was a king-messiah (Rabbi Akiba was positive that he was, but Rabbi Yohanan ben Tortah said he was not of the Davidic line; J. T., *Ta'an.* 4.8.

68d). Eusebius as well as other church fathers denigrated Bar Kokhba because, according to him (*Hist. Eccl.* 4.6.2), Bar Kokhba persecuted Christians who refused to join him in the war against Rome. [*See* 'Ein-Gedi; Judean Desert Caves.]

The Romans were caught by surprise and had to send auxiliary forces to Judea (Judah) in addition to the two standing legions already there. Two legions constituted a substantial force for the Roman army of the period: two legions were stationed only in problematic areas such as Upper Germany, Lower Germany, and Dacia. Because Judea was considered a problematic place by the Romans long before the Bar Kokhba war, roads had been built in strategic places during Hadrian's reign as emperor. The intensity of the revolt can be deduced by the number of troops the Romans used to subdue the rebels (more than fifty thousand), as well as from Cassius Dio's condensed history: he claims that during the war the Romans destroyed 50 of the Jewish strongholds and 985 of their villages (69.14.1). The available sources do not say whether the rebels conquered Jerusalem before or during the war, whether they renewed the sacrifices on the Temple Mount, or whether the revolt extended beyond Judea proper. It is, however, clear from the coins that the main aims of the rebels were to rebuild the Temple and renew its rituals. Some of the symbols on the coins are associated with the Temple cult and with its facade. Other coins minted by the rebels refer to "the Priest Eleazar," who was apparently an important figure in those stormy days, and who may have been considered a candidate for the high priesthood in the eventual Third Temple (Meshorer, 1982). Eleazar is sometimes identified with the uncle of Bar Kokhba who fought with him at Betar and was then put to death because of accusations that he wished to make peace with the Romans (J. T., *Ta'an.* 4.8.68d–69a).

From the little information available, in particular from the epitomized version of Cassius Dio, it appears that the emperor himself came to Palestine during the revolt, and that troops from Roman legions all over the East were sent there. The rebels' coinage and various legal documents reveal that a new "calendar" was created for the emerging Jewish state, and that the years of the revolt were counted according to the "liberation of Israel," or the years of Bar Kokhba's rule ("Third year of Simeon the son of Kosiba the *nasi'* of Israel"), and the years of "the liberation of Jerusalem." There is, however, very little evidence of exactly which territories the rebels succeeded in liberating during the revolt. Conflicting evidence may indicate that the revolt encompassed, along with Judea, parts of the coastal plain, the Galilee, and even the Golan (Kloner and Tepper, 1987).

On the ninth of Ab 135 CE, the last stronghold of the Jewish rebels, called Betar, near Jerusalem, fell. Shim'on Bar Kokhba was among the victims. According to Cassius Dio 580,000 Jews fell in the battle, and many others were sold as slaves in the aftermath of the war. If later Jewish traditions are to be believed, the Romans also enforced restrictive laws on the Jews in Palestine, such as the ban on circumcision and a prohibition against reading the Torah in public. The memories of these terrible days are depicted in the rabbinic literature in a very vivid manner. The story about the ten martyrs, among whom was Rabbi Akiba, is perhaps the most famous (Schäfer, 1981).

Provincia Judaea became Syria Palaestina, and Aelia Capitolina was founded with a pagan temple in its midst. Non-Jews were settled in the new colony in place of Jews, and Jews were forbidden to enter the city. Moreover, any Jew found there was put to death. Pagan cults of Bacchus, Astarte, and Aphrodite were established in Jerusalem, and on the Temple Mount a pagan temple was built that contained a statue of Hadrian.

[*See also* Jerusalem.]

BIBLIOGRAPHY

Applebaum, Shimon. *Prolegomena to the Study of the Second Jewish Revolt, A.D. 132–135.* Oxford, 1976.

Hachlili, Rachel. *Ancient Jewish Art and Archaeology in the Land of Israel.* Leiden, 1988.

Kloner, Amos, and Yigal Tepper, eds. *The Hiding Complexes in the Judean Shephelah* (in Hebrew). Tel Aviv, 1987.

Kuhnen, Hans-Peter. *Palästina in griechisch-römischer Zeit.* Munich, 1990.

Lewis, Naphtali, et al. *The Documents from the Bar Kokhba Period in the Cave of Letters: Greek Papyri, Aramaic and Nabatean Signatures and Subscriptions.* Jerusalem, 1989.

Mendels, Doron. *The Rise and Fall of Jewish Nationalism.* New York, 1992.

Meshorer, Ya'acov. *Ancient Jewish Coinage.* 2 vols. Dix Hills, N.Y., 1982.

Meshorer, Ya'acov. *The Coinage of Aelia Capitolina.* Jerusalem, 1989.

Schäfer, Peter. *Der Bar-Kokhba-Aufstand: Studien zum zweiten jüdischen Krieg gegen Rom.* Tübingen, 1981.

Schürer, Emil. *The History of the Jewish People in the Age of Jesus Christ, 175 B.C.–A.D. 135.* 4 vols. Revised and edited by Géza Vermès et al. Edinburgh, 1973–1987.

Stern, Menachem, ed. and trans. *Greek and Latin Authors on Jews and Judaism.* 3 vols. Jerusalem, 1976–1984.

Yadin, Yigael. *Bar-Kokhba: The Rediscovery of the Legendary Hero of the Last Jewish Revolt against Imperial Rome.* London, 1971.

DORON MENDELS

BARROIS, AUGUSTIN GEORGES, (1898–1987), theologian and archaeologist. Born in Charleville, France, Barrois studied in Louvain. He was ordained a priest and joined the Dominican Order in 1924. The following year he was sent to the École Biblique et Archéologique Française in Jerusalem, where he spent a decade. He returned to France in 1935 to become professor of Old Testament studies at the Dominican Faculty of Saulchoir. In 1939 he moved to the United States, where he taught theology in Washington, D.C., at Princeton University, and at St. Vladimir's Orthodox Theological Seminary in Crestwood, New York.

In 1926–1927, Barrois codirected (with P. Carrière and F. M. Abel) the excavations at Nerab, 7 km (4 mi.) southeast of Aleppo, Syria, where two Aramean stelae had been discovered in 1891. The major discovery of the 1920s had been an important Neo-Babylonian and Achaemenid necropolis. A group of twenty-five cuneiform tablets (Dhorme, 1928) was also found. [See Nerab Inscriptions.] In 1929 he took part, under François Thureau-Dangin, in the excavations at Arslan Tash (ancient Ḥadat[t]u) in northern Syria. The following year, he joined a Harvard University expedition to Serabit el-Khadem in Sinai. Barrois is responsible for having discovered or studied several important monuments: a funerary chapel in the convent of St. Euthyme in the Judean Desert; synagogues at Beth Alpha, east of the Jezreel Valley, and in Jerash, in Jordan; and tombs in Jerusalem and its vicinity. In addition, he published studies on biblical metrology, and on the excavations at Beth-Shean, Caesarea, Megiddo, and Helbon (mod. Khalbun, 25 km north of Damascus). Most of his publications appeared in the *Revue Biblique* and in the journal *Syria* between 1927 and 1939. Barrois's most significant publication is his two-volume *Manuel d'archéologie biblique*, an ambitious enterprise covering the entire field of traditional biblical archaeology.

BIBLIOGRAPHY

Barrois, Augustin Georges. *Précis d'archéologie biblique*. Paris, 1935.
Barrois, Augustin Georges. *Manuel d'archéologie biblique*. 2 vols. Paris, 1939–1953.
Dhorme, Paul. "Les tablettes babyloniennes de Neirab." *Revue d'Assyriologie* 25.2 (1928): 53–82.
Thureau-Dangin, François, and Augustin Georges Barrois, et al. *Arslan-Tash*. 2 vols. Bibliothèque Archéologique et Historique, vol. 16. Paris, 1931.

PIERRE DE MIROSCHEDJI

BASILICAS. Derived from the Greek word *basilike*, "royal house," the basilica is "a roofed hall, usually rectangular or apsidal, and often with inner columns, serving . . . general social and commercial intercourse and the hearing of lawsuits, for which it became the primary location" (Robertson, 1969, p. 268). A tribunal (or dais) for the presiding magistrate was often a feature. Its plan may be simple or have two to four aisles formed by pillars alongside the central nave. Some make use of the clerestory system for illumination. Its apse(s) or rectangular dais(es) may be on the short or the long side, with one or three entrances facing the tribunal. Models of the form are the Greek hypostyle hall (*ibid.*, p. 180), the Stoa Basilike in the agora in Athens, and the audience hall in imperial palaces.

Early Basilicas. The basilica first appears in Italy in republican times. The oldest known structure is the Basilica Porcia (c. 175 BCE) in Rome. Frank E. Brown (1976) points to second-century BCE basilicas at Cosa and Ardua. The basilica at Pompeii (c. 100 BCE), destroyed in 79 CE, had a rectangular central space (possibly unroofed) surrounded by a colonnade that created a corridor. Its raised dais was at its western end. The civil basilica became a standard feature of Roman cities in the early empire, at Augusta Raurica (Augst, Switzerland), Thaumagusta (Timgad), Leptis Magna in North Africa, and at Trier in Germany (now a Lutheran church). Later Roman basilicas include the Basilica Aemilia (first century BCE), the Basilica Julia (first Century CE, rebuilt in third century), and the great Basilica of Maxentius (completed by Constantine after 313 CE).

Eastern Basilicas. The civil basilica first appears in the early Roman Empire, though primarily in what were essentially Roman cities in the east: three in Corinth (all first century CE), in Shaqqa in Syria, north of the Sea of Galilee (c. 280 CE), and in Samaria/Sebaste in Israel. The so-called Royal Stoa at the southern end of the Herodian Temple platform in Jerusalem presents some problems. According to Benjamin Mazar (*The Mountain of the Lord*, Garden City, N.Y. 1975, pp. 124–125), the center of this stoa was "in the shape of a basilica." Josephus (*Antiq.* 15.411–416) describes three rows of monolithic Corinthian columns and one row of engaged columns forming a three-aisled structure whose central nave was half as high as the two aisles. Such a stoa would be unique. Did Josephus confuse a building like the two-story Stoa of Attalos (with its interior colonnade) in the Athens agora with the basilicas he saw in Rome? Its function is unclear as well. Meir Ben-Dov (1982, pp. 124–127) hypothesizes an eastern apse decorated with a menorah. Richard Mackowski (*Jerusalem City of Jesus*, Grand Rapids, 1980, p. 125), however, argues that the Temple functioned as a place where everybody mixed, "either for business or to exchange religious and political news and views," like the basilicas in Rome and at Sebaste and the Stoa of Attalus.

Basilical Synagogues. The basilical plan in synagogues appears in the third or fourth century CE. The location of the Torah shrine distinguishes the longhouse plan (Barʿam, Beth Alpha, Capernaum, Chorazin, Gush Ḥalav, Hammath-Gader, Khirbet Shemaʿ, Meiron, and Tiberias in Israel; on Delos; and in Ostia and Stobi in Italy) from the broadhouse plan (Eshtemoa and Khirbet Susiya in Israel and Dura-Europos in Syria). The longhouse type sometimes has an apse for the Torah shrine, as at Beth-Sheʿarim and Beth Alpha in Israel and at Sardis in Asia Minor.

Christian Basilicas. Constantine began building great basilical churches in the fourth century. Their typological origins have been attributed to the atrium house, secular basilicas or halls, and to the synagogue. Ecclesiastical basilicas use colonnades that divide the structure into aisles and a nave (as at Pompeii), with an eastern apse. They have axial entrances on the west, often with an atrium in front of them. Constantine erected the Church of the Resurrection in Jerusalem, the Church of the Nativity in Bethlehem, and St. Peter's Basilica in Rome to set a standard.

After Constantine, the building of ecclesiastical basilicas

spread rapidly throughout the eastern Mediterranean, especially in Syria-Palestine, which presents a broad spectrum of basilicas, many of which are from the fourth to the sixth centuries CE. Some of the most important are in North Syria (Antioch and inland regions). They range from simple three-aisled basilicas without an apse (Behyo, North Syria) or with a single apse (Kharem Shems, Der Turmanin, and Qalb Louzeh in Syria; Umm er-Rasas and the series of churches at Gerasa—St. Theodore, the cathedral, and Bishop Genesius—in Jordan), to triple-apsed churches (designed by the architect Julianus at Brad; by a series by Marcianus Cyris in the mountains from Antioch to Aleppo; at Rusafa (Sergiopolis), in the desert south of the Euphrates River; and at Petra, in Jordan). The introduction of transepts, coupled with the dome and squinch, led to the gradual abandonment of the basilica plan and the adoption of the Byzantine cross-in-square plan.

The great basilicas at Santa Maria Maggiore, Santa Sabina, and St. Paul outside the walls of Rome were built in the fifth century. In the sixth century, Justinian rebuilt the Church of the Nativity and erected the Nea Church in Jerusalem. The addition to Sancta Sophia of a dome and side apses to the basilical plan influenced subsequent Greek ecclesiastical style.

Basilical churches are numerous, and the basilica form clearly became the standard in both the east and west (Milburn, 1988, pp. 83–201). Basilical churches have been excavated in Israel at Avdat (Oboda), Tabgha (Heptapegon), Herodium, Khirbet el-Kursi (Gergesa?), Latrun, Mamre, Kurnub (Mampsis), Nessana, and Shivtah.

The basilica was also adapted for martyria. The cruciform Martyrion of St. Babylas at Antioch/Kaoussie has four arms without apses. The most grandiose is the cruciform martyrion of St. Simeon Stylites at Qal'at Sim'an in northern Syria, with four basilicas radiating from the octagon built around the saint's pillar. The eastern three-aisled basilica terminated in an apse.

[*See also* Churches; Synagogues; *and* Temples. *In addition many of the Near Eastern sites mentioned are the subject of independent entries.*]

BIBLIOGRAPHY

Ben-Dov, Meir. *In the Shadow of the Temple.* Translated by Ina Friedman. New York, 1985. Useful popular report on recent excavations in Jerusalem.

Brown, Frank E. *Roman Architecture.* New York, 1976. Very clear, brief account of factors influencing Roman architects in planning buildings and cities.

Grimal, Pierre. *Roman Cities.* Translated and edited with a descriptive catalog of Roman cities by G. Michael Woloch. Madison, Wis., 1983. Covers Roman cities in the West only.

Hachlili, Rachel. "The Niche and the Ark in Ancient Synagogues." *Bulletin of the American Schools of Oriental Research,* no. 223 (1976): 43–53. Includes useful synagogue plans.

Krautheimer, Richard, and Slobodan Curcic. *Early Christian and Byzantine Architecture.* 4th ed. New Haven, 1986.

Milburn, Robert L. P. *Early Christian Art and Architecture.* Berkeley, 1988. The most accessible recent discussion of early church architecture.

Robertson, D. S. *Greek and Roman Architecture.* 2d ed., corrected. London, 1945. Classic descriptions, easily accessible to any reader.

Shanks, Hershel. *Judaism in Stone: The Archaeology of Ancient Synagogues.* New York, 1979. Trustworthy popular report on excavated ancient synagogues.

Strange, James F., and Hershel Shanks. "Synagogue Where Jesus Preached Found at Capernaum." *Biblical Archaeology Review* 9 (November–December 1983): 24–31.

White, L. Michael. *Building God's House in the Roman World: Architectural Adaptation among Pagans, Jews, and Christians.* Baltimore, 1990. Fascinating attempt to describe the development of worship centers from modifications of houses to the construction of special buildings for Mithraism, Judaism, and Christianity.

EDGAR KRENTZ

BASSIT, site located on the Syrian coast, as the crow flies about 40 km (25 mi.) north of Latakia, 50 km (31 mi.) from Antioch, and 137 km (85 mi.) from Cape St. Jean on Cyprus (35°51'38" N, 35°49'15" E). The site has been visited by, among others, C. Leonard Woolley, Claude Schaeffer, Henri Seyrig, P. J. Riis (who identified it with ancient Posideion; see below), George Saadé, and John W. Hayes (who studied the site's corpus of stamped clay basins (Fr., *pelves*). Herodotus (3.91.1–3) and then various other authors (Diodorus, Strabo, Ptolemaeus) mention Posideion. The name appears, more and more distorted, on portolanos, medieval (fourteenth–sixteenth centuries CE) navigation manuals; on a 1692 map (Michelet edition, Paris) that reads Possidie and places it on the coast; on an 1859 British Admiralty chart that calls it Ancient Posideion; and as el Bouseit, mentioned at the end of the nineteenth century.

Following a 1969 survey, excavations took place from 1971 to 1984 under the direction of Paul Courbin, and were at first limited to the site's ancient terrace (now called Meidan), the tombs in the Iron Age necropolis, and the Hellenistic and Roman acropolis. In 1973, the western valley was partly excavated and subsequently the tell (Late Bronze Age I–end of the Roman period) itself was excavated.

The first evidence of settlement dates to about 1600 BCE. The surrounding woodland was cleared to cultivate cereals. [*See* Cereals.] The name of the site in that period is unknown, but it appears to have been an advanced outpost of Ugarit. Two important buildings succeeded each other that had been abandoned before the arrival of the Sea Peoples in about 1200 BCE. The site was immediately reoccupied, but only partially. It appears then to belong to the Aramean kingdom of Hama. Many architectural levels follow without interruption during the Early Iron Age. As a small Levantine harbor related by trade to central Phoenicia and Cyprus, and possibly receiving colonists from those areas, Bassit developed contacts with Greece in the tenth century BCE that continued into the ninth and eighth centuries BCE; however, there is no evidence of a Greek presence at Bassit before the first half of the seventh century BCE. The site received its name, *Posideion*, then. Many objects found in the eighth–seventh-century BCE necropolis confirm relations with Phoenicia and Cyprus. The settlement appears to have been small and its inhabitants poor. Some sixth-century BCE child burials were dug *intra muros*. The society appears to have been both exclusive and egalitarian.

Following the end of the seventh century BCE, relations grew steadily with eastern Greece: Aeolis, Ionia, Samos, Miletus (630–520 BCE); mainland Greece: Corinth and Sparta; and even (although doubtless, indirectly) Etruria and then Athens (575–480 BCE). The Persian conquest (539 BCE) brought no change to these relations. The Median wars seem to have slowed trade during most of the fifth century BCE, but it was later resumed. The city may eventually have minted its own coinage, before Alexander's death, as a local coin of Alexander's is known. In that period the acropolis was fortified. Following Alexander's death, the site became part of the Seleucid kingdom and later used the Hellenistic koine. Even after the Roman conquest (64 BCE), the Greek language remained in use.

From the third century CE onward, the town witnessed considerable construction activity: a new pier and harbor facilities, a new town wall made of modular blocks, large houses, new ramparts, a basilica, chamber tombs that eventually held sarcophagi, and a synagogue. It became a Christian cult place. In addition, *pelves* (see above) were produced and exported. The site was inhabited until the Arab conquest at the beginning of the seventh century.

[*See also the biographies of Schaeffer, Seyrig, and Woolley.*]

BIBLIOGRAPHY

Courbin, Paul. "Bassit." *Syria* 63 (1986): 175–220. Includes fifty-five illustrations.

Courbin, Paul. "Bassit-Posidaion in the Early Iron Age." In *Greek Colonists and Native Populations: Proceedings of the First Australian Congress of Classical Archaeology Held in Honour of Emeritus Professor A. D. Trendall, Sydney, 9–14 July 1985,* edited by Jean-Paul Descoeudres, pp. 503–509. Oxford, 1990.

Courbin, Paul. *Les tombes du Fer II à Bassit.* Paris, 1993.

Courbin, Paul. "Fragments d'amphores protogéométriques grecques à Bassit (Syrie)." *Hesperia* 62 (1993): 95–113.

Le Rider, Georges. "L'atelier de Posidèion et les monnaies de la fouille de Bassit en Syrie." *Bulletin de Correspondance Hellénique* 110 (1986): 393–408.

Perreault, Jacques Y. "Céramique et échanges: Les importations attiques au Proche-Orient du VIe au milieu du Ve siècle avant J. C., les données archéologiques." *Bulletin de Correspondance Hellénique* 110 (1986): 145–175.

Perreault, Jacques Y. "Les *emporias* grecs du Levant: mythe ou réalité." In *L'Emporion,* edited by Alain Bresson and Pierre Rouillard, pp. 59–83. Paris, 1993.

PAUL COURBIN

BASTA, site located about 20 km (12 mi.) south of Wadi Musa/Petra, in southern Jordan, 1,460–1,420 m above sea level, at the border between arable land with rich springs and the steppic Artemisia (Artemisia herba alba) regions of the western Arabian plateau, where the mean annual precipitation is 200 mm (30°13′47″ N, 35°32′06″ E). A Neolithic occupation was first recorded in a survey carried out by the Department of Antiquities of Jordan in 1972. Hans Georg Gebel did a sounding in 1984 that revealed a deep Late Pre-Pottery Neolithic B (PPNB) occupation that was excavated from 1986 to 1989 and again in 1992 by the Basta Joint Archaeological Project, directed by Hans J. Nissen and Mujahed Muheisen. Gebel was the project's assistant director.

The settlement was located next to the rich spring of Basta, on a steep wadi slope. The surface distribution of PPNB artifacts was almost 14 ha (36 acres). The area excavated covered about 900 sq m. The evidence at Basta was of a shifting site occupation, with marginal refuse dumps, activity areas for processing food, materials used for construction, and possible cultivated areas. The Late PPNB chipped lithics and architectural phases excavated had radiocarbon dates of the second half of the seventh millennium, with parallels at 'Ain Ghazal, Wadi Shu'eib, 'Ain Gamam, and Nahal Issaron. [*See* 'Ain Ghazal; Shu'eib, Wadi.] The cultural layers and deposits above the PPNB architecture revealed a PPNC- and Yarmukian-related chipped stone industry and artifacts. The layers were more than 6 m deep. Below the surface, predominantly sixth-millennium colluvials were interbedded with cultural layers (Yarmukian-related arrowhead types and a few Pottery Neolithic sherds as well as flimsy installations of a phase between the Late PPNB and the PN) covering an upper Late PPNB architectural phase.

Because of terraced housing on the slopes and rebuilding activities, it is difficult to separate the main architectural phase from even one subphase. The architectural units are assumed to have been used for long periods of time. Built on terraces created by channel-like grids of dry-stone masonry, they were well preserved (up to 4 m high), preplanned, and multiroomed. The substructures have parallels at Çayönü and Nevalı Çori in Turkey. [*See* Çayönü; Nevalı Çori.] These substructures, possibly related to subfloor climatic needs (i.e., air circulation), were covered by stone slabs, a stone fill, and the beds of the first-floor rooms, and sometimes with a finish of burnished plaster stained in a red or cream color. Most of the "channels" were found empty; some had been used as a burial ground and a few at least were accessible. (An entrance into one channel could be traced for more than 12 m.) Some of the well-built walls on the terraces (double rows of dressed stones set in mortar, with smaller stones wedged into the courses) show traces of mud plaster, rarely bearing burnished and painted plaster. In one case a painting appears to represent twigs with berries. The ground plans of the larger units and rooms seemed to follow the contour lines of the slope of the terrace. The central building unit of area B (10 × 15 m), however, was constructed on one level, with two single and double rows of small rooms (1.3–2 sq m) around a central open space. In many cases there was no evidence of how the rooms were connected, and their function remains unclear. True entrances and stairs were rare, but windowlike wall openings (for air circulation, light, and accessibility) are attested. The evidence is of a long-time use of the main walls, and two stories cannot be ruled out. Less well-built structures in the upper architectural phase were related to an early sixth-millennium occupation.

Unmixed debitage dumps of workshops indicated specialized craftsmanship in naviform core technologies (with exclusive use of tabular flint) that gave place to predominantly flake technologies in the Post-PPNB layers. Arrowhead types in the Late PPNB layers are related to the Byblos and 'Amuq shapes; the 'Amuq-related morphology dominates. [*See* Byblos; 'Amuq.] The tool kit comprises all implement classes known from permanent PPNB village sites, with additional types. A rich ground stone industry is represented by marble and limestone vessels, standardized manos and grinding slabs, as well as items with unknown functions. The bone industry is of a Late PPNB standard type, including needles and tubular bone beads. Large marble plates and oval vessels, as well as limestone and tiny chlorite vessels, exist at Basta. Vessels made of tempered sun-dried or low-fired clay are also well attested in the Late PPNB contexts.

All sorts of beads made of greenstones, Red Sea corals and mollusks, local and exotic minerals, pailletts of mother-of-pearl, and tokenlike objects were found. Human faces are represented by two Basta "heads" (green marble, limestone), a stone carving and a mask fragment (limestone). From the Post-PPNB layers (possibly mid-sixth millennium BCE), a hoard of two animal figurines and two pendants carved in different styles and raw materials was found; one represents a ram that resembles a phallus when turned (see figure 1).

Primary burials of complete and incomplete corpses as well as secondary deposits of skulls from disturbed burials were found together with dispersed human remains in architectural contexts. It is likely that uninhabited parts of the settlement (ruins) were used as a burial ground. Multi-individual burials were common. Infant mortality is represented by 38 percent for zero–two years and 38 percent for five–seven years. Well-attested diseases and pathological alterations are dental caries, periodontal diseases, stomatitis, scurvy, transversal enamel hypoplasia, possible anemia and/or A-hypervitaminosis, *cribra oribitalia*, meningitis, osteomyelitis of the skull vault, arthrosis of the large joints, and rheumatic arthritis.

In the Late PPNB, subsistence appears to have been 76 percent domestic sheep/goats, 1–3 percent morphologically wild sheep/goats, 10 percent goitered and mountain gazelle

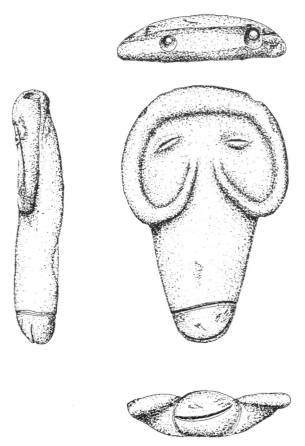

BASTA. Figure 1. *Limestone ram amulet.* From a Yarmukian-related context. Length, 7.8 cm. (Courtesy H. G. Gebel)

(possibly also *G. dorcas*), 4 percent morphologically wild and possibly domestic cattle, very few wild and possibly domestic pigs, fallow deer, onager, and African wild asses. [*See* Sheep and Goats; Cattle and Oxen; Pigs.] Late PPNB arboreal cover and subsistence are represented by juniper, 74 percent; pistachio, 25 percent (most likely *P. atlantica*); and a few poplar and willow trees. The inhabitants of Basta collected almonds and wild figs and cultivated two-row hulled barley and emmer wheat and filed peas. [*See* Cereals; Agriculture.]

BIBLIOGRAPHY

Becker, Cornelia. "The Analysis of Mammalian Bones from Basta, a Pre-Pottery Neolithic Site in Jordan: Problems and Potential." *Paléorient* 17.1 (1991): 59–75.

Gebel, Hans G., et al. "Preliminary Report on the First Season of Excavations at Basta." In *The Prehistory of Jordan*, vol. 1, edited by Andrew N. Garrard and Hans G. Gebel, pp. 101–134. British Archaeological Reports, International Series, no. 396. Oxford, 1988.

Nissen, Hans J., et al. "Report on the First Two Seasons of Excavations at Basta, 1986–87." *Annual of the Department of Antiquities of Jordan* 31 (1987): 79–119.

Nissen, Hans J., et al. "Report on the Excavations at Basta, 1988." *Annual of the Department of Antiquities of Jordan* 35 (1991): 13–40.

HANS GEORG GEBEL and MUJAHED MUHEISEN

BATASH, TEL (Ar., Tell el-Batashi), site located in the Sorek Valley, 7 km (4 mi.) west of Beth-Shemesh and 5 km (3 mi.) northwest of Tel Miqne (Ekron). The site (map reference 141 × 132) can be safely identified with Timnah, a town mentioned in the biblical description of the northern border of Judah as located in the Sorek Valley, between Beth-Shemesh and Ekron/Miqne (*Jos.* 15:10–11). Tel Batash is the only mound between these two points. Timnah is mentioned in several additional biblical texts, the most important of which is the Samson narrative in *Judges* 14–15, where it is described as a Philistine town close to the Danite border. Timnah in *Genesis* 38:13–14 probably also refers to this site. The town is mentioned in the town lists of Dan (*Jos.* 19:43), attributed by many scholars to the time of the United Monarchy. It thus appears that during the time of David and Solomon Timnah changed hands and became an Israelite town. According to 1 *Chronicles* 28:18, the Philistines, probably the Ekronites, took the city back from the Israelites during the time of King Ahaz. A few decades later, during Sennacherib's invasion of Judah, the Assyrians captured Timnah, just before Ekron, which during that time was also under Judean subjugation.

Tel Batash covers 6 acres of a flat alluvial plain south of the Sorek brook. The mound, rising about 15 m above the plain, is square and its sides are oriented to the points of the compass.

Excavations were carried out on the mound in twelve seasons (1977–1989), sponsored by the Southwestern Baptist Theological Seminary, in collaboration with the Institute of Archaeology of the Hebrew University of Jerusalem. The expedition director was George L. Kelm, and the archaeological director was Amihai Mazar. A sequence of twelve major strata was identified, some with several subphases, covering a span of 1,300 years, from Middle Bronze II until the Persian Period.

Middle Bronze Age (Strata XII–X). The town was founded sometime during Middle Bronze II, perhaps in about 1700 BCE. Its founders constructed a square earthen rampart, 200 m long on each side, which subsequently created the mound's geometric configuration. The town developed inside the crater-shaped area. In area B, in the mound's northeastern corner, the rampart was uncovered for a length of more than 30 m. It was preserved to a height of about 6 m, leaning on the massive mud-brick wall of a large structure, perhaps a citadel. Only two rooms of this citadel were excavated, in which two construction phases (denoted strata XII–XI) were observed. The citadel appears to have been destroyed before the final phase of MB III: occupation was resumed on its ruins following its destruction in stratum X. Only fragmentary building remains were preserved from this level, and it appears that the fortifications (or at least the citadel) went out of use then. The pottery suggests a date late in the Middle Bronze Age. Stratum X was heavily destroyed by fire.

Late Bronze Age (Strata IX–VI). Four occupation levels from the Late Bronze Age were identified in area B. Each of the lower three (IX–VII, dated to the fifteenth–fourteenth centuries BCE) was destroyed violently by fire, indicating a period of unrest and instability. It appears that during this period Tel Batash was a town in the kingdom of Gezer, which dominated the fertile land of the Sorek Valley. As at many other LB sites in Israel, no trace of a city wall was found; the outer walls of houses served as a defense line, and where streets reached the end of the mound they were blocked by walls that closed the gaps between houses.

In each of the three strata the remains of substantial buildings were found, including those of large pillared halls with staircases leading to a second floor. The architecture of these houses is unparalleled elsewhere; they probably belonged to upper-class landlords or merchants. Rich assemblages of pottery and other finds were recovered in the destruction layers: considerable amounts of Cypriot pottery (mainly in stratum VII) and cylinder seals, scarabs from Egypt, clay figurines, and metal objects.

It seems that after the destruction of the prosperous stratum VII town (fourteenth century BCE), the site declined. Only poor structural remains and a few finds could be attributed to stratum VI (thirteenth century BCE).

Iron Age (Strata V–II). It is stratum V at Tel Batash that is to be identified with the Philistine town of Timnah in the biblical texts, probably built by the Philistines as a border town in the territory of the city-state of Ekron/Miqne. It was founded sometime in the second half of the twelfth century BCE, when Philistine bichrome pottery was already in use. Unlike nearby Ekron/Miqne, Tel Batash produced no Mycenaean IIIC pottery. The Batash was destroyed in about 1000 BCE or slightly later, perhaps when King David conquered the region. The Philistine town was well built, with mud-brick structures on stone foundations. Evidence for a shallow defensive wall was found in area C. In the residential areas several phases of construction were observed, evidence of the longevity of this stratum. Among the finds were typical Iron I pottery assemblages, including Philistine pottery and some figurines; however, the area of this stratum excavated thus far is too limited to allow an in-depth evaluation of the material culture.

Stratum IV (tenth century BCE) follows the total destruction or abandonment of the previous town. Its new structures were built on a different plan and are mainly domestic, probably belonging to a community of farmers. No city wall was discovered, but two towers and an L-shaped wall are probably the remains of its city gate. It appears that the stratum IV population was Israelite, and the town was part of the kingdom of David and Solomon. The pottery is very similar to that found at other Judean sites of the period and includes vessels covered with a thick, hand-burnished red slip. The stratum IV town came to an end in the late tenth century BCE, perhaps during the invasion of Pharaoh Shishak. Among the finds was an incised inscription on a bowl fragment that mentions "[so]n of Hanan." The name Hanan in this context is interesting because Elon Beth-Hanan is mentioned as one of the cities in this region during the reign of Solomon (1 *Kgs.* 4:9).

Stratum III represents the rebuilding of the town on a large scale. This town was destroyed in 701 BCE during Sennacherib's invasion; however, the date of its foundation is not clear, and it is still not known whether there was an occupation gap in the ninth century BCE. There clearly is no more than one major stratum between the tenth century (stratum IV) and the seventh century (stratum II).

The stratum III city was well fortified by a stone wall on the crest of the mound and a lower wall on its slope. A magnificent city gate led into the town (see figure I). The narrow approach to the town was defended by an outer gate with a large bastion (8 × 24 m). A bent-axis approach in the outer gate and a small piazza led to an inner four-entryway or six-chambered gate structure.

South of the gate complex, on the crest of the mound, the foundation courses of a large public building were discovered. It appears to have been an administrative structure, just inside the city gate. In the northern part of the town, a building was found with large storage spaces in which dozens of smashed storejars, Judean in type, stamped with royal Judean seal impressions (*lmlk*), were found. One jar bears the seal impression of an official, "Tsafan (son of) Abi-

maas." The building was destroyed during Sennacherib's invasion of Timnah in 701 BCE, recorded in his annals. This fits the historical sources, which relate that King Hezekiah took control of the city-state of Ekron/Miqne, exiled its king to Jerusalem, and forced its elders to join him against Assyria. Timnah, which the Philistines had taken from Judah several decades earlier (according to 2 *Chr.* 28), was thus under Judean control, and the jars with royal seal impressions may have belonged to a Judean garrison stationed there.

In Stratum II (seventh century BCE), Timnah prospered, as did its much larger neighbor, Ekron/Miqne. The fortifications of the previous city of stratum III were reconstructed, the city wall thickened, and the gate rebuilt. The building remains indicate that the seventh-century town was well planned and densely built up. The public building south of the gate was replaced by an industrial and commercial complex, which included a finely built oil-pressing installation. In the northern part of the town, a large area was exposed that revealed a series of dwellings and a public building. The dwellings are typical Iron Age pillared buildings, or four-room house, featuring a space on the ground floor that is divided by a row of monolithic pillars. [*See* Four-room House.] A street separated the houses from the northern city wall. Out of the four houses exposed, three had industrial installations: one had an oil press and the two others an in-

BATASH, TEL. Figure I. *View of the outer gate at Tel Batash, looking northeast.* (Courtesy Tel Batash Expedition)

stallation of undefined function, known also from nearby Ekron/Miqne.

Every house contained large quantities of pottery and other finds. Many of the forms of pottery vessels are typical of the region of Philistia and mainly of Ekron/Miqne; the others are Judean. Evidence for long-distance connections is found in the form of Phoenician, Transjordanian, and East Greek pottery. Connections with Judah are also illustrated by inscribed stone shekel weights and rosette seal impressions. Stratum II at Timnah was probably a town in the state of Ekron/Miqne that maintained strong ties with Judah and conducted extensive industrial and commercial activity. It appears that, as at Ekron/Miqne, the production and export of olive oil, part of a "cottage industry," was a major factor in the town's prosperity. It was severely destroyed by fire during the Babylonian conquest of the region, probably in 603 BCE.

The city subsequently fell into ruins and was briefly occupied by few squatters. During the Persian period there was a small settlement on the mound, but only a few walls and pits can be attributed to this period.

[See also Miqne, Tel.]

BIBLIOGRAPHY

Kelm, George L., and Amihai Mazar. "Three Seasons of Excavations at Tel Batash (Timnah): Preliminary Report." *Bulletin of the American Schools of Oriental Research*, no. 248 (1982): 1–36.

Kelm, George L., and Amihai Mazar. "Tel Batash (Timnah) Excavations: Second Preliminary Report (1981–1983)." *Bulletin of the American Schools of Oriental Research*, Supplement, no. 23 (1985): 93–120.

Kelm, George L., and Amihai Mazar. "Excavating in Samson Country: Philistines and Israelites at Tel Batash." *Biblical Archaeology Review* 15.1 (1989): 36–49.

Kelm, George L., and Amihai Mazar. "Tel Batash (Timnah) Excavations: Third Preliminary Report, 1984–1989." *Bulletin of the American Schools of Oriental Research*, Supplement, no. 27 (1991): 47–67.

Mazar, Amihai, and George L. Kelm. "Batash, Tel." In *The New Encyclopedia of Archaeological Excavations in the Holy Land*, edited by Ephraim Stern, vol. 1, pp. 152–157. Jerusalem and New York, 1993.

Mazar, Amihai. "The Northern Shephelah in the Iron Age: Some issues in Biblical History and Archaeology." In *Scripture and Other Artifacts: Essays on the Bible and Archaeology in Honor of Philip J. King*, edited by Michael Coogan, J. C. Exum, and Laurence E. Stager, pp. 247–267. Louisville, 1994.

AMIHAI MAZAR

BATHS. During pre-Hellenistic times in the Near East, the private bath, consisted either of a bathtub or bathing platform. From the Hellenistic through Byzantine periods, public bathhouses became the popular form of bathing. The sources for baths in antiquity are archaeological evidence, ancient depictions, and written sources.

Some of the earliest archaeological evidence comes from Mesopotamia, from the first half of the second millennium BCE. From eighteenth-century BCE Mari, located on the Eu-

phrates River, terra-cotta bathtubs were recovered in the palace. [See Mari; Palace.] Bronze bathtubs have occasionally been uncovered from the first millennium BCE in Mesopotamia. It seems, however, that in ancient Mesopotamia tubs were reserved for the wealthy; the poor bathed on the banks of canals and rivers and in cisterns or poured water over a bather on a plastered or paved surface. [See Cisterns.] In Nebuchadrezzar's Babylon, residences typically included a bathroom located behind the main room of the house. The bathroom consisted of a fired-brick floor, lined with bitumen and powdered limestone. The waste water from the bath flowed into a sump located beneath the lowest section of the floor. No traces of bathtubs have been recovered, indicating that shower water was poured over the bather.

Bathtubs appear on Cyprus in the Late Cypriot II period (fourteenth–thirteenth centuries BCE) and became increasingly popular in the Late Cypriot IIIA period (twelfth century BCE). [See Cyprus.] Both limestone and terra-cotta examples are known from Ayios Iakovos, Kalavasos Ayios Dhimitrios, Enkomi, and Maa-Palaeokastro. [See Kalavasos; Enkomi.] The custom of bathing in tubs is well known in Mycenaean Greece. It is described in the *Iliad* and *Odyssey* (cf. *Odyssey* 10.165) and can be associated with the increasing influence of Late Bronze Age Greece on Cyprus in the Late Cypriot II–III.

Indoor bathing installations in residences were common in Egypt. From Middle and New Kingdom Egypt, excavations at the royal palace of Amenophis III in Thebes and in residences at Lahun and el-Amarna have uncovered numerous examples of bathrooms. [See Amarna, Tell el-.] The typical bathroom was located near the bedroom, in close proximity to a latrine and dressing room. The bathroom consisted of a slightly sloped stone-slab floor and wall-lined with stone slabs. The bathwater drained through a spout located at the lower end of the stone slab or through a drainage channel that ran through the outer wall into a vessel or to the outdoors. A low wall separated the bathroom from the latrine. Similar bathrooms have been excavated on Minoan Crete. [See Crete.]

In addition to the archaeological evidence, a wall painting from a New Kingdom tomb at Thebes depicts a woman bathing in a bath installation that resembles those excavated at el-Amarna. [See Wall Paintings.] The woman is shown with four slaves waiting on her. One removes her jewelry and clothing, a second pours water over her head, the third rubs her arms and body, and a fourth holds a flower to her nose as she is bathed. The Greek historian Herodotus and the Roman author Diodorus mention Egyptian bathing customs, noting that warm and cold baths were used by the Egyptians; for ordinary ablutions, however, cold water was preferred.

Though rare, bathing installations similar to those found in Egypt are known from Canaan. At Tell el-'Ajjul and Beth-Shean, both sites with a strong Egyptian influence, plas-

BATHS. *Hasmonean ritual bath at Jericho.* (Courtesy ASOR Archives)

tered, pebbled, or shell floors have been interpreted by the excavators as bathrooms in which water was poured over the bather. [*See* 'Ajjul, Tell el-; Beth-Shean.] Bathtubs in ancient Philistia and Israel are found only occasionally. Terra-cotta baths or fragments from them have been excavated at several sites, including Tell Qasile, Ashdod, Tel Miqne/Ekron, Tell Abu Hawam, and Tel Dan. [*See* Qasile, Tell; Ashdod; Miqne, Tel; Abu Hawam, Tell; Dan.] It is noteworthy that the first three are Philistine sites, perhaps reflecting an Aegean origin for the custom of bathing. The nearly complete tenth-century BCE tub from Tel Dan was discovered in the sacred precinct and it presumably served a cultic function. [*See* Cult.]

Bathing in the modern, nonreligious sense is seldom mentioned in the Bible. In *Exodus* 2:5, Pharaoh's daughter bathes in the river; in *2 Samuel* 11:2, Bathsheba is observed by David bathing on the roof. However, washing of the face, hands, and feet are mentioned frequently in the Hebrew Bible and New Testament (cf. *Gn.* 43:31, *Sg.* 5:3; *Jn.* 13). Oval pottery footbaths have been found at Iron Age II Israelite levels at Samaria, Tell en-Nasbeh, and Megiddo. [*See* Samaria; Nasbeh, Tell en-; Megiddo.]

Private bathrooms in domestic architecture, located in proximity to lavatories, often including bathtubs, became common among the aristocracy in the eastern Hellenistic and Roman world. Bathtubs, hewn from stone, appear in subterranean rock-cut chambers below houses dating to the Hellenistic period from Mareshah, Israel. Several examples of bathrooms, located on the ground floor of the house and separate from ritual-bath installations, are known from Judea (Judah) during the Herodian period (first century BCE–first century CE). [*See* Ritual Baths.]

The custom of bathing in public baths originated in the classical Greek world with the rise of the public gymnasia and hot baths in the fourth century BCE. The gymnasium provided the inspiration for later bathing complexes throughout the Roman Empire that combined physical exercise with public bathing. The rapid spread and popularity of Roman baths are in a large part the result of the development of hypocaust heating and the ability to transport large quantities of water into cities via an aqueduct. [*See* Aqueducts.] Numerous contemporary Roman and Byzantine authors comment on the custom of public bathing. Bathing in Roman society was a daily habit, and spending the afternoon in the public baths was a well-accepted custom, except among certain groups—philosophers, Jews, and Christians—who frowned upon the decadence of public bathing.

The major features of Roman baths include an exercise courtyard *(peristylum)* or larger gymnasium (palaestra), a dressing room (apodyterium), a cold room (frigidarium), often with a plunge bath, and a warm room (tepedarium) that led to a hot room *(caldarium)*. Because of the great variety in building plans, it has proven difficult to devise a typology for bathing complexes. Public bathing establishments can be divided into two main groups: *thermae* and *balneae*. Publicly funded thermae were exceptionally large baths that incorporated hygienic, athletic, recreational, educational, and social activities. Public baths could also be located near natural hot springs that also served medicinal purposes. One of the largest of these thermomineral complexes in the Roman world was Hammath-Gader, located in the southern Golan along the Yarmuk River in Roman Syria. [*See* Hammath-Gader.] *Balnaea* were smaller baths, either publicly or privately owned. In addition to public baths, bathing complexes are found in military camps, sanctuaries, and private and imperial residences.

In Asia Minor, the Greek gymnasium heavily influenced the plan and function of public bath buildings. At Pergamon, Roman baths were added on to the Hellenistic gymnasium; at Salamis and Samos, Roman baths were built over the Hellenistic gymnasium; and at Miletus Roman baths operated separately from the gymnasium. [*See* Pergamon; Salamis; Miletus.] In the larger centers they were symmetrical and well planned. Smaller baths in towns and villages were more varied in plan.

Most of the baths in North Africa date to the mid-second century CE and later. Almost every major center had more than one public bath. Fikret Yegül (1992) divides the North African baths into three main categories: imperial (e.g., the Hadrianic baths at Leptis Magna in Libya), half-axial (e.g., the Julia Memmia baths at Bulla Regia in Tunisia), and small, asymmetrical establishments (e.g., the Baths of Gallienus at Vollubilis in Morocco). [*See* Leptis Magna.]

In Judea and Roman Syria, public baths were introduced by King Herod and the Roman legions in the late first century BCE–first century CE. However, the majority of the public baths in Syria-Palestine date to the Late Antique and Byzantine periods and belong to the small-bath category. In the Byzantine period, the palaestra and associated athletic events disappeared from the bath. This trend is associated with the rise of Christianity in the fourth century, which frowned upon the gymnasium, an institution associated with pagan culture. Following the Islamic conquest of Syria-Palestine in the seventh century, the bathhouse continued in use, both as public baths in towns (e.g., the baths at Qasr al-Hayr East in Roman Syria) and as private baths in palaces (e.g., Khirbat al-Mafjar in the Jordan Valley in Roman

Syria) and in desert castles (e.g., Quṣayr ʿAmra in the eastern desert of Roman Syria). [*See* Qaṣr al-Ḥayr al-Gharbi; Mafjar, Khirbat al-; Quṣayr ʿAmra.]

[*See also* Medicine; *and* Personal Hygiene.]

BIBLIOGRAPHY

Badawy, Alexander. *A History of Egyptian Architecture*, vol. 2, *The First Intermediate Period, the Middle Kingdom, and the Second Intermediate Period*; vol. 3, *The Empire (The New Kingdom)*. Berkeley, 1966–1968. Excellent general summary of all aspects of Egyptian architecture, including bathing installations.

Courtois, Jacques-Claude. "Une baignoire monolithe en calcaire du Bronze récent à Enkomi." In *Studies in Honour of Vassos Karageorghis*, edited by G. C. Ioannides, pp. 151–154. Nicosia, 1992. Description of bathtubs at Enkomi (Cyprus).

Delaine, J. "Roman Baths and Bathing." *Journal of Roman Archaeology* 6 (1993): 348–358. Critique of recent major publications on Roman baths and bathing.

Graham, J. Walter. "Bathrooms and Lustral Chambers." In *Greece and the Eastern Mediterranean in Ancient History and Prehistory: Studies Presented to Fritz Schachermeyr on the Occasion of His Eightieth Birthday*, edited by K. H. Kinzl, pp. 110–125. Berlin, 1977. Describes Minoan bathrooms and bathing practices; one of the few articles on pre-Hellenistic bathing installations.

Nielsen, Inge. *Thermae et Balnea: The Architecture and Cultural History of Roman Public Baths*. Aarhus, 1990. Catalog of 387 baths in the Roman Empire and an account of the development of Roman public baths.

Saggs, H. W. F. *Everyday Life in Babylonia and Assyria*. London, 1965. Summary of literary, pictorial, and archaeological evidence for daily life in ancient Mesopotamia.

Wilkinson, J. Gardner. *The Manners and Customs of the Ancient Egyptians*. Vol. 3. New ed. London, 1878. Summary of literary, pictorial, and archaeological evidence for daily life in Egypt.

Yegül, Fikret K. *Baths and Bathing in Classical Antiquity*. New York, 1992. Thematic treatment of Roman baths in Italy, North Africa, and the eastern provinces, including a detailed description of the development of public baths from classical Greece through Byzantine times.

ANN KILLEBREW

BE'ER RESISIM (Ar., *Bir er-Resisiyeh*, "well of the morning-dew") is a small hilltop site in the western Negev highlands, near the Naḥal Neṣṣana (30°49′ N, 34°34′ E; map reference 109 × 026). It is one of the largest of the dozens of Early Bronze IV pastoral nomadic encampments (c. 2300–2000 BCE) known in this area of scant rainfall. It was excavated in 1978–1980 by William G. Dever and Rudolph Cohen, sponsored jointly by the University of Arizona and the Israel Antiquities Authority.

The ridge above the wadi and modern well below revealed some eighty circular or elliptical stone huts, averaging 2.00–4.50 m in diameter, with walls well preserved up to 1.50 m (see figure 1). Door jambs and lintels were often intact. The roofs were made of chalk slabs, supported by wooden beams and central stone pillars. Few furnishings were noted, apart from sporadic stone benches, bins, hearths, and saddle querns for grinding grain.

BE´ER RESISIM.   Figure 1.   *Eliptical stone hut.* A portion of the upper walls and slab roof are reconstructed from original materials. (Photograph by Jonathan Kline; courtesy ASOR Archives)

The scant pottery, none of it restorable, consisted of a scattering of Early Bronze IVA red-burnished wares of Transjordanian type, dated about 2300 BCE, but mostly quantities of Early Bronze IVC wares typical of Dever's "Southern/Sedentary" family, about 2100–2000 BCE. Several copper awls and daggers were found, as well as a hoard consisting of a broken dagger and two triangular-section bar ingots. Miscellaneous domestic items included stone and shell ornaments; many *ad hoc* flint tools; two small chalk cups; a piece of leather; and several fragments of Red Sea conch shells and polished pierced bars made from them, perhaps remains of pectorals.

Most of the animal bones recovered came from a few large, unroofed stone circles. They were more than 90 percent sheep and goat, with a few small birds, desert gazelle, and hares also represented. The presence of immature caprids (sheep-goat) indicates winter occupation of the site since that is when they are slaughtered, but that does not, of course, rule out occupation in the summer as well.

Several off-site structures were investigated or excavated, including isolated stone circles, burial cairns with both articulated and disarticulated inhumations, two large rectangular hilltop buildings of enigmatic character, a few remains of run-off irrigation systems, and even a small "satellite village" on a nearby alluvial fan.

The plan of the main hilltop settlement, with many nearly identical round sleeping huts clustering around central courtyards, suggests a relatively egalitarian, polygamous society, with a total population of eighty to one hundred individuals at any one time. They were certainly pastoral nomads, but the copper ingots and a few "exotic" items like the conch shells suggest long-distance trade; the grinding stones are evidence of some primitive irrigation means that agriculture was also an element in a mixed subsistence system. The strong similarities of the pottery to that of the many Hebron hills shaft-tomb cemeteries (as at Jebel Qaʿaqir) probably indicate a pattern of seasonal transhumance over a circuit of roughly 60 km (100 mi).

BIBLIOGRAPHY

Cohen, Rudolph, and William G. Dever. "Preliminary Report of the Pilot Season of the 'Central Negev Highlands Project.'" *Bulletin of the American Schools of Oriental Research,* no. 232 (1978): 29–45.

Cohen, Rudolph, and William G. Dever. "Preliminary Report of the Second Season of the 'Central Negev Highlands Project.'" *Bulletin of the American Schools of Oriental Research,* no. 236 (1980): 41–60.

Cohen, Rudolph, and William G. Dever. "Preliminary Report of the Third and Final Season of the 'Central Negev Highlands Project.'" *Bulletin of the American Schools of Oriental Research,* no. 243 (1981): 57–77.

Dever, William G. "New Vistas on the EB IV ('MB I') Horizon in Syria-Palestine." *Bulletin of the American Schools of Oriental Research,* no. 237 (1980): 35–64.

Dever, William G. "Village Planning at Be'er Resisim and Socio-Economic Structure in Early Bronze Age IV Palestine." *Eretz-Israel* 18 (1984): 18*–28*.

Horwitz, Liora K. "Sedentism in Early Bronze IV: A Faunal Perspective." *Bulletin of the American Schools of Oriental Research*, no. 275 (1989): 15–25.

WILLIAM G. DEVER

BEERSHEBA (Ar., Tell es-Saba'), a small mound about 1 ha (2.5 acres) in area, located in the Beersheba valley, east of the modern city of Beersheba in Israel's Negev desert (map reference 135 × 073). The settlement was built on a hill at the fork of the Beersheba and Hebron riverbeds, which provided the site with natural protection and close proximity to cultivable alluvial soil, as well as to the main crossroad.

Biblical References. The main biblical references to Beersheba come from the patriarchal narratives. The patriarchs appear as pastoral nomads and occasional cultivators in the southern part of the land. God revealed himself to them (*Gn.* 26:24–25, 46:1–2) and they struggled at Beersheba with Abimelech over the wells (*Gn.* 21:22–34, 26:15–33). The name of the site stems from the Hebrew *shebu'a* ("oath") or *shiby'a* ("seven") (*Gn.* 21:31, 26:33). In the late premonarchical period, Joel and Abijah, the sons of Samuel, were stationed in Beersheba as "judges over Israel" (*1 Sm.* 8:1–2). Beersheba appears on the list of cities of Simeon and Judah (*Jos.* 15:28, 19:2; *1 Chr.* 4:28). It demarcates the southern end of the land of Israel that stretched "from Dan to Beersheba" (*Jgs.* 20:1; *1 Sm.* 3:20; *2 Sm.* 3:10, 17:11, 24:15; *1 Kgs.* 5:5). [*See* Judah.] Elijah passed through Beersheba on his journey to Mt. Horeb (*1 Kgs.* 19:3), and Amos

BEERSHEBA. *Plan of the city.* (Courtesy ASOR Archives)

condemned the pagan rites held at Beersheba along with those at Dan, Bethel, and Gilgal (*Am.* 5:5, 8:14).

Identification and Excavations. Although the identification of Tell es-Saba' with biblical Beersheba seems to be confirmed by excavation (Aharoni, 1973; Rainey, 1984), some scholars see a contradiction between the biblical accounts and the finds. Mervyn D. Fowler claims that the absence of Bronze Age and Late Iron Age remains discredits Tel Beersheba as a patriarchal period site and as a city during Josiah's reign, respectively (Fowler, 1982). Nadav Na'aman believes that the location of ancient Beersheba must be sought at Bir es-Saba', while locating biblical Sheba at Tel Beersheba (*Jos.* 19:2; Na'aman, 1980). Patriarchal Beersheba is well represented in the remains dated to the twelfth and eleventh centuries BCE. Anson F. Rainey suggests that two settlements—one at Tel Beersheba and one at Bir es-Saba'—bore the same name (Rainey, 1984). Yohanan Aharoni also suggested identifying Tel Beersheba with the "Hagar of Abra(ha)m" of Shishak's list (Aharoni, 1973, pp. 111–113).

Extensive excavations were conducted at Tel Beersheba by an expedition from the Institute of Archaeology at Tel Aviv University. The project was directed by Yohanan Aharoni from 1969 to 1975 and in 1976, following Aharoni's death, by Ze'ev Herzog. Methodologically, a wide horizontal-exposure approach was applied, aimed at uncovering broad and continuous occupation levels. Indeed, a comprehensive picture of the city planning in stratum II was revealed. Additional seasons, directed by Herzog, have been carried out at the site since 1990 in conjunction with the National Parks Authority's preservation of the site.

Chalcolithic Period. Scattered sherds from the Chalcolithic period were found in the site's debris. It seems that any structures from this stage were removed by later construction operations. The first Iron Age settlers (Iron I, stratum IX) cleaned and reused depressions, or pits, they noticed on the mound that may have belonged originally to the Chalcolithic settlement (see below).

Iron Age I. The best sequence of Iron Age remains was detected on the southeastern slope of the mound, under the outer gate of stratum V. The remains include four strata (IX–VI) dating from the mid-twelfth to the early tenth centuries BCE. The first settlement (stratum IX) consisted of a series of pits hewn into the hill's natural bedrock. The pits range from 5 to 10 m in diameter, and from 2 to 3 m in depth. The excavated area yielded parts of seven pits, most of them used for storage, apparently of grain. One pit, excavated almost in its entirety, had clearly been utilized for habitation. It was hewn into the bedrock at an angle, so that the rock provided natural protection from above. Its floor was paved with pebbles, and storage jars stood in a hewn niche. A cooking oven, surrounded by layers of ash, indicates domestic use of the pit.

A community of about twenty families could have lived

in this settlement in tents or huts alongside the pits. The lack of stone architecture may point to a seminomadic community experiencing the first stage of sedentary life, a shift generated by slightly improved climatic conditions that enabled them to grow yields. Dry farming is indicated from the presence of cattle bones (12 percent), but most of their subsistence was still based on animal husbandry (sheep and goats, 74 percent). [*See* Cattle and Oxen; Sheep and Goats.] Two Egyptian scarabs from the New Kingdom, fragments of Philistine pottery, and local ware date stratum IX to the second half of the twelfth and the first half of the eleventh centuries BCE.

The first houses at the site were erected in stratum VIII, although the pits were still utilized. The single large unit erected near the well (see below) consists of a broad room and a forecourt—a house that might be considered the prototype of the four-room house. [*See* Four-room House.] The meager number of objects found in this stratum include the earliest iron arrowheads found at the site. Stone-built houses indicate a more permanent type of settlement. Stratum VIII is dated to the third quarter of the eleventh century BCE.

The stratum VII settlement was built over the abandoned pits and houses of stratum VIII. Houses with solid stone foundations were erected in a belt covering the eastern slope—about half of the hilltop. The houses, which can be reconstructed as four-room-house types, encircled the settlement, their back walls facing outward, forming an enclosed settlement (Herzog, 1984). The large open space in the center of the settlement was probably utilized for the community's flocks of sheep and goats. However, large quantities of cattle bones discovered at Tel Beersheba, Tel Masos, and other sites in the area may point to the growing role of agriculture in the region's economy, most probably from further-improved climatic conditions. [*See* Agriculture; Masos, Tel.] In the eleventh century BCE, the Beersheba valley witnessed the most dense occupation in its premodern history. Stratum VII yielded rich finds, including pottery vessels, jewelry, iron tools, and fragments of figurines, that date to the late eleventh and early tenth centuries BCE.

The settlement of stratum VII was abandoned and parts of the houses were dismantled. The next stage, stratum VI, is characterized by a partial reuse of the earlier units, once interior partition walls were added. A single new "three-room" house was constructed in this stage. The finds from this stratum are very similar to those from stratum VII and must date to the first half of the tenth century BCE. The remains in stratum VI are interpreted as belonging to an interim stage, during which the new city (of stratum V) was built. The single house on the slope of the hill may have served the commander of the project. The compartments near it could be used as stores for equipment and shelters for work supervisors. These remains were eventually razed toward the final stage of the construction of the new city.

The well. A well 69 m deep was found in the center of the remains of the Iron I settlement. During Iron II, this well was left outside the city fortifications but continued to serve both the city's inhabitants and passers by. Although the well was reused for several centuries, it seems that it was first dug in one of the Early Iron phases. Aharoni (1973) identified this well with the one mentioned in the patriarchal narratives (*Gn.* 21:26). Stratigraphically, the well does not destroy any Iron I structure, and the builders of the outer gate of stratum V clearly took it into consideration when erecting the gate's foundations. During Iron II, the city's drainage system directed rainwater into the well. The finds from the fill indicate that the well was destroyed (apparently in an earthquake) and filled in during the Late Hellenistic period.

Iron Age II. The four strata of the Iron II city include remains of a small fortified city (2.8 acres) built on the top of the mound (strata V–II). The last occupational phase (stratum I) was an attempt to rebuild the city that was eventually halted. Two systems of fortifications were erected at Beersheba in Iron II. The earlier one consisted of a solid city wall with a four-chambered gate built in stratum V and reused in stratum IV. The later fortifications consisted of a casemate city wall and another four-chambered gate built in stratum III and reutilized in stratum II. Each of these strata suffered destruction, but the destruction of strata V and II was clearly caused by a more violent and widespread conflagration. These destructions should be dated, based on the rich pottery finds, to campaigns of Pharaoh Shishak (Sheshonq) in 926 BCE and King Sennacherib in 701 BCE, respectively. Some scholars have, however, challenged the date of stratum II. Kathleen M. Kenyon (1976) dated Beersheba II earlier than Lachish III, whereas Yigael Yadin (1976a) correlated it with stratum II at Lachish. [*See* Lachish.] Na'aman (1979) suggests, on historical grounds, pushing the conquest of Beersheba back to the time of Sargon.

Israelite city. The city of stratum II at Beersheba presents a valuable picture of an administrative center in a marginal region. The oval city is small but carefully planned, with the encircling city wall following the topography of the hill. Only on the eastern side of the mound does the plan extend to a lower level. The water-supply system was erected there, and in order to incorporate it into the city, a colossal earthen rampart was built. A belt of two circular streets, parallel to

BEERSHEBA. *View of the Beersheba Gate.* (Courtesy Pictorial Archive)

the outer contour of the mound, divided the city's interior. An additional street was cut through its center. All the streets converged on the open gate square, the city's only piazza, which could serve as a meeting place and market. The gate itself consisted of chambers with benches used by the city's functionaries in conducting their business.

An elaborate system of drainage channels was uncovered beneath the streets and pavements that conducted rainwater outside the city quickly. This prevented the collapse of the walls, which were made of stones packed with a mud mortar topped by sun-dried mud bricks. The main channel, which ran under the gate, conducted the water into the deep well outside the gate.

Water system. Aharoni (1973) interpreted a wide flight of stairs he exposed in the 1970s as part of a water system. In 1994, the entire area was excavated and a monumental water-supply system unearthed. The system was approached through a square, vertical shaft, about 15 m deep. Stairs with a low parapet led to a stepped tunnel for an additional 5 m, at the bottom of which a series of underground cisterns is entered. [*See* Water Tunnels; Cisterns.] Five cisterns, each about 3 × 6 m and about 6 m high, were hewn into the limestone bedrock and covered with thick layers of water-resistant plaster. The total capacity of the system was about 500 cu m. Water was directed into the system through a tunnel from a nearby riverbed. Because the rivers in the Negev flow only for brief periods in the winter, the planners had to build a dam that directed floodwater into the tunnel. In this respect, the system at Beersheba differs from its counterparts at Hazor and Megiddo—which offer an approach to the underground water level or cistern. [*See* Megiddo; Hazor.] The systems in both regions were adapted to the availability of their water resources. Because the system could be filled only during a limited period of time (when it rained in winter), water was probably spared for emergency use, when the city was under siege. Assuming a population of three hundred in the city and an annual consumption rate of about 1,000 l per person, the city could withstand a siege for as long as one year. The well outside the city gate provided the daily needs of the city's inhabitants as well as of merchants, caravans, and military units passing by and of the livestock.

Pillared buildings. A large (600 sq m) typical pillared building was exposed near the city gate. It consisted of three units, each with three long halls separated by limestone columns that are square in section. Hundreds of pottery vessels found in the building's destruction layer indicate that it was the city's main storehouse. The goods would have been collected as taxes from neighboring villages like *byt 'mm* and *tld* mentioned in an ostracon found in one of the storerooms (see Aharoni, 1973, pp. 71–72). In addition to storejars for cereals, oil, and wine, the inventory also included objects for food preparation and serving, evidence that the storehouse also was used for cooking and serving food to the city's ad-

ministrative or military personnel (functions hinted at in some of the Arad ostraca). [*See* Arad Inscriptions.] Despite such clear-cut information, some scholars are of the opinion that the pillared buildings at Beersheba were horse stables (Yadin, 1976b; Holladay, 1986).

Horned altar. In the fifth season of excavation, unusually well-dressed stones were uncovered that were incorporated into a wall of the storerooms. Peculiar rounded projections at the top of three of the stones (a fourth was cut off) identified them as part of a large horned altar. Additional stones were found in the eighth season that together reconstruct an altar that is a cube of 1.6 × 1.6 × 1.6 m. Aharoni (1973) suggested that the alter had originally stood in the courtyard of a temple, apparently in the place of the later basement building (see below). The dismantling of the temple and demolishing of the alter at both Beersheba and Arad are viewed as part of the cultic reform carried out by Hezekiah, king of Judah. [*See* Arad, *article on* Iron Age Period.] Yadin (1976a) suggested locating the altar in a *bāmâ* near the city gate.

Governor's palace. A large unit (no. 416) in stratum II that controlled the gate square is interpreted as the residence of the city's governor (Heb., *śar hā'îr*). The building is composed of ceremonial, residential, and service wings. Two large halls paved with stone pebbles, located on either side of the entry corridor, served as reception rooms. The doorjambs in the rear of the rooms were adorned with ashlar stones, the only example of such masonry found in Iron Age Beersheba. At the far end of the palace, with a separate wide entrance, was a small kitchen and a storage room. The western wing of the building consisted of two residential units. A narrow stair area offered passage to the upper floor from the entry corridor.

Basement house. The second large structure in stratum II was found on the western side of the city. Its odd wall foundations were sunk 4 m deep into the ground (all others were only about .5 m deep). While in some rooms the space was filled with homogenous earth, two rooms were left empty and served as basements. The building's exceptional wall structure and east–west orientation led Aharoni to conclude that Beersheba's temple had stood there: that in stratum II, after the temple was destroyed down to its oldest foundations, the basement house replaced it. The underground rooms were connected by a door and apparently served as a wine cellar owned by one of the city's chief functionaries.

Residential dwellings and population. Apart from the units listed above, the city's space was allocated for residential buildings. The sections of the city exposed attest that the domestic units were not uniform, however. Although they resemble the four-room-house type (most houses possessed a wall made of stone pillars to support the roof), their sizes differ and their internal division varies. The kitchens appear to have been located in the front room, which was unroofed. The central space, divided by pillars, may have been roofed and used as a storage area and as a stable for the household's livestock. The rear broad room was the family's bedroom. In houses located at the outer belt of the city, this room was also part of the defensive casemate wall. An estimated 300–350 people could live in the seventy-five dwellings at Tel Beersheba.

Its high standard of city planning as well as the vast resources and effort invested in its urban structures—its fortifications, street network, water system, and storehouses—clearly point to an administrative role for it. Such efforts were made for the kingdom's civil service elite; ordinary citizens lived in villages and farms and were engaged in agriculture. The inhabitants of Israelite cities were the region's governor; regional tax collectors who were also responsible also for redistributing taxes in kind; military commanders and local guards; officials responsible for international trade; and the priests who controlled religious rites.

Late periods. After the destruction of stratum II, Tel Beersheba was never rebuilt as a city. Following an unsuccessful attempt to rebuild the fortifications (stratum I), the site was deserted for nearly three hundred years. The majority of the finds from the Persian period are from pits around the mound's perimeter. Forty Aramaic ostraca found in the pits list personal names of Jews, Edomites, and Arabs and mention quantities of wheat and barley. The pits were used, as elsewhere, to store grain, which was then supplied to the Persian army.

Remains of a large Hellenistic fortress with a temple nearby were found on the mound. Numerous objects were uncovered in *favissae,* or pits, dug in the temple's courtyard: a clay figurine (made in a mold) of a pair of goddesses; a Babylonian-style cylinder seal; female figurines in bronze and bone; a bronze bull figurine; and a falcon-shaped faience pendant. In the Herodian period a large palace, including a bathhouse, was built on the mound. The latest structure was a fortress from the Roman period (second and third centuries CE), built as a part of the limes Palaestinae. Following another gap of about five hundred years, the fortress was reused as a way station in the Early Arab period (eighth–ninth centuries CE). In the last few centuries the mound has served as burial place for local bedouin.

BIBLIOGRAPHY

Aharoni, Yohanan, ed. *Beer-Sheba I: Excavations at Tel Beer-Sheba, 1969–1971 Seasons.* Tel Aviv, 1973.
Aharoni, Yohanan. *Investigations at Lachish: The Sanctuary and the Residency (Lachish V).* Tel Aviv, 1975.
Fowler, Mervyn D. "The Excavation at Tell Beer-Sheba and the Biblical Record." *Palestine Exploration Quarterly* 114 (1982): 7–11.
Herzog, Ze'ev, et al. "The Stratigraphy of Beer-Sheba and the Location of the Sanctuary." *Bulletin of the American Schools of Oriental Research,* no. 225 (1977): 49–58.
Herzog, Ze'ev. *Beer-Sheba II: The Early Iron Age Settlements.* Tel Aviv, 1984.
Holladay, John S. "The Stables of Israel: Functional Determinants of Stable Construction and the Interpretation of Pillared Building Remains of the Palestinian Iron Age." In *The Archaeology of Jordan and Other Studies Presented to Siegfried H. Horn,* edited by Lawrence T. Geraty and Larry G. Herr, pp. 103–165. Berrien Springs, Mich., 1986.
Kenyon, Kathleen M. "The Date of the Destruction of Iron Age Beer-Sheba." *Palestine Exploration Quarterly* 108 (1976): 63–64.
Na'aman, Nadav. "The Brook of Egypt and Assyrian Policy on the Border of Egypt." *Tel Aviv* 6 (1979): 68–90.
Na'aman, Nadav. "The Inheritance of the Sons of Simeon." *Zeitschrift des Deutschen Palästina-Vereins* 96 (1980): 136–152.
Rainey, Anson F. "Early Historical Geography of the Negeb." In *Beer-Sheba II: The Early Iron Age Settlements,* edited by Ze'ev Herzog, pp. 88–104. Tel Aviv, 1984.
Yadin, Yigael. "Beer-Sheba: The High Place Destroyed by King Josiah." *Bulletin of the American Schools of Oriental Research,* no. 222 (1976a): 5–17.
Yadin, Yigael. "The Megiddo Stables." In *Magnalia Dei; The Mighty Acts of God; Essays on the Bible and Archaeology in Memory of G. Ernest Wright,* edited by Frank Moore Cross et al., pp. 249–252. Garden City, N.Y., 1976b.

ZE'EV HERZOG

BEHISTUN. *See* Bisitun.

BEIDHA, site located 4.5 km (2.8 mi.) north of Petra, 33 km (20 mi.) from Ma'in, 101 km (63 mi.) from 'Aqaba, and 180 km (112 mi.) from Amman in southern Jordan. It lies along a 4-kilometer-wide shelf comprised of alluvial valleys interspersed between steeply faced Cambrian sandstone outcrops. This north-south shelf interrupts an abrupt westerly descent from the Jordanian plateau to the lowlands of the Wadi 'Arabah, where elevations drop from 1,600 m to fewer than 200 m within a distance of 16 km (10 mi.). The site's elevation is 1,020 m, on and within a remnant terrace formed by alluviation of the Wadi el-Ghurab. A thick sequence of cultural and noncultural deposits, up to 6 m deep, accumulated. Three periods of human occupation were identified; a Natufian encampment (primarily during the eleventh millennium BCE), a Pre-Pottery Neolithic B (PPNB) village (during the seventh millennium), and terraced Nabatean agricultural fields (second century BCE—first century CE).

Beidha, initially called Seyl Aqlat, was discovered by Diana Kirkbride with the aid of B'dul bedouin during a 1956 reconnaissance survey for sites predating the ceramic Neolithic in the Petra area. Stone walls and early Neolithic flints eroding out of the upper talus slope of a seasonal drainage, and white-patinated Natufian artifacts farther downslope revealed the site's research potential. Kirkbride excavated the site for eight seasons; seven between 1958 and 1967 and a final one in 1983. She supervised the excavations, and a series of assistants directly supervised local workers, starting in 1963. The digging was conducted primarily by trained Jericho men using a hand pick and a trowel.

Excavations exposed 54 sq m of the Natufian occupation,

revealing a maximum thickness of 0.6 m of cultural deposits that thinned along the margins. The Natufian occupation, consisting primarily of small lithics, faunal remains, and small hearths and large roasting pits, appears to have been a short-term or seasonal campsite that was occupied repeatedly over a considerable period of time. Minimal evidence of plant processing was discovered, there was an absence of features such as buildings, storage facilities, and burials.

The PPNB settlement lies on top of the alluvial terrace. It consists of a small, low tell more than 3 m thick, along with a shallower deposit of associated cultural material beyond the limits of the village. Excavations exposed 1,425 sq m of Neolithic deposits and sixty-five buildings (1,050 sq m and sixty-one buildings within the limits of the tell, and 375 sq m of indeterminate Neolithic deposits outside the tell, including four buildings and a series of related features 40 m farther east). Final Neolithic stratigraphic modeling distinguished three main phases associated with well-preserved buildings and abundant artifacts on their floors (including bone tools, flaked stone tools, ground-stone axes, pestles, stone grinders, stone beads, raw materials, and subsistence remains, including gazelle, goat, cattle, cereals, legumes, and pistachios). These data allowed for considerable insight into the spatial organization of an Early Neolithic village.

The Neolithic village appears to have been continuously occupied, during which time a unique, indigenous architectural progression took place from clusters of oval post houses, through individual oval and subrectangular buildings, and ultimately to full rectangular buildings complete with two stories (with an open upper story and a basement consisting of a long corridor and up to seven very small rooms).

Initially, the Early Neolithic village consisted of open courtyard spaces and small aggregates of buildings. The distribution of buildings became more compacted over time, and open space was limited to a central courtyard. The earliest buildings were simply organized, interior structural features were absent, and storage and production shared an undifferentiated space used for eating, receiving guests, and sleeping. Production and storage became more spatially segregated within domestic dwellings over time. Interior architectural features increased in frequency and diversity, focusing activities and storage in particular locations within domestic buildings. Storage and production areas were ultimately restricted to the basements of the two-story domestic buildings.

Larger, distinct, nondomestic structures were centrally situated throughout the village's history. They were inferred to have been the venue of suprahousehold decision making and related ceremonial activities. Five uniquely constructed medium-sized buildings off-site were also interpreted as nondomestic, possibly associated with aspects of the rich ideological and ritual tradition that flourished during the PPNB.

Research at this Early Neolithic village has provided considerable insights into how one small community attempted to embrace the social and economic changes initiated by sedentarism and food production.

BIBLIOGRAPHY

Bar-Yosef, Ofer, and François R. Valla, eds. *The Natufian Culture in the Levant.* Ann Arbor, Mich., 1991.

Bar-Yosef, Ofer, and Anna Belfer-Cohen. "From Foraging to Farming in the Mediterranean Levant." In *Transitions to Agriculture in Prehistory,* edited by Anne Birgitte Gebauer and T. Douglas Price, pp. 21–48. Madison, Wis., 1992.

Byrd, Brian F. *The Natufian Encampment at Beidha: Late Pleistocene Adaptation in the Southern Levant.* Jutland Archaeological Society Publications, vol. 23.1. Aarhus, 1989.

Byrd, Brian F. "Public and Private, Domestic and Corporate: The Emergence of the Southwest Indian Village." *American Antiquity* 59.4 (1994): 636–666.

Kent, Susan. *Domestic Architecture and the Use of Space: An Interdisciplinary Cross-Cultural Study.* Cambridge, 1990.

Kirkbride, Diana. "Five Seasons at the Prepottery Neolithic Village of Beidha in Jordan." *Palestine Exploration Quarterly* 98 (1966): 5–61.

Kirkbride, Diana. "Beidha 1965: An Interim Report." *Palestine Exploration Quarterly* 99 (1967): 5–13.

Kirkbride, Diana. "Beidha: Early Neolithic Village Life South of the Dead Sea." *Antiquity* 42 (1968a): 263–274.

Kirkbride, Diana. "Beidha 1967: An Interim Report." *Palestine Exploration Quarterly* 100 (1968b): 90–96.

Rollefson, Gary O., Alan H. Simmons, and Zeidan A. Kafafi. "Neolithic Cultures at 'Ain Ghazal, Jordan." *Journal of Field Archaeology* 19 (1992): 443–470.

Wilson, Peter. *The Domestication of the Human Species.* New Haven, 1988.

BRIAN F. BYRD

BEIRUT, capital of Lebanon, located on the Mediterranean coast (33°54′ N, 35°30′ E). The city's ancient name was Biruta and, in the classical period, Berytus. The name is generally thought to be derived from the common Semitic word for "well" or "pit"—in Akkadian, *būrtu;* Hebrew, *bĕ'ēr;* Arabic, *bīr.* Biruta is a plural form.

Berytus was renowned in the Roman world as a commercial center but most especially for its school of law, which flourished from the third to the sixth centuries CE. The earthquake of 551 CE devastated the city. In turn the medieval city fell into ruins, but its scattered granite columns impressed the Persian traveler Nasr-i-Khusraw, who visited the city in 1047. The early western visitors, Henry Moundrell (1697), Richard Pococke (early eighteenth century), F. B. Spilsbury (1799), and William Thomson (1870), all realized that the scattered remains were the ruins of Roman public buildings.

Early Investigations. Beiruit provides only the barest archaeological evidence of a pre-Roman city. The Roman city itself lies beneath the port area, making regular excavations impossible.

Prehistoric period. Early investigations and limited archaeological activity were begun in 1914 by a group of Jesuit scholars at St. Joseph University, Beirut. In 1946 Henry Fleisch and Louis Dubertret, also from St. Joseph, made a careful study of the marine terraces of Ras Beirut, the promontory, identifying different levels. During this survey of open-air, unstratified sites, Fleisch picked up an Acheulean biface, a water-worn hand ax believed to be the oldest stone tool found in Ras Beirut.

In 1972–1973, Fleisch extracted fifteen Lower and Middle Acheulean bifaces, the oldest stone bifaces found in Beirut in a stratified deposit. Raoul Desribes found similar tools at Furn ech-Chebbak near Nahr (the River) Beirut in about 1914. Fleisch and Paul San-Laville identified the Middle Paleolithic and the Levallois-Mousterian cultures by their core and flake industries, making Ras Beirut the earliest Mousterian site in the eastern Mediterranean basin (see Saidah, 1970).

Fleisch found evidence of the Upper Palaeolithic at two kinds of sites in the vicinity of Ras Beirut: open-air campsites and caves and shelters. Lorraine Copeland's survey in the early 1960s recognized twenty open-air campsites in the sand around Beirut (see Saidah, 1970). The caves and shelter sites belong mainly to Upper Paleolithic Beirut, and they are represented in the Wadi Antelias area, some 6 km (4 mi.) north of Beirut. Ksar 'Akil is a key site for this period and for the prehistory of Lebanon. [*See* Ksar 'Akil.]

In 1930 Auguste Bergy identified the earliest known Neolithic village site, called Tell Arslan, near the Beirut airport. Fleisch rescued a large number of Neolithic flint tools as well as potsherds there that are now part of the collection at St. Joseph's Museum of Lebanese Prehistory. In 1969 Roger Saidah located another Neolithic settlement in the center of the city, at the ancient tell of Beirut. In 1914, Desribes uncovered a Chalcolithic site called Minet ed-Dhalieh on the second headland south of Pigeon Rock. The site was partly excavated. Abundant remains of flints, blades, and flakes litter its surface.

Historical periods. Little is known about Beirut in historical periods before Greco-Roman times. Although kings from Egypt and Mesopotamia had stelae carved in the rock cliffs of Nahr el-Kalb north of the city, recounting their military exploits in the eastern Mediterranean (see figure 1), written documents pertaining to the history of Beirut are

BEIRUT. Figure 1. *Nahr el-Kalb rock-cut stelae.* At left is Assyrian stela no. 13; at right, Egyptian stela no. 14 of Rameses II. (Courtesy I. Khalifeh)

rare. The city is not mentioned by Herodotus and it does not appear in the Hebrew Bible.

Second millennium. In 1926, near the port area, an Egyptian sphinx with a royal inscription of Amenemhet IV (eighteenth century BCE), was uncovered that found its way to the British Museum. In 1954, about 100 m northeast of where the sphinx was found, three tombs were discovered containing burials ranging from the seventeenth to sixteenth centuries BCE. In addition to pottery and metal tools, the scarabs and alabaster vases found are evidence of trade with Egypt and Palestine. Another Middle Bronze Age tomb was discovered at Sin el-Fil, about 2 km east of the ancient tell. At the tell itself, a Late Bronze Age tomb was found containing a stone vase fragment bearing the name of Rameses II. The presence of Mycenaean pottery in this tomb indicates that Beirut was also involved in trade with the Aegean.

First millennium. Written and archaeological records for Beirut from the first millenium BCE are scarce. A small ivory perfume vase in the form of a standing woman, now in the Ashmolean Museum in London, is said to have come from Beirut. It may date as early as the eighth century BCE. In 1930, just east of the Grand Serail, a quantity of baked-clay figurine fragments of horsemen and a small terra-cotta statuette of a woman, perhaps a goddess, with an Egyptian hairstyle were discovered that belong to the Persian period. Several of these fragments are part of the collection of the Museum of the American University of Beirut.

Classical period. From 1907 to the late 1950s, no major archaeological excavations were conducted in Beirut. Mainly rescue operations attempted to salvage certain Hellenistic, Roman, or Byzantine architectural elements. Important suburbs developed on the sandy beaches south of Beirut during the Roman period. Between Jnah and Ouzai several mosaic floors were uncovered belonging to those seaside villas. High on a mountain overlooking Beirut, at Beit Mery, stand the remains of a Roman settlement and a temple. During the 1960s, the Department of Antiquities excavated the area, whose rich finds of Roman Beirut and its environs are now in the Beirut National Museum.

Beirut's urban plan followed the practice of all Roman city planning: it has two major crossroads, a *Decumanus Maximus* and a *Cardo Maximus.* The information available about this city was assembled into a plan from various unrelated sources by Jean Lauffray in 1914. It is still a useful document (see Saidah, 1969).

Recent Excavations. In 1968, the Department of Antiquities commissioned Haroutine Kalayan to excavate certain monuments in Beirut.

1. An extensive Roman bath near the Grand Serail, with a large cistern and rooms decorated with frescoes were uncovered and partly restored
2. A Roman defensive tower that had been reused in the medieval period
3. A stretch of a Roman street complete with its pavement, columns, capitals, and an architrave in the center of Parliament Square

BEIRUT. Figure 2. *Detail of the Roman baths.* (Courtesy I. Khalifeh)

4. A second Roman bath and part of an important municipal building (a basilica?) that probably covers the *Decumanus Maximus*

In 1969, the Department of Antiquities, represented by Roger Saidah, began to clear an area on the ancient tell, near the port area, where in 1954, MB and LB tombs had been found (see above). Surface finds included a Neolithic hammerstone, some EB combed ware, and MB and LB sherds. No Early Iron Age material was recovered, but some sixth-century BCE jar handles were found. This excavation was the last opportunity to work on the ancient tell. Saidah's results remain unpublished, as he died soon thereafter.

In 1977, when the possibility of reconstructing the modern city was being studied, Ibrahim Kawkabani, under auspices of the Lebanese Department of Antiquities, and J. D. Forest, from the Institut Français d'Archéologie du Proche Orient, undertook a series of soundings to look for the city's ancient law school (see above). The work stopped with the onset of Lebanon's civil war. Twenty soundings were made, producing finds from the Hellenistic, Roman, Byzantine, and Mamluk periods. The material culture unearthed included pottery jars, lamps, and figurines; stamped Rhodian and other jar handles; carved bone objects; metal weights, rings, and handles; sculptured and inscribed reliefs, mortars, and capitals; and weaving utensils. Glass, coins, and gold jewelry, mainly from the Byzantine period, were also recovered but remain unpublished.

In 1977 and 1982, several attempts to reconstruct and restore modern Beirut's central business district were stalled by security considerations. In 1983 and 1984, reconstruction and restoration went forward at a considerable pace. A symposium called Beirut of Tomorrow, held at the American University of Beirut in 1983, called for the protection of historic monuments and for attempts to explore the ancient tell of Beirut. UNESCO experts Ernst Will and Rolf Hachmann were invited to the city in 1983 as consultants.

Early in 1993, UNESCO consultants Philippe Marquis, John Schofield, and Jean Paul Thalmann were contracted to work with the Council for Development and Restoration and the Department of Antiquities. On 10 September 1993, work was begun in downtown Beirut in collaboration with teams from the Lebanese University, the American University of Beirut, Britain, France, the Netherlands, and Italy, and the Royal Museum of Belgium. Five soundings were dug in a three-month period in the downtown area, with the objective of exploring the limits of the ancient town. The teams worked during 1994 and 1995 in and around the ancient town in an area of about 500,000 sq m, expanding the number of soundings to find the Prehistoric, Canaanite, Phoenician, Roman, and medieval cities. Archaeological rescue operations accompanied the construction in the downtown area and will continue to do so.

BIBLIOGRAPHY

Badre, Leila. "The Historic Fabric of Beirut." In *Beirut of Tomorrow*, edited by Friedrich Ragette, pp. 65–76. Beirut, 1983. Historical outline and review of archaeological remains unearthed to the date of publication.

Forest, J. D. "Fouilles a municipalité de Beyrouth, 1977." *Syria* 59 (1982): 1–26. Primarily the results of soundings that produced Roman, Byzantine, and later material.

Jidejian, Nina. *Beirut through the Ages*. Beirut, 1973. Useful history of Beirut.

Mouterde, René, and Jean Lauffray. *Beyrouth ville romaine: Histoire et monuments*. Beirut, 1952. Helpful study of the history and archaeology of Beirut in the Roman period.

Mouterde, René. *Regards sur Beyrouth: Phénicienne, hellénistique et romaine*. Beirut, 1966. Good review of Beirut's historical and archaeological monuments and remains.

Saidah, Roger. "Archaeology in the Lebanon, 1968–1969." *Berytus* 18 (1969): 119–142. Useful information on archaeological activities in the late 1960s.

Saidah, Roger. "The Prehistory of Beirut." In *Beirut: Crossroads of Cultures*, pp. 1–13. Beirut, 1970. Good review of archaeological evidence for the prehistoric periods.

Turquety-Pariset, Françoise. "Fouille de la municipalité de Beyrouth, 1977: Les objects." *Syria* 59 (1982): 27–76. Good catalog of objects from the Roman, Byzantine, and later periods.

Ward, William A. "Ancient Beirut." In *Beirut: Crossroads of Cultures*, pp. 14–42. Beirut, 1970. Uses the scant archaeological remains to reconstruct the history of Beirut, with some freewheeling interpretations.

ISSAM ALI KHALIFEH

BEIT MIRSIM, TELL, site located in the chalk foothills of the eastern Shephelah, about 20 km (12 mi.) southwest of Hebron and 13.5 km (8 mi.) southeast of Tell Lachish (31°27′ N, 34°54′ E; map reference 1415 × 0960). In 1924 William Foxwell Albright identified the 3-ha (8-acre) site as biblical Debir (*Jos.* 15:15–17; *Jgs.* 1:11–15). This identification, however, has been contested, most convincingly, by Moshe Kochavi, who identified Debir with Khirbet Rabud. [*See* Rabud, Khirbet.] Tell Beit Mirsim thus remains without a known biblical identification.

The site was first excavated in four seasons (1926–1932) by a joint expedition from Xenia Theological Seminary and the American Schools of Oriental Research, with Albright serving as field director. Excavations were devoted mainly to a broad exposure in the mound's southeast quadrant, reaching bedrock in some parts. In the northwest sector a large, contiguous area of the uppermost stratum (A) was cleared. For many years Albright's excavation at Tell Beit Mirsim was considered a model of scientific accuracy, and his four volumes of final reports (1932, 1933, 1938, 1943) became a cornerstone for the ceramic typology and chronology of biblical Palestine.

In the 1970s extensive looting led to the discovery of the necropolis of Tell Beit Mirsim, and some thirty tombs were investigated between 1978 and 1982 by the Israel Antiquities Authority; as of 1995 these have yet to be published.

The Mound: Stratification and Principal Finds. Ten major strata (A–J), some of them subdivided into phases, were identified on the site, representing nearly continuous settlement from the Early Bronze Age to the Iron Age II. Albright's excavation method and somewhat sketchy stratigraphic analyses, which consist mainly of identifying major burn layers and homogeneous pottery assemblages, have attracted several attempts at a reassessment of the major strata and finds (see bibliography). The following description of the excavations, while based on Albright's most recent summary (1975), incorporates the results of these more recent reevaluations.

Stratum J: Early Bronze Age. No architectural remains were recovered in stratum J, which consisted of pottery deposits in pockets in the bedrock. The bulk of this pottery is EB III in date—large, pattern-burnished platters; combed-ware jars and pithoi; and spouted vats—with possible fragments of earlier EB forms.

Strata I–H: Early Bronze IV. Fragmentary pavements and masonry were attributed to strata I–H, which are separated by ash deposits. The pottery of the two strata is similar and consists of typical southern EB IV forms: ribbed and inverted rim bowls, ovoid jars, jugs, and cups with combed and applied decoration, some forms with vestigial lug and ledge handles.

Strata G–F: Middle Bronze Age I. Strata G–F represent the beginning of intensive occupation on the mound. While stratum G appears to be an unwalled settlement, with generously proportioned houses, stratum F reveals elements of urban planning—a city wall and adjacent structures built at right angles to it. The city wall, with massive stone foundations some 3.3 m wide, is polygonal in plan, with towers placed at each angle. The houses abut the fortification by means of a common rear wall running along its inner face. Despite evidence of considerable building activity in the two strata, their pottery assemblages were indistinguishable, consisting of forms typical of both earlier and later phases within the MBI.

Strata E–D: Middle Bronze Age II–III. Strata E–D, each subdivided into two phases, represent the zenith of Canaanite Urban civilization at Tell Beit Mirsim. In stratum E, the fortification wall was buttressed by a massive beaten-earth glacis, partly faced with stone. Traces of what may have been a three-entryway gate were unearthed beneath the east gate of the Iron Age town. Within the wall and parallel to it, a street furnished with a stone-lined drain was revealed, lined on both sides by several well-built structures. The stratum was characterized by a rich, well-made ceramic repertoire.

Stratum D continued the stratum E layout, with two perimeter streets and connecting radial alleys clearly defined. A large (200 sq m), thick-walled courtyard building, the "palace," was cleared in the west. Finds in this building included many storejars, as well as stone, metal, and ivory objects—including a game board with a die and gaming pieces—and, most important, the lower part of a cultic stela, interpreted by Albright as a "serpent goddess" but now recognized as a representation of a Canaanite dignitary. Additional noteworthy finds in this stratum are royal Hyksos scarabs (one of *yqb*[*ḥr?*]) and fine Syrian-type cylinder seals.

Stratum C: Late Bronze Age. Following the destruction of the MB town in the mid-sixteenth century BCE, there was a considerable hiatus in settlement. The subsequent architectural phases, C1 and C2, both date to Late Bronze Age II and represent a decline in the site's urban character. The thin, fragmentary perimeter wall ascribed to the latter phase (C2), suggests that the town relied on the MB defenses for protection, and many open spaces between the houses are occupied by grain silos. The LB settlement was destroyed in a fierce conflagration, dated by the ceramic assemblage to about 1225 BCE.

Strata B–A: Iron Age. The stratum C destruction was followed closely by a partial rebuilding. Strata B1–B2(Iron I) are characterized by fragmentary architectural remains and a large number of stone-lined silos, many of them superimposed. The pottery recovered from the silos continues Canaanite traditions, with a small amount of Philistine ware, probably imported from the coast, appearing in B2. A major change came about in stratum B3, dated to the period of the United Monarchy. A 4–4.5-meter-wide casemate wall was built, following the line of the MB fortifications. Of the few structures found within the walls, a series of storerooms abutting the wall is the most prominent.

Following the destruction of stratum B3 at the close of the tenth century, possibly by Shishak, an extended period of relative prosperity set in. The fortifications were rebuilt and repaired along B3 lines, and a new two-entryway gate was built in the east. The gate was later rebuilt as an indirect-entry gate, protected by towers. The town itself was densely built up, with perimeter streets and radial alleys reminiscent of the Bronge Age town plan. Houses were mainly of the pillared three- and four-room type, with those at the perimeter utilizing the wall casemates. Public construction included a large building near the center of the town and a large tower (originally identified by Albright as a city gate) built over the casemate fortifications at the western end of the site. Rock-cut cisterns and oil presses (Albright's dye plants) are ubiquitous.

Albright attributed the destruction of this city to the Babylonians, mainly on the basis of a private seal attributed to a servant of Jehoiachin, the penultimate king of Judah. Later studies of the pottery by Yohanan Aharoni ("The Stratification of Judahite Sites," *BASOR* 224 [1976]: 73–90) and of stamped jar handles by David Ussishkin ("Royal Judean Storage Jars and Private Seal Impressions," *BASOR* 223 1976: 6–11) have established that the destruction should be attributed to Sennacherib's 701 BCE campaign. There is slight ceramic and stratigraphic evidence for a partial reoccupation of the site in the seventh or early sixth century BCE.

The Cemetery. Tell Beit Mirsim's cemetery includes hundreds of tombs—most of them recently robbed—extending in an arc on the southwest and northwest slopes of the mound. Salvage excavations by David Alon and Eliot Braun were conducted on the southwest slope. Intact tombs included EBIV shaft tombs; several MB tombs, exceedingly rich in finds; LB tombs with many imported goods (and, possibly, evidence of an LB I occupation); and rectangular Iron II loculus and shelf tombs. Thousands of vessels and other finds looted from the Tell Beit Mirsim cemetery (and from the mound itself) have made their way to the antiquities market and thence to private and public collections all over the world.

[*See also the biography of Albright.*]

BIBLIOGRAPHY

Excavation Reports

Albright, William Foxwell. *The Excavation of Tell Beit Mirsim*, vol. 1, *The Pottery of the First Three Campaigns*; vol. 1A, *The Bronze Age Pottery of the Fourth Campaign*; vol. 2, *The Bronze Age*; vol. 3, *The Iron Age*. Annual of the American Schools of Oriental Research, 12, 13, 17, 21/22. New Haven, 1932–1943. These four volumes of the final excavation report remain the most comprehensive source for information on the site.

Albright, William Foxwell. "Beit Mirsim, Tell." In *Encyclopedia of Archaeological Excavation in the Holy Land*, vol. 1, pp. 171–178. Jerusalem, 1975. Albright's latest synthesis of the Tell Beit Mirsim finds.

Critical Revision of Stratigraphy and Major Finds (in order of strata)

Dever, William G., and Suzanne Richard. "A Reevaluation of Tell Beit Mirsim Stratum J." *Bulletin of the American Schools of Oriental Research*, no. 226 (1977): 1–14.

Eitan, A. "Tell Beit Mirsim G–F: The Middle Bronze IIA Settlement." *Bulletin of the American Schools of Oriental Research*, no. 208 (1972): 19–24. Reassigns the stratum G fortifications to stratum F.

Yadin, Yigael. "The Tell Beit Mirsim G–F Alleged Fortifications." *Bulletin of the American Schools of Oriental Research*, no. 212 (1973): 23–25. Rejoinder to Eitan (above), suggesting a stratum E date for the fortifications.

Merhav, Rivkah. "The Stele of the 'Serpent Goddess' from Tell Beit Mirsim and the Plaque from Shechem Reconsidered." *Israel Museum Journal* 4 (1985): 27–42. Convincing reidentification of one of the most important MB finds at Tell Beit Mirsim.

Greenberg, Raphael. "New Light on the Early Iron Age at Tell Beit Mirsim." *Bulletin of the American Schools of Oriental Research*, no. 265 (1987): 55–80. Stratigraphic discussion and presentation of previously unpublished material.

RAPHAEL GREENBERG

BEIT RAS, site located in northwestern Transjordan, 5 km (3 mi.) north of Irbid (map reference 680 × 105). Beit Ras was known as Capitolias from the first through the sev-

enth centuries CE and was a member of the Decapolis confederation. Following Islamic hegemony over the region (c. 636 CE), the original Aramaic name, Beit Ras, was reinstituted. To date, no stratified deposits earlier than the first century CE have been excavated, although survey has provided some data earlier than the Roman period. These data, primarily pottery, were found on the *rās*, the highest point (about 600 m) in the immediate vicinity of the site, which may indicate the use of the *rās* as a lookout post prior to the formation of the city.

F. Kruse and H. L. Fleischer (1859), commenting on Ulrich J. Seetzen's travels and explorations (1806) were the first to identify Beit Ras with Capitolias. J. S. Buckingham (1816), Selah Merrill (1881), Gottlieb Schumacher (1890), Nelson Glueck (1951) and Siegfried Mittmann (1970) all visited the site and recorded certain of it's elements. G. Lankester Harding, director of antiquities for the area during the British Mandate, noted the site's importance. The Jordanian Department of Antiquities has conducted salvage excavations there, particularly in the necropolis, during the last thirty years. Systematic archaeological research was begun in 1983 with an intensive survey of the site and its immediate vicinity; excavation, begun in 1985, continues. Because the village is inhabited, research combines archaeological strategies with ethnohistorical research, oral history, and text interpretation, with the aim of elucidating all of the site's past.

In antiquity, the site was walled. The excavated portion of the wall, built in the second century CE of local limestone ashlar blocks, consists of three gates that face north. The gates were altered in the following five centuries, perhaps because of seismiturbation. In the early eighth century CE, one gate was turned into a tower. A walled acropolis has been excavated on the *rās*, evidencing the same constructional techniques and alterations throughout the site's occupational periods as the city wall.

Two levels of a three-tiered marketplace, known from literary sources, has been excavated north of the main *decumanus*, known from the city's oral history. The upper level consists of nine vaults that face north, bounded by vaults that face east and west. The region's natural bedrock was used to construct the marketplace. The rear wall of the vaults is continuous. One vault is a Roman barrel vault; the others were periodically reconstructed throughout Beit Ras's history. The vaults' interior and exterior are covered by utilitarian tesselated pavements. Marble facing found inside the vaults suggests that the upper level of the marketplace was used for selling finished products. This second story evidences the same construction. The vaults were altered considerably in the thirteenth/fourteenth century.

The city's main church has been excavated across from the first level of the vaults. Built on the remains of an earlier

Roman structure, this construction dates to the mid-fifth century. It is likely that it was turned into a mosque in the early eighth century. A three-tiered water installation (ablution pool?) was built against the juncture of the church's central and southern apses. The entire area of the vaults and church remained public space until the tenth century CE, when the space was used for domestic and minor industrial activities.

An intricate water system served the city from its inception in 97/98 CE and subsequently. The absence of springs in the vicinity made the city dependent on rainwater and water brought from a distance. Part of a low aqueduct system was surveyed west of the city, outside the city wall. Inside the city, a well-engineered channel run-off system cut into the bedrock debouched into large cisterns. A reservoir was built on the south side of the city and periodically refurbished throughout the city's history.

The archaeological research to date indicates that Beit Ras/Capitolias was a planned Roman city, probably established for military reasons, and that it flourished in the period between the first and tenth centuries. Excavation has yielded quantities of pottery comparable to that at other Decapolis cities. No hiatus in occupation at the site has yet been found, but a gradual decrease in size and change in use from public space to private space seems to begin as early as the tenth century.

[*See also* Decapolis.]

BIBLIOGRAPHY

Works by the nineteenth-century explorers and travelers mentioned in this entry are not listed below. These works are available only in university or other specialized libraries.

Glueck, Nelson. *Explorations in Eastern Palestine.* Vol. 4. Annual of the American Schools of Oriental Research, 25/28. New Haven, 1951.
Lenzen, C. J., et al. "Excavations at Tell Irbid and Beit Ras, 1985." *Annual of the Department of Antiquities of Jordan* 29 (1985): 151–159.
Lenzen, C. J. "Tall Irbid and Bait Rās." *Archiv für Orientforschung* 33 (1986): 164–166.
Lenzen, C. J., and E. Axel Knauf. "Tell Irbid and Beit Ras, 1983–1986." *Liber Annuus/Studii Biblici Franciscani* 36 (1986): 361–363.
Lenzen, C. J., and E. Axel Knauf. "Beit Ras-Capitolias: A Preliminary Evaluation of the Archaeological and Textual Evidence." *Syria* 64 (1987): 21–46.
Lenzen, C. J., and Alison M. McQuitty. "The 1984 Survey of the Irbid/Beit Rās Region." *Annual of the Department of Antiquities of Jordan* 32 (1988): 265–274.
Lenzen, C. J. "Beit Ras Excavations, 1988 and 1989." *Syria* 67 (1990): 474–476.
Lenzen, C. J. "The Integration of the Data Bases—Archaeology and History: A Case in Point, Bayt Rās." In *Bilād al-Shām during the Abbasīd Period: Proceedings of the Fifth Bilād al-Shām Conference,* vol. 2, edited by Muhammad Adnan al-Bakhit and Robert Schick, pp. 160–178. Amman, 1992.
Lenzen, C. J. "Irbid and Beit Ras: Interconnected Settlements between c. A.D. 100–900." In *Studies in the History and Archaeology of Jordan,* vol. 4, edited by Ghazi Bisheh, pp. 299–307. Amman, 1992.

C. J. LENZEN

BENNETT, CRYSTAL-MARGARET (1918–1987), first director of the British Institute at Amman for Archaeology and History and the excavator of those Edomite sites that have been most extensively investigated. Bennett began her archaeological career relatively late, in 1954, at the Institute of Archaeology in London. At first she participated in excavations in England, later joining Kathleen M. Kenyon's final season at Jericho.

In 1958, while taking part in Peter Parr's excavations at Petra, in Jordan, Bennett became interested in the Iron Age "Edomite" site of Umm el-Biyara in the center of Petra. She excavated there (1960–1965), at the Edomite site of Tawilan (1968–1970, 1982), and at Buṣeirah, the probable capital of Edom (1971–1974, 1980). Although she did not produce a final report for any of these sites, her preliminary reports were regular and comprehensive. Her results made the Edomites archaeologically visible for the first time and considerably revised the then generally accepted chronological picture of Edom. The three Bennett excavations clearly dated Edomite pottery to the seventh century BCE, rather than to the thirteenth century BCE, as was previously thought. Her excavations also revealed strong evidence for Edomite settlement continuity into the Persian period.

Bennett's other major contributions were organizational and diplomatic. She was assistant director of the British School of Archaeology in Jerusalem from 1963 to 1965, and director from 1970 to 1980, overseeing the greater part of the mammoth survey of Mamluk Jerusalem that recorded the Islamic buildings in the Old City (Michael H. Burgoyne, *Mamluk Jerusalem,* London, 1987).

By 1970 Bennett had rented space in Amman at her own expense to provide an office and base for British excavations in Jordan. She was the prime mover, with Kenyon, in founding the British Institute at Amman for Archaeology and History and was its first director (1980–1983). During that time she established the institute as a viable body and developed close links with the Jordanian Department of Antiquities and particularly the Jordanian royal family.

[*See also* British Institute at Amman for Archaeology and History; British School of Archaeology in Jerusalem; Buṣeirah; Edom; Tawilan; *and* Umm el-Biyara.]

BIBLIOGRAPHY

Bienkowski, Piotr. "Umm el-Biyara, Tawilan, and Buseirah in Retrospect." *Levant* 22 (1990): 91–109. Appraisal of Bennett's three major excavations, including a bibliography of her principal preliminary reports.
Homès-Fredericq, Denyse, and J. Basil Hennessy, eds. *Archaeology of Jordan,* vol. 1, *Bibliography.* Louvain, 1986. See pages 32–33 for a comprehensive bibliography of Bennett's work.
Talbot, Geraldine. "Crystal-M. Bennett, O.B.E., D. Litt., F.S.A.: An Appreciation." *Levant* 19 (1987): 1–2. Traces Bennett's career in detail.

PIOTR BIENKOWSKI

BENZINGER, IMMANUEL, (1865–1935), German Protestant theologian, born in Stuttgart. In 1894 Benzinger worked as an assistant at Tübingen, and in 1895 as a pastor in Neuenstadt. From 1897 to 1902 he edited the *Zeitschrift* of the Deutscher Palästina-Verein and served on its executive board until 1912. From 1898 to 1902 he was a lecturer (*privatdozent*) at the University of Berlin. He spent the next ten years in Jerusalem. In fall 1903 he replaced Gottlieb Schumacher, who had been called away on a special assignment, as director of the excavations for the Deutscher Palästina-Verein at Tell el-Mutesellim/Megiddo and published a preliminary report of his work. Benzinger was a professor at the University of Toronto from 1912 to 1915; at Meadville, Pennsylvania, from 1915 to 1918; and at the University of Riga in Latvia from 1921 until his death. He published his scholarship on the Hebrew Bible as well as *Bilderatlas zur Bibelkunde* (Stuttgart, 1905; 2d ed., 1912) and revised Karl Baedeker's travel guidebook *Palästina und Syrien* (Leipzig, from the 3d ed., 1890, to the 7th ed., 1910). His principal work, however, is *Hebräische Archäologie*. In its first edition (1894) using "archaeology" as a source meant describing ancient Israel's private, public, and sacred institutions, based chiefly on the biblical texts. However, in its second edition (1907), which he wrote in Jerusalem, Benzinger began to emphasize the importance of excavations and their discoveries in order to reconstruct a history of the civilization of Israel. This is evident in a new discussion on ceramics and new and more illustrations of archaeological artifacts. In its third edition (1927), Benzinger included many of the important results of excavations that had been made since 1907. Benzinger was a pioneer in publishing the discipline of biblical archaeology.

[*See also* Deutscher Palästina-Verein; Megiddo.]

BIBLIOGRAPHY

Adamovičs, Ludvigs. *Latvijas Universitātes: Teologijas Fakultāte, 1919–1939.* 2d ed. Lincoln, Neb., 1981. Information about Benzinger's activities at Riga and his place in the international community.

Avi-Yonah, Michael. "Benzinger, Immanuel." In *Encyclopaedia Judaica*, vol. 4, p. 574. Jerusalem, 1971. Benzinger's professional activities in Jerusalem and a list of his main works.

Mitteilungen und Nachrichten des Deutschen Vereins zur Erforschung Palästinas. Leipzig, 1895–1912. Primary source for the little biographical data available for Benzinger.

DIETHELM CONRAD

BETH ALPHA, also known as Beit Ilfa or Alfa, site located in the eastern part of the Jezreel Valley, at the foot of Mt. Gilboa. Beth Alpha was settled by Ptolemaic Greeks and was part of Scythopolis, one of the cities of the Roman Decapolis. The city is named after the nearby ruins of Khirbet Beit Ilfa; it shows no occupation before the Roman period. The foundation remains and mosaic floor of a synagogue were accidentally discovered there in 1928 and were excavated in 1929 by Eleazar Lipa Sukenik of the Hebrew University of Jerusalem.

The synagogue, built of untrimmed local limestone, is basilical, with two longitudinal rows of columns and stone benches. It includes a courtyard with columns on the south and enclosing walls on the other sides. The courtyard's columns also formed the north side of the narthex. On the north, a large central door is flanked by two smaller entrances. A side door on the west leads into an annex. It is conjectured that there was an upper gallery over the two aisles and the narthex. Stairs leading to the gallery are believed to have been located in the western annex. It is not clear, however, what the function of such a gallery would have been.

A semicircular external apse at the southern end of the basilica faced Jerusalem and was reached via three narrow steps. Two holes on the second step may have held posts for a curtain to close off the Torah shrine. Evidence of an earlier mosaic pavement was discovered below the present mosaic floor. In its present state the entire building complex has mosaic floors.

The nave mosaic has three panels, whose interpretation has found no scholarly consensus. All the panels are surrounded by a wide decorative border. The northern, or lowest, panel features the Binding of Isaac and is to be read from left to right. Abraham's two servants are depicted with the donkey. One leads the donkey by its reins, and the other stands behind it, but his legs are not visible. A hand emerges from above, symbolic of the hand of God, with the Hebrew inscription from *Genesis* 22:12: "Don't stretch forth [your hand]." A ram is shown tethered to a tree with the Hebrew inscription from *Genesis* 22:13: "Here is the ram." Neither the hand of God nor the ram tied to the tree follow the biblical narrative, but they are in keeping with later Jewish and non-Jewish sources (see below). A bearded and haloed Abraham brandishes a long knife in his right hand; he seems to be grasping Isaac, who is suspended in midair, with his left hand. Both Abraham and Isaac have Hebrew labels. A flaming altar is also depicted.

Isaac floating in midair is found in early Christian depictions, but in them Abraham is shown grasping the ends of a blindfold. Apparently, the provincial Beth Alpha artists, Marianos and his son Hanina, misunderstood their Christian model, leaving only the anomalous projections attached to the boy's neck.

The middle panel depicts the zodiac with the pagan god Helios riding his chariot. Personifications of the four seasons are shown in the four corners, but they do not correspond to the twelve signs of the months, which run counterclockwise. Both the seasons and the months carry labels with their Hebrew names on them. The practice of placing the zodiac in synagogues finds striking analogies in contemporary liturgical poems.

The southern, or uppermost, panel shows the Torah

shrine flanked by two three-footed, seven-branched menorahs, lions, and such ceremonial objects as the shofar, lulav and etrog, incense shovel, and Torah shrine curtains. Whether the objects are symbolic of contemporary synagogal celebrations or relate to the destroyed Jerusalem Temple cult has not been resolved. The Torah shrine also has a lamp suspended from it. Although the lamp is frequently called *nēr tāmîd*, its symbolism is uncertain, as the "eternal light" is not known in synagogue furnishings until the seventeenth century CE.

The synagogue is usually dated to the early sixth century CE on the basis of thirty-six coins—the latest dating from the reign of the Byzantine emperor Justinian I—and an Aramaic inscription referring to Emperor Justinian. Recent research places the synagogue in the third quarter of the sixth centry, on both stylistic and iconographic grounds. An earthquake probably destroyed the synagogue shortly after its construction.

[*See also* Decapolis; Mosaics; Synagogues; *and the biography of Sukenik.*]

BIBLIOGRAPHY

Chiat, Marilyn Joyce Segal. *Handbook of Synagogue Literature*. Chico, Calif., 1982. Includes a good descriptive summation of research on the Beth Alpha synagogue.

Goldman, Bernard. *The Sacred Portal: A Primary Symbol in Ancient Judaic Art*. Detroit, 1966. Suggestive interpretation of the upper mosaic panel.

Gutmann, Joseph. "Revisiting the 'Binding of Isaac' Mosaic in the Beth-Alpha Synagogue." *Bulletin of the Asia Institute* 6 (1992): 79–85. Critical study of the mosaic, with an up-to-date bibliography.

Sukenik, Eleazar L. *The Ancient Synagogue of Beth Alpha*. Jerusalem, 1932. Archaeological report of the excavation.

JOSEPH GUTMANN

BETHEL (Heb., "House of [the god] El"), site located 16 km (10 mi.) north of Jerusalem, on the border of ancient Israel and Judah (31°56′ N, 35°14′ E; map reference 172 × 148), at the juncture of the trunk road from the central hills down to the Jordan Valley. Bethel is mentioned in the Hebrew Bible more times than any site except Jerusalem. It figures prominently not only as a border fortress, but in the patriarchal narratives, in the stories of the period of the Judges, and as an important sanctuary in accounts of the Monarchy.

The site was first identified with the modern Arab village of Beitin by Edward Robinson, the American explorer, in 1838. Excavations were carried out at the site in 1934 by William Foxwell Albright and James L. Kelso for the American Schools of Oriental Research, and again by Kelso in 1954, 1957, and 1960. Kelso published these excavations in 1968 as *The Excavation of Bethel, 1934–1960*. The report lacks stratum designations and information on provenience and mixes factual description with imaginative interpretations (usually biblically inspired), making historical reconstruction almost impossible, except in the broadest sense. The following points have been extracted from that report, however.

The site was first occupied briefly in the Late Chalcolithic period (c. 3200 BCE) and then again in the Early Bronze Age III–IV (c. 2400–2000 BCE)—no doubt because of its hilltop location and nearby springs. Kelso's claim for an EB IV "temple" is fanciful, based as it was more on biblical traditions regarding the Patriarchs than on the evidence; the walls in question are no more than the foundations of the Middle Bronze Age city gate.

The Middle Bronze Age occupation witnessed a gradual urban buildup. The MB I (c. 2000–1800 BCE) is attested only by sherds and tatters of walls. Somewhere in the MB II (c. 1800–1650 BCE), the town was defended by a cyclopean city wall and earthen glacis. The dearth of detail in the report precludes saying anymore. Kelso's description of a northeastern "gate" in this wall suggests that this particular structure is Roman, or at least was destroyed in the Roman period. A northwest gate may well be MB II, but its plan, as published, is enigmatic. The masonry of the town's MB II domestic structures was excellent. The MB III period (c. 1650–1500 BCE) apparently continued without interruption, with the building of more houses and additions to the defenses. Another "sacred area" (or Ar., *haram*) claimed for this phase is largely imaginative. The report is ambivalent about a destruction at the end of the MB III, but there does appear to be a gap in occupation in the Late Bronze IA–B (c. 1500–1400 BCE).

The LB II period (c. 1400–1200 BCE), with two phases, seems particularly well attested. Domestic structures are very well laid out, with courtyards and drains, and the masonry is excellent. A destruction by earthquake is claimed between the two phases, which might be Claude F. A. Schaeffer's notorious 1365 BCE earthquake, if it has any credence. Kelso makes much of the final "Israelite destruction" of the Canaanites (as Albright had), but the little evidence presented is neither well dated nor conclusive. The best indication of change may be the new town plan in the Iron Age I, presumably in the early twelfth century BCE. When Kelso published, our knowledge of this transitional Bronze/Iron Age horizon was limited, but today it is possible to show that the Bethel pottery is indeed typical of the Early Iron Age, "proto-Israelite" ceramic repertoire in the hill country. The four Iron I phases (not numbered in the report) apparently extend from the early twelfth to late eleventh/early tenth centuries BCE. No fortifications are mentioned.

The Iron II period (c. 900–600 BCE) is said to have had three phases (also not numbered). The report offers scant material for the entire period, leaving the biblical accounts of Bethel's importance in the Divided Monarchy without a context. Presumably, occupation at the site ends with the Babylonian destructions in the early sixth century BCE; the report discusses a corpus of sixth-century BCE pottery but without a context. There is some Persian occupation, and the town recovered some of its importance by the Hellenistic-Roman period (the pottery treated by Paul W. Lapp). Travelers mention Bethel in the Byzantine period, from which there are some remains.

BIBLIOGRAPHY

Albright, William F. "The Kyle Memorial Excavation at Bethel." *Bulletin of the American Schools of Oriental Research*, no. 56 (December 1934): 2–15.
Dever, William G. "Archaeological Methods and Results: A Review of Two Recent Publications." *Orientalia* 40 (1971): 459–471.
Kelso, James L. *The Excavation of Bethel, 1934–1960.* Cambridge, Mass., 1968.

WILLIAM G. DEVER

BETH-GAN (also Beit Gan), site located at the edge of a subdivision of Moshavah Yavne'el (Jabneel), in the eastern Lower Galilee, astride the Darb el-Hawarneh, an ancient road connecting Akko with the Hauran (32°43′ N, 35°30′ E; map reference 197 × 235). The site is situated on an alluvial fan near the western edge of the Yavne'el Valley, which has 20 sq km (12 sq. mi.) of potential arable land. The site's rich soil and ample water supply are owed to its adjacent location to Wadi Saruneh and numerous nearby springs. The site is listed in the *Survey of Western Palestine* as a "ruined Arab village built of basaltic stone" (Conder and Kitchener, 1881, p. 382) and was subsequently explored by Aapeli Saarisalo (Saarisalo, 1927, pp. 37–39), who reported finding Late Bronze, Early Iron, Roman-Byzantine, Byzantine, and "Early and Late Arabic" sherds, and by Zvi Gal, who reported finding Iron II pottery (Gal, 1992, p. 33). Harold Liebowitz conducted soundings in 1988 and 1989 on behalf of the University of Texas at Austin, and found Iron I, Late Byzantine, and Mamluk sherds. The first small-scale season of excavation was conducted by Liebowitz in 1992 and was followed by excavations in 1994 and 1995, which yielded the following remains.

LB II sherds in association with a wall were found in a probe in square FO2 at the close of the 1995 season of excavation, confirming Saarisalo's report of discovery of Late Bronze Age sherds and confirming that the Late Cypriot Age milk-bowl sherd found on the surface of the tell in 1992 was not a simple chance discovery. Iron I pottery assemblages were found in association with two superimposed domestic structures in the same square. Iron IIA sherds were found in squares EO2 and EO3 in association with poorly preserved architectural remains, the result of Mamluk disturbance, and in a limited probe in square BO3, where debris adjacent to a disturbed 1.9-meter-long and 1.30-meter-

wide wall that rode under the Roman period east–west wall yielded Iron II pottery and a bronze fibula.

The Persian period is represented by a single restored storage jar found at the base of a Roman-period locus in square BO3 and by large thicked-walled bowl sherds with external thickening and prominent everted ring base (moratoria), found in a sounding. The Roman period was reached only in a narrow probe, where part of a wall with an associated surface with second-century CE cooking pots, bowls, storage jars, and casserole sherds were found. However, Roman-period architectural fragments such as a heart-shaped column segment (reused in the subsequent Late Byzantine phase), suggest that there was a synagogue or church in the Roman period inasmuch as heart-shaped columns are generally associated with synagogues or churches. The Late Byzantine period is represented by a large structure in Area A whose walls contained reused architectural fragments (door jams, ashlar blocks, column bases, and a segment of a heart-shaped column in BO1 and two heart-shaped columns in square AO1). The pottery includes terra sigillata bowls, cooking bowls with horizontal handles, and storage jars with white-painted decorations. Coins found on the surface span a possible twenty-three year period, from the reign of Justinian II and Sophia (565–587 CE) to Tiberias (582–602 CE). A flat bronze cross that resembles examples from Pella, in Jordan, suggests a Christian presence or a mixed population at the site in this period that may have had connections with the population east of the Jordan River. Parts of a Byzantine building with large flagstones and well-cut limestone blocks were found below the Mamluk terrace wall in Area B.

Parts of three Mamluk structures, one of which yielded evidence of architectural phases, were excavated in Area A. Pottery from the period is comparable to assemblages of vessels from Yoqne'am and 'Afula. The single coin found confirms a fourteenth-century CE date for the stratum. In Area B, Liebowitz found a Mamluk terrace wall that was traced for about 18 m, and parts of walls that abutted the terrace on the west.

Adjacent to the wadi, at the western edge of the mound, Liebowitz and his team excavated a check point of a dam used for water management datable to the Late Roman/Byzantine period.

Beth-Gan is significant because of its LB occupation, which supports the idea of a significant presence in the eastern Lower Galilee in that period. Unlike the neighboring Tel Yin'am, which was abandoned before the Byzantine period, this site was occupied during the Late Byzantine and Mamluk periods, enabling an understanding of the regional material culture for these periods in the Yavne'el Valley. Finally, Beth-Gan's location along the Darb el-Hawarneh furthers efforts to reconstruct a picture of intercity and international trade in the eastern Lower Galilee in antiquity.

BIBLIOGRAPHY

Conder, Claude R., and H. H. Kitchener. *The Survey of Western Palestine: Memoirs of the Topography, Orography, Hydrography, and Archaeology*, vol. 1, *Galilee*. London, 1881.

Gal, Zvi. *Lower Galilee during the Iron Age*. Winona Lake, Ind., 1992.

Liebowitz, Harold. "Beit Gan, 1988" (in Hebrew). *Hadashot Arkheologiot* 93 (1989): 96; 94 (1990): 7.

Liebowitz, Harold. "Beit Gan, 1992." *Israel Exploration Journal* 43.4 (1993): 259–263.

Saarisalo, Aapeli. *The Boundary between Issachar and Naphtali: An Archaeological and Literary Study of Israel's Settlement in Canaan*. Helsinki, 1927.

HAROLD A. LIEBOWITZ

BETHLEHEM, modern town occupying the site of the ancient town, located 9 km (5.5 mi.) south–southwest of Jerusalem, 21.5 km (13.5 mi.) north–northeast of Hebron, 23.5 km (15 mi.) west of the Dead Sea, and just east of the main north–south ridge road of the central hill country of Judah (31°42′ N, 35°12′ E; map reference 169 × 123).

Bethlehem may appear in the Amarna tablets (fourteenth century BCE) as "Bit-Laḥmu" (J. A. Knudtzon, ed., *Die El-Amarna Tafeln*, 2 vols., Leipzig, 1915, no. 290), apparently meaning "house of Lahmu," an Assyrian god. The name may have been distorted later to *beth-lehem*, meaning "house of bread." While Bethlehem is mentioned in the Hebrew Bible (cf. *Ru.* 1:19; *Jgs.* 12:8) and is the city where Jesus was born (*Mt.* 2; *Lk.* 2), it is also identified as Ephrath(ah) (cf. *Gn.* 35:19; *Ru.* 4:11; *Mi.* 5:1 [Eng. 5:2]).

Extrabiblically, Bethlehem is mentioned by Justin (*Dial. Trypho* 78.5–6), in the *Protoevangelium of James* (18.1), and by Origin (*Contra Celsum* 1.51) refering to a cave in which Jesus was born. Jerome (*Epis. ad Paul* 58:3) records that Hadrian destroyed the Christian site and built a shrine to Adonis in its place. Jerome's remarks are largely the basis upon which the current identification of the Church of the Nativity rests.

Few excavations have been conducted in the town, except in the vicinity of the Church of the Nativity. However, as a result of investigations in the caves beneath the church and in the process of building a new school in Bethlehem, remains from the Iron Age town tenth–eighth centuries BCE have come to light. The data are insufficient, however, to relate to descriptions in the Hebrew Bible indicating the presence of a well and fortifications at Bethlehem (cf. *2 Sm.* 23:15; *2 Chr.* 11:5–6).

Constantine initiated construction of the Church of the Nativity in Bethlehem in 326 CE over the traditional cave of Jesus' birth, and Queen Helena dedicated it thirteen years later. The building was partially destroyed in a Samaritan revolt in 529, but Justinian quickly ordered its reconstruction. The current building reflects that reconstruction with minor modifications.

William Harvey's excavations in 1934 under the auspices of the Mandatory Department of Antiquities proved that the current structure dates from the time of Justinian and not Constantine, although the Justinian structure follows many of the Constantinian foundations. The Constantinian church consisted of a square basilica (about 26.5 m to a side), divided by four rows of nine columns into a 9-meter-wide nave with two aisles on each side. The excavations revealed a patterned mosaic floor above the original column bases but 50–60 cm below the modern floor. Hence, the Constantinian structure appears to have undergone some modification before its destruction at the hands of the Samaritans. An octagonal apse stood over the traditional grotto. The octagon measured 7.9 m on each side. Later alterations to the bedrock in the grotto destroyed the original entrance.

Justinian added an atrium to the western end of the basilica, extending its length by 6.5 m, and strengthened the walls to protect the building from attackers. The central nave was widened to 10.5 m, narrowing the adjacent aisles accordingly. Under Justinian's auspices the octagonal apse was replaced with a triapsal arrangement, and the north and south entrances to the grotto were introduced. All subsequent modifications to the building have been minor.

BIBLIOGRAPHY

Bagatti, Bellarmino. "Bethléem." *Revue Biblique* 72 (1965): 270–272.

Gutman, S., and A. Berman. "Bethléem." *Revue Biblique* 77 (1970): 583–585.

Harvey, William. *Structural Survey of the Church of the Nativity, Bethlehem*. London, 1935.

Saller, Sylvester J. "Iron Age Remains from the Site of a New School at Bethlehem." *Studium Biblicum Franciscanum/Liber Annuus* 18 (1968): 153–180.

Schultz, Robert W., et al. *The Church of the Nativity at Bethlehem*. London, 1910.

Stockman, Eugene. "The Stone Age of Bethlehem." *Studium Biblicum Franciscanum/Liber Annuus* 17 (1967): 129–148.

Vincent, L.-H., and Félix-Marie Abel. *Bethléem, le sanctuaire de la nativité*. Paris, 1914.

DALE W. MANOR

BETH-PELEṬ. See Far'ah, Tell el- (South).

BETHSAIDA, site located 2.5 km (12 mi.) north of the Sea of Galilee and a few hundred meters from the Jordan River (map reference 209 × 257). Following the death of Herod the Great in 4 BCE, the region of Bethsaida became a part of the tetrarchy of his son Philip (Josephus, *Antiq.* 17.189; *Lk.* 3:1). Sometime during the second decade of the first century CE, Jesus withdrew to Bethsaida upon hearing of John the Baptist's death (*Lk.* 9:10) and performed some of his "mighty works" there. Toward the end of Jesus' ministry in the area, when he realized that not many would follow him, he condemned Bethsaida to humiliation, along with

Capernaum and Chorazin (*Mt.* 11:21; *Lk.* 10:13). [*See* Capernaum; Chorazin.]

In 30 CE, Bethsaida was elevated to the status of a Greek polis by Philip Herod and renamed Julias, after Livia-Julia, Augustus's wife and Tiberius's mother, who had died a few months earlier (Josephus, *Antiq.* 18.28; *War* 2.9.1). Josephus's statement that the renaming was after Julia, Augustus's daughter, should be corrected based upon numismatic evidence. Philip died in 34 CE in Bethsaida and was buried in a magnificent funeral (*Antiq.* 18.108).

In 65–66, the Roman armies of Agrippa II clashed with rebels in a series of battles that failed to result in a clear victory for either side (Josephus, *Life* 71–73). The archaeological evidence is that the city was destroyed and never rebuilt.

Bethsaida is mentioned by biblical interpreters and in pilgrims' accounts beginning in the fourth century. Most of these descriptions point to a few locations at the north of the Sea of Galilee, perhaps neither to the correct site. A scholarly controversy over its identification began at the end of the sixteenth century. Based on *John* 12:21, which places Bethsaida in Galilee, and Josephus (*Antiq.* 18.28) and other Gospel citations, which place it in the Golan, scholars deduced that there were two such places: one named Bethsaida in Galilee—namely, on the west side of the Jordan River—and the other, Julias—on the east side. The quest for the proper site reemerged with the rise of modern biblical research. In the first half of the nineteenth century, a few scholars proposed identifying Bethsaida with a large mound named et-Tell at the northern corner of the Bteha plain, 2.5 km (1.5 mi.) from the Sea of Galilee. In the 1880s Gottlieb Schumacher maintained that it was implausible for a fishermen's village to have been located so far from water. He proposed two sites located on the shore: el-Araj, a few hundred meters from the mouth of the Jordan, and el-Mesadiyeh, a small ruin father to the southeast. [*See the biography of Schumacher.*]

In 1987 the archaeological investigation of the site of Bethsaida began on behalf of the University of Haifa. Probes were carried out at Tell Araj and et-Tell. As et-Tell alone yielded levels dating to the period in question, excavations have continued exclusively there. In 1991 a consortium of university scholars for the excavations of Bethsaida was formed, headed by the University of Nebraska at Omaha.

Et-Tell/Bethsaida is the largest mound near the northern Sea of Galilee. Its ancient ruins lie on a basalt hill, an extension of the lava plains that form the Golan Heights. The mound (450 × 200 m) rises 25 m above its surroundings. Two peaks and a saddle form its summit, and steep slopes descend from all sides, except at its northern corner. A spring, now hidden by bushes, flows down its western slope toward the Jordan. Probes opened on the summit revealed four periods of occupation.

The first settlement dates to the Early Bronze I period (3100–2850 BCE) and continued uninterrupted through the EB II (2850–2650 BCE), when the settlement was surrounded by a very thick wall built of huge boulders. Parts of this wall have survived to a height of 1.30 m.

The next period of occupation at the site of Bethsaida occurred during the end of Iron Age I and the beginning of Iron Age II (eleventh century BCE). This was a very intensive period of occupation and constructions. Although segments of the Early Bronze Age city walls were put back into use, particularly as revetment walls, a new city wall was constructed. It was built as a series of offsets and insets on the exterior and the interior faces of the wall. In addition to this, towers were constructed. The width of the city wall varies between 6 and 7 m. The tower that was discovered at the east added 2 m to the city wall.

The northeast area of the mound forms the summit of the site and the upper city. New revetment walls were built there to loop large basalt bedrock boulders that could not be removed. This area was filled with red clay material and formed the platform of the upper city, where new constructions were added. A tower that was excavated at the southern revetment wall may indicate that few other towers were constructed astride this wall. Thus far, excavations at the summit reveal two main structures: one in the north and the other in the south of a large plaza, adjacent to the city wall and tower. The massive structures were of large and heavy basalt boulders that measure 1.4 m in width and indicate that they were built for public purposes.

The building at the north was a rectangular structure of 20 × 30 m in the form of the Aramean-Assyrian palaces known as *bit-ḥilani*. Architectural elements, such as a porch, that preceded the facade were thoroughly destroyed by later constructions and a modern Syrian military trench. At the facade a rectangular vestibule room with two antae and a single large pillar out of presumably two, have survived. Behind the vestibule a large rectangular room was discovered that is interpreted to be a throne room. West of the vestibule a rectangular service room has been discovered and at the east, another room was found. This room contained an Egyptian statuette known as Pataekos, highly competent artistically (see figure 1). A row of four smaller storage rooms were unearthed at the northern side of the palace. One of these rooms contained more than twenty complete vessels; some of them are Cypro-Phoenician and Samarian ware. In addition, an Israelite bulla in Phoenician style testifies correspondence with Samaria and an existence of an archive were also discovered.

In the eighth century the palace may have gone out of use as the modification and alternation of its rooms may imply. The throne room was divided into two halls by a relatively thinner partition wall. Large numbers of loom weights and spindle whorls suggest that some sections of the palace were utilized for a garment industry. Other changes included blocking the entrances to the back storage rooms, installa-

BETHSAIDA. Figure 1. *Faience statuette of the Egyptian dwarf god Pataekos.* Iron Age II period. (Courtesy R. Arav)

tions at the vestibule, and two brick benches in the northern of these aforementioned halls.

In front of this building there was a large, well-paved piazza. The plaza contained a canal that led to a row of three standing stones in the form of stelae. At the east the piazza reached the city wall and at the south there was another public building. The city wall was constructed by large boulders at the exterior and the interior faces. The core of the wall was made of large field stones. The width of the wall varies from 5.5 to 6.5 m. A strong tower was added to the wall east of the piazza and created a majestic width of 8 m to the wall.

The building at the south was built by large boulders and was preserved at one point to an elevation of 2 m. The function of this building is yet unclear. Thus far the facade of the structure has been entirely excavated. It contains an en-

trance 1.7 m wide built in an impressive wall. A large, broad room, divided in a later period into two sections, is behind the entrance. A column base and a column drum that were found in a later deposit may originate from the area of the entrance or belong to the missing porch of the *bit-ḥilani*. A large cavity was excavated in front of the entrance during the last period of the Iron Age and the entire floor and whatever was in front of it were removed.

Bethsaida was not abandoned at the end on the Iron Age. A small but distinctive layer of occupation during the Persian period was discerned during the dig. Unfortunately, this layer was too poor and its remains too fragmentary to retrieve a comprehensive ground plan. However, the settlement resumed to a remarkable extent when the next period, the Hellenistic, emerged. The ancient city walls most probably remained at a fairly high level and therefore were reused, as were other sections and walls of the old Iron Age public buildings. The overall view of the settlement during the Hellenistic and Early Roman periods seems to be thoroughly different from the Iron Age. Simple private homes occupy the summit; the former Iron Age upper city remains were observed and reused. The impression was of a peculiar combination of a fishing village within city walls. A few private houses were excavated thus far. Two of them were preserved fairly well and present a similar ground plan. They were built in the typical courtyard pattern. The main core of the building is a central courtyard where most of the home activities, perhaps, were carried out. The kitchen is the next largest room, occupying the eastern section of the house. The residential quarter is located at the north. The southern courtyard house contains many fishing implements, including lead net weights and other implements indicative that the owner of the house was a fisherman. The northernmost of the houses was preserved to a better state. It contained four iron sickles for harvesting grapes and a wine cellar (see figure 2). These finds imply that the owner of the house was a wine dresser. An interesting discovery at this house was a cross incised on a sherd of pottery, discovered next to the entrance to the residential quarter. In addition, architectural elements and remains of a monumental building were discovered scattered on the surface. The location and the function of this building are still unknown.

The later history of Bethsaida is a history of destruction and ruin. Throughout the fourteenth and fifteenth centuries CE, the site suffered severely from intensive stone looting. Limestone blocks, columns, capitals, architectural elements and decorations, and perhaps statues and sculptures that once adorned the town were taken away. In addition to this, hundreds of bedouin tombs were dug in the mound in the last few centuries. The excavations have uncovered over one hundred tombs dug into the walls and floors of the Iron Age and Hellenistic buildings. However, the most destructive period for the site occurred rather recently, when the mound served as a Syrian military stronghold until 1967. Military

Fourth R 4.1 (January 1991): 1–4. Short summary of Bethsaida research, including a survey of excavation results.

Arav, Rami, and John J. Rousseau. "Bethsaida, ville perdue et retrouvée." *Revue Biblique* (1993): 415–428.

Kindler, Arieh. "The Coins of the Tetrarch Philippus, Son of Herod I, and the Renaming of Bethsaida/Julias." *Cathedra* 53 (1989): 24–26 (in Hebrew). Presents numismatic evidence for the renaming of Bethsaida after Livia-Julia in 30 CE.

Kuhn, H.-W., and Rami Arav. "The Bethsaida Excavations: Historical and Archaeological Approaches." In *The Future of Early Christianity: Essays in Honor of Helmut Koester,* edited by Birger A. Pearson, pp. 77–106. Minneapolis, 1991. Detailed survey of research, including a preliminary report on the first three seasons.

McCown, Chester C. "The Problem of the Site of Bethsaida." *Journal of the Palestine Oriental Society* 10 (1930): 32–58.

Pixner, Bargil. "Searching for the New Testament Site of Bethsaida." *Biblical Archaeologist* 48 (1985): 207–216. The last study prior to the excavations.

Robinson, Edward, et al. *Biblical Researches in Palestine and the Adjacent Regions: A Journal of Travels in the Years 1838 and 1852.* 3 vols. 2d ed. London, 1856. For et-Tell, see volume 2, pages 412–414; for Tabqa as Bethsaida, see volume 2, pages 404–406, and volume 3, page 358.

Rousseau, John J., and Rami Arav. *Jesus and His World.* Minneapolis, 1995.

RAMI ARAV

BETHSAIDA. Figure 2. *Cellar with winejars.* Found adjacent to a Hellenistic-Early Roman courtyard house in area C. (Courtesy R. Arav)

trenches, bunkers, and positions of all kinds crisscross the site, leaving upheaval and destruction.

In antiquity the Bethsaida plain was a bay of the Sea of Galilee. Geological investigations reveal that landslides in the upper Jordan River gorge blocked the river and formed catastrophic floods. Torrents of gravel and mud filled the bay and isolated the fishing town of Bethsaida, leaving only a small lagoon between the town and the Sea of Galilee. Another flood during the second century CE filled the lagoon almost entirely and shifted the seashore away from the city.

BIBLIOGRAPHY

Arav, Rami. "Et-Tell and el-Araj." *Israel Exploration Journal* 38 (1988): 187–188; 39 (1989): 99–100; "Bethsaida, 1989" *Israel Exploration Journal* 41 (1991): 184–186; "Bethsaida, 1992" *Israel Exploration Journal* 42 (1992): 252–254.

Arav, Rami. "A Mamluk Drum from Bethsaida." *Israel Exploration Journal* 43 (1993): 241–245.

Arav, Rami, and Richard Freund. *Bethsaida, A City by the Shore of the Sea of Galilee.* Kirksville, Mo., 1995.

Arav, Rami, and John J. Rousseau. "Elusive Bethsaida Recovered." *The*

BETH-SHEAN (also Beth-Shan; Ar., Tell el-Ḥuṣn), site located at the intersection of two major roads that cross the land of Israel from west to east (through the Jezreel and Beth-Shean Valleys toward Transjordan) and from north to south (along the Jordan Valley). The mound, about 4 ha (10 acres) in area, is located on a steep natural hill on the southern bank of the Harod River, in the midst of a fertile, well-watered valley. The site was settled intermittently from the Late Neolithic period until the Middle Ages. [*See* Jordan Valley.]

Although the appearance of the name *Beth-Shean* in the Egyptian Execration texts of the Middle Kingdom is questionable, it does appear in various Egyptian New Kingdom sources: the topographic lists of Thutmose III, Seti I, and Rameses II; the Amarna tablets (in which it is mentioned only once); and Papyrus Anastasi I also from the reign of Rameses II. During this period (sixteenth–thirteenth centuries BCE) Beth-Shean was an Egyptian administrative center, second in importance only to Gaza. In the Bible, Beth-Shean is one of the cities from which the Israelites, at the time of the conquest, did not rout Canaanites (*Jos.* 17:11; *Jgs.* 1:27), and the city onto whose walls the Philistines "fastened" the body of Saul and those of his sons (*1 Sm.* 31:10). Later, it is a city in the fifth district of Solomon (*1 Kgs.* 4:12) and is on the list of cities Shishak conquered during his campaign in the land of Israel (c. 918 BCE) shortly after the monarchy was divided. In the Hellenistic, Roman, and Byzantine periods, the city was known as Nysa or Scythopolis, during which time it is attested in the written record. It was recorded as well by Theodorich of Würzburg, who visited the town in 1172. During the Early Islamic period, it was once again called by its ancient Semitic name, in the form of Beisan; a nearby Arab town preserved the name, making the identification of the site certain.

The University Museum of the University of Pennsylvania carried out excavations at Beth-Shean from 1921 to 1933, under the direction variously of Clarence S. Fisher, Alan Rowe, and Gerald M. FitzGerald. They exposed the site's uppermost strata (Early Islamic and Byzantine periods) across the mound; their work on the upper part of the mound was more limited, but they cleared an extensive cemetery to the north of it. As the first large-scale stratigraphic excavations conducted in Palestine after World War I, the work contributed significantly to the archaeology of the biblical period despite deficiencies in excavation methods and publication. In 1983, Yigael Yadin and Shulamit Geva of the Institute of Archaeology of the Hebrew University in Jerusalem excavated briefly on the summit. Since 1989, Amihai Mazar has been working there, under the auspices of the university and the tourism authority at Beth-Shean; his on-going excavations have reexamined almost all the site's occupation layers, refining its stratigraphic sequences.

Neolithic–Early Bronze Age: Strata XVIII–XI. An 8.5-meter-deep layer of occupation debris dating from the Neolithic period to the Early Bronze Age attests to the importance of these periods at Beth-Shean. However, very little is known about them. In stratum XVIII, the Pottery Neolithic period (fifth millennium) is represented by pits dug into the bedrock. In stratum XVII, the Chalcolithic period (fourth millennium) is represented by pottery. Strata XVI–XIV, the Early Bronze I (thirty-fifth to thirty-first centuries BCE), produced an oval dwelling, gray-burnished pottery, and bronze axes, all typical of the period. Strata XIII–XI appear to be EB II–III occupation layers (thirtieth to twenty-fourth centuries BCE). A rich assemblage of Khirbet Kerak ware, reflecting Anatolian influences, characterizes its last phase. The latest excavations uncovered a very shallow occupation level, perhaps evidence of a seasonal settlement of the EB IV/Middle Bronze I transitional period (2300–2000 BCE). Pottery typical of the Jezreel and Beth-Shean Valleys has been recovered from many MBI burial caves in the Northern Cemetery.

Middle and Late Bronze Ages: Strata X–VII. A gap existed in the occupation of the tell during the first phase of the Middle Bronze Age (William Foxwell Albright's MB IIA, or MB I, c. 2000–1800 BCE), although the tomb of a warrior from this period was discovered in the Northern Cemetery. Three settlement layers belong to the MB IIB–C periods (MB II–III; mainly seventeenth-sixteenth centuries BCE) were discerned in the recent excavations (stratum X in the nomenclature of the earlier excavations). Dwellings of this period yielded high-quality domestic pottery and luxury objects, indicating an advanced standard of living. No fortifications were discovered. The period's last occupation

phase is characterized by pottery of the so-called chocolate-on-white ware.

Settlement in the Late Bronze Age generally reflects Egyptian hegemony and is divided into five phases. The first settlement phase, in LB I, occurs before the Egyptian occupation. Of the four phases that followed, strata IXB–A date to the fifteenth and fourteenth centuries BCE and strata VIII–VII to the thirteenth century BCE.

Five successive temples of the Late Bronze and Iron Age I periods were found on the summit of the tell. Mazar's excavations revealed the earliest temple in an occupation level later than MB stratum X and earlier than LB IIA stratum IX, which should be dated to LB I. This modest (11.7 × 14.6 m) building's plan is unique: it is tripartite and includes an entrance hall, a central hall with benches and raised platforms, and an inner room (sanctuary) whose walls were lined with benches. The entrances, however, are not on the same axis. In stratum IX (divided into two subphases) a large sacred area was established in which various structures surrounded a central courtyard. On the east, the main part of the complex included a monumental hall and an additional cultic room. The plan of this holy precinct is unique and has no parallel at any known temples in Canaan. Outstanding among the many finds attesting to an Egyptian presence is the Mekal stela, a small stone monument carved with a cultic scene that is Egyptian in style and that was dedicated by an Egyptian official to the memory of his father. The iconography in the scene includes a seated god whose dress and attributes are Canaanite. A large building partially preserved at the edge of the tell south of the sanctuary yielded one of the most outstanding relics of Canaanite monumental art: a basalt orthostat carved with two scenes, each of which depicts a struggle between a lion and a dog (or a lioness).

The stratum IX town was destroyed by a massive conflagration but was soon rebuilt on a new plan (strata VIII–VII, thirteenth century BCE), perhaps during the reign of Seti I. A new temple, with an entrance vestibule, was erected on a north–south axis. The ceiling of its main hall was supported by two pillars, and its holy of holies was raised about 1.5 m above the floor in the main hall. A foundation deposit, found underneath the steps leading to the holy of holies, yielded a rich assemblage of precious objects, including dozens of cylinder seals and numerous pendants. In a residential quarter east of the temple, houses lined the street. Rowe called a massive building southwest of the temple a *migdol*, a "tower" or inner "citadel," which would have been the seat of the representative of the Egyptian government at Beth-Shean; however, both its reconstructed plan and its supposed function are suspect. A large round silo found nearby may have been used by the Egyptians to garrison their soldiers.

Three locally made basalt Egyptian royal (nineteenth dynasty) stelae found in later contexts belong to this stratum, evidence of Beth-Shean's prestige as an Egyptian administrative center in the Late Bronze Age. The text on one of the three stelae relates that during the reign of Seti I, Egyptian units put down a rebellion in the northern Jordan Valley at Hamath (Tell el-Ḥammeh) and Peḥal (Pella). The text also mentions the cities of Reḥob, Yano'am, and Beth-Shean. A second stela from the reign of Seti I preserves the record of military action in the hill country against raiding 'Apiru and Theru. These actions were meant to shore up Egypt's administration of Canaan, which, at the end of the eighteenth dynasty, had been weakened. The third stela bears a standard laudatory inscription of Rameses II.

Iron Age I: Upper and Lower Stratum VI. Two strata (lower VI and upper VI; "lower" and "upper" are the terms used by the University of Pennsylvania excavators) are attributable to Iron I. Lower stratum VI is dated to the time of the twentieth dynasty (twelfth century BCE), namely to the final stage of Egyptian administration in Canaan. In this stratum the buildings of stratum VII were rebuilt, retaining the earlier town plan. The temple of the stratum VII city was rebuilt, but changes were made in its entrance vestibule and holy of holies. To its north were found administrative buildings whose architectural details are Egyptian in style. The most important of these buildings is the Governor's Residence (building 1500), a square structure with a central hall surrounded by rooms (see figure 1). Two monumental pillars supported the ceiling in the hall; door sills and inscribed doorjambs, and two lotus-shaped column capitals found nearby that may belong to it, are all distinctly Egyptian. Additional Egyptian friezes, reliefs, and inscribed door jambs were recovered from adjacent buildings. The inscrip-

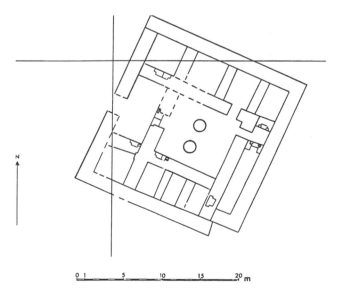

BETH-SHEAN. Figure 1. *Plan of building 1500, the Governor's Residence.* (Courtesy University of Pennsylvania Museum, Philadelphia)

tions are dedications, prayers, vows, personal names, and titles. The most important is a dedicatory inscription of an official named Rameses Weser Khepesh. He may have been the governor of Beth-Shean during the reign of Rameses III, whose life-sized statue, found in the following level, probably originated in this stratum. These finds, as well as locally made Egyptian pottery, attest to the intensive Egyptian presence in the city during the twentieth dynasty.

During the reign of Rameses VI or Rameses VIII, as Egypt's control over Canaan was waning, lower stratum VI was destroyed in a violent conflagration. Among the finds in the destruction level were bronze stands similar to ones known from Cyprus and the Mycenaean IIIC sherds of vessels that most probably were imported from Cyprus.

In the Northern Cemetery many strata VII and VI tombs were found that held fragments from more than fifty anthropoid clay coffins (see figure 2). The lids of most represent human faces, five of them in what is known as the grotesque style reminiscent of the anthropoid coffins from Deir el-Balaḥ in the Sinai Desert. [*See* Deir el-Balah.] An Egyptian funerary influence and contemporary Egyptian funerary customs are clear. On the forehead of three of the lids is a headdress that resembles the one worn by the Sea Peoples in the wall reliefs at Medinet Habu in Egypt. The finds from these tombs include bronze vessels, Egyptian-style Ushabti figurines, jewelry, ivories, and weapons. The coffins were probably used to bury Egyptian officials and military personnel, although some of the coffins with grotesque lids may have been for mercenaries who originated among the Sea Peoples. There are no burials in this cemetery later than the end of the period of Egyptian domination in Canaan (mid-twelfth century BCE).

In upper stratum VI the town was rebuilt following the violent destruction of lower stratum VI. Some of the streets and ruined buildings of the previous city were reutilized, while many others went out of use. The material culture is typical of the eleventh century BCE. During this period, Beth-Shean was probably settled by Canaanites and perhaps by some of the Sea Peoples. The American excavators identified a pair of public buildings they uncovered above the temples of the previous strata as twin temples: "the House of Ashtoreth" (*1 Sm.* 31:10) and "the House of Dagon" (*1 Chr.* 10:10) mentioned in accounts of the Philistines removing Saul's armor and impaling his head on the wall of Beth-Shean. Although attributed by the excavators to stratum V, the buildings may belong to upper stratum VI. These buildings were damaged by later construction work, so that many details of their plans are lost. Access to the southern temple, a long building, was indirect, through its large entrance hall in the front. The building's main room is a large rectangular hall with auxiliary rooms on its two long sides. The ceiling of this central hall rested on two rows of three columns each. Access to the northern temple, which could be reached from the southern temple through a narrow corridor, was also indirect and led to a central hall in which four columns supported the ceiling. The rich assemblage of cultic vessels found in the temples includes an assortment of ceramic cult stands. Many are multitiered, possibly to suggest multistoried temples, and are decorated with human and animal figures. Others are cylindrical with applied decoration of snakes in relief.

Several of the above-mentioned Egyptian monuments of the nineteenth and twentieth dynasties were found in the large courtyard in front of the northern temple. An Egyptian stela dedicated to Antit was discovered in the northern temple. These Egyptian monuments predate the context in which they were found, suggesting that they came to be venerated in local tradition and were passed from stratum to stratum in a cultic context. The recent excavations showed that this town was also destroyed by fire, perhaps during the conquest of Beth-Shean by King David in the early tenth century BCE.

Iron Age II: Strata V and IV. It is difficult to interpret Beth-Shean's development in the tenth–eighth centuries BCE because of the complicated remains in stratum V. The original excavators subdivided the stratum into two phases: lower V and upper V. However, the temples attributed to lower V should probably be dated to the eleventh century BCE (upper VI). A large, well-planned architectural complex north of the temples, apparently an administrative center, may belong to the tenth century BCE, along with a partially preserved public building the recent excavations uncovered. The latter was severely burned, perhaps as a result of Shishak's invasion in about 918 BCE. It may be that the buildings in the northwest section of the excavated area, whose construction with ashlars and stone pillars is characteristically Israelite, were also built in the tenth century BCE. One of the buildings appears to have been used as a city gate through which the administrative complex on the acropolis could be reached. A large hall to the east of this gate was either a royal storehouse or a stable.

The upper phase of stratum V, as well as a few poorly preserved buildings attributed to stratum IV (ninth–eighth centuries BCE), indicates a later date for the town. The new excavations revealed a well-preserved large building that was destroyed by heavy fire, probably during Tiglath-Pileser III's conquest of the region in 732 BCE. A few structures may represent a partial resettlement following the conquest.

Persian–Roman Periods: Stratum III. In the Persian period, the tradition of Beth-Shean as a cultic place may have been perpetuated in the vicinity of the temples, which is indicated by the discovery from that period of several ceramic figurines on the tell itself. The Hellenistic period is represented by a hoard of tetradrachmas, as well as by an occupation layer from the second and first centuries BCE identified by the recent excavations. It appears that the tell was occupied after the Hasmoneans destroyed the nearby large settlement at Tel Istaba. The Early Roman period

BETH-SHEAN.   Figure 2.   *Anthropoid sarcophagus in situ.* (Courtesy University of Pennsylvania Museum, Philadelphia)

(stratum III) is represented by what appears to have been an isolated structure on the summit. Interpreted as the remains of a monumental temple, it towered over the civic center that had grown up around the foot of the mound. Several of its architectural elements were a rectangular stone podium, column fragments, and Corinthian capitals. Late Hellenistic and Early Roman tombs were uncovered in the site's Northern Cemetery.

Byzantine, Islamic, and Crusader Periods: Strata II–I. The entire tell was resettled in the Byzantine period (stratum II). A round church, typical of the fifth century CE, was constructed on the summit and embellished with a mosaic floor and carved capitals. In the northern part of the tell a residential quarter filled with grand houses was clustered on a ledge to the east. On the tell itself, another well-protected neighborhood of large, well-built houses existed, a suburb of the large Byzantine city to the south and west. During the Early Islamic period (stratum I) a residential quarter appeared here as well. At the northwestern corner of the tell a thin circumference wall and a city gate have been identified that probably date to the Crusader period.

BIBLIOGRAPHY

With the exception of Mazar (1993), all of the items below are University of Pennsylvania reports of the excavations.

FitzGerald, Gerald M. *The Four Canaanite Temples of Beth-Shan: The Pottery.* Beth-Shan II.2. Philadelphia, 1930.

FitzGerald, Gerald M. *Beth-Shan Excavations 1921–23: The Arab and Byzantine Levels.* Beth-Shan III. Philadelphia, 1931.

FitzGerald, Gerald M. "The Earliest Pottery of Beth-Shan." *The Museum Journal* 24 (1935): 5–22.

James, Frances. *The Iron Age at Beth Shan: A Study of Levels VI–IV.* Philadelphia, 1966.

Mazar, Amihai. "The Excavations at Tel Beth-Shean in 1989–1990." In *Biblical Archaeology Today: Proceedings of the Second International Congress on Biblical Archaeology, Jerusalem, June–July 1990,* edited by Avraham Biran et al., pp. 606–619. Jerusalem, 1993. Report of the excavations of the Hebrew University.

Mazar, Amihai. "Beth Shean in the Iron Age: Preliminary Report and Conclusions of the 1990–1991 Excavations." *Israel Exploration Journal* 43 (1993): 201–229.

Oren, Eliezer D. *The Northern Cemetery of Beth-Shan.* Leiden, 1973.

Rowe, Alan. *The Topography and History of Beth-shan.* Beth-Shan I. Philadelphia, 1930.

Rowe, Alan. *The Fourth Canaanite Temple of Beth-Shan.* Beth-Shan II.1. Philadelphia, 1940.

AMIHAI MAZAR

BETH-SHE'ARIM (Ar., Sheikh Abreik; map reference 2344 × 1624), site located in southwestern Galilee near modern Tiv'on, some 20 km (12 mi.) east of Haifa, facing the western extremity of the Jezreel Valley. The identification of this site with the Beth-She'arim of rabbinic literature is confirmed by the correlation between the archaeological finds from the enormous necropolis discovered there, several literary sources, and an inscription found at the site that mentions the town's Greek name, Besa[ra] (see below).

Referred to by Josephus as Besara (*Life* 24. 118–119) and in the rabbinic literature as Beth-Sharei and Beth-Sharein, the site is first mentioned in connection with Berenice, the wife of Agrippa II, who owned property in the Jezreel Valley (*Life* 24. 118–119). From the early second century CE onwards, at least one sage, Yohanan ben Nuri, was associated specifically with Beth-She'arim (cf., Tosefta, *Suk.* 2:2). Beth-She'arim, however, achieved its prominence owing to the extended residence there of the editor of the Mishnah, Rabbi Judah I (B.T., *San.* 32b). Although he spent the last part of his ministry in nearby Sepphoris, Rabbi Judah nevertheless left explicit instructions that he wished to be buried at Beth-She'arim. The Jerusalem Talmud describes his funeral cortege in detail (*Kil.* 9.4.32b); for the next century and a half, Beth-She'arim served as the central necropolis for Jews throughout Palestine and the Diaspora (cf., J. T., *Mo'ed Q.* 3.5.82c).

The principal excavations at the site were carried out in the 1930s and 1950s. Between 1936 and 1940, four seasons of excavation were conducted by Benjamin Mazar of the Hebrew University of Jerusalem. Eleven burial complexes were discovered, in addition to the remains of a city wall and a synagogue and its various annexes. Between 1953 and 1958, Nahman Avigad, also of the Hebrew University, discovered an additional twelve catacombs (nos. 12–23, and 30) during his four seasons of excavation at the site. In summer 1956, Mazar returned to Beth-She'arim for one season and uncovered three additional catacombs (nos. 24–26), as well as a large basilica.

Five main building phases have been identified at Beth-She'arim: Period I (first and early second centuries CE), several walls and isolated burials; Period II (late second and early third centuries CE, the period of Rabbi Judah I), extensive expansion of the necropolis and the erection of other public buildings; Period III (mid-third to mid-fourth centuries CE, whose *terminus ad quem* is about 352 CE, evidenced by a destruction layer probably from the aftermath of the Gallus Revolt), construction of the majority of catacombs and a synagogue (only sketchily reported); Period IV (Byzantine era), a small, modest settlement; and Period V (Arab period), a very brief span of settlement.

The various catacombs at the site differ from one another in size and style. Most consist of a series of connected caves (or halls), with burial places (trough-shaped *kôkhîm*, or arcosolia) cut into the walls. Remains of sarcophagi were found in a number of catacombs; the largest concentration was in catacomb 20, which contained the remains of 130 sarcophagi. Several catacombs (nos. 14, 20, and possibly 23) were especially monumental and consisted of a spacious outer courtyard and facade, the latter consisting of four engaged pillars, a large central arch, and two side arches (see figure 1). Within these arches doors are often decorated with panels and studs and crowned by a decorated lintel. Above these burial chambers and carved into the side of the mountain are semicircular benches, probably an element of an assembly place for those who came to memorialize the dead.

Catacombs 14 and 20, the focal points of the necropolis, were the most elaborate burial sites. Catacomb 20 was the densest of all the catacombs, representing the entire range of burial styles, but particularly the use of the sarcophagus: some 65 percent of the two-hundred burials in catacomb 20 were in sarcophagi, of which a third were decorated. These sarcophagi were made primarily of stone, but examples in marble, lead, and wood were also found. Rabbis were buried in this catacomb, and it is therefore not surprising that Hebrew dominates the inscriptions. Catacomb 14 appears to have been a private burial site, as it held far fewer interments. The names Rabban Gamaliel, Rabban Simeon, and Rabbi Aniana (Ḥanina?) discovered in this catacomb point to it as the burial site of the immediate family and circle of Rabbi Judah I (B. T., *Ket.* 103a–b). Indeed, the innermost double-trough burial is very likely the resting place of this patriarch and his wife.

These catacombs are rich both in their ornamentation and epigraphic remains. Many reliefs and carvings, as well as pictures painted and incised on stone, were found throughout the necropolis; they reflect one of the richest depositories of popular Jewish art in late antiquity. Floral and geometric designs are ubiquitous, as are representations of animals (lions, oxen, eagles, birds, horses) and an occasional human figure. Depictions of cuetic objects abound and include the Torah shrine, lulav, ethrog, shofar, and incense shovel. A predominant motif is the menorah, which appears scores of times in a variety of shapes and styles.

The approximately 280 inscriptions found at Beth-She'arim give the names and titles of the Jews interred, as well as their professions and places of origin. Moreover, the distribution of the languages in these inscriptions is most revealing: almost 80 percent are in Greek, 16 percent in Hebrew, and the remainder in Aramaic or Palmyrene.

The monumental catacomb 11, with its many and lavish fragments, indicates that a large building, probably a mausoleum, was located there. In the debris near the mausoleum, a seven-line inscription written in Greek on white marble was found:

> Here I lie, dead, Justus the son of Leontis and Sappho
> After I have picked (the fruits) of all wisdom
> I left the light, my unhappy parents who mourn
> continuously,
> And my brothers, Woe to me in my Besara,
> And after I have descended to Hades, I, Justus, lie here
> With many of my relatives, for so determined the powerful
> Fate
> Be comforted, Justus, for no one is immortal.

There is no question that the importance and centrality of Beth-She'arim to Jewish Palestine in late antiquity were inextricably linked to the presence of the patriarchal family there; Jews from all parts of Israel and the Diaspora wished to be interred there precisely because the necropolis was associated with the patriarch. The centrality of the office in late antiquity has been, however, a controversial subject in modern historiography. On the one hand, rabbinic literature

BETH-SHE'ARIM. Figure 1. *Entrance to catacomb 20.* (Courtesy E. M. Meyers)

following the ministry of Rabbi Judah I takes an increasingly dim view of the patriarchate, and by the fourth century either ignores the office or has only negative things to say about it. On the other hand, non-Jewish sources, such as the Theodosian Code and Libanius, depict the office as the most important one within the Jewish community. Even the church fathers, whose theological motivations led them to be critical of the patriarchate, nevertheless attest to its centrality. Archaeological finds at other sites have corroborated the results of the Beth-She'arim excavations. For example, both a synagogue inscription from Stobi (Yugoslavia) dating to 280 CE and a mosaic floor in the Hammath Tiberias synagogue attest to the importance of this office in the Jewish world. (In the former, the patriarch was designated as the recipient of a sizable fine owed by the party breaking the agreement outlined in the inscription; in the latter, one Severus associated with the patriarch was the principal donor to the synagogue.)

The finds at Beth-She'arim, along with those from ancient synagogues in general, have revolutionized our concept of Jewish art in antiquity. Previously, it had been assumed, on the basis of very explicit sources from the late Second Temple period, that Jews throughout antiquity shied away from all figural representation. The archaeological finds here, however, demonstrate that Jews used figural representation from the biblical period until the Hasmonean era, and that during the centuries of the Late Roman and Byzantine periods they once again depicted humans and animals figurally to decorate their public and private buildings. Beth-She'arim was one of the first and certainly most dramatic expressions of this more liberal posture, paving the way for a reevaluation of the historical attitude of the Jews and Judaism toward figural art.

The necropolis at Beth-She'arim provides evidence of the extent to which Jewish burial customs in late antiquity differed from those of the Second Temple period. Secondary burials, especially in ossuaries, are almost entirely absent at Beth-She'arim. The use of ossuaries was superceded by the trough-shaped burials and sarcophagi, which had been rare in earlier Jewish funerary contexts. Many of the customs evidenced at Beth-She'arim indicate the adoption by the Jews of the forms of burial regnant in late antiquity in general.

Finally, Beth-She'arim is a dramatic example of the extent of Hellenization within the Jewish community in Late Roman Palestine. Its art, architecture, and inscriptions attest to the far-reaching influence of contemporary forms and styles.

[See also Architectural Decoration; Burial Sites; Burial Techniques; Catacombs; Sarcophagus.]

BIBLIOGRAPHY

Avi-Yonah, Michael. "The Leda Coffin from Beth-She'arim" (in Hebrew). Eretz-Israel 8 (1967): 143–148. Detailed description and analysis of a marble coffin with blatantly pagan motifs.
Goodenough, Erwin R. Jewish Symbols in the Greco-Roman Period. Vol.
1. New York, 1953. Contains an overview of the Beth-She'arim finds (pp. 89–102) from the author's particular perspective—the search for mystical, nonrabbinic Judaism in archaeological remains.
Levine, Lee I. "The Finds from Beth-She'arim and Their Importance for the Study of the Talmudic Period" (in Hebrew). Eretz-Israel 18 (1985): 277–281. An attempt to relate the Beth-She'arim finds to a number of larger issues in Jewish history of late antiquity.
Mazar, Benjamin, et al. Beth She'arim. 3 vols. New Brunswick, N.J., 1973–1976. Authoritative report of the excavations and findings from Beth-She'arim. Volume 1 describes Mazar's excavations; volume 2, the Greek inscriptions; and volume 3, the results of Nahman Avigad's work there.
Weiss, Zeev. "Social Aspects of Burial in Beth She'arim: Archeological Finds and Talmudic Sources." In The Galilee in Late Antiquity, edited by Lee I. Levine, pp. 357–371. New York, 1992. An attempt to relate the Beth-She'arim finds with Talmudic literature, elucidating the customs and practices surrounding Jewish burial procedures.

LEE I. LEVINE

BETH-SHEMESH (Heb. "house/temple of the sun"), site located in the northeastern Shephelah, along the inner reaches of the Sorek valley that guarded the major ascent to Jerusalem in antiquity (map reference 1477 × 1286). It is a prominent mound, about 7 acres in size. The Hebrew name apparently preserves the tradition of an older Canaanite temple (cf. Ir-shemash, "city of the sun" in Jos. 19:41). The site's Arabic name is Tell er-Rumeilah; the nearby village of 'Ain Shems ("spring of the sun") preserves the ancient name.

Edward Robinson identified the mound in 1838 and Duncan Mackenzie excavated it in 1911–1912 under the auspices of the Palestine Exploration Fund. Haverford College (Pennsylvania) excavated from 1923 to 1928, under the direction of Elihu Grant, who was assisted by G. Ernest Wright in publishing the final volume of the excavation report. Bar-Ilan University resumed excavations in 1990, under the direction of Shlomo Bunimovitz and Zvi Lederman.

Stratum VI consists only of Early Bronze IV–Middle Bronze I sherds near bedrock. Stratum V represents the well-fortified MB II–III city with a few patrician houses and several tombs (tombs 9, 12, 13, 17). Mackenzie had identified its "strong wall" and triple-entry gate. Stratum IVa–b denotes the prosperous Late Bronze town, which produced some fine domestic structures, many cisterns, a smelting furnace, a Proto-Canaanite ostracon, a jewelry hoard, and several tombs (tombs 10, 11). Its destruction may date to about 1200 BCE, but the causes are unknown.

Beth-Shemesh in the Iron Age I was a large but relatively unplanned village, still somewhat in the LB tradition, but with Philistine Bichrome ware. (It is Mackenzie's "second city," stratum III.) Wright (Grant and Wright, 1938–1939) ascribed its destruction to the Philistines (c. 1050 BCE). The recent excavations have confirmed that it was indeed a massive destruction (Mackenzie's Red Burnt stratum), but it dates somewhat earlier, to the beginning of the eleventh century BCE.

Stratum II, with phases IIa–c, spans the tenth–eighth centuries BCE. In stratum IIa (c. 1000–950 BCE) a casemate wall was constructed around the entire site, and pillared courtyard houses characterized the well laid-out city within it. The structures included industrial installations, a fine "residency," a large silo, and a typical tripartite storehouse (sometimes called stables), which may indicate that Beth-Shemesh was a regional administrative center during the United Monarchy. How much of stratum IIa is Davidic, if any, is debated. The earlier excavations had published a good deal of pottery slipped with an unburnished, streaky red slip. This pottery also occurs in abundance at nearby sites such as Tell Qasile XI and Gezer X–IX, where it characterizes the period from about 1050 to 950 BCE, postdating Philistine bichrome ware and immediately preceding typical Solomonic red-burnished wares. [See Qasile, Tell; Gezer.] This evidence does suggest a Davidic date for stratum IIa.

Stratum IIb (c. 950–700 BCE) and stratum IIc (700–586 BCE) follow stratum IIa rather closely. Many of the houses were reconstructed several times, and some were even built over the stratum IIa casemate wall. The recent excavations have shown, contrary to Mackenzie's and Wright's view, that the city was scarcely fortified in Iron II; there was a massive rebuild of the city wall in this period, including a northern gate complex. Large olive-crushing installations and many Royal stamped jar handles attest to the city's continued importance. Several tombs (tombs 14–16) belong to this horizon. The final destruction of stratum IIc was thought by the earlier excavators to have been carried out by the Babylonians (c. 586 BCE), but the latest excavations have not revealed any seventh-century BCE remains. The destruction is better related to the well-known Judean campaigns of Sennacherib in 701 BCE.

The site's later periods are represented by Hellenistic, Roman, Byzantine, and medieval materials (stratum I). A large Byzantine monastery on the southeast slopes is still visible.

[See also the biography of Mackenzie.]

BIBLIOGRAPHY

Grant, Elihu. *Beth Shemesh (Palestine): Progress of the Haverford Archaeological Expedition.* Haverford, 1929.
Grant, Elihu. *Ain Shems Excavations (Palestine, 1928–1929–1930–1931).* Parts 1 and 2. Haverford, 1931–1932.
Grant, Elihu. *Rumeileh, Being Ain Shems Excavations (Palestine).* Part 3. Haverford, 1934.
Grant, Elihu, and G. Ernest Wright. *Ain Shems Excavations (Palestine).* Parts 4 (pottery) and 5. Haverford, 1938–1939.
Mackenzie, Duncan L. "Excavations at 'Ain Shems." *Palestine Exploration Fund Annual* 1 (1911); 2 (1912–1913).

WILLIAM G. DEVER

BETH-YERAH (Ar., Khirbet Kerak, "the ruins of the castle"), a low, flat tell (25 ha, or 62 acres) located at the southwestern end of the Sea of Galilee, which has eroded some portion of the site (32°43′ N, 35°34′ E; map reference 204 × 236). The present outlet of the Jordan River lies to the south, but in antiquity it was to the north and the river flowed along the site's western edge. Fortifications on the south and west, and a Roman bridge on the north, suggest that the river's southern outlet was dug in the Byzantine period or later.

Four identifications have been suggested for Beth-Yerah/Khirbet Kerak (Maisler [Mazar] et al., 1952, p. 165, n. 1.; Avi-Yonah, 1976, pp. 88, 95; Esse, 1991, pp. 34–35; Hestrin, 1993, p. 255). Pliny and Josephus indicated that the site of Tarichea, Vespasian's campsite during his campaigns in the Galilee in 67 CE, was located at the southern end of the Sea of Galilee (*War* 3.447; 4.455). Most scholars reject this, while some others equate Khirbet Kerak with Philoteria, which Polybius said was built by Ptolemy II Philadelphus (Polybius 5.70.3–4). Others suggest Roman Sennabris or neighboring Beth-Yerah. The Jerusalem Talmud indicates that Beth-Yerah and Sennabris were walled sites at the southern end of the Sea of Galilee (*Meg.* 70a), while the Babylonian Talmud notes that the Jordan River began at Beth-Yerah (*Bekh.* 51a; *Bik.* 55a), which favors the identification with Khirbet Kerak. The name of *Khirbet Kerak* in the Bronze Age is unknown. *Beth-Yerah* is not mentioned in the Hebrew Bible or in other Bronze or Iron Age sources, but the term *bt yrh*, "house of the moon," places the name within Canaanite lunar traditions.

Major excavations at Beth-Yerah include those of Benjamin Mazar for the Jewish Palestine Exploration Society in 1944–1946 (Maisler [Mazar], 1952) and Pierre Delougaz for the Oriental Institute of the University of Chicago in 1952–1953, 1963, and 1964. The unpublished excavations of Pessah Bar-Adon (1951–1955) were the most extensive. William Foxwell Albright's surveys of the site and the Jordan Valley during the 1920s revealed distinctive Early Bronze III red-on-black burnished pottery known as "Khirbet Kerak ware" (Albright, 1926), the southernmost manifestation of the Early Transcaucasian or Kura-Araxes tradition, originating in the Caucasus region (Burney, 1989). [See Jordan Valley; and the biographies of Mazar and Albright.]

The site was densely settled during the Early Bronze Age and also reveals Hellenistic, Roman, Byzantine, and Early Islamic remains. Stratified EB material was recovered in all parts of the site. The Mazar excavation discerned four phases:

Beth-Yerah I: Pit dwellings containing ashes and animal bones. Gray-Burnished Ware, called Late Chalcolithic by the excavators, dates to the early EB I.
Beth-Yerah II: Rectangular mud-brick houses. Grain-Wash or Band-Slipped wares date to the late EB I.
Beth-Yerah III: Rectangular mud-brick buildings with basalt foundations and possibly a mud-brick city wall in three sections (8 m wide). The phase dates to EB II.

Beth-Yeraḥ IV: The thickest phase, with up to 2 m of accumulation and four building stages. Large stone buildings were found along with Khirbet Kerak Ware and animal figurines. Whether the mud-brick fortification wall was used during this phase (EB III) is unclear.

Later excavations revealed EB stratification, in keeping with the strata I–IV sequence, varying in depth and number of structural phases (Esse, 1991, pp. 40–41). Bar-Adon also excavated an EB IV occupation level, including a potter's workshop, houses with courtyards, and a paved street. The Tell el-Yahudiyeh ware found in a grave is the only MB material known at the site. [See Yahudiyeh, Tell el-.]

The three-element mud-brick wall was founded on virgin soil and may date to EB I but is more characteristic of EB II. Bar-Adon's excavation revealed two superimposed gate structures paved with basalt stones, with steps leading down into the city. The latter phase had flanking guardrooms. The early phase was flanked on its exterior by several tall basalt stones, probably *maṣṣēbôt*. These gates remain unpublished (but see photographs in Yeivin, 1955, pl. VI:1; 1955b, pl. 50, fig. 8; and the plan in Eph'al, 1964, pp. 365–366). Mazar also found a poorly built stone wall 4 m wide. Bar-Adon cleared approximately 1,600 m of it along the southern and western edge of the site. The wall was constructed on massive stone foundations up to 7 m wide and 3 m high. The foundation supported a poorly preserved mud-brick superstructure containing alternating round and square towers. Bar-Adon dated this wall to EB IV, but it is Hellenistic.

The most notable structure excavated was the Building with Circles, dated to EB III. It is a rectangular stone structure (30 × 40 m) surrounded on three sides by paved streets. Comprised of a single wall 10 m thick, it surrounds a square courtyard and has a rectangular entrance passage. In the wall are eight or ten circles 7–9 m in diameter, each subdivided by partition walls. The partitions do not reach the center of the circles. The structure was entered through a 7-meter-wide passageway. Narrow paved passages led into two of the circles. The others were entered from a higher level. Large amounts of pottery, including Khirbet Kerak Ware, burnt animal bones, soot, and carbonized olive pits were found. The shape of the circles' mud-brick superstructure is unknown. The Building with Circles is one of the largest EB structures known. The excavators suggested four possible functions for it: fortress, granary, palace, or sanctuary. The building resembles the model of a Helladic granary found on Melos, the model of an Old Kingdom granary from el-Kab, and depictions of granaries from Egyptian tomb paintings of the fourth and fifth dynasties.

Persian remains are reported by excavators but are unpublished. However, considerable Hellenistic material was excavated at Khirbet Kerak. The largest feature is the stone fortification wall with towers. Other materials remain unpublished. Bar-Adon found several Hellenistic houses on the southern part of the site, including a large residence with a courtyard dating to the Ptolemaic period, and houses, decorated with colored plaster, preserved to their windows.

The Roman materials were found on the northern part of the site and include a bathhouse. [See Baths.] Its frigidarium was paved with marble slabs and contained a round pool lined with marble situated in the center of the room and surrounded by a round bench. Beyond the bench were pillars and impressions of smaller pillars, indicating that there had been a dome or pavilion above the pool. The walls were decorated with colored and gilt mosaics. [See Mosaics.] Adjoining the frigidarium was a hypocaust cellar below a caldarium and tepidarium. The hypocaust had thick walls and a cement floor; its burnt-brick and ashlar pillars in the walls had supported floors of upper rooms. Walls containing vertical square ceramic pipes vented the hot air up into the caldarium. The complex was fed by a clay pipe that cut across part of the Building with Circles and connected to an aqueduct from Nahal Yavne'el to Tiberias. The thermal establishment was constructed in the fourth or fifth century CE, repaired in the sixth century, and destroyed in the seventh. It was partially built above a square Roman fortress (60 sq m) with corner and gate towers constructed of dressed stones and with a rubble core and dated to the second or third centuries CE. Within the fortress were foundations of a synagogue, in which two rows of columns created a nave and aisles. The nave was decorated with a mosaic depicting plants and animals and a column base was decorated with carved motifs of a menorah, lulav, etrog, and incense shovel. The apse in the southern wall was oriented toward Jerusalem.

A large church was excavated on the north of the site by Delougaz and Richard C. Haines. This was a basilica (11.5 × 12.5 m) with three apses and a row of pillars along its long axis, creating a nave and aisles. Tombs, possibly reliquaries, were found under the floor of the nave. The narthex led to a large rectangular atrium and narrow loggia, all later additions. A small diaconicon was added to one side of the basilica and decorated with floral and geometric mosaics. The diaconicon was decorated with a mosaic containing a short Greek dedicatory inscription. The basilica was constructed in the early fifth century; the diaconicon was completed in 528; and the complex was abandoned during the late sixth or early seventh centuries. A building from the Early Arab period was partially excavated above the church that consists of well-built small rooms around a courtyard.

BIBLIOGRAPHY

Albright, William Foxwell. "The Jordan Valley in the Bronze Age." *Annual of the American Schools of Oriental Research*, vol. 6, pp. 13–74. New Haven, 1926.

Avi-Yonah, Michael. *Gazeteer of Roman Palestine*. Qedem 5. Jerusalem, 1976.

Bar-Adon, Pessah. "Beth Yerah." *Israel Exploration Journal* 2 (1952): 142; 3 (1953): 132; 4 (1954): 128–129; 5 (1955): 273.

Bar-Adon, Pessah. "Beth Yerah." *Revue Biblique* 62 (1955): 85–88.

Burney, Charles "The Khirbet Kerak Question and the Early Trans-Caucasian Background." In *L'urbanisation de la Palestine à l'âge du Bronze ancien: Bilan et perspectives des recherches actuelles; Actes du Colloque d'Emmaüs, 20–24 octobre 1986*, edited by Pierre de Miroschedji, pp. 331–339. British Archaeological Reports, International Series, no. 527. Oxford, 1989.

Delougaz, Pinhas, and Richard C. Haines. *A Byzantine Church at Khirbat al-Karak*. Oriental Institute Publications, 85. Chicago, 1960.

Eisenberg, Emmanuel. "Beth Yerah" (in Hebrew). *Hadashot Arkeologiyot* 76 (1981): 11–13.

Eph'al, Israel, ed. *The Military History of Eretz Israel during the Biblical Period*. Jerusalem, 1964.

Esse, Douglas. *Subsistence, Trade, and Social Change in Early Bronze Age Palestine*. Studies in Ancient Oriental Civilization, no. 50. Chicago, 1991.

Hestrin, Ruth. "Beth Yerah." In *The New Encyclopedia of Archaeological Excavations in the Holy Land*, vol. 1, pp. 255–259. Jerusalem and New York, 1993.

Maisler [Mazar], Benjamin, et al. "The Excavations at Beth-Yerah (Khirbet el-Kerak), 1944–1946." *Israel Exploration Journal* 2 (1952): 165–173, 218–229.

Mazar, Benjamin, et al. "An Early Bronze Age II Tomb at Beth-Yerah (Kinneret)." *Eretz-Israel* 11 (1973): 176–193.

Ussishkin, David. "Beth Yerah." *Revue Biblique* 75 (1967): 266–268.

Yeivin, Shmuel. *Archaeological Activity in Israel (1948–1955)*. Jerusalem, 1955.

ALEXANDER H. JOFFE

BETH-ZUR, site located 30 km (19 mi.) south of Jerusalem in the hill country of Judah, identified with Khirbet et-Tubeiqah (map reference 159 × 110). The conical mound rises between 22 and 100 m above the valley floor, commanding roads northward to Jerusalem and westward toward the Shephelah. Its ancient Hebrew name is preserved in the Arabic of nearby Khirbet Burj es-Sur.

Beth-Zur was first identified by F.-M. Abel, William Foxwell Albright, and Ovid R. Sellers. Excavations took place in 1931 and in 1957, directed by Sellers for the Presbyterian (McCormick) Theological Seminary and the American Schools of Oriental Research. Albright and H. Neil Richardson served as archaeological advisers. In 1931, some 8,000 sq m were cleared to bedrock; in 1957, fields I and III within the city wall and field II outside of it were opened. [*See the biographies of Albright and Abel.*]

Early Bronze Age sherds suggest some third-millennium occupation, but Beth-Zur's first significant settlement dates to the Middle Bronze II/III period. The hill was inhabited in the seventeenth century BCE, fortified early in the sixteenth century, destroyed in about 1550, and then abandoned until the beginning of the Iron Age.

Israelite Beth-Zur (*Jos.* 15:59; *1 Chr.* 2:45), a rather poor town, was destroyed late in the eleventh century BCE. The biblical description of Rehoboam's fortifying the site (*2 Chr.* 11:7) remains unsubstantiated archaeologically. Excavations attest to an Israelite occupation in the mid-seventh century BCE, at which time the city was undefended. Fifteen *lamelekh* jar handles are among the finds from that period. Archaeological evidence for a 587 BCE destruction is ambiguous.

The Hebrew Bible notes that Beth-Zur was a district center at the time of the rebuilding of the Jerusalem Temple, but remains of the fifth-century BCE town are sparse (*Neh.* 3:16). Numismatic evidence substantiates a fourth-century Hellenistic city. In the third century BCE, Beth-Zur attained new importance, figuring strategically in the conflict between the Ptolemies and the Seleucids. It was then that the site's phase I citadel was constructed.

Beth-Zur, or Bethsura, as it was then called, reached the zenith of its prosperity during the Maccabean wars (stratum II, second century BCE) and the reign of Antiochus IV Epiphanes (175–165 BCE). It was the site of a major battle between Judah Maccabee and the Seleucid general Lysias (*1 Mc.* 4:28–34; Josephus, *Antiq.* 12.7.5). In 164 BCE, the victorious Judah reconstructed its MB wall and built the phase II citadel (*1 Mc.* 4:61, 6:7, 6:26; *Antiq.* 12.7.7).

Lysias retook control of the city almost immediately and strengthened its defenses even further (*1 Mc.* 6:28–31, 47–50; *Antiq.* 12.9.4–5; *War* 1.1.5). The phase III citadel was built in 161 BCE by his successor, Bacchides (*1 Mc.* 9:52). The many Rhodian wine-jar handles found at Beth-Zur are remnants of two decades of Seleucid occupation, an occupation that included both a military garrison and some renegade Jews loyal to the Seleucids (*1 Mc.* 10:14).

In the last years of the Hasmonean king Jonathan's reign (160–143 BCE), his brother Simeon (later high priest) conquered Beth-Zur and posted a Judean garrison there (*1 Mc.* 11:65–66, 14:33). This stratum I city remained an important Judean border fortress until another Hasmonean, John Hyrcanus, annexed Idumea in 129 BCE, thus undermining Beth-Zur's significance. By about 100 BCE, Beth-Zur had been abandoned.

BIBLIOGRAPHY

Funk, Robert W. "The 1957 Campaign at Beth-Zur." *Bulletin of the American Schools of Oriental Research*, no. 150 (1958): 8–20. Primary field report from the 1957 season.

Lapp, Paul W., and Nancy L. Lapp. "A Comparative Study of a Hellenistic Pottery Group from Beth-Zur." *Bulletin of the American Schools of Oriental Research*, no. 151 (1958): 16–27. Study of an assemblage of Hellenistic pottery, with some comparative materials.

Sellers, Ovid R., and William Foxwell Albright. "The First Campaign of Excavation at Beth-Zur." *Bulletin of the American Schools of Oriental Research*, no. 43 (1931): 2–13. Field report from the 1931 season.

Sellers, Ovid R., *The Citadel of Beth-Zur*. Philadelphia, 1933. Final report of the first excavation, presenting both archaeological data and literary references.

Sellers, Ovid R., et al. *The 1957 Excavation at Beth-Zur*. Annual of the American Schools of Oriental Research, 38. Cambridge, Mass., 1968. Report from the 1957 season, which includes a synthesis of the earlier material.

BETH ALPERT NAKHAI

BIBLICAL ARCHAEOLOGY.

BIBLICAL ARCHAEOLOGY. The movement known popularly as biblical archaeology is principally an American phenomenon. Its parent disciplines are Syro-Palestinian archaeology and biblical studies. The history of biblical archaeology can be divided into four phases.

Premodern Period. The emergence of both Syro-Palestinian and biblical archaeology really began in the mid- to late nineteenth century with the rediscovery through exploration of ancient Palestine, following that of Mesopotamia and Egypt. This was also the period that witnessed the birth of modern literary-historical criticism of the Bible. Thus, the romance of discovery and the challenge of vindicating the historicity of the biblical accounts combined to create the movement that came to be called biblical archaeology. Its objective was to bring external "proofs," provided by archaeological discoveries, to bear directly on such problematic issues as the patriarchal and conquest eras, Moses and monotheism, and other issues where faith and history seemed to intersect. The method of biblical archaeology was to excavate (in reality, to "mine") select sites thought to be identified with places and events in the Bible. From their recovered remains a "political history" would be written—of great men and public events—that could be correlated directly with the biblical texts for the purpose of corroborating the texts (or at least the writers' interpretation of the texts). However, despite mounting enthusiasm for archaeology in biblical circles in late nineteenth-century Europe, neither American biblicists nor American scholars in any disciplines, except for the philologist Edward Robinson, were involved in Palestinian archaeology until nearly the end of the century. [*See the biography of Robinson.*]

The first actual fieldwork in Palestine was carried out for the British Palestine Exploration Fund (1865–) by the legendary Sir William Flinders Petrie, at Tell el-Hesi in southern Palestine (possibly biblical Eglon) in a six-week season in 1890. [*See* Palestine Exploration Fund; *and the biography of Petrie.*] American involvement in fieldwork finally materialized when Frederick Jones Bliss directed a follow-up season in 1893. [*See the biography of Bliss.*] It was Bliss who, in 1903, delivered the Ely Lectures at Union Theological Seminary in New York City—Robinson's old school—under the published title *The Development of Palestine Exploration* (New York, 1906). It was the first comprehensive survey of the field. The combination of Bible and archaeology, evident at the beginning of American archaeology in Palestine (dating back in fact to Robinson's explorations in 1838), was to remain characteristic. Some subsequent American excavations, such as those of George Andrew Reisner at Samaria in 1908–1910, were carried out under secular auspices; however, the growing fundamentalist-modernist controversy of the early twentieth century—named for the six-volume series of Evangelical theology called *The Fundamentals* (the first ones published in about 1909—and its divisive impact on American religious life set the scene for the flowering of biblical archaeology.

Heyday: 1920s–1960s. World War I brought a halt to all archaeological fieldwork in the Near East. The year 1919, however, marked the dawn of a new era. In that year the fledgling British Mandatory Government established a Department of Antiquities in Palestine and promulgated a modern antiquities law; and Americans founded the Oriental Institute at the University of Chicago and began to plan for an in-country institute and year-round field operation at Tell Megiddo, in the Jezreel Valley. Perhaps the most significant event, as it turned out, was the arrival in Jerusalem of a young American scholar, William Foxwell Albright, at the American Schools of Oriental Research (ASOR), which had been established in 1900 but had neither a building, a program of fieldwork, nor a long-term director. [*See* American Schools of Oriental Research.] Albright became unarguably the most prominent and influential Orientalist of the twentieth century. [*See the biography of Albright.*]

Albright was the director of ASOR from 1920 to 1929 and again from 1933 to 1936. He also directed field campaigns at Tell el-Ful (biblical Gibeah) in 1922 and Tell Beit Mirsim (biblical Debir?) from 1926 to 1932. His mastery of the pottery of Palestine and his ability to establish the results of excavations in the broad context of the whole of the ancient Near East quickly placed him in the forefront of Palestinian archaeology. Furthermore, it was he who really established biblical archaeology as a legitimate enterprise, at least in principle. Under both his influence and direct tutelage there developed a pattern that included the deliberate choice of biblical sites for excavation; financial and institutional backing drawn from church-related organizations (largely Protestant); field staffs made up almost exclusively of biblical scholars, seminarians, and clerics; and an agenda that subjugated strictly archaeological methods and objectives to what were perceived as the larger issues of biblical interpretation (largely in the Hebrew Bible). Projects of this type were those of Albright himself at Tell el-Ful, Bethel, and Tell Beit Mirsim in 1922–1934; of the Pacific School of Religion at Tell en-Nasbeh in 1926–1935; of Haverford College, Pennsylvania, at Beth-Shemesh in 1928–1933; and, of course, the American excavations in the 1950s–1960s at such sites as Dibon, Heshbon/Hesban, Shechem, Ai, Ta'anach, Gibeon, and other sites in modern Israel and Jordan (see below).

The biblical archaeology movement dominated American Palestinian archaeology (though not continental) from the 1920s through the 1960s, and it still has a few wistful defenders. In retrospect, it appears that the movement constituted a chapter in American religious life, and particularly in theological development, as seen in connection with the biblical theology movement in the 1950s by Albright's protegé G. Ernest Wright and others (Dever, 1985, 1993). [*See the biography of Wright.*]

Albright had furthered the original historical aims of biblical archaeology, such as the attempt to use archaeology to confirm the essential historicity of the patriarchs, of Moses and early monotheism, and of the Israelite conquest of Canaan. Wright, however, went further in deliberately joining the issue of "faith and history"—a characteristic theme of the Neo-Orthodox theology movement of the 1950s—with developments in Syro-Palestinian archaeology. Unlike Albright, Wright was an ordained clergyman and a leading biblical scholar—indeed he was Parkman Professor of Divinity at Harvard. As Wright stated the issue: "Now in Biblical faith everything depends upon whether the central events [i.e., the call of Abraham, the promise of the Land of Canaan, the conquest under Joshua, etc.] actually occurred" (*God Who Acts: Biblical Theology as Recital*, London, 1952, p. 126).

To many, especially in Europe, Wright's position appeared dangerously close to fundamentalism, even more so than Albright's historicism. By the mid-late 1960s, however, the biblical theology movement had waned, and the stage was set for American Syro-Palestinian archaeology to move toward independent status. Nevertheless, up until that time much of postwar American archaeology in the Holy Land remained in the traditional biblical mold. That included Wright's own excavations at Shechem (1956–1968); the work of Joseph A. Callaway, a professor at the Southern Baptist Theological Seminary, at Ai (1964–1969); the work of Paul Lapp, a Lutheran clergyman, at 'Iraq el-Amir (1961, 1962), Ta'anach (1963–1968), Tell er-Rumeith (1967), Bab edh-Dhra' (1965–1967), and elsewhere; the excavations of James B. Pritchard, professor of religious thought at the University of Pennsylvania, at el-Jib (1956–1962) and Tell es-Sa'idiyeh (1967); and the project of Siegfried H. Horn, Lawrence T. Geraty, and others at Hesban (1968–1978).

"New Archaeology": 1970s–1980s. It may be significant that all the above excavations were of sites in Jordan, where Americans with a Christian theological background apparently felt more at home after the partition of Palestine in 1948. Although a vigorous Israeli national school was developing in the new State of Israel, there were no American-directed excavations there until the long-lived project directed by William G. Dever, Joe D. Seger, and others at Gezer (1964–1974, with final seasons in 1984 and 1990). Gezer was followed by other projects under Gezer-trained personnel: at Tell el-Hesi (John E. Worrell, Lawrence E. Stager, and others, 1971–1983); at Galilean synagogue sites and at Sepphoris, in separate projects (Eric M. Meyers and Carol Meyers, and then James F. Strange, 1970–1981 and 1984–, respectively); at Lahav (Seger and Dan P. Cole, 1976–); at Tel Miqne (Seymour Gitin, with Trude Dothan of the Hebrew University of Jerusalem, 1981–); at Ashkelon (Stager and others, 1985–); and other sites. Other American excavations of this and later periods in Israel included large

projects at Caesarea (Robert J. Bull and Lawrence E. Toombs, 1971–); at Tel Anafa (Saul S. Weinberg and Sharon Herbert, 1968–1981); Tel Jemmeh (Gus van Beek, 1970–1982); and Be'er Resisim in the Negev (Dever, jointly with Rudolph Cohen of the Israel Department of Antiquities, 1978–1980).

The Gezer excavations proved to be a microcosm of developments in the field of archaeology. They transformed "biblical" archaeology beyond recognition, gradually bringing about the emergence of the discipline of Syro-Palestinian archaeology by the mid-1970s. There occurred in this enterprise what the scientist/philosopher Thomas S. Kuhn (*The Structure of Scientific Revolutions*, Chicago, 1970), has termed a paradigm shift. In this case it was a practical consensus about improving field and recording techniques. It was not a deliberate and profound intellectual reorientation—the development of a systematic body of theory as this was understood in other branches of archaeology or in the social sciences generally (that is, in fact, yet to occur).

From the late-1960s through the mid-1980s biblical and Syro-Palestinian archaeology borrowed elements of a trend in Americanist New World archaeology that came to be called the New Archaeology. These "external factors," as we shall call them, in the demise of biblical archaeology, need only be enumerated briefly here, since they have been amply treated elsewhere (Dever, 1993; Drinkard et al., 1988). The principal aspects of the New Archaeology follow:

1. An orientation that is more anthropological than historical, away from particularization toward the study of culture and culture change generally
2. A "nomothetic" approach that seeks to formulate and test the lawlike propositions that govern cultural processes (thus, "processualist" archaeology)—and thus to develop a body of theory that qualifies archaeology not only as a discipline but as a science
3. An ecological thrust that emphasizes technoenvironmental factors (rather than simply evolutionary trajectories) in the role of adaptation in culture change
4. A multidisciplinary strategy that involves many of the physical sciences and their statistical and analytic procedures in attempting to reconstruct the ancient landscape, climate, population, economy, sociopolitical structure, and other subsystems (often using the model of General Systems Theory)
5. An insistence on an overall, up-front "research design" for projects that integrate all of the above, and thus advance archaeology as a culturally relevant enterprise.

Radical as these trends were to conventional "biblical archaeologists" in the 1960s, many aspects were prefigured in developments already taking place in the field of Syro-Palestinian archaeology, or "internal factors" in change. These included the following:

1. The recent stratigraphic revolution led by Kathleen M. Kenyon and others that promised total retrieval, automatically generating data so copious and varied they required analysis by specialists
2. The growing complexity and costs of excavation, especially in Israel, which was pushing the field inevitably toward professionalization
3. Field schools and student volunteerism—which not only constituted an intellectual challenge but broke the monopoly of biblical scholars on dig staffs and thus contributed to the secularization of the discipline
4. The increasing sense that "biblical archaeology" was not only parochial but had failed to achieve even its own limited agenda of historical-theological issues.

Another major factor in American Syro-Palestinian archaeology's "coming of age" was competition with other national schools and their approaches. The European schools, while not ignoring the connection between archaeology in the Holy Land and the Bible, had taken differing approaches: some completely secular (the British); others aligned with the religious establishment, largely through a state church that located Palestinian archaeology academically in state university departments of theology (the Germans); and still others viewing clerics and secular scholars alike involved in Near Eastern archaeology generally (the French). The significant difference was that none of the European schools was haunted by the specter of fundamentalism, as the American school had historically been. At the same time, none of these schools possessed the perseverance to enable them to survive as a major force in Syro-Palestinian archaeology as it evolved into a mature discipline in the 1980s.

The Middle Eastern countries themselves had developed national schools only in the 1960s, well after the establishment of the State of Israel and the end of the mandatory governments in Syria, Jordan, and Iraq. Arab countries wanted little to do with either the Bible, the ancient history of Israel, or the search for Western cultural and theological roots in the Holy Land. However, their national schools, as they developed in the 1960s and later, did not manage to avoid bias toward pan-Islamic culture or escape the pull of nationalism. All in all, however, archaeology in Arab countries has developed recently, with all the strengths and weaknesses of the field generally. American involvement from country to country is difficult to assess because of rapidly changing political configurations. In the early 1990s American fieldwork and influence in Jordan are strong, thanks to the work of the American Center for Oriental Research (ACOR) in Amman since 1968. British and German insti-

tutes also exist but are less conspicuous. American and other foreign projects continue in Syria on varying scales, while Lebanon is virtually closed to all archaeologists.

The situation in Israel is in many ways unique. Israelis claim that they connect with the biblical past not necessarily in the sense of formal religion, certainly not theologically—since most of the archaeologists are neither personally observant nor academically trained in Bible and religion—but emotionally and directly. They maintain that the Hebrew Bible is, after all, the virtual constitution of the modern state; that for Jews displaced for centuries, even secular Jews, digging for their past in the soil of the Holy Land is a vital matter of identity, an existential quest no one has the right to deny them. They have a point, although the argument is somewhat disingenuous, and it can lead to nationalist extremes. In any case, Israeli archaeologists who use the phrase "biblical archaeology" for popular consumption, or for an English-speaking audience, do so with a meaning that differs from typical American usage, and partly to avoid the awkward term "Palestinian." (In Hebrew, the common designation is simply "the archaeology of Eretz-Israel, the "Land of Israel," exactly parallel to the archaeology of Jordan or Syria.) The most recent syntheses by Israelis of archaeological results (Amihai Mazar, *Archaeology of the Land of the Bible 10,000–586 B.C.E.*, New York, 1988; Amnon Ben-Tor, ed., *The Archaeology of Ancient Israel*, New Haven, 1992) have not been matched by American archaeologists working in Israel. The 1990s have, however, been witness to several major and a number of smaller American field projects, most coordinated with ASOR through the W. F. Albright Institute of Archaeological Research in Jerusalem. Despite the changing balance of Israeli and foreign-sponsored work, it is obvious that the leadership has shifted to Israeli archaeologists, who now dominate the field through extensive excavations, surveys, and publications. [*See* Israel Antiquities Authority; Israel Exploration Society; Survey of Israel.]

The overall general impact of the American-generated New Archaeology must be assessed. As biblical archaeology moved from a relative backwater into the mainstream of archaeology in the 1970s it was considerably influenced by the New Archaeology then current, especially by its much more anthropological than historical orientation, and its concern with culture and culture change (so-called "processual archaeology"). Yet, if the full impact of the New Archaeology was felt, it was so only belatedly: the antihistorical attitude and theoretical thrust toward positivist philosophies of science were rejected outright; and the actual changes were more a matter of style than of substance. The real contribution of the "New Archaeology" lay first of all in its commitment to multidisciplinary methods and its insistence on explicit, self-conscious statements of methods and purpose, as we have seen. Second, the broad overriding ecological approach placed all archaeological research in the broad context in which it belongs. These aspects of Americanist "New Archaeology" should remain features of Syro-Palestinian archaeology as it moves into the next phase of its own development.

A still newer approach to recovering the past developed in the late 1980s: the postprocessualist archaeology. Specifically identified with several British archaeologists such as Cambridge's Ian Hodder (cf. *Reading the Past: Current Approaches to Interpretation in Archaeology,* Cambridge, 1986), this approach rejects the positivism, scientism, and determinism of the more extreme expressions of the New Archaeology. It returns to more traditional, symbolic, ideological (or "mentalist"), and historical explanations of culture change. It views "context" (Hodder's preferred term) as broader than the ecological setting—as embracing the concept of culture in its widest sense. This more balanced and eclectic approach may be particularly congenial to future Syro-Palestinian and biblical archaeologists.

Current Status: Two Disciplines. The trends of the 1970s and 1980s resulted in sweeping and probably permanent change. American Syro-Palestinian archaeology has emerged as an autonomous academic and professional discipline, often quite independent of biblical studies, with its own appropriate aims and methods. The change of name from biblical to Syro-Palestinian archaeology (reviving Albright's original designation in the 1930s) is now widely used, appropriately reflecting the new reality. That is to say, this field is simply a branch of Near Eastern or Levantine archaeology—the other accepted branches being Egyptian, Anatolian, Mesopotamian, and Iranian archaeology (Cypriot archaeology may straddle the border between Near Eastern and classical archaeology).

The specialization of Syro-Palestinian archaeology focuses primarily on ancient Canaan, which includes biblical Israel in the Iron Age. No longer "the handmaiden of history," as a former generation put it—and especially not of biblical history—Syro-Palestinian archaeology has come of age as a parallel but unique means of investigating the past, based not on texts alone but primarily on material culture remains. The archaeology of ancient Palestine as a cultural entity is still allied with biblical and ancient Near Eastern studies, ancillary and contributory disciplines. Increasingly, however, it is multidisciplinary, linked also with general archaeology, with social and cultural anthropology, with the social sciences, and even with the natural sciences, when analytical procedures are required.

The secularization of Syro-Palestinian archaeology also poses a challenge. The long-dominant understanding of the history of ancient Israel as unique, or *Heilsgeschichte* ("salvation history"), has given way to an approach that sees ancient Israel and Canaan in terms of *Siedlungsgeschichte,* the long, complex settlement history of the ancient Near East generally (similar to *la longue dureé* of Fernand Braudel and historians of the *annales* school). Invoking the deus ex machina of divine purpose does nothing to elucidate the actual phenomena of culture and culture change, even in ancient Palestine. Syro-Palestinian archaeology, as a basically historical discipline, deals with the problem of reconstructing ancient events, or "What happened?" Exegesis and theology deal with the question "What did/does it mean?" These may indeed be complementary tasks; however, honest inquiry demands that they be kept separate, at least initially. Syro-Palestinian archaeology has now matured to where it is ready to assume its proper role in this and other dialogues. Ironically, it is the new "secular" archaeology that promises to contribute most to biblical studies, precisely because it is indifferent, in the best sense of the word (below).

Toward a Dialogue. Biblical archaeology—or "the archaeology of Palestine in the biblical period"—is not a surrogate for Syro-Palestinian archaeology, or even a discipline at all in the academic sense. It is a branch of biblical studies, an interdisciplinary pursuit that seeks to utilize the pertinent results of archaeological research to elucidate the historical and cultural setting of the Bible. In short, biblical archaeology is what it always was, except for the brief Albright-Wright period. The crucial issue for biblical archaeology is properly conceived as a dialogue to achieve the proper relationship between its understanding and use of archaeology on the one hand, and its understanding of the issues in biblical studies that are fitting subjects for archaeological illumination on the other.

What is that relationship? That is, what can archaeology and biblical studies contribute to each other? First, archaeology is unique in providing an immediate context in Canaan in which to situate the places, peoples, and events of the Bible—most of which would otherwise be without any external witness, and therefore are problematic for the historian. In particular, most aspects of the daily lives of ordinary people would not be known because the biblical writers and editors were, rather, preoccupied with the grand schemes of their own brand of theocratic history. The *Sitz im Leben* ("life-setting") that the form-critical and traditio-historical schools of biblical scholarship sought for specific biblical texts and larger blocks of material remains at best a *Sitz im Literatur,* apart from the real-life setting archaeology and archaeology alone can provide.

Second, archaeological discoveries, including the textual evidence recovered through excavation, enable us to paint the broader canvas of ancient Near Eastern peoples and cultures, against which Israel's distinctiveness (if not her uniqueness) can be more accurately portrayed and fully appreciated. Such comparative cultural study, based on archaeological investigation and its unique angle of vision on the past, provides a perspective that no other approach can, certainly not one based on minute internal analysis of the texts alone. Finally, archaeology can contribute to questions of faith and morality, although not by offering "proofs." It does, however, have its limits: archaeology illuminates, but cannot confirm; it brings understanding, but not necessarily belief. Yet, a grasp of the material reality of ancient Israel, in all its variety and vitality, can make the Bible both accessible and credible.

The dialogue can be viewed from the opposite perspective, that is, what can biblical studies contribute to Syro-Palestinian archaeology? It can interpret the texts of the Bible in the light of the best modern tools of philology, literary-critical, exegetic, and hermeneutic principles. Because this is a complex, highly specialized task, teamwork among specialists is required. Here the contribution of biblical scholarship to archaeology is essential because the Hebrew Bible is virtually all the literature there is for Iron Age Palestine. Despite the limitations of theological biases, biblical literature provides a wealth of information on conditions in Palestine, as well as an outline of its political history and ideology—at least of the ruling classes, scribal schools, and theological circles that produced the Bible in its final version. Archaeology is not "mute" without texts, as biblical scholars such as Martin Noth and others have long maintained; however, its voice is amplified considerably when textual records are available and happen to accord well with the interpretation of material culture remains.

There is little to be said about archaeology and New Testament studies in this context. Biblical archaeology has been almost exclusively the province of scholars of the Hebrew Bible—largely because of the long sweep of biblical history, the vast setting of the ancient Near East, the paucity of direct extrabiblical historical testimony, and the complex historiographic issues involved. By contrast, the New Testament covers a brief, extremely well-documented period in Roman Syria-Palestine and Asia Minor. In addition, the theological issues involved in the study of Christian origins have not been thought amenable to archaeological investigation in the same way as the origins of early Israel.

[See also New Archaeology. In addition, the sites mentioned are the subject of independent entries.]

BIBLIOGRAPHY

Albright, William Foxwell. "The Impact of Archaeology on Biblical Research." In *New Directions in Biblical Archaeology,* edited by David Noel Freedman and Jonas C. Greenfield, pp. 1–16. Garden City, N.Y., 1969.
Bar-Yosef, Ofer, and Amihai Mazar. "Israeli Archaeology." *World Archaeology* 13 (1982): 310–325.
Ben-Tor, Amnon, ed. *The Archaeology of Ancient Israel.* New Haven, 1992.
Broshi, Magen. "Religion, Ideology, and Politics and Their Impact on Palestinian Archaeology." *Israel Museum Journal* 6 (1987): 17–32.
Dever, William G. *Archaeology and Biblical Studies: Retrospects and Prospects.* Evanston, Ill., 1974.
Dever, William G. "Syro-Palestinian and Biblical Archaeology." In *The Hebrew Bible and Its Modern Interpreters,* edited by Douglas A. Knight and Gene M. Tucker, pp. 31–74. Chico, Calif., 1985.
Dever, William G. *Recent Archaeological Discoveries and Biblical Research.* Seattle, 1990.
Dever, William G. "Biblical Archaeology: Death and Rebirth?" In *Biblical Archaeology Today, 1990: Proceedings of the Second International Congress on Biblical Archaeology, Jerusalem, June–July 1990,* edited by Avraham Biran and Joseph Aviram, pp. 706–722. Jerusalem, 1993.
Drinkard, Joel F., et al., eds. *Benchmarks in Time and Culture: An Introduction to Palestinian Archaeology Dedicated to Joseph A. Callaway.* Atlanta, 1988.
Glock, Albert E. "Biblical Archaeology: An Emerging Discipline." In *The Archaeology of Jordan and Other Studies Presented to Siegfried H. Horn,* edited by Lawrence T. Geraty and Larry G. Herr, pp. 85–101. Berrien Springs, Mich., 1986.
King, Philip J. *American Archaeology in the Mideast: A History of the American Schools of Oriental Research.* Winona Lake, Ind., 1983.
Kuhnen, Hans-Peter. *Palästina in Griechisch-Römischer zeit.* Handbuch der Archäologie Vorderasiens, 2.2. Munich, 1990.
Mazar, Amihai. *Archaeology of the Land of the Bible, 10,000–586 B.C.E.* New York, 1988.
Meyers, Carol L., and Eric M. Meyers. "Expanding the Frontiers of Biblical Archaeology." *Eretz-Israel* 20 (1989): 140*–147*.
Meyers, Carol L. "The Contributions of Archaeology." In *The Oxford Study Bible,* edited by M. Jack Suggs et al., pp. 48–56. New York, 1992.
Moorey, P. R. S. *A Century of Biblical Archaeology.* Cambridge, 1991.
Noth, Martin. "Die Beitrag der Archäologie zur Geschichte Israels." *Vetus Testamentum Supplement* 7 (1960): 262–282.
Perdue, Leo G., et al., eds. *Archaeology and Biblical Interpretation: Essays in Memory of D. Glenn Rose.* Atlanta, 1987.
Silberman, Neil Asher. *Digging for God and Country: Exploration, Archaeology, and the Secret Struggle for the Holy Land, 1799–1917.* New York, 1982.
Weippert, Helga. *Palästina in Vorhellenisticher zeit.* Handbuch der Archäologie Vorderasiens, 2.1. Munich, 1988.
Wright, G. Ernest. "Biblical Archaeology Today." In *New Directions in Biblical Archaeology,* edited by David Noel Freedman and Jonas C. Greenfield, pp. 149–165. Garden City, N.Y., 1969.

WILLIAM G. DEVER

BIBLICAL LITERATURE. [*To survey the chronological range and literary genres of the books of the Bible and to discuss the formation of the formal canon, this entry comprises two articles:* Hebrew Scriptures *and* New Testament.]

Hebrew Scriptures

The dramatic changes in biblical scholarship during the late twentieth century have shattered the relative consensus that much of the field had enjoyed since the advent of historical criticism in the late 1800s. Feminist, reader-response, deconstructionist, and other new approaches have challenged understandings not only of individual books and passages but indeed of the Bible's very nature and origins.

These heated and on-going debates center on a collection of documents, most of which are believed to have been written in Hebrew, that are accepted as religious canon by Judaism and Christianity. The modern Jewish canon has a tripartite organization: the Torah (the first five books, also called the Pentateuch); Prophets, subdivided into Former

Prophets (*Joshua* through *Kings*) and Latter Prophets (*Isaiah* through *Malachi*); and Writings (a variety of materials, from *Psalms* to *Chronicles*). The early Christian canon retained these books as well as deuteroncanonical writings from the Greek-speaking world; to enhance how the collection would lead to the additional documents about Jesus also accepted by the church, Christianity renamed the earlier collection the Old Testament and moved the Latter Prophets to its end. The Protestant Reformers later removed the deuterocanonicals, labeling them Apocrypha. Hence, while Jews, Roman Catholics, and Protestants rightly may be said to share the books found in the Hebrew Scriptures, each community understands differently the significance of a given book within its respective canon, a reality that is also reflected in the ordering of the books in each tradition.

These modern canons include many different types of literature. The Torah narrates events from the creation of the world through the death of Moses, interspersing judicial and cultic regulations as well as poetry. The Former Prophets are primarily narrative in form and cover Israelite history from the entry into the land of Canaan through the fall of Judah. Poetic oracles dominate the Latter Prophets, although biographical narratives occasionally intertwine. The Writings contain liturgical poetry *(Psalms)*, instructions on "wisdom" *(Proverbs, Ecclesiastes, Job, Song of Songs)*, short narratives *(Esther, Ruth)* and miscellaneous books, such as *Lamentations*.

Getting a Text. Such a straightforward description of the organization and content of these existing canons can, however, obscure the fact that the Hebrew Bible as a whole and its constituent parts have undergone an extended process of collection, canonization, transmission, and translation. As a result of the lack of autographs (originals), even determining the text of the collection can be problematic. Modern translators rely on manuscripts (handwritten copies), some of which are removed from their assumed originals by more than a thousand years. The two principal manuscripts, used exclusively prior to 1940 and still used today, are medieval in date. Manuscripts found in the Judean Desert since the 1940s have given scholars more ancient scraps of biblical materials but no complete copies of the whole. Early translations (versions) in languages such as Greek, Coptic, and Syriac also inform textual judgments.

Because such manuscripts and subsequent codices were created in and preserved by religious communities, determining what is genuinely ancient is a matter of scholarly judgment. During the history of biblical interpretation, scholars interested in the historical information the Hebrew Scriptures can provide have developed a number of critical methodologies, such as source criticism, form criticism, and redaction criticism. Recently, however, these methods have been challenged—both in the results they produce and the assumptions from which they work.

Finding an Author. Although many modern books are the products of a single author writing from a consistent point of view, the great variations in content and style between and within biblical books suggest quite different origins. Alert for inconsistencies in style, vocabulary, and theology, source criticism arose in the 1800s to distinguish the signs of multiple authors. For example, Julius Wellhausen (*Prolegomena to the History of Ancient Israel,* reprint, Gloucester, 1983) argued that the Pentateuch was not the work of Moses but rather a compilation of four discrete sources, the first written during the Monarchy and the last in the postexilic period.

Form criticism as developed in the early 1900s claimed that the biblical materials are yet more ancient. Hermann Gunkel (*What Remains of the Old Testament and Other Essays,* translated by A. K. Dallas, New York, 1928) and his successors interpreted recurring motifs and stereotypical formulae as signs that biblical writings preserve a prior oral stage. Within this framework, some of the writings now found in the Hebrew Bible may be very ancient, perhaps as old as the patriarchs.

Although source and form criticism are still practiced, both have waned in popularity. Myriad literary studies of biblical narrative have argued that source "inconsistencies" exist in the eye of the beholder and that ancient Semitic writers worked within a different aesthetic than that of modern Europeans. While studies of folklore and anthropology continue to trace elements of orality, form criticism has recently been challenged—by John van Seters (*In Search of History: Historiography in the Ancient World and the Origins of Biblical History,* New Haven, 1983) in the case of the Pentateuch, and by other literary studies that attribute formulae and repetitions to creative authors in other portions of the Bible.

Dating the Composition. Describing the time period a text talks "about" is much less difficult than determining "when" it was written, although neither may be readily tied to recognized archaeological time periods. Biblical history is usually divided according to the political history of the Israelite and later Judean nations, and thus does not directly coincide with the archaeological designations of the Bronze or Iron Age.

Using biblical terminology, the Hebrew Bible relates material about an undated prehistory through the Hellenistic period. In regard to when it was written, greater consensus exists for the more recent periods than for early ones. For example, that parts of the Bible were written in the Hellenistic period is generally accepted *(Daniel, Ecclesiastes,* perhaps *Joel)*, and much material is seen to derive from the Persian period (the last of the prophets, some wisdom texts, *Ezra, Nehemiah)*. The Babylonian period is well represented *(Jeremiah, Ezekiel,* parts of the Pentateuch, perhaps the Former Prophets), as is the Assyrian period *(Isaiah, Amos, Hosea)*.

How many of the writings precede the Assyrian period, however, is questioned. Building on Wellhausen, Gerhard von Rad (*The Problem of the Hextateuch and Other Essays,* translated by E. W. Trueman Dicken, London, 1984) dated the first strand of the Pentateuch (J) to the era of Solomon. Few modern scholars place the writing of biblical materials before the Monarchy, although the Song of Deborah (*Jg.* 5) and the Song of Moses (*Dt.* 32) may be earlier compositions.

Making Comparisons. In dating discussions, in analyses of literary genres, and in historical reconstructions, scholars have turned to other literature from the ancient Near East for illumination. Comparisons abound, offering much fodder for scholarly debate. Such parallels provide rich background regarding the cosmological, cultural, and religious milieu of the ancient Near East. Mythological texts from Mesopotamia and Ugarit are particularly helpful in this regard. Concerned with the division of the elements from chaos, the loss of immortality because of a sly snake, and the ability of one man to survive a flood on a boat, the Mesopotamian documents *Enūma elish* and the epics of Gilgamesh and Atraḥasis appear to be the backdrop against which the writers of *Genesis* worked. Ugaritic myths of Baal's ordeal in the underworld illumine some psalmic and prophetic language.

Similarly, comparison of biblical legal material with that of Mesopotamian and Hittite cultures reveals many similarities, both in individual laws and in their underlying values. Laws often considered unique to Israel (such as sabbath observance and an owner's responsibility for a goring ox) have Mesopotamian counterparts. In addition, the covenant ideology in which biblical law is presented employs diplomatic language typical of Hittite and Assyrian treaties.

Much of the Writings section utilizes common ancient Near Eastern literary types. The Psalms, for example, often adapt Mesopotamian, Ugaritic, and Egyptian hymnody to the monotheism of later Israel. Large portions of the *Book of Proverbs* draw from the Egyptian wisdom text "The Instruction of Amenemope," and the books of *Job* and *Ecclesiastes* and the *Song of Songs* bear equally strong literary ties to other forms of Near Eastern literature.

Although scholars have long recognized the benefit of such comparisons in appreciating the intellectual and cultural environment in which the Bible arose, much more debated is the accuracy with which specific events recorded in the Hebrew Bible can be verified in extrabiblical documents. A prime example of such disagreement concerns the date of the Exodus. Followers of William Foxwell Albright (for example, John Bright, *A History of Israel,* 3d ed., Philadelphia, 1981) insist on a thirteenth-century date for the Exodus based on the mention of "Israel" on Pharaoh Merneptah's victory marker (1220 BCE) and on an identification with the store cities mentioned in *Exodus* 1:11 with Egyptian sites. Earlier dates for the Exodus are embraced by scholars who correlate the *ḥapiru* mentioned in the Amarna texts with the Hebrew people: if Canaanite rulers were complaining about marauding "Hebrews" in the fourteenth century BCE, the Exodus would necessarily have taken place earlier. A good number of European scholars today are questioning whether the Exodus actually occurred. Similar debates have arisen as well over dating the nature of the Israelite occupation of Canaan and the historicity of the patriarchal narratives.

Forming a Canon. Understanding how stories and books were gathered into larger units and then into a single collection involves understanding how and why documents came to be understood as canonical. A standard view of this process identifies the first move toward "scripture" with a reform movement recorded in *2 Kings* 22, in which a book found in the Temple in Jerusalem (perhaps *Deuteronomy*) served as a basis for a community covenant. With the concept of canon thus established, Ezra the scribe elevated the Pentateuch in postexilic Judah to the status of "law" and introduced provisions prohibiting exogamy. According to this view of canonical development, the Prophets were accepted as canon by the Maccabean period; the Writings, and hence the whole Hebrew Bible, were ratified by a rabbinic council at Yavneh/Jamnia in about 90 CE.

Alternatives to this understanding of canon development have been offered. According to Martin Noth (English translation: *The Deuteronomistic History,* Sheffield, 1981), since *Deuteronomy* through *Kings* forms a continuous narrative, *Deuteronomy* would have been composed not with the rest of the Pentateuch but as part of a longer historical work called the Deuteronomistic History. David Noel Freedman ("The Formation of the Canon of the Old Testament," in *Religion and Law: Biblical-Judaic and Islamic Perspectives,* edited by Edwin B. Frimage et al., pp. 315–331, Winona Lake, Ind., 1990) posits that a primary history (*Genesis* through *Kings*), along with much of the prophetic corpus, was complete by 540 BCE and, hence, that *Ezra's* contribution was the reorganization of the collections to exalt a Pentateuch devoid of the conquest. Recent studies of Achaemenid governance of the postexilic community suggest that the impetus for codifying the community's laws and membership criteria may have come from Persia.

Discussions since the 1960s have challenged the assumption that the Council of Jamnia finalized the canon, since the "council" model more resembles later Christian councils than it does a first-century Jewish gathering and since the ordering of biblical books remained fluid until at least 400 CE. In the case of Judaism, Talmud *Bava' Batra'* 14b places the book of *Isaiah* after *Ezekiel,* whereas in the modern Jewish canon *Isaiah* precedes *Jeremiah.* In Christianity, different canonical orders are given by Epiphanius, Cyril of Jerusalem, and Jerome.

Understanding the Current Discussion. Recent biblical scholarship has produced many critiques of older views of biblical origins and canonical development without providing a new consensus in their place. Indicative of the late twentieth-century *Zeitgeist*, newer approaches offer less certainty than they do discrete and passionate voices on these fundamental issues in understanding the Hebrew Scriptures.

[*See also* Hebrew Language and Literature.]

BIBLIOGRAPHY

Bright, John. *A History of Israel,* 3d edition. Philadelphia, 1981.

Childs, Brevard S. *Introduction to the Old Testament as Scripture.* Philadelphia, 1979. Explains the processes and movements of canon formation.

Freedman, David N. "The formation of the Canon of the Old Testament." In *Religion and Law: Biblical-Judaic and Islamic Perspectives,* edited by E. B. Frimage et al., pp. 315–331. Winona Lake, Ind., 1990.

Gunkel, Hermann. *What Remains of the Old Testament and Other Essays.* Translated by A. K. Dallas. New York, 1983.

Hayes, John H., and J. Maxwell Miller, eds. *Israelite and Judaean History.* Philadelphia, 1977. Collection of essays balancing the historically optimistic views of Albright and Bright.

Haynes, Stephen R., and Steven L. McKenzie, eds. *To Each Its Own Meaning: An Introduction to Biblical Criticisms and Their Applications.* Louisville, Ky., 1993. Provides explanations and examples of traditional approaches (historical, source, and form criticism), as well as more modern ones (feminist, poststructuralist).

Knight, Douglas A., and Gene M. Tucker, eds. *The Hebrew Bible and Its Modern Interpreters.* Chico, Calif., 1985. Surveys contemporary thought on most of the topics discussed in this article, with a review of each of the Hebrew Bible's major sections.

Noth, Martin. *The Deuteronomistic History.* Journal for the Study of the Old Testament Supplement Series, no. 15. Sheffield, 1981.

Pritchard, James B., ed. *Ancient Near Eastern Texts Relating to the Old Testament.* 3d ed. Princeton, 1969. Standard collection of ancient texts offering few explanatory or critical notes; more helpful for general background to the literature than as a source document for scholars.

Rad, Gerhard von. *The Problem of the Hexateuch and Other Essays.* Translated by E. W. Trueman Dicken. London, 1984.

Van Seters, John. *In Search of History.* New Haven, 1983.

Wellhausen, Julius. *Prolegomena to the History of Ancient Israel.* Gloucester, 1983.

JULIA M. O'BRIEN

New Testament

The New Testament is a collection of twenty-seven individual documents written between about 50 and 150 CE, the period following the initial founding of the Christian movement. They were originally written for small, specific audiences (either congregations or individuals) but were collected during the next two centuries to form a body of literature. Circulation in this form also influenced the development of the codex (or book type) of manuscript production that became popular among Christians in place of scrolls. Of the twenty-seven documents, the majority (twenty were originally written in the form of private letters, and two more (*Hebrews* and *Revelation*) incorporate epistolary features. Because of the diverse and particular nature of the documents, the process of collection and editing to form the present New Testament canon was sometimes complex and contentious.

The earliest New Testament writings are the genuine letters of Paul, dating to the Aegean period of his ministry (c. 50–60 CE). Paul's first letters were written to fledgling house-church congregations of predominantly gentile converts, for whom the letters served as encouragement or to answer questions that arose after Paul had moved on. [*See* House Churches.] The earliest letter is *1 Thessalonians* (c. 51 CE); Paul wrote it while in Corinth, and within a relatively short time after he had left Thessalonike after founding the congregation there. From Corinth, Paul proceeded to Ephesus, which was to become his base of operations for most of this period. [*See* Ephesus.] He continued to make a regular circuit of visits, but in the interim often sent coworkers, such as Timothy and Titus, bearing a letter from him to a community. Letter writing in the Greco-Roman world followed certain highly stylized conventions of form and address. Paul adopted many of them in his writing, adapting them to a given occasion's particular needs or issues. Formal analysis of the genre and conventions has been greatly enhanced by the discoveries of many private letters on papyrus from Egypt and elsewhere. In addition to giving advice and encouragement, Paul's letters often served as formal letters of recommendation in which he sought hospitality for himself (*Phlm.* 22) or his coworkers (*Rom.* 16:2; *Phil* 2:25–29).

The New Testament contains two letters from Paul to Corinth (*1 Cor.,* from c. 54; *2 Cor.,* from c. 56/57), both written in Ephesus. From internal references (cf. *1 Cor.* 5:9; *2 Cor.* 2:3; 7:8), it is clear that Paul also wrote at least two other letters to Corinth that are now lost. The sequence of these letters is, therefore, (1) letter now lost; (2) *1 Corinthians;* (3) letter lost (partially?); and (4) *2 Corinthians.* Moreover, analysis of *2 Corinthians* reveals a later composite of fragments of several letters, especially (3) and (4) and perhaps one or two more. The various Christian groups at Corinth also wrote letters to Paul (cf. *1 Cor.* 7:1). There are other letters by Paul that may incorporate fragments of several letters (e.g., *Philippians*), and there are several other lost letters (cf. *Phil.* 3:1; *Col.* 4:16). All the genuine letters from Paul were written from 50 to 60 CE, in the Aegean; the last was most likely his letter to Rome, which was to prepare the way for his intended mission to Spain.

Following Paul's death there was some concern on the part of his followers in these regions to preserve the apostle's legacy and teachings. This led to the composition of pseudonymous (or pseudepigraphic) letters written in his name. Of the thirteen letters in the New Testament attributed to Paul, the authenticity of seven is debated: *2 Thessalonians, Colossians, Ephesians,* and the so-called Pastoral Epistles (*1, 2 Tm.; Ti.*). *Ephesians* and the Pastorals are the least likely to have been written by Paul. The explicit address "who are at Ephesus" does not appear at all in the oldest manuscripts of the so-called Ephesian letter; it was probably produced nearer the end of the first century, at about the time that a collection of Paul's letters was first being assembled. The Pastoral Epistles may derive from some partially preserved writing by Paul (in *2 Tm.*); however, in their present form, they were probably produced in the early to mid-second century.

There is a wide range of composition, date, and authorship questions relating to letters in the New Testament not attributed to Paul. The *Epistle of James* is generally associated with the brother of Jesus who, according to tradition, led the Jewish Christian community in Jerusalem until his death (c. 64 CE), just prior to the beginning of the First Jewish Revolt against Rome. [*See* First Jewish Revolt.] Some scholars have suggested, however, that it is a later pseudonymous composition, probably dating to near the turn of the second century. The two epistles attributed to Peter are likely by different authors: *1 Peter* is a pseudepigraph with influences from Pauline tradition (especially the debated letters *Colossians* and *Ephesians*) and was probably written sometime in the first decade of the second century, in Asia Minor. The letter *2 Peter* appears to be later still (probably from the 120s or so); it draws on (and is thus later than) the *Epistle of Jude* and seems to reflect an existing collection of Paul's letters (cf. *2 Pt.*, 3:15–17). The situation addressed by *2 Peter* may be similar to that in *2 Thessalonians* because both address disputes and opinions over the delay of the eschaton.

The three Johannine letters are probably the work of two distinct schools. The letter *1 John* was probably written by the same group of followers of John who produced the Gospel. Like the Gospel, it can be dated to between 95 and 125 CE. The place of composition is usually thought to be Ephesus, but a Syrian origin (such as Antioch) has been suggested by some scholars. The two short letters, *2* and *3 John*, seem to be by a single author who is never identified except as "The Elder"; they probably come from early in the second century, from Asia Minor. They might have derived their Johannine attribution from the fact that a figure known as John the Elder, not the same as the apostle, was prominent at Ephesus at the end of the first century. The *Book of Revelation* (which carries the Greek title of *The Apocalypse*) is thought by some to be by this same John the Elder because the traditional attribution to the apostle John was disputed in antiquity; the author is, however, clearly different from that of *2* and *3 John*. The date of *Revelation* is traditionally placed at about 95 CE, from Patmos, but it has been variously dated as early as 70 and as late as the second century.

Despite their position within the canon of the New Testament, the Gospels and *Acts* were products of a long and complex compositional history stretching into the second century. According to prevailing scholarly opinion, the earliest of the canonical Gospels to be written was *Mark*; it is usually dated to between 66 and 75 CE. A date sometime after the destruction of Jerusalem in 70 seems the most likely,

given internal references to these events (cf. *Mk.* 13:14). The dates usually assigned to the other Gospels follow: *Matthew*, 75–85/90 CE; *Lk.*, 80–90/95 CE; and *John*, sometime after 95 CE. The Gospels were composed by authors or groups of authors working with a combination of oral and written source materials that they reworked with their own peculiar stories and concerns. Hence, these authors are properly thought of as redactors (or editors) as well. As with most of the New Testament documents, the actual names of the authors remain unknown. The author of *Mark*, for example, likely had available an early collection of miracle stories and an existing passion narrative; however, the final narrative of Jesus' life was the product of the Markan redactor. Both *Matthew* and *Luke* seem to follow the basic outline of *Mark*, although they alter some sections radically in shape or position and add some new material. Each adds some material peculiar to its author, so that it is not possible to know whether it was derived from earlier sources or from the author's own composition. Some 250 verses are common to both *Matthew* and *Luke* (but are entirely missing from *Mark*); therefore, scholars have proposed the existence of a lost source (called Q), which appears to be an early collection of "sayings" material. Recent work on the Q document suggests that it dates from about 50 to 70 CE and that it, too, was edited in various stages over time, prior to its incorporation in *Matthew* and *Luke*. Further corroboration of the existence of such a collection of sayings has been given since the discovery among the Nag Hammadi (Egypt) library of a complete Coptic text of the *Gospel of Thomas*, a noncanonical sayings Gospel (originally composed in Greek, probably in Syria) variously dated either before about 70 or to between 100 and 140 CE). [*See* Nag Hammadi.]

The editorial process at work in each of these Gospels derives in large measure from the context in which each was used. These earliest narrative compilations of the life of Jesus were told and retold within particular Christian communities. The tone and details of the narrative were shaped according to the circumstances of each community. *Matthew*, for example, was written in Upper Galilee or in Lower Syria (the nearer diaspora) in a context in which emergent Pharisaic and Christian groups were competing to establish their identities. The Christian community of *Matthew*'s Gospel still thinks of itself as completely Jewish, but it feels pressure from other Jewish groups. The vitriolic anti-Pharisaic sentiments attributed to Jesus in *Matthew* are in reality a reflection of this tension in the period of post-70 reconstruction, rather than the situation in Jesus' own day. In sharp contrast, both *Luke* and *John* seem to come from a decidedly Greek environment; each has been claimed as having been written in Antioch and Asia Minor. *John*'s development of the synoptic tradition seems to favor some highly Platonic philosophical speculations, similar to those found in Philo of Alexandria. It has been suggested that *John* went through five stages of editing to achieve its present form sometime after the death of its namesake, the apostle John. *Luke,* on the other hand, comes from a later follower of the Pauline tradition, who adapts the synoptic tradition to meet the more cultured literary tastes of a Greco-Roman audience. *Luke* seems to follow the Greek genres of history writing and novelistic fiction. What sets *Luke* apart in the development of the Early Christian literary tradition is that it was clearly designed from the outset as a two-part narrative that continues in *Acts* (cf. *Lk.* 1.1–4 with *Acts* 1.1). The formal preface and dedication combine with the stylistic features of the writing to make this the most literary document in the New Testament.

None of the writings of the New Testament have survived in their earliest manuscript form: all are copies of copies that were preserved chiefly through the process of collection beginning in the early to mid-second century. The earliest manuscript version of Paul's letters (the Chester Beatty II papyrus [P46], c. end of the second century), however, clearly omits the Pastoral Epistles. The earliest impulse to assemble such a collection seems to have begun around the legacy of Paul in the churches of Asia Minor and Greece. By the 110s, a partial collection of Paul's letters was known by Ignatius of Antioch, but he does not reflect a knowledge of the diverse Gospel traditions. By the 140s, at least a partial collection of Paul's letters (omitting the Pastorals) was known and used by Marcion, but he refused to accept any Gospel other than *Luke.* Marcion was originally from Sinope on the Black Sea but migrated to Rome, where he was eventually excommunicated as a heretic.

The earliest canon list that resembles the shape of the present New Testament comes from the so-called Muratorian fragment; preserved in a later Latin manuscript from Milan, it dates to about 180–200 and is most likely from Rome. The beginning is lost, but the fragment commences by naming *Luke* as the Third Gospel; its strenuous defense of the authorship of John suggests that it was written in response to an ongoing debate. While it includes the deutero-Pauline letters, it omits *Hebrews, James,* and both Petrine letters. It accepts the debated *Apocalypse of John,* but also included the apocryphal *Apocalypse of Peter* and the *Wisdom of Solomon.* While it knew of other churches (notably in Alexandria) that accepted the Shepherd of Hermas, the Muratorian canon list treats it as secondary—that is, suitable for admonition but not worthy of being numbered among the prophets and apostles. It seems that this last twofold designation was the term by which the entire Christian Bible was conceptualized in the Muratorian list, with the "prophets" designating those books of the Hebrew canon, and the "apostles," the equivalent of the New Testament. It is the first clear reference to this two-part structure in the Christian tradition. While a core of works (the four Gospels and the letters of Paul) seem to have been fixed from the mid-second century, other works (notably *Hebrews* and *Revela-*

tion) continued to be debated into the fourth century. At the same time, numerous other writings were being produced, some with purported apostolic authority. These divisive issues were further fueled by the fact that each geographic region and local sectarian group often used different collections or other competing works. By the time of Constantine, therefore, calls for unity were beginning, and these eventually resulted in the establishment of criteria for considering works as Scripture. Eusebius of Caesarea (c. 325) designated three categories: those "accepted" (Gk., *homologoumena*) as Scripture, those disputed (Gk., *antilegomena*), and those that are spurious (Greek., *en tois nothois*). His final list is less than clear, however, because only twenty writings were in the first category, most of the so-called catholic epistles appear in the second, and *Revelation* seems to be in the last. Athanasius of Alexandria (in his *Festal Letter* 39 of 367 CE) produced the first list of New Testament books that corresponds to that used today. This list was eventually ratified by practice rather than dogmatic assertion in later Christian councils, even though some debate continued into the sixth century.

BIBLIOGRAPHY

Aland, Kurt, and Barbara Aland. *The Text of the New Testament.* 2d ed. Leiden, 1989.

Campenhausen, Hans von. *The Formation of the Christian Bible.* Philadelphia, 1972.

Ferguson, Everett. "Canon Muratori: Date and Provenance." *Studia Patristica* 18 (1982): 677–683.

Gamble, Harry. *The New Testament Canon: Its Making and Meaning.* Philadelphia, 1985.

Koester, Helmut. *Introduction to the New Testament,* vol. 2, *History and Literature of Early Christianity.* Philadelphia, 1982.

Koester, Helmut. *Ancient Christian Gospels: Their History and Development.* London, 1990.

McDonald, Lee M. *The Formation of the Christian Biblical Canon.* Nashville, 1988.

Metzger, Bruce M. *The Canon of the New Testament: Its Origin, Development, and Significance.* Oxford, 1987.

Stowers, Stanley K. *Letter Writing in Greco-Roman Antiquity.* Philadelphia, 1986.

L. MICHAEL WHITE

BIBLICAL TEMPLE. The biblical temple is understood to be the Temple of Solomon, completed in about 953 BCE and destroyed in about 587 BCE (commonly known as the First Temple), and the Temple of Zerubbabel, dedicated in 516 BCE, substantially expanded and restored by King Herod beginning in 20 BCE, and destroyed by the Romans under Titus in 70 CE (a long and complex phase of the biblical temple commonly known as the Second Temple). The sole literary source for the First Temple and the Zerubbabel phase of the Second Temple is the Hebrew Bible.

The Herodian transformations of the Zerubbabel Temple

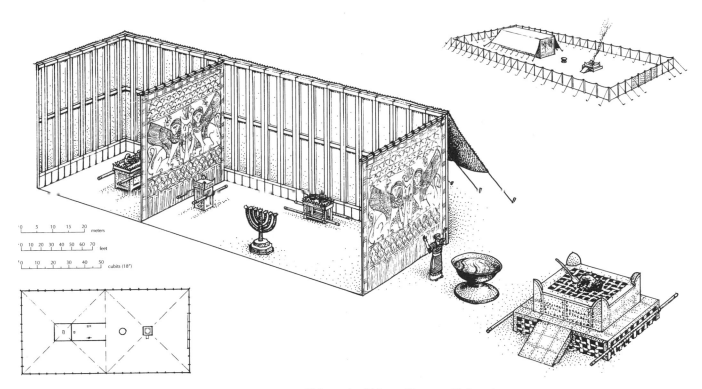

BIBLICAL TEMPLE. *Tabernacle of Moses.* (Courtesy M. Lyon)

are described at length in the writings of the ancient Jewish historian Josephus, who was an eyewitness to the destruction of the Second Temple. There are many other records describing various aspects of the architecture and ritual of the Second Temple, chief among them the Mishnaic tracts *Middot* and *Sheqalim*. Also important are the writings of Philo and the intertestamental Apocrypha and Pseudepigrapha, particularly *Maccabees* (Books 1 and 2). The New Testament also has many references to the Second Temple in its Herodian phase. From among the Dead Sea Scrolls, the Temple Scroll, although visionary in spirit, probably had the Zerubbabel Temple as its point of reference and may have influenced the architecture and decoration of the Herodian temple.

Perhaps the greatest irony regarding the archaeology of the Near East is that the biblical temple, arguably the most famous sacred structure in world history, is entirely absent, in all its phases, in the archaeological record. The primary reason for this is that the Temple Mount in Jerusalem, the building site of the First and Second Temples, is also a Muslim holy site, the location of the Dome of the Rock, and is thus unavailable for archaeological excavation or exploration. In addition, the absence of any archaeological remains of the temples is that they were destroyed more than once in antiquity, which resulted as well in the thorough looting of precious metals and the destruction and looting of ritual objects. The building history of the subsequent phases (in-

cluding the preparation of the foundations for the Dome of the Rock in the seventh century CE), resulted in the clearing away and scattering as rubble the remains of earlier phases.

The unavailability of archaeological remains has led to the extensive use of archaeological analogy, in which the excavated remains of shrines from approximately contemporary sites in Syria and Palestine have been used to achieve a sense of what the First Temple, in particular, may actually have looked like. A comprehensive volume of architectural plans and diagrams by G. R. H. Wright (1985) presents comparative evidence, and a compilation of comparative material relating to the biblical conceptions of the Temple and ritual has been published by Othmar Keel (1978).

First Temple. The best, indeed the only, evidence for the floor plan, construction methods, decoration, and ritual of the First Temple is found in the Hebrew Bible, primarily *1 Kings* 5–6; *2 Chronicles* 2–3; *Ezekiel* 40–47, and *Psalms*. Other related passages include the looting by Pharaoh Shishak (Sheshonq) during the reign of Rehoboam (*1 Kgs.* 14:25–26); expansion the "new court" built by Jehoshaphat, possibly reflecting the time of the Chronicler (*2 Chr.* 20:5); repairs made during the reign of Jehoash (*2 Kgs.* 12); the looting of precious metals by King Hezekiah to collect tribute for Sennacherib (*2 Kgs.* 18:14–17); the additions of non-Israelite altars and rituals to the Temple and its courtyards by King Ahaz, who replaced the Israelite altar with one he had seen in Damascus, and by Manasseh, who introduced

Phoenician altars and pillars (*2 Kgs.* 16:10–16 and 21:1–9, respectively); and the complete repair, cleansing, restoration, and rededication of the Temple under King Josiah (*2 Kgs.* 22–23).

While the Hebrew Bible provides a clear picture, even in the absence of material remains, there are many discrepancies in the biblical record regarding the various stages in the biblical temple and its ritual: in *1 Kings* 6:2, the House is 30 cubits high; in *2 Chronicles* 3:4, it is 120 cubits high; in *Ezra* 6:3, Cyrus decrees that the Temple should be 60 cubits high; and in both the Qumran Temple Scroll and in Josephus the Second Temple is said to be 60 cubits high (*11QT* 4:10; *War* 5:215). These discrepancies are usually attributed to differing social, political, and religious conditions and points of view between the actual events in the time of David and Solomon and those of the two main Hebrew Bible editors, the Deuteronomist (sixth century BCE) and the Chronicler (fifth century BCE). The classic instance of editorial difference as it affects the Temple accounts is *1 Kings* 8, which depicts King Solomon's dedicatory prayer. According to the earlier biblical view, which is more in line with Canaanite ideas, the Temple was the actual dwelling place of Yahweh (*Ps.* 74:2, 76:3). However, the Deuteronomist (see *1 Kgs.* 8:17–20, 44, 48), tones this view down considerably: the Temple is now built to the name of the Deity, and the sanctuary becomes a house of prayer (*1 Kgs.* 8:41–43).

In the biblical record, the Temple is a tripartite building, of the *Langraum* (Ger., "long room") type, constructed on a straight axis: it had three distinct building units, or elements; was longer than it was wide (as a whole); and the most holy place was directly on the same axis as the worshiper standing at the front entrance. The three units, from front to rear, were the *'ûlām*, the "vestibule," or "porch"; the *hêkāl*, the "cella," or "nave"; and the *dēbîr*, the "inner sanctuary," or most holy place. The length of this building was 60 cubits (the royal cubit was about 21 inches), its width was 20 cubits, and its height was 25 cubits. The *'ûlām* was 20 cubits wide and 10 cubits long (defining it as a *breitraum*, or Ger., "broad room," architectural type). The *hêkāl* was 40 cubits long, and the *dēbîr*, the most holy place, was a cube, 20 cubits on each side. The holy of holies was, thus, 5 cubits shorter than the rest of the building. Of the many attempts to explain this difference, the most plausible is that the inner sanctuary stood over the cosmic "Rock of Foundation"— that part of the rock massif on the Temple Mount that stood for the place of original creation in Israelite cosmogony. This does not necessarily place Solomon's Temple over the present-day Dome of the Rock. Convincing arguments have been made placing the Temple north of the Dome of the Rock, on the same line as the Byzantine-period Golden Gate (which, in turn, was built on a much earlier gate) located in the northern quadrant of the eastern wall of the Temple Mount (Yadin, 1975, p. 95). The Temple was oriented east.

In general, the Temple's floor plan must have subsumed

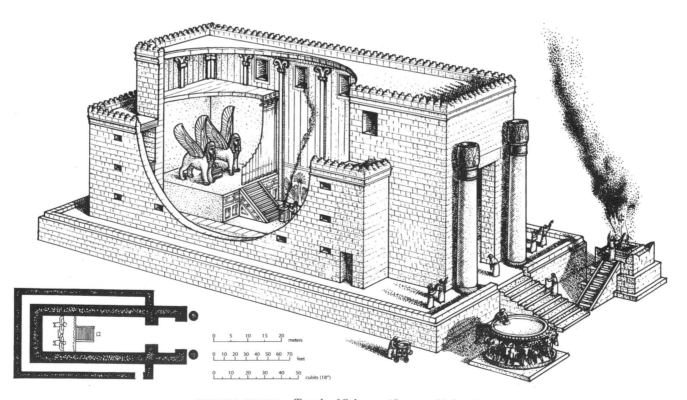

BIBLICAL TEMPLE. *Temple of Solomon.* (Courtesy M. Lyon)

within its walls the location of the biblical Tabernacle. Thus, the *děbîr* housed the Ark of the Covenant and the protective cherubim standing over—and in all probability forming—the cosmic throne of the deity. The *hêkāl* housed the lampstand, table of showbread, and the other ritual objects described for the Tabernacle for the room immediately in front of the inner sanctum. The Tabernacle texts (*Ex.* 25:31, 35:14; 37:17) mention a single lampstand whereas the sources for the First Temple (*1 Kgs.* 7:49) indicate that there were ten lampstands.

A three-story annex surrounded the *hêkāl* and *děbîr* but not the *'ûlām*. Finely dressed ashlars, prepared offsite in a quarry, provided the building material. The entire inner building was lined with cedar and then overlaid with gold. Gilded olive-wood doors formed the entrances both to the *hêkāl* and the *děbîr*. The walls of the nave and inner sanctum were carved with cherubim, palm trees, and flowers and then gilded. According to the Chronicler, a veil of blue, purple, and crimson linen, with cherubim embroidered on it, was hung immediately before the Ark of the Covenant, separating the *děbîr* from the *hêkāl* (*2 Chr.* 3:14). This corresponds exactly to the veil described for the Tabernacle in the desert (*Ex.* 26:31, 36:35). The veil described here stands in place of the olive-wood doors of *1 Kings* and presumably represented the situation at the time of the Chronicler, as it did also in the time of Josephus (*Mt.* 27:51; *Mk.* 15:38; *Lk.* 23:45).

The *'ûlām*, which stood in front of the *hêkāl*, may have been an inner court providing access to the two inner rooms of the divine dwelling. Two hollow, cast-bronze pillars (18 cubits high) stood in front of the *'ûlām*. They were probably freestanding and marked the entry to the inner court (Lundquist, 1982, 1988). The pillars had 5-cubit-high capitals of pomegranates and lotuses and bore enigmatic names, Jachin (the southernmost) and Boaz (the northernmost). They carried cosmic connotations, founding the Temple in the underworld, while uniting it with the heavenly sphere, to tie all three world spheres (heaven, earth, underworld) together in the universal heavenly Temple. The names on the pillars symbolized the cosmic universal rule of Yahweh and of the Davidic dynasty the building of the Temple founded and legitimized: *Jachin* meant that Yahweh founded the dynasty and the Temple, and *Boaz* that Yahweh's power emanates from the Temple (Meyers, 1983). It was this legitimizing power that made possible the promulgation of "law codes" in the temples of the ancient Near East, as well as the enactment of state and dynastic renewal covenant ceremonies, such as that directed by Josiah in front of the pillars (*2 Kgs.* 23:1–3). The pillars as gateposts also signified the entrance of the building's resident, Yahweh, into his dwelling place and of God's sanction of and availability to the national state.

The structural relationship of the *'ûlām* to the pillars may follow the Egyptian model: the pillars may have formed a monumental entrance, the way pylons do in an Egyptian temple, giving way to the open *'ûlām*; or, they may have been structural members of an open porch (the *'ûlām*), either in the North Syrian *bit-ḫilani* style or in the style of the megaron, with the pillars standing in antis.

There were two courts in front of the Temple (*2 Kgs.* 21:5), an inner (*Ez.* 40:28) and an outer (*Ez.* 40:20) court, also known as the upper, and lower courts. At the northeastern corner of the inner court, in front of the Temple, was a wooden altar covered with bronze for burnt offerings, with horns at each of its four corners, according to the prescriptions of *Exodus* 27:1–2, but constructed in the time of David (*2 Sm.* 24:21, 25). In his dedicatory prayer Solomon stood (*1 Kgs.* 8:22) and kneeled (*1 Kgs.* 8:54) before this altar as he prayed. A round bronze basin, 30 cubits in circumference and supported by twelve cast-bronze oxen, stood at the southeast corner of the Temple.

No architect is named, but in the ancient Near East, gods and kings were architects and builders. Kings received architectural plans from the gods through direct revelation, often while spending the night in a sanctuary, as was the case with King Gudea of Lagash (cf. *2 Chr.* 1:7–13: "In that night God appeared to Solomon"—that is, in the high place at Gibeon.) The Temple plan is then presented in *2 Chronicles* 2 (cf. *1 Kgs.* 3:3–5). The beginning of a new dynasty, which often meant the beginning of a new national state, was the time for building a great dynastic temple. According to this ancient pattern, the king went to Lebanon for cedar (*2 Chr.* 2:3–10), for other building materials (*2 Chr.* 2:11–16), and, as is also stated in the biblical records, for the building expertise for which Phoenicia was famed (*2 Kgs.* 7:13–14, 45). Materials and technological assistance may have been accompanied by an architectural plan—which may mean that the First Temple was Phoenician in style—a style strongly influenced by Egypt and that is documented in Lebanon as early as the Egyptian twelfth dynasty (1991–1783 BCE; see Lundquist, 1983b, pp. 205–219).

There was also a long tradition of temple building in Syria and Phoenicia of tripartite, straight-axis temples, with an open *breitraum* porch or vestibule with columns in antis and a *langraum* nave or antecella. In most cases, these temples had a niche in the rear of the nave for the statue of the deity, representing the most holy place. Examples from more recent excavations are Temple D from Middle Bronze Age I Ebla/Tell Mardikh in North Syria, and the three LB temples from Emar/Meskene, on the west bank of the Euphrates River, in Syria, just east of Aleppo (see "Syria and the Temple of Solomon," 1985, pp. 192–193).

The overall impression of the Temple precinct in Jerusalem in the time of Solomon is that of a Near Eastern cosmic temple, sitting on top of the sacred mountain—the ultimate architectural expression of the heavenly temple revealed on the Mountain of God and built after the pattern revealed there (*Ex.* 25:8–9). The primordial waters of the

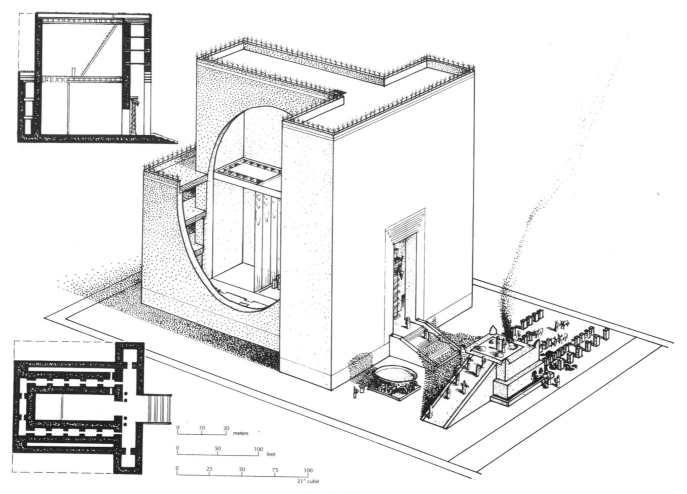

BIBLICAL TEMPLE. *Temple of Herod.* (Courtesy M. Lyon)

abyss from the time of the creation were harnessed, present in the symbolism of the bronze sea. Everywhere were sacred trees and life-giving vegetation, both real-life and carved, representing "the primordial landscape," the state of the world at the creation, whose purpose the temple represents and symbolizes (see Lundquist, 1990, pp. 113–123).

The closer the worshiper came to the inner sanctum, through its sequence of courtyards and chapels, all on a single axis, the holier and more restricted the sacred space became. The most holy place could only be entered by the high priest (once each year on the Day of Atonement) and, during the time of the First Temple, by the king himself (*2 Kgs.* 19:14). Approaching ever nearer to the most holy place, along the axis, the path rose in elevation, perhaps to 5 cubits (see above). This is directly analogous to the situation in Egyptian temples, where the floor level rises at each threshold, until the adyton is reached, which was believed to be built on the primordial mound of creation. In the First Temple, according to this theory, the higher elevation of the *dĕbîr* would have been created by the rock formation below it, the Rock of Foundation, the place creation began.

Second Temple. The Temple Mount lay in ruins for a generation following Nebuchadrezzar's destruction of Jerusalem in 587 BCE. What is known of Zerubbabel's Temple, dedicated in 516 BCE, centers primarily on the difficulties the people had in managing the rebuilding, not on the details of the building itself. *Haggai* gives a sense of how much poorer and less grand the Zerubbabel Temple was in comparison to Solomon's (*Hg.* 2:1–3). At the same time, there is valuable evidence in *Haggai* (e.g., 1:1–11) for the common ancient Near Eastern temple ideology in which the people's dire economic straits are tied directly to their neglect of the Temple (see Lundquist, 1984).

Perhaps the clearest picture of what this phase of the Temple was intended to be, architecturally and in its building methods and decoration, is to be found in Cyrus's decree in *Ezra* 6:1–5: a 60-cubit (broad) by 60-cubit (high) House of God where sacrifices and burnt offerings will be brought, constructed of ashlars and timber, to which the gold and silver vessels taken to Babylon by Nebuchadrezzar will be returned.

As with the biblical accounts of the First Temple, the major sources for the Herodian Temple (Josephus, *Antiq.* 15, *War* 5; Mishnah *Mid.*) provide contradictory information for many important details. Furthermore, the Temple Scroll from Qumran (*11QT*), which stands in roughly the same relationship to the two phases of the Second Temple that *Ezekiel* 40–48 does to the First Temple, provides a visionary source of a future Temple based in some degree—perhaps to a great degree—on the Temple that stood in Jerusalem at the time of the writing of the visionary scripture (Maier, 1989; Delcor, 1989).

The canonical demands of the biblical prescriptions for the Temple determined that Herod's Temple could not be altered in any significant way. Its dimensions were to be 60 cubits long, 60 high, and 20 wide (equivalent dimensions in the First Temple were 60, 25, and 20). The primary way in which Herod altered the Zerubbabel Temple, thereby transforming it into the largest and most spectacular sacred temenos in antiquity, was by greatly expanding the area of the platform (to an area of 67,000 sq m [172,000 sq. yd.]). The temple precinct included an elaborate array of courtyards, beginning with the Court of the Gentiles along the southern perimeter and followed by increasingly sacred courtyards in front of the Temple: from east to west, a Court of the Women, then, passing through the Nicanor Gate, the Court of the Israelites, and finally, just in front of the Temple, the Court of the Priests. Herod also had the outside of the temple covered with gold, which would have created a scene of blinding incandescense in the sunlight (*War* 5:222–223 and passim; *Mid.* 2, 3, 4). The building's implements and furnishings as well were probably crafted on a more sumptuous scale than ever before. Similar arrangements in *11QT* represent part of the evidence for many scholars that *11QT* was a foundation document for the Herodian construction.

[*See also* Jerusalem; Temples.]

BIBLIOGRAPHY

Barker, Margaret. *The Gate of Heaven: The History and Symbolism of the Temple in Jerusalem.* London, 1991. Very important work, exceptionally thorough and insightful.

Busink, Th. A. *Der Tempel von Jerusalem, von Salomon bis Herodes.* 2 vols. Leiden, 1970–1980. Work of vast learning, fundamental to all research on this subject.

Delcor, Mathias. "Is the Temple Scroll a Source of the Herodian Temple?" In *Temple Scroll Studies,* edited by George Brooke, pp. 67–89. Sheffield, 1989.

Gutmann, Joseph, ed. *The Temple of Solomon: Archaeological Fact and Medieval Tradition in Christian, Islamic, and Jewish Art.* Missoula, Mont., 1976. Five articles bringing together fundamental and fairly inaccessible scholarly literature on the Solomonic Temple in the three postbiblical traditions.

Hurowitz, Victor. *I Have Built You an Exalted House.* Sheffield, 1992. Thorough analysis of temple building in ancient Israel in relation to Mesopotamian and northwest Semitic texts.

Keel, Othmar. *The Symbolism of the Biblical World: Ancient Near Eastern Iconography and the Book of Psalms.* New York, 1978.

Lundquist, John M. "The Legitimizing Role of the Temple in the Or-
igin of the State." In *Society of Biblical Literature 1982 Seminar Papers,* edited by Kent H. Richards, pp. 271–295. Chico, Calif., 1982.

Lundquist, John M. "Studies on the Temple in the Ancient Near East." Ph.D. diss., University of Michigan, 1983a. Covers the entire ancient Near East, with heavy emphasis on the First Temple. Very thorough bibliography up to the time of completion.

Lundquist, John M. "What Is a Temple? A Preliminary Typology." In *The Quest for the Kingdom of God: Studies in Honor of George E. Mendenhall,* edited by H. B. Huffmon et al., pp. 205–219. Winona Lake, Ind., 1983b.

Lundquist, John M. "The Common Temple Ideology of the Ancient Near East." In *The Temple in Antiquity,* edited by Truman Madsen, pp. 53–76. Provo, Utah, 1984.

Lundquist, John M. "Temple, Covenant, and Law in the Ancient Near East and in the Old Testament." In *Israel's Apostasy and Restoration: Essays in Honor of Roland K. Harrison,* edited by Avraham Gileadi, pp. 293–305. Grand Rapids, Mich., 1988.

Lundquist, John M. "C. G. Jung and the Temple: Symbols of Wholeness." In *C. G. Jung and the Humanities: Toward a Hermeneutics of Culture,* edited by Karin Barnaby and Pellegrino D'Acierno, pp. 113–123. London, 1990.

Lundquist, John M. *The Temple: Meeting Place of Heaven and Earth.* London, 1993. Application of the author's temple typology in a popular format, with many photographs and illustrations.

Maier, Johann. "The Architectural History of the Temple in Jerusalem in the Light of the Temple Scroll." In *Temple Scroll Studies,* edited by George Brooke, pp. 23–62. Sheffield, 1989. Excellent, detailed account of the relationship of *11QT* to the Second Temple. See also Delcor (above).

Mazar, Benjamin. *The Mountain of the Lord.* Garden City, N.Y., 1975. The most comprehensive coverage of the First and Second Temples, including thorough analysis of ancient evidence and modern archaeology. Exceptionally well illustrated.

Meyers, Carol L. "Jachin and Boaz in Religious and Political Perspective." *Catholic Biblical Quarterly* 45 (1983): 167–178.

Meyers, Carol L. "Temple, Jerusalem." In *The Anchor Bible Dictionary,* vol. 6, pp. 350–369. New York, 1992. Fundamental, comprehensive study of the First and Second Temples.

Ottosson, Magnus. *Temples and Cult Places in Palestine.* Uppsala, 1980. Thorough coverage, with excellent plans and diagrams and extensive presentation of the scholarly literature.

Parry, Donald W., et al., eds. *A Bibliography on Temples of the Ancient Near East and Mediterranean World.* Lewiston, N.Y., 1991. Recent, exhaustive bibliography, with major sections devoted to the biblical temples.

Parry, Donald W., ed. *Temples of the Ancient World: Ritual and Symbolism.* Salt Lake City, 1994. Twenty-four articles dealing with many aspects of biblical, ancient Near Eastern, and Jewish temples, ritual, symbolism, and typology.

Patai, Raphael. *Man and Temple in Ancient Jewish Myth and Ritual.* 2d enl. ed. New York, 1967. One of the most important and interesting books ever written on the subject; brings together the rabbinic material.

Ritmeyer, Kathleen, and Leen Ritmeyer. "Reconstructing Herod's Temple Mount in Jerusalem." *Biblical Archaeology Review* 15 (1989): 23–42. The most thorough compilation and analysis of what is known of the Herodian achievement.

Ritmeyer, Leen. "Locating the Original Temple Mount." *Biblical Archaeology Review* 18 (1992): 24–45, 64–65. Exhaustive and seminal analysis of what is known of the development of the Temple Mount from Solomon's time onward, summarizing and critiquing the various theories of the placement of the temple on the mount.

"Syria and the Temple of Solomon." In *The World Atlas of Archaeology,* pp. 192–193. Boston, 1985. Plans of relevant temples.

Wright, G.R.H. *Ancient Building in South Syria and Palestine.* 2 vols. Handbuch der Orientalistik, vol. 7. Leiden, 1985.

Yadin, Yigael, ed. *Jerusalem Revealed: Archaeology in the Holy City, 1968–1974.* Jerusalem, 1975.

JOHN M. LUNDQUIST

BISITUN (Behistun; Old Pers., **bagastana*, "place of god[s]"), a strategically located, scenically dramatic site in western Iran, some 32 km (20 mi.) east of Bactaran, formerly Kermanshah (34°35′ N, 47°25′ E). The site is variously known for its remains of Paleolithic, pre-Achaemenid, Achaemenid, Parthian, Sasanian, and Islamic date. Preeminently, however, Bisitun is associated with the rock-cut relief and inscriptions the Achaemenid ruler Darius the Great (522–486 BCE) chose to erect, in 520 and 519 BCE, on the precipitous southeast face of the Bisitun mountain (see figure 1). The monument, which provides the only historical account left by an Achaemenid monarch, stands 70 m above the age-old east–west highway that connects the highlands of Media with the Mesopotamian plain. The site appears as Mt. Bagistanon in Diodorus (2.13, after Ctesias).

The relief is approximately 3 m high and 5.5 m wide. It is bordered on three sides by trilingual inscriptions, a circumstance that gives the whole composition a height of about 7 m and an overall width of 18 m. In the earliest stage of the creation of this complex monument, the carved panel was complemented by no more than a single text, in Elamite, which carried the story of Darius's career through the course of his accession year and his first regnal year. Soon after-

ward, a Babylonian version of the text was inscribed on the opposite, left side of the relief. In a stunning innovation that followed the subsequent invention of the Old Persian cuneiform script, Darius chose to introduce, directly beneath the relief, a separate Persian version of the text. Then, in response to fresh triumphs in Darius's second and third regnal years, the existing scheme was arbitrarily expanded. The right-hand limit of the relief was extended into the area occupied by the original Elamite text—and the contents of that text were reinscribed in a new position, to the left of the Old Persian text. In addition, Darius's description of his latest accomplishments came to be accommodated in the final, fifth column of the Old Persian account.

In the beginning of the Bisitun inscription, Darius is clearly concerned about bolstering his claim to the throne. Thus, special stress is laid on his standing as an Achaemenid; and, while his selection as king is ascribed to the divine "favor of Ahuramazda," it is also made clear that it was the personal actions of Darius that were responsible for the downfall of "Gaumata the magus"—an apparent impostor who had abrogated Achaemenid rule. The greater part of the rest of the inscription is taken up with a description of the fate of those who then sought to wrest power from Darius and who were duly overcome, either by Darius himself or by his generals.

As far as possible, the relief offers a single abridged version of the full sweep of these successive events. The tall, commanding figure of Darius, armed with a bow, is shown with his leading foot on the prostrate body of Gaumata, who raises both arms in supplication. Another nine rebel leaders,

BISITUN.   Figure 1.   *Relief of Darius I.* (Deutsches Archäologisches Institut, Abteilung Tehran)

identified, in the fashion of Darius and Gaumata, by trilingual labels, proceed in bonds toward the king. Skunkha, the last of these, was not of course a part of the initial design; his image was cut into the area of the adjacent Elamite inscription after Darius's victory over the pointed-capped Scythians. The scene is completed by three unlabeled figures: two armed (and seemingly noble) attendants, each elegantly attired, like their sovereign, in the full, pleated Persian costume; and a male figure (with a far more ornate crown than that worn by Darius) who rises out of a winged disk and hovers above the row of standing, slightly bowed captives.

The identity of this winged figure in Achaemenid art is today a subject of controversy (see Shapur Shahbazi, "An Achaemenid Symbol. I: A Farewell to 'Frahahr' and 'Ahuramazda,'" *Archäologische Mitteilungen aus Iran* n.s. 7 [1974]: 135–144). Yet, from the way in which the hovering, elaborately crowned figure at Bisitun appears to hold the ring of kingship in one hand and to reciprocate the gesture of the raised right hand of Darius, it does seem warranted, at least in this instance, to identify the winged symbol with Ahuramazda, whose "favor" is so repeatedly acknowledged in the accompanying text. Such an assumption is most specifically supported by Darius's evident quotation of the complementary motifs of investiture and military triumph that appear in the relief, 150 km (93 mi.) away, of the early second-millennium Lullubi monarch Anubanini. Anubanini is depicted with his forward foot firmly lodged on the supine form of his principal opponent, while his gaze rests on the elevated, ring-clasping image of the goddess Inanna.

Darius asserts (in para. 70 of the Old Persian version of the Bisitun inscription) that copies of the text—itself remote, but indubitably safe, in its lofty situation—were sent "everywhere among the provinces." This statement is confirmed by copies of portions of the text in Aramaic (Greenfield and Porten, 1982) and Akkadian (Voightlander, 1978) discovered at Elephantine and Babylon, respectively. Furthermore, the possibility that copies of the sculptured panel also circulated within the empire is raised by the recovery of three apparently related relief fragments from Babylon that are executed in a slightly different style (Ursula Seidl, "Ein relief Darios I in Babylon," *Archäologische Mitteilungen Aus Iran* n.s.9 [1976]: 125–130).

Following a long period of time, during which the true significance of the Bisitun monument was wholly lost, the monument's identity as the handiwork of Darius was reestablished by Henry Creswicke Rawlinson (1846) who, at intervals between 1835 and 1847, was the first to examine and copy the inscriptions. [*See the biography of Rawlinson.*] Moreover, it was this trilingual "empress of inscriptions" that provided, from the time of Rawlinson onward, many of the initial clues that led to the decipherment of the Babylonian and Elamite cuneiform scripts. Subsequent landmarks in the study of the monument include Leonard W. King and

Reginald Campbell Thompson's publication of both the relief and the inscriptions in 1907 (*The Sculptures and Inscription of Darius the Great on the Rock of Behistun in Persia*, London) and the numerous studies contributed by George G. Cameron (e.g., "The Elamite Version of the Bisitun Inscriptions," *Journal of Cuneiform Studies* 14 [1960]: 59–68). Last but not least, the monument was rerecorded and reexamined in many important ways during the course of the exemplary surveys of the locality of Bisitun carried out in the 1960s and the 1970s under the direction of Heinz Luschey on behalf of the German Archaeological Institute in Tehran.

[*See also* Elamites; Persian; *and* Persians.]

BIBLIOGRAPHY

General

Luschey, Heinz. "Bisutun: Geschichte und Forschungsgeschichte." *Archäologische Anzeiger* 89 (1974): 114–149.
Rawlinson, Henry Creswicke. *The Persian Cuneiform Inscription at Behistun Decyphered and Translated*. London, 1846. The pioneer publication.
Schmitt, Rüdiger. "Bīsotūn." In *Encyclopaedia Iranica*, vol. 4, pp. 289–305. London, 1987–.
Weissbach, F. H. "Bagistana." In *Paulys Realencyclopädie der classischen Altertumswissenschaft*, vol. 2, cols. 2769–2771. Stuttgart, 1896.

Archaeology

Borger, Rykle. *Die Chronologie des Darius-Denkmals am Behistun-Felsen*. Göttingen, 1982.
Farkas, Ann E. *Achaemenid Sculpture*. Istanbul, 1974. See pages 25–86 for the beginnings of Achaemenid drapery style.
Kleiss, Wolfram. "Zur Topographie des 'Partherhanges' in Bisutun." *Archäologische Mitteilungen aus Iran* 3 (1970): 133–168. Note especially the detailed site plans in figures 1 and 2.
Luschey, Heinz. "Studien zu dem Darius-Relief von Bisutun." *Archäologische Mitteilungen aus Iran* 1 (1968): 63–94. Admirable, in particular for its fine photographs.
Stronach, David. *Pasargadae*. Oxford, 1978. See pages 96ff. for a discussion of the beginnings of the Achaemenid drapery style.
Trümpelmann, Leo. "Zur Entstehungsgeschichte des Monumentes Darios' I. von Bisutun und zur Datierung der Einführung der altpersischen Schrift." *Archäologische Anzeiger* 82 (1967): 281–298.

Texts

Greenfield, Jonas C., and Bezalel Porten. *The Bisitun Inscription of Darius the Great: Aramaic Version*. Corpus Inscriptionum Iranicarum, part 1, vol. 5: Texts 1. London, 1982. Contains two versions in Aramaic.
Grillot-Susini, François, et al. "La version élamite de la trilingue de Behistun: Une nouvelle lecture." *Journal Asiatique* 281 (1993): 19–59. The Elamite version.
Kent, Roland G. *Old Persian: Grammar, Texts, Lexicon*. 2d ed. New Haven, 1953.
Schmitt, Rüdiger. *The Bisitun Inscriptions of Darius the Great: Old Persian Text*. Corpus Inscriptionum Iranicarum, part 1, vol. 1: Texts 1. London, 1991. Supersedes Kent.
Voightlander, Elizabeth N. von. *The Bisitun Inscription of Darius the Great: Babylonian Version*. Corpus Inscriptionum Iranicarum, part 1, vol. 2: Texts 1. London, 1978.

DAVID STRONACH and ANTIGONI ZOURNATZI

BLEGEN, CARL WILLIAM (1887–1971). American pioneer of Aegean prehistoric archaeology, excavator of Troy and Pylos, and early advocate of interdisciplinary fieldwork and surface survey. Blegen's excavations in the Corinthia at Korakou (1915–1916) and Zygouries (1921–1922) established the relative chronology of prehistoric Greece in pre-Mycenaean times. His stratigraphic excavations at Troy (1932–1938) clarified the stratigraphy of the site and suggested that city VIIa was the Troy of the Homeric epics.

In 1939, Blegen began excavations in Messenia. At Ano Englianos he discovered the Palace of Nestor and its archive room; the rapid transcription of its documents greatly facilitated the decipherment of the Linear B script as Mycenaean Greek. Blegen's scholarly articles were particularly influential. He was the first (1928) to argue that Greek speakers must have entered Greece at the beginning of the Middle Bronze Age and invaded Crete in the Late Bronze Age; later (1958) he sparked the "Knossos controversy" by pointing out discrepancies between the dates of contexts in which Linear B tablets had been found at Pylos, Mycenae, and Knossos. Blegen and his close friend and frequent coauthor A. J. B. Wace saw (1918) Mycenaean civilization as an indigenous development shaped by interaction with Crete (a "fruit of the cultivated graft set on the wild stock of the mainland"), and argued strongly against the then-prevalent theory that the Greek mainland had been controlled by the Minoans in the Late Bronze Age. Already in 1939 they saw the dominance of Mycenaean pottery over Minoan in the Near East and Egypt as evidence that the Greek mainland had by the second phase of the Aegean Late Bronze Age replaced Crete as the politically dominant force in the Aegean; the decipherment of Linear B more than a decade later proved them right.

BIBLIOGRAPHY

Anonymous. "Bibliography of Carl William Blegen." *Hesperia* 35 (1966): 287–294. List of Blegen's publications, with the exception of his final reports on Pylos.

Blegen, Carl W. "The Coming of the Greeks." *American Journal of Archaeology* 32 (1928): 146–154.

Blegen, Carl W. "A Chronological Problem." In *Minoica: Festschrift sum 80. Geburtstag von Johannes Sundwall*, edited by Ernst Grumach, pp. 61–66. Berlin, 1958.

Blegen, Carl W. *Troy and the Trojans.* London, 1963. Summary of the most significant results of Blegen's excavations at Troy.

Blegen, Carl W. *The Palace of Nestor at Pylos in Western Messenia.* 3 vols. Princeton, 1980. Definitive publication of the results of Blegen's excavations.

Blegen, Carl W., and A. J. B. Wace. "The Pre-Mycenaean Pottery of the Mainland." *Annual of the British School at Athens* 22 (1916–1918): 175–189.

Blegen, Carl W., and A. J. B. Wace. "Pottery as Evidence for Trade and Colonisation in the Aegean Bronze Age." *Klio* 32 (1939): 131–147.

Blegen, Carl W., et al. *Troy: Excavations Conducted by the University of Cincinnati, 1932–1938.* 4 vols. Princeton, 1950–1958. Definitive publication of the results of Blegen's excavations.

McDonald, William A. *Progress into the Past: The Rediscovery of Mycenaean Civilization.* 2d ed. Bloomington, 1990. Biography of Blegen and other pioneers of Aegean prehistory.

JACK L. DAVIS

BLISS, FREDERICK JONES (1859–1937), archaeologist, educator, and lecturer. Born in Lebanon, Bliss was the son of American missionaries and educators. Unable to hold standard employment because of marginal health, in 1890 he was asked by the Palestine Exploration Fund (PEF) to continue William Matthew Flinders Petrie's pioneering archaeological excavation at Tell el-Ḥesi in southern Palestine. Bliss trained under Petrie in Egypt before going to Tell el-Ḥesi where, in 1891 and 1892, he conducted the first truly stratigraphic excavation in Palestine. Bliss's work combined Petrie's ceramic chronology with his own original stratigraphic concept, thereby founding the discipline of Palestinian archaeology.

Bliss continued to excavate on behalf of the PEF until 1900: in Jerusalem (1898) and later at Tell Zakariya ('Azekah), Tell es-Ṣafi, Tell el-Judeideh, and Tell Sandahanna (Marisa/Mareshah). For these sites, he produced the first modern archaeological report for Palestine (with R. A. S. Macalister, 1902). In 1900 Bliss was dismissed as excavator for the PEF primarily because his careful excavation methods were too time consuming and did not yield finds thought sufficient to raise funds. Within thirty years William Foxwell Albright recognized this as a tragic mistake. After his dismissal, Bliss prepared one final archaeological monograph (1906), describing the development of Palestinian research from its beginnings until 1902. The theoretical foundations he defined for archaeological research in Palestine are still in use today.

Bliss served as dean of men at the University of Rochester in New York State from 1911 through 1914 and as a tutor at the Syrian Protestant College in Beirut until the end World War I. In 1919 he was an adviser to the British general Allenby on the antiquities of Syria and Palestine, and in 1920 and 1921 he was an archaeological consultant to the American Schools of Oriental Research. He retired in 1921.

[*See also* 'Azekah; Ḥesi, Tell el-; Judeideh, Tell el-; Mareshah; Palestine Exploration Fund; *and the biography of Petrie.*]

BIBLIOGRAPHY

Albright, William Foxwell. "Bliss, Frederick Jones." In *Dictionary of American Biography*, vol. 22, suppl. 2, pp. 44–45. New York, 1958. The basic biographical sketch of Bliss by someone who knew him.

Bliss, Frederick Jones. *A Mound of Many Cities, or, Tell el Hesy Excavated.* London, 1894. The first major archaeological monograph based on stratigraphic excavation in Palestine. Delightful reading, but generally accessible only in major university and research libraries.

Bliss, Frederick Jones. *Excavations at Jerusalem, 1894–1897.* London, 1898.

Bliss, Frederick Jones, and R. A. S. Macalister. *Excavations in Palestine during the Years 1898–1900*. London, 1902.

Bliss, Frederick Jones. *The Development of Palestine Exploration*. New York, 1906.

King, Philip J. "Frederick Jones Bliss at Tell el-Hesi and Elsewhere." *Palestine Exploration Quarterly* 122 (1990): 96–100. Basic review of Bliss's contributions to the field of archaeology.

Matthers, John M. "Excavations by the Palestine Exploration Fund at Tell el-Hesi, 1890–1892." In *Tell el-Hesi, vol. 4, The Site and the Expedition*, edited by Bruce T. Dahlberg and Kevin G. O'Connell, pp. 37–67. Winona Lake, Ind., 1989. Detailed review and modern critical analysis of Bliss's excavations at Tell el-Hesi.

JEFFREY A. BLAKELY

BOATS. *See* Ships and Boats.

BODRUM. *See* Halikarnassos.

BOĞAZKÖY, site of Ḫattuša, the capital of the Hittite Empire. The village of Boğazköy has been renamed Boğazkale and upgraded to a town, but scholars continue to use its former name. Boğazköy (roughly 40°01′ N, 34°40′ E) is in the province (Tk., *il*) of Çorum, Turkey, 200 km (124 mi.) on the road east of Ankara, 80 km (50 mi.) from Çorum; 40 km (25 mi.) from Yozgat; and 19 km (12 mi.) from Alaca Höyük. It is situated at the southern end of a small, fertile plain. The ancient city rises on a slope between two deeply cut streambeds, filling the angle between their converging courses. The ancient city rises toward the south from about 900 m to about 1200 m above sea level on a length of about 2 km (1 mi.). It covers an area of 414 acres. The modern town lies near the northern end of the ancient city, partly encroaching upon it.

Boğazköy was discovered in 1834 together with the nearby rock sanctuary Yazılıkaya by the French explorer Charles Texier. It was later visited by British and German scholars. In 1893 and 1894 another Frenchman, Ernest Chantre, found some fragments of clay tablets inscribed in Babylonian cuneiform script, but in a hitherto unknown language. In 1901, J. A. Knudtzon deciphered two letters found at Tell el-Amarna written in a language he recognized as Indo-European; they belonged to a correspondence between Pharaoh Amenhotep III and a king of the country of Arzawa. It was soon noticed that the language of these letters closely resembled that of Chantre's tablets. Therefore, in 1905, the German archaeologist Hugo Winckler and Theodore Makridi Bey, second director of the Istanbul Museum, went to Boğazköy in search of Arzawa. The following year, they began excavations at the site under the auspices of the museum but financed in part by the Deutsche Orient-Gesellschaft (DOG). They found thousands of tablets and fragments on the west slope of Büyükkale, the royal acropolis. Since the introductory formulas on some tablets were written in Ak-

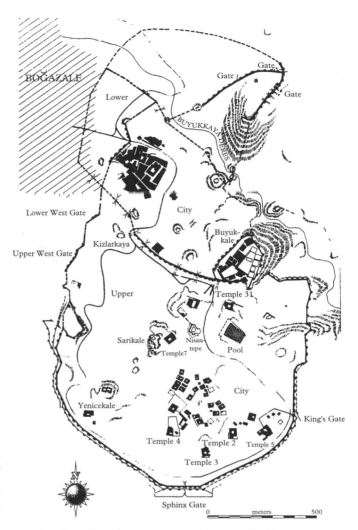

BOĞAZKÖY. *Plan of the ancient city.* (Courtesy ASOR Archives)

kadian (Babylonian), Winckler immediately recognized the title "Great King, King of Ḫatti," which showed that Boğazköy had been the Hittite capital. The excavations continued in 1907, 1911, and 1912 and included some storerooms belonging to the Great Temple. Fieldwork brought the total number of tablets to ten thousand, and these became the source material for Hittitology. In 1907, a team of archaeologists and architects, directed by Otto Puchstein, under the auspices of the German Archaeological Institute, surveyed and partly excavated the city walls, including five gates and five temples.

After World War I the excavations were resumed in 1931 jointly by the German Archaeological Institute and the DOG. Because Winckler had only dug for tablets and Puchstein's work was limited to the great monuments, it became necessary to establish the site's stratigraphy with modern methods. The field director was Kurt Bittel. Interrupted in 1939 by World War II, the work was resumed in 1952 and is still underway. Peter Neve succeeded Bittel upon his retirement and he, in 1994, was succeeded by Jürgen Seher.

In 1931 Bittel started on Büyükkale, because it had an accumulation of debris that would allow for stratigraphic observations. Later, the excavations were extended over most of the city area. Neve concentrated his work on the Upper City. The excavations since 1931 have added several thousand tablets to those Winckler found. Since 1993 the excavation has been extended to Büyükkaya, an elevation east of the Ancient City.

The earliest settlements in the area of the city go back to the late phase of the Early Bronze Age (before 2000 BCE). Finds belonging to the period's earlier phases appeared at sites near Boğazköy, but not in the city. The next major phase at the site is the Middle Bronze Age. It is characterized by the Assyrian merchant colonies then in Anatolia. A settlement found in level 4 of the Lower City contained old Assyrian tablets belonging to the later period of the Assyrian colonies known from level 1b (eighteenth century BCE) at Kültepe. [See Kültepe Texts.] The inscription of the early Hittite king Anitta says that he defeated the king of Ḫatti, destroyed his city, and put a curse on its site. Anitta is at-

tested at Kültepe toward the end of 1b, so the settlement at Boğazköy must antedate this destruction. At that time the city was known by the name Ḫattuš, in the language of the pre-Indo-European population, which scholars call Ḫattic, to distinguish it from Indo-European Hittite. In Hittite, the stem was enlarged by the vowel a to Ḫattuša (nominative Ḫattušaš). About one hundred years later, a Hittite king of another dynasty, disregarding the curse, made Ḫattuša his capital and was given the name Ḫattušili, the man from Ḫattuša. He belongs to what is known as the Old Hittite Kingdom. This is followed by the so-called Middle Kingdom (fifteenth century BCE) and the New Kingdom (fourteenth and thirteenth centuries BCE), also referred to as the Empire period. Almost all buildings visible today belong to this last period. Older levels, particularly those excavated on Büyükkale, have been covered up, so that the buildings of the empire could be restored.

During the Old Kingdom, only the lower part of the city and Büyükkale were settled. The wall separating the Upper and Lower Cities can still be followed. The Upper City was apparently only occupied in the New Kingdom. The southern city wall, with its three monumental gates decorated with

BOĞAZKÖY. *Lion gate.* (Courtesy ASOR Archives)

sculpture—Lion's gate, King's Gate, and Sphinx Gate—also belong to the Empire period.

Shortly after 1200 BCE, Boğazköy was destroyed. Traces of the conflagration have been found in all parts of the city. This event is usually connected with the migrations of the peoples mentioned in Egyptian sources as the Sea Peoples. After the destruction, there is a settlement gap. The next building level is datable by its painted pottery, which strongly resembles that of the Phrygians, known from their capital, Gordion [See Gordion.] It is datable to after 1000 BCE. On Büyükkale, the Phrygian level is superceded by one that lasted into the Hellenstic period. In the third century BCE, the Celtic Galatians entered Anatolia, and one of their tribes, the Trocmai, settled east of the Halys River. Boğazköy probably belonged to their realm, but an earlier theory, according to which a certain class of decorated Hellenistic pottery was Galatian, is no longer accepted. Under the Romans, Galatia became a province, but the Roman period is poorly attested by scattered remnants of buildings, coins, and some objects. The name of the Roman city may have been Pteria.

The Christian era is represented by an apse carved out of a rock called Mihrablı Kaya ("Rock with Prayer Niche") and a small church built of spoils over a Hittite temple in the Upper City. Under the Ottomans, members of a family called Zülkadir Oğulları ruled over a large area in central Anatolia. In the nineteenth century, a branch of this family resided at Boğzaköy. Its last member, Ziya Bey, was a host to Winckler and later to Bittel.

[See also Anatolia, article on Ancient Anatolia; Hittite; and Hittites.]

BIBLIOGRAPHY

Preliminary reports appeared in *Mitteilungen der Deutschen Orient-Gesellschaft*, vols. 70 (1932)–78 (1940) and 86 (1953)–106 (1974) and in *Archaeologischer Anzeiger* for the same years and continued yearly.

Bittel, Kurt. *Kleinasiatische Studien.* Istanbuler Mitteilungen, vol. 5. Istanbul, 1942.

Bittel, Kurt. *Hattusha: The Capital of the Hittites.* New York, 1970.

Bittel, Kurt, et al. *Boğazköy.* 6 vols. Berlin, 1935–1984.

Bittel, Kurt, ed. *Boğazköy-Ḫattuša: Ergebnisse der Ausgrabungen.* 14 vols. to date. Stuttgart and Berlin, 1952–.

Güterbock, Hans G. "Boğazköy." In *Encyclopedia Britannica*, 15th ed., vol. 2, pp. 1181–1183. Chicago, 1974.

Neve, Peter. "Hattuša: Stadt der Götter und Tempel; Neue Ausgrabungen in der Hauptstadt der Hethiter." *Antike Welt*, special issue (1993). Survey of the results of the excavations, containing superb color photographs.

Neve, Peter. "Hattusha, City of Gods and Temples: Results of the Excavations in the Upper City." In *Proceedings of the British Academy (1991 Lectures and Memoirs)* 80 (1993): 105–132.

Puchstein, Otto, et al. *Boghazköi: Die Bauwerke.* Wissenschaftliche Veröffentlichung der Deutschen Orient-Gesellschaft 19. Leipzig, 1912.

HANS G. GÜTERBOCK

BONE, IVORY, AND SHELL. [*This entry surveys the history of bone, ivory, and shell artifacts with reference to* the technologies used to create them, the uses to which they were put, and their overall role in the cultures and societies in which they figure. It comprises four articles:

Typology and Technology
Artifacts of the Bronze and Iron Ages
Artifacts of the Persian through Roman Periods
Artifacts of the Byzantine and Islamic Periods

The first serves as a general overview, while the remaining articles treat the artifacts of specific periods and regions.]

Typology and Technology

A number of animal-derived materials were crafted into artifacts in antiquity. Almost all worked bone was mammalian in origin, although a few pieces of worked bird bone are known from Tell Jemmeh and Ashkelon. [*See* Jemmeh, Tell; Ashkelon.] Ivory came from the incisors and canines of hippopotamus, the tusks of wild boars, but mostly from the upper incisors of the male Asiatic elephant or the male or female African elephant (see figure 1). Artistic and literary evidence suggests the existence of wild elephants in Syria in the second and first millennia BCE until the end of the Late Bronze Age, when they were hunted to extinction. The absence of a fossil record from the Near East leaves open the question of whether these Syrian populations were related to the African or Indian form, or evolved separately from one or the other group. One scholar (Caubet, 1991) believes

BONE, IVORY, AND SHELL: Typology and Technology. Figure 1. *Sections of sawn hippo ivory from Ashkelon.* This is some of the earliest evidence of bone and ivory working, dating to the MB II/LB I levels. (Photograph by Carl Andrews)

that most of the ivory worked at Aegean sites through the end of the Late Bronze Age was from the hippopotamus.

Antler, the bony outgrowth of cervid skulls, is a sturdy raw material for making tools and was preferred for objects subject to heavy-duty use. Numerous sawn tines and sections of antler are known from sites such as Ashkelon, Tel Miqne, and Tel Batash in Israel, but few complete artifacts have been recovered. [See Miqne, Tel; Batash, Tel.] Antler found at Levantine sites could derive from fallow, red, or roe deer, but almost all of the sawn antler documented is from the fallow deer. Antler, shed annually, was probably an item of trade.

Horn, the keratinous sheath surrounding the bony interior, or horn core, of bovids, was also worked in antiquity; however, because it is more susceptible to attritional processes than osseous tissue, it often has not survived the rigors of deposition—although a fragment of worked horn that may have been intended for use as a border inlay has been identified from Ashkelon (Wapnish, 1991). In the absence of the raw material, horn working can be documented from the concentrations of sawn horn cores found belonging to sheep, goat, and cattle. [See Sheep and Goats; Cattle and Oxen.]

Bone was by far the most commonly worked animal-derived material, and ivory a distant second. The documentation for antler is scarce, and for horn, nonexistent—except for the piece mentioned above. Ivory objects have received the greatest attention because they were often luxury items carved with much finesse; yet, little is known about the actual process of manufacture. Studies on ivory lengthily discuss style and typology, but not much else. When archaeologists direct more attention to the systematic collection of all animal remains, it will be possible to document the complex processes of procurement, manufacture, and distribution of many of the objects of daily life crafted from those materials in antiquity. Present information allows the documentation in any detail only of boneworking.

The manufacture of a diverse array of bone artifacts found in the later historic periods in the ancient Near East had its beginnings in Late Paleolithic boneworking. Awls, borers, and scrapers, most likely made by their users, were some of the earliest tools fashioned with stone implements. With the introduction of copper, bronze, and (later) iron, metal tools gradually supplanted stone as the primary shapers of bone.

The tools used to work animal-derived materials were probably borrowed from wood-carvers. Because these tools are rarely found, their use must be inferred from the telltale marks they leave, particularly on the backs of objects and on unfinished pieces. Judging by Late Chalcolithic artifacts, numerous types of tools were already available. Early Egyptian wall reliefs (c. 2500 BCE) show furniture makers using knives, saws (more like large knives with a toothed edge), and bow drills. By the Middle Bronze Age II period, a sophisticated

tool kit existed that included knives, coarse- and fine-toothed (finishing) saws, drills, gouges, chisels, straight- and compass-scribers, rasps, and files. Wet sand, leather and sand (or other minerals), and, by Roman times, the coarse skins of fish, shark, or ray were used to smooth and polish finished pieces.

By about 1500 BCE, simple lathes were in use in the wood-producing and working areas of the eastern Mediterranean. The first lathes were in all likelihood elaborations of the bow drill. The object in preparation became the actual stock of the drill, secured between two fixed points; it was turned by a bow as cutting and shaping tools were applied. Even simple, early lathes could produce pieces with a precise circumference. As they became more technologically sophisticated, lathes were indispensable to bone-carvers of quality items, such as furniture embellishments (see figure 2), round composite boxes, jewelry, and even hairpins. [See Jewelry.]

Bone was used for a wide range of artifacts, from utilitarian to purely decorative. With any bone tool type it is important to distinguish between casually worked bone (pieces

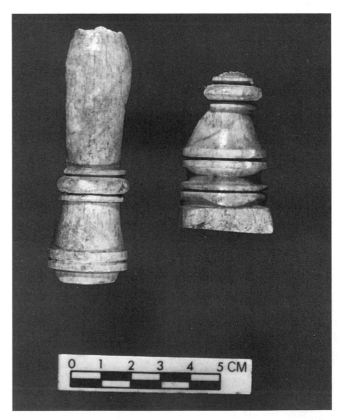

BONE, IVORY, AND SHELL: Typology and Technology. Figure 2. *Lathe-turned furniture mounts.* These pieces were often made from metapodials, or bones from the lower legs. They were attached to the legs of chairs and tables as decoration. Most are sawn longitudinally, leaving either half or two-thirds of the tube as an attachment, perhaps an indication that only the fronts of the legs were decorated. (Photograph by Carl Andrews)

BONE, IVORY, AND SHELL: Typology and Technology. Figure 3. *Lathe-made ligula or handle.* Most of the handle is hollow to hold the tang of the attached implement that was secured by a metal rivet, the hole for which can be seen at one end. This was probably the handle for some sort of spoon. (Photograph by Carl Andrews)

made by the user) and objects resulting from the organized production of professional craftsmen. A fragment of long bone sharpened at one end into a pointed tip to serve as a borer or stylus, ankle bones (astragali) planed and smoothed into gaming pieces thrown like dice, and bone sections minimally modified to scrape and dress hides are examples of casually worked bone known from antiquity that are still being produced. [*See* Games.] They testify to the fact that bone is easy to model, inexpensive, and readily available. User-made tools are found widely and over long periods at most sites because they were made by simple methods and served immediate needs. Casual tools were distinct in form and technique from products of specialized manufacture; they were also heterogeneous in character, whereas items of specialized manufacture are more uniform in shape and appearance. Casual tools were most likely crafted in or around the home, whereas those of specialized manufacture almost certainly were produced in workshops.

Increased community size and degree of urbanization, coupled with more sophisticated boneworking technology and professional organization, led to a proliferation in the types of objects made from bone. Beginning in the Persian period (sixth century BCE) and continuing into the later historical periods, the variety of bone artifacts offers a comprehensive picture of daily life: handles for a range of implements (see figure 3), spoons, whorls, buttons, needles, pins (cloth and hair), spatulas, beads, pendants, amulets and charms, rings and bracelets, composite boxes (pyxides; see figure 4), cosmetic accessories, single- and double-sided combs, gaming pieces, paralleliped and cubical dice, theater tickets, stamp seals, hinges for boxes and chests (see figure 5), composite elements for mechanical devices, flutes,

carved figurines, toy dolls with movable arms (see figure 6), and furniture attachments and inlays, including carved plaques, decorative borders, finials, and mounts to cover furniture legs. [*See* Seals; Musical Instruments; Furniture and Furnishings.]

Gauging the intensity and organization of production is difficult. Because finished pieces recovered at any given site could have been imports, the debris of manufacture—blanks, waste and trim, and unfinished pieces—is a necessary indicator of on-site production. Bone is often not intensively collected during excavation; however, even when it is, scraps and leftovers are likely to be overlooked because of an unfamiliarity with this type of artifact and the tendency to focus on finished pieces. A great deal of potential information is thus lost. In addition, no actual workshop or primary surface littered with bone debris has so far been reported from any site in Israel, where most of the research is presently being carried out on these materials.

Renewed excavations at Ashkelon since 1985, have, however, yielded evidence of a large-scale boneworking industry that began in the Persian period and continued until the thirteenth century CE (Wapnish, 1991). Boneworking is actually documented from the MB II period onward at the site but did not reach industrial proportions until the later pe-

BONE, IVORY, AND SHELL: Typology and Technology. Figure 4. *Two lathe-made composite pyxides with similar turned decorations.* Sections of these hollowed pieces were joined together into a complete box. A flat disc fitted to the bottom formed the floor of the box. The shorter, squatter piece is made of elephant ivory, a precious material. The longer section in bone is most probably a cheaper version, perhaps an ancient "knock-off." (Photograph by Carl Andrews)

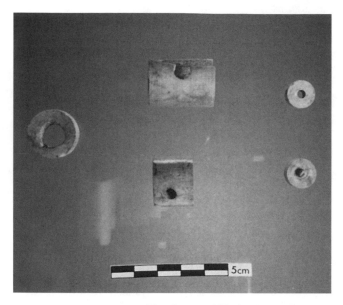

BONE, IVORY, AND SHELL: Typology and Technology. Figure 5. *Hinges (three larger pieces) and spacers for hinges (two smaller pieces).* These were often made of bone for boxes and larger pieces of furniture. They were both hollow and solid, like the small spacer at the lower right. (Photograph by Carl Andrews)

riods. Unfortunately, none of the evidence for manufacture has been found in situ; even concentrations of waste and blanks are secondary and even tertiary deposits. A clear (if incomplete) reduction sequence in the manufacturing pro-

cess of a large variety of artifacts at Ashkelon can be observed, however.

The professional status of Ashkelon's bone-carvers is manifest in a number of factors. The tool kit alone indicates a degree of specialization uncharacteristic of casually modeled bone. So, too, does the kind of bone used: mostly the long bone shafts of cattle and camel, occasionally donkey, and, in the rarest instances, horse. [*See* Camels.] The fact that the raw material derived from the largest domesticates is particularly significant. Small-scale pastoralists raise these animals in small numbers, in quantities insufficient to produce a regular flow of bone into the production system. Only in highly organized supply systems, where bone was not just a raw material but a commodity, would crafters be able to access the bones of camel and equids regularly. At scales of production above the household level, the bones of sheep and goats were used only for casually worked bone, when user and producer were the same.

Standardization is a critical indicator of how specialized craftsmen were. At Ashkelon there is uniformity at a number of points in the reduction sequence. Initial preparation of a whole long bone began when the articular ends (areas of spongy bone unsuitable for working), were sawn off, leaving a tube of dense cortical bone. These tubes were then sectioned into smaller, workable segments that, in turn, were reduced further into blanks of various shape and size, depending on the object to be modeled. Blanks were standardized in form as flat sheets of varying thickness, square and

BONE, IVORY, AND SHELL: Typology and Technology. Figure 6. *Various dolls made from bone.* The first piece is the torso of a composite doll made from the hollow shaft of a cow metacarpal (lower front leg). The carved arms were attached to the torso at the shoulder by rivets, allowing the arms some front and back movement. Neither of the arms shown here goes with this torso. The second and third examples are flat, carved dolls. (Photograph by Carl Andrews)

round rods also of varying thickness, complete and halved tubes, and chunks whittled into somewhat irregular blocks. The preparation of both blanks and artifacts produced standardized waste and trim pieces. The presence of a reduction sequence with uniformity at some nodes argues against one individual creating an object from start to finish. The intensity of production remains a question in the absence of a workshop site. However, because some contexts yielded concentrations of particular unfinished objects and/or off-cuts, it is probable that workshops were specialized by object and that several stages of production existed, with each delegated to a different worker. It is possible that middlemen dealing in bone as a commodity bridged the gap between abattoir and workshop.

The tools used to work bone were also used to model ivory, antler, and horn. However, it is doubtful that the same craftsmen worked both bone and ivory. Bone was readily available, inexpensive, and used for many mundane items, whereas ivory was rare, expensive, and mainly used for luxury goods. In addition, although the carving techniques may be similar, the substances are different. Although bone, antler, and ivory are roughly equal in hardness (1.5–2.5 on the Mohs' scale), elephant ivory is somewhat softer and easier to carve. Because it is comprised of large areas of solid matter, it can be used to make larger items, like furniture panels, figures in the round, and especially circular boxes. On the other hand, hippopotamus ivory is denser and more difficult to carve, and the canines and incisors of which it is comprised cannot be used for large objects. These differences—in carving techniques, suitability for certain objects, and availability of supply—point to a separation of bone and ivory carvers.

Another issue concerning bone and ivory carving for the region is whether craftsmen were itinerant or sedentary. While both would contribute to the economic activity of a settlement, only sedentary craftsmen would be an integral part of the social fabric and organization of the larger community. It is certainly true that all the tools needed, even early lathes, were portable. At least one authority (Barnett, 1982) considers that preindustrial craftsmen were highly mobile. However, just how roving specialists provided themselves with a raw material as expensive and relatively difficult to obtain as ivory is a question not easily answered. Bone, though, as the by-product of meat production, would be at hand in sufficient quantities in any large settlement. "Itinerant workers" implies that one craftsman worked each piece from start to finish because the logistics of moving a group of carvers, each specialized at a certain task, would make it unpracticable at best. However, the elaboration of production argues for the opposite because a manufacturing sequence, such as existed at Ashkelon, could be carried out more efficiently by sedentary craftsmen.

Despite the absence of workshops, it is possible to speculate about some of the organization of bone-tool production. (Until comparable waste materials and a manufacturing sequence are known for ivoryworking, or the working of antler for that matter, it cannot be assumed that it was the same in organization.) Ancient and modern markets in the Near East are characterized by streets or areas given over to the practice of one trade or craft. It is possible that the majority of bone-carvers were so arranged in the urban settings of their work. Craftsmen attached to special interests (e.g., state or temple) could have been clustered near their sponsor. Nor should home crafting on the piecework system be ruled out, with entrepreneurs organizing the production by providing the raw material, dictating what and how much was produced, and handling marketing and distribution. This is obviously far removed from home-based production of casual tools. Although both types of boneworking occur at the household level, they are totally different in organization, scope, and content. Craftsmen in any of these schemes could have been specialized not only by product, but also by the stage of the reduction sequence at which they labored. Because these arrangements are not mutually exclusive, one or several of them could have operated at a given place and time with respect to a variety of artifact types.

A number of other factors may be suggested for the organization of the craftsmen, although none can presently be demonstrated. The opportunity to learn and practice a given profession may have depended on kinship affiliation. Craftsmen may have been organized into professional associations, with various economic and social missions. Such groups are known from Roman sources, such as the *eborarii*, or "ivory workers," recognized as specialized craftsmen in the second century BCE. A professional association of dice and theater ticket makers was also formed at this time (Barnett, 1982). It appears that there were numerous associations of craftsmen and merchants in Asia Minor, especially during the Roman period (37 BCE–324 CE). These may have already existed in Hellenistic times (332–37 BCE) as the successors to extant native guilds prior to the Greek conquest (Koester, 1987). During the Islamic period (610–1919 CE), professional associations of craftsmen and merchants became prominent features of urban economic life, beginning with 'Abbasid rule (750 CE). They continued as a mainstay of economic activity through successive caliphates (Perry, 1983).

BIBLIOGRAPHY

Ariel, Donald T., et al. "Worked Bone and Ivory." In *Excavations at the City of David, 1978–1985, Directed by Yigal Shiloh*, vol. 2, edited by Donald T. Ariel, pp. 119–148. Qedem, vol. 30. Jerusalem, 1990. Important recent summary of worked bone and ivory from the Bronze Age to the Byzantine period.

Barnett, R. D. *Ancient Ivories in the Middle East* (Qedem 14). Monographs of the Institute of Archaeology, The Hebrew University of Jerusalem. Jerusalem, 1982. Still the most comprehensive overall study on ivory working in the Middle East. Many invaluable illustrations of objects.

Caubet, Annie. "Ivoires de Cappadoce." In *Marchands, diplomates et empereurs,* edited by Dominique Charpin and Francis Joannès, pp. 223–225. Paris, 1991. Brief review of the significance of hippopotamus ivory in the Bronze Age.

Hutchinson, V. J., and D. S. Reese. "A Worked Bone Industry at Carthage." In *The Circus and a Byzantine Cemetery at Carthage,* vol. 1.2, edited by John H. Humphrey, pp. 549–594. Ann Arbor, Mich., 1988. One of the few studies to treat boneworking in other than stylistic terms.

Koester, Helmut. *History, Culture, and Religion of the Hellenistic Age.* New York, 1987.

Krzyszkowska, Olga. *Ivory and Related Materials.* Institute of Classical Studies, Bulletin Supplement 59. London, 1990. Excellent comprehensive review of animal-derived products recovered from archaeological contexts.

Perry, G. E. *The Middle East: Fourteen Islamic Centuries.* Englewood Cliffs, N.J., 1983.

Starling, Katherine, and David Watkinson, eds. *Archaeological Bone, Antler, and Ivory.* United Kingdom Institute for Conservation, Occasional Papers, no. 5. London, 1987. Several useful discussions of problems in identification and conservation of animal-derived products found at archaeological sites.

Wapnish, Paula. "Beauty and Utility in Bone: New Light on Bone Crafting." *Biblical Archaeology Review* 17.4 (1991): 54–57. Brief survey of the boneworking industry at Ashkelon.

PAULA WAPNISH

Artifacts of the Bronze and Iron Ages

As opposed to metalwork or glasswork—which involve heat, chemical changes and fusion, molds (for copper and bronze), and hammering—bone-, ivory-, and shellworking involve relatively simple techniques to produce objects of utility and adornment. Worked and unworked ivory and unworked shell were also items of trade, providing evidence of long-distance cultural contact. D. S. Reese (1985) notes that elephant tusks found on Minoan Crete and hippopotamus canines from Bronze Age Greece and Cyprus originated in the Levant or Egypt. Three unmodified hippopotamus incisors were recovered from the thirteenth- or early fourteenth-century BCE Uluburun shipwreck off the coast of Turkey—evidence of trade in unworked animal bone. [*See* Uluburun.]

Bone. In antiquity, bone was used to decorate utilitarian objects and wooden boxes, to fashion figurines and tools, and to serve as handles for tools and weapons. Bone sickle hafts with animals carved in the round are known from the Natufian Mesolithic period (c. 8000 BCE) in the Levant. However, bone sculpture subsequently suffered a decline, and the style of sickle hafts became simplified. Bone strips made from the bones of sheep or goats, were used to decorate wooden boxes in the Middle Bronze Age. Metal saws were used to cut the bone to size and shape. The strips were then incised with a pointed metal instrument. Applied bone silhouettes of birds, *djed* (Egyp., symbol of endurance and stability) columns, and snakes were more complicated to produce, but in all likelihood required the same combination of sawing and incising. Bone objects such as whorls, needles, awls, and club-shaped pendants carved in the round involved a technology that included splintering and smoothing with a stone, in addition to carving and the use of a bow drill with a metal bit for perforation.

Bone is best known for its use for utilitarian objects. In

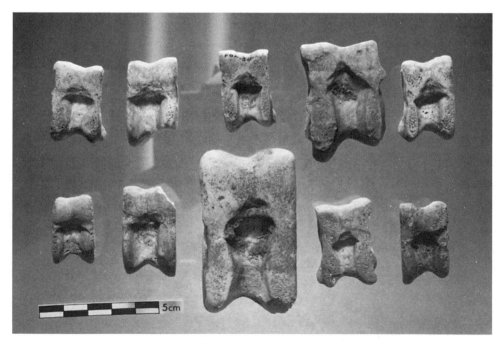

BONE, IVORY, AND SHELL: Bronze and Iron Ages. Figure 1. *Planed astragali (ankle bones), used as gaming pieces.* The two largest astragali are from cattle, the others are from sheep or goats. (Photograph by Carl Andrews)

BONE, IVORY, AND SHELL: Bronze and Iron Ages. Figure 2. *Large and small spatulas made from ribs.* Spatula tools like these date from the prehistoric to late historic periods at sites in Israel. Despite numerous theories, their use remains a mystery, but they most likely had numerous purposes. (Photograph by Carl Andrews)

spite of the increase in the use of metal for tools throughout the Bronze and Iron Ages, bone continued to be used to produce awls, needles, and pins. Bone pins are commonly represented in 'Amuq G and H (third millennium), at which time decorated tubes became popular in Syria. [*See* 'Amuq.] Highly polished, incised bone tubes were popular in Early Bronze III Palestine as well, where they have been found at sites such as Megiddo, Khirbet Kerak/Beth-Yeraḥ, Jericho, and Ai. [*See* Megiddo; Beth-Yeraḥ, Jericho; Ai.] Bone whistles, unknown in the Early and Middle Bronze Ages, are found in Palestine in Late Bronze Age levels at Lachish and 'Ein-Gedi. [*See* Lachish; 'Ein-Gedi.] Bone gaming pieces are also known from this period (see figure 1), as are bone handles for bimetalic knives (also found with some frequency in the tenth century BCE). [*See* Games.] In the Iron Age, bone was used for spatulae that were rounded at one end and pointed at the other (see figure 2)—in all likelihood used for weaving. Dome-shaped, vertically perforated bone spindle whorls are found along with stone spindle whorls in both the Bronze and Iron Ages (see figure 3).

Beginning in MB IIA in Palestine, reaching a zenith in MB IIB, and continuing into the LB I period, bone was used extensively as a decorative element (e.g., as strips with incised geometric motifs and in a variety of silhouettes applied to wooden boxes; see figure 4). The genre is also known in Syria at Ras Shamra/Ugarit and Byblos, in Anatolia, and in Egypt; however, Palestine was the apparent center for this craft. Subsequently, ivory replaced bone for luxury items. [*See* Ugarit; Byblos.] Few examples of bone sculpture in the round are known for the following periods, although a carved bone figurine is known from Iron Age Beersheba. [*See* Beersheba.] Frontal armless, flat bone figurines, whose legs are separated by an incised line and that have other

anatomic features suggested by clusters of incised dotted lines, appear in the Orontes River Valley at Hama (East) in about the eighth century BCE. Club-shaped bone pendants pierced at one end and incised with dotted circles and encircling horizontal incisions were almost ubiquitous in Iron II (ninth–eighth centuries BCE) Palestine.

Ivory. The ivory used in the Levant came from the tusks of African elephants that roamed northern Syria in the second and first millennia BCE and from the canines and incisors of hippopotami, which are superior to elephant ivory. Ivory, like bone, was sawed to the desired size for use. Because ivory is softer and is not hollow, it lends itself more readily to carving in the round, relief carving, openwork, and the hollowing out of square and cylindrical shapes to fashion containers. The carver cut the tusk according to the shape the piece was ultimately to assume: plaques for incision, relief carving, and openwork; or blocks for carving in the round. The tools used in ivoryworking included hacksaws to cut the tusks, finer saws for detail work, bow drills to bore holes, chisels to shape and gouge, compasses to outline arcs, a stylus for incising, and an abrasive for polishing.

Cloisonné, a technique that involves cutting depressions into the ivory that are then filled with substances of varying colors and framed with ivory ribbing, although well known in New Kingdom Egypt, was not popular in Palestine and Syria until the Iron Age. In some instances, such as on the plaques featuring floral forms from Megiddo VIIA, parts of the object were painted. Ivories from Nimrud and elsewhere are known to have been covered with gold foil, either to cover blemishes or make the objects more resplendent. [*See* Nimrud.]

Ivoryworking reached a high point in the Palestinian Chalcolithic period, but went into a decline in the Early Bronze Age and only slowly revived in the latter part of the Middle Bronze Age, when ivory, well-suited for decorating contain-

BONE, IVORY, AND SHELL: Bronze and Iron Ages. Figure 3. *Undecorated whorls.* On the left is a knife cut blank. The whorl at the center is made of bone, the one on the right of ivory. (Photograph by Carl Andrews)

ers, was applied to wooden boxes at least from the sixteenth century BCE onward, demonstrated by examples from Pella in Transjordan and from silhouettes from el-Jisr in Palestine. [See Pella.] However, there was a resurgence at the beginning of the Late Bronze Age that reached its peak in the latter part of the period, when it was used for many kinds of luxury items. The most prominent use was for ivory plaques worked in a variety of techniques and affixed to wooden furniture (see above). The most complex of these plaques feature continuous narrative scenes, such as the military and feast scenes on examples from Megiddo and Tell el-Far'ah (South). [See Far'ah, Tell el- (South).] Less finely worked LB ivory plaques and silhouettes with some affinities to those found elsewhere in Syria-Palestine have been found at Tell Fakhariyah. [See Fakhariyah, Tell.] Although Syro-Palestinian wooden furniture is not preserved, the manner of attachment and the use of the ivory can be reasonably reconstructed based on Egyptian New Kingdom chairs and on an Iron Age chair from Salamis, Cyprus. [See Salamis.]

Ivory was also used in the Late Bronze Age for freestanding objects. An exquisite ivory sculptured figurine was found in the Megiddo VIIA hoard, in which several ivory female figurine heads were also found. A carved ivory hand, apparently from a large sculpture, much of which was made from a different material (probably wood), was found at LB Lachish. In the Iron Age, ivory sculpture in the round was reserved, based on what is currently known, to small-scale objects, such as lion fittings for furniture, as demonstrated by carved lions in the round from Samaria and Nimrud.

Ivory was also used in the Late Bronze and Iron Ages for combs. It was used less commonly for dice (e.g., the eight-sided die from Iron II Shechem). [See Shechem.] Although it is generally assumed that the LB ivories found in Palestine were imported from Syria, a case can be made, on the basis of style, for some of the Levantine-type ivories having been made in Palestine. In addition, unworked tusks were discovered at Megiddo.

A fascinating ivory box with lions and cherubs in bold relief on a projecting ledge encircling the base of a box was found in the Megiddo VIIA hoard (see above). The missing lid may have featured cherubs similar to those on the two opposing sides of the box; they suggest the type of decoration that may have covered the Hebrew tribes' Ark of the Covenant. Lids of cylindrical cosmetic boxes (whose lower parts are generally missing) have been found at Megiddo and elsewhere. A tusk-shaped oil or perfume container with a stopper was also found at Megiddo, with parallels elsewhere. Other types of containers are duck shaped and have movable parts. Scepters or wands in the shape of cylindrical tubes fitted into pomegranate-shaped heads have been found at LB Lachish; an Iron Age parallel is an inscribed pomegranate-shaped miniature ivory head purported to be from King Solomon's Temple in Jerusalem. [See Jerusalem.]

In the Iron Age, ivory carving enjoyed a great resurgence in the Levant. Major collections of worked ivory originating there have been found at Nimrud, Khorsabad, Arslan Tash (Syria), and Samaria; isolated pieces have been found elsewhere in Syria, Assyria, and Mesopotamia, and on Cyprus

BONE, IVORY, AND SHELL: Bronze and Iron Ages. Figure 4. *Bone border inlays and mounts.* The pieces were arrayed around the edges of boxes, caskets, and so forth as decoration. (Photograph by Carl Andrews)

and in the Aegean. [*See* Khorsabad; Samaria; Cyprus.] Richard D. Barnett (1982) has distinguished between those ivories coming from North Syrian workshops and those originating in Phoenicia. [*See* Phoenicia.] In the Syrian style old motifs were continued—animal combat, a hero and a winged griffin, or a procession to a throne—motifs derived primarily from Mesopotamia, and a figural style developed with rather squat bodies and faces with either a prominent nose and eyes or round, chubby faces. The Phoenician ivories almost slavishly imitated Egyptian motifs and proportions and used techniques such as polychromy and open-work. Irene J. Winter (1976) has raised the possibility of the existence of a South Syrian school. The notion of a Palestinian origin for the ivories found at Samaria has been ruled out basically because, in spite of considerable excavation in Israel, a major collection has only been found at Samaria. Yet, literary evidence pointing to Assyrians carting off booty including ivory chairs from Judah suggests the possibility of the existence of a Palestinian school. The richest assemblage (consisting of several thousand pieces) and the finest examples of Iron Age ivories come from Nimrud, where they were used on the backs and sides of beds and chairs and for wall paneling. Another important assemblage, primarily of small fragments, which reflects the complexity of cultural transmission, was found at Hasanlu in Iran, in a settlement of unknown ethnic and linguistic background that was burned before the end of the eighth century BCE. [*See* Hasanlu.] The majority of those ivories were locally made; others originated elsewhere in Iran or are said to have originated in North Syria. The smallest class is Assyrian. Though the influence of the North Syrian, Phoenician, and Assyrian workshops is apparent, the local and otherwise Iranian examples lack the intricacy, precision, and richness of the former.

Ivory was favored for the carving of small luxury items because it was soft and relatively easy to carve; it was even-grained, and its rich, light color was well suited for flesh tones. In the eighth century BCE, when the elephant population dwindled in North Syria, eliminating the locally available supply of ivory, tridacna shells and bone were used as substitutes.

Shell. Shell, readily available along the shores of the Red Sea, the Mediterranean coast, and the shores of the Kinneret (Sea of Galilee), provided the early inhabitants of the Levant with a natural, practically ready-made object for adornment from Mesolithic times onward. In later periods, it was imitated in precious metal or covered with gold foil. Desired for its natural beauty, it was transported over great distances and used both in its natural state and carved into geometric forms. In their natural state, shells require only a perforation to permit stringing. At other times they were cut to conform to varying shapes. Shell beads were sawed into disks and bored with a bow drill.

Used for a variety of purposes, but primarily for jewelry, shell was not a popular material in the Bronze Age. It gained popularity in the Iron Age, when jewelry in precious metal is found with less frequency. Clusters of intact small conch shells with perforations for stringing have been found at several Iron II sites. In other instances, disks cut from tridacna shells (giant clam shells), with central perforations for stringing, were used as filler beads. Engraved tridacna shells that probably come from the Red Sea have been found at numerous sites in the Near East (i.e., Kish, Nippur, Babylon). [*See* Kish; Babylon.] They were widely distributed in Israel, where they have been found at Shechem, Jerusalem, Bethlehem, Tell el-Far'ah (South), and Arad, and in Syria at Alalakh. [*See* Bethlehem; Arad.] These examples may have been used as containers for cosmetics or unguents.

[*See also* Furniture and Furnishings, *article on* Furnishings of the Bronze and Iron Ages; *and* Jewelry.]

BIBLIOGRAPHY

Barnett, Richard D. *A Catalogue of the Nimrud Ivories: With Other Examples of Ancient Near Eastern Ivories in the British Museum.* London, 1957.

Barnett, Richard D. *Ancient Ivories in the Middle East.* Qedem, vol. 14. Jerusalem, 1982.

Caubet, Annie, and Françoise Poplin. "Les objets de matière dure animale: Étude du matériau." In *Ras Shamra–Ougarit,* vol. 3, *Le centre de la ville,* edited by Marguerite Yon, pp. 273–306. Paris, 1987.

Kantor, Helene J. "The Ivories from Floor 6 of Sounding IX." In *Soundings at Tell Fakhariyah, 1906–1950,* by Calvin McEwan et al., pp. 57–68. Oriental Institute Publications, 79. Chicago, 1958.

Krzyszkowska, Olga. *Ivory and Related Materials: An Illustrated Guide.* Institute of Classical Studies, Bulletin Supplement 59. London, 1990.

Liebowitz, Harold. "Bone and Ivory Inlay from Syria and Palestine." *Israel Exploration Journal* 27 (1977): 89–97.

Liebowitz, Harold. "Knochen." In *Reallexikon der Assyriologie und vorderasiatischen Archäologie,* vol. 6, pp. 41–45. Berlin, 1981.

Liebowitz, Harold. "Late Bronze II Ivory Work in Palestine: Evidence of a Cultural Highpoint." *Bulletin of the American Schools of Oriental Research,* no. 265 (1987): 3–24.

Mallowan, M. E. L. *Nimrud and Its Remains.* Vol. 2. London, 1966.

Muscarella, Oscar White. *The Catalogue of Ivories from Hasanlu, Iran.* University Museum Monograph, no. 40. Philadelphia, 1980.

Potts, T. F. "A Bronze Age Ivory-Decorated Box from Pella (Pahel) and Its Foreign Relations." In *Studies in the History and Archaeology of Jordan,* vol. 3, edited by Adnan Hadidi, pp. 59–71. Amman, 1987.

Reese, D. S. "Appendix VII(D): Hippopotamus and Elephant Teeth from Kition." In *Excavations at Kition V,* vol. 2, *The Pre-Phoenician Levels,* edited by Vassos Karageorghis, pp. 391–409. Nicosia, 1985.

Winter, Irene J. "Phoenician and North Syrian Ivory Carving in Historical Context: Questions of Style and Distribution." *Iraq* 38 (1976): 1–22.

HAROLD A. LIEBOWITZ

Artifacts of the Persian through Roman Periods

Virtually nothing is known about the scale, organization, or physical whereabouts of the industries that produce objects from bone, ivory, and shell from the Persian through the Roman periods. The study of the relative uses of these materials at different periods is hampered by a lack of systematic archaeological interest in them. As a result, identification often even of objects, material or species is lacking: primary attention instead has usually been focused on their date, decoration, and possible function. In addition, there is some confusion over how to distinguish between bone, antler, horn, and ivory; without laboratory analysis, it is also difficult to distinguish between hippopotamus and African elephant or Asiatic (male) elephant ivory (although the possible use of fossilized mammoth, walrus, or whale ivory is less likely in the Near East than in northern Europe). An additional problem is that, unless artifacts are particularly distinctive or are found in a single-period context (e.g., a grave), it is difficult to isolate objects—such as beads—as being residual or deliberately reused from earlier periods. Close study of the artifacts themselves, combined with analyses of bone or shell assemblages, can throw some light on the subject. Bone and shell working generally are by-products of food industries, whereas ivory working reflects deliberate procurement of a scarcer resource used to manufacture more valuable ("luxury") goods. Although there is a tendency in the archaeological literature to view bone and shell (let alone antler and horn) as unimportant artifact categories, broad consistencies in style between different regions at specific periods suggest minor but popular craft traditions. Small numbers of professional craftsmen are likely to have worked at or near major centers of demand (e.g., cities, large military garrisons), while itinerant craftsmen may have served rural populations; many of these craftsmen may also have worked seasonally.

Bone. A distinctive category of worked bone found in Achaemenid (Persian period) graves and other contexts from Palestine to southwestern Iran consists of kohl tubes. Occasionally found with applicators in situ, these were usually decorated with incised horizontal registers of lattice, chevron, or herringbone, sometimes with dog's-tooth incision around one end ('Atlit, Hazor, Kamid el-Loz, Deve Höyük, Til Barsip, Nippur, Ur, Susa). They were also copied in bronze at Deve Höyük. Other bone artifacts include decorated handles (Hazor, Shiqmona), spatulae (Tel Haror,

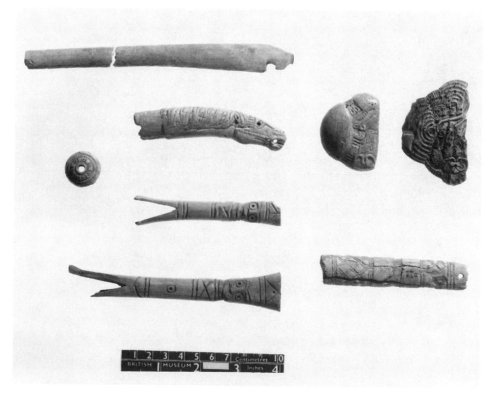

BONE, IVORY, AND SHELL: Persian through Roman Periods. *Assorted carved ivory and bone artifacts from the Persian through Sasanian periods.* Top left: two Persian-period scabbard tips in carved ivory and bone (BM.WAA 132925, 140666). Top right: Persian-period decorated bone cosmetic tube from Deve Höyük (BM.WAA 108684). Middle: Parthian-period bow-tip reinforcement from Nineveh (BM.WAA 138666), a horse's-head handle (BM.WAA 135718), and two "doll" handles from Uruk-Warka (BM.WAA 1856-9-9, 214; 1881-11-3, 38). Bottom: Sasanian incised and colelored bone spindle-whorl from Dailem (BM.WAA 1881-8-30, 558). (Courtesy Trustees of the British Museum)

Tel Michal), coarse-toothed combs (Tel Michal), beaters used in weaving (Susa), perforated tools or objects of uncertain function (Hazor, Tel Michal), pins (Nippur), inlays (Hazor), and simple beads (Tel Michal, Deve Höyük). Corresponding reliably dated Achaemenid evidence from highland Iran is sparse. Simple beads, disks, biconical toggles, a pair of "spatulae," and a point were excavated at Pasargadae (Tall-i Takht) but derive partly from post-Achaemenid contexts; an incised scabbard chape (i.e., a scabbard-tip reinforcement), another toggle, pins, possible gaming pieces, and fragmentary possible containers were found at Persepolis.

Bone was used as a cheaper alternative to ivory during the Seleucid period: a possible workshop has been identified at Alexandria and portraits of Ptolemaic queens appear on bone finger rings. Some utilitarian objects continued to be made of bone, including spindles (Bahrain), beaters for weaving, and spatulae (Larsa, Uruk, Nimrud in Mesopotamia). Plates incised with floral motifs were riveted to handles (Tel Zeror); decorative plaques, carved figures, and double-sided combs also occur (Uruk; Hajar Bin Ḥumeid in South Arabia). As with later Roman work, these were carved using a knife or flat chisel, followed by compass drilling for concentric incision.

The iconography of Roman products in Egypt continued to be heavily Hellenistic in style, although it is possible to distinguish between Egyptian, Syro-Palestinian, Anatolian, and Italian workmanship. Bone plaques and panels, often decorated with scenes from classical mythology, paralleled on sarcophagi, peak in the second–third centuries CE in the eastern Mediterranean (Antinoopolis, Ras el-Soda in Egypt; Ḥesban, Mampsis, Neṣṣana, Oboda [Avdat], Samaria, Amman Airport Cemetery, Pella in Palestine). Some of these may have been carved in Alexandria, where other varieties were carved from ivory. Many of these plaques were glued or riveted together to form larger continuous panels attached to cosmetic boxes, caskets, beds, couches, and other objects. Traces of crimson, dark-red, pink, or black color sometimes survive. Other uses of bone are attested by a coffin with bone and wooden inlays forming circles, rosettes, and pomegranates (Jericho) and a wooden casket decorated with Nereids (Damascus Museum). [See Sarcophagus.]

Bone objects comprise naturalistic human figurines, dolls with movable limbs, cubical die and other gaming pieces, double-sided single-piece combs (also made of wood or iron), handles, spatulae, needles, spoons, spindles, whorls, beads, and pendants (Tel Dor, Jerusalem, Masada, Samaria, Judean Desert caves, Amman Airport Cemetery, Ḥesban, Dura-Europos). Bone pins with knife-cut shanks and turned heads carved in geometric, vegetal, anthropomorphic, or zoomorphic shapes (e.g., birds, nude females), were widespread throughout the Roman Empire (Gush Ḥalav, Samaria, Amman Airport Cemetery, Pella, Jerash, el-Lejjun, Dura-Europos, Anemurium) and are paralleled in metal and

glass. In some cases, bone originals were used to prepare molds to cast bronze specimens. Most pins were cut from the sides of large ungulate limb bones; the process destroyed the identifying characteristics, so that the original species usually cannot be identified—although rare examples survive where gold leaf was applied to the heads (Jerusalem). Similar locally made bone pins are found at Parthian-period sites in Mesopotamia (Kish, Nineveh, Nippur, Nuzi, Seleucia on the Tigris, Uruk), Central Asia (Akhal, Merv, Nysa) and elsewhere (Taxila).

Parthian bone working, especially during the first–second centuries CE, generally seems to have been more extensive than in the later Sasanian period. A possible workshop has been identified at Merv. Bone objects from other Parthian, Kushan, or contemporary sites include belt plates lightly incised with vigorous scenes of animals, combat, or mounted hunters pursuing stags and boars (Dedoplis Mindori in Georgia, Orlat in southern Uzbekistan, Takht-i Sangin). Other plaques depict female dancers and male acrobats plus standing or seated individuals (Olbia on the Black Sea). Decorative carved inlays are found, possibly that originally were attached to small boxes (Seleucia on the Tigris, ed-Dur in southeast Arabia). Small decorative finials or handles carved in the shape of lively horse or other animal heads occur at Parthian (Seleucia on the Tigris) and contemporaneous sites (Petra; Qaryat al-Fau in southwest Arabia); bronze versions also exist. Inscribed Parthian bone knife-handles have been found at Nineveh and Seleucia on the Tigris. A distinctively Parthian type of cylindrical bone handle found in Mesopotamia (Babylon, Nippur, Seleucia on the Tigris, Uruk) and southwest Iran (Masjid-i Suleiman, Susa) is carved in the shape of a crude stylized human face or figure. Traces of paint survive on some of these objects: usually described as bone dolls they are often found in children's graves, but their exact function remains unclear. Other varieties of plain or decorated hollow or flat handles, sometimes made of antler, also occur (Uruk, Masjid-i Suleiman, Susa, Noruz Mahale in Dailaman, Taxila). [See Grave Goods.]

Composite bows were used in the Near East from the fourth millennium onward, but the addition of elongated bone splints in the first–second centuries CE suggests the development of more powerful weapons. These occur in both domestic and funerary contexts at Parthian sites (Nineveh in northern Mesopotamia; ed-Dur, Akhal, Merv). Syrian auxiliaries may have been responsible for introducing these bows into the Roman army: similar splints have been found at several Roman military sites from Egypt (Belmesa) and Palestine (Neṣṣana) to Scotland (Bar Hill on the Antonine wall). Bone arrow nocks and possible arrowheads also occur (Ctesiphon, Nuzi, Uruk, Taxila). Other objects include beaters, spindles, and spindle whorls (Nineveh, Nippur, Nuzi, Seleucia on the Tigris, Uruk; Nush-i Jan in western Iran; Hassan-i Mahale in Dailaman; Merv), spoons, applicators and styli (Taxila), cosmetic containers (Seleucia on the Tigris), plain or incised combs (Nippur, Seleucia on the Tigris, Taxila), finger rings (Uruk), belt buckles (Kampyr-tepe in Uzbekistan), dice (Uruk, Nush-i Jan, Kampyr-tepe, Taxila), astragali (Taxila), flutes (Seleucia on the Tigris), beads and "amulets" (Seleucia on the Tigris). Finally, antler and bone horse-bridle cheek-bars occur in Parthian-period levels at Taxila.

Corresponding Sasanian evidence is rarer. Objects include pins (Tell Barghuthiat, Ctesiphon, Tell ed-Der, Kish, Tell Mahuz, Tell Mohammed Arab, Nippur, Nuzi, Yarim Tepe, plus Kushano-Sasanian sites in Bactria such as Zartepe) and rare beads, mostly found in graves (Barghuthiat, Ctesiphon, ed-Der, Kish, Mahuz, Tell Mohammed Arab, Uruk, Yarim Tepe, Merv). Cubical dice (Tell Mahuz); ground and polished astragali, or knucklebones (Merv); other possible gaming pieces (Kish); bone and horn handles (Tell Ababra, Tell Barghuthiat, Kish, Shahr-i Qumis); spindle whorls (Tell Abu Sarifa, Babylon, Barghuthiat, Coche, Ctesiphon, Kish, Tell Mahuz, Merv, Tell Mohammed Arab, Nineveh, Nippur, Nuzi, Umm Kheshm, plus Qasr-i Abu Nasr in south-central Iran); and miscellaneous tools and other objects (Ctesiphon, Tell ed-Der, Kish, Nippur, Nuzi) also occur.

Ivory. Ivory tusks are shown among East African tribute depicted on reliefs of Darius I (521–486 BCE) at Persepolis: twenty tusks were said by Herodotus (3.97) to be presented every three years. Darius also obtained ivory from Arachosia (western Afghanistan) and Sind, whereas "the ivory workers" employed in his palace at Susa came from Sardis according to a foundation inscription from this building. Finished objects of Achaemenid date include *akinakes* (short sword) "scabbards" (Takht-i Sangin) and dagger chapes. They are carved in low relief at Deve Höyük, are depicted at Persepolis, and are closely comparable to surviving examples in metal and bone. An ivory comb found at Ashkelon was carved with representations of a horseman, ibex, lions, and a contest scene; other decorated combs have been found at Susa. Small studs, presumably for ornate objects (Hazor); incised inlays in Egyptianizing, Greek, and other styles (Persepolis, Susa); handles ('Atlit); and statuettes (Susa) were also made from ivory.

The price of ivory within the eastern Mediterranean fell during the third century BCE, followed by the appearance of a range of naturalistically carved ivories (e.g., a sword-hilt and chape from Takht-i Sangin). An ivory furniture leg dating from the fourth–third centuries BCE was found at Ai Khanoum near Takht-i Sangin. During this period, elephants were frequently depicted in Bactria, particularly on coins, whereas a tomb painting at Marisa/Mareshah in Palestine depicts a saddled African elephant. Alternative ivory sources are suggested by boar tusk fragments (Samaria). Alexandria was an important ivory market during the Seleucid period and ivory plaque fragments, triangular inlays,

pins, and probable spindle whorls occur at various sites (Alexandria, Bahrain, Failaka, Uruk).

There was a heavy demand for both elephants (for the army and circus) and their ivory during the Roman period. These were obtained mainly via Red Sea ports, although a small elephant population still survived in northwest Africa. Associations of ivory workers (Lat., *eborarii*) were formed in Rome and Egypt, and the price of the ivory itself was finally fixed by Emperor Diocletian at 150 denarii per pound. Caligula provided an ivory stable for his horse; Seneca owned five hundred ivory tripod-leg tables; and a friend of Zenobia, queen of Palmyra, had a pair of complete elephant tusks made into a couch. Ivory was reportedly used to make statues, doors, chairs, beds, boxes, chariots, scepters, hilts, scabbards, flutes, lyres, tablets, book covers, birdcages, combs, brooches, and earrings. Archaeological finds from Syria-Palestine are more modest but include carved spindles (Amman Airport Cemetery) and a figurine depicting Ganymede, a subject familiar from Egyptian bone carvings (Samaria). Finished ivory pieces were only rarely traded from India (Pompeii, Hatra).

The most spectacular Parthian evidence consists of more than forty-five large ivory rhyta (hornlike pouring vessels) found within the citadel at the first Parthian capital at Nysa/Mithradatkert (Turkmenistan). These were made from up to four lathe-turned elements carefully jointed with copper pins, lined with wood, inset with semiprecious stones or colored glass, and later repaired with silver wire. They measured up to 60 cm in length and contained between 0.5–1.5 l. The spouts ended in animal protomes, and the upright portions were decorated with classical scenes. Turned ivory furniture legs, cheek pieces with griffins' heads and decorative inlays (Nysa), statuettes, figurines, painted or incised combs, handles, gaming pieces including dice, and beads also occur (Uruk, Bard-i Nishandeh, Masjid-i Suleiman, Susa, Dalverzin-tepe, Kampyr-tepe in Uzbekistan; Begram, Tillya-tepe in Afghanistan; Taxila).

Evidence for Sasanian ivory use is rare, despite sixth-century and later references to its being imported from East Africa: a fine casket carved with hunting and other scenes, formerly attributed to Sasanian workmanship, is probably of Early Islamic date; possible Sasanian pins, beads, pendants, and a stick die (?) from other sites (Tell Mohammed Arab, Qasr-i Abu Nasr) may be bone rather than ivory. Occasional ivory chess pieces have been found in Mesopotamia and Central Asia, but they probably date to the sixth-seventh centuries CE (Late/post-Sasanian periods). A single ivory handle (Tell Dhahab) and ring bezel inset (Tell ed-Der) complete the list of known excavated occurrences of Sasanian ivory.

Shell. Sporadic uses of shell are found at Achaemenid sites, as beads, for instance (Yafit, Tell el-Mazar in the Jordan Valley; Kamid el-Loz, Persepolis): species include cowries (*Cypraea annulus, carneola and moneta*) and horn shell

(Cerithium erithraconense). Horus-type pendants were made of mother-of-pearl (Tel Michal), paralleled in frit at other sites (Kamid el-Loz). Pearl beads were used in Achaemenid jewelry: a hoard of 244 was found at Pasargadae. Coral beads also occur (Kamid el-Loz). Finally, Murex snail and *purpura haemastoma* were crushed in lined pits to produce purple dye (Dor, Tel Mikhmoret).

Pearls are occasionally found in Tylos-period graves in Bahrain; shell from Seleucid contexts includes *Pinctada* (pearl oyster) with holes punched along the edges (Kourion, Paphos) and other species (Nimrud). During the Roman period, perforated Mediterranean (*Arcularia*/Basket shell, *Columbella*, *Cymatium*, *Glycymeris*/dog cockle/comb shell), Indo-Pacific/Red Sea/Gulf (*Conus, Cypraea, Dentalium, Nerita, Pinctada, Strombus*/true conch) and freshwater *(Unio)* shells were used as beads (Quseir el-Qadim on the Red Sea, Jerusalem, Amman Airport Cemetery, Amathus on Cyprus, Alişar Höyük in central Anatolia, Tell Hadidi and Tell Sheikh Hamad in Syria). An exceptional instance from Hesban was the modification of a tiger/panther cowrie into a small bird-shaped cosmetic container with an ivory head and tail. Conch, horn shell, *Charonia tritonis*/triton or trumpet shell, *Drupa, Natica*/Moon or necklace shell, *Olivia*/olive shell, *Tectus*/top shell, *Tridacna*, incised *Pinctada*, a Red Sea whelklike species used in perfume, and pearls are also found (Quseir el-Qadim, Hajar bin Humeid, Hureidha, Samaria, el-Lejjun, Amman Airport Cemetery, Kourion). *Lambis*/spi-

der conch and *Turbo*/turban shell at Quseir el-Qadim probably represent food remains.

Decorated shell inlays, possibly belonging to a small box, were found in a Parthian grave at Shami (western Iran) and depicted archers, horsemen, and a female figure wearing ornate jewelry and an embroidered cloak. A *Pinctada* valve from a third–fourth century CE burial at Mtskheta (Georgia) was incised with an architectural design, a pair of birds, and a ribboned investiture diadem. Large bivalves decorated with dotted outlines of animals were found at Merv and Uruk; simple ringed dot decoration has been found on other shells from Kobadian (Bactria). Finally, shell (including cowrie, *Engina mendicaria*/whelk), mother-of-pearl, and coral beads, rings, and "buttons" occur sporadically at Parthian sites (Seleucia on the Tigris Uruk, Masjid-i Suleiman, Nush-i Jan, Nysa). A wide variety of marine and freshwater species, including Indo-Pacific scallop, were represented by uncut shells at Taxila.

Red Sea coral was a sought-after material for beads in the Roman Empire and may have been traded eastward, judging from archaeological finds (Tell Mohammed Arab, Merv). Sasanian mother-of-pearl geometric inlays occur (Qasr-i Abu Nasr), closely paralleled by stone inlays from Ctesiphon; mother-of-pearl was also used to make beads, pendants, and buckles (Qasr-i Abu Nasr). The extensive Sasanian use of pearls in jewelry (drop earrings, beads) suggests expanded local Gulf pearl fisheries or imports from Sri Lanka: reliable archaeological evidence for Sasanian occupation or trade in these respective areas has hitherto been scarce. Cowry beads are found in graves (Tell Mohammed Arab) and other contexts (Ctesiphon, Qasr-i Abu Nasr). They were regarded in later periods as a means of protection against the Evil Eye, but it is unclear whether similar superstitions were held at this date. Other shells were used as beads, pendants, rings, and spindle whorls, although the varying proportions of shell to other bead materials hints at local fashions (Babylon, Ctesiphon, Kish, Tell Mahuz, Tell Mohammed Arab, Nippur, Nuzi, Umm Kheshm, Uruk, Yarim Tepe, Qasr-i Abu Nasr, Merv). Ostrich-egg cups were sent from Persia to China; one example was excavated at Qasr-i Abu Nasr. Remains of a painted and gilded ostrich egg from Ctesiphon may have served either as a cup or been attached above a hanging lamp: the latter were characteristic of Byzantine and later churches in the southern Levant, the dual purpose being as a counterweight and an obstacle to rodents seeking to drink the lamp oil. The source of both the Sasanian and Levantine examples is likely to have been Arabia.

[*Many of the sites mentioned are the subject of independent entries.*]

BONE, IVORY, AND SHELL: Persian through Roman Periods. *Interior of a Parthian-period pearl-oyster shell from Uruk-Warka.* Note the drilled decoration showing a pair of animals (BM.WAA 1851-1-1, 177). (Courtesy Trustees of the British Museum)

BIBLIOGRAPHY

Ackerman, P. "Ivory and Bone Decoration." In *A Survey of Persian Art*, vol. 3, edited by Arthur Upham Pope, pp. 2659–2663. London and

New York, 1938. A brief section within this classic four-volume reference work, it is now largely superseded by more recent research.

Amiet, Pierre. "Les ivoires achéménides de Suse." *Syria* 49 (1972): 167–191, 319–337. Study of the largest surviving group of Achaemenid ivories.

Barnett, Richard D. *Ancient Ivories in the Middle East.* Qedem, vol. 14. Jerusalem, 1982. Wide-ranging survey including Achaemenid, Seleucid, and Roman material.

Bernard, Paul. "Sièges et lits en ivoire d'époque hellénistique en Asie centrale." *Syria* 47 (1970): 327–343. Comparative study of furniture fragments from Ai Khanum, with material from other sites.

MacGregor, Arthur. *Bone, Antler, Ivory, and Horn: The Technology of Skeletal Materials since the Roman Period.* London, 1985. Standard work dealing with technology and function, based on excavated finds from northern Europe.

Marangou, Lila I. *Bone Carvings from Egypt,* vol. 1, *Graeco-Roman Period.* Tübingen, 1976. Detailed critical survey of the Egyptian evidence.

Reese, D. S. "The Trade of Indo-Pacific Shells into the Mediterranean and Europe." *Oxford Journal of Archaeology* 10 (1991): 159–196. Catalog of excavated evidence from the Epipaleolithic to postmedieval periods, arranged by modern country from Jordan to Norway.

Rosenthal, Renate. "Late Roman and Byzantine Bone Carvings from Palestine." *Israel Exploration Journal* 26 (1976): 96–103. Review of the excavated data with an attempt to distinguish Palestinian from Egyptian products.

Scullard, H. H. *The Elephant in the Greek and Roman World.* Ithaca, N.Y., 1974. Useful historical study focusing on the military and circus roles of elephants, followed by an appendix on ivory.

Zavyalov, V. "Bone Toilet Articles from Central Asian Sites of the Kushan and Post-Kushan Periods" (in Russian). *Kratkie Soobshtseniya Instituta Arkheologii* 209 (1993): 31–41. Situates within a typological framework all Partho-Sasanian–period bone pins from Central Asia published to date.

ST. JOHN SIMPSON

Artifacts of the Byzantine and Islamic Periods

Precious, hard, and resistant—but less hard than marble and therefore easier to cut—ivory is an excellent material for carving planes in relief. The art of carving developed greatly during the last centuries of the Roman Empire when, with the decadence of classical Greek culture and sculptural art, a pictorial tendency prevailed. Important in this and later periods (up to the tenth century) was the influence of miniature painting as a source for theme and style (cf., e.g., the plaque showing "The Washing of the Feet," now in Berlin at the Staatliche Museen, with the painted icon of the same theme in the Monastery of St. Catherine in the Sinai Desert).

Among the most notable masterpieces of late imperial art in carved ivory is the series of diptychs—double small tables joined by hinges, carved on their exterior face, and covered on the interior with wax for writing—used as gifts for special state occasions like the appointment of high state officials, especially consuls, to whom, indeed, the use of diptychs would later be reserved. The several consular diptychs that come mainly from Constantinople are almost all datable to the fifth and sixth centuries. [*See* Constantinople.] On them, the idealized image of the consul exemplifies the original style created by the syncretic art of the eastern empire. Among the best of this group is the diptych of Aerobindus, consul in 506 (now in Zurich, at the Musée National Suisse), and the one representing the empress Ariadne, dated to about 500 (in Florence, at the Museo Nazionale). The diptychs are often very useful in establishing a chronology of comparable ivory objects as they often bear the name of the official they represent. Whereas Italian imperial cities like Rome, Ravenna, Milan, and Monza were once thought to have been the main centers for the ivory craft, it is now clear that many of the best ivories came from peripheral areas (Cutler, 1985).

A well-known pyxis representing the Sacrifice of Isaac and Sts. Peter, Paul, and John, datable to the fourth or fifth century (Berlin, Staatliche Museen), is most probably from Antioch. [*See* Antioch on Orontes.] Egypt as a source of worked ivory is attested by both papyri and excavations and was recently confirmed by the finds at Abu Mina (Engemann, 1987). The sixth-century cathedra of Maximianus (Ravenna, National Museum) seems to come from Alexandria, as do other stylistically cognate artifacts, such as the Barberini ivory dated to about 500 (Paris, Louvre Museum), on which a barbarian is represented offering a giant tusk to the emperor—testimony to the reputation of ivory in late antiquity as an imperial material. [*See* Alexandria.]

The production of carved ivory artifacts in the Byzantine world did not cease with the Islamic invasions in the mid-seventh century. The masterpieces of the ninth century present an iconographic repertoire that looks both toward classical antiquity and the Orient, especially to Sasanian Persia. [*See* Sasanians.] Characteristic products of the eighth and ninth centuries are caskets and hunting horns (oliphants). The caskets are usually rectangular, with a flat or a truncated pyramidal lid, and are decorated with ornamental squares or bands with mythological subjects or zoomorphic subjects in the Persian tradition. One of the best examples is the tenth-century Veroli casket (London, Victoria and Albert Museum).

A large number of Byzantine ivories datable to the ninth and eleventh centuries are carved tablets, mainly intended as icons, and there are also examples of ivories sculpted in the round. Documentation for ivory carving after the sixth century is scanty. Nothing is known of modes of production, and there is no information about how such objects were used. There is only one extant Byzantine ivory tablet. It is presently displayed at the tenth-century great cross/reliquary at San Francesco at Cortona, Italy. It was probably originally exhibited as it is now (except that its elaborate frame is a seventeenth-century work) because the inscription on its back required that it be displayed in the Hagia Sophia so as to show both its front and back.

Ivory objects from the Islamic period include caskets (both rectangular and cylindrical), combs, oliphants, and chess pieces. [*See* Games.] Ivories sculpted in the round are rare. Techniques of decoration were relief carving; the painting or gilding of flat surfaces; intarsia, or mosaic decoration, on ivory plaques countersunk in wood; adhering cut ivory shapes to a wooden surface; and incising dots and concentric circles on a surface, sometimes filling them in with colored pigments.

Excavations at Umayyad and early 'Abbasid sites have yet to reveal ivory objects, and there are very few attributable to the Sasanian period in Persia. In Egypt, on the other hand, Coptic craftsmen kept alive an earlier tradition, and there are pieces that, on stylistic grounds, can be attributed to Coptic craftsmen of the ninth and tenth centuries. For the eleventh and twelfth centuries there are bone and ivory carved panels from Fustat, associated stylistically with Fatimid wood carvings. [*See* Fustat.] Cut in low relief and depicting hunting scenes, isolated animals and human figures are set against a background of scrollwork. These examples were probably either whole panels belonging to caskets or insets for larger wooden panels.

Ivory caskets are mentioned in an eye-witness account of the treasures of the caliph al-Mustansir reported by the fourteenth-century historian al-Maqrizi. Also to be attributed to Fatimid Egypt is a group of panels carved in openwork (Florence, Bargello Museum; Berlin, Staatliche Museen; Paris, Louvre Museum). These are related in style and subject matter to the carved-wood panels from the *maristan* (hospital) at Qala'un and to some Fatimid wooden panels now also in the Louvre.

Another group of objects ascribed to Fatimid Egypt or to Norman Sicily comprises ivory oliphants and caskets. Their style is distinctive and characterized by relief cutting in two planes; the decoration consists of interlaced circles, each containing an animal or bird and, on the caskets, human figures. Similar decorative treatment appears in Muslim Spain, but an attribution to Sicily or southern Italy—whose Norman rulers are known to have employed Muslim craftsmen—is likely, as it presents elements common to the oliphants and caskets manufactured in southern Italy.

A group of ivories that has given rise to much discussion consists of painted and gilded caskets (and combs and crosiers). Many of these found their way to the treasuries of European churches in the Middle Ages, where the caskets were used as reliquaries or pyxes and the combs for liturgical purposes (i.e., used in the ceremony consecration of a bishop). All have certain common stylistic and technical features. Many caskets have inscriptions around the rim of the lid in either Kufic or Naskhi script, generally containing benedictory phrases addressed to the owner. [*See* Arabic.] Occasionally, there are verses of a love poem, suggesting that these particular examples were bridal caskets for jewels and

trinkets. The painted decoration includes floral motifs, birds, falconers, and images of Christian saints. Unfortunately, no surviving inscription contains a date, or the name of either the maker or owner.

While it is generally agreed that the painted ivories can be assigned to the twelfth or thirteenth centuries, opinions differ regarding their place of origin; on stylistic grounds they have been variously attributed to Persia, Mesopotamia, Syria, Egypt, Spain, and Sicily. The decoration of one distinctive group contains interlaced star and geometric ornaments so similar to those found in the art of Nasrid Granada (Spain) that their attribution to a fourteenth-or fifteenth-century Granada workshop seems certain. For the others, however, an attribution to twelfth-century Sicily seems most likely—given the close stylistic connection with the painted pottery of Norman Sicily and with the greatest surviving monument of Fatimid painting, the ceiling of the Cappella Palatina in Palermo.

By far the most remarkable examples of medieval Islamic craftsmanship are the carved ivories made in Muslim Spain that include masterpieces to rival the best Byzantine and Western ivories. Unlike most of the ivories discussed so far, these were produced under royal patronage and include some objects made for presentation to royal personages. They belong to the years of the caliphate of Cordoba, having been produced first in Cordoba itself and then in Madinat az-Zahra'. The three finest examples are two cylindrical pyxes, one, dedicated to al-Mughira, brother of al-Hakam II and dated to AH 357/968 CE (in the Louvre Museum), and the other, dedicated to Ziyad ibn Aflah and dated to AH 359/970 CE (Victoria and Albert Museum), and the casket in the cathedral of Pamplona, dedicated to a son of al-Mansur and dated to AH 399/1008 CE. Scenes include the prince with attendants, servants, and musicians; huntsmen with falcons; men performing rustic tasks; and animals attacking their prey: in one case an elephant carrying a litter is represented. The use to which these domed cylindrical pyxes were put is suggested by an example owned by the Hispanic Society in New York City (D752, c. 966 CE): it bears an inscribed poem identifying it as a container for musk, camphor, and ambergris, which were considered precious substances, on a par with large amounts of gold or silver.

Plentiful amounts of ivory were available in the Mediterranean area from the fourth to the sixth centuries; the supply was cut short, however, by the Persian wars (first half of the seventh century) and the Islamic conquest of Spain (711 CE). An ample flow appears to have been restored by the ninth and especially the tenth centuries. By the middle of the tenth century, it became abundant in Spain, as a result of flourishing trade contacts with North Africa. The main source of ivory in the Islamic period was probably East Africa, also the greatest ivory-producing area in the Middle Ages. Surviving Islamic ivories seem to be of elephant tusk.

Walrus ivory was used for the handles of daggers. Hippopotamus ivory is more elastic and compact than elephant ivory and, in general, is less yellow. It is also harder, and therefore more difficult to work, but it is more suitable for small objects, such as knife handles. A hippopotamus ivory hoard has been discovered in Gao (Mali), that was destined for export, most probably to Islamic Spain. It was found in an archaeological context that dated it to the eleventh century.

The range of application for bone carving exceeded that for ivory. It was probably worked by the same craftsmen, and bone fragments (e.g., plaques attached to caskets and boxes) have often been mistaken for ivory. Bone, usually from cattle and pack animals, was used for buttons, knobs, and struts, as well as for tools, especially in the weaving trade. It was also used to craft gaming pieces, containers, and bird rings. [See Jewelry.] Ornamental handles for fans or flyswatters from many different periods have been found in excavations in Constantinople (Gill, 1986).

Similarly eclectic uses for bone have been found in Islamic-period contexts, and it sufficient here to refer to the Egyptian finds at Karanis and Fustat (which also included Coptic material; see Scanlon, 1976), among which were found figurines, combs, weaving tools, gaming pieces, draughtsmen, and cubic and rectangular dice.

Except for its sporadic use in intarsia decoration, shell does not appear to have been a mainstream material in either the Byzantine or the Islamic period.

BIBLIOGRAPHY

Contadini, Anna. "Islamic Ivory Chess Pieces, Draughtsmen, and Dice in the Ashmolean Museum." *Oxford Studies in Islamic Art* 10 (1995). Survey of the chronology, distribution, and typology of Islamic ivory chess pieces from the ninth to the fifteenth centuries.

Cott, Perry B. *Siculo-Arabic Ivories*. Princeton, 1939. Standard work for the group of Siculo-Arabic painted ivories, illustrating some ninety pieces in which the painted decoration is still visible.

Curatola, Giovanni, ed. *Eredità dell'Islam: Arte islamica in Italia*. Milan, 1993. Catalog of an exhibition at the Doge's Palace, Venice. Includes chapters on Muslim Spain and Fatimid Egypt, with new or known ivory pieces reconsidered. Color illustrations.

Cutler, Anthony. *The Craft of Ivory: Sources, Techniques, and Uses in the Mediterranean World, A.D. 200–1400*. Dumbarton Oaks Byzantine Collection Publications, 8. Washington, D.C., 1985. Important survey of the art and craft of ivory from Roman to late Byzantine times, illustrating a variety of materials.

Cutler, Anthony. *The Hand of the Master: Craftsmanship, Ivory, and Society in Byzantium, Ninth-Eleventh Centuries*. Princeton, 1994. Important study of many ivories (especially icons), their techniques, uses, and importance within the Byzantine world (ninth–eleventh centuries).

Dalton, O. M. *Catalogue of the Ivory Carvings of the Christian Era, with Examples of Mohammedan Art and Carvings in Bone in the Department of British and Mediaeval Antiquities and Ethnography of the British Museum*. London, 1909. Standard catalog on bone and ivory material from both Byzantine and Islamic periods in the British Museum.

Dimand, Maurice S. *A Handbook of Muhammadan Art*. New York, 1947. Examples of objects found in Egypt (now in the Metropolitan Museum of Art, New York City) made by Coptic craftsmen in the ninth and tenth centuries (see fig. 69).

Dodds, Jerrilynn D., ed. *Al-Andalus: The Art of Islamic Spain*. New York, 1992. Catalog of an exhibition held in Granada and at the Metropolitan Museum of Art, New York City. Contains many Islamic ivories from Spain, all reproduced in color, and a survey of the present scholarship.

Engemann, Josef. "Elfenbeinfunde aus Abu Mena/Ägypten." *Jahrbuch für Antike und Christentum* 30 (1987): 172–186. Byzantine ivory finds at Abu Mina (Egypt).

Ferrandis, José. *Marfiles árabes de Occidente*. 2 vols. Madrid, 1935–1940. Standard work on Islamic ivories made in the West, comprising both Siculo-Arabic and Spanish types.

Gill, Margaret V. In *Excavations at Sarachane in Istanbul*, vol. 1, edited by R. Martin Harrison, pp. 226–231, 258–262. Princeton, 1986. Bone objects from many different periods found at Constantinople.

Goldschmidt, Adolph, and Kurt Weitzmann. *Die byzantinischen Elfenbeinskulpturen des X.–XIII. Jahrhunderts*. 2 vols. Berlin, 1930–1934. Standard corpus of Byzantine ivories from the tenth to thirteenth centuries.

Kühnel, Ernst. *Die islamischen Elfenbeinskulpturen VIII.–XIII. Jahrhunderts*. 2 vols. Berlin, 1971. Up-to-date, comprehensive, and well-illustrated survey of Islamic ivories from the eighth to thirteenth centuries. A fundamental work.

Longhurst, Margaret. *Catalogue of Carvings in Ivory*, part 1, *Up to the Thirteenth Century*. London, 1927. Examples of bone and ivory carved panels found in the ruined mounds at Fustat (now in the Victoria and Albert Museum, London, and the Metropolitan Museum of Art, New York City), and associated stylistically with the wood carvings of the Fatimid period (see pl. 28). For examples of comparative items in carved woodwork, see Edmond Pauty, *Les bois sculptes jusqu'à l'époque ayyoubide: Catalogue général du Musée Arabe du Caire* (Cairo, 1931), and Elise Anglade, *Catalogue des boiseries de la section islamique, Musée du Louvre* (Paris, 1988).

Morey, Charles R. *Gli oggetti di avorio e di osso del Museo Sacro Vaticano*. Vatican City, 1936. Good catalog of this important collection.

Pinder-Wilson, Ralph H., and C. N. L. Brooke. "The Reliquary of St. Petroc and the Ivories of Norman Sicily." *Archaeologia* 104 (1973): 261–305. Important article updating Cott (see above), with much new information about the painted Siculo-Arabic ivories, listing some 220 pieces.

Scanlon, George T. "Fustat Expedition: Preliminary Report 1968, Part II." *Journal of the American Research Center in Egypt* 13 (1976): 69–89. Ivory and bone finds from Fustat.

ANNA CONTADINI

BOSRA, site located to the south of the basalt plateau in the Hauran province of Syria (32°31′ N, 36°29′ E), 42 km (26 mi.) east of Der'a and approximately 10 km (6 mi.) from the Jordanian border. Although the population has been reduced in recent centuries, there is no doubt that the city has been inhabited continuously since the Nabatean-Roman period. Before that period, it is uncertain whether the city is to be identified with a site named *bwdznw* in the inscription on a statuette from Saqqara from the late twelfth dynasty; with BDN in a list engraved on the Karnak pylons; with Busruna in two Amarna texts; or with bdrn on a geographic list in the funerary temple of Amenophis III (1408–1372 BCE). The site has sometimes been confused with Bosora in Moab, which may be the one cited in *Deuteronomy* 4:43, and with

Bosora (Buṣeirah) in Edom. The present-day Arab name *Bōṣra* corresponds exactly to the Nabatean and Palmyrene written form *BSR'*, from the root *bāṣar*, "to make inaccessible," when defining, for example, a fortress. The *t* in the Greco-Latin form *Bostra* seems designed to facilitate pronunciation.

The excavations by the American University of Beirut (1980–1984) in the northwest area of the city have attested the occupation of the city from the Early Bronze Age onward. Judging mainly from the ceramic materials found there, Helga Seeden (1986) concluded that the site was first inhabited toward the beginning of the second millennium

BCE. It was not enclosed by a fortification wall, and was situated in the vicinity of a perennial spring, which explains settlement in a region where springs are very rare. Old aerial photographs of the area to the west of Bosra indicate the boundaries of what may have been the Bronze Age settlement. At least one building, constructed on a stone foundation, has been identified at the very edge of the settlement; remains of domestic and agricultural activity, such as ceramics, basalt utensils, and animal bones, were recovered. The excavations conducted by the Franco-Syrian mission since 1981 have revealed traces of older occupation at the site. On the edge of the South Thermae (see plan, no. 14)

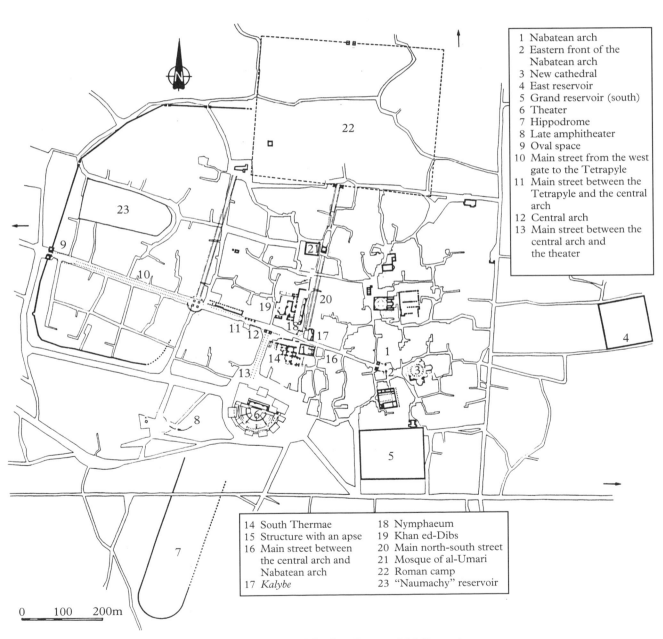

1 Nabatean arch
2 Eastern front of the Nabatean arch
3 New cathedral
4 East reservoir
5 Grand reservoir (south)
6 Theater
7 Hippodrome
8 Late amphitheater
9 Oval space
10 Main street from the west gate to the Tetrapyle
11 Main street between the Tetrapyle and the central arch
12 Central arch
13 Main street between the central arch and the theater

14 South Thermae
15 Structure with an apse
16 Main street between the central arch and Nabatean arch
17 *Kalybe*
18 Nymphaeum
19 Khan ed-Dibs
20 Main north-south street
21 Mosque of al-Umari
22 Roman camp
23 "Naumachy" reservoir

BOSRA. *Plan of the city.* (Courtesy J. M. Dentzer)

and of the main east–west street (nos. 10–11, 16) of the city sherds out of context dating to EB I and lithic material were discovered. Near the Nabatean arch (no. 1), ceramics also out of context date to EB II–III and a few sherds to the Iron Age.

In 162 BCE Judas Maccabeus, coming to the aid of the site's Jewish minority, destroyed the city of Bosor in Gilead (*1 Mc.* 5:26, 28). The identification of Bosor as Bosra is certain, but no trace of this period has been found yet at Bosra.

Bosra and the surrounding region were under the authority of the Nabatean dynasty from at least the beginning of the first century BCE (Aretas III controlled Damascus between 84 and 72 BCE). Under Rabel II's rule (70–106 CE) at the latest Bosra becomes the second capital of the Nabatean kingdom. The Franco-Syrian excavations at the Nabatean arch (plan, no. 2) and in the area to the east of it show the importance of the Nabatean urbanistic activity in Bosra. The arch was conceived as a structure connecting two areas of the town oriented toward different directions. Its western front (no. 1) has the same orientation as the main street whereas the east front (no. 2), which bears two Nabatean half columns, matches the chief orientation of the eastern part of the city. At the same time, the western part of the city, which was already entirely occupied as attested by the Nabatean ceramics found in many places within and beyond the city, must also have been reorganized.

About 100 meters east of the Nabatean arch, the Franco-Syrian mission discovered remains of a large enclosure wall (plan, no. 3) with pilasters, decorated with fine limestone slabs and stucco and dated to the Nabatean period. In front of it a stylobate belonged to a portico. These structures follow the alignment of the eastern front of the structure. It is tempting to explain these structures as parts of a vast sanctuary (temenos) whose architectural elements, for example the Nabatean capitals, were reused in the Christian church built above it. Dushares, god of the Nabatean dynasty, associated with A'ra, a local god, was called by inscriptions "the god of Rabel, our Lord, who is at Busra."

Architectural blocks sculpted in the Nabatean style were discovered in the center of the city. So it is possible to imagine a Nabatean temple not far from the crossroads near the nymphaeum (no. 18).

The role played by Bosra during the period of the Nabatean kingdom explains why, after the kingdom's annexation by Rome in 106 CE, it became the capital of the Provincia Arabia, the headquarters of the camp (plan, no. 22) of the Third Legion Cyrenaica (at the northern end of the city), and the hub of a network of roads, the most important of which was the Via Trajana Nova. The city, to which Alexander Severus gives the status of colony, develops impressively: at least four of the main streets were decorated with ionic capitals of Severan style. Nearby all the buildings were of basalt but in the street (no. 13) that led from the central arch (no. 12) to the theater (no. 6) limestone was used. In the main east–west (no. 11) and in the north–south street (no. 20) porticoes and shops were built at least partly above cryptoporticoes. The ends of the east–west main street and intersections were marked by arches or a tetrapyle; at the western end was an oval-shaped open space (no. 9). Among public buildings the best preserved is the theater constructed entirely on vaulted substructures, with an elaborate system of passageways. The *frons scenae* was completed in the Severan period. Recently an amphitheater (no. 8), probably from a later, not yet determined period, was excavated, as the hippodrome (no. 7) farther south. The two huge thermae in the center of the city had vaulted or domed roofings made of volcanic scoria concrete. In the "South Thermae" (no. 14) the big bay windows were closed with double glass partitions. The rooms were initially arranged on one line; later, in the third–fourth century, the bath was extended on both sides of these rooms in order to allow a symmetrical circulation. A part of it was still in use in the Umayyad period. The so-called Khan ed-Dibs (no. 19) was a second bath complex created with a symmetrical plan. A temple of Zeus Hammon, dedicated to the tutelary god of the Third Legion Cyrenaica is known from an inscription (IGLS, XIII, 9107). An other inscription found in the vicinity of the Nabatean arch is the dedication of a temple to Rome and Augustus (IGLS, XIII, 9143). Further cults are mentioned in inscriptions.

The lower front of the so-called *Kalybe* (no. 17), excavated by the Directorate of Antiquities of Bosra in 1994, was arranged as a monumental fountain. The real use of the so-called nymphaeum (no. 18), which faces it, is not yet proved.

In the surroundings of Bosra the Franco-Syrian mission discovered remains of several antique organized areas of land (gardens near the city, fields farther away). One of these cadasters, based on square units (705 m) must date to the Roman period.

A period of turmoil explains the restoration of the city's ramparts in about 249–250 CE. Their layout is still largely hypothetical, particularly in the southern part of the city, where they were subsequently dismantled to furnish construction materials for the Islamic citadel. In fact, an incursion of Palmyrene troops under Zenobia's direction probably damaged the Temple of Zeus Hammon then, which was restored in about 273–275 CE.

The Christian era saw a new phase of construction. Directly above the Nabatean "temenos" (plan, no. 2) a fourth–fifth-century structure, of which only the mosaic floors remain, was built; it was excavated by the Franco-Syrian mission. In turn, it was overbuilt by a church complex that could be a cathedral, similar to the Church of Sts. Serge, Bacchus, and Leonce but even larger (about 44 × 62 m).

These two churches had a similar plan: a circular central space inscribed in a square, with four exedrae in the corners, and the sanctuary and subsidiary rooms on the east.

In the Byzantine period urban maintenance and improvement continued. An inscription dated to 517 mentions the paving of the portico bordering the street (plan, no. 13) along the south thermal. A large monumental access leading to the eastern palaestra of the south thermae (no. 14) passing under a structure that has an apse (no. 15; church?).

Bosra was the first Byzantine city conquered by the Islamic armies (634 CE) and the first Syrian city to receive a copy of the Qur'an. It occupies a place of eminence in the history of the birth of Islam because the prophet is said to have met the monk Bahira there. The American University excavations in the northwest part of the city have uncovered a farm from the Late Umayyad era. The porticoes of the north–south street (plan, no. 20), excavated in 1994 by the Bosra Directorate of Antiquities, have been overbuilt by crossing walls to a *suq*, probably from the eighth century. An eleventh-century fortress built in and around the Roman theater became the heart of the medieval city. A group of religious buildings (the mosques of al-Umari, al-Mibrak, al-Khidr, and the *madrasah* al-Dabbagha), dated between the Umayyad period and the thirteenth century, is still standing. One of the last major buildings from the Mamluk period is the *hammam* Manjak, recently restored by a German team.

[*See also* Nabateans.]

BIBLIOGRAPHY

Aalund, Flemming, et al. *Islamic Boṣrā: A Brief Guide.* Damascus, 1990. *Berytus* 32 (1984); 33 (1985).

Brünnow, Rudolf-Ernst, and Alfred von Domaszewski. *Die Provincia Arabia auf Grund zweier in den Jahre 1897 und 1898 unternommenen Reisen und der Berichte früherer Reisender.* Vol. 3. Strassburg, 1909. See pages 1–84.

Butler, Howard Crosby. *Ancient Architecture in Syria.* Publications of the Princeton University Archaeological Expedition to Syria, 1904–1905 and 1909, Division 2, Section A. Leiden, 1907. See pages 215–295, plates 1–43.

Cerulli, S. "Boṣrā." *Felix Ravenna,* no. 115 (1978): 77–120.

Dentzer, Jean-Marie. "Les sondages de l'Arc Nabatéen et l'urbanisme de Boṣrā." *Comptes Rendus des Séances de l'Académie des Inscriptions et Belles-Lettres* (1986): 62–87.

Dentzer, Jean-Marie. "Fouilles franco-syriennes à l'Est de l'Arc Nabatéen, 1985–1987: Une nouvelle cathédrale à Bosra?" In *XXXV Corso di cultura sull'arte ravennate e bizantina, Ravenna, 22–24 marzo 1988,* pp. 13–34. Ravenna, 1988.

Dentzer, Jean-Marie, et al. "Nouvelles recherches franco-syriennes dans le quartier est de Bosra ash-Sham." *Comptes Rendus des Séances de l'Académie des Inscriptions et Belles-Lettres* (1993): 117–147.

Dentzer, Jean-Marie, et al. "Le développement urbain de Bosra: Quinze ans de recherches archéologiques." *Annales Archéologiques Arabes Syriennes.* In press.

Farioli [Campanati], Raffaella. "Gli scavi della chiesa dei SS Sergio, Bacco e Leonzio a Bosra." *Berytus* 33 (1985): 61–74.

Farioli Campanati, Raffaella. "Relazioni sugli scavi e ricerche della missione Italo-Siriana a Bosra, 1985, 1986, 1987." In *XXXV Corso di cultura sull'arte ravennate e bizantina, Ravenna, 22–24 marzo 1988,* pp. 45–92. Ravenna, 1988.

Farioli Campanati, Raffaella. "Bosra chiesa dei SS Sergio, Bacco e Leonzio: I nuovi ritrovamenti, 1988–1989." In *La Syrie de Byzance à l'Islam: VIIe–VIIIe siècles,* edited by Pierre Carnivet and Jean-Paul Rey-Coquais, pp. 173–179. Damas, 1992.

Felix Ravenna, nos. 137–138 (1970–1971).

Finsen, Helge. *Le levé du théâtre romain à Bosra, Syrie.* Copenhagen, 1972.

Freyberger, Klaus S. "Zur Datierung des Theaters in Boṣrā." *Damaszener Mitteilungen* 3 (1988): 17–26.

Freyberger, Klaus S. "Einige Beobachtungen zur städtebaulichen Entwicklung des römischen Bostra." *Damaszener Mitteilungen* 4 (1989): 45–60.

Kadour, Muhamed, and Helga Seeden. "Busra 1980: Reports of an Archaeological and Ethnographic Campaign." *Damaszener Mitteilungen* 1 (1983): 77–101.

Maqdissi, Michel al-. "Sites et matériel du sud de la Syrie à l'âge du bronze." In *Le djebel al-ʿArab: Histoire et patrimoine au Musée de Suweidāʿ,* edited by Jean-Marie Dentzer, pp. 13–14. Paris, 1991.

Meinecke, Michael. "Der Hammām Manĝak und die islamische Architektur von Busrā." *Berytus* 32 (1984): 181–190.

Meinecke, Michael, and S. A. al-Muqdād. "Der Hammām Manĝak in Busrā . . . Grabungsbericht 1981–1983." *Damaszener Mitteilungen* 2 (1985): 177–192.

Mougdad, Ryad al-, et al. "Un amphithéâtre à Boṣrā?" *Syria* 67 (1990): 201–204.

Sartre, Maurice. *Bostra: Nos. 9001 à 9472. Inscriptions Grecques et Latines de la Syrie,* vol. 13.1. Paris, 1982.

Sartre, Maurice. *Bostra des origines à l'Islam.* Paris, 1985.

Sartre, Maurice. "Bostra." In *Reallexikon für Antike und Christentum.* In press.

Seeden, Helga. "Bronze Age Village Occupation in Busrā: AUB Excavations on the Northwest Tell, 1983–1984." *Berytus* 34 (1986): 11–81.

Seeden, Helga. "Busra 1983–1984: Second Archaeological Report." *Damaszener Mitteilungen* 3 (1988): 387–411.

XXXV Corso du cultura sull'arte ravennate e bizantina, Ravenna, 22–24 marzo 1988. Ravenna, 1988.

JEAN-MARIE DENTZER
Translated from French by Elizabeth Keller

BOTTA, PAUL-ÉMILE

BOTTA, PAUL-ÉMILE (1802–1870), French consul at Mosul, in Iraq, credited with discovering Assyrian civilization and thus opening the way for the discipline of Mesopotamian archaeology. Born in Turin, Italy, he joined his father, the historian Carlo Botta, in France, where he studied medicine. It was as surgeon on the ship *Héros* that Botta first traveled around the world (1826–1829). He subsequently traveled through Lebanon, Egypt, Senaar, and Yemen, where he perfected his Arabic and gathered collections for the Museum of Natural History in Paris. Following his appointment to Mosul, he began his search for Nineveh on the instigation of the secretary of the French Asiatic Society, Julius Mohl. Botta's first excavations at Kouyunjik were unsuccessful, but in March 1843, on the site of Khorsabad, he discovered the first sculptures of the palace built for the Assyrian king Sargon II in his capital Dur Sharrukin between

717 and 706 BCE. In two excavation campaigns (1843, 1844), with the collaboration of the painter Eugène-Napoléon Flandin, Botta unearthed the greater part of the building. The best-preserved sculptures were transported to Paris to constitute at the Louvre the first Assyrian museum in the world, inaugurated by King Louis-Philippe on 1 May 1847. The results of Botta's work were recorded in the imposing publication *Monument de Ninive découvert et décrit par M. P. E. Botta, mesuré et dessiné par M. E. Flandin* (5 vols., Paris, 1846–1850). Botta pursued his career as a consul in Jerusalem and then in Tripoli in Libya. Exploration of Khorsabad was resumed in 1852–1854 by Botta's successor at Mosul, Victor Place (1815–1875), who completed the excavation of the palace and drew up the map of the city.

The lapidary description the novelist Flaubert made of Botta during his short stay in Jerusalem in 1850: "Man in ruin, man of ruins in the city of ruins; denies everything and gives me the feeling of hating everything except what is dead" is regrettably severe for a man who was austere, timid, and solitary and whose openness of spirit, honesty, and generosity were praised by all who came into contact with him.

BIBLIOGRAPHY

Albenda, Pauline. *The Palace of Sargon, King of Assyria.* Paris, 1986.
Bergamini, Giovanni. "Paolo Emilio Botta e la scoperta della civiltà assira." *Bollettino della Società Piemontese di Archeologia e Belle Arti* 38–41 (1984–1987): 5–16.
Botta, Paul-Émile. *Lettres de Botta sur les decouvertes à Khorsabad pres de Ninive.* Paris, 1945.
Botta, Paul-Émile, and Eugène-Napoléon Flandin. *Monument de Ninive découvert et décrit par M. P. E. Botta, mesuré et dessiné par M. E. Flandin.* 5 vols. Paris, 1846–1850.
Botta, Paul-Émile. *Inscriptions découvertes à Khorsabad.* Paris, 1848.
Botta, Paul-Émile. "Mémoire sur l'écriture cunéiforme assyrienne." *Journal Asiatique* 8.1 (1848): 1–197.
Knowlton, Edgar C. "Paul-Émile Botta, Visitor to Hawai'i in 1828." *Hawaiian Journal of History* 18 (1984): 13–37.

ELISABETH FONTAN

BOUQRAS, Neolithic village site located in Syria on the right bank of the Euphrates River, just below its confluence with the Khabur River (35°5'12" N, 40°23'50" E). Bouqras was the first Neolithic settlement to be identified in the Euphrates valley. It was discovered by a Dutch geomorphologist, Willem J. van Liere. He and a French archaeologist, Henri de Contenson, under the auspices of the Centre National de Recherche Scientifique, exacavated at Bouqras briefly in 1965 to determine the sequence of occupation and to learn something of its material culture and economy. More extensive excavations were conducted from 1976 to 1978 by a Dutch team led by P. A. Akkermans and J. J. Roodenberg of the Universities of Amsterdam and Groningen. Their most significant contribution was to expand greatly what is known of the site's layout.

Bouqras was an oval mound nearly 3 ha (7 acres) in extent and 5 m deep. De Contenson and van Liere dug two trenches through the deposits at its center that revealed a sequence of three phases of occupation (Contenson, 1985, p. 336). No pottery was found in the two earliest phases, I and II, but potsherds were recovered in phase III; thus, it appears that occupation at Bouqras spanned the introduction of pottery to this region. The Dutch excavators defined a sequence of at least ten architectural episodes that could be grouped in four phases, numbered from surface to subsoil. Radiocarbon dates indicate that the village was inhabited from about 6,400 to 5,900 BP in radiocarbon years.

The village was composed of tightly packed, rectangular, mud-brick houses, grouped around open yards and along streets (Akkermans et al., 1983, figure 3). The houses were similar in size and plan, suggesting that there were no great differences in status among the inhabitants. The artifacts from Bouqras were unusually varied for a site of its age, attesting to the versatile craftsmanship of its inhabitants. Among them were figurines of human females and animals made of sun-dried clay, a wide variety of bone tools, and numerous small stone dishes and bowls. Chipped-stone tools, more than 20 percent of which were made of obsidian from eastern Turkey, were ubiquitous.

Bones of domesticated sheep and goats and some wild animals recovered in the 1965 campaign persuaded the excavators that the inhabitants had been herdsmen and hunters (Contenson, 1985). Seeds of domesticated wheats, barley, lentils, and peas found in the more recent excavations indicate that the people of Bouqras had been farmers and herders, although they had still engaged in some foraging for wild foods. Farming cannot be conducted successfully at Bouqras today without the aid of irrigation because the rainfall is too low. Either the climate was a little moister then, or the inhabitants had already developed simple irrigation techniques.

Soon after the development of agriculture in the Levant, farmers expanded their area of settlement eastward, as far as the Euphrates. Bouqras flourished for several centuries, just as this phase of expansion reached its limits. The village attests to the precocious success of the new way of life and the considerable agricultural skills of its inhabitants.

[*See also* Agriculture.]

BIBLIOGRAPHY

Akkermans, P. A., et al. "Bouqras Revisited: Preliminary Report on a Project in Eastern Syria." *Proceedings of the Prehistoric Society* 49 (1983): 335–372. Summary of the results of the second campaign of excavations at Bouqras, with plans of the structures in the Neolithic village and ample illustrations of the artifacts recovered.
Contenson, Henri de. "La campagne de 1965 à Bouqras." *Cahiers de l'Euphrate* 4 (1985): 335–371. Full description of the 1965 season of excavation.

A. M. T. MOORE

BRAK, TELL, site located near Wadi Jaghjagh on the Upper Khabur plains, one of the largest ancient mounds in northeastern Syria, measuring 43 ha (98 acres) in area (c. 800 × 600 m) and 45 m above plain level (36°46′ N, 41°00′ E). While the Upper Khabur triangle is known for its agricultural productivity, Brak's location in the relatively dry southern margins indicates that its importance lay in its strategic position: it served as an entry point onto the Khabur plains from the southeast, controlling access from the Sinjar region and—ultimately—southern Mesopotamia.

Current evidence strongly suggests that the ancient name of Tell Brak was Nagar (Nawar). Excavations of third millennium levels yielded a clay bottle stopper with the inscription *Na-gàr^{ki}*, and a seal impression from the 1937–1938 excavations (see below) in the Aleppo Museum is inscribed with the name of Talpuš-atili, "sun of the land of Nagar." Finally, a tablet from the Mitanni palace (see below) refers to reeds of "Nawar in the province of Ta'idu."

In 1937 and 1938, Max Mallowan conducted three seasons at Brak under the auspices of the British School of Archaeology in Iraq, excavating the Eye Temple and the Naram-Sin "palace." Excavations were resumed in 1976 by David Oates of the Institute of Archaeology, University of London, who, together with his wife Joan Oates, conducted the fourteen seasons (1976–1993) responsible for the majority of what is currently known of the site's history and character. In 1994 and 1995, Roger Matthews directed excavations there for the British School of Archaeology in Iraq.

Ubaid Beginnings and Uruk-Period Urbanization. As a result of the formidable depth of deposit at Brak, virgin soil has yet to be reached. The earliest levels excavated, dating to the sixth millennium, derived from deep soundings in area CH in the southern part of the site and yielded later Ubaid ceramics. Deposited above these were Early Uruk-period materials (late fifth/early fourth millennia), including Gawra XI–IX type stamped and incised pottery and clay "hut symbols," associated with the niched facade of a probable temple.

The subsequent era, the mid to late fourth millennium, was of particular importance in the history of Tell Brak. Judging from the distribution of surface sherds, the entire site was occupied, in addition to a set of smaller surrounding settlements. Moreover, it is in this phase that the relationship of Brak with southern Mesopotamia first comes into sharp focus. The Eye Temple, so-called because of its limestone plaquettes with eye images, had southern characteristics in its tripartite plan and in its colored clay cone and inlaid stone rosette decoration. [*See* Mosaics.] In area TW, the earliest excavated architecture was built of Riemchen (a southern Mesopotamian style of small bricks that are square in section) and contained southern Mesopotamian-style Middle Uruk pottery as well as a local chaff-faced ware. In the succeeding level more Riemchen architecture contained

southern Late Uruk pottery; a final Riemchen phase yielded Jemdet Nasr painted pottery, a rare find outside southern Mesopotamia.

In addition to pottery and architectural characteristics, many other aspects of Uruk southern Mesopotamian material culture have emerged from Brak, including cylinder seals, a clay tablet with numerical notations, and two pictographic tablets in an unusual style. The significance of southern material culture at Brak, as well as Brak's expansion to full-fledged urban size, remains to be fully understood. One view identifies Brak as a southern Mesopotamian "colony" controlling the route to the copper mines of eastern Anatolia; an alternative perspective suggests that local elites were emulating the prestigious styles of southern Mesopotamia in order to reinforce their own status and power. [*See* Colonization.]

Reurbanization and Akkadian Conquest. In the Ninevite 5 period (early third millennium), it appears that Brak did not have the extensive size of the preceding period, and no temples or other public structures have yet been discovered. However, by the mid-third millennium, Brak had again achieved imposing urban dimensions and was probably the political and economic center of a prosperous state. This period ended with a major destruction evident in the burned architecture of five excavation areas (CH, ER, DH, AL, ST), probably to be attributed to the Akkadian rulers of southern Mesopotamia. [*See* Akkadians.]

The Akkadian conquerors made Brak an administrative center for the control of the Khabur plains. To judge from the cuneiform documentation, the Akkadian occupation occurred in later Sargonic times—during the reigns of Naram-Sin and Sharkalisharri. The Naram-Sin palace (95 × 90 m in area, with outer walls 9 m thick), whose association with Naram-Sin was established via stamped inscriptions on mud bricks, was probably a storehouse and administrative locus (see figure 1). Major Sargonic building projects were also revealed in areas FS and SS, both of which included bent-axis temple complexes. The area SS temple produced a calcite figure of a recumbent human-headed bull, perhaps to be associated with the sun god Shamash. Both temple complexes were abandoned, after which they were filled in and provided with ritual deposits including, in the case of area SS, a number of donkeys. After a brief reoccupation, the Akkadian settlement at Brak suffered a fiery destruction.

Late Third/Early Second Millennia BCE. After the Akkadian occupation, the site was reoccupied and the Naram-Sin palace rebuilt. In this period, Brak evidently functioned as one of the capitals of the Hurrian kingdom of Urkeš and Nawar. [*See* Hurrians.] By the early second millennium BCE, however, the southern part of the site was abandoned. Relatively little documentation has been retrieved for the early second millennium BCE thus far, but evidence of defensive architecture has been obtained, as well as a vaulted shrine.

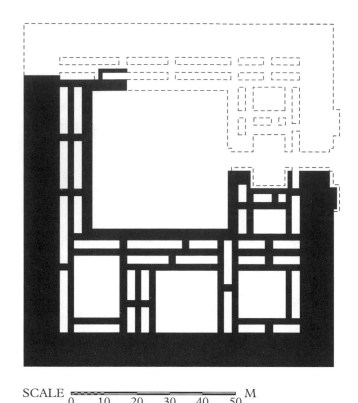

SCALE 0 10 20 30 40 50 M

BRAK, TELL. Figure 1. *The palace of Naram-Sin.* (After Mallowan, 1947, plate LX)

Mitanni Period. In its last period of occupation, Brak was a major center of the Mitanni Empire. Excavations in area HH, on the highest point of the tell, have revealed a residential fortress-palace and adjacent shrine. The palace has produced the oldest extant Mitanni-period text written in Hurrian, as well as legal texts of the time of kings Artaš-ummara and Tušratta. From these contexts also came ivory and wood furniture components, a unique stone statue, and elaborately decorated vessels of glass—a technology apparently first developed in the Mitanni heartland. [*See* Glass.] The palace was destroyed in the thirteenth century BCE, most probably by the Middle-Assyrian kings; Brak itself was abandoned by 1200 BCE.

[*See also* British School of Archaeology in Iraq; Mitanni, *and the biography of Mallowan.*]

BIBLIOGRAPHY

Mallowan, M.E.L. "Excavations at Brak and Chagar Bazar." *Iraq* 9 (1947): 1–266. Publication of the 1937–1938 seasons, including the Eye Temple and Naram-Sin palace.
Matthews, Donald M., and Jesper Eidem. "Tell Brak and Nagar." *Iraq* 55 (1993): 201–207. Discussion of the evidence supporting the identification of Tell Brak as ancient Nagar/Nawar.
Matthews, R. J., et al. "Excavations at Tell Brak, 1994." *Iraq* 56 (1994): 177–194. Report on the first results of Matthews's excavations.
Oates, David. "Tell Brak." In *Fifty Years of Mesopotamian Discovery,*
edited by John E. Curtis, pp. 62–71. London, 1982. Brief description of the site and a summary of early results of the postwar excavations.
Oates, David, and Joan Oates. "Tell Brak: A Stratigraphic Summary, 1976–1993." *Iraq* 56 (1994): 167–176. Synthesis of the site's occupation history from the results of the fourteen postwar seasons of excavation; includes a bibliography.
Oates, Joan. "Some Late Early Dynastic III Pottery from Tell Brak." *Iraq* 44 (1982): 205–219. Pottery from the destruction level at Tell Brak predating the Naram-Sin palace, an important link between ceramic and historical chronology.

GLENN M. SCHWARTZ

BREASTED, JAMES HENRY (1865–1935), the father of American Egyptology. Born in Rockford, Illinois, Breasted received a B.A. from Northwestern (now North Central) College. He then successfully completed a program at Chicago College of Pharmacy, becoming a registered pharmacist in 1886. A personal call to the ministry prompted Breasted to enter the Congregational Institute (now Chicago Theological Seminary), where he excelled in Hebrew. He launched his career as an Orientalist when he decided to continue his studies at Yale University under William Rainey Harper, a brilliant linguist. Having received his M.A. in 1892, Breasted resolved to study under Adolf Erman of the University of Berlin, who held one of the few chairs in Egyptology. In 1894, Breasted received his Ph.D., having written his dissertation on the sun hymns of Akhenaten (*De Hymnis in Solem sub Rege Amenophide IV Conceptis*).

His first trip to Egypt came after his graduate work when he spent his honeymoon there in 1894, undertaking to collate inscriptions for the preparation of the *Wörterbuch der Aegyptischen Sprache*, the great German dictionary of ancient Egyptian language. In subsequent years (1899–1901 and 1905–1907), Breasted continued to copy and collate inscriptions on objects in European museums as well as on monuments in Egypt, contributing significantly to the *Wörterbuch*'s publication. Breasted made significant Egyptological discoveries on these expeditions, including a temple built by Akhenaten at Sesebi in Nubia, and he compiled a large collection of historical inscriptions.

In 1894 Breasted was appointed by the University of Chicago to the first chair of Egyptology ever in the Western Hemisphere. At Chicago, Breasted began his life-long teaching career. William F. Edgerton, Harold H. Nelson, Caroline Ransom Williams, and John A. Wilson were among his most distinguished pupils.

Breasted's collection and translation of historical inscriptions provided an enormous corpus of information for his next two projects. The first, *A History of Egypt* (1905), was a cultural history of ancient Egypt that combined a chronological outline with information about lifestyle. Subsequently, he published five volumes entitled *Ancient Records of Egypt* (1906), a translation of all "historical" texts available to Breasted. Although *Ancient Records* is still in use, the

History is outdated. Breasted continued to publish regularly, often producing popular volumes. Two of his publications have lasting scholarly value. A series of lectures for Union Theological Seminary in New York was published as *Development of Religion and Thought in Ancient Egypt* (1912). In 1930, *The Edwin Smith Surgical Papyrus* appeared. This volume includes a translation of a papyrus that contained treatments for head and chest injuries. Breasted's background in pharmacology as well as his remarkable philological skills resulted in a masterful treatment of this text.

Throughout his career, Breasted's professional goals and his research were dedicated to understanding the connections between the ancient civilizations of Egypt and the Near East and earlier cultures and later Western civilization. He saw these three cultures linked evolutionarily, convinced that Western culture owed a great debt to these early civilizations. This belief resulted in his lifelong conviction that every effort should be expended to preserve and understand them.

In 1919 as a result of a generous gift from John D. Rockefeller, Jr., Breasted formalized his plans for the Oriental Institute at the University of Chicago. The institute's overall direction was different from more traditional institutions because Breasted intended the Oriental Institute to be a place in which information gathered by all disciplines working in ancient Egypt and the Near East would be collected. The projects that Breasted instituted as director (1919–1935) demonstrate the breadth of his interests and interdisciplinary concerns: developing the Assyrian dictionary, copying the *Coffin Texts* in the Cairo Museum, recording inscriptions at Karnak and Medinet Habu temples in Upper Egypt (these endeavors resulted in the permanent establishment, Chicago House, in Luxor), surveying early human remains in the Nile Valley, and excavating Megiddo in Palestine and Ališar in Anatolia.

BIBLIOGRAPHY

Breasted, Charles. *Pioneer to the Past: The Story of James Henry Breasted, Archaeologist*. New York, 1943. Readable and informative biography by his son that includes a list of his books and awards.
Breasted, James H. *A History of Egypt: From the Earliest Times to the Persian Conquest*. New York, 1905.
Breasted, James H. *Ancient Records of Egypt: Historical Documents from the Earliest Times to the Persian Conquest*. 5 vols. Chicago, 1906–1907.
Breasted, James H. *Development of Religion and Thought in Ancient Egypt*. New York, 1912.
Breasted, James H. *Ancient Times: A History of the Early World*. Boston, 1916.
Breasted, James H. *The Edwin Smith Surgical Papyrus*. Oriental Institute Publications, 3–4. Chicago, 1930.
Breasted, James H. *The Oriental Institute*. University of Chicago Survey, vol. 12. Chicago, 1933. Breasted's presentation of his ideas about the origins of civilization and how these thoughts led to the development of the University of Chicago's Oriental Institute.
Bull, Ludlow, et al. "James Henry Breasted, 1865–1935." *Journal of the American Oriental Society* 56 (1936): 113–120. Thorough obituary that discusses Breasted's personality as well as his scholarly achievements.
Dawson, Warren R., and Eric P. Uphill. *Who Was Who in Egyptology*. 2d rev. ed. London, 1972. Highlights important places, dates, and publications in Breasted's career and provides a list of references.
Wilson, John A. *Signs and Wonders upon Pharaoh: A History of American Egyptology*. Chicago, 1964. Devotes significant attention to Breasted's career in the context of the field (see chapters 7, 9, and 10).

DIANA CRAIG PATCH

BRITISH INSTITUTE AT AMMAN FOR ARCHAEOLOGY AND HISTORY.

British scholars and academic institutions have been conducting archaeological research in Jordan since the nineteenth century. The work of such pioneers as Claude R. Conder, George and Agnes Horsfield, and Gerald Lankester Harding was followed by that of Kathleen M. Kenyon, Diana Kirkbride, Peter Parr, Crystal-M. Bennett, and many others. In 1978, largely through the efforts of Dame Kathleen Kenyon and Crystal Bennett, the British Academy founded the British Institute at Amman for Archaeology and History (BIAAH).

The BIAAH sponsors, funds, and provides logistical support for British research on the archaeology, history, languages, ethnography, geography, and natural history of Jordan, Syria, Lebanon, and Saudi Arabia. It publishes this research through the journal *Levant* (London, 1969–) which it sponsors jointly with the British School of Archaeology in Jerusalem, and contributes major reports to the series British Academy Monographs in Archaeology. The BIAAH also presents the work of British research in Jordan through lectures, day-schools, conferences, and exhibitions.

The Institute in Amman provides accommodation and logistical support for visiting individuals and teams. Its library, photographic archive, and reference collections of pottery and animal bones are open to all scholars and students.

The BIAAH sponsors numerous archaeological, epigraphic, paleoenvironmental, ethnographic, historical, and other research projects in Jordan and Syria, covering all periods from the prehistoric to the Islamic. These have included excavations at prehistoric sites in and around Azraq, at Tell Iktanu, Tell Hammam, and Tell esh-Shuna (North), in the Jordan Valley, at the Islamic site of Khirbet Faris near Kerak, and at Tell Nebi Mend/Qadesh and Jerablus-Taḥtani in Syria. Archaeological surveys have been undertaken in the basalt desert and Edom; and epigraphic surveys in the basalt desert and in Wadi Ram. In recent years the BIAAH has also sponsored much ethnographic and ethnoarchaeological work.

Membership of the BIAAH is open to all. Members receive *Levant* and/or the *BIAAH Newsletter*, have priority in the use of the institute's hostel and equipment and are charged at a reduced rate.

M. C. A. MACDONALD

BRITISH INSTITUTE OF ARCHAEOLOGY AT ANKARA.

In 1947, the British Institute of Archaeology at Ankara was founded largely on the initiative of the noted archaeologist John Garstang. It is the only foreign archaeological mission established in Turkey's capital, rather than in Istanbul. The institute undertakes research into Anatolian archaeology, folklore, and anthropology in Turkey and collaborates with Turkish universities in organizing international colloquia. It is a center for the study of Turkey's history, art, archaeology, architecture, and kindred subjects.

Between 1968 and 1990, the institute cooperated with the antiquities authorities in rescue work when development plans for southeast Turkey threatened to drown hundreds of archaeological sites. An excavation was begun at Maltepe-Mut, near Silifke, on the Mediterranean coast, in 1994. The site, an important Hittite regional center, will be lost under the waters of a dam to be constructed on the Göksu, ancient Calycadnus.

The institute also sponsors and offers financial support to survey projects. These include the detailed survey of Roman roads and milestones in Asia Minor; surveys of Hellenistic- and Roman-period remains at Ariassos in Pisidia, at Balbura in Lycia, and at Amasra and Canayer near Trabzon in Pontus; and financial assistance to the excavations at Amorium in Phrygia. The institute's interest in the medieval castles of Anatolia continues in western Turkey, where it sponsors a survey near Nazilli. Research projects carried out in museums and collections include studies into ancient coins and glass, prehistoric pottery, and unpublished material from old British digs, notably at Mersin, Sakçagözü, and Tell esh-Sheikh.

The institute's archaeological library is comprehensive, including Anatolian archaeology and epigraphy, journals, sherd collections from surface survey work, a photographic archive, and perhaps one of the best bone and seed collections for the Near East. The epigraphic squeeze collection (of Neo-Hittite, Neo-Assyrian, Greek, and Latin inscriptions recorded in Turkish museums and on surveys) is the only known collection of its kind in Turkey.

The institute's annual journal, *Anatolian Studies*, first appeared in 1951 (London). A variety of occasional monographs has been published over the years, notably in the British Archaeological Reports series, now replaced by Oxbow Monographs. The Institute contributes to the Oxford University Press/British Academy joint-publication scheme.

[*See also the biography of Garstang.*]

BIBLIOGRAPHY

Foss, Clive. *Survey of Medieval Castles of Anatolia.* British Institute of Archaeology at Ankara, Monograph no. 7–. Oxford, 1985–.

French, David H., ed. *Studies in the History and Topography of Lycia and Pisidia. In Memoriam A. S. Hall.* British Institute of Archaeology at Ankara, Monograph no. 19. London, 1994.

Lightfoot, C. S., ed. *Recent Turkish Coin Hoards and Numismatic Studies.* British Institute of Archaeology at Ankara, Monograph no. 12. Oxford, 1991.

Moore, John. *Tille Höyük 1: The Medieval Period.* British Institute of Archaelogy at Ankara, Monograph no. 14. London, 1993.

Summers, G. D., et al. *Tille Höyük 4: The Late Bronze Age and the Iron Age Transition.* British Institute of Archaeology at Ankara, Monograph no. 15. London, 1993.

DAVID H. FRENCH

BRITISH INSTITUTE OF PERSIAN STUDIES.

Founded in 1961, the British Institute of Persian Studies served as a very active academic center for field research in Iran until the late 1970s. The journal of the institute, *Iran*, first appeared in 1963 and, although the institute's premises in Tehran are no longer formally open, it continues to be published annually. The institute's first director was David Stronach, and the founding president was Max Mallowan. Michael Rogers has been president of the governing council since 1993.

During the 1960s and 1970s, the institute was open to visiting scholars from many countries, often working in varied disciplines, including anthropology, history, and religious studies. It may be best known, however, for the excavations conducted in its name. In chronological order, they include Yarim Tepe on the Gurgan plain (Stronach, early 1960s), Pasargadae, the capital of Cyrus the Great (Stronach, 1961–1963); the prehistoric site of Tall-i Nokhodi (Clare Goff, 1961–1962); the Persian Gulf port of Siraf (David Whitehouse, 1965–1973); the Median site of Tepe Nush-i Jan (Stronach, 1967–1977); the largely Parthian site of Shahr-i Qumis (John Hansman and Stronach), 1967–1978); the late Parthian fortress of Qal'eh-i Yazdigird (Edward Keall, 1976); and the Early Islamic site of Sirjan (Antony Hutt, 1970).

The institute's library continues to be augmented and maintained and its current premises, in Ghulak, in north Tehran, were recently refitted.

[*See also* Pasargadae; *and the biography of Mallowan.*]

KIM CODELLA

BRITISH SCHOOL OF ARCHAEOLOGY IN EGYPT.

Founded in 1905 by Sir William Matthew Flinders Petrie, the BSAE was dependent on the Egyptian Research Account (ERA), another organization that Petrie had launched in 1894 after appealing for funds to employ one of his students as a fieldworker in Egypt. Petrie visualized the transformation of the ERA into a permanent British school in Egypt. The BSAE never had premises there, however, and was run from University College London, where annual exhibitions of the school's finds were held. The BSAE had more ambitious aims than the ERA because it needed to support both Petrie's and his students' work in Egypt. Apart from the Egypt Exploration Fund (later Society) the BSAE was the major British excavating organization in Egypt from its foundation until 1926. In that year Petrie transferred its activities to Palestine, in the belief that he and his coworkers had traced by fieldwork and exploration the main outlines of civilization in the Nile Valley, and the time was ripe to "proceed with the collateral search on the Egyptian remains in the South of Palestine—Egypt over the Border" (Drower, 1985, p. 364). The constitution of the school accorded with these aims because it had been founded "to work in any country that has been subject to Egypt, and so to deal with all branches of the Egyptian civilisation" (Drower, 1985, p. 364). After Petrie's death in 1942 the school, directed by Lady Petrie, ceased fieldwork and was concerned more with publication of field reports. The school terminated in 1954. Its crucial role in the study of Egyptian culture is clear from the large number of publications that bear its imprint. Petrie reckoned that about 100 students passed through the school, and that about half, including Guy Brunton, Reginald Engelbach, and John Garstang, found permanent positions in Egyptology or related disciplines.

[*See also the biography of Petrie.*]

BIBLIOGRAPHY

See Margaret S. Drower, *Flinders Petrie: A Life in Archaeology* (London, 1985), for an authoritative biography of the founder of the British School of Archaeology in Egypt. A list of the school's publications (1906–1953), of which Petrie was author or contributor, is given on pages 467–469. The publishing history of the school and the numbering of volumes in the series is somewhat complicated. For additional lists, see Ida M. Pratt, *Ancient Egypt: Sources of Information in the New York Public Library* (New York, 1925), p. 3; and Pratt, *Ancient Egypt, 1925–1941: A Supplement to Ancient Egypt* (New York, 1942), p. 4.

GEOFFREY T. MARTIN

BRITISH SCHOOL OF ARCHAEOLOGY IN IRAQ.

Founded in 1932 as a memorial to Gertrude Bell, the celebrated explorer and archaeologist who was first director of antiquities in Iraq, "to encourage, support and undertake the study of and research relating to the archaeology of Iraq and neighbouring countries, including excavation," the British School of Archaeology in Iraq has, since that time, supported almost all British archaeological research in Iraq and Syria east of the Euphrates River. The school's first director was Max Mallowan, who excavated at Arpachiyah, Chaghar Bazar, Tell Brak, and, after World War II, at Nimrud.

The School's most important excavations were at Nimrud, both on the citadel and in Fort Shalmaneser, which was investigated by David Oates, who succeeded Mallowan as director in 1961. The most spectacular discoveries were the foundation stela of Ashurnasirpal II and magnificent collections of carved ivory. From 1964 to 1971, Oates excavated the important second-millennium BCE site of Tell er-Rimah and in 1975 reopened Mallowan's excavations at Tell Brak

in Syria. The next director was Diana Kirkbride, who investigated the important Neolithic site of Umm Dabaghiyeh. From 1975 to 1981 Nicholas Postgate was director and started his extensive exploration of the Sumerian city of Abu Salabikh. Beginning in 1977 the School was involved in salvage projects in Iraq: first in the Hamrin, then at Haditha, in Eski Mosul, and in the Northern Jezira. In the 1980s the BSAI embarked on a detailed survey of the Islamic site of Samarra and a reinvestigation of the site of Jemdet Nasr.

In addition to sponsoring excavations, the BSAI has supported other archaeological as well as Assyriological projects, through grants and annual fellowships. The results of research supported by the School are normally published in the journal *Iraq*. In addition, there are various series of monographs which offer definitive reports on excavations and other research. Subscribing members of the British School of Archaeology receive a copy of the journal as well as invitations to the lectures the school organizes.

During the sixty years it has been in existence, the British School of Archaeology in Iraq has played an important role in the development of Mesopotamian archaeology in Britain. Furthermore, scholars of many nationalities have benefited from the hospitality and assistance of the School and its staff in Iraq.

[*See also* Abu Salabikh; Brak, Tell; Eski Mosul Dam Salvage Project; Hamrin Dam Salvage Project; Jemdet Nasr; Nimrud; Rimah, Tell er-; Samarra; *and the biography of Mallowan.*]

BIBLIOGRAPHY

For details of the archaeological fieldwork conducted by the British School of Archaeology in Iraq, see M. E. L. Mallowan, *Twenty-Five Years of Mesopotamian Discovery, 1932–1956* (London, 1956), and John E. Curtis, ed., *Fifty Years of Mesopotamian Discovery: The Work of the British School of Archaeology in Iraq, 1932–1982* (London, 1982). For further information about the school's activities, see its journal, *Iraq*, published annually.

MICHAEL ROAF

BRITISH SCHOOL OF ARCHAEOLOGY IN JERUSALEM.

Founded in 1919 and modeled on its sister institutions in Rome and Athens, the roots of the British School of Archaeology in Jerusalem (BSAJ) are in the Jerusalem Literary Society of 1852 and the Palestine Exploration Fund (PEF) of 1865. Within a month of General Allenby's entrance into Jerusalem in December 1917, during Britain's conquest of Palestine, Sir Flinders Petrie was lecturing on Britain's responsibility to the antiquities of the countries coming under her control. The British Academy responded to an approach from the officers of the PEF and set up an organizing committee in May 1918 chaired by Sir Frederic Kenyon and with Sir Israel Gollancz as secretary. John Garstang was the school's first director, as well as the first director of the Department of Antiquities of the Government of Palestine. The early scholars became core members of the later antiquities service. The earliest government inspectors did their work from a register of sites prepared by the BSAJ's first assistant director, W. J. Phythian-Adams. The school's role was not limited to Palestine; one or two of the more promising students in Jerusalem were sent there to study the antiquities of Mesopotamia as well.

For several years in the 1920s, the British School in Jerusalem shared accommodations with the American School of Oriental Research (ASOR). Way House, near St. George's Cathedral, was home not only to the American library, but also to a museum that would become part of the founding collection of the Palestine Archaeological Museum (now the Rockefeller Museum). Early British hospitality was duly repaid when the Americans housed the British library from the early 1930s to the early 1950s, while first the French and then the museum stored British digging equipment. ASOR participated at Jericho under A. D. Tushingham in the 1950s, as did the École Biblique, under Père Roland de Vaux, in the opening seasons of the excavations in Jerusalem in the 1960s. Tushingham also participated in the Jerusalem excavations, representing the Royal Ontario Museum. By 1927 the Department of Antiquities, with Garstang briefly acting as its director, too, formally became the British school's major tenant, and the Americans moved to a home nearby. J. W. Crowfoot became director of the British school in 1927 and played an important role in fashioning its new character. The school's independence from its erstwhile partners proved financially precarious. In the 1930s a largely American-financed excavation assumed responsibility for Crowfoot's salary while he led the excavations at Samaria jointly with Harvard, the PEF, and the Hebrew University of Jerusalem. It was there that Kathleen M. Kenyon, fresh from her training under Sir Mortimer Wheeler in England, had her first digging experience in Palestine. By 1940, the school's work diminished considerably because of war, tension between P. L. O. Guy (who had become director in the mid-1930s) and the supervisory council, and the death of Sir Robert Mond, who was not only the school's first treasurer, but also its founding and principal benefactor.

In 1950, when Kenyon succeeded to the directorship of the school, plans were already underway to resume the excavation of Garstang's still-open trenches at Jericho. Like Garstang, she would combine her directorship and her leadership of its major excavations—at Jericho in the 1950s and in Jerusalem in the 1960s—with a vigorous academic role in England. Since the mid-1960s the school's directors (Basil Hennessy, Crystal-M. Bennett, John Wilkinson, and Richard Harper) have resided in Jerusalem. In the 1970s, the school concentrated its research on a survey of Mamluk Jerusalem, not just of the imposing facades on the roads leading to the Ḥaram esh-Sharif, but of all its interior details. The survey has encouraged interest in restoration within the Muslim quarter. With the birth of its sister institute in Am-

man the Jerusalem school's role in excavations east of the Jordan River decreased. In the 1980s, the school excavated at the Crusader, Red Tower on the coastal plain, at Upper Zohar in the northern Negev desert (Late Roman/Early Byzantine), and at Belmont Castle, west of Jerusalem (a Crusader castle over a Byzantine village).

A concern with field methodology, with good training, and with accurate publications has been a continuous emphasis at BSAJ. The organization undertook a countrywide survey of medieval and Ottoman architecture in 1989, a major collaborative excavation at Tel Jezreel with the Tel Aviv Institute of Archaeology in 1990; and a wide-ranging study of Ottoman Jerusalem's Islamic monuments with the Waqf (religious trusts) Authority late in 1992. The *Palestine Exploration Quarterly* (*PEQ*) which had long been the vehicle for the school's quarterly reports. However, it launched its own journal, *Levant*, in 1969, now shared with the institute in Amman.

[*See also* British Institute at Amman for Archaeology and History; Palestine Exploration Fund; *and the biographies of Bennett, Crowfoot, Garstang, Guy, Kenyon, Petrie, and Wheeler.*]

BIBLIOGRAPHY

Burgoyne, Michael Hamilton, and D. S. Richards. *Mamluk Jerusalem: An Architectural Study*. London, 1987.

Franken, Henk J., and Margreet L. Steiner. *Excavations in Jerusalem, 1961–1967*, Vol. 2, *The Iron Age Extramural Quarter on the South-east Hill*. Oxford, 1990.

Kenyon, Kathleen M., et al. *Excavations at Jericho*. 5 vols. London, 1960–1983.

Kenyon, Kathleen M. *Jerusalem: Excavating 3000 Years of History*. New York, 1967.

Kraeling, Carl H., ed. *Gerasa, City of the Decapolis: An Account Embodying the Record of a Joint Excavation Conducted by Yale University and the British School of Archaeology in Jerusalem (1928–1930), and Yale University and the American Schools of Oriental Research (1930–1931, 1933–1934)*. New Haven, 1938.

Pringle, Denys, et al. *The Red Tower*. British School of Archaeology in Jerusalem, Monograph Series, 1. London, 1986.

Tushingham, A. D., et al. *Excavations in Jerusalem, 1961–1967*. Toronto, 1985.

GRAEME AULD

BUILDING MATERIALS AND TECHNIQUES. [*To survey the history, distribution, and role of building materials and techniques throughout the Near East, this entry comprises four articles:*

An Overview

Materials and Techniques of the Bronze and Iron Ages

Materials and Techniques of the Persian through Roman Periods

Materials and Techniques of the Byzantine and Islamic Periods

The first provides a general introduction that treats building

materials; the remainder treat the developments of particular historical periods.]

An Overview

Geography and topography affect the availability of construction materials and the methods by which they are utilized. In antiquity as well as in traditional construction methods still in use, clay bricks were the principal construction material in the alluvial valleys of Mesopotamia and Egypt, and a lack of forests compelled the Egyptians to develop sophisticated stone architecture as well. The variety of natural features in ancient Israel and Syria offered builders a choice of materials and generated assorted construction techniques.

The size of political groups and a community's level of technological competence were additional factors that influenced the use of natural materials. Large and centralized political organizations were capable of investing immense resources into constructing formidable fortifications, or of producing costly building materials like ashlar masonry. Affluent nations could overcome the shortage of local sources by importing materials from a great distance: ancient Mesopotamia, Egypt, and Israel imported cedar beams from Lebanon.

Each of the natural materials used in construction had advantages and disadvantages. Sophisticated builders were capable of combining materials to minimize the drawbacks of a single one. Archaeological data (Yeivin, 1954; Reich, 1992), supported by ethnographic evidence (Canaan, 1933; Dalman, 1942), indicate that the most common building techniques made use of wood, clay bricks, and different kinds of stones.

Wood. Tree branches are readily available in nature and are a relatively elastic construction material. The framework of a hut can be easily constructed by tying a few together and then covering the structural skeleton with leaves or animal hides to create an effective shelter. Circular wooden huts have appeared in many parts of the world as the first architectural structures (e.g., in the Natufian and Pre-Pottery Neolithic A (PPNA) periods in the ancient Near East (Bar-Yosef, 1992). Hollow gaps on the inner face of round stone houses at the PPNB site of Beidha in modern Jordan indicate the use there of wooden posts. [*See* Beidha.]

Wood has also been utilized in more complex structures. In orthogonal (right-angled) units, beams were used for roofing. The main beams were placed at intervals across the room and thinner branches were densely laid over and perpendicular to the beams. The top layer was made of mud or lime mortar. In many cases segments of the mortar, bearing the imprints of branches, are observable in the destruction deposits. Tree trunks were commonly used as columns to support the roof beams of large halls. Stone bases, which insulated the wood from moisture in the ground, are testi-

mony to their existence. Wood was also used for door lintels and doors themselves. In monumental buildings, wooden beams were inserted between courses of ashlar masonry (see below). In quality construction the walls and floors were laid with wood, sometimes bearing carved decorations. A detailed description of this method appears in the biblical account of the Solomonic Temple (*1 Kgs.* 6:15). The most serious disadvantage of wood as a construction material is its susceptibility to fire and decay. The severity of the destruction of many ancient cities by fire was the extensive use of wood in their buildings. [*See* Wood.]

Clay Bricks. Sun-dried bricks are a simple and common type of building material. The bricks are produced by mixing soil with water, shaping the mud into the desired form, and drying the final product in the sun. To prevent cracking during drying, cut straw is usually added to the mixture (*Ex.* 5:7–18). The earliest bricks were formed by hand and were elliptical. In PPN Jericho, bricks have been found that bear the fingerprints of the workers (Kenyon, 1957, pl. 11B). Since the Chalcolithic period, to create uniformly sized bricks the mud has been placed in a wooden mold (*mlbn*, lit., "rectangular," *Na.* 3:14). This improvement enabled the construction of level courses and allowed for good wall bonding. Brick size differs depending on the region and the period, but they commonly are 12–15 cm high, a size easily grasped in the hand. Bricks were affixed to each other by a layer of mud mortar. Firing clay bricks required large amounts of fuel and, except for a few cases in Mesopotamia, was not practiced before the Hellenistic period (late fourth century BCE). Unfired bricks were always a risky building material because contact with water turns them back into mud. To prevent this from occurring, bricks were isolated from ground moisture by stone foundations. Additional protection against rain was gained by covering walls with a thick layer of mud plaster, sometimes reinforced by the addition of crushed limestone. Another means for decreasing damage to the walls was water-drainage channels, aimed at quickly conducting rainwater outside a city.

Stone. Used as a building material, stone may be subdivided into the categories of fieldstone and dressed stone.

Fieldstones. In hill country in the ancient Near East, fieldstones were useful as a construction material. The earliest round huts were girdled by low stone walls (e.g., at Natufian 'Einan and Sultanian [PPNA] Nahal Oren). [*See* 'Einan; Nahal Oren.] High standards of construction with tabular stone slabs is noticable in PPNB structures at Beidha, 'Ain Ghazal, and Basta. [*See* 'Ain Ghazal; Basta.] To consolidate walls constructed of irregularly shaped fieldstones, mud mortar and small rocks were set in the spaces between individual stones. Fieldstones were commonly used in later periods as foundations for brick superstructures, providing walls with stability and increasing their resistance to moisture. More formidable walls consisted of at least two rows of stones, about 50–60 cm wide. The top stone courses were leveled to carry the bricks. The weakness of a fieldstone structure could be overcome by the additional width of the walls. In the fortifications of the Early Bronze Age cities at Megiddo, Ai, and Tel Yarmut, solid city walls reached a total width of 8 m or more. [*See* Megiddo; Ai; Yarmut, Tel.] For additional strength, some of those walls were constructed of extra-large blocks (megalithic masonry), and occasionally stones were fitted to adjoining ones in a polygonal method (i.e., not cut at right angles and often with more than four sides).

Dressed stones. The stability of walls could be increased by dressing the building stones into rectangular blocks, using an iron chisel. The straight sides ensured tight contact along the faces of the block without the use of mortar. The earliest appearance of dressed stone is attested in the stone bases of some EBA temples at Ai and Megiddo. During the Middle Bronze Age, huge dressed blocks were utilized as orthostats, mainly facing the entrance piers of city gates, as at Shechem, Gezer, Ebla, Carchemish, and Alalakh. [*See* Shechem; Gezer, Ebla; Carchemish; Alalakh.] A more extensive use of ashlar masonry is apparent in the city gate at Megiddo, already in existence in the Middle Bronze Age (stratum X). Well-dressed basalt orthostats faced the lower parts of walls, which were otherwise made of fieldstones, in the Late Bronze Age temples and palaces at Hazor and Megiddo. [*See* Hazor.]

Ashlar masonry was used extensively in the Iron Age II, mainly in the northern part of Israel—at Hazor, Samaria, Megiddo, and Gezer (Shiloh, 1979). [*See* Samaria.] A more limited use was applied in Judah—in Jerusalem, Lachish, and Ramat Raḥel. A common stone used for building was *nari*, a chalky rock (Shiloh and Horowitz, 1975). [*See* Judah; Lachish; Ramat Raḥel.] Two types of stone dressing are evident in Iron Age ashlar masonry: one in which the stone's entire surface is smooth (e.g., the aboveground courses of the acropolis at Samaria) and dressed margins in which the center of the stone is left as a rough boss and only between one and three of the side margins are smoothed. Marginal dressing was applied to stones in the foundation courses, which indicates that its aim was to economize on construction expenses and not aesthetics. The smooth margins were necessary to maintain a straight line for the wall, both horizontally and vertically. Dressed ashlars became a decorative element in later masonry, especially in the Hellenistic and Herodian periods, when both the margins and the central boss were carefully worked.

The additional strength of ashlar walls was guaranteed by the large size of the building blocks and by their being positioned in alternate layers of headers and stretchers. The 10–20-centimeter-wide gap between ashlar courses observed at Megiddo, Hazor, and Samaria should be interpreted as the location of a wooden (decayed) beam. The long beams probably provided the wall with elasticity, thus minimizing damage to the solid structure by earth-quakes. Examples are found in both the LB (stratum VIII) and Iron Age (stratum IV) city gates at Megiddo. Mason's marks are found on the back sides of many ashlars. Ashlar masonry was also applied in constructing the square pillars used in the "pillared buildings" at Megiddo (accompanied by stone-hewn troughs), Hazor, and Beersheba. [*See* Beersheba.] The explicit method of construction combining ashlar piers and rubble stones to fill gaps has been identified as Phoenician. It appeared in Israel in the tenth century BCE, (apparently introduced by the Phoenicians) and remained popular throughout the Mediterranean region down to the Hellenistic period (Van Beek, and Van Beek, 1981; Stern, 1992). [*See* Phoenicians.]

Worked ashlars were utilized during Iron II for ceremonial and decorative purposes, as well. The design on the most popular type of decorated stone block, the proto-Aeolic capital, consisted of a triangle flanked by two spiraling volutes with upper and lower leaves (Shiloh, 1979). Because these capitals are decorated on either one or both sides, it is clear that some were freestanding and others abutted a wall pilaster or an entrance jamb. The proto-Aeolic capital ornamented the entrances of royal palaces (e.g., Samaria, Megiddo). The windows of such palaces could be decorated by a recessed frame and a stone-carved balustrade, like those found at Ramat Raḥel. At Beersheba (Aharoni, 1974) and Dan (Biran, 1994), beautifully dressed stones were used to construct horned sacrificial altars. [*See* Dan; Altars.] Decorated stone bases in the North Syrian style (like those found at Carchemish, Zincirli, and Tell Taʿyinat) have been found at Tel Dan; the wooden pilars standing on the bases apparently supported a ceremonial canopy. Stepped-stone structures identified as wall crenellations have been found at Megiddo, Samaria, Ramat Raḥel, and Tel Mevorakh (Stern, 1992).

BIBLIOGRAPHY

Aharoni, Yohanan. "The Horned Altar of Beer-sheba." *Biblical Archaeologist* 37.1 (1974): 2–23.

Bar-Yosef, Ofer. "Building Activities in the Prehistoric Periods until the End of the Neolithic Period." In *The Architecture of Ancient Israel: From the Prehistoric to the Persian Periods,* edited by Aharon Kempinski and Ronny Reich, pp. 31–39. Jerusalem, 1992.

Biran, Avraham. *Biblical Dan.* Jerusalem, 1994.

Canaan, Taufik. *The Palestinian Arab House: Its Architecture and Folklore.* Jerusalem, 1933.

Dalman, Gustaf. *Arbeit und Sitte in Palästina,* vol. 7, *Das Haus.* Gütersloh, 1942.

Kenyon, Kathleen M. *Digging Up Jericho.* London, 1957.

Reich, Ronny. "Building Materials and Architectural Elements in Ancient Israel." In *The Architecture of Ancient Israel: From the Prehistoric to the Persian Periods,* edited by Aharon Kempinski and Ronny Reich, pp. 1–16. Jerusalem, 1992.

Shiloh, Yigal, and Aharon Horowitz. "Ashlar Quarries of the Iron Age in the Hill Country of Israel." *Bulletin of the American Schools of Oriental Research,* no. 217 (1975): 37–48.

Shiloh, Yigal. *The Proto-Aeolic Capital and Israelite Ashlar Masonry.* Qedem, vol. 11. Jerusalem, 1979.

Stern, Ephraim. "The Phoenician Architectural Elements in Palestine during the Late Iron Age and Persian Period." In *The Architecture of Ancient Israel: From the Prehistoric to the Persian Periods,* edited by Aharon Kempinski and Ronny Reich, pp. 302–309. Jerusalem, 1992.

Van Beek, Gus W., and Ora Van Beek. "Canaanite-Phoenician Architecture: The Development and Distributions of Two Styles" (in Hebrew). *Eretz-Israel* 15 (1981): 70–77.

Yeivin, Shmuel. "Construction" (in Hebrew). In *Encyclopedia Biblica,* vol. 2, cols. 179–262. Jerusalem, 1954.

ZE'EV HERZOG

Materials and Techniques of the Bronze and Iron Ages

In the early part of the third millennium, the Levant achieved sociopolitical definition as an urbanized region where each town formed a separate unit of government. In roughly the same period, the neighboring regions of Egypt and Mesopotamia also assumed their social and political character, but the power generated was of a different order and vastly greater. However, in spite of the power and resources disposed by these two regions, between which the Levant formed a communications corridor, building construction in the Levant was in no way annexed to the practices in Early Dynastic Mesopotamia and Old Kingdom Egypt.

The tradition of substantial building construction was far older in the Levant than in Egypt or Mesopotamia. At the outset of urban development in the Levant, its building tradition was already about five thousand years old—roughly the same stretch of time that has elapsed since—perhaps twice as long as that for Egypt and Mesopotamia. In addition, the environment of the Levant is overall Mediterranean, which contrasted the region with Egypt and Mesopotamia. Thus whatever the influence Egypt and Mesopotamia exerted there in other contexts, the first towns in the Levant were built with the methods and materials of construction that had specifically evolved in the region during the preceding millennia. So far as can be determined, the scale but not the methods of building changed.

Preurban Building Materials and Methods. The Levant had abundant and varied building material. While good plastic earth is common there, the land is basically rocky and stones are for the gathering. In ancient times, the land was also well wooded. These basic building materials were all thoroughly understood, and were builders' stock in trade about 3000 BCE.

Stone. In the settled areas of Syria-Palestine, the lithology is basically limestone (of mainly secondary but with some tertiary and recent formations). However, between Damascus and Amman, extending across into Upper Galilee, there had been widespread basalt lava flows. While at the southern, desertic limits of the area, a Precambrian granite shield is exposed together with its immediate sedimentary cover of sandstone, often multicolored (Nubian Sandstone is the

"rock" of Petra). The coastal plain, which is extensive in Palestine, is sandy, but where the sand dunes have been compacted into rock, it is virtually a sandy limestone (*kurkar*). Thus, although sandstone and basalt were used on occasion, the region's building stone is generally limestone of some sort. Notable is the "re-formed" or "reprocessed" limestone (*huwwar*), created by the leaching out and subsequent redepositing of calcium carbonate by groundwater under the effect of insolation. This forms a surface layer that can be dug away like marl and readily crushed and powdered to produce a cementitious plaster or mortar.

Mud. Earth of a reasonable constituency for mud construction is available in most areas and predominant in some (e.g., the coastal plain and the central Rift Valley continuum). Mud is virtually a natural material for mortar and plaster, and its use as a manufactured material for building units appears to have developed in the region by way of *tauf,* or puddled mud (coherent balls of earth set in a plastic state). *Tauf* occurs at the beginning of Neolithic settlements, but already in Pre-Pottery Neolithic times, the standard material was hand-modeled mud bricks of various forms (the forms probably derive from characteristic fieldstone shapes). Whereas in other regions (Anatolia, Mesopotamia) hand-modeled mud bricks were replaced fairly soon by molded mud bricks, from the evidence it appears that hand-modeled mud bricks continued in use for long ages, at least in the southern part of the Levant.

Timber. Good building timber was once plentiful in the Levant. Although only a few species employed in very ancient times have been identified, their availability and use in the historical periods allow the following reasoning about species usage. For general purposes (fittings, frames, etc.) sycamore fig, Aleppo pine, and oak (*terebinth*) were used. The same pine and sycamore and also cypress and poplar (in specific instances, date palm) were used in roofing. Mt. Lebanon was then the preeminent logging center of the ancient world, and the cedars of Lebanon were the most prized wood for magnificent construction projects. However, felling and transporting those great timbers posed problems of organization akin to those attendant in quarrying stone. For that reason it is likely that the cedar industry was only developed on a large scale with infusion of Egyptian capital, which became available during the Old Kingdom (c. midthird millennium).

Other materials. One or two other materials may have been used in construction, although there is no evidence for them in earliest times and indeed very little in later periods. Metal, particularly copper, was available from the Sinai area; bitumen from the Dead Sea (Lake Asphaltitis); gypsum, more generally available, was used as an alternative to lime in plaster and mortar.

The earliest round buildings in the region (c. 8000 BCE) appear to have been of framed construction—that is, wood framework with, for example, a wattle-and-daub cladding.

However, it was already understood by builders in that period that masonry walls (of rubble and/or mud brick) were solid enough to bear the load of an entire structure, including its roof. The roof construction proper to the round house is a corbeled mud-brick dome as can be seen in the survivals of the type in traditional modern building. With the introduction of the rectangular plan (c. 7000 BCE), a flat mud roof set over timber beams became standard and remained so ever since in village building.

Urban Building Materials and Methods. The basic materials and methods of construction discussed here survived and sufficed for village-style construction in the region until the middle of this century (i.e. for about five thousand years). It now remains to indicate the developments brought about by political changes in society.

The most salient changes in building techniques and materials appearing with urbanization (about 3000 BCE) were occasioned by the need for massive urban fortifications. Solid walls sufficiently tall to inhibit escalade and with a total run of several kilometers had to be thrown up quickly (e.g., at Arad and Ai). Rubble stone and mud brick were used. However, since there was no basic change in the quality of the masonry, an enormous quantitative change was needed to achieve height with the necessary stability. Thus, these city walls were sometimes 5–10 m deep. This in turn meant organizing laborers into very large gangs. Urban fortifications then became the occasion in the Levant for the forced labor system (*corvée*) endemic in Mesopotamia for canals, bunds, and levees and in Egypt for pyramids. Equally modifications were required in the supply of materials.

At this stage, form-molded mud bricks ousted the hand-modeled type. Whatever other advantages there may be in molded mud bricks (stiffer construction and better bonding), it was the only type of manufacture appropriate for mass producing the enormous quantities required for the great city walls. From the beginning, both square and rectangular molded bricks were used. There was and still is a facile theory that square mud bricks are more proper to Mesopotamia and rectangular bricks to Egypt. Whether there is much significance in this theory, the fact remains that both types were always equally current in the Levant. (Nothing like the plano-convex forms of protodynastic Mesopotamia appeared at any stage.) The bonding pattern was and continued to be in the simple stretcher-bond style. Any evidence of sophisticated bonding (such as at Deir el-Balah) is confined to the southern limits of the region, where it is an Egyptian feature.

The masses of large rubble stone required for the walls also probably affected how supplies were made available. Although there is no evidence for quarrying, simple surface gathering may have involved an uneconomic spreading of the work and a more intensive winning of stone via digging, levering, and detaching is probable.

It is also possible to see the planning of the new public buildings as affecting forms of construction. For example, both palaces and sanctuaries demanded a larger, open-unit plan where the appropriate form of construction is the point support—pillar, post, or column. The principle of primeval framed construction had never been forgotten, but in the main, pillars had been used in doubling and reinforcing walls. Urban public buildings at Ai and Megiddo, however, show some columnar porticoes and halls. At Byblos, as a result of its propinquity to a cedar supply, something like primitive hypostyle halls appear in Early Bronze Age temples and mansions (cf. the Reshef Temple and the Baalat Temple complexes). However, nothing is known as yet of any systematized "order."

Monumental Construction. The highly prosperous city-state regimes of the Middle Bronze II through the Late Bronze Age (the mid-second millennium BCE) changed building construction in the Levant. Whereas the burnt-brick construction of Mesopotamia was never adopted, something like one thousand years after the grandiose buildings of Old Kingdom Egypt, elements of monumental stone masonry appeared in the Levant. At first this was confined to isolated blocks, but during the Late Bronze Age quarried and finely dressed blocks came to be used for more extended passages (cf. the Palace at Ras Shamra/Ugarit, the City Gate at Megiddo, and the Orthostat Temple at Hazor). With the increasing resources of the nation-state, fine stone masonry became a notable feature of building in Palestine (and, according to all circumstantial evidence, in Phoenicia).

This monumental masonry belonged to a very distinctive style of stone dressing. It presented the appearance of finely jointed ashlar on the face of the stone (where much of the dressing was done, in situ). However, all the joints opened widely to the interior, so that in reality it was ashlar-faced, coursed rubble. This was neither the style of pharaonic Egypt nor of the later classical Greek masonry. However, it appeared in a wide continuum extending to the west (Cyprus, Crete) and north (northern Syria, Anatolia). The style remained viable over a long period (down to Hellenistic times) and maintained its rationale vis-à-vis both Egyptian and classical masonry (see figure 1).

Parallel with these developments in stone masonry was the increasing use, from the middle of the second millennium onward, of point supports. Thus, Levantine building styles came to occupy a position between the almost totally astylar tradition of Mesopotamia and the columnar style of Egypt. There were various ramifications to this.

Columns came to be used fairly generally in palaces and temples. For the most part, they continued to be arranged across the length of an internal space—in accordance with broadroom planning concepts. The characteristics of the columns varied. In the native tradition they were probably simple posts devoid of architectural refinements. However, occasionally more formal items appeared, borrowed from neighboring regions. Remains of Egyptian plant-form cap-

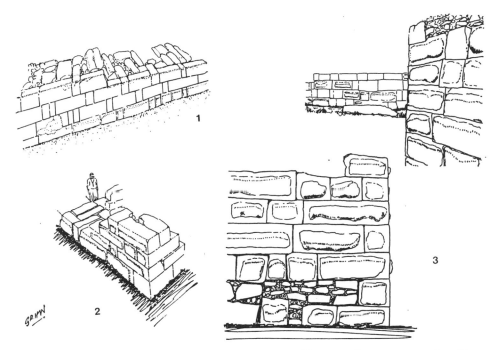

BUILDING MATERIALS: Bronze and Iron Ages. Figure 1. *Monumental stone masonry, Late Bronze and Iron Ages.* (1) Israelite, Samaria Acropolis; (2) Israelite, Megiddo; (3) Late Bronze Age, Ras Shamra Palace. (After Wright, 1985, figs. 315, 317)

itals (e.g., Open Papyriform) have been found in Late Bronze levels at Beth-Shean, Lachish, and Megiddo; the octagonal, or faceted, shafts of Egyptian proto-Doric columns have been found at LB Shechem and Lachish; the north-Syrian ornamental torus pot or bowl base has been found in Iron Age levels at Dan; and Persian-period fragments of the Persepolitan (Bull Protome) order have been found at Sidon.

If the region never developed a columnar style of its own, in the first millennium BCE it developed a pillar/pilaster capital that it exported (e.g., to Cyprus). This was the proto-Aeolic capital used to dignify ceremonial portals by way of engaged piers at the jambs and, occasionally, a freestanding medial pier. This capital form is basically a stylized tree-of-life design and is thus allied to other plant-form capitals (Aeolic and eventually Ionic and Corinthian). All circumstances suggest that it was developed in Phoenicia, but all the evidence for it is in Israelite Palestine and Transjordan (see figure 2).

More notable is the utilitarian structural development of the pier in the Israelite period, in which it took two forms: a long pillared hall (articulated into three aisles) for all-purpose public buildings where privacy was not a requirement—stables, stores, and barracks. A monumental variant was King Solomon's House of the Forest of Lebanon.

A striking pier and panel type of wall construction also was developed (see figure 3). Again, it might seem natural for this form to have come out of Phoenicia because versions

of it are found in the Phoenician colonies of the West, whence it came to be known as *Opus africanum*. However, the bulk of the examples is found in Israelite Palestine (e.g., at Megiddo), where it survived through the Persian period (Tel Mevorakh, Jaffa). It was to remain standard in North Africa until the Arab invasions of the seventh century CE.

Throughout this time, the structural system employed was trabeated: mud roofing on horizontal timber beams (terra-cotta roofing tiles were a Greek invention and do not

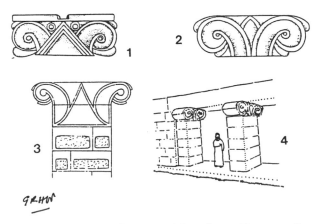

BUILDING MATERIALS: Bronze and Iron Ages. Figure 2. *Proto-Aeolic capital.* (1) standard (Megiddo) form; (2) variant (Hazor) form; (3) broad (Megiddo) form; (4) installation in portal. (After Wright, 1985, figs. 333, 336)

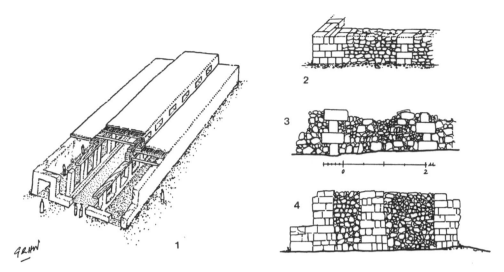

BUILDING MATERIALS: Bronze and Iron Ages. Figure 3. *Pillar construction*. (1) Pillar house stable or stores unit, Iron Age II; (2) ashlar pier and rubble panel masonry, Megiddo general type, Iron Age II; (3) ashlar pier and rubble panel masonry, Megiddo, Southern Palace, Iron Age II; (4) coursed square rubble pier and random rubble panel masonry, Jaffa, Persian period (450-320 BCE). (After Wright, 1985, figs. 245, 322)

appear in the region until the Hellenistic age). Nevertheless, the arch was not unknown. The Middle Bronze City Gate at Tel Dan has its outer portal built as a true arch, with mudbrick voussoirs, but to what degree this was common practice in such monuments is unknown. Also, rubble masonry was used in MB underground tombs at Megiddo to build something like a true dome or saucer vault; whereas at Late Bronze Age Ras Shamra, imposing underground tombs entered from the courtyard of houses were built with ashlar masonry with corbel vaulting. In the Provincial period (c. 600–300 BCE), when the land was ruled from Mesopotamia, practices in mud construction belonging to that region were introduced: tall, conical, corbeled silos and pitched barrel vaulting in residences and stores (e.g., at Tell Jemmeh). A form of pitched vaulting in rubble was also used to roof the Lachish Residency (see figure 4).

Public Works Engineering. Throughout the Bronze and Iron Ages, earthworks of various forms and functions were carried out in connection with the city raised up on its mound. Quite frequently this involved an expert use of lime-plaster surfaces and slicks of crushed *huwwar*. It is not always a straightforward matter to determine the purpose of this kind of installation—whether its purpose was military or it was a civil consolidation of friable earth skirting. Such earthworks are not accurately signified by the term *glacis*, once commonly used to describe them.

Rock-cut shafts and galleries to ensure a city's water supply are another public works enterprise of vast scope that was highly developed in Israelite Palestine. In addition to cisterns and reservoirs to store surface runoff water, quite spectacular schemes were carried out to capture ground-water aquifers outside a city and bring the water into it via subterranean aqueducts (as at Gibeon, Gezer, and Hazor). Analogies to these schemes are best known in Anatolia.

Construction Methods. Little direct evidence is extant of construction methods in the region. Building preurban village houses was very likely a family affair, and the first specialized master builders were probably those who directed and supervised the raising of the first city walls—and throughout antiquity a master builder/engineer possibly recommended himself first as a military engineer. The basic problem of construction technique is how heavy, massive units can be got up into place. Some city walls show heavy boulders set at a considerable height. Those units could have been brought into position only by hauling along and up construction ramps; traces of such earthworks have been reported against several city walls (e.g., at Gibeon and Jericho). Since there is no evidence in Palestine of lifting devices (neither of hoists, winches, and pulley blocks, nor of lifting lugs, or lewis holes), we can assume that all heavy construction basically relied on the same method. This was the method of monumental masonry used in Egypt. It was highly labor intensive and so was not for everyday application in Palestine and Syria. Instead it would appear that massive units were as a rule kept close to ground level (such as a stone socle) and that the superstructure consisted of materials (wood and mud brick) that could be raised and set in place by a few hands and broad backs operating with ladders, planks, and ropes, as in traditional village building.

In summary, it can be said that building construction in the region of Syria-Palestine during the Bronze and Iron Ages was entirely adequate for its utilitarian purpose. The

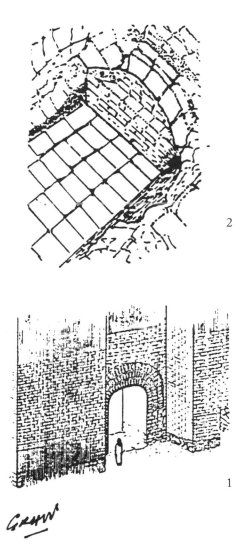

BUILDING MATERIALS: Bronze and Iron Ages. Figure 4. *Arcuated construction in mud brick.* (1) arched portal, city gate, Dan, Middle Bronze II; (2) pitched barrel vaulting, Assyrian Residence, Tell Jemmeh (Provincial period). (After Wright, 1985, figs. 286, 367)

population accepted forced labor for the vital purpose of urban defense (cf. *Neh.* 3), but violently opposed it (cf. *1 Kgs.* 12.18) when the Hebrew monarchy sought to enforce it generally for display purposes (cf. *1 Kgs.* 5.13–16; 9.20–22). This public attitude is probably an underlying reason why the character of construction in the region was so different from that in neighboring Egypt and Mesopotamia.

[*See also* Cisterns; Four-room House; Furniture and Furnishings, *article on* Furnishings of the Bronze and Iron Ages; *and* House. *In addition, many of the individual sites mentioned are the subject of independent entries.*]

BIBLIOGRAPHY

Aurenche, Olivier, ed. *Dictionnaire illustré multilingue de l'architecture du Proche Orient ancien.* Lyon, 1977. Provides well-illustrated definitions of all relevant topics.

Aurenche, Olivier. *La maison orientale: L'architecture du Proche Orient ancien des origines au milieu du quatrième millénaire.* 3 vols. Paris, 1981. Thorough account of the establishment of the region's original building tradition.

Avi-Yonah, Michael, and Ephraim Stern, eds. *The Encyclopedia of Archaeological Excavations in the Holy Land.* 4 vols. Oxford, 1975–1978. Provides extensive coverage of data revealed by excavation. The reader may also consult the updated edition, *The New Encyclopedia of Archaeological Excavations in the Holy Land* (Jerusalem and New York, 1993).

Barrois, A.-G. *Manuel d'archéologie biblique.* 2 vols. Paris, 1939–1953. See especially volume 1, chapter 3, "La technique architecturale."

Busink, Th. A. *Der Tempel von Jerusalem, von Salomo bis Herodes.* 2 vols. Leiden, 1970–1980. An academic architect of enormous learning covers the entire range of building development in the region.

Clarke, Somers, and Reginald Engelbach. *Ancient Egyptian Masonry.* London, 1930. Comparative background to the different traditions in Syria-Palestine.

Hult, Gunnel. *Bronze Age Ashlar Masonry in the Eastern Mediterranean: Cyprus, Ugarit, and Neighbouring Regions.* Göteborg, 1983. Exhaustive survey of the continuum of stone masonry which includes that in Syria-Palestine.

Naumann, Rudolf. *Architektur Kleinasiens.* 2d ed. Tübingen, 1971. Technical account of building techniques in northern Syria-Palestine.

Nylander, Carl. *Ionians in Pasargade: Studies in Old Persian Architecture.* Uppsala, 1970. Good characterization of the later stages in the stone masonry tradition discussed by Hult (see above).

Shiloh, Yigal. *The Proto-Aeolic Capital and Israelite Ashlar Masonry.* Qedem, vol. 11. Jerusalem, 1979. Basic study of Israelite fine stone masonry.

Spencer, A. Jeffrey. *Brick Architecture in Ancient Egypt.* Warminster, 1979. Very good account of the niceties of brick construction, providing a comparative frame of reference.

Stern, Ephraim. *Material Culture of the Land of the Bible in the Persian Period, 538–332 B.C.* Warminster, 1982. Detailed account of the period.

Weippert, Helga. *Palästina in vorhellenistischer Zeit.* Handbuch der Archäologie, vol. 2. Munich, 1988. The latest general manual on the subject.

Wright, G. R. H. *Ancient Building in South Syria and Palestine.* 2 vols. Handbuch der Orientalistik, vol. 7. Leiden, 1985. A compilation of references.

G. R. H. WRIGHT

Materials and Techniques of the Persian through Roman Periods

The period of building development in the millennium from above 650 BCE to 350 CE is the most momentous of all from the present-day point of view. During this period the long-established modes of monumental building extending back across the previous two millennia and more went out of use forever. Some of the new modes of building developed during this period survived in part or were revived in part to remain in currency into modern times. On the other hand, domestic building in the region has a completely different history. It was fully developed several millennia previously and in essentials it remained little changed in nature until the middle of the present century.

Existing Building Traditions. In the middle of the first millennium BCE, three ancient modes of monumental building continued to flourish: Mesopotamian massive mud brick; pharaonic Egyptian large-block stone; and Levanto-Anatolian mixed building. Each had a long history and survived variously for an additional half millennium or more.

Mesopotamian Massive Brick Building. The oldest type of monumental building is found in Mesopotamia and was well established by the beginning of the third millennium BCE. The material of construction was mud brick (also, on occasions, burnt brick) and the structural system was trabeated and noncolumnar, with very massive load-bearing walls. However, the flat terrace roofs on timber beams were supplemented by mud-brick vaulting, generally of the corridorlike peripheral chambers. The main apartments were commonly of broadroom disposition. The individuation of the tradition was a mud-brick artificial mountain, the ziggurat, in the form of a stepped pyramid with a temple at the summit. [*See* Mesopotamia, *Article on* Ancient Mesopotamia; Ziggurat.]

Pharaonic Egyptian Stone Building. Building with stone was fully evolved in Egypt by the middle of the third millennium. The construction was entirely of fine stone masonry out of large and very large blocks, hauled into position and dressed almost entirely in situ. In fact, this system of building has been well characterized as piling up an artificial mountain and then forming a rock-cut monument out of it. The structural system was a columnar, trabeated one—the flat terrace roofs being entirely of stone beams and slabs. Mud brick was used on a large scale in utilitarian structures—for example, for outer precinct enclosure walls—and mud-brick vaulting appeared in magazines and the like, but such construction was never introduced into a monument. Both broadroom and longroom design were known. The individuation of the tradition was a stone mountain, the pyramid, containing the tomb of the deified king and/or, in later times, the obelisk, a tall pier capped by "the pyramidion" (the *benben* stone). [*See* Egypt, *article on* Dynastic Egypt; Pyramids.]

Levanto-Anatolian Mixed Building. Less homogenous than pharaonic stone buildings and of later development (second millennium BCE), Levanto-Anatolian mixed building is something of a residual category. It remained closer to domestic building in style. The materials of construction were mixed: stone, mud brick, and timber (for wall reinforcing or framing and roofing). The (relatively slighter) walls comprised a socle of dressed stone (facing), mud-brick superstructure incorporating varying degrees of timber, and flat, mud-terrace roofing (see figure 1). The structural system was (to some degree) columnar (mainly wooden posts) and trabeated. Vaulting was entirely absent. Both broadroom and longroom design were known. There was no characteristic "individuation" monument.

These three dissimilar modes of monumental building closely maintained their regional distribution—particularly the highly characteristic Mesopotamian and pharaonic structures. Ornamental motifs or elements of these latter two in a limited way may have come into use elsewhere (e.g., the Egyptian cavetto cornice, Mesopotamian[?] crow stepping). However, the monumental building as a complete unit was proper to its region. More especially, pharaonic building was restricted to the Nile Valley, where it was uniform from end to end. Mesopotamian building was subject to some regional modification (cf. Assyrian vs. Babylonian) and to some merger in peripheral regions (e.g., at Mari on the confines of Syria).

Nevertheless, in one important respect, these markedly dissimilar building systems have a uniform expression—the uniformity of ancient Near Eastern society. The projects they embody are confined to the same restricted range of monuments: these are, in the first place, religious monuments, temples (and perhaps with them may be considered monumental tombs); monumental palaces (where applicable); and the monumental features of fortifications (e.g., city gates).

Out of the above background, during the sixth century BCE, two new modes of building (imperial Achaemenid and classical Greek) evolved suddenly and dramatically. Although there were considerable points of contact in the processes, the results were utterly different. In terms of the general historical succession in the Near East, the Achaemenid mode is outlined first, but this does not impute any primacy in influence. The two formative traditions abutted geographically in western Anatolia—namely in the kingdoms of Phrygia and Lydia, where the ancient building tradition was Levanto-Anatolian.

Achaemenid Building. Unlike, for example, the Egyptians and the Greeks, the Persians got an empire before they had a monumental architecture to dignify it. Thus, they had to crash develop their monumental imperial architecture within two generations or so—and the achievement was marvelous and since there was nothing vulgar or banal about the mode, it was both graceful and dignified. (Incidentally, almost nothing is known of the domestic building of the imperial Persians—they could have continued to live in tents for all that is evident to the contrary.)

The imperial (aulic) Achaemenid mode of building is best manifested in two palace-city complexes: that of Cyrus the Great at Pasargadae (c. 550 BCE) and that of Darius and Xerxes at Persepolis (c. 500 BCE). With this instant achievement, the style remained frozen and there were no further developments (nor it seems much central building activity) for the ensuing two centuries, until Persepolis was ceremonially put to flames by Alexander the Great in 331 BCE to mark the end of an old order. This it certainly did, in the architectural sense, since that was the end of the Achaemenid grand manner. Although later Iranian dynasties (Par-

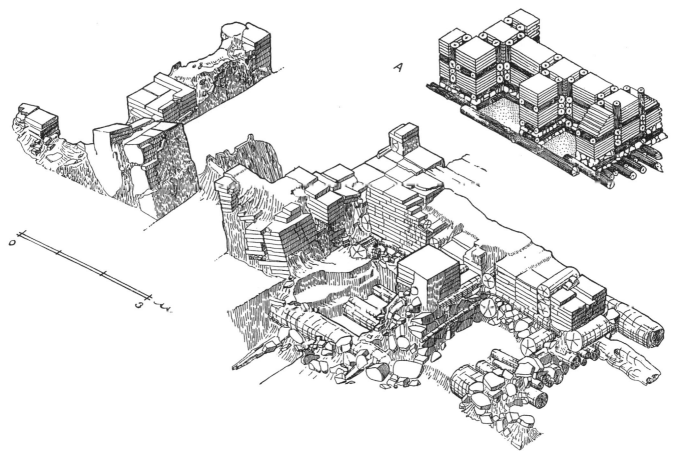

BUILDING MATERIALS: Persian through Roman Periods. Figure 1. *Isometric reconstruction of Bey-cesultan in western Anatolia.* Half timbered mud-brick construction on rubble foundations. Mixed construction is typical of Levanto-Helladic area, but is noteworthy here because of the unbridled use of wood in a (then) heavily forested area. Note the remains of a charred wooden door standing in place. Remains dated to about 1500 BCE. (Courtesy G. R. H. Wright)

thians and Sasanians) regained an empire for the Persian people, their building, however explained, was in no way a revival of the Achaemenid style.

The materials of Achaemenid construction were mixed. Extremely fine ashlar masonry characterizes the building. Very large blocks were used to face the great podia on which the complexes are elevated, while fine stone framing (e.g., door and window frames) articulates the walls of individual buildings. The bulk of the wall was, however, mud brick and the great flat terrace roofs were of mud brick on enormous timber beams. The structural system was an entirely trabe-ated one, and the arch and vault were not used. Perhaps the most notable structural feature is the columnar development and the forests of immensely tall stone columns, some with animal capitals or impost blocks, remain a world wonder. Although a broadroom tradition was evident at Pasargadae, at Persepolis a highly idiosyncratic design principle became dominant—that of centralized (concentric) square planning: square units set concentrically within square units. Perhaps

it might be said that the great masonry podium was the individuation of the system.

The question of the sources for this harmonious composition of elements has always evoked discussion. The palace building inscriptions state that whereas the various operations of construction were carried out by subject peoples, the overall design was exactly as the "Great King" had intended it to be, which has been understood to indicate that the planning of the palace complex was entirely determined by Persian taste. This, however, is not a full explanation of the style; between the client who determines the planning and the craftsman who effects the details of construction is the architect who determines the overall composition of details in elevation. Thus, it remains unclear whether the architect of the complex was a Persian (of whatever background) or the master mason (the office which traditionally gives on to that of architect) who, according to the building inscriptions, should have been a Lydian (from Sardis) or an East Greek (from the neighboring Ionian coast). Certainly the general overall appearance in elevation of the Achaemenid palaces was quite unlike anything known in the contemporary development of Greek monumental building.

The impact of Achaemenid monumental architecture on the building scene of the contemporary Near East is obscure. The archaeological evidence is obviously defective. Some smaller apadana-type "government house" buildings have been discovered in important regional centers (e.g., in Babylon and on the Phoenician coast). However, little can be adduced regarding the significant question of influence and hybridization. What appears clear is that Achaemenid building had a negligible impact on the great monumental traditions of Egypt and Mesopotamia. It is in the Levanto-Anatolian region where there are indications (or possibilities) of interaction with an older tradition, here the most cognate. However, in the light of existing information, traces and effects of Achaemenid building appear most recognizable after the end of the regime—a strange matter which will be mentioned in its historical context (see below). [*See* Persians.]

Classical Greek Building In Ionia. A meaningful part of the development of classical Greek building took place on Near Eastern ground: the Ionian coast of Asia Minor. In this measure it was a native Near Eastern building style and its development must be outlined on that account, quite apart from the momentous role it was eventually to play over the whole region in virtue of later political history.

The material of construction of classical Greek building is uniform, fine stone masonry—but only up to the roof. The highly characteristic roofing was a timber-framed gable roof normally clad with terra-cotta tiling, but on splendid occasions with stone (marble) tiling. The structural system employed was trabeated, and no arches or vaults were included (the ceiling was coffered stone slabbing on stone beams). The system was hyperessentially columnar, and this in a novel manner: the external load-bearing components in major structures were rows of columns. The design form was rigorously "longroom," here supplemented by the peristyle (peripheral colonade), the whole being set on a three-stepped raised platform (the "crepis").

Again, the development of this superb mode of building was rapid (entirely within the seventh and sixth centuries BCE), and anything but obvious. Certainly there is nothing in the building history of Greece during the preceeding three centuries or so to account for it. Thus, the only modes of monumental building which could have influenced the development of classical Greek architecture were the neighboring Levanto-Anatolian or Egyptian building. The ridged tile roof sets the Greek temple apart from all preceeding Near Eastern monumental building—as does the outward-looking peristylar design. The profusely columned Egyptian buildings were inward looking (as essentially was all Near Eastern architecture): the columns were enclosed within halls or internal courts. It is possible to find arrangements something like Greek in antis or prostyle design in Near Eastern building, but nothing like the peristyle. On the other hand, there is a background in the Near East to classical building in the fine stone masonry common to both.

However classical Greek masonry evolved an unsurpassed excellence of its own. Utterly unlike Levanto-Anatolian masonry, it was entirely solid throughout the thickness of the wall, and unlike Egyptian masonry, the blocks were regular orthogonal units of medium size set in regular courses dressed entirely true on all the joints before setting. The blocks were set without mortar and fixed one to the other by horizontal cramping and, on occasion, by vertical doweling. The hairline jointing was facilitated by the process of anathyrosis: the rising joints were hollowed out, leaving a band like a clear frame around three margins to make the lateral contact between adjacent blocks. An integral factor in this stone masonry was the development, in about 500 BCE, of block-and-tackle lifting devices, so that quite massive blocks could be cleanly lifted and lowered into position. The full excellence of this mode was restricted to very monumental walling of marble or hard limestone.

During the fifth and fourth centuries BCE classical Greek masonry spread into regions contiguous with Greek Ionia (cf., e.g., the Temple of Artemis at Sardis; the Nereid monument at Xanthos; the Mausoleum at Halikarnassos). However, with Alexander's conquest of the Achaemenid Empire and the firm establishment of Greek rule in the third century BCE over almost the entire ancient Near East, the stage was set for varied developments in the buildling of the region.

Oriental Hellenistic Building. Before particularizing regional developments, an important general manifestation of hellenization on Near Eastern building must be noted: namely, extension to the scope of monumental building. With hellenization, both newly Greek-founded towns and some old towns were invested with the forms of the Greek city (the polis) to enable their citizens to lead a truly human life—that is, the public one encompassing activities political, judicial, economic, and cultural-recreational. All these activities required facilities, for the most part involving substantial monumental building projects. Thus, in addition to the military, religious, and palatial structures of the ancient Near East (which certainly did not decline in significance), there was a whole new and varied series of design projects: public meetinghouses and law courts (bouleterion, ecclesiasterion, basilica); agorai, stoas, colonnaded streets, nymphaea, triumphal arches; theaters, amphitheaters, stadiums, hippodromes, gymnasia, and baths. These public buildings remained part of the Near Eastern urban scene until they disappeared when the area reverted once more to an eastern way of life under Islamic domination. There were, however, one or two legacies from the Hellenistic interregnum. The two institutions which casual impression associates with the lifestyle of the traditional Near East, the *suq* ("market") and the *ḥammam* ("bath"), are both developments of two Hellenistic features introduced into the region: the agora and the balaneia/thermae.

If Greek architectural forms transformed the Orient, then it is only fair to say that the Orient and its wealth had its effect on Greek architectural forms. Various civic buildings mentioned here were strikingly developed during the Hellenistic period. The theater and the gymnasium, as also the agora (*cum* stoa complexes), were simple, indeed primitive, in the 5th century BCE. It was the wealth put into circulation by the expansion into the Orient which promoted their evolution into the monumental complexes now taken as the norm.

The deployment of all these types of civic building was bound up with probably the most salient feature hellenization brought to the Near East region: rationalized town planning, with its regular orthogonal grid pattern of streets and its organization of urban space on functional lines (i.e., into residential quarters and public quarters of various types). The Greek practice probably originates with the rebuilding of Miletus after the Persian destruction early in the fifth century BCE. However, the original, rather mechanical, concept was much vivified from the third century BCE onward by various monumental features of design incorporated into it. The grid was diversified and articulated into sectors (zoning) by colonnaded major streets and associated devices: the tetrapylon at important street crossings and the triumphal arch (or monumental arched gate) to break the perspective at the entrance to different areas (e.g., the sanctuary area, the agora, the harbor). Such features appeared contemporaneously in Asia Minor, Syria, and Palestine and were doubtless originally an expression of Seleucid enlightenment and munificence (cf. the foundation of Antioch on the Orontes). However, their full and true development took place under Roman rule during the prosperity of the second century CE (cf., e.g., Petra, Gerasa/Jerash, Ephesus), by which time they are to be found uniformly across the whole region to the Atlantic (cf. Ptolemais in Cyrenaica, Leptis Magna in Tripolitania).

One other very generalized mark of hellenization on Near Eastern building was in military engineering. Alexander's empire was won by the superior military science of the Greeks over that of Asiatics, and the Wars of the Successors ensured the maintenance of this superiority. Of particular note here was the development of the science of siegecraft (cf. Demetrios Poliorketes and Philo of Byzantium). In this way fortifications were required to keep pace with ever more and more powerful means of destruction. Greek military engineers saw traditional types of fortification over the whole region but saw nothing in advance of their own practice. Accordingly, when fortifications were required in the hellenized Orient, they were designed on Greek principles. This involved, in the first place, building city walls almost exclusively of finely dressed stone masonry (in the interest both of strength and beauty). Design novelties included the idea of the Great (or extended) Circuit—that is, of enclosing within the walls all the neighboring high ground which potentially could be used to command the terrain (cf. at Priene, Ptolemais in Libya).

Finally, a notable application of the classical Greek mode of building in the East was the architecturally developed monumental tomb. Various traditions of monumental tombs were known in the ancient Near East; however, by the middle of the first millennium BCE, generally speaking, traditional tombs were unobtrusive externally—exceptions were the tumulus tombs of Anatolia (e.g., at Gordion and Sardis) and tombs with architectural facades cut in rock cliffs (e.g., in Lycia and Persia). In contrast, before Alexander's conquests (e.g., the Mausoleum at Halikarnassos, the Nereid Monument at Xanthos) there were monumental tombs in the Near East embodying the classical orders of architecture and afterward these became commonplace. There were several different types, both rock cut (cf. the elaborate rock-cut facade tombs at Petra, the peristyle house tombs in disused quarries at Alexandra and Nea-Paphos), while freestanding built tombs are widespread, for example, in Syria (Suweida), Egypt (Cape Zephyron), and North Africa (Ptolemais).

The regional distribution of hellenization in building across the ancient East is of great historical importance and has hitherto received little close attention. The following is a summary outline.

Anatolia. A very critical region in building development during this period is Anatolia (or, rather, western Anatolia). On the one hand, its western coast was a home ground of classical Greek building; on the other, the bulk of the region was only patchily and sparingly hellenized, contrasting strongly in this respect with geographically more remote regions. However, whether on this account or otherwise, the area came to be one with prolific building in Roman times (and to a degree in Roman manners). In this way, much varied construction (e.g., faced mortared rubble, solid burnt brick) resulted, of importance in the ecumenical history of building.

Alexander's conquests had little effect on the building of the Greek cities of Ionia (he is said to have personally dedicated the Temple of Athena at Priene). They retained their civic status and maintained their building activities in the (largely Ionic) Greek style to form a (perhaps the) focal point for the continuation of the tradition. As some of the earliest Greek temples were erected in this region, so were some of the latest (e.g., at Magnesia on the Meander in the late second century BCE, and the Temple of Domitian at Ephesus, first century CE). Also, such temples continued to be built in Roman times in the interior (cf. the Temple of Rome and Augustus at Ankara). Developments here were ones of stylistic evolution and it was the famous architect of the region, Hermogenes, who was the source for Vitruvius' ideas about the rules of the Ionic order. The new Hellenistic power in the region was Pergamon, and the pro-Roman policy of the local Attalid dynasty was of great historical importance because it gave Rome its early foothold in Asia. Some of the latest monumental Doric building was at Pergamon (e.g., the Temple of Hera, c. 150 BCE). Above all, it was in the Hellenistic building of the region that the true masonry arch is first seen expressed in monumental building (e.g., at Priene and Miletus).

Mesopotamia and Iran. The heartland of the Achaemenid Empire was formed by Mesopotamia and Iran, and in turn the house of Seleucus immediately established its principal capital in (and near) Babylon. However, in 129 BCE the Seleucids definitely lost all control over the eastern part of their vast kingdom when those lands passed into Parthian possession. This does not mean that thereafter hellenized building came to an end in this great tract of land. It did not, and indeed there were Greek communities which survived on the far eastern fringes (i.e., on the confines of central Asia and India). What it does mean is that Rome never established any real footing in the region, and thus building development continued there without any renewed direction from the West via Roman rule, as in other parts of the Near East.

It was Seleucus (the "royalest" of mind among Alexander's successors) who alone carried on Alexander's program for the brotherhood of man, and over recent years astonishing evidence has been found of a symbiosis of Greek architectural forms with others native to the region. This is the architectural expression of what may be called Greco-Oriental art (cf. Greco-Roman art) and it has been considered that it was this style which was adopted and continued by the Parthian successors of the Seleucids and thus has been termed Parthian art (without in fact, having any significant ethnically Parthian component). Much of the evidence occurs in extraordinarily remote areas (e.g., Central Asia, India, the Persian Gulf, the Syrian Desert). The evidence is fragmentary, and it is impossible to reassess it in short compass. Only the main strands are indicated here. [*See* Seleucids; Parthians.]

The Seleucids did not in any way discountenance local styles. They maintained intact the old Mesopotamian massive brick building tradition, providing for the restoration of famous old buildings and the erection of new ones (e.g., at Babylon and Uruk). This tradition survived throughout their regime and only came to an end in Parthian times early in the Christian era. Indeed, the old Mesopotamian broadroom temple plan, atypically and unexpectedly, was made use of far away (e.g., at Ai Khanum). However, Greek forms both of design and construction appeared immediately (by 300 BCE): towns were planned on Hippodamian lines (e.g., at Dura-Europos on the Middle Euphrates), and there were Greek theaters (e.g., at Babylon and Ai Khanum) and recognizable Greek temples (e.g., at Failaka, by modern Kuwait, at the head of the Persian Gulf). While plentiful Greek roofing tiles have been found (e.g., at Babylon). Nonetheless, overall development was such that Greek forms were merged with oriental ones—and increasingly so with time, culminating in the high tide of an "oriental reaction" during the latter part of the first century BCE, when Parthian political power was at its strongest.

The principal fact here was the prevalence in planning of two local forms: the centralized square cella and an open-fronted hall chamber, the iwan. The former is, of course, the typical "Iranian" design noted at Persepolis (whatever be its ultimate origins), while the origins of the latter are difficult to account for. In any event, it was to have a great future, extending on into medieval East Islamic architecture. It was these forms, generally brick built with arched portals and barrel-vaulted rooms, which were dressed with architectural ornament derived from the Greek order. Although in earlier times there were stone columns and entablatures (e.g., in western Iran at Kurrha and Kangavar), the tendency was for this architectural detail to become expressed as engaged facade decoration in stuccoed brickwork; this development thus paralleled the Roman development of transforming the Greek orders from structure to ornament. There were also reminiscences of Achaemenid style in the details: the columns slender and lofty, sometimes with campaniform bases.

This composite style was geographically widespread—from Ai Khanum and Surkh Kotal on the eastern margins to the Nabatean temples of Syria (see below). It is perhaps possible to see a reflex classical influence from romanized Syria in the second century CE in northern Mesopotamia, where, for example, the stone-built monuments of Hatra have affinities with those of contemporary Palmyra but still show the iwan and the centralized square cella pattern. However, the overall line of subsequent development is clear.

In the middle of the third century CE, the collapsing Parthian regime was replaced by the Sasanians—Persians from the province of Fars, centred on the ancient capital of Persepolis. Sasanian building clearly proceeded from Parthian building in a direction away from its Greek component. The oriental planning elements, the square cella and the *iwan*, remained dominant, but the expression evolved markedly. The dome was added to the vault as the focus of design in elevation (cf. the Firuzabad Palace), thus affording grounds for one of architecture's most persistent debates: *Rom oder Orient* (did medieval domical building develop out of Roman or Eastern prototypes?). Alongside brick, mortared rubble came into use as a staple building material, with the strong (gypsum) mortar a basic load-bearing element. However, the aspect remained the stucco rendering, and here virtually all reference to Greek forms disappeared and the stucco decoration assumed an entirely oriental all-over style. As a logical conclusion to this line of development, it is not always easy to differentiate between later Sasanian building and Early Islamic building (cf. the Palace at Sarvestan). [*See* Sasanians.*]

Syria. Greco-Roman Syria is probably the cynosure of building development during the period. The native Levanto-Anatolian style, imperial Achaemenid, Hellenistic Greek, Greco-Oriental (Parthian?), Greco-Roman, all the several monumental styles previously detailed found expression in this region.

Achaemenid rule was long and prosperous and the Phoenician seaboard was a strategically important region to the Persians. Thus, there are to be found a number of Achaemenid building remains, both *disjecta membra* (Persepolitan column fragments from Sidon) and building plans (funerary monuments and sanctuary from 'Amrit, apadana from Byblos). The degree to which this Achaemenid building remained a living force in the land across the next centuries of Seleucid rule is a matter of considerable interest in view of the surprising profusion of Iranian-style building about three hundred years later, at the turn of the eras. At this stage in central southern Syria (the Hauran), then under Nabatean rule, a number of sanctuaries (Seeia, Sahr) occur, showing the Persian square temple design with elements of Persepolitan-type ornament. Similar building can be found at this time at Kalat Fakra in Mount Lebanon. This building activity is generally reckoned to be the result of Parthian influence in the region, which at the time threatened the continuance of Hellenism—and thus the building is put down as pertaining to the Greco-Oriental style. However, there are gainsaying considerations. The very monumental Baris ("stronghold") of the Tobiads at 'Iraq el-Amir, near Amman in Transjordan, belongs to the second century BCE and its massive stone masonry clearly has many Achaemenid affinities. Furthermore, although chronologically compatible with Parthian political influence, the temples in the Hauran are akin to contemporary temples on the far eastern margin of the Iranian world, in India and Central Asia, rather than to Parthian buildings of the period.

It is unfortunate that very little Greek building by the Seleucids has been preserved in Syria. Abundant ancient sources let us know that Antioch on the Orontes (the western capital of the Seleucids) soon came to be the third city in the world (after Rome and Alexandria). However, at the Great metropolitan centers (e.g., Antioch, Apamea), Hellenistic building remains are overlaid by massive Roman and Byzantine remains. As a result, later Roman developments have been projected back or evidence sought in remote areas. A significant feature at issue here is baroque design, where orders are broken up into ornamental elements in conjunction with curvilinear design. This mode is prominent during later Roman building in Syria (cf. the Temple of Venus at Baalbek), but whether it is a development brought from Rome (cf., e.g., the curvilinear Roman-type theaters in Syria), or whether, on the other hand, Roman baroque derived originally from Hellenistic Syrian exemplars is still argued. Exemplifying the debate are the monuments at Petra, where some of the tomb facades manifest postclassical baroque compositions. The date of these monuments has long been in contention—with the so-called Roman temple tombs being variously assigned to the second century CE or the first century BCE.

At all events, the floruit of hellenized Syrian building was in the second century CE during the prosperous Antonine period, when the grandiose remains from, for example, Gerasa, Baalbek, Palmyra, and Apamea, together with temple and sanctuary sites, form one of the most spectacular assemblages of ancient architecture.

The embellished Hippodamian town planning of these Syrian cities is notable, and as surviving this is almost entirely Roman period work. The colonnaded street with its articulating features, while known in other regions, is standard in Syria. These monumental building programs were effected in finely dressed ashlar masonry, close jointed throughout. The material, however, is local stone (limestone, although on occasion other stone, such as basalt, was used), and there is little evidence for the anathyrosis and cramping proper to classical marble masonry. Syria has a long background of fine stone masonry (e.g., Israelite and Phoenician) of the Levanto-Anatolian type and the later ashlar masonry is in some measure a conformable development of this. There are, however, striking examples of another type of masonry. Some blocks (the Trilithon) forming part of the podium of the main temple at Baalbek (early first century CE) are the largest blocks surviving from ancient building. They were hauled into position up long ramps from the quarry and represent another tradition of masonry. This work is often ascribed to a survival of Achaemenid building tradition, but the matter is not obvious.

The great majority of monumental building remains surviving in Syria are of religious buildings, the famous "Roman Temples in Syria" (at, e.g., Baalbek, Niha, and Dmer). These buildings are very interesting, inasmuch as they speak for the strong survival of old Syrian tradition in a central part of the hellenized world. And as opposed to Egypt, this takes the form of hybridization, for whereas in external appearance these temples give the impression, for the most part, of Roman podium temples (generally prostyle or in antis), the reality is quite other. A striking feature of their functional design is that, at the rear of the temple, raised up on a podium of its own, is a unit commonly referred to as the adyton, although in view of its special nature perhaps *thalamos* is better. Its facade received a full architectural development, as befits a separate unit; and in numbers of instances it is exactly this, being an aedicule—a small building set in a larger one. In religious terms it has been looked on as the survivor of the old Syrian shrine set in new hellenized dress. Another telling factor in this connection is the temple roofing. Almost universally, the appearance at least of a classical ridged roof is adverted to by way of a gabled front, but whether and in what manner and to what extent this was carried over into reality is a question which has to be examined in each case on its merits. Often, the pediment and horizontal cornice mask a terrace roof of importance in the cult, to which access is gained by stair towers.

Finally, it may be noted that in view of its status as the Holy Land, some of the earliest (e.g., Constantinian) monumental Christian buildings were erected in the region (at Jerusalem, Bethlehem). It was once considered that the Syrian temples, some of them apsed, played a part in forming Christian church architecture, but this view has not found much favor and the development of Christian church architecture in the region essentially belongs to the succeeding epoch.

Arabia. In the past, the very large geographical region of Arabia has gone almost entirely unnoticed in terms of building history. However, recent discoveries have shown that during the periods under consideration it had an important and diversified building development. It is possible to recognize three provinces: Western Arabia, Eastern Arabia, and Southern Arabia.

Ancient Mesopotamian civilization expanded down the Persian Gulf (cf. the paradisial island of Dilmun), and there are remains of traditional Mesopotamian building in Eastern Arabia (e.g., the Barbar Temple at Bahrain) from early times. Then, in due course, the Seleucids established stations in the area (cf. Ikaros Island sanctuary = modern Failaka, off Kuwait).

It was, however, perhaps via Western Arabia (the Hijaz) that the most significant communication was held with the ancient world. To this degree, ancient Arabia can in some sense be regarded as an outlier of Syria. Without doubt, the most striking Arabian building is in Southern Arabia (the Yemen, Arabia Felix). From Bronze Age times onward, influences had reached the region from Syria and also from Egypt. Thus, by the sixth century BCE a very striking regional school of monumental building in fine stone masonry was already long established there (above all at Marib; cf. the famous Dam and the Haram). The characteristic of this school was the superior large-block masonry, after the Egyptian manner; however, the architectural expression (i.e., the order) was not at all Egyptian inspired. It has a stark, cubist form of its own, marked by lofty monolithic piers of rectangular section. Sometime during the latter half of the first millenium BCE, the technique of stone dressing changed to accord more closely with classical Greek practice; but it would seem that it was not until well on in the Christian era (Roman rule was never established) that naturalistic Hellenic architectural ornament appeared in the region.

On the other hand, Western Arabia (extreme southern Transjordan, the Hijaz, or Arabia Petraea) shows virtually no monumental building prior to the rise of the Nabateans. Tayma' oasis in North Arabia was an outlier of Mesopotamia and a temporary royal residence in later Neo-Babylo-

nian times, but little is known of its building. The Nabatean monuments in the Hijaz are virtually restricted to the rock-cut tomb facades at Meda'in Saleh (Hegra), and it is difficult to see in these anything but regional versions of Hellenistic building (Alexandrian centered).

Egypt and Its Dependencies. It has been a long accepted standpoint that in Egypt there was little commingling of Greek monumental building and Egyptian monumental building. In this respect of existence at least, the Ptolemies, as opposed to the Seleucids, enjoined a type of "apartheid"—they promoted both building modes but did not sanction their hybridization. Certainly Egyptian temple building in the traditional pharaonic manner thrived greatly under the Ptolemies (and on into Roman times). Numbers of the great showpiece Egyptian temples are of this period (e.g., Kom Ombo, Edfu, Dendera); none shows the slightest infection by the Greek style in design—and in all essentials the same might be said for construction, which is still large-block Egyptian masonry (see figure 2). However, it is possible that on close examination some secondary details of construction may show influence from classical Greek masonry. In short, the pharaonic style well survived the period of Ptolemaic rule and died of old age somewhere about 200 CE, after an incredibly extended life of about three thousand years. Hieroglyphs were probably the potent vehicle which conserved the life spirit so long, and when they fell into general disuse it marked the end. [*See* Ptolemies.]

Most of Greek monumental building under the Ptolemies was concentrated in Alexandria, which both in theory and reality was a Greek city by Egypt, not in it. The town plan of ancient Alexandria has been recognized beneath the overlay of subsequent building—it was a very regular checkerboard Hippodamian plan as directed by Alexander himself. Unfortunately, however, almost all the standing monuments have disappeared. Knowledge of such buildings is therefore available almost exclusively from *disjecta membra* and *simulacra* in the rock-cut cemeteries contrived in disused quarries around the town, which frequently represent opulent peristylar houses.

Ancient and Islamic sources speak of the splendor of Alexandrian building, so marbled that it dazzled by day and lighted up the night, but it is extremely probable that much of this marble was revetment dating from later Roman times. At any rate, very little marble of any sort remains; surviving fragments are almost entirely of local limestone. So far as can be judged, such construction was generally of good ashlar masonry; it is doubtful, however, whether anathyrosis or cramping was normal.

What is revealed by the surviving remains at Alexandria is a distinct architectural style—that is, a characteristic manner of using the Greek orders. Its notable features are a heterodox type of Corinthian capital (lacking cauliculi and medial spirals), sometimes presented in draft form (the Nabatean capital), and the appearance of modillions sup-

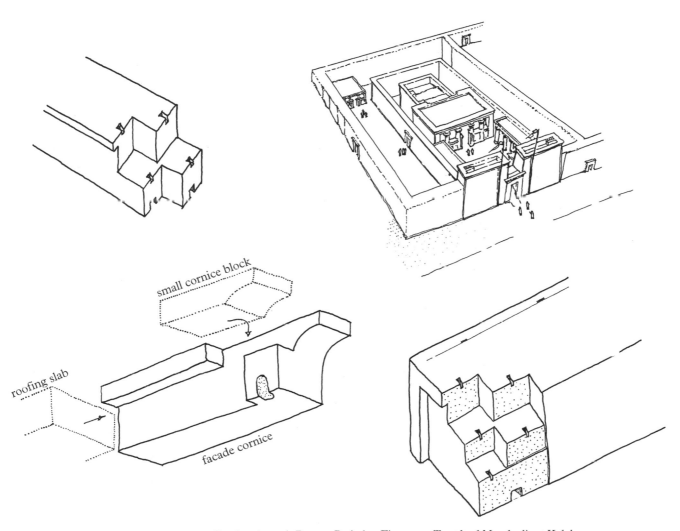

BUILDING MATERIALS: Persian through Roman Periods. Figure 2. *Temple of Mandoulis at Kalab-sha (south of Aswan).* Constructed by the Romans in the first century CE in the traditional pharaonic design. The massive scale of the construction is shown in the perspective drawing at the upper right. Lintels, roofing slabs, and entabulature blocks weigh about 20-25 tons and were hauled up into place on ramps. The detail sketches show how large entabulature blocks rising through two or three courses were trimmed in situ for jointing with the adjacent normal blocks. (Courtesy G. R. H. Wright)

porting the corona of the cornice (simple equivalents of the imperial Roman console). There is also the breaking up and variegating of pediments into decorative compositions of, for example, flanking pinnacles and arcs. Internal colonnades were common and the solution of the angle problem adopted was the cordiform pier, a striking design element. The ultimate origins of these features are various, and some of them are found in other connections; the assemblage is, however, characteristic and can be termed the Alexandrian school. Thus, when it is encountered elsewhere, in Cyrenaica, Cyprus, southern Palestine, and Arabia (all parts of the Ptolemaic Empire or under its influence), it indicates an Alexandrian architectural province. Well-known monuments evidencing this style are the Khazne tomb facade at Petra and the Colonnaded Palace at Ptolemais in Cyrenaica,

both difficult to date and assigned anywhere between later first century BCE to second century CE. This illustrates that the style survived the establishment of Roman rule in some regions and probably was only supplanted by the imperial organized "prefabricated marble" style of the second century onward.

The Alexandrian style was light and graceful and may be thought of as ancient Rococo. It was a well-known and popular image and probably formed the manner of earlier Roman wall-plaster decoration (cf. the Pompeian Second Style). As a concluding remark, it should be noticed that all discussion of this Alexandrian style refers to appearance in elevation; it does not refer to a type of building plan, far less a temple type—again, unlike Syria, with its distinct genre of Roman temples. It may be possible, however, to suggest from the decor that the tholos was used as a planning element.

But this is not the end of the story, although such an impression is often given. Within the Roman Empire, Egypt was a very special and important province—a critical source of grain and monumental building stone (granite); thus, of necessity it was well planted with Roman administrative centers. As a result, a Roman style of monumental building supplemented the "Alexandrian" mode more brusquely in Egypt than in the Ptolemaic provinces of Cyrenaica and Cyprus, both backwaters of the Roman Empire. Certainly by the second century CE (i.e., in Hadrianic and Antonine times) there was much new building in Egypt, and it was virtually entirely in the classical mode; by that time, although relief decoration continued on Egyptian temples together with some very minor alterations and additions, no large-scale new building work was undertaken.

This Roman building was in no way confined to Alexandria or even to the other Greek cities (Naukratis, Ptolemais, Antinoe). It was spread throughout the length of the Nile Valley and further, in the desert margins and the oases. Moreover, at least by the second century CE, this Roman building was in no way derived from or modeled on the Alexandrian school, which had ruled down to the beginning of the Christian era (cf. the temple dedicated to Augustus at Philae). This new building was the Egyptian counterpart of the Imperial "Marble" style which came in earlier or later in the second century through the various provinces of the empire. Only in Egypt, for the most part, it was a "Granite" style, where monolithic granite column shafts were ordered prefabricated from the Aswan and Mons Claudianus quarries and were provided with capitals and bases in white limestone—the capitals, for the most part, being Ionic or orthodox Corinthian. Surviving buildings in the style include Roman podium-type temples, baths, theaters, and a notable profusion of monumental arches, tetrapyla, and honorific columns.

There is also striking evidence for a later stage in this building history. During the third century CE, and particularly in its closing years (cf. the times of Diocletian), there was a very considerable conversion of pharaonic monumental complexes (e.g. the Luxor Temple) into Roman establishments (notably fortresses). This indicates that the vitality of pharaonic Egyptian culture was virtually exhausted. Equally, at a somewhat later time, early Christian energies extended to contriving premises in derelict pharaonic temples and tombs, providing appropriate interior decor by covering the ancient reliefs with painted plaster. However, the architectural development of Christian Egypt, Coptic architecure, is essentially later than Constantinian times.

North Africa. In this era, North Africa was a prosperous, peaceful region with much monumental building, so that present-day remains are notable. Cyrenaica was a very old and wealthy Greek colony. Although Achaemenid armies reached the land, their irruption left no effect on building. Alexander himself arrived at its border on his visit to the oracle of Zeus Ammon but never led his armies into the territory. Shortly afterward it was brought under Ptolemaic control and during this period its old Doric building tradition continued, subject to influence from Alexandria, and probably in turn exercising some influence on Alexandrian building. It passed under Roman control early in the first century BCE, but it was probably not until the late second century CE that large-scale importation of prefabricated marble elements began to change the building scene.

Tripolitania was colonized by Phoenicians, but its monumental building eventually came to bear a Hellenistic aspect. Incorporation into the empire (first century BCE) brought no radical change until the Imperial Marble style arrived in the first half of the second century CE. In this connection a notable development was at Leptis Magna during the reign of Septimius Severus, a native of the town. Thereafter, monumental building was "international" in expression.

Circumstances were somewhat different in the extensive western areas (Tunis, Algeria, Morocco). This was very thinly urbanized by Phoenician colonization. Thus, when it came under Roman rule (from 146 BCE onward), much of it was land more akin to Western European provinces. In this way Roman settlement of the hinterland was marked by the establishment of colonies (e.g., Timgad) which came to resemble Roman towns in Europe more than cities of the Eastern provinces (n.b., bath buildings, when on a large enough scale, were modeled on the Roman thermae and concrete construction was introduced). Eventually here also during the second century CE, imperial marble building appeared. The region is of note as preserving its building energies well on into the fourth century CE. It also preserved to the end of the ancient world the highly characteristic mode of construction which the Romans called *opus africanum* (see figure 3). This was the old Canaanite System (introduced by the Phoenician colonists) of superior stone piers with a paneling of lower-grade rubble.

Roman Building in the Orient: A Summary. Roman rule in the hellenized Orient did not radically alter developments in building there. The impact of Roman rule was quite other than in those provinces previously without monumental building (e.g., the western provinces in Europe). Nonetheless, in the overall sense, certain modifications to building resulted in the eastern provinces, and it is necessary to summarize them.

The epochal building development in Rome during late Republican times (first century BCE) was *opus caementicium* (walls formed with a core of mortared aggregate laid in between faces of small stones or of flat, brick tiles). This is today loosely called Roman concrete, but the term is misleading because the core was not poured as a viscous mass like modern concrete. The construction was in fact essentially similar to traditional walling in Levanto-Anatolian building, whether monumental or nonmonumental, and differed only to the degree that the (pozzolana) mortar was of superior adhesive strength. This construction was very flexible and soon its logic revolutionized design—it ousted columns as principal load-bearing elements, thus reducing the orders essentially to nonstructural ornament; and it promoted curvilinear form, both in plan and elevation (viz., the arch and the vault). Thus, by the second century CE, much monumental building in Rome was of this nature (e.g., the Pantheon). This new type of construction was not to become accepted in the eastern provinces of the empire, although a number of exceptional instances have been found, mainly in Syria. Nevertheless, baroque design certainly became prominent in some eastern provinces, but this was carried out in ashlar masonry, not in "Roman concrete."

On the other hand the next major building development in Rome equally affected the eastern provinces. During the second century CE, Roman imperial resources promoted the development of marble quarrying on a new, extended scale at quarries in the northern Aegean (e.g., Prokonesos) with adjacent harbor facilities. Mechanized masons' yards were established so that elements of the architectural orders could be dressed into nearly finished forms and dispatched to monumental building sites all over the empire. Thus, from this time onward monuments at many sites in the hellenized Orient were dignified by prefabricated marble architectural ornament. The trademark of this development was that such columns were monolithic (often of colored marble shafts with contrasting white-marble bases and capitals). In principal, this development was to outlast the age and to continue into Byzantine times.

There was, of course, a further way in which Roman rule changed the picture of building in the hellenized Orient: by the direct expedient of introducing new and radically changed building projects. Certainly the achievements of Roman engineering on roads, bridges, and above all on aqueducts were highly conspicuous. The aqueduct was associated with other projects which necessitated this urban water supply on a new scale—primarily the vastly increased use of public baths. Although the great leisure establishments of the Roman thermae were not transplanted to the East, public baths (either independent or associated with gymnasia) became endemic. Another very popular monument was the ornate nymphaeum, a pleasant amenity in the hot and dusty East. Also an additional Roman monument which became popular in the eastern provinces was the triumphal arch, or arched gate. Then there were new types of leisure projects in addition to theaters (where the more monumental Roman design became common), namely amphitheaters and hippodromes. Also a rather unexpected development in Roman times was the more frequent provision of public libraries. In review, it may be noted here that virtually all such projects in their design involved a movement away

BUILDING MATERIALS: Persian through Roman Periods. Figure 3. *Example of western Roman building construction in the province of Africa (Tunisia).* Note the opus africanum with the panel infill of opus reticulatum, a very interesting construction technique. (Courtesy G. R. H. Wright)

from the old rectilinear Greek orders structure toward curvilinear design and arcuated structure. [*See* Aqueducts; Baths; Roads; Arches.]

Conclusion. Constantine's political and religious settlement of the Roman world was a watershed in building development. Whether they had endured for several millennia or several centuries, all the building systems described here had become or became extinct within a short period. The marble perfection of the Greek temple did not essentially survive the massive stone or brick of Egypt and Mesopotamia, and Roman concrete construction was not to be continued in Constantinople. Elements of construction survived: walls of dressed stone or baked brick, the framed timber roof, domes and vaults, marble columns and associated ornament, plastered decoration. These elements were fashioned into styles: Islamic, Byzantine, Romanesque, Gothic architecture, to be followed by Renaissance, and revivals. None of these styles was a direct descendant of any one ancient building style, but each new style was recognizably Eastern or Western. The ecumenical Roman monumental building of the high empire (second or third century CE) was never paralleled. Only modern ferroconcrete building is again an international mode, unlimited in scope and provenance but unloved.

[*See also* House; Palace; Temples. *In addition the regions and sites mentioned are the subject of independent entries.*]

BIBLIOGRAPHY

Mesopotamian Building

There has been little systematic study of structures and construction in Mesopotamian building. Hitherto inquiry has concentrated on design types.

Egyptian Building

Arnold, Dieter. *Egyptian Building*. New York, 1990. Recent review of subject matter, extending both scope and detail, but not changing the basics.

Clarke, Somers, and Reginald Engelbach. *Ancient Egyptian Masonry*. London, 1930. The original vigorous and clearcut exposé of elements, based on good observation.

Levanto-Anatolian Building

Hult, Gunnel. *Bronze Age Ashlar Masonry in the Eastern Mediterranean: Cyprus, Ugarit, and Neighbouring Regions*. Göteborg, 1983. Detailed, itemized survey establishing the existence of a system of masonry widespread in space and time; the system did not go out of use at the end of the Bronze Age.

Naumann, Rudolf. *Architektur Kleinasiens*. 2d ed. Tübingen, 1971. Very systematic and comprehensive account to the end of Syro-Hittite building.

Wright, G. R. H. *Ancient Building in South Syria and Palestine*. 2 vols. Handbuch der Orientalistik, vol. 7. Leiden, 1985. Supports an account of building development to the end of Persian times, with analytical definitions of basic categories of construction and design.

Wright, G. R. H. *Ancient Building in Cyprus*. Leiden, 1992. Covers the period down to 200 CE, during which time Cyprus both conserved

its Bronze Age Levantine tradition and also received Achaemenid and Hellenistic Greek styles.

Achaemenid Building

Herzfeld, Ernst. *Iran in the Ancient East*. London, 1941. Assessment by a man (both architect and philologist) of great genius and experience in the field.

Nylander, Carl. *Ionians in Pasargadae: Studies in Old Persian Architecture*. Uppsala, 1970. Detailed study of masonry tools and techniques, serving to establish the interconnection between Achaemenid and Classical Greek masonry.

Classical Greek Building

Coulton, J. J. *Greek Architects at Work*. London, 1977. Deals with Greek building from the contemporary animating point of view.

Martin, Roland. *Manuel d'architecture grecque*. Paris, 1965. The most convenient and precise analysis of the structural elements of Greek building.

Scranton, Robert L. *Greek Walls*. Cambridge, Mass., 1941. Old typological study of wall masonry lacking depth but providing a useful assemblage of examples.

Oriental Hellenistic Building

Busink, Th. A. *Der Tempel von Jerusalem, von Salomo bis Herodes*, vol. 2, *Von Ezechiel bis Middot*. Leiden, 1980. Surveys in extensive detail all the developments in Oriental Hellenistic building which could have contributed to Herod's Temple.

Colledge, Malcolm A. R. "Greek and Non-Greek Interaction in the Architecture of the Middle East." In *Hellenism in the East*, edited by Amélie Kuhrt and Susan Sherwin-White. Berkeley, 1987. Resume and development of author's previous studies of Parthian art and architecture.

Stucchi, Sandro. *Architettura cirenaica*. Monografie di Archeologia Libica, vol. 9. Rome, 1975. Shows the effects of the interregionalism of the Hellenistic age on regional building in the Doric tradition.

Roman Building in the East

Adam, Jean-Pierre. *La construction romaine*. 2d ed. Paris, 1989. The most recent in a long line of excellent manuals, providing a convenient review and resume of established data.

Crema, Luigi. *L'architettura romana*. Turin, 1959. Encyclopedic survey presenting the buildings of each successive age according to structural categories and functional types. The exposition is based on citation of individual monuments, profusely illustrated.

Dodge, H. "The Architectural Impact of Rome in the East." In *Architecture and Architectural Sculpture in the Roman Empire*, edited by M. Henig, pp. 108–120. Oxford, 1990. An up-to-date survey of current discoveries and investigations.

Kreneker, D. M., and W. Zsoheitzschmann. *Römische Tempel in Syrien*. Berlin-Leipzig, 1938. A full and precise study of an interesting category representing the adaptation of Roman temples to an old Near Eastern tradition of temple building.

Lezine, A. *Architecture romaine d'Afrique*. Tunis, 1961. Of special use as dealing with a region often overlooked.

Macready, S., ed. *Roman Architecture in the Greek World*. London, 1987. A recent survey containing contributions on many different aspects of the subject, including developments in methods and materials of construction.

Ward-Perkins, J. B. *Roman Imperial Architecture*. 2d ed. Harmondsworth, 1989. General analytical account, of utility in the present context for its regional framework.

Early Christian Building

Krautheimer, Richard. *Early Christian and Byzantine Architecture*. 3d ed. Harmondsworth, 1981. Standard, very detailed manual.

White, L. Michael. *Building God's House in the Roman World: Architectural Adaptation among Pagans, Jews, and Christians*. Baltimore, 1990. Recent examination of the subject, based on social considerations explaining a tradition of "nonmonumental" construction.

G. R. H. WRIGHT

Materials and Techniques of the Byzantine and Islamic Periods

Building techniques in early Byzantine and Islamic lands were learned from the Roman and, to a lesser extent, Sasanian empires. In the formation of an Islamic vocabulary, the first Muslim dynasty, the Umayyads (640–750 CE), adopted Byzantine plans such as the centralized martyrium, as seen in the Dome of the Rock, Jerusalem (692), and architectural ornament such as the Dome of the Rock's mosaic and drilled-marble capitals, for example, those at Madinat az-Zahra', near Cordoba (936–976). Counterinfluences, which were minimal, did not occur until the late eighth century. The decorative manipulation of brick in the Middle Byzantine period, such as the sawtooth-brick bands on the facade of St. Mary of the Coppersmiths at Thessalonike (1028) and the glazed tiles excavated at the monastery of Constantine Lips in Istanbul (908), may have been a response to Islamic ornamental brickwork.

Surviving Byzantine architecture consists mostly of brick and stone churches, virtually all of the domestic and civil architecture built before 1100 having vanished. As an unfortunate result, the following description of early Byzantine architecture is skewed toward a type of religious building that was in fact outnumbered by, for example, the Justinianic fortifications described by Procopius (c. 555). This situation contrasts with the Islamic context, in which quite a number of agricultural estates, palaces, baths, fortifications, and hydraulic structures remain, giving a fair idea of both secular and religious architectural building types.

According to Glanville Downey's study (1948), the Byzantine architect, trained in geometry and physics as well as construction skills, was called either a *mechanikos* (architect) or *architekton* (master builder) until the sixth century, when the terms changed to *oikodomos* (builder) and *protomaister* (guildmaster). As stated in Leo Mayer's study (1956), the Islamic architect was variously called a *muhandis* (engineer or even designer), *banna* (builder), or a *mi'mar*, which was roughly equivalent to a mason or skilled builder. Master rank indicated by the title of *sahib* and *mu'allim* (in North Africa and western Asia) or *ustadh* (Iran, Iraq, Asia Minor).

Because of the simplicity and economy of rubble-core wall construction, most Byzantine and Islamic buildings were erected quickly by a single team of builders. Their plans were rarely innovative: Byzantine architecture improvised on conventional formulas, and Islamic architecture relied on a limited number of plans that served a variety of functional purposes. A significant problem in the study of early Byzantine and Islamic architecture is that no working drawings have survived. Given the relative simplicity of early Islamic building with its small domes and thick-walled towers, it is believed that Islamic builders relied upon a simple, numerically based system of geometrical notation for buildings such as the Great Mosque of Qayrawan (836). In contrast, Byzantine architects erected churches such as Hagia Sophia (532–537) in which the volumetric realization of a dome appended by half domes and buttresses was technically sophisticated and daring. Such complex designs would have required working drawings that may have been generated from geometrical constructions that, in turn, could be applied at the building site.

Little is known about the quantity of wood available before the eleventh century in Byzantine and Islamic Syria-Jordan-Palestine. In Lebanon, the forests diminished sometime after the sixth century; natural forests were more plentiful in Cyprus, Anatolia, and the Balkans. In the Islamic context wood was available where irrigation was practiced, as attested by the ubiquitous use of wood in tie beams, scaffolding, centering forms, and furnishings. In Byzantine architecture through the eighth century, truss-timber roofing was used for spans of 6 m (20 ft.) or less. Although the shift to the domed and vaulted church in the ninth and tenth centuries has been attributed to a lack of wood, this theory is speculative until more is known about the economics of the early Byzantine lumber industry.

The Mediterranean regions supplied ample stone, which was quarried in large blocks and sent to the construction yard to be trimmed more finely. In particular, both Islamic and Byzantine architecture used marble from the rich quarries along the Mediterranean rim, from where it was transported by ship. Marble was used for columns, carved capitals and cornices, lintels, window grilles, fountains, furnishings, pavements, and wall revetments. The variation in grain, vein, embedded crystals, color, and translucency, made marble an important decorative element. The most commonplace was an off-white marble with a blue-gray vein from the island of Proconnesus in the Sea of Marmara; red porphyry from Egypt was the most prized; green, yellow, and ivory marble came from Laconia, Tunisia, and Phrygia respectively. Because of the expense of obtaining rare marble, its presence added considerable prestige to a building. Marble was the preferred material for the revetment of interiors in Byzantine architecture, although painting and mosaic were also used. Islamic architecture also valued exotic imported marble but did not hesitate to use *spolia* (reused earlier material) where available.

Byzantine and Islamic bricks were made according to traditional practice that has been studied by contemporary ethnoarchaeologists. Bricks were made of clay (hydrated oxide of aluminum and iron, hydrated silicates of aluminum), some sand to reduce shrinkage during firing, and organic bacteria for plasticity. Limestone and gypsum were naturally occurring impurities and, because they cause cracking, were removed manually. The clay was pressed into a wooden form and fired at 900–1,000°C (1,652–1,832°F) in an oxidizing atmosphere. Byzantine and Islamic builders often decorated their buildings with glazed or natural terra cotta. Because terra cotta is modeled, the clay body is finer than ordinary brick and must be free of impurities to prevent distortion during firing.

Ceramic glaze, like glass, was made of ground silica, soda or potash, and chalk. Glassmaking was known in the ancient Near East and Roman Empire and used in Byzantine and Islamic architecture for glazing windows: Hagia Sophia had 18-centimeter panes set in marble grilles, and Ibn al-Faqih in 903 stated that the Dome of the Rock had "fifty-six windows, glazed with glass of various hues" (as quoted by Creswell, 1989, p. 24). Although the archaeological evidence is inconclusive, it is possible that colored glass was also used in windows in the Early and Middle Byzantine periods (fourth–twelfth centuries).

The tiny units used in wall mosaics were made of colored marble and glass. The units, called *tesserae*, were set in a lime-plaster ground to form a continuous surface. For floors, stone and marble were favored; for walls, a mixture of marble, and glass—including gilded glass—was used to create rich figural and decorative representations such as the reknowned mosaics in the Church of S. Apollinare Nuovo in Ravenna (c. 490). Islamic patrons decorated some of their finest early monuments with mosaics; however, Muslims were not able to equal the skill of their Byzantine neighbors, as indicated by the importation of Byzantine masters and *tesserae* to create the mosaics for the Dome of the Rock, the Great Mosque of Damascus, and the Great Mosque of Cordoba. Both the Byzantines and Muslims also decorated architectural interiors with wall painting on plaster, which, though not as durable as mosaic, was certainly less expensive and faster.

Byzantine buildings were generally made of a mixture of ashlar (dressed stone) masonry, brick, and rubble core. Walls were made of two vertical faces of ashlar sometimes mixed with brick and filled with rubble that was held together with plenty of mortar. One common technique was to bind the ashlar faces horizontally with courses of brick laid across the entire wall at regular intervals. Walls were usually two bricks thick or about 76 cm (30 in.). Byzantine brick size varied according to region; in Constantinople, bricks measured 35.6–38 cm (14–15 in.) on each side and about 5 cm (2 in.) thick. Arches, vaults, and domes were usually made entirely of brick, an outstanding exception being the huge (11 m or 36 ft. in diameter) stone roof of the tomb of Theodoric, Ravenna (c. 530). Buildings could be constructed entirely of brick, although more commonly mixed with stone (in courses) or on stone foundations.

The mortar was made of lime, sand, and crushed brick. Perhaps as a measure of economy, the mortar layer was thicker than the brick, with the unfortunate result that structural deformation could occur as mortar dried and buildings settled. Conversely, the intended effect may have been visual because mortar was often grooved (*falsa corona*) or in the tenth–twelfth centuries made to appear even thicker by recessing alternate courses of brick. Cyril Mango states (1976, p. 10) that Byzantine construction was derived from practices in western Asia Minor and the Balkans of the second and third centuries CE. Byzantine construction differed from Roman; whereas buildings such as the Pantheon had a cement core that formed a monolith when set (the wall surfaces and internal arches serving structurally only until the cement hardened), Byzantine rubble was loose and depended upon wall surfaces to contain it; hence the importance of bonding courses.

Although Byzantine churches were generally plain on the exterior, a style of decorative brickwork appeared in the tenth century in buildings such as the Theotokos Church at Hosias Lukas (946–955) where sawtooth bands alternate with courses of brick imitating a Kufic (Arabic) inscription and stone framed with brick (called *cloisonné*). This revival of Roman decorative brick technique was clearly stimulated by the extraordinarily textured brick facades of Islamic buildings such as the tomb of Ismail the Samanid in Bukhara (first half of the tenth century) and the Bib Mardum Mosque in Toledo (999).

Islamic buildings rested on stone foundations (except where stone was scarce) that were sunken well below ground and rose .5 m (1.6 ft.) or more above ground. A wood frame was built on this socle, the walls filled in with mud brick or baked brick. In very tall towers, such as Gunbad-i Qabus in Gurgan (1006/07), the foundations were 11 m (36 ft.) below ground. In two-story complexes, like the buildings inside the large enclosure at Qaṣr al-Ḥayr East in Syria (begun 728/29), the lower story was stone and the upper was brick. Mortar, made of gypsum or lime, was used more to lubricate the stone during positioning than to hold it in place. A concrete of mortar and pebbles with an exterior revetment of stucco or marble panels replaced brick in the 'Abbasid period beginning in 749. The use of colored marble for dados and floors, as in the Great Mosque of Damascus (714/15) was adopted from Byzantine practice.

Islamic bricks followed the Roman and Sasanian preference for the square unit, although the unit varied in size according to time and place. Unbaked brick was made of earth trampled with an admixture of chaff, straw, and water, packed into a wooden form, baked by the sun on both sides, and used immediately. The same mud-straw mix formed the bond between brick courses. Afterward the walls were coated with mud mixed with lime for greater durability.

Terre pisé, or rammed earth, consisted of earth trampled with chaff and minimal water. The mixture was applied to the wall in large globs, each course being allowed to dry for a few days before the addition of the next layer. The walls were battered (sloped up and back) diminishing in width with height. Such apparently impermanent building materials could, with proper maintenance, prove structurally solid and durable. For example, both mud brick and *terre pisé* were used in Lashkari Bazar, the eleventh-century palace city of the Ghaznavids. Floors could also be made with the *terre pisé* technique, leveling and either beating or flooding the earth to harden its surface. A coating of lime might then be applied.

Fired brick was dried more slowly than mud brick and burned for three days in a kiln fueled with dung (wood being too scarce and expensive). Islamic ornamental brickwork, called *hazarbaf*, appeared in Syria in the eighth century in monuments such as the great gate of Raqqa (772) and was probably originally a Roman technique. The technique consisted of bricks laid in patterns, protruding and recessed to create a woven effect when light played over the surface. Often the plaster joints between bricks were ornamented with a wedge-shaped instrument pressed directly in the soft plaster, and the insertion of carved ceramic plugs and molded plaster plugs in the interstices of the bricks.

The use of glazed brick in building was an ancient Mesopotamian practice revived by the 'Abbasids at least as early as the early tenth century. Rarely were surfaces totally glazed; usually glazed and unglazed brick were used together to make lively patterns. Cut brick added to the complexity and crispness of the design. These bricks were cut and their edges ground smooth and then arranged face down in a vegetal or geometric design. Next liquid plaster was poured liberally over the reversed composition to form a glue. When dry, the whole piece was lifted, and the glazed surface was revealed in a negative ground of plaster. The tile panel was then affixed to the building interior or facade.

An important Islamic innovation in glazed ceramic was luster, an expensive technique, which nonetheless was considerably cheaper than the silver and gold it imitated. First developed for use on glass, it appears on ceramic in ninth-century Iraq. Luster consisted of the application of a silver or copper compound to a tile surface with an oxidized glaze; the tile was refired in a reduction atmosphere until the glaze began to soften and the metallic compound burned away leaving an iridescent stain ranging in color from red to golden yellow. Lusterware tiles from the 'Abbasid palace-city of Samarra were used to decorate the *mihrab* niche of the Great Mosque of Qayrawan in Tunisia (836).

Early Islamic architects often reused Roman, Visigothic, and Byzantine columns, capitals, decorative or epigraphic fragments, and sculpture. Spolia was abundantly available in abandoned Roman and fifth–sixth-century buildings, and its use probably reflected a taste for older pieces at a time in which Islam was searching for aesthetic models. Occasionally the spolia was inverted, as in the minaret of the Great Mosque of Qayrawan, where a block of stone with Latin letters was deliberately placed upside down, or used in new combinations, as in the entrance to the cistern of the

BUILDING MATERIALS: Byzantine and Islamic Periods.   Figure 1. *Great Mosque of Cordoba.* Eighth-tenth century. The red and white alternating voussoirs of the arches were derived from a Roman aqueduct in Merida and soon became a sign of royalty and legitimacy that was copied in later Islamic architecture of the Mediterranean and Near East. (Courtesy D. F. Ruggles)

Merida Alcazaba (early eighth century) in Spain, perhaps implying the superiority of Islam over older religions. Marble spolia was favored by the Umayyads but the supply ran out for 'Abbasids, who, building on a much greater scale, often resorted to stucco imitations.

Stucco was made of either ground gypsum or lime, sometimes mixed with finely ground marble, and served as a cheap substitute for carved marble. It could be modeled in three-quarter relief for engaged statuary, as in Khirbat al-Mafjar's baths (c. 739–744), carved or modeled (while soft) directly on walls and vaults (as in the mid-ninth-century palaces of Samarra) or prefabricated in carved or pierced slabs that were affixed to walls in the manner of marble. As a medium for wall decoration, stucco had the advantage of being an inexpensive material that could be worked more quickly and easily than solid stone.

Early Islamic architects preferred lavish surface decoration to structural or spatial sophistication. However, beautiful spatial effects were achieved using the arch as a rhythmically repeating element, as evident in arcades of stilted arches at the Cordoba and Qayrawan mosques (see figure 1). But although Islamic architecture is known for its vast array of arch profiles—round, pointed, stilted, and cusped—all have Byzantine precedents. Even the horseshoe arch, which dominated Islamic hypostyle architecture around the Mediterranean, appeared first in Byzantine churches of the third through sixth centuries. Two-centered parabolic arches are seen at the Byzantine church of Qsar Ibn Wardan, near Homs in Syria (561–564). Such pointed arches are structurally superior to round arches because they send the thrust downward instead of laterally, reducing the need for a counterthrust of heavy masonry and allowing taller, more stable buildings. Wooden tie beams were usually used to strengthen and support arches during construction.

Although Byzantine and Islamic walls were made of ashlar or brick or a combination thereof, the arches, vaults, and domes were all made of brick. Whereas Roman arches rested on wooden frames that were removed after the mortar was set, Muslims followed the eastern technique of building uncentered arches without frames (see figure 2). In the latter, the barrel or pointed barrel vault was built as a series of arches, each leaning on the previous one; as the sides met, the central space was filled by a brick plug that functioned like a keystone. Vaults made by this method could and did reach enormous size; an outstanding Sasanian example that was known both to Byzantine and Muslim architects was the great arch of Ctesiphon in Iraq (third–mid-sixth century?). Domes and groin vaults were built similarly but on four arches.

One important difference between Roman vaults and Byzantine and Islamic ones was the change in material. Beginning in the fourth century, a gradual transition was made from heavy concrete mass to thin membranes of brick. The result was lighter vaults with fewer supports and wider interior spans. To lessen the weight further in Byzantine buildings, inverted earthenware vases were often placed in the poured mortar of the extrados of the vault to create a light cellular mass. In early Byzantine buildings on the Italian Peninsula, vaults were made of tubular ceramic vessels laid end to end in progressively smaller courses, as was the case in the apse of S. Apollinaire Nuovo.

Early Byzantine architects experimented with huge domes spanning large unimpeded interiors. The domes rested on a system of arches, supporting half-domes, and pendentives, the latter often serving as a surface for figural representation. The first monumental Byzantine dome on four pendentives was the Hagia Sophia. Following in the footsteps of the Sasanians, Islamic builders from Iraq eastward excelled in vaulting, specifically domes and iwans (large vaulted halls open on one side, having the appearance of a monumental niche). Islamic domes generally relied on squinches (arched corners) rather than pendentives for support, the squinches contributing to the decorative articulation of the interior (see figure 3). In buildings such as the mausoleum of Ismail the

BUILDING MATERIALS: Byzantine and Islamic Periods. Figure 2. *A maqarnas vault section.* The stucco vault is suspended from above by means of a complicated system of timber hangers attached with lumps of gypsum mortar to the brick or stone structural arches—and to each other. (From G. Michell, ed., *Architecture of the Islamic World*, London, 1978, p. 142; courtesy Thames and Hudson)

BUILDING MATERIALS: Byzantine and Islamic Periods. Figure 3. *Drawing showing a series of squinches resting upon one another in the mausoleum of Umm Qulthūm. This Islamic method of bridging the gap between a square base and a circular dome takes advantage of both squinch and pendentive. (From G. Michell, ed., Architecture of the Islamic World, London, 1978, p. 142; courtesy Thames and Hudson)*

Samanid, four squinches alternate with four arches, above which is a sixteen-sided band, the whole forming a perfectly conceived zone of transition from square base to diminutive dome.

The many shared building practices and materials of Byzantium and Islam is explained by their history and geography. Both societies received significant legacies from imperial Roman architecture and were essentially Mediterranean societies that confronted and competed with each other in the Levant. Until after the Islamic conquest of Constantinople in 1453, Byzantium amply provided Islam with typological models, building techniques, and methods of decoration; in contrast, Islam's contribution to Byzantine architecture was less significant and principally in the area of nonfigural decoration.

BIBLIOGRAPHY

Choisy, Auguste. *L'art de bâtir chez les Byzantines*. Paris, 1883. Outdated in some respects but still fundamental.

Creswell, K. A. C. *Early Muslim Architecture*. 2 vols. 2d ed. Oxford, 1969. Essential, detailed survey of the architectural method, style, and typological development in the first three centuries of Islamic architecture.

Creswell, K. A. C. *A Short Account of Early Muslim Architecture*. Rev. ed. Aldershot, 1989. Useful updated abridgment of the original.

Davey, Norman. *A History of Building Materials*. New York, 1971. Describes construction materials and techniques from antiquity to the nineteenth century. Excellent descriptions but historically nonspecific.

Downey, Glanville. "Byzantine Architects: Their Training and Methods." *Byzantion* 18 (1948): 99–118. Definitive study of the role of the architect, based on Greek texts.

Grabar, Oleg, and Renata Holod. "A Tenth-Century Source for Architecture." In *Harvard Ukrainian Studies, Eucharisterion: Studies Presented to Omelian Pritsak* 3–4 (1979–1980): 310–317. Discusses the paucity of primary sources on Islamic architecture and examines a rare description of building practice in Khurasan.

Hassan, Ahmad Y. al-, and Donald Hill. *Islamic Technology: An Illustrated History*. Cambridge, 1986. Basic but useful source.

Hill, Donald. *A History of Engineering in Classical and Medieval Times*. LaSalle, Ill., 1984. Basic but useful source.

Krautheimer, Richard. *Early Christian and Byzantine Architecture*. 3d ed. Harmondsworth, 1981. Standard and authoritative work.

Lewcock, Ronald. "Architects, Craftsmen, and Builders: Materials and Techniques." In *Architecture of the Islamic World*, edited by George Michell, pp. 112–143. London, 1978. Useful description of Islamic building based on a study of "traditional" methods practiced today.

Mango, Cyril. *Byzantine Architecture*. New York, 1976. Chapter 2 presents an excellent description of materials and methods in Byzantine construction.

Mayer, Leo. *Islamic Architects and Their Works*. Geneva, 1956. Begins with a brief but important discussion of the nomenclature for architects.

Ward-Perkins, J. B. "Notes on the Structure and Building Methods of Early Byzantine Architecture." In *The Great Palace of the Byzantine Emperors: Second Report*, edited by David Talbot Rice, pp. 52–104. Edinburgh, 1958. Useful for the early period.

Wilber, Donald N. "Builders and Craftsmen of Islamic Iran: The Earlier Periods." *Art and Archaeology Research Papers*, no. 10 (December 1976): 31–39.

Wulff, Hans E. *The Traditional Crafts of Persia*. Cambridge, Mass., 1966. Ethnographic study of traditional building methods in Iran, not always historically reliable but essential nonetheless.

D. Fairchild Ruggles

BULL SITE, located on the ridge of Daharat et-Tawila, in the northern Samaria hills, east of Dothan (map reference 1807 × 2016). The chance discovery of a fine bronze figurine (18 cm long) showing a zebu bull, lent this site its name (see figure 1). Excavations carried out at the site between 1978 and 1981 by Amihai Mazar under the auspices of the Hebrew University of Jerusalem revealed what appears to be a unique example of a *bāmâ*, or "high place," dated to about 1200 BCE. This is a single-period site, with only one structure: a circular enclosure surrounded by a wall constructed of large stones about 20 m in diameter. The wall is

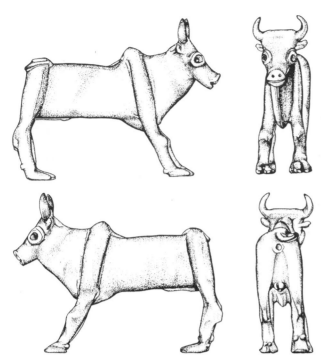

BULL SITE. Figure 1. *Drawings of the bronze bull figurine.* (Courtesy ASOR Archives)

poorly preserved as a result of erosion. The bedrock is exposed in most of the enclosure except on the east, where a standing stone is fronted by a small paved area that may be interpreted as a *maṣṣēbâ*. There may have been a sacred tree at the center of the enclosure. The site is thus a unique illustration of a Canaanite-style high place, like those mentioned frequently in the Bible (*1 Sm.* 9: 13; *Dt.* 12: 2), and the bull figurine may have served an important cultic function. While the bull is known as the attribute and symbol of both El and Baal, the main Canaanite gods, it was also adopted by the northern tribes of Israel as a symbol of Yahweh (e.g., the golden calves Jeroboam set up in the temples at Dan and Bethel). The Bull Site may thus have been a high place serving the cluster of Iron Age I sites found in archaeological surveys in the vicinity. These sites represent what is generally identified as part of the wave of initial Israelite settlement in the central hill country of Palestine.

BIBLIOGRAPHY

Mazar, Amihai. "The 'Bull Site': An Iron Age I Open Cult Place." *Bulletin of the American Schools of Oriental Research*, no. 247 (1982): 27–42.

AMIHAI MAZAR

BURIAL SITES. In the ancient Near East, burial grounds usually reflected either tribal or familial affiliations (tribal in less complex societies and familial in more com-

plex, more urbanized societies). Most large settlements were surrounded by cemeteries, but many societies maintained practices of intramural burial—in prehistoric periods and the Middle Bronze Age in the southern Levant, and throughout preclassical history in Mesopotamia. Successive interment of the dead in a particular burial site from one "period" to the next (as defined by material culture) most probably testifies to continuity in settlement as well. The reuse of Intermediate Bronze Age shaft tombs in the Middle Bronze Age and Late Bronze Age for example (see below) may point to long-term lineage stability and cultural continuity. Cemeteries of rural agriculturalists and pastoralists that featured conspicuous tomb monuments such as dolmens or tumuli may have served as territorial markers.

The meager human skeletal remains ascribed to the Paleolithic, Epipaleolithic, and Early Neolithic periods originate chiefly in subfloor contexts of cave, hut, or village occupations. From the Neolithic onward, a combination of intramural and extramural interment was normative for sedentary occupation in Syria and Mesopotamia, although the intramural aspect is often better represented archaeologically. By the Chalcolithic period, part of the mortuary process (secondary burial of defleshed bones for the most part) had moved beyond the limits of settlement, and the concept of a necropolis separate from the domicile became firmly established in the southern Levant, as can be seen at sites such as Shiqmim, Ghassul-Adeimeh, and the necropoli on the southern coastal plain. Infants continued to be buried beneath the surfaces of rooms and courtyards, but more mature individuals were interred in burial circles (Shiqmim), in pits around and within mortuary temples (Gilat), around elite tombs (Kissufim), in cist tombs (Adeimeh), and in rock-hewn and cave tombs along the coastal plain (Hadera, Azor, Ben-Shemen), in the highlands (Naḥal Qanah), and in the Judean Desert.

In the southern Levant, Early Bronze Age cemeteries seem to lie almost exclusively beyond settlement limits. Some burial sites—highland cave tombs in particular—show continuity in utilization from the Chalcolithic to the Early Bronze Age (at Naḥal Qanah, Beit Sahur). At Byblos, too, subfloor, intramural burial—particularly in large jars—seems to carry through. The circles, stone constructed grave or *nawamis*, in the Sinai Desert have been dated to EB I, but the *nawamis* cemeteries probably date back to the Chalcolithic as well. In the burial grounds on the east bank of the southern Jordan Valley, the Chalcolithic cist-tomb tradition seems to give way to the tumulus and dolmen tradition in more pastoralist societies. In a more sedentary context, at Bab edh-Dhraʿ, early EB I shaft tombs were gradually supplanted by above-surface, round burial structures (EB Ib–EB II) and finally by large rectangular "charnel houses" (EB III). In the EB IV, the shaft-tomb tradition was revived. However, the Bab edh-Dhraʿ above-surface burial structures and the length of the burial sequence are unique thus far for the Early Bronze Age.

One of the hallmarks of the Intermediate Bronze Age in the southern Levant is the existence of large cemeteries of shaft, dolmen, or tumulus tombs often associated with the small, non-nucleated settlements characteristic of this period (at Dhahr Mirzbaneh, Jebel Qaʿaqir). In the central highlands this phenomenon was maintained into the Middle Bronze Age (many of the IB cemeteries show continued use) and the Late Bronze Age (when cave tombs containing multiple, successive burials seem to have been the norm—e g , at Dothan, Shechem, Jerusalem). From the Iron Age onward, burial sites are generally allied with settlements, aside from bedouin cemeteries in marginal zones.

In the Middle and Late Bronze Age of the southern Levant both extramural and intramural burial were practiced, sometimes coinciding in the same settlement, as, for example, at Megiddo and Jericho. It has been suggested that intramural burial was reintroduced from the northern Levant, where the practice had never died out. Some sites seem to show either exclusively intramural (Tel Dan) or extramural (Tel Nagila) interment; however, most settlements of the second millennium BCE possess subfloor jar burials of infants, regardless of whether their main cemetery is extra- or intramural.

The above features persevere into the Early Iron Age in the lowland sites of the southern Levant, where the material culture shows continuity from previous periods. The hill country sites of the "Israelite" type are oddly lacking in burial sites, it is generally suggested that normative burial practices changed, shifting to simple inhumation in the earth or rock-heap burials without offerings. In the first millennium BCE, burial sites are comprised of rock-hewn tombs beyond settlement bounds. Contemporary biblical references imply the social status inherent in tomb ownership (e.g., *Is.* 22, 57) and indicate the prohibition against intramural inhumation by excepting royalty (*1 Kgs.* 2:10, 11:43; *2 Chr.* 9:31). One of the largest and best-known first-millennium BCE necropoli in the southern Levant is in Jerusalem, most of whose Iron Age tombs were carved into the malleable limestone scarps and layers to its east and north, though some of the later Iron Age tombs were placed to the west as well (e.g., Ketef Hinnom, Mamilla). [*See* Necropolis.] The number of known tombs and skeletons from this necropolis cannot account for the city's total population, and it is assumed that only the social elite could afford or were permitted such tombs. [*See* Demography.] It was also during this period that the city's cemetery became inextricably linked with both quarrying and water storage. Quarries became convenient venues for tomb carving, and tombs were often reused as cisterns or reservoirs. [*See* Cisterns; Reservoirs.] These patterns continued into modern times.

The Iron Age cemeteries in the Phoenician cultural sphere (e.g., at ʿAtlit, Achziv, Tyre, and on Cyprus) featured shaft and cist tombs and cremations in kraters. At Achziv these different tomb types seem to be organized in groupings (by kin?), sometimes enclosed by a wall. They can include above-surface tomb construction; funerary stelae *(maṣṣēbôt)* and altars; perforations in roofs; and extramural, postburial offerings, all of which point to ancestor veneration (or other interaction) and beliefs in an afterlife.

The cemeteries of the Persian period initially continue Iron Age traditions. They are uniformly located outside settlements but generally in close association with them. Most of the known cemeteries of this period, and certainly the largest ones, are found on the Levantine and Cypriot coasts at sites such as ʿAin Hilweh, Achziv, ʿAtlit, and Tell el-Farʿah (South) and Tsambres and Aphendrika, respectively. The dominant tomb type in this coastal "Phoenician" tradition is the shaft tomb. Other cemeteries, more often inland (at Gezer in Palestine, Kamid el-Loz in Lebanon, and Til Barsip and Ur in Mesopotamia) are characterized by cist tombs or pit graves.

Of the many and often extensive Syro-Palestinian Hellenistic-, Roman-, and Byzantine-period necropoli, several have been studied and reported on in depth: Palmyra, Jericho, Jerusalem, Petra, Beth-Sheʿarim, and Mareshah (Marisa). Other important necropoli have been underexcavated, underreported, and/or widely plundered or damaged: Gaza, Ashkelon, Beth-Shean, Caesarea, Sepphoris, Tiberias, and Caesarea Phillipi (Banias). Starting with this period, chalk seems to have been a favored material in which to quarry out cave or chamber tombs with loculi (burial niches) and/ or arcosolia (recessed, arched benches or troughs)—in Jerusalem, Beth-Guvrin, and Beth-Sheʿarim. Where large chalk exposures were not immediately available or convenient, constructed cist tombs and mausolea were more common (e.g., Akko, Beth-Shean, Neapolis, Caesarea, Reḥovot in the Negev, Gush-Ḥalav, Mesillot). The great necropolis at Palmyra included very large and ornate tomb structures of three kinds: subterranean hypogea with loculi (the most frequent), tower tombs (originally perhaps serving as monuments for hypogea) and atrium tombs (the least frequent). [*See* Mausoleum.]

During the Late Roman and Byzantine periods, great catacombs developed at Beth-Sheʿarim and Beth-Guvrin that included large halls and corridors filled with numerous arcosolia, burial troughs, and sarcophagi. Those at Beth-Sheʿarim were intended for the interment of Jews from afar, as well as for local denizens, but by this time kinship was not a prerequisite. Their cosmopolitan decoration includes figurative portrayals and multilingual inscriptions. The Beth-Guvrin catacombs, in contrast, show little decoration and almost no figurative art. They also accommodated an admixture of Jewish and Christian interment. Several cemeteries of this period reveal structures and tables for the preparation and consumption of funerary meals (e.g., at Elusa [Ḥaluṣa] and Gerasa [Jerash]). Beyond the limits of large cities, at both Beth-Shean and Gerasa, for example, large, ornate tomb monuments and mausolea lined the main roads, as they did the Appian Way in Rome.

It is still an open question for most periods as to whether known burial sites represent the dead of an entire population, with all its attendant social statuses, or only its elite. In cemeteries associated with large settlements, the total number of tombs and skeletons seldom corresponds to total populations calculated over long periods of occupation. This may indicate that only part of the population was interred in the associated cemetery and lead to the inference of a measure of social stratification. In cemeteries in frontier zones not clearly associated with settlements—or only with lower ranking settlements—a more egalitarian order may be expressed and a larger proportion of the total population represented. Tomb type and decoration have been used to determine class division (wealthy, middle, and poor classes) at Roman Abila in Jordan, though such claims can only be substantiated by further evidence. Other cemeteries may reflect particular ideologies or lifestyles—examples being the simple cist burials at Qumran or the interments of Byzantine monks in caves scattered throughout the Judean desert, both of which reveal a predominance of males.

[See also Burial Techniques; Catacombs; Cave Tombs; Cist Graves; Dolmen; Grave Goods; and Tombs. In addition, many of the sites mentioned are the subject of independent entries.]

BIBLIOGRAPHY

Bloch-Smith, Elizabeth. *Judahite Burial Practices and Beliefs about the Dead*. Journal for the Study of the Old Testament, Supplement 123. Sheffield, 1992. Comprehensive study of Iron Age burial practices, tomb form, and mortuary ideology in Judah, with a strong biblical emphasis.

Campbell, S., and A. Green, eds. *The Archaeology of Death in the Ancient Near East*. Oxford, 1994. Articles dealing with mortuary practices from prehistory to the modern era, including a trove of new data.

Gonen, Rivka. *Burial Patterns and Cultural Diversity in Late Bronze Age Canaan*. American Schools of Oriental Research, Dissertation Series, 7. Winona Lake, Ind., 1992. Synthetic analysis that chiefly covers tomb typology and patterns of geographical distribution, but little analysis of grave goods or belief systems.

Hachlili, Rachel. *Ancient Jewish Art and Archaeology in the Land of Israel*. Leiden, 1988. See chapter 4, "Funerary Customs and Art," for a good synopsis of late Second Temple period burial practices; weak on Jewish mortuary behavior of the later Roman and Byzantine periods.

Rahmani, L. Y. "Ancient Jerusalem's Funerary Customs and Tombs." *Biblical Archaeologist* 44 (1981): 171–177, 229–235; 45 (1982): 43–53, 109–119. Delves into religious beliefs and the social and psychological setting of burial, in addition to illuminating the evolution of the Jerusalem necropolis archaeologically.

Stern, Ephraim. *Material Culture of the Land of the Bible in the Persian Period, 538–332 B.C.* Warminster, 1982. Contains a typological, geographical, and chronological analysis of Persian-period tomb forms and burial goods.

Zohar, Mattanyah. "Megalithic Cemeteries in the Levant." In *Pastoralism in the Levant: Archaeological Materials in Anthropological Perspectives*, edited by Ofer Bar-Yosef and Anatoly Khazanov, pp. 43–63. Madison, Wis., 1992. The most up-to-date synthesis of megalithic burial fields in the Levant that also attempts a socioecological explanation.

DAVID ILAN

BURIAL TECHNIQUES. The consistent pattern for ancient Syro-Palestinian burial techniques is the practice of multiple burials—both primary and secondary—in subterranean chambers. Despite periodic changes in tomb architecture and methods of interment, the prevailing custom was to bury family members together in an underground cave. Early Bronze shaft graves held single burials. Middle Bronze tombs were larger circular underground chambers containing multiple primary and secondary burials, as well as miscellaneous grave goods—including jewelry, pots, jars, and juglets (representative sites include Gibeon and Jericho). The custom of multiple burial in small caves of this type continued into the Iron Age, albeit with slight architectural improvements—plastered walls and flooring (at Lachish, for example).

Significant changes in both tomb architecture and methods of interment occurred during the Iron Age, with the appearance of the "bench" tomb, an underground chamber with waist-high benches around three sides, entered by a stairway (e.g. the St. Etienne tombs in Jerusalem). Often, the area under one of the benches was hollowed out as a repository for secondary burial: corpses were laid on the benches to decompose, and when desiccation was complete, the bones were gathered into the repository. Over time, the repository came to hold the bones of a family's ancestors, a fact vividly captured in the biblical idiom "to be gathered to one's fathers" (2 Kgs. 22:20 and elsewhere). Bench tombs and secondary burial remained characteristic into the sixth century BCE.

The conquest of Syria-Palestine by the Persians, Greeks, and Romans introduced foreign cultures and brought about changes in burial techniques, but the tradition of multiple burial in underground chambers was not erased. Cist graves, individual graves lined with stone slabs, appeared when the exiles returned from Babylon in the sixth century BCE and during the Roman occupation. Wooden coffins and stone sarcophagi were used during the Hellenistic and Roman periods (exemplary specimens of each have been found at Jericho and on Mt. Scopus), but burial within niches in the walls of subterranean chambers was more typical. Two types of Greco-Roman niches proliferated during the Roman period (37 BCE–323 CE): the arcosolium, a broad, arch-shaped shelf carved along the wall of a cave, used for primary burial (e.g. the Tomb of the Kings in Jerusalem, and the tombs at Khirbet Shema'), and the koḥ, a deep, narrow slot carved perpendicular to the cave wall for primary or secondary burial (e.g., the "Caiaphas" tomb in Jerusalem and the "Goliath" tomb in Jericho). In *kokhim* caves in the Roman period, ossuaries or other repositories—pits, niches, and even separate chambers and charnel rooms—were frequently used for secondary burial. These various forms of secondary burial are illustrated by Jason's Tomb, the first-century tombs at Jericho, the cemetery at Dominus Flevit, and the excavated tomb at Meiron.

Ancient Syro-Palestinian concepts of the afterlife cohere closely with these burial techniques. The Israelites, for example, called the afterlife *Sheol* and described it as a dark underground place where the souls of the dead reposed (*Gn.* 37:35; *Jb.* 17:13; and elsewhere)—not unlike Bronze and Iron Age subterranean burial caves. During the Roman period, beliefs in the resurrection of the body and expiation by decomposition motivated the widespread practice of secondary burial, especially in ossuaries. Syro-Palestinian burial techniques never included efforts to preserve flesh through mummification, a practice known in Egypt as early as 2600 BCE.

[See also Burial Sites; Ossuary; *and* Sarcophagus.]

BIBLIOGRAPHY

Bloch-Smith, Elizabeth. *Judahite Burial Practices and Beliefs about the Dead.* Journal for the Study of the Old Testament, Supplement 123. Sheffield, 1992. Exemplary study of Iron Age burial techniques, particularly of the development and use of the bench tomb.
Greenhut, Zvi. "The 'Caiaphas' Tomb in North Talpiyot, Jerusalem." *'Atiqot* 21 (1992): 63–71. Report from a recent excavation of an Early Roman period tomb containing ossuaries, including one marked with the name *Caiaphas*.
Meyers, Eric M. "Secondary Burials in Palestine." *Biblical Archaeologist* 33.1 (1970): 2–29. The most comprehensive survey of the practice of secondary burial, including all the relevant periods and sites as well as beliefs about afterlife.
Rahmani, L. Y. "Ancient Jerusalem's Funerary Customs and Tombs." *Biblical Archaeologist* 44.3 (1981): 171–177; 44.4 (1981): 229–235; 45.1 (1982): 43–53; 45.2 (1982): 109–119. Readable four-part series by the dean of Israeli tomb archaeologists, with a useful bibliography. Covers only the area in and around Jerusalem.
Spencer, A. Jeffrey. *Death in Ancient Egypt.* New York, 1982. Lively introduction to the archaeology of Egyptian burial practices, particularly mummification.

BYRON R. MCCANE

BURROWS, MILLAR (1889–1990), biblical scholar and theologian. A professor of Bible at Brown University (1934–1938) and of biblical theology at Yale University (1934–1958), Burrows also served as director of the American School of Oriental Research (ASOR) in Jerusalem (1931–1932, 1947–1948) and as president of ASOR (Jerusalem and Baghdad, 1934–1948). His dissertation, "The Literary Relations of Ezekiel" (Yale University, 1925), was printed privately. He completed and edited the last volume of C. F. Kent's *Student's Old Testament* (*Proverbs, Job,* and *Ecclesiastes*). His *Founders of Great Religions* (1931) presents

sketches of the lives and teachings of leaders of the world's major religions. Burrows excavated in the ASOR garden in Jerusalem, where he uncovered Byzantine tombs (1932). His 1941 work, *What Mean These Stones?*, on the purpose of archaeology and its relation to the Bible and the history of culture, remains a landmark in the field. His work on the Dead Sea Scrolls, published in 1955, was a best seller and translated into many languages; its sequel (1958) was equally successful. Eschewing sensationalism, these scholarly, balanced studies deal with all the material available at the time.

Burrows contributed to the Revised Standard Version (RSV) of the Hebrew Bible. In its ongoing correction and revision, his *Diligently Compared* (1964) presents numerous discrepancies previously overlooked. His last book, *Jesus in the First Three Gospels* (1977), is a masterly survey of the content of the Synoptic Gospels, with critical comment and an appraisal of scholarly opinions.

In 1961, Burrows was awarded an honorary degree by Yale. The opening sentence of the citation appropriately praised his career: "As archaeologist of the Near East and master of its language, as a friend of both Jews and Arabs, as interpreter of the Dead Sea Scrolls and translator of the Revised Standard Version of the Bible, you have made a notable contribution to the life and learning of our time."

BIBLIOGRAPHY

Burrows, Millar. "The Byzantine Tombs in the Garden of the Jerusalem School." *Bulletin of the American Schools of Oriental Research,* no. 47 (1932): 28–35.
Burrows, Millar. *What Mean These Stones? The Significance of Archeology for Biblical Studies.* New York, 1941.
Burrows, Millar. *An Outline of Biblical Theology.* Philadelphia, 1946.
Burrows, Millar. *The Dead Sea Scrolls.* New York, 1955.
Burrows, Millar. *More Light on the Dead Sea Scrolls.* New York, 1958.
Burrows, Millar. *Diligently Compared: The Revised Standard Version and the King James Version of the Old Testament.* London, 1964.
Burrows, Millar. *Jesus in the First Three Gospels.* Nashville, 1977.
Hyatt, J. Philip, and Raymond P. Morris. "A Bibliography of Millar Burrows' Works." In *Essays in Honour of Millar Burrows,* pp. 87–96. Leiden, 1959.
Pope, Marvin H. "Millar Burrows, 1889–1990, in Memoriam." *Biblical Archaeologist* 44.2 (1991): 116–121.

MARVIN H. POPE

BUSEIRAH, site located about 10 km (6 mi.) south of Tafila, 4 km (2.5 mi.) west of the King's Highway, and 45 km (28 mi.) north of Petra in modern Jordan (31°10′ N, 35°40′ E; map reference 208 × 018). Lying to the north of the present-day village, the ancient site, on a spur running north-northwest along the 1,100-meter contour line, is dominated by a mound about 3,200 sq m in area. It is surrounded on three sides by deep ravines and is connected to the main land mass only to the south. Feinan, the largest copper-production area in the southern Levant, heavily exploited during the Iron Age, is to its southwest, which helps to explain Buseirah's importance.

The modern site of Buṣeirah was first identified with biblical Bozrah by Ulrich Jasper Seetzen, following his trip to the southern end of the Dead Sea in 1806 (*Reisen durch Syrien, Palästina, Phönicien, Transjordan-länder, Arabia Petraea und Unter-Aegypten*, Berlin, 1854–1859). However, there is no inscriptional evidence to confirm or deny this equation. Bozrah as a city of Edom appears several times in the Hebrew Bible (*Gn.* 36:33; *1 Chr.* 1:44; *Am.* 1:12; *Is.* 34:6, 63:1; *Jer.* 49:13, 22). It may well have been Edom's capital, al-

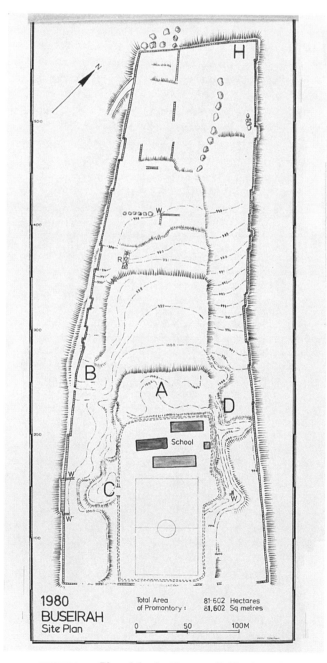

BUṢEIRAH. *Plan of the site* (Courtesy P. Bienkowski)

though this is not explicitly stated anywhere. The prophet Amos predicted Bozrah's overthrow, which was taken as symbolic of the defeat of powerful Edom and of God's vengeance on his enemies (*Am.* 1:12). Two other places named Bozrah exist, one in Moab and one in the Hauran, the latter a provincial capital of Roman Arabia.

Nelson Glueck was the first to survey Buṣeirah. He at first thought the site was small and that its major occupation was in the Nabatean period. For this reason, he felt that the identification of Buṣeirah with biblical Bozrah was problematic and instead identified Tawilan with Bozrah ("Explorations in Eastern Palestine and the Negev," *Bulletin of the American Schools of Oriental Research* 55 [1934]: 14). [*See* Tawilan.] Later, though, he changed his mind and accepted the equation Buṣeirah = Bozrah (*Explorations in Eastern Palestine* 2. Annual of the American Schools of Oriental Research 15 [1935]: 83). The size of the site and the nature of the remains, more impressive than any other Iron Age site in Edom, together with the apparent preservation of the ancient name, make the identification reasonably secure.

Crystal-M. Bennett excavated at Buṣeirah from 1971 to 1974 and again in 1980. Her four principal reasons for excavating the site were its probable identification with biblical Bozrah; the passages in *Numbers* 20 that tell of the king refusing passage through his land to the Israelites, an event generally dated to about 1230 BCE; Buṣeirah's proximity to Feinan; and Buṣeirah's seeming the most likely site to provide the first chronological sequence for Edom.

Bennett's excavations revealed a major Edomite site dating to the Iron II period, and possibly continuing into the Persian period (c. seventh–sixth or fifth centuries BCE), with some evidence of reuse in the Nabatean and Roman periods. Iron II Buṣeirah was a substantial administrative center dominated by two or three large buildings and fortified by a town wall. The area excavated probably embraced only the central part of the ancient city, the rest being hidden under the modern village to the south. No water source has been found within the site; the water supply probably came from the 'Ain Jenin spring about one kilometer to the east.

Bennett excavated four main areas: A–D, and a small sounding, area H. Area A, the highest point on the site, has a palatial and/or temple building in two main phases built on a deep fill or mound. Building B, the earlier phase, had overall dimensions of 77 × 38 m, with two entrances on the northeast, both off-center and approached by a ramp. In the main central courtyard water flowed into a cistern through one or two drains, one emerging from another room. At the end of the courtyard was a flight of shallow steps, flanked by plinths which may have served as the bases of two columns. The steps led into a long narrow room. All the floors and walls were plastered. There was some evidence for a mud-brick superstructure. Building B shows evidence of destruction by fire.

Building A was built on top of building B but was smaller

(48 × 36 m). It had a large central space surrounded by rooms or corridors. The corners of the exterior walls seem to curve outward—hence, its colloquial title, the Winged Building. The main entrance was now on the opposite, southwest, side. Building A also showed evidence of destruction by fire.

Buildings B and A have a generic similarity to the so-called Assyrian open-court buildings in Palestine and to Neo-Assyrian palaces and residencies in Mesopotamia and the North Syrian provinces, both in plan and in their being situated on a raised artificial citadel. These resemblances strongly suggest that the Buseirah buildings should be considered palaces, even though they do not necessarily attest to direct influence from Assyria. The battered enclosure wall traced between areas A and B suggests a deliberate division into upper and lower towns.

Area B, adjacent to area A to the southwest, consisted of ordinary domestic buildings, a postern, and a section of the town wall. No complete plans of the buildings were recovered, and the stratigraphy is very complex on the uneven bedrock. The impression is of a series of rebuildings of individual houses, not of unified building phases. The stone town wall in area B is 3.80 m high and pierced by a small gate. It may be a casemate wall, but the evidence is inconclusive: the "casemates" may be later Iron Age houses built over the wall. The gate was blocked in the final phase and the whole area used as a pottery dump.

Area C lies southeast of area A and measures about 67 × 105 m. It contained a monumental building with a bathhouse that bears some similarity to the area A complex, although its complete plan was not recovered. Its two main phases include a large quantity of pottery from stratified contexts (once analyzed, it may prove to be significant to understanding the repertoire of Edomite pottery). The later phase contained a cooking pot dated to the Persian period. This is so far the only direct evidence from Buseirah for continuity of occupation into the Persian period. The similarity of the town plans in areas C and A led Bennett to suggest that the later phase in area A may also have continued into the Persian period.

Area D, adjacent to area A to the northeast, apparently was also residential, again with no complete plan recovered. The two small trenches Bennett excavated have a stratified sequence of three phases. However, the stratified pottery does not enable meaningful conclusions: there is a low incidence of painted Iron II pottery in the earliest phases, but this may be related to the low sample size.

A small sounding in area H, in the far northeast corner of the site, revealed a massive wall about 4 m wide of coursed rubble with a rubble core. A later phase of the wall appears to be Roman.

Taken as a whole, there appear to be several major architectural phases at Buseirah, although each area and trench has distinct subphases.

1. *Phase 1.* The earliest town wall in area B is impossible to date accurately; it may be no earlier than the seventh century BCE.

2. *Phase 2.* The possible casemate town wall in area B, building B in area A, and the earlier building in area C appear to date to the seventh century BCE.

3. *Phase 3.* There is an intermediate phase between buildings B and A in area A.

4. *Phase 4.* The later building in area C, and possibly building A in area A, may date to the Persian period, or continue into it.

5. *Phase 5.* Following the possible Persian period occupation, the site was abandoned. An inscribed Nabatean altar and scatters of Roman sherds from the first/second centuries CE, possibly connected to some rebuilding, are the only evidence of later reuse.

The major buildings at Buseirah remain unique in Edom, although they fit the pattern of palace plans known from Mesopotamia, Syria, and Palestine in the Late Iron Age. They are probably to be interpreted as an example of selective borrowing by the kings of Edom and suggest that Buseirah was indeed their royal city. However, the excavations revealed little evidence of luxury items. Only a small number of inscribed ostraca, seals, weights, and seal impressions on pottery were recovered, all of which were dated to about 700 BCE. The painted pottery from Buseirah is particularly fine and certainly has the widest repertoire of forms in Edom.

The dates of occupation at Buseirah are subject to revision by future discoveries. Much of this uncertainty hinges on the dating of Iron II pottery in Edom. While the pottery from Buseirah cannot at present be dated earlier than the seventh century BCE, an earlier date, perhaps in the eighth or even ninth centuries, cannot be conclusively excluded. There is no Iron I pottery from Buseirah, so a date earlier than 1000 BCE is definitely excluded. The end of occupation at Buseirah is similarly uncertain. Although the Iron II period traditionally ends with the Persian conquest in 539 BCE, the current understanding of Iron II pottery in Transjordan suggests that it continued largely unchanged into the Persian period. If this was so, occupation at Buseirah may have continued beyond the sixth century BCE, perhaps down to about 400 BCE.

[See also Edom; Feinan; *and the biography of Bennett.*]

BIBLIOGRAPHY

Bartlett, John R. *Edom and the Edomites.* Sheffield, 1989. Most up-to-date and comprehensive work on the Edomites, including critical evaluation of the data on Buseirah and Bozrah.

Bennett, Crystal-M. "Excavations at Buseirah." *Levant* 5 (1973): 1–11; 6 (1974): 1–24; 7 (1975): 1–19; 9 (1977): 1–10. Preliminary reports that should now be read in conjunction with the reappraisals by Bienkowski (below).

Bennett, Crystal-M. "Excavations at Buseirah (Biblical Bozrah)." In *Midian, Moab, and Edom: The History and Archaeology of Late Bronze* and Iron Age Jordan and North-West Arabia, edited by John F. A. Sawyer and David J. A. Clines, pp. 9–17. Sheffield, 1983. General overview.

Bienkowski, Piotr. "Umm el-Biyara, Tawilan, and Buṣeirah in Retrospect." Levant 22 (1990): 91–109. Reevaluates the excavations ten years after the last season and suggests slight changes in the dating proposed by the excavator (see pp. 101–103).

Bienkowski, Piotr. "The Date of Sedentary Occupation in Edom: Evidence from Umm el-Biyara, Tawilan, and Buseirah." In Early Edom and Moab: The Beginning of the Iron Age in Southern Jordan, edited by Piotr Bienkowski, pp. 99–112. Sheffield, 1992. Surveys the evidence for the earliest Iron Age occupation at Buṣeirah (see pp. 101–104).

Oakeshott, Marion F. "The Edomite Pottery." In Midian, Moab, and Edom: The History and Archaeology of Late Bronze and Iron Age Jordan and North-West Arabia, edited by John F. A. Sawyer and David J. A. Clines, pp. 53–63. Sheffield, 1983. Useful overview of the repertoire of pottery from Edom, and particularly that from Buṣeirah.

Puech, Émile. "Documents épigraphiques de Buṣeirah." Levant 9 (1977): 11–20. Preliminary report.

PIOTR BIENKOWSKI

BUTLER, HOWARD CROSBY (1872–1922), prominent American archaeologist and architectural historian. Butler became a professor of art and archaeology at Princeton University in 1905 and in 1920 was named the first director of its School of Architecture. In 1899–1900 he led a survey expedition to north-central Syria, where he located all of the monuments that had been noted earlier by the Marquis de Vogüé, in addition to many more, mostly Roman and Early Christian structures of the first century BCE to the seventh century CE. In subsequent expeditions (1904–1905, 1909), he studied the more important sites in detail and explored southern Syria, particularly Philadelphia (Amman, in modern Jordan), and the Nabatean sites in the Hauran, such as Suweida and Seeia, which yielded numerous inscriptions and sculptures. Butler contributed several volumes to the two publication series resulting from these expeditions: Publications of an American Archaeological Expedition to Syria in 1899–1900 (1903); and Publications of the Princeton University Archaeological Expedition to Syria in 1904–1905 and 1909 (1907–1920).

At the invitation of the Ottoman authorities, Butler excavated at Sardis, the capital of Lydia, from 1910 to 1914, with a brief season in 1922. Excavation of the city of Croesus, particularly the famous temple of Artemis, attracted worldwide attention. Butler inaugurated the Publications of the American Society for the Excavation of Sardis (1922). A later monograph in this series appeared posthumously (1925).

Butler's pioneering success cleared the way for American archaeology in Syria and Turkey. A popular teacher, he emphasized practical studies of architectural technique. In addition to his major works, he authored several popular books.

[See also Amman; Sardis; and Suweida.]

BIBLIOGRAPHY

Butler, Howard Crosby. Scotland's Ruined Abbeys. New York, 1899. Leisurely, anecdotal survey with engraved illustrations.

Butler, Howard Crosby. The Story of Athens: A Record of the Life and Art of the City of the Violet Crown Read in Its Ruins and in the Lives of Great Athenians. New York, 1902. Athens from mythological to modern times. Dated.

Butler, Howard Crosby. Architecture and Other Arts. Publications of an American Archaeological Expedition to Syria in 1899–1900, Part 2. New York, 1903. Selective survey of pre-Roman, Roman, and early Christian architecture of southern and south-central Syria, with notes on sculpture, mosaics, and wall paintings.

Butler, Howard Crosby. Ancient Architecture in Syria. 2 vols. Publications of the Princeton University Archaeological Expedition to Syria, 1904–1905 and 1909, Division 2. Leiden, 1907–1920. Results of surveys and excavations at several sites in southern and north-central Syria, including Seeia, Amman, Bosra, and Umm el-Jimal, with emphasis on Nabatean, Roman, and early Christian architecture. Numerous plans and drawings, including some fanciful reconstructions.

Butler, Howard Crosby. Sardis: The Excavations, 1910–1914. Publications of the American Society for the Excavation of Sardis, vol. 1.1. Leiden, 1922. Foundation for later research at Sardis (Harvard-Cornell excavations, 1958–). Devoted primarily to excavation of the Temple of Artemis, but also Lycian and Roman tombs.

Butler, Howard Crosby. The Temple of Artemis. 2 vols. Publications of the American Society for the Excavation of Sardis, vol. 2.1. Leiden, 1925. Still the basic work on the architecture, but the historical conclusions (archaic and Persian phases) have now been discredited.

Collins, V. Lansing, ed. Howard Crosby Butler, 1872–1922. Princeton, 1923. Includes full bibliography.

J. MICHAEL PADGETT

BYBLOS, seaport located in Lebanon, on the eastern coast of the Mediterranean Sea, at the foot of the Lebanese mountains 60 km (25 mi.) north of Beirut on the Tripoli highway, (approx. 34° N, 36° E). The site has been known throughout its long history in several variants on its name: in modern Arabic as Jebail, Jebeil, Jubail; by the Crusaders as Gibelet; in biblical Hebrew as Gebal (1 Kgs. 5:18, 32; Ez. 27:9; Jos. 13:5); in Egyptian as kbn, kpny, kbny; and in Babylonian as Gubla. The Greeks probably gave the city its name at about the end of the second millennium BCE—the Greek bublos, "papyrus scroll." Egyptian papyrus came to Greece through Phoenicia and Byblos for transshipment to the Aegean area. The English word Bible is derived through medieval Latin from the Greek ta Biblia, "the books." [See Papyrus.]

In Naples, Italy, in 1881, a sandstone bust from Byblos surfaced in the antiquities market. It was of Osorkon I, pharaoh of the twenty-second dynasty (924–889 BCE), and it had on it a cartouche and a Phoenician alphabetic dedicatory inscription by King Elibaal of Byblos. It was sold in Paris in 1910 and subsequently donated to the Louvre Museum (where it remains); in 1925 René Dussaud translated the inscription. Also in the Drehem archives (the Ur III archives in Drehem, just south of Nippur) and dated to about 2050 BCE is the earliest cuneiform economic text referring to Byblos, mentioning Ibdadi, the *ensi* (a title meaning "ruler" in Sumerian) of Byblos (Ward, 1963). [*See the biography of Dussaud.*]

In 1860 the French savant Ernest Renan, representing Napoleon III's mission in Phoenicia, located Byblos, made several soundings (even though twenty-nine houses occupied the site), and sketched the site and the sacred spring, the arched, roofed "Pool of the Phoenician Princess." In 1864 he published his findings and inscriptions, including the Renan bas-relief now also in the Louvre. The city was recognized as Byblos certainly by 1899. French archaeologist Pierre Montet undertook four campaigns (1921–1924) there, which uncovered the so-called Egyptian and Syrian temples (later identified as the single Temple of Baalat Gebal), along with three mutilated limestone colossi and many Egyptian Old Kingdom inscriptions, which he published in 1928 (Montet, 1928). A landslide in 1922 revealed the sarcophagus of a Byblite king with gifts from the Egyptian pharaoh Amenemhat III (c. nineteenth century BCE); eight other tombs were excavated in this royal necropolis. In 1930 the Lebanese government expropriated the houses built on the site. In 1926 the commissioner of France in Syria reopened the excavations, sponsored by the Lebanese government and the French Academy of Inscriptions and under the direction of French archaeologist Maurice Dunand. Dunand excavated from 1928 until the Lebanese civil war in the 1970s, under the auspices of the Lebanese government and the Louvre. [*See the biographies of Renan, Montet, and Dunand.*]

Major Remains. Byblos is one of the few remaining walled cities in Lebanon. The walls have massive rectangular towers, pierced by two almost-intact arched gates on the east and the north; part of the port defenses extends 1,000 m to the Mediterranean. There are four entrances: the east gate is the main entry and the northwest tower (of six *barlongue* towers) is the most important. Constructed in 1197 CE, the walls are of mediocre construction. Only from the north can Byblos be viewed as a walled city. A deep excavation marks the position of the sacred spring or well that was reached by a descending ramp. The site is guarded by a Crusader citadel (on the north, facing the sea), with its original east gate, under the twelfth-century CE chapel of Notre Dame de la Porte.

Occupational History. Built on a promontory with two harbors, close to Lebanon's cedar-bearing mountains, Byblos has been occupied for more than seven thousand years. Although one legend states that Byblos was founded by the first of the Semitic gods, El, according to Philo of Byblos, "Kronos put a wall about his habitation and founded Byblos in Phoenicia" (Felix Jacoby, *Die Fragmente der Griechischen Historiker*, Leiden, 1958, no. 790). Although Byblos has been occupied since the Neolithic period (6000 BCE), there are no early architectural remains. In about 4500 BCE small monocellular houses appear with crushed-limestone floors

and shallow graves in which the deceased were placed on their back or in a half-flexed position. Incised pottery was found in one such grave. Other dwellings with beaten-earth floors held "cradle," or cyst, burials in which the deceased, in a semiflexed or flexed position, were surrounded by upright stones associated with ceramic bowls with so-called chicken-scratched decorations. Also known from this period are a pebble idol and a fine tool repertoire. The site's Chalcolithic levels (3500–3000 BCE) are known for their numerous (1,207) jar burials (with the deceased in a flexed position accompanied by ceramic offerings) and large monocellular houses with beaten-earth or pebble floors, some having interior partitions.

By the Early Bronze Age (3000–2300 BCE), Byblos was an important Canaanite West Semitic coastal city-state and a timber and shipbuilding center. Close ties to Old Kingdom Egypt are revealed in numerous inscriptions of the Egyptian pharaohs Cheops, Chephren, Mycerinus, Wenis, and Sahure, as well as in thirty-six inscriptions bearing the names of Pepi I and Pepi II. Egyptians dominated the coastal plain and sent to Byblos for cedar wood for their shipbuilding, royal sarcophagi, tomb, and palace construction, as well as for cedar oil used in mummification. The houses dated to 3000 BCE are rectangular with sandstone slab superstructures constructed in a herringbone pattern. The houses have interior partitions and beaten-earth floors and some incorporate a courtyard and used wood posts to support the roof. The temple of Balaat Gebal, "lady of Byblos" (Dunand's building 40 [Dunand, 1937–1958]; and Montet's Syrian temple [Montet, 1929]), is among the earliest monumental structures in Phoenicia. The lady of Byblos has a known relationship to the Egyptian goddess Hathor, and the temple produced many inscribed Egyptian offerings.

By 2800 BCE, Byblos was a planned city with massive walls and two gates, one on the land side and one at the seaport; the city wall had a sloping glacis with cobblestones on the north exterior surface and square buttresses on the interior (see figure 1). By 2600 BCE, Dunand's tripartite *Temple en L* (L-shaped temple) was constructed facing the Temple of Balaat Gebal but separated from it by a sacred lake. (See Jidejian, 1968, pp. 209–212, for the local dynasty of rulers who were dependent on Egypt from 2350 to 2333 BCE.)

An Amorite invasion destroyed Byblos between about 2300 and 2100 BCE. A wave of newcomers succeeded it and the city was rebuilt. A jar with nearly one hundred valuable objects, buried in about 1950 BCE (seals, amulets, cylinder seals, baboon figurines, and more than forty bronze and silver torques), was recovered by Montet in his excavations in the 1920s (Montet, 1929).

In the Middle Bronze Age (1900–1600 BCE), the Byblites generally sided with the Egyptians against common enemies. Byblos, an international center, also traded with Crete, as evidenced by the Kamares wares found. The MB period is distinguished by the nine royal necropolis sarcophagi

BYBLOS.   Figure 1.   *Early Bronze Age city walls.* (Courtesy M. Joukowsky)

found in underground chambers reached by 12-meter-long tunnels hewn into the cliff. In this period the Temple of Balaat Gebal underwent modifications. The Obelisk temple which was constructed above Montet's Syrian temple, was moved to its present site in the 1930s; it had been erected over the ruins of the larger EB temple, and Dunand rebuilt the Obelisk temple a short distance away from the EB temple so he could excavate it (see figure 2). The Obelisk temple contains more than twenty-six votary obelisks in its courtyard. Many precious articles were found in all of these contexts.

During the Late Bronze Age (1600–1200 BCE), Byblos, like her coastal neighbors, felt the impact of the Hittites (1380–1355 BCE). During the Iron Age (1200–539 BCE), Byblos was the center for an extensive papyrus trade with Egypt and an important Phoenician settlement. An active seaport, it was referred to by Tiglath-Pileser I (*ANET*, no. 274), the hapless Wenamun (*ANET*, nos. 25–29), and the Egyptian text of Thutmose III (Breasted, 1906–1907, no. 492). The principal find from the Phoenician period is the Ahiram sarcophagus (now in the Beirut National Museum), which dis-

plays a variety of artistic influences (Egyptian lotus designs, Hittite crouching lions, a Syrian rope design) as well as the earliest Archaic Phoenician alphabetic inscription, which is incised around the lid. [*See* Ahiram Inscription.] Under Ashurnasirpal II the Assyrians conquered Byblos around 877 BCE and held the city until the Persian period (after about 529 BCE).

The city was a vassal of the Achaemenids from 539–332 BCE. They reinforced the city walls with yet another glacis (the last of seven successive layers extending from the Early Bronze Age to the fifth century BCE). A fifth-century stela of Yehawmilk, king of Byblos has been recovered, found shortly after Renan's excavations in 1869. Except for a large platform, there are few Persian traces in the city.

In 333–332 BCE, Alexander the Great conquered the coast and Byblos voluntarily became part of his empire. Under the Seleucids, after the conquest of Antiochus III in 200 BCE, the city became completely hellenized. In the second century, this was the home of Philo. By 64 BCE, or the end of the Hellenistic period, the city had lost most of its importance.

Roman Byblos (64 BCE–330 CE) was threatened by the Itureans in the first century BCE. It was a hellenized and romanized classical city resplendent with temples, shrines, a surrounding colonnade, grand avenues, villas, and monuments; during that time, the settlement spread to the adjacent countryside. The Roman settlement developed along the same plan as the Hellenistic city: its Roman street extended east from the acropolis, through the Crusader-Arab castle moat, and into the modern town. To the north and east of the acropolis was the commercial and residential sector. Twelve meters below the acropolis a second-century CE colonnaded street is positioned going northeast, extending to meet the port street. At a bend in the road, east of the castle's bridge, is an apsidal nymphaeum out of which water flowed into a fluted pool. Sculpture adorned its niches, the best-preserved of which is of Hygeia and a group made up of Achilles and Penthesilea and Orpheus with animals (the fountain is in the Beirut National Museum). To the east of the nymphaeum was a four-columned portico. Little of the Greek, Roman, and Byzantine eras remains, except for paved streets, a Corinthian colonnade, a theater, a nymphaeum, and some sculpture and mosaics from the third century CE. Roman mosaics illustrating the legendary Atalanta were unearthed by Dunand and a large villa to the southeast contained mosaics dated to the second century CE. All that remains from classical Byblos are reused stones in the citadel; scattered granite columns, of which six have been reerected as part of the colonnade that extended from the Adonis temple to the lower town to the north; the nymphaeum; a number of tombs; and part of a temple/church structure. The best surviving example of classical architecture is the late second-century CE restored hemicycle theater with seven sectors of steps that was moved by Dunand in the 1930s and reconstructed in reduced form in its present position overlooking the sea west of the acropolis. The theater's orchestra, which was built about 218 CE, was embellished with a delicately crafted mosaic of the bust of Bacchus, surrounded with white tesserae and a black border, which also is now in the Beirut National Museum. The ramparts of the city were once reconstructed with the aid of Herod the Great (Josephus, *War* 1.422).

In the Roman period Byblos was the pilgrim center of the Adonis cult and was known for his tomb site. The main temple to Adonis, which was constructed around a central cone-shaped altar, or baetyl, is pictured on Roman coins of the emperor Macrinus (217–218 CE). It is not clear where this temple stood in antiquity. A Greco-Roman necropolis of multistoried rock-cut tombs lies south of the present-day excavations, in the rock cliffs between the highway and the sea.

The Byzantine period (330–634 CE) is poorly represented at Byblos because of the later reuse of its buildings. Remains are found in only three areas: seven rows of flagstones at the Temple of Baalat Gebal, an area near the Roman colonnade with a circular basin and a wall, and an east–west street associated with shops. In the time of Justinian (551 CE), a severe earthquake rocked all the Phoenician cities, including Byblos. In the Early Arab period (636–1108 CE), Byblos was under the control of Banu Ammar of Tripoli. The bridge from the site to the Crusader castle was erected then.

Stratification. The reuse of architectural elements of earlier periods has disturbed the stratigraphy, or archaeological levels, at Byblos. Mixed deposits abound and modern houses are built all over the site. Byblos also served as a quarry for later builders; even modern builders use the old blocks. The topography is so complicated that Chalcolithic and Roman remains of gray or rose-red granite can be found at the same level. Remains are scattered on the land and on the sea floor, and many are built into the Crusader castle, the port's defense walls, and modern houses.

BIBLIOGRAPHY

Albright, William Foxwell. "The Eighteenth-Century Princes of Byblos and the Chronology of the Middle Bronze." *Bulletin of the American Schools of Oriental Research*, no. 176 (Nov. 1989): 38–46.

Breasted, James H. *Ancient Records of Egypt: Historical Documents from the Earliest Times to the Persian Conquest*. 5 vols. Chicago, 1906–1907.

Dunand, Maurice. *Fouilles de Byblos*. 5 vols. Paris, 1937–1958.

Dunand, Maurice. "Rapport préliminaire sur les fouilles de Byblos." *Bulletin du Musée de Beyrouth* 9 (1949–1950): 53–74; 12 (1955): 7–23; 13 (1956): 73–86; 16 (1964): 69–85. Reports by the site's most prolific excavator.

Dunand, Maurice. *Byblos: Its History, Ruins, and Legends*. 2d ed. Beirut, 1968.

Jidejian, Nina. *Byblos through the Ages*. Beirut, 1968. Comprehensive history of Byblos through the ages, with strong coverage of ancient, classical, and contemporary references. Includes a good bibliography through the late 1960s.

Joukowsky, Martha Sharp. *The Young Archaeologist in the Oldest Port City in the World*. Beirut, 1988. Children's book exploring the history and archaeology of Byblos.

Montet, Pierre. *Byblos et l'Égypte: Quatre campagnes de fouilles à Gebeil 1921–1924*. Paris, 1929. Comprehensive publication of four early expeditions.

Pritchard, James B. *Ancient Near Eastern Texts Relating to the Old Testament*. 3d ed. with supp. Princeton, 1978.

Renan, Ernest. *Mission de Phénicie*. Paris, 1864. One of the earliest works on Phoenician sites.

Tufnell, Olga, and William A. Ward. "Relations between Byblos, Egypt, and Mesopotamia at the End of the Third Millennium B.C." *Syria* 43 (1966): 165–241. Specialized study of the Montet jar and

BYBLOS. Figure 2. *Temple of the Obelisks*. (Courtesy M. Joukowsky)

BYZANTINE EMPIRE

its contents; see Ward and Dever (below) for a recent study of the jar.

Ward, William A. "Egypt and the East Mediterranean in the Early Second Millennium B. C." *Or* 30 (1961): 22–45, 129–155.

Ward, William A. "Egypt and the East Mediterranean from Pre-Dynastic Times to the End of the Old Kingdom." *Journal of Economic and Social History of the Orient* 6 (1963): 1–57. Survey of political and cultural relations between Egypt, Asia, and the Aegean world.

Ward, William A., and William G. Dever. *Studies on Scarab Seals.* Vol. 3, *Scarab Typologies and Archaeological Context.* San Antonio, 1994. See chapter 4 for the most recent study of the Montet jar and its contents.

MARTHA SHARP JOUKOWSKY

BYZANTINE EMPIRE. The term *Byzantium,* originally the name of the ancient Greek colony on which Constantinople was founded, is used conventionally to designate the eastern part of the Roman empire, which survived after the fall of Rome in 476 CE. The Byzantines called themselves *Romaioi* (i.e., Romans), and their country *Romania,* indicating the historical continuity with the Roman empire. The fundamental cultural elements of Byzantine civilization were three: Greek language and education, Roman political theory and legal system, and Orthodox religion.

History, Society, Economy, Culture. Constantine I (324–337) founded the new empire when he transferred his capital to Byzantium, renamed Constantinople, on the Bosporus and recognized Christianity. In the course of the early Byzantine period (324–c. 600) the empire gradually became Christian. This early period is also called "late Roman" or "late antiquity" by those scholars who emphasize the continuity with the Roman past. Julian the Apostate (361–363) in vain tried to restore paganism. Theodosius I (379–395) strengthened the Christian Church with a series of measures, and at his death the empire was permanently divided between the Greek East and the Latin West. The Byzantine emperors successfully diverted the numerous barbaric invaders with war or diplomacy. In 476 Rome fell to the Ostrogoths, the Roman Empire in the West collapsed, and Constantinople became Rome's heir, the second Rome. The pressure of the barbarians increased and Anastasius I (491–518) attempted the reconstruction of the defense system. Justinian I (527–565) undertook large-scale building activity described in Procopius's *Buildings.* The major wars to restore the frontiers of the Roman Empire, however, weakened the state's resources, and the recovery of large districts in the West was temporary. After the Justinianic *renovatio* (reconstruction) the empire suffered serious losses: the Danubian frontier collapsed because of the invading Avars and Slavs. The permanent installation of the Slavs in the Balkan peninsula from the late sixth century created a profound crisis in the area, and its northern territories were lost forever. To the south in the Greek mainland a slow process of assimilation and christianization of the Slavs began.

The early Byzantine period is the period of the great Christological controversies. In the fourth century the fathers of the Orthodox Church shaped the Orthodox dogma in their theological works. Ecclesiastical synods condemned the heresies and defined the dogma with accuracy. The controversies that were dealt with by the ecumenical councils were Christological (they tried to define the nature of Christ). The Council of Nicaea I (325) and that of Constantinople I (381) condemned the Arian heresy, which proclaimed the subordination of the Son to the Father, and defined Christ as consubstantial with the Father. The Council at Ephesus (431) condemned Nestorius, who emphasized Christ's human nature. The Council of Chalcedon (451) defined Christ's two natures united without confusion or division. The second Council of Constantinople (553) attempted to reconcile monophysitism with Orthodoxy, while the third Council of Constantinople (681) was an attempt to settle the controversy of monothelitism. The second Council of Nicaea (787) brought an end to the first period of Iconoclasm. The canons of the ecumenical councils were accepted as deriving from and expressing the bishops' consensus (B. Botte, H. Marat, et al., *Le concile et les conciles,* Chevetogne, 1960; *Histoire des conciles oecuméniques,* 12 vols., Paris, 1962–; P. L'Huillier, *The Church of the Ancient Councils,* Crestwood, N.Y., 1986). The role of certain emperors in this process was decisive. Classical education was accepted by the Church in spite of the radical views of some ecclesiastics, and although some elements of Greek philosophy and literature were rejected, classical tradition remained until the end the cornerstone of Byzantine civilization.

Archaeological excavations show with certainty that in all the provinces of the empire there was great prosperity and an unprecedented increase of population (see Foss, 1977; Russell, 1986). Agriculture, industry, and trade flourished. Great building activity is attested everywhere, particularly in the fifth and sixth centuries. Large basilicas were constructed, although their size does not correspond with the size of the settlements. Signs of profound transformation of urban life, however, appear already in the fourth century in the literary sources and at all excavated sites. The principles of ancient urbanism were gradually abandoned: public monuments, theaters, hippodromes, temples, and forums fell out of use, and a long process of dilapidation started. Orthogonal city-planning was replaced by irregular configurations, and the ancient social and political center of the cities *(forum)* was broken up into parochial districts around churches, which became the nucleus of economic and social activity. The municipal aristocracy (*decurion*s) declined, and the responsibility for public works and defense was transferred to the provincial governors. The cities lost their financial independence, and together with the new ideological orientation promoted by the Church the interest in public life gradually diminished. Monasteries became urban institutions, accumulated great wealth, and established philanthropic foundations. The Roman form of exploitation of land, the *villa*, was still the basis of the agrarian economy. Imperial legislation indicates that the large estates were increasing and that the *coloni* (peasants attached to the land) were becoming dependent peasants. The villages, however, according to archaeological evidence from Syria and Palaestine, were flourishing (Tchalenko, 1953–1958).

Absolute monarchy was reinforced and supported by Christian principles of order and philanthropy. A career in the state administration was a way to social recognition and wealth. Ethnic languages and cultures promoted diversity and national literatures appeared (Syriac, Coptic). In spite of the profound hellenization of the provinces in the East and in Egypt, national differences and resentment for the ruling Orthodox Greek administration of Constantinople were reinforced by the religious opposition with significant consequences: the monophysite populations of the East did not resist the invading Arabs in the seventh century.

The seventh and eighth centuries are the Dark Ages of Byzantine history. Early in the seventh century the Persians occupied Egypt, Palestine, and Syria. Heraclius (610–641) recovered these territories (629), but they were lost again to the Arabs in 636 at the decisive battle of Yarmuk. Most of the cities in the East surrendered peacefully. The Umayyad Arabs, with their capital at Damascus, established a strong navy and raided Asia Minor every year. Constantinople was besieged twice (in 669 and 717–718) and threatened during the war of 674–680. The new caliphate of 'Abbasids (750–1258) moved their capital to Baghdad, and the pressure was lifted. The consequences of the Arab occupation of the eastern provinces of the empire were decisive: the empire lost the areas with the greatest resources, but it gained a religious, linguistic, and ethnic uniformity. In the last quarter of the sixth century the first signs of a crisis appeared; archaeological evidence shows that building activity ceased. In the seventh century a dramatic decrease of population is attested everywhere. Many cities that had flourished earlier were abandoned or reduced to insignificant settlements. Economic activity, as illustrated in the interrupted numismatic series from excavated sites and coin hoards was diminished. Barter economy had apparently replaced monetary in many daily transactions. Most of the urban centers that survived resembled rural settlements with agrarian social and economic structure. The reform in the administrative system introduced with the institution of the *themes* (provinces) led to the militarization of the empire: both military and civil powers were concentrated in these administrative units. Their army was composed of peasants-soldiers. The new system strengthened the defensive forces of the empire, and it was efficient in repelling the enemies and consolidating Byzantine rule in the reoccupied territories. The class of independent peasants increased.

Overall, however, Byzantine society acquired a strong medieval character. The religious controversy of iconoclasm supported by the emperors of the Isaurian dynasty (717–802) has been seen from various angles: as a conflict between cultural and religious traditions of the East and the West (the Jewish and Muslim aniconic [nonrepresentational] concept of God versus the anthropomorphic representation of God of the Greek culture) or as an effort of the state to diminish the power of the Church, especially the monasteries. In the course of the controversy the classical tradition was attacked and interest in it was diminished. Many objects of art were deliberately destroyed.

A recovery started with the Macedonian dynasty (867–1025). Syria and Crete were conquered from the Arabs, and several wars against Bulgaria brought that new state into the Byzantine sphere of ecclesiastical and political influence (King Boris I, 852–889, was christianized). In the ninth century the glagolitic alphabet (the earliest alphabet used for writing Church Slavonic) was invented by Cyril and Methodius (apostles of the Slavs), who were sent to Moravia as missionaries in 863. Thus the first Slavic literary language, Church Slavonic, was created. The Rus (Scandinavians in origin, who had settled along the rivers of Russia and were assimilated with the local Slavic population, founding several principalities centered on Kiev) also were christianized—Christianity was officially accepted in 988. The Russian attacks against Constantinople were successfully repelled, and commercial relations were established and sanctioned with treaties. The metropolitan (bishop) of Kiev was placed under the patriarch of Constantinople. The Church became the vehicle for Byzantine cultural influence on the Rus: Byzantine artists, architects, painters, and craftsmen were sent to Russia. Archaeological evidence suggests that a growth of the urban population started in the ninth century and that the economy was slowly recovering. Imperial legislation and other sources testify to the increase of large estates, secular and ecclesiastic, which the Macedonian emperors tried to control with restrictive measures. The emperors exercised a remarkable power over the Church. The interest in classical antiquity was revived. The so-called Macedonian Renaissance in literature was marked by encyclopedism, the copying of ancient texts and selections in anthologies. The work of the intellectuals was practical: to organize and codify the knowledge of the earlier centuries (treatises on military art, administration, imperial ceremonies, and codification of imperial legislation).

In the eleventh century the schism between the Orthodox and Catholic Churches became permanent. The split of the two Churches is dated to the early Byzantine period, when the question of primacy of Rome and the privilege of honor attributed to the bishop of Constantinople on political grounds (Constantinople was the city of New Rome) were raised at the first Council of Constantinople. Doctrinal differences also appeared in various heretical controversies, especially over Arianism and monophysitism (Akakian Schism in 484–519). The controversy over the *filioque* emerged in the conflict between Patriarch Photios and Pope Nicholas I (858–867). In the eleventh century new conflicts appeared over disciplinary questions (the celibacy of western clergy) and the use of the azymes in the liturgy. In 1054 the anathems spelled against Patriarch Michael I Keroularios and the papal legates (under Cardinal Humbert) finalized the split of the two Churches, which were already separated by different institutional traditions, theological views, and cultural reality. The political developments in the following centuries and the fall of Constantinople to the Crusaders in 1204 broadened the distance between them. In the middle of the eleventh century economic prosperity naturally coincided with the development of the middle class, represented in Constantinople by the emperors of the civil party. A further social evolution was prevented by the establishment of a military aristocracy represented by the dynasty of the Komnenoi (1081–1185). They developed institutions similar to those of western feudal society: ties of kinship appeared in the aristocracy, and the large estates were increased. The defeat of the Byzantines by an emerging new power, the Seljuk Turks, in Manzikert in 1071 marked the beginning of the troubled years ahead. The dynasty of the Komnenoi attempted a major renovation of the empire. Their rule was in many respects successful. The commercial privileges granted to the Italian cities, Venice, Pisa, and Genoa, in exchange for military and naval support, however, further weakened the resources of the state and mark the beginning of dependency on foreign aid. In 1176 a second defeat by the Seljuk Turks in Myriokephalon radically changed the situation in Anatolia: independent Armenian states were established in Cilicia, and a large part of Asia Minor was definitively lost to the Turks. In the same period the Latin West threatened Byzantium for the first time. The Normans repeatedly attacked the empire, threatened Constantinople, and occupied Thessalonike (1185). The Crusaders were successfully diverted to the East by means of diplomacy. The second Bulgarian Empire was established in 1186, and the Serbs became independent. In the interior the polarization of the ruling aristocracy in Constantinople and the heavy taxation led to the alienation of the provinces. Ambitious local magnates tried to become independent, and dynastic conflicts and corruption of the dynasty of the Angeloi (1185–1204) weakened the empire. In this climate the resistance to the Latins of the Fourth Crusade was unsuccessful.

The fall of Constantinople to the Crusaders in 1204 marks the beginning of the last period of Byzantine history (1204–1453): the empire was divided between Latin states, colonies of the Italian merchant cities, the Byzantine empires in Nicaea and Trebizond, and the Despotate of Epiros. In 1261 Michael VIII Palaeologos (1259–1282) from Nicaea liberated Constantinople and restored the empire. The period is marked by the advance of the Serbs, who by 1355 controlled most of Greece, and by the constant progress of the Ottoman Turks, who by 1340 had occupied all of Asia Minor, and then advanced into the European territories. Thessalonike, the second most important city of the empire was occupied by the Turks in 1387 and 1430. The support that the Western powers gave to the Palaeologoi by recognizing the union of the churches (synods in Lyon in 1274 and in Ferrara-Florence in 1439) was limited. The civil wars between the Palaeologoi Andronicus II and Andronicus III (1321–1328) and between John V Palaeologos and John VI Kantakouzenos (1341–1347) weakened the constantly diminishing resources of the empire. Mercenaries were used in the army; the state finances could not recover; trade was controlled by the Italians; and territories were given to the sons of emperors as appanages (independent, nonhereditary administrative districts) and became autonomous. Although the power of the state was diminishing, the Church took control of many aspects of life. The fourteenth-century theological controversy of hesychasm (promoting a method of monastic prayer and contemplation through which communion with God could be attained) revived tendencies toward spirituality, and it is often seen as a reaction to the Palaeologan Renaissance. The Church nourished the anti-Latin feelings of the common people and often promoted the idea that submission to the Turks was preferable to submission to the Latin Church. The intellectuals, however, tried to establish bridges with the West and the renewed interest in classical antiquity gave birth to Greek national consciousness and to dreams of a national rebirth. Constantinople fell to the Turks in 1453. The Despotate of Morea in the Peloponnesos, which flourished in the fifteenth century fell in 1460, and the empire of Trebizond one year later.

Archaeology, Art. Byzantine archaeology was for many years defined as Christian archaeology: the study of the architectural styles of churches, the influence of the liturgy on their development, their mosaic or fresco decoration, their sculptural ornaments, their implantation in the urban fabric. Interest in secular buildings, urban centers or rural settlements appeared only recently. A major restriction on Byzantine archaeology was that for a long time it remained a branch of classical archaeology. Because the excavators focused on classical sites and their monuments, Byzantine remains were often destroyed in order to reach the classical strata or were disposed of because they supposedly had no significant artistic value. The excavations on major sites focused primarily on identification of sites and monuments. Attention to the evolution of sites has finally been paid, and the imposition of modern cities limits the archaeological investigation to small-scale rescue excavations.

Interest in cities, particularly in the period of transition from the early to the middle Byzantine period, has been a late development. The debate on the discontinuity of urban life in the dark ages among historians since the 1950s, has opened the way for the archaeological investigation of early Byzantine cities. In most cities, however, the excavations have been limited to the classical city centers or in and around important monuments, for example, pagan temples, hippodromes, and theaters. Obviously in all sites the archaeological evidence is fragmentary. Another difficulty consists of inadequate reports of earlier excavations, which were not conducted according to the principles of modern scholarly investigation. This situation has often been observed in Athens and Corinth, the best excavated sites in Greece. The Byzantine remains are very poor, not precisely dated, and inaccurately described. Promising sites for the study of the changing character of the early Byzantine cities are places that were destroyed and abandoned in the end of this period: Nea Anchialos in Greece and Caričin Grad in the former Yugoslavia. The latter, built by Justinian, represents the trends of Byzantine urbanism in the sixth century. Numerous forts have been investigated along the Danube and the hinterland. The best excavated sites in Asia Minor are Ephesus, Sardis, Miletus, Priene, and Aphrodisias. [See Ephesus; Sardis; Miletus; Priene; Aphrodisias.] Excavations in Byzantine Palestine and Syria have revealed several cities and towns that ceased to exist after the Arab conquest. The most important sites are Caesarea Maritima, Gerasa (Jerash), Scythopolis (Beth-Shean), Pella, and the cities of the Negev desert. [See Caesarea; Jerash; Beth-Shean; Pella; Negev.] In the latter local elements were maintained next to the Byzantine features of urbanism. Since the 1960s new technology has allowed underwater investigation of sunken coastal sites and shipwrecks. Shipwrecks provide evidence for trade: the sixth century shipwreck at Marzamemi in southeast Sicily contained a load of marble church furnishings, and the wrecks at Serçe Limanı (eleventh century) and Pelagonnesos (twelfth century) had cargoes of glasses and ceramic vessels, respectively. [See Serçe Limanı.] The archaeological survey of large areas without excavation has been widely used to establish settlement pattern, network of forts, villages, and agricultural installations.

Of all branches of art, architecture is most intimately related with archaeological work. Byzantine architectural types naturally developed from ancient prototypes such as the basilica. Other types are the martyria (shrines honoring martyrs), baptisteries, and mausolea. [See Basilicas; Martyrion; Baptisteries; Mausoleum.] The great innovations of the sixth century were the domed basilica and the very elaborate sculptural ornaments. The best example of both is the church of St. Sophia in Constantinople. In the middle Byzantine period the churches were smaller, centralized with domes, and adjoined by many attached chapels. From the twelfth century local characteristics are notable in the churches built in the provinces, and Byzantine art was disseminated in Slavic countries. Although iconography continued earlier traditions, it developed a new repertory of

Christian themes from the Old and New Testaments and the lives of saints. Decoration of secular buildings derived mainly from the early centuries. Mosaics, the most expensive mural or floor decoration, were primarily used to embellish domes and apses of churches. [See Mosaics.] From the sixth century they were also used to adorn the walls. The best preserved examples are found at Hagia Sophia, St. Catherine at Sinai, and Ravenna.

[See also Anatolia, articles on Anatolia from Alexander to the Rise of Islam and Anatolia in the Islamic Period; and Constantinople.]

BIBLIOGRAPHY

Brown, Peter R. L. The World of Late Antiquity. 2d ed. New York, 1989.

Deichmann, F. W. Einführung in die christliche Archäologie. Darmstadt, 1983. History of Christian archaeology and treatment of major subjects (architecture, development of Christian motives, etc.).

Foss, Clive. "Archaeology and the 'Twenty Cities' of Byzantine Asia." American Journal of Archaeology 81 (1977): 469–486. Account of the archaeological evidence of twenty major cities in Anatolia, demonstrating that the changing character of seventh-century cities can be reconstructed from the archaeological finds alone.

Frend, W. H. C. The Rise of the Monophysite Movement: Chapters in the History of the Church in the Fifth and Sixth Centuries. 2d ed. Cambridge, 1979.

Grabar, André. Sculptures byzantines de Constantinople, IVe–Xe siècle. Paris, 1963. Major study of the Byzantine sculptural ornaments of churches and tombs of Constantinople.

Grabar, André. Sculptures byzantines du moyen âge II, XIe–XIVe siècle. Paris, 1976. Major study of Byzantine sculpture mainly in churches.

Harvey, Alan. Economic Expansion in the Byzantine Empire, 900–1200. Cambridge, 1989. Comprehensive study of the Byzantine economy and related subjects, such as demographic growth, taxation, monetary circulation, and agricultural production.

Hendy, Michael F. Studies in the Byzantine Monetary Economy c. 300–1450. Cambridge, 1985. Technical study of the Byzantine monetary economy, coin circulation and production, and imperial policy, based on literary sources and excavation finds.

Hussey, John M., ed. The Cambridge Medieval History. Vol. 4.1–2. Cambridge, 1966. Comprehensive history of Byzantium covering history, economy, society, and culture.

Krautheimer, Richard, and Slobodan Curcic. Early Christian and Byzantine Architecture. 4th ed. New Haven, 1986. Standard study of Byzantine architecture focusing mainly on religious buildings.

Lemerle, Paul, ed. Villes et peuplement dans l'Illyricum protobyzantin: Actes du colloque organisé par l'École Française de Rome, Rome, 12–14 mai 1982. Rome, 1984. Collection of studies on Byzantine cities of the western Balkan peninsula based primarily on the archaeological evidence.

Mango, Cyril. Byzantium: The New Order of Rome. New York, 1980.

Mango, Cyril. Byzantine Architecture. 2d ed. New York, 1985. Broad synthesis including study of materials, techniques, architects, and architectural styles of religious and secular buildings.

Obolensky, Dimitri. The Byzantine Commonwealth: Eastern Europe, 500–1453. London, 1971. Major study of the political and commercial relations and cultural and religious influence of Byzantium on the Slavic world.

Ostrogorsky, George. History of the Byzantine State. Rev. ed. New Brunswick, N.J., 1969. The most authoritative history of Byzantium.

Russell, James. "Transformations in Early Byzantine Urban Life: The Contribution and Limitations of Archaeological Evidence." In The

Seventeenth International Byzantine Congress: Major Papers, Dumbarton Oaks/Georgetown University, Washington, D.C., August 3–8, 1986, pp. 137–154. New Rochelle, N.Y., 1986. Fundamental work demonstrating the importance of archaeological finds for the study of Byzantine historical periods which are not adequately documented by literary sources. Also analyzes the limitation of the archaeological evidence, especially in dating the finds with accuracy.

Sellers, R. V. *The Council of Chalcedon: A Historical and Doctrinal Survey.* London, 1967.

Tabula imperii byzantini. Vienna, 1976–. Exhaustive list of all known sites from Greece and Asia Minor, with reference to all literary sources, archaeological reports, and bibliography.

Tchalenko, Georges. *Villages antiques de la Syrie du Nord: Le massif du Bélus à l'époque romaine.* 3 vols. Paris, 1953–1958. Major work on village communities in North Syria based primarily on archaeological survey.

HELEN SARADI

C

CAARI. *See* Cyprus American Archaeological Research Institute.

CAESAREA, site of an ancient Greek and Roman port city, Caesarea Maritima, located on the coast of Israel, about 40 km (25 mi.) north of Tel Aviv (32°30′ N, 34°53′ E; map reference 1400 × 2120). Herod the Great founded the city above remains of a Hellenistic town called Straton's Tower. He named it Caesarea for Caesar Augustus, his patron, and its adjacent port Sebastos, Greek for Augustus. Josephus (*War*, 7.20) calls it Caesarea by the Sea, whereas other Greek and Latin authors specified "Caesarea near Sebastos," "Straton's Caesarea," or "Caesarea of Palestine" to distinguish it from numerous homonyms. Rabbinic authors call it Qisri or Qisrin, and Arabic Qaisariya survived into modern times, leaving no doubt about the site's identification.

History. Straton's Tower was a Phoenician fortified town (Heb., *Migdal Shorshon*), not just a fortress. Although the earliest ceramics date from the fourth century BCE, and scholars have suggested one of two fourth-century Sidonian kings as the founder, the earliest textual reference is a papyrus from 259 BCE (*P Cairo Zeno* 59004), attesting commercial activity and a harbor. A local tyrant named Zoilus may have fortified Straton's Tower near the close of the second century BCE, but this did not prevent Alexander Jannaeus from seizing it in about 100 BCE for the expanding Hasmonean kingdom and introducing a Jewish population. To weaken the Hasmoneans, the Roman general Pompey attached Straton's Tower and other coastal towns to Syria in 63 BCE; in 31 BCE, however, Octavian restored it to Herod's kingdom. By this time Straton's Tower lay depopulated and in ruins.

Herod the Great built Caesarea and its harbor between 22 and 10/9 BCE (see figure 1); it ranks with the Second Jewish Temple as his most spectacular building project. In two succinct passages (*War* 1.408–415; *Antiq.* 15.331–341) the historian Josephus describes a typical city (*polis*) of the late Hellenistic age, including a theater, an amphitheater "along the shore," a "royal palace," marketplaces, and streets laid on a grid plan. However, he devotes most of his attention to the harbor, Sebastos—to its breakwaters extending out into the sea, vaulted warehouses for trade goods, statues apparently of the emperor's family on columns at the harbor entrance, and a tower (lighthouse?) named Drusion, for the son of Augustus. On an elevated platform above the inner harbor, Herod erected a temple to Roma and Augustus.

After 6 CE, when Herod's grandson died, the Romans ruled Judaea directly through a governor and an administration headquartered at Caesarea. The site remained the capital of the province, later renamed Palestine, until it fell to the Muslims in 641 CE. A Latin inscription found in the theater records that Pontius Pilate, governor in about 30 CE, dedicated a temple at Caesarea to the emperor Tiberius (*Annales épigraphiques* 1963, no. 104). During the First Jewish War (66–70 CE), the Roman commander, Vespasian, wintered his troops there, and after it, as emperor, he refounded Caesarea as a Roman colony. For the next three centuries, Roman governors, soldiers, and veterans dominated the city. The bulk of inscriptions from this period are in Latin. The city's constitution was of a western type, with two chief magistrates (*duumviri*) and a municipal senate (*decuriones*). Caesarea profited from close links with Rome: the emperors expanded its aqueduct system (Hadrian, in c. 130 CE) and built an amphitheater for gladiators and a hippodrome for chariot racing, both of western type.

Christianity emerged at Caesarea soon after the Crucifixion, when St. Peter converted the centurion Cornelius (*Acts* 10). The Jewish War had eradicated the large Jewish population, and most of the Christians as well, but after the Bar Kokhba revolt (132–135 CE), when Rabbi Akiba was martyred at Caesarea, both groups began to resettle, attracted by the city's prosperity. The rural population was mostly Jews and Samaritans. In the third century, Caesarea was the site of a celebrated rabbinic academy and the Christian school of Origen, the scholar and theologian, who assembled a notable library and compiled the hexapla text of the Christian Bible.

Caesarea reached its apogee of population and prosperity between the fourth and late sixth centuries, under the Christian Empire. A Christian church replaced Herod's Augustus temple on the Temple Platform (see figure 2). The authorities repaired and expanded the aqueducts and built new

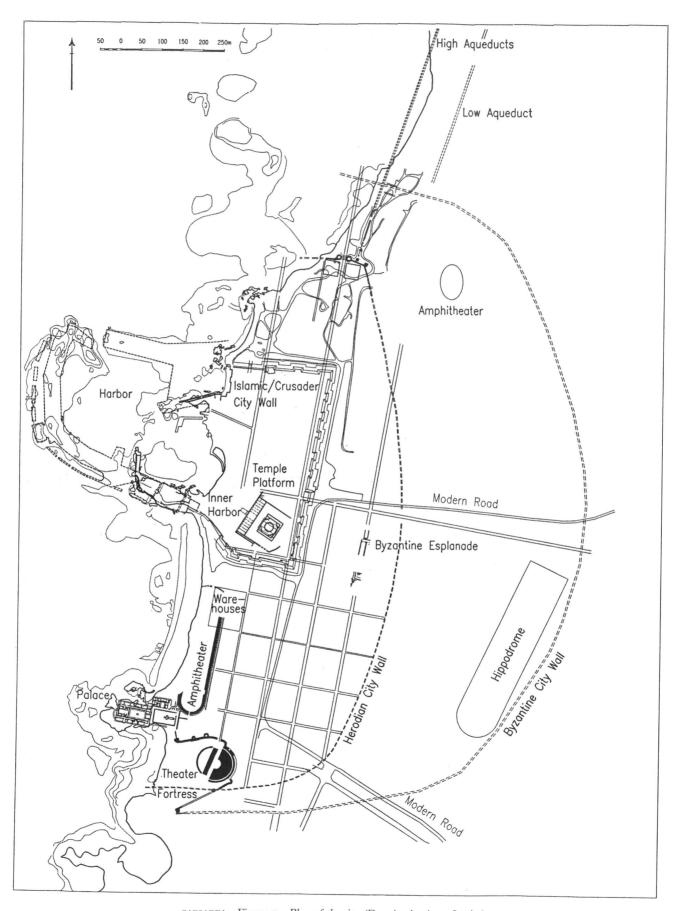

CAESAREA. Figure 1. *Plan of the site.* (Drawing by Anna Iamim)

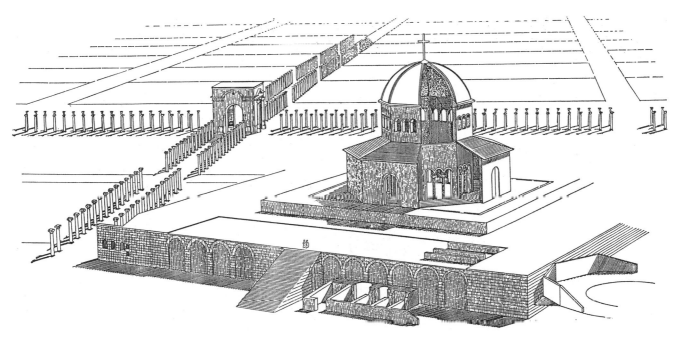

CAESAREA. Figure 2. *Sixth-century octagonal church on the Temple Platform, looking east.* (Drawing by Will Andalora and Anna Iamim)

fortifications to enclose a much larger inhabited space. Among the city's bishops, metropolitans of Palestine, was Eusebius (bishop c. 315–339), who wrote an ecclesiastical history and recorded Christian martyrdoms in Caesarea's amphitheater during the Great Persecution. His Jewish counterpart, Rabbi Abbahu, frequented the baths and taught his daughters Greek, which was then the predominant language. The classical historian Procopius (sixth century) was a product of the city's schools.

Although tectonic action and the coastal surge had damaged the breakwaters of Herod's harbor severely, Caesarea remained an important seaport until the seventh century. Emperor Anastasius restored the harbor about 500 CE (Procopius of Gaza, *Penegyricus* 19; *Patrologia graeca* 87, col. 2817); trade through the port helps account for the intense urban construction of churches, streets, and public buildings, attested archaeologically and in inscriptions throughout the sixth century. In the meantime, a series of Samaritan rebellions caused severe dislocations in the rural economy, the other source of Caesarea's prosperity. Like other cities, Caesarea suffered from recurrences of plague after 541–542, and from crushing imperial taxation demanded for the wars of the emperor Justinian (d. 565). Deurbanization had probably set in before the seventh-century invasions.

In 614, a Persian army invaded Palestine. Caesarea capitulated and suffered no physical damage but remained under Persian rule until 627. In 641 or 642, Caesarea fell to the Muslims, and the Roman city came to a precipitous end. Many of the landholding aristocracy, who had supported urban life, went into exile during the invasions. The Muslim conquerors did not favor Caesarea. During the Umayyad age (to 750) it was reduced to little more than a coastal defense station.

By the tenth and eleventh centuries, however, under Fatimid rule, a prosperous town had emerged on the site, with new fortifications encompassing a much-reduced urban space (see figure 3). The geographers el-Muqaddisi and Nasr-i-Khusrau praise the water supply of Muslim Qaisariya, its luxuriant gardens and orchards outside the walls, and its Great Mosque, positioned on what had been Herod's Temple Platform (Palestine Pilgrims' Texts Society, vol. 3.3 [1971], p. 55; vol. 4.1 [1971], p. 20). In 1101 European Crusaders took the Fatimid town by storm, and it became a Christian principality that lasted, despite episodes of reconquest and destruction, until 1265. A church of St. Peter succeeded the Great Mosque on the Temple Platform. In 1251–1252 the French king Louis IX rebuilt the fortifications. However, only fourteen years later, the Mamluk sultan Baybars seized Caesarea from the Crusaders; in 1291 his successor leveled the walls to make them useless to subsequent invaders. Caesarea then remained desolate until modern times, although squatter villages sometimes inhabited the ruins.

In 1884, Bosnian refugees from Europe resettled ancient Caesarea. Their town survived until 1940, and some of its buildings, including a mosque, still exist within the medieval fortification perimeter, now called the Old City.

Archaeology. Recently, archaeological exploration has begun to enrich our understanding of Caesarea's history, known previously from literary sources. Archaeologists rec-

CAESAREA. Figure 3. *Islamic/Crusader fortifications, eastern range, looking north.* (Photograph by Aaron Levin)

ognize six periods of occupation, corresponding to the history outlined above: Hellenistic (fourth–first century BCE), Roman (first–third century CE), Byzantine (fourth–seventh centuries), Islamic (seventh–eleventh centuries), Crusader (twelfth–thirteenth centuries), and Mamluk to modern (fourteenth–twentieth centuries).

Until thirty years ago the site was known only from the reports of nineteenth-century explorers, chance finds, and a few rescue excavations. Among the explorers, most important were Claude R. Conder and Horatio Herbert Kitchener, who visited Caesarea briefly in 1873. They studied and mapped the aqueducts, the theater, the outer (Byzantine) perimeter wall, which they dated to the Roman period, and also the medieval (Islamic and Crusader) fortifications. In 1945, J. Ory reported remains of a Byzantine synagogue exposed during winter storms to the north of the Old City, which Michael Avi-Yonah examined briefly in 1956 and 1962. In 1950 Benjamin Reifenberg recognized, in an aerial photograph, an amphitheater (not the one mentioned by Josephus) to the northeast of the Old City. In 1951 Shmuel

Yeivin excavated a site to the east of the Old City, where a tractor from the neighboring kibbutz had struck one of two colossal Roman statues that had flanked the entrance (propylaeum) to an unidentified building from the Byzantine period. A tessellated pavement (11.5 × 13.4 m) exposed accidentally in 1955, is decorated with medallions displaying eleven species of birds. This has recently been identified plausibly as part of a suburban villa from the Byzantine period. [*See the biographies of Conder, Kitchener, and Yeivin.*]

Excavation on a large scale dates only from 1959, when archaeologists first comprehended Caesarea as an urban, maritime site and began systematic recovery of all phases of occupation. In 1960, Edwin A. Link, a pioneer of underwater exploration, brought a team of divers that identified the ruins of Herod's harbor. In five campaigns (1959–1964) the Italian Missione Archeologica, directed by Antonio Frova, explored the outer perimeter wall, proving it to be Byzantine; the team also exposed part of an inner perimeter to the north of the medieval fortifications, which it failed to date convincingly. The Missione also excavated the Herodian theater, to the south of the Old City, and the ruins of an imposing fortress that succeeded it in the sixth or seventh century. Between 1960 and 1964, Avraham Negev supervised clearing within the Old City that brought to light barrel-vaulted substructures forming the western facade of the Herodian Temple Platform and, on the platform itself, the ruins of a triple-apsed Crusader basilica. He also cleared the moats in front of the medieval fortifications and removed dune sand from the southern preserved section of the twin high-level aqueducts, northward along the shore, that date to the Roman period.

The 1970s and 1980s brought a higher level of archaeological sophistication to research at Caesarea, including stratigraphic excavation using balks, scientific ceramic analysis, and modern underwater techniques useful for studying the harbors. Between 1971 and 1987, the American Joint Expedition to Caesarea Maritima, directed by Robert J. Bull, conducted twelve summer seasons of excavation. This team explored sectors to the south, east, and north of the Old City, including the low-level aqueduct, which it dated to the fourth century; a well-preserved suburban bath from the Byzantine period; and a Byzantine public building that appears, from inscriptions in its tessellated pavements, to have been part of the governor's headquarters (Gk., *praitorion*). In 1973 and 1974, John Humphrey studied Caesarea's hippodrome, now one of the best-known facilities of its type from the Roman East. Among other outstanding finds were a marble statue of the city goddess, Tyche (see figure 4), of Caesarea and, to the south of the Old City, a cult center of the Roman god Mithras, located in a barrel-vaulted warehouse (Lat., *horreum*), one of a complex of such vaults dating from Herod's time. The Joint Expedition also restudied the inner perimeter wall, which it dated to Herod's original foundation, and devoted special attention to Caesarea's

The project established that Josephus (*War* 1. 408–413; *Antiq.* 15.332–338) had described the breakwaters accurately and recovered details of their design and construction. In building Sebastos, Herod's engineers had employed imported materials and the technology of hydraulic concrete developed in Italy. Still under debate is the later history of Herod's harbor and whether it continued to function in the Roman and Byzantine periods, despite tectonic action and the destructive force of the sea.

In 1989 Kenneth G. Holum and the University of Maryland joined Raban and Haifa's Center for Maritime Studies in the Combined Caesarea Expeditions, a project that continues the strategy and methods of the former Joint Expedition and Harbour Project. This team has devoted its attention again to the underwater exploration of Sebastos and to the outer (Byzantine) perimeter wall and has conducted submarine and field surveys, remote sensing, and geological studies inside the ancient site and to its north and south along the coast. Within the Old City, it has expanded the limits of the Hellenistic and Herodian inner harbor; identified and studied an important Early Christian church on the Temple Platform, octagonal in plan, that Negev's clearing operation had first exposed; and excavated Islamic and Crusader dwellings and public buildings both above the inner harbor and on the Temple Platform. To the south of the Old City, this team has undertaken the excavation of a complete insula of Roman and Byzantine Caesarea to study diachronically the development of the urban plan and the urban infrastructure in antiquity. Under the Combined Expeditions' auspices, Jeffrey A. Blakely has begun excavation of another Herodian *horreum* vault to exploit the ceramics found in its well-stratified and protected context for evidence of trade goods passing through Caesarea's port. Under the auspices of the University of Pennsylvania, Kathryn Gleason and Barbara Burrell are excavating the Promontory Palace.

In 1992 the Israel Antiquities Authority organized a large project to excavate extensive sectors of ancient Caesarea, both within the Old City and to the south along the coast, for the purpose of establishing an archaeological park. Director of the IAA excavations is Yosef Porath, who had earlier conducted important research on the Roman aqueduct system and rescue excavations within the Old City. In the meantime both the University of Pennsylvania team and the Combined Caesarea Expeditions have joined the expanded project, the latter adding Joseph Patrich to its directorate of Raban and Holum. Inside the Old City, the project has identified a sea wall that may represent the harbor restoration of Emperor Anastasius (c. 500), has begun excavation and restoration of one of the vaults that formed the western facade of the Temple Platform, and has exposed a well-preserved Early Islamic dwelling quarter above the landlocked Inner Harbor. To the south of the Old City, the expanded excavations have uncovered, among other finds, a complex of

CAESAREA. Figure 4. *Marble statue of Tyche and the god Sebastos to the right.* Height, 1.52 m. (Courtesy Israel Antiquities Authority)

streets. By excavating numerous street fragments in various sectors, mostly Byzantine in date, the team recovered the orientation of the original Herodian grid and the dimensions of some of the city blocks (insulae).

In 1975–1976 and 1979, a team from the Hebrew University of Jerusalem, directed by Lee I. Levine and Ehud Netzer, excavated a sector in the northwest of the Old City that contained a well-preserved Islamic dwelling quarter and, beneath it, remains of a large Byzantine public building of unknown function. Netzer also began exploring the Promontory Palace jutting into the sea northwest of the theater, which may be the royal palace of Herod's city. In 1986, Ronny Reich and Michal Peleg, in a rescue excavation, identified a south gate of the outer (Byzantine) perimeter wall beneath a factory in the neighboring kibbutz. Meanwhile, in 1975, Avner Raban and Haifa University's Center for Maritime Studies had begun systematic exploration of Caesarea's harbors. In 1980 Raban joined with Robert M. Hohlfelder, John Oleson, and later R. Lindley Vann in the Caesarea Ancient Harbour Excavation Project. That team explored Caesarea's harbors intensively for a decade. It studied shipwrecks and anchorages to the north and south— from the Hellenistic, Roman, and Byzantine periods—but devoted most of its attention to Herod's harbor, Sebastos.

Byzantine warehouses used for storage and marketing of grain, wine, oil, and other trade goods; a Roman/Byzantine public bath; luxurious Roman and Byzantine dwellings; and the spectacular ruins of the amphitheater that Herod built, as Josephus reports (*Antiq.* 15. 341), when he founded Caesarea.

Work in the last two decades demonstrates that Caesarea is a major site for research on the evolution of ancient urbanism—especially its maritime component—from the Hellenistic period through the Crusader occupation. Research is also advancing on floral and faunal remains, glass, metal and bone objects, and other categories of material culture, including ceramics. Current projects are deploying a full range of scientific strategies and techniques to exploit Caesarea's past.

BIBLIOGRAPHY

Blakely, Jeffrey A. *Caesarea Maritima: The Pottery and Dating of Vault 1—Horreum, Mithraeum, and Later Uses.* The Joint Expedition to Caesarea Maritima, Excavation Reports, vol. 4. Lewiston, N.Y., 1986. Important for ceramic studies.

Bull, Robert J. "The Mithraeum of Caesarea Maritima." *Textes et mémoires* 4 (1978): 75–89.

Bull, Robert J., Edgar Krentz, and Olin Storvick. "The Joint Expedition to Caesarea Maritima: Ninth Season, 1980." In *Preliminary Reports of ASOR-Sponsored Excavations, 1980–84,* edited by Walter E. Rast, pp. 31–55. Bulletin of the American Schools of Oriental Research, Supplement no. 24. Winona Lake, Ind., 1986. This and the following item are comprehensive but sketchy preliminary reports with useful photographs and plans.

Bull, Robert J., Edgar Krentz, Olin Storvick, and Marie Spiro. "The Joint Expedition to Caesarea Maritima: Tenth Season, 1982." In *Preliminary Reports of ASOR-Sponsored Excavations, 1982–89,* edited by Walter E. Rast, pp. 69–94. Bulletin of the American Schools of Oriental Research, Supplement no. 27. Baltimore, 1991.

Fritsch, Charles T., ed. *Studies in the History of Caesarea Maritima.* Bulletin of the American Schools of Oriental Research, Supplemental Studies, vol. 19. Missoula, 1975. Essays on Jewish, Christian, and Crusader Caesarea, written from literary sources.

Frova, Antonio, et al. *Scavi di Caesarea Maritima.* Rome, 1966. Final report of the Italian Missione Archeologica.

Holum, Kenneth G., Robert L. Hohlfelder, Robert J. Bull, and Avner Raban. *King Herod's Dream: Caesarea on the Sea.* New York, 1988. Good introduction to the site for the general reader, but outdated in part by recent discoveries. Includes a bibliography.

Holum, Kenneth G. "Archaeological Evidence for the Fall of Byzantine Caesarea." *Bulletin of the American Schools of Oriental Research,* no. 286 (1992): 73–85. Interpretive essay on the reasons for ancient Caesarea's decline.

Levine, Lee I. *Caesarea under Roman Rule.* Leiden, 1975. Authoritative study of the Roman period from the literary sources, especially the rabbinic material.

Levine, Lee I. *Roman Caesarea: An Archaeological-Topographical Guide.* Qedem, vol. 2. Jerusalem, 1975. Scholarly guide to the monuments of Roman and Byzantine Caesarea, partly outdated by recent finds.

Levine, Lee I., and Ehud Netzer. *Excavations at Caesarea Maritima, 1975, 1976, 1979: Final Report.* Qedem, vol. 21. Jerusalem, 1986. Includes a helpful guide to earlier excavations.

Peleg, Michal, and Ronny Reich. "Excavations of a Segment of the Byzantine City Wall of Caesarea Maritima." *'Atiqot* (English Series) 21 (1992): 137–170.

Raban, Avner, et al. *The Harbours of Caesarea Maritima: Results of the Caesarea Ancient Harbour Excavation Project, 1980–1985,* vol. 1, *The Site and the Excavations.* Edited by John Peter Oleson. British Archaeological Reports, International Series, no. 491. Oxford, 1989. Comprehensive report on the harbor project's main seasons, with important topographical and geological studies.

Vann, R. Lindley, ed. *Caesarea Papers: Straton's Tower, Herod's Harbour, and Roman and Byzantine Caesarea.* Journal of Roman Archaeology, Supplementary Series, no. 5. Ann Arbor, Mich., 1992. Collection of interpretive essays reflecting current scholarship, including recent reports of the Combined Caesarea Expeditions and ceramic studies.

Wenning, Robert. "Die Stadtgöttin von Caesarea Maritima." *Boreas* 9 (1986): 113–129. Detailed study of the Caesarea Tyche.

Wiemken, Robert C., and Kenneth G. Holum. "The Joint Expedition to Caesarea Maritima: Eighth Season, 1979." *Bulletin of the American Schools of Oriental Research,* no. 244 (1981): 27–52. Important for the discovery of the street grid south of the Old City; includes coins and ceramics.

KENNETH G. HOLUM

CAIRO, capital of Egypt (30°04′ N, 31°15′ E). The Fatimids, a Shi'i Muslim group, invaded Egypt in 967 CE and founded Cairo as their capital two years later. Like all Shi'is, the Fatimids were strongly inclined to mysticism, which often led to a deep dependence on astrology. They chose the time of the conjunction of Mars and Jupiter in the sign Aries (the ram) for their conquest. Apparently the capital's original name was to have been al-Mansuriyah ("the victorious"), named after a suburb of Kairouan (Qayrawan, the capital of the Shi'i sect at that time in Tunisia). The name al-Kahira (Cairo), which was given to the city later, derives from *Kahir el-Falak* ("the conqueror of the planets"), the designation of the planet Mars. After the Byzantine general Jawhar captured al-Fustat (the early Islamic city founded by the Arabs in Egypt), he immediately began building an enclosure of very large unbaked bricks, measuring about 1,188 sq m (12,915 sq. ft.), which would include a palace, barracks, and administrative buildings.

A major north–south street of al-Kahira linked the old gates of Bab al-Futuh and Bab Zuwayla; both are named after gates at al-Mansuriyah (the Fatimids' headquarters in Tunisia). Part of this street survives in the modern Sharia al-Muizz Li-din Illah. On either side of this sheet, north of the Mosque of al-Azhar, stood the eastern palace, which was laid out by Jawhar, and the western palace built by al-Aziz (975–996). Between them was a very large open square called the Bayn al-Kasrayn ("between the two palaces"). No trace remains of the eastern palace, but literary sources inform us that it consisted of a walled enclosure with nine gates of stone and burned brick.

The gates were the most important architectural feature of this period. At the southern side of the city were the doors of Bab Zuwayla and Bab al-Farag. These portals are prime examples of medieval military fortification. To the west were the gates of Bab Saada and Bab al-Kantara. Bab el-Futuh ("the conquest gate") and Bab el-Nasir ("the victory gate") were at the north. Bab el-Futuh contained two cylindrical towers, and Bab al-Nasir had two square towers. The two eastern doors, Bab Barquyah and Bab el-Qarratin, were connected by two vaulted galleries with domed chambers. Bab Zuwayla was named after a tribe of the same name that lived nearby. During the Mamluk period, the door was called Bab el-Metwalli, "the gate of the tax collector." According to tradition, the revenue official would sit by the door to collect the annual levy. Bab Zuwayla is considered architecturally the most beautiful gate.

Among the most important monuments that the Fatimids erected is the mosque of al-Azhar, which was built in the center of Cairo. Al-Azhar became an institution for the Shi'i rite and a famous Islamic university. During the Ayyubid rule, prayers were not permitted at al-Azhar. The Ayyubids, who were Sunni, terminated Fatimid rule in Egypt. They stopped the Shi'i ritual and closed al-Azhar as a center for Shi'i teaching. Although they ruled for only eighty years, they had a remarkable influence on the arts, and particularly on architecture. The mosque was restored during the eighteenth and nineteenth centuries CE, but the central part still preserves its original brick form.

Many Fatimid mosques remain in Cairo, such as al-Aqmar at Nahasein, as-Salih Talai near Bab Zuwayla, al-Fakahani, and al-Hakim, which follows the same plan as al-Azhar. At the end of the Fatimid period, Cairo reached its peak in terms of art and culture, and became a large city with beautiful mosques, parks houses, palaces and markets.

The first expansion of the city occurred when Salah ad-Din (Saladin) extended the original walls of Cairo farther south to enclose such early Islamic cities as al-Fustat, which was built by the Arab General Amr ibn al-'As in 641, al-Askar, founded by the 'Abbasids in 750, and el-Qatai, founded by Ahmed ibn Tulun in 870.

The origin of the name al-Fustat is not clear; some find that it derives from the Arabic word meaning "camps," and other scholars suggest that it is from the Greek word *phossaton* (Lat., *fossatum*), meaning "fortress" or "town." It is also called "the city of the tent." The site of the new capital, al-Fustat, was protected by natural hills to the east and north. On the west, the city was protected by the Nile, which at that time was the link between the northern and southern Egypt. Early historians and travelers, such as al-Kudai, wrote that there were 3,600 mosques, 8,000 roads, and 1,700 public baths at al-Fustat. Writers may have exaggerated the numbers to show the progress of this new capital in the Islamic world.

Amr ibn al-'As built the al-Atique (old) mosque in 641 in the center of the city. It is the oldest mosque in Egypt and is regarded as the first building of Islamic architecture. The mosque was expanded to its current size in the tenth century during the Umayyad period, and many additions were made by succeeding governors. The most impressive character-istics of early Islamic architecture as seen in this mosque are the magnificent large open court, the colonnades, and the marble columns. Early Arab historians named the mosque "the crown of the mosques" and "the mosque of conquest." Amr built a house for himself to the north of the mosque and another one to the west for his son.

Wanting to prevent the conquest of the city by the Crusaders, the governor of al-Fustat in the twelfth century ordered it to be burned. The fire lasted for fifty-four days and destroyed almost the entire capital, creating a beneficial situation for archaeologists because the event preserved the entire stratigraphic record. Scientific excavation of the debris of al-Fustat settlement could provide us with information about the socioeconomic status of the people, as well as details of early Islamic art and architecture.

Despite its status, al-Fustat for many decades went without scientific excavation. In 1912–1913, Ali Bahgat excavated approximately fifty acres and found the wall that surrounded al-Fustat, the Citadel, and Cairo, built by Salah ad-Din. Hassan el-Hawary and A. Marzouk conducted an excavation at the site. K. A. C. Creswell, in cooperation with Mehriz, also worked at the site. Although the Egyptian Antiquities Organization excavated for many seasons, most of their archaeological reports are unpublished. A team from the American University in Cairo under the direction of George Scanlon, as well as a Japanese group, has been working at al-Fustat.

After the 'Abbasids defeated the last Umayyad caliph in Egypt in 750, they ordered their governor in Egypt to build another capital for their troops. This new site was called al-Askar, "the barracks." It was built as a suburb to the northeast of al-Fustat, in an area known as al-Hamra al-Kuswa and extended to the Yashkur Hills. The 'Abbasids built their houses and the governor's headquarters, known as Dar el-'Imarah, in al-Askar. The soldiers' barracks and the mosque of al-Askar were established by al-Fadl ibn Salih; during his tenure the two cities al-Fustat and al-Askar merged to form one large city. With the destruction of al-Fustat, al-Askar became the principal city. A series of sixty-five governors ruled Egypt from al-Askar on behalf of the 'Abbasids for a period of approximately 118 years. The significance of the new capital al-Askar did not affect al-Fustat, which was still an important trade center.

Ahmed ibn Tulun founded the new city of al-Qata'i, "the wards," in 870. The city was built in a one-square-mile area located between al-Askar and el-Mokattam. Ibn Tulun built his palace, and ordered his people to build new houses, in the new city. He built one of the finest mosques in Egypt and in the Islamic world. It took him two years to finish it, from 879 to 891. The mosque covers approximately 6.5 acres and is the largest mosque in the Islamic world. It is known as Ka'lat el-Kabsh or "fort of the ram." The court measures ninety-nine m (325 ft.) on each side and is surrounded by arcades resting on massive square brick pillars.

There are three hundred pointed horseshoe arches, constructed of brick and covered with stucco decorated with arabesque carvings. Some architectural features used in this mosque (such as brick pillars) were new to Islamic architecture. The minaret with external corkscrew stairs shows Mesopotamian influence. The pointed arches and handmade arabesque carvings are the best example of the Islamic style of decoration.

Salah ad-Din commissioned many important monuments that can still be seen today. The Citadel (intended to house his administration at el-Mokattam) and its aqueduct were built in 1177. Several buildings were added to the Citadel during the Ottoman period. Muhammad Ali Pasha expanded the Citadel, beginning with his mosque, which dominates the area, in 1845. The Citadel later served as the royal palace until Khedive Ismail moved it to the Abdeen Palace in 1850.

Salah ad-Din also introduced the architectural design known as el-Madrasa, which he adapted from Syria. *Madrasah*s were Islamic institutions used both as schools for Sunni Muslim subjects and as mosques for prayer services. The earliest known *madrasah* had two *iwan*s (porticoes). The only surviving *madrasah* in Egypt was built by Sultan as-Salih Najm ed-Din (the last ruler of the Ayyubid period) and is an example of the important Ayyubid style, which was followed by the Mamluks. They built *madrasah*s on a cruciform plan to accommodate the four orthodox schools of Islam. The *madrasah* complex also contained a school, dormitory space, mausoleum, and mosque. The Mamluk "collegiate mosque" style of *madrasah* was a distinctive feature in the Islamic architectural vocabulary in Egypt. An extant example is the mosque of Sultan Hasan (1356), which stands in front of the Citadel. The best statement to describe that mosque was written by the historian Makrizi, "(it) surpassed all the mosques ever built in any part of the world."

The Mamluks ruled for about one hundred years, leaving a large number of important and beautiful artifacts and buildings. Forty mosques are known from this period, and their art and architecture are considered by Islamic scholars and historians to be the most refined in all of Egypt's Islamic history. The minaret was introduced in this period and became an important architectural element of the mosques. Many artists and artisans from Syria and Iraq came to Egypt and introduced other new features. Cairo attained its current size during the Mamluk period. No monuments of distinction were added to Cairo during the reign of the Ottomans.

Today Cairo is the most famous Islamic city, because of its role in the politics of the Middle East as well as its central role in Islam. Al-Azhar Mosque remains the oldest and largest Islamic educational institution and the seat of Dar al-Fatwa ("the house of constitutions") for all Muslims. A thriving urban center with fifteen million inhabitants, it has endured centuries of change to prove worthy of its glorious history.

[*See also* Egypt, *article on* Islamic Egypt; Fatimid Dynasty; *and* Fustat.]

BIBLIOGRAPHY

Abu Lughod, Janet. *Cairo: 1001 Years of the City Victorious.* Princeton, 1971.
Butler, Alfred J. *The Arab Conquest of Egypt and the Last Thirty Years of the Roman Dominion.* Oxford, 1902.
Creswell, K. A. C. *Early Muslim Architecture,* vol. 2, *Umayyads, Early 'Abbasids, and Tulunids.* Oxford, 1940.
Desmond, Stewart. *Great Cairo, Mother of the World.* Cairo, 1981.
Guest, A. R. "The Foundation of Fustat and the Khittahs of That Town." *Journal of the Royal Asiatic Society* (1907): 49–83.
Hasan, Hasan Ibrahim. *Al-Fatimiyun fi Misr.* Cairo, 1932.
Hoag, John D. *Islamic Architecture.* New York, 1975.
Kubiak, Wladyslaw. *Al-Fustat: Its Foundations and Early Development.* Cairo, 1987.
Lane-Poole, Stanley. *A History of Egypt in the Middle Ages.* London, 1901.
MacKenzie, Neil D. *Ayyubid Cairo: A Topographical Study.* Cairo, 1992.
Parker, Richard B., and Robin Sabin. *Islamic Monuments in Cairo: A Practical Guide.* 3d ed., revised and enlarged by Caroline Williams. Cairo, 1985.
Rivoira, Giovanni T. *Moslem Architecture.* London, 1918.
Rogers, John M. "Al-Kahira." In *Encyclopaedia of Islam,* vol. 4, pp. 424–441. New ed., Leiden, 1960–.
Sanders, Paula. *Ritual, Politics, and the City in Fatimid Cairo.* Albany, 1994.
Staffa, Susan Jane. *Conquest and Fusion: The Social Evolution of Cairo, A.D. 642–1850.* Leiden, 1977.

ZAHI HAWASS

CALLAWAY, JOSEPH ATLEE (1920–1988), American archaeologist and principal excavator of Ai/et-Tell, in Israel, a representative of the "biblical archaeology" movement; and leading figure in the American Schools of Oriental Research (ASOR). Callaway was born and educated in Arkansas, where he graduated from Ouachita College. He prepared for the Christian ministry at the Southern Baptist Theological Seminary in Louisville. In addition to his special interests in the Hebrew Bible and language, Callaway developed an interest in Near Eastern archaeology under the tutelage of William H. Morton, professor of Old Testament and biblical archaeology. After earning an M.Div. degree in 1954 and a Ph.D. in Old Testament studies in 1957, Callaway returned to Southern Seminary to teach Old Testament and Near Eastern archaeology from 1958 until his retirement in 1982.

Callaway's desire to relate archaeological findings to biblical study is best illustrated in his general essays and in his extensive fieldwork at the site of et-Tell (1964–1972), which he and most scholars identified as biblical Ai. Over a period of twenty years, Callaway modified his views on the historical accuracy of the conquest narrative (Callaway, 1968), concluding that if there was a "conquest" of Ai, it was accomplished by other Canaanites in the eleventh century BCE.

Callaway published a number of influential articles and books about et-Tell's Early Bronze Age Canaanite culture (cf. Rust, 1988, for a bibliography). He was also deeply concerned with methodological issues, including pottery analysis and the application of the sciences to archaeological research. His attention to refinements in controlled stratigraphic excavation (i.e., the Wheeler-Kenyon method) stemmed from his pre-Ai field experiences at Bethel/Beitin (1960, under James L. Kelso), Shechem (1960, 1962, and 1964, under G. Ernest Wright), and Jerusalem (1961 and 1962, under Kathleen M. Kenyon and Roland de Vaux). Indeed, Kenyon's suggestion that he study the Early Bronze tombs at Ai/et-Tell was the catalyst in his decision to excavate that site.

Joseph Callaway earned a reputation as a captivating speaker, capable administrator, and skilled excavator, all of which were evidenced in his roles as minister, professor, president of the Albright Institute of Archaeological Research in Jerusalem, trustee of the American Schools of Oriental Research, officer in the Society of Biblical Literature, and director of the Joint Expedition to Ai.

[See also Ai; American Schools of Oriental Research; and Biblical Archaeology.]

BIBLIOGRAPHY

Callaway, Joseph A. "Biblical Archaeology." Review and Expositor 58 (1961): 155–172.
Callaway, Joseph A. "The Emerging Role of Biblical Archaeology." Review and Expositor 63 (1966): 199–209.
Callaway, Joseph A. "New Evidence on the Conquest of 'Ai." Journal of Biblical Literature 87 (1968): 312–320.
Callaway, Joseph A. "Archaeology and the Bible." In The Broadman Bible Commentary, vol. 1, edited by Clifton J. Allen, pp. 41–48. Nashville, 1969.
Drinkard, Joel F. "In Memoriam." Biblical Archaeologist 51 (1988): 67.
Rust, Eric C. "Biographical Sketch of Joseph A. Callaway: Christian Minister, Old Testament Professor, and Field Archaeologist." In Benchmarks in Time and Culture: An Introduction to Palestinian Archaeology Dedicated to Joseph A. Callaway, edited by Joel F. Drinkard, Gerald L. Mattingly, and J. Maxwell Miller, pp. 456–464. Atlanta, 1988. The most complete source of information on Callaway's life and work, including a bibliography of his publications through 1985.
Shanks, Hershel. "Joseph A. Callaway, 1920–1988." Biblical Archaeology Review 14.6 (1988): 24.

GERALD L. MATTINGLY

CAMELS. Modern camels are of two types, Camelus dromedarius—the one-humped dromedary—and C. bactrianus—the two-humped Bactrian, both of which are known only as domestic or feral populations. Modern dromedaries are distributed from Morocco to western India, and Bactrians from Anatolia to Mongolia. Their ranges overlap in Anatolia, Azerbaijan, and regions to the east of the Caspian Sea. It is likely that these distributions were different in antiquity, having now shifted somewhat in response to environmental change. No wild camels exist save for a possible relic pop-

ulation in the Gobi Desert. Pleistocene remains in the Near East and Egypt include specimens from the Paleolithic in modern Jordan, Egypt, Syria, and Israel (best referred to as Camelus spec., given nomenclatural complications and an uncertain fossil history, and C. thomasi, a large form known from southern Egypt and northern Sudan). In the early Holocene, evidence for the animal is limited to a small collection from Sihi on the southern Red Sea coast of Saudi Arabia. It has been radiocarbon dated to 8200 BCE (uncalibrated), although the archaeological deposit within which the bones were found dates stratigraphically to the end of the second millennium BCE. Evidence for camels becomes more abundant in the third millennium BCE with specimens from Jericho, coastal sites around the Arabian Peninsula, and Shahr-i Sokhta in eastern Iran. These last are probably Bactrian.

Dromedaries are usually assumed to have been domesticated in Arabia before the third millennium, but no clear archaeological evidence exists to support the claim. The often-cited camel-bone collections from late third millennium Umm an-Nar, Hili 8, and Ras Ghanada on the gulf coast of the United Arab Emirates cannot be shown to contain domestic animals. In fact, the associated bone finds suggest that they were hunted. Rock art depicting camels is known in Arabia and the Sinai but is difficult to date. Therefore, the use of this evidence to support a third-millennium date for domestication is inconclusive. Only further excavation in the region will settle the question of the domestication of the one-humped camel. A tiny number of camel bones is known from third-millennium sites in the Levant (Arad, Jericho)—information insufficient to determine wild or domestic status. The discovery of dung and woven camel hair in association with the bones at Shahr-i Sokhta (2700–2500 BCE) reinforces the suppositions that these are domestic stock and that the Bactrian was domesticated slightly earlier at the border of Turkmenistan and Iran. A camel-hair rope and a series of Old Kingdom depictions suggest the presence of the animal in Egypt but do not provide certain evidence for local domestication. Even later, the evidence for the camel in Egypt is sporadic. It is not until the Hellenistic period that the animal was used extensively there.

In the second millennium BCE, a two-humped camel was depicted on a Syrian cylinder seal (c. 1800 BCE), and the animal is mentioned in cuneiform texts from Mesopotamia from the Old Babylonian period onward. Clay figurines from Yemen showing dromedaries with saddles may be as old as the second millennium BCE. One theory suggests that camels had become numerous in western Arabia by 1500 BCE, contributing to the rise of oases states. However, this pattern of sharp increases in camel use is not reflected at Levantine sites. Only a very few camel-bone finds from Middle Bronze Age sites in the Levant have been reported (Megiddo, Gezer, Ta'anach, el-Jisr, Be'er Resisim). Only the bones from the last site were excavated using modern techniques and are stratigraphically reliable. However, none of these bones have been radiocarbon dated and none can be shown to be domestic. In the Late Bronze Age, camels are still rare. Several specimens are known from Tell Jemmeh. Although it has been reported that a large number of camel bones were found in thirteenth–twelfth-century BCE sites at the copper mines of Timnaʿ, no report of this material has been forthcoming to allow an evaluation. At Ḥesban in Transjordan, only a few camel bones are known from thirteenth–twelfth-century levels.

William Foxwell Albright argued that dromedary domestication and the spread of its use did not much precede the twelfth century BCE. This would mean that the mention of camels in the *Genesis* narrative (12:16; 24:10 ff.) is anachronistic. The archaeological evidence from the Levant still bears out his point about the late spread of camel use. During the Iron Age, camel bones begin to increase in frequency. Although substantial collections have been reported from fortress sites dated to the tenth century BCE in Israel's Negev desert (Har-Saʿad, Qadesh-Barnea), the most dramatic and sustained increase in the use of the camel, as documented from the bones, is found at Tell Jemmeh during the Assyrian occupation in the seventh century BCE. This is coincident with the textual evidence indicating that camels were used by the Assyrian army as pack animals during military campaigns. In the Persian period, the number of camel bones increased even more, as camels were used to carry the international trade in aromatics from the Arabian Peninsula. This further increase in camels at Tell Jemmeh is roughly paralleled by a similar change at the other end of the route, in Yemen. From the textual evidence it is clear that camel management was a specialty of the Arab tribes inhabiting the Syro-Arabian desert and northern Sinai. From the Persian period until the advent of gasoline-powered vehicles, as their use on trade routes expanded, camels became more frequent at sites in the better-watered parts of the Near East. It is also from the Persian period that the animal found another use: their bones became important as a raw material in the large-scale manufacture of bone tools and objects, an industry abundantly evidenced at the port city of Ashkelon in Israel.

[*See also* Animal Husbandry; Ethnozoology; *and* Paleozoology. *In addition, most of the sites mentioned are the subject of independent entries.*]

BIBLIOGRAPHY

Beebe, H. Keith. *The Dromedary Revolution.* Institute for Antiquity and Christianity, Occasional Papers, 18. Claremont, Calif., 1990. Discusses the relationship between the camel and trade in the ancient Near East.

Bulliet, Richard W. *The Camel and the Wheel.* Cambridge, 1975. Classic exposition of camels and camel use in the ancient world.

Grigson, Caroline, et al. "The Camel in Arabia: A Direct Radiocarbon Date, Calibrated to about 7000 BC." *Journal of Archaeological Science*

16 (1989): 355–362. Discussion of the earliest Holocene evidence for camels in Arabia.

Hakker-Orion, D. "The Role of the Camel in Israel's Early History." In *Animals and Archaeology,* vol. 3, *Early Herders and Their Flocks,* edited by Juliet Clutton-Brock and Caroline Grigson, pp. 207–212. Oxford, 1983. Review of the camel in southern Israel and Sinai.

Midant-Reynes, Beatrix, and Florence Braunstein-Silvestre. "Le chameau en Égypte." *Orientalia* 46 (1977): 337–362. Presents the archaeological evidence from Egypt, emphasizing artistic and textual records.

Uerpmann, Hans-Peter. *The Ancient Distribution of Ungulate Mammals in the Middle East.* Wiesbaden, 1987. Thorough review of the early archaeological and osteological record for the camel.

Wapnish, Paula. "Camel Caravans and Camel Pastoralists at Tell Jemmeh." *Journal of the Ancient Near Eastern Society of Columbia University* 13 (1981): 101–121. Links the spread of camel use and political and economic processes in the Iron Age and Persian period in the Levant.

Wapnish, Paula. "Beauty and Utility in Bone: New Light on Bone Crafting." *Biblical Archaeology Review* 17 (1991): 54–57. Illustrates the use of camel bone as a raw material.

PAULA WAPNISH

CANAAN. In Hebrew, Ugaritic, and Phoenician/Punic Canaan is spelled *knʿn,* in Akkadian cuneiform it is spelled *ki-na-aḥ-nu(m)* (at Mari, Byblos, and Tyre), *ki-in-a-nim* (at Alalakh), *māt ki-na-ḥi* (in Assyria and Ugarit), or *māt ki-in-na-aḥ-ḥi* (in Egypt, Mitanni, Boğazköy/Ḥattuša, Babylon); and in Egyptian it is spelled *k-3-n-ʿ-n-3* or *k-i-n-ʿ-nw* (with many variations). The Septuagint generally simply transliterates into Greek as Chanaan. The etymology of the name has been much discussed, and the discussion revolves around whether *knʿn* should be understood as derived from the Semitic root *k-n-ʿ,* "to bend, be subdued," with the *-n* suffix (the consensus at present; see Astour, 1965); or whether the same word as the place name *Canaan* (also spelled *kinaḥḥu* in several cuneiform sources) should be seen in *kinaḥḥu,* "blue cloth" from Nuzi (in Hurrian or hurrianized Akkadian; see Speiser, 1936, disputed in Landsberger, 1967). *Kinaḥḥu* would present a parallel (though opposite) process to the Greek use of a derivative of a word for red-purple to name the Phoenicians.

The term *Canaan* or *Canaanite* appears in the extant evidence for the first time in an eighteenth-century BCE text from Mari in Syria. A man named Mut-Bisir complains to his lord in a letter written from the town of Rāḥiṣum that "thieves and Canaanites are in Rāḥiṣum." (Doubt has recently been cast on a suggestion that the term is to be seen in *ga-na-na(-um)* in third-millennium texts from Ebla in Syria; see Archi et al., 1993, pp. 229–230.) Other than this text, nothing appears in writing about Canaan or the Canaanites until the late fifteenth century (in a booty list, Amenophis II declares that he had deported Canaanites) and then several times in the fourteenth-century BCE Amarna letters. "Ammia in the land of Canaan" shows up in the "autobiography" of Idrimi (of Alalakh), dated variously by scholars to the fifteenth–thirteenth centuries BCE. At Ugarit, in about 1200 BCE, a list of merchants includes one *Y'l*, described as a Canaanite *(kn'ny)*, along with other people with ethnic identifiers, such as Egyptian and Ashdodite. Because the Ugaritians bothered to label these people with gentilics, it is generally deduced that they were in some sense outsiders and that, therefore, Ugarit did not consider itself a part of Canaan. At about the same time, the "Israel stela" of Pharaoh Merneptah lists Canaan as one of the conquered lands.

The land of Canaan is described in several ancient texts, with predictably varying boundaries. Through most of the second millennium BCE, Canaan's boundaries began in the south at Wadi al-'Arish and reached north to the Lebanon and the Anti-Lebanon Mountain ranges. The western border was, of course, the Mediterranean, and the eastern was Transjordan (mostly the Bashan) and the Jordan River and Dead Sea farther south. These boundaries accord with the area covered by the eighteenth-century BCE Saqqara group of Egyptian Execration texts and with the descriptions of the land of Canaan in *Numbers* 34:1–12 and the future inheritance in *Ezekiel* 47:13–20; 48:1–7, 23–29. (See also the southern boundary in *Jos.* 15:2–4 and the northern one in 19:24–31.) The table of nations gives a rather more restricted picture of Canaan in *Genesis* 10:19: from Sidon in the north to Gaza in the south; to the east, the area of Sodom and Gomorrah.

Biblical traditions about the land of Canaan cluster in the genealogies and in the stories of promise and conquest. The word *Canaan* occurs largely in *Genesis* and *Numbers*, a few times in *Exodus, Leviticus,* and *Deuteronomy,* and then many times in *Joshua* and *Judges* (including the earliest-dated biblical attestation, *Js.* 5:19). *Canaanite* occurs frequently in *Genesis* and *Exodus* and a few times in *Numbers* and *Deuteronomy,* but most commonly in *Joshua* and *Judges.* These mentions, of course, refer to the land in which Israel settled (conquered, according to biblical tradition) and to the inhabitants of that land. Neither word appears very many times outside the Pentateuch and *Joshua* and *Judges,* although a few later occurrences are interesting for their apparent use of phrases with the word *Canaan* (once *Canaanite*) to mean "merchant, trader" (*Jb.* 40:30; *Ez.* 16:29, 17:4; *Hos.* 12:8; *Zep.* 1:11).

Extrabiblical uses of the terms *Canaan* and *Canaanite* end for the most part with the Iron Age, with a few exceptions. In the third century BCE, coins from Beirut read *l'dk' 'š bkn'n* (in Phoenician, "Laodikea which is in Canaan"—the Greek equivalent of *Laodikeia hē en Phoinikē,* "Laodikea which is in Phoenicia." The Phoenician priest Sakkunyaton (perhaps mid- or late first millennium BCE), in excerpts from Philo of Byblos (first or second century CE), quoted by Eusebius (fourth century), says that Chna was the first person to call himself Phoenician. Both Herodianus Grammaticus (second century CE; *Peri monērous lexeōs,* 8.5–9) and Stephanus

of Byzantium (fifth century CE; see under Chna) note that Phoenicia was formerly called Chna.

[*See also* Canaanites; Phoenicia; *and* Phoenicians.]

BIBLIOGRAPHY

Aharoni, Yohanan. *The Land of the Bible: A Historical Geography.* Rev. & enl. ed., translated and edited by Anson F. Rainey. Philadelphia, 1979. A densely packed presentation of the geography of Israel and of what is known of the identification of sites.

Archi, Alfonso, Paola Piacentini, and Francesco Pomponio. *Archivi Reali di Ebla.* Vol. 2, *I nomi di luogo dei testi di Ebla.* Rome, 1993. Listing of occurrences of place names in the Ebla texts, with comment where appropriate.

Astour, Michael C. "The Origin of the Terms 'Canaan,' 'Phoenician,' and 'Purple.'" *Journal of Near Eastern Studies* 24 (1965): 346–350. Discussion and evaluation of alternative arguments for the origins of the three terms.

Attridge, Harold W., and Robert A. Oden Jr. *Philo of Byblos. The Phoenician History.* Washington, 1981. Fine, accessible version of Sakkunyaton, with introduction and notes.

Landsberger, Benno. "Über Farben im Sumerisch-Akkadischen." *Journal of Cuneiform Studies* 21 (1967): 139–173. Wide-ranging discussion of the precise referents of color words.

McCarter, P. Kyle, Jr. "The Patriarchal Age." In *Ancient Israel,* edited by Hershel Shanks, pp. 1–29. Washington, 1988. An up-to-date introduction to the possible background of the patriarchal stories in *Genesis,* in the course of which Middle Bronze and Late Bronze Age Canaan are discussed.

Mazar, Benjamin. "Canaan and the Canaanites." In *Biblical Israel: State and People,* edited by Shmuel Ahituv, pp. 16–21. Jerusalem, 1992. Extensive presentation of the evidence bearing on the meaning of the name *Canaan.* The entire work is a collection of Mazar's essays.

Rainey, Anson F. "The Kingdom of Ugarit." *Biblical Archaeologist* 28.4 (December 1965): 102–125. Summary of the excavations, history, administration, and religion at Ugarit; includes the evidence (through the mid-1960s) that Late Bronze Ugarit did not consider itself part of Canaan.

Speiser, Ephraim A. "The Name *Phoinikes.*" *Language* 12 (1936): 121–126. Discussion and evaluation of three theories about the origin of the Greek name for the Phoenicians.

JO ANN HACKETT

CANAANITES. There are several ways to distinguish the ancient Canaanites: as people who lived in Canaan (Lebanon, southern Syria, Israel, and Transjordan); people who spoke a Canaanite language; people identified in antiquity by other groups as Canaanites; and people who identified themselves as Canaanites. [*See* Canaan.] For the period before there is any evidence of the individual Canaanite languages, the term *Canaanite* simply designates people who lived in (or came from) Canaan. It is not known when, exactly, the peoples who will later speak Canaanite languages arrived in Canaan, or where they came from. The first certain extant mention of "Canaanites" is in an eighteenth-century text from Mari in Syria. [*See* Mari Texts.] The clear break in culture in the region seen at about the beginning of the second millennium BCE, known as the beginning of the Middle Bronze Age I, and some ties between MB I culture

CANAANITES. *Relief showing Canaanite vassals.* From the Memphite tomb of general Horemheb at Saqqara. Eighteenth dynasty. (Courtesy Rijks Museum van Oudheden, Leiden)

on the coast of Syria and Palestine and the slightly earlier culture in the interior of Syria, suggest that the "Canaanites" of the second millennium BCE came to Canaan from Syria. At any rate, it is now evident that there was a major shift at the beginning of the second millennium BCE away from rural pastoralism and toward living in large, fortified urban centers, such as Megiddo, Jericho, Tell Beit Mirsim, Gezer, Shechem, and Hazor. [*See* Megiddo; Jericho; Beit Mirsim, Tell; Gezer; Shechem; Hazor.] Established urban centers were growing, new settlements were being founded, and trade was on an international scale, including the islands of the Mediterranean, another sign of prosperity.

The three-tiered settlement pattern typical of an urbanized culture can be seen: most people lived in large urban areas; most of the settlements outside the urban areas were small villages (many were 2 acres or less); and in between the villages were a few medium-sized towns. This information has been gleaned largely from archaeological surveys; adding to it what has been learned from full-scale excavations at a few sites and comparing settlement patterns in other areas of the world and in other periods of time to

help us reach conclusions about life in MB Canaan. These conclusions are much broader than what we can learn from text finds or from the few tells that have been excavated intensely and well.

The massive fortifications around the urban areas usually included a rampart (e.g., Akko, Tel Zeror, Hazor, Tel Dan, Dor, Shechem, Ashkelon, Megiddo, Lachish, Gezer). Such fortifications could only be undertaken where there was surplus wealth, a workforce free from subsistence activities, central control of natural resources outside urban areas, and central planning. They also indicate that there was a perceived enemy or enemies to warrant such precautions, as do the more modest city walls found as defenses at small farming and pastoral villages (such as Mevorakh and Shiloh). The labor that went into huge fortifications was probably forced labor—an assumption that accords well with the archaeological indicators of a stratified society: large numbers of rather poor living arrangements alongside a very few large domestic structures as at Hazor and Tell Beit Mirsim.

The transition from the Middle to Late Bronze Age in Canaan entailed some destruction, especially in the hill country and in the south, but that destruction was not complete and, in the Late Bronze Age (especially LB II, the "Amarna age"), the old sites were largely resettled: Hazor, Megiddo, Shechem, Gezer, Tell Beit Mirsim, and Tell el-Far'ah (North) retained their prominence. [*See* Far'ah, Tell el- (North).] In general, the LB city-states did not build new fortifications: where they could, they used those that still stood. This is also an urban period in Canaan, but much reduced from the Middle Bronze Age. There were fewer sites and they were generally smaller, and most settlement was along the coast and in the valleys, along the trade routes (there was very little settlement in the central hill country). Until the very end of the Late Bronze Age, there is clear evidence of trade with Cyprus and the Aegean. [*See* Cyprus; Aegean Islands.]

Agriculture combined with pastoralism was the way of life for most Canaanites—in what was probably a kind of dimorphic society, like the one known from eighteenth-century BCE Mari. [*See* Mari; Agriculture; Pastoral Nomadism.] Rural pastoralists had close ties to the urban areas, from which they were supplied with agricultural and manufactured products. The urban areas, in turn, depended on the pastoralists for animal products. There is evidence of the cultivation of wheat and barley, as well as olives, grapes, and other horticultural products. [*See* Cereals; Olives; Viticul-

ture.] Cattle, sheep, goats, and pigs were herded. [*See* Cattle and Oxen; Sheep and Goats; Pigs.] By the Middle Bronze Age the technology existed to make tools sharper and of sturdier bronze than was possible in the Early Bronze Age. In addition, the quality of Canaanite pottery was extremely fine as a result of advances in ceramic technology.

There is no indication that the Canaanite urbanized three-tiered settlement pattern, or city-state system, was ever organized on a larger scale, into a true nation-state system. (No capital city of all Canaan has so far presented itself.) Canaan was ruled by Egypt from at least the time of Thutmosis III (early fifteenth century BCE), although Egyptian control of the province was sometimes very loose. The Canaanites of the fourteenth-century Amarna letters lived in feuding city-states that depend on Egypt to settle their disputes, and there is archaeological evidence of periodic Egyptian sorties, especially in the south. [*See* Amarna Tablets.] As the era proceeded, the evidence for Egyptian fortress sites and "governors' residencies" increases (e.g., Haruvit, Tel Mor, Jaffa, Deir el-Balah, Tell esh-Shari'a, Aphek, Tell el-Far'ah [South], and Tell Jemmeh), suggesting that the city-states' pleas for more protection from Egypt were heeded.

A weakened Egypt lost control of Canaan in the mid-twelfth century BCE, and the vacuum left by its withdrawal

CANAANITES. *Copy of a mural from a tomb at Beni Hasan.* Semitic tribespeople dressed in colored striped costumes ask permission to enter Egypt. Dated to the nineteenth century BCE, Middle Kingdom. Kunsthistorisches Museum, Vienna. (Erich Lessing/Art Resource, NY)

allowed for the establishment there of independent political units: Israel, Moab, Ammon, Edom, the Philistine pentapolis, and the Phoenician cities in the north. This process in Israel and Judah seems to have been a gradual sedentarization of the population, helped along by deforestation and terracing for agriculture, and often in areas not heavily settled in the Late Bronze Age. [*See* Moab; Ammon; Edom; Philistines, *article on* Early Philistines; Phoenicians.]

Writing and Languages. There is evidence that the Canaanite peoples used several writing systems in the Middle Bronze Age and later. Akkadian syllabic cuneiform texts have been found at Taʿanach, Megiddo, Aphek, and Hazor. [*See* Akkadian; Cuneiform; Taʿanach; Aphek.] One of them, a literary text found at Megiddo, is part of the Epic of Gilgamesh, suggesting the existence of a traditional cuneiform scribal school there in which students learned to write in part by copying "the classics." [*See* Writing and Writing Systems; Scribes and Scribal Techniques.] What is known as Peripheral Akkadian was the lingua franca of much of the Near East (outside Mesopotamia proper) in the Late Bronze Age. Many letters from Amarna in Egypt (ancient Akhetaten) exist that were sent to and from Canaanite cities (e.g., from Akko, Ashkelon, Beirut, Byblos, Gezer, Hazor, Jerusalem, Lachish, Megiddo, Shechem, Sidon, and Tyre) and are written in several of these Peripheral Akkadian dialects. [*See* Amarna, Tell el-; Akko; Ashkelon; Beirut; Byblos; Jerusalem; Lachish; Sidon; Tyre.]

A much-simplified cuneiform writing system is also known from such Canaanite sites as Taʿanach, Sarepta, and Beth-Shemesh, although the vast majority of the texts in this system come from the Syrian city of Ugarit (modern Ras Shamra) and its environs. [*See* Sarepta; Beth-Shemesh; Ugarit.] Because not all such texts are from Ugarit, there has been a tendency in recent scholarship away from calling this writing system Ugaritic cuneiform. [*See* Ugaritic.] It is referred to it instead as Canaanite cuneiform (although this usage also has its problems: strictly speaking, Ugarit was not a part of Canaan). Unlike the Akkadian syllabary, with its hundreds of signs, this Canaanite cuneiform writing system (also writing wedge-shaped characters with a stylus on clay tablets) has only thirty characters, each of which represents a consonant in the Ugaritic language—or, in the case of the phoneme *ʾaleph*, represented by three signs, a consonant plus a vowel. It is, therefore, an alphabet rather than a syllabary.

The system for which the Canaanites are best remembered, however, is the linear alphabet, first encountered on a single sixteenth-century BCE sherd from Gezer and then in large numbers of fifteenth-century BCE inscriptions from Serabit el-Khadem, a turquoise-mining site in western Sinai where Canaanite-speaking slaves were the labor force. (The name *Proto-Sinaitic* was given to the corpus.) [*See* Alphabet; Proto-Canaanite; Proto-Sinaitic.] Some of the signs resemble Egyptian hieroglyphs, but no consistent system of influ-

ence has ever been demonstrated. Each of the original twenty-seven symbols represents a consonantal phoneme. The linear alphabet operates according to the acrophonic principle: each symbol originated as the picture of something whose name in Canaanite was a word that began with the sound the picture represents. A picture of a house was the original *b* because the Canaanite word for house, *bayt-*, begins with the *b* sound. The *k* is a picture of a hand, because in Canaanite "(palm of) hand" is *kapp-*. This linear alphabet—incised in stone, metal, and gemstones and drawn in ink on potsherds (ostraca), papyrus, and leather—is the forerunner of all modern Western alphabets, spread through the Mediterranean by Phoenician traders. [*See* Ostracon; Papyrus; Leather.] Some of the signs in the earlier Canaanite cuneiform alphabet resemble this linear alphabet—it is as if the cuneiformists had attempted to draw the pictographs rather abstractly with a stylus on clay. It has therefore been suggested that the Canaanite cuneiform alphabet developed under the influence of the linear alphabet. The order of the alphabet is the same for both, as witnessed by the several complete and partial abecedaries discovered in both systems (e.g., from Ugarit, ʿIzbet Sartah, and Lachish).

This linear alphabet is the source of the later Phoenician, Hebrew, and Aramaic scripts (including subsets of each, such as Ammonite and Edomite); it is also the source of the South Semitic alphabet—the letter shapes in this series suggest that it must have broken off from the rest by the thirteenth century BCE. [*See* Phoenician-Punic; Hebrew Language and Literature; Aramaic Language and Literature; Ammonite Inscriptions.] The earliest inscriptions in this linear alphabet so far recovered include (in addition to some largely dedicatory Proto-Sinaitic inscriptions) several short inscriptions likely representing claims to ownership: bronze arrowheads inscribed with personal names; several dedicatory inscriptions, usually written on the dedicated objects; and an abecedary from ʿIzbet Sartah.

The word *Canaanite* is also used as the name of a group of Northwest Semitic languages: Israelite and Judahite Hebrew; Phoenician and Punic; Ammonite; Edomite; and Moabite. Also Northwest Semitic languages, but differentiated from Canaanite, are Ugaritic, Aramaic, and the language of the plaster text from Tell Deir ʿAlla. [*See* Deir ʿAlla Inscriptions.] (Cf. the reference to Hebrew as the "language of Canaan" in *Is.* 19:18.) The Canaanite languages are differentiated from other Northwest Semitic languages in at least the following three ways.

1. The suffix-conjugation forms for the D ("intensive"; Heb., *piʿel*) conjugation and C ("causative"; Heb., *hipʿil*) conjugation are **qattila* and **haqtila* in Proto-Northwest Semitic, but they become **qittila* and **hiqtila* in Hebrew, in Phoenician, and in at least one of the Amarna Canaanite dialects.

2. The first-person singular independent pronoun, originally **ʾanākŭ*, becomes **ʾanōkŭ* ([ā] > [ō] (the so-called

Canaanite shift), and then dissimilates to *'anōkī. Corresponding to this new form comes the change from *-tŭ to *-tĭ in the suffix-conjugation ending for the first-person singular.

3. Proto-Canaanite leveled *-nŭ for all first-person plural suffixes (on suffix-conjugation verbs, on nouns, and in the objective verbal suffixes), from an earlier mixture of *-nŭ and *-nă. (Proto-Aramaic, on the other hand, leveled *-nă.) Obviously, evidence for all these features is not to be found in the traditions that exist only in unvocalized form (e.g., Moabite, Edomite, Ammonite); where there is evidence, however, it supports these suggested divisions.

Religion and Cult. The picture of Canaanite religion is often drawn from the texts found at ancient Ugarit (in spheres outside religion, however, most scholars do not include Ugarit within the scope of Canaan). While the Ugaritians distinguished themselves from Canaanites, Ugaritic religious literature has enough links with later biblical literature to place Ugarit on a cultural continuum with Canaan. The copious amounts of material from Ugarit may, then, suggest what LB Canaanite religion was like. Because the later political entities of Israel, Moab, Ammon, Edom, and the Phoenician cities were also Canaanite, their religious traditions also constitute "Canaanite religion," although many biblical texts, for instance, distinguish between Israelite religion and the religion of "the Canaanites," with the latter seen as the pre-Israelite inhabitants of the land.

Canaanite religion was a religion of blood sacrifice, as can be seen not only in the Bible but also on the lists of sacrifices to various deities found at Ugarit and in the number of altars found in the vicinity of animal remains at archaeological sites throughout the region. [See Altars.] The harvest festivals known from the Bible are thought to be general Canaanite, and not specific Hebrew, festivals. Several other religious features known especially from the Bible are also confirmed by the archaeology and historical geography of the area: outside worship at installations called bāmôt; the erection of standing stones; and the veneration of mountains and hills. [See Cult.]

A large number of male and female deities was worshiped throughout the area, known from Ugarit, the Bible, various Canaanite personal names, and inscriptions. The high god 'El, the father-god, head of the council of gods, lived on top of a mountain at the foot of which was the source of fresh water. Of the same "generation" was Asherah, a marine goddess ('atiratu yammi at Ugarit); the gods at Ugarit are called her children and she is called creator of creatures. Asherah was also known as Qudshu, "holiness" (in Egypt as well as at Ugarit), and as 'Elat, "goddess" (e.g., on a ewer from Lachish; see Cross, 1954, pp. 19–22). The storm god, Ba'al Hadad, a warrior-god, fights battles with both the Sea (Yamm) and Death (Mot). 'Anat, a warrior goddess, is also typical of the Near Eastern goddess represented as an adolescent—no longer a child but not yet a woman (like some descriptions of Mesopotamian Ishtar). She is described in a manner reminiscent of some iconographic representations of the Indian goddess Kali, adorned with skulls and hands (KTU 1.3.2.9–11). The goddess 'Ashtart is not very well developed at Ugarit or in the Bible, but she is the head deity at Sidon in the sixth and fifth centuries BCE, where her cult is presided over by the royal family. Dagon, god of grain (known also from Ugarit), is said in the Bible to be worshiped by the Philistines (e.g., 1 Sm. 4), and so may have been more important in second-millennium BCE Canaan than the texts suggest.

These deities demonstrate continuity with those of the national religions of the Iron Age: Yahweh in Israel, for instance, is a storm god as well as an 'El figure (patriarch, head of the council). There is no evidence that Chemosh in Moab, Milkom in Ammon, and Qaws in Edom were any different. In fact, there is some slight evidence that they were similar; they were also national gods from the same time period, and the onomastica are similar; and the Mesha stela shows Chemosh leading Mesha in war and requiring a kind of "holy war" destruction.

The Phoenician gods vary in name and/or function from city to city. Ba'al Shamêm ("lord of heaven," probably a local name for Ba'al Hadad) is the god who legitimizes and blesses the ruling families of several Phoenician (and Aramean) cities; the Lady of Byblos seems to have the same function at Byblos. [See Arameans.] 'Ashtart, mentioned above, was also one of the gods, along with Melqart, Eshmun, Bethel, 'Anat-Bethel, and various Ba'al figures, who served as Tyrian guarantors of Tyre's seventh-century BCE treaty with the Assyrian king Esarhaddon. [See Assyrians.] Eshmun is the Phoenician god of healing, and Melqart ("king of the city") appears largely in Tyrian or Tyrian colonial settings. Tanit (or Tinnit), presumably a local name for Asherah, is at home in seventh-century BCE Sarepta in Phoenicia and throughout the Mediterranean, especially in North Africa in the third–second centuries BCE. [See Phoenicia; North Africa.]

No local evidence presently exists for the kind of sexual magico-sympathetic religion so often asserted for the Canaanites—even though the fertility of humans, animals, and crops was of course a concern of ancient Near Eastern religions (including that of the Israelites and Ugaritians). At Ugarit, Ba'al Hadad was the provider of rain as well as the god of fertility for crops; and 'El was the deity appealed to for human fertility, just as Yahweh was the god of fertility in Israel.

In addition to the cults of the national or city gods of Canaan, other forms of religious activity existed throughout the area. Both the goddess figurines excavated by archaeologists in Israel and the inscriptions from Kuntillet 'Ajrud in Sinai offer evidence of goddess worship officially or unofficially alongside the worship of Yahweh. [See Kuntillet 'Ajrud.] From the coastal areas there is some evidence, mostly iconographic and architectural, of a religion peculiar to seafarers: anchors included in temple architecture, temples on isolated promontories, and what appear to be divinized ships portrayed on coins. [*See* Seafaring; Anchors.] Moreover, there appears to be a form of ancestor religion attested in texts and in burials from Israel (e.g., *Ps.* 106:28) and Ugarit (especially *KTU* 1.161 and the Duties of the Ideal Son repeated several times in *KTU* 1.17), as well as farther afield in Syria and Mesopotamia. [*See* Burial Techniques.] (Ancestor religion, which exists primarily in patrilineal societies, generally includes blood sacrifice; it functions to tie males to ancestors in the genealogy, while seeking blessings as a reward for keeping up the cultic ties.)

The gruesome practice of child sacrifice was also a part of Canaanite religion. It is best known from the Punic colonies in North Africa, but inscriptions related to Phoenician child sacrifice have also turned up on Malta, Sicily, and Sardinia. [*See* Malta; Sardinia.] There are many biblical references to the practice in Israel and its environs (e.g., *Dt.* 12:31, 18:9–10; *2 Kgs.* 3:26–27, 16:3; *Jer.* 7:31; *Ps.* 106:37–38).

Hebrew Bible. In the Hebrew Bible, the word *Canaanite(s)* is sometimes used as a general term for the pre-Israelite inhabitants of the land (*Ex.* 13:11; throughout *Jgs.* 1); the term *Amorite(s)* is also used (*Gn.* 15:16; *Jgs.* 6:10). More often, several peoples are said to have lived in the land before the Israelites, and the Canaanites are mentioned as one among them (e.g., *Gn.* 15:19–21; *Ex.* 3:8; *Jos.* 3:10). In a few of these cases, the Canaanites are specifically located along the coast—perhaps a reflection of the position of Phoenicia in the first half of the first millennium BCE (*Nm.* 13:29; *Jos.* 5:1, cf. 7:7–9). In the genealogy of *Genesis* 10:6, Canaan is the son of Noah's son Ham and the brother of Ethiopia (Cush), Egypt, and Libya (Put); and in 10:15–18 it is the father of Sidon, the Hittites (Heth), and the Jebusites and Amorites (who are elsewhere listed as pre-Israelite peoples in the land), as well as the father of the Arkites, Sinites, Arvadites, Zemarites, and Hamathites.

The term *Canaanite* fell out of use for the most part in about 1000 BCE, when it was replaced by the gentilics of the various Iron Age nations that grew out of Canaan. Trade in the coastal cities continued to be active, however, and the Phoenicians (see above) eventually set up a long-distance trade network in the Mediterranean world. Carthage, initially a Phoenician colony, became the head of a commercial empire of its own in the late first millennium BCE. [*See* Carthage.] In the fourth century CE its people, according to Augustine, still called themselves Canaanites (Migne 35, 2096).

BIBLIOGRAPHY

Clifford, Richard J. "Phoenician Religion." *Bulletin of the American Schools of Oriental Research*, no. 279 (1990): 55–64. Brief but excellent presentation of current thinking about the religion and gods of the Phoenicians.

Coogan, Michael D. *Stories from Ancient Canaan.* Westminster, 1978. The best English translation of the three major mythic narratives from Ugarit.

Cross, Frank Moore. "The Evolution of the Proto-Canaanite Alphabet." *Bulletin of the American Schools of Oriental Research*, no. 134 (1954): 15–24.

Cross, Frank Moore. *Conversations with a Bible Scholar*, edited by Hershel Shanks. Washington, 1994. A recent and informal exposition of Canaanite and biblical religion by the scholar who defined the parameters of the discussion in the United States.

Dever, William G. "The Middle Bronze Age: The Zenith of the Urban Canaanite Era." *Biblical Archaeologist* 50.3 (1987): 148–77. Comprehensive presentation of the era, plus a discussion of the New Archaeology.

Halpern, Baruch. *The Emergence of Israel in Canaan.* Chico, Calif., 1983. Painstaking exposition of the beginnings of Israel in Canaan, as revealed in Israel's earliest literature.

Huehnergard, John. "Languages (Introductory)." *Anchor Bible Dictionary.* Vol. 4, pp. 155–170. New York, 1992. Extensive overview of the languages of the biblical world, the time periods in which they are attested, and the kinds of texts written in each.

Mazar, Amihai. *Archaeology of the Land of the Bible, ca. 10,000–586* B.C.E. New York, 1990. Readable and thorough introduction to the archaeology of Israel and its environs.

Miller, Patrick D., Jr. "Ugarit and the History of Religions." *Journal of Northwest Semitic Languages* 9 (1981): 119–28. The best short treatment of the subject of Ugaritic religion.

Miller, Patrick D., Jr., Paul D. Hanson, and S. Dean McBride, eds. *Ancient Israelite Religion: Essays in Honor of Frank Moore Cross.* Philadelphia, 1987. More than thirty scholars address Israel's religion in the context of the ancient Near East.

Moran, William L. *The Amarna Letters.* Baltimore, 1992. The definitive translation, with introduction and notes, of the fourteenth-century BCE diplomatic letters, found at el-Amarna in Egypt, between the pharoah and his vassals in Syria-Palestine. The correspondence is the source of much of what is known of LB Canaan.

Na'aman, Nadav. "Economic aspects of the Egyptian occupation of Canaan." *Israel Exploration Journal* 31.3–4 (1981): 172–185. Discussion of the logic of the administration of Canaan during the Amarna age.

Naveh, Joseph. *Early History of the Alphabet.* Jerusalem, 1987. Readable survey of the earliest known West Semitic inscriptions and the later first-millennium BCE evolution of the script traditions.

JO ANN HACKETT

CAORC. *See* Council of American Overseas Research Centers.

CAPE GELIDONYA, sometimes also Khelidonya, or Şilidonya Burnu, and more recently known as Taşlık Burun or Anadolu Burnu, the Chelidonian promontory of Pliny (*Natural History* 5.27.97) in Lycia. The cape marks the western extremity of the Bay of Antalya. Running south from the cape is a string of five small islands, the Chelidoniae of antiquity, called Celidoni by Italian sailors, and later Şelidonlar by the Turks, but today known simply as Beşadalar (Tk., "five islands"). Strabo (14.2.1, 14.3.8) noted only three of them and Pliny (*Natural History* 5.35.131) only four.

In about 1200 BCE, a merchant vessel apparently ripped its bottom open on a pinnacle of rock that nears the surface of the sea just off the northeast side of Devecitaşı Adası, the largest of the islands (36°11′40″ N, 30°24′27″ E). Spilling artifacts in a line as she sank, the ship eventually settled with her stern resting on a large boulder 50 m or so away to the north; the bow landed on a flat sea floor of rock. At some point during the hull's disintegration, the stern slipped off the boulder into a natural gully formed by the boulder and the base of the island.

In 1954, a sponge diver from Bodrum, Kemal Aras, stumbled on the wreck's main concentration of cargo, between 26 and 28 m deep. Four years later, he described it to American journalist and amateur archaeologist Peter Throckmorton, who was cataloging ancient wrecks along the southwest Turkish coast. Throckmorton was able to locate the site in 1959 and, recognizing its great age, asked the University Museum of the University of Pennsylvania if it would organize its excavation.

The subsequent excavation by the museum of this Late Bronze Age site (June–September 1960) was the first shipwreck excavation carried to completion on the seabed, the first directed by a diving archaeologist, and the first conducted following the standards of terrestrial excavation. Visits to the site in the late 1980s by a team from the Institute of Nautical Archaeology (INA) at Texas A&M University, led by the original excavation director, George F. Bass, showed, after more artifacts were recovered, how the ship had sunk. The sinking has been dated to the late thirteenth century BCE by two nearly intact Mycenaean IIIB stirrup jars discovered on these visits and by a radiocarbon date of 1200 BCE ± fifty years from brushwood on the wreck.

Because of a lack of protective sediment, most of the ship's hull had been devoured by marine borers, especially teredos. However, its brushwood dunnage gave, for the first time, meaning to the brushwood Odysseus placed in a vessel he had built (*Odyssey* 5.257). The distribution of cargo originally led to a published estimate of not much longer than 10 m for the hull, but recent discoveries suggest that this estimate was low.

The bulk of the cargo consisted of the ingredients for making bronze implements, including both scrap bronze tools from Cyprus, intended to be recycled, and ingots of both copper and tin, meant to be mixed to form new bronze. The scrap, at least partly carried in wicker baskets, included broken plowshares, axes, adzes, chisels, pruning hooks, a spade, knives, and casting waste. The copper, mined on Cyprus, was shipped as thirty-four flat, four-handled ingots, weighing on average 25 kg apiece, of the type once thought to imitate dried ox hides in a premonetary form of currency (see figure 1); discoid "bun ingots," averaging only about 3 kg each; and fragments chiseled from each type. The tin ingots were too badly corroded to reveal their original shapes, but seabed evidence suggests that at least one was a

CAPE GELIDONYA. Figure 1. *Three oxhide copper ingots.* (Copyright Frey/INA)

rectangular bar. In addition, there were eighteen much smaller, flat, ovoid ingots, at least one of them bronze, that seem to have been cast in multiples of 0.5 kg.

The discovery on the wreck of a bronze swage, stone hammerheads of the kind sometimes used for metalworking, many stone polishers and a whetstone, and a large, flat, close-grained stone that could have served as an anvil suggest that a tinker may have been on the voyage.

The wreck's importance derives from the historical conclusions drawn from it. At the time of its excavation, it was generally accepted that Mycenaean Greeks had a monopoly on maritime commerce in the eastern Mediterranean during the latter part of the Late Bronze Age, and that Phoenician sailors did not begin their great tradition of seafaring until the following Iron Age. Indeed, the main reason that Homer has been commonly dated to the eighth century BCE by twentieth-century classicists is his frequent mention of Phoenician sailors and bronzesmiths.

The Cape Gelidonya shipwreck suggests new possibilities. The southeast end of the wreck, most probably its stern, held what may be considered personal possessions of the crew or passengers, as opposed to the mostly Cypriot cargo and the shipboard mixture of Mycenaean, Cypriot, and Syrian pottery. These possessions included four scarabs and a scarab-shaped plaque, an oil lamp, stone mortars, more than sixty stone pan-balance weights (including Egyptian *gedets*, and Syrian *nesefs* and *shekels*), and a merchant's cylinder seal (see figure 2), all apparently of Syrian, or Canaanite, origin; a razor is of Egyptian rather than Mycenaean type.

The excavator concluded that the ship was probably Canaanite, or early Phoenician (the Canaanites being simply Bronze Age Phoenicians), although because so many Near Eastern artifacts are found on Cyprus from the same period, there was the possibility that the ship was Cypriot. Library research revealed that, with a single exception, contemporary Egyptian artists associated the trade in four-handled copper ingots, and tin ingots, solely with Syrian merchants (the only known mold for casting four-handled copper ingots was found after the Cape Gelidonya excavation, in a palace at Ras Ibn Hani, the port of Ras Shamra/Ugarit, the greatest of Late Bronze Age Syrian port cities). [*See* Ras Ibn Hani; Ugarit.] Furthermore, the only foreign merchant ships depicted in Egyptian art of the time are Syrian. All this suggested that Homer's Phoenicians are not anachronistic in the Late Bronze Age of the Trojan War. The discovery in 1994 of the Cape Gelidonya ship's Syro-Canaanite or Cypriot stone anchor bolstered the excavator's contention that the ship was of Near Eastern origin.

BIBLIOGRAPHY

Bass, George F. *Cape Gelidonya: A Bronze Age Shipwreck*. Transactions of the American Philosophical Society, 57.8. Philadelphia, 1967. The full excavation report.

Bass, George F. "Cape Gelidonya and Bronze Age Maritime Trade." In *Orient and Occident: Essays Presented to Cyrus H. Gordon*, edited by Harry A. Hoffner, Jr., pp. 29–38. Kevelaer, 1973. Additions to the excavation report.

Bass, George F. *Archaeology Beneath the Sea*. New York, 1975. See pages 1–59. A popular account of the excavation.

Bass, George F. "Return to Cape Gelidonya." *INA Newsletter* 15.2 (June 1988): 2–5. Discoveries made on site decades after its excavation.

Bass, George F. "Evidence of Trade from Bronze Age Shipwrecks." In *Bronze Age Trade in the Mediterranean*, edited by N. H. Gale, pp. 69–82. Studies in Mediterranean Archaeology, vol. 90. Göteborg, 1991. The wreck in light of discoveries made at Uluburun.

Muhly, James D., et al. "The Cape Gelidonya Shipwreck and the Bronze Age Metals Trade in the Eastern Mediterranean." *Journal of Field Archaeology* 4.3 (1977): 353–362.

Pulak, Cemal, and Edward Rogers. "The 1993–1994 Turkish Shipwreck Survey." *The INA Quarterly* 21.4 (Winter 1994) 17–21. The discovery of the ship's anchor.

Throckmorton, Peter. "Thirty-Three Centuries under the Sea." *National Geographic* 117 (May 1960): 682–703. A popular account of the discovery of the wreck.

Throckmorton, Peter. "Oldest Known Shipwreck Yields Bronze Age Cargo." *National Geographic* 121 (May 1962): 696–711. A popular account of the excavation.

Throckmorton, Peter. *Lost Ships: An Adventure in Undersea Archaeology*. New York, 1964. A popular account of the discovery and excavation of the site.

GEORGE F. BASS

CAPE GELIDONYA. Figure 2. *A Syrian cylinder seal and its impression in clay.* (Copyright Frey/INA)

CAPERNAUM (Heb., Kefar Naḥum), site located on the northwest shore of the Sea of Galilee (map reference 255 × 204), 16 km (9 mi.) northeast of modern Tiberias, 3 km (2 mi.) northeast of ancient Heptapegon (modern Tabgha), 3 km southeast of ancient Khorazin, and 5 km (3 mi.) west of the upper Jordan River. The site is called Talhum by local Arabs.

The location of the site matches data provided by the ancient literary sources. Eusebius (fourth century CE) sets Capernaum 3 km from Khorazin (*Enchiridion Locorum Sanctorum* [*ELS*], p. 305, n. 459), whereas, according to Theodosius (530 CE), it was between Heptapegon and the Jordan River—more precisely, 3 km from Heptapegon and 10 km (6 mi.) from Bethsaida across the river (*ELS*, p. 267, n. 381). The archaeological remains stretch for a considerable distance along the lake shore, with the Sea of Galilee to the south side and the hills to the north, precisely as described by Arculphus in 670 CE (*ELS*, p. 176, n. 404).

Archaeological excavation at the site has not only provided full confirmation of all the periods of occupation recorded by the literary sources, but brought to light specific buildings. The monumental synagogue and the churches built upon the traditional house of Simon Peter attracted, in the Byzantine period, the attention of such pilgrims as Egeria, in 384 CE, and the Anonymus Placentinus, in 570 CE (*ELS*, p. 299, n. 443, and p. 297, n. 436).

The identification of the ruins of Talhum with ancient Kefar Nahum is also indirectly strengthened by the fact that no other ancient settlement exists in this area of the lake to vie with Talhum: in fact, Khirbet al-Minyeh, in the Ginnosar valley, which several scholars once took for ancient Capernaum, turned out to be an Umayyad castle, with no remains earlier than the seventh century CE. In addition, no other ancient settlements have so far been recorded along the lake shore between the Jordan and Heptapegon, except for the evidence of some isolated potsherds from the third millennium BCE collected in surveys.

The original Semitic name Kefar Nahum (meaning "village of Nahum") is known from a Byzantine inscription found in the synagogue at Hammath-Gader; in some passages in the Mishnah (*Midrash Qoh Rabba* 1:8 and 7:26); and, as late as the year 1333, when Rabbi Ishak Chelo visited the site (*ELS*, p. 301, n. 451).

In non-Semitic languages the composite name Kefar Nahum is always rendered as a single name, and the guttural *h* is dropped altogether. In the Greek manuscripts of the Gospels two spellings occur: Capharnaum and Capernaum. The Greek spelling Capharnaum, closely following the Hebrew pronunciation and attested also by Flavius Josephus (*War* 3.519), is to be preferred; the spelling Capernaum (followed in modern English) was probably introduced as an idiom in the district of Antioch in Syria. It is difficult to tell when, if ever, this old name went out of use among the local Arab population to indicate the remains today called again Kefar Nahum. Significantly, as late as the year 1668, Michel Nau, a scholar who asked the local bedouins to accompany him to the site of ancient Capernaum, was indeed led to Talhum, and could write: "Capernaum is called at present Telhoum" (*ELS*, p. 304, n. 458).

It is equally difficult to know when the new name Talhum was applied to the ruins of Capernaum, although its first occurrence is so far not earlier than 1537, the year Uri of Biel wrote: "Tanhum. Here Rabbi Tanhum is buried." Probably, the presumed tomb of R. Tanhum gave the new name to the ruins. (In a parallel way, the village of Bethany, near Jerusalem, was renamed el-Azariyeh in Arabic because of the Lazarium—the tomb of Lazarus.) The local bedouins subsequently softened the pronunciation of Tanhum to

Talhum. Finally, several modern scholars, beginning with Nau, understood the Arab pronunciation of Talhum as Tell Hum, and someone went so far as to conclude that Tell Hum could mean "the ruins (*tell*) of (Na)hum." Certainly the very preservation of the original name Kefar Nahum, even under the name Talhum is additional support for the identification of the ruins. The interpretation of Talhum as Tell (Na)hum seems rather weak, although etymologically possible.

Surveys and Excavations. In 1816 J. S. Buckingham published a sketch of Talhum, showing what seems to be the remains of the Byzantine octagonal church. The American clergyman Edward Robinson visited Talhum in 1838 and correctly identified "the prostrate ruins of an edifice which, for expense, labour, and ornament, surpasses any thing we have yet seen in Palestine" as the remains of a synagogue. In 1864 Sir Charles W. Wilson described two monumental tombs, one of which is a Roman mausoleum. His limited soundings in the synagogue yielded no significant results, but they were significant to the local bedouins, who started pillaging the remains, looking for treasure. The site robbing ended in 1894, when two-thirds of the ruins, including the remains of the monumental synagogue, were acquired by the Franciscan Custodians of the Holy Land; the remainder of the site, on the east side, became the property of the Greek Orthodox Patriarchate of Jerusalem.

In 1905, H. Kohl and Carl Watzinger began an excavation of the synagogue that Wendelin von Menden expanded between 1906 and 1915. Gaudenzio Orfali worked on an octagonal structure in 1921 that he tentatively interpreted as a Byzantine baptistery. He partially restored the synagogue, which William Foxwell Albright considered "one of the most satisfying places to visit in all Palestine." From 1968 to 1986, Virgilio Corbo and Stanislao Loffreda conducted nineteen seasons of excavation on the Franciscan property, attempting to understand both the synagogue and the octagonal church in stratigraphic context and in the context of the ancient settlement, which had been extensively excavated. Finally Vassilios Tzaferis directed four seasons of excavation (1978–1982) on the Greek property. [*See the biographies of Watzinger and Corbo.*]

Periods of Occupation. Capernaum is mentioned for the first time in first-century CE sources, namely in Flavius Josephus, and particularly in the Gospels. Excavation has, however, pushed back the settlement's origins by three thousand years by recovering sporadic sherds (band-slip ware) from the third millennium BCE. Some walls, pavements, and a considerable amount of pottery from the second millennium BCE (Middle and Late Bronze) have also been recorded. After a complete break during the Israelite period (1200–587 BCE), the site was resettled in the fifth-century BCE and expanded progressively in the following centuries, reaching its peak in the Late Roman and Byzantine periods fourth–seventh centuries CE. The town began to decline in the eighth century. Some structures were built as late as the twelfth and thirteenth centuries, and even later, but the town as such was already in ruins.

Material Culture. The ruins cover an area of approximately 6 ha (13 acres) suggesting a population of about 1,500 during the town's maximum expansion in the Byzantine period. The settlement's center, which reveals town planning during that period of great prosperity, is marked by the monumental synagogue, and only 30 m to the south, by the octagonal church. Both structures share the main north-south street, intersected at right angles by several alleys that form small quarters. Although the two public buildings were constructed of white limestone blocks brought from some distance, the private structures were both unpretentious and of local basalt.

Capernaum was crossed by an imperial highway leading to Damascus. It was also a border town that received revenue from collecting customs. Its additional economic resources were fishing, agriculture, industry, and trade. It was commercially linked with the northern regions in particular and, beginning in the fourth century CE, was flooded with elegant wares from Africa, Greece, and Cyprus. It was also a prominent center of Christian pilgrimage, being considered "the town of Jesus" (*Mt.* 9:1).

Excavation provided archaeologists with sealed and superimposed strata, through which it is was possible, for the first time, to classify and date the regional ware.

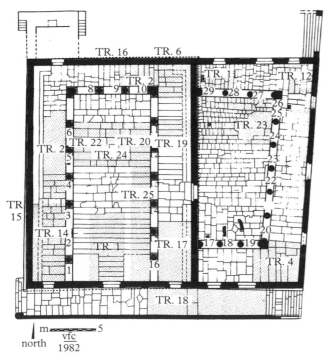

CAPERNAUM. *General plan of the fourth-century CE synagogue.* (After Loffreda, 1985, p. 34)

The in-depth excavations, both in the synagogue and in the octagonal church, clarified several problems but raised many questions. It is indisputable that the synagogue and the church were not built on virgin soil, but on previous strata dating back at least to the Hellenistic period (under the octagon) and the Late Bronze Age (under the synagogue). Scholars agree that the late fifth-century octagonal church was preceded by a fourth-century *domus ecclesia* (a house used for religious gatherings by a Christian community). The excavators suggest that this change had already taken place in the late first century CE. At the same time, several structures and pavements appear under the monumental synagogue that may belong to earlier synagogues. Finally, the two public buildings were certainly in use for the span of the Byzantine period: the earliest clear evidence of some stones from the synagogue being reused in private buildings in the village is well after the eighth century.

In sum, the synagogue and the Christian shrines built on the traditional house of Peter were not only close to one another, sharing the same street, but were in use side by side for several centuries. It is true that in the late fifth–early seventh centuries the synagogue was completely encircled by private houses, in which a considerable number of terra sigillata bowls with stamped crosses were found, but no direct evidence whatsoever exists to indicate that the synagogue was used as a church. What is still highly debated is the original dating of the monumental synagogue. On the basis of architectural, stylistic, and historical considerations, several archaeologists consider the synagogue at Capernaum to be the best example of the basilica-style synagogues that flourished in Galilee in the second–third centuries CE. On the contrary, however, the excavators, on the basis of stratigraphic material, conclude that the synagogue's prayer hall was built in the late fourth century CE and that the east courtyard was added a century later. Although they admit that several decorative elements from the synagogue can be dated to the third century, they reject the idea that the late material found in sealed levels is to be explained as the result of minor repairs in the building.

The fifth-century octagonal church and the fourth-century *domus ecclesia* are Christian shrines. The excavators suggest that some of the fragmentary, but numerous, graffiti (in Greek, Aramaic, and Syriac) predate the fourth-century *domus ecclesia*, the structure described by the pilgrim Egeria in 384, when she wrote: "The house of the Prince of the Apostles was changed into church. The walls however, are still standing as they were" (*ELS*, p. 299, n. 443). They also suggest that the octagonal church is the structure visited by the Anonymus Placentinus in 570, who wrote: "We came to Capernaum in the house of St. Peter, which is now a basilica" (*ELS*, p. 297, n. 436). To date, the assertion that the recent excavations have identified the traditional house of St. Peter remains uncontested. Is the traditional house of St. Peter the true house of Peter? How reliable is the tradition

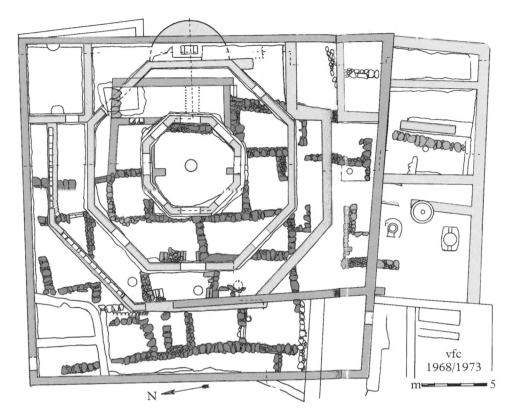

CAPERNAUM.   *General plan of the Insula Sacra.* ■■■■: Private houses of the Hellenistic-Roman period. ■■■■: The fourth-century CE Domus-Ecclesia. ▭▭▭: The mid-fifth-century CE Octagonal Church. (After Loffreda, 1985, pp. 50-51)

concerning the house of Peter, where Jesus lived? The excavators are certain of the identification, based on the considerable body of circumstantial evidence.

BIBLIOGRAPHY

Corbo, Virgilio. *The House of St. Peter at Capharnaum: A Preliminary Report of the First Two Campaigns of Excavations, April 16–June 19/September 12–November 26, 1968.* Studium Biblicum Franciscanum, Collectio Minor, 5. Jerusalem, 1972.

Corbo, Virgilio. *Cafarnao,* vol. 1, *Gli edifici della città.* Studium Biblicum Franciscanum, no. 19. Jerusalem, 1975.

Enchiridion Locorum Sanctorum: Documenta S. Evangelii Loca Respicientia (1955). Edited by Donato Baldi. Jerusalem, 1982.

Loffreda, Stanislao. *Cafarnao,* vol. 2, *La ceramica.* Studium Biblicum Franciscanum, no. 19. Jerusalem, 1974.

Loffreda, Stanislao. *Recovering Capharnaum.* Studium Biblicum Franciscanum Guides, 1. Jerusalem, 1985.

Orfali, Gaudenzio. *Capharnaüm et ses ruines d'après les fouilles accomplies à Tell-Houm par la Custodie Franciscaine de Terre Sainte, 1905–1921.* Paris, 1922.

Spijkerman, Augusto. *Cafarnao,* vol. 3, *Catalogo delle monete della città.* Studium Biblicum Franciscanum, no. 19. Jerusalem, 1975.

Testa, Emmanuele. *Cafarnao,* vol. 4, *I graffiti della casa di S. Pietro.* Studium Biblicum Franciscanum, no. 19. Jerusalem, 1972.

Tzaferis, Vassilios, et al. *Excavations at Capernaum,* vol. 1, *1978–1982.* Winona Lake, Ind., 1989.

STANISLAO LOFFREDA

CAPITOLIAS. *See* Beit Ras.

CAPPADOCIA. A land dominated by volcanic tuffs in what is central Turkey, the region of Cappadocia was home to Hittite, Greek, Roman, Christian, Seljuk, and Islamic civilizations in that order. Evidence for occupation in the area extends back to the Stone Age. Small settlements developed later into trading posts that increasingly served as places of exchange as traffic headed east–west and north–south.

At one point the region covered a large area that extended from Lake Tatta to the Euphrates River and from the Black Sea to Cilicia. [*See* Euphrates; Cilicia.] The northern section came to be known as Pontus and the middle and southern part, Greater Cappadocia. Often, the passes, which are the principal access to the area, were closed by snow in the winter. The region is almost in the center of ancient Anatolia. The Assyrians understood the area as part of the kingdom of Kaneš. The Persians called it Katpatuka. In the classical period it came to be called Cappadocia. Its boundaries varied through history, but basically the region includes an area bounded by volcanic formations on the south and east (with Mt. Argaeus at the northeast corner and Hasan dağ on the south), a middle valley formed by the Kizil İrmak (Red River), and a depression created in the Tuz gölü (Salt Lake) on the southwest.

Few of its areas became urbanized. The site of Kaneš, located on the Hittite town of Kültepe near Kayseri, traded with the region of present-day Iran and Syria, primarily exchanging copper and lead for cloth and skins. [*See* Kaneš.] A Late Hittite text refers to an early coalition (c. 2300 BCE) that included seventeen local kings from this region who organized the "Great Revolt" against the Assyrian king Naram-Sin, Sargon's successor, and offers the earliest evidence of urban development in the region (Frayne, 1991). [*See* Hittites.] Boğazköy (ancient Ḥattuša) the Hittite capital, indicates the importance this central region held for the Hittite Empire until the latter's demise in 1200 BCE. [*See* Boğazköy.] In the sixth century BCE the region was incorporated into the kingdom of Lydia and shortly thereafter into the Persian Empire, but few new settlements are found until 350 BCE under Persians hegemony. [*See* Persians.] The region's rich pastures are apparent in the Persian kings' demand of fifteen hundred horses, fifty thousand sheep, and two thousand mules and the fact that Roman emperors kept stud racehorses there. It also had quartz, salt, and silver mines (Strabo 12.533–540). In the Hellenistic and Roman periods large estates controlled much of the good land; some of the estates were temple territories (e.g., Ma of Comana [modern Gümenek] and Zeus of Venasa). The strategic importance of the region for the Romans is evidenced by the continual beneficence of the Romans toward building projects, beginning with Pompey. He provided significant funds

to help reconstruct several urban centers after the destructive Mithridatic Wars (88–63 BCE). Kings ruled the area for a time in the Hellenistic period, including Archelaus, put into power by Mark Antony, who renamed Mazaca Caesarea (modern Kayseri) and founded Archelais, formerly Garsaura (modern Aksaray). In 17 CE Cappadocia was annexed as a procuratorial province. Vespasian brought Galatia and Cappadocia together as an administrative unit, which lasted until Trajan combined it with Pontus, a situation that lasted until Diocletian's reign.

During the Hellenistic and Roman periods, the main towns and cities in the region that occupied ancient sites included the capital, Caesarea (Mazaca-Eusebeia), Tyana (Hittite Tuwanuwa), and Soandos (between Garsaura and Mazaca). Two main roads running north–south through the region connected the main southern (east–west) coastal road with the road linking Assyria and the western coast of Asia Minor in the eighth century BCE.

Little remains from the Hellenistic and Roman periods by way of architecture, even in the towns directly under Greek or Roman control. A few cult buildings and tombs have been discovered in some outlying areas (e.g., Sivasa, where the octagonal martyrium described by Gregory of Nysa was built; and Mavrucan, modern Güzelöz, the site of the Church of the Stratilates)—notably remnants of a tomb at Avcilar. [*See* Martyrion; Tombs.] Marcus Aurelius built a temple for his wife, Faustina, at the town in Cappadocia where she died, renamed Faustinopolis. In addition, a temple established under Septimius Severus was built at Caesarea, as indicated by a coin dated to the year 206 CE. A

CAPPADOCIA.   *Northwest interior wall and arcade of the main church at Tokali Kilise.* (Courtesy Pictorial Archive)

CAPPADOCIA.   *Earlier style section of church decor at Tokalı Kilise, exposed by the collapse of the rock face.* (Courtesy Pictorial Archive)

second *neocorate* (a provincial imperial cult complex) was established under Gordian (Price, 1984, p. 269). Unfortunately, most of the early periods have been obliterated by Christian building activities extending through the Byzantine period (roughly from the fourth through the thirteenth centuries). The numerous Byzantine churches carved into the rock follow the architectural patterns established in the east and apparently do not represent any unique local traditions. [*See* Churches.]

In the Byzantine period the primary cities—Andaval, Nazianzus (Diocaesarea), Garsauritis (Colonia Archealis), Soandos (Hittite Ḫupišpa, modern Ereğli), Cybistra, and Caesarea (Mazaca)—played critical roles as part of the military and trading road network that linked the plateau region with the larger empire, and especially the city of Byzantium. [*See* Roads.] A key road protected by a series of fortresses ran along the southern slope of Hasan dağ. Beyond the main traffic patterns a series of villages were cut out of rock and linked by local roads. Numerous wells, gardens, vineyards, olive presses, and other remnants of small agricultural communities have been located. Monastic centers of the eastern church and part of the diocese of Caesarea in Cappadocia (which included Sogani, Hasan, Göreme, and the chief town of the diocese, Caesarea Cappadociae) have also been discovered. Two Byzantine emperors (Zeno the Isaurian and Michael II) came from the region, as did several famous theologians, including Gregory of Nysa, Basil of Caesarea, and Gregory of Nazianzus.

Home to Christian and later Muslim mystics, the area is dotted with churches, monasteries, and chapels carved in the soft stone. [*See* Monasteries.] Some structures lent themselves to use by ascetics (both Christian and Muslim), notably the sites at "Monk's Valley" along the Zilve road, in the Peristrema valley (the monastery of Karanlık Kale, the "Dark Fort"), and Göreme, near the village of Avcilar (the location of such churches as Tokalı Kilise (the "Boss Church") and Karanlık Kilise (the "Dark Church"). During the Muslim period, a series of caravanserais, or well-fortified way stations that often had baths, stables, and lodging, were created for traders who helped maintain the links between the east and the west. [*See* Baths.] Key market towns such as the citadel of Kayseri served as the foundation for such important trade networks.

Settlement in the region tended to follow a fairly set pattern from an early period. The accessible and flat region of the plateau saw the development of the larger settlements, which were often devoted to trade and generally were the place of residence for the elite classes. In the more rugged mountainous areas, smaller villages built of stone or carved out of the rock predominated. Temples to local deities have been found throughout the region, especially in the rural areas. Numerous Christian communities developed in these rugged areas, often in isolation from the more official structures found in the larger towns, such as the capital, Caesarea. The remoteness of the area often provided a refuge from political authority as well as religious persecution. Some of the earliest Christian art from the iconoclastic period survives because of this isolation.

Perhaps best known are the spectacular underground complexes of interconnecting rooms and chambers hewn out of the tuffaceous rock (e.g., at Kaymaklt and at Ortahisar, site of Cambazli Kilise, the "Church of the Acrobat"). Some underground towns extend for more than ten floors in depth and cover many kilometers. Round stone slabs often blocked off passages, indicating the need for security in the region. Xenophon, in his *Anabasis* (4.5.25–26) shows that such underground complexes were important in this area as early as the fifth century BCE: "The dwellings in these villages are underground: they have an entrance like the mouth of a well, but the rooms are spacious. The livestock lives in separate apartments hollowed out of the ground; the men go down into them with ladders. Here they rear goats, sheep, cows, and hens, together with their progeny; and all these beasts are fed solely on hay. They keep stores of corn, rice, vegetables, and barley wine in large jars. . . ."

The coming of the Seljuk Turks in the eleventh and twelfth centuries altered the landscape in Cappadocia. Private houses had few of the embellishments sometimes found in their Byzantine counterparts. They did develop elaborate water systems (cisterns, aqueducts, canals) to irrigate orchards, parks, and gardens and to provide plentiful water to bath complexes. [*See* Cisterns; Aqueducts; Irrigation.] Caesarea remained the leading city and capital of Cappadocia and continued its significant military and trading role. Niğde and Bor took on increasing importance as well because they controlled a critical crossing on the main road to the Cilician gates and the Mediterranean Sea.

[*See also* Anatolia.]

BIBLIOGRAPHY

Arts of Cappadocia. Geneva, 1971. Series of essays that collectively provide one of the best discussions in English on this region.
Frayne, Douglas R. "Historical Texts in Haifa: Notes on R. Kutscher's 'Brockman Tablets.'" *Biblioteca Orientalis* 48 (1991): 378–409.
Gwatkin, William Emmett, Jr. *Cappadocia as a Roman Procuratorial Province.* University of Missouri Studies, vol. 5.4. Columbia, 1930.
Kostof, Spiro. *Caves of God: Cappadocia and Its Churches.* Oxford, 1989.
Mitford, Terence B. "Cappadocia and Armenia Minor: Historical Setting of the Limes." In *Aufstieg und Niedergang der römischen Welt,* vol. II.7.2, edited by Wolfgang Haase, pp. 1169–1228. Berlin and New York, 1980.
Orlin, Louis L. *Assyrian Colonies in Cappadocia.* The Hague, 1970.
Price, S. R. F. *Rituals of Power: The Roman Imperial Cult in Asia Minor.* Cambridge, 1984.
Sullivan, Richard D. "The Dynasty of Cappadocia." In *Aufstieg und Niedergang der römischen Welt,* vol. II.7.2, edited by Wolfgang Haase, pp. 1125–1168. Berlin and New York, 1980.
Teja, Ramon. "Die römische Provinz Kappadokien in der Prinzipatszeit." In *Aufstieg und Niedergang der römischen Welt,* vol. II.7.2, edited by Wolfgang Haase, pp. 1083–1124. Berlin and New York, 1980.

DOUGLAS R. EDWARDS

CAPPADOCIAN TEXTS. *See* Kültepe Texts.

CARAVANSERAIS. Denoting a variety of commercial, residential, and pilgrimage structures in the Islamic world, caravanserais reflect the importance of trade routes in the history of the Islamic lands of the Near East. Caravanserais served as staging posts on major roads between towns, or as secure commercial storage with residential facilities within towns. Terminology varies in different contexts and related buildings include *khan*s, *wakala*s, *fundug*s, and *ribaṭ*s. The involvement of central governments in the construction of many of these caravanserais has led to a degree of stylistic uniformity in their design.

The commercial routes of the pre-Islamic world may have given rise to caravanserailike architecture, but it is in the Islamic period that the provision of facilities for travelers led to a significant body of architecture. The early Islamic geographers often refer to way stations as *manzil,* which may be presumed to have been buildings. *Khan*s have also been identified at the Umayyad sites of Qaṣr al-Ḥayr al-Gharbi (724–727 CE) and Qaṣr al-Ḥayr ash-Sharqi (728–729) in Syria and the location of other Umayyad desert sites suggests that some may have encompassed a caravanserai role.

In the late eighth century, the 'Abbasid caliphs developed the Darb Zubaydah, the road from Iraq to Mecca, building *quṣur* (enclosures, palaces), and *mazil* at staging posts. There are numerous settlements on the road, and excavations at ar-Rabadha east of Medina show a major eighth–ninth century settlement with several secure courtyard buildings with storage facilities. The presence of lusterware and other early 'Abbasid glazed pottery points to a luxurious level of provisioning of the way stations.

The Seljuks were munificent builders of caravanserais, reflecting their interest in maintaining commerce and security along the extensive road system under their control. The Ribaṭ-i Malik (c. 1068–1080), southeast of Bukhara in central Asia is the earliest extant Seljuk caravanserai. It has a courtyard enclosure preceded by a great portal of a type found in contemporary mosques, and its lavish brick decoration is in keeping with the finest architectural decoration of the period. Another early Seljuk caravanserai is the twelfth-century Ribaṭ-i Sharaf in northeastern Iran that also has monumental portals, *iwan*s and chambers around the courtyards, in a manner reminiscent of Seljuk mosques.

The tradition of the caravanserai is continued in later times in Iran, Central Asia, and the Near East. The Timurids, Ottomans, and Safavids were all involved in maintaining and improving commercial facilities along the roads. Examples of royal or aristocratic foundations on major roads include the series of twelfth–thirteenth-century Seljuk *khan*s along the Anatolian road system; a group of fifteenth-century caravanserais associated with a Timurid official, 'Ali Shir Navai, concentrated in northeastern Iran; and the seventeenth-century Mader-i Shah caravanserai near Isfahan, built by Shah 'Abbas II.

Related to such caravanserais are urban *khan*s or *wakala*s, which constituted the distribution points for goods, as well as the collection point for customs duties. In many cases, these urban depots specialized in particular commodities, such as oil or soap. This situation is well demonstrated in Damascus and Aleppo, where a number of *khan*s still survive within the extensive market areas.

At Jerusalem, commercial caravanserais were established to support religious foundations in the Mamluk period. The *Khan as-Sultan*, or *al-Wakala* at Jerusalem, built under Sultan Barquq (1386–1387) has a covered market hall: in a neighboring two-story courtyard structure, the lower floors were for storage and the selling of goods to local merchants, the courtyard was for animals, and the upper rooms accommodated visiting merchants. Such urban *wakala*s have parallels in Asia Minor, Syria, Egypt, the Hijaz, and North Africa.

A quite different type of caravanserai occurs in Mamluk and Ottoman times, to guard pilgrim roads in desert regions. On the Red Sea coast of Arabia, fortications at 'Aqaba, al-Muwayliḥ, al-Azlam, and al-Zurayb reflect attempts to protect the coastal route from Egypt to the Hijaz. In the sixteenth century, the Ottomans also built a series of fortified caravanserais through Syria to the Hijaz to garrison the pilgrim road and disperse payments to tribal leaders during the *hajj* march. Such structures are more more closely related to the caravanserai's security role than its commercial purpose.

[*See also* Camels; Transportation. *In addition, many of the sites mentioned are the subject of independent entries.*]

BIBLIOGRAPHY

Aslanapa, Oktay. *Turkish Art and Architecture.* New York, 1971.
Burgoyne, Michael Hamilton, and D. S. Richards. *Mamluk Jerusalem: An Architectural Study.* London, 1987.
Elisséeff, Nikita. "Khān." In *Encyclopaedia of Islam,* new ed., vol. 4, pp. 1010–1017. Leiden, 1960–.
Erdmann, Kurt. *Das anatolische Karavansaray des 13. Jahrhunderts.* Istanbuler Forshungen, 21. Berlin, 1961.
Golombek, Lisa, and Donald Wilber. *The Timurid Architecture of Iran and Turan.* Princeton, 1988.
Pope, Arthur Upham. *A Survey of Persian Art.* London, 1938.
Sauvaget, Jean. "Les caravansérails syriens du Ḥadjdj de Constantinople." *Ars Islamica* 4 (1937): 98–121.
Sauvaget, Jean. "Caravansérails syriens du moyen-âge." *Ars Islamica* 6 (1939): 48–55; 7 (1940): 1–19.
Siroux, Maxime. *Caravansérails d'Iran, et petites constructions routières.* Mémoires de l'Institut Français d'Archéologie Orientale, vol. 81. Cairo, 1949.

G. R. D. KING

CARCHEMISH, ancient Hittite city and its territory located on the west bank of the upper Euphrates River (37°10′ N, 38°01′ E). To the south of the site circles the Aleppo-Mosul railway, which also defines the modern Turkish-Syrian frontier. The Syrian village of Jerablus ad-

joins the site to the southwest, and a more recent Turkish village named Kargamiş has grown up to the northwest.

The site, under the name of Jerablus (or Jerabis), attracted the notice of travelers from the eighteenth century onward because of its citadel mound, walls, and surface monuments. It was identified in 1876 by the famous Assyriologist George Smith as the Karkamiš known from Assyrian, Egyptian, and Hebrew sources. The spelling "Carchemish" represents the anglicization of *krkmyš* in the Hebrew Bible.

Carchemish is known from limited archaeological investigations; its history is much more fully documented by the historical sources. The British Museum has sponsored three archaeological expeditions there: (1) P. Henderson, a British consul in Aleppo, dug intermittently from December 1878 to July 1881 to recover sculpture and inscriptions for the museum; (2) regular excavations were conducted between March 1911 and spring 1914 under the direction first of D. G. Hogarth, then Campbell Thompson, and then C. Leonard Woolley, but these were broken off by the outbreak of World War I; (3) Woolley's attempt to resume operations in spring 1920 was again interrupted by the Turkish occupation of the area in the autumn. The subsequent peace settlement established the Turkish-Syrian frontier, as already noted. The site's strategically sensitive position has precluded any resumption of excavations up to and including the present time (1995).

Only the operations of 1911–1914 resulted in any significant exposure of parts of the site, which include three main areas: (1) the citadel mound, (2) the outer town and its fortifications, and (3) the inner town and its fortifications.

On the citadel mound, little coherent architecture was recovered, except for a poorly preserved building first identified, incorrectly, as Assyrian ("Sargon's Fort") and subsequently identified, without supporting evidence, as the Temple of Kubaba.

The rubble foundations of the outer city wall were located at certain points by sondage, permitting a reconstruction of its course. Within this wall, a number of private houses designated A–H were excavated, and a west gate was examined.

The inner city wall, a high earthen rampart, was surveyed and its west and south gates excavated. Within this wall lay the main area of the site to be exposed, which extended westward from the Water Gate along the southwest foot of the citadel. Even here few complete buildings were recovered: the Storm God Temple complex, including its exterior facade (the Long Wall of Sculpture), the Great Staircase with its Gatehouse ascending to the citadel, and the poorly preserved *ḥilani* (as buildings with columned porticoes are designated by archaeologists, using the Assyrian term). Besides these, only facades faced with sculptured and inscribed orthostats were revealed: the Herald's Wall, the Processional Entry (later remodeled by the addition of the Royal Buttress), and the King's Gate.

All excavated monuments at the site belong to its Neo-

Hittite floruit (c. 1000–717 BCE). The excavation reports often mention damage done to these by Roman foundations, although they were neither recorded nor published.

The sculpture and inscriptions found in situ and other pieces found out of context give information on two dynasties, the houses of Suhi and of Astiruwa, dating apparently to the tenth and eighth centuries BCE, respectively. The former seems to have built most of the excavated monuments, to which the latter added the Royal Buttress and, also according to an inscription, rebuilt the Temple of Kubaba.

These excavated remains represent only a small period in the site's recorded history. Carchemish is already attested in the Ebla archives of the mid-third millennium as a part of the trading network of the period, and in the Mari archives of the early second millennium as an independent kingdom enjoying good relations with Mari. In the mid-second millennium, the site was an important outpost of the upper Mesopotamian kingdom of Mitanni. Most important, however, is its position under the Hittite Empire, when Šuppiluliuma I, after his conquest of Syria, captured Carchemish and installed his son Piyassili as king. This dynasty lasted for at least five generations, surviving the fall of the Hittite Empire. Its kings acted as Hittite viceroys of Syria, and in the absence of any remains of this period from the site itself, their activities are documented in the archives of Ugarit and Emar. This important position in the Late Bronze Age made Carchemish the most prominent of the Neo-Hittite states.

The Assyrians terminated the power of Carchemish. In 717 BCE they conquered and annexed the city, constituting it a province of their empire, which it remained until the fall of Assyria in 612 BCE and beyond. Carchemish was the site of the final battle between the Babylonian and Egyptian armies in 605 BCE, at which the remnant of Assyria was obliterated. This was the city's last appearance in history.

[See also Anatolia, article on Ancient Anatolia; Hittites; Neo-Hittites; and Syria, articles on Syria in the Bronze Age and Syria in the Iron Age.]

BIBLIOGRAPHY

Hawkins, J. D. "Karkamiš." In *Reallexikon der Assyriologie und Vorderasiatischen Archäologie,* vol. 5, pp. 426–446. Berlin and New York, 1980. Comprehensive encyclopedia entry with full bibliography to date of publication.

Hawkins, J. D. "Kuzi-Tešub and the 'Great Kings' of Karkamiš." *Anatolian Studies* 38 (1988): 99–108. Important new evidence for political and cultural continuity at Carchemish beyond the fall of the Hittite empire.

Hawkins, J. D. "Karkamiš." In *Corpus of Hieroglyphic Luwian Inscriptions.* Berlin and New York, forthcoming. Translation of all the hieroglyphic inscriptions from Carchemish, with historical and philological commentary.

Hogarth, David G. *Carchemish: Report on the Excavations at Djerabis,* part 1, *Introductory.* London, 1914. The first excavation report, containing background information on the site and its name and a preliminary section on the excavated inscriptions and sculpture.

Orthmann, Winfried. *Untersuchungen zur späthethitischen Kunst.* Bonn,
1971. Detailed analysis of neo-Hittite sculpture, including prominently that of Carchemish, grouped according to style for the purpose of dating.

Winter, Irene J. "Carchemish *ša kišad puratti.*" *Anatolian Studies* 33 (1983): 177–197.

Woolley, C. Leonard. *Carchemish: Report on the Excavations at Djerabis,* part 2, *The Town Defences.* London, 1921. The second excavation report, concentrating on the fortifications but including a further selection of excavated inscriptions and sculpture.

Woolley, C. Leonard. "The Iron-Age Graves of Carchemish." *Liverpool Annals of Archaeology and Anthropology* 26 (1939): 11–37. Publication of the Carchemish cemetery excavated at Yunus, northwest of the mound.

Woolley, C. Leonard, and R. D. Barnett. *Carchemish: Report on the Excavations at Djerabis,* part 3, *The Excavations in the Inner Town; The Hittite Inscriptions.* London, 1952. The final excavation report, published many years after the work ended.

J. D. HAWKINS

CARMEL CAVES. Mount Carmel is a limestone mountainous block that stretches as a triangular mass over about 350 sq km. It was surveyed intensively and all visible prehistoric sites were recorded (Olami, 1984). A series of prehistoric caves is located in the western escarpment of Mount Carmel, facing the narrow coastal plain (1–3 km wide), which even during glacial regression periods did not exceed 10 km in width. Excavated sites include Naḥal Meʿarot (Wadi Mughara), es-Skhul, El-Wad, Jamal, and et-Tabun and Kebara caves. In the wadis that descend westward, Sefunim, Naḥal Oren, and Abu Usba caves were excavated as well as Rakefet cave, which is located in Naḥal Yoqneʿam, which flows eastward into the Jezrel Valley.

Excavations at Mount Carmel were first undertaken by Dorothy A. E. Garrod in a project that lasted from 1929 to 1934. Subsequent excavators included Francis Turville-Petre (Kebara), Moshe Stekelis (Kebara, Sefunim, Naḥal Oren), Arthur Jelinek (Tabun), Avraham Ronen (Sefunim and Tabun), Tamar Noy and Eric Higgs (Rakefet), Ofer Bar-Yosef and Bernard Vandermeersch (Kebara), Mina Weinstein-Evron (El-Wad and Jamal). These excavations uncovered remains from the Lower, Middle, Upper and Epi-Paleolithic, as well a few Neolithic assemblages described in the following pages.

Tabun Cave. Originally excavated by Dorothy Garrod (1929–1934) in a joint expedition of the British School of Archaeology in Jerusalem and the American School of Prehistoric Research and later by Arthur J. Jelinek (1967–1972) for the University of Arizona, Tabun Cave is still under excavation by Avraham Ronen of the University of Haifa. The cave lies 45 m above sea level; the lower part of its sequence of layers (G, F, half of E) is filled by fine-grained, well-sorted sand, resembling a modern dune. The upper part of layer E is increasingly siltier, and the layer D deposit resembles loess. Layer C contains the remains of brush fires in the form of ash lenses. The sediments are mainly clays that were washed in through the "chimney" that was formed by the dissolution of the limestone from the Mt. Carmel plateau. Layer B and the "chimney" were filled in with similar deposits with numerous limestone cobbles and blocks. The old shoreline next to the cave, 39 m above sea level, was probably the source of the sand. It has been suggested, but not confirmed, that the cave was lifted to its present location by the tectonic movements that characterized the Pleistocene era.

The chronological placement of Tabun's various layers is an unresolved debate. Pollen evidence is rather scanty but indicated fluctuations from warmer to wetter conditions. Thermoluminescent (TL) dates suggest an average age of 170,000 years old for layer C; 270,000 years old for layer D; and 300,000 years old for the upper part of layer E. Electron spinresonance (ESR) indicates somewhat later dates, such as about 80,000–100,000 years old for layer B; about 100,000 years old for layer C; 130,000–150,000 years old for layer D; and more than 200,000 years old for layer E. There are no dates yet for layers F and G. The previously held chronological scheme that viewed most of the sequence in Tabun as lasting from the last interglacial (c. 130,000 years ago) to about 45,000 years ago is therefore not accepted, although disagreement still exists about the ages of the older layers. It has also become evident that the kurkar ridge about 2 km west of Tabun, where the red loam soil is known as Mousterian *hamra*, is much older—150,000–175,000 years old.

Lithic industries began in layer G with what was defined as Tayacian by Garrod and later as Tabunian by F. C. Howell (1959). It is a core-chopper assemblage with a few retouched pieces. Layer F contains an Upper Acheulean industry with ovate and cordiform bifaces, side scrapers, and other stone tools.

Layer E was originally called Micoquian by Garrod and later Acheulo-Yabrudian or the Mugharan by Jelinek. The Acheulo-Yabrudian is limited to the northern and central Levant. It contains three industrial facies, once considered independent archaeological entities, defined on the basis of quantitative and qualitative studies:

The Yabrudian facies contains numerous side scrapers, often made on thick flakes, which results in relatively high frequencies of Quina and semi-Quina retouch; a few Upper Palaeolithic tools; rare blades; and few or no Levallois products.

The Acheulean facies has up to 15 percent bifaces, with numerous scrapers fashioned in the same way as the Yabrudians.

The Amudian facies—including end scrapers, burins, backed knives, and rare bifaces—seems, as the result of the Tabun excavations, to be closer to the Acheulean than the Yabrudian and contains evidence for limited practice of the Levallois technique.

The Mousterian sequence begins with layer D and contains blades and elongated points predominantly removed from Levallois unipolar convergent cores and perhaps some blade cores with minimal preparations of the striking platforms. Elongated retouched points, numerous blades, racloirs, and burins are among the common tool types. Layer C is characterized by large, oval flakes that were removed from Levallois cores through radial or bipolar preparation. Levallois points appear in small numbers. In layer B, blanks were mainly removed from unipolar convergent Levallois cores with a minority of radial preparation. Broad-based Levallois points and, often, short, thin flakes and some blades were all made by the same Levallois recurrent method. The chimney seems to have contained a similar industry and numerous bones. Jelinek (1973) has suggested at that time the hole of the chimney served for trapping deer.

Human remains include a broken femur in layer E and the burial of a woman, the exact provenience of which remains uncertain. It is traditionally attributed to layer C but could have originated in layer B. An isolated jaw resembles modern humans in the Qafzeh cave, while the woman is considered to have more robust features.

Jamal Cave. Garrod believed that the Jamal cave was empty, but in recent years, in the course of conservation activities, the cave was found to contain Acheulo-Yabrudian industry in brecciated deposits. It is currently being excavated by Mina Weinstein-Evron for the University of Haifa.

Skhul Cave. The ceiling of Skhul cave, which is located on the northern face of the same escarpment in which Tabun and el-Wad are found, collapsed in prehistoric times, and the archaeological remains are mostly the residues of two Mousterian layers. Layer C was found in small pockets in the bedrock with a small lithic assemblage, mostly abraded. Layer B was about 2 m thick and contained the remains of several Mousterian burials. The remains of ten individuals were uncovered. The best known are the burial of Skhul V, with a pig's mandible incorporated in the grave; Skhul I, the skeleton of an infant; Skhul IV, a semiflexed burial; and Skhul IX. The skeletal remains of this group served as the basis for the identification of early modern human anatomical characteristics. Stratigraphically, the remains of the Skhul II and V seem to be later than the others. The lithic industry essentially resembles that of Tabun C. ESR and TL dates indicate an age in the range of 80,000–117,000 years old. Layer A contained some Upper Paleolithic artifacts.

El-Wad Cave. An elongated karstic corridor that lies 44.5 m above sea level, the El-Wad cave and its terrace were first excavated by Garrod from 1929 to 1933. In 1981 the terrace was reexamined by François R. Valla and Ofer Bar-Yosef, and from 1988 to 1990 salvage excavations were carried out in the interior chamber by Weinstein-Evron. The earlier layers were found only in the cave. Layer G contained a late Mousterian industry that resembles the upper part of the Tabun sequence. Layer F was in part mixed, and some of the artifacts were abraded by water. The mixture of tool types, together with Emireh points, is related to the earliest phase of the Upper Paleolithic. Layer E contained a Levantine Aurignacian assemblage with scrapers, carinated and nosed scrapers, burins, and el-Wad points. In addition, seven bone and antler points were recovered. Layer D contained a Levantine Aurignacian assemblage (D2 and D1). Carinated and nosed scrapers, together with ordinary scrapers, are most frequent, with a small number of el-Wad points. Layer C was characterized by numerous burins and scrapers, originally called the ʿAtlitian culture. In this industry, the production of flakes is more dominant than blades, while numerous bladelets were removed from carinated cores.

Layer B contained the remains of a Natufian (c. 10,000–8,000 BCE) settlement and cemetery and covered both the frontal chamber of the cave as well as the entire terrace. The remains of more than one hundred skeletons were mostly recovered on the terrace, but also in the cave. Garrod identified the collective burials as typical of the Early Natufian and the isolated, often flexed burials as Late Natufian. In a few cases, body decorations were found attached to the remains (remains of headgear, necklaces, belts). Most of the decorations were made of dentalium shells but also of bone. In the bedrock of the terrace, four mortars were recovered; next to them Garrod identified the remains of a terrace wall constructed of large cobbles. The lithic industry included numerous microliths, among which lunates were dominant. The high frequencies of bifacially retouched Helwan lunates is representative of the Early Natufian, while subsequently the backed lunates are more common. Other tool types include scrapers, burins, borers, and awls, as well as many sickle blades. The bone industry includes points, a few harpoons and fishhooks, spatulas, and sickle hafts, one of which was preserved with two blades still adhering. Ground-stone artifacts include pestles, often of basalt, which were brought from the Galilee or the Golan, and fragments of bowls and portable mortars. With regard to artistic expression, the site is known for a sickle blade with a carving of a young ungulate, a small model of a human head in limestone, and some schematic human figurines. Information concerning subsistence activities was obtained from animal bones, which indicate the hunting of gazelle and fallow and roe deer, the trapping of birds, and fishing; reptiles were also collected. Pollen spores indicate the importation of branches with flowers of olive and tamarisk; firewood was identified, indicating that the cave was occupied during spring and summer. Cementum increments of gazelle teeth reflect hunting during both winter and summer, and it therefore seems that el-Wad was a sedentary to semisedentary campsite. Layer A contained remains from the Neolithic to historical periods. Also worth noting is a Hellenistic clay statue of Aphrodite. Since Medieval times, the cave has been occupied mainly by shepherds.

Kebara Cave. Located at the western escarpment of Mt. Carmel, the Kebara cave is about 13 km (8 mi.) south of Naḥal Meʿarot, at about 60–65 m above sea level (map reference 1442 × 2182). The first sounding near the cave entrance was made by Moshe Stekelis in 1927 (Schick and Stekelis, 1977). While excavating the caves in Wadi el-Mughara in 1930, Garrod, unaware of Stekelis's test pit, dug a small trench in Kebara, where, below the historical deposits, she encountered remains of the Natufian culture. In 1931, together with C. A. Baynes, Francis Turville-Petre excavated at Kebara, revealing about 300 sq m of surface area to a depth of 3 m. Stekelis carried out additional excavations from 1951 to 1965, and a joint project coordinated by Bar-Yosef and Bernard Vandermeersch was conducted from 1982 to 1990 under the auspices of the Hebrew University and the French Mission in Jerusalem. The combined stratigraphy, from which the first three layers were removed in their entirety by Turville-Petre, follows:

Layer A: From the Bronze Age to the modern period, layer A was a mixed stony layer, quite variable in its thickness.

Layer B: About one meter thick, layer B contained an Early Natufian assemblage with numerous bone tools, pendants, ornaments, and decorated sickle hafts. The lithic assemblage, collected without sieving, included approximately five hundred lunates and one thousand sickle blades. Turville-Petre (1932) also listed a few mortars and pestles and a variety of other stone tools, such as shaft straighteners and whetstones. A pit with several badly damaged Natufian skeletons was uncovered close to the cave's entrance.

Layer C: A microlithic assemblage in layer C (20–40 cm thick) serves as the type-site for the definition of the Kebaran. The dominant tool types were the obliquely truncated backed bladelet and some curved backed bladelets. At the rear of the cave, some fragmentary charred human remains were found, but recent radiocarbon dates on the bones relate them to the Early Natufian.

Layer D1: A Levantine Aurignacian assemblage dominated by end scrapers, steep (carinated) scrapers, and some burins, mostly made of flakes, was found in layer D1.

Layer D2: Currently units I–II, layer D2 was similar in its contents to layer D1; it had a Levantine Aurignacian assemblage with mainly flake end scrapers, steep scrapers (both nosed and carinated), a few burins, and El-Wad points. Two bone tools were recovered in this layer, one a point with the tibia articulation still intact and the other a broken point with parallel incisions encircling its width. The new excavations found a typically Aurignacian split base point and provided several radiocarbon dates indicating a time span of 36,000–28,000 years ago.

Layer E: Currently units II–IV, layer E contained a few Mousterian elements, most of which differ in their patination from the typical Upper Palaeolithic elements. The industry is dominated by blade production; the main tool types are end scrapers, some steep (carinated) scrapers with a few burins, and el-Wad points. A series of radiocarbon dates ranges from 43,000–36,000 years ago.

Layer F: Originally termed Levalloiso-Mousterian, layer F remained largely untouched until the 1951–1965 Stekelis excavations. The Upper Palaeolithic layers (D–E) contained several hearths and a series of peculiar installations built of limestone slabs laid over small stones near the northern cave wall. The Mousterian layers were excavated to varying depths and contained large quantities of debitage and bones. The major discovery was the skeletal remains of a baby (eight–nine months old) found close to the northern wall at a level of 6.83–6.90 m.

Bedrock was reached near the northern wall in the 1982–1990 excavations and in Stekelis's original sounding. Upper Paleolithic levels still in place were in the southern portion of the dig and were radiometrically dated to 43,000–28,000 years ago.

In 1983, the excavation in the Stekelis deep sounding uncovered a human burial. The skull is missing, but the post-cranial skeleton is complete. This robust individual, TL dated to about 60,000 years ago, is included with the other so-called Near Eastern Neanderthals. The central area was chosen for "horizontal" excavation (exposing everything, leaving it in place for mapping and photography). Plotted artifacts and bones indicate that the hearths were located toward the entrance and the dumping zones toward the rear of the cave. Diagenetic processes caused by intensive water percolation destroyed all bones in the southern sector of the cave.

The lowermost unit is an accumulation of sterile, sandy-silty deposits (units XV–XIV) above the uneven bedrock. Subsidence into a sinkhole and subsequent erosion were followed by sedimentation of a depositional admixture created by intervening activities of biogenic and natural agencies. Unit XIII was the first to accumulate the admixture. It contains numerous well-delineated hearths and rare artifacts, but no bones. Following an unconformity, units XII–VII accumulated as a continuum, containing ashy deposits, hearths, bone accumulations, isolated human bones, a human burial, and rich Mousterian lithic assemblages. An additional major event of subsidence in the sinkhole led to slumping and microfaulting of the Mousterian layers at the rear of the cave, followed by erosion and burrowing. Thus, the cave floor during the early Upper Palaeolithic formed a basin slanting steeply toward the cave's rear wall. Continuous erosion and burrowing led to the mixed accumulation of Upper Paleolithic and Mousterian artifacts in the lower part of this basin. Some Upper Palaeolithic lithics infiltrated into units V and VI, which primarily contain Mousterian artifacts, and some Mousterian elements found their way into unit III, primarily Upper Palaeolithic. Unit IV is a thin lense; together with unit II, it may be similar to what Turville-Petre (1932) called layer E.

Lithic studies of the Mousterian period demonstrate that blank production was frequently done by the convergent recurrent Levallois method. Short and broad-based Levallois points and triangular flakes were often the end products. Despite the site's proximity to sources of raw materials, the sequence of flake removals was repeated until the cores were exhausted. The upper units (VII–VIII) exhibit a proliferation of Levallois flakes obtained by unidirectional or radial removals. Retouched pieces in Kebara are quite rare and include a few side scrapers and Upper Palaeolithic tool types. Levallois points and triangular flakes are rarely retouched but bear traces of hafting and impact fractures caused by their use as projectiles. Other stone tools demonstrate signs of use for woodworking and butchery. Bone accumulations in Kebara cave reflect the hunting of gazelle and fallow and roe deer and the gathering of reptiles. Carbonized plant remains were mainly of vetch—indicating gathering activities in late spring. Firewood from the Tabor oak and common oak were collected from the cave's immediate environment.

[*See also* British School of Archaeology in Jerusalem; Paleobotany; Paleozoology; Tabun; *and the biographies of Garrod, Stekelis, and Turville-Petre.*]

BIBLIOGRAPHY

Arensburg, Baruch. "The Hyoid Bone from the Kebara 2 Hominid." In *Investigations in South Levantine Prehistory,* edited by Ofer Bar-Yosef and Bernard Vandermeersch, pp. 337–342. British Archaeological Reports, International Series, no. 497. Oxford, 1989.

Arensburg, Baruch, L. A. Schepartz, A. M. Tillier, Bernard Vandermeersch, and Yoel Rak. "A Reappraisal of the Anatomical Basis for Speech in Middle Palaeolithic Hominds." *American Journal of Physical Anthropology* 83 (1990): 137–146.

Bar-Yosef, Ofer, et al. "The Excavations in Kebara Cave, Mt. Carmel." *Current Anthropology* 33.5 (1992): 497–550.

Bar-Yosef, Ofer. "Middle Paleolithic Human Adaptations in the Mediterranean Levant." In *The Evolution and Dispersal of Modern Humans in Asia,* edited by Takeru Akazawa et al., pp. 189–216. Tokyo, 1992.

Bar-Yosef, Ofer. "The Role of Western Asia in Modern Human Origins." *Philosophical Transactions of the Royal Society of London, Series B* 337 (1992): 193–200.

Bar-Yosef, Ofer, and Bernard Vandermeersch. *Le Squellete Moustérien de Kebara 2.* Paris, 1991.

Bar-Yosef, Ofer, and Bernard Vandermeersch, eds. *Le Squelette Moustérien de Kébara 2.* Paris, 1992.

Farrand, William R. "Chronology and Palaeoenvironment of Levantine Prehistoric Sites as Seen from Sediment Studies." *Journal of Archaeological Science* 6 (1979): 369–392.

Farrand, William R. "Confrontation of Geological Stratigraphy and Radiometric Dates from Upper Pleistocene Sites in the Levant." In *Late Quaternary Chronology and Paleoclimates of the Eastern Mediterranean,* edited by Ofer Bar-Yosef and R. Kra, pp. 21–31. Tucson and Cambridge, 1994.

Garrod, Dorothy A. E., and Dorothea M. A. Bate. *The Stone Age of Mount Carmel: Excavations at the Wady al-Mughara.* Oxford, 1937.

Garrod, Dorothy A. E. "Excavations at the Mughuret Kebara, Mount Carmel, 1931: The Aurignacian Industries." *Proceedings of the Prehistoric Society* 20 (1954): 155–192.

Grün, Rainer, et al. "ESR Dating of Teeth from Garrod's Tabun Cave Collection." *Journal of Human Evolution* 20.3 (1991): 231–248.

Howell, F. C. "Upper Pleistocene Stratigraphy and Early Man in the Levant." *Proceedings of the American Philosophical Society* 103 (1959): 1–65.

Jelinek, Arthur J., et al. "New Excavations at the Tabun Cave, Mount Carmel, Israel, 1967–1972: A Preliminary Report." *Paléorient* 1.2 (1973): 151–183.

Jelinek, Arthur J. "The Middle Palaeolithic in the Southern Levant with Comments on the Appearance of Modern *Homo sapiens*." In *The Transition from Lower to Middle Palaeolithic and the Origin of Modern Man,* edited by Avraham Ronen, pp. 57–104. British Archaeological Reports, International Series, no. 151. Oxford, 1982a.

Jelinek, Arthur J. "The Tabun Cave and Paleolithic Man in the Levant." *Science* 216 (1982b): 1369–1375.

McCown, Theodore D., and Arthur Keith. *The Stone Age of Mount Carmel,* vol. 2, *The Fossil Human Remains from the Levalloiso-Mousterian.* Oxford, 1939.

McDermott, F., et al. "Mass Spectrometric U-Series Dates for Israeli Neanderthal/Early Modern Hominid Sites." *Nature* 363 (1993): 252–255.

Meignen, L., and Ofer Bar-Yosef. "Variabilité technologique au Proche Orient: L'exemple de Kébara." In *L'homme de Néandertal,* edited by Marcel Otte, pp. 81–95. Études et Recherches Archéologiques de l'Université de Liège, no. 34. Liège, 1988.

Meignen, L., et al. "Les structures de combustion moustériennes de la grotte de Kébara (Mont Carmel, Israël)." In *Nature et fonction des foyers préhistoriques: Actes du colloque international de Nemours, 12–13–14 mai 1987,* edited by Monique Olive and Yvette Taborin, pp. 141–146. Mémoires du Musée de Préhistoire d'Ile-de-France, no. 2. Nemours, 1989.

Mercier, N., H. Valladas, G. Valladas, J.-L. Reyss, Arthur Jelinek, L. Meignen, and J.-L. Joron. "TL Dates of Burnt Flints from Jelinek's Excavations at Tabun and Their Implications." *Journal of Archaeological Science* 22 (1995): 495–510.

Rak, Yoel, and Baruch Arensburg. "Kebara 2 Neanderthal Pelvis: First Look at a Complete Inlet." *American Journal of Physical Anthropology* 73 (1987): 227–231.

Ronen, Avraham. *Sefunim Prehistoric Sites, Mount Carmel, Israel.* British Archaeological Reports, International Series, no. 230. Oxford, 1984.

Schick, Tamar, and Moshe Stekelis. "Mousterian Assemblages in Kebara Cave, Mount Carmel." In *Moshé Stekelis Memorial Volume,* edited by Baruch Arensburg and Ofer Bar-Yosef, pp. 97–150. Eretz-Israel, vol. 13. Jerusalem, 1977.

Smith, Patricia and Baruch Arensburg. "A Mousterian Skeleton from Kebara Cave." In *Moshé Stekelis Memorial Volume,* edited by Baruch Arensburg and Ofer Bar-Yosef, pp. 164–176. Eretz Israel, vol. 13. Jerusalem, 1977.

Smith, Patricia, and A. M. Tillier. "Additional Infant Remains from the Mousterian Strate, Kebara Cave (Israel)." In *Investigations in South Levantine Prehistory,* edited by Ofer Bar-Yosef and Bernard Vandermeersch, pp. 323–335. British Archaeological Reports, International Series, vol. 497. Oxford, 1989.

Tchernov, Eitan. "The Biostratigraphy of the Levant." In *Préhistoire du Levant: Chronologie et organisation de l'espace depuis les origines jusqu'au VIe millénaire,* edited by Jacques Cauvin and Paul Sanlaville, pp. 67–97. Paris, 1981.

Tchernov, Eitan. "Biochronology of the Middle Paleolithic and Dispersal Events of Hominids in the Levant." In *L'homme de Néandertal,* edited by Marcel Otte, pp. 153–168. Études et Recherches Archéologiques de l'Université de Liège, no. 34. Liège, 1988.

Tchernov, Eitan. "Biological Evidence for Human Sedentism in Southwest Asia during the Natufian." In *The Natufian Culture in the Levant,* edited by Ofer Bar-Yosef and François R. Valla, pp. 315–340. Ann Arbor, Mich., 1991.

Tchernov, Eitan. "The Afro-Arabian Component in the Levantine Mammalian Fauna: A Short Biogeographical Review." *Israel Journal of Zoology* 38 (1992): 155–192.

Turville-Petre, Francis. "Excavations in the Mugharet el-Kebarah." *Journal of the Royal Anthropological Institute* 62 (1932): 271–276.

Valla, François R., et al. "Un nouveau sondage sur la terrasse d'El-Ouad, Israël." *Paléorient* 12.1 (1986): 21–38.

Weinstein-Evron, Mina. "New Radiocarbon Dates for the Early Natufian of el-Wad Cave, Mt. Carmel, Israel." *Paléorient* 17.1 (1991): 95–98.

Weinstein-Evron, Mina, and A. Tsatkin. "The Jamal Cave is Not Empty: Recent Discoveries in the Mount Carmel Caves, Israel." *Paléorient* 20 (1992): 119–128.

Weinstein-Evron, Mina, and Anna Belfer-Cohen. "Natufian Figurines from the New Excavations of the el-Wad Cave, Mt. Carmel, Israel." *Rock Art Research* 10.2 (1993): 102–106.

Weinstein-Evron, Mina. "Provenance of Ochre in the Natufian Layers of el-Wad Cave, Mount Carmel, Israel." *Journal of Archaeological Science* 21 (1994): 461–467.

OFER BAR-YOSEF

CARTER, HOWARD

CARTER, HOWARD (1873–1939), English Egyptologist, discover of Tutankhamun's tomb. Trained in drawing and painting by his father, Carter was introduced to Egyptology by a coincidence. In 1891, while visiting the renowned collections of paintings and Egyptian antiquities of Lord and Lady Amherst at Didlington Hall, their home in Brandon, Norfolk, not far from the Carter residence in Swaffham, both father and son were introduced to the Egyptologist Percy Edward Newberry. Subsequently Lady Amherst recommended young Howard to the Egypt Exploration Fund in London, which sponsored archaeological work in Egypt. Thus, at the young age of seventeen, Carter found himself in Egypt employed as a draftsman for Newberry's work in the decorated tombs and Beni Hasan. Following Newberry's method of facsimile recording, Carter hung sheets of tracing paper on the walls directly over the decorated surfaces in order to trace in pencil what was visible. In time Carter devised his own technique, which in his own words "created scientifically exacting facsimile(s) from the originals with a free and understanding hand" (quoted in James, 1992, p. 22). Carter's later watercolors, which were made for the tourist trade, command respectable prices when occasionally offered on the art market.

Carter learned as much about all aspects of Egyptology as possible. His perseverance was rewarded in 1900 when he was appointed chief inspector of antiquities (or archaeologist) for Upper Egypt. In time he was introduced to Lord Carnarvon, who had come to Egypt to convalesce after a near-fatal automobile accident, perhaps by Gaston Maspero, the then head of the Egyptian Antiquities Organization. From that moment in 1908 on they forged a partnership, excavating sites in Thebes until that fateful day,

26 November 1922, when Carter peered through a small hole in what proved to be King Tutankhamun's treasure-laden tomb, and replied to Carnarvon's query about whether he could see anything with, "Yes, wonderful things." Subsequently political maneuvering and disputes between Carter and various officials caused him personal pain that mitigated the success he now enjoyed. In fact, his life as an Egyptologist has been characterized as a "sad success."

BIBLIOGRAPHY

James, T. G. H. *Howard Carter: The Path to Tutankhamun*. London, 1992. Sober account with copious notes.

Reeves, Nicholas. *The Complete Tutankhamun: The King, The Tomb, The Royal Treasure*. London, 1990. Brief discussion of Carter's career. Profusely illustrated narrative about the discovery of the tomb.

Reeves, Nicholas, and John H. Taylor. *Howard Carter before Tutankhamun*. London, 1992. Thorough account of Carter's early career. Contains many illustrations.

ROBERT STEVEN BIANCHI

CARTHAGE, city on the North African coast, now a suburb of Tunis (36°51′ N, 10°20′ E), founded around the end of the ninth century BCE by settlers from Tyre, who called it Qart Ḥadasht ("new town"). Centuries later, Tyre in Phoenicia was still honored as the mother city, its gods receiving from Carthage an annual offering of the first fruits (Polybius, 31.12). The Phoenician ancestry of Carthage is reflected in the Latin term *Punicus*, which is an adjectival derivation from the Greek for "Phoenician." The designation *Punic* describes anything pertaining to Carthage.

The traditional date for the foundation, 814/13 BCE, thirty-eight years before the first Olympic games, goes back at least to Timaeus, a Sicilian Greek who wrote in the third century BCE. In the next century Menander of Ephesus, who had access to Phoenician sources, gives a similar date. Cicero and other Latin writers follow the same tradition, which recent excavations tend to confirm. A variant that sets the foundation before the Trojan War must be rejected.

Sources and Early History. No Punic literature survives, the city's libraries having been dispersed when Carthage was taken by the Romans (Pliny, *Natural History* 18.22). There is material in the works of more than forty Greek or Latin writers, but these sources must be treated with skepticism. Polybius, one of our fullest sources, who had traveled in Africa and was present at the sack of Carthage in 146, is overtly pro-Roman and mentions Greek historians who wrote from a Carthaginian standpoint only to dismiss them as worthless (Polybius, 3.20). The Carthaginians, he says, are ashamed of nothing if it makes money (6.56), and Plutarch calls them harsh and gloomy, caring nothing for pleasure or the arts (*Moralia* 799D). Such negative stereotypes have been accepted uncritically all too often. Classical writers are also often negative and ill-informed

about the Jews or Syrians as well. For the Greeks and Romans, peoples of Semitic culture were "the other."

Punic inscriptions, however, survive in some quantity. Carthage itself has yielded more than six thousand, and one thousand more come from other sites in Africa or elsewhere in the western Mediterranean. Most are merely standard formulae, such as votive or funerary inscriptions and documents regarding sacrifice and religious cult, but they give us more than five hundred personal names, plus names of magistracies, trades, and professions. Otherwise little historical information can be gleaned from them, and when it comes to the longer texts, there is often considerable dispute among experts as to the meaning, because the Punic language is not perfectly understood. Texts in Punic or in the later script known as "neo-Punic" continue into the Roman period.

Attempts to reconstruct the form of government and the internal politics of Carthage from this literary and epigraphic material are very hazardous, especially for the early centuries. Whether there were kings in Carthage's early years is hotly disputed. Oligarchic factions subsequently disputed the power, and the literary tradition suggests that the leading families were successively the Magonids, the Hannonids, and the Barcids, founded by Hamilcar Barca, father of the great Hannibal, but again the family names and the dynastic concept may owe something to the Greek historiographic tradition.

Carthage had extensive trading interests in the western Mediterranean and beyond and fought to defend them. We thus find Carthage in the early sixth century unsuccessfully contesting the foundation of a Phocaean colony at what is now Marseilles (Thucydides, 1.13), but succeeding around 535 in alliance with the Etruscans in driving the Phocaeans from their Corsican base at Alalia (Herodotus, 1.166). By the fourth century Carthage was a major power, striking gold and silver coinage, importing pottery and luxury goods from Greece, and exporting her own manufactured goods and agricultural surpluses (her agricultural expertise was famous). Punic amphorae of the fourth and still more the third century are particularly common in Spain and southern Italy. Punic vessels sailed down the west coast of Africa, though how far they reached is much disputed, as well as northward, perhaps as far as Britain. Treaties between Carthage and Rome in 509/08 (Polybius, 3.22) and on subsequent occasions recognized the two cities' respective spheres of interest, but Rome's expansion eventually brought them into conflict over Sicily and the three Punic Wars (264–241, 218–202, 149–146), so named from the Roman standpoint, ended with the total destruction of Carthage, whose site thereafter lay abandoned for over a century.

Archaeological Evidence and Topography. The urban development of Carthage down to 146 can be traced from well over a century of archaeological excavation, culminating since 1972 in the UNESCO-sponsored Save Carthage campaign, described below. Excavations have now shown that the earliest city lay between the Byrsa hill and the sea, where the occupation sequence goes back to at least the first quarter of the eighth century, dated by imported Euboean pottery. The Byrsa and adjacent hills were first used as cemeteries, but in fourth century the Byrsa became an industrial zone with extensive metal-working operations, and from the end of the third century it was a residential area. Excavation corroborates Appian's account (*Punica* 96, 128) of the steep streets descending from the Byrsa toward the ports, which comprised a circular inner harbor for warships with an island in the center and shipsheds all around, and an outer, rectangular, commercial harbor. The latest reports ascribe the construction of the harbors to the second century, in flagrant violation of the peace treaty at the end of the Second Punic War. The original port of Carthage must presumably have been within what is now the Lake of Tunis, then much more extensive.

Religion. Alongside the commercial harbor lay the religious precinct known today as the *tophet*, by analogy with the Old Testament site in the valley of Hinnom (*Jer.* 731–32). Here were found urns dating from the seventh century onward, containing the cremated remains of babies, small children, and animals, and steles referring to sacrifice (*molk*) and dedicated to the goddess Tannit ("face of Baal") and her consort, Baal Hammon. Most scholars see this material as corroborating what the literary sources attest—that the Carthaginians practiced infant sacrifice, which according to Tertullian (*Apology* 9.2) continued clandestinely even into the Roman period. Child sacrifice was certainly practiced by the Phoenicians, as the Hebrew Bible makes clear (e.g., *Jer.* 19:5, references assembled by Brown, 1991, pp. 27–29), and attempts to explain away the evidence and to interpret the *tophet* as a cemetery for children who died naturally do not carry conviction. This aspect of Punic culture shocked Greeks and Roman writers, who may be suspected of piling on the horror, although the same writers accepted complacently the Greco-Roman practice of exposing unwanted infants to die on dungheaps.

Baal Hammon is frequently celebrated in theophoric personal names like Hannibal and Hasdrubal; he was identified in the Roman period with Saturn, as was Tannit with Juno, and his cult is widely attested. Other divinities of Punic Carthage include Ashtart (Astarte), here subordinate to Tanit, and Eshmun, identified with the Greek Asclepius, god of healing, whose temple crowned the Byrsa and was the site of the final Punic stand in 146; both appear in theophoric names, as in a dedication from the *tophet* by Bodashtart, son of Abdeshmoun. Inscriptions mention Melqart, the patron deity of Tyre, Shadrapa, Sid, Sakon, and Rašap (Resheph) and attest the preponderant role of sacrifice in worship. The terminology often recalls that of the Old Testament, but parallels must not be pushed too far. [*See* Cult.]

Art. Punic art has generally been dismissed as unimaginative, unoriginal, and just plain bad. Nothing could be more totally damning than M. P. Charlesworth's account in the original *Cambridge Ancient History* (vol. 8, 1930, pp. 484–494) concluding, "It is hard to name anything which mankind can be said to owe to Carthage." A reappraisal, however, is long overdue. Two magnificent statues of a so-called priest and priestess on sarcophagus lids in the Carthage Museum reveal a synthesis of Egyptian, Hellenistic, and local elements that cannot be dismissed as merely imitative. Typically and without evidence, earlier scholars pronounced them as the work of Greek immigrants! Some stelae are very fine, though most are rough work, the local sandstone did not lend itself to sculpture. Apotropaic (protective) masks and pendants of human heads show great vigour. Bone and ivory, glass, and metalware reached a high standard, and Punic furniture was renowned. The swan-necked, so-called razors found in tombs are most elegantly engraved, and Punic jewelry is magnificent. Carthage adapted Greek and Egyptian models to serve her own needs and values, as did Rome later.

Foundation of the Roman Colony. For a century after the destruction of Carthage in 146, BCE, neighboring Utica served as capital of the new Roman province of Africa. Carthage was abandoned, although the story that the site was sown with salt was apparently invented for the *Cambridge Ancient History* (vol. 8, 1930, p. 484). Literary sources ascribe to Gaius Gracchus the project of founding a colony in 122, but there is no evidence of urban settlement, though Gracchus is probably responsible for the Roman division of the Carthage peninsula into units of two hundred *iugera*, which survives in the modern field boundaries. Caesar revived the idea of a colony, but it was probably Augustus who realized it, laying out a street grid parallel to the coast and leveling the summit of the Byrsa to create a rectangular esplanade, building massive retaining walls around it, and covering the late Punic houses on its slopes beneath many meters of fill. A peculiarity of the grid was that the blocks were four times as long from north to south as from east to west. In the flat ground between the Byrsa and the coast, the orientation was that of the late Punic city, and elements of this, such as the cisterns, were reused in Roman structures.

Public buildings. Of the city under Augustus and in the first century CE archaeology tells us little. None of the great public buildings in its present form goes back that far, though an earlier phase is not excluded. The amphitheater has been ascribed to the late first or early second century, the circus was given monumental form in the Antonine period, and the top of the Byrsa was also rebuilt under Antoninus Pius. Both the Antonine basilica on the Byrsa and the circus are the largest of their kind outside Rome. The theater goes back to the early second century and may be earlier, and the neighboring Odeon, the largest in the whole Roman world, is described as new in the early third century (Tertullian, *On the Resurrection of the Dead*, 42.8). In Punic times, the whole Odeon hill had been a cemetery. The vast Antonine Baths on the seashore take their name from an inscription that probably records Antoninus's completion or refurbishing of baths started by Hadrian. To supply these baths Hadrian had commissioned the aqueduct that brought to Carthage the waters from Jebel Zaghouan.

This aqueduct is one of the greatest works of Roman engineering. It is over 90 km (56 mi.) in length from its source at Zaghouan and falls almost 265 m (870 ft.) to the cisterns on the hill of Bordj Djedid in Carthage, which supply the Antonine Baths. It loses nearly half this height, however, in the first 6 km (3.7 mi.) as it descends rapidly to the plain of the Oued Miliane at Moghrane, where it is joined by another branch, possibly of Severan date, coming from Aïn Djoukar more than 33 km (20.5 mi.) away. Thereafter from Moghrane to Bordj Djedid the aqueduct channel falls only 127.93 m (419.7 ft.) in 84.418 km (52.34 mi.), a gradient of .15 percent, and its capacity has been calculated at 370 l (98 gal.) per second. Where it enters the city, the aqueduct bifurcates, one branch feeding eighteen cisterns at Bordj Djedid, the other twenty-four at La Malga, each some 102 m (335 ft.) long and 7.40 m (24.3 ft.) wide.

Christianity and culture. By the second century CE, only Alexandria rivaled Carthage as the empire's largest and wealthiest city after Rome. It was beginning to be a center of Christianity and produced some notable martyrs. When the serious persecutions of the third century began, the whole of Africa was divided on how to respond. One result was the Donatist movement, rigorist and intransigent on doctrinal matters, and at the same time a movement of social protest, poor against rich and country against town (Frend, 1952). Carthage lay at the heart of the controversy, and was split between the two parties. When the emperor Constantine himself adopted Christianity in 312, both Donatists and Catholics began to build, and Carthage acquired its first basilicas and other Christian buildings, such as the late fourth century martyrium on the Odeon hill.

At the same time, Carthage was an intellectual center, second only to Rome in the Latin-speaking West. The works of Tertullian and Apuleius in the late second century give some of the flavor. In the fourth century, Augustine naturally gravitates there from a small town in the interior and finds his intellectual milieu. He also finds it a city of luxury and pleasure: "there seethed about me a cauldron of unholy lusts" (*Confessions* 3.1). His subsequent career led him to Italy, where he converted to Christianity, then returning to Africa to find himself bishop of Hippo (Annaba) from 395 until his death in 430. Augustine spent half the year in Carthage battling for the faith, the outstanding personality, and intellect of the Catholic church in Africa.

Vandal and Byzantine Carthage. By the end of the fourth century, the Roman Empire in the West was falling apart. In 410 the Goths sacked Rome. Africa, protected by the Mediterranean, received refugees, but the remission was short-lived. The Vandals crossed the Straits of Gibraltar in 429, swept along the coast, besieged Hippo as Augustine lay dying within the walls, and finally took Carthage in 439, despite the so-called Theodosian Wall, which had been built around the city about 425 in anticipation of the attack. The Vandal king occupied the proconsul's palace on the Byrsa hill, and Vandal notables took over the grand houses on the seaward slope of the Odeon hill. Some public buildings were allegedly destroyed (Victor Vitensis in J.-P. Migne, *Patrologia Latina*, Paris, 1862, vol. 58, col. 184), and archaeology suggests that, although there was no sudden dramatic change in the city's condition, within a generation its trade and prosperity had fallen off and soon the outlying parts of the city were being abandoned.

The Theodosian Wall was also allowed to fall into disrepair, and in 533 the Byzantine general Belisarius captured the city with no great difficulty, repairing the wall thereafter. Economic recovery and new building ensued under Byzantine rule, but little less than a century later the first Arab invasions culminated in the battle of Sbeïtla (647), in which the governor Gregory fell. The Arabs departed for a time, but their foundation of Kairouan (Qayrawan) in 670 symbolized their intention to stay, and around this time the reoccupation of areas of Carthage that had earlier been abandoned may betoken the arrival of refugees seeking the security of the city. If so, it was in vain, because Carthage fell to the Arabs in 695, and after a rebellion it was retaken and destroyed in 698. The site may not have been completely abandoned, but organized urban life ceased, and Tunis replaced Carthage, subsequently becoming the capital of Ifriqiya, the former Roman Africa, modern Tunisia.

Destruction of Carthage in Middle Ages and History in Modern Times. Carthage became a stone quarry. Because there is no good building stone on the peninsula, much of the Roman stone was either limestone from the Jebel Zaghouan region or sandstone brought by sea from the quarries at El Haouaria on the tip of Cap Bon. It was easier to "recycle" Roman stone than to bring in more. Carthage supplied the columns and capitals for the Zaytouna Mosque in Tunis and the great blocks of the fort of Charles V at La Goulette guarding the entrance to the Lake of Tunis. Stone was also exported: al-Idrisi in the twelfth century says that no boat left Carthage without a cargo of stone, and marbles were shipped from Carthage to build the cathedrals of Pisa and Genoa. Memoirs and archaeological accounts right up to World War II speak of stone-robbing as an honorable local profession nor is it yet totally extinct. It is to be hoped that recent legislation and the establishment of a national archaeological park will save what remains.

The UNESCO "Save Carthage" Campaign. The site of Carthage was virtually uninhabited in the nineteenth century, but construction of a suburban railway along the coast from Tunis to La Marsa in 1907 opened it up for development, which increased after independence in 1956. By 1972 the danger that the site might become totally built over led the Tunisian authorities to launch an international campaign of excavation and conservation under the patronage of UNESCO before it was too late. About a dozen countries took part, and the results have been summarized in a volume of articles (see Ennabli, 1992). The campaign officially closed in 1992, and although excavation continues, the emphasis is now more on conservation and the creation of an archaeological park.

The campaign added more to our knowledge of Punic Carthage and of late Roman, Vandal, and Byzantine Carthage than to that of the early empire. For the Punic period, the German excavations at a number of points between the Byrsa hill and the sea revealed the original Punic settlement, going back at least to the first quarter of the eighth century BCE; the French laid bare several blocks of late Punic housing on the Byrsa itself, overlying an earlier industrial quarter, and preserved under later Roman fill; and British and American teams excavated in the area of the Punic ports, backed up by geophysical prospection and underwater exploration along the coast, while the Americans also excavated in the *tophet.*

The British and German excavations also cast light on the early Roman period, and a second French team worked out the topography of the monumental first- and second-century forum on the summit of the Byrsa. The Americans helped clarify the history of the circus, following geophysical prospection by a Polish team, and the Italians in the northwest and Canadians in the northeast of the city added to our knowledge of the urban topography. A second British team carried out a number of rescue excavations and made observations during the construction of a new sewage system. Most of the great monuments of the early empire, however, had been excavated long ago, like the amphitheater, the theater, the Odeon, the vast cisterns at La Malga and Bordj Djedid, and the Antonine baths, along with the houses on the east slope of the Odeon hill, and much of the information that they might have yielded to modern excavation techniques is lost forever.

From later periods a number of Christian basilicas and their adjacent cemeteries, previously excavated at least in part, were reinvestigated, and the Americans also dug a major Byzantine cemetery behind the circus and one of the Vandal period just outside the city to the northwest. Germans studied the enigmatic underground structure known only as the Kobbat Bent el Rey, dating from the early fourth century, and a Canadian team showed the "Circular Monument" west of the theater to be a Christian *memoria* of the later fourth century. A University of Michigan team excavated an ecclesiastical complex linked to a basilica in the southeast sector of the city and built an exemplary site museum to display their results. The Swedes excavated a house with a bath complex at the foot of the Byrsa and the Danes a late Roman villa on the coast in the extreme northeast of the city. The British, Americans, Italians, and Canadians all excavated stretches of the Theodosian Wall, built around 425 in anticipation of the Vandal invasion, and the Canadians and Danes in the northeast, like the Michigan team in the southeast, found evidence of squatter occupation in the final years before the Arab capture of the city in 695.

This summary necessarily omits much, and particularly the Tunisian contribution in numerous rescue excavations, but it indicates how important the UNESCO campaign has been, utterly transforming our knowledge of the city, although adding little to its history in the Arab period, when pottery suggests that it was largely but not completely abandoned.

[*See also* Phoenician-Punic; *and* Phoenicians.]

BIBLIOGRAPHY

The best known Greek and Latin writers are available in the Loeb series, published by Harvard University Press, with the original text and translation on facing pages. For inscriptions, see the following: *Corpus inscriptionum semiticarum* (Paris, 1881–); *Répertoire d'épigraphie sémitique* (Paris, 1990–); *Corpus inscriptionum latinarum*, vol. 8 (Berlin, 1981–); Maria Giulia Amadasi Guzzo, *Le iscrizioni fenicie e puniche delle colonie in Occidente* (Rome, 1967); and Alfred Merlin, *Inscriptions latines de la Tunisie* (Paris, 1944). Secondary sources include the following:

Bartoloni, Piero, et al., eds. *Atti del I congresso internazionale di studi fenici e punici, Roma, 5–10 novembre 1979.* 3 vols. Rome, 1983. International collection of essays covering a variety of topics in Punic-Phoenician material culture, history, and language. Useful resource on recent scholarly interests and controversies and primary and secondary sources; state-of-the-field summaries.

Benichou, Hélène. *Les tombes puniques de Carthage: Topographie, structures, inscriptions et rites funéraires.* Paris, 1982. Painstaking and invaluable account of over a century of excavation reports, with analyses of tomb types, inscriptions, and funerary rites.

Bomgardner, David L. "The Carthage Amphitheater: A Reappraisal." *American Journal of Archaeology* 93 (1989): 85–103. Study of the amphitheater as currently visible, listed here because this is one of the few major monuments of the city not touched in the UNESCO campaign.

Brouillet, Monique Seefried, ed. *From Hannibal to Saint Augustine: Ancient Art of North Africa from the Musée du Louvre.* Atlanta, 1994. Exhibition catalog with eighteen specialist articles on Carthage and North Africa, about half translated from French and often conveying ideas and information otherwise inaccessible in English.

Brown, Susanna Shelby. *Late Carthaginian Child Sacrifice and Sacrificial Monuments in Their Mediterranean Context.* Sheffield, 1991. Survey of literary, epigraphic, and archaeological evidence for child sacrifice, with typological and iconographic study of stelae from the Carthage *tophet.*

Cintas, Pierre. *Manuel d'archéologie punique.* 2 vols. Paris, 1970–1976. Historical and archaeological evidence for western Phoenician, especially Carthaginian, civilization. Volume 1 contains a useful overview of classical and Christian sources, focusing on the foundation of Carthage and other sites, but generally taking ancient sources too literally. Volume 2 deals with the archaeology of Carthage. Both volumes are now largely out of date as far as the archaeology is concerned, and Cintas is just plain wrong about the ports. Good bibliography through 1975.

Ennabli, Abdelmajid, ed. *Pour sauver Carthage: Exploration et conservation de la cité punique, romaine et byzantine.* Paris and Tunis, 1992. Twenty-four articles summarizing the results of the UNESCO team, mostly by the directors of the excavations themselves, with complete bibliography to date, which in most cases will lead the reader to more detailed reports on which summaries are based.

Fantar, M'hamed Hassine. *Carthage: Approche d'une civilisation.* 2 vols. Tunis, 1993. Detailed discussion of the history and civilization of Punic Carthage; up to date, full of excellent information, but lacks a decent index. There is nothing remotely comparable in English. On the *tophet* and infant sacrifice, see volume 2, pages 302–306.

Frend, W. H. C. *The Donatist Church: A Movement of Protest in Roman North Africa.* Oxford, 1952. Still the fundamental account, although Frend's views on the social basis of Donatism have been challenged by more recent scholarship.

Gsell, Stéphane. *Histoire ancienne de l'Afrique du Nord.* 8 vols. Paris, 1921–1928. Still the basic survey of evidence for Phoenicians and natives, Stone Age to Roman conquest. Often methodologically and archaeologically out of date, but never superseded by equally comprehensive work, and nothing comparable exists in English.

Lancel, Serge. *Carthage.* Paris, 1992. Account of Punic Carthage, particularly strong on the history of French research, with good bibliography. An English translation is in preparation (Oxford: Blackwell).

Moscati, Sabatino. "Il sacrificio punico dei fanciulli: Realtà o invenzione?" *Rendiconti dell'Accademia Nazionale dei Lincei* (1987): 3–15. The fullest statement to date of the case for supposing that infant sacrifice is a myth.

Pedley, John G., ed. *New Light on Ancient Carthage.* Ann Arbor, 1980. Series of articles by UNESCO participants reporting on early stages of the campaign. See especially Stager on the *tophet,* Wightman on the layout of the city, and Humphrey on Vandal and Byzantine Carthage.

Rakob, Friedrich. "Die römische Wasserleitung von Karthago." In *Journées d'études sur les aqueducs romains/Tagung über römische Wasserversorgungsanlagen, Lyon, 26–28 mai 1977,* edited by Jean-Paul Boucher, pp. 309–332. Paris, 1983. The definitive account of the Zaghouan aqueduct.

Raven, Susan. *Rome in Africa.* 3d ed. London, 1993. The only book on North Africa in English that is both readable and reliable, with Carthage playing a prominent role.

Soren, David, et al. *Carthage: Uncovering the Mysteries and Splendors of Ancient Tunisia.* New York, 1990. Chatty and popular in approach, and occasionally already out of date, but very useful in the absence of any recent scholarly account in English.

Sznycer, Maurice. "Carthage et la civilisation punique." In *Rome et la conquête du monde méditerranéen, 264–27 avant J.-C.,* vol. 2, *Genèse d'un empire,* edited by Claude Nicolet, pp. 545–593. Paris, 1978. Invaluable survey by a Semitic linguist, covering evidence (especially epigraphic) and the main controversies, with a summary of modern bibliography.

COLIN M. WELLS

CARTS. Wheeled vehicles apparently developed in Sumer during the Uruk period, perhaps as early as 3000 BCE. The earliest type was a heavy, four-wheeled, ox-drawn wagon featuring a boxlike body and four solid wheels. Excavated remains reveal that these early wagons were relatively small, with bodies less than half a meter wide and wheels 50–100 cm in diameter. Covered wagons, with leather or linen covers, are represented in Sumerian models as early as 2500 BCE, as well as at Carchemish and Aššur. Examples of some of the earliest remains and models of various types of wagons and carts are presented by Armas Salonen in his *Die Landfahrzeuge des alten Mesopotamien* (Helsinki, 1951, pp. 157–158, with accompanying plates). From this cumbersome wagon developed the somewhat lighter two-wheeled cart, which was still a ponderous affair, also borne on solid wheels.

Such wagons and carts appear to have been extensively used in the ancient Near East. In the code of Hammurabi, for example, two laws (nos. 271, 272, *ANET,* p. 177) deal with the rental of a wagon with or without a driver and oxen, and at Alalakh, in Syria, "twenty wagons" are mentioned in a Hurrian list of objects. Shamshi-Adad sent instructions that the inhabitants of Qattunan were to transport some goods from Qattunan to Shubat-Enlil in wagons. The Akkadian term for wagon, *eriqqu,* occurs frequently in Mesopotamian literature and in records from the earliest times through the Neo-Babylonian period (626–539 BCE). Wagons and carts are also frequently represented in the art of the region, particularly during the Neo-Assyrian period (900–612 BCE). For example, a relief from Nimrud, depicting a city under attack, shows several two-wheeled, ox-drawn carts carrying away women and children prisoners (cf. *ANEP,* no. 367, and the similar relief of Sennacherib's siege of Lachish, which shows a two-wheeled cart transporting women and children who are sitting on top of some bundles). A closed, four-wheeled, covered wagon is depicted on Ashurnasirpal's obelisk. (For other Mesopotamian examples, see *ANEP,* nos. 167, 169, and 303). Carts and wagons were used especially to transport heavy loads, such as large quantities of metal, timber, or military supplies (see Annals of Sennacherib 1.25).

After the introduction of the horse as a draft animal in about 2300 BCE, a lighter type of two-wheeled cart was needed. This lighter vehicle, the precursor to the chariot, eventually evolved, thanks to a new technological development: by about 1500 BCE, Mesopotamian craftsmen had learned the technique of bending wood with heat, which enabled them to replace heavy disc wheels with much lighter spoked wheels. These wheels comprised four or six spokes connected to a rim of curved, joined felloes. The cart's cumbersome all-wood body was redesigned with a curved wooden frame overlaid with a hide or wicker covering. The new, light conveyance became highly popular, and within two or three centuries it had not only become a standard means of transportation in the Near East, but also penetrated as far away as Greece, northern Europe, India, and even China.

The type of harness used throughout the ancient world was the yoke, originally designed for hitching a team of oxen.

It comprised a draft pole extending from the center of the vehicle's front side, with a horizontal crossbar near the outer end. One ox would be positioned on either side of the pole, and the crossbar (the yoke) would sit on the oxen's protruding shoulders. When horses became draft animals, the same yoke was used. Because the horse lacks prominent shoulders, the yoke was secured by a band that passed over the animal's breast, which unfortunately pressed against the windpipe and prevented it from using its full strength. This design flaw was never rectified in antiquity.

During the Roman period the most common means of transportation was the ox-drawn wagon, normally drawn by eight oxen or horses in the summer, ten in the winter. Heavy goods, such as army supplies, were transported by heavy *clabulariae*, a large, open wagon that could carry as much as 1,500 Roman pounds. Lighter vehicles included the *rheda*, a mule-drawn, four-wheeled cart using eight to ten mules, which could bear a maximum load of 450 kg; the *carrus*, a four-wheeled cart, which carried 270 kg; the *verreda*, drawn by four mules, which carried two to three persons and up to 135 kg of goods; and the two-wheeled *birota*, drawn by three mules, which carried one to two passengers and a maximum of 90 kg.

[*See also* Roads; Transportation; Wheel.]

BIBLIOGRAPHY

Casson, Lionel. *Travel in the Ancient World.* London, 1974. New ed. Baltimore, 1994. Carts and wagons are discussed throughout, but especially on pages 23ff.

Casson, Lionel. *Ancient Trade and Society.* Detroit, 1984. Good, up-to-date overview of trade and transportation in the ancient world.

Childe, V. Gordon. "Wheeled Vehicles." In *A History of Technology,* vol. 1, *From Early Times to the Fall of Ancient Empires,* edited by Charles Singer et al., pp. 716–729. London, 1954. Good survey of the technological development of the cart, wagon, and chariot.

Jope, E. M. "Vehicles and Harness." In *A History of Technology,* vol. 2, *The Mediterranean Civilizations and the Middle Ages, c. 700 B.C. to c. 1500 A.D.,* edited by Charles Singer et al., pp. 537–562. London, 1956. Well-documented study of the ancient technology of vehicles drawn by draft animals.

Littauer, M. A., and J. H. Crouwel. *Wheeled Vehicles and Ridden Animals in the Ancient Near East.* Leiden, 1979. Relatively up-to-date study of the technology of carts and wagons in the ancient Fertile Crescent.

Piggott, Stuart. *The Earliest Wheeled Transport: From the Atlantic Coast to the Caspian Sea.* London, 1983. Up to date and especially valuable for the pre-Roman periods.

Pritchard, James B., ed. *The Ancient Near East in Pictures Relating to the Old Testament (ANEP).* Princeton, 1954.

Pritchard, James B., ed. *Ancient Near Eastern Texts Relating to the Old Testament (ANET).* Princeton, 1969.

Salonen, Armas I. *Notes on Wagons and Chariots in Ancient Mesopotamia.* Helsinki, 1950. Dated, but still of some value.

Salonen, Armas I. *Die Landfahrzeuge des alten Mesopotamien.* Helsinki, 1951.

DAVID A. DORSEY

CATACOMBS. Large underground cemeteries, catacombs typically consist of a network of long, subterranean galleries whose walls have been cut as graves. Sometimes galleries open into rectangular or quadrangular rooms *(cubicula).* Such rooms usually contain rock-cut graves; occasionally, they also contain sarcophagi (stone containers used as coffins). [*See* Sarcophagus.] In the ancient Near East, catacombs normally consisted of galleries situated on one level. In the early Christian catacombs in Rome, by contrast, it is not unusual to find as many as four galleries one on top of the other.

The term *catacomb* derives from the Greek *kata kumbēn,* a toponym that means "near the hollow." In the Roman period it was used to denote a particular spot on the Via Appia, near the Catacomb of Sebastiano and the Circus of Maxentius, where the terrain suddenly drops tangibly. In exceptional cases, as in Hellenistic and Roman Egypt, catacombs were used to deposit the remains of mummified animals. Normally, however, catacombs served in the burial or reburial of the mortal remains of human beings. Discoveries in Roman Palestine and in Rome itself show that both the Jewish and the early Christian communities used catacombs. It is not clear, however, whether the idea of burial in catacombs first originated in Jewish or in early Christian circles.

Burial in catacombs was customary from the late second to the early sixth centuries CE. Extensive remains of catacombs have been found throughout the Mediterranean area, including the Near East. Yet, in Late Antiquity, burial in catacombs seems to have been particularly popular in Italy (e.g., at Rome, Naples, Venosa) and on the islands adjoining it (particularly Sicily and Malta).

Catacombs differ from other types of underground tombs in size, formal appearance, and, consequently, in function. In the ancient Near East, subterranean tombs were usually mere underground structures (hypogea). They offered a final resting place to a restricted group of people only—the members of an extended family. Compared to burial in such family tombs, burial in catacombs always remained exceptional in the eastern provinces of the Roman Empire. Occurring during a relatively short period of time only, the use of catacombs must be taken to reflect a particular attitude toward burying the dead. With their long underground galleries, catacombs were designed from the outset to accommodate the remains of large groups of people that either had to be or wanted to be buried or reburied together in a given locality.

In contrast to Rome, where more than sixty catacombs are known, only a few catacombs have been discovered in the Near East. Among the sparse finds, the dozen or so Jewish catacombs at Beth-She'arim (Lower Galilee) are certainly the most important because of the abundance of archaeological and epigraphic remains preserved there. [*See* Beth-She'arim.] No less significantly, Beth-She'arim is the only catacomb complex in the region that was studied systematically by its excavators (Avigad, 1971; Mazar, 1973).

In the Near East a few early catacombs believed to be Christian, but that may be Jewish-Christian, have also been discovered. One such catacomb came to light in the late nineteenth century CE on the Mt. of Olives in Jerusalem at a site known as Viri Galilei (Schick, 1889). The so-called Tomb of the Prophets, also located on the Mt. of Olives, has also been known since the nineteenth century and is still accessible (Vincent, 1901). It consists of several short, semicircularly shaped galleries. Despite its unusual plan, it too must be considered a catacomb. An early Christian catacomb was discovered and partially excavated in the late 1960s, at Emesa/Homs in Syria (Bounni, 1970). In Alexandria (Egypt), many subterranean Christian tombs, often referred to as early Christian catacombs, were discovered from 1820 to 1890; most of them are now destroyed (Leclercq, 1924). Although adequate documentation on the formal appearance of these Alexandrinian tombs is often lacking, the use of the term *catacomb* to describe them is incorrect. Characteristic of Alexandria's early Christian funerary architecture is the hypogeum—in this case a collection of subterranean rooms arranged around a central courtyard. Such hypogea were dug in proximity to one another. Not unusually, they were interconnected to form large underground complexes. Yet, they lack a catacomb's most distinguishing feature: galleries dug specifically for the deposition of the deceased members of an entire community.

Because ancient tombs have often been robbed, it is usually difficult to establish when precisely a given catacomb came into use or when burial ceased there. Archaeological small finds can, however, point to the approximate period of its use. Thus, it was ascertained that the Jewish catacombs at Beth-She'arim were in use mainly from the late second to the middle of the fourth centuries CE. The precise dating of the catacomb on the Mt. of Olives has not been achieved. It is not unlikely though that burials took place there in the third–fifth centuries CE. The Tomb of the Prophets is dated to the fourth and fifth centuries. The Christian catacomb at Emesa Homs has been dated by its excavator to the third–seventh centuries (Bounni, 1970).

The size and layout of a catacomb's complex network of underground galleries and cubicula are determined by several factors: the workability of the rock, the amount of space needed, and the degree of planning involved. In Rome, for example, the earliest catacombs frequently consist of a network of irregular galleries (curvilinear galleries that seem to go into every direction). Galleries in later Roman catacombs, on the other hand, display a much more systematic layout (Brandenburg, 1984). Such developments in planning testify to a rise in the popularity of burial in catacombs, as well as to the need to dispose of the ever-increasing number of dead in the most rational way. This explains why in many of the catacombs at Beth-She'arim, too, a tendency toward symmetry and the economic use of space is discernible.

Rock-Cut Graves. In catacombs, different types of rock-cut graves were used. Some graves are long, rectangular slots that were cut parallel to the wall. These loculi take up little wall space, and so it is not unusual to find rows of up to seven or eight loculi, one on top of the other. Another rectangular grave, the *kokh*, is cut at right angles to the wall and goes right into it. The term *kokh* has a clear association with the practice of secondary burial in the Near East and is borrowed from the East Semitic language groups (Meyers, 1971). Despite a clear difference in formal appearance, the terms *loculus* and *kokh* are often used interchangeably in scholarly literature, which may lead to confusion. A third type of wall-cut grave, known as an acrcosolium, consists of one or more rectangular containers that are dug into the rock and overarched by a vault. The fourth and by far the simplest type of rock-cut grave is also rectangular: dug into the

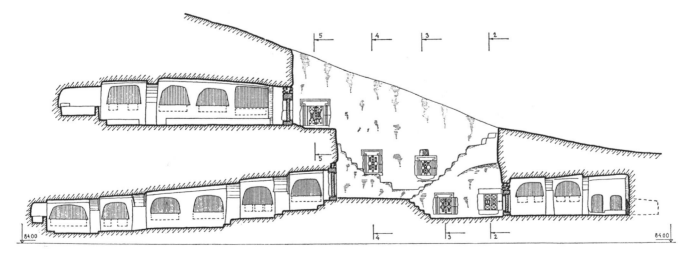

CATACOMBS.   *Cross-section of catacomb 13 at Beth-She'arim.* (After Avigad, 1971; courtesy Massada Press, Ltd.)

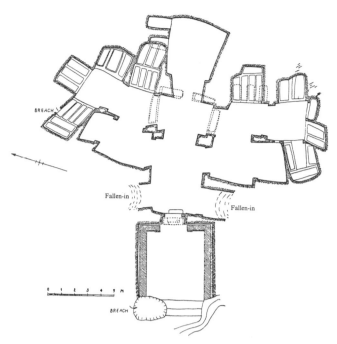

CATACOMBS.   *Plan of Mugharet el-Jehennem, a catacomb at Beth-She'arim.* (After Mazar, 1973; courtesy Massada Press, Ltd.)

floor of a gallery or burial room, it is known as a pit grave, or *forma.*

Rock-cut graves of the kind listed above normally offered enough space for one person only, though in some instances they were used for multiple reburials. They were sealed in various ways: with stones, bricks, rubble, or with a marble plate that sometimes carried a funerary inscription. In catacombs, burial in sarcophagi (coffins made of either stone, terra cotta, wood, or lead) is not very common. Unexpectedly, the underground galleries of catacomb 20 at Beth-She'arim were found filled with 125 well-preserved specimens of large sarcophagi, the great majority of which are of local limestone (Avigad, 1976). Another peculiarity confined to the catacombs at Beth-She'arim is the use of ossuaries—small stone or wooden containers used for secondary burial. [*See* Ossuary.] Together with sarcophagi and loculi, the vast majority of burials at Beth-She'arim were reburials, testifying to the Jewish idea of the importance of burial or reburial in the land of Eretz-Israel, where resurrection would occur and where the land had atoning powers (Zlotnick, 1966).

With the exception of ossuaries, which reflect a typically Jewish funerary philosophy (at least in Roman Palestine), the grave forms listed above occur in Jewish and Christian catacombs alike. In fact, in the second–fourth centuries CE, there are no major differences between catacombs and hypogea, either in terms of grave types or burial customs. The tombs in the Jewish catacombs at Beth-She'arim and in the early Christian catacombs at Viri Galilei are remarkably sim-

ilar in both shape and selection of tomb types to those found in contemporary hypogea, such as the chamber tombs of the Dominus Flevit cemetery in Jerusalem. Evidence from these catacombs and hypogea shows cumulatively that in second–fourth-century Palestine, the arcosolium slowly but steadily replaced the *kokh* as the most popular grave form. Similarly, archaeological materials from the catacombs at Beth-She'arim and from hypogea at Meiron, Khirbet Shema', Gezer, Ramat Rahel, and Horvat Thala in Roman Palestine document that in the period under discussion the same trends in burial customs affected the funerary customs in catacombs and hypogea. It is now known, for example, that secondary burial continued to be practiced in different parts of Roman Palestine throughout antiquity, but that it lost much of the popularity it had enjoyed in first-century CE Jerusalem.

The single most important factor leading to the genesis and subsequent evolution of burial in catacombs was that large numbers of people could be buried together without taking up too much space. The various stages of this process can best be seen in Rome. There, the earliest Christian catacombs are nothing but a collection of irregularly shaped galleries. Originating in deserted quarries, cisterns, and water channels, these subterranean galleries maintained the character of privately owned tombs until more space and more systematic planning were needed. In the third and fourth centuries, Rome's Christian community—all people who had to be buried—rapidly increased in size, and many Christians wanted to be buried near the remains of their martyrs. Beginning in the period of Pope Zephyrinus (199–217), who appointed one Callistus as overseer of a catacomb, the Christian community was enabled to fulfill an obligation it had taken upon itself—to bury the Christian poor. Planned catacombs were dug that were no longer privately owned and offered room for all members of the Early Christian community (Brandenburg, 1984).

It is not clear whether similar factors shaped the contemporary development of catacomb architecture in the Near East. It is clear, however, that in the eastern part of the Mediterranean, catacombs were constructed because this form of burial offered the same advantages the inhabitants of Rome had come to appreciate. Beginning in the second century CE, Beth-She'arim replaced Jerusalem as the most prestigious Jewish necropolis. This happened, in part, because many Palestinian and Diaspora Jews alike believed that burial in the land of Israel was to be preferred over burial in the Diaspora (cf. Tosefta, *A.Z.* 4:3: "He who is buried in the Land of Israel is as though he were buried under the altar"). The presence, in the Beth-She'arim catacombs, of the earthly remains of important Jewish religious and political leaders of the time must have been a major attraction as well. In the historical development of the Christian catacombs of Jerusalem, other, comparable factors are likely to have played a role. Inscriptions indicate that the people buried in the Tomb of the Prophets were pilgrims who had either died accidentally in Jerusalem or who had traveled there with the intention of securing their last resting place in proximity to the Holy City.

Little is known about those responsible for the exploitation and administration of catacombs. In fourth- and early fifth-century Rome, specialized gravediggers *(fossores)* can be shown to have worked by order of the church. At the same time, however, some of these *fossores* are known to have operated as independent entrepreneurs. Whether individual Roman parish churches each administered their own catacomb is a hypothesis that has frequently been advanced but never been proved conclusively (Guyon, 1987). The inscriptional evidence from Beth-She'arim and Acmonia (Asia Minor) as well as rabbinic literature suggest the existence of Jewish burial societies, but it is impossible to determine whether such colleges were also responsible for excavating and supervising catacombs (Schwabe and Lifschitz, 1974).

The same factors that led to the development of catacombs also caused its abandonment in Late Antiquity. With the dramatic drop in population in sixth-century Rome, burial shifted from catacombs to the exterior of churches within the Aurelian city wall. Beth-She'arim, perhaps destroyed during the Gallus Revolt of 351–352, had already ceased to be a center of importance. A decrease in the number of Christian pilgrims to Jerusalem must have been the determining factor that led to the discontinuation of burial in catacombs there.

From the Hellenistic and Roman Near East, several underground complexes are known whose walls are dotted with small niches, known as columbaria, measuring, on average, 20 × 20 × 15 cm. Examples of these columbaria are preserved in, among other places, Roman Palestine (Beth-Guvrin, Dor, Gezer, Masada, Ramat Rahel, Samaria); Roman Arabia (Petra); and Asia Minor (Sebaste in Cilicia). Such complexes are normally located in the same general areas as tombs. For that reason and because the niches they contain resemble somewhat the niches of subterranean constructions in Rome whose funerary function is beyond doubt, scholars have suggested that cremated human remains were placed in these Near Eastern counterparts. Inasmuch as there is no archaeological evidence to show that the niches in the columbaria ever contained ashes, the conclusion is problematic. Other scholars have suggested that these complexes may have been used to raise and keep pigeons.

Burial of hundreds or even thousands of animals in catacombs is an exclusively Egyptian phenomenon. Such animals were first mummified, wrapped in embroidered cloth, and then deposited in either limestone sarcophagi or pottery jars. They were layed to rest in winding underground galleries that could be hundreds of meters long. In Alexandria (Rhacotis), such "animal catacombs" were found to contain the mummified remains of dogs. In Memphis they contained the cadavers of bulls, while catacombs in Saqqara, Baklija (near Hermopolis), and Tuna el-Gebel testify to the cultic veneration of the ibis and, at the latter sites, also to that of the baboon. The practice of burying mummified animals in catacombs seems to have begun as early as the thirtieth dynasty (380–342 BCE) but did not gain widespread popularity until the Hellenistic and Roman periods (Kessler, 1983).

Iconography and Inscriptions. The artistic remains from catacombs represent not only the development of art in antiquity but also burial customs, ideas about death and afterlife, social relations, the economy, and gender (Peskowitz, 1993). For example, the discovery and scientific study of the Beth-She'arim catacombs profoundly changed the ways in which scholars view the genesis of rabbinic Judaism and the interaction of Jewish and non-Jewish cultures in antiquity.

Little is known about the aesthetics of the few catacombs discovered so far in the Near East, except at Beth-She'arim, where the iconography represented on the walls includes menorahs, the Ark of the Law, human figures, animals, ships, and geometric designs. Impressive portals with elaborately rendered stone doors and courtyards with mosaic floors lend monumentality to the entrances to its catacombs. [*See* Mosaics.] Inside, many of the sarcophagi, mostly of local production, show a rich iconographic repertoire consisting of crudely carved human figures and animals. A combination of three elements characterizes Beth-She'arim's artistic corpus: a lack of narrative themes, the absence of scenes taken from the Hebrew Bible, and a preference for motifs that are not only often religiously neutral, but that sometimes (especially on sarcophagi) are of clear pagan derivation. That the users of these catacombs were indeed vividly aware of the artistic achievements of non-Jewish workshops located on the Phoenician coast, or in Greece and Asia Minor, can also be inferred from the remains of imported marble and lead sarcophagi (Avigad, 1976). Another noticeable feature about the Beth-She'arim catacombs is that elaborate cycles of wall paintings are absent; this contrasts markedly with the evidence preserved in the Jewish and Early Christian catacombs in the western Mediterranean, where such wall paintings do decorate most catacombs.

At Beth-She'arim, many small finds—lamps, pottery, glass vessels, bronze and iron artifacts, and items of personal adornment—further enrich what is known of ancient art, manufacturing techniques, and Jewish burial customs and have enabled the dating of individual catacombs.

Often characterized by great conciseness, painted and incised funerary inscriptions as well as graffiti inform about a wide variety of issues, including the deceased's social, economic, and religious status, place of origin, onomastic practices, language, and religious beliefs and practices. Thus, it is known that the people buried in the Tomb of the Prophets and in the catacomb of Viri Galilei spoke Greek, and that some of them hailed from such cities as Harpagia (Asia Minor), Bostra, Palmyra, and Batanea (Schick, 1989; Vincent, 1901).

The inscriptions from the Beth-She'arim catacombs document the extent to which the Greek language, Greek literary form, and Greek ideas about death and afterlife had made inroads into a community in which the rabbinic element was unmistakable, if not dominant. Eighty percent of the Beth-She'arim inscriptions are in Greek, one of them a metric inscription composed in Homeric hexameters. Other inscriptions found at Beth-She'arim are in Hebrew, particularly in catacomb 14, which may contain the grave of Judah I the Patriarch, a well-known rabbinic figure traditionally regarded as the redactor of the Mishnah. Still other inscriptions are in Palmyrene. [See Palmyrene Inscriptions.] Together with the Greek inscriptions, the Palmyrene epitaphs indicate that Beth-She'arim rapidly evolved into a funerary center of supraregional importance: leaders of Jewish Diaspora communities as far apart as Byblos, Sidon, Tyre, Beirut, Antioch, Palmyra, Nehardea (Mesopotamia), and southern Arabia all had their mortal remains brought to Beth-She'arim for final interment (Schwabe and Lifschitz, 1974; Nagakubo, 1974).

[See also Burial Sites; Burial Techniques; Grave Goods; Necropolis; Sarcophagus; and Tombs. In addition, many of the sites mentioned are the subject of independent entries.]

BIBLIOGRAPHY

Avigad, Nahman. Beth She'arim: Report on the Excavations during 1953–1958, vol. 3, Catacombs 12–23. Jerusalem, 1971. Standard treatment on the second part of the excavations in the catacombs of Beth-She'arim.

Bounni, Adnan. "Les catacombes d'Émèse (Homs) en Syrie." Archeologia 37 (1970): 42–49. The only preliminary report presently available on the excavations.

Brandenburg, Hugo. "Überlegungen zu Ursprung und Entstehung der Katakomben Roms." Jahrbuch für Antike und Christentum 11 (1984): 11–49. Standard review essay on the origin and development of the Christian catacombs in Rome.

Buhagiar, Mario. Late Roman and Byzantine Catacombs and Related Burial Places in the Maltese Islands. British Archaeological Reports, International Series, no. 302. Oxford, 1986. Comprehensive study of underground cemeteries on Malta and of their inscriptions; richly illustrated and with references to earlier studies on the subject.

Fasola, Umberto M. La catacombe di San Gennaro a Capodimonte. Rome, 1975. Monographic study of the building history of the largest Early Christian catacomb in Naples.

Garana, Ottavio. Le catacombe siciliane e i loro martiri. Palermo, 1961. Somewhat outdated account of catacomb burial on Sicily; useful for its comprehensiveness and illustrations.

Guyon, Jean. Le cimetière aux deux lauriers: Recherches sur les catacombes romaines. Rome, 1987. Authoritative work on the building history of the catacomb of Sts. Marcellinus and Peter in Rome; especially important for its general methodological observations.

Kessler, Dieter. "Die Galerie C von Tuna el-Gebel." Mitteilungen des Deutschen Archäologischen Instituts, Kairo 39 (1983): 107–124. Excavation report on the ibis catacombs in Tuna el-Gebel; richly illustrated and with references to earlier literature on the subject.

Leclercq, Henri. "Alexandrie: Archéologie." In Dictionnaire d'archéologie chrétienne et de liturgie, vol. 1.1, cols. 1098–1182. Paris, 1924. Comprehensive survey of otherwise difficult-to-locate excavation reports on the early Christian funerary architecture of Alexandria.

Marinone, M., et al. "Cimetières inconnus d'Italie." Les Dossiers de l'Archéologie 19 (1976): 68–81. Brief account of Early Christian hypogea and catacombs discovered in Tuscany, Abbruzzo, and Latium and on Sardinia.

Mazar, Benjamin, et al. Beth She'arim: Report on the Excavations during 1936–1940, vol. 1, Catacombs 1–4. Jerusalem, 1973. Standard treatment on the first part of the excavations.

Meyers, Eric M. Jewish Ossuaries: Reburial and Rebirth. Rome, 1971. Major study of Jewish reburial into containers and various cavities and its theological significance.

Meyers, Eric M. "Report on the Venosa Catacombs, 1981." Vetera Christianorum 20 (1983): 455–459. English summary of the discovery of a hitherto unknown catacomb complex in southern Italy.

Nagakubo, Senzo. "Investigation into Jewish Concepts of Afterlife in the Beth-She'arim Greek Inscriptions." Ph.D. diss., Duke University, 1974. Detailed review of the extent to which Greek concepts of afterlife entered Jewish epigraphic formulae at Beth-She'arim.

Peskowitz, Miriam. "The Work of Her Hands: Gendering Everyday Life in Roman-Period Judaism in Palestine (70–250 CE), Using Textile Production as a Case Study." Ph.D. diss., Duke University, 1993. Methodologically interesting study (esp. pp. 244–294) on how grave gifts can be used for writing social history.

Rutgers, Leonard V. "Überlegungen zu den jüdischen Katakomben Roms." Jahrbuch für Antike und Christentum 33 (1990): 140–157. Critical review of the origin and chronology of the Jewish catacombs in Rome.

Schick, Conrad. "Katakomben auf dem Ölberg." Zeitschrift des deutschen Palästina-Vereins 12 (1889): 193–199. The only available report on an Early Christian catacomb in Jerusalem that has since disappeared.

Schwabe, Moshe, and Baruch Lifshitz. Beth She'arim, vol. 2, The Greek Inscriptions. New Brunswick, N.J., 1974. Standard corpus that should be consulted in conjunction with Avigad (above).

Vincent, L.-H. "Le tombeau des prophètes." Revue Biblique 10 (1901): 72–88. The only substantial study on this Early Christian catacomb in Jerusalem.

Zilliu, G. "Antichità paleocristiane di Sulcis." Nuovo Bullettino Archeologico Sardo 1 (1984): 283–300. Description of Early Christian hypogea and wall paintings on Sardinia.

Zlotnick, Dov. The Tractate "Mourning" (Semahot). Yale Judaica Series, vol. 17. New Haven, 1966. Critical edition of a treatise that is basic to any understanding of Jewish burial customs.

LEONARD V. RUTGERS and ERIC M. MEYERS

ÇATAL HÖYÜK, ancient name unknown, a double mound located at 37°06′ N, 32°08′ E, on the Konya Plain in south-central Turkey, about 260 km (156 mi.) south of Ankara and about 40 km (24 mi.) southeast of the town of Konya. Çatal Höyük, the largest Neolithic site known on the Anatolian plateau, was discovered by James Mellaart of the British Institute of Archaeology at Ankara and his colleagues during a field survey in 1958. Subsequent excavations, mainly directed by Mellaart between 1961 and 1963 and again in 1965, revealed extensive evidence of a large Neolithic settlement on the east mound; small-scale excavation

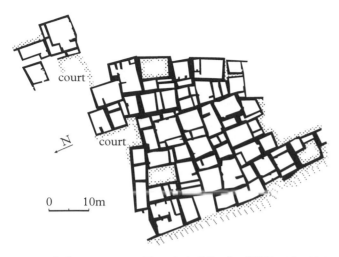

ÇATAL HÖYÜK. Figure 1. *Plan of a building, level VI B.* (After Mellaart, 1967, fig. 9)

on the west mound indicated the presence of a sizable Early Chalcolithic village, but the full sequence of occupation of the site as a whole remains to be established. No evidence has been found for occupation of the immediate area in the Aceramic Neolithic, but more extensive excavation may reveal its presence. Fieldwork on the site was resumed by another British team under the auspices of Cambridge University in 1993.

The oval east mound (500 × 300 m) rises to a height of 17.5 m above the plain. It is situated 28 km (17 mi.) from the nearest edge of the plain, in an agriculturally rich region, at an elevation of about 1000 m. The nature of the soils upon which the settlement was established is uncertain; it is likely that a branch of the Çarsamba Çay river flowed nearby in the Neolithic period, perhaps in the area now between the east and west mounds; the village may have been founded on the alluvial fan delta of that river. Proximity to a perennial river or stream may have made settlement feasible in this area of low average annual rainfall (249 mm).

Excavation on the east mound was principally concentrated on a one-acre area on its west side. Virgin soil was not reached in the deepest excavation area; approximately fifteen building levels were encountered (0–XIII, in descending order, with two phases in level VI). A sounding in 1963, close to the edge of the mound, is stated to have revealed occupation deposits to a depth of 5 m below the present plain level; if this is correct, a total depth of occupation of 22.5 m or more is to be found on the site.

Information about the settlement's architecture was predominantly obtained from levels VIII–II. Despite the paucity of evidence for the earliest and latest phases, no radical architectural changes could be discerned, and many aspects of the site indicate continuity. In all levels, the building plans are rectilinear (see figure 1). In the best-represented levels, houses and associated storerooms were built against each other, with abandoned houses and open areas serving as courtyards and dumps. A general tendency toward a more open plan is visible after level VI. The buildings are constructed of sun-dried, mold-made mud bricks; extensive use was made of a wooden framework, especially in the earlier levels. Floors and walls were plastered, and the flat roof was constructed of beams, lighter timber, and a thick mud coating. Most of the buildings were entered from the roof by means of a ladder; there are no doorways, except between a house and its associated storeroom. A degree of standardization is visible in many structures: the ladder is placed against the south wall, in association with hearths and ovens, benches and lower platforms appear in all houses.

One of the site's most notable features, in addition to the excellent state of preservation of some of the architecture and artifacts, is the elaborate decoration evidenced in a considerable number of buildings Mellaart classified as shrines (see figure 2). Decoration takes the form of wall paintings, plaster reliefs, cut-out figures, and other features that, in some cases, combine several techniques. The subjects of the wall paintings are geometric designs, sometimes reminiscent of textile patterns; animal and human figures, sometimes in combination; and, in one case, a possible landscape with the settlement shown with a mountain in the background. Several hunting scenes depict various species of birds and animals, especially a large red bull, in association with numerous human figures, each dressed in a kind of spotted loincloth. Some of the figures may be dancing, and a general atmosphere of levity is indicated. More macabre are scenes showing large red birds (perhaps vultures) hovering over headless human figures, no doubt alluding to the excarnation of bodies before burial.

The main subjects depicted in plaster relief are animal

ÇATAL HÖYÜK. Figure 2. *Shrine VI.B.10, restored.* (After Mellaart, 1967, fig. 38)

heads, human figures (sometimes in association with animal heads), complete animal figures, and rows of what seem to be human breasts, often molded over the jawbones or skulls of animals. The face, hands, and feet of the human figures are always damaged and appear to have been intentionally mutilated. The bodies are arranged parallel-sided with their arms and legs branching out at right angles to the body and turning up at the ends. One figure bears extensive linear painted decoration, perhaps representing a netlike dress. The figures may be goddesses, in a birthing position. In some cases a figure is shown immediately above a plaster bull's head. Pairs of leopardlike animals in relief and painted with spots or rosettes appear on the walls of several buildings. A representation of a stag looking behind him was found, as were silhouettes of animal heads and complete animal figures, also cut into the plaster on walls where the plaster was thick enough. The features in some buildings are complex: pairs of bull's horns were sometimes set into the sides of benches or into the top of small, rectangular, free-standing mud-brick pillars.

Burial customs are well evidenced by the 480 or so complete or partial burials found within the settlement below the floors of houses. The dead were usually placed under the platforms, in a contracted position, on their left side, with the head toward the center of the room and the feet near the wall. Some, if not all, of the bodies were wrapped in skins or textiles, placed in baskets, or laid on mats. The skeletons were sometimes found in rather chaotic heaps; later burials disturbed earlier interments. Clear evidence for secondary burial (burial after the flesh had at least partially decomposed) was found, and some skeletons (both male and female) were decorated with ocher or paint. A wall painting that may portray a lightly built structure with schematic human skulls shown below it has been interpreted as a charnel house, where the dead were laid out for excarnation. Grave goods of various types were buried with the dead, including wooden vessels that were preserved in carbonized form by the fire that destroyed the overlying building.

Handmade pottery in simple shapes was found in all levels at the site; the most characteristic product is a hole-mouth jar with a dark, streakily burnished surface. Baked clay was also used in the manufacture of stamp seals. Male and female figurines made of clay and stone were sometimes found in association with animal figurines. Other artifacts include quantities of finely fashioned tools, weapons, and some mirrors made of obsidian; ground stone tools; and objects made of animal bone. Despite the application of the term *Neolithic* to the site, copper and lead had been used to manufacture small items such as beads, pendants, and rings; a lump of copper slag in level VI suggests that the initial steps toward true metallurgy had already been taken.

According to a series of twenty-seven uncalibrated radiocarbon dates, the earlier excavated levels are to be dated to the late seventh millennium, whereas level VI and the later

levels fall after 6,000 BCE. The latest levels at Çatal Höyük East may just overlap with the beginning of the Late Neolithic occupation of Hacılar in the Anatolian Lake District to the west of the Konya Plain.

The excavations at Çatal Höyük East cast a completely new light on Neolithic civilization on the Anatolian plateau and in the Near East as a whole. Subsequent excavations in Turkey and elsewhere have still not revealed a contemporary site with more advanced art forms, religious ideology, or general level of sophistication than were found at Çatal Höyük.

[*See also* Hacılar.]

BIBLIOGRAPHY

Mellaart, James. "Excavations at Çatal Hüyük, 1965: Fourth Preliminary Report." *Anatolian Studies* 16 (1966): 165–191. The finds of this season are not covered in Mellaart (1967).

Mellaart, James. *Çatal Hüyük: A Neolithic Town in Anatolia.* London, 1967. Well-illustrated account of the first three seasons of excavation.

Todd, Ian A. *Çatal Hüyük in Perspective.* Menlo Park, Calif., 1976. Brief summary of the site, including environmental and other aspects to the extent that they were known at the time of writing.

Todd, Ian A. *The Prehistory of Central Anatolia,* vol. 1, *The Neolithic Period.* Studies in Mediterranean Archaeology, vol. 60, Göteborg, 1980. Publication of sites with contemporary material in central Anatolia, north of the Konya Plain. Contains a summary of the Anatolian Neolithic, including Çatal Höyük, and a useful bibliography as of 1975.

Yakar, Jak. *Prehistoric Anatolia: The Neolithic Transformation and the Early Chalcolithic Period.* Tel Aviv, 1991. Valuable, up-to-date summary of sites in all areas of Turkey, against which the excavations at Çatal Höyük must now be viewed. See also supplement no. 1 (1994) by the same author.

IAN A. TODD

CATON-THOMPSON, GERTRUDE (1888–1985), pioneering British archaeologist in Egyptian and East African prehistory. Caton-Thompson was born in London and in 1921 began to study archaeology there with Flinders Petrie at University College. From 1921 to 1926, she attended the British School of Archaeology in Egypt, where she continued to work with Petrie. From 1934 to 1951, she was a fellow at Newnham College, Cambridge. Caton-Thompson also did research on Malta (1921–1924) and in Yemen, her work established for the first time some of the prehistoric sequences in Egypt, and her thorough archaeological publications usually included excellent geological studies as well.

In Egypt, she excavated at Abydos (1921–1922) and at Qau and Badari (1923–1925). She also conducted archaeological and geological surveys in the Faiyum (1924–1928). From 1930 to 1933, she excavated at the Khargah oasis. In 1928–1929 she excavated at Zimbabwe, demonstrating that the culture was not as ancient as had been proposed. Her archaeological and geological work in the Hadhramaut (now in Yemen) was important: she excavated a pre-Islamic temple and tomb site at Ḥureidha (1937–1938).

Caton-Thompson received a number of awards and honors, including the Cuthbert Peek Award from the Royal Geographical Society in 1932, the Rivers Medal from the Royal Anthropological Institute in 1934, and the Burton Medal from the Royal Asiatic Society in 1954. In 1944 she became a fellow of the British Academy and in 1954 was awarded an honorary doctorate from Cambridge University.

[See also Abydos; Faiyum; Hadhramaut; Ḥureidha; Malta; Yemen; and the biography of Petrie.]

BIBLIOGRAPHY

Caton-Thompson, Gertrude, and Guy Brunton. The Badarian Civilisation and Predynastic Remains near Badari. London, 1928. Excellent final report dealing primarily with the predynastic villages and tombs at Badari, Qau, and Hemamieh.

Caton-Thompson, Gertrude. The Zimbabwe Culture: Ruins and Reactions. Oxford, 1931. Based on careful excavations and artifact parallels; correctly dates the Zimbabwe culture.

Caton-Thompson, Gertrude, and E. W. Gardner. The Desert Fayum. 2 vols. London, 1934. Major final reports combining geological and archaeological history.

Caton-Thompson, Gertrude, et al. Lake Moeris: Re-Investigations and Some Comments. Cairo, 1937. A small study of the Fayum that argued against a high Lake Moeris in the area.

Caton-Thompson, Gertrude. The Tombs and Moon Temple of Hureidha (Hadhramaut). Oxford, 1944. Important early archaeological excavation of a South Arabian temple and tomb site, together with early geological observations about the area.

Caton-Thompson, Gertrude. The Aterian Industry: Its Place and Significance in the Palaeolithic World. London, 1946. Small study assigning the Aterian to the Upper Paleolithic period.

Caton-Thompson, Gertrude. Kharga Oasis in Prehistory. London, 1952. Major final report describing the site's Paleolithic-Neolithic remains.

Caton-Thompson, Gertrude. The Zimbabwe Culture: Ruins and Reactions. 2d ed. London, 1971. Updated publication of her results, together with radiocarbon data supporting the later date for the Zimbabwe culture.

JAMES A. SAUER

CATS. The principal ancestor of the domestic cat, the wild cat *Felis silvestris*, is a single species with a worldwide distribution that varies in appearance and behavior across the northern and southern extensions of its range. Behavioral studies suggest that the African/Arabian form of wild cat, *F. s. libyca*, is the most amenable to forming commensal relationships with humans and habiting their settlements. This behavioral trait, as well as alloenzyme analyses and philological and archaeological evidence, strongly suggests that the *libyca* form was the direct ancestor of the domestic cat, formally designated *F. s. catus*.

Cat domestication probably began in Egypt, but because the skeleton of *libyca* differs little from the domestic form, it is difficult to document the earliest stages of the process. The first purposeful interments of *F. s. libyca* are found with Egyptian human burials from the early fourth millennium. Although there is no evidence to indicate that these cats were domestic, the burials may signal the beginning of the domestication process. Other wild cats from the region, notably the larger jungle or marsh cat *F. chaus*, have been identified in early burials as well, but in smaller numbers. This led some authorities to suggest that *chaus* may also have contributed to the domestic cat genome, but recent genetic studies show that any significant contribution is unlikely. The ancient Egyptians kept wild animals in captivity without domesticating them, and this was probably the case with the jungle cat.

A fifth-dynasty (c. 2494–2345 BCE) tomb painting from Saqqara depicts a cat with a band that may be a collar around its neck. This may demonstrate human control of the animal but is not proof of domestication. However, by the early Middle Kingdom period (c. 2050–1785 BCE), pictorial and textual evidence point to the cat as a domesticate. Both functional and religious reasons are advanced to account for its domestication. As with most domestic animals, however, a primary stimulus, assuming there was one, eludes archaeological detection.

Animals played a prominent role in Egyptian religion from the predynastic period or even earlier. Most deities were associated with one or more animals that were intrinsic to the performance of their cult. Cats, large and small, were sacred to a number of Egyptian gods. The goddess Sekhmet was usually represented by a lioness, the goddess Pakhet by lions and cats. The most popular cat deity, the fertility goddess Bast was portrayed as a lioness from the protodynastic period (c. 3100–1700 BCE) until the Second Intermediate period (c. 1800–1570 BCE) and thereafter mostly as a female cat. In the New Kingdom (sixteenth–twelfth centuries BCE), the solar deity Re is associated with male cats. Cats, and other animals, were kept and raised within the confines of the temples of their special deities.

When Bubastis, a center for the worship of Bast, assumed leadership of the country is the early first millennium BCE, the cat gained new prominence. Prior to this time, cats appear to have been pets of the elite. As the symbol of a national protectress, however, the cat as a pet became extremely popular across all classes.

By the Hellenistic period (c. 332–200 BCE), cats had become big business. Priests raised them by the thousands in and around temple precincts, to be used as votive offerings by pilgrims. Herodotus (2.65–68) described at length the affection of the Egyptian populace for their pet cats and the sacred burial grounds that received their mummified remains. Archaeologists have discovered enormous numbers of cats in cemeteries at Abydos, Giza, Bubastis, and Saqqara, to name a few examples.

Nowhere in the ancient world were cats as beloved or important to religion as in Egypt. Indeed, their religious role may have hindered their export, as it greatly overshadowed the utilitarian role they played in vermin control. Except for Egypt, the domestic cat is not mentioned in the region's ancient texts, and there is no evidence for it beyond Egypt's borders until the first millennium BCE. Its popularity appears to have spread rather slowly, reaching Crete in the ninth century, mainland Greece during the sixth century, and China only in the second century BCE.

In neighboring Syria-Palestine, there is little early evidence for the domestic cat. An ivory statuette from Lachish, dated to about 1700 BCE, may be of a wild or domestic cat. Osteological evidence for cats of all forms is sparse. Several bones of a small wild cat (probably the sand cat, *F. margarita*) were found in Middle Bronze II levels (c. 1900–1600 BCE) at Tell Jemmeh in Israel's northern Negev desert. Cut marks consistent with skinning reveal that the animals were hunted for their pelts. A small number of bones referred to *F. chaus* has been recovered at the coastal site of Ashkelon in Israel from various periods, some with cut marks. Not until the Persian period (c. 538/39–332 BCE) do several bones of domestic cat appear. In the ensuing Hellenistic period the numbers began to rise, and about one hundred specimens of domestic cat have been identified to date from Hellenistic to Islamic deposits at Ashkelon. Domestic cat bones, and the occasional skeleton, have been reported from historic-period sites throughout the ancient Near East. The numbers are always small, however, perhaps an indication that dogs, whose bones are much more common, were preferred as pets.

BIBLIOGRAPHY

Armitage, P. L., and Juliet Clutton-Brock. "A Radiological and Histological Investigation into the Mummification of Cats from Ancient Egypt." *Journal of Archaeological Science* 8 (1981): 185–196. Important modern evaluation of domestic cat mummies from nineteenth- and early twentieth-century excavations.

Baldwin, James A. "Notes and Speculations on the Domestication of the Cat in Egypt." *Anthropos* 70 (1975): 428–448. A useful survey of the relevant evidence and offers a cogent, if not always demonstrable, timetable of cat domestication.

Bradshaw, John W. S. *The Behaviour of the Domestic Cat.* Wallingford, 1992.

Malek, Jaromir. *The Cat in Ancient Egypt.* London, 1993. A handsome book with a comprehensive study of cats, domestic and wild.

Morrison-Scott, T. C. S. "The Mummified Cats of Ancient Egypt." *Proceedings of the Zoological Society of London* 121 (1952): 861–867. Comprehensive discussion of cat mummies, although some of the conclusions have been superseded by later findings.

Randi, Ettore, and Bernardino Ragni. "Genetic Variability and Biochemical Systematics of Domestic and Wild Cat Populations (*Felis silvestris*: Felidae)." *Journal of Mammology* 72.1 (1991): 79–88. The most up-to-date genetic study of wild and domestic cats.

Robinson, R. "Cat." In *Evolution of Domestic Animals*, edited by Ian L. Mason, pp. 217–225. London, 1984.

PAULA WAPNISH

CATTLE AND OXEN. During the Late Pleistocene and Early Holocene, the aurochs (*Bos primigenius*), the wild

ancestor of domestic cattle, ranged over diverse environments across the Near East. Aurochs remains are common in Upper Paleolithic levels at sites in the southern and eastern Levant. According to artistic evidence, the aurochs was still present in this region during historic times. It is unclear just when the animal finally became extinct.

With few exceptions, the number of identified large bovid bones in Neolithic sites is small. Therefore, criteria based on mortality are rarely available and the evidence for domestic cattle is primarily osteometric. [*See* Animal Husbandry.] Domestic stock are considerably smaller than their aurochs ancestors. However, the application of this criterion is complicated by sexual dimorphism and the resulting danger of identifying a bone from a wild female as one from a domestic bull. Furthermore, dependence on morphological signs means that the earliest phases of domestication will not be recognized. It is not clear how the incorporation of such a large and powerful animal as an aurochs into human settlements was managed. Perhaps the provision of salt to wild herds was a strategy for conditioning the animals to human presence and initiating the process of taming.

However it was accomplished, the first claim for "predomestication," on the basis of mortality data, comes from Pre-pottery Neolithic A (PPNA) Tell Mureybet in Syria. Osteometric evidence has been cited to assert that the cattle from sixth-millennium deposits from Çatal Höyük and Hacılar, Neolithic sites in central Anatolia, were domestic, but this has been challenged. Domestic or wild, the cattle at Çatal Höyük are particularly interesting because the site also yielded extensive evidence for the animal in a ritual context. Not only are aurochs included in the spectacular mural art, but horns were mounted on a bench and associated with human figurines and what may be fertility symbols. On the basis of size diminution, domestic cattle are certainly present in central Anatolia, northern Syria, and the Levant by 5000 BCE, though the process must have started earlier. The sex ratio of morphologically wild PPNB (late seventh millennium BCE) cattle favors females, which may be evidence for the onset of husbandry. There is insufficient evidence to pinpoint the appearance of domestic cattle in Iran and Iraq prior to the fourth millennium. [*See* Mureybet; Çatal Höyük; Hacılar.]

Because cattle are extremely adaptable to diverse habitats, a degree of isolation between regional populations arose. This resulted in stock of varied appearance by the end of the second millennium BCE. The zebu, or humped cattle (*Bos indicus*), is present in Jordan in the Late Bronze Age on the basis of osteological evidence. Figurines found at Tell Jemmeh in Israel's northern Negev, as well as the vertebrae distinctive of this bovid, place it there in this period as well. Because zebu cannot always be reliably distinguished from their taurine cousins, there is a possibility that they were both earlier and more important than is currently recognized. [*See* Jemmeh, Tell.]

Aurochs were hunted for their meat and hides. It is not

known how long it took before domestic cattle produced sufficient quantities of milk or became sufficiently tractable to mark a significant change in how they were used. The earliest reliable evidence for dairying is from fourth-millennium sites in Egypt and Mesopotamia. Similarly from the fourth millennium comes the earliest (artistic) evidence for the plow in southern Mesopotamia. Osteological evidence for cattle as plow or draft animals at this time is noted in collections from the Levant and Anatolia. The advent of plow agriculture utilizing cattle as motive power was a major threshold. Because cattle assumed much of the work previously supplied by humans, surplus labor could be redirected to other pursuits in the community, thereby enhancing the potential for increased socioeconomic complexity.

In historic periods cattle were usually the third most common domesticate at a site, after sheep and goats. However, their larger size and utility for draft made them much more valuable, animal for animal, than either of the "small cattle." Oxen (neutered bulls) began to be employed in the fourth millennium BCE, based on osteometric data. However, textual evidence from Mesopotamia and the Hebrew Bible is equivocal about whether the technique was actually practiced in all periods.

[See also Agriculture; Animal Husbandry; Ethnozoology; Leather; and Paleozoology.]

BIBLIOGRAPHY

Clutton-Brock, Juliet. *Domesticated Animals from Early Times.* Austin, 1981. Excellent discussion of domestic bovids.
Grigson, Caroline. "Size and Sex: Evidence for the Domestication of Cattle in the Near East." In *The Beginnings of Agriculture,* edited by Annie Milles et al., pp. 77–109. British Archaeological Reports, International Series, no. 496. Oxford, 1989. The most critical, up-to-date review of the problems of cattle domestication in the Near East.
Mellaart, James. *Çatal Hüyük: A Neolithic Town in Anatolia.* London, 1967. The most comprehensive popular book on the site, including many excellent illustrations.
Uerpmann, Hans-Peter. *The Ancient Distribution of Ungulate Mammals in the Middle East.* Wiesbaden, 1987. Clear and comprehensive review of ancient faunal distributions.

BRIAN HESSE

CAVE TOMBS. Burial in cave tombs was practiced from the Chalcolithic period onward, primarily in the hill country of Canaan, where caves occurred naturally. Both natural and hewn caves appear to have been conceived of as an ancestral dwelling for families and generations, based on the selection of mortuary provisions: common household ceramic vessels and assorted items used for food production, clothing, hunting and warfare, farming, fishing, amusement, personal grooming, symbolic protection (amulets), and personal identification (seals). In undisturbed examples, individuals lay extended on their back, with objects positioned around their body, near the center of the cave. Bones and objects scattered around the cave's periphery suggest that

bodies were later moved to the sides to clear a space in the center for additional burials.

Extramural cemeteries first appeared in the Chalcolithic period (4300–3300 BCE). Individual remains buried in caves were frequently collected and deposited in a ceramic receptacle shaped like a jar or a house, called an ossuary (Azor, Hadera, Jerusalem, Palmaḥim, near Shechem). [See Ossuary.] Objects and vessels found in the caves accompanying the dead include V-shaped bowls, pedestaled bowls, holemouth jars, and flint tools, many characteristic of the Ghassulian culture. Ossuaries were not used in the three cave tombs at the Judean Desert site of Naḥal Mishmar. the cave 2 man, woman, and four children, aged 2–6 years old, were wrapped in blood-stained linen cloth and covered with mats. The deceased are thought to have been family members who met with violence.

Highland settlers in the Early Bronze I (3300–3050 BCE) buried from five to up to two hundred "kin" together in caves (Ai, Tell el-Farʿah [North]), Gezer, Jericho, Tell Taʿanach), along with pottery vessels, jewelry, weapons, and other personal items. At several sites (Bab edh-Dhraʿ, Gezer, Jericho, Tell Taʿanach) skulls were separated from the other bones, continuing a Neolithic practice interpreted as an element in an ancestor cult. It is commonly assumed that multiple burial in caves was the practice of extended families in sedentary agrarian societies, yet no settlement has been located in the vicinity of the Tell el-Farʿah (North) cemetery.

After a paucity of burials in EB II–III, and divergent practices during EB IV–Middle Bronze I, cave burial resumes in MB II (2000–1550 BCE) with the reuse of earlier burial caves at sites including Tell el-Farʿah (North), Jericho, and Megiddo. By the Late Bronze Age (1550–1200 BCE), the distribution of cave tombs was concentrated in the hill country (Tell el-Farʿah [North]), Gezer, Hebron, Jericho, Jerusalem, Lachish). As in the preceding periods, new or used caves accommodated multiple burials with a modest assemblage of domestic pottery and few imports or metals. Gibeon and Hebron provide further examples of cemeteries with no nearby settlements.

Through all the social and political upheavals of the Iron Age, the pattern of burial practices changed little from that in the Bronze Age. Cave tomb burials continued as before, and in several tombs (Tel Aitun, Jericho, Lachish) skulls were separated from the remaining bones, recalling the earlier practice. A commensurate number of gifts accompanied the large numbers of individuals buried in cave tombs. Locally made bowls, lamps, jars, jugs, and juglets predominate, with a wide assortment of other ceramic forms, household items, and personal possessions. Through the course of the Iron Age, as the number of sites employing the bench tomb increased, a decreasing number of sites buried their dead in cave tombs. There are two likely explanations for the decreasing use of the cave tomb. One possibility is that adherents of LB highland culture, the Amorites and others, lived among the bench-tomb-burying population (later the Judahites) and continued to bury their dead in caves. A second possibility is that highland settlers, regardless of ethnic or religious affiliation, continued to bury their dead in caves because caves required less of an investment of time and labor than did hewing a bench tomb.

[*See also* Burial Sites; Burial Techniques; Catacombs; *and* Grave Goods. *In addition, most of the sites mentioned are the subject of independent entries.*]

BIBLIOGRAPHY

Avi-Yonah, Michael, and Ephraim Stern, eds. *Encyclopedia of Archaeological Excavations in the Holy Land.* 4 vols. Englewood Cliffs, N.J., 1975–1978. Summary of excavations, including results of all earlier expeditions to the sites.

Ben-Tor, Amnon, ed. *The Archaeology of Ancient Israel.* Translated by R. Greenberg. New Haven, 1992. Essays with differing emphases on the Neolithic through the Iron Age II–III periods.

Bloch-Smith, Elizabeth. *Judahite Burial Practices and Beliefs about the Dead.* Journal for the Study of the Old Testament, Supplement 123. Sheffield, 1992. Summary and comprehensive catalog of the Iron Age burials.

Mazar, Amihai. *Archaeology of the Land of the Bible, 10,000–586 B.C.E.* New York, 1990. Comprehensive, detailed, well-illustrated survey of biblical archaeology, limited only by the traditionalist biblical interpretation.

Stern, Ephraim, ed. *The New Encyclopedia of Archaeological Excavations in the Holy Land.* 4 vols. Jerusalem and New York, 1993. Supplements Avi-Yonah and Stern (above), with results of more recent excavations and revised interpretations.

ELIZABETH BLOCH-SMITH

ÇAYÖNÜ, type-site of a Neolithic culture in southeastern Turkey (38°16′ N, 39°43′ E), with a long and uninterrupted sequence from 8250 to 5000 BCE (in uncalibrated years), located along the foothills of the East Taurus range, in the plain of Ergani, 60 km (37 mi.) north of the district center of Diyarbakır. The site is a low, flat mound (300 × 150 m) along a small tributary of the Tigris River. Evidently, the paleotopography of the terrain was significantly different in antiquity. A second stream, forming a brook or a pond, encircled the site on the north, and the settlement developed on two natural hills, separated by a shallow depression. Çayönü was recovered in 1963 during an extensive surface survey of the region. It was excavated for sixteen field seasons from 1964 to 1991, within the framework of the Joint Prehistoric Project, initially founded by the Prehistory Department of the University of Istanbul and the Oriental Institute of the University of Chicago, and later joined by Karlsruhe and Rome Universities. The project was run initially by Halet Çambel and Robert J. Braidwood (1963–1985) and later by Mehmet Özdoğan.

Culturally, earlier parts of the Çayönü sequence represent the era of Incipient Food Producing, more commonly known as the Pre-Pottery Neolithic A (PPNA), which in time gradually develops into Effective Food Producing

(PPNB) and into Developed Village Communities (Early Pottery Neolithic). This represents almost the entire range of the transition from a food-collecting to a food-producing way of life and to the formation of a village economy. With an exposure exceeding 7,000 sq m, Çayönü is the most extensively excavated Neolithic site in the Near East. The well-preserved and stratified architectural remains evince every stage in the development of village architecture, from simple, round huts in wattle and daub, to very complex rectangular structures in mud brick. The site is also unique in revealing some remarkable aspects of this transitional period: strict rules in the plans and measurements of buildings; preplanned functional and status areas; sophisticated building techniques, such as "terrazzo" flooring (see below); and monumental buildings with special functions, all of which are indicative of a rigid but complex social system. Also significant at Çayönü is the earliest known practice of metallurgy, mainly native copper and malachite.

Archaeological Sequences. The Çayönü sequence is divided into three main phases: the Pre-Pottery Neolithic (PPN), or Main Çayönü Phase (I); the Pottery Neolithic (II); and later occupations of minor importance, ranging from Late Chalcolithic to medieval (III). During the later part of the Early Bronze Age, the settlement shifts to the other side of the river, and the site was used as a burial ground.

Phase I. Çayönü phase I is subdivided into six subphases. Each subphase is named after its prevailing building type.

Round building subphase. The earliest structures at Çayönü are radiocarbon dated to 10,230 BP and are round or oval huts, of wattle and daub construction, with semisubterranean floors. In the course of this long-lasting period, covering at least a thousand years, there is a gradual development in construction techniques to structures with stone-lined foundations.

Grill plan subphase. As a further development of round huts with stone foundations, living floors were raised on multiple rows of stones laid parallel to each other, almost resembling a large grill (see figure 1). Twigs and branches were laid over the grill-like foundations and then coated with a thick layer composed of a mixture of lime and clay. This insulation from groundwater increased the amount of living area available. The grill technique was a revolutionary architectural concept in the transition from round to rectangular plans.

The grill plan at Çayönü developed gradually. The standard model had a tripartite layout, a large living area raised on low-lying grill foundations, a closed inner court, and a small binlike storage area. Wattle and daub were still the main materials used to construct the buildings' vaulted upper structures. The grill plan subphase constitutes numerous building layers, each layer manifesting further elaboration of the building plan. However, at any given layer, all buildings are arranged in a checkerboard pattern, were all

ÇAYÖNÜ. Figure 1. *Cell and grill buildings.* Excavated foundations of grill buildings appear at the upper right, cell buildings to the left. (Courtesy M. Özdoğan)

alike in size, plan, and orientation, suggesting a communal construction effort according to a preset plan.

Channeled building subphase. Gradually, the openings between the grill-like foundations became narrower, merging into subfloor drainage channels. Mud, as a prototype of mud brick, was used on walls for the first time. There was also a substantial change in settlement pattern: the houses became more sparsely scattered and the area of the settlement expanded considerably.

Cobble-paved building subphase. Additional innovation in building techniques included high stone walls, small buttresses, and possibly a flat roof. Drainage channels disappeared and insulation from groundwater was ensured by a cobble fill.

Cell building subphase. Cell-like small compartments with living floors raised on stone basements were used for burials and storage (see figure 1). The buildings are considerably larger than in the previous phase, with high standing-stone and mud-brick walls. Houses were arranged around large courtyards in which all domestic and industrial activity took place. There was considerable diversity in plan, size, and in the artifactual yield of these buildings, implying social and functional differentiation.

Large-room building subphase. The last subphase of the PPN settlement is poorly documented. The buildings consisted of one or two large rooms with claylike floors and the settlement itself became smaller.

Phase II. Pottery appears suddenly at Çayönü (c. 8,020 BP), indicating that the concept was borrowed from elsewhere. There are no indications of a break in the sequence,

as most elements in the material assemblage continue. The settlement, then restricted to the eastern part of the old PPN mound, seems to have developed as a conglomerate of houses and narrow passages with numerous annexes and alterations. Three distinct horizons are apparent within this phase. Settlement seems to cease completely during the Halafian period, just before 7,000 BP.

Communal Buildings and Areas. Only the Large-room Building subphase and the Pottery Neolithic occupation lacked communal buildings. The earliest one, a large round structure, was followed by a large rectangular building, named the Flagstone Building because of the large polished slabs used for its flooring. Megalithic stones were set upright into its floor. The next public building is the so-called Skull Building, named for the recovery of seventy human skulls during the first exposure of the building (see figure 2). The building was rebuilt at least six times, with considerable changes in plan—but it held numerous human skeletons or skeletal fragments in each phase. Bones of 295 individuals were collected from the building, some placed carefully and others tossed in. The last of the public buildings is the Terrazzo Building, a large single room with inner buttresses; its floor is of pinkish limestone, elegantly burnished and set into a thick lime mortar.

During the channeled building subphase a large part of the eastern area of the settlement was reserved as an open area for special functions that are not yet understood. Two rows of huge standing stones were set into its meticulously leveled and prepared clayey floor, which was was kept very clean. During the cells subphase, the most important build-

ÇAYÖNÜ. Figure 2. *"Skull building."* (Courtesy M. Özdoğan)

ings in the settlement encircled this open area, which had been empty of buildings. Later, during the large-room building subphase, it was turned into a refuse area.

Subsistence and Social Structure. When settlement began on Çayönü it was a sedentary village hosting a considerable population. Up to the end of the cell subphase, however, subsistence depended mainly on hunting wild animals and gathering wild fruit—though cultivation of some cereals, including wheat and lentils, had been known by the latter part of the round-house subphase. By the end of the cell subphase, herds of domestic sheep and goat were suddenly introduced to the site from elsewhere, resulting not only in a sharp decline in hunting activities, but also in the collapse of the traditional social structure. During the hunting stage the site must have been tightly controlled by a socially stratified society. Status objects, as well as public buildings and the appearance of an organized settlement, disappear almost completely by the time of the large-room building subphase.

Technology, Assemblages, and Trade. The artifactual assemblage includes bone and ground, polished, or chipped stone (mainly basalt, flint, and obsidian) objects. The latter were traded from a distance of at least 150 km (93 mi.). Long obsidian blades with retouched steep sides, also known as the Çayönü blade, are the most significant implements in

this assemblage. The presence of seashells also indicates long-distance trade. Beads, numbering in the thousands, must have been a specialized craft at Çayönü. Native copper and malachite, available in the vicinity of the site, were used in the grill building subphase, but there was an upsurge in metallurgy in the period of the channeled buildings. Metal was shaped by heating and used in making either simple tools or beads and inlays. Pyrotechnology included burning lime, which was used both in producing primitive vessels and constructing the terrazzo floor. The earliest known "lime vessels" are from Çayönü. Among specialized crafts, weaving is significantly documented at Çayönü by the recovery of a cloth impression made of domestic linen, being the earliest known cloth.

Dating. Çayönü is dated by a series of radioactive dates. As noted above, the earliest dates for the round house subphase are around 10,230 BP and 8,020 BP for the pottery phase. It is clear that the "Çayönü culture" is a part of the "Near Eastern" Neolithic tradition, developing along the same lines, and sharing numerous cultural innovations. However, in contrast to the other Near Eastern cultures of the southern semiarid zones, an almost completely different model of subsistence seems to have developed in the environmentally rich areas of the East Taurus range. Recent excavations of sites such as Hallan Çemi, 150 km east of Çayönü, has clearly indicated the autochthonous character, as well as the antiquity of this culture, going as early as the Proto-Neolithic Period. The earliest subphase of Çayönü, being a direct descendant of Hallan Çemi culture, also shares typical elements of Near Eastern PPNA horizon, such as the round buildings, the so called "Nemrik points," and so forth. Of the other excavated Neolithic sites in the region, Nevalı Çori revealed architectural layers parallel with the "channeled building" and "cobble-paved building" subphases of Çayönü, while Cafer Höyük layers parallel the "cell" subphase and those at Gritille the terminal part of the pre-pottery sequence.

[*See also* Çatal Höyük; Hacılar; *and* Nevalı Çori.]

BIBLIOGRAPHY

Braidwood, Linda S., and Robert J. Braidwood, eds. *Prehistoric Village Archaeology in South-Eastern Turkey.* British Archaeological Reports, International Series, no. 138. Oxford, 1982.

Browman Morales, Vivian. *Figurines and Other Clay Objects from Sarab and Çayönü.* Oriental Institute Communications, 25. Chicago, 1990.

Çambel, Halet, and Robert J. Braidwood, eds. *Prehistoric Research in Southeastern Anatolia.* Istanbul, 1980.

Muhly, James D. "Çayönü Tepesi and the Beginnings of Metallurgy in the Ancient World." In *Old World Archaeometallurgy,* edited by Andreas Hauptmann et al., pp. 1–11. Bochum, 1989.

Özdoğan, Mehmet, and Aslı Özdoğan. "Çayönü: A Conspectus of Recent Work." In *Préhistoire du Levant: Processus du changements culturels,* edited by Olivier Aurenche et al., pp. 387–396. Paris, 1990.

Özdoğan, Mehmet, and Aslı Özdoğan. "Pre-Halafian Pottery of Southeastern Anatolia, with Special Reference to the Çayönü Sequence." In *Between the Rivers and Over the Mountains: Festschrift for Alba*

Palmieri, edited by Marcella Frangipane et al., pp. 87–103. Rome, 1993.

MEHMET ÖZDOĞAN

CENTRAL MOAB. The region immediately east of the Dead Sea, known as Moab in ancient times, consists of a narrow strip of cultivable land between the rugged Dead Sea escarpment and the Syrian (or North Arabian) desert. This is rolling plateau for the most part, but it is interrupted by the deep Wadi el-Mujib canyon that separates northern Moab from central Moab, and the less steep but equally formidable Wadi el-Hasa canyon that bounds Moab on the south. Northern Moab is much better known from epigraphic sources, the Hebrew Bible, and archaeological exploration, but presumably central Moab, the region between the Mujib and the Hasa, would have been the heartland of ancient Moabite settlement. Later, central Moab was part of the Nabatean realm, until 106 CE, when Trajan joined Nabatea with Perea and the Decapolis to form the Roman province of Arabia Petraea. Written sources from the Roman period indicate that Rabbathmoba (present-day er-Rabbah) and Charachmoba (present-day Kerak) were important cities at the time. Because central Moab is situated between Mecca and Damascus, it would have been central to the Umayyad caliphate. The Crusaders built a major castle at Kerak to protect the southeastern flank of the Latin kingdom of Jerusalem. The Mamluks expanded the castle and Kerak flourished during the thirteenth and early fourteenth centuries CE, when it served as a favored city of political exiles from the Mamluk court in Cairo. Central Moab experienced increasing urban decline thereafter, especially during the Ottoman period, when it was dominated by fiercely independent bedouin tribes. All towns and villages had been abandoned by the beginning of the nineteenth century CE, except for four straggling settlements (Kerak, 'Iraq, Kathrabba, and Khanzira), and outsiders entered the region at risk. [*See* Kerak; 'Iraq el-Amir.]

This situation continued throughout the nineteenth century; the results were that while other parts of Palestine were being mapped and explored for archaeological remains, central Moab was largely bypassed. Among the travelers who did enter the region and noted in their travel accounts its many abandoned ruins were Ulrich J. Seetzen (1805), Johann Ludwig Burckhardt (1812), Charles L. Irby and James Mangles (1818), Félicien de Saulcy (1851), C. Mauss and Henri Sauvaire (1866), Henry Baker Tristram (1872), Charles M. Doughty (1875), and Grey Hill (1890, 1895). As the century drew to a close, however, even the topography of central Moab remained poorly understood, and none of its ruins had been examined in any detail. Then, between 1894 and 1910, the Ottoman government reasserted its authority in southern Transjordan, rendering central Moab and its archaeological ruins more accessible for investiga-

tion. During that brief period Rudolf-Ernst Brünnow and Alfred von Domaszewski conducted a systematic study of the Roman road system and associated fortifications, while Alois Musil explored the geography of southern Transjordan and prepared a 1:300,000 scale map that included the names and approximate locations of more than one hundred ruins between the Mujib and the Hasa.

Thereafter, except for a brief excursion by William Foxwell Albright in 1924, the archaeological remains of central Moab received no further attention of consequence until 1930, when Reginald Head discovered the Balu' stela [*See* Balu'.] This discovery prompted John Winter Crowfoot and Albright to mount a two-week expedition in 1933, at which time Crowfoot made soundings at Khirbet el-Balu' and Albright conducted soundings at Ader. That same year Nelson Glueck began his important survey of Transjordan. Paul W. Lapp excavated Bab edh-Dhra' in 1965–1967 and Fawzi Zayadine cleared a first-century BCE Nabatean tomb near Dhat Ras in 1968. [*See* Bab edh-Dhra'.] Otherwise, Glueck's survey report, published in the *Annual of the American Schools of Oriental Research* (1934, 1935, 1939), stood as the final word on the archaeology of central Moab until the late 1970s.

Specifically, in 1976 (and returning in 1982), Emilio Olávarri (1983) conducted soundings at Medeinet el-Mu'arrajeh (i.e., Khirbet el-Medeineh north overlooking Wadi Lejjun), which proved to be an Early Iron Age fortress. [*See* Medeineh, Khirbet el-.] That same year S. Thomas Parker (1987) began a study of the Roman *limes Arabicus* in Transjordan; the project has involved, beginning in 1980, excavations at the Late Roman legionary fortress of Lejjun and a survey (led by Frank Koucky) of archaeological features in the immediate vicinity. [*See* Limes Arabicus.] Meanwhile, from 1978 to 1983, J. Maxwell Miller (1991) conducted a general survey of the whole plateau between the Mujib and the Hasa, complemented by less extensive surveys along the wadis leading from the plateau to the Dead Sea. Siegfried Mittmann and Linda K. Jacobs explored Wadi 'Isal in 1979 and 1981, respectively (Mittmann, 1982; Jacobs, 1983). Udo Worschech examined sites in Wadi Ibn Hammad and the northwest quadrant of the plateau in 1983–1985. Worschech also (1986) began new excavations at Khirbet el-Balu' in 1985 that produced primarily Iron Age remains. Robin M. Brown (1989) conducted a sounding in the Palace Reception Hall in the Kerak citadel in 1987 and distinguished Mamluk and Ottoman phases. Jeremy Johns and Alison M. McQuitty (1989) examined several medieval Islamic sites on the plateau in 1986 and have excavated Khirbet Faris [*See* Faris, Khirbet.]

Although attention from archaeologists to central Moab increased, its archaeological features remain poorly known. Much of what is known is derived from surface surveys conducted with benefit of very little stratified pottery from the region itself to provide control. It does seem clear, however, that central Moab was occupied to some degree throughout historical times. Moreover, to the extent that the relative density of sites with surface pottery from a given period corresponds to the density of sedentary population during that period (which may not be the case), some trends are noticeable. Central Moab seems to have had significant sedentary occupation during the Early Bronze Age, for example, with the strongest showing during EB II–III and slightly less during EB IV. Fewer sites present surface pottery for the Middle Bronze Age, a trend that seems to have continued well into the Late Bronze Age. At that time, an upward trend in sedentary population seems to have begun, probably near the end of the Late Bronze Age, that continued until Iron II. The transition from Iron II to the Hellenistic/ Nabatean period is unclear, but the latter period is strongly represented, especially with Nabatean pottery, throughout central Moab. Numerous sites with Roman and Byzantine pottery indicate a continuation of relatively dense sedentary population until early Islamic times. Relatively few sites produced surface pottery clearly attributable to the early Islamic periods, in contrast to the Ayyubid/Mamluk, which is well represented.

Two intriguing basalt stelae have been discovered in central Moab, the Baluʿ stela mentioned above and the so-called Shihan stela, which actually was discovered at Rujm el-ʿAbd/Faquʿ by de Saulcy in 1851. The Baluʿ stela bears an illegible inscription and depicts three figures, apparently a local ruler flanked by a god and a goddess. The script and language are uncertain, but the scene reflects Egyptian influence suggestive of the New Kingdom period—for example, the central figure wears a headdress of the sort usually worn by Shasu in Egyptian scenes, while the god wears the double crown of upper and lower Egypt and the goddess wears a crown similar to that of Osiris. The Shihan stela presents in bas-relief a man in helmet and short skirt, holding a spear, with an animal, possibly a lion, at his left. Stylistic similarities with monumental art of the "Neo-Hittite" cities in northern Syria suggest an Iron Age date. An inscription fragment, reportedly discovered at Kerak, exhibits parts of four lines in Canaanite (Moabite) script similar to that of the famous Mesha inscription discovered at Dibon. In one of the broken lines it is possible to read "K]mšyt king of Moab." [See Dibon; Moabite Stone.] Finally, a large proto-Ionic pilaster capital was found at Medeibi that resembles those found at several Iron Age sites west of the Jordan River (Hazor, Jerusalem, Megiddo, Ramat Raḥel).

[See also Moab.]

BIBLIOGRAPHY

Brünnow, Rudolf-Ernst, and Alfred von Domaszewski. *Die Provincia Arabia auf Grund zweier in den Jahre 1897 und 1898 unternommenen Reisen und der Berichte früherer Reisender.* 3 vols. Strassburg, 1904–1909. Surveys all published materials relevant to the archaeology of Moab, up to and including their own study of the Roman road and fortification system.

Glueck, Nelson. *Explorations in Eastern Palestine.* Vols. 1–3. Annual of the American Schools of Oriental Research, 14, 15, 18/19. New Haven, 1934–1939.

Miller, J. Maxwell, ed. *Archaeological Survey of the Kerak Plateau.* American Schools of Oriental Research, Archaeological Reports, 1. Atlanta, 1991. A comprehensive gazetteer of archaeological sites on the central Moabite plateau, with full bibliography for each site through 1990.

Recent Field Reports

Brown, Robin M. "Excavations in the Fourteenth Century A.D. Mamluk Palace at Kerak." *Annual of the Department of Antiquities of Jordan* 33 (1989): 287–304.

Jacobs, Linda K. "Survey of the South Ridge of Wadi ʿIsal, 1981." *Annual of the Department of Antiquities of Jordan* 27 (1983): 245–274, figs. 1–15.

Johns, Jeremy, and Alison M. McQuitty. "The Fâris Project: Preliminary Report upon the 1986 and 1988 Seasons." *Levant* 21 (1989): 63–95.

Mittmann, Siegfried. "The Ascent of Luhith." In *Studies in the History and Archaeology of Jordan,* vol. 1, edited by Adnan Hadidi, pp. 175–180. Amman, 1982. Reports Mittmann's survey of Wadi ʿIsal.

Olávarri, Emilio. "Sondeo arqueológico en Khirbet Medeineh junto a Smakieh (Jordania)." *Annual of the Department of Antiquities of Jordan* 22 (1977–1978): 136–149.

Olávarri, Emilio. "La campagne de fouilles 1982 à Khirbet Medeinet al-Mu'arradjeh près de Smakieh (Kerak)." *Annual of the Department of Antiquities of Jordan* 27 (1983): 165–178.

Parker, S. Thomas, ed. *The Roman Frontier in Central Jordan: Interim Report on the Limes Arabicus Project, 1980–1985.* 2 vols. British Archaeological Reports, International Series, no. 340. Oxford, 1987.

Parker, S. Thomas. "Preliminary Report on the 1987 Season of the *Limes Arabicus* Project." In *Preliminary Reports of ASOR-Sponsored Excavations, 1983–87,* edited by Walter E. Rast, pp. 89–136. Bulletin of the American Schools of Oriental Research, Supplement no. 26. Baltimore, 1990.

Worschech, Udo F. Ch., et al. "The Fourth Survey Season in the North-West Arḍ el-Kerak, and Soundings at Baluʿ, 1986." *Annual of the Department of Antiquities of Jordan* 30 (1986): 285–310.

Inscriptions and Artistic Representations

Reed, William L., and Fred V. Winnett. "A Fragment of an Early Moabite Inscription from Kerak." *Bulletin of the American Schools of Oriental Research,* no. 172 (1963): 1–9.

Ward, William A., and M. F. Martin. "The Baluʿa Stele: A New Transcription with Palaeographic and Historical Notes." *Annual of the Department of Antiquities of Jordan* 8–9 (1964): 5–29.

Warmenbol, Eugène. "La stèle de Ruğm el-ʿAbd (Louvre AO 5055): Une image de divinité moabite du IXème-VIIIème siècle av. N. È." *Levant* 15 (1983): 63–75.

J. Maxwell Miller

CERAMIC ETHNOARCHAEOLOGY.

Archaeologists who study living peoples and their pottery for the purpose of addressing problems encountered with ancient pottery engage in ceramic ethnoarchaeology. In contrast to the social and political topics ethnographers investigate among extant communities, ethnoarchaeologists examine material culture to document sources of variation in contemporary artifacts. This enables them to make inferences about the diversity detected in excavated artifacts. One goal is to understand better the human behavior responsible for the artifacts. All material culture is suitable for examination. Ceramic ethnoarchaeology among potters practicing traditional technologies (i.e., without the use of electrical or other modern conveniences) and whose finished products (cooking pots, jugs, jars, lamps) are for use by local clientele rather than tourists, is especially relevant given the abundance of pottery archaeologists find in excavations.

In the ancient Near East and Mediterranean basin, the material used most commonly to produce containers of all sizes and shapes was clay. Pottery was inexpensive and highly breakable. Because fired clay becomes rock-hard, sherds of broken pots, which litter ancient sites, are virtually indestructible.

Ancient pottery is important to archaeologists both because of its high rate of survival and the rapidity with which changes in shape and decoration occur. It has been used to establish relative chronologies; to establish the function of buildings; to trace the social and economic implications of the repertoire of forms; and to make inferences about cultic practices. Ceramic ethnoarchaeology enhances these studies because it can explain sources of diversity in form and finish that may have little to do with chronology but, rather, reflect cultural preference: archaeologists want to know whether two jugs with similar but distinct painted patterns reflect different, yet coexisting, sources or two consecutive time periods.

The goal of ethnoarchaeology is not only to observe and record potters and their society, but to do so with the intention of addressing the specific questions ancient ceramics pose. Ethnoarchaeologists initially state the questions under investigation and then select an appropriate community for a long-term field project. During the project, wares of a representative sample of potters are recorded using quantitative means whenever possible. A sample ideally includes people of different generations, gender, and families and those born in the community as well as newcomers. It is essential to learn if and how the manufacturing technique, division of labor, family association, and potter's age and gender impact on the finished product. Interviews with potters and other members of the community are part of the field research. Rather than rely on verbal accounts alone, ethnoarchaeologists systematically observe whatever occurs relating to pottery. On the next level, the ethnoarchaeologist might conduct a similar study at a nearby community, a contemporaneous production location, to compare wares and dynamics of production.

Without long-term field work and a representative sample, the result may be a distorted and incomplete picture.

Representative samples ideally include as many variables as possible—a difficult task because the number of potters is decreasing steadily in many parts of the world. Unless an appropriate community is selected, the results may not be suitable for addressing the issues archaeological materials raise. An industry of wheel-thrown tourist wares is not suitable for comparisons with ancient handmade wares produced and used by household potters and sold or bartered with a neighboring community.

Ethnoarchaeologists examine topics related to clay procurement and processing; manufacturing techniques; surface treatments; firing techniques; breakage rates; sales and distribution; seasonality; organization of the industry; discard and reuse of newly made and used wares; the artifacts, layout, and remains (material correlates) associated with pottery production locations; and the sources of variation in all aspects of the industry. Attention is focused on issues such as vessel longevity, use, and reuse; the relationship between wealth and the number of pots in individual homes; the number of people and pots in a home; the presence and use of nonceramic containers; the potters' social status; and local names and pottery classification systems. Ethnoarchaeologists can test the validity of terms (such as *full-time* or *part-time craft specialists*) archaeologists use in describing ancient potters. The considerable ambiguity in these terms, in light of the data from ethnoarchaeological studies, suggests that the terms are too rigid and divisive.

One outcome of recent research suggests that at any given time in antiquity the ceramics industry was never a monolithic, static, homogeneous enterprise characterized by potters working at a single level of production; it is more accurately represented as different traditions coexisting. On Cyprus today, for example, potters in a secluded rural village continue to make goat-milking pots and jars to store cheese and water; at the same time these old-fashioned vessels have disappeared from the repertoire of rural village potters who live and work close to an urban center, yet the two villages coexist (London, 1989, p. 227). In Jordan, village women continue to build pots by hand from locally available clays, while male potters nearby throw pots made of imported clays and surface treatments (London and Sinclair, 1992). Diversity characterizes the industry rather than uniformity.

Broken pottery was recycled throughout antiquity: sherds were suitable surfaces for writing transactions and notes with ink. [*See* Ostracon.] Ethnoarchaeological research on Cyprus (London, 1989) demonstrates that sherds are also suitable building materials; animal feeders; protection for seedlings; carriers (of charcoal from the kitchen to the kiln); wind protection for candles in cemeteries; and for separating pots from kiln walls during firing.

Potters in traditional societies are able to identify the work of individual potters by considering a vessel's overall proportions, its surface treatment, and its finish. These same criteria can help archaeologists identify the work of individual potters in antiquity in order to address the issues that concern how society and the industry were organized.

[*See also* Ethnoarchaeology.]

BIBLIOGRAPHY

Kramer, Carol. "Ceramic Ethnoarchaeology." *Annual Review of Anthropology* 14 (1989): 77–102. Overview of the subject.

London, Gloria Anne. "Past and Present: The Village Potters of Cyprus." *Biblical Archaeologist* 52 (1989): 219–229.

London, Gloria Anne, et al. *Traditional Pottery in Cyprus.* Mainz am Rhein, 1990. Account of one of the few remaining countries in the region with rural potters practicing a traditional technology to produce wares for local use.

London, Gloria Anne, and Marlene Sinclair. "An Ethnoarchaeological Survey of Potters in Jordan." In *Madaba Plains Project 2: The 1987 Season at Tell el-'Umeiri and Vicinity and Subsequent Studies,* edited by Larry G. Herr et al., pp. 420–428. Berrien Springs, Mich., 1992. Brief report on two groups of Jordanian potters.

Longacre, William A., ed. *Ceramic Ethnoarchaeology.* Tucson, 1991. The most recent collection of articles dealing with ceramic ethnoarchaeology worldwide.

Nicholson, Paul, and Helen Patterson. "Pottery Making in Upper Egypt: An Ethnoarchaeological Study." *World Archaeology* 17 (1985): 222–239. Unlike other places in the Near East, pottery production in Egypt remains a viable livelihood.

GLORIA ANNE LONDON

CERAMICS. [*This entry surveys the history of ceramic artifacts with reference to the technologies used to create them, the uses to which they were put, and their overall role in the cultures and societies in which they figure. It comprises seven articles:*

Typology and Technology
Mesopotamian Ceramics of the Neolithic through Neo-Babylonian Periods
Syro-Palestinian Ceramics of the Neolithic, Bronze, and Iron Ages
Ceramics of the Persian Period
Ceramics of the Hellenistic and Roman Periods
Ceramics of the Byzantine Period
Ceramics of the Islamic Period

The first serves as an overview, providing a discussion of the importance of typology for dating purposes and the development of specific typologies. The remaining articles treat the artifacts of specific periods and regions.]

Typology and Technology

Archaeologists excavating ancient sites find thousands of artifacts that must be described, defined, and interpreted in order to reconstruct the societies responsible for them. Ceramic wares, or pottery, represent one of the most abundant finds throughout the ancient Near East and the eastern Mediterranean. Given the plastic nature of clay, the raw material of pottery, a range of basic shapes can be formed, and when the clay is fired it becomes virtually indestructible. To describe the pots and sherds (broken pieces of pottery) they find, archaeologists have created typologies, or classifications, that group pieces based on stylistic similarities. Today, new technological considerations (how and of what a pot was made) are contributing to the construction of those typologies. The first goal of a typological ordering is to generate types defined by specific attributes and then to discern the meaning or significance of the types. The concept of "type" refers to a group of artifacts that resemble each other and that can be differentiated from other groups. Distinguishing attributes include aspects of form: morphology, or shape, and size; style: surface treatment and decoration; and technology: a pot's materials and method of manufacture. Each typology addresses specific questions and serves a different, specific purpose.

Ceramic Typologies. Initially, ceramic typologies were devised to address chronology. Because ceramic wares are fragile, the rate of breakage is high; thus, there is a constant need to replace what breaks. As forms are replaced over time, the tendency is to change their shape and surface treatment. It is the periodic changes during replacement that make pottery a chronological marker: sequences can be discerned for the local culture or for the history of a region. Comparative chronological studies focus on the superficial modifications in vessel morphology and surface treatment (decoration)—the most obvious changes over time. Because shape and decoration can change relatively quickly, archaeologists can assign a relative date to each pottery style. Once the pottery is dated, archaeologists can date the deposit in which it is found. Based on ethnoarchaeological studies in Cyprus, the life span of portable jugs used for drinking water is no more than six months to two years before the walls become clogged with rock and mineral deposits (G. London, F. Egoumendiou, and V. Karageorghis in *Traditional Pottery in Cyprus,* Mainz, 1989, p. 33). In contrast, immobile water storejars could last for more than a century. As a consequence of the differences in their daily use, the former change more rapidly than the latter. However, finding similar pots at two different sites does not mean that the sites were either contemporaneous or similar. The pottery may have been curated or saved from one generation to the next, or types may have reached one site a decade or more later. Such relative ceramic chronologies are important, but they cannot address the complex issues of where, how, and by whom pottery was made. Answers to those questions have important implications for understanding how ancient societies and economies functioned.

The earliest typologies focused on style—on both form and finish (morphology and decoration)—rather than on manufacturing technology. Aspects related to form are body shape and function (bowl, jug, etc.) and the shape of the rim, base, handles, and other accessory elements, such as a spout or a lid. Surface finish involves decoration and various treatments such as adding paint, slip, or clay appliqué; removing clay by incising and carving; texturing by scoring, stamping, impressing, and rouletting; rubbing, polishing, and burnishing with a tool; and treatments created by the firing process, such as mottling. While most stylistic attributes and changes are apparent to the eye, subtleties exist that are sometimes understood subjectively, with experience. In contrast, the technological aspects of manufacture require sophisticated laboratory techniques (mineralogical and chemical analysis, radiography) and an understanding of how pottery is made. A ceramic technologist investigating why a pot looks the way it does (its form and finish) considers its stylistic *and* technological features. The resulting analysis is therefore more objective than a reliance only on form and finish. For a typology to be useful for making comparisons, each type of pot must be accurately and concisely defined and described, based on objective criteria: the steps that led to its final form and surface finish.

Ceramic Technology. A technological study involves discovering the potter's choice of clay and nonplastic inclusions; manufacturing technique; surface treatment; and drying and firing. In creating a ceramic typology, the raw materials must be characterized—including the type, frequency, and condition of the nonplastic elements, rather than the clay particles (when fired, plastic clay particles shrink, while aplastic, or nonplastic, rock and mineral tempering materials remain virtually unchanged at low temperatures).

Reconstructing an ancient ceramic technology reveals how each stage of pot creation influences subsequent stages. Thus, the factors that combined to produce the final pot—as well as its range of potential variations—emerge. In particular, clay type influences each of the potter's successive decisions. The clay's texture determines manufacturing technique, surface treatment, drying, and firing. For example, certain clays are best suited for constructing pots using the coiling process. These are known as lean clays, and they contain relatively large quantities (more than 30 percent) of aplastic material (tempering material or inclusions) in the form of rocks, minerals, and organic materials. When a potter works with lean clay, the nature of the surface treatment has already been determined: any tool used to incise patterns into the surface will pull up and drag with it some of the aplastic material protruding from the surface, unless a slip layer is first applied. A slip is a thin coating of very watery clay (with or without the addition of a coloring agent) that covers either all or part of a pot's surface. A slip layer allows the potter greater decorating choices with a pot made of heavily tempered clay than would otherwise be feasible. Paint (slip to which a pigment has been added) is applied in a pattern rather than over an entire surface because paint does not adhere well to a surface from which inclusions protrude. Surfaces to be burnished similarly benefit from an

initial application of a slip to coat and cover the inclusions and alleviate "drag" lines. For this reason, intentionally burnished pots are usually slipped. However, primary manufacturing can produce burnishing as well. When pots are made in the process known as turning, the potter first shapes a thick-walled vessel and allows it to dry slightly. When the potter judges the pot ready, it is returned to the turntable and thinned, or "turned down," to the desired thinness. This process will produce a burnish only if the clay has reached a particular stage of drying and if the pot is fired at a certain temperature. If the clay is too wet when it is turned, burnishing is less likely to occur. It is the clay that largely determines the two final stages of the work, drying and firing. Heavily tempered pots require shorter and less carefully controlled drying and firing. Certain aplastic inclusions, especially of the limestone group, do not tolerate a high temperature unless they have been finely ground before being added to the clay.

By assessing technological features, questions can be addressed about where certain pottery was made and who made it (whether it was local, regional, or arrived at a site via international trade), the continuity and breaks in ceramic traditions, and the organization of the ceramics industry. These issues and others are relevant to understanding ancient societies. Typologies based on style and technology not only address issues about relative chronology, but can also explain why and how some shapes changed through time—some quickly and others barely at all. Numerous revisions are necessary during the initial stages of creating a typology, which can be expanded at any time to include new information. It is, however, difficult to use typologies to address issues for which they were not initially designed. For example, by arranging pottery in terms of what is earlier or later based on shape and decoration, it can be difficult to identify other potential causes for differences in appearance. Pottery that looks different can be the work of two workshops operating at the same time, but in different communities. Differences in the shape of rims or bases, or other diagnostic parts might reflect two distinct pottery production locations rather than chronological differences. By classifying pottery with chronology as the prime consideration, one can overlook evidence of the organization of the pottery industry, or the signatures of individual potters who worked at the same time, but in different villages.

Once the functional pottery (bowls, jars, jugs, etc.) belonging to a single period at a site are collected, typologies can be designed to provide relative chronologies. Two questions are traditionally posed: how does the collection differ or coincide with the assemblages from the periods that precede and follow it; and how similar or different is the collection to contemporaneous material from nearby sites? The results are chronological/functional typologies. Such typologies allow archaeologists to establish relative dating schemes, which are critical for sites and deposits that lack other internal dating evidence, such as inscriptional remains (names or references to kings) and organic material.

Development of Ceramic Typologies. The first ceramic typology was designed by William Flinders Petrie in 1890, based on pottery he had excavated from Tell el-Ḥesi in southern Israel. There, stream action had cut a vertical section into the tell, providing a roughly stratified chronological sequence at the site. By recognizing pottery similar to the wares he had excavated in Egypt, Petrie could accommodate the Ḥesi material into the system of sequence dating he had developed for Egyptian funerary ceramics and epigraphic data. Pottery at Tell el-Ḥesi provided a stratified sequence of both plain and decorated wares that enabled Petrie to draw attention to the chronological value of domestic undecorated pottery. Until this development, classical archaeologists had relied exclusively on decorated wares. Nevertheless, undecorated and coarser wares continued to receive far less attention than decorated wares in subsequent pottery studies and typologies. [*See* Ḥesi, Tell el-; *and the biography of Petrie.*]

As more sites were excavated and new pottery forms were discovered, an emphasis was placed on improving and completing Petrie's initial chronological typology. J. Garrow Duncan compiled the *Corpus of Dated Palestinian Pottery* (London, 1930) to provide a system for identifying well-known pottery types and to alleviate the repetitious publication of such pots in future reports. In later excavation reports, pottery was sometimes listed according to Duncan's *Corpus* identifications, but it soon became outdated. Its emphasis was on whole vessels (sherds belonged only if they bore a special surface treatment). However, increasing reliance on stratigraphic methods of excavation and recording the precise location of sherds and pots, as exemplified by the work at Samaria of George Reisner (see Reisner et al., 1924), resulted in an increased appreciation and use of sherds in the Near East and in the New World. Reisner later influenced his students at Harvard to study sherds. [*See the biography of Reisner.*]

Chronological typologies enabled archaeologists to compare and cross-date assemblages from different sites, especially in the early days of archaeological research. A cross-cultural study by Henri Frankfort (London, 1924) dealt with pottery from Mesopotamia to Egypt. However, it emphasized chronological questions, ignoring variation within and among local and regional wares. Local cultural uniformity (ceramic similarity) characterized the basis for research with few exceptions. Ceramic typologies continued to revise the functional/chronological typologies over the years. G. E. Wright's important study *The Pottery of Palestine from the Earliest Times to the End of the Early Bronze Age* (New Haven, 1937) dealt with chronological issues of Early Bronze Age material while noting ceramic analysis's potential to deal with other issues. An unusual typology, based on geometric-shape analysis, by Pinhas Delougaz (1952) for Mesopota-

mian pottery, and analyses of clays by other researchers, unfortunately has a minimal impact on how ancient pottery was studied and published. [*See the biographies of Frankfort and Wright.*]

In 1963 Ruth Amiran and her associates published *Ancient Pottery of the Holy Land,* first in Hebrew and then in an English translation (Jerusalem, 1970). In it, they collected examples of whole pots and some sherds typical of different regions in Israel from the Neolithic period to the Late Iron Age. Little was known then about the pottery of more recent periods, although publications since have helped to construct typologies for them: Ephraim Stern's *Material Culture of the Land of the Bible in the Persian Period, 532–332 B.C.* (Warminster, 1982); and Paul W. Lapp's *Palestinian Ceramic Chronology, 200 B.C.–A.D. 70.* (New Haven, 1961). Amiran's widely used typology was the guide for all subsequent studies, as local heterogeneity became recognized with the ever-increasing number of sites excavated. Studies of specific types of decorated pottery, from Cyprus to Mesopotamia, are too numerous to mention. Most, but not all, concentrate on stylistic features, with little or no reference to the wares' technological aspects.

Technological Studies. An exceptional study for its day is the Iron Age pottery from Tell Beit Mirsim excavated by William Foxwell Albright. James L. Kelso and J. Palin Thorley (1943) studied it, addressing various aspects of its manufacturing techniques. Their technological analysis was separate from the functional/chronological typology Albright devised for the assemblage. William F. Badè developed an approach for studying pottery that drove the methodology and techniques he used in his excavation at Tell en-Nasbeh (*A Manual of Excavation in the Near East,* Berkeley, Calif., 1934). He advanced the idea of pottery's local and regional heterogeneity, rather than follow the established view of cultural homogeneity in ancient Israel. [*See* Beit Mirsim, Tell; Naṣbeh, Tell en-; *and the biographies of Albright and Badè.*]

With the first edition of Anna O. Shepard's *Ceramics for the Archaeologist* (Washington, D.C., 1956) a text to explain ceramic technology became available. It had considerable impact in New World archaeology but less elsewhere. Frederick R. Matson worked in the Near East with both ancient pots and with contemporary potters using traditional techniques. As the editor of Robert Ehrich's *Ceramics and Man* (Chicago, 1965), among many other publications, Matson focused on the technology available to the people responsible for making and using ceramic wares. Despite the number of studies that concentrate on nonchronological issues, most ceramic typologies continue to present catalog formats of pottery, used for chronological purposes, that are classified according to stylistic criteria alone.

An important exception accompanied the publication of the excavations at Tell Deir 'Alla in Jordan. The archaeologist H. J. Franken and the potter Jan Kalsbeek (1969) introduced an approach to ceramic analysis that avoids classification based on stylistic criteria. It considers pottery-making techniques to be critical to the presentation of the material. After examining the clays at Deir 'Alla from the perspectives of a potter and a geologist, Kalsbeek systematically described and defined the ancient pottery and manufacturing techniques in potters' terminology. The result is a typology based on form and function. It begins by explaining how each form was created. Thus, pots that may appear to be different can be understood to represent a single technique. Knowing how vessel bodies, rims, bases, and handles are made enables an understanding of the ancient potters decisions and the variations in excavated pottery: if the rim is the last part of the body to be made, its length may simply be the result of how much clay remained by the time the potter reached the rim. Variations in rim forms, thus, do not always need to represent chronological differences, and this applies to virtually all of a pot's features, including surface treatment and decoration. [See Deir 'Alla, Tell.]

In addition, Franken and Kalsbeek redefined the terms archaeologists commonly use to describe pottery: wheel thrown, well levigated, and self-slip, to name a few. The vast majority of ancient wares published as "wheel made" were made on a turntable capable of movement but lacking momentum—consequently, the pots technically were not wheel thrown. Imprecise use of terminology in archaeological reports generally characterizes descriptions of the firing process, as well. Archaeologists tend to describe wares as poor or well fired depending on clay color: if the entire piece has fired one color, the pot is well fired, but if more than one color is present in the cross section the ware is said to be poorly fired. Nevertheless, the end result was a usable pot, made and fired by a potter who may have been conscientious about not wasting precious fuel. Potters could have learned from experience that burnished wares fired too high lost their sheen. As a result, many burnished vessels are not fired red throughout—of little significance to a pot's use-life—but have a darkened core visible only in the profile of a sherd.

The goal is to create a more objective typology based on style and technology, which are inseparable. The ultimate objectives are to find the potter behind the pot, the people who used it, and the society in which they lived. One achievement of technological analyses, which has been demonstrated repeatedly in recent ethnoarchaeological studies of traditional potters, is that more than one tradition and technology can and will coexist; they are not always replaced by a new technique. This discovery has considerable implications for every chronological typology.

BIBLIOGRAPHY

Delougaz, Pinhas. *Pottery from the Diyala Region.* Chicago, 1952. Unusual ceramic typology arranged according to geometric-shape analysis.

Franken, H. J. "Analysis of Methods of Potmaking in Archaeology." *Harvard Theological Review* 64 (1971): 227–255. General statement on ceramic technology and its application to ancient pottery.

Franken, H. J., with contributions by Jan Kalsbeek. *Excavations at Tell Deir 'Allā,* vol. 1, *A Stratigraphical and Analytical Study of the Early Iron Age Pottery.* Leiden, 1969. Pioneering excavation report using ceramic technology to construct typologies; offers a new way to analyze, describe, and present ancient pottery.

Franken, H. J., and Jan Kalsbeek. *Potters of the Medieval Village in the Jordan Valley: Excavations at Tell Deir 'Alla, a Medieval Tell, Tell Abu Gourdan, Jordan.* New York, 1975. Application of ceramic analysis to medieval pottery with an explanation of many ceramic terms for archaeologists.

Frankfort, Henri. *Studies in the Early Pottery of the Near East,* vol. 1, *Mesopotamia, Syria, and Egypt and Their Earliest Interrelations.* London, 1924. Early cross-cultural analysis.

Kelso, James L., and J. Palin Thorley. "The Potter's Technique at Tell Beit Mirsim, Particularly in Stratum A." In *The Excavations of Tell Beit Mirsim,* vol. 3, *The Iron Age,* edited by William Foxwell Albright, pp. 86–142. Annual of the American Schools of Oriental Research, 21/22. New Haven, 1943. Albright's typological study of Iron Age pottery; separate chapter on technology by Kelso and Thorley.

London, Gloria A. "Decoding Designs: The Late Third Millennium B.C. Pottery from Jebel Qa'aqir." Ph.D. diss., University of Arizona, 1985. History of ceramic analysis in the ancient Near East, with an emphasis on Israel. Available from Ann Arbor: University Microfilms.

Petrie, W. M. Flinders. *Tell el Hesy (Lachish).* London, 1891. Pioneering study in ceramic typology that influenced archaeological research worldwide.

Reisner, George A., et al. *Harvard Excavations at Samaria, 1908–1910.* 2 vols. Cambridge, Mass., 1924. Oversized format, difficult to obtain.

Rice, Prudence M. *Pottery Analysis: A Sourcebook.* Chicago, 1987. Most recent and comprehensive text describing techniques available for ceramic analysis.

GLORIA ANNE LONDON

Mesopotamian Ceramics of the Neolithic through Neo-Babylonian Periods

A group of crude, low-fired clay containers found at the Syrian site of Mureybet and dating to about 8000 BCE is the earliest known in the Near East. [See Mureybet.] During the latter half of the eighth millennium, the inhabitants of Ganj Dareh in west-central Iran also began making vessels of fired clay, but another half-millennium would pass before pottery came into more general use across the Near East.

Proto-Hassuna through Halaf Periods. In lowland northern Mesopotamia, the first ceramics were produced early in the seventh millennium. They represent the earliest phase of the Hassuna sequence, known as the proto-Hassuna. Like the type-site of Hassuna, located near the Tigris River south of Mosul, sites with proto-Hassuna and/or Hassuna levels have, for the most part, been found within the dry-farming region of northern Iraq. The best-known proto-Hassuna site, Umm Dabaghiyeh, was located well beyond the southern edge of the rainfall zone, however. [See Hassuna; Tigris.]

The characteristic proto-Hassuna pottery, consisting of

low-fired vessels formed by hand from heavily vegetable-tempered clay, belongs to what is known as the Coarse group. Jars in this group typically had a low carination separating a convex upper body profile from a lower body that frequently had a concave profile. Small lumps of clay, sometimes shaped to represent animal heads or human faces, were often added to a vessel's surface. Among the most elaborate of these applied designs were whole animals (onagers) and the upper bodies of women. Simple painted designs—dots, circles, lines, and squiggles—appeared in early levels at Umm Dabaghiyeh.

Pottery from the small site of Ginnig in northwestern Iraq may represent the earliest stage in the evolution of Mesopotamian ceramics because typologically and technologically it is the simplest assemblage of Coarse ceramics. Confirmation of this, however, must await further excavation (Campbell and Baird, 1990). Sherds of a thin, well-fired shell- or sand-tempered ware with a burnished red or gray slip have been found alongside typical proto-Hassuna ceramics. This pottery, which represents a separate, more advanced ceramic tradition, may have been imported from Syrian and Anatolian sites to the west.

The pottery of the Standard Hassuna group, the principal assemblage for the Hassuna period proper, represents a technological advance over the Coarse ceramics of the proto-Hassuna. Domed, two-chambered kilns, examples of which have been excavated in Hassuna levels at Yarim Tepe I, permitted higher firing temperatures, which produced less porous, more durable vessels (Merpert and Munchaev, 1973). The use of such relatively sophisticated kilns indicates that pottery making was becoming a specialized craft at a very early date. The Standard Hassuna assemblage has been divided into incised, painted, and painted-and-incised groups. The most common was the incised group, with vessels typically coated with a thick, light-colored slip and incised with simple geometric designs like cross-hatching, chevrons, and sprigs.

Archaic Painted Ware, a separate pottery group, characterized by highly burnished surfaces and glossy red-painted decoration, was first produced in later proto-Hassuna levels and continued into the Hassuna, thus linking the ceramic assemblages for the two periods. The distinctive "husking tray," an oval basin with a corrugated bottom, chronologically overlapped the proto-Hassuna and Hassuna as well.

Painted Samarra Ware appeared in northern Mesopotamia toward the end of the seventh millennium. Although it has been found together with Standard Hassuna pottery on sites in the Hassuna heartland, the Samarra, with its geometric and naturalistic designs in fugitive brown or gray paint, stemmed from a ceramic tradition that originated in the region to the south and southeast, at sites like Samarra, Tell es-Sawwan, and Chogha Mami. [See Samarra, article on Chalcolithic Period.] Characteristic of Samarra designs were horizontal bands filled with a variety of geometric pat-

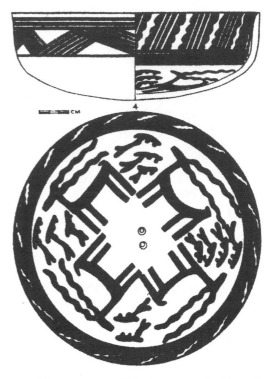

CERAMICS: Mesopotamian. *Painted Samarra bowl from Tell Hassuna.* (After S. Lloyd and F. Safar, "Tell Hassuna: Excavations by the Iraq Government Directorate General of Antiquities in 1943 and 1944, with Prefatory Remarks by Robert J. Braidwood," *Journal of Near Eastern Studies* 4 [1945]: fig. 1)

terns, some of which may have been taken from textiles. [See Textiles, article on Textiles of the Neolithic through Iron Ages.] Among other typical motifs is the centrifugal arrangement of horned animals around the bottom of large, shallow bowls.

The latest Samarra pottery from Chogha Mami showed technological improvements both in terms of its firing and in the quality of its paint. However, it was still similar to the classic Samarra in shape and decoration, although naturalistic designs had largely disappeared. Dubbed Chogha Mami Transitional, this last stage in the evolution of the Samarra had close affinities with pottery from both Chogha Sefid in Iranian Khuzistan and Tell el-'Oueili in southern Iraq. [See 'Oueili, Tell el-.]

The Halaf culture, named for the site in northeastern Syria where its distinctive pottery was first discovered, succeeded the Hassuna in the northern rainfall zone. [See Halaf, Tell.] It has frequently been interpreted as intrusive, but work in northern Mesopotamia and Syria suggests that it may have developed indigenously out of local cultures, including the Hassuna, during the early part of the sixth millennium (Campbell, 1992). The lustrous painted pottery of the Halaf period represents a high point in the history of Mesopotamian pottery in terms of both technical and aesthetic achievement. As the potters achieved mastery over their medium of expression, their geometric designs became increasingly elaborate. Animals occasionally appear on early Halaf vessels, while stylized bucrania are a common element in later designs. The surpassing skill of the Halaf potters is best represented by a group of intricately decorated polychrome plates from the latest Halaf level at Tell Arpachiyah, a site near Mosul. This was clearly a luxury ware produced for trade and export by highly skilled artisans. Neutron activation analysis of potsherds has identified major regional centers of production at Arpachiyah and at Chaghar Bazar in northeastern Syria. These centers dominated the local pottery trade and apparently exported ceramics to locations as far as 200 km (124 mi.) away (Davidson and McKerrell, 1976, 1980).

In the latter part of the sixth millennium, locally made pottery bearing designs characteristic of the Ubaid 3 culture of southern Mesopotamia began to appear alongside the Halaf in northern Mesopotamia. After a transitional period during which ceramics of both types were produced, the Halaf was finally completely supplanted by the Ubaid.

Ubaid. The Ubaid culture, which has been traced back as far as the early sixth millennium, takes its name from the small site near Ur where its distinctive ceramics (belonging to the phases now called Ubaid 3 and 4) were originally recognized. [*See* Ubaid.] Ubaid pottery was characterized generally by geometric decoration in dark paint (black, brown, red) on a light-colored surface. Changes over time in the designs on the pottery have been used to divide the period variously into five or six phases.

Tell el-'Oueili, near the ancient city of Larsa in southern Iraq, has yielded the earliest known phase of the Ubaid sequence, sometimes referred to as the 'Oueili phase of the Ubaid. More frequently, however, it is called Ubaid 0, because the pottery assemblage found at 'Oueili was both earlier than and developmentally related to the Ubaid 1. Until the mid-1980s, Ubaid 1 had been believed to be the earliest pottery in southern Mesopotamia. The lowest levels at 'Oueili have not yet been reached, and the presence of Neolithic-looking sherds out of context in higher levels make it almost certain that still-earlier phases will have to be added

to the southern Mesopotamian ceramic sequence (Huot, 1992).

Ubaid 0 vessels were decorated with simple geometric designs—zigzags, crosses, and parallel vertical lines—in a dull, powdery black paint. Sherds belonging to this phase have thus far been identified at only a few sites in a relatively small area in southern Mesopotamia. However, affinities with ceramics from Chogha Mami east of Baghdad and Chogha Sefid in Khuzistan (see above) indicate that the geographic range of Ubaid 0 ceramics must have been significantly larger.

Ubaid 1 (Eridu phase) pottery was first identified in the lowest levels at the site of Eridu, where archaeologists were able to excavate a stratigraphic sequence containing all the post-Ubaid 0 phases. [*See* Eridu.] Ubaid 1 decoration included elaborate geometric designs (particularly on the interiors of open forms) delicately rendered with a shiny, strongly adhering dark-brown paint. By this phase, Ubaid material culture had definitely spread across southern Mesopotamia and into the western foothills of the southern Zagros Mountains.

Ubaid 2 (Hajji Mohammed phase) ceramics were discovered at Hajji Mohammed, a small site near ancient Uruk. The site had been completely buried by several meters of alluvial deposits but had been cut through by an arm of the Euphrates River, so that it was visible in the riverbank only when the water was low. [*See* Euphrates.] Because of heavy alluviation, only a fraction of the earliest sites in southern Mesopotamia have been located. In Ubaid 2 there was a marked change in pottery decoration. In contrast to the delicate designs of Ubaid 1, surfaces were typically almost completely covered by purplish-black paint, creating a reserve pattern of numerous small, pale areas. Ubaid 2 vessels manufactured in southern Mesopotamia have been found along the eastern coast of the Arabian Peninsula, perhaps indicating the activities of Ubaid traders or fishermen.

In the latter phases of the period (Ubaid 3–4, Terminal Ubaid) the Ubaid cultural tradition extended across both southern and northern Mesopotamia and into northern Syria. Though they display some regional differences, northern and southern ceramics were closely related during

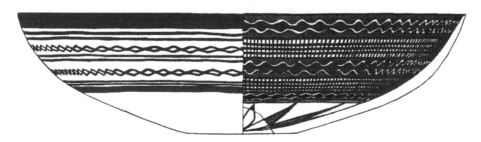

CERAMICS: Mesopotamian. *Polychrome Halaf plate from Arpachiyah.* (After M. E. L. Mallowan and J. Cruikshank Rose, "Excavations at Tall Arpachiyah, 1933," *Iraq* 2 [1935]: pl. 13)

CERAMICS: Mesopotamian. *Late Ubaid bowl from Eridu.* (After F. Safar, M. A. Mustafa, and S. Lloyd, *Eridu*, Baghdad, 1981, fig. 84)

the later phases of the Ubaid. For example, a vessel of unusual shape, the so-called tortoise jar, was a part of both the southern and northern assemblages. The designs on the later Ubaid pottery—lines, scallops, chevrons, and triangles—became simpler and more horizontally oriented. The use of more intricate decoration was abandoned in the face of an evolving technology for the mass production of pottery. Instead of being painstakingly applied stroke by stroke, later Ubaid designs were frequently created simply by holding the brush to the surface of a vessel that was turned slowly in front of the potter. Toward the end of the Ubaid period in the south, the quality of the painted designs deteriorated markedly as vessel painting in general became increasingly rare. Ubaid pottery from Mesopotamia continued to be used at sites along the Arabian coast, though no other elements of Ubaid material culture have been found there. Affinities in ceramic decoration indicate that there were links with Khuzistan as well (Oates, 1983, 1987).

Uruk–Early Dynastic I. The similarity of material culture that characterized southern and northern Mesopotamia during the latter part of the Ubaid period did not endure as southern Mesopotamia began to outpace the north in terms of both political and technological development. The introduction of the fast wheel during the latter half of the fifth millennium vastly increased the speed and scale of pottery production in the south in order to meet the growing demands of a newly urbanized population. The widespread adoption of the fast wheel, together with the not-unrelated demise of painted decoration, heralded the advent of the Uruk period. The period is named for the ancient Sumerian city where the trend toward urbanized life manifested itself most spectacularly. [*See* Uruk-Warka.] It is the only site where the entire Early, Middle, and Late Uruk sequence has been excavated stratigraphically. Paradoxically, the most frequently encountered and most readily recognizable component of the Uruk ceramic repertory was not thrown on a potter's wheel; it was shaped by pressing coarsely mixed, chaff-tempered clay into a mold. This was the beveled-rim bowl, tens of thousands of which have been found across the Near East from southern Iran to southeastern Anatolia. Its discovery attests to the economic penetration of neighboring regions by the new cities of southern Mesopotamia.

The reappearance of monochrome and polychrome ceramic decoration toward the end of the fourth millennium marked the transition to the Jemdet Nasr period, itself a short-lived transitional period between the Late Uruk and Early Dynastic periods (Wilson, 1986). These and other Jemdet Nasr characteristics disappeared early in the third millennium with the emergence of new ceramic features that are diagnostic for the Early Dynastic I: fenestrated stands, solid-footed goblets, and, in the Diyala River valley and areas to the east, Scarlet Ware, with its geometric and naturalistic designs (plants, fish, birds, quadrupeds, humans) in red and black paint (Delougaz, 1952). [*See* Jemdet Nasr; Diyala.]

Post-Ubaid Developments. In the north, the period that followed the end of the Ubaid is sometimes referred to as the Gawra period. It is named for the site with the longest excavated sequence of Ubaid and post-Ubaid levels, Tepe Gawra. [*See* Tepe Gawra.] However, the Gawra assemblage is not typical for the north as a whole; indeed, each site excavated thus far appears to have unique ceramic characteristics (Roaf and Killick, 1987). Adding to an already complicated situation, there is ample ceramic evidence from sites along rivers and other trade routes attesting to the presence of people from southern Mesopotamia in the north toward the end of the Gawra period (the Late Uruk in southern terms). The presence of Late Uruk pottery influenced ceramic development in the north, but the post-Ubaid northern tradition remained distinct from that of the south and followed its own evolutionary trajectory. The fast wheel began to be used in the north much later than it had been in the south. Wheelmade pots first appeared at Tepe Gawra and elsewhere during the fourth millennium, contemporary with the Late Uruk period in the south, when connections between south and north were at their closest.

CERAMICS: Mesopotamian. *Scarlet-ware jar (Early Dynastic I) from Tell Agrab in the Diyala.* (From P. Delougaz, *Pottery from the Diyala Region,* Chicago, 1952, pl. 11; courtesy Oriental Institute, University of Chicago)

The next northern cultural assemblage, Ninevite 5, was named for stratum 5 of the Prehistoric Pit at Nineveh, in which several styles of decorated pottery were identified—although their chronological relationships could not be established. [*See* Nineveh.] More recent work has shown that the painted style was the earliest, apparently having developed from a painted northern variant of Late Uruk pottery at about the beginning of the third millennium (Roaf and Killick, 1987). Painted Ninevite 5 vessels were decorated with all-over geometric designs, as well as birds and horned animals, in red or brown paint. Ceramics with incised and excised decoration, divided into early and late subgroups, appeared only later in the sequence. They continued to be produced until the middle of the third millennium, after the painted pottery had gone out of use.

Historical Periods. Several factors combine to make it more difficult to present a period-by-period ceramic survey for the historical periods than it is for the prehistoric. First, the later ceramic sequences—post-Early Dynastic I in the south and post-Ninevite 5 in the north—are inadequately documented and poorly understood, especially in the case of northern Mesopotamia. One of the most crucial tasks confronting the field of Mesopotamian archaeology is to remedy this situation. Although progress is being made, the

present state of affairs will persist until additional multiperiod stratigraphic sequences are excavated and published.

Second, the historical periods, in contrast to the prehistoric periods surveyed here, are not defined by their ceramic assemblages but by political events. Ceramics were, of course, sometimes indirectly affected by such events—as, for example, when the unification of a region resulted in an increasing homogenization of its pottery. However, even when certain ceramic features happened to be characteristic for a particular historical period, the temporal range of such features was only coincidentally coterminous with the events that defined that period.

Finally, the pottery of the historical periods, with several notable exceptions, consisted of undecorated, mass-produced vessels in plain wares. Their shapes evolved only gradually, creating, at least in the south, what appears to be a continuous sequence that extended well beyond the final political eclipse of Babylonia in the sixth century BCE. Aesthetically, the nadir in southern Mesopotamian pottery production was reached in the Kassite period, during the fourteenth and thirteenth centuries BCE. [*See* Kassites.] At this time the ceramic corpus was reduced to a regionwide homogenized assemblage of only six principal forms, none of them decorated and all of them indifferently, and sometimes even crudely, manufactured (Ayoub, 1982; Armstrong, 1993).

Although a thorough presentation of the ceramic sequence for the historical periods is beyond the scope of this discussion, developments in the ongoing evolution of ceramic technology can be highlighted. From finds at Nuzi, a Hurrian city in northern Mesopotamia, it is clear that, by the fourteenth century BCE, at the same time the potter's craft in southern Mesopotamia was reaching its low point, northern potters had mastered the ability to throw vessels with walls of near-eggshell thinness. [*See* Nuzi; Hurrians.] Having such thin walls, these vessels could not be removed from the wheel without being dimpled, so the potter would add more indentations to create a pattern. In the early first millennium BCE, elegant dimpled cups continued to be produced for use by the wealthy classes of the Late Assyrian Empire; examples of these cups have been found at sites stretching from the border of Egypt to southern Mesopotamia (Oates, 1959). [*See* Assyrians.]

Glazed ceramic objects began to appear at Nuzi in the fourteenth century BCE, concurrently with the emergence of a substantial glass industry in northern Mesopotamia. [*See* Glass.] Glaze technology at that time seems to have been at an early experimental stage, not fully under the potter's control. Moreover, the pale blue-green glaze developed was used at Nuzi only on items associated with the religious cult, including numerous ceramic wall decorations (nails, plaques), several small statues, other sculptural items, and an offering table, but surprisingly few vessels (Vandiver, 1982.

CERAMICS: Mesopotamian. *Glazed bottles from Nippur (c.* 600 BCE). (Courtesy J. Armstrong)

However, it was soon recognized that glazed pottery vessels, because their walls were completely sealed against transpiration, were a relatively inexpensive alternative to stone or glass vessels for storing valuable liquids like perfumes and oils. By the early first millennium BCE, both Assyrian and Babylonian potters were producing large numbers of glazed vessels, especially small bottles and jars. [*See* Babylonians.] Decoration in both the north and the south consisted mainly of geometric designs in white, yellow, blue, green, and brown. On larger Assyrian vessels, stylized flowers and even animals sometimes appeared. After the end of the Neo-Babylonian period in the sixth century BCE, the polychrome geometric designs in Babylonia were replaced by solid-color glazes of blue-green, green, and gray during the Achaemenid (Persian) period.

[*See also* Mesopotamia, *articles on* Prehistoric Mesopotamia *and* Ancient Mesopotamia.]

BIBLIOGRAPHY

Armstrong, James L. "Pottery." In *Nippur III: Kassite Buildings in Area WC–1,* edited by Richard L. Zettler, pp. 67–80. Oriental Institute Publications, 111. Chicago, 1993. Offers a ceramic chronology for southern Mesopotamia in the late second millennium BCE.

Ayoub, Sa'ad. *Die Keramik in Mesopotamien und in den Nachbargebieten: Von der Ur III–Zeit bis zum Ende der kassitischen Periode.* Mittenwald, 1982. Pottery typology for the late third–late second millennium BCE; problematic because the excavations on which it is based frequently lacked sufficient stratigraphic control and because the excavators' attributions of ceramic types to specific periods are adopted uncritically.

Campbell, Stuart, and Douglas Baird. "Excavations at Ginnig: The Aceramic to Early Ceramic Neolithic Sequence in North Iraq." *Paléorient* 16.2 (1990): 65–78.

Campbell, Stuart. "The Halaf Period in Iraq: Old Sites and New." *Biblical Archaeologist* 55 (1992): 182–187.

Davidson, T. E., and H. McKerrell. "Pottery Analysis and Halaf Period Trade in the Khabur Headwaters Region." *Iraq* 38 (1976): 45–56.

Davidson, T. E., and H. McKerrell. "The Neutron Activation Analysis of Halaf and 'Ubaid Pottery from Tell Arpachiyah and Tepe Gawra." *Iraq* 42 (1980): 155–167.

Delougaz, Pinhas. *Pottery from the Diyala Region.* Oriental Institute Publications, 63. Chicago, 1952. Provides the framework for the third millennium BCE ceramic chronology of southern Mesopotamia, updated and corrected in detail by more recent studies.

Huot, Jean-Louis. "The First Farmers at 'Oueili." *Biblical Archaeologist* 55 (1992): 188–195. Popular account of the recent discoveries at 'Oeuili, which has yielded the earliest ceramics in southern Mesopotamia.

Merpert, N., and R. Munchaev. "Early Agricultural Settlements in the Sinjar Plain, Northern Iraq." *Iraq* 35 (1973): 93–113.

Oates, Joan. "Late Assyrian Pottery from Fort Shalmaneser." *Iraq* 21 (1959): 130–146.

Oates, Joan. "Ubaid Mesopotamia Reconsidered." In *The Hilly Flanks and Beyond: Essays on the Prehistory of Southwestern Asia,* edited by T. Cuyler Young, Jr., et al., pp. 251–281. Studies in Ancient Oriental Civilization, no. 36. Chicago, 1983.

Oates, Joan. "Ubaid Chronology." In *Chronologies in the Near East,* edited by Olivier Aurenche et al., pp. 473–482. British Archaeological Reports, International Series, no. 379. Oxford, 1987. This and the article above represent recent analyses of the Ubaid by one of the foremost scholars of the prehistoric periods in Mesopotamia.

Porada, Edith, et al. "The Chronology of Mesopotamia, ca. 7000–1600 B.C." In *Chronologies in Old World Archaeology,* vol. 1, edited by Robert W. Ehrich, pp. 77–121. 3d ed. Chicago, 1992. Essential reference for Mesopotamian archaeology, providing thorough discussions of the ceramic evidence and an extensive bibliography.

Roaf, Michael, and R. G. Killick. "A Mysterious Affair of Styles: The Ninevite 5 Pottery of Northern Mesopotamia." *Iraq* 49 (1987): 199–230. Convincing new analysis of the relative chronology of Ninevite 5 pottery.

Vandiver, Pamela B. "Mid-Second Millennium B.C. Soda-Lime-Silicate Technology at Nuzi (Iraq)." In *Early Pyrotechnology: The Evolution of the First Fire-Using Industries*, edited by Theodore A. Wertime and Steven F. Wertime, pp. 73–92. Washington, D.C., 1982. Presentation of the evidence for glass technology at Nuzi, including the early glazed ceramics.

Wilson, Karen L. "Nippur: The Definition of a Mesopotamian Gamdat Nasr Assemblage." In *Gamdat Nasr: Period or Regional Style?*, edited by Uwe Finkbeiner and Wolfgang Röllig, pp. 57–89. Beihefte zum Tübinger Atlas des Vorderen Orients, Reihe B, vol. 62. Wiesbaden, 1986.

JAMES A. ARMSTRONG

Syro-Palestinian Ceramics of the Neolithic, Bronze, and Iron Ages

This article will treat the pottery of ancient Syria-Palestine with specific reference to the history of its analysis; technology, form, decoration, and typology; and the distinguishing characteristics of archaeological phases from the Neolithic to the Iron Age.

Uses of Pottery in Archaeology. Archaeologists in many fields, not just Syro-Palestinian archaeologists, seem almost obsessed with pottery, for good reasons. Pottery, once it is invented, is relatively abundant on all archaeological sites; when fired it is virtually indestructible; even broken sherds are diagnostic enough for analysis; and its plastic qualities and almost limitless possibilities for form and decoration are particularly expressive of human ideas, behavior, and even socioeconomic organization. As the well-known archaeologist Robert Ehrich has put it: "Pottery is our most sensitive medium for perceiving shared aesthetic traditions—in the sense that they define ethnic groups—for recognizing culture contact and culture change, and for following migration and trade patterns" (1965, pp. vii, viii).

Brief History of Ceramic Analysis. Although scattered over the surface of innumerable mounds in what was ancient Palestine, pottery was not appreciated at first by early explorers. Even Edward Robinson, the father of Palestinology, who visited and correctly identified dozens of long-lost biblical sites in 1838, failed to recognize pottery as a clue to the antiquity of places. The great British Survey of Western Palestine (1871–1878) paid no attention to pottery (and did not, in fact, recognize tells, or mounds, for what they were). Not until the brief field trip to Palestine made by the legendary Sir William Flinders Petrie in 1890 did pottery analysis begin to play a role in archaeology.

Petrie had already applied his own intuitive typological instincts to a large corpus of pottery from predynastic tombs in Egypt. He had worked out the fundamental principles of what is now known as seriation (his sequence dating), to yield a reasonably accurate relative ceramic chronology. Noting the abundance of local, undecorated pottery on the multilayered mounds of Palestine, he argued that the systematic and detailed classification of the common pottery could yield a suitable chronology. He argued, furthermore, that such a ceramic typology would be a useful guide in excavating mounds stratigraphically (creating the twin principles of all subsequent archaeological method: typology and stratigraphy). As Petrie put it with characteristic verve: "Pottery is the essential alphabet of archaeology." To appreciate Petrie's achievement, it must be recalled that before he laid the foundations for ceramic typology, almost nothing from archaeological sites in Palestine could be dated, even within centuries. Nevertheless, Petrie, who did not return to Palestine to excavate until the 1920s, did not follow through on his own original insights. [*See the biography of Petrie.*]

In their excavations in the Judean Shephelah (1898–1900), Frederick J. Bliss and R. A. S. Macalister developed the first ceramically based scheme of absolute chronology, departing from Petrie's suggested dates, but their idiosyncratic dates were several centuries off. Macalister's own work at Gezer (1902–1909), based on very faulty stratigraphy, represented something of a retrogression. [*See the biographies of Bliss and Macalister.*]

Little progress in ceramic analysis was made until the work of William Foxwell Albright, who in his excavations at Tell Beit Mirsim (1926–1932) had worked out a ceramic sequence, with suggested terminology and a range of dates. With minor modifications, it still serves as the basic chronological framework for Palestine in the Bronze and Iron Ages. This brilliant achievement alone would qualify Albright to be regarded as the father of modern Palestinian archaeology. [*See the biography of Albright.*]

Albright also encouraged others in ceramic analysis. During Albright's tenure as director of the American School of Oriental Research in Jerusalem in the 1920s and 1930s, Clarence S. Fisher followed up Petrie's typical nineteenth-century notion of developing a complete catalog, or corpus, of pottery. This had been attempted in Petrie's own two corpora of Egyptian pottery and in J. Garrow Duncan's corpus, (1930), based on Petrie's later excavations at Tell Jemmeh. Although Fisher's work, "A Corpus of Palestinian Pottery," was never finished (the manuscript exists at the Smithsonian Institution, however), it had some valuable features, such as classification according to function, and it gave impetus to the ideal of a corpus. [*See the biography of Fisher.*]

Albright's own protegé, G. E. Wright, worked out the Neolithic, Chalcolithic, and Early Bronze Age pottery, as it was then known, in his doctoral dissertation (1937). Later, several of Wright's students at Harvard and elsewhere sought to complete this enterprise with dissertations on the Early Bronze IV, Middle Bronze, Iron Age, and Hellenistic periods (based largely on Wright's excavations at Shechem). Only Paul W. Lapp (1961) and Dan P. Cole (1984) ever published, however. [*See the biographies of Wright and Lapp.*]

Meanwhile, Israeli archaeologists, particularly after the establishment of the State of Israel in 1948 and the flowering of the Israeli national school, were mastering the pottery of ancient Palestine, also in the Albrightian tradition. This research culminated in the only published effort at a complete corpus, Ruth Amiran's handbook *Ancient Pottery of the Holy Land* (1970), but it stops short of the Persian period. Amiran's work remains, however, the indispensable handbook and basis for all future studies. Beyond this general compendium, there are now detailed studies of individual periods and problems, as well as many exhaustive comparative studies that are published in the course of preliminary and final field reports. There also are newer methods supplementing traditional typological approaches, to which we now turn.

Ceramic Typology and Its Application. Typological principles in general can be applied to pottery, metals, house forms, tombs, and even ideas. "Type" refers to a cluster of essential attributes that occur frequently enough that they serve to characterize an object, enable it to be recognized in other examples, and distinguish it from objects of another class. The attempt to isolate those attributes that capture the "essence" of a thing or category of things often involves the postulation of an ideal "prototype," either real or imagined, from which all the actual variations can have derived—a kind of theme, on which there are many possible variations. Such a procedure, however, is much debated among archaeologists, who tend to divide themselves on the question of "discovered," or empirical, types that actually exist; and "designed" types, invented for the convenience of the cataloger, that do not necessarily correspond to actual reality. Archaeologists who hold to the latter view are often skeptical about the value of typological analyses of any sort. They are usually reacting, however, to the excesses of typology, which is always somewhat subjective and can indeed go to absurd extremes. Nevertheless, typology, reasonably utilized and with presuppositions that are clearly spelled out and tested against adequate stratified data, can be a useful tool.

Typological analysis of pottery in Syro-Palestinian archaeology has from the beginning been largely preoccupied with questions of chronology. This is undoubtedly because of the dominance of biblical archaeology, with its overriding interest in "political history," and the concomitant problem of fixing dates for great public events that could be correlated with biblical history. There are, however, other, more sophisticated aspects of typology that are typical of general archaeology and are increasingly appreciated in the discipline. Following David H. Thomas's *Predicting the Past* (1974), several uses of typology can be distinguished, depending on the questions being asked.

1. *Morphological typology.* What is indeed most fundamental in Palestinian pottery is form. Morphological typology is therefore largely descriptive; it is an attempt to define what a thing is, in terms of such basic attributes as shape: an ovoid storejar, flat-based cooking pot, and piriform juglet, for example.

2. *Technological typology.* The investigation of how a vessel is made and finished reveals its technological typology. It is an attempt to determine ways in which a vessel can be distinguished from other vessels: is the vessel coil made, wheel thrown, or hand burnished? It includes the study of clay types and sources, tempering agents *(dégraissant),* forming methods, kiln usage, and finishing or decorative techniques. Ceramic technology is a relatively new specialization, aided substantially by sedimentological and petrological studies; kiln refiring experiments; use-wear analysis under a high-powered electron microscope; and especially by neutron activation analysis to "fingerprint" clays and pinpoint their sources.

3. *Temporal typology.* More familiar in Syro-Palestinian archaeology, temporal typology is an analysis of the evolving shape of ceramic vessels over time, charting the changes along a time line and assuming that the observed evolution of form (and often of decoration) corresponds, more or less, to historical-cultural developments and can help to date these. In practice, the relative chronology that is first established is concerned only with determining which are the earlier and which are the later developments. With multiple tomb groups or other mixed deposits (such as Petrie started with), intuition and/or theoretical principles may be the only recourse. However, stratified materials—preferably from large and representative samples on short-lived living surfaces—yield the only reliable sequences. Then, at some stage of research, an absolute chronology must be developed by fixing as many pegs as possible on which to hang the entire framework. This can be done only by correlating archaeological assemblages (or groups of stratigraphically related and contemporaneous materials) to events known in history through datable texts. In the case of ancient Palestine, the biblical texts are of some value chronologically. These depend in turn on Mesopotamian and Egyptian king lists and the like, which are often dated precisely through ancient astronomical observations. Thus, gradually there is built up an elaborate network of synchronisms that date pottery groups; and the basic types of the repertoire known in these fixed contexts can then yield relatively accurate historical (i.e., calendrical) dates when the same ceramic forms are encountered in different and otherwise undatable contexts. If imported pottery or other artifacts are found that are datable in their country of origin, these can be incorporated into the synchronism. Best of all are written remains found in situ, which can be independently or epigraphically dated, but these are exceedingly rare for ancient Palestine. Radiocarbon-14 dates promise scientific precision, but their range is too broad to improve much on historically determined dates. For most periods, the common pottery of ancient Palestine can now be dated to the century, and often to one half or the other.

4. *Functional typology.* The attempt to determine how an artifact is used defines functional typology. In the case of pottery vessels, the objective is to catalog separate groups of

vessels on the basis of supposed function. Distinguishing some types is largely a matter of observation and common sense—separating cooking pots, storejars, and dipper juglets, for example. The use of some vessels, may remain enigmatic, however, unless they are subjected to laboratory analysis that can identify food or other remains in skims or they are duplicated and actually used experimentally. Of course, many vessels may have had multiple uses. Finally, it should be cautioned that some functional terms are either whimsical (Early Bronze IV "teapots") or based largely on guesswork. Note that the Cypriot Late Bronze Age bilbil carries an ad hoc onomatopoeic name that duplicates the sound of pouring from the restricted neck of the juglet (although it may in fact have been for opium use). Vessels thought to have been designed for cultic usage are sometimes so designated; but apart from obvious vessels like kernoi ("trick vessels" with deceptive pouring spouts) or censers, cult vessels may be difficult to identify positively. Functional typology is surprisingly undeveloped in Syro-Palestinian archaeology. There is, however, the pioneering effort of James L. Kelso (1948), a biblical scholar, who, under Albright's influence, worked with a professional potter in an attempt to identify excavated Iron Age vessels with terminology in the Hebrew Bible.

5. *Cognitive typology.* Developing a cognitive typology (getting at the ancient artisan's "mental template") is the most difficult of the typological challenges. It is usually achieved by extrapolating from all the known individual examples of a presumed type, to arrive at a theoretical prototype on the basis of which all the variations can be explained. This effort, moving beyond description toward explanation, reaches the outer limits of the archaeological inquiry. It asks: Why is a particular vessel made the way it is? What was the intent of the maker? What cultural and aesthetic values does the vessel embody? Ultimately, answers are needed to such questions as: Why was the pottery of Iron Age Palestine "utilitarian," while that of Cyprus was "exotic"? Do the presence of many vestigial features, as in the pottery of the Early Bronze IV period, suggest that the period in general was one of decline—that is, does ceramic degeneration signal cultural degeneration? As has been seen, some more functionalist investigators are skeptical at this point—perhaps mindful of Lewis R. Binford's oft-stated observation that "archaeologists are poorly equipped to be paleopsychologists." Clearly, however, artifacts do express human behavior and the thought behind it; and there were cultural norms in ancient Palestine, as in all societies, that governed both. Formidable as the task may seem, the ultimate goal of ceramic typology is precisely to discover what cultural values did lie behind ceramic production, not just to fix the dates of pottery forms.

This leads to a concluding observation on ceramic typology. Attempting to "read" pottery may be compared to mastering the grammar of a language. Children and native speakers may use the language properly without any formal knowledge of the principles of grammar. The latter are worked out inductively by linguists, for their own purposes, in order to analyze the language and compare it with others, as well as to enable non-native speakers to learn it. Thus, even though the ancient potters would have been puzzled by modern attempts to impose order on what appears to be chaos, the effort is legitimate, indeed essential, for an understanding of ceramics. At its best, typology may actually enable the grasping of something of the reality of an extinct social system, its technology, its aesthetic values, and its contacts with other cultures.

Some practical advances in fieldwork, analysis, and publication have been made in recent years, many of them largely mechanical: thin-section microscopic observation of tempers, or ingredients, in the clay, and the neutron activation analysis of clays. Improvements in processing pottery include simple sectioning and profile drawing techniques that speed up preparation for publication, even in the field; more sophisticated descriptive methods, such as the use of the *Munsell Soil Color Charts* to describe clay and paint colors, and the Moh's Hardness Scale to determine how brittle the ware is; kiln refiring to establish the original temperature at which the vessel was fired; microscopic examination to determine both how a vessel was made and how it may have been used or reused (use-wear analysis); and the use of scanning computers and sophisticated multivariate statistical analyses to produce complete comparative corpora of certain classes of vessels (such as all the Mycenaean wares found in Palestine and their prototypes). Some of these recent attempts to make ceramic study more precise and objective, more "scientific," actually go back many years, to the simple "punch-card" hand sorting of the 1960s, which anticipated computerization. Notable attempts were made to reduce analysis of form, always somewhat subjective, to mathematical principles as early as 1952 by Pinhas Delougaz in Iran (*Pottery from the Diyala Region,* Chicago, 1952). Anna O. Shepard (1956) has attempted to work out a comprehensive catalog of virtually all possible ceramic shapes, based on easily recognizable geometric forms.

Pottery from the Neolithic to the Iron Age. The major ceramic developments for each period in the long archaeological history of Palestine are highlighted here.

Neolithic period (c. 6000–4000 BCE). Pottery appears almost simultaneously throughout the Levant in about 6000 BCE, at the beginning of what was called by Kathleen M. Kenyon the Pottery Neolithic A (PNA) and by others Neolithic 3 or Developed Neolithic. This is some two to three millennia after the early Neolithic domestication of plants and animals, the beginnings of village life, and the transition from hunting and gathering to a food-producing society and economy. The long delay is surprising, considering the unique utility of ceramic vessels for so many domestic functions, as well as for artistic purposes, cultic and other sym-

bolic uses, and trade. Nevertheless, once introduced, pottery seems to have caught on very quickly throughout the ancient Near East, Cyprus, and Egypt (for the latter two, in c. 5000 BCE); and it developed rapidly, in technology, form, and decoration. Thus, the delicate polychrome wares of the Hassuna, Samarra, and Halaf Neolithic phases in Mesopotamia are astonishingly sophisticated.

The origins of pottery production probably lie in the highly developed pyrotechnic capabilities of the earlier Neolithic, which had already experimented with minerals and clays, as well as with advanced kiln-firing techniques, to produce the period's ubiquitous fine plaster. It was only a step farther to apply this technology of clays to produce ceramic vessels. The actual stages in the experimental process are probably reflected in the *vaissals blanches,* or "white wares"—unfired plasterlike containers of the Prepottery Neolithic (PPN)—found at several sites in Syria.

The Neolithic pottery of Palestine is relatively crude: handmade, with coarse, low-fired clays; with straw or heavy grit temper; limited to a simple, utilitarian repertoire of shapes; and having decoration that consists of heavy slip applied like paint in geometric patterns, sometimes with incised chevron patterns. Little improvement distinguishes the Pottery Neolithic B (PNB) pottery from that of PNA, except for a slight improvement in wares and the addition of some new forms.

Chalcolithic period (c. 4000–3300 BCE). The Chalcolithic period in Palestine—the transition between the Stone Age and the fully developed urban Early Bronze Age (overlapping with Kenyon's Proto-Urban phase)—witnesses the flourishing of the ceramic industry. A whole new repertoire of forms is introduced, most of them innovative and not directly related to the Neolithic tradition. These include a large range of pithoi (storejars), with a variety of ledge and loop handles; large kraters of several kinds; holemouth jars, some of them cooking pots; a family of globular and flaring bowls; cornets and other globular chalices; pedestal chalices; churns modeled after goatskins; and even crucibles for copperworking. Decoration includes incision, scalloping, thumb molding, and other plastic devices, as well as quite

◀ CERAMICS: Syro-Palestinian. *Examples of Palestinian pottery of the Chalcolithic, Bronze, and Iron Ages.* (1) Late Chalcolithic cornet; (2) EB I painted jug; (3) EB II Abydos-style pitcher; (4) EB III burnished platter bowl; (5) EB IV "teapot"; (6) EB IV corrugated cup; (7) MB I-II "Tell el-Yehudiyeh" juglet; (8) MB III trumpet-footed chalice; (9) LB I bichrome jug; (10) LB II "Canaanite" storejar (half-scale); (11) LB II cooking pot; (12) LB II lamp; (13) Early Iron I "collar-rim" storejar; (14) twelfth-century BCE Philistine bichrome krater; (15) Iron II neckless jar; (16) Iron II decanter; (17) Iron II burnished juglet; (18) Iron II "beerjug"; (19) Iron II Phoenician flask. (After Amiran, 1970)

exotic geometric patterns in red and/or black paint over a cream-colored ground. Clays are well levigated, especially the kaolin-rich "cream ware" of the Beersheba region; and high kiln temperatures produced some thin, quite metallic wares. Some vessels, like the small flaring bowls with a thinned rim, are finished, if not actually formed, on a rotation device, probably a simple wooden platform or mat that could be rotated. Reed impressions on the bases of some vessels give evidence of the latter.

A striking phenomenon of the Late Chalcolithic period (c. 3600–3300 BCE) is the development of several regional assemblages that, although they overlap somewhat, have distinctive diagnostic features. These assemblages include, at a minimum (1) the original Ghassulian culture of the Dead Sea area, together with the related complex from the Beersheba valley; (2) a central coastal culture around modern Tel Aviv and somewhat inland; (3) the central hill-country sites, still poorly known; and (4) the Golan Heights group, only recently discerned.

Early Bronze I–III period (c. 3300–2400 BCE). The Early Bronze Age is conveniently divided into an initial proto-urban EB I phase and then the urban EB II–III phases that are followed by a decline and transition in EB IV (treated separately below). The pottery of EB I (c. 3300–3200/3100 BCE) follows somewhat in the Late Chalcolithic tradition, indicating a basic cultural continuity. There are, however, many new forms that herald the full-fledged EB II–III era, as well as a decorative tradition that signifies several regional cultures—not peoples, and certainly not newcomers, as Kenyon maintained. (1) Red-painted wares with parallel bands of decoration (line-group or multiple-brush techniques) are largely confined to the south and parts of the Jordan Valley, while streaky grain-wash wares dominate in the north; (2) a gray-burnished class of knobbed bowls and footed chalices, possibly a descendant of the earlier widespread dark face-burnished ware, is found at sites around the Jezreel Valley (giving it the name Esdraelon ware, first thought to be Late Chalcolithic); and (3) red-burnished wares occur throughout the country, now widespread for the first time. Among the diagnostic EB I forms are storejars with simple thumb-indented ledge handles; high loop-handled mugs or juglets; omphalos-based bowls; and ear-handled juglets. While wares are less well made than those of the Chalcolithic, the earliest known potter's wheel (i.e., the basalt bearing stone) belongs to this period, found at Beth-Yerah (Khirbet Kerak) on the Sea of Galilee. [*See* Beth-Yerah.]

The pottery of EB II–III, which can be considered together, develops out of the EB I repertoire in basic form. However, the gray burnish and most of the red geometric paint disappear, while a heavy red burnish predominates on many forms. The latter include, in particular, storejars with wavy and pushed-up/scalloped ledge handles; large shallow platters; small carinated bowls in metallic ware; large hole-mouth storejars and cooking pots; two-handled amphorae; and footed chalices. Particular mention should be made of a class of graceful handled pitchers and jugs in fine red-burnished ware (sometimes a painted geometric decoration) called Abydos ware because it was first found by Petrie as imported ware in royal tombs of the first dynasty at Abydos in Egypt. It thus gives a valuable synchronism: the first dynasty (c. 3200/3100 BCE onward) equals the floruit of EB II in ancient Palestine. A complete potter's workshop found at Tell el-Far'ah (North) includes a wheel, burnishing tools, clays and coloring agents, and a kiln.

The EB III phase (c. 2650–2400 BCE) is marked principally by the further development of many forms, such as platters; a few new forms, like spouted jars and flaring goblets; and especially by the brief appearance in the north of exotic red- and black-burnished vessels of Anatolian-Caucasian inspiration and the distinctive Khirbet Kerak ware (named after the site on the Sea of Galilee where it was first distinguished).

Early Bronze IV (c. 2400–2000 BCE). The pottery of Early Bronze IV (Albright's Middle Bronze I and Kenyon's Intermediate Early Bronze–Middle Bronze), a transitional nonurban interlude that represents a major socioeconomic decline, is of interest chiefly because of its many distinctive features. These include a combination of hand forming and wheel finishing; many unique vestigial features, such as nonfunctional handles and spouts; very strong and consistent regional "families"; and a clear influence from the calciform repertoire (cuplike shapes) of central and southern Syria. Red burnish and paint are rare, except in the north; and many wares are incised and/or band combed, especially in the south. Distinctive EB IV forms include ovoid storejars with vestigial handles; "teapots" and other spouted jars; many kinds of cups, goblets, and chalices; flasks; one-handled flask-pitchers; offset-shoulder bowls; and four-spouted lamps. It has been argued that EB IV pottery has some links with that of the first phase of the Middle Bronze Age; but in fact it represents the last, dying gasp of the long Early Bronze Age tradition.

Middle Bronze I–III period (c. 2000–1500 BCE). Albright's MB IIA, B, and C are termed here, as increasingly by others, MB I–III (his MB I having become the EB IV here). This is the second urban period in ancient Palestine and represents the zenith of the Canaanite culture. The pottery, which is entirely new in every regard, clearly reflects the wealth, sophistication, and international connections of the country in this period. Although there are recognizable inner divisions (thus the MB I–III phasing), the strong continuity throughout allows the Middle Bronze Age pottery to be treated as a whole. It begins in MB I with a new repertoire of exquisite wheelmade forms (the first use of the fast wheel), many of them related to Syrian styles, as well as fine red-burnished and painted wares. The basic repertoire,

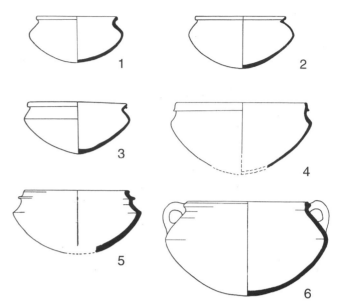

CERAMICS: Syro-Palestinian. *Typical development of cooking pots.* (1) MB III; (2) LB I; (3) LB II; (4) twelfth-eleventh century BCE; (5) ninth century BCE; (6) eighth century BCE. (After Amiran, 1970)

which continues until the end of MB III (and even into the Late Bronze Age), consists mainly of large, tapering ovoid storejars; globular cooking pots; large kraters; many styles of graceful jugs and juglets (e.g., dipper, piriform, cylindrical, and Tell el-Yahudiyeh ware), many of them slipped and burnished; platter bowls; globular bowls; sharply carinated bowls (with a shoulder or cyma profile), some footed; and single-spouted saucer lamps. Syrian styles of paint are evident (the North Syrian simple wares); and the first imports from the Mediterranean now occur, principally in Cypriot White-Painted IV–VI styles.

The MB II–III phases are marked by general continuity, but also by a certain degeneration in form and finish. Imports from Cyprus increase, however, and in the late MB III a number of new Syrian imports appear, such as Gray Lustrous ware. Cypriot Bichrome (and its local versions), Monochrome, Base-Ring I, and White-Slip I wares accompany the transition to LB I (below), as does a local Chocolate-on-White ware that may be of Cypriot inspiration.

Late Bronze Age (c. 1500–1200 BCE). The Late Bronze Age represents a final revival of urban Canaanite culture, by then in decline. It extends from the Egyptian destructions in about 1530–1460 BCE until the end of the Bronze Age (c. 1200 BCE). The pottery, as expected, continues the MB tradition, but it is exhausted by the end of the period. Virtually no new forms appear, except for flasks, kraters, and chalices; but there are imports. The imports are surprisingly numerous, and they include more from Cyprus: White-Painted IV–VI, White-Slip I–II, White-Shaved, and Base-Ring I–II wares; a few from Syria: red-burnished flasks; Mycenaean IIIA–B wares, and even a few Late Minoan vessels; and an occasional vessel from Egypt. The local wares, while rather poorly made, now feature relatively common painted decoration, with both geometric and naturalistic and animal motifs (e.g., a pair of ibexes and the sacred tree; a palm tree and panel).

Iron Age (c. 1200–600 BCE). The Iron Age witnesses a succession of new, local peoples and cultures, replacing the Bronze Age Canaanite culture, including "Sea Peoples," or Philistines, and the biblical Israelites. The common Iron I pottery of the twelfth–eleventh centuries BCE is, however, still strongly in the LB tradition. Philistine bichrome ware, a locally made offshoot of Late Mycenaean IIIC:1b ware, with beautiful geometric and bird designs, appears in about 1150, principally along the coast. Diagnostic ceramic forms for the Iron I proto-Israelite settlements now increasingly being brought to light include collar-rim storejars, as well as certain types of flanged-rim cooking pots (neither exclusively Israelite, however).

By the tenth century BCE (styled either Iron IC or Iron IIA), the Israelite state emerges, and with it a standardized ceramic repertoire that has few LB reminiscences and represents the fully developed local Iron Age cultures. Imported wares are now extremely rare, except for several Cypriot fabrics of the tenth century (e.g., Black on Red II, White Painted, Bichrome, Red Slip) and occasional Greek imports, which begin sporadically in the late eighth century. Some Phoenician ware appears along the coast, as early as the tenth century that has locally made derivatives in such luxury wares as the ninth–eighth-century BCE Samaria Ware. Apart from imports, painted decoration is rare in the tenth–seventh centuries BCE. Red slip and burnish, however, characterize much of the repertoire, particularly on bowls; in the tenth century it is done by hand, but in the ninth century wheel burnish takes over, gradually dying out toward the end of the period. The somewhat different repertoires of the Iron II coastal or "Neo-Philistine" culture along the southern coast, as well as the repertoires of the Transjordanian states of Ammon, Moab, and Edom, are now beginning to be better known to researchers.

All in all, the utilitarian pottery of the Iron II period represents the culture of a series of relatively isolated, petty regional states. When the Neo-Assyrians advance in the late eighth century, their presence is felt in Assyrian Palace Ware. By and large, the local pottery continues, even after the Babylonian destructions in 586 BCE (in what might be called an Iron III phase), throughout the 6th century).

Later periods. The Persian, Hellenistic, and Roman-Byzantine periods see Palestine becoming part of a larger international, imperial world. Thus, the pottery of these periods is both part of the classical tradition in the eastern Mediterranean and a separate study beyond the purview here. For the subsequent Arabic and Turkish periods, from the seventh to the nineteenth century CE, Palestine is part of the Islamic world, and the local pottery reflects that reality.

BIBLIOGRAPHY

Amiran, Ruth. *Ancient Pottery of the Holy Land* (1963). New Brunswick, N.J., 1970.
Cole, Dan P. *Shechem I: The Middle Bronze IIB Pottery.* Winona Lake, Ind., 1984.
Dever, William G. "Vestigial Features in MB I: An Illustration of Some Principles of Ceramic Typology." *Bulletin of the American Schools of Oriental Research,* no. 200 (December 1970): 19–30.
Dever, William G. "New Vistas on the EB IV ('MB I') Horizon in Syria-Palestine." *Bulletin of the American Schools of Oriental Research,* no. 237 (Winter 1980): 35–64.
Dever, William G., and H. Darrell Lance, eds. *A Manual of Field Excavation: Handbook for Field Archaeologists.* Cincinnati, 1978.
Duncan, J. Garrow. *Corpus of Dated Palestinian Pottery.* London, 1930. Based on Petrie's excavations at Tell Jemmeh.
Ehrich, Robert W., ed. *Chronologies in Old World Archaeology.* Chicago, 1965.
Homès-Fredericq, D., and H. J. Franken, eds. *Pottery and Potters, Past and Present: 7000 Years of Ceramic Art in Jordan.* Tübingen, 1986.
Kelso, James L. *The Ceramic Vocabulary of the Old Testament.* New Haven, 1948.
Lapp, Paul W. *Palestinian Ceramic Chronology, 200 B.C.–A.D. 70.* New Haven, 1961.
Magness, Jodi. *Jerusalem Ceramic Chronology, circa 200–800 CE.* Sheffield, 1993.
Orton, Clive, Paul Tyers, and Alan Vince. *Pottery in Archaeology.* Cambridge, 1993.
Sauer, James A. *Heshbon Pottery, 1971: A Preliminary Report on the Pottery from the 1971 Excavations at Tell Hesban.* Berrien Springs, Mich., 1973.
Shepard, Anna O. *Ceramics for the Archaeologist.* Washington, D.C., 1956.
Stern, Ephraim. *Material Culture of the Land of the Bible in the Persian Period, 538–332 B.C.* Warminster, 1982.
Thomas, David H. *Predicting the Past: An Introduction to Anthropological Archaeology.* New York, 1974.
Wood, Bryant G. *The Sociology of Pottery in Ancient Palestine.* Sheffield, 1990.
Wright, G. Ernest. *The Pottery of Palestine from the Earliest Times to the End of the Early Bronze Age.* New Haven, 1937.

WILLIAM G. DEVER

Ceramics of the Persian Period

Local Palestinian pottery in the Persian period was made of three different clay compositions, two of which were characteristic of the coastal region, while the third was found mainly in the mountain regions of Judah and Samaria. On the coastal plain the pottery was composed most frequently of a yellowish-green or a reddish clay. The visible differences in the clay (used for pottery in other periods as well) may have been created during firing. This pottery is for the most part crudely made, and the clay is not finely levigated; its most distinctive feature is its very poor firing, which left the clay extremely porous. Most of the pottery from Judah and Samaria, by contrast, is made of a brown-gray clay (a continuation of the material used earlier, in the Iron Age), is well fired, and is pleasing in its shapes.

The pottery types of the Persian period can be divided into three major groups: (1) local pottery that continues the ceramic tradition of the end of the Iron Age; (2) local imitations of imported pottery of "eastern" origin; and (3) local imitations of "western" prototypes.

The first group comprises most of the bowls, cooking pots, hole-mouth jars (an important jar family, especially those jars that continue the tradition of the *lamelekh* type), flasks, certain types of jugs and juglets, lamps, twin vases, funnels, and stands. Because the production and use of these vessels were generally confined to the areas of Judah and Samaria, the Israelite ceramic traditions persisted longer there than in the other parts of Palestine.

Vessels belonging to the second group, imitations of "eastern" prototypes, exhibit Assyrian, Persian, Phoenician, and Egyptian influences. The Assyrian pottery, especially the Palace Ware from the close of the seventh century BCE, is now well known from the excavations at Nimrud. The original vessels and the Palestinian copies appear almost simultaneously at the end of the Israelite period; by the Persian period they are already a constant feature in the local pottery repertoire. An Assyrian influence is evident mainly in the carinated bowls, in both pottery and metal, as well as in most of the bottles. However, in their crude shapes and especially in their lack of typical painted decoration, the vessels of the Persian period are inferior to both the Assyrian originals and their Iron Age imitations. No attempts were made in Palestine to duplicate the Achaemenid pottery, for its quality was generally very poor and it was not commonly found outside the borders of Persia. Among all the pottery finds in Palestine, only two or three vessels can be designated with any certainty as direct Persian imports. The magnificent Achaemenid metalware, on the other hand, was a significant source of inspiration for Palestinian potters, who imitated it in clay. The most outstanding imitations are the rhytons. It is also possible that the impressed wedge and reed decoration, which appears on a ramified class of Palestinian pottery in the Persian period, is modeled after the decoration on this metalware. Other Palestinian vessels can be attributed to a Phoenician origin by analogy with the earlier Phoenician vessels (from the end of the Iron Age) discovered at Phoenician sites and in tombs. The Phoenician influence is particularly marked in the jugs and juglets, in the face and Bes vases, in several types of jars, and in the lamps. Egyptian influence, on the other hand, can be observed only in the alabastra, which seem to be copies of an alabaster original.

The imported pottery of the period was mainly Greek. The earliest Greek vases found in Palestine are Late Proto-Geometric, which dates to the end of the eighth century BCE. Later Greek vessels came from a variety of regions. In the Babylonian and Early Persian periods, most came from Corinth, which then possessed mastery of the seas. Those ves-

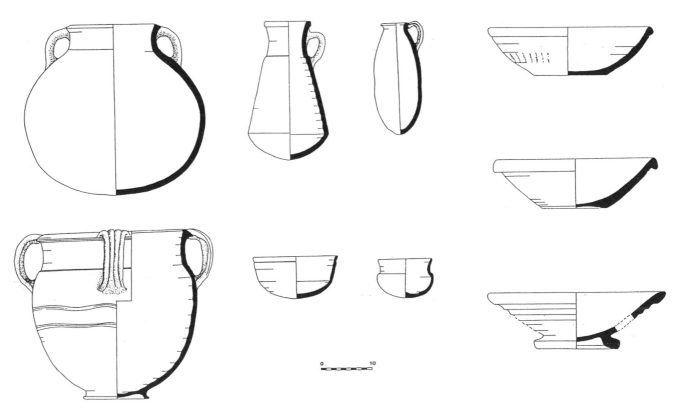

CERAMICS: Persian Period. *Pottery types from Qadum.* (a) cooking pot; (b) krater; (c) jug; (d) dipper juglet; (e) five examples of bowls. (Courtesy ASOR Archives)

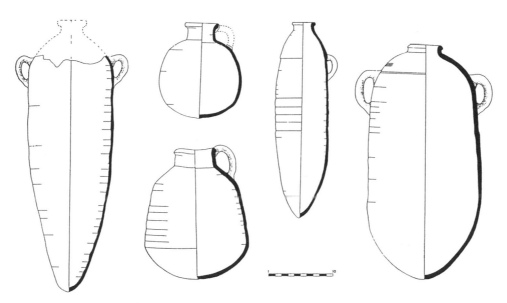

CERAMICS: Persian Period. *Pottery types from Qadum.* (a) torpedo jars; (b) jugs; (c) storage jar. (Courtesy ASOR Archives)

sels were still rare in Palestine, and only a few have been found. It is only from the sixth century BCE onward that imports from the eastern Greek islands increased: from Rhodes, Kos, Cnidus (Knidos), Chios, Samos, and Lesbos, for example, as well as from the Greek settlements along the northeastern Mediterranean coast, such as Al-Mina. These East Greek vases included bowls with painted bands and horizontal handles, jugs with black-painted decoration or geometric designs on their upper part, and vessels in the Wild Goat style. During the sixth century BCE, especially toward its close, Greek vessels from Athens began to arrive. Although initially they only reached Palestine in small numbers, they were quickly integrated with the vessels in common use.

The first Greek vessels to arrive were painted in black on a red background (black figured). Later, the colors were reversed: figures painted in red on a black background (red figured). Last to arrive were plain black-glazed types. The changes in the source of the imported Greek ware and the absolute dominance of the Attic pottery throughout the Persian period in Palestine is conclusively proven by comparable finds in neighboring lands and throughout the Mediterranean area, as well as on the Mediterranean islands.

The influx of Greek goods to coastal sites in the eastern Mediterranean brought with it Greek colonization on the coasts of Phoenicia and Palestine. Clear evidence for this process was recently recovered at Al-Mina, Tell Sukas, Tabat el-Hammam, and elsewhere along the Phoenician coast.

There also is evidence for the settlement of Greek merchants in Israel. At Tel Akko, a rich assemblage of Attic-Greek pottery was discovered in a well-planned quarter on the western part of the mound; on the basis of this find, the excavator, Moshe Dothan, proposed that the mound's northwest section had, in the Persian period, contained a quarter of rich merchants, most of them Greek, and that it had been the finest section of the town. In excavations at Jaffa, a large warehouse from the Persian period was found to have close affinities with the plan of the recently published warehouses at Al-Mina. A sizable amount of pottery was found on the floor of one of the rooms. All the vessels were of a single type and all bore similar red-figured decoration. It is very likely that, as at the northern Phoenician port city of Al-Mina, a group of Greek merchants resided in Jaffa during the Persian period and engaged in the wholesale trade of the products of Athenian potteries.

Athenian pottery apparently was also brought to Tell Jemmeh. The discoveries there included about a dozen of the red-figured cups that were evidently painted by the Pithos Painter; although not found on the same site, they may have been purchased at the same time in Athens and carried over on the same vessel to the eastern Mediterranean coast, whence they were distributed to several merchants. The best examples to date of the phenomenon of Greek settlers are perhaps the finds from Tel Dor, Meṣad Ḥashavyahu, and Migdol. At many other sites—Tel Michal, Tell el-Ḥesi, and Ashkelon, among them—also produced rich assemblages of imported Greek pottery, have been unearthed, however.

Undecorated everyday ware from Greece also began to appear in Palestine during the Persian period. It included heavy bowls, cooking pots, and, prominently, wine amphorae from the eastern Greek islands. It seems that even though Palestine produced large quantities of excellent wine,

CERAMICS: Persian Period. *Imported Attic vases from Tel Dor.* Dated from fifth to fourth century BCE. (Courtesy E. Stern)

a considerable amount still had to be imported from abroad, undoubtedly for consumption by the increasing numbers of Greeks who had settled there.

In the Babylonian-Persian periods, and even before, Greek pottery was plentiful in Palestine, exerting a strong influence on local ceramics. However, while the eastern vessels were for the most part merely imitations, and often very late ones, the western pottery comprised both imported ware and contemporary local copies. This pottery was widely imitated, especially the types of vessels, though the Palestinian potters did not succeed in duplicating the excellent quality and exquisite decoration. The East Greek bowls probably were the original models for the small bowls and kraters with horizontal handles that were widespread in Palestine. The locally produced closed lamps, made of coarse clay without the typical burnish, were certainly patterned after Attic lamps. Juglets found at Tel Megadim bear a close resemblance to the Attic lekythos, and one from Tel Mevorakh imitates the *laginos*.

In most cases, the difference between the imported ware

and the Palestinian imitations can be readily distinguished. It is also possible to detect the source of the copies. There is a large group of vessels whose form is nearly identical to the above-three imported western groups; however, because they lack distinctive decoration, it is impossible to determine whether they are imports or local products. This group includes the "Persian" bowls with a flat base, a large group of straight-shouldered jars, jars with basket handles, and amphorae that were the prototype of the Rhodian amphorae of the Hellenistic period. These vessels were all used in transporting goods by sea and are found widely dispersed along the eastern Mediterranean coast. Only mineralogical and petrographic analyses can provide more exact conclusions as to their place of origin. Nevertheless, even if the majority of these jars, bowls, and amphorae were indeed locally manufactured, their origins are to be sought on the East Greek islands and on Cyprus. Their appearance in the eastern Mediterranean is certainly connected with the early Greek trading colonies: Al-Mina and Tell Sukas in Syria; Meṣad Ḥashavyahu in Palestine; and Migdol, Daphnae, and Naukratis in Egypt.

Cypriot pottery, of which only a small part has been studied, is among the pottery imported from the west. The following survey is based on Einar Gjerstad's summary. It includes only examples that are clearly Cypriot types, with painted decoration. Cypriot vessels were often also found in context with local ware of the Persian period, but their dates are as yet unverified. Some have been attributed, apparently incorrectly, to earlier periods. It seems, however, that most belonged to the White-Painted V group.

Only one vessel among all of the pottery from the Persian period has been interpreted as an Achaemenid import: it is a cup made of a light-greenish clay with high, very thin ribbed sides. Fragments of another cup were found lying next to it in an unstratified context at Samaria. Even though direct imports of Achaemenid ware were nonexistent in the Persian period—the ware was not outstanding either for its quality or beauty—Achaemenian metal vases specifically had an indirect influence on rhyta and several types of local Palestinian pottery (see above). Because Achaemenid pottery was almost uniformly dull, and because the Achaemenids were not colonizers, the advent of the Persians did not change the local styles of pottery in use in the Near East.

[*Many of the sites mentioned are the subject of independent entries.*]

BIBLIOGRAPHY

Boardman, John. *The Greeks Overseas.* Harmondsworth, 1973. Study of the Greek expansion toward the eastern Mediterranean.

Lapp, Paul W. "The Pottery of Palestine in the Persian Period." In *Archaeology und Altes Testament,* pp. 179–192. Tübingen, 1970.

Stern, Ephraim. *Material Culture of the Land of the Bible in the Persian Period, 538–332 B.C.* Warminster, 1982. Study of local Palestinian pottery in the Persian period. See pages 93–142.

Stern, Ephraim. "The Beginning of the Greek Settlement in Palestine in the Light of the Recent Excavations at Tel Dor." In *Recent Excavations in Israel: Studies in Iron Age Archaeology*, edited by Seymour Gitin and William G. Dever, pp. 107–124. Annual of the American Schools of Oriental Research, 49. Winona Lake, Ind., 1989.

EPHRAIM STERN

Ceramics of the Hellenistic and Roman Periods

Vast amounts of pottery for the period from about 300 BCE to 300/400 CE (the periods covered in this survey) have been found in Israel/Palestine, but many questions remain unanswered. Numerous preliminary reports, illustrating a few select items, often assigned to unrealistically precise, historically based periods, have been the norm. Synthetic studies of the regional wares by ware and/or shape are few. Finds from Jordan have generally been handled similarly. In other regions (e.g., Syria and Egypt), detailed pottery reports exist on the finds from a few widely separated sites; the reports in local journals are generally of poor quality. A good understanding of the wares in these countries is not close at hand. Throughout the Near East, the care lavished on Bronze and Iron Age wares has not generally been extended to the wares of the later periods. Statistics of frequency are available for relatively few sites, and many excavators have not recorded the bulk of their finds before discard. A lack of excavations on kiln sites impedes our understanding of sources and of production techniques.

In general, the pottery of the region mixes local traditions (seen in coarse and cooking wares and the storage jar series) with Mediterranean Hellenistic and Roman-type fine tablewares and amphorae (transport containers), both locally made and imported from farther west. Eastern (Seleucid, Parthian) wares are generally absent, except on sites on the Roman frontier on the Euphrates River, and at Palmyra, in Syria. The Nabatean region has its own distinctive local wares, generally thin-walled: a series of round-bottomed painted vessels not matched elsewhere, made alongside a series of close copies of Italian Roman vessels (and clay lamps), owing little to Levantine models. A similar coexistence of "native" painted wares and imitation Roman products—in thin, whitish wares—is evidenced in Meroitic Nubia. Egypt, commercially largely isolated during the Roman period, is a special case: there, traditional wares and Ptolemaic derivatives were supplied to a large local market.

During the third century BCE, Greek-derived fineware types appear throughout the region. True Greek black-gloss wares appear as imports (from Athens and, although rarely, from southern Italy, early in the third century BCE, and thereafter from various ill-defined Aegean and Asia Minor sources). The numerous local copies from the Levant, including Cyprus—Jerusalem wares are a notable exception—generally have a dull, darkish slip coating over a buff fabric. Subsequently, the major regional tableware is the red-slipped (red-gloss) Eastern Sigillata A ware (once

CERAMICS: Hellenistic and Roman Periods. *Hellenistic bottles.* Standard bottle is shown at left, spindle bottle is shown at right. Dated c. 100 BCE. (Courtesy Pictorial Archive)

termed Pergamene), from unlocated sources (Lebanon?, southern Syria?), current from about 150 BCE to about 150 CE. This is well studied: a Late Hellenistic phase is typified by platters with very heavy feet and small floral stamps around the center (not unrelated to the black-gloss Campana B platters of Tuscany in Italy). These probably were formed with the aid of molds. Small hemispherical footed cups (not modeled on imports) accompany them. The red gloss surface here appears earlier than on other Mediterranean wares; it is applied by a double dipping process, leaving a darker stripe across the middle of the vessel (seen later on some other eastern fine wares). A Cypriot(?) counterpart (Cypriot sigillata) has a more pinkish- or purplish-red clay and slip coloration; the slip tends toward a metallic luster. Eastern Sigillata A is abundant throughout the Near East, whereas the Cypriot ware is sporadic outside Cyprus (except in the lower Nile Delta and in Israel's Negev desert—where, dubiously, local production has been claimed).

Between about 10 and 80 CE, the classic Eastern Sigillata A ware shapes are replaced by ones modeled on those of Italian red-gloss terra sigillata ware, perhaps indirectly through the products of Asia Minor (Eastern Sigillata B and Pergamon-region wares). The Asia Minor wares also bear

CERAMICS: Hellenistic and Roman Periods. *Terra sigillata juglets.* (Courtesy Pictorial Archive)

stamps inscribed in Greek—a rather short-lived fashion. Cypriot sigillata shows similar changes. Thereafter, new shapes (mainly flat-based, with decoratives moldings on the interior) seem to owe more to Roman metalware. Some late Eastern Sigillata A ware vessels with a sponged mottled slip treatment (current from about 70 to 120 CE) also attest to these new influences. Similar trends are present throughout Eastern Sigillata B ware (which can be fired black or dark brown).

Red-gloss (sigillata) tablewares and thin-walled ware imports, mainly from Italian and Aegean sources, are quite common during the first century CE, particularly at coastal sites, but also as far afield as Petra, in Jordan. Some serve to mark the early Red Sea trade links with India (where a few specimens have been found); many are present at Quseir el-Qadim, one of the Egyptian departure points. Adaptations of these imported shapes are seen in other local products, from Cilicia and Syria to Egypt (but rarely, if at all, in Mesopotamia).

Some lead-glazed cups, mimicking decorated silverware, were made at Tarsus from about 1 to 100 CE. These match types made in western Asia Minor and are quite distinct from the essentially Parthian alkaline-glazed wares made in Mesopotamia, of which some forerunners are seen in later Hellenistic Antioch. Finds from Dura-Europos in Syria show that the Parthian series, typically rather heavy amphora jars with peaked handles and gouged ornament, lasted beyond 250 CE.

Other fine wares include a series of buff-ware bowls with partial two-tone (red/black) slip and double-bulge horizontal handles below the rim, common in second-century BCE

deposits at Paphos and at Shiqmona in Israel and elsewhere. Many versions of the Hellenistic *lagynos* shape (an angular-bodied, narrow-necked jug with silhouetted floral patterns and horizontal bands painted in brown on a cream slip or surface) appear from about 175 to 50 BCE on Cyprus (probably a major source); Egyptian and other versions are also known. Small figured vessels and lamps made in molds (some depicting heads) were produced in the Nile Delta region (e.g., at Memphis) from about 100 BCE to 100 CE; also found at this time are red-ware painted jars with erotic motifs and busts of favored youths half-hidden on the interiors. Later Egyptian wares bear floral patterns in paint or added raised slip (barbotine); a particular group of shallow beige-ware cups depicts silhouetted pygmylike figures in black. Corresponding treatments occur on the Meroitic wares of Nubia.

Recorded Hellenistic to Roman imports include thin carinated bowls from Knidos, later relief-ware bowls from Corinth, and moldmade relief-ware "novelty" figured vases from Knidos (notably a cache in the form of parts of the human body, possibly for medical use, discovered on Paphos). In contrast to the Mediterranean-type wares, Jerusalem products show a range of thin, well-fired plain wares in the tradition of the preceding Persian period.

Thin-walled Greek-influenced cooking vessels in sandy wares appear in Hellenistic times. A large Cypriot series and those from the Nile Delta show typically Greek features such as internally ledged rims (to support lids) and, on the shallower "casseroles," striplike handles along the exteriors of rims. The typical Palestinian version is fairly shallow, with a sagging bottom and a short neck flanked by small handles;

Early Roman examples are particularly thin. Horizontal ribbing is a feature of these and of related round-bottomed jugs and flasks, as from the later second century BCE; the treatment is copied in Egypt, and, much later, in the Aegean region, and is widespread on later Roman/Byzantine wares from the Levant. In about 170–50 BCE, portable braziers set on tall stands, with three internal knobs set obliquely to support a pot, were made in quantity in the Alexandria region and also in the Aegean; some copies of them appear on Cyprus and elsewhere. Their most distinctive feature, the internal knobs, is regularly molded in the form of plaques (sometimes inscribed) bearing Greek-style Silenos masks or bulls' heads.

The traditional Palestinian storage jars with ringlike handles at the shoulder continue unabated, being commonly accompanied by imported wine and oil amphorae—in Hellenistic times mostly from Rhodes and in Roman times from Italy (Campania, Istria, and elsewhere) and even Spain. Enormous numbers of Hellenistic wine amphorae from Aegean sources (identified by the stamps on their handles) are documented at Alexandria. These spawned local imitations, at first along Lake Mareotis and then throughout Egypt. Similar copies appear on Cyprus and elsewhere. These normally have ovoid or long cylindrical bodies and distinctive necks flanked by two long, upright handles; they taper at the base to a solid toe of variable length. A distinctive version of this shape, with ribbing added and the handles reduced to mere loops under the rim, is seen in Egypt in Roman times. Elsewhere, the most common local amphora types in Early Roman times are modeled on the Italian "pseudo-Koan" type (copied from an Aegean Hellenistic product), with tall handles formed of two rolls of clay set side by side. In Cilicia, a bulging version of the Palestinian torpedo-shaped jar is supplied with handles of this type. Later Roman types, apparently more diverse, are still inadequately studied. Painted commercial "labels" (*tituli picti*) are seen on both imports and copies; those from Masada in Israel include some labels in Latin, indicating the arrival of Italian wines there by about 20 BCE.

Clay mixing bowls with gritted interiors (*mortaria*) are present only sporadically: some wide-rimmed Italian imports bearing potters' stamps (first–second centuries CE) are known from Caesarea and Paphos. In the third–fourth centuries, versions of the Italian type, in a distinctive deep-brown ware with volcanic grits, were made on the northern Syrian coast (in the area of Ras el-Bassit). These bear multiple name stamps in Greek (and occasionally in Latin). They, and later unstamped narrow-rimmed versions, circulated widely around the Levantine coastlands.

BIBLIOGRAPHY

Adan-Bayewitz, David. *Common Pottery in Roman Galilee: A Study of Local Trade.* Ramat Gan, 1993. Fine all-around study of a regional cooking ware, with clay analyses and ancient textual references.

'Amr, Khairieh. *The Pottery from Petra: A Neutron Activation Analysis Study.* British Archaeological Reports, International Series, no. 324. Oxford, 1987. Provides a selection of wares found at Petra and a review of the existing literature.

Blakely, Jeffrey A., et al. "Roman Mortaria and Basins from a Sequence at Caesarea: Fabrics and Sources." In *Caesarea Papers: Straton's Tower, Herod's Harbour, and Roman and Byzantine Caesarea,* edited by R. Lindley Vann, pp. 194–213. Journal of Roman Archaeology, Supplementary Series, no. 5. Ann Arbor, Mich., 1992. Discusses *mortaria* (Syrian and Italian imports).

Cahiers de la Céramique Égyptienne. Cairo, 1987–. Series issued by the Institut Français d'Archéologie Orientale du Cairo, which includes studies of Ptolemaic and Roman-period wares. Supplemented by *Bulletin de Liaison du Groupe International d'Étude de la Céramique Égyptienne,* which contains brief reports on current excavation finds.

Cotton, Hannah M., and Joseph Geiger. *Masada.* vol. 2, *The Latin and Greek Documents.* Jerusalem, 1989. Greek and Latin *dipinti.*

Gunneweg, Jan, et al. *The Provenience, Typology, and Chronology of Eastern Terra Sigillata.* Qedem, vol. 17. Jerusalem, 1983. Study based on selected clay analyses.

Hayes, John W. "Sigillate orientali." In *Enciclopedia dell'arte antica: Atlante delle forme ceramiche romane,* vol. 2, pp. 1–96, pls. 1–23. Rome, 1986. Typology of the eastern sigillata wares.

Hayes, John W. *Paphos,* vol. 3, *The Hellenistic and Roman Pottery.* Nicosia, Cyprus, 1991. Presents a wide range of ware found throughout the region.

Herbert, Sharon, et al. *Tel Anafa.* 2 vols. Ann Arbor, 1994 Covers ceramics from an important Late Hellenistic site in Israel.

Negev, Avraham. *The Late Hellenistic and Early Roman Pottery of Nabatean Oboda: Final Report.* Qedem, vol. 22. Jerusalem, 1986. Discusses local and imported products.

Toll, N. P. *The Excavations at Dura-Europos,* vol. 4.1, fasc. 1, *The Green Glazed Pottery.* New Haven, 1943. Covers Parthian-style glazed wares.

Tushingham, A. D., et al. *Excavations in Jerusalem, 1961–1967.* Vol. 1. Toronto, 1985. For fine wares, see the contribution by John W. Hayes (pp. 183–194).

Vanderhoeven, Michel. *Fouilles d'Apamée de Syrie,* vol. 9.1, *Les terres sigillées, 1966–1972.* Brussels, 1989. Covers Eastern Sigillata A and more, with color photos.

Vitto, Fanny. "Potters and Pottery Manufacture in Roman Palestine." *Bulletin of the Institute of Archaeology* (University College, London), no. 23 (1986): 47–64. Discusses Jewish ceramic use (and some later Roman use?).

Whitcomb, Donald S., and Janet H. Johnson. *Quseir al-Qadim, 1978: Preliminary Report.* Cairo, 1979. See W. R. Johnson on Roman pottery (pp. 67–103).

For more general works on the categories mentioned, not restricted to the region, see the following titles:

Ettlinger, Elisabeth, et al. *Conspectus formarum terrae sigillatae Italico modo confectae.* Bonn, 1990. New typology.

Magness, Jodi. *Jerusalem Ceramic Chronology, circa 200–800 CE.* Sheffield, 1993.

Peacock, D. P. S., and D. F. Williams. *Amphorae and the Roman Economy.* London and New York, 1986. Contains a partial typology.

JOHN W. HAYES

Ceramics of the Byzantine Period

Pottery of the fourth to seventh century found in the Levant is generally labeled Byzantine; elsewhere in the Mediterranean the same wares are normally designated Late Roman (the term *Byzantine* being reserved for later, typically lead-glazed wares). The modern Levantine usage implies close links with political history. Actual fashions in pottery tend to lag behind political changes, relying on the creation or extinction of markets (which are, in part, affected by major natural disasters such as plagues and earthquakes). Thus, Roman-derived wares continued to be produced through the Umayyad period; the major break in tradition occurred in around 800 CE. Similarly, in Egypt, the religious term *Coptic* is used to designate pottery of this period, although, in Nubia at least, the same tradition can be traced down to the fourteenth century. *Late Roman* as a designation should be viewed here in cultural rather than political terms—for much of the period Rome (or its successor, Constantinople) did not directly rule all the areas under consideration. The influence of (Roman) Christianity was generally strong, however, and this influenced pottery decoration.

The universal fine ceramic wares of the period are fine textured and red bodied, with a reddish slip finish (not a glazed treatment). A few major centers of production in North Africa, western Turkey, and (probably) Cyprus led the way, in due course providing models for other, more local wares. This concentration of production in a few major centers may reflect the tendency to centralized control and specialization found in the age of Diocletian and Constantine. While the potters themselves remained free agents, the marketing of their products seems to have become more regulated, with a view to maintaining steady supplies to ma-

jor urban centers such as Constantinople. Eventually, the monetary economy of imperial Rome shrank, and organizations such as the church and local magnates seem to have assumed more control over the circulation of these cheap everyday products.

The various fine wares have attracted the bulk of scholarly attention, mainly from the standpoints of typology and art history. Trade amphorae have also become well known in recent years. The coarser wares are generally more poorly served by the scholarly literature. Statistics of frequency are available for relatively few sites; many excavators have not troubled to record the bulk of their finds before discard. A lack of excavations on kiln sites impedes our knowledge of sources and of production techniques. Chemical and petrological techniques of analysis have not yet been widely used on the wares in question.

Fine Red Wares. The fine red-gloss (terra sigillata) wares of earlier Roman times, represented in the Levant chiefly by Eastern Sigillata A and Cypriot(?) products, died out during the late second century. A general scarcity of well-dated deposits for the period from 150 to about 300 or so containing fine wares may signal reduced use of such imports. With the fourth century, new trade patterns emerged: African Red-Slip Ware, a medium-to fine-grade tableware with a red slip, made in the region of modern Tunisia, circulated widely in the Levant and also in Egypt (a region previously partly closed to imports, owing to its

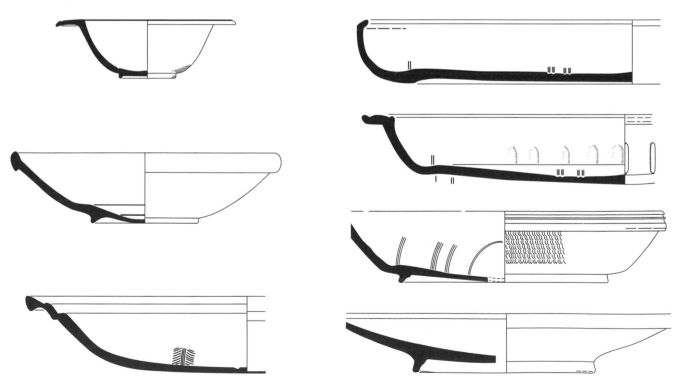

CERAMICS: Byzantine Period. Figure 1. *African Red-Slip Ware types.* Fourth-seventh centuries. (Courtesy J. W. Hayes)

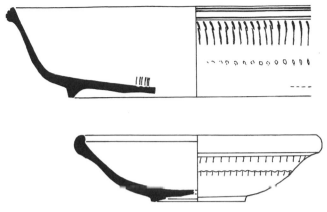

CERAMICS: Byzantine Period. Figure 2. *Examples of Cypriot Red-Slip Ware.* (Courtesy J. W. Hayes)

pre-Diocletianic monetary isolation; see figure 1). Some African wares had already appeared at Dura-Europos (before 256), but their main influx was later. The fourth-century African products (Terra Sigillata africana C and D) are mostly blatant copies of metalware shapes, with analogous decoration, either applied or stamped; these "metallic" types (flat-based dishes and small bowls with wide rims, for example) may generally have been wheel-thrown within molds. Throughout the fourth century floral stamped patterns, mostly based on radiating palm-branch motifs—not derived from metalware—persisted. The stamped patterns of the fifth and sixth centuries, largely Christian in content, more closely match the decor of contemporary silverware.

The primacy of the African wares throughout the Mediterranean region is proved by numerous imitations; in the East, these are noted throughout Egypt, in Jordan, and in Athens. Two major fine-ware competitors, widely traded, appeared in around the 360s: Phocean Red-Slip Ware (former name: Late Roman C) from western Asia Minor, and Cypriot Red-Slip Ware (a revival of the earlier Cypriot Sigillata, whose source remains unlocated; see figure 2). The latter ware—current in Cyprus, western Cilicia, the Alexandria region, and parts of Palestine—is first attested in deposits from 365 CE(?) at Kourion on Cyprus and on a contemporary wreck at Yassıada in southwest Turkey. Its principal fifth-century shape mimics an African type. Phocean Red-Slip Ware, at first influenced by the earlier regional (Çandarlı) ware and by the stamped African products, soon developed a characteristic shape—a shallow bowl with an overhanging (often rouletted) rim—along with distinctive stamps (see figure 3). The classic version (c. 450–550) is common on Levantine sites (e.g., at Antioch, in deposits associated with the earthquake in 526, but not in Egypt, where local stamped copies of the African wares predominated. The principal dated contexts for this period are those at Antioch (Turkey), Kourion (Cyprus), Tell Keisan

(Israel), Lejjun (Jordan), Kellia and Karanis (Egypt), and Ballana (Nubia); their dates are confirmed by finds from more distant sites such as Athens (the Agora), Constantinople, and Carthage. An alternative dating scheme (for the 350s–380s) has been proposed for Jalame (northern Israel), although exact contexts for the pottery finds there are unspecified. A suspicious absence at Jalame of the African types elsewhere current between 360 and 390, and the frequency of Phocean and other products elsewhere assigned to the early/mid-fifth century, may here point to a need for reassessment. Cypriot Red-Slip Ware of unusual types is common on this site.

Reduced imports of the Phocean ware and a revival of the Cypriot ware (after fifty or more years of decline), accompanied by changes in their vessel forms, occur in the mid-sixth century. The new pattern, already just evident at Lejjun (a probable victim of the 551 earthquake), could be a consequence of the plague of 540–542. Imports of the African ware, at a low ebb for a century, now resume in quantity. All three wares are widespread on numerous Palestinian church sites for the period from about 550 to 625 (cf. also the Beth-She'arim catacombs). The later Cypriot products, typified by flat-based dishes bearing single cross stamps, are particularly common in and around Alexandria.

Renewed imitation of, chiefly, the African wares is seen in various places. In northern Jordan (at Jerash and Pella), dishes in a local thin-walled red-slipped fabric bear painted figures or floral ornaments in two tones (purple and yellow-cream); some early examples have the traditional stamps. In Egypt, the Aswan fine-ware factories continued to produce derivatives of late fifth-/early sixth-century African products (the latest to be imported there) for two centuries or more (see figure 4). These exhibit a flaky pink fabric and a burnished red slip (often obscuring the stamps). Examples were exported to Cyprus and elsewhere in the late seventh century, when the other fine red wares were disappearing. In due course, painted cream-bodied wares supplanted them, particularly in Nubia.

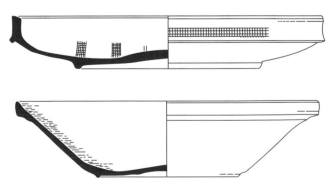

CERAMICS: Byzantine Period. Figure 3. *Examples of Phocean Red-Slip Ware.* (Courtesy J. W. Hayes)

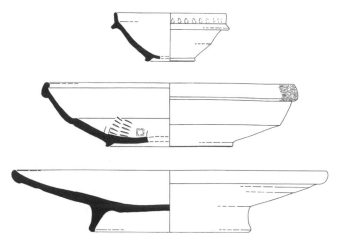

CERAMICS: Byzantine Period. Figure 4. *Egyptian Red-Slip A (Aswan Ware)*. (Courtesy J. W. Hayes)

Lead-Glazed Wares. Until the seventh century lead-glazed wares are absent from the eastern Mediterranean. It is then that utilitarian lead-glazed vessels began to be produced in the neighborhood of Constantinople. This functional lead glazing, of uncertain origins (various short-lived wares are noted in Thrace, the Balkans, and the Alpine regions from the fourth century), seems quite distinct from the ornamental tradition of Islamic glazed wares in the period after 775/800. A mid-seventh-century deposit in Istanbul proves medium-scale production (chiefly of internally glazed jars); the earliest closely dated examples of the series come from the Yassıada wreck (c. 625). [*See* Yassıada Wrecks.] Production en masse, chiefly of white-bodied tablewares, such as dishes, followed in about 700, initiating a conservative tradition of plain or minimally decorated wares that persisted for some four centuries. A few early examples of the Constantinople wares, along with occasional derivatives, are noted from Cyprus and elsewhere on the Mediterranean littoral in the seventh–eighth-century contexts. No comparable wares are yet known from Anatolia.

Plain Wares. Marked differences between regional traditions blur the picture for plain wares. Painted decoration is not common in the late Roman/Byzantine period, except in parts of Egypt, where lively figural scenes in two colors are known. A ribbed treatment is more common. In Egypt and Palestine, flasks and jugs often feature internal strainers (to keep out flies?), and small spouts on the shoulder; a few have lids attached by a loop set on the handle (a feature later copied in Constantinople). Combed grooving (mostly wavy lines) appears on sixth–seventh-century Aegean wares. By the sixth century, declining standards are evident in many provincial products; simple squat jugs and jars, lacking any decoration, become frequent. Their bases may be hollowed, with a central knob. On the mold-made clay lamps of the period, the ornament becomes more linear

and schematic; the Palestinian Syrian series survive into 'Abbasid times.

Cooking Wares. Thin-walled cooking vessels, normally with small handles, reflect Roman traditions. The ribbed treatment originating on Palestinian products now becomes universal. A range of typical fifth–sixth-century shapes appears on the Dhiorios kiln site on Cyprus. Deeper vessel types appear in western Asia Minor and the Aegean. Jewish culinary practices are evident in a class of steep-sided casseroles with close-fitting lids—actually thrown by the potter in a single piece and then partly sliced open. The abrupt knife-cut separation of the two elements, found first in Roman times, is seen on "Byzantine" examples from Palestine, Cyprus, and the Nile Delta region until the eighth century. It is possible that Jewish concerns for purity influenced Christian usage also.

Special Types. Small mold-made clay flasks, "souvenirs" from Christian pilgrim shrines, presumably meant to hold sanctified oil or water, were current from about 450 to 650. These imitate precious versions in silver and other materials and bear crude representations of saints or simple Christian symbols in relief, sometimes with an identifying inscription. Best known are the St. Menas flasks from Egypt, but other Egyptian and Palestinian series exist whose sources are unknown; a series with string holes replacing small handles is native to western Asia Minor. Related in function are some spindly flasks with signet-impressed stamps (origin unknown). Like the Menas flasks, they were widely transported. Their stamps embrace monograms that are Christian and also Gnostic/magical symbols.

Commercial Amphorae. Within the Mediterranean orbit, large two-handled clay jars remained the preferred transport containers for wine, olive oil, and certain dry goods (often indicated by markings, mostly undeciphered, made in red paint). The Byzantine examples tend to be rather smaller and more round bodied than their predecessors. Cylindrical storage jars bearing two small ring handles on the shoulder remain the standard Palestinian type; the examples from this period are normally finely ribbed. Among the Palestinian storage jars, buff to orange-brown wares predominate, but one widely exported type, from the Beth-Shean region in Galilee, has a hard gray fabric bearing multiple loops painted in white. Both buff- and gray-ware types survived through the Umayyad period. In Egypt, the standard local type is a slender carrot-shaped vessel with irregular ribbing and crude handles, made of coarse dark-brown Nile silt.

During the period from about 380 to 650, a small number of distinctive amphora types of Levantine and Aegean origin circulated widely throughout the eastern Mediterranean and beyond (e.g., to Constantinople, Nubia, and even distant Britain). The prime types are, in Riley's (1979) Benghazi classification: Late Roman Type 1 (cylindrical, with a sandy buff ware, uneven ridging, and unevenly grooved handles), made in Cilicia and Cyprus; Late Roman 2 (nearly globular, with a cupped mouth, slanted handles, and straight or wavy close-set grooving covering the upper part), from various Aegean sources; the Gaza type (Late Roman 3), a long, bullet-shaped variant of the common Palestinian ring-handled shape, in a dull-brown ware; and Late Roman 10 (small, spindly, and ribbed, in a silky, micaceous brown ware), from western Asia Minor. In addition, some large cylindrical oil amphorae from North Africa (in brick-red wares, often fired buff on the outer surface) appear everywhere. The successors of these amphorae in the seventh and eighth centuries are less widely distributed, documenting a general decline in Mediterranean trade during that period.

BIBLIOGRAPHY

Adams, William Y. *Ceramic Industries of Medieval Nubia.* 2 vols. Lexington, Ky., 1986. Conspectus of fifth- to fourteenth-century wares.
Catling, H. W. "An Early Byzantine Pottery Factory at Dhiorios in Cyprus." *Levant* 4 (1972): 1–82. Dhiorios kiln site.
Egloff, Michel. *Kellia: La poterie copte.* 2 vols. Geneva, 1977. Important for Lower Egypt; datable groups.
Emery, Walter B., and L. P. Kirwan. *The Royal Tombs of Ballana and Qustul.* 2 vols. Cairo, 1938. Classic study for fourth- to sixth-century Nubia (see, especially, vol. 1, pp. 386–405).
Hayes, John W. *Late Roman Pottery* and *A Supplement to Late Roman Pottery.* London, 1972–1980. Basic classification of fine Red-Slip Wares.
Hayes, John W. *Excavations at Saraçhane in Istanbul,* vol. 2, *The Pottery.* Princeton, 1992. The Constantinople sequence.
Johnson, Barbara. *Pottery from Karanis.* Ann Arbor, 1981. Egyptian wares to about 500 CE.
Johnson, Barbara. "The Pottery." In *Excavations at Jalame: Site of a Glass Factory in Late Roman Palestine,* edited by Gladys Davidson Weinberg, pp. 137–226. Columbia, Mo., 1988. Alternative dates for fourth- to fifth-century wares.
Landgraf, J. "Keisan's Byzantine Pottery." In *Tell Keisan, 1971–1976,* edited by Jacques Briend and Jean-Baptiste Humbert, pp. 51–99. Fribourg, 1980. Study of fifth- to sixth-century wares in northern Israel.
Metzger, Catherine. *Les ampoules à eulogie du Musée du Louvre.* Paris, 1981. Recent survey of pilgrim flasks.
Riley, John A. "Pottery from the First Season of Excavation in the Caesarea Hippodrome." *Bulletin of the American Schools of Oriental Research,* no. 218 (April 1975): 25–63. Statistical treatment of finds at Caesarea.
Riley, John A. "The Coarse Pottery from Berenice." In *Excavations at Sidi Khrebish, Benghazi (Berenice),* edited by J. A. Lloyd, vol. 2, pp. 91–467. Libya Antiqua, Supplement 5. Tripoli, 1979. Classification of standard amphora types (see especially pp. 112–236 and appendices, pp. 419–449).
Smith, Robert H., and Leslie P. Day. *Final Report on the College of Wooster Excavations in Area IX, the Civic Complex, 1979–1985.* Pella of the Decapolis, vol. 2. Wooster, Ohio, 1989. Useful for sixth- to eighth-century regional wares in Jordan (especially pp. 100–117).
Vitto, Fanny. "Potters and Pottery Manufacture in Roman Palestine." *Bulletin of the Institute of Archaeology, London,* no. 23 (1986): 47–64. Covers Jewish usages in the Late Roman period.
Waagé, Frederick O., ed. *Antioch-on-the-Orontes,* vol. 4.1, *Ceramics and Islamic Coins.* Princeton, 1948. The type site for Syria (especially pp. 4, 43–59).
Watson, P. M. "Jerash Bowls: Study of a Provincial Group of Byzantine Fine Ware." In *Jerash Archaeological Project,* vol. 2, *Fouilles de Jérash, 1984–1988,* edited by Fawzi Zayadine, pp. 223–261. Paris, 1989. Covers late regional painted wares.

JOHN W. HAYES

Ceramics of the Islamic Period

The seventh to eleventh centuries in the Near East is not a monolithic period in either historical or ceramic terms. In Palestine, these centuries cover the end of Byzantine rule (up to 640), the Umayyad period (c. 640–750), the 'Abbasid period (c. 750–969, during the latter part of which the country was ruled by the Tulunids and Ikhshidids), and the Fatimid period (c. 969–1099). To date neither comprehensive ceramic sequences covering these centuries in all parts of the Near East nor definitive regional typological distinctions have been established.

The study of Islamic pottery has been plagued by problems of terminology and historical biases. Historically based typological divisions (e.g., Umayyad, 'Abbasid, Fatimid) are inaccurate because changes in pottery rarely coincide with political events. Though excavations in Israel have demonstrated that the Muslim conquest was not accompanied by widespread destructions, it is still generally held that the transition from Umayyad to 'Abbasid rule in the mid-eighth century marked the beginning of a dramatic decline in Palestine's prosperity because the capital was transferred from Damascus to Baghdad. In archaeological terms, however, this has been a self-fulfilling prophecy: post-Umayyad remains have not been found because it was assumed that they do not exist. Part of the failure to identify these remains in the archaeological record in Israel has been the misdating of Islamic ceramic types by archaeologists, many of whom have ignored the clearer sequence in Jordan (e.g., Pella, Amman, Ḥesban, 'Aqaba).

Islamic pottery has traditionally been studied from an art historical perspective, with an emphasis on whole glazed vessels, at the expense of the fragmentary and often unglazed material recovered on excavations. Palestinian sites from which important Islamic ceramic material is published include Ḥesban, Pella, 'Aqaba, the Amman Citadel, Khirbat al-Mafjar, Abu Ghosh, Capernaum, Ramla, Caesarea, Tiberias, Khirbet Kerak, and Neṣṣana. Key sites outside Palestine include Usais in Syria, Samarra and Susa in Iraq, Fustat in Egypt, Istanbul/Constantinople in Turkey, and Siraf in Iran. This article focuses on the Islamic types characteristic of Palestine. The lack of well-excavated and published material leaves open the question of whether some of the eighth- and ninth-century types described here continued into the tenth and eleventh centuries.

Seventh-Century Types. Byzantine ceramic types continued without significant changes until the end of the seventh century: Late Roman Red Wares; Fine Byzantine Ware

CERAMICS: Islamic Period. Figure 1. *Islamic pottery types.* Black stone bowl (no. 8); red-painted basin fragments (no. 4); and a channel-nozzle oil lamp (no. 11). (After P. V. Corbo, *Gli scavi di Kh. siyar el-Ghanam (campo dei Pastori) e I Monasteri dei Dintorni,* Jerusalem, 1995, fig. 40)

bowls (see below) with incised wavy lines and jars, jugs, and juglets with incised gashes; "Gaza" amphoras, the latest of which have a very short neck and pointed base; and large candlestick lamps, "Persian" (wheelmade) lamps, and Jerash lamps. Painted decoration was rare, except in the case of dark-surfaced, white-painted bag-shaped storejars from Palestine and painted Coptic wares from Egypt and their imitations (e.g., Jerash bowls). Aside from the painted wares, all of these types disappeared sometime between the late seventh and mid-eighth centuries.

Fine Byzantine Ware. A group of vessels of the mid-sixth–tenth centuries, distinguished in form, fabric, and surface treatment, are known as Fine Byzantine Ware. In the early eighth century, the repertoire of open vessels was expanded to include a wide variety of shallow dishes and plates. The burnishing characteristic of the Byzantine period continued, but painted black, white, and/or red designs were sometimes added, perhaps reflecting Coptic ceramic influence. The walls of the vessels tend to be thinner and more delicate than was usual in the sixth and seventh centuries. Islamic small bowls and cups also differ from Byzantine examples in having rounded, flat, or disk bases, and in lacking the incised wavy-line decoration. Some have deep, hemispherical bodies and eggshell-thin walls. Local variants of these deep cups, with thicker walls and combed bands, are common at Islamic sites in Israel's Negev desert.

Black Stone and Ceramic Bowls. One of the characteristic bowl types of the eighth and ninth centuries is the black bowl with a broad, flat base and straight walls (see figure 1). Many have ledge handles and are decorated on the exterior with incised linear designs. The material is either a hard, dark-colored stone described as steatite, or soapstone, or a dark, burnished, handmade ceramic. A related and contemporary group of bowls that seems to have been used as cooking vessels is distinguished by its lack of decoration, large size, and blackened exterior. The type may have its origins in the northwest Hijaz, where similar unfinished bowls have been found in association with 'Abbasid pottery at steatite mines.

Kerbschnitt Bowls. *Kerbschnitt,* which means "cut-ware," describes a group of thick-walled, handmade bowls decorated with deeply cut patterns (see figure 2). The decorative technique seems to be inspired by woodcarving, while the form is clearly related to the contemporary black bowls described above. The cut patterns became cruder during the course of the 'Abbasid period.

Red-Painted Ware. Red-painted jars and basins made of a thick, buff fabric were common in northern Israel, Jordan, and Syria during the eighth and ninth centuries (see figure 1). Their painted designs often consist of spirals, wavy lines, and branch or tree motifs. Bowls are also found decorated with red-painted designs, though they usually

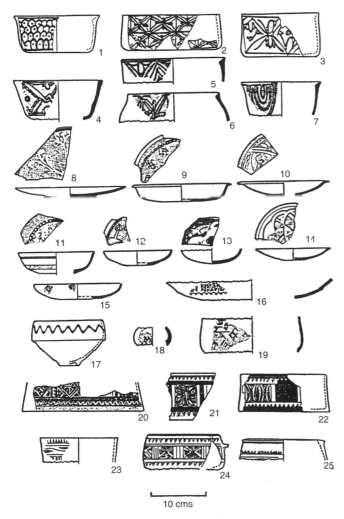

CERAMICS: Islamic Period. Figure 2. *Islamic pottery types.* Examples of painted Islamic variants of Fine Byzantine ware bowls (nos. 8-16, 19); red-painted bowls (1-3); and Kerbschnitt bowls (nos. 20-25). (After Baramki, 1944, fig. 6)

by the Ummayads in the first half of the eighth century. However, these "earliest levels" at Ramla probably represent an expansion of the site in the ʿAbbasid period because neither Mefjer ware nor glazed pottery has been found in Umayyad levels at sites in Jordan, such as Pella, Amman, and Hesban. Even at Khirbat al-Mafjar, the earliest glazed pottery and Mefjer ware were assigned by Baramki to the ʿAbbasid period (Baramki, 1994).

This type of buff ware was probably introduced into Palestine from ancient Mesopotamia (areas of modern Iran and Iraq), where it is found in seventh–eighth-century contexts. It continued to be produced through the Mamluk period, as indicated by its presence at Samarra in the ʿAbbasid period and at Hama in contexts dating to the twelfth–fourteenth centuries. Though no typology of Mefjer ware exists, changes can be distinguished over time. The carinated shapes of the ʿAbbasid jars and jugs are clearly inspired by metallic prototypes, as are the protruding knobs on the tops

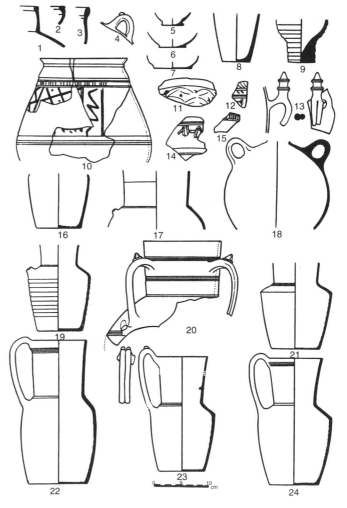

CERAMICS: Islamic Period. Figure 3. *"Mefjer Ware."* (After de Vaux and Steve, 1950, pl. C)

have thinner, hard-fired walls and more elaborate painted motifs. Some have the same flat-based, straight-walled form as the black bowls and *kerbschnitt* bowls described above (see figure 2). The designs on this group also recall the latter's cut patterns and the incisions on the former.

Buff Ware. Sometime in the second half of the eighth century, a new group of vessels made of a porous buff, cream, or greenish-white fabric appeared in Palestine. Archaeologists in Israel use the term *Mefjer ware* to describe jars and jugs made of this fabric, which often have molded, impressed, incised, and/or applied decoration (see figure 3). The ware takes its name from the site Khirbat al-Mafjar, where it was found by D. C. Baramki (who did not use the term). According to Myriam Rosen-Ayalon and Avraham Eitan (1969), both glazed pottery and Mefjer ware were present in the earliest levels at Ramla, which was founded of their handles and their incised or impressed decoration. The jars and jugs of the twelfth–fourteenth centuries have rounded bodies and elaborate, barbotine decoration that combines incised and molded designs and applied and impressed clay strips.

Though the term *Mefjer ware* is sometimes used by archaeologists in Israel to describe any Islamic vessel made of a light-colored fabric, it properly refers only to the decorated jars and jugs described above. Mahesh ware, which was identified by Donald S. Whitcomb at 'Aqaba, represents another group of light-colored Islamic vessels (Whitcomb, 1989b). Like Mefjer ware, Mahesh ware is characterized by its light-colored fabric. However, it includes such open shapes as cups, bowls, and basins and has simple decoration consisting of occasional comb-incised bands. Mahesh ware dates to the 'Abbasid period and has been found at many of the eighth–ninth-century settlements in the southern Negev.

Glazed Pottery. Aside from an occasional piece of Parthian glazed ware and the seventh-century lead-glazed wares from the area of Constantinople, glazed pottery is rarely found outside Iran and Iraq before the eighth century. Glazing is usually applied to the interiors of bowls, though it also occurs on the exteriors of jars, jugs, and oil lamps. [*See* Lamps.] In the eighth and early ninth centuries, Coptic glazed ware was produced in Egypt. It is decorated with brown and black painted designs on a white slip, with or without a transparent glaze, and covered with a green or brown glaze. The earliest locally produced glazed pottery in Palestine has a monochrome green or yellow glaze or is decorated with polychrome splash glaze (including any combination of brown, yellow, white, green, purple, and black).

Monochrome and splash glazes made their first appearance in Palestine during the 'Abbasid period, perhaps in the early ninth century. Whitcomb (1989a) has noted that similar polychrome splash-glazed wares were produced elsewhere during the ninth and tenth centuries. One of these is Egyptian Faiyumi ware, which is characterized by its bold, radiating stripes of color (see figure 4). Another is Hijazi ware, which, as its name suggests, seems to have been produced in Arabia. Its dark, red-orange fabric is decorated with bold polychrome spirals and cross-hatched designs. The Red Splash wares common at 'Aqaba, which also fall into this category, include examples decorated with incised (sgraffito) designs. The ceramic types characteristic of Samarra in this period include white-glazed wares, and blue-green glazed barbotine storage jars, which may have served as specialized containers for *dibs*, or "date honey." The Samarran wares, which are common at sites like Siraf, may derive from Sasanian prototypes. [*See* Sasanians.] During the Fatimid period, luster ware (glazed) was a popular luxury item, with local variants produced in Egypt and around the Near East. It derives its name from its shiny metallic gold designs on a white background. During the ninth and tenth centuries, glazed cooking wares appeared in Palestine.

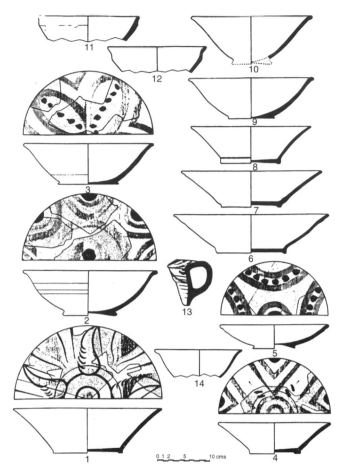

CERAMICS: Islamic Period. Figure 4. *Polychrome splash-glazed ware.* (After de Vaux and Steve, 1950, pl. A)

They are represented by globular cooking pots and open casseroles made of a brittle, dark, red-brown ware with a dark-brown or dark-purple glaze on the interior.

Oil Lamps. Mold-made "channel-nozzle" oil lamps were common in Palestine during the Islamic period (see figure 1). The name refers to a channel that connects the filling hole and the wick hole. Though these lamps vary from region to region within Palestine, general morphological changes can be distinguished during the course of the period. The lamps of the seventh and early eighth centuries still have the low circular ring base and elongated, oval body of their Byzantine predecessors. They have a small knob handle and are sometimes decorated with a Greek or an Arabic inscription, in the Byzantine tradition. During the course of the eighth–tenth centuries, the body became taller and shorter, and the nozzle became more pointed. The handle grew larger and became tongue shaped. The low ring base, which often contains delicate relief patterns, mirrored the outline of the pointed oval body. The relief decoration on the upper half of the body usually consists of floral or geometric motifs, such as the grapevine (Arndt, 1987). By the ninth and tenth centuries, these lamps were sometimes covered with a monochrome green glaze.

Conclusion. Many of the changes that occurred in the ceramic repertoires of the seventh–eleventh centuries should be understood in light of the reorientation of trade away from the Mediterranean world to the Near and Far East. The fine red-slipped pottery of the Roman world was superceded by Egyptian-inspired painted wares and glazed pottery influenced by Sasanian wares and Chinese imports. By the eleventh century, the subtle interplay of these changes had transformed the pottery of the Near East, especially in the western areas, where contacts with the Mediterranean world had formerly been strongest.

[*Many of the sites mentioned are the subject of independent entries.*]

BIBLIOGRAPHY

Arndt, M. B. "Lucerne arabe con decorazione 'a vite' dallo scavo della Probatica." *Studium Biblicum Franciscanum/Liber Annuus* 37 (1987): 241–289. Survey of Islamic channel-nozzle oil lamps decorated with the grapevine motif.

Baramki, Dimitri C. "The Pottery from Kh. el Mefjer." *Quarterly of the Department of Antiquities in Palestine* 10 (1944): 65–103. This site provides the most important published corpus of Islamic pottery in Palestine.

Hodges, Richard, and David Whitehouse. *Mohammed, Charlemagne, and the Origins of Europe: Archaeology and the Pirenne Thesis.* Ithaca, N.Y., 1983. Reevaluation of the evidence for contacts between the Mediterranean world and the Near East after the Muslim conquest, with a description of the excavations at Siraf.

Magness, Jodi. *Jerusalem Ceramic Chronology, circa 200–800 CE.* Sheffield, 1993. Typology of the late Roman, Byzantine, and Islamic pottery of Jerusalem.

Magness, Jodi. "The Dating of the Black Ceramic Bowl with a Depiction of the Torah Shrine from Nabratein." *Levant* 26 (1994): 199–206. The starting point for a reevaluation of the dating of Islamic pottery.

Rosen-Ayalon, Myriam, and Avraham Eitan. *Ramla Excavations: Finds from the VIIIth Century C.E.* Jerusalem, 1969. Catalog of an exhibition at the Israel Museum in Jerusalem; the only publication to date of the finds from the Ramla excavations.

Sarre, Friedrich P. T. *Ausgrabungen von Samarra,* vol. 2, *Die Keramik von Samarra.* Berlin, 1925. The capital of the 'Abbasid Empire from 836–882 CE, Samarra thus provides a fixed point for the pottery (especially the glazed wares) found there. Still the basic publication.

Sauer, James A. "The Pottery of Jordan in the Early Islamic Period." In *Studies in the History and Archaeology of Jordan,* vol. 1, edited by Adnan Hadidi, pp. 329–337. Amman, 1982. Synthetic overview of the pottery types of Jordan from the Umayyad to Fatimid periods.

Vaux, Roland de, and A.-M. Stève. *Fouilles à Qaryet el-'Enab, Abū Gôsh, Palestine.* Paris, 1950. Abu Ghosh is still the type-site for 'Abbasid pottery in Israel.

Walmsley, Alan. "The Umayyad Pottery and Its Antecedents." In *Pella in Jordan 1: An Interim Report on the Joint University of Sydney and the College of Wooster Excavations at Pella, 1979–1981,* edited by Anthony W. McNicoll et al., pp. 143–157. Canberra, 1982. The excavations at Pella provide one of the most accurately dated corpora of Umayyad pottery.

Walmsley, Alan. "Architecture and Artefacts from 'Abbasid Fihl." In *Bilād al-Shām during the Abbāsīd Period: Proceedings of the Fifth Bilād al-Shām Conference,* vol. 2, edited by Muhammad Adnan al-Bakhit

and Robert Schick, pp. 1–19. Amman, 1991. Up-to-date discussion of eighth- and ninth-century ceramic types, based on the evidence from Pella.

Watson, P. M. "Ceramic Evidence for Egyptian Links with Northern Jordan in the Sixth–Eighth Centuries AD." In *Trade, Contact, and the Movement of Peoples in the Eastern Mediterranean: Studies in Honour of J. Basil Hennessy,* edited by Stephen Bourke and Jean-Paul Descoeudres, pp. 303–320. Sydney, 1995. Attempt to define and date some of the Early Islamic ceramic types of Egypt and Palestine, including Egyptian Red Slip A, B, and C Wares; Coptic Painted Ware; and bag-shaped storejars.

Whitcomb, Donald S. "Khirbet al-Mafjar Reconsidered: The Ceramic Evidence." *Bulletin of the American Schools of Oriental Research,* no. 271 (1988): 51–67. Reevaluation of the dating of the site's pottery.

Whitcomb, Donald S. "Coptic Glazed Ceramics from the Excavations at Aqaba, Jordan." *Journal of the American Research Center in Egypt* 26 (1989a): 167–182. Discussion of Coptic glazed ware and related wares.

Whitcomb, Donald S. "Mahesh Ware: Evidence of Early Abbasid Occupation from Southern Jordan." *Annual of the Department of Antiquities of Jordan* 33 (1989b): 269–285. Defines this category of Islamic pottery on the basis of evidence from his excavations at 'Aqaba.

JAMES A. SAUER and JODI MAGNESS

CEREALS. The greatest proportion of the diet of the ancient Near East, as today, was supplied by cereals. These annual grasses were likely the first plants cultivated for food: the signs of domestication appear earliest for wheat and barley. Rye may also have been domesticated in the Near East (probably in Anatolia), though, like oats (whose origin is uncertain), it did not become a substantial crop. Millet cultivation appeared only in the first millennium BCE. Two other cereals, rice and sorghum, were transplanted from Asia and Africa, respectively, during the Hellenistic and Roman centuries.

Cereals were initially gathered from bounteous naturally occurring stands during the Epipaleolithic period for thousands of years prior to domestication. Gathering unconsciously selected for ears that resisted shattering, a crucial characteristic for the seed's dissemination among wild grains. Some carbonized seed remains from Pre-Pottery Neolithic (PPN) villages show fracture patterns produced by human threshing rather than natural shattering—unambiguous proof of cultivation. What motivated the transition from cereal gathering in the wild to deliberate cultivation remains an open question. Nevertheless, human sowing, harvesting, and threshing cemented the shift to nonshattering (nonbrittle) ears and brought about other changes in growth habit (abandonment of germination inhibition so that seeds sprout upon planting at any time) and morphology (increased size of grains and decreased attachment of grains in their spikelets). Morphological changes permit paleoethnobotanists to differentiate between wild and domesticated types in the archaeological record. [*See* Ethnobotany; Paleobotany.] Because wheat and barley are self-pollinating, the changes wrought by domestication were more readily secured from one generation to the next.

Morphologically distinct cereals appear at about 9000 BCE: Netiv ha-Gedud and Gilgal in Israel's Jordan Valley have produced domesticated barley, as has Ganj Dareh in western Iran. [See Jordan Valley.] Domesticated wheat (einkorn and emmer, see below) occurs at the Syrian steppe region sites of Aswad and Abu Hureyra, as well as at Çayönü in Turkey. [See Çayönü.] Prior to this PPN emergence of farming, wild grain seeds are known from the Epipaleolithic period in Jordan at Abu Hureyra, to its north at Mureybet, and at Naḥal Oren on Israel's Mt. Carmel spur. [See Mureybet; Naḥal Oren.] Paleoethnobotanists can trace the subsequent spread of agriculture throughout the Near East and beyond. Before the end of the Neolithic period, villages cultivated grain on Cyprus and in Greece. [See Cyprus.] By the end of the third millennium, barley and wheat had spread throughout the western Mediterranean basin, the Nile Valley, and central Europe.

Seeds and floral parts are preserved predominantly in carbonized form, accidentally (over)heated but not burned. Occasionally, seed impressions are found in baked clay. More rarely, fully desiccated kernels are recovered. Vegetal remains are routinely retrieved through simple flotation, in which water is used to separate carbonized material from soil samples.

Morphology. At the head of the cereal stalk stands the ear: an arrangement of flowers in a compound spike. The ear consists of spikelets arranged on a central axis or rachis. If brittle (shattering as in wild species), the ear breaks up into its component spikelets. If tough (nonshattering, as in most domesticated forms), the rachis remains intact until threshing, which produces random fractures. Thus, rachis fragments can be diagnostic of domestication. The spikelet contains the flower enfolded by the glumes, which can be strong and hold the grain tightly in the spikelet (glume wheats), or weak, permitting the grain to separate readily from the spikelet (free-threshing wheats). The floral parts themselves are surrounded by two protective layers (lemma and palea), which are either fused to the grain as it develops (hulled barley) or fail to adhere (naked barley). The grain itself is a layered structure in which the active seed is encased by a number of coats, the outermost of which is called the bran.

Wheat (*Triticum* L.). Archaeological literature catalogs an assortment of wheats by a variety of names: the older literature possesses even more terminology, as the botanical classification scheme has been recently simplified. Three of the four chromosomally distinct species of wheat regularly appear in ancient Near Eastern contexts. Within each species, subspecies differentiate themselves by the characteristics of their glume attachment.

Einkorn (*T. monococcum* L.) varieties, both wild (subspecies *boeoticum*) and cultivated (subspecies *monococcum*), are diploid glume wheats. A crucial component of the earliest agriculture, einkorn's place in the village pantry gave way to more productive species. Better suited to poorer soils, einkorn does not have attractive rising qualities when baked as bread.

Emmer and durum (*T. turgidum* L.) appear as wild emmer (subspecies *dicoccides*), cultivated emmer (subspecies *dicoccum*), and durum (subspecies *durum*). These are tetraploid wheats that include both glume (emmer) and free-threshing varieties (durum). Emmer belongs to the preagricultural and early agricultural crop medley and constitutes the principal wheat of the prehistorical period. It continued to sustain Egypt until Hellenistic times. Durum (hard wheat, macaroni wheat) evolved from emmer early on and became the dominant wheat of the Mediterranean basin, probably because of its free-threshing quality.

Bread wheat and spelt (*T. aestivum* L.) appear in cultivated varieties only, likely derived from a cross between a wheat of the species *turgidum* and a wild grass; bread wheat (subspecies *vulgare*) and spelt (subspecies *spelta*) are hexaploid wheats. Bread (common, vulgar) wheat is free-threshing. Finds indicate its availability to Neolithic farmers. Apparently, bread wheat did not become an important crop in the Near East until modern times, perhaps because of its susceptibility to bird predation or seed loss during harvest. Spelt appeared in about 5000 BCE, but finds are numerous only in Europe.

Barley (*Hordeum sativum* var. or *Hordeum vulgare* L.). Although terminological ambiguity exists, barley is taxonomically much simpler than wheat: a single diploid species with variants based on the number of grains that develop at each site on the rachis. Apart from the wild variety (*H. spontaneum*), the barleys also differentiate themselves on the basis of the fusion of the hull and the grain.

In two-row barley (*H. sativum* var. *distichum*) only one grain develops at each attachment on the rachis, resulting in two rows of fruitful spikelets, like its wild progenitor. Most two-row barleys are hulled. Their grains appear among the earliest cultivars at the inception of agriculture. Six-row barley (*H. sativum* var. *hexistichum*) also appeared early, yet subsequent to the two-row variety at a number of sites (e.g., Ali Kosh in southwest Iran). [See Ali Kosh.] The six rows are produced by three fertile spikelets at each attachment of the rachis and may have arisen as a mutation under irrigated conditions, which meet the water needs of the extra flowers. By the fourth millennium, it had replaced the two-row variety as the dominant cereal throughout Mesopotamia, presumably because of its higher yield. The occasional preservation of triplet spikelets and subtle differences in seed shape permit paleoethnobotanists to differentiate between the two varieties. Six-row also occurs as a naked grain (var. *nudum*) in the prehistoric periods but declines inexplicably later on.

Production. Wheat demands better soil conditions than barley: well-drained clayey soils that hold more moisture and possess greater nitrogen content. Barley does better than wheat on less fertile soils and those with higher salinity or alkalinity and under more arid conditions. Both cereals are broadcast sown or deposited by dibbling or seed plow, usually after the tilling of the field in early winter (approximately November–January). Harrowing covers the seed, if broadcast. Repeated irrigations follow in Mesopotamia, while rain-fed agriculture hopes for abundant and well-timed precipitation. Weeding heightens yields, reduces undesirable seeds in the harvest, and provides a fodder resource.

Harvest takes place by uprooting or reaping with a sickle. Barley matures more rapidly than wheat, and its harvest is first. Thus, sowing both barley and wheat can serve to stretch the harvest season in order better to accommodate the labor supply. Sheaves are transported to the threshing floor, and the stalks are beaten, trampled, or sledged to separate ears from straw and to disarticulate the ears. Raking and winnowing ensue, successively refining the product, followed by various grades of sieving. The grain is then packed for transport and storage.

Archaeology can identify numerous tools and installations employed in grain growing. These include plowpoints, hoes, sickles and sickle blades, threshing floors, and storage facilities such as pithoi, stone-lined or plastered grain pits, silos, and granaries. [See Granaries and Silos.]

Depending upon the species of grain, a variable number of additional steps intercede before consumption. Kernels of glume wheats must be removed from the spikelets. This process normally involves parching in an oven. The brittle chaff is then broken away by pounding in a mortar. Additional episodes of sieving and hand sorting result in clean grain ready for food preparation. Free-threshing wheat and barley obviate parching and pounding. The most common species of barley, however, requires dehulling for most foods. The hull is removed by pounding moistened kernels. Sieving cleans the grain from the husks. Freed of spikelets and hulls, cereals are processed into a huge variety of foodstuffs, from bulgur to bread and porridge to beer. Mortars and pestles, cooking pots, ovens, bread molds, beer strainers, and saddle querns are notable artifacts of grain processing.

The ancient Near East's preoccupation with cereals extends beyond their cultivation, of course, to their control. Its agrarian societies were based chiefly on the wealth of cereal fields. Grains were the fundamental building block of the economy and principal medium of taxation as well. Cereal production and distribution also underlie an enormous range of ideas and their literary and artistic expression.

[See also Agriculture.]

BIBLIOGRAPHY

Charles, M. P. "Introductory Remarks on the Cereals." *Bulletin on Sumerian Agriculture* 1 (1984): 17–31. Compact and lucid treatment of botanical terminology and characteristics of wheat and barley.
Hillman, Gordon. "Traditional Husbandry and Processing of Archaic Cereals in Recent Times: The Operations, Products, and Equipment which Might Feature in Sumerian Texts. Part I: The Glume Wheats," and "Part II: The Free-Threshing Cereals." *Bulletin on Sumerian Agriculture* 1 (1984): 114–152; 2 (1985): 1–31. Meticulous and detailed presentation of cereal production and processing, from fieldwork to food preparation, based on ethnographic work in Turkey.
Miller, Naomi F. "The Origins of Plant Cultivation in the Near East." In *The Origin of Agriculture: An International Perspective*, edited by C. Wesley Cowan and Patty Jo Watson, pp. 39–58. Smithsonian Series in Archaeological Inquiry, 16. Washington, D.C., 1992. Review of the latest archaeobotanical finds, with an emphasis on the methodological aspects of theories of agricultural origins.
Renfrew, Jane M. *Palaeoethnobotany: The Prehistoric Food Plants of the Near East and Europe*. New York, 1973. Classic text introduces its discipline and discusses with illustrations each of the major genera and species of domesticated and edible wild plants, their origins, identification (with detailed morphology), cultivation, and use.
Zohary, Daniel, and Maria Hopf. *The Domestication of Plants in the Old World: The Origin and Spread of Cultivated Plants in West Asia, Europe, and the Nile Valley*. 2d ed. Oxford, 1993. Synthesis of crop-plant evolution combining data from archaeology and the distribution of living plants. Covers cereals, pulses, oil and fiber crops, fruit trees and nuts, vegetables and tubers, condiments and dyes, as well as wild fruits.

DAVID C. HOPKINS

CHALCEDON (modern Kadiköy), site located on a small peninsula on the Asiatic side of the southern end of the Bosporus, on a strait 32 km (20 mi.) long, between the Black Sea and the Propontis, or Sea of Marmara. The city was founded in 685 BCE by colonists from the Dorian city of Megara, reportedly led by the colony's founder, Archias. Chalcedon was only a short distance across the Bosporus from Byzantium (modern Istanbul), which the Megarians also founded in about 668 BCE, on the Thracian-European side (Herodotus, *Hist.* 4.144; Strabo, *Geog.* 12.4.2). Two rivers, the Himeros and the Chalcedon, flowed into the Bosporus on the east and west side of the peninsula, respectively, forming small natural harbors that have since silted up. The peninsula and part of the mainland (where Chrysopolis was located, farther north, across from Byzantium) were called Chalcedonia (Xenophon, *Anabasis* 6.6.38) and, later, Bithynia.

Byzantium had a large natural harbor and was in an ideal position to control the Bosporus and impose tolls on traffic entering and leaving the Black Sea. The ancients called Chalcedon the "city of the blind" because its Megarian founders had not selected that more advantageous site (Herodotus, 4.144; Strabo 7.6.2; Tacitus *Ann.* 12.63; Pliny, *Nat. Hist.* 5.149). However, it appears likely that Chalcedon was settled as an agricultural rather than a trading colony. Prehistoric remains suggest that it may originally have been a Thracian settlement. Chalcedon and her sister colony, Byzantium, controlled the Black Sea trading traffic (Dionysius of Byzantium, *Anaplus Bospori* 19–20). Chalcedon's prosperity was also based on copper mines and on semiprecious stones from the island of Chalcitis. Throughout much of their history, Chalcedon and Byzantium were closely allied. Participation in the Ionic rebellion against Persia resulted in the sacking and burning of Chalcedon in 494 BCE by the Phoenician fleet allied with Persia; the colonists then temporarily abandoned the city and, with the Byzantines, founded Mesambria on the west coast of the Black Sea (Herodotus 6.33). During the ascendancy of Athens following the Persian wars, Chalcedon was a member of Athen's Delian League; it paid an extremely large tribute to Athens derived from tolls exacted from Black Sea trade. In 416, Chalcedon's forces defeated the Bithynians (Diodorus 12.82.2). During the late fifth century BCE, Chalcedon was one of the Greek cities that sided with Sparta. The city was again subjugated by Persia in 387 BCE but was later liberated by Alexander (Arrian, *Anabasis* 3.24.5). Lysimachos, one of Alexander's successors, controlled Chalcedon until his overthrow in 281 BCE. The fact that Byzantium and Chalcedon minted copper coins in common during the third century BCE indicates that they had formed a *sympoliteia* (a "civic union") that may have been in effect in the fourth century BCE.

Chalcedon maintained its freedom through much of the fifth and fourth centuries BCE. It became a free city in 74 BCE, when Nicomedes IV of Bithynia bequeathed his kingdom to the Romans. Freedom did not mean independence, but rather the privilege of maintaining ancestral laws and customs and immunity from tribute and a military garrison. Pompey organized the Roman province of Bithynia-Pontus in 65–64 BCE. Byzantium was also part of it, although technically it was located on the Thracian-European side of the Bosporus. The Goths sacked Chalcedon during the reigns of Valerian (c. 258 CE) and Gallienus (267 CE).

When, in 330 CE, the emperor Constantine founded Constantinople as the *Roma Nova*, "New Rome," on the site of Byzantium Chalcedon was relegated to little more than its suburb. In 365–366 CE, Chalcedon supported Procopius, the imperial rival of Valens. After Procopius was overthrown, Emperor Valens had Chalcedon's walls taken apart and used the stone to construct Roman baths, the *Constantinianae thermae*, at Constantinople, as well as an aqueduct (Ammianus Marcellinus, *Historia Augusta* 31.1.4; Socrates, *Historia Ecclesiastica* 4.8). Chalcedon is chiefly known from late antiquity as the site of the Fourth Ecumenical Council, the Council of Chalcedon, convened on 8 October 451 CE in the church of St. Euphemia (martyred under Diocletian in Chalcedon in 303). More than five hundred bishops and imperial representatives attended. The Chalcedonian creed was presented during the fifth session on 22 October. In its final form it emphasized that Jesus Christ was fully human and fully divine and that these two natures should not be confused. Chalcedon was captured by the Persians in 615 and in 626 was taken by the Arabs during their siege of Constantinople.

The site of Chalcedon-Kadiköy has never been systematically excavated. The remains of the ancient city still visible in the sixteenth century have since disappeared. Greek and Latin inscriptions from Chalcedon, now widely scattered, have been collected and edited by Reinhold Merkelbach (1980). Four inscriptions from the hieron, or sanctuary, of Zeus Ouranios and the Twelve Gods have survived, some in the Chalcidian dialect (Merkelbach, 1980, pp. 26–34), but it is a matter of dispute whether this hieron, which existed as early as the third century BCE, was located on the Asiatic (Polybius 4.39.5–6) or European side (scholion on Apollonius Rhodius 2.531–533) of the Bosporus (Long, 1987, pp. 55–57, 153–155). Marble fragments from an ancient temple were incorporated into a castle built in about 1150 CE in a village called Anadolu Kavağli, but the site from which the fragments were taken has never been identified. An oracle of Apollo is also known to have existed in Chalcedon. The Byzantine remains of Chalcedon, including a palace, a hippodrome, and several churches, including St. Euphemia, were destroyed by the Persians when they captured Chalcedon in 615 CE.

BIBLIOGRAPHY

Grant, Michael. *A Guide to the Ancient World: A Dictionary of Classical Place Names.* New York, 1986. See pages 137–138.

Jones, A. H. M. *The Cities of the Eastern Roman Provinces.* 2d ed. Oxford, 1971. Definitive study of the Greek cities of the eastern Roman Empire. See pages 148–152, 159, 164–165.

Long, Charlotte R. *The Twelve Gods of Greece and Rome.* Études Préliminaires aux Religions Orientales dans l'Empire Romain, vol. 107. Leiden, 1987. Discusses the hieron, or sanctuary, to the Twelve Gods, which may have been located in or near Chalcedon. See pages 55–57, 153–154, 186, 217–218.

Magie, David. *Roman Rule in Asia Minor to the End of the Third Century after Christ.* 2 vols. Princeton, 1950. The most important study of Asia Minor under the Romans, with a brief, but important, discussion of Chalcedon (see vol. 1, pp. 304–305).

Merkelbach, Reinhold. *Die Inschriften von Kalchedon.* Bonn, 1980. The only complete collection of Greek and Latin inscriptions, papyri, coins, and literary notices associated with Chalcedon.

Merle, Heinrich. *Die Geschichte der Städte Byzantion und Kalchedon von ihrer Gründung bis zum Eingreifen der Römer in die Verhältnisse des Ostens.* Kiel, 1916. The only extensive monograph on Chalcedon.

DAVID E. AUNE

CHALDEANS.

CHALDEANS. The Chaldeans were a group of tribes first clearly attested in the ninth century BCE in southern Mesopotamia. The name *Chaldeans* comes from the Greek *chaldaioi* (cf. Hebrew *kaśdîm*) and goes back to the term *kaldu* in Mesopotamian cuneiform sources. The Mesopotamians used the latter term to refer to both a people and a land.

Outside of a possible mention in an administrative document from the reign of the Assyrian king Tiglath-Pileser I (1114–1076 BCE), the Chaldeans appear first in an inscription of the Assyrian king Ashurnasirpal II (883–859 BCE) which refers to the land of Chaldea in connection with the king's military campaign into southern Mesopotamia in 878 BCE. The Chaldeans are best attested from the second half of the ninth century through to the middle of the seventh century BCE, but continue to be mentioned into the Persian period. The latest reference to a Chaldean tribe in cuneiform sources probably comes from the time of the Persian ruler Darius II (423–405 BCE). In biblical and classical sources the term *Chaldeans* came to refer to Babylonians in general and priests, magicians, astrologers, diviners, and other such scholars in particular.

When the Chaldeans first appear in the ninth century BCE, they are already well settled in southern Babylonia. Their origin and the manner in which they moved into southern Mesopotamia are not known, although it has sometimes been proposed that they came from eastern Arabia. Nothing is known of their language beyond a few names which appear to be West Semitic in origin. All the Chaldean kings of Babylonia bore traditional Babylonian names, as did most Chaldeans whose names are known. It has often been stated that the Chaldeans were a subgroup of the Arameans, but there is insufficient evidence to decide on this matter. The Mesopotamian sources clearly distinguished between the two groups, while frequently mentioning them next to one another. The Arameans first appear in southern Babylonia about a century after the Chaldeans; they were split into many more smaller tribes and were less inclined to adopt Babylonian customs and manners than Chaldeans. At times the two groups acted in alliance (generally against Assyria) and at other times were at enmity with one another. Aramaic was likely the predominant language in Mesopotamia from about the middle of the first millennium BCE and Chaldeans appear to have spoken either this or a dialect of it. This language came to be associated with them and was even on occasion called Chaldee. The Chaldeans spoke in Aramaic in *Daniel* 2:4, and *Daniel* 1:4 presumably intends to indicate Aramaic when referring to the "writings and language of the Chaldeans." [*See* Arameans; Aramaic Language and Literature.]

The Chaldeans were located primarily in southern and eastern Babylonia, and rarely appear outside of Babylonia. The Sealand, an area of swamps and marshes around the head of the Persian Gulf, and likely corresponding to the modern Hor el-Hammar marshes, came to be particularly identified with the Chaldean tribe of Bit-Yakin, and its rulers were sometimes called "king of the Sealand" in Assyrian sources. Because Elam bordered on the Sealand to the east, the Bit-Yakin were in frequent contact with that country and often turned to it for military support against the Assyrians and for refuge in time of flight from Assyrian punishment. [*See* Assyrians.]

Most Chaldeans probably lived a nomadic or seminomadic existence dependent upon animal husbandry, hunting, and small-scale agriculture. From the earliest times, at least some lived a settled existence. They are found dwelling in the major urban centers of Babylonia (Cutha, Hursagkalama, Kish, Nippur, Sippar, Uruk), and are said to have had numerous settlements. Sennacherib claims to have conquered 88 walled towns and 820 villages belonging to them, but some of these may simply have been settlements located in the general areas inhabited by the individual Chaldean tribes because several old Babylonian cult centers are included among the towns named by Sennacherib. [*See* Kish; Nippur; Uruk-Warka.]

Five Chaldean tribes are known: Bit-Amukani, Bit-Dak(k)uri, Bit-Yakin(i), Bit-Ša'alli, and Bit-Šilani. The latter two, however, are only attested from the reign of the Assyrian king Tiglath-Pileser III (744–727 BCE) through to that of Sennacherib (704–681 BCE). Many Chaldeans seem to have become "babylonianized," taking traditional Babylonian names, becoming involved in Babylonian political life, and turning to agriculture for their livelihood. Nevertheless, they maintained their tribal structure and distinct identity. Tribes were referred to as the "House of PN," with PN standing for the personal name of the eponymous ancestor of the tribe (e.g., Bit-Amukani, "house of Amukani"). Each tribe was headed by one individual, whose power and authority was such that Assyrian royal inscriptions sometimes referred to him as a "king." Led by their own sheikhs and less settled in particular locations than most Babylonians, the Chaldean tribes remained semi-independent of the central government. They often play a disruptive role in events and frequently led the opposition to Assyrian control of Babylonia. [*See* Babylon; Babylonians.]

The first quarter of the first millennium BCE was a time of political instability and economic weakness in Babylonia and the Chaldeans made use of this situation. Several tribal leaders gained control of the throne and came to be included in the canonical lists of Babylonian rulers. None of these individuals, however, succeeded in establishing a lasting dynasty. Each of the three major tribes provided at least one ruler who was recognized as king of Babylonia: Marduk-apla-usur (end of the ninth or early eighth century BCE); Eriba-Marduk of Bit-Yakin (at least nine years, ending no later than 760 BCE); Nabu-šuma-iškun of Bit-Dakkuri (c. 760–748 BCE); (Nabû)-mukin-zeri of Bit-Amukani (731–729 BCE); Marduk-apla-iddina II of Bit-Yakin (721–710 and 703 BCE), the Merodach-Baladan of the Hebrew scriptures; and Mušezib-Marduk of Bit-Dakkuri (692–689 BCE).

In addition to these individuals, the tribes provided several important rebel leaders in the fight against Assyria, in particular Nabu-zer-kitti-lišir (c. 680 BCE), Nabu-ušallim (c. 680–675 BCE), and Nabu-bel-šumati (during the Šamaš-šuma-ukin Revolt, 652–648 BCE); all three were descendents of Marduk-apla-iddina II, who was himself a descendent of the earlier ruler Eriba-Marduk. Although the time of the Neo-Babylonian Empire (625–539 BCE) has often been called the Chaldean period, there is in fact no evidence that the rulers of that time were Chaldeans or that Chaldeans played a major role in affairs of the period. It is unlikely, however, that their influence just disappeared after the installation of the new ruling dynasty.

The Chaldean tribes are frequently found in opposition to the central Babylonian administration and in particular in opposition to Assyrian forces who were trying either to gain or maintain control of Babylonia. The Chaldean tribes were thus targeted for punishment by Assyrian rulers. Assyrian royal inscriptions often mention the destruction of Chaldean settlements. They claim that almost a quarter of a million Chaldeans were deported from Babylonia during the reigns of Tiglath-Pileser III and Sargon II, and these deportations are known to have continued under Sennacherib. The deportees were resettled in Assyria proper and in other parts of the Assyrian Empire. The tribes of Bit-Ša'alli, Bit-Šilani, and Bit-Yakin were particularly hurt by deportations in the eighth century BCE. The various Chaldean tribes did not as a rule act in unison with other groups in Babylonia against Assyria, and this facilitated Assyrian domination. The Chaldeans were not always in opposition to Assyria; at times some served in the Assyrian army.

No archaeological remains have been discovered which can be assigned to the Chaldeans with any degree of certainty. Assyrian reliefs depict them engaged in animal husbandry (horses and cattle), and Assyrian inscriptions state that Chaldean leaders provided a wealth of goods as tribute to the Assyrian rulers (e.g., gold, silver, tin, bronze, precious stones, ivory, elephant hides, valuable woods, colored garments, and aromatic plants). Undoubtedly, the tribal leaders had profited handsomely from the trade routes which ran through the territories controlled by them, and in particular from the sea trade up the Persian Gulf.

Very little is known of Chaldean religious matters. Those rulers of Babylonia who were of Chaldean ancestry referred to the old, traditional gods of Babylonia in their inscriptions and built or restored temples for them. An unusual inscription vilifying the Chaldean ruler Nabu-šuma-iškun states that he despoiled Esagila, the temple of Marduk, the head of the Babylonian pantheon, at Babylon, and then installed in that temple the gods of the Sealand, the Chaldeans, and the Arameans. Nothing more is known specifically as to who these Chaldean gods were. Chaldeans appear to have honored their ancestors and were concerned for their remains. Marduk-apla-iddina II, for example, took the bones of his deceased ancestors with him when he fled to Elam from Assyrian forces in 700 BCE.

(There is no evidence of a connection between the modern people in Iraq known as Chaldeans, who speak a Neo-Aramaic dialect sometimes referred to as "Chaldean," and their ancient namesakes [see Solomon I. Sara, *A Description of Modern Chaldean*, Janua Linguarum, Series Practica, vol. 213, The Hague, 1974].)

BIBLIOGRAPHY

Brinkman, John A. "Merodach-Baladan II." In *Studies Presented to A. Leo Oppenheim, June 7, 1964*, edited by Robert D. Biggs and John A. Brinkman, pp. 6–53. Chicago, 1964. Detailed study of the career of the most fascinating of all Chaldean leaders.

Brinkman, John A. *A Political History of Post-Kassite Babylonia, 1158–722 B.C.* Analecta Orientalia, vol. 43. Rome, 1968. Definitive study of Babylonia during the twelfth through eighth centuries which includes a discussion of the various tribal groups in that country.

Brinkman, John A. "Babylonia, c. 1000–764 B.C." In *The Cambridge Ancient History*, vol. 3.1, edited by John Boardman et al, pp. 282–313. 2d ed. Cambridge, 1982.

Brinkman, John A. *Prelude to Empire: Babylonian Society and Politics, 747–626 B.C.* Occasional Publications of the Babylonian Fund, vol. 7. Philadelphia, 1984. Separately printed version of the author's chapter "Babylonia in the Shadow of Assyria, 747–626 B.C." in *The Cambridge Ancient History*, vol. 3.2, pp. 1–70, 2d ed. (Cambridge, 1991), with expanded notes and references.

Edzard, D. O. "Kaldu." In *Reallexikon der Assyriologie und Vorderasiatischen Archäologie*, vol. 5, pp. 291–297. Berlin and New York, 1977. Concise overview of the Chaldeans written by a noted German scholar in the standard reference work for Mesopotamian studies.

Frame, Grant. *Babylonia, 689–627 B.C.: A Political History*. Uitgaven van het Nederlands Historisch-Archaeologisch Instituut te Istanbul, vol. 69. Istanbul and Leiden, 1992.

Leemans, W. F. "Marduk-apal-iddina II, zijn tijd en zijn geslacht." *Jaarbericht van het Vooraziatisch-Egyptisch Genootschap "Ex Oriente Lux"* 10 (1945–1948): 432–455. Deals mainly with the Chaldean leader Marduk-apla-iddina II but also presents a useful summary of the history of the Chaldeans and a bibliography of earlier studies.

Zadok, Ran. "Zur Geographie Babyloniens während des sargonischen, chaldäischen, achämenidischen und hellenistischen Zeitalters." *Die Welt des Orients* 16 (1985): 19–79. Presents details about the areas and settlements inhabited by the Chaldean tribes (pp. 49–63).

GRANT FRAME

CHAMPOLLION, JEAN FRANÇOIS (1790–1832), first person to reconstruct the ancient Egyptian language. Having been a child prodigy with an insatiable appetite for languages, Champollion is generally credited with deciphering ancient Egyptian hieroglyphs (picture writing) in 1822 when he presented his paper *Lettre à Monsieur Dacier relative à l'alphabet des hiéroglyphes phonétiques* to the French Academy. Previous attempts at decipherment by Europeans were thwarted by the widely held opinion that hieroglyphs were allegorical cryptograms with encoded arcane information, which had to be "interpreted" rather than translated. This symbolic approach was so rooted in academic circles that Champollion himself was its proponent as late as 1821.

The discovery of a stela (commemorative stone) at Rosetta, near Alexandria, in July 1799 by Pierre Bouchard, an engineer in Napoleon's army and its subsequent surrender to the British after their defeat of the French forces in Egypt in 1801 made such an impression on Europeans that this monument, now known as the Rosetta Stone, became the focus of intense academic scrutiny.

The Rosetta Stone contains a decree issued by Egyptian priests in honor of the Macedonian Greek pharaoh of Egypt, Ptolemy V Epiphanes, in 196 BCE. The text is written in hieroglyphs, demotic (a cursive script), and ancient Greek. Working on the inscription from 1814 to 1818, Thomas Young, a British polymath, identified about eighty words appearing in all three versions. He communicated his findings to Champollion by letter and published them in a supplement (1819) to the *Encyclopedia Britannica*. Champollion never admitted in print his indebtedness to Young. However, Champollion's knowledge of Coptic (the latest form of the ancient Egyptian language) and Greek enabled him to surpass Young's work and to lay the scientific foundations upon which the systematic study of ancient Egyptian as a language is based. The initial work by Young and its perfection by Champollion are astounding because of the great number of hieroglyphs—more than seven thousand—that existed when the Rosetta Stone was written. By contrast, the earlier, classical periods of the ancient Egyptian language used seven hundred signs.

[*See also* Egyptian; Hieroglyphs.]

BIBLIOGRAPHY

Andrews, Carol. *The Rosetta Stone.* London, 1981.
Ziegler, Christiane. "Champollion et le déchiffrement des hiéroglyphes." In *Naissance de l'écriture: Cunéiformes et hiéroglyphes,* edited by Jean-Paul Boulanger, pp. 369–375. 4th ed. Paris, 1982.

ROBERT STEVEN BIANCHI

CHARIOTS. In the Near East the chariot was a light, open vehicle with two spoked wheels, drawn by horses yoked on either side of a draught pole. It was used primarily in warfare, but also in hunting and processions. The first known examples with these features appear in Anatolian glyptics of the early second millennium BCE, followed by those depicted on Syrian seals of the eighteenth and seventeenth centuries BCE.

In Mesopotamia the chariot had been preceded by disk-wheeled vehicles with both two and four wheels, pulled by asses or ass/hemione or ass/horse crosses. Five innovations gave the true chariot its superiority: the spoked wheel; the exclusive use of horse draft (with an adaptation of the yoke for this purpose); the replacement of the old nose-ring control by a proper horse bit; the use of the bow as a primary chariot weapon; and proportions permitting a crew of two to stand abreast.

Details of dimensions and construction before about 1000 BCE come from New Kingdom Egypt, where the chariot had been introduced from the Levant at some time during the Second Intermediate period. Large numbers of Egyptian and Asiatic chariots are illustrated in reliefs and paintings, and (all or parts of) eight actual chariots have survived, six of them from the tomb of Tutankhamun. These were con-

structed entirely of heat-bent wood and rawhide. Their D-shaped floors (about 1.00 m wide × 0.50 m deep) were made of interwoven thongs that not only helped to keep the bent-wood frame in tension, but also provided some springiness. The approximately hip-high siding, in profile shown as rounded or rectangular, extended around the sides and front, leaving the rear open for rapid mounting or dismounting. The siding was solid or fenestrated. Parade and royal chariots might have gilded and decorated sidings.

The light, fast vehicle was given stability by a rear axle and a wide wheel base (1.54–1.80 m). The long draft pole, which ran all the way under the body and helped to support it, was attached only at the front, by being lashed to the floor frame there. A pair of rods, dropped diagonally from the front railing to the draft pole, restricted the tendency of the floor frame and pole to pull apart in rough going and braced the front of the chariot. Two thongs (so-called yoke braces) extended from the pole to each arm of the yoke in order to keep the latter at right angles to the pole and to distribute tractive stress. The yoke, an element originally designed for bovids, was adapted to equine anatomy by means of yoke saddles. These wooden Y-shaped objects were fastened by their "handles" to the yoke, while their "legs," secured at either end by a crescentic strap across the front of the neck, lay along the shoulders of the horse and took the pull in a manner similar to that of the later horse collar.

Chariotry was an important military arm in this period. Two-man Asiatic and Egyptian chariots carrying archers were used as mobile firing platforms to run along the face of infantry to soften it up or to play a flanking or pursuing role (figure 1). Bow cases and quivers of arrows attached outside the chariot body provided reserve arms. The three-man chariots of the Hittites and their allies at the battle of Qadesh, depicted in Egyptian temple reliefs, carry driver, shield bearer, and spearman (quivers are absent) and must have served essentially as transports.

Evidence is scarce in the late second and early first millennia BCE, but Assyrian palace reliefs of the ninth–seventh

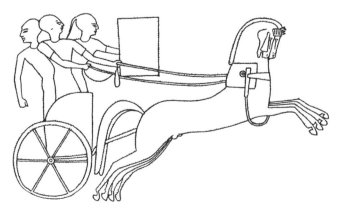

CHARIOTS. Figure 1. *Detail of a stone relief of Rameses III, from Medinet Habu.* (After Littauer and Crouwel, 1979, fig. 44)

centuries BCE furnish plentiful documentation. Cypriot chariot models and actual chariot remains of the eighth and seventh centuries BCE provide additional information. They illustrate solid-sided bodies strengthened by a central front-to-back partition. The partition was supported at its rear by a standing loop that could serve as a handhold for mounting as well as a fixture on which to hang a shield. Evidence persists for the woven-thong flooring of the body, which sometimes was large enough to accommodate a third or even a fourth man at the rear.

Ninth-century BCE Assyrian chariots (figure 2) appear to have had draft poles in the Y form documented by some later models from Cyprus and the Levant: two poles, one from each side of the chariot, come together in front to become a single pole to the yoke. The pole support/breastwork brace of the previous period was exchanged for a metal rod. A peapod-shaped, apparently rigid element, extending from the breastwork top to the yoke, further strengthened the traction system. By the ninth century BCE, draft teams appear to consist of three or four horses. Only two horses were under yoke, the third and fourth being outriggers.

The rear-axled chariot is still shown as a fast, mobile firing platform for flanking, pursuing, and harnessing. Because only two of the horses were under yoke, the vehicle remained quite maneuverable. Crossed quivers (containing bows and arrows and sometimes axes) were fixed outside the body, and a thrusting spear stood at the rear; the two last, being short-range weapons, were for use dismounted or from a standing vehicle. Protective armor was sometimes worn by both crew and horses.

Reliefs of Tiglath-Pileser III (745–727 BCE) and later Assyrian kings document a marked change in the chariot. The body evidently had a rectangular floor plan and was large enough to accommodate four men (two and two abreast). The iconographic evidence shows only a single pole with the then-prevailing four-horse team under one yoke; however, the fuller Cypriot documentation indicates that two poles might go to a single four-horse yoke or, more often, to two two-horse ones. The yoke saddles were then abandoned in favor of a shaped yoke, with bays for each horse's neck. A bow case was vertically attached at the chariot's front corners and a spear is still shown at the rear. The solid siding is often depicted as armored with small metal plates.

Assyrian chariots of the late eighth and seventh centuries BCE continue to be shown as firing platforms for archers, although they were less mobile, as a result of their greater size, heavier fabric, and the restrictions on maneuverability imposed by four horses under yoke. Under Ashurbanipal (668–627 BCE) archers are, for the first time, shown shooting from a stationary chariot.

Throughout the first half of the first millennium BCE, the chariots of other Near Eastern states (Urartian, Neo-Hittite, and Levantine) are usually shown resembling, in appearance and function, Assyrian models. By late in the first millennium BCE, military chariotry was largely replaced by mounted troops who had greater mobility, the ability to function in more rugged terrain, and economies of man- and animal power. The turreted and scythed chariots of the Achaemenids and others, mentioned by classical authors, are nowhere illustrated; it is known, however, that at the

CHARIOTS. Figure 2. *Detail of a stone relief of Ashurnasirpal II, from Nimrud.* (After Littauer and Crouwel, 1979, fig. 53)

battles of Cunaxa (401 BCE) and Gaugamela (331 BCE) they proved useless against prepared and disciplined Greek infantry. The chariots remaining in use were either processional ones or ones used in the traditional hunt, in which beaters drove the game from cover and across terrain suitable for the chariot to negotiate.

[*See also* Carts; Equids; Transportation; *and* Wheel.]

BIBLIOGRAPHY

Crouwel, J. H. "Chariots in Iron Age Cyprus." *Report of the Department of Antiquities, Cyprus* (1987): 101–118.

Littauer, M. A., and J. H. Crouwel. *Wheeled Vehicles and Ridden Animals in the Ancient Near East.* Leiden, 1979.

Littauer, M. A., and J. H. Crouwel. *Chariots and Related Equipment from the Tomb of Tut'ankhamūn.* Tut'ankhamūn Tomb Series, 3. Oxford, 1985.

Nagel, Wolfram. *Die mesopotamische Streitwagen und seine Entwicklung im ostmediterranen Bereich.* Berlin, 1966.

Piggott, Stuart. *Wagon, Chariot, and Carriage: Symbol and Status in the History of Transport.* New York, 1992. Includes a chapter on chariots and chariotry (pp. 337–368).

Spruytte, J. *Early Harness Systems.* Translated by M. A. Littauer. London, 1983. Includes experiments with reconstructions of Egyptian New Kingdom chariots (pp. 23–51).

J. H. CROUWEL and MARY AIKEN LITTAUER

CHOGHA ZANBIL (mod. Pers., "hill of the basket"; Elam., al Untash-Napirisha, "city of Untash-Napirisha"; Akk., Dûr Untash, "fortress of Untash"), Elamite royal city and religious center located on the plain of Khuzistan (Iran), some 40 km (25 mi.) southeast of Susa, on the bank of the Ab-e Diz River (32° N, 48°30′ E). The site covers about 100 ha (247 acres) and is composed of a central ziggurat (still standing at 25 m above the level of the plain) surrounded by three concentric walls (see figure 1). Built by King Untash-Napirisha (c. 1340–1300 BCE) early in his reign, in a previously unsettled area, it was mostly abandoned after the king's death. Discovered in 1935, Roland de Mecquenem excavated it on a limited scale (1935–1939, 1946) and Roman Ghirshman uncovered most of its remains (1951–1962).

Functionally, the site consists of two parts: a nearly 16-ha (40 acres) central temenos, or sacred precinct, enclosed by a wall and occupied by a ziggurat and several temples, that its incriptions (see below) call *Siyan-kuk* ("holy place")—the heart of the city and its *raison d'être;* and a royal city of about 85 ha (210 acres) that is protected by a rampart 4 km (2.5 mi.) long.

Ziggurat Compound. The center of the temenos is occupied by a ziggurat that is itself demarcated by a wall and surrounded by several cultic buildings. Built in mud brick with a baked-brick casing, the ziggurat is a square building measuring almost 100 m on each side, with its angles oriented to the cardinal points. Inscriptional and archaeological evidence indicates that its construction went through different phases, of which two have been clearly identified by Ghirshman.

Initially, it was not a ziggurat, but a monumental square building consisting of a large open court surrounded by rooms (see figure 2a).Access to the court was through large doors in the middle of each side that were guarded by bulls and winged griffons in glazed terra cotta. The rooms served as magazines, except on the southeast, where they composed two temples, A and B, both dedicated to the god Inshushinak (originally the god of the city of Susa). Presumably, different rituals were performed in each temple. This square building of the first phase, as well as the entire temenos, was dedicated to Inshushinak, distinguished by the epithet "lord of the *Siyan-kuk*."

Later in the king's reign, this unusual building was transformed into a ziggurat in the strict sense of the term (see figure 2b). Three concentric blocks of brick were erected in the central court to form the second, third, and fourth stories of the ziggurat. As the original square building became the first story, some of its rooms and Inshushinak's temple A were filled up and blocked; Inshushinak's temple B, however, remained in activity because it was entered from the parvis (enclosed court). The doors in the middle of each side of the original building were transformed into inner vaulted stairwells leading to the top of the first story—except on the southwest, where the stairwell went directly to the top of the second story; from there, another stairwell, possibly located on the southeast, led to the summit of the ziggurat. The ziggurat's appearance was thus quite different from its Mesopotamian counterparts, which had external stairways applied against one side of the tower.

The ziggurat was crowned by a high temple, called the *kukunum* in its inscriptions (see below). Culminating at a height of some 50 m, it was lavishly decorated with silver- and gold-colored glazed bricks. It was dedicated jointly to the gods Napirisha (originally the god of the city of Anshan in Fars) and Inshushinak, who both received the epithet of "lord of the *Siyan-kuk*." Thus, the dedication of the ziggurat and that of the entire temenos had changed between the first and the second phase of construction.

The ziggurat compound contained several shrines and cultic installations located at the foot of the monument. Along the northwest facade a temple complex with shrines was dedicated to Ishnikarab (a god of Susiana), Nabu (a god of Babylonian origin), and Kiririsha (Napirisha's consort). These temples have no striking architectural characteristics but resemble ordinary dwellings with an inner courtyard, except for Nabu's temple, which is T-shaped. A large collection of votive objects, including several silver and bronze axes and more than one hundred mace heads, was found in Kiririsha's temple. Along its southwestern side a row of four rooms was interpreted as "chapels"; more than one hundred votive cylinder seals were discovered in them.

Several gates gave access to the ziggurat compound

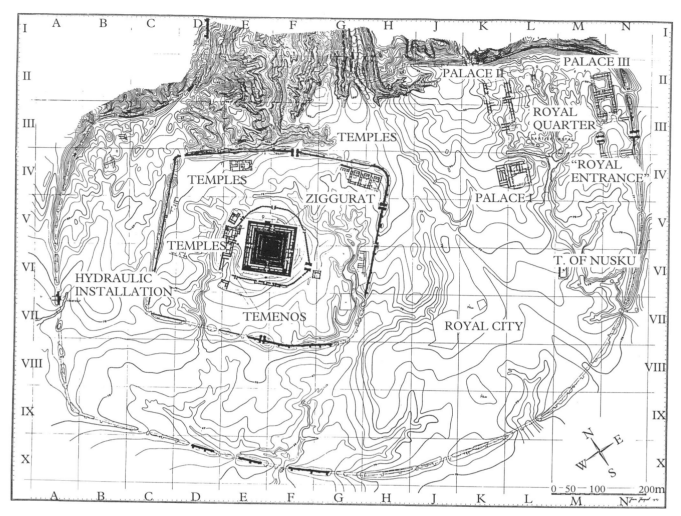

CHOGHA ZANBIL. Figure 1. *Topographic plan of the site.* (Courtesy P. de Miroschedji)

through the enclosure wall; pavement remains indicate that they were linked to the gates of the temenos wall by large processional ways. Immediately outside three of the gates were square temples of unknown designation, except for the northern one, which was dedicated to Napirisha; it is larger than the other and may have had a towerlike appearance.

Temenos. Extending around the ziggurat compound, the temenos was enclosed by a thick mud-brick wall with outer buttresses. It was occupied by a series of temples dedicated to divinities originating from all parts of the empire. Only some of these temples were preserved and cleared.

A complex of four temples existed near the east corner. Three were built side by side with an identical plan (a courtyard surrounding a small building composed of an antecella and a cella) and dedicated to Pinikir (an Elamite goddess) and to two divine couples originating from Susiana (Adad and Shala, Shimut and Nin-ali/Manzat). The fourth temple consisted of a row of four small chapels, each containing a

pair of altars, and was dedicated to the Napratep (a group of local divinities).

Along the northeastern side of the temenos two other temples were dedicated to the goddess Hishmitik and to the god Ruhuratir (divinities from Shimashki in the Zagros highland); one was comparable to the three temples to the east, while the other was an enlarged version of Napirisha's square temples.

Royal city. The royal city extended around the temenos. It may have been entirely built up, although not necessarily densely. The major buildings were concentrated in the northeast, also the location of the main city gate, called the Royal Entrance. The gate was a double gate with an inner courtyard (64 × 62 m) bordered on three sides by elongated rooms. It opened into a sort of "royal quarter" occupied by three large buildings, presumably palaces.

The most elaborate is palace I (70 × 56 m) also called the palace-*hypogeum* (see below). It is composed of three parts:

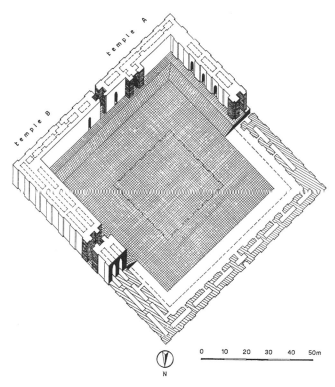

CHOGHA ZANBIL. Figure 2a. *Plan of the ziggurat.* Initial phase of construction. (After Ghirshman, 1966-1968, vol. 1)

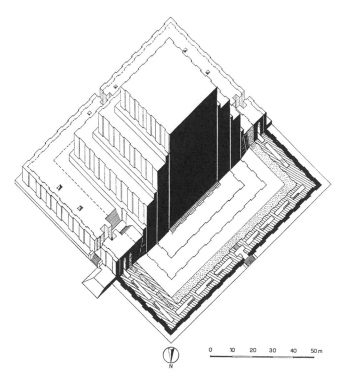

CHOGHA ZANBIL. Figure 2b. *Plan of the ziggurat.* Second phase of construction. (After Ghirshman, 1966-1968, vol. 1)

an official section with a large courtyard decorated with glazed polychrome bricks and surrounded by long rooms; a private section with apartments around two small courtyards; and a (domestic?) section with a series of elongated rooms. The building is exceptional because there are several tombs under the private and domestic rooms. Built in baked brick set in bitumen and plaster, the tombs were reached by means of a steep staircase and consist of one or two vaulted rooms up to 4 m high and 5–6 m long. With a single exception, all the bodies in the tombs had been cremated with their funerary offerings, a unique example of cremation in Elam.

The two other palaces may have served as quarters for the royal entourage. They are quite different from the palace-*hypogeum* but resemble each other in plan and organization. Both consist of a series of separate apartments (including several bathrooms) organized around two or three square courtyards placed side by side (palace III) or at a right angle (palace II); the organization of each unit is original and recalls that of the first phase of the ziggurat complex.

Some 100 m southwest of the palaces, the sanctuary of Nusku is an unusual building, called *ipillati* instead of *siyan* ("temple") by the inscriptions (see below): it is T-shaped, composed of a transversal anteroom and a large longitudinal hall with a high mud-brick podium in its center; considering its size (30 m × 13 m), the hall was probably unroofed. Because of Nusku's connection with fire and light, this sanctuary is sometimes interpreted as a sort of fire temple.

A hydraulic installation was built on both sides of the city wall to the southwest of the royal city to ensure Chogha Zanbil's water supply. Located at the end of a canal, it is composed of two basins that communicate through small channels—a large basin of decantation on the outside and a smaller basin on the inside.

Finds. The vast majority of the thousands of inscriptions found in the excavations are building inscriptions on baked bricks; they consist of fifty-two different Elamite texts and only five Akkadian texts and represent an invaluable source of information on Elamite language and religion.

The excavations have yielded numerous objects, but no large monuments. A large collection of glazed objects in terra cotta or in frit was uncovered. Many are decorative architectural elements in the shape of glazed plaques with knobs or large pegs of the same material; some seven hundred were found in one of the rooms in the first story of the ziggurat. Glazed sculptures (bulls and winged griffons), figurines (human and animal), and vessels of various kinds were also found.

A cache in palace III has yielded a group of alabaster jugs of Syro-Egyptian type. Noteworthy from palace I is a mosaic panel of ivory showing a winged goddess and a frieze of wild goats alternating with a sacred tree. Metal objects are represented by axes, daggers, arrowheads, plaques, and personal ornaments. A large collection of stone mace heads, inscribed and plain, and about 160 cylinder seals, the majority in faience and in glass, were found. They illustrate the range of glyptic styles in use in fourteenth-century BCE Susiana. Other examples of such seals were exported as far as Marlik in northern Iran. [See Marlik.]

There are relatively few finds from Chogha Zanbil because the site was generally abandoned after Untash-Napirisha's reign and cleared of its major monuments by the twelfth-century Elamite kings. An inscription of King Shutruk-Nahhunte (c. 1185–1155 BCE) specifically mentions the transfer of a stela from the *Siyan-kuk* (i.e., Chogha Zanbil) to Susa. Therefore, monuments found in Susa that, based on inscriptional and/or stylistic and iconographic evidence, originally stood in Untash-Napirisha's city should be added to the finds from Chogha Zanbil. [See Susa.] Among these are Untash-Napirisha's stela, a divine bust holding two dragon snakes, the lower part of a divine statue showing intertwined dragon snakes, various fragments of sculptures and reliefs, a large bronze sacrificial table, and, possibly, a bronze statue of Queen Napir-Asu.

Interpretation of the Finds. Chogha Zanbil is best understood as a new capital city built around a federal sanctuary in which the major divinities of the empire resided together under the aegis of the gods of Anshan and Susa. It entails on the part of its founder a political vision of unusual magnitude, aiming to achieve the unity of the Elamite Empire.

The foundation of the new city marks a break from the past: built on new ground and without any direct relationship to the old capital of Susa, all members of the empire could claim it equally as their capital. The temenos was the federal sanctuary that united the major gods of the empire's main cities and provinces. With its concentric plan (the ziggurat compound surrounded by a religious city and it in turn by a royal city) the site was an ideal image of Elam.

The fact that the center of this Elamite microcosm was a ziggurat initially dedicated to Inshushinak suggests that at first Susiana was perceived as the center of the empire. Only later did Untash-Napirisha change his plan and rededicate the ziggurat jointly to Napirisha and to Inshushinak. This placed the new capital city (and by the same token the whole empire) under the joint auspices of the god of Anshan and the god of Susa. The new scheme may imply that the empire was thereafter conceived as the union of the highland and the lowland—a union further expressed by Untash-Napirisha's parallel title "king of Anshan and Susa."

This grandiose enterprise seems to have ended in failure, however. The king died and the construction of Chogha Zanbil was never completed. In the historic record, there is a gap during most of the thirteenth century BCE. When Elamite kings reappear on the scene in the twelfth century BCE, they have abandoned Chogha Zanbil in favor of Susa and again chosen Inshushinak as the major deity of the empire.

[*See also* Elamites; Ziggurat; *and the biography of Ghirshman.*]

BIBLIOGRAPHY

Amiet, Pierre. *Elam.* Auvers-sur-Oise, 1966. Classical synthesis of Elamite archaeology, with illustrations of the main monuments of Chogha Zanbil.

Aynard, Jeanne-Marie. *Le prisme du Louvre AO 19.939.* Paris, 1957.

Ghirshman, Roman. *Tchogha Zanbil (Dur Untash)*, vol. 1, *La ziggurat;* vol. 2, *Téménos, temples, palais, tombes.* Mémoires de la Mission Archéologique en Iran, vols. 39–40. Paris, 1966–1968. Final publication of Ghirshman's excavations.

Harper, Prudence, Oliver, et al., eds. *The Royal City of Susa: Ancient Near Eastern Treasures in the Louvre.* New York, 1992. Includes an up-to-date presentation of the Middle Elamite monuments.

König, Friedrich W. *Die elamischen Königsinschriften.* Archiv für Orientforschung, vol. 16. Graz, 1965. Although many translations become outdated, this book is not yet superseded.

Luckenbill, Daniel D. *Ancient Records of Assyria and Babylonia*, vol. 2, *From Sargon to the End.* Chicago, 1927.

Mecquenem, Roland de, and J. Michalon. *Recherches à Tchogha Zembil.* Mémoires de la Mission Archéologique en Iran, vol. 33. Paris, 1953. Publication of de Mecquenem's pioneering work at Chogha Zanbil.

Miroschedji, Pierre de. "Le dieu élamite Napirisha." *Revue d'Assyriologie* 74 (1980): 129–143. Study of the god Napirisha and his significance.

Miroschedji, Pierre de. "Le dieu élamite au serpent et aux eaux jaillissantes." *Iranica Antiqua* 16 (1981): 1–25. Includes a study of Untash-Napirisha stela and the publication of fragmentary monuments originating from Chogha Zanbil and found in Susa.

Porada, Edith. *Tchogha Zanbil (Dur-Untash)*, vol. 4, *La glyptique.* Mémoires de la Délégation Archéologique en Iran, vol. 42. Paris, 1970. Masterly study of the Chogha Zanbil glyptic.

Roche, Claude. "Les ziggurats de Tchogha Zanbil." In *Fragmenta historiae elamicae*, edited by Leon De Meyer et al., pp. 191–197. Paris, 1986.

Stève, M. J. *Textes élamites et accadiens de Tchogha Zanbil.* Mémoires de la Délégation Archéologique en Iran, vol. 41. Paris, 1967. *Editio princeps* of the inscriptions found in Chogha Zanbil, with references to parallel inscriptions found earlier in Susa.

Vallat, François. "L'inscription de la stèle d'Untash-Napirisha." *Iranica Antiqua* 16 (1981): 27–33.

PIERRE DE MIROSCHEDJI

CHORAZIN (also Chorazim), a Jewish village in the Galilee in the Greco-Roman period identified with Khirbet Karazeh and located approximately 4 km (2.5 mi.) north of the Sea of Galilee (map reference 2031 × 2575). Chorazin is first mentioned in the New Testament (*Mt.* 11:21–24; *Lk.* 10:13–16) in regard to Jesus' ministry. It is mentioned in Tosefta *Menahot* 9:2 (and parallels), a text that dates to the second or perhaps third century CE. Eusebius (c. 260–340 CE) reports that the site of Chorazin is 2 Roman miles from Capernaum and that the town was in ruins in his day (*On-*

omasticon 174.23). The first modern scholar to identify the town as Chorazin was Charles Wilson in 1869. From 1905–1907 Heinrich Kohl and Carl Watzinger partially excavated the synagogue on behalf of the Deutsche Orient-Gesellschaft; it was completely cleared on behalf of the Mandatory Department of Antiquities in 1926. From 1962–1964 Zeev Yeivin conducted a survey of the town on behalf of the Israel Department of Antiquities, and between 1980 and 1984 excavations were carried out under his direction.

The synagogue at Chorazin is of the Galilean type, which also includes the synagogues of Capernaum, Bar'am, Meiron, Arbel, and Merot. [*See* Synagogues.] Although Michael Avi-Yonah dated this group to the second century, it is now generally accepted that Galilean-type synagogues belong to the third–sixth centuries CE. The building was constructed in the town center of local basalt ashlars on a broad podium. A flight of steps led up to the podium. The facade, which is aligned toward the south, has been partially reconstructed under Yeivin's supervision. In antiquity an exedra was constructed along the length of the facade. The building had three entrances: a large central portal that led into the nave and two smaller portals that led into the side aisles. A wolf, a Medusa, and other figures appear in bas-relief on architectural members of the synagogue. Remains of two aediculae as well as a basalt chair bearing a dedicatory inscription were discovered near the southern wall of the synagogue. The interpretation of this inscription has been the subject of considerable dispute. A translation of this text, following the reading of Joseph Naveh (1978) is as follows:

> Remembered for good Yudan son of Ishmael
> Who made (or, donated) this stoa
> and its steps from his (own) property. May
> he have a portion with the righteous.

The extensive excavations of the Byzantine-period town of Chorazin between 1964 and 1984 disclosed that its shape conformed to the topography of the hill on which it was built. Its housing units are reminiscent of housing excavated in the neighboring Golan Heights. Units A and B are contiguous rooms constructed around a central courtyard, an arrangement reminiscent of the communal courtyards mentioned in numerous rabbinic sources (e.g., Mishnah *B. B.*, ch. 1, and parallels) The town is divided into housing units by streets that join the main street on the east and west. The civic center, which included the synagogue, was built on a broad natural platform in the center of the town. The outer walls of the buildings in the center seem to have been contiguous and enclosed the civic complex. An elaborate ritual bath complex was uncovered in building E, on the northern side of the town.

[*See also* Bar'am; Capernaum; Deutsche Orient-Gesellschaft; Galilee, *article on* Galilee in the Hellenistic through Byzantine Periods; Merion; Synagogue Inscriptions; *and the biographies of Avi-Yonah, Watzinger, and Wilson.*]

BIBLIOGRAPHY

Chiat, Marilyn Joyce Segal. *Handbook of Synagogue Literature.* Chico, Calif., 1982. Surveys the architectural history of the Chorazin synagogue.

Hirschfeld, Yizhar. *Dwelling Houses in Roman and Byzantine Palestine* (in Hebrew). Jerusalem, 1987. Utilizes both archaeological and literary sources (see esp. pp. 35–36, 167).

Naveh, Joseph. *On Mosaic and Stone: The Aramaic and Stone Inscriptions from Ancient Synagogues* (in Hebrew). Tel Aviv, 1978. Discusses the Chorazin inscription and the various scholarly attempts to decipher it (pp. 36–38).

Yeivin, Zeev. "Chorazin." In *The New Encyclopedia of Archaeological Excavations in the Holy Land,* vol. 1, pp. 301–304. Jerusalem and New York, 1993. Survey of the site's archaeological history, written by its principal excavator.

STEVEN FINE

CHUERA, TELL, site located almost midway between the valleys of the Balikh and Khabur Rivers in the province of Raqqa, Syria, (36°40′ N, 39°30′ E). The site belongs to a special type of settlement named *kranzhügel* (Ger., "wreath-like mound") by Max von Oppenheim, who, during his travels in Upper Mesopotamia between 1911 and 1913, was the first to recognize them. The settlements occur mainly on the steppe between the upper courses of the Balikh and the Khabur and on both sides of the Abd al-Aziz Mountains. They are usually almost circular, with a line of low hills at their outer edge, indicating the existence of a fortification wall, and with a flat lower city and a central elevated citadel mound.

Tell Chuera is the largest of these settlements, covering a surface of about 650,000 sq m. Excavation began with a sounding in 1955 carried out by Jean Lauffray on behalf of the Syrian Antiquities Department. In 1958, the Max von Oppenheim Foundation began a long-term excavation project at Tell Chuera, first under the directorship of Anton Moortgat (1958–1976), then of Ursula Moortgat-Correns (1982–1985), and since 1986, of Winfried Orthmann.

Settlement history at Tell Chuera may be divided into two main phases. Period 1 extends from about 2800 to 2300 BCE, and, after a hiatus, period 2 lasts from 1600 to 1100. Settlement reached its largest expanse during period IC. The site was surrounded by a mud-brick fortification wall and a ditch. The lower city, which covered an area of about 220,000 sq m, was apparently completely built up with private houses. Recent excavations have shown that the citadel mound was at least partly surrounded by an inner fortification.

An important sanctuary complex has been identified at the southeastern part of the citadel. It consists of a high terrace, built with rather large stone boulders, accessed from the east via a ramp or staircase; the temple, of which only a few remains are preserved, probably stood on this terrace. Several side terraces were added to the building during its existence. A second stone building seems to have been a kind of gate to the sanctuary. Another temple on the north side of the citadel is the oldest known example of the traditional North Syrian type of sanctuary: the building, which was erected on a low terrace, consists of a rectangular cella, entered from an open porch on its east side. A small temple in the central part of the citadel, surrounded by private houses, is of the same general type; in the cella and its immediate neighborhood, several stone statuettes have been found that resemble figures from the Diyala region in Mesopotamia, dating from the Early Dynastic II period. They show that at the time northern Mesopotamia was already influenced by the Sumerian culture to the south.

The remains of a large palace (about 70 × 60 m) have been identified in the western part of the citadel. Excavation revealed several courtyards and a large hall with a dais built against its east wall (probably the throne room). In the southern part of the citadel, a quarter with private houses was excavated. The houses were built one against the other along narrow streets. Each house had a courtyard, accessed from the street through a narrow corridor, and a reception room built between the courtyard and the street. About 200 m to the east of the settlement, a double row of irregularly shaped large stelae resembles a megalithic structure. Nearby, a sanctuary with two North Syrian-style shrines has been excavated.

During the period of Mitanni beginning in period 2, Tell Chuera was resettled following a long hiatus. Except for a small shrine, few building remains have been recovered from this period. The Middle Assyrian period, which followed, is represented by two main building levels in the northern part of the citadel. To the earlier of these levels belongs a well-fortified manor house that was the seat of the local Assyrian governor. A small archive of cuneiform tablets found in one of its rooms belongs to the thirteenth century BCE; it made possible the identification of Tell Chuera with the city of Ḫarbe (or Ḫurbe), mentioned in Middle Assyrian texts from Dur Katlimmu.

BIBLIOGRAPHY

Kühne, Hartmut. *Die Keramik vom Tell Chuera und ihre Beziehungen zu Funden aus Syrien-Palästina, der Türkei und dem Iraq.* Berlin, 1976. Full account of the pottery found up until 1964, with a useful summary of the stratigraphy.

Moortgat-Correns, Ursula. *Die Bildwerke vom Djebelet el Beda in ihrer räumlichen und zeitlichen Umwelt.* Berlin and New York, 1972. General background information on the *kranzhügel* type of settlements (see pp. 26–52).

Moortgat-Correns, Ursula. *Tell Chuera in Nordost-Syrien: Vorläufiger Bericht über die neunte und zehnte Grabungskampagne 1982 und 1983.* Berlin, 1988. Preliminary report on the Tell Chuera excavations; see, as well, Moortgat-Correns (1988) and Orthmann et al. (1986).

Moortgat-Correns, Ursula. *Tell Chuera in Nordost-Syrien: Vorläufiger Bericht über die elfte Grabungskampagne 1985.* Berlin, 1988.

Orthmann, Winfried, et al. *Tell Chuera in Nordost Syrien, 1982–1983.* Berlin, 1986.

Orthmann, Winfried. *Tell Chuera: Ausgrabungen der Max Freiherr von Oppenheim-Stiftung in Nordost-Syrien.* Damascus, 1990. Summary of the excavations up until 1989.

WINFRIED ORTHMANN

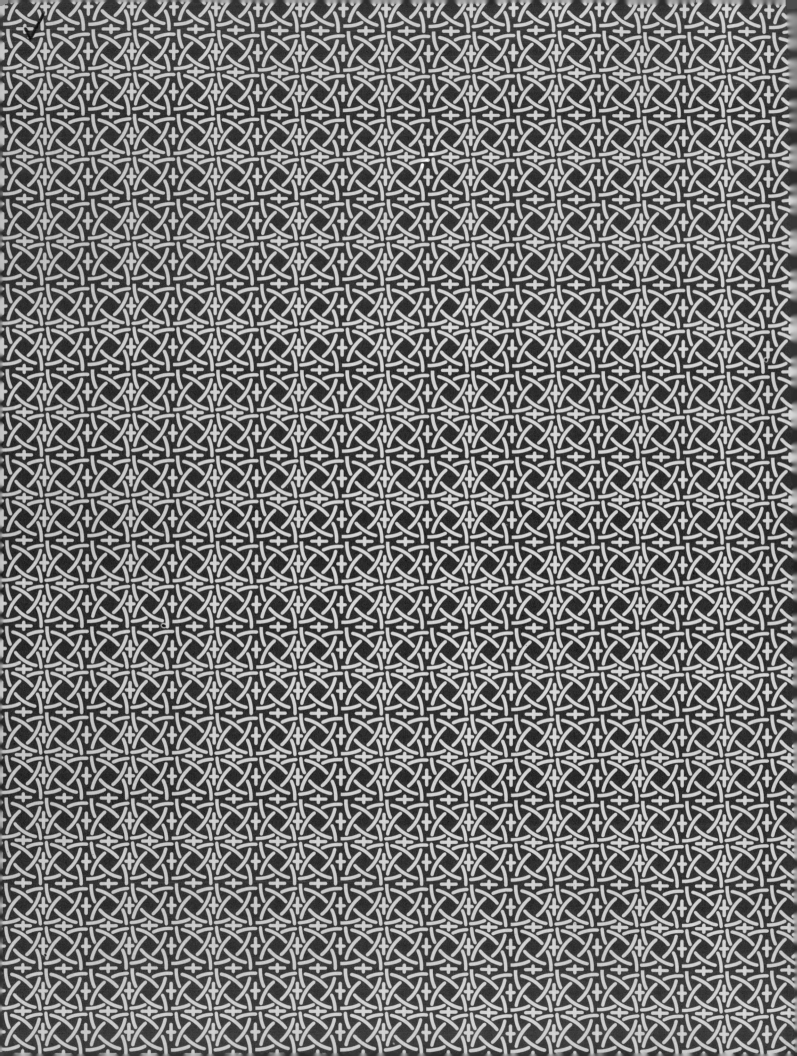